NORTH CAROLINA

Extant Voter Registrations

of

1867

FRANCES HOLLOWAY WYNNE

HERITAGE BOOKS
2014

HERITAGE BOOKS
AN IMPRINT OF HERITAGE BOOKS, INC.

Books, CDs, and more—Worldwide

For our listing of thousands of titles see our website
at
www.HeritageBooks.com

Published 2014 by
HERITAGE BOOKS, INC.
Publishing Division
5810 Ruatan Street
Berwyn Heights, Md. 20740

Heritage Books by the author:

Holloways of the South and Allied Families
C.J. Stevens, editor; Frances Wynne, Edith Stevens, Peggy Brown, Thomas Brown
North Carolina Extant Voter Registrations of 1867
Register of Free Negroes and of Dower Slaves, Brunswick County, Virginia, 1803–1850

International Standard Book Numbers
Paperbound: 978-1-58549-646-4
Clothbound: 978-0-7884-6029-6

Acknowledgments

This book represents the efforts of many people from George Stevenson, Frank Gatton, James Sorrell, and the other staff at the Archives in Raleigh who told me of these records, helped me get them transcribed, saw to it that I had space to work, and answered frantic phone calls with long-distance assistance, to my husband who acted as my technical and editorial advisor. Michael Musick and Willna Uebrick-Pacheli at the National Archives made it possible to locate the record group that had the information I needed to give additional background and to determine that any other of these records, if indeed there are any others, are cleverly hidden beyond the knowledge of the National Archives. James Dent Walker let me use his microfilm equipment to permit my working on this at home rather than in Raleigh. Sandra Lawson and my friend Tom Blakslee at the Library of Congress located the law that set the mechanism for the voting procedure and saw to it that I had it to include in the book. Wilma Perry contributed expertise in getting the maps in usable form. My friend Bonnie Smith Almond is responsible for stimulating my interest in genealogy and local history many years ago, an interest that sustained me through many agonizing hours of bad microfilm and worse handwriting. I thank all of you for your help.

Frances Holloway Wynne

30 June 1992

North Carolina Extant Voter Registrations of 1867
INTRODUCTION

That wars have an impact upon all people of a society and not merely the military alone can be attested to by anyone who has ever read of or lived through such upheavals, no matter where or when, and the American South after the Civil War was no exception. The task of restoring order in the South Congress gave to five military districts into which all secessionist states were divided. On March 2, 1867, Chapter 153 of the Statutes at Large of the United States (Appendix A) set the provisions for an orderly return to a more efficient government.

North and South Carolina were placed in the Second of the five districts with headquarters in Charleston, South Carolina. All governmental details came under the jurisdiction of the commanding general, from reestablishing local and state government and seeing that all people were treated fairly, to overseeing the everyday details of local business, such as the issuing of a license to sell liquor by the glass in a country store (Appendix B). The big problem facing the military government was that of registering newly-enfranchised black voters who met the legal requirements set by Congress. The copy of the correspondance from the office of the general 15 November 1867 detail the instructions in General Order 119 of getting the registration accomplished:

> Boards of Registration will provide each polling place with one ballot box, with lock and key, not to exceed two dollars per box. Name and residence of persons voting to be entered on poll lists. At close of election managers of election count votes polled, compare with poll lists and correct errors if possible.
>
> Tickets <u>for Convention</u> and those <u>against convention</u> will be placed in packages by themselves number contained to be marked thereon. Those that are informal but same in substance by themselves in separate packages for and against. Tickets which do not contain the inscription FOR or AGAINST CONVENTION to be put by themselves number in each package to be marked.
>
> Thereupon packages will be replaced in boxes by and seal with the seal of the managers of election and will be delivered by the chairman with poll lists and books of registration to chairman of Board of Registration to which such polling place belongs.
>
> The Board of Registration count the votes in respective packages, compare them with poll lists and will canvass votes for or against convention and for deligates and enter summary of votes in printed canvass lists and will replace votes in same packages in which they were placed by managers and forward same to these Headquarters through Post Commander packages of votes for each polling place will be returned with poll lists and registration books for such polling place in one parcel.
>
> By command BVT Major General Canby

North Carolina Extant Voter Registrations of 1867

INTRODUCTION

These voting lists were to have been made up of all males, age twenty-one and over, who had lived in the precinct for one year or more. The registrars had to sign the oath of allegiance and had to be assured that the registrant had not given aid and comfort to the enemy, the Confederate government (Appendix C). Many people were not allowed to vote for any number of reasons as the notes on the lists show.

The voter lists found in the papers of the Secretary of State in the Archives of North Carolina in Raleigh that comprise this book are the only lists that have been found to date, either there or in the papers of the Second Military District of Charleston in the National Archives. The whereabouts of other lists are unknown at either repository. Even though we do not have the lists for the entire state (Appendix D), the lists are historically interesting because it is the first showing of full names of black voters, many of whom were former slaves and give for some a record of residence and an indication of age. Some entries have comments that show involvement with the war; some show changes of residence; a few show ages; and in rare cases even parentage is noted. It is unfortunate that more of these records did not survive or have not been located.

The usual problems of transcription exist when old records are involved -- water stains, faded ink, poor handwriting, worm holes, and the ever-present <u>creative spellings</u>. To get these transcribed necessitated either many hours in the North Carolina Archives or working from microfilmed copies at home. Both approaches were used when time dictated the procedure. Every attempt was made to minimize errors, but as surely as there is a record, there is the possibility of error, unintentional to be sure, but still a possibility.

There were discrepancies caused by the registrars themselves, <u>i.e.</u>, Brownstone in one place and Brownstown in another; Rhyners/Ryners in one place, Rhymers/Rymers in another. Brownstown was a former town in Davidson County, according to <u>The North Carolina Gazetteer</u> by William S. Powell, but there is no reference to Rhyners/Rymers. There were other oddities. When the law definitely required a one-year residency, one wonders why some potential voters were accepted after showing less time. Some voters were challenged and rejected with no explanation while on others the registrars went into great detail to explain the rejection, such as those in Gaston County (<u>q.v.</u>). One wishes the registrars had been equally conscientious in all precincts. There was no explanation for some names' being stricken but yet there were indications of acceptance for voting. In one precinct a man might be rejected for conviction of a felony while in another county this may not have been cause to deny voting. Even though the voting age was supposedly twenty-one, there are a few indications that not all voters were that age. From the wording on some items it is evident a duplicate copy of the lists was taken and checked against the original, but either one or the other has survived with no record of what happened to the others. When a residence in the state of less that a year is noted, one wishes the orignal state has been given in each instance. Someone named Gallagher will be happy to know that their ancestors may have come to Duplin County from Ireland in 1866 because three of them were denied the right to vote since they had not met the year's residency requirement.

North Carolina Extant Voter Registrations of 1867
INTRODUCTION

It is readily understandable why a militia officer during the rebellion would be denied the privilege of voting, but one wonders why an overseer of highways, a lighthouse keeper, or a post master. These latter hardy seem to be key governmental decision-making positions. Of all the reasons that were given for rejecting a voter, probably the most provocative is that of William B. Tooly of Hyde County, who was stricken at his own request. One cannot help wondering what visual pictures of the past his "reflections" produced, especially when at the bottom of the LATE WHITE REGISTRANTS one sees that his political disabilities were removed, and he was permitted to vote.

In an effort to save space, repetition of the directions to registrars that appeared at the beginning of each precinct book has been avoided by including only one copy here for the benefit of the reader:

Directions To Registrars

1. The Books must be carefully preserved, so as to allow no unauthorized entries or alterations therein.

2. The Books marked on the covers "Original," are the official record of Registration, and all question of the right of Registration must be determined by reference to such original.

3. All names hereafter recorded in either Book, must be placed below the red line (marked February or March, 1868.)

4. The first duty of the Registrars, on receiving the Books, will be to examine whether there is a list of names accompanying them found in the duplicate Books, and not contained in the "Originals." If such a list accompanies the Books, it will be examined, and if the persons whose names are therein set forth are entitled to Registration, such names will be entered upon the "Original" in their due place after the red line, and a note will be made, showing each name so copied, as follows: Copied from duplicate.

5. When a person already registered is decided not to be entitled to registry, the following note will be inserted after his name: "Stricken out April...., 1868"; but the name will not be erased.

6. Where there is not space left in the Books for continuing the Registration, a note will be found at the end of the column of names indicating another letter, where the entries will be continued. A red line will be found at such new letter, where the entry of names will commence.

7. When two books are attached together, one of them blank, the entries will be made in the blank Book.

8. When a certificate is given on account of change of residence, an entry thereof will be made opposite to the name of the person to whom the same was given, stating his present place of residence.

North Carolina Extant Voter Registrations of 1867
INTRODUCTION

The following recapitulation will be filled up by the Board:
Recapitulation of Revision of Registration
April........ 1868

	WHITES	BLACKS	TOTAL
Stricken out from Registration			
Applications for Registry accepted			
Application for Registry rejected			
Certificates given to persons who have changed their residence			

We, the undersigned Board of Registrars for the .... Registration Precinct, County of ...., State of North Carolina, do certify that the following is a correct list of votes registered in said Precinct, as per revision of ...., 1868.
Dated ...., 1868.

The lists show those "below the red line" as LATE BLACK REGISTRANTS or LATE WHITE REGISTRANTS. A certificate may have been given to a person to vote elsewhere and is so indicated, sometimes with new or previous precinct given, sometimes no indication. The books were arranged by color with black on the left leaf and white on the right leaf. Occasionally a name would be entered on the wrong page and a note made to indicate the registrar's error. Such errors and notes have been preserved here. Occasionally the registrars wrote notes or made tally sheets at the end of a book, and as one would expect, there are some discrepancies in these totals, giving cause to wonder at the registrars' ability to count as well as write and spell.

The North Carolina Legislature in 1868 called for township descriptions. Some of these have been found for a few counties and included with the county histories and registration totals in Appendix E. Any peculiarities for a county either in registrations or precinct divisions are noted there. The number appearing in the left margin indicates the county number designated by the N.C. Archives. The SS number after the name is the number of the box of the Secretary of State papers where the book may be found.

Abbreviations found in the text

A - accepted for voting
Board - Board of Registrars
"C" - certificate
cert res - certificate of residence
Chal - challenged
Chm - chairman
debt shff - deputy sheriff
R or rej - rejected for voting
Recon. - Reconsidered
trans - transferred
(X) - signed name with an X
1st - 1st person by the name
2nd - 2nd person by same name
? - could not be read clearly
--- - illegible
[ ] - author remarks

North Carolina Extant Voter Registrations of 1867
CARTERET COUNTY

Carteret County, was formed in 1722 from Craven, was named in honor of Sir John Carteret who became the Earl of Granville. In the eastern section of the State, it is bounded by the Atlantic Ocean, the counties of Onslow, Jones, and Craven, and on the banks by Hyde County. In 1770 part of Hatteras Banks was annexed to Carteret. In 1779 and 1788 parts of Carteret went to Jones and in 1845 part went to Hyde. The boundaries between Craven and Carteret were under discussion from 1806 to 1885. The present area of the County is 532 square miles.

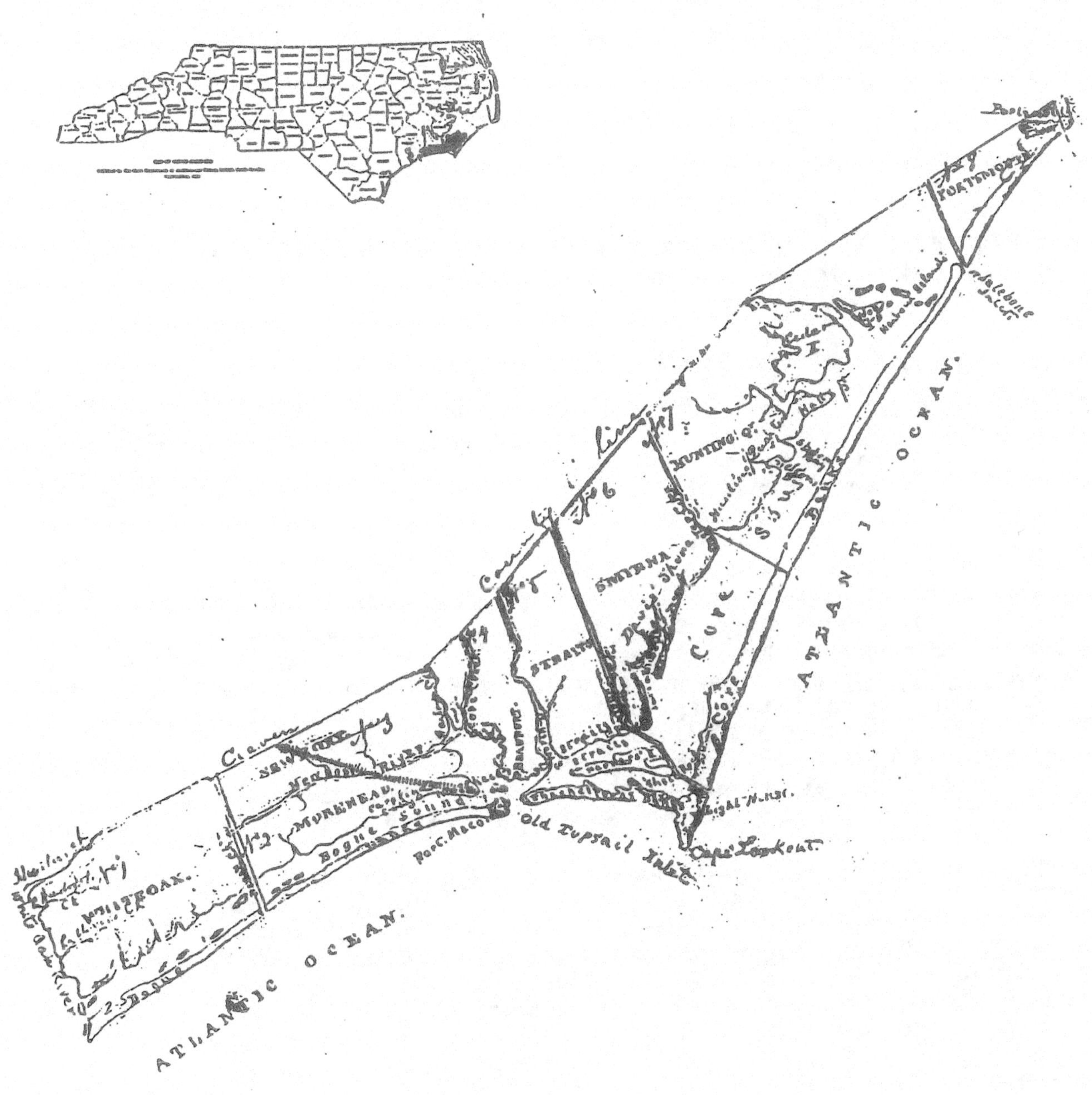

North Carolina Extant Voter Registrations of 1867
CARTERET COUNTY

19	CARTERET COUNTY SS991-2	WHITES	BLACKS	AGGREGATE
19 BE1	BEAUFORT (1)	315	389	604
19 BE2	BEAUFORT (2)	37	29	66
19 CED	CEDAR ISLAND	40	1	41
19 DAV	DAVIS SHORE	42	7	49
19 HAD	HADNOTS CREEK	128	63	191
19 HAR	HARLOWS CREEK	43	61	104
19 HUN	HUNTING QUARTERS	128	0	128
19 MOR	MOREHEAD CITY	110	105	215
19 NEW	NEWPORT	144	141	285
19 POR	PORTSMOUTH	69	0	69
19 SHA	SHACKLEFORD BANKS	54	1	55
19 SMY	SMYRNA	100	8	108
19 STR	STRAIGHTS	118	21	139
19	CARTERET TOTALS	1,328	826	2,154

The County was divided and laid off into Townships by the County Commissioners 1 January 1869, John Primley, Ex-officio Clerk. Some of the 1867 voting precincts do not appear in the 1869 division. From the registrars one is able to get some idea of the location of precincts.

Carteret County Township Descriptions

Whiteoak Township. To begin at the mouth of Hunters Creek on Whiteoak River, running down the river and with the Onslow County line to Bogue Inlet, then along the seashore eastwardly to a point bearing due south from the mouth of Broad Creek on Bogue Sound, thence north to the mouth of said Broad Creek, thence up the various courses of said creek to the main road thence north to the Craven County line, then with said line westwardly to the head of Hunters Creek, and then down the various courses of said creek to the beginning. [No election precinct by this name in 1867. Included Hadnots Creek Precinct where all entries carried notation of CHALLENGED but show acceptance.]
Board: Jno J Henshaw Chm., Thomas Daniels, Oliver T Henry 16 Nov 1867

Beaufort Township. Beginning at the N.E. corner of Newport Township, running with the lines of said Township to the mouth of Core Creek, then with the waters of Newport River and Beaufort Harbour to the mouth of North River, then up the various courses of North River to the head thereof thence north to the Craven County line, and thence with said line to beginning.
Board: Thos C Allen Chm, James E Whitehurst, David M Fenderson 24 Sep 1867

Hunting Quarter Township. Beginning at the N.E. corner of Smyrna Township on Craven County line, running south to the head of the Oyster Creek then down the creek to its mouth then southeast to the sea side; then along the sea eastwardly to the Whalebone Inlet then north to the Craven County line, and with the same to the beginning. [Included Cedar Island precinct.]
Board: Thos C Allen Chm, James E Whitehurst, David M Fenderson 23 Sep 1867

Morehead Township. Beginning at the corner of Whiteoak Township on the seashore, running along the sea eastwardly to the corner of the United States land on which Fort Macon stands, then with the line of said land to the sound, thence up the various courses of Newport River to the head thereof; thence west to the line of Whiteoak Township and thence with the line of said Township to the beginning.

Board: Jno J Henshaw Chm, Thomas Daniels, Oliver N Henry 16 Nov 1867

Newport Township. Beginning at the mouth of Core Creek on Newport River running up the creek to its head; then north to the Craven County line; then with said line westwardly to the corner of Morehead Township; then with said line south to the corner of Morehead, then with the lines of the same and Newport River to the beginning, including all the land on the north side of Newport between Core Creek and Whiteoak Township. [Included Harlows Creek Precinct where all entries carried notation of CHALLENGED but show acceptance.]

Board: Jno J Henshaw Chm, Thomas Daniels, Oliver N Henry 16 Nov 1867

Portsmouth Township. Beginning at Whalebone Inlet, running north to Craven County line, then with said line to Ocracoke Inlet, and from thence the various courses of the sea to the beginning.

Board: Thos C Allen Chm, James E Whitehurst, David M Fenderson 24 Sep 1867

Smyrna Township. Beginning at the N.E. corner of Straits Township, running with the lines of the same to the corner on the seashore; then along the sea eastwardly to a point bearing southeast from the mouth of the Oyster Creek; then northwest to the mouth of the Oyster Creek; then up the creek to its head; thence north to the Craven County line and with the same to the beginning. [Included Davis Shore Precinct.]

Board: Thos C Allen Chm, James E Whitehurst, David M Fenderson 24 Sep 1867

Straits Township. Beginning at the N.E. corner of Beaufort Township in the Craven County line, running with the lines of Beaufort to the mouth of North River; then with the waters of Beaufort Harbour to old Topsail Inlet; then along the sea eastwardly to a point bearing south east from the shell rock on Harkers Island; from thence to the eastward mouth of the straits; then along the straits to the mouth of Fulfords Creek; then up the creek to its head then north to the Craven County line; and with the same to the beginning. [Included Shackleford Bank Precinct.]

Board: Thos C Allen Chm, James E Whitehurst, David M Fenderson 24 Sep 1867

North Carolina Extant Voter Registrations of 1867
CHOWAN COUNTY

Chowan was formed in 1670 as a precinct in Albemarle County. It is in the northeast section of the State, bounded by Albemarle Sound, the Chowan River, and Bertie, Hertford, Gates, and Perquimans Counties. There have been many changes in its boundary lines. Bertie County was formed from it in 1722. Parts of it were taken to help form Tyrrell in 1729, Hertford in 1759, and Gates in 1779. Boundaries between Chowan, Perquimans, Gates, Washington, and Tyrrell have been disputed from 1805 to 1911. The present area is 180 square miles.

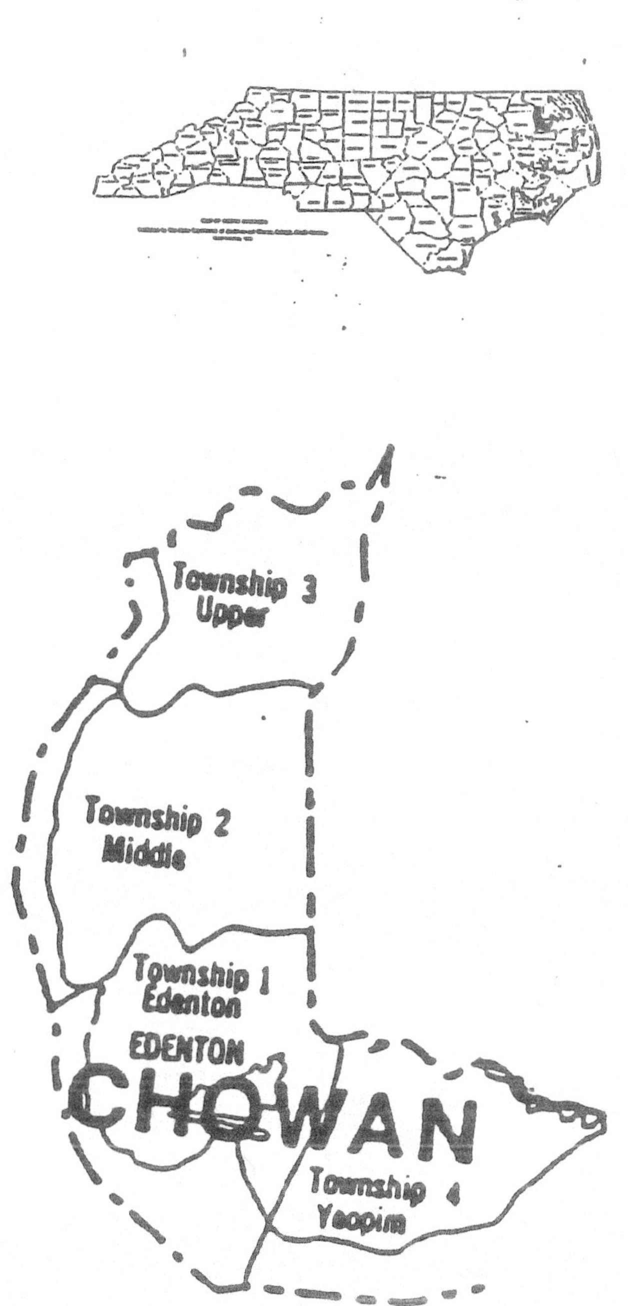

24	CHOWAN COUNTY SS993	WHITES	BLACKS	AGGREGATE
24 EDE	EDENTON	272	549	821
24 MID	MIDDLE GROUND	181	82	263
24 UPP	UPPER GROUND	162	45	207
24	CHOWAN TOTALS	615	676	1,219

[There were no township descriptions found for this county.]

Edenton Precinct. Note at the beginning of the Edenton book reads as follows:

Blacks 537
Blacks Rejected
1. Bond Chas
2. Crasy Jacob
3. Davis Harry
4. Jones Wm
5. Moor Chas
6. Skinner Jacob
7. Coffield Rubin
Did not take the Oath

Whites 261
Whites Rejected
1. Badham Wm Did not take the oath
2. Evans Thos " " " " "
3. Hall John " " " " "
4. Skinner Wm R " " " " "
5. Waff T J " " " " "
6. White Peter F " " " " "

Hackett S Holland Chal but accepted

Note at the end of the book reads as follows:

Names of Whites Rejected

1. W E Burton
2. Wm Badham
3. Thos Evans
4. John Hall
5. Richard Keough
6. Richard Keough Second time
7. Geo B McDowell
8. J W Rogersson
9. Chas E Robinson
10. Wm R Skinner
11. T J Waff
12. Peter F White

Names of Blacks Rejected

1. Jacob Skinner
2. Haywood Pettigrew
3. Elias B White

Board: T T Brice, D V Etheridge, J A Beebe 28 Sep 1867

Middle Ground Precinct. Note at the beginning of Middle Ground book reads as follows:

Whites Rejected
1. Holly David A Did not take the Oath
2. Leary West " " " " "
3. Simpson Henderson " " " " "
4. Goodwin Miles Rejected

Joseph Z Pratt Chm, J A Beebe, Sylvester Dunston 28 April 1867
Board: T T Brice, D V Etheridge, J A Beebe 26 Sep 1867

Upper Ground Precinct.

Board: T T Brice, D C Etheridge, J A Beebe 28 Sep 1867
Joseph Z Pratt Chm, J A Beebe, Sylvester Dunston 25 April 1868

North Carolina Extant Voter Registrations of 1867
CLAY COUNTY

Clay County was formed in 1861 from Cherokee County. It is in the western part of the State, bounded by the State of Georgia and Cherokee and Macon Counties. Portions of the county were annexed from Macon in 1872, and the boundary lines between Clay and Cherokee were adjusted in 1883, 1885, and after an annexation of part of Cherokee in 1891, finally settled in 1897. The present area is 219 square miles.

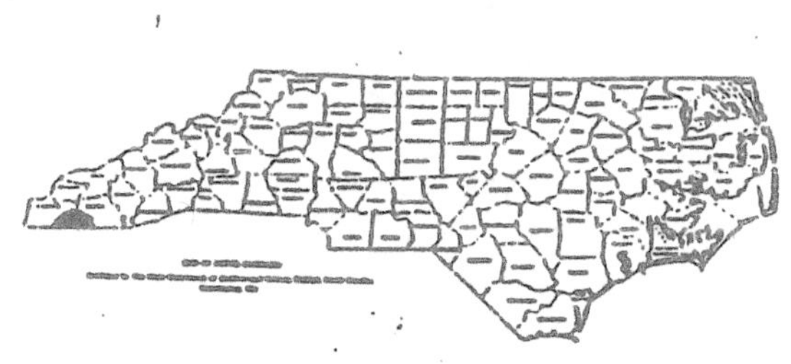

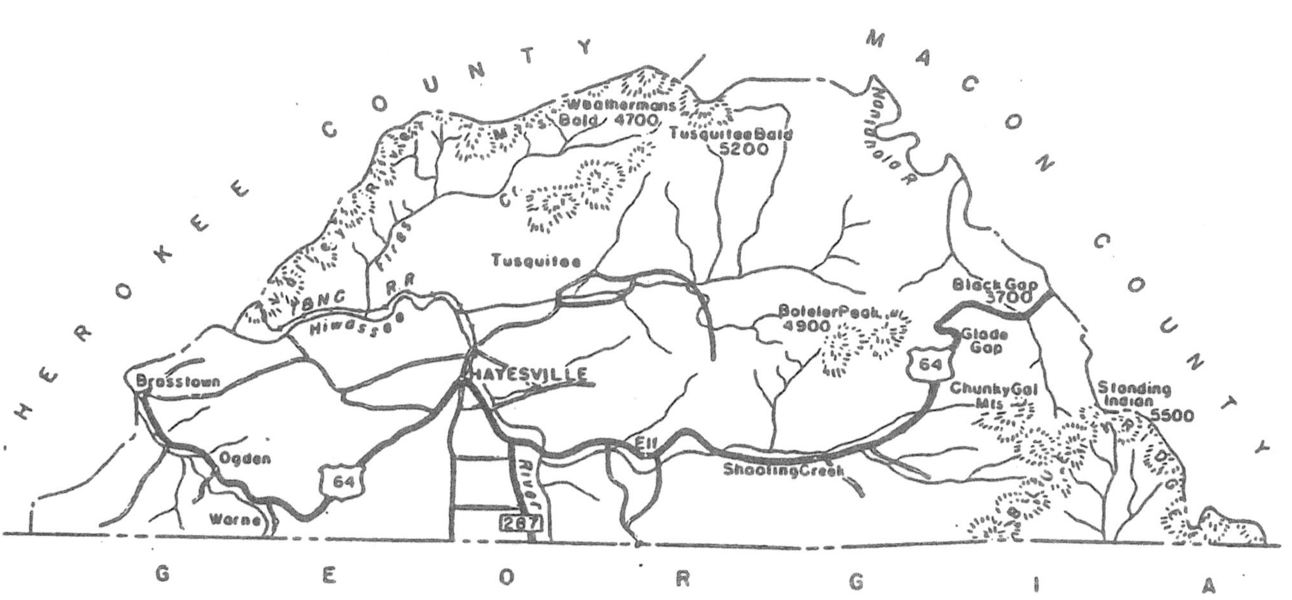

25	CLAY COUNTY SS994	WHITES	BLACKS	AGGREGATE
25 HAY	HAYESVILLE	198	5	203
25 PIN	PINE LOG	27	0	27
25 SHO	SHOOTING CREEK	138	5	143
25 TUS	TUSQUITEE	73	4	77
25	CLAY COUNTY TOTALS	336	14	450

Clay County Township Descriptions

Hayesville Township. Beginning on the north side of Hiwassee River on the Cherokee and Clay line thence up said river to the mouth of Sweet Water Creek crossing the river and up said creek near Center Ledford's including said Ledford thence south west to the top of the mountain between Sweet water and Brasstown then along the top of the ridge to near Wm. Fleming's thence a south east direction down said Fleming's Branch to the mouth; said Fleming living in the forks of said Branch and will therefore take choice of townships. Thence south so as not to include Alfred Patton & Albert Phillips to the Ga. line, thence east with said line to the Hiwassee River thence down said river to the Island in A Barnard's field. Thence running to the south east corner of W.H. McClure's land thence north with said land line to the top of the ridge that divides Downings Creek and Bristol's Branch, thence around the ridge so as to include said Branch to the corner of John C. Moore's and A.O. Lyon land, thence north crossing Tusquittee Creek & continuing north (so as not to include J.H. Johnson's land) to the Cherokee County line thence west with said line to the beginning.
Board: H W Penland, Allen Sherer, S J Bell 13 Sep 1867

Pine Log Precinct. [There was no township by this name in 1869.]
Board: H M Penland Ch, Allen Sherer, S N Bell 13 Sep 1867

Shooting Creek Township. Beginning on the top of the mountain above Jason McClure's and runs with the Tusquittee Township line east to the Macon County line thence with said line south to the Georgia line, thence with said line west to the corner of Hiwassee Township thence with said Hiwassee Township line to the beginning.
Board: J M Galloway Ch, Amos Ledford, Charles Moore 12 Sep 1867

Tusquittee Township. Beginning on top of the ridge between N.W. Moore's and Stamey's then with the Hayesville Township line a south direction to the Cherokee County line, thence east with said line to the Macon County line, thence with said line to the dividing ridge between Tusquittee and Shooting Creek thence with said dividing ridge to the beginning.
Board: J M Galloway Ch, Amos Ledford, Charles Moore 14 Sep 1867

Brasstown Township. Beginning at the mouth of Sweet Water Creek and running up the said creek near Center Ledford's so as to leave said Ledford in the Hayesville township thence a south west course to the top of the mountain dividing Brasstown waters and Sweet Waters thence along the top of said mountain in a south east direction to near William Fleming's thence a south east course down said Fleming's branch to the mouth at A. Patton's including said Patton; thence sounth east so as to include Albert Phillips, thence south to the Georgia line. Thence west with said line to the Cherokee County line thence with the Cherokee and Clay line to the Hiwassee River thence up said river to the beginning. [There was no voting precinct by this name in 1867.]

Hiwassee Township. Beginning on Hiwassee River at the Georgia line down said river to the Hayesville Township line, thence with said line to the top of the ridge between N.W. Moore's and Stamey's thence with the to top of said ridge to the top of the mountain above Jason McClure's thence south so as to include the lands of Riley Jones and C M Penland to the Georgia line near John Loyd's thence west with said line to the beginning. [There was no voting precinct by this name in 1867.]

CLEVELAND COUNTY

Cleveland was formed in 1841 from Rutherford and Lincoln Counties. It is in the southwestern section of the State, bounded by South Carolina and Rutherford, Burke, Lincoln, and Gaston Counties. Parts of Rutherford were annexed in 1841 and 1845, and parts of Gaston in 1915, 1917, and 1921.

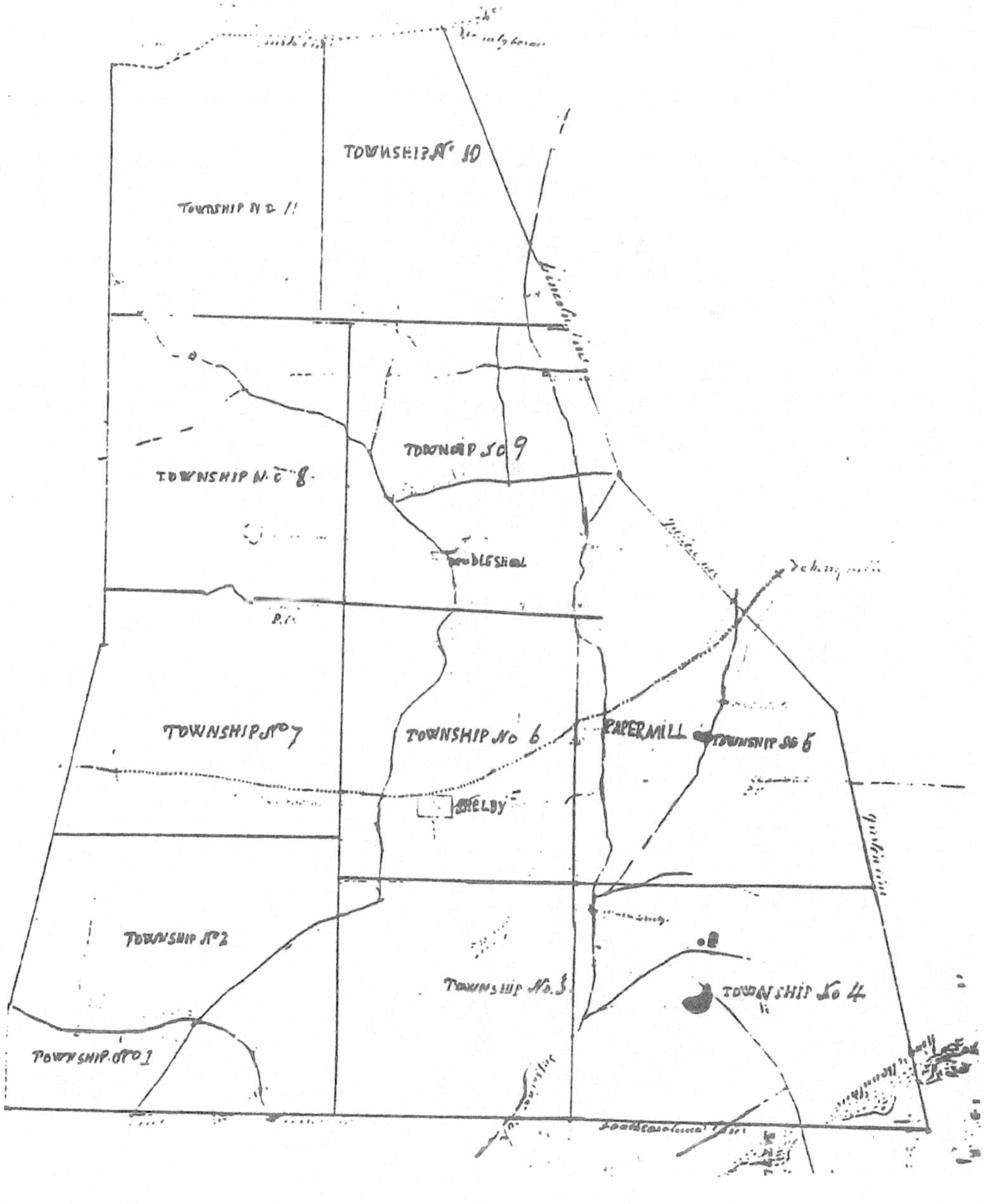

North Carolina Extant Voter Registrations of 1867
CLEVELAND COUNTY

26	CLEVELAND COUNTY SS995-6	WHITES	BLACKS	AGGREGATE
26 BLA	BLANTONS	145	25	170
26 BOR	BORDERS STORE	104	46	150
26 BUR	BURTOWN	96	27	123
26 CAR	CARPENTERS	83	23	106
26 GOF	GOFORTHS	131	35	166
26 GRI	GRIGGS	162	46	208
26 HOL	HOLLAND'S MILL	75	11	86
26 MOO	MOORESBORO	132	15	147
26 MOU	MOUTH OF SANDY RIVER	103	14	117
26 PEE	PEELERS	103	22	125
26 SHE	SHELBY	286	97	383
26 SWA	SWANS	57	15	72
26 WAR	WARLICK	136	19	155
26	CLEVELAND TOTALS	1,613	395	2,008

The board consisting of P D Grigg, Chm, J W Williams, and L S Wright registered voters in the following precincts and signed books on the dates given:

Blanton's 9 & 10 Sep 1867 | Griggs 23 & 24 Aug 1867
Borders Store 19 & 20 Sep 1867 | Peelers 13 Sep 1867
Carpenters 21 & 22 Aug 1867 | Warlick 4 & 5 Sep 1867

The board consisting of John Y Aydlotte, N D Davis, and L A Botts registered voters in the following precincts and signed books on the dates given:

Burtown 28 Sep 1867 | Moorsboro 25 Sep 1867
Goforth 26 Sep 1867 | Mouth of Sandy River 28 Sep 1867
Holland's Mill 25 Sep 1867 | Shelby 26 Sep 1867
Swans 26 Sep 1867

North Carolina Extant Voter Registrations of 1867
CRAVEN COUNTY

Craven, first called Archdale, was later renamed for Lord Craven, one of the Lords Proprietors of Carolina. It is in the eastern part of the State, bounded by Carteret, Jones, Lenoir, Pitt, Beaufort, and Pamlico Counties. Many other courties were formed from Craven: Carteret in 1722, New Hanover in 1729, Johnston in 1746, Jones in 1778. Parts of Beaufort were annexed in 1757 and 1801. Other counties annexed parts of Craven: Dobbs in 1764; Pitt in 1787; Lenoir in 1798, 1808, and 1819; and Greene in 1801. Boundary lines were established between Carteret and Craven in 1809, 1883, and again in 1885; between Craven and Beaufort in 1851 and 1852. Parts of Craven and Beaufort formed Pamlico in 1872 with more land from Craven in 1875.

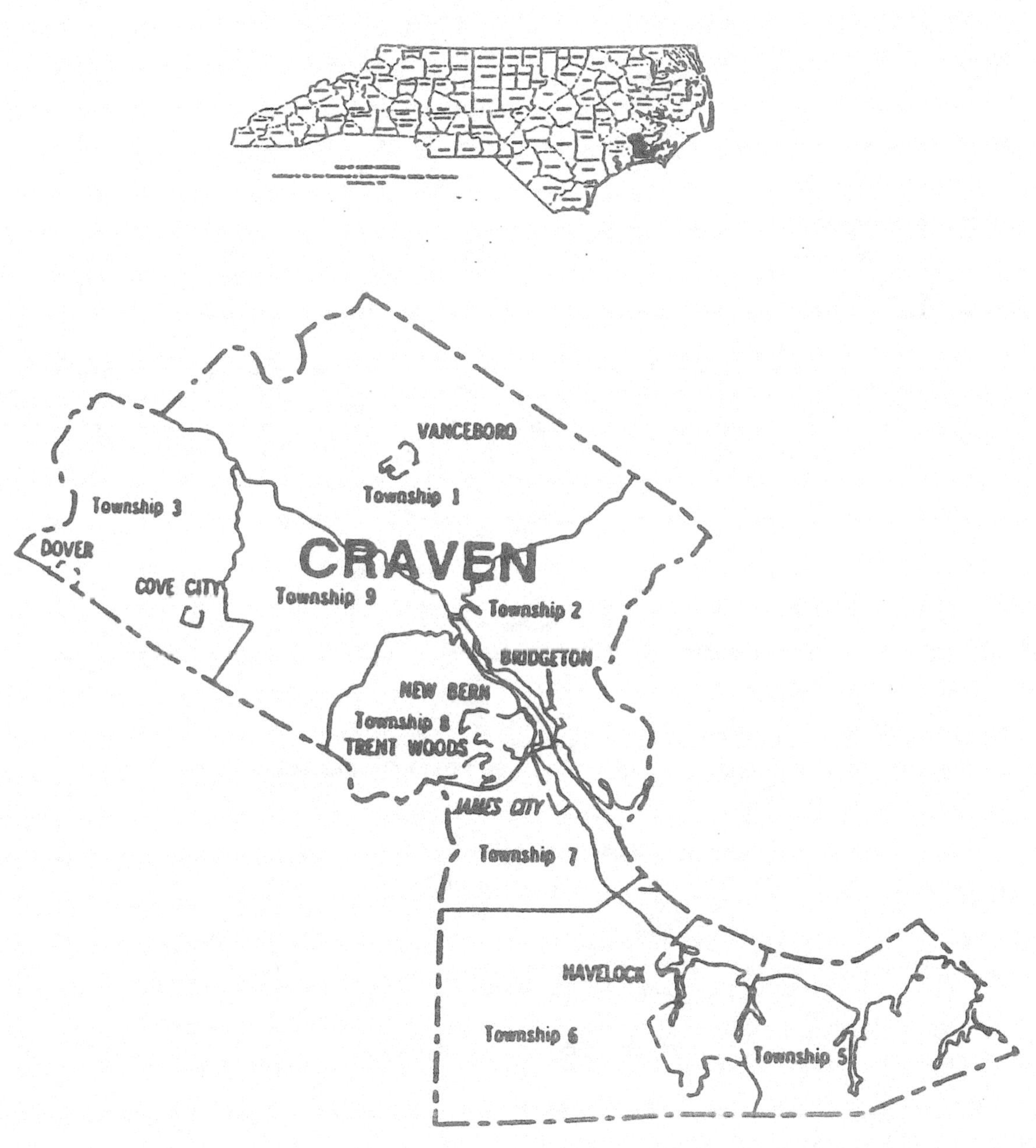

28	CRAVEN COUNTY SS999-11	WHITES	BLACKS	AGGREGATE
28 01A	1ST book 1	221	162	383
28 01B	1ST book 2	76	31	107
28 02N	2ND	131	126	257
28 03A	3RD book 1	92	477	569
28 03B	3RD book 2	20	41	61
28 04A	4TH book 1	35	729	764
28 04B	4TH book 2	23	93	116
28 05A	5TH book 1	6	604	610
28 05B	5TH book 2	2	30	32
28 06T	6TH	120	132	252
28 07T	7TH	95	131	226
28 08T	8TH	77	97	174
28 09T	9TH	69	232	304
28 10T	10TH	85	226	311
28 11T	11TH	220	124	344
28 12T	12TH	61	41	102
28 13T	13TH	94	13	107
28 14T	14TH	134	41	175
28 15T	15TH	98	45	143
28 16T	16TH	221	99	320
28 17T	17TH	53	6	59
28	CRAVEN TOTALS	1933	3480	5416

The board consisting of N P Angen, H P Doane, and R Tucker registered voters in the following precincts and signed books on the date given:

First 26 Sep 1867
Second 26 Sep 1867
Third 26 Sep 1867
Fourth 26 Sep 1867
Fifth 26 Sep 1867
Sixth 26 Sep 1867

The board consisting of C A Nelson, Fredk D Shlachter, M D Hill registered voters in the following precincts and signed books on the date given:

First (2nd bk) 9 Nov 1867
Seventh 25 Sep 1867
Eighth 9 Nov 1867
Ninth 9 Nov 1867
Tenth 9 Nov 1867
Eleventh 9 Nov 1867
Twelfth (Little Creek) 9 Nov 1867

The board consisting of E C Tunis, J W Day, and W H Johnson registered voters in the following precincts and signed books on the date given:

Thirteenth 25 Sep 1867
Fourteenth 25 Sep 1867
Fifteenth 25 Sep 1867
Sixteenth 25 Sep 1867
Seventeenth 25 Sep 1867

Craven County Township Descriptions

[Since the precincts numbered 17 with no names given, there is a question which township refers to which precinct.]

CRAVEN COUNTY

We the undersigned, composing the Board of Commissioners of the County of Craven, do hereby certify that we have divided the same into nine townships which are bounded and described as follows:

No. 1. Beginning on the Neuse River at the Pitt County line, and running along said line to the intersection of the Beaufort County line, thence along Beaufort County line to the road to Blount's Creek on said line, thence down said road to Little Swift Creek, thence along said Creek to Big Swift Creek, thence down Big Swift Creek to Neuse River, thence up Neuse River to the Pitt County line, the beginning.

No. 2. Beginning at the mouth of Big Swift Creek on Neuse River, and running up Big Swift Creek to Little Swift Creek, thence along and up Little Swift Creek to Blount's Creek Road, thence along said road to the Beaufort County line, thence along said county line to the Old Pamlico Road, thence along said road to Neuse River, near Wilkinson's Point, thence up Neuse River to Big Swift Creek, the beginning.

No. 3. Beginning at the intersection of the Beaufort County line and the Old Pamlico Road, and running along the Beaufort County line and the Old Pamlico Road, and running along the Beaufort County line to the head of Jones' Bay, thence down Jones' Bay to Bay River, thence up Bay River to Bay River Mills, thence up Bay River Road to the Old Pamlico Road, thence up said road to Beaufort County line, the beginning.

No. 4. Beginning at the intersection of the Bay River Road and the Old Pamlico Road, and running along the Bay River Road to Bay River Mills, thence down Bay River to Pamlico Sound, thence along said Sound to Neuse River, thence along and up Neuse River to the Old Pamlico Road, thence up said road to the beginning.

No. 5. Beginning at the mouth of Hancock's Creek and running down Neuse River to Turnaghin Bay, thence up Turnaghin Bay to the Carteret County line, thence along said County line to Hancock's Creek, thence down said Creek to Neuse River, the beginning.

No. 6. Beginning at the mouth of Otter Creek and running down Neuse River to the mouth of Hancock's Creek, thence up said Creek to the Carteret County line, thence along the said county line to the west prong of Brice's Creek, thence down said creek to the intersection of the Pollocksville Road, thence along said road to the old Beaufort Road, thence along and with said Beaufort Road to Otter Creek, thence down said Creek to Neuse River, the beginning.

No. 7. Beginning at the Jones County line on Trent River and running down said River to Neuse River, thence down Neuse River to the mouth of Otter Creek, thence up Otter Creek to the Beaufort Road, thence up said road to the Pollocksville Road to Brice's Creek, thence up and with Brice's Creek to the Jones County line, thence along said county line to Trent River, the beginning.

No. 8. Beginning at the mouth of Bachelor's Creek and running down Neuse River to Trent River, thence up Trent River to the mouth of Deep Gully Branch, thence up Deep Gully Branch to the head of Bachelor's Creek, thence down said creek to Neuse River, the beginning.

No. 9. Beginning at the Lenoir County line on Neuse River, and running down said River to the mouth of Bachelor's Creek, thence up Bachelor's Creek to its head, thence direct from said Creek to Deep Gully branch, thence down Deep Gully branch to the junction with the Jones County line, thence along and with said county line to the Lenoir County line, thence along said Lenoir County line to Neuse River, the beginning.

In testimony whereof, we have hereunto set our hands and affixed the official seal of the county, in New Berne, this 30th day of November A.D. 1868. E.H. Stanly, Act. Chm., John L. Smith, Ethelbert Hubbs.

North Carolina Extant Voter Registrations of 1867

CUMBERLAND COUNTY

Cumberland was formed in 1754 from Bladen. It was settled by many of the Scottish Highlanders who had been defeated at the Battle of Culloden. It is in the southeastern section of the State, bounded by Sampson, Bladen, Robeson, Hoke, Harnett, and Johnston Counties. There have been many boundary changes between Cumberland and contiguous counties. Wake was formed from Johnston, Cumberland, and Orange in 1770; Moore in 1784; Harnett in 1855; and Hoke in 1911 from Cumberland and Robeson. Much land was annexed from Bladen in 1789 and 1824 and from Robeson in 1791.

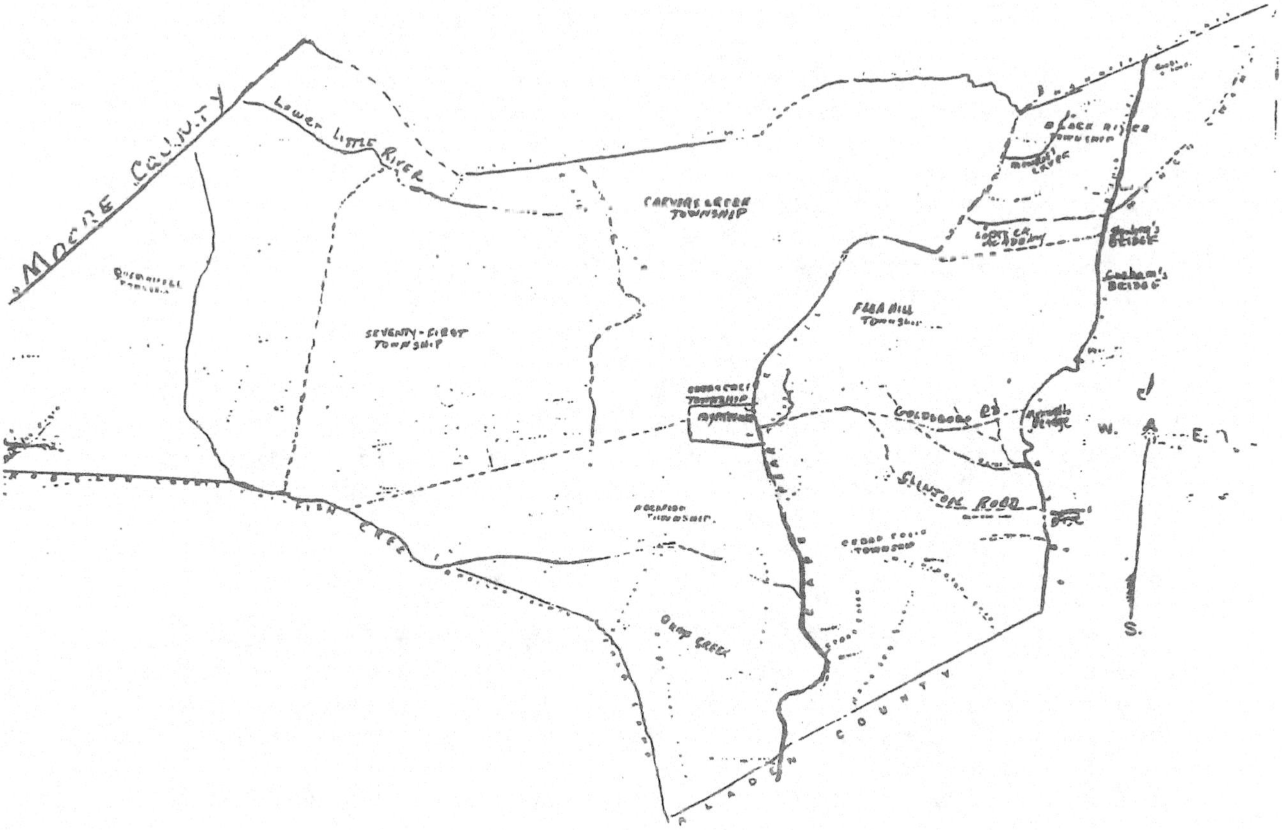

North Carolina Extant Voter Registrations of 1867
CUMBERLAND COUNTY

29	CUMBERLAND CO SS997-8	WHITES	BLACKS	AGGREGATE
29 BLA	BLACK RIVER	79	25	104
29 CAR	CARVERS CREEK	99	117	216
29 CED	CEDAR CREEK	131	40	171
29 FA1	FAYETTEVILLE 1	560	802	1,362
29 FA2	FAYETTEVILLE 2	101	84	185
29 FLE	FLEA HILL	123	149	272
29 GRA	GRAYS CREEK	109	161	270
29 LOC	LOCKS CREEK	154	108	262
29 MON	MONROES	35	32	67
29 QUW	QUWHIFFLE	74	38	112
29 ROC	ROCKFISH	164	44	208
29 SEV	SEVENTY FIRST	131	105	236
29	CUMBERLAND TOTALS	1,760	1,705	3,465

Cumberland County Township Descriptions

Black River Township. Beginning at Kyle's Landing on Cape Fear River thence the road leading to Mrs. Mary William and following said road to Starling's bridge on Black River then up Black River to the confluance of said river and Mingo Swamp. Then up the channel of said Swamp to the corner of Johnston County thence with the line of Harnett County to Cape Fear River at the mouth of Lower Little River thence down Cape Fear to the beginning.

D.G. McDuffie, Surveyor

Board: David McDuffie, James Bowars, W A Mann Chairman 1 Oct 1867

Carver's Creek Township. Beginning at the mouth of the big Fully in Strange's plantation below his fishery thence up Cape Fear River to the mouth of Little River thence up said river to Elliott's bridge thence with the county line to the Fayetteville and Western Plank road thence down said road to the 9 mile post (excluding Daniel McDearmed and Manchester) thence to the head of Little Cross Creek thence down said creek to Cross Creek Township at Martine's vineyard thence with that line to Porterfield's old mill on the other prong of Cross Creek thence a direct line to the beginning.

Board: T A Byrnes Chm, Jno C Collahan, Jno G Minor 1 Oct 1867

Cedar Creek Township. Beginning on Cape Fear River on the Bladen County line nearly opposite the mouth of Willis Creek thence following the Bladen County line to Black River thence up said river to Maxwell's old bridge thence with the old Scotch road to Cape Fear River at the mouth of Lord's Creek thence down Cape Fear River to the beginning.

[This township includes the old districts of Cedar Creek and Lock's Creek.]

Board: James Boman Chm, David McDuffie, Robt Royal 1 Oct 1867

Flea Hill Township. Beginning at Kyle's Landing on Cape Fear River thence following the road leading to Mrs. Mary Williams to Starling's Bridge on Black River thence down Black River to the old Maxwell Bridge thence following the old "Scotch road" to the Clarenden Bridge on Cape Fear River, thence up said river to the beginning.

Board: James Boman, David McDuffie, W A Maner Chm 1 Oct 1867

Gray's Creek Precinct. [There was no township by this name, but it may have been part of Rockfish in 1869.]
Board: Jno C Collahan, Jno G Minor, T A Byrnes Chm 1 Oct 1867

Locks Creek Precinct. [Part of Cedar Creek, q.v., in 1868.]
1 Oct 1867 Board: James Boman, David McDuffie, W A Maner Chm

John Monroe's Precinct. [There was no township by this name in 1869.]
Board: M N Leary Jr Chm, John S Leary, Walker Pearce 30 Sep 1867

Quewhiffle Township. Beginning at the Robeson County line on Big Rockfish at the mulatto road thence with the Robeson County line to Drowning Creek thence up Drowning Creek to the Moore County line thence with said line to the corner of Harnett County on the William's road thence with said road to the ford on Hector's Creek thence down said creek to Little River thence up the river to the mouth of Deep Creek thence with the Mulatto road to the beginning.
Board: M N Leary Jr Chm, John S Leary, Walker Pearce 30 Sep 1867

Rockfish Township. Beginning at the lower corner of Cross Creek township on Cape Fear River it being the old district corner thence down Cape Fear River to the Bladen County line near the mouth of Willis Creek thence with the Robeson County line to Johnson's bridge on Big Rockfish Creek thence with the line of Seventy First to Branson's old mill on Blount's Creek thence down said creek to Mims pond thence to the fork thence S 70 E to the beginning. D.G. McDuffie, Surveyer Cumberland Co.
Board: Jno C Collahan, Jno G Minor, T A Byrnes Chm 1 Oct 1867

Seventy First Township. Beginning at Branson's old mill on Blounts Creek at the turnpike road thence direct to Johnson's bridge on Big Rockfish thence up said creek to the Mulatto road thence with said road to Deep Creek thence to the mouth of Deep Creek thence down Little River to the mouth of Hector's Creek thence up said creek to the William's road thence with the Harnett County line to the Fayetteville and Western Plank road thence down said road including the residence of Daniel McDearmed and the village of Manchester to the 9 mile post thence to the head of Little Cross Creek and down said creek to the line of Cross Creek Township at Martin's vineyard thence s 20 m to the 2 mile post on the plank road thence to the center plank road at Blount's Creek thence down Blount's Creek to the beginning.
Board: M N Leary Jr Chm, John S Leary, Walker Pearce 30 Sep 1867

Cumberland County Townships that were not a part of the voting districts in 1867:

Cross Creek Township. Beginning at the mouth of a large gully on Cape Fear River in Strange's plantation thence down the river to the corner of Rockfish Township near the lower corner of the Town of Fayetteville thence N 70 W to the fork of Mims Millpond thence up Blount's Creek to the centre Plank road thence to the 2 milepost on the Western plank road thence a direct line to Porterfield's old mill on a prong of Cross Creek thence direct to the beginning.

Fayetteville Books 1 and 2. [There is no separate township description for the town of Fayetteville. It may have been included with Cross Creek.]
Board: John C Collahan, Jno G Minor, T A Byrnes Chm 1 Oct 1867

North Carolina Extant Voter Registrations of 1867

CURRITUCK COUNTY

Currituck County was formed in 1670 as a precinct in Albemarle County. It is in the northeastern section of the State and is bounded by the Atlantic Ocean, Albemarle Sound, Camden County, and the state of Virginia. From its formation in 1670 until 1873, three other counties were formed from the original county and parts of Chowan, Bertie, and Pasquotank: Tyrrell (1729), Hyde (1745 and 1823), and Dare (1870). The establishment of the Currituck-Camden dividing line was authorized in 1784.

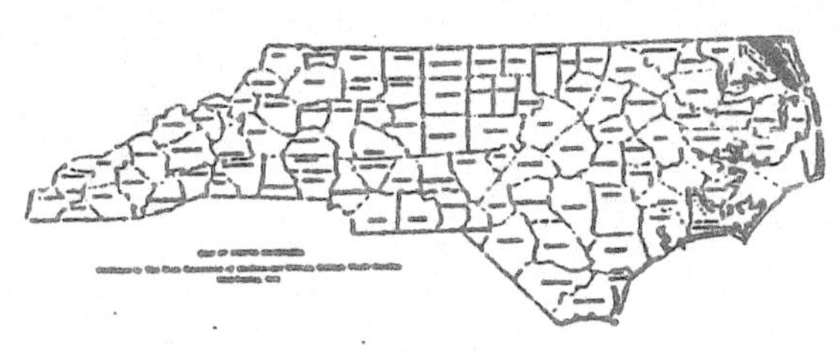

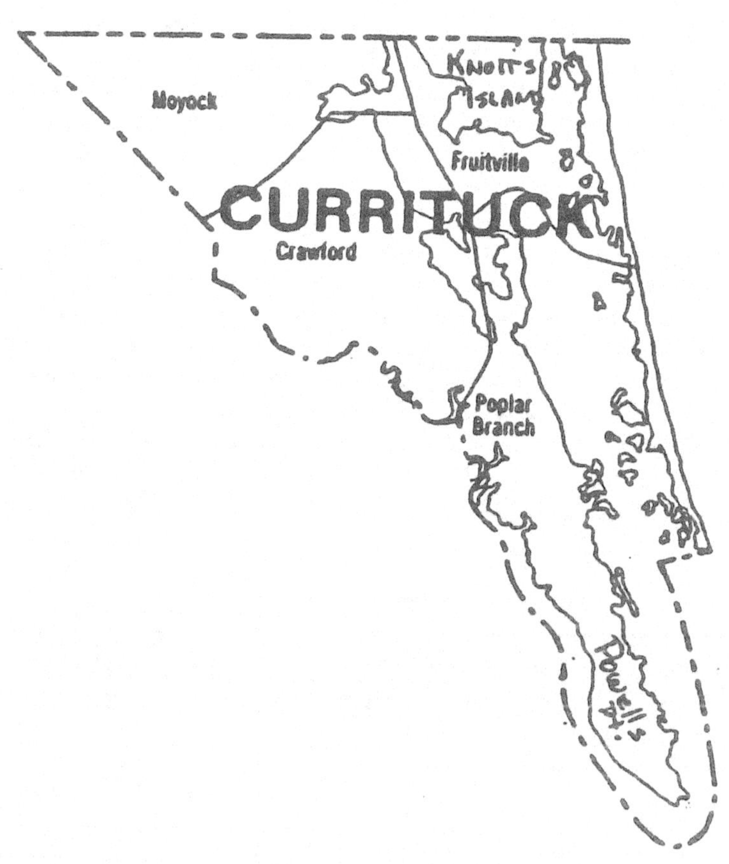

30	CURRITUCK COUNTY SS1003	WHITES	BLACKS	AGGREGATE
30 COI	COINJOCK	78	16	94
30 CUR	CURRITUCK COURT HOUSE	114	67	181
30 GIB	GIBBS WOODS	33	6	39
30 IND	INDIAN RIDGE	183	94	277
30 KNO	KNOT ISLAND	104	7	111
30 MOY	MOYOCK	121	72	193
30 NAR	NARROW SHORE	41	6	47
30 NOR	NORTH BANKS	78	6	84
30 POP	POPLAR BRANCH	82	30	112
30 POW	POWELLS POINT	72	20	92
30 ROA	ROANOKE ISLAND	96	82	178
30 TUL	TULLS CREEK	74	14	88
30	CURRITUCK TOTALS	1,232	526	1,758

Currituck County Township Descriptions

The county is so formed, being intersected by water courses, and by islands detached from the mainland, the commissioners, N.E. Baxter, Chm. Board Commiss., have thought it best, for the convenience of the inhabitants, to divide it into five townships as follows:

Moyock Township. Commencing on North Landing River on the Virginia line, following said river and Currituck Sound in a southern direction up to a place known as the Launch, thence west across Tulls Creek bay to the mouth of Tulls Creek thence up said creek to the head of New Bridge creek thence west to the Camden Co. line, thence along said county line to the Virginia line, thence along said line to the beginning. This Township includes the precincts of Moyock, Tulls Creek and Gibbs Woods.
Board: W H Cowell, Jno W Evans, Richard Etheridge 14 Sep 1867

Gibbs Woods Precinct 13 Sep 1867 Tulls Creek Precinct 15 Sep 1867

Poplar Branch Township. Commencing on the Atlantic Ocean at the south line of Fruitville Township running south along said ocean to Caffees Inlet from thence a due west course across the beach to Currituck Sound thence south across said sound to the south end of Powells Point, thence around said point to Camden Co. line, thence down said line to the south boundary of Crawford Township, thence from the west mouth of Albemarle & Chesapeake canal through said canal across Currituck Sound touching the north end of Churches Island to the head of Ship Bay, thence from the head of Ship Bay running a due east course to the beginning. This township embraces Narrow Shore, Church's Island, Poplar Branch, Powells Point and that portion of the beach beginning from the head of Ship Bay running south to Caffees Inlet.
Board: Robert S D Holbrooke, Samuel Dowdy, George Baum 19 Sep 1867
Narrow Shore Precinct 19 Sep 1867 Powells Point Precinct 19 Sep 1867

Crawfold Township. Beginning at the Launch, binding Currituck sound, running in a southern direction to the Albemarle & Chesapeake canal, thence down said canal to North River, thence down said river to the Camden line, thence along said line until it intersects the line of Moyock township. This township includes the precincts of the Court House & Indian Ridge, and that portion Coinjock precinct lying north of the canal. [There was no election precinct by this name in 1867.]

Coinjock Precinct Board: Robert S D Holbrooke, Samuel Dowdy, George Baum
19 Sep 1867

Currituck Court House Board: W H Cowell, Jno W Evans, Richard Etheridge
16 Sep 1867

Interleaved between the letters M and N of Tulls Creek was the following form:

STATE OF NORTH CAROLINA)
County of Currituck)

Personally appeared before me .. Thos G. Munden.. A Manager of Election for .. C. H. .. election precinct, 1st registration precinct, County aforesaid. .. A. B......., who, being by me duly sworn, did depose and say that deponent was duly accepted as a qualified voter by the Board of Registrars for the County of .. Camden...., and was registered by said Board at ... Old Trap.... in said last named County: that this deponent has resided in this County ten days next previous to this election, and has not previously voted at such election.

Sworn to before me this ...21...)
day of ... April...., 1868)

Thos. G. Munden
Manager of Election,
C House Precinct.

Penciled note says "go by this form vary according to circumstances."

Indian Ridge Precinct Board: W H Cowell, Jno W Evans, Richard Etheridge
16 Sep 1867.

Fruitville Township. Commencing on the Atlantic Ocean at the Virginia line, running south along said ocean to a point due east from Ship Bay in Currituck Sound, thence running across the beach due west to said bay, thence across Currituck Sound to the Launch, thence following the eastern boundary of Moyock Township to the Virginia line, thence along said line to the beginning. This township embraces Knotts Island, Mackeys Island, Crow Island, Morse's Point, Monkey Island, and that portion of the beach land, from the Virginia line south to the head of Ship Bay.

Knotts Island Precinct Board: W H Cowell, Jno W Evans, Richard Etheridge
13 Sep 1867

Nags Head Township. Commencing at Caffees Inlet on the Atlantic Ocean running south along said ocean to the Hyde Co. line, thence across the beach along the Hyde Co. line to Pamlico Sound, thence north up said sound to the south end of Roanoke Island, thence up Croatan Sound along the west side of said island, thence across the mouth of Albemarle Cound, thence up Currituck Sound to Caffees Inlet, thence a due east course to the beginning. This township embraces North Banks, Roanoke Island, Nags Head, and Bodys Island. [There was no voting precinct by this name in 1867.]

North Banks Precinct Board: Robert S D Holbrooke, Samuel Dowdy, George Baum
19 Sep 1867

Roanoke Island Precinct Board: Robert S D Holbrooke, Samuel Dowdy, George Baum
19 Sep 1867

North Carolina Extant Voter Registrations of 1867
DAVIDSON COUNTY

Davidson was formed in 1822 from Rowan. It is in the central section of the State and is bounded by Randolph, Montgomery, Rowan, Davie, Forsyth, and Guilford counties. Acts to amend the act establishing Davidson County were passed in 1822 and 1835, setting the boundary line between Davidson and Rowan. An act to empower the commissioners of Randolph and Davidson to establish the dividing line was passed in 1871. A part of Davidson was annexed to Forsyth County in 1889 and again in 1921.

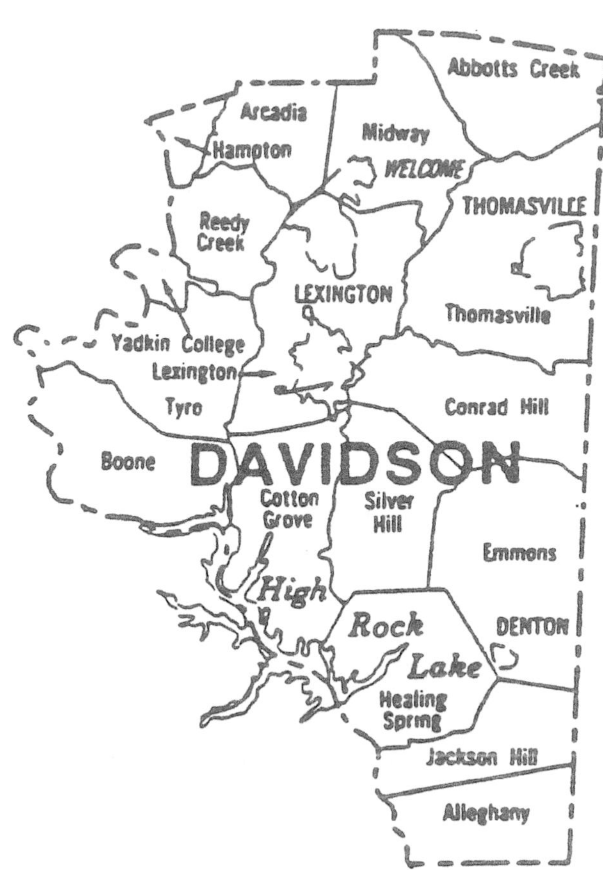

32	DAVIDSON COUNTY PRECINCTS SS1004-1005	WHITES	BLACKS	AGGREGATE
32 BRO	BROWNSTOWN	128	18	146
32 CLE	CLEMMONSVILLE	101	36	137
32 COT	COTTON GROVE	133	41	174
32 JAC	JACKSON HILL	235	47	282
32 LEE	LEES	93	2	95
32 LEX	LEXINGTON	553	278	831
32 LOF	LOFLIN	138	14	152
32 POS	POSSUMTOWN	234	47	281
32 SHE	SHELTONS	210	20	230
32 THO	THOMASVILLE	385	90	475
32 TYR	TYRO	177	97	274
32 YAD	YADKIN INST.	45	23	68
32	DAVIDSON TOTALS	2432	713	3145

[Box SS1006 is labeled Davidson County, but the book inside are Duplin County. Since precinct names and township descriptions do not match, precincts have been grouped according to registrars.]

The Board, consisting of John T Cramer, Chm, Philip Ball, and Richard Ayeres, registered voters in the following precincts and signed the books on the dates given:

Browntown Precinct 25 Sep 1867
Clemmonsville Precinct 25 Sep 1867
Possumtown Precinct 25 Sep 1867
Sheltons Precinct 25 Sep 1867
Thomasville Precinct 25 Sep 1867
Yadkin Inst. Precinct 25 Sep 1867

The Board, consisting of L E Johnson, Wm A Berrier, and J Kinney, Chm, registered voters in the following precincts and signed the books on the dates given:

Cotton Grove Precinct 12 Sep 1867
Jackson Hill Precinct 14 Sep 1867
Lees Precinct 19 Sep 1867
Lexington Precinct 24 Sep 1867
Loflin Precinct 17 Sep 1867
Tyro Precinct 10 Sep 1867

Davidson County Township Descriptions

Abbotts Creek Township. Beginning at the corner of Davidson Co. where Guilford and Forsyth corners running thence west with the Forsyth line near Mount Vernon thence south with the Cuecumber Road as said Militia line to Madison Lindsays thence east to the old State Road thence with the old state road also with the militia line to the Davidson and Guilford line near Pennsfields Post Office.

Thomasville Township. Beginning on the Guilford line near Pennsfield Post office running thence down the state Road the line between Abbotts Creek and Thomasville Township continuing on with said road to Abbotts Creek thence down said creek with the same to the mouth of Hambys Creek thence up said creek east to Clodfetters sawmill continuing on east with the Asboro Road to George Helpers on the Randolph line thence north with said line to the beginning.

Conrad Hill Township. Beginning on the Randolph line running thence west with the Asboro Road to Clodfetters sawmill on Hamby Creek thence down said creek nearly east to Abbotts Creek thence down Abbotts Creek to David Swings thence east to Mary Amis the old Militia line thence south east to the Three Hat Mountain thence east to the Randolph line near Plummers thence north with said line to the beginning.

Emmans Township. Beginning on the Randolph line near Plummers running thence west to Bosses Branch near David Headricks thence down said branch to William Williams thence southeast to Widow Styers with the old militia line thence east to the Randolph line Siloam Church thence north with the county line to the beginning.

Silver Hill Township. Beginning at the Three Hat Mountain running thence northwest to Mary Smiths thence west to Abbotts Creek thence down the same to the mouth of Jacobs Creek thence up said creek with the miltia line at or near William Workmans on the four mile branch thence up said four mile branch to the fork of Bosses Branch with said militia line thence east to the Three Hat Mountain.

Healing Springs Township. Beginning at Widow Styers running thence northwest to the four mile branch at William Workmans thence west with the militia line down Jacobs Creek to Abbotts Creek thence down said creek to the Yadkin River thence down the River to the mouth of Lick Creek thence up said Cole Lick Creek to Brinkles Ferry Road thence east with said militia line to John Loflins thence north to the beginning.

Jacksons Hill Township. Beginning at Siloam Church on the Randolph line running thence west to Widow Styers thence south with the Big Road to John Loflens thence west with the Brinkles Ferry road to Lick Creek thence down said creek to the Yadkin River thence down said River to James Thayers mill on said River thence east with the old militia line to James Skeens on the Randolph line thence north with said line to the beginning.

Allegany Township. Beginning on the Randolph at James Skeen running thence west with said old militia line to the Yadkin River thence down the river to Stokes ferry Montgomery line thence east to the corner of Davidson County on the Randolph line thence north with said line to the beginning.

Midway Township. Beginning on the Forsyth line at Mount Vernon church running west with said line to a point --- thence west of south to Welks line south to Henry Wagoners thence South of east Abbotts Creek near Pleasant Murfreys line North east with said creek to where the Abbotts Creek Township line crosses said creek thence north west with the Cucumber Road to the beginning.

Arcadia Township. Beginning near Stoners on the Forsyth line and and running thence west with said line to Muddy Creek thence with said creek south west to the --- Yadkin River thence south with said river to a point near G.W. Grimes' thence south of east to Henry Wagoner's thence north with the Midway Township line to the beginning.

Clemmonsville Township. Beginning at Muddy Creek on the Forsyth line and running thence with said line to the Yadkin River thence with said river south east to Muddy Creek thence up Muddy Creek to the beginning.

Yadkin Township. Beginning at a point on the Yadkin River near G.W. Grimes' thence down said river to Fulton Ferry thence south of east with the old militia district line to Waitman's thence north with said militia line to Henry Wagoner's thence north of west with Arcadia Township line to the Yadkin River.

Tyro Township. Beginning at Fultons Ferry on the Yadkin River thence down the said river to Galloway and Kindley's line thence with said line to Kindley's ferry road thence with said road to John Barne's lane thence south east with the old Militia line to Potts's Creek thence north east with said Militia line to Waitman's thence north of West with said Militia line to the beginning on the Yadkin River.

Lexington Township. Beginning at Abbotts Creek near Pleasant Murpheys and running thence north of west with the old Militia line to Henry Wagoner's thence south of west with old Militia line to Potts' Creek thence east to Abbotts Creek thence east of north with said Creek to the beginning.

Cotton Grove Township. Beginning at S--- Mill on Abbotts Creek and running thence west with the Old Militia line to Pott's Creek thence south with said creek to the Yadkin River thence with said river to the mouth of Abbotts Creek thence up said creek to the beginning.

Boone Township. Beginning at the mouth of Potts Creek where it enters into the Yadkin River running thence up said Potts Creek to Holts Mill thence north west with the Old Militia line to the Danville Road in John Barnes lane thence with said road to the fork John Grubbs thence with the old Salem Road to the fork at Elisabeth Wyattes thence with the Kindleys Ferry Road commonly called the Buncome Road to Kindleys & Dr Galloway line thence with said line to the river thence down the river to the beginning.

Commissioners: Wm Loflin, John L. Snider, W. Bodenhamer, B.L. Bukenhite (?) and J.C. Taylor

North Carolina Extant Voter Registrations of 1867
DUPLIN COUNTY

Duplin was formed in 1750 from New Hanover. It is in the eastern section of the State and is bounded by Jones, Onslow, Pender, Sampson, Wayne, and Lenoir counties. Part of New Hanover was annexed to Duplin in 1751 with the authorization for the boundary line in 1766. Part of Duplin was annexed to Johnston in 1777 and Sampson was formed from it in 1784. Since the boundary line between Duplin and Wayne had not been established in 1806, the legislature authorized the establishment of the line according to the acts which established the said counties. The establishment of the dividing lines between the counties of Duplin and Onslow and Duplin and Lenoir were authorized in 1819. In 1824, 1826, 1831, 1833, and as late as 1883 the legislature authorized the dividing line between Duplin and Wayne. The boundary lines between Duplin and Onslow were in contention as they were between Duplin and Wayne for almost as many years, up to 1924.

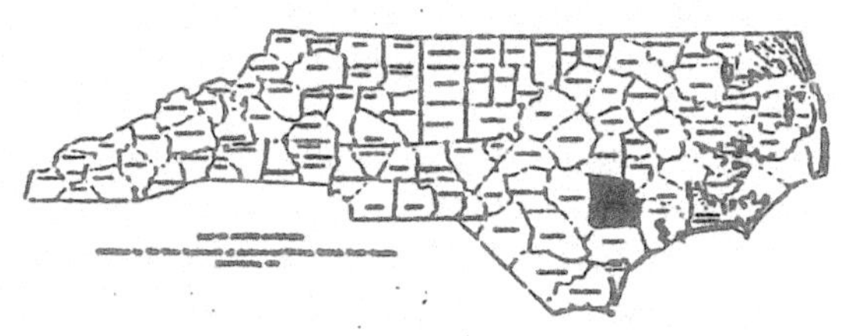

35	DUPLIN COUNTY PRECINCTS SS1006-1007	WHITES	BLACKS	AGGREGATE
35 ALB	ALBERTSONS	90	17	107
35 CYP	CYPRESS CREEK	117	58	175
35 FAI	FAISON'S	98	100	198
35 GLI	GLISSON'S-	64	27	91
35 ISL	ISLAND CREEK	151	98	249
35 KEN	KENANVILLE	207	265	472
35 LIM	LIMESTONE-	161	38	199
35 MAG	MAGNOLIA	229	196	425
35 ROC	ROCKFISH	140	124	264
35 SMI	SMITH'S-	82	42	124
35 WAR	WARSAW	156	143	299
35 WOL	WOLFES CRAPE	119	57	176
35	DUPLIN TOTALS	1,614	1,165	2,779

Albertson's District. Beginning on the Wayne County line at the north east River, then the Wayne line to the Lenoir line --- to the Newbern Road, then that Road to Burncoat then down Burncoat to the north east river then up the road to the beginning.
Board: S B Woodmansee, Henry F Brandis, Edward Martin 30 Sep 1867

Cypress Creek District. Beginning on the Onslow County line then back Swamp Road then the Onslow to the New Hanover County line, then the New Hanover line to the north east River then up the river to the mouth of Muddy Creek, then up Muddy Creek to the Back Swamp Road, then that road to the beginning.
Board: John M Graham, Patrick C Oates 20 Aug 1867

Faison's District. Beginning at the corner of Sampson and Wayne County lines thence with the Wayne line to the head of Bear Marsh then down Bear Marsh to Goshen, down Goshen to the mouth of Nahunga then up Nahunga to Mrs. Cooper's mill race, then the road by Dr. Blount's to the Sampson line then the Sampson line to the beginning.
Board: S B Woodmansee, Henry F Brandis, Edward Martin 30 Sep 1867

Glisson's District. Beginning at Carroll's Point on the southeast River then to the mouth of Goshen then up Goshen to Ward's Bridge, then the main road to Glisson's Crossroads, then a straight line to Kinsey Jones's, then a straight line to the head of Ground nut, then to the beginning.
Board: S B Woodmansee, Henry F Brandis, Edward Martin 30 Sep 1867

[Note at bottom of last page: out of 550 white persons registered in the first registration precinct 230 coult not sign their names.]

Island Creek District. Beginning on the North East River at the mouth of Rockfish Creek then up Rockfish to the Kitty Landing, then a direct line to Rockfish Church then a straight course to the ---- Creek on the Rail Road, then the Rail Road to the yellow cut, then a straight line to Maxwell Creek at the mouth of Beaver dam, then down Maxwell to the North East River, then the river to the beginning.
Board: John N Graham, Daniel Kline, P C Oates 12 Sep 1867

Kenansville District. Beginning at Mrs. Cooper's Mill Race, then down Nahunga to Goshen, down Goshen to the North East River down the River to Murray's landing thence a direct line to the ------ beyond the Widow Carr's, then the road to the Jo. Chasten's ford, then up Maxwell to the head, then to the beginning.
Board: John M Graham, Patrick C Oates 3 Sep 1867

Limestone District. Beginning on the Jones County line at Glade Branch then the Jones to the Onslow County line, then the Onslow line to the Buck Swamp -- then down that road to Muddy Creek then Muddy Creek to the north east River, then up the River to the mouth of Maxwell Creek, then up Maxwell to the Jo. Chasten ford then the road to a point near the Widow Carr's then a direct line to Murray's landing then down the river to the mouth of Glade Branch, then up the branch to the beginning.
Board: S B Woodmansee, Henry F Brandis, Edward Martin Dated 30 Sep 1867

[Note at the beginning of Limestone precinct:
Of 144 white persons registered 80 could not sign their names.]

Magnolia District. Beginning on the Sampson County line, at Beaverdam then the Sampson line to the New Road, then that road to Maxwell's Creek to the mouth of Beaver dam, then a straight line to the yellow cut on the Rail Road, then a straight line to Ben's Creek at Elizabeth Wells's line then down Ben's Creek to Rockfish Creek then down Rockfish to the mouth of Beaver dam, then up Beaverdam to the beginning.
Board: John M Graham, Daniel Klein, Patrick C Oates Dated 27 Aug 1867

Rockfish District. Beginning at the Kitty Landing on Rockfish Creek then the New Hanover to the Sampson County line, then the Sampson line to Beaverdam Creek then down said Creek to Rockfish Creek, then up Rockfish to Ben's Creek then up Ben's Creek to Elizabeth Wells's line, then a straight line to the yellow cut on the Rail Road, then the Rail Road to the head of Fussell's Creek, then a straight line to Rockfish Church, then to the beginning.
Board: John M Graham, Daniel Klim, Patrick C Oates Dated 23 Aug 1867

Smith's District. Beginning on the Lenoir line at the Fayetteville and Newbern Road down the Lenoir to the Jones County line, then that line to Glade branch, down that branch to Limestone Creek, down Limestone to the North East River, then up the River to the mouth of Burncoat, then up Burncoat to the Fayetteville and Newbern Road, then that road to the beginning.
Board: S B Woodmansee, Henry F Brandis, Edward Martin Dated 30 Sep 1867

[There were two notes in the front of the Smith Precinct book, as follows.]

NOTE AT THE BEGINNING OF THE DIRECTIONS TO REGISTRARS:
of 82 white persons registered 32 could not sign their names.
Written at the beginning of SMITHS Precinct:
OF 75 WHITE PERSONS REGISTERED 26 COULD NOT SIGN THEIR NAMES

North Carolina Extant Voter Registrations of 1867
DUPLIN COUNTY

Warsaw District. Beginning on the Sampson line at the New Road then the Sampson line to the road which forms the southern boundary of Faison's District, then that road to Mrs. Cooper's mill race, then a direct course to the head of Maxwell, then down Maxwell to Cicero Bourden's then the New Road to the begining.
Board: John M Graham, Patrick C Oates, H H Foster Dated 30 Aug 1867

Wolfscrape District. Beginning on the Wayne Co. line at the head of Bear Marsh, then the Wayne line to Carroll's Point on the northeast River then a straight line to the head of Ground nut; then a straight line to Kinsey Jones's; then a straight line to Glisson's Cross Roads; then the main road to Ward Bridge, then up Goshen to the mouth of Bear Marsh, then up Bear Marsh to the beginning.
Board: B Woodmansee, H F Brandis, Edward Martin Dated 30 Sep 1867

D T McMillan, C D Hill, John E Fussell, Jno Peterson, D T Best, were the commissioners 17 Dec 1868 who divided the county into townships.

The undersigned citizens of Wolfscrape District, having learned that in laying off the territory of this county the Commissioners had made the main road from Ward's Bridge and Goodson's Bridge to be the dividing line between Wolfscrape and Gilsson's district stated that they would thereby be transferred to Gilsson's district to their very great inconvenience both in relation to schools and elections. They felt the commissioners had been mislead in making the new boundary for the township, and they petitioned to have it changed to read as it does above.

Henry Sullivan	Benjamin Bizzell	W B Bowden
Needham Southerlin	John W Whitfield	Luther Dail
Kinsey Jones	B H Whitfield	John G Arnett
James Dail	C Hill	C C Buchan
Hinson Jones	Henry Garner	Joseph E Kornegay
Alford Dail	Calvin Herring	

The undersigned citizens of Wolfscrape and Glisson's districts recommended that the petition be granted:

David Reaves	Henry Dail	E B Herring
Thaddeus Jones	Benj F Kornegay	Philip L Sumerlin
Haskill Jones	S R Winders	Basil Garner
Samuel Sullivan	F M Garner	Gaston Kelly
Nathian Garner	Jas A Jones	Haywood Glisson
John T Whitfield		

Commissioners: P H Blaylock, W L Kelly, J R Reaves, Watson Jernigan, Simpson Sullivan, F M Keathley, Luke Kornegay

North Carolina Extant Voter Registrations of 1867
EDGECOMBE COUNTY

Edgecombe was formed in 1741 from Bertie. It is in the eastern section of the State is bounded by Martin, Pitt, Wilson, Nash, and Halifax counties. Between 1746 and 1777 three other counties were formed from Edgecombe: Granville (1746), Halifax (1758), and Nash (1777). Other changes in the boundary lines between Tyrrell, Halifax, Martin, Pitt, and Nash occurred in 1741, 1779, 1784, 1793, 1801, 1876, and as late as 1883. Wilson County was formed from it in 1855.

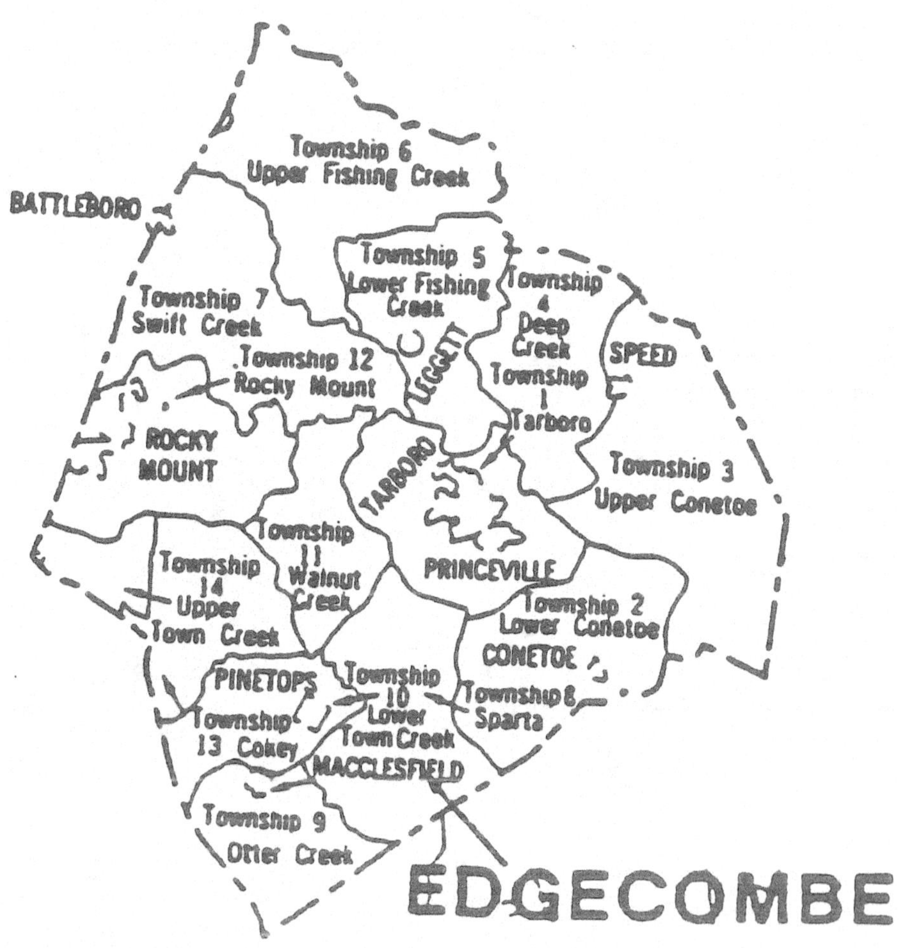

37	EDGECOMBE COUNTY PRECINCTS SS1008-1009	WHITES	BLACKS	AGGREGATE
37 EDW	EDWARDS	88	320	408
37 HIC	HICKORY FORK	68	150	218
37 HIG	HIGH LEVEL	117	230	347
37 HOL	HOLLY GROVE	43	69	112
37 MAN	MANNER HILL	75	225	300
37 PEN	PENDER'S MILL	75	236	311
37 PIN	PINEY GROVE	84	280	364
37 ROB	ROBERTSONS STORE	139	253	388
37 ROC	ROCKY MOUNT	195	361	556
37 SHA	SHARPE'S STORE	96	59	155
37 SPA	SPARTA	98	100	198
37 TA1	TARBORO (FIRST)	125	315	440
37 TA2	TARBORO (SECOND)	55	67	122
37 WEB	WEBBE'S	75	16	91
37 WHI	WHITLEY'S	48	120	168
37	EDGECOMBE TOTALS	1,381	2,801	4,182

[Even though the voting precincts and the townships are not the same, both are here for the benefit of the reader who may be familiar with the areas and able to put the proper ones together.]

The Board, consisting of S B Woodmansee, Henry F Brandis, and Edward Martin registered voters in the following precincts and signed books on the days given:

Edwards Precinct 30 Sep 1867
Hickory Ford Precinct 30 Sep 1867
Tarboro First and Second Precinct 30 Sep 1867
Sharpes Store Precinct 30 Sep 1867

The Board, consisting of Francis (Frank) Bennett, Robert John Dixon, and John (X) Vaughn, registered voters in the following precincts and signed books on the days given:

High Level Precinct 7 Oct 1867
Holly Grove Precinct 10 Oct 1867
Manner Hill Precinct 27 Sep 1867
Robertsons Store Precinct 28 Sep 1867
Rocky Mount Precinct 10 Oct 1867
Sparta Precinct 12 Oct 1867
Webbes Precinct 10 Sep 1867
Whitleys Shop Precinct 10 Sep 1867

The Board, consisting of A McCabe, Charles S Bartlett, and Thomas Newton registered voters in the following precincts and signed books on the days given:
Penders Mill Precinct 30 Sep 1867
Piney Grove Precinct 30 Sep 1867

Edgecombe County Township Descriptions

<u>Tarboro District.</u> Beginning at the mouth of Indian Creek on Tar River, thence up the said creek its various courses to John H Daniel's canal; thence up said canal, to its intersection with the Black Acre Canal, thence down the latter canal to Tar River; thence up the River to the mouth of Hatcher's Swamp; thence up the various courses of said swamp to the public road leading directly from Tarboro to Stantonsburg; thence along the southern boundary

line of the respective lands of Robt. Norfleet, Margaret E. Bridgers and Jannetta Staton (formerly Baker Staton's) to Crooked Creek; thence down the various courses of said creek to Tar River thence down the river to the mouth of Indian Creek at the beginning.

Lower Coneto District. Beginning on the Tar River in the Pitt County line; thence along the said line to Great Coneto Creek; thence along the various courses of said creek to the confluence of Mill and Crisp's Creeks, thence up the various courses of Mill Creek to the mouth of Little's Swamp; thence up Little's Swamp to the Devil's Ferry (a pond) thence up the pond to the Gum Swamp; thence up said Swamp to the Ballahack Swamp; thence up the said swamp to the most direct public road leading from Tarboro to the Cross Road Meeting house; thence down said road to a big ditch crossing said road; thence down said ditch to the Black Acre Canal; thence down the canal to the main ditch that connects said canal with John H. Daniel's canal; thence down the said ditch and J H Daniel's canal to Indian Creek; thence down said creek to Tar River; thence down the River to the Pitt County line to the beginning.

Upper Coneto District. Beginning on Great Coneto Creek on the Pitt County line thence up the various courses of said creek to the confluence of Mill and Crisp's Creeks; thence up the various courses of said Mill Creek to the mouth of Little's Swamp; thence up said swamp to the Devil's Ferry (a pond) thence up the pond to the Gum Swamp; thence along said swamp to Ballahack Swamp; thence up said Ballahack Swamp to the most direct road leading from Tarboro to the Cross Roads Meeting House; thence down said road and including said road to a big ditch (Jones) Crossing said road; thence down said ditch to the Black Acre Canal; thence down the said canal to the public road at the bridge near Clark's Mill; thence down the said road in the direction of Hamilton to a private cart or wagon way, beginning at or near Mary A. Howell's; thence along said wagon way to Hill's Ferry Road, at or near the residence of the late Peter E Knight; thence along the said Hill's Ferry Road to the Halifax County line; thence along the Martin County line to the Pitt Co. line; thence along the Pitt County line to the beginning on Coneto Creek.

Deep Creek District. Beginning on the Tar River at the mouth of Clark's Mill River; thence up the said river to the public road, leading from Tarboro to Hamilton at the Mill Bridge; thence along the said road and including the said road to a private cart and wagon way beginning at or near Mrs. M.A. Howell's; thence along the said cart and wagon way to the Hill's Ferry Road at or near the residence of the late Peter E Knight's; thence down said road and including said road to the Halifax County line; thence along the Halifax Co. line to Fishing Creek; thence down said creek to Tar River; thence down the River to the mouth of Clark's Mill Race to the beginning.

Lower Fishing Creek District. Beginning on the Tar River at the upper corner of the land of David Hinton Esq.; thence along the Western and Northern boundaries of his said land to the land of James H Williams and thence along the Western and Northern boundaries of his land (said to include the land of the said Hinton and Williams) to Swift Creek; thence up the various courses of said creek to the mouth of White Oak Swamp; thence up said swamp to George's ford; thence running therefrom along a path or cartway to the Spins Bridge Road; thence up said road to another path or cartway commencing near the residence of the Cate Henry mansion; thence along said path leading by the residence of William Atkins, Merritt Weeks, and William Weeks, crossing Maple Swamp and out to the new road, leading to Coffield's Bridge; thence a straight line through a pocoson the the head of Cabin Branch, thence down said branch to Fishing Creek thence down Fishing Creek to Tar River the beginning.

Upper Fishing Creek District. Beginning at the mouth of White Oak Swamp in Swift Creek; thence up said swamp to George's Ford; thence along a path or cartway leading therefrom to the Spice's Bridge Road; thence up said road to another cart or pathway commencing near the residence of the late Henry Newsom; thence along said path or way leading by the residence of William Atkins, Merritt Weeks, and William Weeks, crossing Maple Swamp and out to the New Road, leading to Coffield Bridge; thence a straight line through a pocosin to the head of Cabin Branch; thence down the said branch to Fishing Creek; thence up said creek to the Halifax County line; thence along said line to the Nash County line; thence along said line to Swift Creek; and thence down said creek to the mouth of White Oak Swamp at the beginning.

Swift Creek District. Beginning on Tar River at the upper corner of the land of David Hinton Esq; thence along the western and northern boundaries of his land to the land of Jas H Williams and along the northern and western boundaries of the land of the said Williams to Swift Creek; thence up said creek its various courses to the Nash County line; thence along said line to Tar River; thence down the river to the beginning.

Sparta District. Beginning on Tar River on the Pitt County line; thence up the river to the mouth of Crooked Creek; thence up said creek until it leaves the lands of Mrs Jannette Staton (formerly Baker Staton's); thence along the southern boundary lines of the respective lands of Jannette Staton, Margaret E Bridgers, and Robert Norfleet, to the direct road leading from Tarboro to Stantonsburg; thence along said road to town creek at the bridge near Town Creek Meeting House including the road; thence down said creek to Bynum's Mill Swamp; thence up said swamp to the road leading from Town Creek Meeting House to Otter Creek Meeting House; thence down and along said road to a private cart or wagon way or path near Dunford School House; thence down said cart or wagon way to the Cow Branch; thence down the said creek to the Fish Pond Branch; thence up the said Fish Pond Branch to the Pitt County line; thence along the Pitt County line to the beginning.

Otter Creek District. Beginning on the Pitt County line at the Fish Pond Branch; thence along said line to the Wilson County line; thence along the Wilson County line to the direct public road leading from Tarboro to Stantonsburg; thence along said road to Carter and Bynum's canal; thence down said canal to Bynum's Mill Swamp thence down said swamp to the road leading from Town Creek Meeting House to Otters Creek; thence down the creek to the Fish Pond Branch; thence up the Fish Pond Branch to the Pitt County line at the beginning.

Lower Town Creek District. Beginning at the mouth of Bynum's Mill Swamp in Town Creek; thence up the said creek to the Wilson Co. line; thence along said Co. line, to the direct road leading from Stantonsburg to Tarboro; thence down said road (including said road) to Carter's and Bynum's Mill canal; thence down the canal to Bynum's Mill Swamp, and thence down the swamp to the beginning at its mouth.

Walnut Creek District. Beginning at the public bridge over Town Creek near Town Creek Meeting House; thence up Town Creek to the mouth of Cokey Swamp;

thence up said swamp to C B Killebrew's canal; thence up said canal, to Deloache's Branch; thence up said branch to a private path or cart way leading from C B Killebrew's to the Pork Island Plantation; thence along said path or way to Brake's Branch; to its head near the residence of John Peel; thence east of John Peel a straight line to the head of the east prong of Walnut Creek; thence down Walnut Creek to Tar River; thence down the river to the mouth of Hatcher's Swamp; thence up said swamp to the public road leading from Tarboro to Stantonsburg; thence along said road to Town Creek Bridge at the beginning.

Rocky Mount District. Beginning at the mouth of Walnut Creek on Tar River; thence up said river to the Nash Co. line; thence along said county line to the direct public road leading from Tarboro to Raleigh; thence down the said road (including said road) to Proctor's Mill Swamp, near the Curl place; thence down the said mill stream (a prong of Cokey Swamp) to Cokey Swamp; thence down said Cokey Swamp to C B Killebrew's canal; thence up said canal to Deloach's Branch; thence up Deloach's Branch to a private cart or wagon way, leading from C B Killebrew's to Pork Island Plantation; thence along said pathway to Brake's Branch; thence up Brake's Branch to its head near the residence of John Peel; thence east of John Peel's a straight line to the head of the east prong of Walnut Creek; thence down Walnut Creek to the beginning at its mouth on Tar River.

Cokey District. Beginning at the confluence of Town Creek and Cokey Swamp; thence up Town Creek to the mouth of Williams Branch; thence up the said branch to the public road, leading from Tarboro to upper Town Creek Meeting House; thence down the said road to Temperance Hall thence along the new road to Cokey Swamp; at Armstrong's Bridge; thence down the said swamp to it mouth at the beginning.

Upper Town Creek District. Beginning at the mouth of Williams Branch on Town Creek; thence up the said creek to the Wilson County line; thence along the Wilson Co. line to the Nash Co. line; thence along the Nash Co Line to the direct public road leading from Tarboro to Raleigh; thence down the said road to Proctor's Mill Run (or stream); thence down said stream to Cokey Swamp thence down Cokey Swamp to the road at Armstrong's Bridge; thence along said road to Temperance Hall, (including said road) to the upper Town Creek Meeting House road; thence along said road and including the same to the Williams Branch thence down the Williams Branch to it mouth on Town Creek the beginning.

Bryan J. Keech Register and Ex. Off. Clerk

North Carolina Extant Voter Registrations of 1867

FRANKLIN COUNTY

Franklin was formed in 1779. It is in the northeastern part of the State and is bounded by Nash, Wake, Granville, Vance, and Warren counties. Part of Wake was annexed to Franklin in 1787 with much contention about the boundary existing until 1810. In 1817 the establishment of the dividing line between Franklin and Nash was authorized. Part of Granville was annexed to Franklin in 1875. Vance was formed in 1881 from Granville, Warren, and Franklin. An act to change the boundary between Vance and Franklin was passed in 1909.

North Carolina Extant Voter Registrations of 1867
FRANKLIN COUNTY

39	FRANKLIN COUNTY PRECINCTS SS1011	WHITES	BLACKS	AGGREGATE
39 DAV	DAVIS CROSS ROAD	152	176	328
39 FRA	FRANKLINTON	149	256	405
39 FRE	FREEMAN'S CROSS ROAD	82	155	237
39 GRI	GRIFFIN	127	80	207
39 HAR	HARRIS CROSS ROAD	108	117	225
39 HAY	HAYESVILLE	94	171	265
39 JOR	JORDAN COOK'S	159	136	295
39 LOU	LOUISBURG	179	229	408
39 PUG	PUGHES' HILL	97	147	244
39 SPE	SPEED'S STORE	111	101	212
39	FRANKLIN TOTALS	1,258	1,568	2,825

Franklin County Township Descriptions

We the undersigned commissioners of Franklin County beg leave to make the following report of townships of our county. We have caused to be made a survey of the township lines from a survey of the county made by Jos. Bridgers in the year 1840 into school districts (which were despensed with). There were originally ten districts in the county but the boundaries could not be ascertained so as to make a map of the county and we caused a survey of all the inside lines to be made and laid off the county into ten townships as laid down on the accompanying map, and have numbered and named the townships beginning in the northwest corner of the county next to Granville and Warren and named the first Haysville, the 2nd Sandy Creek, the 3rd The Gold Mines, the 4th Cedar Rock, the 5th Louisburg, the 6th Franklinton, the 7th Freemans, the 8th Harris', the 9th Cypress Creek; the 10th Dunn's. All which is respectfully submitted to your Honorable body this 3rd day of December 1868.

Fenner Tharrington Chairman, James W Fuller, A W Pearce Jr, James C Reid, and J E Tharrington.

[No other descriptions nor any map was found with this report. The registrations precincts and the township designations are inconsistent with each other.]

The Board consisting of J T Harris, Chm, J E Tharrington, and Hilliard Dunston registered voters in the following precincts and signed books on the dates given:

Franklinton Precinct 9 Nov 1867 Harris Cross Roads Precinct 9 Nov 1867
Freemans Cross Roads Precinct 9 Nov 1867 Griffins Precinct 30 Sep 1867

The Board, consisting of James N Uzzel, Chm, and Nathaniel T Harriss registered voters in the following precincts and signed books on the dates given:

Hayesville Precinct 9 Nov 1867 Pughes Hill Precinct 11 Nov 1867
Jordan Cook's Precinct 11 Nov 1867 R A Speed's Store Precinct 11 Nov 1867
Louisburg Precinct 11 Nov 1867 Davis Cross Roads 11 Nov 1867

North Carolina Extant Voter Registrations of 1867
GASTON COUNTY

Gaston was formed in 1846 from Lincoln. It is in the southwestern section of the State and is bounded by the state of South Carolina and Cleveland, Lincoln, and Mecklenburg counties. Part of Gaston was annexed to Lincoln in 1875 and the establishment of the dividing line was authorized in 1909. Part of Gaston was annexed to Cleveland in 1915 and other parts in 1917 and 1921.

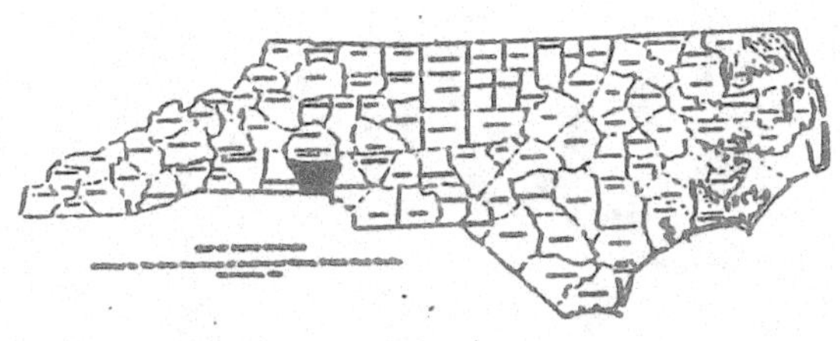

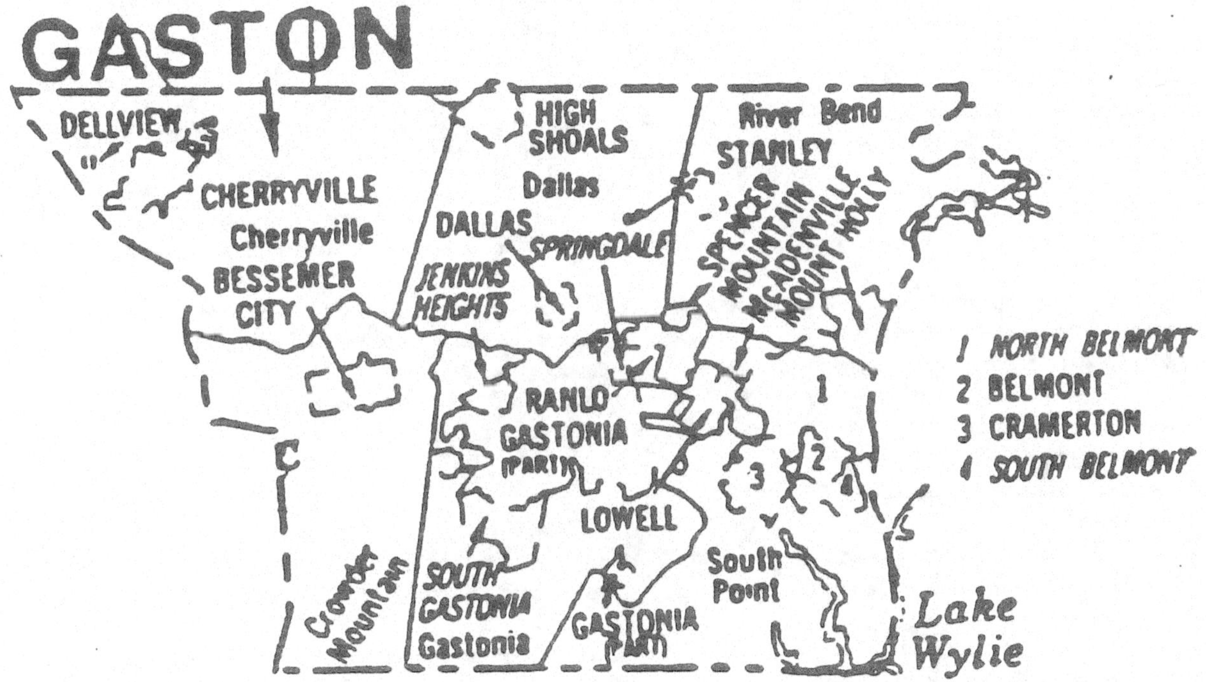

40	GASTON COUNTY PRECINCTS SS1012-1013	WHITES	BLACKS	AGGREGATE
40 BLA	BLACK'S	122	10	132
40 CAN	CANSELER'S	103	66	169
40 DA1	DALLAS (FIRST)	283	161	444
40 DA2	DALLAS (SECOND)	45	12	57
40 DEC	DECK'S	97	24	121
40 FER	FERGUSON'S	92	37	129
40 MAU	MAUNEY'S	82	16	98
40 RHY	RHYMER'S	65	37	102
40 SAN	SANDEFER'S	162	52	214
40 STO	STOWE'S	112	55	167
40	GASTON TOTALS	1163	470	1633

Gaston County Township Descriptions

Gentlemen,

I have the honor to transmit herewith a report from the commissioners for said county, that they did on the 17th day and days following divide said county in (5) five townships about equal territory and population. 1. Chenyville; 2. Dallas; 3. River Bend; 4. South Point; 5. Crowders Mountain.

It is believed by said commissioners that the above named townships are laid off convenient to the citizens of each district. Cyrus C. Wethers, Clk.

[The registration precincts and the township designations are inconsistent, nor were any other descriptions found for this county.]

The Board, consisting of E Pasour, Andrew Long, and James Hoffman, registered voters in the following precincts and signed the books on the dates given:

M J Aydlot instead of Andrew Long served on the board in Mauney's:

Black's Precinct 7 Sep 1867
First Dallas Precinct 7 Sep 1867
Ferguson's Precinct 7 Sep 1867
Mauney's Precinct 7 Sep 1867

The Board, consisting of E Parsons, Chm, M J Aydlott, and James Hoffman registered voters in the following precincts and signed the books on the dates given:

Deck's Precinct 24 Sep 1867

The Board, consisting of Wm McKee, A Titman, and James Rhyne, registered voters in the following precincts and signed the books on the dates given:

Cansler's precinct 7 Sep 1867
Second Dallas Precinct 7 Sep 1867
Rhymer's Precinct 7 Sep 1867
Sandifer's Precinct 7 Sep 1867
Stowe's Precinct 7 Sep 1867

North Carolina Extant Voter Registrations of 1867
GRANVILLE COUNTY

Granville was formed in 1746 from Edgecombe. It is in the northeastern section of the State and is bounded by Vance, Wake, Franklin, Durham, and Person counties and the state of Virginia. Orange was formed in 1752 from Johnston, Bladen, and Granville. Bute was formed in 1764. Part of Granville was annnexed to Warren in 1786. The establishment of the boundary line between Granville and Person was authorized in 1871. Part of Granville was annexed to Franklin in 1873 and in 1875. Vance was formed in 1881 from Granville, Warren, and Franklin.

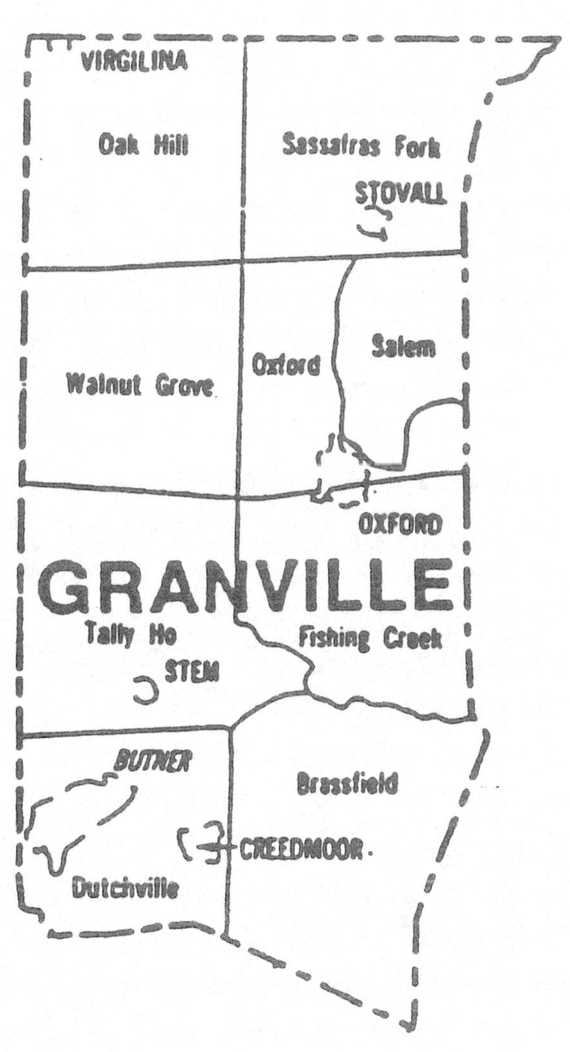

44	GRANVILLE COUNTY PRECINCTS SS1014-1015	WHITES	BLACKS	AGGREGATE
44 BEA	BEAVER DAM	81	36	117
44 BR1	BRASSFIELD (1)			
44 BR2	BRASSFIELD (2)	302	258	660
44 DUT	DUTCHVILLE	157	105	262
44 FIS	FISHING CREEK	140	79	219
44 FOR	FORT CREEK			
44 HEN	HENDERSON	253	447	700
44 ISL	ISLAND CREEK	66	72	138
44 KIT	KITTRELL	93	32	125
44 KNA	KNAPP OF REEDS	42	39	81
44 LED	LEDGE OF ROCK	216	111	327
44 OXF	OXFORD	276	543	819
44 RAG	RAGLAND	56	52	108
44 SAS	SASSAFRASS FORK	97	260	357
44 TAR	TAR RIVER	119	92	211
44 TOW	TOWNSVILLE	78	210	288
44 YXR	YOUNG'S CROSS ROAD	107	97	204
44 YXS	YOUNG'S STORE	113	220	333
44	GRANVILLE TOTALS	2,196	2,653	4,849

Granville County Township Descriptions

Gentlemen. In obedience to the Constitution of North Carolina Article 9 Section 3 the Commissioners of Granville County do most respectfully present to your Honorable body a map and survey of the said county of Granville shewing therein eleven townships or school districts marked and named as follows: to wit; Townsville, Sassafras Fork, Oak Hill, Walnut Grove, Oxford, Henderson, Kittrells, Fishing Creek, Tally Ho, Dutchville, Brassfields.

Your commissioners beg to report that the townships as marked are all eight miles square excepting only Townsville and Brassfields and some small points on the Wake County line also a small dificiency in Kittrells township on the corner at Tar river. Your commissioners could not lay off the county otherwise with out loosing the old public school houses now standing. The townships are herein represented generally embrace from of the old original school districts of four miles square each with the school houses now standing in the center of those old districts.

Townsville and Brassfields townships are larger but the prevailing opinion is that for some years those were by no occasion to alter them and when if should be desired or important to do so the survey to redraw them will not be laborious or very expensive.

All of which is most respectfully submitted.

Lewis H. Kittle Chairman Board County Commissioners
15 Dec. 1868

North Carolina Extant Voter Registrations of 1867
GRANVILLE COUNTY

[No other township descriptions nor map was found with this report. Additional note states that Fort Creek and Brassfields voted together and that totals were included with Brassfields. Although the box of voter lists numbered SS 1014 is labeled Gaston County, the contents are Granville.]

The Board, consisting of F J Tilley Chm, John Peed, and Aaron Pratcher, registered voters in the following precincts and signed books on the dates given:

Beaver Dam Precinct 30 Sep 1867
Brassfield's Precinct 30 Sep 1867
Dutchville Precinct 30 Sep 1867
Fishing Creek Precinct 30 Sep 1867
Ledge of Rock Precinct 30 Sep 1867

The Board, consisting of John Gallagher, Thos W Pool, and William Tyler registered voters in the following precincts and signed books on the dates given:

Townsville Precinct 9 Nov 1867
Island Creek Precinct 30 Sep 1867
Sassafrass Fork Precinct 9 Nov 1867
Young's Cross Roads 30 Sep 1867
Young's Store Precinct 30 Sep 1867

The Board, consisting of Lewis H Kittle, C Betts, and Abraham Hinton registered voters in the following precincts and signed books on the dates given:

Henderson Precinct 30 Sep 1867
Kittrell Precinct 30 Sep 1867
Knapp of Reeds Precinct 30 Sep 1867
Oxford Precinct 23 Sep 1867
Ragland Precinct 30 Sep 1867
Tar River Precinct 30 Sep 1867

North Carolina Extant Voter Registrations of 1867
GUILFORD COUNTY

Guilford was formed in 1770 from Rowan and Orange. It is in the north central section of the State and is bounded by Alamance, Randolph, Davidson, Forsyth, and Rockingham counties. Randolph County was formed from Guilford in 1779 and Rockingham in 1785.

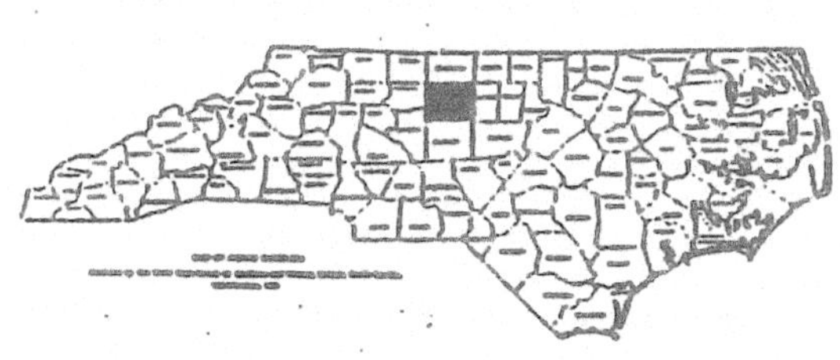

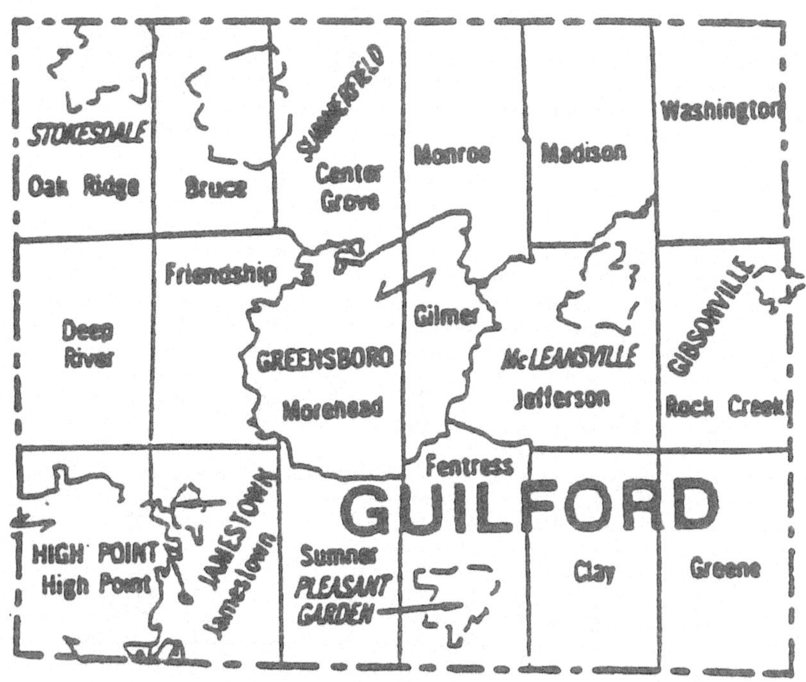

46	GUILFORD COUNTY PRECINCTS SS1019-1020	WHITES	BLACKS	AGGREGATE
46 COB	COBLE	197	35	232
46 FRI	FRIENDSHIP	271	81	352
46 GIB	GIBSONVILLE	138	51	189
46 GRE	GREENSBORO	528	391	919
46 HIG	HIGH POINT	238	42	280
46 JAM	JAMESTOWN	246	64	310
46 KIN	KING'S	134	39	173
46 MCL	MCLEANSVILLE	203	70	273
46 MON	MONTECELLO	165	118	283
46 RAG	RAGAN'S	165	37	202
46 ROS	ROSS'S	158	50	208
46 SUM	SUMMERFIELD	214	119	333
46	GUILFORD TOTALS	2657	1097	3754

[No township descriptions nor map was found with this report. There were two total pages for Greensboro Precinct, and no way to separate the numbers of registrants by precinct.

The Board, consisting of P S Benbow, D H La Pish, and Harmon Unthank, registered voters in the following precincts and signed books on the dates given:

Second Greensboro Precinct 25 Sep 1867
Friendship Precinct 11 Sep 1868
Gibsonville Precinct 11 Sep 1868
First Greensboro Precinct 25 Sep 1867
Coble Precinct 30 Sep 1867
Ragan's Precinct 30 Sep 1867
Ross's Precinct 11 Sep 1867

The Board, consisting of John T Poe, T C Starbuck, and R Y Davis, registered voters in the following precincts and signed books on the dates given:

High Point Precinct 30 Sep 1867
Jamestown Precinct 30 Sep 1867
Kings Precinct 17 Sep 1867
Monticello Precinct 30 Sep 1867
Summerfield's Precinct 30 Sep 1867

The Board, consisting of M Porcher, P S Benbow, and Hiram Unthank registered voters in the following precincts and signed books on the dates given:

McLeanesville Precinct 30 Sep 1867

North Carolina Extant Voter Registrations of 1867
HYDE COUNTY

Hyde was first called Wickham, the name being changed about 1712. It is in the eastern section of the State and is bounded by Pamlico Sound and Beaufort, Washington, Tyrrell, and Dare counties (and on the banks by the Atlantic Ocean and Dare and Carteret counties.) Part of Currituck was annexed to Hyde in 1745. The establishment of the boundary line between Hyde and Tyrrell was authorized in 1784. Part of Hyde was annexed to Beaufort in 1819; part of Currituck was annexed in 1823; and part of Carteret was annexed in 1845. Dare was formed in 1870 from Currituck, Hyde, and Tyrrell.

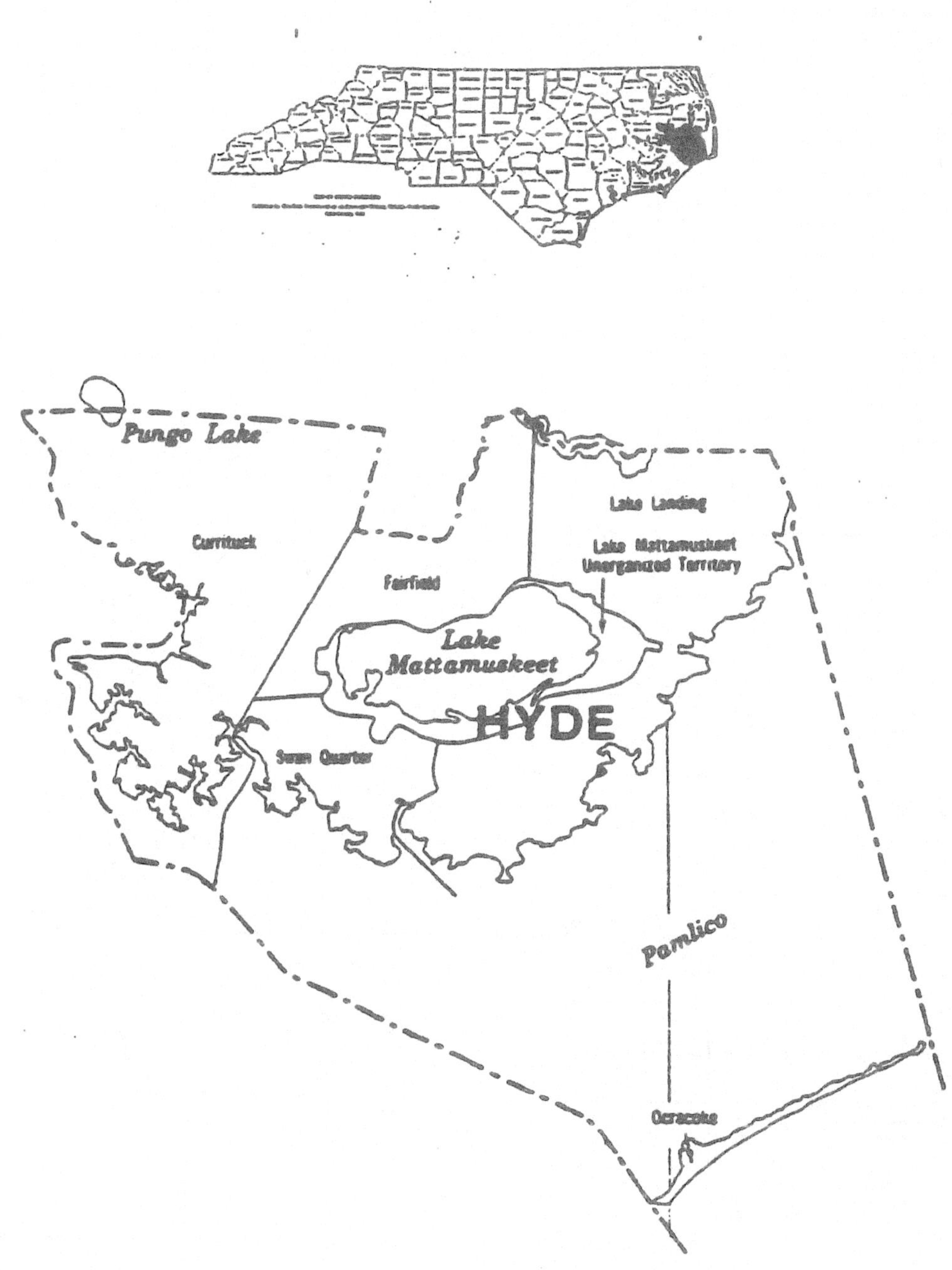

53	HYDE COUNTY PRECINCTS SS1016-1017	WHITES	BLACKS	AGGREGATE
53 BUR	BURGESS MILL	37	7	44
53 CHI	CHICKAMACOMICO	42	0	42
53 FAI	FAIRFIELD	155	103	258
53 GER	GERMANTOWN	156	150	306
53 HAT	HATTARAS	73	6	79
53 KEN	KENNEKEET	52	0	52
53 LA1	LAKE LANDING (FIRST)	249	224	473
53 LA2	LAKE LANDING (SECOND)	46	16	60
53 OCR	OCRACOKE	43	1	44
53 SWA	SWAN QUARTER	166	122	288
53	HYDE COUNTY TOTALS	1017	629	1646

Hyde County Township Report

Wm S Carter, Chm, R.P. Kahab, John J. Fulford, and J.S. McClaud, Coms. made this report 19 Oct 1868. Immediately following the township descriptions is a petition requesting readjustment of the boundaries.

Fairfield Township. Beginning at the Hyde & Tyrrell line at the line of the Lake Landing Township running with the Hyde & Tyrrell to the line of Swan Quarter Township thence with the Swan Quarter Township line to the line of Lake Landing Township then with the line of the Lake Landing Township to the beginning.
Board: B Midyett, Joseph Hodges, Jesse D Mason 30 Sep 1867

Hatteras Township. Beginning at the north end of Ocracoke Township line on the Ocean beach at the waters edge running with said beach across Hatteras Inlet to Cape Hatteras from thence with said beach two miles north of Hatteras Light House, thence west to Pamlico Sound then with the Sound back to the Ocracoke Township line and then with said line to the beginning. Voting Precinct Hatteras.
Board: Benja C Jennett, A J Stow, Iram W Styron 30 Sep 1867

Kinnekeet Township. Beginning at the north end of Hatteras Township line on the Atlantic Ocean at the waters edge running with said Ocean to the Hyde and Currituck line, then with said line to the Pamlico Sound, then with the Sound to the Hatteras Township line then with said line to the beginning. Voting Precinct Kinnekeet & Chickamacomico.
Board: M B Washington, B C June 30 Sep 1867
Chickamacomico Precinct Board: Benja C Jennett, A J Stow, Thomas W Styron 30 Sep 1867

Lake Landing Township. Beginning at the Lake water near the fork of the Juniper Bay Road running with the Juniper Bay Road & Canal to Pamlico Sound then with the Sound to the Hyde & Tyrrell line then with said line to the nearest point on said line to the line between Andrew Shanklin & Thos Jarvis then with said line to the lake water thence across the Mattamuskeet Lake to the beginning. Voting Precinct Lake Landing.
Board: B Midyett, Joseph Hodges, Jesse S Mason 24 and 30 Sep 1867

Ocracoke Township. Beginning at the Hyde and Carteret line on the Atlantic Ocean running with said ocean beach to within one half a mile of the Hatteras Inlet, thence north west to the Pamlico Sound then with the Sound back to the Hyde and Carteret line then with the said Hyde and Carteret line to the beginning. Voting Precinct Ocracoke.
Board: Benjamin C Jennett, A J Stow, Hiram W Styron 30 Sep 1867

Swan Quarter Township. Beginning at the mouth of Rose Bay Creek, and running with said Creek to its head then with the Currituck Township line to the Tyrrell line, then with the Hyde and Washington line to the nearest point to the old Turnpike Bridge at the Lake thence across the Matamuskeet Lake to the Juniper Bay Road, thence with the Juniper Bay Road and Canal to the Pamlico Sound, then with the windings of said sound to the beginning. Voting Precinct Swan Quarter.
Board: B Midyett, Joseph Hodges, Jesse Mason 30 Sep 1867

Currituck Township. Beginning at the head of Pungo River that being the line between Hyde, Beaufort, and Washington Counties running with said River to its mouth, then with the windings of Pamlico Sound to the mouth of Rose Bay Creek then with said Creek to its head, thence the nearest line to the line between Hyde and Tyrrell Counties, thence to the beginning. Voting Precincts Burgesses Mill & Germington [Germantown].
Board: B Midyett, Jesse G Mason, Joseph Hodges 24 and 30 Sep 1867

Sladesville, Hyde Co. Jan. 11, 1869. Mr. John Rispess, Der Sir

I enclose you a pertison covering the townships in Hyde County I hope you will attend to it. I shall bee to Raileght to see you with in 10 days. Very respeficley, John Conklin.

Hyde County, N.C. December 1st, 1868. To the Hon. Members of the General Assembly, Raleigh, N.C. Gentlemen, We the undersigned citizens of Hyde County: having heard of the report of the Commissioners, in regard to dividing the County into convenient districts, determine the boundaries, and prescribe the names of the said districts, do enter our protest and objections; and pray, that the General Assembly will not approve of the report. To divide into convenient districts, would be to have eight on the mainland, and four on the Banks. The Currituck district as it now stands is about sixty-five miles in circumference and the others equally as inconvenient. We do not hesitate in saying that the division of districts, in our opinions, is more for Party purposes than convenience to the people. Very respectfully your obedient servants:

John J McGowan
Benjamin Franklin
Wm A Carawan
Zachs Emery
William Hudson
Eli H Gurkins
Levi McGowan
Augustus R Whitney
John Berry
S B Emery
Richard T Berry
A J Glover

George Bell
John C Dunbar
Lewis Taylor
S C Dredle
B D Gills
Samson Barne
Esics Spencer
Thomas Whitney
Scott Lovel
Reden Hollowell
Frederic McElvain
Anthony Hollowell

Jesper Mackey
Besor Spencer
Jesse Cavel
John Jennitt
Dory Fontiscue
James Harris
Pealeg Oneal
William King
Anson Fortescue
Samul Miller
Bejon Gray
Samul L Gray

North Carolina Extant Voter Registrations of 1867
HYDE COUNTY

Henry Gibbs
John Conklin
James Chase
William H Geven (?)
Beniaj Selby
Walless Selby
E P Hudson
George W Davis
Granderson Whitfield
Samuel Locker
James Daniels
David M Credle
George F Credle
T M Stakebony
Warner Baners
David Covell
Willey Hodgs
Nathan Fremond
Richard Olison
James Bell
Fred Y Spencer
Wm R Simons
Neadham Freemon

Garrison Hudson
Kiah Hudson
James E Gurkins
Thomas Newby
Ormon Gibbs
Elden Midgett
Athony Morris
Richard Morris
Samuel Barrow
Spiens Fortiscue
William Cavell
Danil Silverthorne
Solmon Hawood
Britton Jiner
Edward Jones
William Maning
Richard Spencer
Samuel Barber
Scott Oats
Looke Tonley
James P King
Frank Yonge
Danil Slade

Henry Fortescue
Robert Brinkley
Ed More
Jasy Blont
Sam Hill
Ben Griffen
Eligia Gray
Dence Credle
Dr. Nathan Cambel
George Mackey
Harrison Boion
Thomas Barrow
Major Barrow
Sutton Spencer
Alford Wats
Jabez Barrow
Frederick Barnes
Henry Barrow
M T Harris
S D Owens
Henry Gibbs
John Conklin

North Carolina Extant Voter Registrations of 1867
ONSLOW COUNTY

Onslow was formed in 1734 from New Hanover. It is in the southeastern section of the State and is bounded by the Atlantic Ocean and Pender, Duplin, Jones and Carteret counties. The establishment of the dividing line between the counties of Duplin and Onslow was authorized in 1819. In 1905, 1915, 1921, 1923, and 1924 acts were passed to establish the lines lines between Onslow and Pender, Jones, and Duplin counties because the many disputes over the years had not been resolved. Only Swansboro Precinct records presently available.

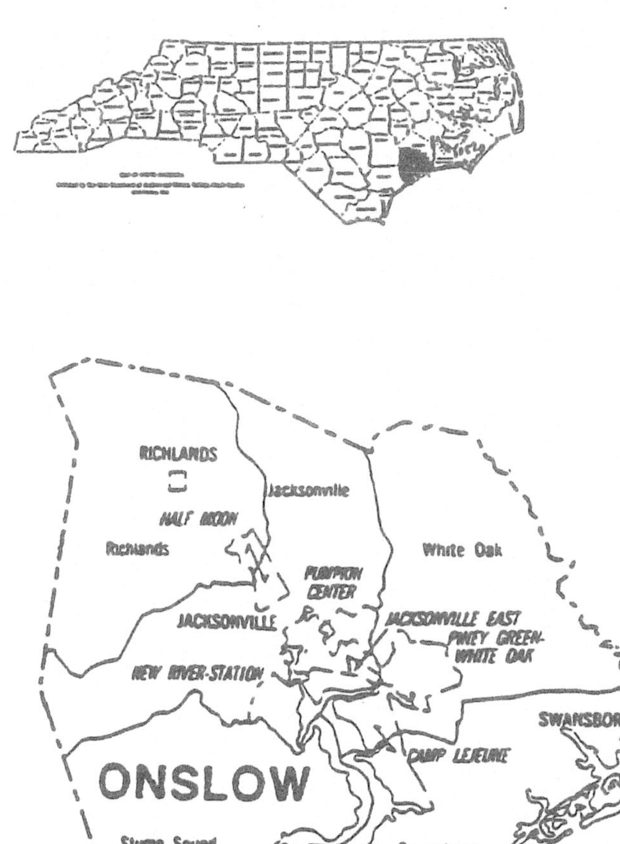

72	ONSLOW COUNTY PRECINCT SS1018	WHITES	BLACKS	AGGREGATE
72 SWA	SWANSBORO	119	56	175

Swansboro Precinct
Board: M C Hoyt Pris Board, John Monroe, Louis A Sharren 20 Sep 1867

North Carolina Extant Voter Registrations of 1867

WAKE COUNTY

Although Wake was formed in 1770 from Johnston, Cumberland, and Orange, the act was not to become effective 12 March 1771. The County is in the east central section of the State and is bounded by Johnston, Harnett, Chatham, Durham, Granville, and Franklin counties. In 1805 the establishment of the boundary line between Franklin and Wake was authorized according to the act which established Granville county. In 1810 the establishment of the boundary line between Franklin and Wake was authorized. Durham was formed in 1881 from Orange and Wake, and another part of Wake was annexed to Durham County in 1911.

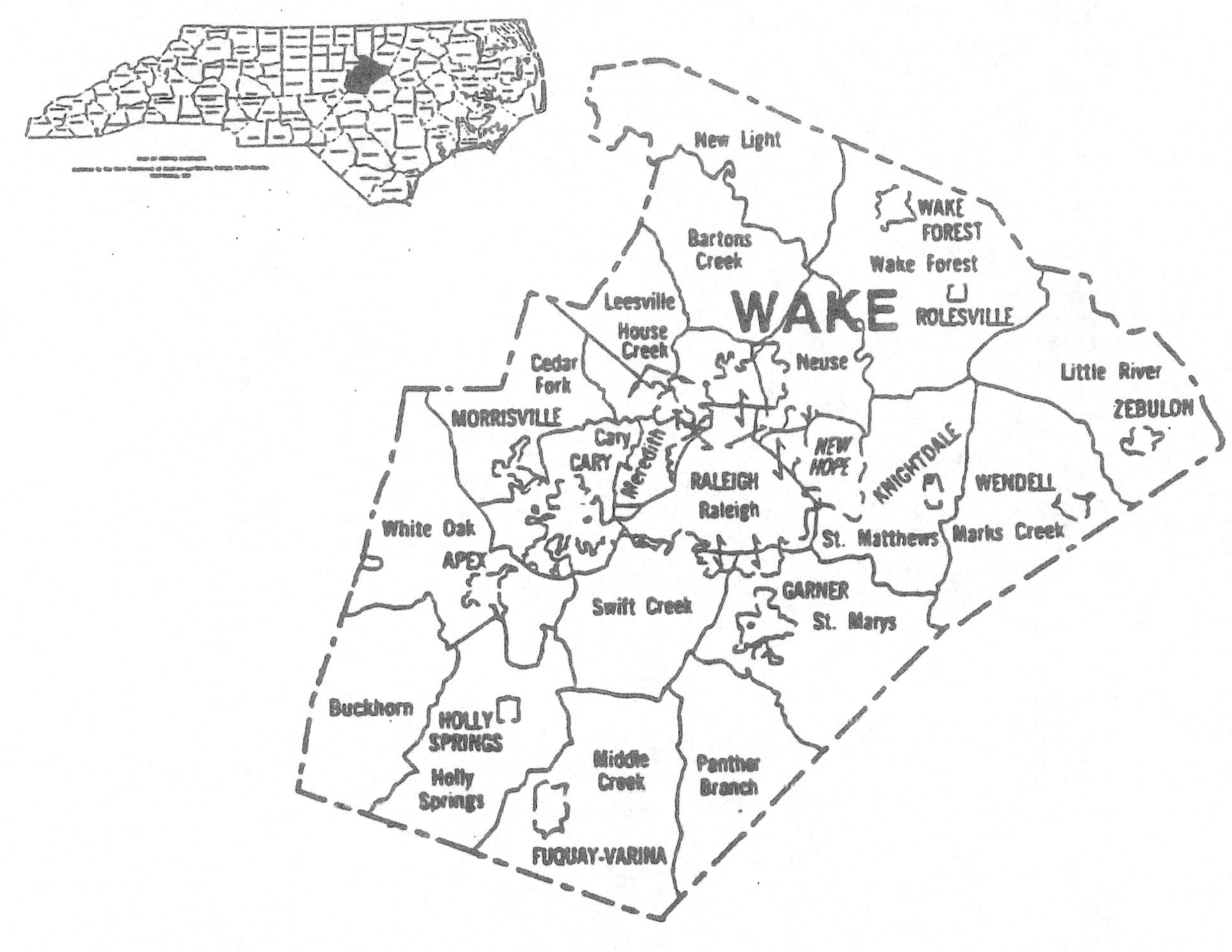

99	WAKE COUNTY PRECINCT SS1018	: WHITES	: BLACKS	: AGGREGATE :
99 BUS	BUSBEE'S - - - - - - - - - - - - -	: 216	: 132	: 348 :

[Of 18 precincts, only Busbee's has been found to date, and it is clearly marked as a "duplicate register."]

Busbee's Precinct
Board: Thomas Hampson, Francis Lamson, Isaiah Hardee 30 Sep 1867

North Carolina Extant Voter Registrations of 1867
COUNTY AND PRECINCT KEYS FOR ALL REGISTRANTS

19 CARTERET COUNTY
19 BE1 BEAUFORT (1)
19 BE2 BEAUFORT (2)
19 CED CEDAR ISLAND
19 DAV DAVIS SHORE
19 HAD HADNOTS CREEK
19 HAR HARLOWS CREEK
19 HUN HUNTING QUARTERS
19 MOR MOREHEAD CITY
19 NEW NEWPORT
19 POR PORTSMOUTH
19 SHA SHACKLEFORD BANKS
19 SMY SMYRNA
19 STR STRAIGHTS

24 CHOWAN COUNTY
24 EDE EDENTON
24 MID MIDDLE GROUND
24 UPP UPPER GROUND

25 CLAY COUNTY
25 HAY HAYESVILLE
25 PIN PINE LOG
25 SHO SHOOTING CREEK
25 TUS TUSQUITEE

26 CLEVELAND COUNTY
26 BLA BLANTONS
26 BOR BORDERS STORE
26 BUR BURTOWN
26 CAR CARPENTERS
26 GOF GOFORTHS
26 GRI GRIGGS
26 HOL HOLLAND'S MILL
26 MOO MOORESBORO
26 MOU MOUTH OF SANDY RIVER
26 PEE PEELERS
26 SHE SHELBY
26 SWA SWANS
26 WAR WARLICK

28 CRAVEN COUNTY
28 01A 1ST book 1
28 01B 1ST book 2
28 02N 2ND
28 03A 3RD book 1
28 03B 3RD book 2
28 04A 4TH book 1
28 04B 4TH book 2
28 05A 5TH book 1
28 05B 5TH book 2
28 06T 6TH
28 07T 7TH
28 08T 8TH
28 09T 9TH
28 10T 10TH
28 11T 11TH
28 12T 12TH
28 13T 13TH
28 14T 14TH
28 15T 15TH
28 16T 16TH
28 17T 17TH

29 CUMBERLAND CO
29 BLA BLACK RIVER
29 CAR CARVERS CREEK
29 CED CEDAR CREEK
29 FA1 FAYETTEVILLE 1
29 FA2 FAYETTEVILLE 2
29 FLE FLEA HILL

CUMBERLAND (Cont)
29 GRA GRAYS CREEK
29 LOC LOCKS CREEK
29 MON MONROES
29 QUW QUWHIFFLE
29 ROC ROCKFISH
29 SEV SEVENTY FIRST

30 CURRITUCK COUNTY
30 COI COINJOCK
30 CUR CURRITUCK COURT HOUSE
30 GIB GIBBS WOODS
30 IND INDIAN RIDGE
30 KNO KNOT ISLAND
30 MOY MOYOCK
30 NAR NARROW SHORE
30 NOR NORTH BANKS
30 POP POPLAR BRANCH
30 POW POWELLS POINT
30 ROA ROANOKE ISLAND
30 TUL TULLS CREEK

32 DAVIDSON COUNTY
32 BRO BROWNSTOWN
32 CLE CLEMMONSVILLE
32 COT COTTON GROVE
32 JAC JACKSON HILL
32 LEE LEES
32 LEX LEXINGTON
32 LOF LOFLIN
32 POS POSSUMTOWN
32 SHE SHELTONS
32 THO THOMASVILLE
32 TYR TYRO
32 YAD YADKIN INST.

35 DUPLIN COUNTY
35 ALB ALBERTSONS
35 CYP CYPRESS CREEK
35 FAI FAISON'S
35 GLI GLISSON'S
35 ISL ISLAND CREEK
35 KEN KENANVILLE
35 LIM LIMESTONE
35 MAG MAGNOLIA
35 ROC ROCKFISH
35 SMI SMITH'S
35 WAR WARSAW
35 WOL WOLFES CRAPE

37 EDGECOMBE COUNTY
37 EDW EDWARDS
37 HIC HICKORY FORK
37 HIG HIGH LEVEL
37 HOL HOLLY GROVE
37 MAN MANNER HILL
37 PEN PENDER'S MILL
37 PIN PINEY GROVE
37 ROB ROBERTSONS STORE
37 ROC ROCKY MOUNT
37 SHA SHARPE'S STORE
37 SPA SPARTA
37 TA1 TARBORO (1)
37 TA2 TARBORO (2)
37 WEB WEBBE'S
37 WHI WHITLEY'S

39 FRANKLIN COUNTY
39 DAV DAVIS CROSS ROAD
39 FRA FRANKLINTON
39 FRE FREEMAN'S CROSS ROAD
39 GRI GRIFFIN

FRANKLIN (Cont)
39 HAR HARRIS CROSS ROAD
39 HAY HAYESVILLE
39 JOR JORDAN COOK'S
39 LOU LOUISBURG
39 PUG PUGHES' HILL
39 SPE SPEED'S STORE

40 GASTON COUNTY
40 BLA BLACK'S
40 CAN CANSELER'S
40 DA1 DALLAS (1)
40 DA2 DALLAS (2)
40 DEC DECK'S
40 FER FERGUSON'S
40 MAU MAUNEY'S
40 RHY RHYMER'S
40 SAN SANDEFER'S
40 STO STOWE'S

44 GRANVILLE COUNTY
44 BEA BEAVER DAM
44 BR1 BRASSFIELD (1)
44 BR2 BRASSFIELD (2)
44 DUT DUTCHVILLE
44 FIS FISHING CREEK
44 FOR FORT CREEK
44 HEN HENDERSON
44 ISL ISLAND CREEK
44 KIT KITTRELL
44 KNA KNAPP OF REEDS
44 LED LEDGE OF ROCK
44 OXF OXFORD
44 RAG RAGLAND
44 SAS SASSAFRASS FORK
44 TAR TAR RIVER
44 TOW TOWNSVILLE
44 YXR YOUNG'S CROSS ROAD
44 YXS YOUNG'S STORE

46 GUILFORD COUNTY
46 COB COBLE
46 FRI FRIENDSHIP
46 GIB GIBSONVILLE
46 GRE GREENSBORO
46 HIG HIGH POINT
46 JAM JAMESTOWN
46 KIN KING'S
46 MCL MCLEANSVILLE
46 MON MONTECELLO
46 RAG RAGAN'S
46 ROS ROSS'S
46 SUM SUMMERFIELD

53 HYDE COUNTY
53 BUR BURGESS MILL
53 CHI CHICKAMACOMICO
53 FAI FAIRFIELD
53 GER GERMANTOWN
53 HAT HATTARAS
53 KEN KENNEKEET
53 LA1 LAKE LANDING (1)
53 LA2 LAKE LANDING (2)
53 OCR OCRACOKE
53 SWA SWAN QUARTER

72 ONSLOW COUNTY
72 SWA SWANSBORO

99 WAKE COUNTY
99 BUS BUSBEE'S

AARONS LIPPMAN A 35 WAR W
ABBAT CHARLES H A 19 BE1 W
ABBOTT GEO A 28 04A B
ABBOTT J A R A 39 LOU W
TRNS FROM P HILL
ABBOTT J B A 28 04A B
ABBOTT JAS R A 39 PUG W
TRANS TO LOUISBURG
ABBOTT JEREMIAH A 19 POR W
ABBOTT JOHN A 28 03A B
ABBOTT P G A 44 HEN W
ABBOTT RICHARD A 28 04B B
ABBOTT SYLVESTER A 28 04A B
ABBOTT WM A 39 LOU W
ABERNATHY ALBERT A 40 DA1 B
5 MOS RESIDENCE
15 AUGUST 1867
ABERNATHY C B A 40 RHY W
ABERNATHY C M A 40 STO W
ABERNATHY C W A 40 RHY W
ABERNATHY COLEMAN A 40 DA1 W
ABERNATHY D M A 40 CAN W
ABERNATHY DANIEL A 40 CAN B
ABERNATHY G W A 40 STO W
ABERNATHY GREEN A 40 CAN B
ABERNATHY
HARTSWELL S A 40 DA1 B
ABERNATHY J M A 40 STO W
ABERNATHY J P A 40 RHY W
ABERNATHY JAMES DR A 40 CAN W
ABERNATHY JAMES W C A 40 DA1 W
ABERNATHY JESS A 40 CAN B
ABERNATHY
JOSEPH R A A 40 DA1 W
ABERNATHY LEWIS A 40 RHY B
ABERNATHY MILES A 40 RHY W
ABERNATHY STARLING A 40 DA1 W
ABERNATHY W L A 40 RHY W
ABERNATHY W M A 40 CAN W
ABERNATHY WILLIAM A 40 DA1 B
5 MOS RESIDENCE
15 AUG 1867
ABERNETHY WILLIAM A 37 PIN W
ABRAHAM FERDINAND A 53 GER W
ABRAMS JOSEPH A 37 PIN W
ABSHUR ASA A 28 11T W
ACHAM W E A 44 DUT W
ACKLING JOHN A 30 POP W
ACKLING WHEELER A 30 POP W
ACREE GEORGE A 39 DAV W
ADAIR JAMES J A 19 BE1 W
ADAMS A T A 19 BE1 W
ADAMS ALFRED A 46 GRE B
ADAMS ANTHONY A 40 FER B
ADAMS AUGUSTUS A 28 10T B
ADAMS BARKLEY A 19 NEW W
ADAMS BEN A 32 DAV B
ADAMS BENJAMIN A 53 LA1 B
ADAMS CHARLES A A 35 MAG W
ADAMS CHARLES H A 37 ROC B
ADAMS DANL A 46 GRE W
ADAMS E A 19 HAD W
ADAMS FRANCIS A 26 SWA W
ADAMS FRANK A 40 FER B
ADAMS FRANK A 44 DUT W
ADAMS GEO A A 19 BE1 W
ADAMS GEO M A 19 BE1 W
ADAMS GEORGE M A 46 GRE W
ADAMS GILBERT A 28 05A B
ADAMS GOLER A 29 CED B
ADAMS HAYWOOD A 37 ROC B

ADAMS HENDERSON CHALA 32 DAV W
FOR HOLDING OFFICE
BEFORE AND DURING WAR.
ADAMS HENRY A 40 DA1 B
ADAMS ISAAC A 44 DUT W
ADAMS J A 26 BOR W
ADAMS J F A 32 DAV W
ADAMS J H A 32 DAV W
ADAMS J J A 28 11T W
CERTIF GIVEN IN CARTERET
ADAMS J P A 44 DUT W
ADAMS J Q A 32 DAV W
ADAMS J QUINCY A 29 ROC W
ADAMS J W A 19 BE1 W
ADAMS JAMES A 28 10T B
ADAMS JAMES A 29 FLE W
ADAMS JAMES A 32 THO W
ADAMS JAMES JR A 46 SUM W
ADAMS JAMES JR A 53 LA1 W
ADAMS JAMES SR A 46 SUM W
ADAMS JAS P A 46 GRE W
ADAMS JERRY A 37 EDW B
ADAMS JOHN A 26 SWA W
ADAMS JOHN A 53 LA1 B
ADAMS JOHN E A 99 BUS W
ADAMS JOHN H A 40 FER W
ADAMS JOHN Q A 28 6TH B
ADAMS JOSEPH A 28 15T B
ADAMS JOSEPH A 28 9TH B
ADAMS KEY A 28 11T W
ADAMS LEWIS A 28 7TH W
ADAMS MARCUS C A 19 MOR W
ADAMS NAT A 44 HEN W
ADAMS NATHAN D A 19 BE1 W
ADAMS NATHANIEL A 99 BUS B
ADAMS NATHL A 28 03A B
ADAMS NELSON A 46 GRE B
ADAMS PETER A 37 ROC B
ADAMS PETER H A 46 GRE W
ADAMS PLENTY A 28 8TH B
ADAMS ROBERT L A 40 FER W
ADAMS ROLAND A 28 11T B
ADAMS RUFUS A 40 DA1 B
ADAMS SALOMON N A 19 BE1 W
ADAMS SAM'L A 29 FA1 B
FLEA HILL
ADAMS SAMUEL A 40 SAN B
ADAMS SAMUEL A 53 FAI B
ADAMS SAMUEL B A 40 DA1 B
ADAMS SETH A 28 10T B
ADAMS SIMON A 28 11T B
ADAMS THOMAS R A 28 02N W
ADAMS W C A 46 GRE W
ADAMS W H A 19 MOR W
ADAMS WATSON A 28 03A B
ADAMS WILLIAM D A 40 FER B
ADAMS WILLIAM H A 28 11T W
ADAMS WILLIS A 37 SHA B
ADAMS WM A 46 GRE B
ADAMS WM S A 24 EDE W
ADCOCK ABSOLAM A 44 YXS W
ADCOCK BIRD A 44 YXS W
ADCOCK BOLDEN A 39 FRA W
ADCOCK DAVID A 44 YXS W
ADCOCK ESQUARE A 44 TAR B
ADCOCK H C A 29 SEV W
ADCOCK H C A 44 YXS W
ADCOCK J J A 44 LED W
ADCOCK JAS W A 44 YXS W
ADCOCK JNO A 44 YXS W
ADCOCK JNO H A 44 TAR W
ADCOCK JOHN A 44 BRA B

ADCOCK JOHN A 53 BUR W
CERT RES SWAN QUARTER
ADCOCK LITTLETON A 44 TAR W
ADCOCK THOS A 44 LED W
ADCOCK W A 44 BEA W
ADCOCK W H A 44 BEA W
ADCOCK WM A 29 ROC W
ADCOCK WM H A 39 PUG W
ADDAMS CHARLES A 32 DAV B
ADDAMS GEORGE A 32 DAV B
ADDAMS ROBERT A 32 LOF W
ADDERHOLDT DAVID A 40 MAU W
ADDERHOLDT EMANUEL R 40 MAU W
NAME LINED OUT
MILITIA OFFICER BEFORE
THE REBELLION & GAVE AID
AND COMFORT TO THE ENEMY
* REJECTED
ADDERHOLDT EMANUEL * 40 MAU W
ACEPTED
ADDERHOLDT JOHN F A 40 MAU W
ADDERSON WHITMOND A 37 PEN B
ADDERTON JACOB A 32 JAC B
ADDERTON JOHN A 32 JAC W
ADDERTON RICHARD S A 32 DAV W
ADDERTON SAM A 32 JAC B
ADDERTON SILAS A 32 JAC B
ADDISON ABRAHAM A 37 SHA B
ADER D C A 32 SHE W
ADER JOHN H A 32 DAV B
ADER LEVI A 32 SHE B
ADER PETER A 32 SHE W
ADERTON S L A 32 JAC W
ADERTON W S A 32 JAC W
ADKEN AULANDER A 37 MAN W
ADKINS ALLEN A 44 BRA B
ADKINS CASY A 29 BLA X
ADKINS DAVID A 37 EDW W
ADKINS JAS A 29 FA1 W
ADKINS ROBERT A 37 ROB B
ADKINS ROBERT A 37 ROB W
ADKINS SAMUEL A 37 ROC W
ADKINS SAMUEL A 37 ROC W
ADKINS WILLIAM A 37 ROB W
ADKINS WILLIAM A 39 PUG W
ADKINS WILLIAM H A 37 ROB W
ADKINSON CALVIN A 29 FA1 W
ADKINSON HENRY A 37 WHI B
ADKINSON JOSEPH J A 37 SPA W
ADKINSON LONDON A 53 GER B
ADKINSON ROBERT W A 37 SPA W
ADKINSON ROBT A 29 FA1 W
ADKINSON WILLIAM A 37 ROB B
ADKISON BENJ A 29 FA1 W
ADNERSON ELEAS B A 19 BE1 W
AGE ALFRED A 37 HIG B
AGGERSON JESSEE A 30 IND B
AGOSTINE F M A 28 01A W
AGOSTINE J M A 28 02N W
AHERN JAS J A 29 FA1 W
AIKINS JOHN A 26 WAR W
AKIN B T A 44 DUT W
AKIN DANIEL C A 46 MCL W
AKIN FRANCIS A A 46 MCL W
AKIN H C A 44 DUT W
AKIN J A A 44 DUT W
AKIN J A A 44 LED W
AKIN JOHN A 44 LED W
AKIN JOS A A 46 MCL W
AKIN R P A 44 DUT W
AKIN WM M A 46 RAG W
ALBA SY A 32 DAV B

ALBERSON LOUIS A 35 LIM W
CERTIF GIVEN REMOVED
TO JONES COUNTY
ALBERTINE DAN'L R 29 FA1 W
NOT NATURALIZED
ALBERTSON E NEWTON A 32 THO W
ALBERTSON ISAAC A 32 LEE W
ALBERTSON JASPER A 32 THO W
ALBERTSON JOHN H A 32 THO W
ALBERTSON JOSIAH A 32 THO W
ALBERTSON P H A 35 SMI W
ALBERTSON SAMEUL A 35 KEN W
ALBERTSON THOMAS A 46 HIG W
ALBRIGHT ALEX A 46 GIB W
ALBRIGHT ANDERSON A 46 GRE B
ALBRIGHT CHARLES T A 46 GRE B
ALBRIGHT DANIEL A 46 COB W
ALBRIGHT DANIEL M A 46 GRE W
ALBRIGHT DANL A 46 GRE W
ALBRIGHT DANL M A 28 01A W
SWORN TO BY JAS H POOL
DEAF & DUMB
ALBRIGHT GABRIEL A 46 COB W
ALBRIGHT GEORGE A 46 GRE W
ALBRIGHT GEORGE W A 46 GRE W
ALBRIGHT HENRY C A 46 GRE B
ALBRIGHT J RUFUS A 46 GRE B
ALBRIGHT JAMES W A 46 GRE W
ALBRIGHT JOHN A 46 COB W
ALBRIGHT JOHNSON A 46 GRE B
ALBRIGHT LAMB A 46 GRE B
ALBRIGHT LOUIS A 32 DAV B
ALBRIGHT ROBERTH A 46 GRE W
ALBRIGHT WILLIAM A 46 COB W
ALBRIGHT WM M A 46 GRE W
ALBRITTON ISAM A 28 05A B
ALBRITTON TIMAN A 28 11T B
ALBROOKS JESSE A 37 HIG W
ALCORN JOSEPH A 40 CAN W
ALCOWT HARDY S A 28 15T W
ALDERMAN AMOS A 35 ROC W
ALDERMAN DANIEL A 29 GRA W
AFFADAVITT WILMINGTON
ALDERMAN HOSEA A 35 MAG W
ALDERMAN JESSY A 29 CED B
ALDERMAN JOSEPH A 35 ROC W
ALDERMAN P F A 29 GRA W
ALDERMAN THOMAS A 35 ROC B
ALDERMAN W F A 39 LOU W
ALDRED JOHN W A 46 JAM W
ALDRED NELSON A 32 COT W
ALDRED WALKER A 46 JAM W
ALDRIDGE AQUILLA S A 28 15T W
ALDRIDGE HAYWOOD A 28 04A B
ALDRIDGE ISAAC A 28 04A B
ALDRIDGE JAMES A 25 HAY W
ALDRIDGE JAMES A 28 04A B
ALDRIDGE JOHN W A 28 15T W
ALDRIDGE ROBERT A 28 16T B
ALDRIDGE THOS A 28 04A B
ALEXANDER A W A 40 CAN W
ALEXANDER AARON A 28 05A B
ALEXANDER DAVID A 26 SHE W
ALEXANDER GIDEON JR A 46 ROS W
ALEXANDER HENDERSON A 46 ROS W
ALEXANDER J H A 25 TUS W
ALEXANDER J L A 26 SHE W
ALEXANDER J M A 25 SHO W
ALEXANDER JAMES A 24 EDE W
ALEXANDER JAMES A 28 03B B
ALEXANDER JAMES A 28 14T B
ALEXANDER JAMES C A 46 MCL W
ALEXANDER JNO A 44 TOW B

ALEXANDER KIT A 44 SAS B
ALEXANDER MARCUS F A 40 DA1 W
ALEXANDER MINGO A 28 03A B
ALEXANDER MORRIS W A 28 17T W
ALEXANDER NELSON A 28 05A B
ALEXANDER NOAH A 40 MAU W
ALEXANDER R V A 25 HAY W
ALEXANDER SALEM A 28 05B B
ALEXANDER SANDY A 32 JAC B
ALEXANDER SANDY A 46 GRE B
ALEXANDER SOLOMON A 28 9TH B
ALEXANDER SPENCER A 28 05A B
ALEXANDER STEPNEY A 37 TA1 B
ALEXANDER W S A 26 SHE W
ALEXANDER WILLIAM A 25 HAY W
ALEXANDER WM A 19 BE1 W
ALEXANDER WM M A 26 SHE W
ALEXANDRE COOPER A 19 HAR B
ALEXANDRE GEORGE A 19 HAR B
ALFORD ADAM A 46 HIG B
ALFORD DANIEL A 39 FRE B
ALFORD DAVID A 39 GRI B
ALFORD EDMUND A 37 EDW W
ALFORD ELI A 39 FRA W
ALFORD G S A 39 GRI W
ALFORD H B A 39 FRE W
ALFORD HENRY A 39 FRE B
ALFORD J E A 39 FRA W
ALFORD JAMES R A 39 HAR W
ALFORD JOHN JR A 39 GRI W
ALFORD JOHN SR A 39 GRI W
ALFORD JULIUS A 38 FRE W
ALFORD KESER A 39 GRI W
ALFORD LITTABERRY A 39 DAV W
ALFORD MADISON A 39 FRE B
ALFORD SIMON W A 39 GRI W
ALFORD THOS A 38 FRE W
ALFRED SIDNEY J A 24 EDE B
ALISON S H A 25 TUS W
ALISON W L A 25 TUS W
ALLAN ALBERT A 26 SHE W
ALLAN CHAMPION A 26 CAR W
ALLDRED THOMAS A 46 HIG W
ALLEN A J A 39 FRA W
ALLEN ABNER CHAL A 26 BUR W
MILITIA OFFICER &
ENGAGED IN REBELLION
ALLEN ALBERT A 44 OXF B
ALLEN ALEXANDER A 29 FA1 B
ALLEN ALVEUS A 46 GRE W
ALLEN AMBROSE A 44 KNA B
ALLEN ANTHONY A 44 YXS B
ALLEN B H A 44 OXF W
ALLEN BEN A 44 OXF B
ALLEN BENJAMIN A 28 17T W
ALLEN BENJAMIN A 37 TA1 B
ALLEN BRYANT A 44 FOR W
ALLEN C E A 44 OXF W
ALLEN CAGER A 44 FIS B
ALLEN CHARLES A 39 PUG B
ALLEN CHARLES A 44 TAR B
ALLEN CHARLES N A 99 BUS W
ALLEN CHAS A 29 FA1 B
ALLEN CHASTEEN A 44 OXF W
ALLEN D S A 44 BRA W
ALLEN DANIEL A 37 ROB B
ALLEN DAVID S A 53 FAI W
ALLEN E C A 44 KNA W
ALLEN E G A 44 FOR W
ALLEN ELIJAH A 44 OXF B
ALLEN ENOCH A 44 OXF B
ALLEN ERASMUS A 44 FOR W
ALLEN FERRILL A 44 BRA B

ALLEN FRANCIS A 39 FRA W
ALLEN FRANCIS A 44 FOR W
ALLEN FRANK A 29 FLE B
ALLEN FRANK A 44 TAR B
ALLEN FRED A 19 NEW B
CERT TO HADNOT CREEK
ALLEN GEO A 28 02N W
ALLEN GEO A 29 CAR B
ALLEN GEORGE A 37 ROB B
ALLEN H Y A 44 YXR W
ALLEN HALE A 40 DA1 W
ALLEN HANNABILL A 44 OXF B
ALLEN HAYWOOD A 44 KIT B
ALLEN HENDERSON A 44 RAG B
ALLEN HENRY A 39 PUG B
ALLEN HENRY A 44 OXF B
ALLEN HORACE A 44 OXF B
ALLEN IRVIN A 29 FLE B
ALLEN ISAAC A 29 FLE B
ALLEN ISAAC A 46 JAM B
ALLEN ISAIAH JAMES A 28 05A B
ALLEN J J A 39 LOU W
ALLEN J W A 29 SEV W
ALLEN J Z A 44 FIS B
ALLEN JACKSON A 39 HAR W
ALLEN JAMES A 26 SHE W
ALLEN JAMES A 28 04B B
ALLEN JAMES A 28 05A B
ALLEN JAMES A 44 OXF B
ALLEN JASPER A 30 IND B
ALLEN JERRY A 38 FRE B
ALLEN JERRY A 44 FOR B
ALLEN JIM A 37 ROB B
ALLEN JNO L A 44 OXF W
ALLEN JOEL A 46 GIB W
ALLEN JOHN A 24 EDE B
ALLEN JOHN A 37 PEN B
ALLEN JOHN A 40 DA1 W
ALLEN JOHN A 44 BRA B
ALLEN JOHN A 44 FOR B
ALLEN JOHN A 44 YXS B
ALLEN JOHN H A 37 HIC A
ALLEN JOHN P A 28 03B W
ALLEN JOHN SR A 44 FOR B
ALLEN JOSEPH A 44 FOR W
ALLEN JOSEPH F A 39 LOU W
ALLEN JOSIAH J A 30 POP B
ALLEN L S A 39 DAV W
ALLEN LARKIN A 26 CAR W
ALLEN LEVI A 44 BRA B
ALLEN LEVI CHAL R 35 WAR B
CONVICTED OF BURGLARY
ALLEN LEWIS A 44 BRA B
ALLEN LOYD A 29 FA1 W
ALLEN MARK A 44 KNA B
ALLEN MATHEW A 37 ROB B
ALLEN MICHL A 29 FLE B
ALLEN NATHANIEL A 37 ROB B
ALLEN PETER A 28 14T B
ALLEN PRESLEY J A 39 DAV W
ALLEN RICHARD A 44 DUT W
ALLEN ROBT A 29 FA1 B
ALLEN ROBT A 44 BRA B
ALLEN ROBT A 44 LED W
ALLEN ROBT A 44 OXF B
ALLEN S S A 39 LOU W
TRNS FROM DAVIS X ROADS
ALLEN SAML A 29 FLE B
ALLEN SAML A 39 FRA B
ALLEN SAMUEL A 44 DUT B
ALLEN SIMEON A 44 KIT B
ALLEN SOLOMON A 28 9TH B
ALLEN T B A 44 BRA W

ALLEN T R	A	44	FOR	W
ALLEN T W	A	44	FOR	W
ALLEN THOMAS D	A	32	LOF	W
ALLEN THOMAS M	A	53	FAI	W
ALLEN THOS	A	44	TAR	B
ALLEN THOS C	A	19	BE1	W
ALLEN THOS H	A	28	01A	W
ALLEN VENABLE	A	44	OXF	W
ALLEN VIRGIL D	A	53	FAI	W
ALLEN W L	A	44	OXF	W
ALLEN W P	A	29	FLE	B
ALLEN W S	A	39	PUG	W
ALLEN W T	A	44	KNA	W
ALLEN WARREN	A	44	OXF	B
ALLEN WESLEY	A	44	LED	B
ALLEN WILLIAM	A	39	PUG	B
ALLEN WILLIAM	A	39	SPE	B
ALLEN WILLIAM	A	44	OXF	B
ALLEN WM H	A	24	EDE	B
ALLEY THOMAS J	A	39	JOR	W
ALLIGOOD NAT	A	40	RHY	B
ALLISON G B	A	40	STO	W
ALLISON J H	A	26	MOU	W
ALLISON J M	A	26	MOU	W
ALLISON NEWTON	A	40	STO	W
ALLISON THOMAS	A	28	10T	B
ALLISON W T	A	40	STO	W
ALLRED ELIAS	A	46	HIG	W
ALLRED WILLIAM	A	46	RAG	W
ALLRED WILLIAM	A	46	RAG	W
ALLRED WILLIAM C	A	46	RAG	W
ALPHIN JORDAN J	A	35	MAG	W
ALPHIN KING D	A	35	SMI	W
ALSBROOK LEWIS M	A	37	EDW	W
ALSTON A	A	39	FRE	B
ALSTON AARON	A	44	TAR	B
ALSTON ABRAM	A	39	HAY	B
ALSTON ALLEN	A	39	JOR	B
ALSTON ALLEN	A	44	TOW	B
ALSTON ANTHONY	A	39	JOR	B
ALSTON BEN	A	39	HAY	B
ALSTON BILLY	A	39	JOR	B
ALSTON BRISTER	A	44	TOW	B
ALSTON BROCKSTON	A	39	HAY	B
ALSTON C P	A	39	JOR	B
ALSTON CHARLES	A	39	PUG	B
ALSTON D	A	38	FRE	B
ALSTON DANIEL	A	39	HAY	B
ALSTON DAVID	A	28	03A	B
ALSTON DAVID	A	39	HAY	B
ALSTON DENNIS	A	39	HAY	B
ALSTON DOCK	A	46	HIG	B
ALSTON DOCTOR	A	39	HAY	B
ALSTON DOCTOR	A	39	JOR	B
ALSTON DUNAM	A	38	FRE	B
ALSTON DUTY	A	39	JOR	B
ALSTON EATON	A	39	LOU	B
TRNS FROM SPEEDS STORE TO LOUISBURG				
ALSTON EATON	A	39	SPE	B
ALSTON EDMOND	A	44	TOW	B
ALSTON EDMOND CHAL	A	39	JOR	B
(NO REASON GIVEN)				
ALSTON ELIHAN	A	39	HAY	B
ALSTON ELLICK	A	39	JOR	B
ALSTON EMANUEL	A	39	JOR	B
ALSTON GEORGE	A	39	JOR	B
ALSTON GEORGE	A	39	JOR	B
ALSTON GEORGE	A	39	PUG	B
ALSTON HAL	A	39	HAY	B
ALSTON HARRIS	A	39	HAY	B
ALSTON HARRY	A	39	HAR	B
ALSTON HARRY	A	39	JOR	B
ALSTON HARRY	A	39	PUG	B
ALSTON HENDERSON	A	38	FRE	B
ALSTON HENRY	A	39	HAY	B
ALSTON HOWARD	A	44	ISL	B
ALSTON HOWARD	A	44	ISL	W
ALSTON JAMES	A	39	FRE	B
ALSTON JAMES	A	44	LED	B
ALSTON JEFFREYS	A	39	LOU	B
ALSTON JIM	A	39	JOR	B
CERT WARREN CO				
ALSTON JOHN	A	39	HAY	B
ALSTON JOHN	A	39	JOR	B
ALSTON JOSEPH	A	44	TOW	W
ALSTON LEROY	A	39	SPE	B
ALSTON LITTLETON	A	39	JOR	B
ALSTON LOBE CHAL	A	39	JOR	B
(NO REASON GIVEN)				
ALSTON MATHEW	A	46	GRE	B
ALSTON MINER	A	39	PUG	B
ALSTON MOSES	A	39	HAY	B
ALSTON NED	A	39	LOU	B
ALSTON PHILL	A	39	DAV	B
ALSTON PHILL	A	39	DAV	B
ALSTON PHILL	A	39	DAV	B
ALSTON PLEASANT	A	39	JOR	B
ALSTON PORTER	A	39	JOR	B
ALSTON RANDOL	A	39	JOR	B
ALSTON REDICK	A	39	LOU	B
ALSTON REUBIN	A	44	TOW	B
ALSTON RICHARD	A	39	HAY	B
ALSTON RICHARD JR	A	39	HAY	B
ALSTON RICHD	A	44	OXF	B
ALSTON ROBT	A	39	LOU	B
ALSTON ROBT	A	44	TOW	B
ALSTON SAM	A	44	TOW	B
ALSTON SAML	A	44	RAG	B
ALSTON SIM	A	39	HAY	B
ALSTON SOLOMON	A	39	HAY	B
ALSTON THOMAS	A	39	JOR	B
ALSTON WARREN	A	44	TOW	B
ALSTON WASHINGTON	A	39	JOR	B
ALSTON WHITT	A	39	PUG	B
ALSTON WILLIAM	A	39	JOR	B
AMAN JOHN S	A	35	LIM	W
AMBERS WILLIAM	A	46	FRI	W
AMBROSE AMBROSE	A	19	MOR	B
AMBROSE DAVID	A	19	MOR	B
AMBROSE EDWARD	A	19	MOR	B
AMBROSE JOHN	A	19	NEW	B
AMBROSE LEWIS	A	72	SWA	B
AMDELL J E	A	26	BUR	W
AMDELL L D	A	26	BUR	W
AMEY ARMESTEAD	A	44	OXF	B
AMEY DAVID	A	37	PIN	B
AMEY DONEHAM	A	37	PIN	B
AMEY GRANVILLE	A	44	KIT	B
AMEY SAM	A	44	OXF	B
AMFIELD RICHARD	A	46	SUM	B
AMFIELD WASHINGTON	A	46	SUM	B
AMICK ALSON G	A	46	COB	W
AMICK FREDERICK	A	46	COB	W
AMICK GEORGE	A	46	COB	W
AMICK ISAAC	A	46	RAG	W
AMICK JOHN	A	46	COB	W
AMICK JOHN M	A	46	COB	W
AMICK SAML	A	46	COB	W
AMICK WM	A	46	COB	W
AMICK WM W	A	46	COB	W
AMIS ALEX	A	44	YXR	B
AMIS ALEXR	A	44	YXS	B
AMIS JNO JR	A	44	YXS	W
AMIS JNO SR	A	44	SAS	W
AMIS JOHN	A	44	OXF	B
AMIS LEWIS E	A	44	SAS	W
AMIS RUFUS	A	44	YXS	W
AMIS SAM	A	44	OXF	B
AMIS WASHINGTON	A	44	YXS	B
AMMOND D J	A	29	BLA	W
AMOS ARTHUR	A	37	WHI	B
AMOS RICHD	A	39	GRI	W
AMOS W T	A	46	GRE	W
AMY BURL	A	37	TA1	B
AMY HARRIS	A	37	PIN	B
AMYETT ELIJAH	A	28	03A	B
AMYETT JOHN E	A	28	01A	W
ANBER WILLIAM	A	37	ROC	B
ANDER JOHN	A	19	BE1	B
ANDERS ISAAC	A	28	9TH	B
ANDERS WILLIAM	A	28	9TH	B
ANDERSON ALFRED	A	44	OXF	B
ANDERSON ANDREW	A	46	RAG	W
ANDERSON ARON	A	46	GRE	B
ANDERSON BENJAMIN	A	37	PIN	B
ANDERSON BRICE	A	28	03A	B
ANDERSON C M	A	25	HAY	W
ANDERSON CHARLES	A	28	01B	W
ANDERSON CHARLES M	A	35	KEN	W
ANDERSON CHAS	A	29	FA1	B
ANDERSON D W	A	29	CED	W
ANDERSON DAN'L	A	29	FA1	B
ANDERSON DAVID	A	19	BE1	B
ANDERSON E	A	25	HAY	W
ANDERSON EDMOND	A	44	TOW	B
ANDERSON ELIAS	A	39	FRA	B
ANDERSON ELIJA	A	28	11T	W
ANDERSON EMANUEL	A	46	GRE	B
ANDERSON EPPS	A	39	DAV	B
ANDERSON GABL	A	40	RHY	B
ANDERSON GEO	A	19	BE1	B
ANDERSON GEORGE	A	37	PEN	W
ANDERSON H W	A	28	05A	B
ANDERSON HENDERSON	A	46	SUM	B
ANDERSON HENRY	A	35	FAI	W
ANDERSON ISAAC	A	35	ROC	B
ANDERSON J J	A	25	HAY	W
ANDERSON J W	A	25	SHO	W
ANDERSON JAMES	A	32	TYR	B
ANDERSON JAMES	A	37	EDW	W
ANDERSON JAMES	A	37	HIG	W
ANDERSON JAMES	A	46	JAM	W
ANDERSON JAS R	A	44	OXF	B
ANDERSON JERRY	A	44	OXF	B
ANDERSON JESSIE	A	37	HOL	B
ANDERSON JOHN	A	25	HAY	W
ANDERSON JOHN	A	35	WOL	B
ANDERSON JOHN	A	37	TA2	W
ANDERSON JOS A	A	28	05A	B
ANDERSON JOSHUA	A	28	11T	W
ANDERSON JOSIAH	A	37	EDW	W
ANDERSON L	A	25	SHO	W
ANDERSON LINDSEY	R	44	OXF	B
RES 10 MONTHS REJ				
ANDERSON MARTIN	A	44	RAG	B
ANDERSON MIKE K	A	37	ROB	W
ANDERSON MOSES	A	28	6TH	B
ANDERSON MOSES	A	53	GER	B
ANDERSON ROBT	A	39	GRI	B
ANDERSON ROYAL	A	44	OXF	B
ANDERSON SANDY F	R	44	OXF	B
RES STATE 10 MONTHS REJ				
ANDERSON SOLOMON	A	44	LED	B
ANDERSON SQUARE	A	44	LED	B
ANDERSON THOMAS	A	28	11T	W
ANDERSON THOMAS	A	37	HIG	W
ANDERSON THOMAS	A	37	ROB	B
ANDERSON THOMAS	A	37	ROC	B

ANDERSON THOMAS A 37 TA1 B
ANDERSON THOMAS A 46 GRE W
ANDERSON THOS A 28 03A B
ANDERSON TOM A 39 DAV B
ANDERSON WILLIAM JR A 35 MAG W
ANDERSON WM A 29 FA1 W
CERTIFICATE GIVEN
RESIDENCE WILMINGTON
NEW HANOVER CO
ANDERSON WM A 44 OXF B
ANDERSON WM J A 29 FA1 W
NOTARY PUBLIC MILITIA
OFFICER AFTER AIDED
IN REBELLION
ANDERSON WM V A 44 OXF B
ANDERSON ZADRICK A 39 PUG B
ANDERSON ZEUS A 19 BE1 B
ANDESON M L A 26 GRI B
ANDRERAS S G A 46 MON W
ANDRERSON CHARLES A 35 KEN B
ANDREW ALEX A 29 GRA B
ANDREW CHARLES G A 46 RAG W
ANDREW DAVID S A 46 GRE W
ANDREW J M A 46 MON W
ANDREW JAMES W A 46 MCL W
ANDREW JAS A 39 FRA W
ANDREW JESSE A 46 RAG W
ANDREW JESSE F A 46 RAG W
ANDREW JOHN A 46 GRE W
ANDREW JOHN M A 46 RAG W
ANDREW SAMIEL A 46 RAG W
ANDREW THOMAS D A 46 GRE W
ANDREW TILGHMAN A 46 JAM W
ANDREW WILLIAM A 46 MCL W
ANDREW WILLIAM A 46 RAG W
ANDREW WM Y A 46 GRE W
ANDREWS A B A 44 HEN W
ANDREWS ALEXANDER A 46 MON W
ANDREWS ALFRED A 37 HIC B
ANDREWS ANDREW A 19 MOR B
ANDREWS BRITTON A 44 KIT B
ANDREWS CAPE A 28 04A B
ANDREWS CASWELL A 99 BUS W
ANDREWS DAVID A 32 LEE W
ANDREWS EDWARD A 29 SEV W
ANDREWS EDWARD A 37 PIN B
ANDREWS ELIAS M A 40 DA1 W
ANDREWS GEO A 19 NEW B
ANDREWS GEORGE A 37 HIC B
ANDREWS GRAY A 37 HIC A
ANDREWS GUILFORD A 37 HIC A
ANDREWS HENRY A 37 HIC A
ANDREWS HENRY A 39 JOR W
ANDREWS ISAAC R A 30 ROA W
ANDREWS ISREAL A 19 HAR B
ANDREWS JACOB A 37 PEN B
ANDREWS JACOB A 39 LOU B
ANDREWS JAMES T A 39 JOR W
TRANS FROM COOKS DIST
ANDREWS JAMES W A 37 HIC A
ANDREWS JOHN A 35 CYP B
ANDREWS JOHN A 35 LIM W
ANDREWS JOHN A 35 ROC B
ANDREWS JOHN A 37 TA2 B
ANDREWS JOHN G A 99 BUS W
ANDREWS JOSEPH A 37 PEN B
ANDREWS JULIUS A 28 8TH W
ANDREWS LEROY A 39 LOU B
ANDREWS MOSES A 37 HIC B
ANDREWS NOAH A 37 HIC B
ANDREWS ROBERT A 37 HIC B
ANDREWS SAMUEL A A 99 BUS W
ANDREWS SHERIDAN A 37 TA1 B
ANDREWS STEPHEN A 37 PEN B
ANDREWS THOMAS A 28 9TH B
ANDREWS W H A 37 PIN W
ANDREWS W J A 35 LIM W
ANDREWS W P A 26 SHE W
MILITIA OFFICER &
ENGAGED IN REBELLION
ANDREWS WHIT A 39 PUG B
ANDREWS WM A 29 SEV B
ANDREWS WM G A 46 GRE W
ANGE H P A 28 04A W
CERTIFICATE GRANTED
TO WIGGINS
ANGE R J A 28 6TH W
ANGE ROBT B A 28 04A W
CERTIFICATE GRANTED
2 WIGGINS
ANGEN NELSON P A 28 01A W
ANSELL A J 1 A 30 KNO W
ANSELL A J 2 A 30 KNO W
ANSELL C B A 30 KNO W
ANSELL CALEB A 30 KNO W
ANSELL JONATHAN A 30 KNO W
ANSELL LEVI A 30 KNO W
ANSELL SAM'L A 30 KNO W
ANSELL WILLIAM A 30 KNO W
ANSTEAD WILLIAM A 39 JOR W
ANTHONEY CHARLES A 44 OXF B
ANTHONEY HENRY A 37 EDW B
ANTHONY GEORGE L A 46 GRE W
ANTHONY GIDEON A 40 BLA W
ANTHONY HENRY A 32 DAV B
ANTHONY HENRY A 46 KIN W
ANTHONY JAMES C A 40 FER W
ANTHONY JAMES C A 46 ROS W
ANTHONY JAMES M A 46 ROS W
ANTHONY JOHN A 26 GOF W
ANTHONY JONATHAN A 46 JAM W
ANTHONY JONATHAN G A 46 ROS W
ANTHONY OBED C A 46 ROS W
ANTHONY PETER A 26 GOF B
ANTHONY PHILIP A 26 GOF B
ANTHONY WILLIAM A 46 KIN W
ANTNA ALEXANDER A 32 TYR B
APLE JAMES A 46 MON W
APPLE D A A 46 MON W
APPLE DANIEL A 44 YXR B
APPLE HENRY A 46 GIB W
APPLE JAMES M A 46 GIB W
APPLE JAMES W A 46 MON W
APPLE JOHN A 46 GIB B
APPLE LEWIS J A 46 GIB W
APPLE MACON V A 46 GIB W
APPLE MEBANE A 46 MON W
APPLE PATTERSON H A 46 GIB W
APPLE PETER A 46 GRE W
APPLE PINKNEY A 46 MON W
APPLE SAMUEL A 46 MON W
APPLE WM L A 46 GIB W
APPLE WM M A 46 GIB W
ARCHA JOHN A 30 MOY B
ARCHA STEVEN A 30 MOY B
ARCHABALD HENRY S A 19 NEW B
ARCHER BILL A 37 PEN B
ARCHER HANSE A 32 THO W
ARCHER HENRY A 37 ROC B
ARCHER JAMES A 32 TYR B
ARCHER JOHN A 32 THO W
ARCHER JOHN A 37 HIG B
ARCHER W J A 39 SPE W
ARCHER W M A 46 SUM W
ARCHIBALD FRANK A 28 05A B
ARCHY SAMUEL A 26 BUR B
ARDEN WILLIS A 35 MAG B
ARENDELL B R 19 MOR W
ARENDELL SAMUEL A 19 NEW B
ARENDELL THOS A 19 MOR W
AREY JOS G A 29 FA1 W
AREY S S A 29 FA2 W
ARLINE DAVID W A 28 13T W
ARMES CHARLES B A 28 9TH W
ARMFIELD ITHAMER A 46 JAM W
ARMFIELD D A A 46 JAM W
ARMFIELD EMSLEY A 46 GRE W
ARMFIELD FRANKLIN A 46 FRI B
ARMFIELD FRANKLIN A 46 GRE B
ARMFIELD J A A 46 JAM W
ARMFIELD J C A 46 JAM W
ARMFIELD JONATHAN A 46 JAM W
ARMFIELD JOSEPH B A 46 JAM W
ARMFIELD JOSEPH T A 46 JAM W
ARMFIELD MADISON L A 46 GRE W
ARMFIELD N S A 46 JAM W
ARMFIELD OLIVER A 46 GRE W
ARMFIELD R B A 46 JAM W
ARMFIELD WM A 46 GRE B
ARMISTEAD HENRY A 37 SHA B
ARMNEY CHESTER A 28 03A B
ARMS J W A 28 9TH W
CERT GIVEN LIVES NOW
NEAR JAMES CITY
ARMSTEAD EDWARD A 37 TA2 B
ARMSTEAD JOE A 39 HAY B
ARMSTEAD PETER A 28 10T B
ARMSTRONG ABRAM A 40 SAN B
ARMSTRONG ALBERT A 37 ROC B
ARMSTRONG ALEXANDER A 29 MON B
ARMSTRONG ALEXANDER A 29 SEV B
ARMSTRONG ARTHUR A 40 STO W
ARMSTRONG AUGUSTINE A 37 ROC B
ARMSTRONG
BENJAMIN A J A 53 SWA B
ARMSTRONG BERRY A 37 ROC W
ARMSTRONG BERRY A 37 ROC W
ARMSTRONG BERRY D A 37 ROC W
ARMSTRONG BERTON A 37 WHI B
ARMSTRONG CALVIN A 37 ROC B
ARMSTRONG CHAS A 29 FA1 B
ARMSTRONG DOSSEY A 37 ROC B
ARMSTRONG EDWIN A 24 UPP B
ARMSTRONG EPENETUS GA 37 ROC W
ARMSTRONG F W A 40 CAN W
ARMSTRONG G S A 40 CAN W
ARMSTRONG GEO W A 29 FA1 B
ARMSTRONG GEORGE A 37 ROB W
ARMSTRONG GEORGE W A 37 SHA W
ARMSTRONG GRANDBERRYA 37 ROC B
ARMSTRONG GRANVEL A 40 SAN B
ARMSTRONG GRAY A 37 ROC W
ARMSTRONG GUS A 37 WHI B
ARMSTRONG HALL A 28 16T W
ARMSTRONG HARRISON A 37 ROC B
ARMSTRONG J M A 40 RHY W
ARMSTRONG J M A 40 STO W
ARMSTRONG J MATHEW A 40 STO W
ARMSTRONG JACINTH A 37 ROC B
ARMSTRONG JACK A 29 FLE B
ARMSTRONG JESSIE A 37 ROC B
ARMSTRONG JNO A 29 FA1 B
REMOVED TO BLADEN CO
ARMSTRONG JOHN A 40 SAN W
ARMSTRONG JOHN L A 40 STO W
ARMSTRONG JOLLIE A 37 ROC W
ARMSTRONG JOS A 29 FLE B
ARMSTRONG JOSEPH A 37 WHI B
ARMSTRONG KING A 29 SEV B

ARMSTRONG M R A 40 CAN W
ARMSTRONG MATHEW A 40 SAN W
ARMSTRONG MATHEW A 40 STO W
ARMSTRONG N E A 35 LIM W
ARMSTRONG NED A 37 ROC B
ARMSTRONG NED A 40 STO B
ARMSTRONG NELSON A 53 BUR W
ARMSTRONG PETER A 28 03A B
ARMSTRONG PETER R 40 DA1 B
NAME LINED OUT
CAUSE CONVICTED OF FELON
ATER REGISTERING
ARMSTRONG R A 29 LOC B
ARMSTRONG RICHD A 29 FA1 B
ARMSTRONG ROBERT A 37 PEN W
ARMSTRONG SAML A 29 FLE B
ARMSTRONG THOMAS J A 35 LIM W
ARMSTRONG THOS A 29 FA1 B
ARMSTRONG W C DEAD 28 02N W
ARMSTRONG WM A 29 FA1 B
ARMSTRONG WM A 29 FLE B
ARMSWORTHY JAMES A 32 CLE W
ARMWOOD HENRY A 29 GRA B
ARMWOOD JAMES A 35 FAI B
ARNETT ALLEN A 29 FA1 W
ARNETT JNO A 29 ROC W
ARNETT JOHN F A 46 GRE W
ARNETT JOHN G A 35 KEN W
ARNETT NEILL A 29 GRA W
ARNETT WILLIAM A 29 SEV W
ARNETT WILLIAM A 35 GLI W
ARNEY ADMIRAL P A 40 DA2 W
ARNOCK A A 46 SUM W
MALITIA OFFICER BEFORE
WARE. REJ BY OWN REQ.
ARNOLD A N A 28 04A B
ARNOLD AARON A 28 03A B
ARNOLD ABRAM A 28 01A B
ARNOLD ALEXR A 28 04A B
ARNOLD CAIN W A 28 9TH B
ARNOLD CHESLY A 44 DUT W
ARNOLD E F A 28 7TH W
ARNOLD EDWARD A 28 7TH W
ARNOLD ELISHA A 28 8TH W
ARNOLD GABRIEL A 28 12T B
ARNOLD J A A 44 DUT W
ARNOLD J J A 25 HAY W
ARNOLD J N A 25 SHO W
ARNOLD JAMES A 28 7TH W
ARNOLD JAMES A 29 FA2 W
COPIED FROM DUPLICATE
ARNOLD JOHN A 28 8TH W
ARNOLD JOSEPH H A 28 03A W
ARNOLD JULY A 28 12T B
ARNOLD MOSES D A 28 7TH W
ARNOLD S B A 28 7TH W
ARNOLD STEPHEN A 28 7TH W
ARNOLD STEPN A 28 04A B
ARNOLD WILLIAM A 28 7TH W
ARNOLD WILLIAM A 32 THO W
ARNOLD WILLIAM W A 28 7TH W
ARNOLD WM S A 29 FA2 W
COPIED FROM DUPLICATE
ARRENDAL WILLIAM A 39 LOU B
ARRENDELL DANIEL A 39 LOU B
ARRINGTON BRADFORD A 37 ROC B
ARRINGTON CEZAR A 44 OXF B
ARRINGTON EOCH A 44 OXF B
ARRINGTON EPHRAIM A 39 DAV B
ARRINGTON JACOB A 37 SHA B
ARRINGTON SAMUEL A 37 ROC B
ARRINGTON WILLIS M A 44 HEN W
ARROWOOD DRURY M A 40 DEC W
ARROWOOD WILLIAM A 40 DEC W
ARTEST ISAAC A 37 TA1 B
ARTHUR BENJN A 28 02N B
ARTHUR ELIJAH A 72 SWA W
ARTHUR G G A 28 12T W
ARTHUR GEORGE A 19 HAD W
ARTHUR HARVEY A 28 12T W
ARTHUR J G A 28 04A W
ARTHUR JAMES A 19 HAD W
ARTHUR MARTIN A 28 13T B
ARTHUR MICHAEL A 28 12T W
ARTHUR SETH A 19 MOR W
ARTIS BENAGER A 29 FLE B
ARTIS GRAY A 28 05B B
ARTIS HAYWOOD A 29 FA1 B
ARTIS IRVIN A 29 FLE B
ARTIS JONATHAN A 29 FA1 B
ARTIS WILLIAM A 28 7TH B
ARTIS WM A 29 FA1 B
ARWOOD L C A 26 BOR B
ASBELL CORNELIUS A 24 EDE W
ASBELL ELISHA A 24 UPP W
ASBELL JAMES A 24 UPP W
ASBELL JOHN A 24 EDE W
ASBELL MARTIN D A 24 UPP W
ASH HENRY A 29 FA1 B
ASH JESSEE A 44 FIS B
ASH JULIUS A 28 01A W
STRICKEN OUT APR 1, 86
ASH THOMAS A 46 JAM B
ASH WILLIAM A 46 MON B
ASH WM A 29 FA1 B
ASH WM A 29 FA1 B
ASHBEE ABIL C A 30 ROA W
ASHBEE BENJAMIN A 30 ROA B
ASHBEE DANIEL A 30 CUR B
ASHBEE HENRY A 30 ROA B
ASHBEE JACOB A 30 ROA B
ASHBEE LAMB A 30 TUL B
ASHBEY JORDEN A 19 BE1 B
ASHBY BAKER A 24 MID W
ASHBY BUSHWAY A 24 MID W
ASHBY PEVAY A 24 MID W
ASHBY THOMAS M A 24 MID W
ASHE CHARLES A 46 GRE B
ASHE GEORGE A 46 GRE B
ASHE M A 26 BOR B
ASHER MAX R 28 01A W
NOT NATURALIZED
ASHFORD THOMAS A 37 ROB B
ASHLEY BENJAMIN R A 53 LA1 W
ASHLEY HENDERSON M A 24 MID W
ASHLEY JEREMIAH A 24 EDE W
ASHLEY MEADE R 24 MID W
CONVICTED OF FELONY
THEREFORE CANNOT VOTE
ASHLEY MILES A 24 EDE W
ASHLEY WILLIAM T A 53 GER W
ASKEW B F A 39 PUG W
ASKEW BENJ A 46 RAG B
ASKEW BRONT A 28 03A B
ASKEW CHARLES E A 39 PUG W
ASKEW GEORGE A 39 PUG W
ASKEW ISAAC A 28 04A B
CERTIFICATE GRANTED
2 WIGGINS
ASKEW J H A 39 PUG W
ASKEW OSBORN L A 39 JOR W
ASKEW SOLOMON A 39 HAY W
ASKEW THOMAS A 39 SPE W
ASKEW W M A 39 HAY W
ASKEW WILLIAM E A 39 PUG W
ASKEW WILLIE A 39 PUG W
ASKEW WILLIS A 39 PUG W
ASKIN JAMES A R 28 12T W
WAS A CONSTABLE
APPOINTED BY CO.
CONST. & A SOLDIER
ASKINS JOHN S A 28 12T W
ASKINS THOMAS H A 28 13T W
ATHERLEY JESSE A 28 14T W
ATKINS JAMES A 46 SUM W
ATKINS L C A 25 HAY W
ATKINS WATSON A 25 HAY W
ATKINSON ARNOLD A 28 7TH B
ATKINSON BENJAMIN A 28 11T W
ATKINSON BENJAMIN A 37 PIN B
ATKINSON CAESAR A 28 7TH B
ATKINSON CHARLES A 28 11T W
ATKINSON CURTIS A 28 7TH B
ATKINSON DANNIEL A 28 11T B
ATKINSON DAVID A 28 7TH B
ATKINSON HARDY A 37 WEB B
ATKINSON JACOB A 28 03B W
ATKINSON JERRY A 28 7TH B
ATKINSON JOHN A 28 7TH B
ATKINSON LEMON A 37 PEN W
ATKINSON M B A 37 WHI W
ATKINSON MARK A 28 11T B
ATKINSON MATTHEW A 29 FA2 W
ATKINSON MINGO A 28 7TH B
ATKINSON THEOPHILUS A 37 WHI W
ATKINSON THOMAS A 28 7TH B
ATKINSON WILLIAM A 28 11T W
ATKINSON WILLIAM A 37 WHI W
ATMORE GEORGE A 28 9TH B
ATTENBRIDGE ANDREW A 28 03A B
ATTMORE GEO S A 28 01B W
ATWATERS ANDREW A 44 LED B
ATWELL S S A 19 HUN W
AUGUSTUS P F A 24 EDE W
AUGUSTUS SOLOMON A 28 02N B
CERTIFICATE GRANTED
TO RALEIGH
AURTHER ANSON A 19 BE1 W
AURTHER GILBERT A 19 STR W
AURTHER JACOB A 19 STR W
AURTHER JACOB C A 19 STR W
AURTHER JOHN A 19 STR W
AURTHER RICHARD A 19 STR W
AUSTAND SYMPSON A 32 DAV W
AUSTELL A P A 26 BUR W
AUSTEN BENJ A 29 FA1 B
AUSTIN ABRAM A 28 04B B
AUSTIN BENJ A 29 GRA B
AUSTIN CHARLES J A 37 TA1 W
AUSTIN DALLAS A 29 FA1 B
AUSTIN DANIEL A A 53 GER W
AUSTIN DANIEL B A 30 ROA W
AUSTIN FRANCIS M A 53 HAT W
AUSTIN GEORGE A 24 EDE B
AUSTIN GRANVILLE A 37 TA1 B
AUSTIN HENRY A 37 TA1 B
AUSTIN ISAAC A 37 TA1 B
AUSTIN ISAAC F A 53 HAT W
AUSTIN JERRY A 37 TA2 B
AUSTIN JOHN A 37 PEN W
AUSTIN JOHN A 53 HAT W
AUSTIN JOHN L A 53 HAT W
AUSTIN JOUSHA D A 53 HAT W
AUSTIN MAJOR A 28 04A B
AUSTIN MOSES R A 53 HAT W
AUSTIN NELSON A 29 FA1 B
AUSTIN NELSON A 39 FRA B
AUSTIN WALLACE A 53 HAT W
AUSTIN WARREN A 39 FRA B

AUSTIN WILLIAM D A 30 ROA W
AUSTIN WM D A 53 HAT W
AUSTON CORNELIOUS A 53 GER W
AUSTON URIAH G A 53 FAI W
AUTERY C W A 29 ROC W
AUTHER ABRAM A 19 STR W
AUTHER DAVID F A 19 STR W
AUTRY A R A 29 FLE W
AUTRY ALEXR A 29 LOC W
AUTRY ALLEN A 29 LOC W
AUTRY DANIEL A 29 LOC B
AUTRY DAVID B A 29 LOC W
AUTRY GEO A 29 LOC W
AUTRY HARY A 29 FLE B
AUTRY JACOB A 29 LOC W
AUTRY JOHN A 29 LOC W
AUTRY M T A 29 LOC W
AUTRY NEWSOM A 29 ROC W
AUTRY RAFORD A 29 LOC W
AUTRY VAN A 29 ROC W
AUTRY W W A 29 LOC W
AUTTREY JNO A 29 FA1 W
AVANT A P A 26 BLA W
AVENT THOMAS A 37 ROC W
AVERAGE CUDJOE A 28 10T B
AVERETT HIRAM R A 29 CED W
AVERETT JOEL A 44 OXF W
AVERETT S S A 29 CED W
AVERETT T R A 44 OXF W
AVERETTE JOSHUA A 44 SAS B
AVERIES ADAM A 29 LOC B
AVERITT ENOCH A 28 11T W
AVERITT LUTHER A 28 11T W
AVERY CALVIN A 99 BUS B
AVERY CHARLES A 29 GRA B
AVERY ELIJAH A 44 OXF W
AVERY JAMES A 28 6TH W
AVERY JAMES A 44 OXF B
AVERY JOHN E A 28 7TH W
AVERY LAWRENCE A 99 BUS B
AVERY RUBEN A 44 OXF B
AVERY WILEY A 28 7TH W
AVERY WILLIAM A 28 8TH W
AVIN GEO A 29 GRA B
AVSHUR JESSE A 28 11T W
AVY LEWIS A 99 BUS B
AWATERS ALFORD A 44 LED B
AXIOM ALEXANDER A 37 PIN B
AXIOM DREW A 37 PIN B
AXIONS DANIEL A 37 EDW B
AXIONS LEWIS A 37 EDW B
AXUM GIDEON A 37 ROB B
AXUM IRVIN A 37 ROB B
AXUM WILLIAM A 28 04B W
AYCOCK A S A 39 SPE W
AYCOCKE D L A 39 SPE W
AYCOCKE SAM A 39 SPE B
AYDELOTT JOHN A 30 POW B
AYDLETT L D A 46 MON W
AYDLETT LEVIN A 46 MON W
AYDLOTTE JOHN F A 26 SHE W
AYDLOTTE MILTON J A 40 DA1 W
AYDLOTTE THOMAS D A 30 POW W
AYECOCK AMBROSE A 39 SPE W
AYERES RICHARD A 32 THO B
AYRES BARRY A 37 HOL B
AYRES JOHN A 37 HOL B
AYRES THOMAS T A 46 JAM W
AYSCUE J D A 39 SPE W
AYSCUE WILLIE A 39 SPE W
AYSCUE WILLIS A 39 HAR W
AYSCUE WM JAMES A 39 SPE W
AYSKEW THOS S A 39 SPE W

- B -

BABBINGTON ELISHA J A 40 MAU W
BABBIT CHARLES M A 28 16T W
BABBIT THOMAS A 28 16T B
BACHELOR JAMES D A 37 SHA W
BACHELOR REDIN A 37 MAN B
BACK TIMOTHY A 37 HIC B
BACON ISAAC A 29 CED B
BADGER LOVELESS A 28 03A B
BADGER MANUEL A 28 03A B
BADGER W H R 32 DAV W
FOR HOLDING OFFICE OF
MAGISTRATE BEFORE AND
DURING THE WAR
BADGER WM A 28 03A B
BADGET C L A 32 JAC W
BADGET CALVIN A 46 MON B
BADGET WILLIS A 46 MON B
BADGET WILSON A 32 JAC W
BADGETT J D A 44 OXF W
BADGETT JAMES W A 44 YXS W
BADGETT W S A 32 DAV W
BADGETT WM J A 44 TAR W
BADHAM MILES A 24 EDE B
BADHAM WILLIAM R 24 EDE W
REJECTED BY THE BOARD
CAUSE WAS NOTARY PUBLIC
BEFORE THE WAR
WAS CAPT IN CONFEDERATE ARMY
DID NOT TAKE THE OATH
BADHAMS THOS C A 24 EDE W
BADY HENRY A 44 OXF B
BADY J W A 32 COT W
BAER KAUFMAN A 28 01A W
BAER LEOPOLD A 28 01A W
BAER LOUIS N A 28 01A W
BAGBY G K A 28 02N W
BAGBY ROBERT A 44 YXS B
BAGGETT W A 29 LOC W
BAGGINS JOE A 37 ROB B
BAGLEY LEWIS A 37 ROC B
BAGLEY R A 29 BLA W
BAGWELL BERY A 99 BUS W
BAGWELL GRANBERY R A 99 BUS W
BAGWELL N J A 99 BUS W
REMOVED TO JOHNSON CO
CERTIFICATE GIVEN
BAGWELL NEEDHAM B A 99 BUS W
BAGWELL WILLIAM S A 99 BUS W
BAHAN W B A 46 FRI W
BAIL D J A 19 NEW W
BAILEY D D A 44 FOR W
BAILEY HARDEE A 28 16T W
BAILEY J A A 44 FOR W
BAILEY J R A 28 01A W
BAILEY J T A 44 FOR W
BAILEY JAMES A 37 HIG B
BAILEY JAMES B A 28 16T W
BAILEY JOSEPH A 28 02N B
BAILEY LEVI A 44 KIT W
BAILEY R C A 46 JAM W
BAILEY RANSOM A 44 FIS W
BAILEY ROBT A 44 FOR W
BAILEY SAML H A 39 HAR W
BAILEY STOKES A 32 TYR W
BAILEY SUSSEX A 44 SAS B
BAILEY W D A 39 DAV W
BAILEY W P A 44 FOR W
BAILEY WILEY A 99 BUS W
BAILEY WILLIAM A 26 BLA W
BAILEY WM D A 44 FOR W
BAILEY WM H A 37 ROC W
BAILY JOHN A 24 EDE B

BAILY JOHN M A 25 HAY W
BAILY STEVEN A 32 JAC W
BAILY THOMAS A 32 JAC W
BAILY THOMAS A 46 GRE B
BAILY W W A 32 JAC W
BAIN A G A 29 BLA W
BAIN ALLEN A 28 6TH B
BAIN ANGUS A 29 BLA W
BAIN CALVIN A 29 FLE B
BAIN DANIEL A 29 BLA W
BAIN DANL JR A 29 BLA W
BAIN ENERY J A 37 WHI W
BAIN ISAAC A 29 FA1 B
BAIN ISAAC JR A 29 FA1 B
BAIN J JR A 29 FLE W
BAIN J W A 29 BLA W
BAIN JNO A 29 LOC B
BAIN JNO 2ND A 29 BLA W
BAIN JOHN A 29 BLA W
BAIN JOHN A A 46 HIG W
BAIN PATK A 29 BLA W
BAIN RICHD A 29 FA1 B
BAINBRIDGE DEMPSEY A 37 EDW B
BAINES JAMES A 46 SUM W
BAINES LINDSAY A 46 SUM B
BAINY LEVI A 29 FA1 B
BAIRD BENJAMIN A 44 YXS B
BAIRD CHARLES A 44 YXS B
BAIRD JOHN N A 40 DEC W
BAIRDELL TONY A 32 CLE B
BAIRLE WILLIE A 37 MAN B
BAISDON ALFRED A 19 BE1 W
BAISON J M A 35 WOL B
BAISON LEMUEL A 46 SUM W
BAITMAN BENJAMIN A 24 MID W
BAITY A G A 26 BOR W
BAITY JOSEPH A 35 LIM B
BAITY TAYLOR A 35 LIM B
BAKER A H A 39 LOU W
BAKER ALEXANDER A 28 02N B
BAKER ALEXANDER A 28 16T B
BAKER ALFRED A 29 LOC B
BAKER ALFRED A 38 FRE B
BAKER ALLAN A 26 CAR W
BAKER AMOS A 37 ROC B
CERT NASH CO REJECTED
BAKER ANTHONEY A 24 EDE B
BAKER ARCHD A 29 FLE W
BAKER BENJAMIN A 37 HIG B
BAKER BLAKE A 37 EDW W
BAKER BRIANT A 39 FRE B
BAKER BRYAN A 28 11T W
BAKER BRYANT A 39 GRI B
BAKER CARY A 37 HIG B
BAKER D J A 29 FLE W
BAKER DAN'L A 29 FA1 B
BAKER DANIEL A 29 FLE W
BAKER DANIEL A 40 MAU W
BAKER DERRY A 39 HAR W
BAKER DORRIS A 37 HIG B
BAKER DORSEY A 28 05A B
BAKER DORSON A 37 EDW B
BAKER EDWARD A 40 BLA W
BAKER ELI A 40 MAU W
BAKER FREDERICK A 37 HIG B
BAKER GEO B A 29 FA2 W
BAKER GEORGE S A 39 LOU W
BAKER HARRY A 37 HOL B
BAKER HENRY A 39 HAR W
BAKER HOGAN A 35 SMI W
BAKER HYRAM A 25 HAY W
BAKER J A A 39 GRI W
BAKER J B A 29 FA1 W

BAKER J C A 39 GRI W
BAKER J ELLITT A 24 UPP W
BAKER J W A 29 FA1 W
BAKER JACOB A 35 MAG W
BAKER JAMES A 29 FLE W
BAKER JAMES A 35 SMI W
BAKER JAMES A 39 HAR W
BAKER JAMES L A 24 UPP W
BAKER JAS A 29 FA1 B
BAKER JAS A 29 FA1 W
BAKER JEPTHA A 28 01B W
BAKER JERRY A 39 GRI B
BAKER JESSEE A 39 HAR B
BAKER JNO W A 29 BLA W
BAKER JOHN A 37 HIG B
BAKER JOHN A 39 HAR W
BAKER JOHN A 44 FIS W
BAKER JOHN A A 46 FRI W
BAKER JOHN R A 35 SMI W
BAKER JONAS A 26 CAR W
BAKER JOSEPH A 24 EDE B
TRANSFERRED TO
MIDDLE GROUND ORIGINAL
REGISTERED BACK AS A
SUPPERINTENDANT OF ELEC
TION AND MUST VOTE AT THE
MIDDEL GROUND PRECINCT
BAKER JOSEPH H A 37 TA1 W
BAKER LONDON A 37 TA1 B
BAKER LOUIS A 39 HAR B
BAKER M A A 29 FA1 W
BAKER M C A 39 GRI W
BAKER MARSHAL A 39 LOU W
BAKER MICHAEL A 40 BLA W
BAKER MILES N A 29 FA1 W
BAKER O J A 29 FLE W
BAKER OTTAWAY A 37 EDW B
BAKER PETER A 39 GRI B
BAKER R J A 29 BLA W
BAKER R S A 39 HAR W
BAKER RICHARD A 29 CAR W
BAKER RICHARD A 37 ROB W
BAKER RICHD A 39 HAR B
BAKER SEWELL A 39 GRI B
BAKER SIDNEY A 39 HAR B
BAKER SIMON A 39 HAR W
BAKER SOLOMON A 37 HIG B
BAKER THOS A 39 GRI B
BAKER THOS J A 29 FA1 W
FLEA HILL
BAKER WILLIAM A 37 EDW B
BAKER WILLIAM A 37 HIG B
BAKER WILLIAM A 37 TA1 B
BAKER WILSON A 37 HIG B
BAKER WM B A 29 CAR W
BAKER WM J A 28 8TH W
BALANCE BENJAMIN A 53 LA1 W
BALANCE HENDERSON A 53 LA1 W
BALARD ELI F A 46 FRI W
BALARD J A 46 FRI W
BALARD PINKNEY A 46 FRI W
BALCHAR B B A 44 YXR W
BALDWIN ANDREW A 40 DA1 W
BALDWIN BENJ A 29 FA1 B
BALDWIN EMANUAL A 37 TA2 B
BALDWIN HARRIS A 29 FA1 B
BALDWIN ISAAC A 29 FA1 B
BALDWIN ISAAC A 29 FA1 B
BALDWIN PHILLIP P A 46 GIB W
BALDWIN PRESTON A 24 EDE B
BALDWIN S A A 29 FA1 W
BALDWIN SHERIDAN A 29 FA1 B
BALDWIN SIMON A 28 04A B

BALE S R A 28 01A W
BALENGER J F A 46 FRI W
BALENGER M H A 46 FRI W
BALENTINE AMERICO A 30 CUR B
BALES J C A 46 JAM W
BALES JOHN W A 46 JAM W
BALES WARNER A 53 GER B
BALL ADAM A 39 SPE W
BALL C R A 44 BRA W
BALL EDWIN A 44 BRA W
BALL ELIJAH A 44 BRA W
BALL G N A 44 BRA W
BALL H N A 39 SPE W
BALL J N A 39 SPE W
BALL J R A 39 FRA W
BALL JAMES A 35 WAR B
BALL JOHN O A 35 LIM W
BALL JOSEPH W A 28 16T W
BALL L D A 44 FOR W
BALL LEMUEL A 30 COI W
BALL MARTIN V A 53 LA2 W
BALL PHILLIP A 32 THO W
BALL TONY A 32 POS B
BALL W H A 28 04B W
BALL WM A 44 HEN W
BALL Y R A 39 HAY W
BALLAN D A A 19 SMY W
BALLANC WESLEY A 30 MOY W
BALLANCE ALEXANDER A 53 LA2 W
BALLANCE BETHUEL JR A 30 CUR W
BALLANCE BETHUEL SR A 30 CUR W
BALLANCE CALEB A 30 CUR W
BALLANCE DANIEL R 53 SWA B
STRICKEN OUT APRIL 16
1868 NOT 21 YEARS OLD
BALLANCE DAVID W A 53 HAT W
BALLANCE EDWARD A 53 SWA B
BALLANCE EUGENE A 30 COI W
BALLANCE JACKSON A 30 CUR W
BALLANCE JAMES C R 53 SWA W
CHALLENGED
NAME LINED OUT
WAS POST MASTER BEFORE
THE WAR FOR THE
CONFEDR GOVERMENT REJ
BALLANCE JOHN A 30 CUR W
BALLANCE LEVI A 30 COI W
BALLANCE LEVI A 30 CUR W
BALLANCE LEVIN A 30 CUR W
BALLANCE LEWIS A 53 LA1 B
BALLANCE MECHANT A 53 HAT W
BALLANCE ROBERT A 30 IND W
BALLANCE STEPHEN A 28 17T W
BALLANCE STEVEN A 30 TUL W
BALLANCE THOMAS P A 53 FAI W
BALLANCE W J A 30 IND W
BALLANCE W S A 30 CUR W
BALLANCE WILLIAM D A 53 LA1 W
BALLANCE WILLOUGHBY A 30 COI W
BALLANCE WILSON A 30 COI W
BALLANCE WM A A 53 HAT W
BALLANCE WM A A 53 HAT W
BALLANCE WM B A 53 HAT W
BALLANCE WM PELEG A 28 01B W
BALLANCE WM W A 53 OCR W
BALLANCE ZION S A 30 COI W
BALLARD ABNER A 46 FRI W
BALLARD ANTHONY A 24 EDE B
BALLARD B T A 39 LOU W
BALLARD G M A 29 FLE W
BALLARD JAMES A 29 ROC W
BALLARD JUNIOUS A 39 LOU W
BALLARD NEPTURE A 39 LOU B

BALLARD R W A 28 03B W
BALLARD W H A 39 LOU W
TRNS TO DAVIS X ROADS
BALLENCE HENRY A 32 THO B
BALLENGER J D A 28 8TH W
CERTIFICATE GIVEN
LIVES AT SMITHFIELD
BALLIANCE G W A 32 THO W
BY CERTIF
BALLINGER W A A 28 6TH W
BALLMORE NORFLEET A 37 ROB B
BALLMORE WILLIAM A 37 ROB B
BALSLEY BENJ A 46 GRE B
BALSLEY
RICHARD HENRY A 46 RAG B
BALSLY J B A 46 GRE W
BALTHORP J W A 39 DAV W
BALTHROP WILLIS A 39 JOR B
BANDY OFFIE A 37 ROB B
BANE ALEXANDER A 46 GRE B
BANE NEEDHAM A 37 SPA B
BANES ALEXANDER A 37 WHI B
BANES ALLEN A 37 WHI B
BANES ANTHONY A 46 GRE B
BANES H J A 39 GRI W
BANES JAMES A 37 WHI B
BANES SIM A 37 WHI B
BANES WILLIS A 37 WHI B
BANETT M C (8 M) A 26 SHE W
MILITIA OFFICER &
ENGAGED IN REBELLION
BANGERT F S A 28 03A W
BANGERT JOHN D A 28 01A W
BANGERT SEBASTIAN A 28 01A W
BANISTER JOHN A 40 SAN W
COPIED FROM DUPLICATE
BANKE EDMOND A 32 POS W
BANKS ADAM A 37 TA2 B
BANKS ALFRED A 28 14T W
BANKS AMOS A 28 03A B
BANKS ANDREW A 24 EDE B
BANKS CASWELL A 28 14T W
BANKS CASWELL A 37 PIN B
BANKS CHAS R A 29 FA1 W
WILMINGTON NC 4-10-68
BANKS EDWARD A 28 02N B
BANKS ENOCH A 30 CUR W
BANKS GEO F A 28 04A B
BANKS GEORGE A 28 02N B
BANKS HARRISON A 37 TA1 W
BANKS HARRY A 28 03A B
BANKS JACOB A 28 02N B
BANKS JAMES A 28 16T W
BANKS JAMES A 30 GIB B
8-MOS-RESIDENCE
BANKS JAS A 29 FA1 B
BANKS JOHN A 28 04A B
BANKS JOHN A 46 GRE B
BANKS JOHN A 99 BUS B
BANKS JOHN D A 28 10T W
BANKS JOHN D A 28 14T W
BANKS MATTHEW A 28 04A B
BANKS MILTON A 46 GRE B
BANKS OBEDIAH A 19 HAD B
BANKS OFFA A 99 BUS B
BANKS OLIVER P A 28 14T W
BANKS PETER A 28 14T W
BANKS SYLVESTER A 28 14T W
BANKS THOS A 28 04A B
BANKS WALKER A 37 TA1 B
BANKS WASHINGTON A 24 EDE B

BANKS WILLIAM A 39 HAY B
OXFORD PRE
GRANVILLE CO
BANKS WILLIAM A 44 OXF B
BANNER ALFRED A 37 WHI B
BANTON BENJAMIN A 28 14T B
BANTON HENRY A 53 LA1 B
BANTON JOHN A 28 01A B
BARBARY ISAAC A 35 FAI W
BARBEE HENRY A 46 SUM W
BARBEE W G A 46 HIG W
BARBEE Y W A 46 JAM W
BARBER ALDEY A 35 MAG W
BARBER DAVID A 53 LA1 B
BARBER DAVID A 53 LA1 B
BARBER HEZKIAH A 53 LA1 B
BARBER JOHN A 28 01A B
BARBER JOHN A 28 05B B
BARBER JOHN A 28 10T B
BARBER JOHN W JR A 53 LA1 B
BARBER JOHN W SR A 53 LA1 B
BARBER MOSES A 28 04A B
BARBER NOAH A 28 16T W
BARBER SAMUEL A 53 GER B
BARBER SAMUEL A 53 LA1 B
BARBER SAMUEL S A 53 LA1 W
BARBER SPENCER A 53 FAI B
BARBER WM A 28 03A B
BARBURY DOC A 37 PEN B
BARCLEY SAML E A 30 CUR W
BARCLIFT DEMPSEY A 24 MID W
BARCO BALEY A 30 NOR W
BARCO BENJIMAN F A 30 COI W
BARCO CALEB A 30 NOR W
BARCO LUKE JR A 30 NOR W
BARCO LUKE SR A 30 NOR W
BARCO SYLVANUS A 28 10T W
BARDEN BUCKNER C A 35 KEN W
BARDEN EDWARD A 35 KEN B
BARDEN GILES A 28 04A B
BARDEN HENRY A 28 05A B
BARDEN JERRY A 28 7TH B
BARDEN JOHN F A 19 NEW B
BARDEN PRIMUS A 35 MAG B
BARDEN RICHARD A 35 MAG B
BARDEN RICHARD A 53 LA1 B
BARDEN SAMEUL J A 35 MAG W
CERTIFICATE TO
KENANSVILLE 11 APRIL 1868
BARDEN THOMAS A 35 KEN B
BARDY DENNIS A 28 05A B
BAREFOOT WILEY A 29 BLA W
BARETT GEORGE A 37 MAN B
BARETT JAMES A 37 MAN B
BARFIELD BLOUNT A 37 HIC A
BARFIELD EPHRIHAM A 37 HIC A
BARFIELD HORACE E A 37 HIC A
BARFIELD ISAAC A 37 HIC B
BARFIELD ISAM A 28 7TH B
BARFIELD JACOB A 28 7TH B
BARFIELD JOHN A 35 ALB W
BARFIELD JOHN A 37 HIC A
BARFIELD JOHN A 37 HIC B
BARFIELD KAIN A 37 HIC B
BARFIELD LEWIS A 37 HIC A
BARFIELD NELSON A [illegible] HIC B
BARFIELD RICHARD A 35 GLI W
BARFIELD WILLIAM A 35 WOL B
BARGE EDWARD W A 29 FA2 W
BARHAM G S A 39 HAR W
BARHAM GEORGE A 28 02N B
BARHAM SANDY A 28 02N B
BARKER CALEB A 46 JAM W
BARKER D J A 46 FRI W
BARKER D T A 44 RAG W
BARKER DAVID J A 28 10T W
BARKER ENOCH A 46 FRI W
BARKER FRANK A 44 RAG B
BARKER H C A 44 ISL W
BARKER HENRY A 46 FRI W
BARKER JOHN C A 37 HIG W
BARKER JOHN G A 44 RAG W
BARKER JOSEPH A 28 10T W
BARKER MAJOR A 44 RAG B
BARKER STEPHEN T A 46 FRI W
BARKER WESLEY A 44 OXF B
BARKLEY JOHN A 46 JAM W
BARKUM N G A 39 LOU W
BARLER JOHN A 26 GOF W
BARLEY CALVIN A 39 HAR W
BARLOW AMOS DON A 37 PEN B
BARLOW BRYANT A 19 BE1 B
BARLOW DOUBLEN A 37 ROC B
BARLOW FRANK A 37 PIN B
BARLOW LEWIS A 37 TA1 B
BARLOW SAMPSON A 37 TA1 B
BARLOW SANDY A 37 ROC B
BARN HENRY A 29 BLA X
BARNARD ANDREW JR A 25 HAY W
BARNARD CHALES A 30 MOY B
BARNARD GRANDY A 30 MOY W
BARNARD HOMER A 25 HAY W
BARNARD ISHMAL A 30 MOY B
BARNARD J S A 28 02N W
BARNARD J T A 44 HEN W
BARNARD JOHN JR A 30 MOY W
BARNARD
JOHN SR CHAL A 30 MOY W
BARNARD JOHNSON A 30 NAR B
BARNARD MUSTIPHER A 30 IND B
BARNARD NED A 30 CUR B
BARNARD ORSAN R 25 HAY W
AFTER BEING OVERSEER OF ROAD
AIDING IN REBELLION BY
HIRING SUBSTITUTE AND
ACTING IN HOME GUARD
BARNARD SAML A 30 MOY B
BARNARD SAML A 30 MOY B
6-MONTH-RESIDENCE
BARNARD THOS A 30 IND B
BARNARD VILGIL A 25 HAY W
BARNARD
WILLOUGHBY D A 30 IND W
BARNELL WILLIAM A 37 WHI W
BARNER JACOB A 37 ROC B
BARNER MICHAEL A 28 9TH B
BARNER SOLLY A 37 ROC B
BARNES A L A 39 DAV W
TRNS TO NASH CO
APR 17 1868
BARNES ALEXANDER A 32 TYR W
BARNES ALEXANDER A 32 TYR W
BARNES ALEXANDER A 37 HIG B
BARNES ALLEN A 28 01A B
BARNES ALLEN A 28 05A B
BARNES ALLEN A 37 HIG B
BARNES ANDREW P A 28 17T W
BARNES ANTHONY A 28 01B B
BARNES ASA A 28 7TH W
BARNES BARRELL WM A 37 SHA W
BARNES BRISTER A 37 HIG B
BARNES BURRELL A 28 05A B
BARNES C A A 32 TYR W
BARNES CHARLES A 37 ROC W
BARNES DAIRY A 28 03A B
BARNES DAMON A 28 05A B
BARNES DENNY A 37 SPA W
BARNES ELI A 37 MAN B
BARNES FRANCIS M A 37 HIG W
BARNES FRANK A 44 HEN B
BARNES G A 29 LOC B
BARNES GEO W A 44 HEN W
BARNES GEORGE A 35 FAI B
BARNES GREEN A 29 FA2 B
BARNES HARRY A 44 RAG B
BARNES HILMAN A 44 OXF W
BARNES HILRED A 37 WHI B
BARNES J M A 44 HEN W
BARNES JACK A 37 ROC B
BARNES JAMES A 37 HIG B
BARNES JAMES A 37 HIG B
BARNES JAMES A 37 ROC B
BARNES JOHN A 19 NEW B
BARNES JOHN A 28 9TH B
BARNES JOHN D A 37 ROC W
BARNES JOHN W A 44 HEN W
BARNES LION A 37 HIG B
BARNES MONROE A 37 HIG B
BARNES RICHARD A 37 EDW B
BARNES RICHARD A 37 HIG B
BARNES RICHARD A 37 SHA B
BARNES ROBERT A 28 8TH W
BARNES SAML A 28 05A B
BARNES SAMUEL W A 32 TYR W
BARNES T H A 29 FA2 W
BARNES WASHN A 28 05A B
BARNES WILLIAM A 32 TYR W
BARNES WM A 28 6TH B
BARNES ZACHARIAH A 53 HAT W
BARNET B D A 35 ALB W
BARNET WILLIAM A 30 ROA B
BARNETT AARON A 53 HAT W
BARNETT ALLEN A 40 SAN B
BARNETT ALX A 44 OXF W
BARNETT C M A 26 MOO W
BARNETT DENIS A 30 IND B
BARNETT FRANCIS A A 28 17T W
BARNETT G A 26 BOR W
BARNETT GREEN A 46 HIG B
BARNETT HEZEKIAH F A 53 HAT W
BARNETT HOWARD N A 53 HAT W
BARNETT JAMES A 35 SMI W
BARNETT JAMES L A 53 FAI W
BARNETT JOHN A 25 HAY W
BARNETT OLIVER N A 53 HAT W
BARNETT R H A 26 MOO W
BARNETT T K A 26 SHE W
BARNETT W J A 44 YXR W
BARNETT W S A 44 OXF W
BARNETT WILLIAM A 26 MOO W
BARNETT WILLIAM A 35 SMI W
BARNETT WILLIAM L A 53 FAI W
BARNETT WM A A 44 OXF W
BARNEY JOHN A 53 LA1 B
BARNHART LEVI A 46 GIB W
BARNHILL JAMES A 40 BLA W
BARNHILL JOHN J A 37 TA2 W
BARNHILL LEMUAL E A 37 TA2 W
BARNHILL RICHARD M A 35 KEN W
BARNS CHRISTOPHER A 53 KEN W
BARNS FRANCIS A 19 BE1 B
BARNS GABRIEL A 46 GIB B
BARNS H A A 26 GOF W
BARNS JOHN A 53 KEN W
BARNS JOSEPH A 19 BE1 B
BARNS PETER A 19 BE1 B
BARNS ROBT A 46 GIB B
BARNS SALATHIEL A 46 ROS W
BARNS WILLIAM A 19 BE1 B

BARNS Y T A 26 GOF W
BARNS ZEBDEE A 25 TUS W
BARNUM STEPHEN A 37 ROB B
BARR GEORGE A 46 MON B
BARREN MALLE A 37 HIG B
BARREN NATHAN A 37 HIG B
BARRET SILAS A 28 6TH B
BARRETT AZOR A 40 DA1 B
BARRETT FRANKLIN A 26 SHE W
BARRETT PERRY A 29 FA1 B
BUNN LEVEL, HARNET CO
APRIL 11 1868
BARRETT THOMAS A 30 POW W
BARRETT W H A 26 SHE W
BARRINGER EDMOND A 28 03A B
BARRINGTON FREEMAN A 28 13T B
BARRINGTON FURNEY O A 28 11T W
BARRINGTON ISAAC A 28 11T W
BARRINGTON J J A 28 11T W
BARRINGTON JAMES A 19 BE1 W
BARRINGTON JESSE S A 28 13T W
BARRINGTON NOAH A 28 13T W
BARRINGTON RICHARD A 28 13T W
BARRINGTON WM A 28 13T W
BARRINGTON WM R A 28 14T W
BARRINGTON WM T A 28 13T W
BARRON CHARLES H A 37 HIG W
BARRON JESSE A 28 05A B
BARROW BENJAMIN A 28 11T W
BARROW ELI A 28 10T B
BARROW FREDRICK A 53 GER B
BARROW GEORGE A 53 FAI B
BARROW GEORGE A 53 GER B
BARROW HENRY A 53 GER B
BARROW J S A 39 LOU W
BARROW JABIN A 53 GER B
BARROW JABIN C A 53 FAI B
BARROW JOHN H A 32 YAD W
BARROW N M A 39 FRA W
BARROW REUBEN A 28 16T W
BARROW SAMPSON A 53 GER B
BARROW SAMUEL A 53 GER B
BARROW THOMAS A 53 GER B
BARRUM HENRY A 44 BRA B
BARRY TONY A 19 MOR B
BARSWILL JAMES A 39 DAV W
BARTEE JOHN A 28 04A B
BARTER DIVER A 24 EDE B
BARTHOLOMEW
BENJAMIN CHAL 39 JOR W
BARTHOLOMEW CHARLES A 39 SPE W
BARTHOLOMEW
GEORGE W A 39 JOR W
BARTHOLOMEW S C A 39 SPE W
BARTLET LEVI A 19 HAD W
BARTLEY CLARKSON A 46 ROS W
BARTLEY MARTIN A 46 GRE W
BARTLEY PETER A 46 GRE B
BARTOLE PETER A 29 FA2 W
BARTON H M A 46 HIG W
BARTON J R A 46 HIG W
BARTON JAMES A 46 COB B
BARTON JOHN R A 46 HIG W
BARUM HARRISON A 37 TA2 B
BARUM W H A 46 SUM W
BASBOURN
NATHANIEL B A 46 GRE B
BASDEN BRANTLEY A 35 LIM W
BASDEN KENIAN A 35 WAR W
BASKENVILLE MOSIS A 44 HEN B
BASKERVILLE
CHARLES JR A 44 YXS B
BASKERVILLE
CHARLES SR A 44 YXS B
BASKERVILLE ROBT A 44 HEN B
BASKERVILLE RUFFIN A 44 HEN B
BASKERVILLE STARLIN A 44 HEN B
BASKERVILLE THOMAS A 44 TOW B
BASKET A M A 44 HEN W
BASKET JOSEPH A 44 HEN W
BASNET BOSSON A 28 05A B
BASNIGHT DAVID A 53 HAT W
BASNIGHT JACK A 24 EDE B
BASNIGHT JAMES A 28 05A B
BASNIGHT JESSE A 28 05A B
BASNIGHT MARTIN A A 53 HAT W
BASNIGHT ROBERT B A 53 HAT W
BASNIGHT WILLOWBY A 53 HAT W
BASNIGHT ZACHARIAH A 53 HAT W
BASS ALVER A 28 04A B
BASS ARTHER A 44 KIT B
BASS BONEY A 44 OXF B
BASS ELIJAH A 39 DAV W
BASS ELIJAH A 39 JOR W
BASS HARRY A 37 EDW B
BASS HILLIARD A 37 PIN B
BASS HINTON A 44 FOR B
BASS HORATIO A 24 EDE W
BASS JACK A 44 OXF B
BASS JAMES A 24 EDE W
BASS JAMES A 29 FA1 B
BASS JAMES A 46 COB B
BASS JAMES W A 24 EDE W
BASS JOHN A 24 EDE W
BASS JOHN A 46 GRE B
BASS JOHN L A 24 EDE W
BASS KADER A 24 EDE W
BASS LARY A 35 MAG B
BASS LEWIS A 28 16T B
BASS LEWIS G A 35 MAG W
BASS PETER A 28 05B B
BASS PETER A 35 MAG B
BASS PEYTON A 24 EDE W
BASS QUINTON A 24 EDE W
BASS ROBERT A 29 LOC B
BASS RUFUS R A 44 FOR B
BASS SILAS A 35 WAR W
BASS THOS E A 24 EDE W
BASS WASHINGTON E A 46 GRE B
BASS WILLIAM A 44 TAR B
BASS WILLIAM H A 35 MAG W
BASS WM A 44 KIT B
BASS WM A A 44 OXF B
BASSETT JOSPH A 37 HIC B
BASSETT RICHARD B A 37 TA1 W
BASSETT WILLIAM A A 37 TA1 W
BASTON EDWARD A 19 BE1 B
BASTON JAMES A 19 BE1 B
BASWELL ALFRED 19 BE1 W
BATANHAMER DAVID A 46 FRI W
BATCHELLOR ALFORD A 39 DAV B
BATCHELLOR JOHN A 39 DAV B
BATCHELOR DAVID A 39 DAV B
BATCHERLOR N J A 39 LOU W
BATEMAN ASA A 28 01A W
BATEMAN J A 28 01A W
BATEMAN JOHN A 53 LA2 W
BATES ALEXANDER A 32 DAV W
BATES JACOB A 32 DAV W
BATHEY SANDY A 29 GRA B
BATRI JOHN T A 26 SHE W
BATS BRICE A 19 BE1 B
BATTEN BENJAMIN A 37 HIG B
BATTEN HIRAM A 40 CAN B
BATTEN J A A 46 FRI W
BATTLE ABEL A 37 ROC B
BATTLE ABRON A 37 MAN B
BATTLE ALBERT A 37 ROC B
BATTLE ALEXANDER A 37 ROC B
BATTLE ALFRED A 28 03A B
BATTLE ALFRED A 37 ROC B
CERT RES NASH CO
BATTLE ALLEN A 37 PEN B
BATTLE ANDREW A 37 TA1 B
BATTLE ANTONY A 37 MAN B
BATTLE ARNOLD A 37 ROC B
BATTLE BEN A 37 ROC B
BATTLE BENJAMIN A 37 MAN B
BATTLE BENJAMINE A 37 HOL B
BATTLE BENNETT A 37 ROC B
BATTLE BENTON A 37 ROC B
BATTLE BICY A 37 MAN B
BATTLE BRISTOW A 37 TA1 B
BATTLE CADMUS A 37 HIG B
BATTLE CAGER A 37 ROC B
BATTLE CALHUN A 37 WHI B
BATTLE CARY A 37 ROC B
BATTLE CHAS A 39 FRE B
BATTLE CLINTON A 37 MAN B
CERT RES NASH CO
BATTLE CROWELL A 37 ROC B
BATTLE CRUMWELL A 37 ROC B
BATTLE DALLAS A 37 ROC B
BATTLE DANIEL A 37 ROC B
BATTLE DAVID A 37 ROC B
BATTLE DERRY A 37 HIG B
BATTLE DIXON A 37 ROC B
BATTLE DORSEY A 37 ROC W
BATTLE EDWARD A 53 GER B
BATTLE EFFERT A 37 ROC B
BATTLE ELIAS A 37 ROC B
BATTLE ELISHA A 37 ROC B
BATTLE EPHRIHAM A 37 TA1 B
BATTLE FRANK A 37 TA1 B
BATTLE FRIDAY A 37 MAN B
BATTLE GAHRAN A 37 ROC B
BATTLE GEORGE A 37 ROC B
BATTLE GUILFORD A 37 ROC B
BATTLE GUY A 37 TA1 B
BATTLE HANDY A 37 ROC B
BATTLE HENDERSON A 37 ROC B
BATTLE HENRY A 37 ROC B
BATTLE HEYWOOD A 37 TA2 B
BATTLE HILLIARD A 37 PIN B
BATTLE HORACE A 37 ROC B
BATTLE IRVIN A 37 HIG B
BATTLE ISAAC A 19 BE1 B
BATTLE ISAAC A 37 ROB B
BATTLE ISAAC A 37 ROC B
BATTLE JACK A 37 ROC B
BATTLE JACOB A 37 ROC B
BATTLE JACOB A 37 ROC B
BATTLE JAMES A 37 MAN B
BATTLE JAMES A 37 ROC B
BATTLE JAMES A A 37 PEN W
BATTLE JAMES L A 37 TA1 W
BATTLE JAMES S A 37 TA1 W
BATTLE JASON A 37 PEN B
BATTLE JATHA A 37 PEN B
BATTLE JESSE A 37 SHA B
BATTLE JESSY A 37 ROC B
BATTLE JOB A 37 ROC B
BATTLE JOHN A 37 PIN B
BATTLE JOHN A 37 ROC B
BATTLE JOHN A 37 ROC B
BATTLE JOHN N A 37 ROC B
BATTLE JORDAN A 37 HIG B
BATTLE JORDAN A 37 ROC B

BATTLE JOSEPH A 37 ROB B
BATTLE JOSEPH A 37 ROC B
BATTLE JOSEPH A 37 ROC B
BATTLE JOSEPH J A 37 MAN W
BATTLE JOYNER A 37 ROC B
BATTLE KING A 37 ROC B
BATTLE LEVI A 37 ROC B
BATTLE LUKE A 37 ROC B
BATTLE MADISON A 37 ROC B
BATTLE MARCUS A 37 ROB W
BATTLE NATHAN A 37 ROC B
BATTLE NELSON A 37 ROC B
BATTLE ORAN A 37 ROC B
BATTLE PETER A 19 BE1 B
BATTLE PETER A 37 ROC B
BATTLE PETER A 37 TA2 B
BATTLE POLD A 37 ROC B
BATTLE RANSOM A 37 PEN B
BATTLE RICHARD A 37 ROC B
BATTLE RICHARD A 37 ROC B
BATTLE RICHMOND A 37 ROC B
BATTLE RICHMOND A 37 ROC B
BATTLE RILEY A 37 ROC B
BATTLE RUFUS A 37 ROC B
BATTLE SAMUEL A 37 HIG B
BATTLE SEZOR A 37 ROC B
BATTLE SOLOMON A 37 ROC B
BATTLE SPENCER A 37 ROC B
BATTLE STARLING A 37 ROC B
BATTLE TEMPY A 37 HOL B
BATTLE THOS C A 28 04A B
BATTLE TONY A 37 MAN B
BATTLE TURNER A 37 MAN B
BATTLE TURNER A 37 TA1 B
BATTLE TURNER W A 37 ROC W
BATTLE VAN A 37 MAN B
BATTLE W H A 39 LOU W
BATTLE
WASHINGTON NO 1 A 37 ROC B
BATTLE
WASHINGTON NO 2 A 37 ROC B
BATTLE WIL A 37 ROC B
BATTLE WILEY A 37 ROC B
BATTLE WILEY A 37 ROC B
BATTLE WILLIAM A 37 MAN B
BATTLE WILLIAM A 37 ROC B
BATTLE WILLIAM A 37 ROC B
CERT REIDENCE NASH CO
BATTLE WILLIAM A 37 ROC W
BATTLE WILLIAM A 37 ROC W
STRICKEN APRIL 10, 1868
BATTLE WILLIAM A 37 TA1 B
BATTLE WRIGHT A 37 ROC B
BATTLLE GEORGE C A 37 MAN W
BATTS ABEL A 35 CYP B
BATTS ALFRED A 37 PEN B
BATTS ALPHONZO A 37 EDW B
BATTS DAVID A 37 EDW B
BATTS DAVID N A 37 WEB W
BATTS DEMPSEY B A 37 EDW W
BATTS EARNEST A 37 EDW B
BATTS HARRY A 37 EDW B
BATTS HILLRED A 37 MAN B
BATTS ISAAC A 37 ROC B
BATTS ISAAC F A 37 EDW W
BATTS JACOB A 37 EDW B
BATTS JAMES A 35 CYP B
BATTS JAMES A 37 WHI W
BATTS JEREMIAH A 37 PEN W
BATTS JEREMIAH A 37 SHA W
BATTS JESSE A 35 CYP W
BATTS JOHN A 37 HIG B

BATTS JOHN R 37 EDW B
NAME LINED OUT
BATTS JOSEPH A 37 HIG B
BATTS LONDON A 35 KEN B
BATTS NATHAN A 35 CYP W
BATTS NATHAN A 35 ISL W
BATTS RANDALL A 37 EDW B
BATTS WILLIAM J A 37 SHA W
BATTS WILLIAM L A 37 ROC W
BATTS WRIGHT A 35 CYP B
BATTS YORK A 37 EDW B
BAUCOM ELIJAH A 99 BUS B
BAUCOM HENRY A 99 BUS B
BAUCOM PLENTY A 99 BUS B
BAUCOM RICHARD A 99 BUS B
BAUCOM YORK A 99 BUS B
BAUER HARRY A 24 EDE B
BAUGH JNO A 29 FA1 B
BAUGH JOS A 29 FA1 B
BAUGH P P A 29 FA1 B
BAUM ABRAM A 30 POP W
BAUM AMOS A 37 HIG B
BAUM DANIEL A 30 ROA W
BAUM DEMPSEY A 30 ROA B
BAUM EDWARD S A 53 FAI W
BAUM GEORGE A 30 ROA B
BAUM JAMES A 30 ROA B
BAUM JAMES A 53 FAI B
BAUM JOHN A 30 NOR W
BAUM JOHN A 30 ROA B
BAUM JOSIAH B A 53 FAI W
BAUM NORRIS H A 30 NOR W
BAUM ROBERT A 53 LA1 B
BAUM RULENE A 30 POW B
BAUM SAMUEL A 30 ROA W
BAUM SAMUEL L A 53 FAI W
BAUM THOMAS T A 30 NOR W
BAUM WILLIAM L A 30 NOR W
BAUM YORK A 30 POP B
BAXLEY ELIAS A 29 GRA W
AFFIDAVIT "HOLLOW"
CUMBERLAND CO
BAXLEY JNO A 29 FA1 W
BAXTER B M A 30 IND W
BAXTER CAMERON A 30 MOY B
BAXTER DALLIS A 30 IND B
BAXTER EDWARD A 28 05A B
BAXTER EDWARD A 30 ROA B
BAXTER H E A 30 CUR W
BAXTER ISAAC A 30 MOY B
BAXTER J J DR CHALA 30 CUR W
BAXTER J W A 28 01A W
BAXTER J W CHALR 30 CUR W
ASSISTING IN REB.
BAXTER JEFFREY A 30 ROA B
BAXTER JNO A 30 CUR B
BAXTER JOHN A 30 COI W
BAXTER JOSEPH A 30 COI W
BAXTER JUBITER A 30 IND B
BAXTER MILES A 30 TUL B
BAXTER MORIS A 30 MOY B
BAXTER SAM'L A 30 KNO W
BAXTER WALLACE A 30 MOY B
BAXTER WILL J A 30 CUR W
BAXTER WILLIAM N A 32 DAV W
BAXTER WM F A 30 CUR W
BAYATT FERDINAND A 37 PIN W
BAYLOR BENNETT A 46 JAM B
BAYLOR JOHN H A 28 02N W
BAYNES O P A 46 SUM W
BAYSMORE RILEY A 28 14T B

BEACH J T R 25 HAY W
FOR HOLING OFFIC
BEACHAM JESSE H A 28 16T W
BEACHER W M A 32 JAC W
BEACHUM E F A 44 OXF W
BEACHUM KADOR A 30 NOR W
BEACHUM MATHIAS A 30 NOR W
BEADIE ZION A 53 GER B
BEAL J W A 44 SAS W
BEAL W F A 29 FA1 W
BEALE JESSE D A 28 01A W
BEALL JAMES F A 32 COT W
BEALS ENOCH F A 30 NOR W
BEALS HENRY S A 19 BE1 W
BEALS MORIS A 30 NOR W
BEALS WILSON A 30 IND W
BEAM ANDREW A 26 CAR W
BEAM D C A 26 BOR W
BEAM D H A 26 CAR W
BEAM D M A 26 SHE W
BEAM DANIEL A 26 SHE B
BEAM DAVID C A 40 BLA W
BEAM E F A 26 CAR W
BEAM EDWARD A 40 MAU B
BEAM HENRY S A 40 BLA W
BEAM J A A 26 BOR W
BEAM J B A 26 BLA W
BEAM J H A 26 GRI W
BEAM J T A 26 CAR W
BEAM JOHN F A 40 BLA W
BEAM JOHN T A 40 BLA W
BEAM LAWSON A 40 BLA B
BEAM M L A 26 MOO W
BEAM M R A 26 GRI W
BEAM MARTIN A 26 GRI W
BEAM MICHAEL A 40 BLA W
BEAM MICHAEL L A 40 BLA W
BEAM S M A 26 GRI W
BEAM STARLING A 26 CAR B
BEAMAN DUNCAN J A 35 WAR B
BEAMAN IRVIN A 35 WAR B
BEAMON
[NO FIRST NAME] A 32 DAV B
BEANER D R A 26 WAR W
BEARD EGBERT M A 29 GRA W
BEARD ELAM A 46 JAM W
BEARD J S A 29 FLE W
BEARD MICHAEL A 29 FA1 B
BEARD W A A 29 FLE W
BEARD WM S A 46 JAM W
BEARSE EDOM A 28 03A B
BEASLEY -?- A 35 MAG W
BEASLEY ALFRED A 28 14T B
BEASLEY AMBROSE A 30 KNO W
BEASLEY BENJ A 28 01A B
BEASLEY BENJAMIN F A 30 ROA W
BEASLEY BREUSTER A 28 16T B
BEASLEY CHARLES A 44 DUT B
BEASLEY DANIEL A 99 BUS W
BEASLEY DANIEL J A 35 MAG W
BEASLEY E A A 30 KNO W
BEASLEY ED J A 30 KNO W
BEASLEY EVERETT A 35 MAG B
BEASLEY FRANCIS A 24 EDE B
BEASLEY HENRY A 24 EDE B
BEASLEY HENRY A 29 FLE B
BEASLEY HENRY A 30 KNO W
BEASLEY HEZEKIAH W A 30 NOR W
BEASLEY J P A 44 DUT W
BEASLEY JOACHUM A 30 KNO W
BEASLEY JOHN A 30 NOR W
BEASLEY JOSEPH A 24 EDE B

BEASLEY JUDGE A 44 SAS B
BEASLEY MAJOR A A 35 MAG W
BEASLEY MALICHI JR A 30 COI W
BEASLEY R B A 44 DUT W
BEASLEY RICHARD A 28 15T B
BEASLEY ROBT A 24 EDE W
BEASLEY ROBT A 44 YXR B
BEASLEY S J A 44 DUT W
BEASLEY SAMUEL H A 30 COI W
BEASLEY STEAPHEN A 30 NOR W
BEASLEY STEPHEN H A 44 YXS W
BEASLEY TIMOTHY A 35 MAG B
BEASLEY W C A 30 KNO W
BEASLEY W R A 44 OXF W
BEASLEY WASHINGTON A 44 YXS B
BEASLEY WILLIAM A 44 YXS B
BEASLEY WILLIAM J A 30 KNO W
BEASLEY WM A 28 03A B
BEASLY ALLEN A 38 FRE B
BEASLY BENJAMIN A 37 ROB B
BEASLY J M A 29 FA2 W
BEASLY JOHN A 24 EDE B
BEASON ARCHABLE A 26 GOF W
BEASON JOHN A 26 MOU W
BEASON JOSEPH A 26 MOU W
BEASON R E A 46 FRI W
BEASON ROBERT A 26 MOU W
BEATIE PINKNEY A 26 BUR W
BEATTIE FRANCIS A 40 FER W
BEATTIE JAMES O A 40 FER W
NAME LINED OUT
MILITIA OFFICER BEFORE
THE REBELLION & GAVE AID
& COMFORT TO THE ENEMY
DID NOT QUALIFY
BEATTIE WILLIAM W A 40 FER W
BEATTY ABRM A 29 FA1 B
BEATTY CALVIN A 29 FA1 B
BEATTY HENRY S A 29 FA1 B
BEATTY J P A 40 STO W
BEATTY JAMES A 37 ROC B
BEATTY THOS A 29 FA1 B
BEATTY WILLIAM A 29 FA2 B
BEATY ANDREW A 40 STO W
BEATY CYRES A 40 STO B
BEATY J W A 40 STO W
BEATY JACOB A 40 STO B
BEATY R J A 40 STO W
BEATY ROBERT A A 40 STO W
BEATY S E A 40 SAN W
BEATY SAMUEL A 40 STO W
BEATY SHERREL L A 40 STO B
BEATY WILLIAM A 40 SAN W
BEATY WM F A 40 STO W
BEAUFORT STEPHEN A 28 05A B
BEAVER JAS W A 44 TAR W
BEAVER RICHARD A 37 ROC B
BEBEE EDWD A 29 FA1 B
BEBEE EDWD SR A 29 FA1 B
BECK AMBROSE A 32 THO W
BECK C F A 44 DUT W
BECK CHRISTIAN A 32 DAV W
BECK CHRISTIAN A 32 LOF W
BECK D H A 44 DUT W
BECK DANIEL A 32 DAV W
BECK DAVID A 32 COT W
BECK DAVID A 32 DAV W
BECK DAVID A 32 LOF W
BECK DAVID A 32 LOF W
BECK DAVID M A 32 COT W
BECK G M A 32 LOF W
BECK GEORGE A 32 COT W
BECK GEORGE A 32 DAV W
BECK GEORGE A 32 LOF W
BECK GEORGE CHAL A 32 TYR W
FOR HOLDING OFFICE OF
COMPTROLLER BEFORE THE
WAR AND ENGAGED IN THE
WAR. RECON.
BECK J B A 44 DUT W
BECK J L A 32 COT W
BECK J R A 32 LOF W
BECK J W A 44 DUT W
BECK JACOB CHAL A 32 DAV W
FOR HOLDING OFFICE OF
MAGISTRATE BEFORE THE
WAR AND ENCOURAGED THE
WAR. RECON.
BECK JAMES A 44 DUT W
BECK JOHN A 25 SHO W
BECK JOHN A 32 COT W
BECK JOHN A 32 THO W
BECK LENARD A 32 LOF W
BECK MICHAEL A 44 DUT W
BECK OBADIAH A 32 DAV W
BECK OBADIAH A 32 LOF W
BECK PETER A 32 DAV W
BECK PETER A 32 LEE W
BECK R H A 44 FOR W
BECK RICHARD A 32 TYR W
BECK SOLOMON A 32 DAV W
BECK T B A 32 COT W
BECK W A A 32 LOF W
BECK WILLIAM L A 32 LEE W
BECKERDITE A A 32 POS W
BECKERDITE B F A 32 POS W
BECKERDITE JOHN A 32 POS W
BECKERDITE WILLIAM A 32 POS B
BECKHAM JOSEPH A 44 HEN W
BECKTON JOHN A 19 BE1 B
BECKWITH ALLEN A 28 8TH B
BECKWITH DAVID A 53 LA1 B
BECTON A A 19 MOR B
BECTON ALLEN A 28 04A B
BECTON ALLEN A 28 04A B
BECTON CAESAR A 28 8TH B
BECTON DENNISON A 28 04A B
BECTON EPHRAIM A 28 8TH B
BECTON GEORGE A 28 04A B
BECTON GEORGE A 28 6TH B
BECTON JAMES H A 28 04A B
BECTON JOE A 28 04A B
BECTON LUKE A 19 MOR B
BECTON MOSES A 28 05A B
BECTON NORRIS A 28 8TH B
BECTON PRIMUS A 28 03A B
BECTON RIGHT A 19 MOR B
BECTON SIMON A 28 6TH B
BECTON SIMON A 29 LOC B
BECTON WM J A 19 MOR W
BEDDINGFIELD C A 39 FRA W
BEDDINGFIELD HENRY A 38 FRE W
BEDDINGFIELD J M A 39 FRA W
BEDDINGFIELD JOHN A 39 FRE W
BEDDINGFIELD THOS A 38 FRE W
BEDDINGFIELD WM H A 44 HEN W
BEDENHAMMER JOHN D A 32 POS W
BEDLIN BARTLETT A 39 GRI W
BEDSOLE LARKINS A 29 CED W
BEDSOLE THOS A 29 LOC W
BEDSOLE TRAVIS A 29 LOC W
BEEBE JOSEPH A A 24 MID B
BEEBE SAMUEL A 29 FA2 B
BEEKER SAMUEL A 32 COT W
BEELS BENJ F A 30 IND W
BEENBLOSOM ABRIHAM A 32 COT W
BEENBLOSSOM ABSLAM A 32 LOF W
BEENBLOSSOM
FREDRICH A 32 COT W
BEENBLOSSOM WM L A 32 COT W
BEERS DANIEL A 32 JAC W
BEERS GIDEON A 32 JAC W
BEERS J C A 32 JAC W
BEERS JAMES A 32 JAC W
BEERS JOHN A 32 JAC W
BEERS L A 32 JAC W
BEERS PETER A 32 JAC W
BEERS R W A 32 JAC W
BEESLEY JAMES M A 28 8TH W
BEESLEY JOSEPH A 30 IND W
BEESLEY M W A 30 CUR W
BEESON ISAAC A 46 JAM W
BEGHAM JESS A 40 STO B
BEIRD ABRAM A 40 SAN B
BEIRD J W A 40 SAN B
BEIRD ROBERT A 40 SAN W
BELAND HENRY P A 37 SHA W
BELAND JAMES A 37 SHA W
BELAND WILLIAM B A 37 SHA W
BELANGA ELISHA A 28 9TH W
BELANGA WILLIAM A 28 9TH W
CERT GIVEN NOW
LIVES IN NEW BERN
BELCH MILLS A 24 EDE B
BELCHER JAMES A 37 TA2 B
BELCHER ROBERT A 28 16T W
BELIMA ALFRED A 37 MAN B
BELIMA CARY A 37 MAN B
BELIMA HENRY A 37 MAN B
BELKER BLOUNT A 37 SPA B
BELKER GEORGE A 37 SPA B
BELKER HUITING A 37 SPA B
BELKER JEREMIAH A 37 SPA B
BELKER SAMUEL A 37 SPA B
BELL ALEX A 39 GRI B
BELL ALEXANDER A 19 NEW B
BELL ALFRED L A 46 MCL W
BELL AMARIAH A 19 NEW W
BELL AMMON G A 19 SMY W
BELL AMOS G JR A 28 10T W
BELL AMOS G SR A 28 10T W
BELL ANDREW J A 53 GER W
BELL AUGUSTUS A 44 OXF B
BELL B F A 46 HIG W
BELL B J A 28 10T W
CERTIF GIVEN NOW LIVES
AT BEAUFORT NC
BELL BENJ A A 19 HAR W
BELL BENJAMIN A 53 GER B
BELL BRANSON C A 30 IND W
BELL C C A 19 HAD W
BELL CALEB A 30 IND B
BELL CALEB A 30 IND W
BELL CALVIN C A 29 FA1 B
BELL CANE A 19 NEW B
BELL CHARLES A A 19 BE1 B
BELL CICERO S A 19 BE1 W
BELL CUFFEE A 19 MOR B
BELL D B A 19 NEW W
BELL D R A 26 SWA W
BELL D S A 19 HAD W
BELL D W A 19 NEW W
BELL DANIEL A 19 MOR B
BELL DANIEL A 19 MOR W
BELL DANIEL A 44 SAS B
BELL DAVID A 19 MOR B
BELL DAVID W A 19 DAV W
BELL DERRY A 28 12T B
BELL DUKE A 30 TUL W

Name		Age	Area	Race
BELL E S	A	19	HAD	W
BELL EDWARD	A	19	BE1	B
BELL EGBERT	A	44	OXF	B
BELL ELI	A	40	FER	W
BELL ELIJAH G	A	28	10T	W
BELL ELIJAH P	A	53	SWA	W
BELL ELISHA	A	46	MCL	W
BELL ELYAS	A	35	WOL	B
BELL EMANUEL	A	28	10T	B
BELL ENOCH P	A	30	TUL	W
BELL FELIX	A	35	WOL	B
BELL FRANCIS M	A	53	GER	W
BELL FRANKLIN	A	26	SWA	B
BELL FRANKLIN	A	28	16T	W
BELL FULDEN	A	26	SWA	W
BELL G C	A	19	HAR	W
BELL GEO R	A	19	SMY	W
BELL GEO W	A	30	MOY	W
BELL GEORGE	A	19	NEW	W
BELL GEORGE	A	37	ROB	B
BELL GEORGE	A	37	TA1	B
BELL GEORGE	A	53	GER	B
BELL GEORGE R	A	53	FAI	W
BELL GEORGE T	A	28	10T	W
BELL GEORGE W	A	19	STR	W
BELL GIBBONS	A	19	HAD	W
BELL GIDEON	A	37	SHA	B
BELL H J	A	39	GRI	W
BELL HANSEL C	A	19	HAD	W
BELL HARDEE	A	37	HIG	B
BELL HARRY	A	28	03A	B
BELL HARRY	A	30	IND	B
BELL HAYWOOD D	A	30	KNO	W
BELL HENRY	A	53	GER	B
BELL HENRY H	A	19	BE1	B
BELL HIRAM	A	19	NEW	W
BELL HIRAM R	A	19	NEW	W
BELL HORACE	A	29	FA1	B
BELL IRVING	A	37	PIN	B
BELL ISAAC	A	29	CAR	B
BELL ISAAC	A	44	KIT	B
BELL ISAAC	A	72	SWA	B
BELL ISAAC T	A	30	TUL	W
BELL ISRAEL F	A	53	LA1	W
BELL J A	A	28	01A	W
BELL J B	A	26	SWA	W
BELL J S	A	19	NEW	W
BELL JABEZ W	A	19	HAD	W
BELL JAMES	A	28	03B	B
BELL JAMES	A	53	GER	B
BELL JAMES E	A	53	GER	W
BELL JAMES H	A	30	MOY	W
BELL JAMES M	A	19	BE1	B
BELL JAMES M	A	25	PIN	W
BELL JAMES M	A	39	GRI	W
BELL JAMES W	A	19	MOR	W
BELL JARVIS	A	19	NEW	B
BELL JAS	A	29	CAR	B
BELL JAS	A	29	CAR	B
BELL JASON	A	30	IND	W
BELL JEFFERSON	A	37	EDW	B
BELL JERRY	A	28	6TH	B
BELL JNO B	A	30	MOY	W
BELL JOHN	A	19	NEW	B
BELL JOHN	A	37	ROB	B
BELL JOHN C	A	72	SWA	W
BELL JOHN JR	A	40	DA1	W
BELL JOHN SEN	A	40	DA1	W
BELL JOS	A	29	CAR	B
BELL JOSEPH	A	46	MCL	W
BELL JOSEPH	A	72	SWA	W
BELL JOSEPH C	A	30	IND	W
BELL JOSEPHUS C	A	40	DEC	W
BELL JOSHUA	A	28	10T	W
BELL JOSUAH	A	19	HAD	B
BELL KILLIS	A	28	6TH	B
BELL KIT	A	28	11T	B
BELL L M DR	A	30	CUR	W
BELL LABEN	A	53	BUR	B
BELL LARKIN	A	29	CAR	B
BELL LEROY	A	46	MCL	W
BELL LEVI	A	19	NEW	W
BELL LORANZO M	A	40	FER	W
BELL M R	A	19	MOR	W
BELL MALICHI	A	30	MOY	W
BELL MARTIN	A	37	EDW	B
BELL MATHIAS	A	53	GER	W
BELL MATHIAS D	A	30	IND	W
BELL MILES MINOR	A	30	IND	B
BELL MILS	A	30	IND	B
BELL MONROE	A	40	DA1	W
BELL MOSES	A	28	05A	B
BELL N A	A	19	MOR	W
BELL N A	A	19	NEW	W
BELL N D	A	19	MOR	W
BELL NIGA	A	29	CAR	B
BELL NOAH	A	28	10T	B
BELL OBA	A	32	DAV	B
BELL OCHRE	A	19	NEW	B
BELL ORPHES	A	19	HAR	B
BELL ORRIN D	A	19	STR	W
BELL OSCOE	A	44	OXF	B
BELL OTWAY S	A	19	BE1	W
BELL P H	A	24	EDE	W
BELL PETER	A	29	CAR	B
BELL PRIMUS	A	28	04A	B
BELL R W	A	19	HAR	W
BELL RALPH	A	19	NEW	W
BELL RICHD R	A	29	CAR	W
BELL RILEY	R	19	MOR	B
DOUBTFUL AS TO AGE				
BELL ROBERT	A	25	PIN	W
BELL ROBERT	A	25	PIN	W
BELL ROBERT	A	28	03A	B
BELL ROBERT	A	37	TA1	B
BELL ROBERT H	A	40	FER	W
BELL ROBT	A	28	05A	B
BELL ROBT	A	29	CAR	B
BELL RUFUS	A	29	CAR	B
BELL S N	A	25	PIN	W
BELL SAML	A	28	05A	B
BELL SAMUEL	A	46	MCL	W
BELL SAMUEL	A	53	GER	B
BELL SAMUEL	A	53	LA1	B
BELL SANDY	A	28	03B	B
BELL SANDY	A	32	COT	B
BELL SETH R	A	53	GER	W
BELL SPENCER	A	30	IND	B
BELL STARLIN	A	37	EDW	B
BELL STEWART	A	37	TA1	B
BELL THOMAS	A	32	COT	W
BELL THOMAS F	A	35	WAR	W
BELL THOMAS SEN	A	40	DEC	W
BELL THOS	A	26	SWA	W
BELL TURNER	A	37	ROC	B
BELL W H	A	39	SPE	W
BELL W T R	A	19	NEW	W
BELL WILEY	A	30	IND	W
BELL WILLIAM	A	35	WOL	B
BELL WILLIAM	A	40	DA2	W
BELL WILLIAM H	A	29	SEV	B
BELL WILLIAM H	A	53	GER	W
BELL WILLIAM H	A	72	SWA	W
BELL WILLIAM J	A	53	GER	W
BELL WILLIAM S SR	A	19	NEW	W
BELL WILLIE	A	44	OXF	B
BELL WILLIS	A	30	IND	B
BELL WM	A	44	OXF	B
BELL WM B	A	19	HAR	W
BELL WM B	A	28	9TH	W
BELL WM F	A	19	HAD	W
BELL WM F 3RD	A	19	HAD	W
BELL WM N	A	19	BE1	W
BELL WM P	A	19	STR	W
BELL WM S JR	A	19	NEW	W
BELLAMY JOHN	A	37	ROB	B
BELLAMY JOHN T DR	A	37	ROB	W
BELLAMY JOSEPH	A	37	ROB	B
BELLAMY LEWIS	A	37	ROB	B
BELLAMY NAPOLEON B	A	37	EDW	W
BELLAMY NOAH	A	37	ROB	B
BELLEMAN AUSTON	A	37	MAN	B
BELLEMAN CARTER	A	37	MAN	B
BELLEMAN DAVID	A	37	MAN	B
BELLEMAN DRED	A	37	MAN	B
BELLEMAN GEORGE	A	37	MAN	B
BELLEMAN HORTON	A	37	MAN	B
BELLEMAN JOHN	A	37	MAN	B
BELLEMAN JOHN	A	37	MAN	B
BELLEMAN LEWIS	A	37	MAN	B
BELLEMAN NEDD	A	37	MAN	B
BELLEMAN OFFA	A	37	MAN	B
BELLEMAN ROBERT	A	37	MAN	B
BELLEMAN THOMAS	A	37	MAN	B
BELLINGRATH D	A	29	FA1	W
BELLMAN JACOB	A	37	ROB	B
BELLMORE CAR	A	37	ROB	B
BELLOWMY PINKNEY	A	19	BE1	B
BELVIN N C	A	44	HEN	W
BELVIN W A	A	44	HEN	W
BELVIN WILSON	A	37	ROB	B
BEMBERRY WM	A	28	05A	B
BEMBRAY LEON	A	30	ROA	B
BEMBRIDGE JOHN	A	28	05A	B
BEMBRY GEORGE	A	46	FRI	B
BEMBY WILSON	A	28	05B	B
BENBERRY GRANVILLE	A	99	BUS	B
BENBERRY WILSON	A	99	BUS	B
BENBOW ANDREW	A	46	KIN	B
BENBOW C R	A	46	KIN	W
BENBOW D W C	A	46	GRE	W
BENBOW JESSE	R	46	KIN	W
NAME LINED OUT				
MAGISTRATE BEFORE WAR &				
CONTINUED DURING WAR				
COULD NOT TAKE OATH WITHOUT				
THE WORD VOLUNTARY REJ				
BENBOW P S	A	46	GRE	W
BENBOW THOMAS J	A	46	KIN	W
BENBOW WIATT	A	46	KIN	B
BENBRIDGE NOAH	A	24	EDE	B
BENBURG CHARLES	A	24	EDE	B
BENBURY ABRAM	A	24	EDE	B
BENBURY AUGUSTUS	A	24	EDE	B
BENBURY CAIN	A	24	EDE	B
BENBURY CHANCE	A	24	EDE	B
BENBURY CHARLES	A	24	EDE	B
BENBURY CHESHIRE	A	24	EDE	B
BENBURY DAVID	A	24	EDE	B
BENBURY EDWARD	A	24	EDE	B
BENBURY HENRY	A	24	EDE	B
BENBURY JOHN	A	24	EDE	B
BENBURY LAWRENCE	A	24	EDE	B
BENBURY LEMUEL C	A	24	EDE	W
BENBURY LEON	A	24	EDE	B
BENBURY SAMUEL	A	24	EDE	B
BENBURY SHADIS	A	24	EDE	B
BENBURY SHADRICK	A	24	EDE	B
BENBURY WILLIAM	A	24	EDE	W

BENBURY WILSON A 24 EDE B
BENCENE H C A 46 HIG W
BENDERS BENJ A 28 01B B
BENDERS BENJN A 28 03A B
BENDERS PARKER D A 53 SWA B
BENDERS PHILIP A 28 03A B
BENDERS YORK A 28 01B B
BENEFIELD THOS A 46 GIB W
BENEY THOMAS A 29 CED W
BENIT LEVI A 53 FAI W
BENJAMIN ALEXANDER A 24 MID B
BENJAMIN W S A 28 03A W
BENNERS ALEXR A 28 05A B
BENNERS WM A 28 04A B
BENNERS WM L A 28 14T W
BENNET CHAS A 39 HAR W
BENNETT ALLEN A 35 FAI B
BENNETT BELL W A 37 SPA W
BENNETT BENJAMIN A 28 14T W
BENNETT BRYANT A 35 FAI W
BENNETT C W A 44 DUT W
BENNETT CALVIN A 29 FA1 B
BENNETT CALVIN O A 46 SUM W
BENNETT CHARLES A 46 SUM W
BENNETT CHARLES E A 37 TA1 W
BENNETT DANIEL A 46 ROS W
BENNETT DANIEL F A 46 COB W
BENNETT DORRIS M A 46 GRE W
BENNETT E J A 44 SAS W
BENNETT FRANK Y A 37 ROC W
BENNETT G T A 35 WOL B
BENNETT H F J A 28 01A W
BENNETT HARDY A 28 9TH B
BENNETT HARPER H A 46 ROS W
BENNETT ISAC A 35 WOL B
BENNETT ISHAM A 44 SAS B
BENNETT J J A 30 MOY W
BENNETT JAMES A 24 EDE B
BENNETT JAMES M R 28 04A W
CONSTABLE PRIOR TO WAR
BENNETT JEPTHA B A 28 14T W
BENNETT JESSE A 28 14T W
BENNETT JESSE JR A 28 16T W
BENNETT JOHN A 35 WOL B
BENNETT JOHN A 37 HIG B
BENNETT JOHN C A 28 14T W
BENNETT JORDAN A 29 QUW B
BENNETT JORDEN A 35 WOL B
BENNETT JOSEPH H A 37 ROC W
BENNETT JOSIAH A 28 14T W
BENNETT LABEN A 28 14T W
BENNETT LONNAR A 19 BE1 B
BENNETT NORFIEL A 19 NEW B
BENNETT RICHARD A 28 14T B
BENNETT RICHARD A 37 HIG W
BENNETT S L A 35 WOL B
BENNETT S W A 44 KNA W
BENNETT SAMUEL A 35 WOL B
BENNETT SIMEON A 28 14T W
BENNETT THOMAS A 35 WAR W
BENNETT W H A 39 SPE W
CERT TO FRANKLINTON
BENNETT WILLIAM A 26 GOF W
BENSON BRIANT A 53 LA1 B
BENSON GEORGE W A 53 SWA W
BENSON IREDELL A 32 THO W
BENSON JAMES O A 37 ROC W
BENSON JOHN G A 53 SWA W
BENSON LEWIS A 53 SWA B
BENSON MARTIN V A 53 SWA W
BENSON W F A 32 DAV W
BENSTON JOSEPH A 28 05A B
BENTLEY BENJAMIN A 28 11T W
BENTLEY JOHN A A 28 11T W
BENTON CALVIN A 39 DAV W
BENTON GEORGE D A 35 MAG W
BENTON HENRY A 39 DAV W
BENTON ISAAC A 28 7TH B
BENTON JONATHAN A 32 THO W
BENTON JOSEPH A 28 04B B
BENTON LAVOS A 28 7TH B
BENTON NATHANIEL A 53 GER B
BENTON ROBT A 29 FA1 B
BENTON RUFUS A 35 MAG W
BERNARD ALXANDER A 29 FA2 W
BERNARD CHURCHELL A 29 SEV B
BERNARD STEPHEN A 29 FA1 B
BERNETT ALEXANDER A 29 FLE B
BERRET RICHARD A 19 HAR B
BERRIER ANDREW A 32 SHE W
BERRIER B A 32 DAV B
BERRIER CHARLES A 32 DAV W
BERRIER F L A 32 DAV W
BERRIER H R A 32 DAV W
BERRIER HENRY A 32 DAV W
BERRIER HENRY A 32 SHE W
BERRIER JACOB A 32 DAV W
BERRIER LOUIS A 32 DAV W
BERRIER WILLIAM A A 32 DAV W
BERRIMAN JOHN F A 24 UPP W
BERRY ABNER M A 30 IND W
BERRY BAILEY A 37 HIG W
BERRY BENJAMIN A 53 FAI W
BERRY BUBIN S A 53 LA1 W
BERRY CAIN A 28 9TH B
BERRY CHRISTOPHER A 53 LA1 W
BERRY E M A 40 SAN W
BERRY E M A 40 SAN W
BERRY E MILTON A 40 SAN W
BERRY ESAU A 30 ROA W
BERRY GEORGE A 28 9TH B
BERRY HENRY A 29 GRA B
BERRY IRA A A 53 LA1 W
BERRY ISAAC N A 30 IND W
BERRY JAMES E A 53 SWA W
BERRY JOHN A 26 SHE W
BERRY JOHN A 53 GER W
BERRY JOHN A 53 SWA W
BERRY JOHN M A 30 IND W
BERRY LANDGON A 53 FAI W
BERRY LANLEE A 29 FA2 B
BERRY LOUIS A 19 MOR B
BERRY REDDING A 53 LA1 W
BERRY RICHARD A 28 01A W
BERRY RICHARD A 53 LA1 W
BERRY RICHARD M A 30 IND W
BERRY RICHARD T A 53 SWA W
BERRY RICHD T A 28 01A W
COMMISSIONER OF
4TH WARD NEW BERN
BERRY ROLLINS C A 29 CAR B
BERRY SETH A 53 LA1 B
BERRY W R A 40 SAN W
BERRY WILLIAM A 30 IND W
BERRY WILLIAM A 53 FAI W
BERRY WILLIAM M A 30 IND W
BERRY WILLIAM W A 53 GER W
BERRY Z D A 28 01B W
BERRYMAN S A A 32 SHE W
BERTES RENO A 46 GRE W
BERTIN LONEY A 37 ROC B
BESS DANIEL A 28 9TH B
BESS HILARY A 28 9TH B
BESS MAC A 28 9TH B
BESS SAMUEL A 37 PIN B
BESSA JOSHUA A 28 01A W
BESSE JOSEPH P A 24 EDE W
BEST ABSALOM A 35 WAR W
BEST ABSALOM A 35 WAR W
BEST ANTHONY A 28 04A B
BEST BENJAMIN A 35 WAR W
BEST BLANY J A 19 HAD W
CERT TO NEWPORT
BEST DANIEL T A 35 KEN B
BEST FIELDING K A 39 LOU W
TRNS FROM GRIFFINS
IN NASH CO
BEST GEORGE H A 35 KEN W
BEST HARDY A 35 WAR B
BEST HARTLESS A 37 HIC B
BEST HENRY A 35 KEN B
BEST HENRY A 35 WAR W
BEST ISAAC A 28 05A B
BEST ISAAC A 28 05A B
BEST ISAAC A 35 MAG B
BEST JACKSON A A 40 DEC W
BEST JAMES A 37 HIC B
BEST JNO A A 19 HAD W
BEST JOHN A 35 WAR B
BEST JOHN A 35 WAR B
BEST JOHN G A 35 WAR B
BEST JOHN H L A 37 TA1 W
BEST JOHN W A 35 WAR W
BEST JOSEPH A 30 NOR W
BEST JOSEPH A 35 WAR B
BEST JOSEPH A 35 WAR B
BEST JOSEPH A 37 TA1 W
BEST JOSEPH B A 37 PEN W
BEST KENAN A 35 WAR B
BEST LEWIS A 35 WAR B
BEST MERET A 35 WAR B
BEST MICHAEL A 40 DEC W
BEST NICODEMUS A 30 NOR W
BEST NOAH A 24 EDE B
BEST OLLIN A 35 WAR B
BEST REDDIN A 35 WAR B
BEST ROBERT A 35 WAR B
BEST ROLLAND J A 28 7TH W
BEST SAMEUL A 35 KEN B
BEST SAMUEL A 40 DEC W
BEST SAMUEL 1ST A 35 WAR B
BEST SAMUEL 2ND A 35 WAR B
BEST TONEY A 35 KEN B
BEST TONEY A 36 KEN B
BEST WILLIAM A 35 KEN B
BEST WILLIAM H A 35 KEN W
BEST WILLIAM L A 37 PEN W
BEST WILLIAM R A 35 WAR W
BEST WM D A 53 HAT W
BETHA STEPHEN A 29 FA1 W
BETHEA NOR C A 29 ROC W
PRESENT PLACE OF RESI-
DENCE HORSE SHOE BLADEN
CO, NC APRIL 6, 1868
BETHUNE A J A 29 QUW W
BETHUNE BENAJMIN A 29 SEV B
BETHUNE COLIN A 29 QUW W
BETHUNE ISAAC A 29 SEV B
BETHUNE LAUCHLIN R 29 QUW W
MEMBER OF CONGRESS
MEMBER OF STATE LEGIS-
LATURE AFTERWARDS AID &
COMFORT TO THE ENEMIES
PARDONED BY THE PRESI-
DENT OF U.S.
OATH NOT TAKEN
BETHUNE WM J A 29 QUW W
BETTS C A 44 HEN W
BETTS JNO W A 44 HEN W

BETTS WILLIAM	A	29	SEV	B
BETTY JOHN	A	44	OXF	B
BEUFF ALFORD	A	32	DAV	W
BEVANS BENJAMIN F	A	24	EDE	W
BEVEL ANDREW	A	46	GRE	B
BEVEL SPENCER G	A	46	MON	W
BEVELS ARCHIBALD	A	46	GRE	W
BEVERIDGE JOHN	A	19	BE1	W
BEVIL LAWSON	A	46	ROS	B
BEVILL ARCHEBALD JR	A	46	SUM	W
BEVILL DANIEL	A	46	SUM	B
BEVILL GREEN	A	46	SUM	B
BEVILL J H	A	46	SUM	W
BEVILL JACKSON	A	46	SUM	B
BEVILL LEVIN	A	46	SUM	B
BEVILL MADISON	A	46	SUM	B
BEVILL MARTIN	A	46	SUM	B
BEVILL PETER	A	46	SUM	B
BEVILL THOS	A	46	SUM	W
BEXELY NATHANIEL	A	28	11T	W
BIBBY WM	A	39	FRA	B
BIDDING ANTHONY	A	46	GRE	B
BIDDLE ALONZO	A	28	7TH	B
BIDDLE BENJAMIN	A	28	7TH	B
BIDDLE EDWARD	A	28	7TH	B
BIDDLE JAMES W	A	28	8TH	W
BIDDLE SAMUEL S JR	A	28	7TH	W
BIESON N M	A	32	BRO	W
BIGGERS ZIMRI P	A	40	FER	W
BIGGS ALEXANDER	A	29	ROC	W
BIGGS AMOS	A	28	05A	B
BIGGS BUNTON	A	29	ROC	W
BIGGS DEMPSEY	A	37	HIC	B
BIGGS GEORGE	A	37	TA1	B
BIGGS ISAAC	A	28	05A	B
BIGGS JOHN	A	44	KIT	W
BIGGS NEIL G	A	29	ROC	W
BIGGS PHILLIP	A	29	ROC	W
BIGGS WILEY	A	28	04A	B
BIGGS WILLIAM	A	30	IND	B
BIGGS WILLIAM	A	37	TA1	W
BIGGS WILLIS	A	44	KIT	W
BIGGS WILLIS L	A	44	KIT	W
BIGGS WM H	A	29	ROC	W
BILBER DAVID	A	37	HIG	B
BILBRO JACOB	A	46	JAM	B
BILBRO PEYTON	A	46	GRE	W
BILLBURY NED	A	37	EDW	B
BILLING HENRY	A	32	COT	W
BILLINGS B F	A	32	COT	W
BILLINGS R A	A	32	COT	W
BILLIS ALLEN	A	26	SWA	W
BILLSBERRY WINDSOR	A	37	TA1	B
BINGHAM CHRISTIE	A	26	WAR	W
BINGHAM MARTIN	A	26	GRI	W
BINGHAM S	A	26	GRI	W
BINGHAM WM	A	26	GRI	W
BINKE RANSOM JR	A	28	11T	W
BINSTON JOHN	A	19	BE1	B
BINUM ANDERSON	A	37	HIG	B
BINUM SAMPSON	A	37	WEB	B
BINUM THOMAS	A	37	HIG	B
BINUM THOMAS	A	37	SHA	B
BIRCH JOHN K	A	28	15T	W
BIRCH SAMUEL	A	19	HAD	B
BIRCHETT ASBURY	A	26	SHE	B
BIRCHETT C R	A	44	BEA	W
BIRCHETT DAVID	A	44	BEA	W
BIRCHETT HENRY	A	26	SHE	B
BIRD JOSEPH	A	99	BUS	B
BIRD MATTHEW	A	28	6TH	B
BIRD PETER	A	29	FLE	B
BIRDSONG GEORGE	A	44	HEN	B

BIRELEY JACOB	A	32	DAV	W
BIRELY A H	A	32	LOF	W
BIRELY AMOS	A	32	DAV	B
BIRELY GEORGE	A	32	LEE	W
BIRELY PETER	A	32	COT	W
BIRELY PETER	A	32	LOF	W
BIRELY ROBERT	A	32	YAD	B
BIRELY SIMSON	A	32	DAV	W
BIRELY W T	A	32	LOF	W
BIRHALL WM J	A	19	BE1	W
BIRKHART ALEXANDER	A	32	DAV	W
BIRKHART ANDREW	A	32	DAV	W
BIRKHART HYRAM	A	32	COT	W
BIRKHEAD WILLIAM	A	32	JAC	W
BIRKHEAD WM C	A	32	JAC	W
BIRNEY CHURCHWELL	A	28	03B	B
BIRNEY WILLIAM	A	46	JAM	W
BIRTCHETT GREEN	A	44	LED	W
BIRTCHETT J W	A	44	DUT	W
BISHOP BENNETT	A	46	MON	W
BISHOP BRYAN	A	35	LIM	W
BISHOP BURAGE	A	53	BUR	W
BISHOP CHRISTOPHER	A	19	BE1	B
BISHOP DANIEL	A	24	EDE	B
BISHOP GEO W	A	19	BE1	B
BISHOP GEORGE	A	28	03A	W
BISHOP ISAAC T	A	35	LIM	W
BISHOP JACKSON	A	53	SWA	W
BISHOP JAMES C	A	37	ROC	W
BISHOP JAMES H	A	35	LIM	W
BISHOP JOHN T	A	53	GER	W
BISHOP M R	A	46	GRE	W
BISHOP PETER	A	28	04A	B
BISHOP RICHARD	A	28	04B	B
BISHOP RICHARD	A	46	MON	W
BISHOP RILEY M	A	35	MAG	W
BISHOP SAML	A	28	03A	W
BISHOP SAMUEL C	A	53	BUR	W
BISHOP SAMUEL E	A	53	BUR	W
BISHOP TONEY	A	28	04A	B
BISHOP WILLIAM	A	24	EDE	B
BISSEL GEORGE	A	28	05A	B
BISSEL WM	A	28	05A	B
BISSELL E H	A	40	CAN	W
BISSELL JIM	A	28	6TH	W
APRIL 7TH				
BISSNER JAMES	A	37	SPA	B
BITTEN ASHLEY	A	39	DAV	W
TRNS BY AFFIDAVIT FROM				
WELDON PRE JOHNSON CO				
TO DAVIS X ROADS				
BITTEN HELERY R	A	39	DAV	W
TRNS BY AFFIDAVIT FROM				
WELDON PRE JOHNSON CO TO				
DAVIS X ROAD FRANKLIN CO				
BITTEN RUFFIN	A	39	DAV	W
TRNS BY AFFIDAVIT FROM				
WELDON PRE JOHNSON CO TO				
DAVIS X ROAD FRANKLIN CO				
BIZZELL B E	A	35	WOL	W
BLACK ALFRED JR	A	40	BLA	W
BLACK ALFRED SEN	A	40	BLA	W
BLACK ANDREW	A	32	DAV	W
BLACK ARCHD G	A	29	FA1	W
BLACK CALVIN	A	29	GRA	B
BLACK DUNCAN J	A	29	ROC	W
BLACK DUNNELL	A	29	FA1	W
BLACK EPHRAIM CHAL	R	40	BLA	W
NAME LINED OUT				
CONSTABLE NOT QUALIFIED				
HOME GUARD UNION MAN				
TILL CONSCRIPTION REJ				
BLACK EPHRAIM JR	A	40	BLA	W

BLACK GEORGE	A	32	DAV	W
BLACK HENRY	A	28	03A	B
BLACK HENRY	A	37	PIN	B
BLACK HENRY	A	46	COB	W
BLACK HENRY M	A	46	COB	W
BLACK J F	A	40	CAN	W
BLACK J S	A	29	SEV	W
BLACK J S	A	40	CAN	W
BLACK J W	A	32	DAV	W
BLACK JACOB	A	40	BLA	B
BLACK JAMES	A	19	HAD	B
BLACK JAMES	A	26	PEE	W
BLACK JEFFERSON	A	26	SHE	W
BLACK JNO G	A	29	FA2	W
BLACK JOHN	A	28	9TH	B
BLACK JOHN	A	29	QUW	W
BLACK JOHN	A	32	THO	W
BLACK JOHN	A	46	COB	W
BLACK JOHN F	A	26	PEE	W
BLACK JOHN T	A	72	SWA	W
BLACK K A	A	29	FA1	W
BLACK LAWSON	A	40	BLA	W
BLACK MARTIN	A	28	04A	B
BLACK MARTIN	A	40	BLA	B
BLACK MATTHEW	A	40	BLA	W
BLACK NATHAN	A	37	EDW	B
BLACK P L	A	29	FA1	W
BLACK PETER	A	28	10T	B
BLACK PHILIP	A	32	DAV	W
BLACK PHILLIP	A	29	GRA	B
BLACK ROBERT	A	32	THO	W
BLACK SAMUEL	A	26	BUR	B
BLACK SAMUEL	A	32	LEE	W
BLACK SAMUEL JR	A	40	BLA	W
BLACK SOLOMON	A	32	THO	W
BLACK SOLOMON R	A	32	DAV	W
BLACK STEPHEN	A	28	9TH	B
BLACK THOMAS	A	40	BLA	W
BLACK THOMAS	A	40	BLA	W
BLACK VINCENT	A	40	DA1	W
BLACK W M	A	40	CAN	W
BLACK WILLIAM	A	28	11T	B
BLACK WILLIAM	A	29	MON	B
BLACKBURN BURRELL	A	35	WAR	W
BLACKBURN COSTON	A	32	CLE	W
BLACKBURN DAN	A	26	GRI	W
BLACKBURN E	A	32	CLE	W
BLACKBURN H	A	32	THO	W
BY CERTIF				
BLACKBURN J A	A	32	CLE	W
BLACKBURN J A	A	32	SHE	W
BLACKBURN RIGDEN	A	35	KEN	B
BLACKBURN ROBT	A	46	SUM	W
BLACKBURN WILEY	A	35	ISL	B
BLACKLEDGE DAVID	A	28	6TH	B
BLACKLEGE CAIN	A	19	BE1	B
BLACKLEY A P	A	44	OXF	W
BLACKLEY B J	A	44	FOR	W
BLACKLEY C C	A	44	FIS	W
BLACKLEY J H	A	44	BRA	W
BLACKLEY JOSEPH S	A	44	FIS	W
BLACKLEY W D	A	44	FIS	W
BLACKLEY WILLIAM	A	44	FIS	W
BLACKLY C R	A	39	FRA	W
BLACKLY S C	A	39	FRA	W
BLACKMAN ADAM	A	29	FA2	B
BLACKMAN CHARLES	A	99	BUS	B
BLACKMAN ELIAS	A	29	LOC	B
BLACKMAN F M	A	29	FA1	B
BLACKMAN JNO	A	29	FA1	B
BLACKMAN JNO B	A	29	FA1	B
BLACKMAN JOEL W	A	29	CAR	W
BLACKMAN L D SR	A	29	CAR	W

BLACKMAN LEONARD A 29 CAR W
BLACKMAN W C A 29 CAR W
BLACKMAN W P A 29 CAR W
BLACKMAN WILLIAM A 19 HAR B
BLACKMAN WILLIS A 29 FA1 B
BLACKMORE BUCK S A 35 WAR W
BLACKMORE HAROLD A 35 WAR W
BLACKMORE HEROD A 35 WAR W
BLACKMUN STEPHEN A 35 KEN B
BLACKNAL SPRIGG A 44 BRA B
BLACKNALL BIRD A 44 KIT B
BLACKNALL CHARLES A 39 PUG B
BLACKNALL DANIEL A 44 OXF B
BLACKNALL DR G W A 44 KIT W
BLACKNALL ELLIC A 44 KIT B
BLACKNALL EPHRAIM A 39 PUG B
BLACKNALL FERNY A 39 HAY B
BLACKNALL GABRIEL A 39 PUG B
BLACKNALL HILLIARD A 39 HAY B
BLACKNALL JOHN A 44 OXF W
BLACKNALL JONATHAN A 44 FIS W
BLACKNALL NATHAN A 44 HEN B
BLACKNALL RICHARD A 72 SWA W
BLACKNALL RICHARD D A 72 SWA W
BLACKNALL SPENCER A 44 FIS W
BLACKNALL STARLING A 39 PUG B
BLACKNALL T H A 44 KIT W
BLACKSHER FRANK A 28 03A B
BLACKWELDER J P A 40 STO W
BLACKWELDER M B A 40 STO W
BLACKWELL ARMSTEAD A 44 SAS B
BLACKWELL CHARLES A 44 KIT B
BLACKWELL EDWARDS L A 53 FAI W
BLACKWELL EWD A 44 YXR B
BLACKWELL GEO A 44 BRA B
BLACKWELL HARLY A 44 BRA B
BLACKWELL HARRY A 44 YXS B
BLACKWELL HENRY A 44 BRA B
BLACKWELL ISAAC A 44 YXR B
BLACKWELL JAS A 44 YXR W
BLACKWELL JNO A 44 YXR B
BLACKWELL JOHN A 44 HEN B
BLACKWELL JOHN P A 44 TOW W
BLACKWELL JOHN P W A 44 TOW W
BLACKWELL LEWIS A 44 TOW B
BLACKWELL MOSES A 44 BRA B
BLACKWELL PETER A 44 BRA B
BLACKWELL PRIMUS A 44 FOR B
BLACKWELL PUMFRET A 44 YXS W
BLACKWELL ROBERT A 44 TOW B
BLACKWELL SILAS A 53 FAI B
BLACKWELL STEPHEN A 44 TOW B
BLACKWELL THOS A 44 BRA B
BLACKWELL WESLEY A 44 BRA B
BLACKWELL WM H A 44 YXS W
BLACKWELL WM M A 44 BRA W
BLACKWELL WM M A 44 HEN W
BLACKWOOD CHARLES A 40 DA1 B
BLACKWOOD J A 26 MOU W
BLACKWOOD J J A 26 SHE W
BLACKWOOD J T A 26 MOU W
BLACKWOOD J T A 26 WAR W
BLAGG SAML A 28 01A W
BLAGMON JOSEPH B A 24 EDE B
BLAIR CHARLES A 24 EDE B
BLAIR HENDERSON A 24 EDE B
BLAIR HENSON A 32 THO W
BLAIR J F A 32 THO W
BLAIR J M A 32 THO W
BLAIR JOURDAN A 24 EDE B
BLAIR L A A 46 HIG W
BLAIR PRIMUS A 24 EDE B
BLAIR S J A 46 HIG W
BLAIR W F A 32 THO W
BLAIR WILLIAM A 24 EDE B
BLAKE HENRY C A 29 FA2 W
BLAKE ISHAM A 29 FA2 W
BLAKE JNO H A 29 FA2 W
BLAKE JOS W A 29 FA1 W
BLAKE MATHIAS A 53 SWA W
BLAKE RICHARD A 28 9TH B
BLAKE WILLIAM H A 53 FAI W
BLAKELEY THOMAS F A 40 BLA W
BLALAR FABIUS A 99 BUS B
BLALOCK DANIEL A 26 GOF B
BLALOCK DANIEL A 32 DAV B
BLALOCK H A 29 BLA W
BLALOCK J B A 26 GOF W
BLALOCK JEREMIAH A 26 GOF W
BLALOCK JOSEPH A 44 KNA B
BLALOCK LEWIS A 44 TAR B
BLALOCK M A 44 TAR W
BLALOCK W A A 26 GOF W
BLANCHARD ABNER A 24 UPP W
BLANCHARD ABRAM W A 35 WAR W
BLANCHARD DAVID J A 35 MAG W
BLANCHARD EDWIN A 24 EDE B
BLANCHARD HENRY A 29 FA1 W
BLANCHARD JAMES M A 35 WAR W
BLANCHARD JOHN A 24 EDE B
BLANCHARD JOHN L A 35 WAR W
BLANCHARD JOSIAH H A 24 UPP W
BLANCHARD W A M A 24 UPP W
BLANCHARD WM A 24 UPP W
BLANCHETT J J A 29 FLE W
BLAND ABRAM F A 35 MAG W
BLAND ALFRED A 46 GRE B
BLAND AMANAH A 35 MAG W
BLAND BALAAM A 35 ROC B
BLAND DAVID A 35 ROC W
BLAND DAVID W A 35 ROC W
BLAND EVERETT A 35 ROC B
BLAND GABRIEL A 35 MAG B
BLAND GEORGE A 35 ROC B
BLAND GEORGE W A 35 MAG W
BLAND HARMAN A 35 ROC W
BLAND ISRAEL A 35 ROC B
BLAND JAMES A 29 MON W
BLAND JAMES T A 35 ROC W
BLAND JAS A 29 FA1 B
BLAND JAS A 29 FA1 B
BLAND SAMUEL J A 35 ISL W
BLAND TIMOTHY A 35 ISL W
BLAND WILLIAM W A 35 ROC W
BLANGER THOMAS A 28 11T B
BLANGO EDWARD A 28 10T B
BLANGO GABRIEL A 28 10T B
BLANGO JOHN A 28 05A B
BLANGO ROSS A 28 10T B
BLANGO SAMUEL A 28 10T B
BLANGO THOS A 28 05A B
BLANGO TONEY A 28 05A B
BLANGY WARREN A 28 16T W
BLANKENSHP L A A 44 YXR W
BLANKS J B R 44 YXR W
IN STATE 7 MONTHS REJ
BLANKS J T A 44 HEN W
BLANKS W T A 39 LOU W
BLANKS WM A 44 KIT W
BLANTON ABRAHAM A 35 ISL W
BLANTON ABRAM A 35 ROC W
BLANTON ALBERT A 26 BLA W
BLANTON ALEXANDER A 35 ROC W
BLANTON AMOS A 35 ISL W
CERTIF GIVEN APRIL
APRIL 9, 1868
BLANTON ANDREW A 26 HOL B
BLANTON B SR A 26 HOL B
BLANTON BACHUS A 26 GRI B
BLANTON BLANEY A 35 ROC W
BLANTON BUNNELL A 26 BLA W
BLANTON CASTILO A 26 BUR W
BLANTON CHARLES 26 BUR W
BLANTON D A A 26 HOL B
BLANTON DAVID A 35 ROC W
BLANTON DOCTOR A 26 SHE B
BLANTON E J A 26 BUR W
BLANTON G W A 26 SHE W
MILITIA OFFICER &
ENGAGED IN REBELLION
BLANTON H I A 26 HOL B
BLANTON HARMON A 26 GOF B
BLANTON J B A 26 MOO W
BLANTON J H A 26 HOL B
BLANTON J M A 26 HOL B
BLANTON J M JR A 26 HOL B
BLANTON J W A 26 HOL B
BLANTON JACKSON A 26 HOL B
BLANTON JACOB O A 35 ROC W
BLANTON JOHN A A 35 ROC W
BLANTON JOHN T A 35 ROC W
BLANTON JOSEPH A 26 GOF B
BLANTON JOSHUA A 35 ISL W
BLANTON JOSHUA A 35 ROC W
BLANTON MOSES N A 35 ROC W
BLANTON R A A 26 MOU W
BLANTON REWBEN SR A 26 BUR W
BLANTON REWBEN SR A 26 BUR W
BLANTON RICHARD A 26 GRI B
BLANTON THOMAS A 35 ROC W
BLANTON W L A 26 MOU W
BLANTON WILLIAM A 26 HOL B
BLANTON WILLIAM A 26 MOO W
BLANTON WILLIS A 26 SHE W
BLANTON Z CHAL A 26 BUR W
MILITIA OFFICER &
ENGAGED IN REBELLION
BLAYLOCK CHARLES A 46 ROS B
BLAYLOCK J H A 35 WOL B
BLAYLOCK J M R 46 FRI W
CAUSE WAS MILITIA
OFFICER BEFORE THE
REBELION AND VOLUNTARY
AIDED AND IS REJECTED
BLAYLOCK JAMES H A 46 HIG W
BLAYLOCK MARTIN A 46 KIN W
BLAYLOCK R A A 46 KIN W
BLAYLOCK W B A 35 SMI W
BLEDSO HARRY A 39 PUG B
BLEDSOE A A 44 HEN W
BLEDSOE JAMES A A 39 SPE W
BLEDSOE JOHN A 39 SPE W
BLESSET WILLIAM A 46 FRI W
BLINSON GASTON W A 99 BUS W
BLINSON JAMES R A 99 BUS W
BLIVEN ALFRED A 30 ROA W
BLIVEN GEORGE B A 30 ROA W
BLIZARD A S A 29 ROC W
BLIZARD FARRIS A 35 MAG W
CERT TO
SMITHS 13 APR 68
BLIZZARD A BA A 35 ALB W
BLIZZARD HENRY R A 35 SMI W
BLIZZARD HEZEKIAH A 35 SMI W
BLIZZARD JOHN H A 35 ALB W
BLIZZARD SAMUEL A 35 ALB W
BLOCKER C H A 29 CED W
BLOCKER ISAAC A 29 FA1 B

BLOCKER J C R 29 CED W
MAIL CONTRACTOR BEFORE THE WAR AND AFTER AIDED REBELLION
BLOCKER MILES A 29 CED B
BLOCKER O H A 29 CED W
REMOVED TO BLADEN
BLOODGOOD JAMES A 72 SWA W
BLOODGOOD JOSEPH A 72 SWA W
BLOODWORTH WASHINGTON A 37 PIN B
BLOSSOM BENJ A 28 04A B
BLOUNT AARON A 35 WAR B
BLOUNT ALBERT A 35 WAR B
BLOUNT ANDREW A 37 TA1 B
BLOUNT EPHRAM A 35 WAR B
BLOUNT IRY A 35 WAR B
BLOUNT ISAAC A 35 KEN B
BLOUNT JAMES S A 53 GER W
BLOUNT JAMES W A 35 FAI W
BLOUNT JAREIAH A 53 GER B
BLOUNT JOHN G A 37 TA2 W
BLOUNT OBEDIAH A 37 WHI B
BLOUNT ROBERT A 35 WAR B
BLOUNT ROSOM A 37 ROB B
BLOUNT SAMUEL A 53 SWA B
BLOUNT THOMAS A 37 TA1 B
BLOUNT THOMAS A 40 DA1 B
BLOUNT WILLIAM A 53 FAI B
BLOUNT WM A 46 GRE B
BLUE ANDW A 29 CAR B
BLUE DANL A 29 CAR W
BLUE DUNCAN A 29 SEV W
BLUE GEO A 29 CAR B
BLUE JACOB A 29 QUW B
BLUE JNO A 29 CAR B
BLUE JNO A 29 CAR B
BLUE JOHN L A 29 QUW W
BLUE JOS A 29 CAR B
BLUE L A A 29 QUW W
BLUE MILES 29 QUW B
DEAD
BLUE NEILL M K A 29 QUW W
BLUE SIMON A 29 FA1 B
BLUE SIMON A 29 FA1 B
BLUNT ALBERT A 44 ISL B
BLUNT ALEN A 24 EDE B
BLUNT ALEX A 28 01A B
BLUNT ALFRED A 24 EDE B
BLUNT ALFRED A 28 05A B
BLUNT ALFRED A 72 SWA B
BLUNT AMOS A 28 01A B
BLUNT ANTHONY A 24 EDE B
BLUNT AUGUSTUS A 24 EDE B
BLUNT AUSTIN A 28 05A B
BLUNT BENJAMIN A 28 05B B
BLUNT CHARLES A 19 NEW B
BLUNT CHARLES A 24 EDE B
BLUNT DAVID A 24 EDE B
BLUNT EDWARD A 28 8TH B
BLUNT EDWARD A 37 HIG B
BLUNT EPHRAIM A 28 05A B
BLUNT FRANK A 19 MOR B
BLUNT FRANK A 28 8TH B
BLUNT FRANK A 28 9TH B
BLUNT GANSEY A 28 05A B
BLUNT GEORGE A 24 EDE B
BLUNT GEORGE A 28 05A B
BLUNT GEORGE A 28 9TH B
BLUNT HARRY A 24 EDE B
BLUNT HENRY A 24 EDE B
BLUNT HENRY A 28 9TH B
BLUNT HENRY A 32 DAV B

BLUNT ISAAC A 28 03A B
BLUNT ISAM A 28 05A B
BLUNT JAMES A 24 EDE B
BLUNT JAMES A 24 EDE B
BLUNT JAMES A 28 05A B
BLUNT JOSEPH B A 24 EDE B
BLUNT MAXWELL A 24 EDE B
BLUNT MILLS A 24 EDE B
BLUNT MILLS A 24 EDE B
BLUNT MOSES A 24 EDE B
BLUNT NELSON A 24 EDE B
BLUNT NELSON A 28 03A B
BLUNT NELSON A 72 SWA B
BLUNT ORANGE A 30 IND B
BLUNT OSSIAN A 28 04A B
BLUNT PETER A 24 EDE B
BLUNT PETER A 28 05B B
BLUNT RIGDON A 28 11T B
BLUNT ROBT A 24 EDE B
BLUNT SHADRACK A 28 05A B
BLUNT THOS A 28 05A B
BLUNT VIRGIL A 24 EDE B
CERT GIVEN TO PERQUIM MANS CO. APR 18
BLUNT WHITMELL A 24 EDE B
BLY FRANKLIN A 28 16T W
BOBBETT J C A 44 HEN W
BOBBETT THOS E A 44 OXF W
BOBBITT A E A 39 JOR W
BOBBITT ASSANIAH A 39 SPE W
BOBBITT BENJ A 44 OXF B
BOBBITT C J A 44 FIS W
BOBBITT D E A 44 FIS W
BOBBITT DAVID A 39 DAV B
BOBBITT F H A 39 SPE W
BOBBITT F M A 44 FOR W
BOBBITT GEO A 44 BEA B
BOBBITT J J A 44 BRA W
BOBBITT J R A 44 FIS W
BOBBITT JOHN R A 39 SPE W
BOBBITT JOHN T A 44 OXF W
BOBBITT LEWIS A 44 BRA B
BOBBITT PATRICK H A 44 OXF W
BOBBITT RANDOLPH A 39 SPE W
BOBBITT RUFUS A 44 BRA W
BOBBITT SAMUEL A 19 DAV W
BOBBITT T H A 44 OXF W
BOBBITT W A A 44 BRA W
BOBBITT W O A 44 BRA W
BOBBITT WILLIAM A 44 FIS B
BOCK FRANKLIN A 32 COT W
BODDIE BURWELL A 39 SPE B
BODDIE PRINCE A 39 DAV B
BODDIE WM A 39 LOU B
BODDY ALFRED A 37 ROC B
BODDY HENRY A 37 ROC B
BODENHAMER C F A 32 BRO W
BODENHAMER CHRISTIANA 32 BRO W
BODENHAMER J B A 46 HIG W
BODENHAMER J F A 46 HIG W
BODENHAMER J P A 32 BRO W
BODENHAMER JACOB A 32 BRO W
BODENHAMER JACOB JR A 32 BRO W
BODENHAMER JOHN A 32 BRO W
BODENHAMER M V A 32 BRO W
BODENHAMER PETER R A 32 BRO W
BODENHAMER RANDALL A 32 BRO W
BODENHAMER W H A 46 HIG W
BODENHAMER W W A 32 BRO W
BODENHAMER WILLIAM A 32 BRO W
BODENHAMMER ANDERSONA 32 POS W
BODENHAMMER ELICKS A 32 POS W
BODENHAMMER J B A 32 POS W

BODENHAMMER J C A 32 POS W
BODENHAMMER JACOB A 32 POS W
BODENHAMMER P N A 32 POS W
BODIE ELLICK A 39 SPE B
BODSFORD FREDERICK A 32 POS W
BODSFORD J H A 32 SHE W
BOESSER FRED A 28 02N W
BOESSER GEO C A 28 01A W
BOGAR ROBERT R 46 MCL B
HE WAS A SLAVE BEFORE THE WAR AND WAS ACCUSED AND CONVICTED OF STEALING BACO AND WHIPPED LAWFULLY SINS FREE HE MADE ALL NECESSARY CONCESSIONS & PROMISES FOR THE FUTURE. AND WE RELEASED HIM REJECTED
BOGART WM R A 46 GRE W
BOGER THOMAS A 26 SHE B
BOGES MILES A 53 LA1 B
BOGEY M C A 28 6TH W
BOGGINS SAML A 29 FA1 B
BOGGS A G A 32 LOF W
BOGGS A M A 26 WAR W
BOGGS ADAM A 32 POS W
BOGGS M C A 26 WAR W
BOGGS N E A 26 WAR W
BOGGS SIMSON A 32 LOF W
BOHANAN B A 46 FRI W
BOHANAN SIMON A 32 DAV B
BOID JOHN A 30 GIB W
BOLABAUGH B A 32 TYR W
BOLES WM A 29 FA1 W
BOLES WM A A 29 FA1 W
BOLIN JOSEPH A 53 LA1 B
BOLING A J A 46 KIN W
BOLING CEPHUS A 44 KIT B
BOLING JOHN M A 46 HIG W
BOLLEN JACOB A 46 FRI B
BOLLEN REYPTON A 37 TA2 B
BOLLOCK ALFRED A 44 TOW B
BOLLOCK BOOKER A 44 TOW B
BOLLOCK EDMOND JR A 44 TOW B
BOLLOCK EDMOND SR A 44 TOW B
BOLLOCK HENDERSON JRA 44 TOW B
BOLLOCK HENDERSON SRA 44 TOW B
BOLLOCK HENRY A 44 TOW B
BOLLOCK LEWIS A 44 TOW B
BOLLOCK MOSES A 44 TOW B
BOLLOCK WM A 44 TOW B
BOLNEY J W A 44 TAR W
BOLTON BRYANT A 39 HAR W
BOLTON HENERY H A 29 CAR W
BOLTON PETER A 29 CAR W
BOLTON PETER L A 29 CAR W
BOLTON WILSON A 39 HAR W
BOMAN DANIEL A 46 RAG W
OF SOLOMON
BOMAN DANIEL SR A 46 RAG W
BOMAN G W A 46 FRI W
BOMAN JOHN M A 46 KIN W
BOMAN JOSEPH A 46 RAG B
BOMAN PETER A 46 RAG W
BOMAN SAMUEL A 46 RAG W
BOMAN WILLIAM W A 46 COB W
BOMMER CALEB A A 53 LA1 W
BON JOHN A 28 04A B
BONAR JOHN A 24 EDE W
BOND ALEXANDER H A 24 EDE W
BOND ALLEN A 32 TYR B
BOND ANTHONY A 24 EDE B
BOND ANTHONY SR A 24 EDE B
BOND AUGUSTUS A 24 EDE B

BOND BENJN A 28 01A B
BOND CATO A 28 05A B
BOND CHARLES A 24 EDE B
CHALLENGED BY J R B
HATHAWAY CONVICTED OF
LARCENY RECORDS OF
COUNTY COURT SHOWS IT
CONVICTED BEFORE HE HAD
THE RIGHT OF SUFFRAGE,
THEREFORE COULD NOT LOSE
WHAT HE NEVER HAD
FINAL REVISION ACCEPTED
BOND DANEIL A 24 EDE B
BOND DANIAL A 37 TA1 B
BOND DANIEL A 28 03B B
BOND EDWARD A 24 EDE B
BOND F W A 24 EDE W
BOND GASKIN A 24 EDE B
BOND GEORGE A 24 EDE B
BOND GEORGE A 24 EDE W
BOND H L A 32 TYR W
BOND HANNIBAL A 28 05A B
BOND HENDERSON A 24 EDE B
BOND HENRY A 24 EDE B
BOND HENRY A JR A 24 EDE W
BOND HENRY A SR A 24 EDE W
BOND J C A 29 FA1 W
BOND J L B A 46 SUM W
BOND JOHN A 24 EDE B
BOND JOHN A 24 EDE W
BOND JOSEPH JR A 24 EDE B
BOND JOSEPH SR A 24 EDE B
BOND MAJOR A 24 EDE B
BOND ORRIN A 29 FA2 B
BOND PETER A 24 EDE B
BOND RICHD A 28 04A B
BOND SAMUEL T A 24 EDE W
BOND SIMON A 28 03B B
BOND T J A 24 EDE W
BOND THOMAS A 24 EDE B
BOND WALLACE A 24 EDE B
BOND WILLIAM E A 24 EDE W
BONER J W A 32 CLE W
BONER JACOB A 32 CLE W
BONER JOHNATHAN A 32 CLE W
BONEY ANDREW A 35 ISL B
BONEY BRYANT A 35 ISL B
BONEY CHRISTOPHER C A 35 ISL W
BONEY DANIEL T A 35 ISL W
BONEY DANIEL W A 35 ISL W
BONEY DAVID W A 35 ISL W
BONEY ELI A 35 ROC B
BONEY EPHRAM A 35 ISL B
BONEY EPHRAM A 35 ISL W
BONEY FELIX A 35 ROC B
BONEY FRANK A 35 ISL B
BONEY GABRIEL A 35 ISL W
BONEY GABRIEL J A 35 ISL W
BONEY HARRY A 37 ROC B
BONEY HIRAM S A 35 KEN W
BONEY JAMES M A 35 ISL B
BONEY JAMES W A 35 ISL W
BONEY JAMES W A 35 ISL W
BONEY JOHN A 35 ISL B
BONEY JOHN A A 35 ISL W
BONEY JOHN Q A 35 MAG W
BONEY JOHN Q A A 35 ISL B
BONEY JOHN W A 35 ROC W
BONEY JOSEPH A 35 ISL B
BONEY JOSEPH DANIEL A 35 CYP B
BONEY LIBERTY A 35 ISL B
BONEY OBED A 35 ISL B
BONEY PATRICK A 28 03A B

BONEY PETER A 35 ROC B
BONEY ROBERT A 35 ISL B
BONEY ROBERT A 35 ISL B
BONEY SAMUEL A 35 ISL B
BONEY SAMUEL A 35 ISL B
BONEY STEPHEN A 35 LIM W
BONEY SUTTON A 35 ISL B
BONEY TIMOTHY W A 35 ISL W
BONEY WELLS A 35 ISL W
BONEY WILLIAM A 35 ISL B
BONEY WILLIAM A 35 ISL B
BONEY WILLIAM A 35 ROC B
BONEY WILLIAM B A 35 ISL W
BONEY WILLIAM J A 35 ISL W
BONHAM JACK A 35 MAG B
BONHAM JAMES R A 35 ISL W
BONNAR JACK A 24 EDE B
BONNER AARON A 28 14T B
BONNER C C A 37 ROC W
BONNER EDWARD A 28 05A B
BONNER HENRY A 40 BLA W
BONNER JAMES A 24 EDE W
BONNER JOHN J A 53 LA1 W
BONNER LINNER A 28 05A B
BONNER LUKE A 28 04A B
BONNER SELBY A 53 LA1 W
BONNER SILFAX A 28 01A B
BONNER SIMON A 28 05A B
BONNER W H A 24 EDE W
BONNER WILLIAM V A 53 LA1 W
BONNER WILLIS A 28 04B B
BONNEY FERDINAND A 30 KNO W
BONNEY HENRY W A 30 KNO W
BONNY JOHN A 30 MOY B
BOOKER GEORGE A 28 03A B
BOOKER HENRY A 46 GRE B
BOOKER PETER A 44 ISL B
BOOKMAN SIDNEY S A 24 EDE B
BOOKOUT L A 26 BOR W
BOOKOUT SILAS A 26 GOF W
BOOKRAM J M A 39 FRA B
BOOKRAM SOLOMON A 38 FRE B
BOOKRAM W A A 39 FRA B
BOOKRAM W H A 39 FRA B
BOOM ELISHA A 19 BE1 B
BOOMER BENJAMIN E A 53 LA1 W
BOOMER CALEB S A 53 SWA W
BOOMER DENNIS A 53 LA2 B
BOOMER HENRY G A 53 SWA W
BOOMER ISREAL A 53 LA1 B
BOOMER MATTHEW A 53 GER W
BOOMER RICHARD A 53 LA1 B
BOOMER THOMAS R A 53 LA1 W
BOOMER WILLIAM H A 53 GER W
BOOMER WILLIAM W A 53 LA1 W
BOON ALFRED A 28 04A B
BOON ALSON A 46 GIB W
BOON AUSTIN A 35 WAR B
BOON C J A 29 FA2 W
BOON DANL L A 46 GIB W
BOON DEMPSEY W A 99 BUS W
BOON GEORGE A 28 04A B
CERTIFICATE GRANTED
POLLOKSVILLE
BOON GEORGE A 35 KEN B
BOON IRVIN A 46 GIB W
BOON J C A 29 FA2 W
BOON J LEVI A 46 COB B
BOON JACOB C A 46 GIB W
BOON JACOB N A 46 GIB W
BOON JAMES A 39 DAV B
BOON JAMES P A 46 GRE W
BOON JARRETT A 29 FA1 B

BOON JIM JR A 39 DAV B
BOON JOHN A 46 GIB W
BOON JOHN A D A 29 FA1 W
BOON JOHN H A 35 MAG W
BOON JOHN T A 46 GIB W
BOON JOSEPH A 35 ROC W
BOON JOSHUA S A 37 ROC W
BOON LEWIS H A 46 GIB W
BOON LOUIS A 39 HAR B
BOON MARTIN A 46 GIB W
BOON OLIVER L A 46 MCL W
BOON R R A 39 DAV W
BOON RANDALL A 30 MOY B
BOON RANKIN A 46 GIB B
BOON S M A 39 DAV W
BOON SAMUEL A 29 CED B
BOON UMPHRY A 37 ROB B
BOON WILLIAM A 24 EDE B
BOON WILLIAM J M A 39 DAV W
BOONE B F A 44 HEN W
BOONE JAMES A 28 8TH B
CERTIF GIVEN NOW
LIVES AT NEW BERN
BOONE MADISON A 28 03A B
BOONE MARTIN A 24 EDE B
BOONE MILLS A 28 12T B
CERTIF GIVEN LIVES
NOW AT CEDAR GROVE
BOONE W S A 25 SHO W
BOONE WILLIS A 44 OXF B
BOOTH CHARLES A 28 03A B
BOOTH JNO B A 44 LED W
BOOTH PETER A 44 FIS B
BOOTH S D A 44 LED W
BOOTHE DANIEL A 44 RAG B
BOOTMAN STEPHEN A 29 QUW B
BOOTS L A A 26 SHE W
BORDEN B F JR A 28 9TH W
BORDEN B F SR A 28 9TH W
BORDER H J A 26 BUR W
BORDERS A J CHAL A 26 BUR W
MILITIA OFFICER &
ENGAGED IN REBELLION
BORDERS ANDREW A 26 HOL B
BORDERS BURKE 26 SHE B
BORDERS HENDISON A 26 SHE W
BORDERS HUGH A 26 SWA W
BORDERS JOHN A 26 BUR W
BORDERS MICHAEL A 26 SHE W
BORDERS MICHAIL A 26 SWA W
BORDERS T G CHAL A 26 BUR W
MILITIA OFFICER &
ENGAGED IN REBELLION
BORDERS WILLIAM A 26 SWA W
BORDORS ANDERSON A 26 SWA B
BORDORS JOSEPH A 26 SWA B
BORDORS ROBERT A 26 SWA B
BOREN A P A 46 FRI W
BORMEN RICHARD A 37 WHI B
BORNES DANIEL A 37 ROC B
BORUM GEORG R A 46 GRE W
BORWELL FRANK A 44 KIT B
BOSEMAN ISAAC A 37 ROB W
BOSEMAN JOHN A 37 ROB W
BOSEMAN JOHN A 37 ROC B
BOSEMAN LIMON A 28 9TH B
BOSEMAN MOSES A 37 ROC B
BOSEMAN THOMAS E A 37 ROB W
BOSKET SIMON A 19 NEW B
BOSMAN JOHN D A 37 ROC W
BOSS WILLIAM A 19 BE1 B
BOSSHART G A 32 TYR W
BOSTICK CHESLY A 26 MOO W

BOSTICK DANIEL A 35 KEN W
BOSTICK DANIEL A 35 KEN W
BOSTICK DANIEL J A 35 LIM W
BOSTICK DAVID A 26 MOO W
BOSTICK DAVID R A 35 KEN W
BOSTICK DAVID R A 35 LIM W
BOSTICK JACOB A 35 KEN W
BOSTICK JAMES A 26 MOO W
BOSTICK JOHN M A 35 LIM W
BOSTICK OWEN D A 35 KEN W
BOSTICK SAMEUL T A 35 KEN W
BOSTICK STEPHEN D A 35 KEN W
BOSTICK WILLIAM A 35 KEN W
BOSTON DANL A 28 04A B
BOSTWICK BRYANT W A 35 MAG W
BOSWELL J J A 19 BE1 W
BOSWELL JOHN A 39 HAY B
BOSWELL JOHN A 44 OXF B
BOSWELL SOLOMON A 44 BRA B
BOSWOOD GIDEON A 30 IND W
BOSWOOD WILLOUGHBY A 30 COI W
BOTTOM JAMES A 37 PEN B
BOTTOMS WM A 29 CAR W
BOTTS GRAVES A 26 SHE B
BOTTS R M A 26 SHE W
BOUCHAN JOHN A 29 MON B
BOUIE D A A 29 CAR W
BOUIE D MCD A 29 FA1 W
BOUIE J D A 29 CAR W
MILLITIA OFFICER AFTER
ENGAGED IN REBELLION
BOUIE JNO R A 29 CAR W
BOUIE M J A 29 CAR W
BOUIE WM A 29 GRA B
BOUNDIE DAVID A 29 FLE W
BOWDEN BENJAMIN C A 35 KEN W
BOWDEN BENJAMIN C A 35 WAR W
BOWDEN BOSAN A 35 WAR B
BOWDEN DAVID A 35 KEN B
BOWDEN DEMSEY A 39 DAV W
BOWDEN J C A 35 FAI W
BOWDEN J L A 39 DAV W
BOWDEN JOHNATHAN A 35 WAR B
BOWDEN M B A 39 DAV W
BOWDEN MOSES A 35 WAR B
BOWDEN ROBERT A 35 FAI B
BOWDEN ROBERT JR A 35 WAR B
BOWDEN ROBERT SR A 35 WAR B
BOWDEN SAMEUL A 35 WAR B
BOWDEN SAMUEL R A 35 WAR W
BOWDEN SEDRICK A 35 WAR B
BOWDEN SIMON A 35 WAR W
BOWDEN SUNNUN A 28 05A B
BOWDEN THOMAS A 30 KNO W
BOWDEN THOMAS A 35 WAR B
BOWDEN TIMOTHY JR A 30 KNO W
BOWDEN TIMOTHY SR A 30 KNO W
BOWDEN W B A 39 DAV W
BOWDEN W M A 35 WOL B
BOWDEN W S A 35 FAI W
BOWDEN WILLIAM A 35 KEN B
BOWDEN WILLIAM A 35 WAR B
BOWDEN WILLIAM A 35 WAR B
BOWDEN WILLIAM SR A 35 WAR B
BOWDEN WILLIS A 35 MAG B
BOWDEN WILLIS A 39 DAV W
BOWDEN WILOBEY A 39 DAV W
BOWDEN WM A 44 KNA W
BOWDIN ABEL A 39 DAV W
BOWDIN ARCH A 39 LOU B
BOWDIN J W A 39 DAV W
BOWDIN JNO W A 29 CAR W
BOWDIN JOHN A 39 DAV W

BOWDIN R D A 39 DAV W
BOWDITCH JOSEPH H A 37 TA1 W
BOWEN BENJAMIN A 26 HOL B
BOWEN CHARLES C A 28 14T W
BOWEN DANIEL A 19 BE1 W
BOWEN G W A 26 HOL B
BOWEN JNO A 44 SAS W
BOWEN JOHN A 26 HOL B
BOWEN JOHN W A 35 ISL W
BOWEN L C A 26 SHE W
BOWEN LEWIS A 29 FA1 B
BOWEN MOSES A 53 GER B
BOWEN OSCAR A 28 05A B
BOWEN S S A 28 01A B
BOWEN SAML A 28 03A B
BOWEN THOS H A 28 14T W
BOWEN WILLIAM A 30 TUL W
BOWENS WM A 28 04A B
BOWERS A R A 32 THO W
BOWERS ANDREW A 32 THO W
BOWERS D M A 25 HAY W
BOWERS GEORGE A 32 THO W
BOWERS H L A 32 THO W
BOWERS J C A 25 HAY W
BOWERS JAMES A 39 SPE W
BOWERS LAZ W A 32 THO W
BOWERS THOMAS A 25 HAY W
BOWERS WILLIAM A 32 THO W
BOWERS WILLIAM A 32 THO W
BOWIE JNO A 29 FA1 W
BOWIN DANIEL K A 35 SMI W
BOWIN MADISON A 32 CLE B
BOWIN WILLIAM A 35 LIM B
BOWLES W H A 44 LED W
BOWLIN GEORGE A 28 04B B
BOWLIN P T A 44 LED W
BOWLIN SAMUEL A 46 ROS B
BOWMAN CHAS A 29 FA1 B
BOWMAN JAS A 29 FA1 B
BOWMAN JAS JR A 29 FA1 B
BOWMAN JOHN A 46 HIG B
BOWMAN MADISON A 46 COB W
BOWMAN N R A 46 COB W
BOWMAN RICHARD R 46 FRI W
WAS A CONSTABLE
BEFORE WAR ENGAGED IN
REBELLION COULD NOT TAKE
THE OATH WITH THE WORD
VOLUNTARY OMITTED REJ
NAME LINED OUT
BOWMAN ROBERT A 46 HIG B
BOWMAN RODY A 46 RAG W
BOWMAN SYDNEY A 46 HIG B
BOWMAN W F A 46 HIG W
BOWMAN WASHINGTON R 46 COB W
HE WAS A MAGISTRATE BEFORE
THE WARE AND CONTINUED TO
ACT DURING THE WARE WITHOUT
A CHANGE OF OATH. REJECTED
BOWMAN WILLIAM A 28 6TH W
BOWMAN WM A 46 HIG W
BOWMAN WM M A 46 SUM W
BOWSER EDIN A 39 FRA B
BOWSER GEORGE W A 30 ROA B
BOWSER JOHN A 30 MOY B
BOWSER JONAS A 30 POW B
BOWSER JOSEPH C A 30 ROA B
BOWSER SPENCER A 30 ROA B
BOWSER WILLIAM H A 30 TUL B
CHAL NON RESIDENCE
APRIL 16, 1868
BOYCE B F A 24 MID W
BOYCE B P JR A 24 MID W

BOYCE B P SR A 24 MID W
BOYCE HENRY A 24 MID W
BOYCE HENRY H A 24 UPP W
BOYCE J D A 24 MID W
BOYCE JNO R A 24 MID W
BOYCE JOSEPH A 24 MID B
BOYCE JOSEPH A 24 MID W
BOYCE JOSEPHUS A 24 MID W
BOYCE JOSIAH A 24 EDE W
BOYCE MARTIN A 24 UPP W
BOYCE MILES A 24 UPP B
BOYCE REV E E A 40 FER W
BOYCE THEOPHS A 24 MID B
BOYCE THOMAS A 24 UPP W
BOYCE W M A 24 MID W
BOYCE WILEY A 24 UPP B
BOYCE WILLIS A 24 MID B
BOYCE WM F A 24 MID W
BOYD A A 44 ISL W
BOYD ABNER A 28 11T W
BOYD AMBROSE A 19 HAR B
BOYD ANDREW A 40 DA1 W
BOYD BENJAMIN A 28 10T B
BOYD BRICE A 44 ISL W
BOYD CHARLES A 28 05A B
BOYD CHARLES A 53 LA1 B
BOYD CHARLES P A 46 KIN W
BOYD DANIEL A 53 SWA B
BOYD DAVID A 24 EDE B
BOYD EDWARD A 44 ISL W
BOYD EDWARD STANLEY A 28 11T B
BOYD GEORGE W A 53 SWA W
BOYD HALL A 44 TOW B
BOYD HARRY A 44 HEN B
BOYD HENRY A 19 BE1 B
BOYD HENRY A 28 05A B
BOYD HENRY A 44 TOW B
BOYD J A A 44 ISL W
BOYD JACOB A 40 FER B
8 MOS RESIDENCE
1ST SEPT 1867
BOYD JOHN A 40 DA1 B
BOYD JOHN A 44 YXR W
BOYD JOS H A 44 ISL W
BOYD JOSHUA A 40 DA1 B
BOYD LEWIS A 37 PIN B
BOYD MALACHI A 30 GIB W
BOYD MERRICK A 28 05A B
BOYD MICHAEL A 28 9TH B
BOYD MICHL A 28 05A B
BOYD MINGO A 28 05A B
BOYD OSBORN A 44 TOW B
BOYD OTIS A 28 05A B
BOYD ROBERT F R 40 FER W
BOYD ROBERT M A 40 FER W
BOYD ROD A 39 JOR B
BOYD RODON A 28 6TH B
BOYD SILUS A 37 MAN B
BOYD STEPHEN A 19 NEW B
BOYD THOMAS A 28 11T W
BOYD TONEY A 28 05A B
BOYD W S A 28 02N W
BOYD WILEY A 28 05A B
BOYD WILLIAM H A 44 TOW W
BOYD WM A 44 TOW B
BOYD WM A 44 YXR W
BOYED ALFRID A 19 BE1 B
BOYED JAMES A 19 BE1 B
BOYED JOHN O A 53 SWA W
BOYED LEE A 40 CAN B
BOYET JOHN W A 35 SMI W
CERTIF GIVEN REMOVED
TO KENANSVILLE

BOYET WILLIAM A 35 SMI W
CERTIF GIVEN REMOVED
TO KENANSVILLE
BOYETT BUCK A 37 TA1 B
BOYETT JOHN E A 37 EDW W
BOYETT NATHAN A 37 TA2 B
BOYETT TOM A 37 TA2 B
BOYETTE ANCRAM A A 35 WAR W
BOYETTE BALAAM A 35 MAG B
BOYETTE HENRY A 35 KEN B
BOYETTE HINTON A 35 KEN W
BOYETTE JOHN A A 35 MAG W
BOYETTE JONAS A 35 WAR W
BOYETTE WILLIAM A 35 WAR W
BOYKIN ANTHONY A 35 ROC B
BOYKIN JOHN A 37 MAN W
BOYKIN MARCH A 35 WAR B
BOYKINS HENRY A 35 MAG B
BOYLE ALANDA A 30 ROA B
BOYLES JOHN A 26 WAR W
BRABBLE BENJAMIN A 30 COI W
BRABBLE DENNIS A 30 CUR W
BRABBLE JAMES A 30 CUR W
BRABBLE JAMES J A 30 CUR W
BRABBLE JNO W A 30 CUR W
BRABBLE JOHN F A 28 15T W
BRACKER JOSEPH A 40 STO B
BRACKET E A 26 PEE W
BRACKET JOSEPH A 26 PEE W
BRACKET WILLIAM A 26 PEE W
BRACKET WILLIAM A 26 PEE W
BRACKET WM SR A 26 PEE W
BRACKETT PETER A 30 IND B
BRACKNALL T J A 39 HAY W
BRACKWOOD LEANDER A 40 DA1 B
BRADARD HARRY A 28 01B B
BRADCHER A A 44 LED W
BRADDICK AYRES A 28 04A B
BRADDICK FRED A 28 01A B
BRADDICK JOHN A 28 04B B
BRADDIE MOSES A 37 PIN B
BRADDY K J A 29 LOC W
BRADDY W E A 29 FA1 W
BRADEY L K A 29 FA1 W
BRADFORD ANDREW A 44 BEA B
BRADFORD ELY A 29 FA2 W
BRADFORD J R A 44 FIS W
BRADFORD J W A 44 FIS W
OXFORD DIST
BRADFORD JOHN A 39 HAY B
BRADFORD THOS A 39 FRA B
BRADFORD WM A 39 FRA B
BRADIE BARNEY A 53 FAI B
BRADIE MOSE A 37 PIN B
BRADLEY A S A 40 CAN B
BRADLEY ALBERT A 40 SAN W
BRADLEY ALEXANDER A 37 ROC B
BRADLEY ALEXANDER S A 40 DA1 W
BRADLEY BENJAMIN G A 40 DA1 W
BRADLEY CALEB A 40 DA1 W
BRADLEY CHALON A 40 DA1 W
BRADLEY CHARLES A 35 WAR W
BRADLEY CHAS A 30 GIB W
BRADLEY COLLINS A 37 ROB W
BRADLEY ELI H A 40 DA1 W
BRADLEY ELIAS A 37 ROB W
BRADLEY ESSA A 37 ROB W
BRADLEY FRANCIS A 37 ROB W
BRADLEY HARDIE A 37 ROB W
BRADLEY HAZARD A 35 WAR B
BRADLEY HENRY A 26 BUR B
BRADLEY JAMES A A 26 MOU B
BRADLEY JOHNATHAN A 37 ROB W
BRADLEY JOSEPH W A 40 DA1 W
BRADLEY JOSHUA A 26 SHE W
BRADLEY LORANCE A 37 HOL W
BRADLEY REUBIN A 30 GIB W
BRADLEY SIMON B A 37 ROB W
BRADLEY STALLINGS A 37 ROB B
BRADLEY STEPHEN A 37 ROB W
BRADLEY THOS A 26 BUR B
BRADLEY WILLIAM A 37 ROB W
BRADLEY WILLIAM E A 37 PEN W
BRADLEY WILLS A 37 ROB W
BRADLY JOHN A 37 MAN B
BRADOCK TIMOTHY A 53 FAI B
BRADSHAW A M A 46 FRI W
BRADSHAW ALEX M A 46 GRE W
BRADSHAW ALFORD A 32 CLE B
BRADSHAW BRYANT D A 35 ISL W
BRADSHAW CALVIN J A 35 KEN W
BRADSHAW DAVID W A 35 MAG W
BRADSHAW DAVID W R 35 ISL W
FOR HAVING BEEN A
MILITIA OFFICER BEFORE
THE WAR AND AFTERWARDS
ENGAGED IN REBELLION
BRADSHAW EDMON A 40 CAN B
BRADSHAW FRANKLIN A 32 DAV B
BRADSHAW HANDY A 35 ISL B
BRADSHAW JACOB B A 35 MAG W
BRADSHAW JAMES B A 35 MAG W
BRADSHAW JOHN A 35 ISL W
BRADSHAW JOHN S A 35 MAG W
BRADSHAW ORSTER A 32 COT W
BRADSHAW PRIDE A 40 RHY W
BRADSHAW SAMEUL A 35 MAG W
BRADSHAW SAMUEL A 35 ISL B
BRADSHAW SAMUEL W A 35 ISL W
BRADSHAW SEABORN A A 35 KEN W
BRADSHAW SETH A 40 DEC W
BRADSHAW WELLS A 35 KEN W
BRADSHAW WILLIAM D A 35 ISL W
BRADSHAW YORK A 32 COT B
BRADY ALLEN A 37 EDW B
BRADY CEASER A 37 PIN B
BRADY JAMES A 28 01A B
BRADY RICHD A 28 05A B
BRADY SPRINGS A 24 EDE W
BRADY THOMAS A 28 7TH W
BRADY W A 29 LOC B
BRADY WALTON A 35 FAI B
BRAG HENRY A 39 HAY B
BRAGG A H A 44 LED W
BRAGG DAVID A 44 FOR W
BRAGG GEORGE A 28 01A B
BRAGG J H A 44 BEA W
BRAGG J T A 44 BEA W
BRAGG JAMES A 19 BE1 B
BRAGG JOEL A 44 FOR W
BRAGG JOHN A 53 OCR W
BRAGG JOHN V A 19 POR W
BRAGG KILLIS A 28 04A B
BRAGG SAMUEL D A 53 OCR W
BRAGG STEPHEN A 44 FOR W
BRAGG THOS W A 44 FOR W
BRAGG W A 39 FRA W
BRAGG W W A 44 BEA W
BRAHAM DAVID E A 28 02N B
BRAHME JOHN A 39 FRA B
BRAK-- JOS J--- A 37 ROC W
BRAKE HENRY A 37 ROC W
BRAKE JACOB A 37 ROC W
BRAKE JESSE A 37 ROC W
BRAKE JOHN A 37 ROC W
BRAKE JOSIAH A 37 ROC W
BRAMBLE WILEY A 29 GRA W
BRAMBLE WM H A 29 GRA W
BRAME CALEB A 44 HEN B
BRAME DAVID A 44 HEN B
BRAME HAYWOOD A 44 HEN B
BRAME J L A 44 HEN W
BRAME J W A 44 HEN W
BRAME JAS A A 44 HEN W
BRAME JAS A JR A 44 HEN W
BRAME JEREMIAH A 44 HEN B
BRAME JOHN A 44 HEN B
BRAME LUNDON A 44 HEN B
BRAME NELSON A 39 HAY B
BRAME SAML A 44 HEN B
BRAME SAMUEL A 44 HEN B
BRAME STEPHEN A 44 HEN B
BRAME T H A 44 HEN W
CERT TO VOTE OUT COUNTY
BRAME W H A 44 HEN W
BRAME W L A 44 HEN W
BRAME WARREN A 44 HEN B
BRAME WM A 44 HEN B
BRAME WM A A 39 PUG W
BRANCH A B A 35 GLI W
BRANCH ALLEN A 35 GLI B
BRANCH BEN A 39 LOU B
BRANCH BOOKER A 39 HAY B
BRANCH CASWELL A 39 SPE B
BRANCH DAMPIER A 39 SPE B
BRANCH EDMOND A 19 BE1 B
BRANCH ESAFE A 39 SPE B
BRANCH FRANK A 39 SPE B
BRANCH GUILFORD A 38 FRE B
BRANCH GUY A 39 LOU B
TRNS TO SPEEDS STORE
BRANCH HENRY A 35 SMI B
BRANCH HILLIARD A 37 EDW B
BRANCH ISIAH A 39 HAY B
BRANCH JETHRO A 39 HAY B
BRANCH JOHN A 37 EDW B
BRANCH JOHN A 46 JAM B
BRANCH JORDAN A 29 FA1 W
BRANCH JR A 39 FRE B
BRANCH MARSHAL A 35 FAI W
BRANCH MOORE A 35 GLI B
BRANCH NELSON A 39 SPE B
BRANCH NEWTON A A 99 BUS W
BRANCH NOFTER A 39 FRA B
BRANCH NORPHLET A 39 SPE B
BRANCH PETER A 35 WOL B
BRANCH ROBERT A 37 EDW B
BRANCH ROBERT E A 29 FA1 W
BRANCH ROBT A 39 PUG B
BRANCH RUBAN A 35 FAI W
BRANCH RUFFIN A 39 SPE B
BRANCH RUFUS A 35 GLI B
BRANCH SAMUEL A 35 GLI B
BRANCH SAMUEL A 35 WOL B
BRANCH THOMAS A 35 WOL B
BRANCH THOS A 39 FRA B
BRANCH THOS H A 39 SPE W
BRANCH W A 39 FRE W
BRANCH W L A 39 FRA W
BRANCH WASHINGTON SRA 39 LOU W
TRNS FROM FREEMANS
BRANCH WILLIAM A 37 PIN B
BRANDEN JOHN B A 44 HEN B
BRANDIS HENRY F A 35 KEN W
BRANDLIN UMBLESTON A 44 KIT B
BRANDON ABRAM A 44 FIS B
BRANDON CHESLEY A 44 FIS B
BRANDON JACOB A 44 HEN B
BRANDON RICHD A 44 KIT B

BRANDON WILLIS A 37 SPA B
BRANDOW DANIEL A 37 HOL W
BRANDT GEO R 29 FA1 W
NATURALIZED CITIZEN &
VOLUNTARILLY ENGAGED
IN REBELLION
BRANDT HENERY A 29 FA1 W
BRANDT SIMON A 29 FA1 W
NATURALIZED CITIZEN &
VOLUNTARILLY ENGAGED
IN REBELLION
BRANHAM NEEDHAM A 99 BUS W
BRANNAM W G A 39 GRI W
BRANNAM WILLIAM A 53 LA1 B
BRANNAN WILLIAM A 99 BUS W
BRANNOCK ANDREW A 46 MON B
BRANNON ABRAM A 40 SAN B
BRANNON ABRAM A 40 SAN W
BRANNON GREEN A 40 SAN B
BRANNON JNO A 29 FA1 W
BRANSON DANIEL B A 46 COB W
BRANSON HENRY A 29 FA1 W
BRANSON HENRY A 46 GRE B
BRANSON MARK A 29 FA1 B
BRANTAN T A 26 BOR W
BRANTLEY ROBERT B A 30 NOR W
BRANTON DAVID A 26 SHE W
BRANTON ELLIS A 28 04A B
BRANTON WM H A 19 BE1 B
BRANY HENRY A 37 EDW B
BRASEL ALEX A 44 FOR B
BRASEL JORDON A 44 FOR B
BRASFIELD JOS A 29 FLE B
BRASHUM TILMON A 53 HAT W
BRASINGHOW S M A 32 SHE W
BRASS GEORGE A 37 HOL W
BRASSFIELD CHAS A 38 FRE B
BRASWELL ABNER A 37 PEN W
BRASWELL ALFRED A 37 ROB B
BRASWELL AMOS A 37 SHA B
BRASWELL ARTHUR A 37 ROB W
BRASWELL ASHBURY A 37 SHA W
BRASWELL BAKER W A 37 TA1 W
BRASWELL BEN A 37 ROB B
BRASWELL BULLOCK A 37 ROC W
BRASWELL CELLEY S A 37 SHA W
BRASWELL DAVID A 37 ROC W
BRASWELL DISBONEY ? A 37 ROC B
BRASWELL GEORGE A 37 HOL B
BRASWELL ISAAC A 37 SHA W
BRASWELL JAMES A 37 SPA W
BRASWELL JESSE A 37 ROC W
BRASWELL JOHN D A 37 HIG W
BRASWELL JOHN H A 37 SHA W
BRASWELL
NATHAN BUSHROD A 37 SHA W
BRASWELL NEUSOM A 37 PEN W
BRASWELL PATRICK H A 37 HIG W
BRASWELL PEMILEY A 37 SHA B
BRASWELL PROCTOR A 37 HIG B
BRASWELL RIGHT R 37 ROC B
CONVICTED FOR LARCENY
BRASWELL ROBERT A 37 SHA W
BRASWELL RUBIN A 37 ROC B
BRASWELL WILEY C A 37 SHA W
BRASWELL WILIE H A 37 ROC W
BRASWELL WILLIAM A 37 SHA W
BRASWELL WILLIAM H CA 37 EDW W
BRASWELL ZEDOCK R A 37 SHA W
BRASWILL RICHARD A 37 PEN W
BRASWWELL HANDY A 37 ROB B
BRATCHER ANDREW A 46 SUM W
BRATCHER D A 28 6TH W
BRATCHER EDMUND A 40 FER B
BRATCHER JOHN L D A 28 6TH W
BRATCHER LEWIS A 28 6TH W
BRATCHR J P A 28 6TH W
BRATTEN FEDRICK A 40 CAN B
MOVED TO LINCOLN CO
BRATTIAN ROBERT A 32 BRO W
BRATTON C A A 32 THO W
BY CERTIF
BRATTON JOHN L SR A 24 EDE W
BRATTON JOSEPH A 24 EDE W
BRAXTON CHARLES A A 37 HIC B
NAME LINED OUT
BRAXTON PETER A 44 TOW B
BRAY ANDREW A 30 CUR W
BRAY B M A 30 CUR W
BRAY BITTON A 30 IND B
BRAY HOMES A 30 TUL B
BRAY JORDAN A 30 CUR B
BRAY JOSIIAN A 30 TUL B
BRAY N A A 28 01A W
BRAY NOAH A 30 IND W
BRAY OWEN A 30 CUR B
BRAY PETER A 30 IND B
BRAY SAML A 30 CUR B
BRAY SKINNER A 30 CUR B
BRAY THOMAS A 30 CUR B
BRAYMAN POLEMUS A 28 03A W
BRAZESFIELD JOSEPH A 37 ROB B
BRAZILL JOSEPH A 24 EDE B
BRAZWELL EDWARD A 37 ROB B
BRAZWELL HILLIARD A 37 ROB B
BRAZWELL ROBERT A 37 ROB B
BRAZZEL JOHN A 44 FOR B
BRAZZEL JORDON A 44 FOR B
BRAZZEL RIGHT A 44 FOR B
BREACE THOMAS A 29 LOC B
BREADLOVE H T A 39 PUG W
BREADLOVE J W A 39 PUG W
BREADLOVE S A 39 PUG W
BREADLOVE W A A 39 DAV W
BREADLOVE WILLIAM A 39 LOU W
BREDGES HARRY A 39 HAR B
BREECE J S A 29 LOC W
BREECE J S A 29 LOC W
BREECE JOS A 29 FLE W
BREECE L R A 29 FLE W
BREECE SAML A 29 LOC B
BREECE SQUIRE A 29 FLE B
BREEDELOVE HENRY A 46 GRE W
BREEDING W C A 26 MOO W
BREEDLOVE BENJA J A 44 SAS W
BREEDLOVE BENNETT A 44 FIS W
BREEDLOVE DAVID A 44 FIS W
BREEDLOVE EMAUNEL A 44 FIS W
BREEDLOVE J A A 44 OXF W
BREEDLOVE J P A 44 FIS W
BREEDLOVE JNO H A 44 RAG W
BREEDLOVE M H A 44 SAS W
BREEDLOVE N H A 44 FIS W
BREEDLOVE WM A 44 FIS W
BREEHN JAMES A 46 COB B
BREESE CHARLES A 29 CED B
BREHN GEORGE D A 46 ROS B
BREHN PHILLIP A 46 ROS B
BRENDT FISHER A 37 EDW B
BREWER ELI M A 46 MON W
BREWER J E A 32 DAV W
BREWER J J A 39 JOR W
BREWER J M A 32 LOF W
BREWER JAMES M A 46 MON W
BREWER JAS S A 29 FA1 W
BREWER JOHN JR A 39 JOR W
BREWER JOHN SR A 39 JOR W
BREWER JOSEPH A 32 SHE W
BREWER JOURDAN A 28 9TH W
BREWER N C A 28 11T W
BREWER NOAH W A 46 MON W
BREWER SAMUEL A 19 BE1 B
BREWER THOMAS A 28 11T B
BREWER W R A 32 CLE W
BREWER W T A 39 JOR W
BREWINGTON GEO R A 29 FA1 B
BREWINGTON JNO R A 29 FA1 B
BREWINGTON WM A 29 FA1 B
BREWR DUMAS A 29 ROC W
BRIAN HENRY A 19 BE1 B
BRIAN LAMB A 19 BE1 B
BRIAN SAMUEL A 28 02N B
BRIANT JAMES A 37 SPA B
BRIANT JOHN A 32 LEE W
BRIANT JOHN A 53 LA2 B
BRIANT KELLY A 32 LEE W
BRIANT S A A 26 CAR W
BRIANT W P A 26 CAR W
BRIANT WASHINGTON A 44 YXS B
BRIANT WILLIAM A 32 LEE W
BRICE FRANCIS A 35 ISL W
BRICE GEORGE A 28 04A B
BRICE JAMES A 46 GRE B
BRICE JESSE A 28 10T B
BRICE JOHN J A 35 ISL W
BRICE POMPY A 19 BE2 B
BRICE WILLIAM A 35 MAG W
BRIDGERS A W A 39 DAV W
BRIDGERS CHARLES A 37 EDW B
BRIDGERS CHARLES A 37 EDW B
BRIDGERS DANCY A 37 EDW B
BRIDGERS DANIEL A 37 EDW B
BRIDGERS DAVID A 40 DEC W
BRIDGERS FRANK A 37 EDW B
BRIDGERS GEORGE A 37 EDW B
BRIDGERS HARRY A 37 EDW B
BRIDGERS HEUBERT A 37 EDW B
BRIDGERS HINES A 37 EDW B
BRIDGERS HIRAM A 37 EDW B
BRIDGERS IRVING A 37 EDW B
BRIDGERS ISAAC A 37 PEN B
BRIDGERS ISAH A 44 HEN B
BRIDGERS JACKSON A 39 HAY W
BRIDGERS JAMES A 37 EDW B
BRIDGERS JERRY A 37 EDW B
BRIDGERS JOHN L A 26 SWA W
BRIDGERS JOSEPH A 37 EDW B
BRIDGERS LEWIS A 37 EDW B
BRIDGERS LEWIS A 37 EDW B
BRIDGERS LIBERTY A 37 EDW B
BRIDGERS MEDIEUS A 44 HEN B
BRIDGERS RAIMOND A 37 EDW B
BRIDGERS S H A 39 LOU W
BRIDGERS SILAS A 37 EDW B
BRIDGERS SILAS A 37 EDW B
BRIDGERS STEWART A 37 EDW B
BRIDGERS THOMAS G A 53 SWA W
BRIDGERS WASHINGTON A 37 EDW B
BRIDGERS WILLIAM A 40 DEC W
BRIDGERS WILSON A 37 EDW B
BRIDGERS ? WILLIAM A 39 LOU B
BRIDGES A B A 26 MOU W
BRIDGES AARON A 26 MOU W
BRIDGES AARON A 37 TA1 B
BRIDGES ASHLEY A 37 HIC B
BRIDGES ATLAS A 38 FRE B
BRIDGES B H A 26 MOU W
BRIDGES BENJAMIN A 37 TA1 B
BRIDGES BOONE A 37 PEN B

BRIDGES CHARLES A 28 04A B
BRIDGES D K A 26 GOF W
BRIDGES D R A 26 BLA W
BRIDGES D S A 26 BLA W
BRIDGES DOLPHIN A 44 BRA B
BRIDGES DRURY A 26 MOU W
BRIDGES E A 26 BLA W
BRIDGES EDMOND A 26 MOU B
BRIDGES EDWARD A 37 TA1 B
BRIDGES F H A 26 SWA W
BRIDGES F M A 26 BLA W
BRIDGES FRANK A 37 TA1 B
BRIDGES G B A 26 BLA W
BRIDGES GEORGE A 40 DEC W
BRIDGES H H A 26 SHE W
BRIDGES I J A 26 BLA W
BRIDGES ISAAC A 37 WHI B
BRIDGES J S A 26 BLA W
BRIDGES JACKSON A 26 MOU B
BRIDGES JAMES A 40 DEC W
BRIDGES JAMES M A 26 MOO W
BRIDGES JAMES M A 37 WEB W
BRIDGES JAS A 39 FRA W
BRIDGES JASPER A 44 ISL B
BRIDGES JERRY A 37 HIG B
BRIDGES JESSE W A 26 MOO W
BRIDGES JOHN A 26 MOO W
BRIDGES JOHN M A 26 BLA W
BRIDGES JULIUS A 99 BUS B
BRIDGES L A A 26 BLA W
BRIDGES L H A 26 SHE W
BRIDGES M A A 26 BOR W
BRIDGES NATHAN A 26 MOU B
BRIDGES PRESTON A 26 MOU W
BRIDGES REDICK A 37 TA1 B
BRIDGES S J A 26 BLA W
BRIDGES S J A 26 PEE W
BRIDGES SG A 26 MOU W
BRIDGES T H A 44 FOR W
BRIDGES T S A 26 BLA W
BRIDGES T S A 26 MOO W
BRIDGES T W A 26 MOO W
BRIDGES W A A 26 BLA W
BRIDGES W A A 26 BUR W
BRIDGES W B A 26 BLA W
BRIDGES W W A 26 MOO W
BRIDGES WASHINGTON A 26 HOL B
BRIDGES WASHINGTON A 44 BRA B
BRIDGES WELCOME A 28 10T B
BRIDGES WILLIAM A 37 SPA B
BRIDGES WM A 29 CAR W
BRIDGES WM P A 39 GRI W
BRIDGETT NELSON A 44 KIT B
BRIDGMAN HENRY A 53 FAI W
BRIDGMAN HIRAM T A 53 GER W
BRIDGMAN JAMES E A 53 SWA W
BRIDGMAN JOHN L A 53 FAI W
BRIGG ENOCH A 32 LOF W
BRIGGS ALLEN A 40 DA2 B
BRIGGS ANDREW A 24 EDE W
BRIGGS CALVIN A 37 PEN B
BRIGGS DANIEL A 32 LOF W
BRIGGS GEORGE A 37 ROC B
BRIGGS H M A 46 JAM W
BRIGGS HENRY A 26 WAR W
BRIGGS HENRY A 44 KNA W
BRIGGS HOWELL A 44 KNA W
BRIGGS ISAAC A 28 10T W
BRIGGS JAMES A 24 EDE W
BRIGGS M A 26 BOR B
BRIGGS NELSON JR A 26 GOF B
BRIGGS PETER A 28 03A B
BRIGHT ANSON H A 28 16T W

BRIGHT GEORGE A 28 11T W
BRIGHT HANSON A 30 GIB W
BRIGHT JOHN A 28 11T W
BRIGHT JOSEPH A 35 MAG B
BRIGHT MAJOR A 30 IND B
BRIGHT PINCKNEY A 19 HAR B
BRIGHT RILEY A 28 05A B
BRIGHT W T A 28 05A W
BRIGHT WM A 28 14T B
BRIGS NELSON SR A 26 GOF B
BRILES ALEXANDER A 32 THO B
BRILES DAVID A 32 THO W
BRILES J O A 32 DAV W
BRILEY WILLIAM B A 37 PIN W
BRILL JOSEPH J A 37 HOL W
BRILLIPS JOSEPH A 37 HOL W
BRIM J H A 28 01A W
BRIMAGE DAVID A 28 05B B
BRIMAGE JOHN F A 53 SWA B
BRIMAGE JOHN JR A 53 SWA B
BRIMAGE JOHN SR A 53 SWA B
BRIMAGE ROBERT A 53 LA1 B
BRIMER C P A 40 CAN W
BRIMER J P A 40 SAN W
BRIMER JOHN A 40 SAN W
BRIMER JOHN A 40 STO W
BRIMER MOSES A 40 STO W
BRIMER WILLIAM A 40 SAN W
BRIMMAGE JOHN A 28 03A B
BRIMMAGE JOHN A 28 7TH B
BRIMMAGE MINGO A 28 04A B
BRIMMIDGE JAMES A 28 7TH B
BRIN SAMUEL T A 53 FAI W
BRINAGE HARRY A 28 04A B
BRINCKLY ROBERT A 53 GER B
BRINDDLE AL A 32 SHE B
BRINDDLE WITTS A 32 SHE B
BRINDELL FRANKLIN A 32 CLE W
BRINDELL JOHN JR A 32 CLE W
BRINDILL JOHN A 32 CLE W
BRINKLEY CALVIN R A 24 UPP W
BRINKLEY DANIEL A 32 POS W
BRINKLEY EDWARD A 24 UPP B
BRINKLEY G W A 44 LED W
BRINKLEY GILBERT A 37 EDW B
BRINKLEY H A 44 LED W
BRINKLEY ISAAC A 29 FA1 B
BRINKLEY ISHAM A 44 LED W
BRINKLEY J A 28 6TH W
BRINKLEY JAS M A 24 UPP W
BRINKLEY JOHN B A 35 CYP W
BRINKLEY JOHN H A 32 DAV W
BRINKLEY JOHN S A 32 POS W
BRINKLEY JOSEPH A 28 6TH W
BRINKLEY M C A 24 EDE W
BRINKLEY MARTIN L A 24 UPP W
BRINKLEY R A 28 6TH W
BRINKLEY RUFFIN A 44 LED W
BRINKLEY SAMPSON A 19 NEW B
BRINKLEY SOLOMON A 24 UPP B
BRINKLEY W J A 44 LED W
BRINKLEY WILLIAM A 28 04A B
BRINKLEY WILLIAM T A 30 ROA W
BRINKLEY WM D A 40 CAN W
BRINKLY DANIEL A 32 DAV W
BRINKLY HARISON A 32 DAV W
BRINKLY HENRY A 32 TYR W
BRINKLY JAMES A 24 MID B
BRINN ABNER A 53 FAI W
BRINN ALBERT A 28 10T B
BRINN ISAAC W A 37 PEN W
BRINN JOHN D A 53 LA1 W
BRINN JOSEPH A 24 MID W

BRINN JOSEPH A 53 LA1 W
BRINN PETER A 37 ROB B
BRINN SAMUEL T A 53 LA1 W
BRINN STEPHEN R A 24 MID W
BRINSFIELD G H A 46 MON W
BRINSON AFFRICA A 53 LA1 B
BRINSON ALEXR A 28 03A B
BRINSON B H A 28 03A W
BRINSON BENJAMIN F A 28 14T W
BRINSON BRYANT A 35 KEN B
BRINSON CASON D A 28 14T W
BRINSON D J A 35 LIM W
BRINSON DANIEL A 28 16T W
BRINSON DAVID B A 28 13T W
BRINSON DAVID H A 28 14T W
BRINSON DAVID H A 28 14T W
BRINSON EDWARD A 28 14T W
BRINSON EDWARD T A 35 LIM W
BRINSON GREEN C A 28 14T W
BRINSON HARPER A 35 KEN B
BRINSON HENRY B A 28 14T W
BRINSON HILLERY T A 35 LIM W
BRINSON J G A 28 03A W
BRINSON J W A 35 LIM W
BRINSON JAMES A 28 16T W
BRINSON JAMES A 30 NOR W
BRINSON JEROME B A 28 14T W
BRINSON JOHN A 35 LIM W
BRINSON JOHN S R 28 16T W
CONSTABLE BEFORE THE WAR
GAVE AID & COMFORT TO THE
ENEMIES OF THE U.S.
BRINSON JONATHAN A 35 LIM W
BRINSON NATHANIEL G A 28 16T W
BRINSON NATTHEW A 28 10T W
BRINSON OLIVER P A 28 14T W
BRINSON ROBERT A 35 KEN B
BRINSON SAMUEL R 28 14T W
MAGISTRATE GIVEN
AID & COMFORT
BRINSON SIMON S A 28 7TH W
CERTIF GIVEN LIVES
NOW AT NEWBERN
BRINSON STEPHEN D A 28 14T W
BRINSON WILLIAM N A 35 LIM W
BRINSON WM A 28 13T W
BRINSON WM G A 28 03B W
BRINSON WM GEO A 28 01A W
BRINSON WM H A 28 16T W
BRINT CHRISTOPHER A 19 HAD B
BRINTON TIMOTHY A 37 PEN W
BRISCOE ANDREW A 26 GRI B
BRISENDINE H A 26 CAR B
BRISON G R A 40 SAN W
BRISON J F A 40 SAN W
BRISTOL GAYLORD A 25 HAY W
BRISTOL T B A 25 HAY W
BRISTON SAMUEL A 24 EDE B
BRITT CHARLES A 99 BUS B
BRITT CHAS G A 24 EDE W
BRITT DAVID T A 37 PIN W
BRITT HARDY A 99 BUS W
BRITT JAMES H A 37 PEN W
BRITT JAS P A 24 EDE W
BRITT MARION D A 99 BUS W
BRITT MILES A 44 KIT B
BRITT W G A 24 EDE W
BRITTAIN JEREMIAH A 46 KIN B
BRITTAN JOHN M A 46 FRI W
BRITTAN WIATT A 46 FRI W
BRITTENHAM J W A 32 DAV W
BRITTON CHARLES A 28 12T B
BRITTON J H A 46 JAM W

BRITTON JOHN A 46 JAM B
BRITTON JOHN W A 53 GER W
BRITTON JOSEPH A 46 SUM B
BRITTON LEWIS A 46 SUM B
BRITTON OWEN W A 35 LIM W
BRITTON SAMUEL A 46 SUM B
BRITTON SAMUEL T A 35 LIM W
BROADAWAY W A 40 CAN W
BROADFOOT C W A 29 FA2 W
BROADFOOT ROBT A 29 FA1 B
BROADHURST D J A 35 WOL B
BROADHURST R C A 35 WOL B
BROADHURST SHEPPARD A 35 FAI B
BROADNAX HENRY A 46 SUM B
BROADSTREET GEO A 28 03A W
BROADSTREET WM A 46 JAM W
BROADSTREETS ADISON A 46 FRI W
BROADWAY ANDREW A 32 TYR W
BROADWAY JOHN A 32 TYR W
BROADWAY JOHN A 32 TYR W
BROADWAY SAMUEL D A 32 TYR W
BROADWAY THOMAS A 32 COT W
BROADWAY THOMAS W A 32 TYR W
BROADWAY W H A 32 TYR W
BROADWAY W M A 40 CAN W
BROADWAY WILLIAM A 32 COT W
BROADWAY WILLIAM A 32 TYR W
BROCK ALLEN J A 28 7TH W
BROCK AMOS A 19 MOR W
CERT TO HADNOT CREEK
BROCK BARNETT A 35 LIM W
BROCK BRINKLEY A 35 WOL B
BROCK BURRELL A 35 WOL B
BROCK CHARLES A 35 WOL B
BROCK CHAS A 28 6TH B
BROCK DAVID A 35 ISL W
BROCK HARDY A 28 04A B
BROCK HENRY A 32 DAV B
BROCK ISAAC A 35 SMI B
BROCK JAMES A 28 7TH B
BROCK JESSE A 35 GLI W
BROCK JESSE H A 35 WOL W
BROCK JOHN A 28 03A B
BROCK JOHN A 30 POW W
BROCK JOSEPH A 28 6TH W
BROCK LEVEN A 35 WAR W
BROCK LEVY A 35 WOL B
BROCK MARTIN F A 28 9TH W
BROCK R J A 28 7TH W
BROCK R M A 28 7TH W
BROCK STEPHEN A 19 NEW B
BROCK STEPHEN A 35 KEN W
BROCK W M A 32 DAV W
BROCK WM A 29 BLA W
BROCKER JOHN A 28 03A B
BROCKMAN AUGUSTUS J A 46 GRE W
BRODGON J W A 32 TYR W
BRODIA ALFORD A 39 LOU B
BRODIA HARRY A 39 DAV B
BRODICK HARRY A 28 04A B
BRODIE CASWELL A 44 HEN B
BRODIE CHARLES A 39 DAV B
BRODIE DR W A 44 SAS W
BRODIE E G A 44 HEN W
BRODIE EDMOND A 44 RAG B
BRODIE HOWARD A 44 HEN B
BRODIE JOE A 39 HAY B
BRODIE KID A 44 HEN B
BRODIE LORENZA A 39 DAV B
BRODIE NATHAN A 44 HEN B
BRODIE S W A 39 DAV W
BRODIE SAM A 39 DAV B
BRODIE THOS A 44 HEN B
BRODIE WASHINGTON A 44 HEN B
BRODIE WESLEY A 44 RAG B
BRODIE WILLIS A 44 HEN B
BRODIS LARKIN A 28 03A B
BROGDAN DAVID A 44 DUT W
BROGDEN ELISHA A 44 DUT W
BROGDEN JAMES A 44 DUT W
BROGDEN JORDAN A 25 HAY W
BROGDEN OLIVER R 19 MOR W
BROGDON ELIAS A 44 DUT W
BROMWELL H W CHAL R 32 DAV W
FOR BEING OUT OF PRECINCT
BROOCK W M A 26 MOO W
BROOK FRANKLIN A 35 GLI B
BROOK JOHN S A 53 LA2 W
BROOKBANK H T A 46 SUM W
BROOKBANK THOMAS A 46 SUM W
BROOKBANK WILLIAM A 46 KIN W
BROOKBANK WILLIAM H A 46 KIN W
BROOKENS ISAAC A 37 TA2 B
BROOKFIELD JOHN A 28 01B W
BROOKFIELD RAYNOR A 28 01B W
BROOKINS WILLIAM A 39 HAY B
BROOKS ANDREW A 37 ROB B
BROOKS ASA A 28 16T W
BROOKS BILL A 37 HIC B
BROOKS CALEB F A 53 LA1 W
BROOKS CASSE A 37 HOL B
BROOKS CHARLES A 46 KIN B
BROOKS CICERO K A 53 LA1 W
BROOKS D M A 26 SHE W
BROOKS DANIEL A 26 PEE B
BROOKS DANIEL A 40 DA1 B
BROOKS DANNIL A 26 WAR B
BROOKS DAVID H A 19 STR W
BROOKS DAVID J A 35 ROC B
BROOKS EDWARD J A 28 15T W
BROOKS ELIJAH A 53 LA1 B
BROOKS GARRISON A 28 04A B
BROOKS GEORGE A 19 STR W
BROOKS GEORGE A 53 LA1 B
BROOKS GEORGE A 53 LA1 B
BROOKS H A 32 TYR W
BROOKS H M A 32 TYR W
BROOKS HARRISON A 46 KIN B
BROOKS HENRY A 19 HAD B
BROOKS HENRY A 44 HEN B
BROOKS J A 26 BOR B
BROOKS J J W A 46 MON W
MALITIA OFFICER BEFORE
WARE AIDED REBELLION
BROOKS JACK A 30 MOY B
BROOKS JAMES A 28 16T B
BROOKS JAMES A 28 7TH B
BROOKS JAMES M A 19 STR W
BROOKS JEREMIAH A 35 ROC B
BROOKS JESSE A 28 05A B
BROOKS JESSE A 28 05A B
BROOKS JOHN A 19 STR W
BROOKS JOHN A 28 16T B
BROOKS JOHNSON A 28 03A B
BROOKS JONAS A 40 DA1 B
BROOKS JOSEPH A 35 LIM W
BROOKS JOSEPH A 35 MAG W
BROOKS JOSEPH A 37 TA1 B
BROOKS JOSEPH S A 28 15T W
BROOKS LAYFAITT A 46 FRI B
BROOKS MADISON A 37 HIC B
BROOKS MARTIN C A 19 STR W
BROOKS MOSES A 28 9TH B
BROOKS NATHAN A 26 BLA B
BROOKS OSCAR A 19 STR W
BROOKS PARDON F A 53 LA1 W
BROOKS PETER A 35 MAG B
BROOKS ROBERT A 28 7TH B
BROOKS SAMUEL A 19 HAD B
BROOKS SAMUEL A 46 GRE B
BROOKS SAMUEL A 53 LA1 B
BROOKS SIMON A 37 MAN B
BROOKS THOMAS A 32 TYR W
BROOKS THOMAS A 37 HIC B
BROOKS THOMAS A 53 LA1 B
BROOKS THOS A 28 04A B
BROOKS WILLIAM A 19 BE1 W
BROOKS WILLIAM A A 35 MAG W
BROOKS WM A 39 FRA B
BROOKS WM L A 46 MON W
BROOKS WM R A 28 15T W
BROOKS WM W A 29 FA1 B
BROTHERS ALFRED A 46 COB W
BROTHERS ED A 28 03A B
BROTHERS ELBRIDGE G A 46 COB W
BROTHERS JEREMIAH A 28 05A B
BROTHERS JOHN A 46 COB W
BROTHERS JONATHAN A 30 CUR W
BROTHERS MILES A 28 15T W
BROTHERS TOM A 28 01A B
BROTHERS WM H A 30 CUR W
BROTHERS WM H A 46 ROS W
BROUGHTON GEORGE W A 28 16T W
BROUGHTON JAMES W A 28 16T W
BROUGHTON LEVI D A 28 16T W
BROUGHTON MAJOR A 28 14T W
BROUGHTON SOLOMON S A 28 14T W
BROUGHTON WILEY A 28 14T W
BROWDER CHRISTOPHER A 37 ROC B
BROWER JOHN W A 46 COB W
BROWER PRESTON A 46 COB B
BROWING R H A 46 KIN W
BROWN A B A 25 HAY W
BROWN A J A 25 PIN W
BROWN A J A 35 LIM W
BROWN A J A 46 MON W
BROWN ABRAM A 28 03A B
BROWN ALFORD A 46 FRI B
BROWN ALFRED A 46 COB W
BROWN ALLEN A 28 05A B
BROWN AMON M A 28 03A B
BROWN AMOS A 35 CYP W
BROWN ARMISTEAD A 28 05A B
BROWN ARTHUR A 40 BLA W
BROWN AUSTIN A 28 05A B
BROWN B CHAL A 26 BOR W
CHARGED WITH FELONY
BROWN B S A 46 FRI W
BROWN BADGER S A 35 WAR W
BROWN BENJAMIN J A 39 FRA W
BROWN BENJAMIN P A 46 FRI W
BROWN BRINDEL A 37 SHA B
BROWN BURELL A 32 CLE W
BROWN BYTHEL G A 37 HIG W
BROWN CALVIN A 28 05A B
BROWN CATO A 29 FA1 B
BROWN CHARLES A 35 LIM B
BROWN CHARLES A 46 ROS B
BROWN CHAS A 29 FA1 B
BROWN CHAS A 29 FA1 B
BROWN CHAS S A 28 01B B
BROWN CLEMONS A 35 KEN B
BROWN D F A 46 FRI W
BROWN DANL A 28 01A B
BROWN DANL A 28 04B B
BROWN DANL A 29 GRA W
BROWN DAVID A 35 ISL W
BROWN DAVID A 35 LIM B
BROWN DAVID A 35 WAR W

BROWN DAVID A 44 SAS B
BROWN DAVID A 46 MCL W
BROWN DAVID B JR A 35 LIM W
BROWN DAVID J A 35 KEN W
BROWN DAVID M A 46 GRE W
BROWN DAVID W A 29 FA1 B
BROWN DENING A 37 SPA B
BROWN DUNCAN A 29 SEV W
BROWN E S A 46 HIG W
BROWN E W A 46 MON W
BROWN EDMUND A 37 PEN B
BROWN EDWARD A 35 LIM W
BROWN EDWD A 28 04A B
BROWN EDWD A 29 FA1 B
BROWN ELIJAH B A 28 04A B
BROWN ELIJAH R A 28 04A B
BROWN EMANUEL A 24 EDE B
BROWN ENOCH A 28 6TH B
BROWN ENOS A 25 PIN W
BROWN ESQUIRE A 35 ISL B
BROWN FAYETTE A 24 EDE B
BROWN FELIX A 35 CYP W
BROWN FRANK A 28 03B B
BROWN FRANKLIN A 28 01B W
BROWN FRANKLIN A 37 HOL B
BROWN FRANKLIN A 46 SUM B
BROWN G W A 35 LIM W
BROWN G W A 46 MON W
BROWN G W R 46 SUM W
CONSTABLE BEFORE THE
WAR INVESTED IN CONFED
RATE BONDS REJ
BROWN G WASHINGTON A 46 KIN W
BROWN GEO A 19 NEW B
BROWN GEO A 29 FA1 B
BROWN GEORGE A 28 6TH W
BROWN GEORGE A 35 KEN W
BROWN GEORGE A 46 GRE B
BROWN GEORGE A 46 KIN W
BROWN GEORGE J A 37 SPA W
BROWN GEORGE W A 28 9TH B
BROWN GEORGE W A 53 SWA W
BROWN GILES A 46 SUM B
BROWN GRAY JR A 37 HIG W
BROWN GREEN A 37 TA1 B
BROWN GREGON A 35 ISL W
BROWN H C A 46 MON W
BROWN H F CHAL A 25 PIN W
FOR BEING IN SERVICE
BROWN HARBERT A 37 SPA B
BROWN HENRY A 28 03A B
BROWN HENRY A 28 04A B
BROWN HENRY A 35 LIM W
BROWN HENRY A 53 LA1 B
BROWN HEZAKIAH A 53 SWA W
BROWN HEZEKIAH A 35 WAR W
BROWN HILLIARD A 28 6TH B
BROWN HOWELL A 35 CYP W
BROWN HOWELL A 35 CYP W
BROWN ISAAC A 28 03A B
BROWN ISAAC A 39 FRA B
BROWN ISAAC JR A 35 WAR W
BROWN ISAAC SR A 35 LIM W
BROWN ISHAM A 29 FA1 B
BROWN J B A 29 FA1 W
BROWN J C A 32 POS W
BROWN J H A 46 FRI B
BROWN J L A 46 HIG W
BROWN J LOGAN A 40 DA1 W
BROWN J M A 25 SHO W
BROWN J W A 19 HAD B
BROWN J W A 28 04A B
BROWN J W A 35 LIM W

BROWN JACKSON A 37 PIN B
BROWN JACOB A 35 LIM W
BROWN JACOB A 44 SAS B
BROWN JACOB T A 32 DAV W
BROWN JAMES A 19 HAR B
BROWN JAMES A 29 ROC W
BROWN JAMES A 32 DAV B
BROWN JAMES A 35 CYP W
BROWN JAMES A 35 ROC W
BROWN JAMES A 37 PIN B
BROWN JAMES A 46 GRE W
BROWN JAMES D A 35 ISL W
BROWN JAMES E A 30 POP W
BROWN JAMES H A 46 SUM W
MALITIA OFFICER BEFORE
WARE. REJ BY OWN REQ.
AIDED IN REBELLION
BROWN JAS A A 29 FA1 W
BROWN JAS W A 29 FA1 W
BROWN JEFFERSON A 40 DA1 B
BROWN JESSE A 35 KEN W
BROWN JESSE A 35 SMI W
BROWN JESSE A 46 KIN W
BROWN JESSY A 32 TYR B
BROWN JNO A 44 SAS B
BROWN JNO H A 44 HEN W
BROWN JOEL A 44 SAS B
BROWN JOHN A 19 SMY W
BROWN JOHN A 26 BOR W
BROWN JOHN A 28 01A B
BROWN JOHN A 28 02N B
BROWN JOHN A 29 SEV W
BROWN JOHN A 35 LIM B
BROWN JOHN A 46 KIN W
BROWN JOHN B A 28 01A B
BROWN JOHN C A 53 SWA W
BROWN JOHN E A 46 SUM W
BROWN JOHN F A 40 BLA W
BROWN JOHN M C A 28 6TH B
BROWN JOHN W A 35 LIM W
BROWN JONAS A 40 BLA W
BROWN JOSEPH A 32 BRO W
BROWN JOSEPH A 44 YXS B
BROWN JOSEPH A A 40 DA2 W
BROWN JOSEPH J A 46 FRI W
BROWN JOSEPH L A 37 PIN W
BROWN JULIUS A 28 16T B
BROWN KIMBROL A 32 DAV B
BROWN LAFAYETTE A 35 LIM W
BROWN LAWRENCE A 29 FA1 B
BROWN LELAND R A 25 HAY W
NAME LINED OUT
FOR NOT HAVING LIVED
IN THE STATE 12 MONTHS
BROWN LEWIS A 28 03A W
BROWN LEWIS A 29 FLE B
BROWN LEWIS A 46 GIB B
BROWN LEWIS W A 35 CYP W
BROWN LITTLE BERRY A 37 PIN W
BROWN LONDON A 35 ISL B
BROWN LOUIS A 19 BE2 B
BROWN LOUIS A 35 LIM B
BROWN LOUIS A 35 LIM W
BROWN M A 39 FRA W
BROWN M W A 35 LIM W
BROWN MADISON A 46 ROS W
BROWN MARK A 24 EDE B
BROWN MICHAEL A 35 KEN W
BROWN MICHAEL A 35 WAR W
BROWN MICHAEL A 46 GRE W
BROWN MILTON E A 25 PIN W
BROWN MONROE A 40 DA1 W
BROWN NEEDHAM A 35 LIM W

BROWN NELSON A 29 FA1 B
BROWN NICHOLAS A 29 FA1 B
BROWN NORRIS A 35 LIM B
BROWN OBEDIAH A 46 HIG W
BROWN OLIVER A 28 16T B
BROWN P J JR A 39 LOU W
BROWN PAUL A 29 GRA B
BROWN PETER A 37 HIC B
BROWN PETER A 39 LOU B
TRNS TO BLADEN CO
10 APR 1868
BROWN PETER A 46 MCL W
BROWN PETER M A 46 HIG W
BROWN PHILIP P A 28 03A W
BROWN PHILLIP A 24 EDE B
BROWN PRIMUS A 35 KEN B
BROWN R H A 35 LIM W
BROWN R J A 28 01A W
BROWN RILY A 46 COB W
BROWN ROBERT A 28 7TH B
BROWN ROBERT C A 37 TA1 W
BROWN ROBERT F A 40 BLA W
BROWN ROBERT G A 40 BLA W
BROWN ROBERT H A 40 BLA W
BROWN ROBT A 29 FA1 B
BROWN RUCH A 44 KIT B
BROWN RUFFIN A 46 KIN W
BROWN SAML A 28 01A B
BROWN SAMUEL A 29 FA2 B
BROWN SHADRACK A 28 04A B
BROWN SIDNEY M A 46 MCL W
BROWN SIFFORD A 28 02N B
BROWN SILAS A 37 EDW B
BROWN SILAS TWICE A 28 03A B
BROWN SIMON A 19 MOR B
BROWN SPENCER A 39 HAY W
BROWN SPENCER A 46 SUM B
BROWN STEVEN A 40 RHY B
BROWN T H A 39 LOU W
TRNS FROM HENDERSON
GRANVILL CO BY CERT
BROWN THOMAS A 19 MOR B
BROWN THOMAS A 29 FA2 B
BROWN THOMAS A 32 DAV B
BROWN THOMAS A 37 PEN B
BROWN THOMAS A 39 HAY B
JACKSON PRE
NORTHAMPTON CO NC
BROWN THOMAS A 40 RHY B
BROWN THOMAS A 53 FAI W
BROWN THOMAS B A 28 7TH W
BROWN TULLEY A 30 IND W
BROWN VIRGIL A 29 FA1 B
BROWN VIRGIL A 29 FA1 B
BROWN W C A 32 BRO W
BROWN W C A 39 FRA W
BROWN W L A 26 BOR W
BROWN W P A 32 DAV W
BROWN WASHINGTON A 29 FA2 B
BROWN WASHINGTON A 44 SAS B
BROWN WASHINGTON A 46 GRE B
BROWN WASHN A 28 04A B
BROWN WILLIAM A 24 EDE B
BROWN WILLIAM A 28 04B B
BROWN WILLIAM A 35 KEN B
BROWN WILLIAM A 37 HIG W
BROWN WILLIAM A 39 JOR W
BROWN WILLIAM J A 35 WAR W
BROWN WILLIAM M A 25 PIN W
BROWN WILLIS A 44 HEN B
BROWN WM A 29 FA1 B
BROWN WM A 46 GIB W
THIS SHOULD BE BOON not BROWN

BROWN WM A A 32 POS W
BROWN WN W A 46 COB W
BROWNE JOSEPH N A 30 COI W
BROWNE WILLIAM W A 30 ROA W
BROWNHILL WM A 32 COT W
BROWNHILL WM A 32 COT W
BROWNING MOSES A 37 SHA W
BROWNRIGG BENJAMIN A 24 UPP B
BROWNRIGG HENDERSON A 24 UPP B
BRUCE SAMUEL P A 46 FRI W
BRUMFIELD J DIDLEY A 40 DA2 W
BRUMFIELD JAMES A 40 DA1 W
BRUMITT W C A 44 BRA W
FISHING CREEK DIST
BRUMLEY DAVID A 30 KNO W
BRUMMELL ALFERD A 32 THO B
BRUMMELL AMOS A 32 THO B
BRUMMELL DAVID A 32 THO W
BRUMMELL GEORGE A 32 POS B
BRUMMELL H W A 32 THO W
BY CERTIF.
BRUMMELL HENRY A 32 THO B
BRUMMELL JOHN A 32 THO B
BRUMMELL NORMAN A 32 THO B
BRUMMELL RANSOM A 32 THO B
BRUMMELL ROBERT A 32 THO B
BRUMMETT J H A 44 OXF W
BRUMMIT THOS S A 44 FOR W
BRUMMITT J R A 39 LOU W
BRUMMITT J R A 44 FIS W
BRUMMITT J V A 44 FIS W
BRUMMITT JOHN A 44 FIS W
BRUMMITT S D A 44 FIS W
BRUMMITT T J A 44 FIS W
BRUMMITT W T A 44 FIS W
BRUMMITT WESLEY A 44 OXF W
BRUMSEY AUG W A 30 CUR W
BRUMSEY AUGUSTUS A 30 CUR W
BRUMSEY MAJOR A 30 CUR B
BRUMSEY MALACHI J A 30 COI W
BRUMSEY THOMAS A 30 COI W
BRUNNER JNO A 29 FA1 W
BRUTON D R A 32 THO W
BRYAN A C A 28 01A B
BRYAN AFFIT A 28 03A B
BRYAN ALEXR A 28 03A B
BRYAN ALEXR A A 28 02N B
BRYAN ALFRED A 28 04A B
BRYAN AMOS A 28 04A B
BRYAN AMOS A 28 9TH B
BRYAN ANDREW A 28 11T B
BRYAN ANTHONY A 37 TA1 B
BRYAN ASA A 28 03A B
BRYAN AUGUSTUS A 28 03A B
BRYAN BARRK B A 37 WEB W
BRYAN BATTLE A 37 PEN W
BRYAN BLUNT A 37 MAN W
BRYAN C J A 28 01A W
BRYAN CAESAR A 28 03A B
BRYAN CAESAR A 28 05A B
BRYAN CALVIN A 28 7TH B
BRYAN CHARLES A 28 03A B
BRYAN CHAS A 28 05B B
BRYAN
COLLISON HENRY A 28 9TH B
BRYAN DANL A 28 04A B
BRYAN DANL A 28 04A B
BRYAN DAVID A 28 04A B
BRYAN DOSEY A 28 11T B
BRYAN ELLIS A 28 04A B
BRYAN FATE A 28 03A B
BRYAN FERNEY A 28 04B B
BRYAN FRANK A 28 04A B

BRYAN FRANK A 28 04A B
BRYAN FREDERICK A 28 7TH W
BRYAN GEORGE A 28 01A B
BRYAN GEORGE A 28 03A B
BRYAN GEORGE A 28 04A B
BRYAN GEORGE A 28 04A B
BRYAN GEORGE A 37 TA1 B
BRYAN
GEORGE WASHINGTON A 28 9TH B
BRYAN HARRISON A 53 GER B
BRYAN HENRY A 28 03A B
BRYAN HENRY A 28 04A B
BRYAN HENRY A 37 MAN W
BRYAN HENRY A 53 GER B
BRYAN IRVING A 28 04A B
BRYAN ISAAC A 28 03A B
BRYAN ISAAC A 28 03A B
BRYAN ISAAC A 28 03A B
BRYAN ISAAC A 28 05A B
BRYAN ISAAC A 40 SAN B
BRYAN ISREAL A 19 BE1 B
BRYAN J J A 28 04A B
BRYAN J W A 28 04A B
BRYAN JAMES A 28 04A B
BRYAN JAMES A 28 11T B
BRYAN JAMES A A 28 01A W
BRYAN JARVIS A 28 03A B
BRYAN JAS A 28 05A B
BRYAN JERRY A 28 04A B
BRYAN JESSE A 28 05A B
BRYAN JOHN A 19 SMY B
BRYAN JOHN A 28 02N B
BRYAN JOHN A 28 03A B
BRYAN JOHN A 28 04A B
BRYAN JOHN A 37 WEB W
BRYAN JOHN R 28 11T W
DID NOT TAKE OATH AND
WAS MAGISTRATE AND
AIDED THE REBELLION
BRYAN JOHN A A 35 KEN W
BRYAN JOHN HENRY A 28 03A B
BRYAN JOSEPH A 28 03A B
BRYAN JOSEPH A 28 6TH B
BRYAN JOSEPH A 37 EDW B
BRYAN JUNIUS A 28 6TH B
BRYAN LEVI A 37 MAN W
BRYAN LEWIS A 28 01A B
BRYAN LEWIS H A 28 04A B
BRYAN LOUIS A 28 11T W
BRYAN LYN W A 99 BUS W
BRYAN M A 28 11T W
BRYAN MILES A 28 11T B
BRYAN MITCHELL A 28 04A B
BRYAN MOSES A 28 04A B
BRYAN MOSES A 28 04A B
BRYAN MOSES A 28 7TH B
BRYAN MUSTAPHA A 28 05A B
BRYAN NATHAN A 28 05A B
BRYAN NELSON A 28 02N B
BRYAN OLIVER A 28 11T B
BRYAN OWEN A 28 04A B
BRYAN P A 28 6TH B
BRYAN POMPEY A 28 7TH B
BRYAN PRINCE A 28 05A B
BRYAN PROVIDENCE A 28 04B B
BRYAN R T A 28 03A B
BRYAN RICHARD A 28 04A B
BRYAN RICHARD T A 28 7TH W
PATROLLER
BRYAN RICHD A 28 03A B
BRYAN ROBERT A 28 04A B
BRYAN ROBERT A 28 04B B
BRYAN SAML A 28 05A B

BRYAN SHADRACK A 28 04A B
BRYAN SILAS A 28 9TH B
BRYAN STEPHEN A 28 04A B
BRYAN SYLVESTER A 28 02N B
BRYAN THOMAS A 28 10T B
BRYAN THOMAS A 28 15T B
BRYAN THOMAS A 28 7TH B
BRYAN THOMAS A 28 7TH B
BRYAN THOMAS A 28 7TH W
BRYAN THOMAS A 99 BUS W
BRYAN THOS A 28 04A B
BRYAN THOS A 28 04A B
BRYAN WASHINGTON A 37 ROC B
BRYAN WESTON A 28 7TH B
BRYAN WILLIAM A 28 9TH B
BRYAN WILLIAM A 99 BUS W
BRYAN WM A 28 04A B
BRYAN WM C R 28 16T W
MAGISTRATE, GAVE AID AND
COMFORT TO THE ENEMY
BRYAN WM G A 28 02N W
BRYAN WM HENRY A 28 03A B
BRYAN WRIGHT A 28 7TH B
BRYANT A S A 32 DAV W
BRYANT AARON A 28 05A B
BRYANT AARON A 29 FA1 B
BRYANT ABE A 28 04B B
BRYANT ADAM A 29 LOC B
BRYANT ALBERT A 37 EDW B
BRYANT ALBERT A 53 GER B
BRYANT ALEXANDER H A 40 FER B
BRYANT ALEXR A 28 6TH B
BRYANT ALFRED A 28 11T B
BRYANT ALFRED A 37 ROC B
BRYANT ALLAN A 37 ROC B
BRYANT ALLEN A 37 EDW B
BRYANT AMON A 37 ROB B
BRYANT AMOS A 35 KEN B
BRYANT ANGUS N A 99 BUS W
BRYANT AUGUSTUS A 37 EDW B
BRYANT BENJAMIN A 28 9TH B
BRYANT BENJAMIN B A 35 ISL W
BRYANT BLUNT A 37 MAN B
BRYANT BOB A 44 TOW B
BRYANT BRITTAN A 29 LOC B
BRYANT C A 32 DAV W
BRYANT CEASAR A 29 LOC B
BRYANT CHARLES A 28 02N B
BRYANT CHARLES A 37 ROB B
BRYANT CYRUS A 28 01A B
BRYANT CYRUS A 37 EDW W
BRYANT DANIEL A 19 MOR B
BRYANT DAVID A A 29 FA1 B
BRYANT DEMSY A 37 MAN B
BRYANT DEMSY A 37 MAN B
BRYANT DEWELL A 37 MAN B
BRYANT DOYLE A 29 FA1 B
BRYANT DURAND A 28 01B B
BRYANT ETHELDRED A 37 EDW W
BRYANT FRANK A 37 ROB B
BRYANT FREDERICK A 28 11T B
BRYANT FREDK A 28 03A B
BRYANT FREDK A 28 04A B
BRYANT GEORGE A 28 04A B
BRYANT GEORGE A 37 TA1 B
BRYANT GRAY A 37 EDW W
BRYANT HENRY A 28 03A B
BRYANT HENRY A 35 KEN B
BRYANT HENRY A 37 ROB B
BRYANT HORACE A 29 FA2 B
BRYANT HUNT A 30 MOY B
BRYANT ILLEY A 29 GRA B
BRYANT ISAAC A 35 KEN B

BRYANT ISAAC A 35 MAG B
BRYANT ISAAC A 37 TA1 B
BRYANT ISHAM A 35 ISL B
BRYANT J B A 44 KIT W
BRYANT JACOB A 35 MAG B
BRYANT JAHAS A 32 THO W
BY CERTIF
BRYANT JAMES A 19 MOR B
BRYANT JAMES A 28 05A B
BRYANT JAMES A 29 FA1 B
BRYANT JAMES A 35 KEN B
BRYANT JAMES A 37 ROB B
BRYANT JAMES A 99 BUS W
BRYANT JAS H A 44 KIT W
BRYANT JAS L A 29 FA1 B
BRYANT JEFFREY A 28 10T B
BRYANT JERRY A 37 ROB B
BRYANT JNO A 29 FA2 W
BRYANT JOHN A 19 MOR B
BRYANT JOHN A 28 02N B
BRYANT JOHN A 35 ROC B
BRYANT JOHN A 37 EDW B
BRYANT JOHN J A 37 HIC A
BRYANT JOS B A 28 04A B
BRYANT JOSEPH A 35 MAG B
BRYANT JOSEPH A 35 ROC B
BRYANT JOSEPH CHAL R 35 MAG B
NOT LIVING IN COUNTY
BRYANT K A 29 LOC W
BRYANT KAGER A 37 EDW B
BRYANT L A 29 LOC W
BRYANT LARKIN A 40 DA1 B
BRYANT LENARD A 29 LOC W
BRYANT LEWIS A 19 NEW B
BRYANT LEWIS A 35 KEN B
BRYANT LEWIS A 35 ROC B
BRYANT LEWIS H CERTA 35 MAG W
FAISONS 13 APRIL 1868
BRYANT LONDON A 19 NEW B
BRYANT LOT A 28 04A B
BRYANT LUCIEN A 29 FA1 B
BRYANT M A 29 FLE W
BRYANT MARCH A 28 03A B
BRYANT MICHAEL A 35 KEN B
BRYANT MICHL A 28 04A B
BRYANT NATHAN A 28 11T B
BRYANT NATHAN A 28 8TH B
BRYANT NELSON A 29 FA1 B
BRYANT NORFLEET A 37 EDW B
BRYANT NORRIS A 28 8TH B
BRYANT PETER A 35 MAG B
BRYANT PETER A 99 BUS B
BRYANT PETER CHAL R 35 MAG B
NOT LIVING IN COUNTY
BRYANT PETER W A 46 GRE B
BRYANT R H A 29 LOC W
BRYANT RALPH A 37 ROB B
BRYANT REUBEN A 28 04A B
BRYANT RICHARD A 28 12T B
BRYANT ROBT A 29 FA1 B
BRYANT ROBT A 29 FA1 B
BRYANT ROBT A 29 LOC B
BRYANT ROBT A 44 KIT B
BRYANT SAML A 28 05A B
BRYANT SAMUEL A 37 ROB B
BRYANT SAMUEL A 37 TA1 B
BRYANT SHADE A 29 GRA B
BRYANT SILAS A 29 FA1 B
BRYANT SIOLAS A 28 05A B
BRYANT STIRLIN A 37 MAN B
BRYANT THOS A 28 6TH W
BRYANT THOS A 29 GRA B
BRYANT TILMON A 40 FER B
BRYANT TURNER A 37 ROB B
BRYANT W H A 24 EDE W
BRYANT WALTER B A 35 KEN W
BRYANT WILLIAM A 24 EDE B
BRYANT WILLIAM A 37 ROB B
BRYANT WILLIAM D A 35 ISL W
BRYANT WILLIAM S A 37 ROB W
BRYANT WM S A 29 FA1 B
BRYANT WM W W A 29 FA1 B
BRYNE JESSEE A 29 GRA B
BRYSON WM P A 40 SAN W
BUCHAN GEORGE C A 35 FAI W
BUCHANAN CHARLES A 46 MON B
BUCK DAVID A 19 HAD W
BUCK ENOCH A 28 11T W
BUCK FRANCIS A 19 HAD W
BUCK JAMES A 28 13T W
BUCK JOHN R A 28 11T W
BUCK MARION A 44 LED B
BUCK RANSOM JR A 28 11T W
BUCK SPENCER A 28 13T W
BUCK THOMAS A 19 HAD W
BUCK THOMAS R 28 11T W
BUCK WILOBY A 19 HAD W
BUCK WM A 28 13T W
BUCKHANAN THOMAS A 46 GRE W
BUCKHANAN WM A 46 MCL W
BUCKHANNON J R A 44 OXF W
BUCKHANON CALVIN A 46 GRE W
BUCKHANON GEORG W A 46 MCL W
BUCKHANON JAS H A 46 GRE W
BUCKHANON T F A 46 GRE W
BUCKHANON WM H JR A 46 GRE W
BUCKINGHAM JNO A 29 FA1 W
BUCKLER JOHN A 37 HOL B
BUCKLIN WM S A 28 15T W
BUCKMAN EDW S A 19 BE1 W
BUCKMAN HENRY J A 19 BE1 W
BUCKMAN JOHN C A 19 BE1 W
BUCKRUM ALFRED A 44 DUT B
BUCKS WASHINGTON A 19 HAD W
BUCKSTON JOHN A 35 ISL W
BUDD RICHARD A 28 10T B
BUDDEN THOS A 28 02N W
BUFF CHRIS. A 26 WAR W
BUFF DAVID A 26 WAR W
BUFF DAVID A 26 WAR W
BUFF JOSEPH A 26 WAR W
BUFF PETER A 26 WAR W
BUFF PETER A 26 WAR W
BUFF PETER SR A 26 PEE W
BUFF WILLIAM A 26 PEE W
BUFFALO ANTHONY A 53 LA1 B
BUFFALO EDWARD A 35 MAG B
BUFFALO ISRAEL A 35 ISL B
BUFFALOE ALLEN A 99 BUS B
BUFKIN HENRY A 24 UPP W
BUFKIN SAML M A 24 UPP W
BUIE ARCHD A 29 SEV W
BUIE CHAS A 29 FA1 B
BUIE D MCD 29 FA2 W
SEE CARVER CK BOOK
BUIE G MCD A 29 CAR W
BUIE GILBERT E A 29 ROC W
BUIE J A A 32 JAC W
BUIE JOHN A 29 FLE B
BUIE JOHN A 29 SEV W
BUIE JOHN B A 29 SEV B
BUIE M J 29 FA2 W
SEE CARVERS CK BOOK
BUIE MC J A 29 CAR W
BUIE N MCD A 29 CAR W
BUIE NEILL A 29 SEV W
COUNTY ASSESSOR & HOME
GUARD (ERROR)
BUIE S J A 32 JAC W
BUIE SIMON A 29 FLE B
BUIE WM C A 32 JAC W
BUIS GEORGE A 32 DAV B
BULL WM A 44 SAS W
BULLA ALEXANDER A 32 JAC W
BULLA JACOB A 29 LOC B
BULLA THOAS J A 29 FA1 W
MILLITIA OFFICER AFTER-
WARDS ENG IN REBELLION
BULLARD JOS A 29 CED W
BULLARD W H A 29 LOC W
BULLOCH THOS A 29 CED W
BULLOCK ABNER A 37 HIG B
BULLOCK ALBERT A 44 KNA B
BULLOCK ALEX A 44 SAS B
BULLOCK ALFRED A 37 EDW B
BULLOCK ALFRED A 37 ROC B
BULLOCK ALFRED A 44 DUT B
BULLOCK ALLEN A 37 SHA B
BULLOCK AMOS A 37 ROC B
BULLOCK ANDERSON A 44 TOW B
BULLOCK ANDREW A 37 PIN B
BULLOCK ANDREW A 44 TOW B
BULLOCK B F JR A 44 DUT W
BULLOCK B T SR A 44 BEA W
BULLOCK B W A 44 KNA W
BULLOCK BEVELEY A 44 HEN B
BULLOCK BILL A 37 EDW B
BULLOCK BLUNT A 37 HIG B
BULLOCK CARDLETON A 37 SHA B
BULLOCK CEASER 2ND A 37 PIN B
BULLOCK CEASOR 1ST A 37 PIN B
BULLOCK CHARLES A 28 05A B
BULLOCK CHARLES A 37 EDW B
BULLOCK CHARLES A 37 PEN B
BULLOCK CHARLES A 44 BRA B
BULLOCK D T A 44 LED W
BULLOCK DANIEL A 37 HOL W
BULLOCK DANIEL A 44 HEN B
BULLOCK DANIEL A 44 SAS B
BULLOCK DANIEL N A 37 WHI W
BULLOCK DANL A 44 BEA B
BULLOCK DAVID A 37 EDW B
BULLOCK DAVID A 37 HOL W
BULLOCK DAVID A 39 FRA B
BULLOCK DAVID A 44 HEN B
BULLOCK DAVID A 44 HEN B
BULLOCK DAVID A 44 ISL B
BULLOCK DAVID A 44 LED B
BULLOCK DAVID A 44 SAS B
BULLOCK DEMPSEY A 37 PIN B
BULLOCK DRED A 44 FIS B
BULLOCK E D A 44 BEA B
BULLOCK EDMOND A 44 HEN B
BULLOCK EDWARD A 37 WHI B
BULLOCK EPHRAM A 44 HEN B
BULLOCK EVERETT A 37 EDW B
BULLOCK EVERETT A 37 PIN B
BULLOCK GENERAL A 37 PEN B
BULLOCK GEO B A 44 KIT W
BULLOCK GEORGE A 37 ROC B
BULLOCK GEORGE A 44 HEN B
BULLOCK GRAY A 37 WHI B
BULLOCK H A A 44 LED W
BULLOCK H G A 29 LOC W
BULLOCK HAL A 44 BEA B
BULLOCK HARRISON A 44 DUT B
BULLOCK HAYWOOD A 44 BEA B
BULLOCK HAYWOOD A 44 HEN B

BULLOCK HENRY A 37 HIG B
BULLOCK HENRY A 37 HIG B
BULLOCK HENRY A 37 ROC B
BULLOCK HENRY A 37 WHI B
BULLOCK HENRY A 44 FOR B
BULLOCK HERBERT A 44 HEN B
BULLOCK HERNDON A 44 HEN B
BULLOCK HILLIARD A 37 ROC B
BULLOCK HORATIO A 37 TA2 W
BULLOCK HORRACE A 44 ISL B
BULLOCK HUMPHREY A 44 ISL B
BULLOCK J D A 44 BEA W
BULLOCK J T A 44 BEA W
BULLOCK JACK A 37 ROB B
BULLOCK JACOB A 37 HIG B
BULLOCK JACOB A 37 ROC B
BULLOCK JAS A A 44 SAS W
BULLOCK JERRY A 37 HIG B
BULLOCK JERRY A 37 WHI B
BULLOCK JETER A 37 HIG B
BULLOCK JNO A 29 LOC W
BULLOCK JNO A 44 HEN B
BULLOCK JNO A 44 ISL B
BULLOCK JOHN A 44 SAS B
BULLOCK JOHN A 44 YXS B
BULLOCK JOHNATHAN H A 37 HIG W
BULLOCK JONATHAN A 37 ROC W
TRNS TO HIGH LEVEL
BULLOCK JORDAN A 44 HEN B
BULLOCK JOS A 44 BEA B
BULLOCK JOSHUA A 37 WHI B
BULLOCK KEMP A 44 HEN B
BULLOCK L H A 44 LED W
BULLOCK LEONARD A 44 ISL B
BULLOCK LEWIS A 37 HIG B
BULLOCK LEWIS A 37 HOL B
BULLOCK LORANCE A 37 SPA B
BULLOCK LUEY A 44 DUT B
BULLOCK LUSTER A 44 DUT B
BULLOCK MACK A 44 HEN B
BULLOCK MAT A 44 HEN B
BULLOCK MICHAEL A 37 WHI B
BULLOCK MIKEL A 37 HIG B
BULLOCK MOSES A 24 EDE B
BULLOCK MOSES A 37 EDW B
BULLOCK MOSES A 44 SAS B
BULLOCK NATHAN A 44 HEN B
BULLOCK NEAL A 37 HIG W
BULLOCK NED A 44 KIT B
BULLOCK NEEL A 37 WHI B
BULLOCK NORFLEET A 37 HOL B
BULLOCK ORANGE A 44 HEN B
BULLOCK ORVELL A 44 HEN B
BULLOCK PETER A 37 SHA B
BULLOCK PETER A 39 LOU B
BULLOCK PHILOMEL A 44 HEN B
BULLOCK R A A 44 HEN W
BULLOCK R H A 44 BEA W
BULLOCK RANDAL A 44 HEN B
BULLOCK RANSOM A 44 SAS B
BULLOCK REDIC A 37 WHI B
BULLOCK REUBEN A 44 BEA B
BULLOCK RICHARD A 37 PIN B
BULLOCK RICHARD A 37 WHI W
BULLOCK RICHD A 44 HEN B
BULLOCK RICHD A 44 LED B
BULLOCK RUFFIN A 44 OXF B
BULLOCK RUFUS A 44 FOR B
BULLOCK RUFUS A 44 SAS B
BULLOCK SAM A 44 TOW B
BULLOCK SAML A 44 BEA B
BULLOCK SAMUEL A 37 PEN B
BULLOCK SAMUEL A 37 PIN B

BULLOCK SAMUEL A 44 HEN B
BULLOCK SIMEON A 44 HEN B
BULLOCK SIMON A 37 HIG B
BULLOCK SPENCER A 37 ROC B
BULLOCK SQUARE A 44 HEN B
BULLOCK STEPHEN A 37 HIG B
BULLOCK STEPHEN A 44 TOW B
BULLOCK STEPHEN A 44 SAS B
BULLOCK THOMAS R 44 SAS B
NAME LINED OUT
NOT OF AGE REJ
BULLOCK W E A 44 BEA W
BULLOCK W G A 44 LED W
BULLOCK WALTER A 44 ISL W
BULLOCK WELDON E A 44 BEA W
BULLOCK WILLIAM A 37 EDW B
BULLOCK WILLIAM A 37 HIG B
BULLOCK WILLIAM A 44 LED B
BULLOCK WILLIAM J A 53 GER W
BULLOCK WM A 44 BRA B
BULLOCK WM A 44 FIS B
BULLOK DANIEL V A 37 HIG W
BULLOK FREDERICK E A 37 HIG W
BULLOK HENRY C A 37 HIG W
BULLOK JESSE A 37 HIG W
BULLOK JOSHUA A 37 HIG W
BULLOK LORENZO A 37 HIG W
BULLOK RICHARD A 37 HIG W
BUMGARNER JOHN A 26 PEE W
BUMGARNER WILLIAM A 26 PEE W
BUMPASS FRANK A 44 TAR B
BUMPASS GREEN A 44 YXS B
BUMPUS JERRY A 37 ROC B
BUNCE HENRY A 29 BLA W
BUNCH ABNER A 30 POW W
BUNCH CORNELIUS B 24 EDE B
BUNCH CULLEN A 24 EDE W
BUNCH ELIJAH A 24 MID W
BUNCH ELIJAH A 24 UPP W
BUNCH EPHRAIM A 24 UPP W
BUNCH ESEX A 39 HAY B
BUNCH FRANK A 24 EDE B
BUNCH FREDERICK A 24 EDE W
BUNCH HUMPHRY H A 24 MID W
BUNCH ISAIAH A 24 MID W
BUNCH J A A 24 MID W
BUNCH J J A 24 MID W
BUNCH J W A 24 MID W
BUNCH JAMES A 24 EDE W
BUNCH JAMES JR A 24 EDE W
BUNCH JESSE A 24 EDE W
BUNCH JOHN C A 46 GRE W
BUNCH JOSEPH A 24 MID B
BUNCH JOSEPH S A 24 EDE W
CERT GIVEN TO PERQUIMANS CO
BUNCH JOSIAH A 24 UPP W
BUNCH KING S A 24 EDE W
BUNCH LEMUEL A 24 MID W
BUNCH N N A 99 BUS W
BUNCH NEHEMIAH A 24 MID W
BUNCH NELSON A 53 SWA B
BUNCH P J A 46 SUM W
BUNCH PAUL A 24 MID W
BUNCH PERY A 24 MID W
BUNCH PETER A 28 10T B
BUNCH ROBT D A 24 EDE W
BUNCH SAMUEL A 24 EDE B
BUNCH SOMERSET A 28 04A B
BUNCH STEPHEN A 24 MID B
BUNCH THOMAS V A 99 BUS W
BUNCH TIMOTHY A 24 UPP W
BUNCH VIRGIL A 24 EDE B
BUNCH W A A 46 SUM W

BUNCH W H A 46 SUM W
BUNCH W M A 24 UPP W
BUNCOMB JAMES A 28 03A B
BUNDY HARMON A 46 JAM W
BUNDY JOSEPH A 46 HIG W
BUNDY MORDICAI A 46 HIG W
BUNDY SHUBAL A 46 JAM W
BUNN AMOS A 37 ROC B
BUNN ARNOLD A 28 10T B
BUNN ASA A 37 PIN B
BUNN BENNETT A 37 ROC W
BUNN BUNKIUM A 37 MAN B
BUNN CHAMPION A 39 GRI B
BUNN CHAPMAN A 37 ROB B
BUNN D J A 39 GRI W
BUNN ELIAS A 39 GRI W
BUNN GILFORD A 37 PIN B
BUNN HANDY A 39 FRE B
BUNN HENRY A 37 SHA B
BUNN J H A 39 GRI W
BUNN JAMES A 37 ROC B
BUNN JNO T A 39 DAV W
BUNN JOHN A 37 MAN B
BUNN JOHN A 37 ROC B
BUNN JORDAN A 37 ROC B
BUNN KARY A 37 MAN B
BUNN LEWIS A 37 EDW B
BUNN LEWIS A 37 MAN B
BUNN MOSES A 39 GRI B
BUNN NED A 37 ROC B
BUNN REDMUN A 37 MAN B
BUNN ROBERT C A 37 EDW W
BUNN SAMUEL A 37 ROC B
BUNN W J A 39 GRI W
BUNNEL JOHN A 30 NAR W
BUNNEL SMART A 30 MOY B
BUNNELL JORDAN C A 30 TUL W
BUNNELL S D A 30 MOY W
BUNTER ARCEN A 37 MAN B
BUNTIN LAWRENCE A 37 PIN W
BUNTING JESSIE W A 37 PIN W
BUNTING RICHARD A 37 TA2 W
BUNTING WILLIAM T A 37 PIN W
BURCH ALLEN A 25 SHO W
BURCH CHARLES E A 28 10T W
BURCH F M A 25 TUS W
BURCH JOSEPH A 25 TUS W
BURCH M C A 25 SHO W
BURCHET JOSEPH A 26 SHE B
BURDEN BALAM A 19 HAD B
BURDEN CATO A 28 01A B
BURDEN EDMOND A 28 05A B
BURDEN ELIAS A 19 HAD B
BURDEN GEO 19 HAD B
(DECEASED)
BURDEN LEWIS A 28 05A B
BURDEN SUTTON A 19 HAD B
BURFOOT JNO F A 30 IND W
BURFOOT W P A 30 IND W
BURGE W H A 39 LOU W
BURGES WILLIAM E A 53 GER W
BURGESS A C A 32 THO W
BURGESS BENJAMIN A 25 HAY W
BURGESS EMANUEL A 39 JOR B
BURGESS GIDEON A 28 05A B
BURGESS HARRISON A 37 HOL W
BURGESS HENRY A 30 IND B
BURGESS JAMES A 26 MOU W
BURGESS JOHN A 26 MOU W
BURGESS JOHN A A 19 POR W
BURGESS MOSES A 53 GER B
BURGESS OSTEN A 37 PEN W
BURGESS PELIDGE A 28 05A B

BURGESS W L A 26 BOR W
BURGESS WILLIAM A 53 GER B
BURGETT DANIEL A 72 SWA W
BURHS HESSICK A 29 GRA B
BURK HARRY A 24 MID B
BURK MAGOR A 24 MID B
BURKE ELISHA J A 24 MID W
BURKE HENNY A 24 MID B
BURKE JOHN A 32 SHE W
BURKE LUKE A 24 EDE B
BURKHARDT LEMIL A 29 FA1 W
BURKHARDT RICHD A 29 FA1 W
BURKHART BRYANT A 29 FA1 W
BURKHART JAS F A 32 DAV W
BURKHART OBE A 32 DAV W
BURNES JAS B A 44 TOW W
BURNES M C A 32 THO W
BURNET ANTHONY A 28 05A B
BURNET ISAAC A 19 MOR B
BURNET JOHN A 35 WAR B
BURNETT ABRAHAM A 19 HAD B
BURNETT ALEX A 29 FA1 B
BURNETT ALEX A A 29 FA2 B
BURNETT ANDERSON A 44 LED B
BURNETT ARCHD A 39 SPE W
BURNETT CESAR A 19 BE1 B
BURNETT DAVID A 19 BE1 W
BURNETT DAVID A 29 FA1 B
BURNETT DAVID A 29 SEV B
BURNETT EDWARD A 19 MOR B
BURNETT ELBERT A 39 SPE W
BURNETT GAINY A 44 SAS B
BURNETT GEORGE A 29 GRA B
BURNETT GILFORD A 29 FLE B
BURNETT GREEN A 39 SPE W
BURNETT HENRY A 28 9TH B
BURNETT J E A 44 SAS W
BURNETT JACOB A 44 ISL B
BURNETT JAMES H A 39 SPE W
BURNETT JAS A 29 FA1 B
BURNETT JESSEY A 29 FLE B
BURNETT JOHN A 35 FAI B
BURNETT JOHN A 39 SPE W
BURNETT LEWIS A 19 NEW B
CERT TO HADNOTS CREEK
BURNETT LEWIS A 72 SWA B
BURNETT MADISON A 44 OXF B
BURNETT MATHEW A 29 FA1 B
BURNETT NEEDHAM A 29 FA1 B
BURNETT PRIMUS A 29 FA1 B
BURNETT ROBT A 39 PUG W
BURNETT RUNALS A 39 LOU W
BURNETT SAMUEL T A 29 QUW B
BURNETT SANDY 29 GRA W
BURNETT SANDY A 29 FA2 W
SEE GRAYS CK BOOK
BURNETT SIDNEY A 39 SPE W
BURNETT W M A 29 FA1 B
BURNETT WARREN A 44 YXR B
BURNETT WASHINGTON A 44 YXS B
BURNETT WESLEY A 39 SPE W
BURNETT WILLIAM A 37 TA1 W
BURNETT WILLIAM T A 53 GER W
BURNETT WILLIE A 39 SPE W
BURNETT WILLIS A 44 ISL B
BURNETT WM A 29 FA1 B
BURNETT WOODSON A 44 SAS B
BURNETT Z H A 44 LED W
BURNEY CHURCHILL A 29 FA1 B
BURNEY JOSEPH A 28 6TH B
BURNEY L D A 46 JAM W
BURNEY LEARY A 28 13T B
BURNEY ORIS A 28 13T B
BURNEY SAMUEL M A 19 BE1 B
BURNEY SIMON A 28 03A B
BURNEY YANCEY A 46 JAM W
BURNHAM JOHN A 35 FAI W
BURNHAM WILLIAM A 35 KEN W
BURNS ABRAM R 46 GIB B
CHALENGED FOR FELONY
FREEMAN PROVED TO
HAVE BEEN CONVICTED &
WHIPED BY ORDER OF COURT
FOR LARCENY IN 1862.
BURNS ALFRED A 46 JAM B
BURNS CAESAR A 29 GRA B
BURNS CARLILE A 28 03A B
BURNS CHAS A 29 GRA B
BURNS DAVID A 19 NEW B
BURNS HENRY A 72 SWA B
BURNS JOHN B A 99 BUS W
BURNS JOSHUA A 46 MON B
BURNS JULIUS A 29 GRA B
BURNS L M A 46 HIG W
BURNS PETER A 29 GRA B
BURNS RANSOM A 28 04A B
CERTIFICATE GRANTED
ONSLOW CO
BURNS RANSOM A 29 FA1 W
BURNS SAMSON A 72 SWA B
BURNS SOLOMAN A 72 SWA W
BURNS THOMAS A 46 HIG W
BURNS Z A A 46 HIG W
BURNSIDE DAVID A 46 MCL W
BURNSIDES BENJ F A 46 GIB W
BUROUGHS J A A 44 ISL W
BURR WILLIAM A 19 BE1 B
BURREL NELSON A 44 FIS B
BURRELL BURTON A 46 HIG W
BURRELL LEWIS A 44 SAS B
BURRELL OSBORN A 44 SAS B
BURRELL WILLIAM A 37 ROB B
BURRIOUS TILSON A 53 SWA B
BURRISS JOHN A 30 ROA B
BURROUGHS B A 44 HEN W
BURROUGHS C G A 44 HEN W
BURROUGHS GILBERT A 44 ISL B
BURROUGHS HAYWOOD A 44 HEN W
BURROUGHS J E A 44 HEN W
BURROUGHS WILLIAM L A 44 HEN W
BURROUS DAVID A 53 SWA B
BURROUS GEORGE A 53 FAI B
BURROUS MARTIN A 53 SWA B
BURROUS WILLIAM A 53 FAI B
BURROW L T A 44 SAS B
BURROW PETER A 44 OXF B
BURROWS BENJAMIN A 53 FAI B
BURROWS FLYNN A 37 ROB B
BURROWS QUASH A 53 FAI B
BURROWS SIMON A 53 FAI B
BURROWS WILLIAM A 53 FAI B
BURRUS ALLEN A 53 LA2 W
BURRUS DANUM A 53 LA1 B
BURRUS ROBERT M A 53 LA1 W
BURT DANIEL A 39 JOR B
BURT JORDAIN A 37 ROB B
BURT SOLOMAN A 39 SPE B
BURT WESLEY A 39 JOR B
BURT WYATTE A 39 JOR B
BURTCHET J F A 44 KNA W
BURTON ALSA A 44 DUT B
BURTON CALVIN A 46 HIG W
BURTON DAVID F A 46 HIG W
BURTON DEMPSEY A 30 NAR B
BURTON DENNIS A 30 COI B
BURTON DURANT A 46 RAG B
BURTON E G A 32 THO W
BY CERTIFICATE
BURTON EATON A 44 RAG B
BURTON EDMOND A 44 RAG B
BURTON EDMOND A 44 TAR B
BURTON FRIDAY A 44 HEN B
BURTON GEORGE A 44 SAS B
BURTON GEORGE W A 35 CYP W
BURTON GUSS A 44 HEN B
BURTON HENRY A 44 HEN B
BURTON HOSEA A 35 CYP W
BURTON J C A 46 JAM W
BURTON J O A 32 TYR W
BURTON J W A 32 THO W
BURTON JOHN A 44 HEN B
BURTON JOHN B A 32 THO W
BURTON JOHN W A 35 ROC W
BURTON LEMUEL A 30 COI B
BURTON MARCH A 30 COI B
BURTON MOSES A 44 OXF B
BURTON OWEN T A 35 CYP W
BURTON P W A 44 RAG W
BURTON R W A 44 RAG W
BURTON RAPP A 44 HEN B
BURTON RICHARD C M A 24 EDE W
BURTON ROBERT A 37 ROC B
BURTON SANDY A 44 HEN B
BURTON SOLOMON A 32 THO W
BURTON THOMAS A 35 CYP W
BURTON THOS R 46 JAM W
BURTON W V R 24 EDE W
ERASED BY HIS OWN REQUEST
CAUSE TOO YOUNG FINAL
FINAL REVISION
BURTON WM A 39 FRE B
BURTON WM A 44 HEN B
BURTON WM A 46 GRE W
BURTON WM H A 28 01A B
BURTON WM S A 32 THO W
BURTT ALFORD A 39 JOR B
BURTT SAM A 39 JOR B
BURUS JOHN A 46 GRE B
BURWELL A R A 44 OXF W
BURWELL AARON A 44 FIS B
BURWELL ABSOLUM A 44 TOW B
BURWELL ALLEN A 44 TOW B
BURWELL BENJ A 44 OXF B
BURWELL BILLY A 44 KIT B
BURWELL BULDER A 44 ISL B
BURWELL CARGILL A 44 TOW B
BURWELL DAVID A 44 OXF B
BURWELL EDMOND A 44 FIS B
EPPING FOREST
BURWELL EDWIN A 44 TOW B
BURWELL EMANUEL A 44 KIT B
BURWELL ENOCH A 44 ISL B
BURWELL HARRY A 44 TOW B
BURWELL HENRY A 44 TOW B
BURWELL J S A 44 FIS W
BURWELL JAMES A 44 KIT B
BURWELL JETHRO A 44 KIT B
BURWELL JIM A 39 HAY B
BURWELL JNO A 44 TOW B
BURWELL JOHN A 44 OXF B
BURWELL LYMUS A 44 FIS B
BURWELL MICHAL A 44 SAS B
BURWELL MIKE A 44 RAG B
BURWELL OSBUN A 44 BRA B
BURWELL OTTOWAY A 44 OXF B
BURWELL ROBT R A 44 TOW W
BURWELL STEPHEN A 44 OXF B
BURWELL SYRUS A 44 FIS B
BURWELL WILLIS A 44 HEN B

BURWELL WM A 44 TOW B
BURWELL WORREN A 44 TOW B
BURWILL DAVID A 44 TOW B
BURWRUS WILLEY A 37 MAN W
BUSBEE JAMES T A 99 BUS W
BUSBEE JOHN A 99 BUS B
BUSBEE URIAS A 99 BUS B
BUSBEE WASHINGTON S A 99 BUS W
BUSH ABRAM A 24 MID W
BUSH ELISHA T A 24 MID W
BUSH JAMES P A 24 MID W
BUSH LIVI A 28 13T W
BUSH QUINTON T A 24 MID W
BY AFFADAVIT
PERQUIMANS COUNTY
BUSH RICHARD A 24 MID B
BUSH W M H A 24 MID W
BUSIC DURANT W A 46 GRE W
BUSICK A J A 46 MON W
BUSICK BRYAN A 28 03A B
BUSICK G L A 46 MON W
BUSICK J P A 46 MON W
BUSKERVILLE ARCHER A 44 TOW B
BUSKERVILLE JERRY A 44 SAS B
BUSKERVILLE PLUMMER A 44 SAS B
BUSNEY JOSEPH A 44 SAS B
BUTLER ALBERT A 28 05A B
BUTLER ALX A 29 GRA B
BUTLER ANDW A 29 GRA B
BUTLER CAESAR A 28 03A B
BUTLER CALVIN A 28 11T W
BUTLER CHARLES C R 28 11T W
DID NOT TAKE OATH WAS
AN OVERSEER OF ROADS
AND AFTERWARDS TOOK
PART IN THE WAR
BUTLER CHARLES C SR A 28 11T W
BUTLER CHARLES JR A 28 11T W
BUTLER CHAS A 29 FA1 B
BUTLER DANL A 29 GRA W
BUTLER DANL A 29 GRA W
BUTLER E G A 44 OXF W
BUTLER ELIJAH A 35 CYP W
BUTLER EMANUEL A 28 05A B
BUTLER FRANK A 29 GRA B
BUTLER G W A 44 TOW W
BUTLER GEORGE A 28 04A B
BUTLER H B A 29 GRA W
BUTLER HEZEKIAH A 35 CYP W
BUTLER JOHN A 28 03A B
BUTLER JOHN A 46 GRE B
BUTLER JOHN C A 28 11T W
BUTLER NATHAN A 28 03A B
BUTLER PETER A 29 GRA B
BUTLER RICHARD A 28 11T B
BUTLER ROBT A 29 GRA B
BUTLER SOLOMAN A 44 YXR B
BUTLER THOS A 29 GRA B
BUTLER W C A 28 11T W
BUTLER WILLIAM A 29 GRA B
BUTLER WILLIAM B A 28 11T W
BUTLER WM A 29 GRA W
BUTT JOHN J A 30 IND W
BUTT SAML A 30 MOY B
BUTTS DORY A 19 MOR B
BUXTON ALX A 29 FA2 B
BUXTON DAN'L A 29 FA1 B
BUXTON FORTUNE A 29 FA1 B
BUXTON JESSEE A 29 FA1 B
BUXTON JONAS A 29 FA1 B
BUXTON RALPH P A 29 FA2 W

BYARS E A R 26 MOU W
WAS MAGISTRATE & POST
MASTER STRICKEN OUT
BYARS JOHN S A 26 MOU W
MILITIA OFFICER &
ENGAGED IN REBELION
BYERELY ISAIAH A 32 YAD W
BYERELY J F A 32 YAD W
BYERELY WESLEY A 32 YAD W
BYERLY ANDREW A 32 DAV W
BYERLY GEORGE A 32 DAV W
BYERLY JACOB A 32 DAV W
BYERLY JESSE A 32 DAV W
BYERLY OBADIAH A 32 DAV W
BYERLY STIMSON A 32 DAV W
BYERS D T A 25 HAY W
BYLE JOSEPH A 37 HOL B
BYNUM A S A 28 04A W
BYNUM ALBERT A A 40 MAU W
BYNUM ARTHUR A 37 WHI W
BYNUM BALUM A 37 HIG B
NAME LINED OUT
BYNUM BENJAMIN A 28 9TH W
BYNUM EDWIN A 24 EDE W
BYNUM FRANK A 37 WHI B
BYNUM HENRY A 37 WHI B
BYNUM HENRY A 37 WHI B
BYNUM ISAAC A 37 TA2 B
BYNUM ISAAC S A 24 EDE W
BYNUM J W A 24 EDE W
BYNUM JACK A 37 WHI B
BYNUM JACOB A 37 WHI W
BYNUM JACOB D A 24 EDE W
BYNUM MARTIN A 37 SPA B
BYNUM NELSON A 37 SPA B
BYNUM S B A 28 04A W
BYNUM SAML A 28 05A B
BYNUM THOMAS D A 24 MID W
BYNUM WILLIAM A 37 WHI B
BYRD ALEX A 44 DUT W
BYRD ALFRED A 35 FAI B
BYRD CHARLES A 44 FIS B
BYRD CHAS A 29 CAR B
BYRD CHAS H H A 29 CAR B
BYRD GEO J A 29 CAR W
BYRD H R A 29 CAR W
BYRD HARRY A 29 CAR B
BYRD J W A 44 DUT W
BYRD JOHN A 40 BLA W
BYRD L D A 29 CAR W
BYRD LEWIS A 29 FA1 W
BYRD MICHAEL A 35 FAI W
BYRD NATHAN A 35 ALB W
BYRD NATHAN A 35 WAR B
BYRD OLIVER P A 40 BLA W
BYRD ROBERT A 35 FAI W
BYRD ROBT J A 29 CAR W
MILLITIA OFFICER AFTER
ENGAGED IN REBELLION
BYRD TIMOTHY S A 35 MAG W
BYRD WILLIAM A 35 ROC B
BYRD WILLIAM B A 35 MAG W
BYRD WM A 29 CAR B
BYRELEY COLUMBUS A 32 SHE W
BYRELY E A 32 THO W
BY CERTIF
BYRELY FRANCIS A 32 YAD W
CERTIFICATE GIVEN
BYRNE DAVID A 29 GRA B
AFF KELLEY GROVE
BLADEN CO
BYRNE ISAAC A 29 GRA B
BYRNE JAS A 29 GRA B

BYRNE JNO F A 29 GRA W
BYRNE MARCUS A 29 GRA B
BYRNE SAML A 29 GRA B
BYRNES T A A 29 FA1 W
BYRNES THOMAS A 29 GRA B
CERT TO BLADEN APR 11 68
BYRNS WM A 29 CED B
BYRUM ALLEN A 24 MID B
BYRUM CORNELIUS A 24 UPP W
BYRUM DR W A 44 BRA W
BYRUM FRANCIS A 24 MID W
BYRUM GEORGE F A 24 MID W
BYRUM GIDEON A 24 MID W
BYRUM H K A 44 KIT W
BYRUM ISAAC A 24 UPP W
BYRUM ISAAC J A 24 UPP W
BYRUM JACOB R A 24 UPP W
BYRUM JAMES J A 24 MID W
BYRUM JESSE A 24 MID W
BYRUM JESSE W A 24 UPP W
BYRUM JOHN W A 37 PIN W
SPARTA
BYRUM JOSEPH J A 24 MID W
BYRUM JOSEPH R A 24 MID W
BYRUM JOSIAH A 24 UPP W
BYRUM KADER A 24 UPP W
BYRUM LEWIS A 24 MID B
BYRUM WHITMAL A 24 MID W
BYRUM WILLIAM A 24 MID W
BYRUM WILLIS A 24 UPP W
BYRUM WM C A 24 UPP W
BYRUM WM J A 24 MID W

\- C -

CABANIS A M A 26 SHE W
CABANIS D K A 26 SHE W
CABANIS JOSEPH A 26 SHE W
CABANISS J P A 26 SHE W
CABANISS JOHN A 26 BLA W
CABARRUS FREEMAN A 24 EDE B
CABARRUS NOAH A 24 EDE B
CABARRUS PRIMUS A 24 EDE B
CABARRUS PULLEM A 24 EDE B
CABE W J A 25 SHO W
CABELL ADAM A 24 EDE B
CABELL ISUM A 37 WHI B
CABINESS EDMUND A 26 BLA B
CABNISS FRANKLIN A 26 SHE B
CADE JOS A 29 LOC W
CADE PIER A 29 FA1 B
CADER G F A 24 EDE B
CADUGAN ROSWELL D A 30 ROA W
CADY LEMUEL A 24 EDE W
CAFFY MICHAEL A 46 SUM W
CAHOON BENJAMIN A 53 LA1 W
CAHOON DAVID A A 53 LA2 W
CAHOON GEORGE A 28 16T W
CAHOON JESSE A 28 16T W
CAHOON MATTHIAS A 30 ROA W
CAHOON MILLARD A 28 16T W
CAHOON SAMUEL A 53 SWA B
CAHOON SYLVENIUS A 53 FAI W
CAHOON WILLIAM A A 53 FAI W
CAHOON WILLIAM H A 53 FAI W
CAHOON WM H A 28 16T W
CAHOON WM T A 28 16T W
CAHOUN NATHAN A 28 15T W
CAIN BLOUNT A 37 EDW B
CAIN CHAS G A 29 CED W
CAIN DANIEL A 46 KIN W
CAIN E P A 29 FA1 W
CAIN ISAAC A 37 HIC B
CAIN JAMES A 29 CED W
CAIN JNO W A 29 FA1 W

CAIN PETER A 24 EDE B
CAIN WILLIAM A 44 FIS B
CAIN WM A 29 CED W
CAINE GEORGE C A 37 TA2 B
CAINE J E J A 29 FLE W
CALCUTT HENRY A 29 FA1 W
CALDCLEUGH ANDREW A 32 DAV W
CALDCLUEGH E W A 32 THO W
CALDER JOHN A 29 FA2 B
CALDWELL ARTER A 46 JAM B
CALDWELL CORNELIUS A 46 GRE B
CALDWELL DAVID A 46 SUM B
CALDWELL GABRIEL A 46 MCL B
CALDWELL HENRY A 46 GRE B
CALDWELL HENRY A 46 MCL B
CALDWELL JAMES A 46 GRE B
CALDWELL MILTON A 46 GRE B
CALDWELL NELSON A 46 GRE B
CALDWELL ROBT C A 46 GRE W
CALDWELL W ADDISON R 46 GRE W
WAS A CLERK OF CORT
BEFORE THE WARE DURING
THE REBELLION GAVE IT
AID & COMFORT
CALDWELL WM A 46 GRE B
CALHON MEEDY A 37 HIG B
CALHOON BLUNT A 37 HIG B
CALHOON CHARLES A 37 HIG B
CALHOON JOHN E A 37 ROC W
CALHOUN ABLE A 28 16T W
CALHOUN ALLEN A 29 FA1 B
CALHOUN J H A 29 ROC W
CALHOUN J M A 46 SUM W
CALHOUN JAMES A 29 ROC W
CALHOUN MOSES A 46 SUM W
CALHOUN OREN A 37 ROC W
CALHOUN W A A 46 SUM W
CALHOUN WILLIAM J A 37 PEN W
ROCKY MOUNT
CALIVAN REUBEN A 28 03A B
CALLAHAN JNO C A 29 FA1 W
CALLAWAY PETER A 28 12T W
CALLICUTT THOMAS A 46 HIG B
CALLIHAN D H A 29 FLE W
CALLIS CHAS W A 44 HEN W
CALLIS JOHN E A 44 HEN W
CALLIS RICND R A 44 HEN W
CALLOWAY DAVID A 28 05A B
CALLOWAY JAMES T A 40 DA1 W
CALPEPPER HARDY A 30 TUL W
CALRTON COLUMBUS A 35 MAG B
CALVIN ISAAC A 29 FA1 B
CALVIN ROSS A 28 05A B
CALVIN WM A 46 ROS B
CALWELL ISOM A 37 HIG B
CAMBRIDGE JOHN A 28 01A W
CAMBRY JOHN A 37 HIG W
CAMERN AMOS A 32 JAC B
CAMERN AUGUSTUS A 32 JAC B
CAMERN WILLIAM A 32 JAC W
CAMERON ALEX A A 29 MON W
CAMERON BENJAMIN A 37 HIG B
CAMERON H D A 29 CAR W
CAMERON J A A 29 QUW W
CAMERON JACKSON A 29 FA1 B
CAMERON JACOB A 29 FLE B
CAMERON JAS A 29 ROC W
POSTMASTER BEFORE &
DURING THE WAR WAS GOOD
UNION MAN
CAMERON JOHN A A 29 MON W
CAMERON JOHN T A 29 MON W
CAMERON LAUCHLIN A 29 MON W
CAMERON SIDNEY A 37 HIG B
CAMERON STALBRED A 37 HIG B
CAMERON STEPHEN A 29 SEV B
CERTIFICATE HARNETT CO
CAMERON WM M A 29 ROC W
CAMERON ZAC A 29 FA1 B
CAMMACK CHARLES A 46 GRE B
CAMMACK JOHN A 46 ROS W
CAMMERON GEO W A 29 ROC W
CAMMERON N A A 29 FA1 W
CAMMERON OWEN A 29 FA1 B
REMOVED TO HARNETT CO
CAMP BILLY A 44 OXF B
CAMP CHALS A A 39 DAV W
TRNS FROM NASH CO
GRIFFINS PREC.
CAMP JOHN A 26 SHE W
CAMP JOSEPH A 26 SHE W
CAMP JOSEPH A A 26 SHE W
CAMP L A A 26 GOF W
CAMP L H A 26 SHE W
CAMP NATHAN A 26 SWA W
CAMP TYRRELL A 26 SHE W
CAMP WILLIAM A 26 SHE W
CAMPBALL D M A 29 BLA X
CAMPBELL A A 29 BLA W
CAMPBELL A M A 29 FA1 W
CAMPBELL A M A 29 QUW W
CAMPBELL ALEX A 29 ROC W
CAMPBELL ALEXANDER A 46 FRI W
CAMPBELL AMOS A 46 HIG B
CAMPBELL CALVIN A 32 TYR B
CAMPBELL CICERO A 28 05A B
CAMPBELL COLIN M P A 29 SEV W
CAMPBELL COUNCIL A 28 11T B
CAMPBELL D K A 29 SEV W
CAMPBELL DUNCAN B A 29 SEV W
CAMPBELL ELVIN A 29 QUW B
CAMPBELL GEO S A 28 01A W
CAMPBELL HARRIS A 19 NEW B
CAMPBELL J A A 44 TOW W
CAMPBELL JACOB A 29 FA1 B
CAMPBELL JAMES A 28 01A W
CAMPBELL JAMES A 40 DEC B
CAMPBELL JAMES A A 46 HIG W
CAMPBELL JAMES N A 46 GRE W
CAMPBELL JARVIS A 28 9TH B
CERTIFICATE GIVEN LIVES
NOW AT BIG SWIFT CREEK
CAMPBELL JOHN A 29 SEV B
CAMPBELL JOHN A 29 SEV W
CAMPBELL JOHN K A 29 SEV W
CAMPBELL JOS A 29 FA1 B
CAMPBELL M N A 29 FA2 W
CAMPBELL MILES A 29 QUW B
CAMPBELL MURDOCH A 29 QUW W
CAMPBELL NEILL A 29 ROC W
CAMPBELL NELSON A 29 CAR B
CAMPBELL NELSON A 29 FA1 B
CAMPBELL NORMAN A 29 SEV W
CAMPBELL NORMAN A 32 TYR B
CAMPBELL NORMAN M A 29 QUW W
CAMPBELL PETER A 28 04A B
CERTIFICATE GRANTED
JONES CO
CAMPBELL R B A 29 FA1 W
CAMPBELL REUBEN B A 28 9TH B
CAMPBELL SAMUEL A 46 SUM W
CAMPBELL SANDY A 29 CED B
CAMPBELL THOS J A 29 FA1 W
CAMPBELL WM F A 29 FA1 W
CAMPER KAVAN A 37 TA1 B
CAMPTON WM H H A 28 11T B
CAMWELL M A 26 CAR W
CANADA DAVID A 53 LA1 B
CANADA SQUIRE A 28 9TH B
CANADA THOMAS A 28 10T B
CERTIF GIVEN NOW
LIVES IN NEW BERN
CANADAY DANL A A 29 GRA W
CANADAY ELIJAH A 72 SWA W
CANADAY EVANS A A 29 GRA W
CANADAY HENRY A 29 GRA W
CANADAY JAMES A 72 SWA W
CANADAY NEEDHAM A 72 SWA W
CANADAY RICHARD A 72 SWA W
CANADAY SIMON A 32 DAV W
CANADY A J A 44 DUT W
CANADY ALLEN A 19 HAD B
CANADY CHARLES A 44 OXF B
CANADY HENRY A 37 EDW B
CANADY NEVISON A 44 OXF B
CANADY W J A 29 LOC W
CANADY WM A 46 SUM W
CANE JNO H A 29 FA1 B
CANIDA JACK A 39 HAY B
CANIPE CLINSTEN A 26 GRI W
CANIPE DANIEL A 26 WAR W
CANIPE J C A 26 PEE W
CANIPE JACOB A 26 WAR W
CANIPE JOSEPH A 26 WAR W
CANNADY ABEL A 28 01A B
CANNADY ALLEN A 28 05A B
CANNADY BENJ A 28 6TH B
CANNADY DAVID A 44 FOR B
CANNADY DAVID A 44 YXS B
CANNADY EPHM A 44 FOR B
CANNADY FRANK A 28 01A B
CANNADY GUILFORD A 44 FOR B
CANNADY HINTON A 44 FOR B
CANNADY J F A 44 BRA W
CANNADY JAMES A 44 FOR B
CANNADY JESSE A 28 05A B
CANNADY LEM A 44 FOR B
CANNADY MAJOR A 44 BRA B
CANNADY OTAWAY A 44 BRA B
CANNADY RANSOM A 44 BRA B
CANNADY RICHARD R 44 FOR B
NOT 20 YEARS OLD 18
YRS OLD NEXT JUNE
CANNADY SIGH A 44 DUT B
CANNADY SOLOMON A 44 BEA B
CANNADY THOS A 39 FRA B
CANNADY WILSON S A 19 NEW W
CANNADY WM A 44 BEA B
CANNADY WM A 44 FOR B
CANNON ABRAM A 28 01A B
CANNON D E A 40 CAN W
CANNON HENRY A 28 05A B
CANNON J F A 40 RHY W
CANNON JAMES A 28 6TH B
CANNON JAMES A A 40 DA1 W
CANNON JAS J A 24 MID W
CANNON JOHN A 28 6TH B
CANNON JOHN C A 46 GRE W
CANNON MARTIN A 46 GRE B
CANNON NED A 44 HEN B
CANNON SAML A 28 05A B
CERTIF GRANTED RALEIGH
CANNON W A 40 CAN W
CANNON W S A 40 CAN W
CANNON WILLIAM A 28 10T B
CANON JAMES M A 28 15T W
CANON THOMAS A 19 HAD W
CANPHIN JOHN A 35 ROC W
CANSLER M L A 40 CAN W

CANSLER PETER A 40 CAN W
CANSLER R T A 40 CAN W
CANVILLE J S A 30 CUR W
CAPEHART B A A 44 FIS W
CAPEHART THOS A 44 KIT W
CAPEHART WM R A 24 EDE W
CAPEL WM A 44 BRA W
CAPOT GEO W A 28 04A B
CAPPLE HENRY A 32 THO W
CAPPS CALEB M A 30 KNO W
CAPPS HENRY A 46 SUM W
CAPPS ISIAH A 30 KNO W
CAPPS J C A 26 CAR W
CAPPS JNO C A 30 MOY W
CAPPS MALICHI A 30 KNO W
CAPPS NEDHAM A 29 FLE B
CAPPS T L A 30 KNO W
CAPPS TULLY A 30 KNO W
CAPS BRYANT A 29 FA1 B
CAPS GRAY A 28 04B B
CAPS HEYWOOD A 28 04A B
CARAVAN WILLIAM A 28 11T W
CARAWAN JAMES G A 53 SWA W
CARAWAN RICHARD B A 53 LA1 W
CARAWAN WILLIAM A A 53 SWA W
CARAWAY ALLEN A 19 BE1 B
CARAWAY JNO A 19 MOR B
CARBY JACOB A 53 LA1 B
CARD D C A 39 HAY B
2ND REGISTRA BORD
FRANKLIN CO
CARD D W A 39 SPE W
CARD J R A 39 FRA W
CARD S H A 39 FRA W
CARD SAMUEL A 37 ROC W
CARDEN JOHN A 46 RAG W
CARDEN WILLIAM A 46 RAG W
CARELL CHARLES A 32 DAV B
CARENIAN NATHAN A 53 GER B
CARFIELD JOHN A 46 GRE W
CARGER JOHN A 28 01A W
CARIL CALEP A 32 TYR B
CARIL MORGON A 32 TYR B
CARISON SIMON A 32 TYR B
CARKER JAMES A 32 DAV W
CARLETON ADAM A 35 MAG B
CARLETON ALFRED A 35 WAR B
CARLETON HENRY A 35 MAG W
CARLETON J G S A 28 01A W
CARLETON LEWIS A 35 MAG B
CARLETON WILLIAM C A 35 MAG W
CARLILE BURWELL A 39 GRI W
CARLILE T H A 39 GRI W
CARLILE T N A 39 LOU W
CARLISLE J W A 29 FA1 W
CARLISLE JAS C A 37 ROB W
CARLISLE JNO H A 37 ROB W
CARLISLE STERLING A 37 ROB W
CARLTON A W A 35 MAG W
CARLTON ABRAM A 35 MAG B
CARLTON BENNETT A 35 WAR B
CARLTON DAVID A 35 MAG B
CARLTON ELIAS A 35 MAG B
CARLTON EMANEUL A 35 WAR B
CARLTON GEORGE A 35 MAG B
CARLTON ISAAC A 35 MAG B
CARLTON JACOB A 35 WAR B
CARLTON JOHN H A 35 MAG B
CARLTON JOHN S A 35 WAR W
CARLTON JOSEPH A 35 KEN B
CARLTON OWEN A 35 WAR B
CARLTON PRIMUS A 35 MAG B
CARLTON RIAL A 35 MAG B
CARLTON SAMEUL A 35 WAR B
CARLTON THIROYAL A 35 MAG W
CARLTON THOMAS A 35 MAG B
CARLTON TONEY A 35 WAR B
CARLYLE BENNETT W A 37 TA1 W
CARLYLE
EDWARD THOMAS A 37 PEN W
CARMACK THOMAS A 28 8TH W
CARMADY ABNER B A 28 14T W
CARMAN JOSH A 29 FA1 W
CARMAN JOSHUA A 29 FA1 W
CARMAN RILEY A 28 13T B
CARMAN WM A 28 04A B
CARMER C A 26 CAR W
CARMER JAMES A 26 CAR W
CARMER JAS W A 28 02N W
CARMER W W A 26 CAR W
CARMER WM A 26 CAR W
CARMERN ROBERT A 32 LOF B
CARMICHAEL ARCHD A 29 SEV W
CARMICHAEL JOHN A 29 SEV B
CARMICHAEL MANUEL A 29 SEV B
CARMICHAEL ROBERT A 29 SEV B
CARMON DAVID A 19 BE1 B
CARMON JOHN A 46 MCL W
CARNAL L J A 44 TAR W
CARNALL J W A 44 TAR W
CARNELL PAUL J A 19 POR W
CARNEY J B A 28 02N W
CARNISH ANDREW A 32 TYR W
CARNWELL S A 26 CAR W
CARPENTER ABEL A 40 MAU W
CARPENTER ALFRED A 40 MAU W
CARPENTER ALFRED G A 40 MAU W
CARPENTER B F A 40 RHY W
CARPENTER BENJ M A 40 BLA W
CARPENTER CALEB C A 40 MAU W
CARPENTER D A 26 CAR W
CARPENTER D C A 28 01A W
CARPENTER DANIEL A 26 GRI W
CARPENTER DANIEL A 26 PEE B
CARPENTER DANIEL A 40 MAU W
CARPENTER E A 26 BOR B
CARPENTER E M A 28 02N W
CARPENTER EMANUEL A 40 MAU W
CARPENTER F L A 46 JAM W
CARPENTER
FREDERIC SEN R 40 MAU W
NAME LINED OUT
CHAL CAUSE: JUSTICE
OF PEACE BEFORE THE
REBELLION AND GAVE AID
& COMFORT TO THE ENEMY
REJECTED.
CARPENTER
FREDERICK JR A 40 MAU W
CARPENTER GABE A 40 MAU B
CARPENTER GEORGE A 40 MAU W
CARPENTER HENRY A 40 BLA W
CARPENTER HENRY S A 40 MAU W
CARPENTER ISAAC A 40 MAU B
CARPENTER ISAAC A 40 RHY B
CARPENTER J L A 26 GRI W
CARPENTER J M A 26 GRI W
CARPENTER J O A 26 CAR B
CARPENTER JACOB A 26 GRI W
CARPENTER JOHN A 26 WAR W
CARPENTER JOHN JR A 40 MAU W
CARPENTER JOHN SEN A 40 MAU W
CARPENTER JOHN T A 40 MAU W
CARPENTER JOSEPH A 40 MAU W
CARPENTER L P A 26 CAR B
CARPENTER LEVI A 26 GRI B
CARPENTER M A 26 CAR W
CARPENTER MARCUS L A 40 MAU W
CARPENTER MARCUS L A 40 MAU W
CARPENTER P Z A 26 GRI W
CARPENTER PETER A 26 GRI W
CARPENTER PETER SR A 26 GRI W
CARPENTER R C A 26 CAR W
CARPENTER S A 26 CAR W
CARPENTER SAMUEL A 46 HIG W
CARPENTER SCIMON A 24 EDE B
CARPENTER THOMAS A 40 DA1 B
CARPENTER W H A 29 FA1 W
CARPENTER WILLIAM A 40 MAU W
CARPENTER
WILLIAM A J A 40 BLA W
CARPENTER WILLIAM B A 40 MAU W
CARR A J A 39 SPE W
CARR AUSTIN A 35 KEN B
CARR B B A 35 FAI W
CARR BARNET G A 35 ROC W
CARR BARNETT A 35 ROC W
CARR BARNETT J A 35 ROC W
CARR BENJAMIN A 37 SPA B
CARR CLAIBORN A 35 ISL B
CARR DANIEL T A 35 ISL W
CARR DAVID A 35 KEN W
CARR ELIAS SPARTA A 37 TA1 W
CARR GABRIEL B A 35 ROC W
CARR GASKIN A 28 01A B
CARR GORTIN A 35 FAI B
CARR HENRY A 35 ISL B
CARR HOWARD A 35 KEN B
CARR ISAAC A 35 KEN B
CARR JACOB O A 35 ROC W
CARR JACOB W A 35 KEN W
CARR JAMES A 35 ISL W
CARR JAMES B A 35 KEN W
CARR JAMES O A 35 ISL W
CARR JOHN A 35 ISL W
CARR JOHN A 35 WOL B
CARR JOHN J A 35 ISL W
CARR JOSEPH A 35 FAI B
CARR JOSEPH CHAL R 35 KEN B
CONVICTED OF LARCENY
CARR JOSEPH H A 35 KEN W
CARR JOSEPH W A 35 ROC W
CARR M H A 28 7TH W
CARR MOSES A 37 SPA B
CARR OZBORN A 35 KEN W
CARR PETER A 35 KEN B
CARR PETER A 35 MAG B
CARR R B A 39 SPE W
CARR RICHARD A 35 ISL B
CARR ROBERT A 35 FAI B
CARR ROBERT A 35 ISL B
CARR SAMEUL A 35 KEN B
CARR SIMEON A 35 ISL B
CARR SOLOMON A 35 WOL B
CARR TIRZMAN A 35 KEN B
CARR VIRGIL A 35 KEN B
CARR WILLIAM A 39 HAY W
CARR WILLIAM D A 35 KEN W
CARRAWAN JOHN G A 53 LA1 W
CARRAWAN JOSEPH G A 53 LA1 W
CARRAWAN PHILLIP B A 53 LA1 W
CARRAWAN WILLIAM A 53 LA1 W
CARRAWAY BENJAMIN A 28 16T W
CARRAWAY CHRISTOPHERA 28 15T W
CARRAWAY D T A 28 02N W
CARRAWAY FRANCIS P A 28 17T W
CARRAWAY GEORGE W A 28 15T W
CARRAWAY JOSHUA A 28 15T W
CARRAWAY MASON A 28 15T W

CARRAWAY MINOS	A	28	10T	B
CARRAWAY PETER F	R	28	10T	W
CHALLENGED WAS AN OFFICER OF PATROL & OVERSEER OF ROADS & A CAPTAIN OF REBEL VIGILANCE COMPANY				
CARRAWAY SIMON	A	28	10T	B
CERTIFICATE GIVEN NOW LIVES AT NEW BERN				
CARRAWAY THOMAS	A	28	15T	W
CARREL B	A	32	JAC	W
CARREL B F	A	32	JAC	W
CARREL ELI	A	32	JAC	W
CARREL PETER	A	32	JAC	W
CARREL STEVAN	A	32	JAC	W
CARREWAY WARREN	A	19	NEW	B
CARRICK JAMES	A	32	JAC	W
CARRICK JOHN	A	32	JAC	W
CARRICK JOHN	A	32	JAC	W
CARRICK JOHN F	A	32	COT	W
CARRICK JOSEPH	A	32	JAC	B
CARRICK JOSEPH	A	32	JAC	W
CARRICK RICHARD	A	32	JAC	W
CARRICK WM B	A	32	COT	W
CARRINGTON ANDERSON	R	44	SAS	B
8 MOS REJ				
CARRINGTON BUTTRICK	A	44	SAS	B
CARRINGTON COLMAN	A	44	OXF	B
CARRINGTON JNO	A	44	SAS	B
CARRINGTON T R	A	44	SAS	W
CARRISON GEORGE	A	32	DAV	B
CARRISON SIDNEY	A	44	OXF	B
CARROL ALEXR.	A	32	DAV	W
CARROLL ANTHONY	A	35	KEN	B
CARROLL BARBEE	A	25	HAY	W
CARROLL BOSTON	A	35	MAG	B
CARROLL E C	A	32	THO	W
CARROLL E J	A	29	GRA	W
CARROLL EDWARD	A	40	BLA	W
CARROLL J L	A	44	OXF	W
CARROLL JAMES	A	28	04B	B
CARROLL JAMES	A	29	ROC	W
CARROLL JAMES JR	A	29	ROC	W
CARROLL JAMES T	A	35	KEN	W
CARROLL JAS	A	29	FA1	B
CARROLL JOE	A	28	03A	B
CARROLL JOHN	A	35	KEN	B
CARROLL JOHN	A	40	BLA	W
CARROLL JOHN D	A	35	KEN	W
CARROLL LEWIS	A	35	KEN	B
CARROLL LEWIS	A	35	KEN	B
CARROLL LUTHER R	A	35	MAG	W
CARROLL MARCUS L	A	40	BLA	W
CARROLL MARLEY	A	35	KEN	B
CARROLL MATHES	A	99	BUS	W
CARROLL MYER	A	35	KEN	B
CARROLL OWEN J	A	35	KEN	W
CARROLL PELEG R	A	35	MAG	W
CARROLL RICHARD	A	35	KEN	B
CARROLL ROBERT	A	35	KEN	W
CARROLL SAMEUL	A	35	MAG	B
CARROLL SANDY	A	46	COB	W
CARROLL T S	A	39	PUG	W
CARROLL THOS	A	29	FA1	W
CARROLL WILLIAM	A	29	FA2	B
CARROLL WILLIAM C	A	35	MAG	W
CARROLL WILLIAM D	A	35	WAR	W
CARROLL WILLIS	A	35	KEN	B
CARROLL WM	R	29	CAR	W
NATURALIZED CITIZEN VOLUNTEERED IN THE CONFED SERVICE				
CARROLL WM	A	46	ROS	W
CARROW DOCTOR	A	46	HIG	B
CARROW JOSEPH	A	28	15T	W
CARROW JOSEPH	A	46	HIG	W
CARROWAN GEORGE D	A	53	SWA	W
CARROWAN WILLIAM R	A	53	FAI	W
CARROWON BENAJAH	A	53	SWA	W
CARROWON GEORGE W	A	53	SWA	W
CARROWON JOHN A	A	28	17T	W
CARROWON RICHARD	A	28	17T	W
CARROWON WILLIAM M	A	53	LA1	W
CARSES WILLLIAM	A	25	SHO	W
CARSON BENJ	A	26	PEE	B
CARSON EDWARD W	A	40	FER	W
CARSON GEORGE	A	32	DAV	B
CARSON J F	A	39	FRE	W
CARSON JAMES M	A	40	FER	W
NAME LINED OUT CAPT OF MILITIA BEFORE THE REBELLION & GAVE AID OR COMFORT TO THE ENEMY DID NOT QUALIFY REJ				
CARSON JOHN B	A	40	DA1	W
CARSON JOS T	A	46	GRE	W
CARSON JOSEPH W	A	40	FER	W
CARSON ROBERT	A	40	FER	W
CARSON RUFUS W	A	40	FER	W
CARTEN JACOB	A	28	04B	B
CARTER A B	A	39	GRI	W
CARTER AARON	A	46	SUM	B
CARTER ABEL	A	28	10T	B
CARTER ABEL	A	28	9TH	B
CARTER ABRAHAM	A	35	SMI	W
CARTER ALEX	A	29	ROC	W
CARTER ALEXANDRE	A	53	GER	W
CARTER ALFIERD	A	53	GER	B
CARTER ALFRED	A	35	ROC	B
CERTIFICATE FOR SAMPSON COUNTY APRIL 17, 1868				
CARTER AMBERS	A	46	SUM	B
CARTER AMOS	A	28	10T	B
CARTER B F	A	25	HAY	W
CARTER BURNEY	A	19	BE1	B
CARTER C N	A	46	FRI	W
CARTER CLEM	A	37	ROB	B
CARTER D M	A	32	THO	W
CARTER D N	A	29	LOC	W
CARTER DAVID	A	19	HAR	B
CARTER DAVID	A	29	LOC	W
CARTER DORSEY	A	28	01A	B
CARTER E H	A	28	02N	W
CARTER F M	A	32	BRO	W
CARTER GEORGE	A	24	EDE	B
CARTER GEORGE	A	28	04A	B
CARTER GEORGE	A	53	GER	B
CARTER GEORGE 1ST	A	28	9TH	B
CARTER GEORGE 2ND	A	28	9TH	B
CARTER H C	A	29	LOC	W
CARTER HAYWOOD	A	28	05A	B
CARTER HAYWOOD	A	37	HOL	B
CARTER HENRY	A	28	9TH	B
CARTER HENRY	A	29	LOC	B
CARTER HENRY	A	29	LOC	W
CARTER HENRY A	A	53	OCR	W
CARTER HENRY C	A	53	FAI	W
CARTER HINTON E	A	35	ISL	W
CARTER ISAAC	A	28	01A	B
CARTER ISAAC	A	28	10T	B
CARTER ISAAC	A	37	TA2	W
SPARTA				
CARTER ISAIAH S	A	53	FAI	W
CARTER J B	A	40	STO	W
CARTER J C	A	29	CED	W
CARTER J E	A	25	SHO	W
CARTER J J	A	35	ALB	W
CARTER J OSBORN	A	46	GRE	B
CARTER J R	A	29	SEV	W
CARTER JABIN	A	53	FAI	B
CARTER JAMES	A	28	05A	B
CARTER JAMES	A	28	9TH	B
CARTER JAMES	A	29	CAR	W
CARTER JAMES	A	29	FA1	W
CARTER JAMES	A	29	GRA	B
CARTER JAMES	A	29	LOC	B
CARTER JAMES	A	29	LOC	W
CARTER JAMES P	A	28	10T	B
CARTER JEFFERSON	A	32	TYR	B
CARTER JNO II	A	29	LOC	B
CARTER JOEL A	A	35	CYP	W
CARTER JOHN	A	37	WHI	W
CARTER JOHNATHAN	A	29	LOC	W
CARTER JOHNATHAN	A	29	LOC	W
CARTER JORDAN	A	28	16T	B
CARTER JOSEPH	A	19	BE1	B
CARTER JOSEPH	A	24	EDE	B
CARTER K D	A	44	BEA	B
CARTER KINCHIN	A	35	ISL	W
CARTER MARTIN	A	53	FAI	B
CARTER NELL	A	29	FA1	B
CARTER OBED	A	35	ISL	W
CARTER PETER	A	29	LOC	B
CARTER PETER	A	46	FRI	B
CARTER RICHARD	A	44	HEN	B
CARTER ROBERT	A	19	NEW	B
CARTER ROBERT	A	37	WHI	B
CARTER RUFUS L	A	28	10T	B
CARTER S	A	29	FA1	W
CARTER SOLOMON	A	53	FAI	B
CARTER STEPHEN	A	29	FA1	B
CARTER STEPHEN D	A	53	GER	W
CARTER THAD	A	44	OXF	B
CARTER THOMAS	A	28	10T	B
CARTER THOMAS	A	35	ISL	W
CARTER THOMAS H	A	35	ISL	W
CARTER THOMAS T	A	46	KIN	W
CARTER THOS	A	29	FA1	W
CARTER TONEY	A	53	FAI	B
CARTER W R	A	25	HAY	W
CARTER WALLACE	A	28	01A	B
CARTER WILLIAM	A	26	GRI	W
CARTER WILLIAM	A	32	BRO	W
CARTER WILLIAM	A	99	BUS	B
CARTER WILLIAM H	A	28	9TH	B
CARTER WILLIAM S		53	FAI	W
STRICKEN OUT APRIL 17TH 1868				
CARTER WM	A	29	FA1	W
CARTHERAL PLEASANT	A	32	CLE	B
CARTHEY HARRY	A	28	01A	B
CARTHURAL CHARLES	A	32	CLE	B
CARTR ALEXR	A	28	03A	B
CARTWRIGHT ALBERT	A	53	FAI	W
CARTWRIGHT GEO	A	30	TUL	W
CARTWRIGHT JESSE	A	30	COI	W
CARVER A R	A	29	FA2	W
CARVER ADAM	A	29	FA1	B
CARVER C	A	29	FLE	W
CARVER CALVIN	A	29	FA1	W
CARVER E P	A	29	FA1	W
CARVER H M	A	29	LOC	B
CARVER H N	A	29	LOC	W
CARVER HESSICK	A	29	GRA	B
CARVER J D	A	29	FA1	W
CARVER JAMES B	A	29	ROC	W

CARVER JAS W A 29 GRA W
CARVER JESSE B A 29 GRA W
CARVER JNO A 29 ROC B
CARVER JNO E A 29 ROC W
CARVER JOHN A 29 FA1 B
CARVER JOHN G A 28 01A W
CARVER JOHN M A 29 ROC W
CARVER JOS B A 29 FA1 W
CARVER M R A 29 FA1 W
CARVER RANDALL A 29 FA1 B
CARVER SOLIMON A 29 LOC B
CARVER THOS A 29 CAR B
CARVER THOS A 29 FA1 B
CARVER WARREN A 29 ROC W
CARVER WM A 29 LOC B
CARVER WM H A 29 FA1 W
CARY JAMES A 32 THO W
CARY RICHARD A 28 15T W
CASE CHARLES A 46 KIN W
CASE CHARLES L R 28 17T W
NOT A NATURALIZED CITIZEN
STRICKEN OUT APR 9/68
CASE IVEY A 30 POP B
CASE JESSE A 46 SUM W
CASE JESSEE A 46 SUM B
CASE JONATHAN A 30 POP B
CASE JOSEPH A 30 POP B
CASE NEEDHAM A 28 02N W
CASE THOMAS A 46 SUM W
MALITIA OFFICER BEFORE
WARE. VOLUNTARILY
AIDED IN REBELLION. REJ
BY HIS OWN REQUEST.
CASE W H A 46 SUM W
CASE WILLIAM A 46 SUM B
CASEY BENJAMIN A 28 16T W
CASEY BRYAN A 35 GLI W
CASEY DAVID A 28 13T W
CASEY ELIJAH A 28 16T W
CASEY FRANK A 28 16T W
CASEY JOHN A 28 14T W
CASEY MICAJH A 28 16T W
CASEY WILLIAM A 19 BE1 W
CASH ANDERSON A 44 LED W
CASH BRIANT A 44 DUT W
CASH EDWARD A 44 LED W
CASH ISAAK A 44 DUT W
CASH J Y A 44 DUT W
CASH JACOB A 44 DUT W
CASH JAMES A 44 DUT W
CASH JAMES A 44 DUT W
CASH JAMES R A 44 TAR W
CASH JOSEPH A 44 DUT W
CASH MOSES A 44 DUT W
CASH N C A 44 DUT W
CASH SPIVY A 40 FER W
CASH VOLENTINE A 44 DUT W
CASH W B A 44 DUT W
CASH WASHINGTON A 44 DUT W
CASHWELL A A 29 CED W
REMOVE TO BLADEN
CASHWELL HUGH J A 29 GRA W
CASHWELL JNO N A 29 GRA W
CASHWELL MARSHALL A 29 GRA W
CASHWELL R W A 29 LOC W
CASHWELL SANDERS A 29 CED W
CASON BENJAMIN F A 53 SWA W
CASON CALVIN B A 30 KNO W
CASON HENRY D A 53 SWA W
CASON SAMUEL R A 53 SWA W
CASON WILLIAM A 30 COI W
CASPER J S A 25 HAY W
CASSELL SILAS A 29 SEV B

CASTEEN KENAN A 35 CYP W
CASTER HENRY A 29 LOC W
CASTER W J A 26 GRI W
CASTLES JERRY A 40 DEC B
CASTLETT LEWIS A 39 HAY B
CASTNER DANIEL A 26 CAR W
CASTNER JACOB A 26 CAR W
CASTNER JOSEPH A 26 GRI W
CASTRUR JOSEPH A 26 CAR W
CATES P C A 32 THO W
CATHEY JAMES A 40 BLA B
CATHY JAMES A 40 CAN B
CATHY T A A 40 SAN W
CATLETT A A A 44 FOR W
CATLETT B G A 44 FOR W
CATLETT G W A 44 BRA W
CATLETT JOHN A 44 BRA W
CATLETT S T A 44 FOR W
CATLETT TABON A 44 BRA W
CATLETT WM A 39 FRA B
CATLETT WM A 39 FRA W
CATON ALEX A 28 11T W
CATON DAVID B A 28 12T W
CATON GEORGE W A 28 13T W
CATON JAMES A 30 CUR W
CATON JAMES A 30 CUR W
CATON JAMES B A 28 13T W
CATON JOHN A 30 CUR W
CATON JOHN S A 28 13T W
CATON NOAH G A 28 11T W
CATON RICHARD A 30 CUR W
CATON WM Z A 28 03A W
CATTON CHELSEA A 37 EDW B
CAUDLE H H A 32 DAV W
CAULDER WM A 29 FA2 W
CAULEY SAMUEL A 40 DA1 W
CAUSEY BURTON A 46 JAM B
CAUSEY CHARLES C A 46 RAG W
CAUSEY DAVID B A 46 RAG W
CAUSEY JACOB A 46 GRE B
CAUSEY JAMES A A 46 GRE W
CAUSEY JOHN G A 46 GRE W
CAUSEY JOHNATHAN A 46 RAG W
CAUSEY JOSEPH F A 46 GRE W
CAUSEY JOSHUA JR A 46 RAG W
CAUSEY JOSHUA SR A 46 RAG W
CAUSEY LEVI W A 46 RAG W
CAUSEY OLIVER S A 46 GRE W
CERT TO HIGH POINT
GUILFORD COUNTY
CAUSEY RILEY A 28 11T W
CAUSEY ROBT D A 46 ROS W
CAUSEY ROGER L A 46 RAG W
CAUSEY WILEY A 28 11T W
CAUSEY WILLIAM A 46 RAG W
CAUSEY WILLIAM RILEYA 28 11T W
CAUSEY WM C A 46 RAG W
CAUSEY WM P A 46 GRE W
CAUSEY WM W A 46 GRE W
CAVANAUGH JNO A 29 CAR W
CAVENAUGH BRYANT A 35 CYP W
CAVENAUGH DAVID W A 35 ISL W
CAVENAUGH HALSEY A 35 ISL W
CAVENAUGH JACOB W A 35 ISL W
CAVENAUGH JAMES D A 35 ISL W
CAVENAUGH JOHN A 35 SMI W
CAVENAUGH JOHN E A 35 CYP W
CAVENAUGH JOSEPH A 35 ISL W
CAVENESS DAVIDSON A 46 FRI W
CAVER JOSHUA A 29 ROC W
CAVNESS L D A 29 ROC W
FELONY 15 YRS AGO DIS-
ABILITY REMOVED 1860

CAWTHIN W T A 25 TUS W
CAWTHORN JNO C A 44 OXF W
CAWTHORN ROBT A 44 TAR B
CAWTHORN W H A 44 OXF W
CAWTHORNE C R A 44 FIS W
OXFORD DIST
CECIL A L A 46 HIG W
CECIL B A 32 LEE W
CECIL BARTLETT A 32 THO B
CECIL C L A 32 THO W
CECIL C W A 32 SHE W
CECIL DANIEL L A 32 THO W
CECIL J W A 32 THO W
CECIL JOHN B A 32 THO W
CECIL OLIVER A 32 LOF W
CECIL PHELIX A 32 LEE W
CECIL PHILLIP A 32 THO W
CECIL REILY A 32 THO W
CECIL RICHARD J A 32 DAV W
CECIL SAMUEL A 32 SHE W
CECIL SAMUEL A A 32 THO W
CECIL SAMUEL L A 32 SHE W
CECIL SOLOMON A 32 THO W
CECIL W H A 32 BRO W
CECIL W L A 32 THO W
CELEMENT CHARLES A 32 TYR B
CELLERN JACOB A 24 EDE B
CENTER A J A 25 SHO W
CENTER J L A 25 SHO W
CENTER JONAS A 40 MAU W
CENTRE R J A 35 FAI W
CHADDIC WILLIAM W A 30 POW W
CHADDWICK RICHD A 28 01A B
CHADWICK ALFRED H A 19 HUN W
CHADWICK ANTHONY A 19 BE1 B
CHADWICK BARNABAS A 19 BE1 W
CHADWICK BASWELL A 28 01A B
CHADWICK BEDFORD B A 19 STR W
CHADWICK BENJ F A 19 BE2 B
CHADWICK BENJAMIN A 19 HAD B
CHADWICK C B A 46 HIG W
CHADWICK CHARLES A 28 9TH B
CHADWICK CHARLES D A 19 STR W
CHADWICK CISCERO A 19 HAD B
CHADWICK DAVID A 19 BE1 B
CHADWICK DEMPSEY A 19 BE1 B
CHADWICK DRIGGONS A 19 BE2 B
CHADWICK EDWARD A 19 BE1 W
CHADWICK EUGENE A 19 STR W
CHADWICK FRANCIS T A 19 STR W
CHADWICK FRANK A 28 05B B
CHADWICK GAYER A 19 BE1 W
CHADWICK HASTY A 28 9TH B
CHADWICK HOMER A 19 BE1 B
CHADWICK JACOB A 19 BE1 B
CHADWICK JACOB A 19 STR W
CHADWICK JAMES A 19 STR W
CHADWICK JERRY A 19 BE1 B
CHADWICK JOHN A 19 BE1 B
CHADWICK JOHN A 28 01A B
CHADWICK JOHN A 53 GER B
CHADWICK JOHN D A 19 SMY W
CHADWICK LEWIS A 19 BE1 B
CHADWICK LEWIS A 19 BE1 B
CHADWICK LEWIS A 19 STR B
CHADWICK MOSES A 19 BE1 B
CHADWICK N M A 28 02N W
CHADWICK OLIVER A 19 STR W
CHADWICK OWEN A 19 BE1 B
CHADWICK PETER A 19 BE1 B
CHADWICK RICHARD A 19 BE1 B
CHADWICK ROMAN A 19 HAR B
CHADWICK SAML A 28 04B B

CHADWICK SAMUEL A 19 BE1 B
CHADWICK SAMUEL A 19 STR W
CHADWICK SEXTY A 19 BE1 B
CHADWICK SIMEON A 19 STR W
CHADWICK STEPHEN A 19 BE1 W
CHADWICK STEPHN A 28 02N W
CHADWICK SUTTON A 19 BE1 B
CHADWICK SUTTON JR A 19 BE1 B
CHADWICK THOMAS A 19 STR W
CHADWICK THOS P A 19 STR W
CHADWICK WM W A 19 BE1 W
CHADWWICK SOLOMON N A 19 STR W
CHAFFEE EUGENE M A 30 POP W
CHAFIN JAMES A 32 YAD B
CHAISON JAS J A 29 CED W
CHALKLEY E E A 44 SAS W
CHALKLEY GILES A 44 YXR W
CHAMBERLAIN BARNA A 32 DAV W
CHAMBERLAIN LEWIS A 37 TA1 W
CHAMBERLAIN MARTIN A 32 THO W
BY CERTIF
CHAMBERLAIN
SPENCER W A 37 TA1 W
CHAMBERS ABNER A 32 BRO W
CHAMBERS ALEXANDER A 35 KEN W
CHAMBERS BOSSON A 35 KEN B
CHAMBERS CAPT A 35 GLI B
CHAMBERS DAVID F A 35 KEN W
CHAMBERS E P A 26 BUR W
CHAMBERS G C A 35 ALB W
CHAMBERS H A A 29 FA1 W
CHAMBERS JAMES A 28 8TH B
CHAMBERS JOHN A 35 KEN W
CHAMBERS JOHN W A 35 KEN W
CHAMBERS JONAS A 35 KEN B
CHAMBERS KENAN A 35 KEN B
CHAMBERS LEWIS A 35 KEN B
CHAMBERS MARTIN A 46 GRE W
CHAMBERS RICHARD A 35 KEN B
CHAMBERS ROBERT A 35 KEN B
CHAMBERS THURSMAN A 35 GLI B
CHAMBERS W D A 35 ALB W
CHAMBERS WILLIAM A 28 6TH B
CHAMBERS WILLIAM A 32 BRO W
CHAMBERS WM A 29 FA1 B
CHAMBLEE BALDIE A 39 GRI B
CHAMBLEE ISHMAEL A 39 GRI B
CHAMBLEE JNO A 39 HAR W
CHAMBLEE TONY A 39 GRI B
CHAMBLEE WM A 39 GRI W
CHAMPION ALEX M A 44 HEN W
CERT TO VOTE OUT COUNTY
CHAMPION B R A 44 FOR W
CHAMPION BENJ A 44 FOR W
CHAMPION C B A 44 HEN W
CHAMPION C H A 39 PUG W
CHAMPION D O P A 26 MOO W
CHAMPION G H A 26 BUR W
CHAMPION H R A 26 MOO W
CHAMPION J H A 44 FOR W
CHAMPION J M A 39 FRE W
CHAMPION J M A 44 FIS W
CHAMPION JOHN W A 26 BUR W
CHAMPION N A M A 26 MOO W
CHAMPION R C A 26 BUR W
CHAMPION RICHARD A 26 MOU W
CHAMPION THORNTON A 44 HEN B
CHAMPION W J A 44 FOR W
CHAMPLIN JOHN A 46 JAM B
CHANCE EVANS A 29 CAR B
CHANCE EZEKIEL A 28 14T B
CHANCE GRIFFIN A 29 FA1 B
CHANCE HENRY A 29 CAR B

CHANCE JAMES A 53 LA1 B
CHANCE JOS A 29 FA1 B
CHANCE LOFTIN A 28 9TH B
CHANCE MAJOR A 53 LA1 B
CHANCE NATHAN A 29 CAR B
CHANCE
NIXON ASHFORD A 29 CAR B
CHANCE NOAH A 37 HIC B
CHANCE RUFUS A 28 9TH B
CHANCE SOLOMON A 28 9TH B
CHANCE SOMON A 37 HIC B
CHANCE WILLIAM A 53 FAI B
CHANCE WM E A 29 FA1 B
CHANCE WM EVERETT A 29 CAR B
CHANCY E A 19 MOR B
CHANCY SAMUEL A 53 GER B
CHANCY WILSON A 19 HAD W
CHANDLER CHESTEFIELDA 44 YXR B
CHANDLER GRIFFITH A 29 FA1 B
CHANDLER JAS A 44 YXS W
CHANDLER JAS H A 44 YXS W
CHANDLER JOHN A 24 MID B
CHANDLER M L R 44 YXR W
IN STATE 7 MONTHS REJ
CHANDLER NEWTON V A 40 DA2 W
CHANDLER R T A 44 YXR W
CHANDLER REUBIN A 44 YXS W
CHANDLER ROBT A 44 YXR B
CHANDLER SIMON A 44 YXS W
CHANDLER SPOTS A 44 YXR B
CHANDLER THOMAS A 44 YXS W
CHANDLER WILLIAM A 44 YXS B
CHANDLER WILLIS A 44 YXR B
CHANDLER WM A 44 YXR B
CHAPEL D A A 44 BEA W
CHAPEL GILBERT A 46 GRE W
CHAPEL JOHN A 46 ROS W
CHAPELL A J A 44 BEA W
CHAPELL FRANCIS A 24 UPP W
CHAPELL J W A 44 DUT W
CHAPELL S J A 24 UPP W
CHAPIE GEORGE A 26 BOR B
CHAPIN A R DR A 46 GRE W
CERT TO RALEIGH
CHAPLAIN CALEB T A 30 NAR W
CHAPLAIN JASPER A 30 POW W
CHAPMAN AMOS A 28 10T B
CHAPMAN BOSTON A 19 MOR B
CHAPMAN GEORGE A 28 11T B
CHAPMAN HILLIARD A 37 TA1 B
CHAPMAN JARVIS 19 HAR B
CERT. TO BEAUFORT
CHAPMAN JERRY A 28 11T B
CHAPMAN JOHN A 28 01A B
CHAPMAN JOHN G A 44 TOW W
CHAPMAN L H A 44 TOW W
CHAPMAN LOUIS A 28 11T B
CHAPMAN PERRY A 28 11T B
CHAPMAN PETER A 28 10T B
CHAPMAN RICHARD S A 28 11T W
CHAPMAN RICHARD S R 28 11T W
CHALLENGED
DID NOT TAKE OATH WAS A
PATROLLER & CONSTABLE
AND GAVE AID TO SOLDIERS
DURING THE WAR
CHAPMAN SAMUEL A 28 11T B
CHAPMAN SILAS A 28 11T B
CHAPMAN SLADE A 28 11T W
CHAPMAN STANLY A 28 04B B
CHAPMAN W H A 28 11T W
CHAPMAN W R A 26 PEE W
CHAPMAN WILLIAM A 26 PEE W

CHAPMAN WILLIAM A A 44 TOW W
CHAPMAN WM A 28 6TH W
CHAPPAL HENRY A 24 MID W
CHAPPEL JONATHAN A 24 MID W
CHAPPELL A R A 44 DUT W
CHAPPELL CALEB A 24 UPP W
CHAPPELL CALEB W A 24 UPP W
CHAPPELL JAS C A 24 UPP W
CHAPPELL JESSE A A 24 UPP W
CHAPPELL M B A 44 DUT W
CHAPPELL ROBT A 24 UPP W
CHAPPELL SILAS W A 24 UPP W
CHAPPELL THOMAS F A 24 UPP W
CHAPPELL THOS C A 30 GIB W
CHAPPELL WILLIAM A 24 UPP W
CHARLES A S A 46 FRI W
CHARLES ADISON A 46 FRI B
CHARLES ALBERT A 28 04A B
CHARLES ALBERT A 53 SWA B
CHARLES ELISHA SR A 46 HIG W
CHARLES G W A 46 HIG W
CHARLES GEORGE W A 32 BRO B
CHARLES HENRY A 32 BRO B
CHARLES ISAAC A 35 KEN B
CHARLES JAMES G A 37 TA1 W
CHARLES JOHNATHAN A 32 POS W
CHARLES LORIN A 32 POS W
CHARLES MILTON A 28 03A B
CHARLES NEWTON A 32 POS W
CHARLES R F A 32 POS W
CHARLES ROBERT A 32 BRO B
CHARLES S M A 32 TYR W
CHARLESTON PETER A 44 OXF B
CHARLOTT GEO W A 19 BE1 W
CHARLOTT W E A 28 03A W
CHARLS A P A 46 FRI W
CHARLTON GEORGE A 24 EDE B
CHARLTON GEORGE W A 28 8TH W
CHARLTON JOB A 24 EDE B
CHARLTON THOMAS A 30 MOY W
CHARLTON W H A 30 MOY W
CHASE FURNEY A 28 9TH B
CHASE GABRIEL A 28 9TH B
CHASE JAMES A 37 ROB B
CHASE JAMES A 53 SWA B
CHASE RICHARD A 28 9TH B
CHASE SAML A 28 03A B
CHASE WILLIAM A 28 9TH B
CHASON ISAAC A 35 ISL B
CHASON JAMES A 29 CED W
CHASON JAS A 29 GRA W
CHASON JNO H A 29 ROC W
CHASON LOT A 35 ISL B
CHASON WM A 29 CED W
CHASON YORK A 35 ISL B
CHASTAIN B S A 25 HAY W
CHASTAIN E H A 25 HAY W
CHASTAIN J P A 25 HAY W
CHASTAIN JOHN G A 25 HAY W
CHASTAIN S B A 25 HAY W
CHATHAM WM A 46 GIB W
CHATMAN ROBT A 28 04A B
CHATWOOD GASTON A 28 03A B
CHAVERS EDMOND A 29 SEV B
CHAVERS JOHN W A 29 SEV B
CHAVERS PHILLIP A 72 SWA B
CHAVIS ALEX A 44 OXF B
CHAVIS BENNETT A 44 FOR B
CHAVIS DANL A 28 04A B
CHAVIS DAVID A 37 ROC B
CHAVIS DEWITT A 44 DUT B
CHAVIS HENRY A 44 LED B
CHAVIS HENRY A 44 OXF B

CHAVIS J H A 44 BRA B
CHAVIS JEFF A 44 YXR B
CHAVIS SAML A 44 OXF B
CHAVIS WM A 44 BRA B
CHAVIS WM A 44 HEN B
CHAVIS WM A 46 GRE B
CHAVOUS MOSES A 44 YXS B
CHAVOUS WILLIAM A 44 DUT B
CHAVUS CASWELL A 39 HAY B
CHEATHAM D T A 44 OXF W
CHEATHAM DANIEL A 44 OXF B
CHEATHAM DR W T A 44 HEN W
CHEATHAM EDMOND A 44 HEN B
CHEATHAM GABE A 44 HEN B
CHEATHAM GREEN A 44 FIS B
CHEATHAM HENDERSON A 44 KIT B
CHEATHAM HENRY A 44 ISL B
CHEATHAM HILMAN A 44 HEN B
CHEATHAM ISHAM A 44 HEN W
CHEATHAM ISHAM A 44 OXF B
CHEATHAM J J A 44 TOW W
CHEATHAM JACK A 44 OXF B
CHEATHAM JAMES A 44 HEN B
CHEATHAM JAMES A 44 OXF B
CHEATHAM JAMES SR A 44 HEN B
CHEATHAM JAMES T A 44 OXF W
CHEATHAM JOHN A 44 HEN B
CHEATHAM JOSEPH A 44 FIS B
CHEATHAM PETER A 44 HEN B
CHEATHAM ROBT A 44 HEN B
CHEATHAM RUBEN A 46 KIN W
CHEATHAM STEPHEN A 44 TOW B
CHEATHAM THOMAS A 44 KIT B
CHEATHAM W A A 44 OXF W
CHEATHAM W H H A 44 FIS W
CHEEK A C A 32 THO W
CHEEK ADKIN A 39 PUG B
CHEEK BILLY A 39 JOR B
CHEEK HENRY A 32 LEE W
CHEEK HENRY A 37 HIC B
CHENEY BRISTOW A 37 EDW B
CHENEY JOHN A 37 EDW B
CHENEY SIMON A 37 EDW B
CHERRY ALBERT A 40 DA1 W
CHERRY ANDREW A 37 PIN B
CHERRY ARDEN A 37 HIC B
CHERRY EDMUND A 37 PIN B
CHERRY ELISHA A 30 MOY B
CHERRY G J A 24 EDE W
CHERRY GENERAL A 37 HIC B
CHERRY GEO W A 35 WOL B
CHERRY GEORGE W A 35 KEN W
CHERRY HENRY A 19 MOR B
CHERRY HENRY C A 37 TA1 B
CHERRY JAMES A 28 03A B
CHERRY JAMES A 37 MAN B
CHERRY JAMES P A 25 HAY W
CHERRY JEREMIAH A 37 ROB B
CHERRY JOHN A 30 TUL W
CHERRY JOHN A 37 MAN B
CHERRY JOHN A 40 DA1 W
CHERRY JOHN R A 37 ROB W
CHERRY JOHN T A 25 HAY W
CHERRY JOSEPH A 28 05A B
CHERRY LANCASTER A 37 PIN B
CHERRY LOUIS A 35 WOL B
CHERRY LUNSFORD A 37 ROB W
CHERRY MACK A 19 BE1 B
CHERRY MARK JR A 30 CUR B
CHERRY MARK SR A 30 CUR B
CHERRY NEWBERN A 37 HIC B
CHERRY ORRIND A 37 ROB B
CHERRY PATRICK A 37 PIN B
CHERRY PETER A 37 PIN B
CHERRY RISHMOND A 37 ROB B
CHERRY ROBERT C A 25 HAY W
CHERRY SOLOMAN T A 37 HIC A
CHERRY STEPHEN A 28 05A B
CHERRY W A A 35 FAI W
CHERRY W H A 40 STO W
CHERRY WARREN A 19 HAR B
CHERRY WARREN A 37 HIC B
CHERRY WM W A 29 FA1 B
CHESHIRE FRANK N A 24 EDE B
CHESHIRE JAMES O A 24 EDE W
CHESHIRE P B A 39 LOU W
CHESHIRE THOMAS A 24 EDE B
CHESNEY JERRY A 28 04A B
CHESNEY JOE A 28 04A B
CHESNUT A J A 29 FA1 B
CHESNUT D A 29 FA1 B
CHESNUT G F A 35 FAI W
CHESNUTT DANIEL H A 35 WAR W
CHESNUTT JAMES A 35 ROC W
CHESNUTT JONATHAN A 35 KEN W
CHESNUTT WILLIAM C A 35 KEN W
CHESSON MARTIN A 37 PIN B
CHESSON PHILLIP A 37 PIN B
CHESSON SAMUEL A 37 HOL B
CHESTER WILLIAM A 53 SWA W
CHESTNUT R L A 28 9TH W
CHESTNUT THOMAS A 35 FAI W
CHESTNUTT EDWARD J A 35 MAG W
CHESTNUTT WILEY A 35 ROC B
CHETHAM T G A 44 FIS W
CHEVES J H A 39 GRI W
CHEVES J L A 39 GRI W
CHEVIS GILES A 26 SHE B
CHILCUTT B G A 46 MON W
MALITIA OFFICER BEFORE
WARE AIDED REBELLION
CHILCUTT ELIJAH A 46 MON W
CHILCUTT F D A 46 MON W
CHILCUTT R L A 46 MON W
MALITIA OFFICER BEFORE
WARE AIDED REBELLION
CHILCUTT T G A 46 MON W
CHILDS DAVID A 40 DA1 B
CHIPMAN ANDREW A 46 JAM B
CHIPMAN JOSEPH A 46 FRI W
CHIPMAN PARIS JR A 46 FRI W
CHISDEN JACKSON A 24 EDE B
CHAL BY J R B HATHAWAY
REASON TOO YOUNG
NO EVIDENCE AGAINST HIM
CHITWOOD W M A 26 BLA W
CHORDEN THEODORE A 24 EDE B
CHRISMAN DAVID A 46 MON W
CHRISMAN LEWIS C A 46 GIB B
CHRISMAN ZACHARIAS A 46 MON W
CHRISTMAN R D A 39 HAR W
CHRISTMAS EDMOND A 44 SAS B
CHRISTMAS HENRY A 37 SPA B
CHRISTMAS SAML A 44 HEN B
CHRISTMAS THOMAS A 28 01A B
CHRISTOPHER
HENDERSON A 46 KIN W
CHRISTOPHER JAMES A 37 TA1 B
CHRISTOPHER SIMON A 46 MON W
CHURCH H F A 46 HIG W
CHURCH J J M R 46 HIG W
CAUSE MILITIA OFFICER FOR
THE REBELLION AIDED
VOLUNTARILY IS REJECTED
CHURCH LUCIUS A 37 TA1 W
CHURCHILL Q ? A 28 01B W
CHURCHILL EPHRAIM A 24 MID W
CHURCHILL JOHN A 24 MID W
CHURCHILL JOHN JR A 24 MID W
CHURCHWELL DAVID A 35 KEN W
CIVIL R S A 28 03A W
CIVILS STEPHN A 28 6TH W
CIVILS W J A 28 6TH W
CIVILS W T A 28 6TH W
CIVILS WM F A 30 IND W
CLACK JAMES A 44 YXR B
CLACK JOHN A 44 SAS B
CLACK SAMUEL A 44 SAS B
CLAGON PETER A 28 05A B
CLAGON WILLIS A 28 05A B
CLANSEY M A 19 NEW W
CLANTON ISAAC A 40 RHY W
CLANTON L A A 40 RHY W
CLAPP ALPHEUS G A 46 GIB W
CLAPP ASA R 46 MCL W
WAS AN OVERSEER OF
A HIGHWAY BEFORE THE
WARE AND SERVED IN THE
MILITIA TO KEEP FROM
GOING TO THE ARMY OF CS.
IS ACCEPTED
CLAPP AUSTEN A 46 MCL B
CLAPP BENJAMIN T A 46 COB W
CLAPP DANIEL A 46 MCL B
CLAPP DANIEL F A 46 COB W
CLAPP DANIEL M A 46 RAG W
CLAPP DANIEL
OF JACOB A 46 COB W
CLAPP DAVID JR A 46 COB W
CLAPP DENNY C A 46 COB W
CLAPP ELIJA A 46 COB B
CLAPP EMANUEL A 46 MCL B
CLAPP F MADISON A 46 COB B
CLAPP F ZWINGLIUS A 46 GIB W
CLAPP GEORG W A 46 MCL B
CLAPP GEORGE M R 46 MCL W
WAS AN OVERSEER OF A
HIGHWAY BEFORE THE WARE
AND CONSCRIBED AND APPO-
INTED CAPTAIN BUT REFUSED
TO SERVE. HE CALLED OUT
THE COMPANY ONE TIME ONLY
HE ALSO TOOK A GOVERNMENT
CONTRACT TO KEEP OUT OF
THE ARMY. ACCEPTED
CLAPP GEORGE M R A 46 MCL W
CLAPP GEORGE W A 46 RAG W
CLAPP HENRY A 46 COB W
CLAPP HENRY A 46 HIG W
CLAPP HENRY C A 46 COB W
CLAPP ISAAC A 46 COB B
CLAPP ISAAC A 46 COB W
CLAPP ISRAELE M A 46 MCL W
CLAPP JACOB A 46 MCL W
CLAPP JACOB (OF EVE)A 46 GIB W
CLAPP JAMES A 46 COB W
CLAPP JAMES A 46 GRE B
CLAPP JAMES F R A 46 MCL W
CLAPP JEREMIAH A 46 COB W
CLAPP JOHANN G A 46 GIB W
CLAPP JOHN C A 46 COB W
CLAPP JOHN E A 46 GIB W
CLAPP JOHN J A 46 COB W
CLAPP JOHN OF JACOB A 46 COB W
CLAPP JORDAN A 46 COB B
CLAPP JOSHUA A 46 COB W
CLAPP JOSHUA A 46 GIB W
CLAPP LEWIS A 46 COB W
CLAPP MADISON A 46 COB W

CLAPP PETER A 46 MCL W
CLAPP PINKNEY W A 46 MCL W
CLAPP PLEASANT S A 46 GRE W
CLAPP REUBIN A 46 MCL B
CLAPP RICHARD A 46 COB B
CLAPP SAMUEL A 46 MON W
CLAPP SIMEON R A 46 GIB W
CLAPP THOMAS T A 46 MCL W
CLAPP WESLEY A 46 MCL B
CLAPP WILLIAM A 46 COB W
CLAPP WILLIS A 46 MCL B
CLARDY ABRAM A 44 TOW B
CLARDY HENRY A 44 TOW B
CLARETY DANIEL A 19 MOR B
CLARK A M K A 29 FA2 W
CLARK ALEX A 44 YXR W
CLARK ANDERSON A 46 FRI B
CLARK ANDREW A 44 HEN B
CLARK ARCHY A 29 FA1 W
CLARK ASSIC A 37 HIC B
CLARK B F A 39 HAY W
CLARK B Y A 46 FRI W
CLARK BENJAMIN A 44 DUT W
CLARK C C A 46 FRI W
CLARK C H A 44 ISL W
CLARK CHARLES A 28 05A B
CLARK CHARLES L A 37 ROC W
CLARK CHESTERFIELD A 37 TA1 B
CLARK CILVESTER A 37 HIG B
CLARK DANIEL A 19 NEW W
CLARK DANUL A 26 SHE B
CLARK DAVID A 46 GRE W
CLARK E E A 28 02N W
CLARK E J A 28 02N W
CLARK EDMOND A 46 KIN W
CLARK EDWARD M A 53 LA1 W
CLARK ELISHA JR A 46 FRI W
CLARK FRANK A 29 MON B
CLARK GEORGE A 32 DAV B
CLARK GREEN A 28 6TH B
CLARK GUST A 37 ROC B
CLARK HARRY A 29 FA1 B
CLARK HARVEY A 28 11T W
CLARK HENERY A 29 GRA W
CLARK HENRY A 28 04A B
CLARK HENRY A 28 04B B
CLARK HENRY A 28 05A B
CLARK HENRY A 46 JAM B
CLARK HIROL A 46 SUM B
CLARK J B A 46 SUM W
CLARK J C A 26 SHE W
CLARK JABIN A 28 9TH B
CLARK JACK A 37 HIC B
CLARK JACKSON A 28 04A B
CLARK JACKSON A 28 11T W
CLARK JAMES A 24 EDE B
CLARK JAMES A 44 ISL B
CLARK JAMES A A 26 GOF B
CLARK JAMES F A 28 01A W
CLARK JAMES M A 40 BLA W
CLARK JOHN A 37 PEN W
CLARK JOHN A 46 FRI W
CLARK JOHN A 46 MCL W
CLARK JOHN A A 29 SEV B
CLARK JOHN J A 44 DUT W
CLARK JOHN JR A 46 FRI W
CLARK JOHN R A 24 EDE B
CLARK JOSEPH A 24 EDE B
CLARK JOSEPH A 28 6TH B
CLARK JOSEPH A 44 DUT W
CLARK JOURDAN A 37 HIC B
CLARK L D A 46 HIG W
CLARK L S A 28 01A W
CLARK MALCOM D A 29 FA1 W
CLARK MATHEW A 37 TA1 B
CLARK MILING A A 40 DEC W
CLARK MOSES A 28 05B B
CLARK MOSES 2ND A 28 05B B
CLARK NATHANIEL A 46 KIN W
CLARK NEILL A 29 ROC W
CLARK NELSON A 37 TA1 B
CLARK PETER A 37 PEN B
CLARK PHILIP A 37 MAN B
CLARK PHILLIP A 37 SHA W
CLARK PRINCE A 28 6TH B
CLARK R G A 29 LOC W
CLARK REUBEN A 28 03A B
CLARK RICHAMOND A 29 FA1 B
CLARK RICHD A 28 6TH B
CLARK RODEN A 32 THO B
CLARK RUFUS A 44 SAS W
CLARK SAMUEL A 44 DUT W
CLARK SAMUEL A 46 MCL W
CLARK SANDY A 44 YXR W
CLARK SIMUEL A 32 THO B
CLARK SOLOMAN A 37 TA1 B
CLARK STEPHEN A 37 EDW B
CLARK STEPHN A 28 03A B
CLARK THOMAS A 28 15T W
CLARK W L A 46 JAM W
CLARK W Y A 46 JAM W
CLARK WALLIS A 28 03A B
CLARK WATSON A 28 05A B
CLARK WILEY A 28 8TH B
CLARK WILLIAM A 37 EDW B
CLARK WILLIAM A 37 PEN W
CLARK WILLIAM A 40 DEC W
CLARK WILLIAM A 53 HAT W
CLARK WILLIAMS S A 37 HOL W
CLARK WM H A 28 16T W
CLARK WM P A 32 THO W
CLARK WM R A 29 FA1 W
CLARKE A S A 44 YXR W
CLARKE ALEX A 44 HEN W
CLARKE DAVID A 44 HEN B
CLARKE EDWARD A 53 GER W
CLARKE ENOCH R 44 YXR B
9 MOS RES REJ
CLARKE GEORGE A 29 SEV B
CLARKE HENRY A 44 YXS B
CLARKE J L A 44 YXR W
CLARKE J S R A 44 KIT W
CLARKE JACOB A 44 YXR B
CLARKE JAMES A 44 HEN W
CLARKE JAMES A 44 YXR W
CLARKE JNO D A 44 HEN W
CLARKE JNO E A 44 HEN W
CLARKE JOHN A 53 GER B
CLARKE JOLIN A 28 11T W
CLARKE JOS A A 44 HEN W
CLARKE JOSEPH A 44 HEN W
CLARY D D A 26 BUR W
CLAVER THOMAS A 32 DAV B
CLAY A M A 44 OXF W
CLAY ABRAHAM A 44 OXF B
CLAY ALEX A 44 FOR B
CLAY C W A 44 FOR W
CLAY HENRY A 28 02N B
CLAY HENRY A 29 FA1 B
CLAY HENRY A 44 BRA B
CLAY ISAAC A 44 OXF B
CLAY J G A 44 BEA W
CLAY J M A 44 FOR W
CLAY MERIDA A 44 FOR B
CLAY PLEASANT A 44 FOR W
CLAY WM A 44 OXF W
CLAYBORN SQUIRE A 46 GRE B
CLAYTON DAVID A 28 05A B
CLAYTON E J A 28 02N W
CLAYTON R P A 28 7TH W
CLAYTON R R A 44 KNA W
CLAYTON RICHARD C A 24 EDE W
CLAYTON WILLIAM P A 53 FAI W
CLEMANS GARSON A 32 TYR B
CLEMENT GILES A 32 TYR B
CLEMENT JAMES A 44 OXF B
CLEMENT SAMEUL W A 35 KEN W
CLEMENT W A A 44 DUT W
CLEMENTS AMIS G A 44 KNA W
CLEMENTS ANDERSON A 44 KNA B
CLEMENTS GEORGE A 44 OXF B
CLEMENTS J K A 44 OXF W
CLEMENTS T D A 44 KNA W
CLEMENTS WM A 44 KNA W
CLEMER ADAM A 40 DA1 W
CLEMER ANDREW A 40 DA1 W
CLEMER HENRY A 40 DA1 B
CLEMER J LARKIN A 40 DA1 W
CLEMER JAMES A 40 DA1 B
CLEMER JOHN A 40 DA1 W
CLEMER JONAS A 40 DA1 W
CLEMER LAFAYETTE M J A 40 DA1 W
CLEMER LARKIN D A 40 DA1 W
CLEMER LEMUEL L A 40 DA1 W
CLEMER LEVI A 40 DA1 W
CHALLENGE CAUSE:
POSTMASTER BEFORE THE
REBELLION AND ENGAGED IN
INSURRECTION OR GAVE AID
& COMFORT TO THE ENEMY
CHALLENGE NOT SUSTAINED
CLEMER LEWIS J A 40 DEC W
CLEMER LEWIS L A 40 DA1 W
CLEMINS OWEN A 29 CAR B
CLEMMENT W B A 32 YAD W
CLEMMENTS ELIJAH A 44 SAS B
CLEMMER G P A 40 SAN W
CLEMMONS PLEASANTS A 44 SAS B
CLEMOND LLOYD A 32 BRO B
CLEMONS ALEXANDER A 37 EDW B
CLEMONS HARDY A 28 03A B
CLEMONS RUFFIN A 44 LED B
CLENDENIN JOHN C A 46 GRE W
CLENDENNIS PETER A 24 EDE B
CLESSON GEORGE A 37 TA2 B
CLEVE EDWARD CHAL R 28 11T W
A NATURALIZED CITIZEN WHO
FURNISHED TRANSPORTATION
TO REBEL SOLDIERS
CLEVE WILLIAM A 28 02N W
CLIBORNE CHAS L A 44 RAG W
CLIBORNE N T A 44 RAG W
CLIBORNE R F A 44 RAG W
CLICK JOHN A 32 TYR W
CLICK JOHN M A 32 TYR W
CLIFFORD JOHN A 28 16T W
CLIFTON B P A 39 LOU W
CLIFTON BEB A 39 HAR B
CLIFTON J B A 39 LOU W
CLIFTON JAMES A 39 HAR B
CLIFTON JOHN A 39 HAR W
CLIFTON NED A 39 HAR B
CLIFTON SAMUEL A 39 FRA B
CLIFTON STEP A 39 HAR B
CLIFTON T T A 39 LOU W
CLIFTON TILMAN A 39 FRA W
CLIFTON WILLIE V A 39 HAR W
CLIFTON WM A 38 FRE B

CLIMER J D A 46 MON W
CLIMER W G A 46 MON W
CLINARD A C A 32 POS W
CLINARD AHART A 32 POS W
CLINARD ANDREW A 32 POS W
CLINARD ANDREW A 32 THO W
CLINARD D B A 32 POS W
CLINARD H F A 32 POS W
CLINARD JOHN A 32 THO W
CLINARD MARTINE A 32 THO W
CLINARD PHILLIP A 32 POS W
CLINARD PHILLIP A 32 THO W
CLINARD R B A 32 THO W
CLINARD S Y A 32 POS W
CLINE DAVID A 26 GRI W
CLINE HENRY A 26 WAR W
CLINE ISAAC A 32 CLE W
CLINE JOHN A 26 WAR W
CLINE JOSEPH A 26 GRI B
CLINE LONDON A 26 GRI B
CLINORD J M A 32 BRO W
CLINORD WILLIAM A 32 BRO W
CLINTON FREDRICK R 40 SAN B
NAME LINED OUT
CHALLENGED
CLINTON THADEUS A 40 SAN W
CLODFELTER ADAM A 32 LOF W
CLODFELTER
ALEXANDER A 32 POS B
CLODFELTER ANDREW A 32 DAV W
CLODFELTER ANDREW A 32 LEE W
CLODFELTER ANDREW A 32 LEE W
CLODFELTER DANIEL A 32 POS W
CLODFELTER DANIEL A A 32 DAV W
CLODFELTER DAVID A 32 DAV W
CLODFELTER DAVID A 32 POS W
CLODFELTER ELIAS A 32 LOF W
CLODFELTER FRANKLIN A 32 DAV B
CLODFELTER G H A 32 DAV W
CLODFELTER GEORGE A 32 JAC W
CLODFELTER GEORGE A 32 POS W
CLODFELTER GEORGE A 32 TYR W
CLODFELTER
HAMILTON L A 32 POS W
CLODFELTER HENRY A 32 POS W
CLODFELTER J A A 32 POS W
CLODFELTER J L A 32 DAV W
CLODFELTER JACOB A 32 POS W
CLODFELTER JESSE A 32 LEE W
CLODFELTER JOHN A 32 LOF W
CLODFELTER JOHN A 32 THO W
CLODFELTER JOSEPH A 32 DAV W
CLODFELTER JOSEPH A 32 POS W
CLODFELTER JOSEPH JRA 32 SHE W
CLODFELTER LEASON A 32 DAV W
CLODFELTER LEWIS A 32 CLE W
CLODFELTER LEWIS A 32 POS B
CLODFELTER PHILIP A 32 DAV W
CLODFELTER RANSOM A A 32 DAV W
CLODFELTER ROBERT A 32 DAV B
CLODFELTER SELAM A 32 DAV W
CLONEGAR WM A 40 RHY W
CLONEGER D R A 40 RHY W
CLONINGER EMANUEL A 40 DA1 W
CLONINGER JACOB C A 40 DA1 W
CLONINGER JONAS A 40 DA1 W
CLONINGER JONAS S A 40 DA1 W
CLONINGER MICHAEL A 40 DA1 W
CLONINGER MOSES A 40 DA1 W
CLONTS JEREMIAH A 40 STO W
CLOPLAN J D A 39 FRA W
CLOPTON THOMAS A 39 LOU W
CLOSE MADISON A 46 MCL B

CLOSE THOMAS D A 46 GRE W
CLOSE WM A 46 GRE B
CLOUSE LEWIS A 32 THO B
CLOUSE ORSBORN A 32 DAV B
CLUTTS JULIUS A 32 DAV W
COAL JOSEPH A 37 ROB B
COALTRAIN AHI W A 46 GRE W
COART W F A 28 04A B
COATES ROMEO A 28 02N B
COATS ANDREW A 28 01B W
COATS JAMES A 28 01B W
COATS WILLIS A 32 TYR W
COBB ALLEN A 37 PIN B
COBB AVERY A 37 SPA W
COBB BENJAMIN F A 35 KEN W
COBB BOSTON H A 46 MCL W
COBB CEASER A 46 MON B
COBB DAVID A 35 FAI W
COBB DAVID A 46 GIB W
COBB DAVID M A 37 PIN W
COBB EDWARD A 37 SPA W
COBB EGHAM A 37 WHI W
COBB ELI A 28 12T B
COBB GEORGE A 46 MON B
COBB GEORGE W A 46 GRE B
COBB HENRY A 46 MCL W
COBB HENRY A 46 MCL W
COBB ISRAEL A 46 GIB W
COBB IVORY A 37 TA1 B
COBB J A A 26 GOF W
COBB JACK A 46 GIB B
COBB JACK A 46 MCL B
COBB JACOB A 37 TA1 B
COBB JACOB H A 46 MCL W
COBB JAMES A 37 WHI W
COBB JOHN A 46 GIB W
COBB JOHN B A 37 SPA W
COBB JOHN G A 26 GOF W
COBB JOSEPH A 37 PIN B
COBB JOSEPH A 37 TA1 W
COBB JOSEPH A 46 MCL B
COBB LEWIS A 46 MON W
COBB LEWIS JR A 46 MON B
COBB LEWIS SR A 46 MON B
COBB LUKE A 28 04B B
COBB M H A 46 FRI W
COBB MILES A 37 WHI B
COBB PETER A 37 PEN B
COBB PETER A 46 MCL W
COBB POMPEY A 37 WHI B
COBB REUBEN A 37 TA1 W
COBB RICHARD A 44 FIS B
COBB RICHARD G A 28 7TH W
COBB ROBERT A 37 PIN B
COBB SAMUEL A 46 MON B
COBB SIMON A 37 PIN B
COBB THOMAS JR A 46 MON B
COBB THOMAS SR A 46 MON B
COBB TIMOTHY A 37 PIN B
COBB VOLANTINE A 46 MCL W
COBB WILLIAM A 26 GOF W
COBB WILLIAM A 44 TOW B
COBB WILLIAM F A 30 ROA B
COBB WILLIAM T A 37 PIN W
COBB WM A 46 GIB W
COBB WM A 46 GIB W
COBB WM G A 46 MCL W
COBB WM W A 26 GOF W
COBBIN JOHN A 28 7TH B
COBERN JOSIAH A 53 GER W
COBLE ABNER A 46 COB W
COBLE ABNER A 46 ROS W
COBLE ALFRED A 46 GRE W

COBLE AMBROSE A 46 RAG W
COBLE ARINGTON A 46 COB W
COBLE CONRAD A 46 RAG W
COBLE DANIEL M A 46 COB W
COBLE DANIEL P A 46 ROS W
COBLE DAVID A 46 GIB B
COBLE DAVI OF TOME A 46 COB W
COBLE DAVID S A 46 COB W
COBLE ELI A 46 RAG W
COBLE EMERY A 46 COB W
COBLE GEORGE A 46 ROS W
COBLE GEORGE A 46 RAG W
OF PETER
COBLE GIDEON A 46 RAG W
COBLE HENDERSON A 46 COB B
COBLE HENRY A 32 TYR W
COBLE HIRAM A 46 RAG W
COBLE HIRAM M A 46 MCL W
COBLE J JOHN A 46 COB W
COBLE JACOB A 46 MCL W
COBLE JACOB A 46 ROS W
COBLE JAMES F A 46 COB W
COBLE JAMES R A 46 RAG W
COBLE JERRY A 46 COB B
COBLE JILES H A 46 RAG B
COBLE JOHN A A 46 COB W
COBLE JOHNATHAN A 46 COB W
COBLE JULIUS S A 46 RAG W
COBLE MICHAEL A 46 RAG W
COBLE NATHANIEL A 46 RAG W
COBLE PETER A 46 COB W
OF GEORGE
COBLE PETER OF ELI A 46 RAG W
COBLE PETER OF PAUL A 46 RAG W
COBLE ROBERT L A 46 RAG W
COBLE RODDY A 46 ROS W
COBLE SIMON P A 46 RAG W
COBLE WESLEY A 46 ROS W
COBLE WM OF FREDERA 46 COB W
COBLE WM A A 46 COB W
COBLE WM M A 46 RAG W
COBLE WM OF ABRAM A 46 RAG W
COBLE WM OF TOM A 46 COB W
COBLES ALFRED A 19 BE1 B
COBURN ALISON A 46 FRI W
COBURN WILLIAM A 53 GER W
COCHRAN CHARLES P A 25 HAY W
COCHRAN JOSEPH A 24 MID B
COCHRAN SAMUEL A 24 MID B
COCHRAN THOMAS A 24 MID W
COCHRANE SAML A 29 FA1 B
COCKER JOSEPH L A 37 PIN W
COCKS GEO A 19 BE1 B
CODNER JNO C A 19 MOR W
CODY HARMAN A 32 DAV W
CODY JESSE A 32 LOF W
COE JOHN P A 46 GRE W
COE JOHN R A 46 JAM W
COE JOHN W A 46 GRE W
COE SAML F A 46 GRE W
COE WESLEY A 46 GRE W
COFFEY JAMES A 25 PIN W
COFFEY JOHN A 25 PIN W
COFFEY JOHN R A 25 HAY W
COFFEY LEVI A 25 HAY W
COFFEY ROBERT A A 25 HAY W
COFFIELD ALBERT A 37 ROB B
COFFIELD ASTON A 37 MAN B
COFFIELD EDWALD A 37 ROB B
COFFIELD HENRY A 24 EDE B
COFFIELD JAMES T A 24 MID W
COFFIELD JNO W A 24 EDE B
COFFIELD JOHN A 24 EDE W

COFFIELD JOHN A 37 ROB B
COFFIELD JOSEPH A 37 MAN B
COFFIELD JOSEPH B A 37 TA1 W
COFFIELD JOSHUA A 24 MID B
COFFIELD JOSIAH A 24 MID W
COFFIELD MARTIN V A 24 UPP W
COFFIELD MCDOWELL A 37 ROB B
COFFIELD OFFICE A 37 ROB B
COFFIELD RAY A 37 ROB B
COFFIELD REUBIN 24 EDE B
CHALLENGED BY
J R B HATHAWAY CONVICTED
OF LARCENY RECORDS
OF COURT SHOW IT
DID NOT TAKE THE OATH
CONVICTED BEFORE HE HAD
THE RIGHT OF SUFFRAGE
THEREFORE COULD NOT LOSE
WHAT HE NEVER HAD.
TOOK THE OATH AND WAS
ACCEPTED BY THE BOARD
COFFIELD THOMAS K A 37 ROC W
COFFIELD WILLIS A 37 ROB B
COFFIELD WILSON A 37 EDW B
COFFIELD WM A 24 EDE W
COFFIN ABNER A 46 JAM W
COFFIN C C A 46 JAM W
COFFIN L S R 46 JAM W
NAME LINED OUT
MAGISTRATE BEFORE WAR AND
DURING WAR COULD NOT TAKE
THE OATH WITH THE WORD
VOLUNTARY OMITTED
IS REJECTED
COFFIN WM S A 46 GRE W
COFIELD GILBERT A 37 ROB B
COFIELD JNO T A 24 MID W
COFIELD NORFLEET A 37 ROB B
COFIELD WARREN R 44 OXF B
RES STATE 7 MONTHS REJ
COGDELL ALLAN A 26 BLA W
COGDELL DANIEL A 29 LOC B
COGDELL JOHN A 28 6TH B
COGDELL PERRY A 26 BLA W
COGDELL THOMAS A 26 BLA W
COGDELL TONEY A 28 01A B
COGDELL WASHINGTON A 28 7TH B
COGDELL WILTON A 29 LOC B
COGDON HILARY A 28 7TH B
COGG JACOB D A 46 MCL W
COGGIN JOHN A 32 JAC W
COGGINS R A 32 JAC W
COGHILL C Y A 39 SPE W
COGHILL HAYWOOD A 44 OXF B
COGHILL HENDERSON A 44 OXF B
COGHILL J F A 44 HEN W
COGHILL K W A 44 KIT W
COGHILL LEVI A 44 HEN B
COGHILL RUFUS A 44 OXF B
COGIN W R A 32 JAC W
COGINS F A 32 JAC W
COGINS G W A 32 JAC W
COGINS WILLIAM A 32 JAC W
COGSDELL WM A 29 GRA B
COGWELL VINCENT A 44 OXF B
COHAN BLUNT A 37 WHI B
COHAN MINGO A 37 ROC B
COHEN A D A 28 02N W
COHN ADOLPH A 28 12T W
COKE GEO H A 24 EDE W
COKER HENRY T A 37 HOL W
COKER WILLIAM A 37 ROB W
COLBERT ALBERT A 46 GRE B
COLBERT E CHAL A 28 11T W
CERT LIVES NOW IN
BEAUFORT CO
COLBERT J H A 39 JOR W
COLBERT JOHN P A 39 JOR W
COLBY JAMES J A 40 DA1 W
COLDER JAMES A 29 FA1 W
COLDWELL JESSE A 46 GRE B
COLDWELL R NEWTON A 46 GRE W
COLDWELL S P A 40 STO W
COLE BAZEL A 35 CYP W
COLE H P A 29 FA1 W
COLE ISAAC A 24 EDE W
COLE JAS A 29 FA1 B
COLE JESSE A 35 CYP W
COLE JOHN L DR A 46 GRE W
COLE JOHNE A 46 GRE B
COLE JOSEPH A 35 CYP W
COLE JOSHUA A 35 CYP W
COLE MAJOR A 28 04A B
COLE ROBERT N A 35 CYP W
COLE THOMAS A 32 JAC W
COLE THOMAS A 35 LIM W
COLE THOMAS CALVIN EA 46 HIG B
COLE WILLIAM A 44 SAS B
COLE WILLIAM F A 35 CYP W
COLE WM A 29 FA1 B
COLE WM P A 32 JAC W
COLEMAN ALBERT A 44 SAS B
COLEMAN ARMSTEAD A 37 ROC B
COLEMAN D B A 29 FLE W
COLEMAN ELI A 25 HAY W
COLEMAN GEORGE A 25 HAY W
COLEMAN H E A 44 SAS W
COLEMAN HENRY A 28 9TH B
COLEMAN ISAAC A 53 GER B
COLEMAN J P A 25 HAY W
COLEMAN JOSEPH A 40 DEC B
8 MOS RES 1ST SEPT 1867
COLEMAN LENON A 28 9TH B
COLEMAN THAD A 46 GRE W
COLEMAN THOMAS A 46 GRE B
COLEMAN W H A 25 HAY W
COLEMON JAMES A 44 SAS B
COLETRAIN SANDY A 46 ROS B
COLEY ABRAM A 44 DUT B
COLEY C F A 44 DUT W
COLEY EDMOND A 44 DUT W
COLEY G W A 44 DUT W
COLEY GEORGE A 28 03A B
COLEY GILBERT A 44 DUT B
COLEY GREEN A 39 JOR W
COLEY HENRY A 28 04A B
COLEY ISHAM A 44 DUT W
COLEY J A A 44 DUT W
COLEY J B A 44 DUT W
COLEY JOHN P A 46 COB W
COLEY JOSEPH A 44 DUT B
COLEY JULIUS B A 46 COB W
COLEY LEWIS A 32 THO B
COLEY LOVIT A 39 JOR W
COLEY PLEASANT A A 39 JOR W
COLEY RICHARD A 44 DUT W
COLEY T B A 44 DUT W
COLEY W D A 44 DUT W
COLEY WM R A 46 COB W
COLEY WM SR A 44 DUT W
COLIER ISAAC J A 46 GRE W
COLLENS GEORGE F A 53 GER B
COLLETT JAMES A 32 POS W
COLLETT JOHN A 32 POS W
COLLEY ABRAHAM A 28 8TH B
COLLEY ARREN A 39 JOR W
TRNS TO WARREN CO
APRIL 10TH
COLLIER SAML P A 28 01A W
COLLIFER BENJAMIN A 24 EDE W
COLLIGAN WM A 28 02N W
IS NOT NATURALIZED BUT
TAKES OATH TO THAT EFFECT
COLLINS A J A 39 JOR W
COLLINS A N A 32 BRO W
COLLINS AMOS A 29 FA1 B
COLLINS ANDREW A 28 7TH W
COLLINS BERRY A 39 HAY W
COLLINS BRYANT A 28 6TH B
COLLINS CHARLES A 53 GER B
COLLINS CHARLEY A 28 03A B
COLLINS CHAS A 28 03A B
COLLINS CLIFTON A 39 JOR W
COLLINS DAVID A 24 EDE B
COLLINS DAVID A 37 TA1 W
COLLINS DAVID A 53 LA1 B
COLLINS EDMUND A 30 IND W
COLLINS ELISHA A 39 HAY W
COLLINS FELSON A 44 OXF B
COLLINS FRANK A 39 SPE B
COLLINS GEORGE A 28 05B B
COLLINS HARDY A 46 GRE B
COLLINS HARRY A 26 SHE B
COLLINS HENRY A 19 BE1 B
COLLINS HENRY A 29 FA1 B
COLLINS HENRY A 37 MAN B
COLLINS ISAAC A 24 EDE B
COLLINS J S A 26 SHE W
COLLINS JAMES A 19 BEI B
COLLINS JAMES P A 39 JOR W
COLLINS JOHN A 53 FAI B
COLLINS JOHN B A 39 JOR W
COLLINS JOHN JR A 53 LA1 B
COLLINS JOHN SR A 53 LA1 B
COLLINS JOHN W A 29 MON W
COLLINS JOHNSTON A 26 GOF W
COLLINS JONES A 28 04B B
COLLINS JOSEPH A 19 BE1 B
COLLINS JOSEPH A 24 EDE B
COLLINS JOSEPH A 39 JOR W
COLLINS JOSEPH A A 28 04A B
COLLINS JOSIAH A 39 DAV W
COLLINS LEROIS A 35 MAG W
COLLINS LEVY A 39 SPE B
COLLINS LEWIS A 28 04A B
COLLINS MILLS A 24 EDE B
COLLINS MOUNTGOMMRY A 53 GER B
COLLINS PETER A 39 JOR W
COLLINS ROBERT E A 39 JOR W
COLLINS SAMUEL A 24 EDE B
COLLINS SAMUEL A 37 HOL B
COLLINS SAMUEL A 53 GER B
COLLINS SOLOMON A 24 EDE B
COLLINS THOMAS A 19 BE2 B
COLLINS W G A 39 LOU W
COLLINS W T A 39 JOR W
COLLINS WASHINGTON A 24 EDE B
COLLINS WELLINGTON A 53 LA1 B
COLLINS WILLIAM A 26 CAR W
COLLINS WM A 28 04A B
COLLINS WM A 46 GRE W
COLLINS WM G JR A 39 LOU W
COLLOTT WILLIAM A 32 DAV W
COLLY DIAMOND A 28 6TH B
COLLY L R A 46 SUM W
COLMAN WM A 29 FLE W
COLPEPER JETHROE D A 37 SHA W
COLSON WM S A 46 GRE W

COLTON LARINCE A 28 04A B
COLTRAIN GEORGE A 46 ROS B
COLTRAIN HENDERSON A 32 THO B
COLTRAIN LINDSAY A 46 ROS W
COLTRANE JOSEPH A 46 JAM W
COLVIN CHAS A 29 CAR B
COLVIN D B A 29 CAR W
COLVIN DUBLIN A 29 CAR B
COLVIN GLASCOW A 29 CAR B
COLVIN JAMES A 29 CAR B
COLVIN JNO A A 29 BLA W
COLVIN NATHAN A 29 CAR B
COLVIN NATHAN A 29 FLE B
COLVIN ROBT A 29 CAR B
COLVIN SADDY A 29 CAR B
COLVIN THOS A 29 CAR B
COLVIN WM A 29 CAR B
COLWELL AARON A 35 MAG B
COLWELL ALBERT S A 35 ROC W
COLWELL PETER A 35 KEN B
COLY ABRAM C A 46 COB W
COLYER R W A 29 CAR W
COLYER ROBT A 29 CAR W
COLYER ZAC A 29 CAR W
COMBEST WM M A 40 STO W
COMBS BALEY A 53 LA1 B
COMBS WILLIAM N A 30 POW W
COMEGAR STEPHEN A 53 GER B
COMINS BRYANT A 28 04A B
COMINS WM A 28 04A B
COMMAC SAML A 28 6TH W
COMMACK GEORGE A 28 6TH W
COMMANDER ALFRED A 28 7TH B
COMMANDER FRANK A 28 05A B
COMMANDER HENRY A 28 16T B
CERTIF GIVEN. RESIDENCE
NEW BERN CRAVEN CO. NC
CONALLY MALCOM A 29 FA2 B
CONARD WILLIAM A 32 DAV B
CONAWAY ALBERT A 28 04B W
CONAWAY GEORGE W A 72 SWA W
CONAWAY LUKE A 28 04A B
CONAWAY THOMAS R A 72 SWA W
CONE G W A 39 DAV W
CONE GELBERT A 39 DAV W
CONE W W A 39 DAV W
CONEGA CHARLES A 28 7TH B
CONEGA ISAAC A 28 7TH B
CONEGA LEWIS A 28 7TH B
CONEGA REDDICK A 28 10T B
CONGLETON ABRAHAM A 19 BE1 W
CONGLETON ABRAHAM A A 19 BE1 W
CONGLETON BENJ C A 19 BE1 W
CONGLETON JAMES A 19 BE1 W
CONGLETON W H A 19 BE1 W
CONGLITON D W A 19 BE1 W
CONKLIN JOHN A 53 GER W
CONLEY NELSON A 29 SEV B
CONN ANDREW A 39 SPE W
CONN EDWARD A 39 PUG W
CONNEGA ABRAM A 28 03A B
CONNEGA ADDICK A 28 04A B
CONNEGA ALFRED A 28 04A B
CONNEGA IRVING A 28 04A B
CONNEGA JACOB A 28 6TH B
CONNEGA JOHN A 28 6TH B
CONNEGA JOSEPH A 28 04A B
CONNEGA LEVI W A 28 03A B
CONNEGA LOUIS A 28 6TH B
CONNEGA MARTIN A 28 03A B
CONNEGA THOS A 28 05A B
CONNEL DAVID A 40 CAN W
CONNEL ROBERT A 40 CAN W
CONNEL SIMON A 46 HIG W
CONNELL A S A 39 PUG W
CONNELL GEORGE A 44 FIS W
CONNELL J C A 44 OXF W
CONNELL J H A 40 CAN W
CONNELL WYATT A 44 OXF W
CONNER ARISTOTTLE A 19 HAR W
CONNER BRYAN W A 28 9TH W
CONNER GEORGE D A 28 9TH W
CONNER JAMES A 26 SHE W
CONNOR CAESAR A 28 04B B
CONNOR JOHN D A 28 8TH W
CONNOR SHADE A 35 KEN B
CONNOR W H A 28 10T W
CONNOWAY DAVID A 19 NEW W
CONOWAY LAWRENCE A 37 HIC B
CONRAD (?) WM A 32 THO W
CONRAD ALEX. A 32 THO W
CONRAD D W A 32 DAV W
CONRAD E F A 32 DAV W
CONRAD H H A 32 DAV W
CONRAD H L CHAL A 32 DAV W
CONRAD JAMES N A 32 DAV W
CONRAD JAS M A 32 DAV W
CONRAD JOHN H A 32 DAV W
CONRAD JOSEPH A 32 DAV W
CONRAD JOSEPH FOR R 32 DAV W
HOLDING OFFICE OF MAGIS-
TRATE BEFORE THE WAR AND
ENCOURAGING MEN TO ENLIST
CONRAD S S A 32 DAV W
CONWAY A B A 39 FRA W
CONYERS HILLIARD A 39 GRI B
CONYERS JOHN R A 39 FRE W
CONYERS NELSON A 39 LOU B
TRNS BY AFF
FROM GRANVILLE
CO TO LOUISBURG
CONYERS NELSON A 44 FOR B
CONYERS RICHARD A 39 HAR W
CONYERS SAML A 39 HAR B
CONYERS SAVE R 39 FRA B
CONVICTED BY COMPENT
JURRY OF BURGLARY
CONYERS THOS H A 39 LOU W
COOCK AARON A 46 KIN W
COOCK HENRY A 46 KIN W
COOD J M A 46 FRI W
COOD M S A 46 FRI W
COOK A B A 19 NEW W
COOK A B A 39 FRA W
COOK AARON A 26 PEE W
COOK AARON A 26 WAR W
COOK ARON A 26 WAR W
COOK ARTHUR A 39 LOU W
COOK BENJAMIN A 39 JOR W
COOK BRYANT A 29 FLE W
COOK C M A 38 FRE W
COOK C S A 29 FA1 W
COOK CHARLES A 46 KIN B
COOK CHARLES A A 35 MAG W
COOK CHAS A 28 05A B
COOK CHAS B A 29 FA1 W
MILLITIA OFFICER AFTER-
WARDS ENG IN REBELLION
COOK D L A 32 JAC W
COOK DANIEL A 46 HIG B
COOK ELIAS A 46 GIB W
COOK ELIJAH A 39 LOU W
COOK EUGINE T A 39 PUG W
COOK FRANK A 39 FRA B
COOK GEORGE A 46 KIN W
COOK H M A 35 FAI W
COOK HARRISON A 26 WAR W
COOK HENRY A 39 HAY B
COOK HENRY A 46 GRE B
COOK HOWELL A 39 FRA W
COOK ISIAH A 25 SHO W
COOK J B A 29 FA1 W
COOK J E A 26 CAR W
COOK J T A 29 CED W
COOK JAMES A 26 PEE W
COOK JAMES D A 39 DAV W
COOK JAMES H A 39 DAV W
COOK JESSE A 46 MCL W
COOK JOHN A 26 WAR W
COOK JOHN A 39 DAV W
COOK JOHN A 46 FRI B
COOK JOHN F A 46 JAM W
COOK JOHN H A 46 KIN W
COOK JORDAN JR A 39 JOR W
COOK JORDAN SR A 39 JOR W
COOK JOS A A 39 HAR W
COOK JOSEPH A 39 JOR W
COOK JOSHUA P A 39 SPE W
COOK JOSIAH A 29 FLE W
COOK JOURDAN A 37 PEN B
COOK MADISON A 40 FER W
COOK MADISON A 46 ROS W
COOK MARTIN A 46 MCL W
COOK N A 26 WAR W
COOK PRESTON JR A 38 FRE W
COOK R O A 29 FLE W
COOK R P A 39 PUG W
COOK ROBT A 29 FLE W
COOK ROBT A 39 FRA B
COOK S A A 46 KIN W
COOK SAML A 28 04B W
COOK SAMPSON A 37 SPA B
COOK SANDERS A 19 MOR B
COOK SHEM A 44 BEA W
COOK SIMON A 46 MON B
COOK STEPHEN A 46 JAM B
COOK THOMAS E R 46 FRI W
WAS A CONSTABLE
AND MAGISTRATE BEFORE
WAR AIDED IN REBELLION
COULD NOT TAKE THE OATH
WITH THE WORD VOLUNTARY
OMITTED REJECTED
COOK THOMAS W A 39 DAV W
COOK THOS A 39 FRA B
COOK THOS H A 46 JAM W
COOK THOS Y A 44 FOR W
COOK VINCENT A 39 HAR W
COOK W H A 28 01A W
COOK WASH A 39 HAR B
COOK WASHINGTON A 32 JAC W
COOK WILLIAM A 37 EDW B
COOK WILLIAM R A 35 ROC W
COOK WM A 29 FA1 W
COOK WM P A 46 GIB W
COOKE ADAM A 39 GRI B
COOKE ANTHONY A 39 FRE B
COOKE BEN A 39 FRE B
COOKE BRIANT A 39 FRE B
COOKE CLATON A 39 FRA B
COOKE EPHRAIM A 39 HAR B
COOKE H H A 44 BRA W
COOKE HENDERSON A 38 FRE B
COOKE HENRY A 39 HAR B
COOKE ISAAC A 39 FRE B
COOKE ISAIAH A 38 FRE B
COOKE J J A 44 BRA W
COOKE JERRY A 39 FRA B
COOKE JOHN A 39 FRA B

COOKE SQUIRE A 44 BRA B
COOKE STEPHEN A 38 FRE B
COOKE THOS A 38 FRE B
COOKE WALLACE A 39 FRE B
COOLEY ALLEN A 39 GRI B
COOLEY FENNER A 39 HAR W
COOLEY G M A 39 HAR W
COOLEY JOHN A 39 GRI B
COOLEY NOFLET A 39 HAR W
COOLEY NORPHLET A 39 LOU W
TRNS FROM HARRIS X
ROADS TO LOUISBURG
COOLEY S H A 28 01A W
COOLEY W J A 29 FA1 W
COOLEY WM A 39 GRI B
COOLY THOS S A 39 HAR W
COONRAD ANDREW A 32 THO W
BY CERTIF
COONRAD PORTER A 32 THO B
COOPE WILSON W A 30 KNO W
COOPER A N A 26 CAR B
COOPER ALBERT A 44 HEN B
COOPER ALDEN A 28 15T B
COOPER ALEX A 44 OXF W
COOPER ALEXANDER A 37 ROC B
COOPER ALLEN A 28 05A B
COOPER ALLEN A 39 JOR B
COOPER BANISTER A 46 MON B
COOPER BEN A 44 OXF B
COOPER BENJAMIN A 28 16T B
COOPER BENJAMIN R A 35 KEN W
COOPER BRYON A 53 SWA B
COOPER BURTON A 37 ROC B
COOPER CHAS A 44 OXF B
COOPER CHESLEY A 44 OXF B
COOPER CLAIBORN A 35 KEN B
COOPER CYRUS A 44 OXF B
COOPER D Y A 44 OXF W
COOPER DANL A 28 04A B
COOPER DAVID A 28 03A B
COOPER DOCTOR A 35 KEN B
COOPER DONAM A 35 KEN B
COOPER DORHAM A 35 KEN B
COOPER EDMOND A 44 OXF B
COOPER EDWARD A 44 HEN B
COOPER ELI A 37 MAN B
COOPER ELIJAH A 28 15T B
COOPER FREDERICK A 28 14T B
COOPER GASTON A 35 CYP B
CERT. TO KENANSVILLE
APRIL 16, 1868
COOPER GEORGE A 39 SPE W
COOPER GREEN A 44 OXF B
COOPER HARRY A 44 OXF B
COOPER HARRY A 44 YXS B
COOPER HENRY A 28 11T B
COOPER HENRY A 44 TAR B
COOPER HENRY A A 32 CLE W
COOPER ISAAC A 28 11T B
COOPER ISAAC A 35 KEN B
COOPER JAMES A 28 04B B
COOPER JAMES A 28 05A B
COOPER JAMES A 44 HEN B
COOPER JAMES A 44 YXS B
COOPER JAS A 44 OXF B
COOPER JOHN A 28 04A B
COOPER JOHN A 28 05A B
COOPER JOHN A 35 CYP B
COOPER JORDAN A 44 HEN B
COOPER JOSEPH A 30 MOY W
COOPER JOSEPH A 44 OXF B
COOPER KITT A 44 OXF B
COOPER LAWRENCE A 44 RAG B
COOPER LEWIS A 28 05A B
COOPER LEWIS A 32 CLE B
COOPER MOSES JR A 35 KEN B
COOPER MOSES SR A 35 KEN B
COOPER NED A 28 04B B
COOPER NORVELL A 44 OXF B
COOPER OLIVE A 44 YXR B
COOPER PERRY A 37 ROC B
COOPER PHILIP A 44 YXS B
COOPER PRINCE A 28 03A B
COOPER RICHARD A 35 KEN B
COOPER RICHARD A 37 PIN B
COOPER RICHD A 28 04A B
COOPER ROBERT A 44 HEN B
COOPER ROBT A 39 SPE W
COOPER ROMULUS A 28 05B B
COOPER S A A 30 KNO W
COOPER SAM A 39 JOR B
COOPER SHOCK A 44 HEN B
COOPER SOLOMON JR A 35 KEN B
COOPER SOLOMON SR A 35 KEN B
COOPER T S A 28 01A W
COOPER THOMAS A 29 LOC W
COOPER THOMAS A 37 PIN B
COOPER TIM A 44 YXS B
COOPER TURMIC A 44 SAS B
COOPER W A A 30 KNO W
COOPER WATT A 44 OXF B
COOPER WILLIAM A 39 JOR B
COOPER WILLIAM A 39 SPE W
COOPER WILSON A 30 KNO W
COOPER WM A 28 16T W
COOPER WM G A 28 13T W
COOPPER SAMUEL A 37 MAN B
COPE JOE A 39 DAV B
COPELAND ALEXANDER A 24 UPP W
COPELAND ANDREW A 24 UPP W
COPELAND B T A 46 FRI W
COPELAND BENJAMIN A 24 UPP B
COPELAND BENJAMIN D A 24 UPP W
COPELAND DAVID L A 24 UPP W
COPELAND DEMSEY A 24 UPP W
COPELAND ELISHA A 24 UPP W
COPELAND HENRY A 39 JOR B
COPELAND JAMES A 24 UPP W
COPELAND JERRY A 24 EDE B
COPELAND JOHN W A 24 UPP W
COPELAND JOSEPH A 24 UPP W
COPELAND JOSEPH G A 24 UPP W
COPELAND JOSEPH JR A 24 EDE W
COPELAND JOSIAH A 24 UPP W
COPELAND JOSIAH R A 24 UPP W
COPELAND MILES A 24 MID B
COPELAND ROBT B A 24 UPP W
COPELAND THOMAS A 24 UPP W
COPELAND THOS E A 19 BE1 W
COPELAND THOS J A 24 UPP W
COPELAND WM A 39 FRA B
COPELANDS SLAAT A 28 03A B
COPELIN JAMES M A 28 04A B
COPELIN JOHN A 26 SHE W
COPELIN JOHN A A 26 GOF W
COPES GEORGE A 28 05A B
COPES JACOB A 28 10T B
COPES PARSON A 28 10T B
COPES WILLIAM A 28 10T B
COPLAND WM A 26 GRI W
COPLE A K A 32 LEE W
COPLEY GEO W A 37 ROB W
COPLY SIMSON A 32 JAC W
COPPAGE W B JR A 39 JOR W
COPPEDGE G W A 39 DAV W
COPPEDGE HENRY A 39 JOR B
COPPEDGE JIRDON A 39 DAV W
COPPEDGE MOSES A 39 DAV B
COPPEDGE PERRY A 39 JOR B
COPPEDGE ROBT A 39 JOR B
COPPEDGE T C A 39 DAV W
COPPEDGE W B JR A 39 DAV W
COPPEDGE WILLIAM A 39 JOR B
COPPER JAMES A 72 SWA B
COPPIDGE ELLICK A 39 DAV B
COPPLE JOSHUA A 32 LEE W
CORBEL MALICHI A 30 POW W
CORBERT ROBT A 28 03A B
CORBET JORDAN A 26 SHE B
CORBET W S A 26 SHE W
CORBETT C A 26 BOR B
CORBETT HENRY A 29 SEV W
CORBIN LEONARD A 29 FLE B
CORDELL J C A 25 HAY W
CORDELL J M A 44 HEN W
CORDEN PRINCE A 53 SWA B
CORDEN SYLVESTER A 28 05A B
CORE ALFRED A 28 7TH B
CORE WILLIAM A 46 HIG W
CORL DANIEL W A 46 GRE W
CORLIE ISAAC A 37 WEB B
CORNELISON J F CHALA 32 DAV W
RECONSIDERED
CORNELIUS ISAAC A 24 UPP B
CORNELL JOHN W A 19 POR W
CORNEY ROBERT A 72 SWA W
CORNISH ADAM A 32 BRO B
CORNISH JAMES A 32 DAV W
CORNWELL A C A 26 SHE W
CORNWELL A H A 26 SHE W
CORNWELL RHANDERSON A 26 CAR B
CORPREE WASHINGTON A 30 MOY B
CORRAN JAMES A 30 COI W
APRIL 10, 1868
CORSBIE GEORGE A 46 COB B
CORSBIE JOHN A 46 COB W
CORSBIE WM W A 46 COB W
CORSLIE DAVID M A 46 COB W
CORSLIE LEMUEL E A 46 COB W
COSAND JOHN A 46 JAM W
COSNER ARON A 40 SAN W
COSNER JOSEPH A 40 SAN W
COSTEN JAMES A 35 WOL W
COSTIN HARDIE A 40 DA1 B
COSTIN JAMES A 35 MAG W
COSTNER ABSALOM A 40 FER W
COSTNER ELI S A 40 DA1 W
COSTNER HENRY M A 40 DA1 W
COSTNER JACOB A 40 DEC W
COSTNER JOSEPH A 40 DA1 W
COSTNER MOSES
(RAN'S SON) A 40 DA1 B
COSTNER MOSES JR A 40 DA1 B
COSTNER RANDALL A 40 DA1 B
COSTNER RUFUS O A 40 DA2 W
COSTNER SIMON P A 40 MAU W
COSTNER SYLVANNUS P A 40 DA1 W
COSTNER WILLIAM M A 40 DA2 W
COTLER HENRY A 37 ROB W
COTLER W H A 35 CYP W
COTRELL D D A 39 LOU W
COTRELL THOMAS A 39 HAY W
COTTEN CHARLES A 37 WHI B
COTTEN JOHN W A 37 TA1 W
COTTEN ROBERT R A 37 TA1 W
COTTER JOHN A 30 IND B
COTTER Q T A 30 CUR W
COTTLE BRANTLEY A 35 CYP W
COTTLE J D A 35 LIM W

COTTLE J W A 35 LIM W
COTTLE WILLIAM T A 35 ISL W
COTTLE WILLIAMS A 35 LIM W
COTTMAN CALEB A 29 FA1 B
COTTON ALFRED A 37 WHI B
COTTON ANDREW A 37 WEB B
COTTON BRISTON A 37 SHA B
COTTON CALVIN A 37 PEN B
COTTON CORNEALOUS A 37 PEN B
COTTON DAVID A 29 GRA B
COTTON DAVID A 32 DAV B
COTTON DEMPSEY A 37 TA1 B
COTTON FREDRICK A 37 SHA B
COTTON GEN'L WASHINGTON A 37 PEN B
COTTON GEORGE A 28 03A B
COTTON GILBERT R 37 PEN B
CONVICTED
COTTON GREEN A 37 PEN B
COTTON IRVING A 37 TA1 B
COTTON JACKSON A 37 TA1 B
COTTON KAJER A 37 PIN B
COTTON LEWIS A 37 HIC B
COTTON MULLIN A 37 WHI B
COTTON NICHOLAS A 30 MOY B
COTTON VIRGIL A 37 PEN B
COTTON WHITMOND A 37 PEN B
COTTON WHITWELL A 28 04A B
COTTON WILLIAM A 44 OXF B
COTTON WILLIAM H A 53 GER B
COTTON WM A 28 05A B
COTTRELL ARMSTEAD A 44 OXF B
COTTRELL JAMES A 44 HEN W
COTWELL JOHN W A 46 GRE W
COUCH J Q A A 46 FRI W
COUCH WM F A 46 FRI W
COUD HENRY A 19 BE1 B
COUNCIL ANDREW A 29 FA1 B
COUNCIL BAKER A 37 HIC A
COUNCIL CIP A 29 GRA B
COUNCIL CUFFIE A 29 FA1 B
COUNCIL HENRY A 29 FA1 B
COUNCIL ISHAM A 29 FA1 B
COUNCIL JAMES A A 29 GRA W
COUNCIL JAS A 29 FA1 B
COUNCIL JNO M A 29 GRA W
COUNCIL JOSH A 29 FA1 B
COUNCIL JOSIAH A 37 HIC A
COUNCIL N A 29 LOC B
COUNCIL SAM'L A 29 FA1 B
COUNCIL WESLEY A 29 FA1 B
COUSEN CALVIN H A 46 ROS W
COUSINS ARTHER A 44 KIT B
COUSINS DANIEL A 44 HEN B
COUSINS ELIJAH R 44 OXF B
RES STATE SINCE
10 APRIL REJ
COUSINS HARRISON A 44 HEN B
COUSINS HENRY A 44 HEN B
COUSINS ISAAC A 44 HEN B
COUSINS J A A 44 FOR W
COUSINS JOHN A 46 FRI B
COUSINS LARKIN R A 44 YXR B
COUSINS WILIE A 44 SAS B
COUSINS WILLIAM A 44 KIT B
COUSINS WM A 44 YXS B
COVE J H A 29 LOC W
COVEL JESSE A 53 GER B
COVEL MARTIN A 53 SWA B
COVEL WILLIAM A 53 GER B
COVEL ZION A 53 GER B
COVELL DAVID A 53 GER B
COVELL JAMES A 28 04A B
COVINGTON A M A 26 GRI B
COVINGTON ANDW A 29 FA1 B
COVINGTON BETTS A 29 SEV B
COVINGTON C S A 26 GRI B
COVINGTON CHARLES A 40 CAN B
COVINGTON FRANK A 28 6TH B
COVINGTON HARRY A 26 GRI B
COVINGTON J T A 26 SHE W
MILITIA OFFICER &
ENGAGED IN REBELLION
COVINGTON LUKE A 28 04B B
COVINGTON W D H A 26 BLA W
COVIRT HENRY A 28 03A W
COWAN J G A 29 CED W
COWAN T B A 29 CED W
COWARD BENJAMIN A 28 7TH W
COWARD E M A 25 SHO W
COWARD J A A 25 SHO W
COWARD J V A 25 SHO W
COWARD LUKE A 28 04A B
COWARD ROBERT A 28 7TH B
COWEL AMOS A 28 16T W
COWELL GEORGE A 30 IND B
COWELL ISAAC A 30 CUR B
COWELL JAMES F A 30 IND W
COWELL JOHN A 30 IND B
COWELL JOHN B A 30 IND B
COWELL JOSEPH F A 30 IND W
COWELL MILES A 30 IND B
COWELL SOLOMON CHALR 30 IND W
DOES NOT ACT FOR HIMSELF
HAVING A GUARDIAN NOT
ENFRANCHISED BY RECON-
STRUCTION ACT.
COWEN JACK A 32 TYR B
COWEN WM A 29 FA1 B
COWLES CHARLES L A 35 MAG W
COWLES T M A 28 02N W
COWLS JOHN A 30 POW W
COWPER SAMPSON A 28 9TH B
COX A L A 32 THO W
COX ALPHEUS A 30 MOY W
COX AMOS A 19 MOR B
COX B B A 30 MOY W
COX BENJAMIN A 28 8TH B
COX BURL A 37 ROC B
COX CHRIS B A 28 6TH W
COX DAVID A 28 6TH B
COX DAVID A 35 LIM B
COX DAVID A 39 FRA B
COX DENNIS A 28 05A B
COX E J A 28 7TH W
COX E S A 30 MOY W
COX EDWARD A 30 IND W
COX ELI E A 40 SAN W
COX FRANKLIN A 28 03A B
COX GREEN A 28 05A B
COX HARRY A 24 EDE B
COX ISAAC A 24 EDE B
COX J B A 30 TUL W
COX J J A 46 FRI W
COX JABEZ A 30 IND W
COX JACK A 53 LA2 B
COX JAMES A 30 MOY W
COX JAMES A 32 DAV W
COX JAMES W A 28 02N W
COX JARREMIAH T A 53 LA1 W
COX JNO A A 44 OXF W
COX JNO T A 30 MOY W
COX JOHN CHAL A 32 JAC W
FOR HOLDING OFFICE OF
MAGISTRATE BEFORE AND
DURING THE WAR. RECON
COX JOHN A 30 IND W
COX JOHN A 32 DAV W
COX JOHN L A 30 MOY W
COX JOHN W A 30 TUL W
COX JOHNATHAN A 53 LA1 W
COX JONATHAN E A 46 FRI W
COX LEWIS A 28 03A B
COX LEWIS H A 72 SWA W
COX LODWICK A 28 11T B
COX ORANGE A 28 7TH B
COX PATRICK A 40 CAN W
COX PRINCE A 28 01A B
COX PROVIDENCE JR A 24 EDE B
COX PROVIDENCE SR A 24 EDE B
COX RICHARD P A 53 GER W
COX ROBERT A 28 7TH B
COX SHARP K A 30 TUL W
COX SILAS A 28 7TH B
COX SMITH A 30 MOY B
COX SPARROW A 28 05A B
COX STARLING A 37 ROC B
COX W C A 30 MOY W
COX WILLIAM A 32 JAC W
COX WILLIAM H A 53 GER W
COX WILLIAM S A 53 LA1 W
COZART B H A 44 KNA W
COZART BRAWDY A 44 LED W
COZART CALVIN A 44 KNA B
COZART CHARLES A 44 LED B
COZART DANIEL A 44 KNA B
COZART DAVID A 44 LED B
COZART DUDLEY A 44 TAR B
COZART GILBERT A 44 LED B
COZART J H A 44 KNA W
COZART SAMUEL A 44 KNA B
COZART W W A 44 DUT W
COZART WILLIAM A 44 KNA B
CRAB JOHN A 19 HAR B
CRABTREE J L A 44 OXF W
CRABTREE WM C A 44 OXF W
CRADLE DINSON A 53 GER B
CRADLE GEORGE L A 53 LA1 W
CRADLE HENRY W A 53 FAI W
CRADLE HOSEA A 53 FAI B
CRADLE JOHN J A 53 GER W
CRADLE MOSA A 53 GER B
CRADLE NOAH A 28 10T B
CRADLE SAMUEL L A 53 FAI B
CRADLE WILLIAM D A 53 GER W
CRADLES ABRAHAM A 53 GER B
CRAFFORD T D A 44 OXF W
CRAFT ADAM P A 40 BLA W
CRAFT JOHN P A 40 BLA W
CRAFT WILLIS A 44 OXF W
CRAIG J M A 40 SAN W
NAME LINED OUT
CRAIG J S A 40 SAN W
CRAIG JAMES M A 40 DA2 W
CRAIG JOHN H A 40 FER W
CRAIG R H A 40 SAN W
CRAIG ROBT Y A 40 SAN W
CRAIG WM A 40 SAN W
CRAIGE WILLIAM A 26 WAR W
CRAIGIE HUGH A 46 GRE W
CRAIN JOHN A 46 GRE W
CRAIN JOHN H R 40 FER W
NAME LINED OUT WAS AN
ADJ ON MILITIA STAFF BEFORE
THE WAR ALSO WARDEN OF POOR
BEFORE THE WAR. HELD AS COM-
MISSIONER GAVE AID & COMFORT
TO THE ENEMY.
DID NOT QUALIFY IS REJECTED

CRAIN RODGER A 29 FA1 W
CRAMER JOHN T A 32 THO W
CRAMMELL GEORGE A 37 EDW B
CRANCE WILLIAM A 26 CAR W
CRANDAL PETER A 28 05A B
CRANDLE JOHN A 19 BE1 B
CRANE HENRY A 28 04A B
CRANE JAMES A 30 COI W
CRANE THOMAS A 30 POP W
CRANFORD B F A 32 JAC W
CRANFORD J D A 32 JAC W
CRANFORD JOEL A 32 JAC W
CRANFORD L D A 32 JAC W
CRANFORD RICHARD A 32 JAC W
CRANFORD T G A 32 JAC W
CRANFORD WILLIAM A 32 JAC W
CRANFORD WILLIS A 32 JAC W
CRANK CALEB T CHAL R 30 POW W
CONSTABLE PRIOR TO WAR
CRANK LEVI A 30 NOR W
CRATCH BENJ A 28 01A B
CRATCH GEORGE A 28 16T B
CRAVEN D H A 32 BRO W
CRAVEN DANIEL A 32 BRO W
CRAVEN E P A 32 BRO W
CRAVEN J W A 32 BRO W
CRAVEN O A A 32 BRO W
CRAVEN SAMUEL A 32 BRO W
CRAVEN SAMUEL A 32 THO W
CRAVER A A 32 CLE W
CRAVER ANDREW A 32 YAD W
CRAVER BRANAN A 32 TYR B
CRAVER DAVIDSON A 32 SHE W
CRAVER GEO N A 32 SHE W
CRAVER J H A 32 CLE W
CRAVER JOHN A 32 TYR B
CRAVER W F A 32 SHE W
CRAVOR JOHN N A 32 DAV W
CRAVOR L P A 32 DAV W
CRAWFORD A VIRGEL A 28 04A B
CRAWFORD ADAM A 28 05A B
CRAWFORD BALAAM A 28 04A B
CRAWFORD BANTON A 28 04A B
CRAWFORD CHAS A 28 05A B
CRAWFORD CHAS W H A 28 01A B
CRAWFORD DALLOUS H A 99 BUS W
CRAWFORD DANIEL A 40 RHY B
CRAWFORD E G A 26 SHO W
CRAWFORD EDWARD A 40 FER B
CRAWFORD EPHRAIM A 28 03A B
CRAWFORD F F A 28 04A B
CRAWFORD GUSTUS A 32 DAV B
CRAWFORD HENRY A 40 FER B
CRAWFORD ISAAC A 40 FER B
CRAWFORD J F A 25 SHO W
CRAWFORD J H A 44 HEN B
CRAWFORD J M A 25 SHO W
CRAWFORD J W A 25 HAY W
CRAWFORD JAMES A 25 HAY W
CRAWFORD JAMES A 44 TOW B
CRAWFORD JAMES L A 37 PIN W
CRAWFORD JOAB L A 25 HAY W
CRAWFORD JOHN F A 25 HAY W
CRAWFORD JULIUS A 99 BUS W
CRAWFORD LAWSON A 40 FER B
CRAWFORD P JR A 25 SHO W
CRAWFORD WILLIAM A 72 SWA B
CRAWFORD WM A 29 FA1 B
CRAWFROD FRANK A 28 14T B
CRAWLEY RAMSON A 29 SEV B
CRAY DAVID A 28 04B B
CREACEMOND JOSEPH A 40 RHY W
CREAL SION A 29 ROC W

CREASY ALFRED A 24 EDE B
CREASY FRAMCIS A 24 EDE B
CREASY JOHN A 24 EDE B
CREDLE ANSON A 53 SWA W
CREDLE BENJAMIN F A 53 SWA W
CREDLE DANIEL A 53 GER B
CREDLE DAVID A 53 SWA B
CREDLE DAVID M A 53 SWA B
CREDLE ELIJAH A 53 SWA B
CREDLE FRANKLIN A 53 SWA W
CREDLE GEORGE F A 53 SWA B
CREDLE GEORGE V A 53 SWA W
POLITICAL DISABILITIS
REMOVED
CREDLE GEORGE W A 53 SWA B
CREDLE GRIFFIN A 53 SWA W
CREDLE JAMES A 53 SWA B
CREDLE JOHN 53 SWA B
STRICKEN OUT
APRIL 17 1868
CREDLE JOHN E A 53 SWA W
CREDLE MARTIN A 53 SWA B
CREDLE MINGSELS A 53 GER W
CREDLE OSCAR A 53 SWA B
CREDLE PETER A 53 SWA B
CREDLE THOMAS M A 53 GER W
CREDLE TILLSON G A 53 SWA W
CREDLE WELDEN A 53 SWA B
CREDLE WILLIAM G A 53 SWA B
CREDLES SAMUEL G A 53 GER W
CREDLES TILSON A 53 GER W
CREDLES WILLIAM M A 53 GER W
CREECH EZEKIEL M A 99 BUS W
CREECY ROBERT A 19 BE1 W
CREEKMORE JOSIAH A 30 IND W
CREEKMUR JNO F A 30 TUL W
CREEKMUR SAML E A 30 TUL W
CREEKMUR WILSON A 30 IND W
CREEL JOHN A 35 ALB W
CREESY AUGUSTUS R A 24 EDE W
CREESY JACOB A 24 EDE B
CHAL BY J R B HATHAWAY
SEE HIS OATH
CONVICTED BEFORE HE HAD THE
RIGHT OF SUFFRAGE THEREFORE
COULD NOT LOSE WHAT HE NEVER
HAD FINAL REVISION ACCEPTED
CREESY SPENSER A 24 EDE B
CREIGHTON ALBERT A A 24 EDE B
CREIGHTON WM A 24 EDE W
CREIL CHAS B A 29 ROC W
CRENSHAW PRINCE A 44 HEN B
CRENSHAW WM M A 39 LOU W
CREWS A A 44 OXF W
CREWS A W A 46 KIN W
CREWS ALBERT A 46 KIN B
CREWS B F A 44 OXF W
CREWS BARTLETT A 44 SAS B
CREWS CARVELL A 44 OXF B
CREWS D G A 44 LED W
CREWS DOCTOR A 44 SAS B
CREWS E H A 44 LED W
CREWS E T A 44 OXF W
CREWS E W A 44 OXF W
CREWS EDMAND A 46 FRI B
CREWS HARRY A 44 LED B
CREWS HORACE A 44 OXF B
CREWS HOROD A 44 OXF B
CREWS ISAAC A 44 OXF B
CREWS J A A 44 LED W
CREWS J B A 44 OXF W
CREWS JAMES A 44 OXF B
CREWS JAS A 44 OXF W

CREWS JAS A A 44 OXF W
CREWS JOHN A 44 OXF B
CREWS JOHN M A 46 KIN W
CREWS M C A 46 KIN W
CREWS MERIDETH A 44 OXF W
CREWS R L A 44 OXF W
CREWS R T A 44 LED W
CREWS S A A 44 DUT W
CREWS SAM A 44 OXF B
CREWS SOLOMAN A 44 OXF B
CREWS SOLOMAN A 44 RAG B
CREWS T J A 44 FIS W
CREWS THOMAS A 44 OXF B
CREWS TIM A 44 OXF B
CREWS W B A 44 LED W
CREWS WILLIAM A 44 OXF B
CREWS WILLIAM W A 46 KIN W
CREWS WM F A 44 RAG W
CREWS WM H A 44 RAG W
CRIBB KYLE A 29 FLE W
CRICHTON H R A 39 LOU W
CRICKMAN J G A 39 DAV W
CRIDDLEBOW THOMAS A 32 BRO W
CRIDER JEREMIAH A 46 SUM B
CRIER NOBLE G A 46 GRE W
CRIMMOND ABRAHIM A 32 YAD B
CRISCO J H A 32 THO W
CRISFIELD JAMES A A 32 DAV B
CRISP BENJAMIN A 37 PIN W
CRISP JESSIE A 37 HIC A
CRISP JOHN D A 37 PIN W
CRISP JOHN W A 37 HIC A
CRISP SILAS E A 37 WEB W
CRISP STEPHEN W A 37 TA2 W
SPARTA
CRISP THOMAS N A 37 PIN W
CRISPY DANL A 28 05A B
CRIST LEWIS A 37 WHI W
CRISTENBERRY A B A 40 CAN W
CRITCHELOW
GENL JACKSON A 28 04A B
CRITCHER A J A 44 OXF W
CRITCHER ANSON A 44 OXF W
CRITCHER J A A 44 OXF W
CRITCHER JNO H A 44 KIT W
CRITCHER W H A 44 OXF W
CRITCHER WM A 44 OXF W
CRITSFEEZER DANIEL A 32 CLE W
CRITTENDEN RICHARD A 46 GRE W
CRITZ WILLIAM A 26 SHE W
CRITZPHIZER HENRY A 32 SHE W
CROCKER BENJAMIN A 38 FRE W
CROCKER ELIJAH A 39 JOR W
CROCKER MADISON A 28 04A B
CROCKER T J A 39 FRE W
CROCKER WILLIAM L A 99 BUS W
CROCKET RANSOM A 40 RHY B
CROELL ROBERT A 37 ROC B
CROFIET JOSEPH A 28 15T B
CROITES J W A 25 SHO W
CROKER BENJIMIN F A 37 TA1 W
CROMADAY GREEN A 19 BE1 B
CROMWELL ARCHER A 37 PIN B
CROMWELL DANIEL A 37 PEN B
CROMWELL ISRIAL A 37 TA1 B
CROMWELL JAMES A 37 TA1 B
CROMWELL LEWIS A 37 EDW B
CROMWELL WILLIAM A 37 SHA B
CROMWELL WILLIS A 37 EDW B
CROOK WILLIAM A 32 COT W
CROOM BRIGHT A 19 BE1 B
CROOM JOHN F A 35 MAG W
CROOM MINGO G A 28 03A B

CROOM SAML A 28 04A B
CROOM SIMON A 28 03A B
CROOM WILLIAM H A 35 MAG W
CROOME JAMES D A 29 FA2 W
CROOMS HAYWOOD A 35 WOL B
CROOMS SIMON A 28 03A B
CROSLAND S T A 29 FA1 W
CROSLIN JNO A 29 GRA B
CROSS ABRAHAM A 32 COT W
CROSS ABRIHAM CHALA 32 LOF W
FOR HOLDING OFFICE OF
MAGISTRATE BEFORE AND
DURING THE WAR. RECON.
CROSS ALEXANDER A 32 JAC B
CROSS ANDERSON A 32 COT W
CROSS DAVID A 32 JAC W
CROSS GEORGE A 32 COT W
CROSS GEORGE W A 32 COT W
CROSS H J A 32 LOF W
CROSS J A A 32 LOF W
CROSS J M A 32 DAV W
CROSS JOHN A 32 COT W
CROSS LENARD A 32 COT W
CROSS MOSES A 32 DAV W
CROSS PETER A 32 COT W
CROSS PETER A 32 JAC W
CROSS SILAS A 32 JAC W
CROSS SMITH A 32 COT W
CROSS SPRUCE A 32 LOF W
CROTTS AMOS A 32 LOF W
CROTTS DAVID A 32 DAV W
CROTTS DAVID A 32 DAV W
CROTTS EDWARD A 26 WAR W
CROTTS EMANUEL A 26 WAR W
CROTTS EMANUEL SR A 26 WAR W
CROTTS JOHN A 32 DAV W
CROTTS JOHN H A 26 WAR W
CROTTS MICHAEL A 32 DAV W
CROTTZ ANDREW A 32 SHE W
CROTTZ JACOB A 32 SHE W
CROTTZ VALENTINE A 32 POS W
CROUCH C A 32 BRO W
CROUCH GEORGE A 32 BRO W
CROUCH M F A 32 BRO W
CROUCH QUDER JOHN ? A 32 SHE W
CROUCH R H A 46 HIG W
CROUGE GEORGE A 37 PEN B
CROUSE G W A 32 DAV W
CROUSE HAMILTON A 32 CLE W
CROUSE J RUFUS R 40 MAU W
NAME LINED OUT
MILITIA OFFICER BEFORE
THE WAR AND GAVE AID &
COMFORT TO THE ENEMY *
REJECTED
CROUSE JOHN A 32 LEE W
CROUSE JOSEPH A 32 COT W
CROUSE WILEY A 32 COT W
CROW BRYANT A 46 JAM B
CROW J O A 26 PEE W
CROW J S A 26 PEE W
CROW JAMES W A 46 JAM W
CROW JOHN A 40 FER W
CROW JOHN D A 40 FER W
CROW JORDAN A 35 FAI B
CROW JOSEPH A 40 FER W
CROW L S A 29 FLE W
CROW R A A 26 BOR W
CROWDER ABRAM A 26 BLA W
CROWDER ALLAN A 26 BLA W
CROWDER ANDERSON A 26 BLA W
CROWDER BARTLETT A 26 GRI W
CROWDER G F A 26 GRI W

CROWDER HERMAN A 37 ROC W
CROWDER ISAAC A 99 BUS W
CROWDER J N A 25 TUS W
CROWDER J W A 26 PEE W
CROWDER JACOB A 99 BUS B
CROWDER JAMES A 26 GRI W
CROWDER JOHN A 26 GRI W
CROWDER JOHN K A 26 BLA W
CROWDER JOSEPH A 99 BUS B
CROWDER M W A 26 GRI W
CROWDER MATTHEW A 26 BLA W
CROWDER S A A 26 GRI W
CROWDER SANDY A 44 TOW B
CROWDER T F A 26 GRI B
CROWDER W J A 25 TUS W
CROWDER W N A 26 GRI W
CROWDER WILLIAM A 25 TUS W
CROWDER WILLIAM D A 99 BUS W
CROWDER WILLIE A 39 DAV W
CROWELL ALBERT A 19 BE1 B
CROWELL P J A 46 JAM W
CRUDUP A D A 39 GRI W
CRUDUP ALFRED A 39 GRI B
CRUDUP ALFRED A 39 HAY B
CRUDUP ANDY A 44 KIT B
CRUDUP CHARLES A 44 KIT B
CRUDUP CLARKE A 44 KIT B
CRUDUP EMSLY A 39 GRI B
CRUDUP HILLIARD A 44 KIT B
CRUDUP ISAAC A 39 HAY B
CRUDUP J B A 44 KIT W
CRUDUP JERRY A 39 GRI B
CRUDUP JOHN A 39 GRI B
CRUDUP JORDAN A 44 KIT B
CRUDUP JUKE A 39 HAY B
CRUDUP NATHAN A 39 GRI B
CRUDUP OSBORN A 39 GRI B
CRUDUP PATRICK A 44 KIT B
CRUDUP POLADO A 44 BRA B
CRUDUP ROBIN A 39 FRA B
CRUDUP SAM A 39 LOU B
CRUDUP SOLOMON A 44 KIT B
CRUMLLEY THOMAS A 29 FA2 B
CRUMP ALEXANDER A 32 YAD B
CRUMP GEORGE A 32 DAV B
CRUMP GILES A 32 YAD B
CRUMP JAMES E A 32 YAD B
CRUMP JOHN A 32 DAV B
CRUMP MOSES A 46 GRE B
CRUMP O C A 44 HEN W
CRUMP ORSBON A 37 ROC B
CRUMP PLEASANT A 32 TYR B
CRUMP WATSON B A 46 GRE W
HERE 9 MOS ACCEPTED
CRUMPLE HENRY C A 37 SHA W
CRUMWELL MAJER A 37 HOL B
CRUTCHFIELD JAMES A 46 KIN W
CRUTCHFIELD MILTON A 46 SUM W
CRUTHIS WILLIAM A 46 HIG W
CUCHIN THOMAS A 37 ROB W
CUFFEE WILLIAM A 30 MOY B
CULBERSON JERRY A 46 GRE B
CULBERSON WESLEY A 46 GRE W
CULBRETH BURNICE B A 35 MAG W
CULBRETH DUNCAN J A 29 ROC W
CULBRETH GREEN A 44 TOW W
CULBRETH H C A 29 CED W
CULBRETH HENRY A 29 CED W
CULBRETH HUGH A 29 FA1 B
CULBRETH ISAAC A 29 FLE W
CULBRETH JAMES A 29 CED B
CULBRETH JNO A 29 FA1 W
CULBRETH JNO A 29 FLE W

CULBRETH JNO A 29 LOC W
CULBRETH N A 29 FLE W
CULBRETH SALOMON A 29 ROC W
CULBRETH W H A 29 FLE W
CULBRETH WILLIAM A 35 WAR B
CULBRETH WM A 29 FLE W
CULBRITH W H A 29 CED W
CULBUTH JOB A 32 THO W
CULLAM DAVID A 30 MOY W
CULLEN Z T A 30 IND W
CULLENS EDGAR A 24 UPP B
CULLEPHIN WILLIAM A 19 HUN W
CULLEY BENJAMIN A 28 10T B
CULLEY WILLIAM A 28 10T B
CULLIN WM A 46 GRE B
CULLINS ALFRED A 46 JAM B
CULLY ABRAM A 28 04A B
CULLY WASHN A 28 01A B
CULP DAVID H A 26 GOF W
CULP JAMES H A 26 GOF W
CULPEPER S D A 30 MOY W
CULPEPPER HARDY A 30 MOY W
CULPEPPER HENRY A 30 MOY W
CULPEPPER J M A 39 DAV W
CULPEPPER JESSEE A 30 MOY W
CULPHIER JORDON A 19 BE1 W
CULPPEPER JAMES A 30 MOY W
CUMING W E A 46 FRI W
CUMING W M A 46 FRI W
CUMINGHAM J C A 46 KIN W
CUMINGS LEMUEL A 46 KIN B
CUMINGS NEWTON A 46 KIN W
CUMMINGS DENNIS A 46 KIN B
CUMMINGS JAMES M A 35 WAR W
CUMMINGS JAMES T A 35 MAG W
CUMMINGS NELSON A 46 GIB B
CUMMINS BENJAMIN A 46 MON B
CUMMINS CALVIN A 46 MCL B
CUMMINS ENOS A 46 GRE W
CUMMINS GEORGE A 46 SUM B
CUMMINS HENRY A 28 10T B
CUNNINGGIM J A A 39 LOU W
CUNNINGHAM ABRAHAM A 32 THO B
CUNNINGHAM ANTHONY A 46 MON B
CUNNINGHAM BENAJMIN A 46 MON B
CUNNINGHAM CLIMER A 46 MON B
CUNNINGHAM DANIEL A 44 HEN B
CUNNINGHAM FRANK A 46 GRE B
CUNNINGHAM G W A 44 KIT W
CUNNINGHAM HARPER A 46 MON B
CUNNINGHAM JAS C A 46 GRE W
CUNNINGHAM JOHN A 46 GRE W
CUNNINGHAM JOSEPH A 37 MAN B
CUNNINGHAM ROBERT A 19 MOR B
CUNNINGHAM WM A A 39 PUG W
CUPMAN A T A 32 DAV W
CURELL ALBERT A 53 FAI W
CURGERLIN D A 19 MOR B
CURL SIMON A 37 ROC B
CURLE GEORGE W A 30 ROA W
APRIL 15, 1868
CURLES THOMAS A 30 ROA W
CURLES WILLIAM A 30 NOR W
CURREN DAVID A 44 YXR B
CURREN EDWARD A 44 YXR B
CURREN J W A 44 OXF W
CURREN JAS A 44 OXF W
CURREN JNO B A 44 YXR W
CURREN JOSEPH F A 35 MAG W
CURREN MITCHELL A 44 KNA W
CURREN RALPH A 44 YXS W
CURREN W R A 44 YXS W
CURREN W S A 44 YXS W

CURRIE D A A 29 SEV W
CURRIE DANL C A 29 FA1 W
CURRIE J H A 29 SEV W
CURRIE JOHN B A 35 WAR W
CURRIE JOHN C A 29 QUW W
MILITIA OFFICER AFTER-
WARDS GAVE AID AND COM-
FORT TO THE REBELLION
HAS TAKEN AN OATH TO
SUPPORT CONSTITUTION
OF THE U.S.
CURRIE JOHN M R 29 SEV W
DIST CONST BEFORE REBE
AFTERWARDS GAVE AID
AND COMFORT TO ENEMIES
OATH NOT TAKEN
CURRIE WM J A 29 QUW W
CURRIEN JOHN A 44 YXS B
CURRIEN ROBERT A 44 YXS B
CURRIN ANDERSON A 44 SAS B
CURRIN C F A 44 SAS W
CURRIN CHESLEY A 44 SAS W
CURRIN E T A 44 RAG W
CURRIN J M A 44 OXF W
CURRIN JAS P A 44 YXR W
CURRIN L W A 44 OXF W
CURRIN R L A 44 YXR W
CURRIN R S A 44 YXR W
CURRIN S J A 44 RAG W
CURRIN STEPHEN A 44 SAS W
CURRIN W A A 44 OXF W
CURRY A M C A 29 FA1 W
CURRY CALVIN A 32 DAV W
CURRY EVANDER A 29 FA1 W
CURRY HECTOR A 29 QUW B
CURRY JAMES A 32 DAV W
CURRY JOB A 40 DEC B
CURTIS A W A 25 HAY W
CURTIS AARON A 44 OXF B
CURTIS ABRAHAM A 39 FRA B
CURTIS ALEX A 44 KNA B
CURTIS ANDREW A 25 HAY W
CURTIS BERRY A 46 GRE W
CURTIS BERRY A 46 GRE W
CURTIS CALDWELL C A 46 GIB W
CURTIS CHARLES A 44 OXF B
CURTIS CYLUS L A 44 OXF B
CURTIS EDWARD A 37 MAN B
CURTIS ELIAS A 44 LED B
CURTIS F N M A 46 MON W
CURTIS GEO H A 28 04A W
CURTIS HAWKINS A 44 OXF B
CURTIS HENRY A 44 OXF B
CURTIS JAMES A A 46 RAG W
CURTIS JAMES H A 46 GRE W
CURTIS JOSEPH A 44 HEN B
CURTIS LONDEN A 44 KIT B
CURTIS PAUL A 44 KNA B
CURTIS PETER A 44 KNA B
CURTIS PETER A 44 LED B
CURTIS SIMEON A 44 YXS B
CURTIS SMITH A 44 TOW B
CURTIS TERRELL A 44 OXF B
CURTIS THOMAS A 44 OXF B
CURTIS THOS J A 29 FA1 W
CURTIS W H A 46 GRE W
CURTIS WM A 44 YXR B
CURY DANIEL A 32 DAV B
CURY SAMUEL A 46 FRI B
CURY SHEPARD A 32 DAV W
CURY SMITH A 32 DAV W
CURY WILLIS A 32 DAV B
CUSHING ISAAC L A 37 EDW W

CUSTIS P R A 28 04A W
CUSTIS ROBERT A 28 01A B
CUTCHAN JAMES A 37 ROB W
CUTCHEN FRANK A 37 MAN B
CUTCHIN ELIJAH A 37 HIC A
CUTCHIN HENRY A 37 ROB B
CUTCHIN ISAAC A 37 ROB B
CUTCHIN JOHN A 37 EDW B
CUTCHIN JOSIAH A 37 ROB W
CUTCHIN NORFLEET A 37 ROB W
CUTCHINS GREEN A 37 MAN B
CUTCHINS THOMAS A 37 ROB B
CUTERAL SYLVESTER A 53 LA1 W
CUTERRAL JESSE A 53 LA1 W
CUTHBERT E C A 28 02N W
CUTHBERT EDGAR G A 28 02N W
CUTHRELL BENJAMIN F A 28 13T W
CUTHRELL GEO W A 28 13T W
CUTHRELL THOMAS A 28 13T W
CUTLER EDWARD A 28 05A B
CUTLER LYCURGUS H A 28 01B W
CUTLER WM A 44 YXR W
CUTREL CHARLES A 53 SWA W
CUTREL ELEAZAR R A 53 LA2 W
CUTREL WILLIAM A 53 FAI W
CUTRELL BURAGE A 53 FAI W
CUTRELL DAVID C A 53 FAI W
CUTRELL ELEAZAR A 53 FAI W
CUTRELL JACKSON A 53 GER W
CUTRELL ROBERT H A 53 FAI W
CUTRELL SETH A 53 LA1 W
CUTRELL STEPHEN A 53 FAI W
CUTRELL WILLIAM R A 53 FAI W
CUTS URIAH A 44 ISL W
CUTTER SYLVESTER A 28 05B B
CUTTS JNO G A 44 OXF W
CUYKENDAL W B A 28 02N W

- D -

DABBINS LEWIS A 26 BLA W
DAGITT SAM'L A 26 PEE B
DAGITT SQUIRE A 26 PEE B
DAGWOOD T A 26 CAR B
DAIL ALFRED A 35 WOL B
DAIL BRYAN A 35 WOL B
DAIL HENRY A 35 WOL B
DAIL JAMES A 35 WOL B
DAIL JULIUS V A 35 FAI W
DAIL LUTHER A 35 WOL B
DAIL MARSHAL A 35 GLI W
DAIL THOMAS A 35 FAI W
DAILEY B D A 25 TUS W
DAILEY JOHN J A 26 MOO W
DAILY BENJAMIN B A 53 HAT W
DAILY J K A 29 FA2 W
DAILY JACK A 29 FA1 B
DAILY JNO A 29 FA1 B
DAILY JOHN A 30 MOY W
DAILY MARTEN A 30 CUR B
DAILY WM A 28 04A B
DALBY E A 44 BEA W
DALBY HENRY A 44 LED B
DALBY SILAS A 44 DUT B
DALE DANIEL A 24 MID W
DALE ELISHA A 24 MID W
DALE HENRY S A 29 FA1 W
DALE ISAH A 24 MID W
DALE J F M A 25 TUS W
DALE J M A 25 HAY W
DALE JULIOUS A 25 HAY W
DALE NATHAN A 24 UPP W
DALE THOMAS A 25 HAY W
DALE WILLIAM A 24 MID W
DALMAN HENRY A 28 01B W

DALSON JAMES A 28 05A B
DALTON BENJAMIN A 46 GRE B
DALTON CALEB A 46 KIN B
DALTON JAMES A 46 MON B
DALTON JEREMIAH A 46 KIN B
DALTON WM A 26 CAR W
DALY WILLIAM A 32 CLE W
DAMERON ALFRED A 40 DA1 B
DAMERON CHARLES A 26 GOF B
DAMERON EPHAM A 26 GOF B
DAMERON HICKS CHAL A 26 BOR B
ACCUSED OF THEFT--
NOT SUSTAINED
DAMERON JAMES T R A 40 DEC W
DAMERON JOHN A 26 BOR W
DAMERON JOHN A 40 STO W
DAMERON JOHN D A 40 MAU W
DAMERON R A 26 BOR B
DAMERON SOLOMON A 40 DEC B
DAN'L JNO A 29 FA1 B
DANCEY SHEDRICK A 37 MAN B
DANCY ALFRED A 37 EDW B
DANCY ALFRED A 37 ROC B
DANCY ALLEN A 37 PEN B
DANCY ANDERSON A 37 TA1 B
DANCY AUSTIN A 37 TA1 B
DANCY BANJAMIN A 37 TA1 B
DANCY BENJAMIN A 37 TA2 B
DANCY CALEB A 37 ROC B
DANCY CAREY A 37 PIN B
DANCY CHARLES A 29 LOC B
DANCY CICERO A 37 TA1 B
DANCY CRAFFORD A 37 ROC B
DANCY DALLAS A 37 TA1 B
DANCY DANIEL A 37 PEN B
DANCY DAVID A 37 TA1 B
DANCY EDMUND A 37 PIN B
DANCY EDWARD A 37 TA1 B
DANCY ELANDER A 37 TA1 B
DANCY EVERETT A 37 TA1 B
DANCY FRANK A 37 TA1 B
DANCY GEORGE A 37 EDW B
DANCY GEORGE A 37 TA1 B
DANCY GLEN A 37 TA1 B
DANCY GRANVILLE A 37 ROC B
DANCY HARRIS A 37 PIN B
DANCY HENDERSON A 37 PEN B
DANCY HENRY A 37 PIN B
DANCY HENRY A 37 TA2 B
DANCY HEYWOOD A 37 TA1 B
DANCY HILLIARD A 37 ROC B
DANCY JACKSON A 37 TA1 B
DANCY JACOB A 37 EDW B
DANCY JERRY A 37 EDW B
DANCY JOHN A 37 EDW B
DANCY JOHN A 37 TA1 B
DANCY JOHN C A 37 TA1 B
DANCY JOURDAN A 37 TA2 B
DANCY KADER A 37 TA1 B
DANCY LEWIS A 37 PIN B
DANCY LEWIS A 37 TA1 B
DANCY LUKE A 37 TA1 B
DANCY MOSES A 37 ROC B
DANCY NED A 37 PEN B
DANCY RIDICK A 37 TA1 B
DANCY ROBERT A 37 EDW B
DANCY RUBIN A 37 PIN B
DANCY SAMUEL A 37 EDW B
DANCY SAMUEL A 37 TA1 B
DANCY SANDY A 37 TA1 B
DANCY SILAS A 37 ROC B
DANCY TASTUS A 37 TA1 B
DANDY TURNER A 37 HIG B

DANFORD WILLIAM C A 37 WEB W
DANFORT JACOB A 37 WEB B
DANIEL AARON A 37 ROC B
DANIEL ANDREW A 46 MON B
DANIEL ARMSTEAD A 44 SAS B
DANIEL BENJAMIN T A 30 ROA W
DANIEL BEVELLY A 44 OXF W
DANIEL BEVERLEY A 44 SAS B
DANIEL CHARLES A 44 TAR B
DANIEL CHESLEY A 44 SAS B
DANIEL CHESLEY A 44 YXS W
DANIEL DAVID A 44 OXF B
DANIEL DAVID A 44 TAR B
DANIEL DENNIS A 44 YXS B
DANIEL EDMUND A 44 YXS B
DANIEL ELIJAH A 44 YXR W
DANIEL ETHERIDGE G A 30 ROA W
DANIEL F D A 46 SUM W
DANIEL FRED A 44 KIT B
DANIEL FRED A 44 OXF B
DANIEL GEO S A 44 YXR W
DANIEL GEORGE A 44 RAG B
DANIEL GORDON A 44 SAS B
DANIEL HANSEY A 37 HIG B
DANIEL HENRY A 30 ROA B
DANIEL HENRY A 37 ROC W
DANIEL HENRY A 44 OXF B
DANIEL HENRY A 44 TAR B
DANIEL ISAH A 44 KIT B
DANIEL JAMES A 44 SAS B
DANIEL JAMES A 44 YXS B
DANIEL JAMES O JR A 35 SMI W
DANIEL JAMES O SR A 35 SMI W
DANIEL JAS B A 44 SAS W
DANIEL JEFF A 44 TAR B
DANIEL JOHN B A 46 MON W
DANIEL JOHN H A 37 PIN W
DANIEL JOHN T A 30 ROA W
DANIEL JOHN W A 32 SHE W
DANIEL JORDON A 44 YXS B
DANIEL JOSEPH A 44 HEN B
DANIEL JOSEPH A 44 SAS B
DANIEL JOSEPH A 44 YXS W
DANIEL JOSEPH G A 30 ROA W
DANIEL JOSEPH M CHALA 30 ROA W
KEEPER OF LIGHTHOUSE
PRIOR TO THE WAR
DANIEL JUNIUS A 44 LED B
DANIEL LAWSON A 44 YXS B
DANIEL MOORE A 46 SUM W
DANIEL MORRIS S A 44 YXR W
DANIEL MOSES A 44 FOR B
DANIEL PRINCE A 37 ROC B
DANIEL R J A 44 HEN W
DANIEL R M A 44 YXS W
DANIEL RICE A 35 MAG B
DANIEL RICHD A A 44 YXS W
DANIEL RUBIN A 44 SAS B
DANIEL RUSMUS A 44 SAS B
DANIEL SAML A 44 OXF W
DANIEL SAMUEL M A 30 ROA W
DANIEL SANDY A 37 ROC B
DANIEL SILAS A 29 FA2 B
DANIEL STEPHEN A A 44 ISL W
DANIEL T L A 44 KNA W
DANIEL TAMY A 37 HOL B
DANIEL THOMAS A 44 YXS B
DANIEL THOMAS S A 53 HAT W
DANIEL THOMAS W A 30 ROA W
DANIEL THOS B A 44 OXF W
DANIEL W ? A 32 THO W
DANIEL W H A 44 RAG W
DANIEL WASHINGTON A 44 HEN B

DANIEL WHITFIELD A 44 TOW B
DANIEL WILLIAM A 44 SAS B
DANIEL WILLIAM R 44 SAS B
NAME LINED OUT
FOR FELONY,
NON RESIDENT
DANIEL WILLIAM B A 30 ROA B
DANIEL WILLIAM J A 30 ROA W
DANIEL WILLIAM J W A 30 ROA W
DANIEL WILLIS A 44 RAG W
DANIEL WM A 44 HEN B
DANIEL WM A 44 TAR W
DANIEL WM A 53 HAT W
DANIEL WM H A 44 SAS W
DANIEL WM R A 44 SAS W
DANIEL WOODSEY A 30 ROA W
DANIEL ZAC A 44 OXF W
DANIEL ZACHRIAH Y A 44 YXS W
DANIELS A E A 32 CLE W
DANIELS ALEXAMDER A 37 ROC B
DANIELS ANDREW J A 37 TA1 B
DANIELS ASA E A 28 17T W
DANIELS BAIRNER A 28 17T W
DANIELS BRIAN A 19 CED W
DANIELS BUTTON A 37 PEN B
DANIELS C M A 32 LOF W
DANIELS CAESAR A 28 11T B
DANIELS CANNY A 28 04A B
DANIELS CHARLES S A 30 ROA W
DANIELS CLEMENT JR A 53 FAI W
DANIELS CLEMENT SR A 53 FAI W
DANIELS DANIEL A 53 GER W
DANIELS EASON A 19 CED W
DANIELS EDWARD J A 28 17T W
DANIELS F H CHAL A 32 JAC W
FOR HOLDING OFFICE OF
DEP SHERIFF BEFORE AND
DURING THE WAR. RECON.
DANIELS GEO W A 19 CED W
DANIELS GEORGE W A 28 16T W
DANIELS HENRY A 28 7TH B
DANIELS HIRAM A 28 15T W
DANIELS ISAAC A 30 ROA B
DANIELS J H A 32 JAC W
DANIELS JAMES A 28 17T W
DANIELS JAMES A 53 SWA W
DANIELS JAMES T A 28 16T W
DANIELS JESSE A 19 CED W
DANIELS JESSE W JR A 53 FAI W
DANIELS JESSE W SR A 53 FAI W
DANIELS JOHN A 19 BE1 B
DANIELS JOHN A 28 15T W
DANIELS JOHN A 28 16T B
DANIELS JOHN D A 19 CED W
DANIELS JOHN D A 53 FAI W
DANIELS JONAH A 28 03A B
DANIELS JOSIAH A 19 CED W
DANIELS NELSON A 28 7TH B
DANIELS NELSON A 32 SHE W
DANIELS RANDOLPH A 19 CED W
DANIELS RICHARD A 28 16T W
DANIELS RICHARD A 53 FAI W
DANIELS RICHARD S A 28 15T W
DANIELS SAMUEL A 53 LA1 B
DANIELS THOMAS A 19 MOR W
DANIELS THOS A 28 02N B
DANIELS THOS A 28 04A B
DANIELS WILLIS A 37 TA1 B
DANIELS WILSON A 28 16T W
DANIELS WILSON A 53 FAI W
DANIELS WILSON W A 28 16T W
DANIELS WOODSON A 32 JAC W
DANKINS JOE A 28 03A B

DANL GEORGE A 44 YXR W
DANOHOO JOHN A 26 BLA B
DANRICH ROBERT A 37 HIC B
DARDEN ESAW A 28 6TH B
DARDEN GAMBER A 28 6TH B
DARDEN GEO F A 28 03A W
DARDEN ISAAC A 28 6TH B
DARDEN JACOB A 28 6TH B
DARIEY OLLIVER A 29 FLE B
DARK ANDERSON A 46 GRE B
DARKS WALLES A 37 SHA W
DARLING JOSEPH W A 19 BE1 W
DARR ADAM A 32 DAV B
DARR GEORGE A 32 TYR W
DARR GEORGE L A 32 THO W
DARR H C A 32 POS W
DARR HENDERSON A 32 POS B
DARR HENRY A 32 DAV W
DARR HENRY A 32 TYR W
DARR JULIUS A 32 DAV W
DARR LEWIS A 32 THO B
DARR OBEDIAH A 32 DAV B
DARR ROBERT A 32 THO B
DARR SAMUEL A 32 THO W
DARR SOCRATES A 32 THO W
DARR SOLOMON A 32 THO W
DARR W A A 32 DAV W
DARRELL N M A 39 GRI W
DARROCH ALEXANDER A 29 MON W
DARROCH ANGUS A 29 MON W
DARROCH DANIEL A 29 MON W
DARROCH DANIEL A 29 SEV W
DARWIN AMZI R 40 DA1 B
NAME LINED OUT
CHAL CAUSE: CONVICTED OF
FELONY AGAINST STATE LAW
TOOK THE OATH REJECTED
DASEN MOSES A 32 DAV B
DASSETT H W A 32 POS W
DAUGHERTY DANL A 28 6TH W
DAUGHERTY EDWARD A 28 6TH W
DAUGHRIDGE ALFRED A 37 ROC W
DAUGHRIDGE JOHN A 37 ROC W
DAUGHRIDGE
JOHNSTON H A 37 ROC W
DAUGHRIDGE REDMOND A 37 ROC W
DAUGHTREY WILLIAM A 29 BLA W
SMITHFIELD JOHNSON CO
BY AFFIDAVIT
DAUGHTRIDGE
WILLIAM M A 37 ROC W
DAUGHTRY DREW A 37 ROC B
DAUGHTRY HENRY H A 37 ROC W
DAUGHTRY JOEL P A 37 MAN W
DAUGHTRY LUKE A 37 ROC B
DAUGHTRY MILLS A 30 MOY B
5-MONTH-RESIDENCE
DAUGHTRY REDIN A 37 ROC W
DAUGHTRY WILLIAM A 37 SHA W
DAUGHTY GEORGE T A 28 16T W
DAUGHTY ISAAC P A 28 16T W
DAUGHTY WM A 28 16T W
DAUTRY JNO A 29 BLA W
DAVAULT GEORGE A 46 MON B
DAVAULT GIDEON R 46 GIB W
NAME LINED OUT HAS NOT
QUALIFIED. WAS AN OVERSEER
OF HIGHWAY BEFORE THE WARE
& ALTHO HE DID NOT ENGAGE IN
THE REBELLION; HIS SONS WENT
INTO THE ARMY VS HIS WILL
THEIR SYMPATHIES WERE WITH
THE SOUTH

DAVENPORT DAVID A 25 SHO W
DAVENPORT FRANKLIN A 40 RHY B
DAVENPORT HARRY A 28 16T B
DAVENPORT J A A 40 CAN W
DAVENPORT J MC A 25 SHO W
DAVENPORT J P A 25 SHO W
DAVENPORT M W A 25 SHO W
DAVENPORT MACK A 28 04A B
DAVENPORT MACK G A 37 HIC A
DAVENPORT MARTIN W A 24 EDE W
DAVENPORT PETER A 40 STO B
DAVENPORT R W A 25 SHO W
DAVENPORT ROBERT A 40 CAN B
DAVENPORT WILLIAM A 24 EDE W
DAVENPORT WM J A 37 EDW W
DAVES JAMES A 26 BLA W
DAVICE SUTTON A 19 HAR B
DAVID GREEN A 44 FOR W
DAVIDS LOT A 28 03A B
DAVIDS LOT JR A 28 03A B
DAVIDS LOT SR A 28 03A B
DAVIDSON AARON A 29 FA2 W
DAVIDSON J S A 40 CAN W
DAVIDSON JESSE A 26 MOU W
DAVIDSON JOS A 46 GRE B
DAVIDSON R R 44 OXF W
RES STATE 7 MOS REJ
DAVIDSON THOMAS A 40 CAN B
DAVIDSON VURGEL A 40 CAN B
DAVIDSON WILLIAM A 26 MOU W
DAVIES DANIEL A 28 8TH W
DAVINS M B A 26 BUR B
DAVIS A F A 19 BE1 W
DAVIS A F A 46 HIG W
DAVIS A H A 26 BLA W
DAVIS A H A 44 HEN W
DAVIS A J A 30 TUL W
DAVIS A M A 32 JAC W
DAVIS A S A 35 WOL B
DAVIS A S A 46 FRI W
DAVIS ABEL A 19 BE1 B
DAVIS ABRAHAM A 39 DAV B
DAVIS ABRAM B A 19 DAV W
DAVIS ALBERT A 39 DAV B
DAVIS ALBERT A 40 DEC W
DAVIS ALEXANDER A 32 CLE W
DAVIS ALEXANDER A 44 SAS B
DAVIS ALEXANDER A 46 KIN W
DAVIS ALEXANDER C A 19 BE1 W
DAVIS ALFORD A 32 DAV W
DAVIS ALFRED A 19 DAV W
DAVIS ALFRED A 28 04A B
DAVIS ALFRED A 44 DUT W
DAVIS ALFRED S A 19 DAV B
DAVIS ALLEN A 19 BE1 W
DAVIS ALLEN A 28 9TH B
DAVIS ALLEN A 29 FA1 W
DAVIS ALLEN A 39 LOU B
DAVIS ALLEN A 44 FOR W
DAVIS ALLEN A 44 SAS B
DAVIS ALLEN JR A 19 BE1 W
DAVIS AMOS A 28 03A B
DAVIS AMOS A 53 GER B
DAVIS ANANIAS A 19 DAV B
DAVIS AND J A 29 ROC W
DAVIS ANDERSON A 44 HEN B
DAVIS ANDREW A 44 RAG B
DAVIS ANDREW JR A 19 BE1 B
DAVIS ANSON G A 19 SMY W
DAVIS ANTHONY A 39 DAV B
DAVIS ANTHONY A 39 SPE B
DAVIS ARCHD A 44 HEN W
DAVIS ARMISTED A 24 EDE B
DAVIS AUSTIN A 39 LOU B
DAVIS AUSTIN A 39 SPE B
DAVIS B P A 26 HOL B
DAVIS BENJAMIN A 19 MOR W
DAVIS BENJAMIN A 19 SMY B
DAVIS BENJAMIN A 28 10T B
DAVIS BENJAMIN A 53 GER W
DAVIS BENJAMIN H A 53 BUR W
DAVIS BENJAMIN P A 19 SMY W
DAVIS BENTON A 39 JOR W
DAVIS BIN A 39 JOR B
DAVIS BRIAN A A 19 BE2 W
DAVIS BRIGHT A 28 04A B
DAVIS BRISTER B A 19 BE1 B
DAVIS BRISTOE A 28 05A B
DAVIS BRYANT A 29 FA1 W
DAVIS BURWELL A 44 OXF B
DAVIS CALVIN A 29 FA1 W
DAVIS CANELLIEM A 53 GER W
DAVIS CEAZER A 19 BE1 B
DAVIS CEPHAS A 40 FER B
DAVIS CHRISTOPHER C A 19 SMY W
DAVIS CICERO W A 19 DAV W
DAVIS CIL A 39 HAY B
DAVIS CLEM A 39 DAV B
DAVIS COLUMBUS A 39 LOU B
DAVIS D J A 29 CED W
DAVIS D L A 46 FRI W
DAVIS DANIEL A 39 DAV B
DAVIS DANIEL W A 19 DAV W
DAVIS DAVID A 28 9TH B
DAVIS DAVID A 37 PEN B
DAVIS DAVID A 39 SPE B
DAVIS DAVID W A 19 SMY W
DAVIS DEMPSY A 29 SEV W
DAVIS DEWIT C A 19 DAV W
DAVIS DICK A 39 DAV B
DAVIS DICK A 39 HAY B
DAVIS DOLPHIN A 38 FRE W
DAVIS DOUBLIN A 53 GER B
DAVIS DUDLEY A 44 HEN B
DAVIS DUKE A 29 FA1 B
DAVIS DUNCAN A 28 05A B
DAVIS DUNCAN A 29 ROC W
DAVIS E A 26 GRI W
DAVIS E A 32 THO W
DAVIS E M A 25 SHO W
DAVIS EDMOND A 28 03B B
DAVIS EDWARD G A 19 DAV W
DAVIS ELIJAH A 19 SMY W
DAVIS ELIJAH A 26 BLA W
DAVIS EPHRAIM A 39 SPE B
DAVIS ESSIC A 44 HEN B
DAVIS EUGENE O A 19 SMY W
DAVIS EVEN A 32 CLE W
DAVIS FRANCIS S A 46 ROS W
DAVIS FRANK A 44 OXF B
DAVIS FREDRICK A 39 DAV B
DAVIS FRIDAY A 39 DAV B
DAVIS G P A 26 WAR W
DAVIS G R A 44 FIS W
DAVIS G W A 29 SEV W
DAVIS GEORGE A 28 03A B
DAVIS GEORGE A 28 04A B
DAVIS GEORGE A 28 10T B
DAVIS GEORGE A 29 CED W
DAVIS GEORGE A 35 ALB B
DAVIS GEORGE A 39 DAV B
DAVIS GEORGE A 44 HEN B
DAVIS GEORGE A 44 OXF B
DAVIS GEORGE O A 39 DAV B
DAVIS GEORGE W A 40 DA1 B
DAVIS GEORGE W A 53 SWA W
DAVIS H C A 29 FA1 W
DAVIS H J A 32 YAD W
DAVIS HANSON A 29 FA2 W
DAVIS HARRIL A 19 BE1 B
DAVIS HARRY 24 EDE B
CHALLENGED
CONVICTED OF LARCENY
COUNTY COURT RECORDS
SHOW IT CONVICTED BEFORE
HE HAD THE RIGHT OF SUF
FRAGE THEREFORE COULD NOT
LOSE WHAT HE NEVER HAD
ACCEPTED IN FINAL REVISION
DAVIS HARRY A 35 ALB B
DAVIS HARRY A 37 ROB B
DAVIS HARRY A 44 SAS B
DAVIS HAYWOOD A 39 HAY B
DAVIS HENRY A 19 DAV B
DAVIS HENRY A 28 04A B
DAVIS HENRY A 28 04A B
DAVIS HENRY A 32 DAV W
DAVIS HENRY A 32 TYR W
DAVIS HENRY A 39 DAV B
DAVIS HENRY A 39 FRA B
DAVIS HENRY A 39 PUG B
DAVIS HENRY A 40 DA1 B
DAVIS HENRY A 44 ISL B
DAVIS HENRY A 46 JAM W
DAVIS HENRY CHAL R 35 MAG B
NOT OF AGE
DAVIS HENRY A A 46 KIN W
DAVIS HENRY D A 53 BUR W
DAVIS HENRY R A 39 DAV B
DAVIS ISAAC A 19 MOR B
DAVIS ISAAC A 30 ROA W
DAVIS ISAAC A 32 DAV B
DAVIS ISAAC A 35 ALB B
DAVIS ISAAC A 35 FAI W
DAVIS ISAAH A 39 HAY B
DAVIS ISAIAH A 19 DAV W
DAVIS ISAIAH A 19 SMY W
DAVIS ISHAM A 30 MOY B
DAVIS ISHAM A 39 HAY B
DAVIS ISHAM A 46 GRE B
DAVIS ISRAEL A 19 BE1 B
DAVIS J A A 44 FIS W
DAVIS J B A 26 GRI W
DAVIS J B A 29 FA1 W
DAVIS J B A 30 TUL W
DAVIS J C A 26 WAR W
DAVIS J C A 28 6TH W
DAVIS J C A 40 SAN W
DAVIS J E A 26 PEE W
DAVIS J H A 40 STO W
DAVIS J H A 44 FIS W
DAVIS J H A 44 SAS W
DAVIS J HENRY A 19 BE1 W
DAVIS J J A 39 LOU W
DAVIS J L A 40 SAN W
DAVIS J M A 26 HOL B
DAVIS J M A 44 BEA W
DAVIS J N A 32 TYR W
DAVIS J P A 44 ISL W
DAVIS J R A 44 HEN W
DAVIS J W A 29 CED W
DAVIS J W A 35 ALB W
DAVIS J W A 40 SAN W
DAVIS J W A 44 LED W
DAVIS J W M A 39 HAR W
DAVIS J W S A 39 PUG W
DAVIS JACK A 53 SWA B
DAVIS JACKSON A 29 FA1 W
DAVIS JACOB A 19 BE2 B

DAVIS JACOB A 19 MOR B
DAVIS JACOB A 28 05A B
DAVIS JAMES A 28 05A B
DAVIS JAMES A 32 JAC W
DAVIS JAMES A 44 YXS B
DAVIS JAMES A 44 YXS B
DAVIS JAMES A 46 ROS W
DAVIS JAMES R 40 DA1 W
NAME MARKED OUT
MILITIA OFFICER BEFORE
THE REBELLION AND GAVE
AID AND COMFORT TO THE
ENEMY * SEE BELOW
REJECTED
DAVIS JAMES * R 40 DA1 W
DAVIS JAMES A A 19 SMY W
DAVIS JAMES B A 19 DAV W
DAVIS JAMES C A 19 BE1 W
DAVIS JAMES G A 19 SMY W
DAVIS JAMES H A 46 MON W
DAVIS JAMES L A 19 MOR W
DAVIS JAMES M A 46 ROS W
DAVIS JAMES O A 39 PUG W
DAVIS JAMES W A 19 DAV W
DAVIS JAMES W A 19 DAV W
DAVIS JAS R A 29 ROC W
DAVIS JASPER A 19 NEW B
DAVIS JEFFERSON A 39 HAY B
DAVIS JEREMIAH A 30 ROA B
DAVIS JERRY A 44 OXF B
DAVIS JERRY A 46 GRE B
DAVIS JESSE A 39 LOU B
DAVIS JESSE A 39 PUG B
DAVIS JESSE H A 19 DAV W
DAVIS JESSE H A 53 LA2 W
DAVIS JNO A 29 FA1 W
DAVIS JNO D A 19 MOR W
DAVIS JNO M A 29 FA1 W
DAVIS JNO O A 29 GRA W
DAVIS JOEL H A 19 BE1 W
DAVIS JOHN A 19 BE1 B
DAVIS JOHN A 19 BE1 B
DAVIS JOHN A 32 DAV B
DAVIS JOHN A 32 LOF W
DAVIS JOHN A 35 WAR B
DAVIS JOHN A 37 ROB B
DAVIS JOHN A 44 YXS B
DAVIS JOHN A 46 FRI W
DAVIS JOHN A 53 LA1 B
DAVIS JOHN A A 28 04A B
DAVIS JOHN B A 32 BRO W
DAVIS JOHN C A 39 SPE W
DAVIS JOHN E A 32 CLE W
DAVIS JOHN EVERETT A 37 EDW B
DAVIS JOHN H A 32 THO W
DAVIS JOHN L A 35 WOL B
DAVIS JOHN P C A 19 BE2 W
DAVIS JOHN S A 37 ROC W
DAVIS JOHN W A 19 BE1 W
DAVIS JONATHAN A 44 FOR W
DAVIS JOSEPH 32 DAV W
NAME LINED THROUGH
DAVIS JOSEPH A 28 04A B
DAVIS JOSEPH A 44 KIT B
DAVIS JOSEPH J A 19 BE1 W
DAVIS JOSEPH P A 19 STR W
DAVIS JOSEPH W A 19 BE1 W
DAVIS JOSHUA A 28 05A B
DAVIS JOSHUA A 44 SAS B
DAVIS JOSIAH B A 19 BE1 W
DAVIS K A 29 CED W
DAVIS KELSEY A 28 9TH B
DAVIS L F A 46 FRI W

DAVIS LARENZO W A 19 DAV W
DAVIS LEWIS A 19 BE1 B
DAVIS LEWIS A 19 SMY B
DAVIS LEWIS A 28 8TH B
DAVIS LEWIS A 32 SHE B
DAVIS LEWIS A 39 SPE B
DAVIS LEWIS A 46 HIG B
DAVIS LORENZA A 39 DAV B
DAVIS M H A 26 GRI W
DAVIS M O A 32 TYR W
DAVIS M S A 39 LOU W
DAVIS MAC A 28 8TH B
DAVIS MACLIN A 28 03A W
DAVIS MADISON A 32 CLE W
DAVIS MALLERY A 24 EDE B
DAVIS MANGRUM A 39 LOU B
DAVIS MARTIN T A 19 SMY W
DAVIS MATTHEW A 28 15T B
DAVIS MELVIN J JR A 19 SMY W
DAVIS MIKE A 32 CLE B
DAVIS MILES A 37 PEN B
DAVIS MONROE A 28 04A B
DAVIS MOSES A 19 BE1 B
DAVIS MOSES A 19 DAV B
DAVIS MOSES A 35 ALB B
DAVIS MOSES A 39 JOR B
CERT NASH CO
DAVIS MOSES A 53 GER B
DAVIS N D A 26 HOL B
DAVIS NAPOLEON A 19 BE1 B
DAVIS NATHAN A 19 MOR W
DAVIS NATHAN A 44 HEN B
DAVIS NATHAN JR A 19 DAV W
DAVIS NATHANIEL A 53 BUR W
DAVIS NATHANUEL A 30 MOY B
DAVIS NED A 39 DAV B
DAVIS NELSON A 28 05A B
CERTIFICATE GRANTED
NEW HANOVER CO
DAVIS OLIVER W A 40 DA1 W
DAVIS OSBORN A 44 OXF B
DAVIS OSCER A 39 DAV B
DAVIS OTAWAY B A 19 SMY W
DAVIS OTTOWAY A 46 ROS B
DAVIS OWEN A 39 LOU W
DAVIS PALMER A 19 BE1 B
DAVIS PETER A 19 BE1 B
DAVIS PETER A 35 ALB B
DAVIS PETER A 39 DAV B
DAVIS PETER A 40 STO B
DAVIS PETER A 44 HEN B
DAVIS PETER A 46 HIG W
DAVIS PHILIP A 26 WAR W
DAVIS POMPEY A 39 DAV B
DAVIS PROCTOR A 19 DAV B
DAVIS R Y A 46 SUM W
DAVIS REUBEN A 37 TA1 B
DAVIS REUBEN W A 19 SMY W
DAVIS RICHARD A 26 BUR W
DAVIS RICHARD A 30 ROA B
REMOVED TO PLYMOUTH
WASHINGTON CO
DAVIS RICHD A 28 6TH W
DAVIS RICHD A 29 FA1 W
DAVIS RICHD A 29 GRA B
DAVIS ROBERSON A 39 DAV B
DAVIS ROBERT A 32 LOF W
DAVIS ROBERT A 37 WHI W
DAVIS ROBT A 28 05A B
DAVIS RODNEY F A 19 STR W
DAVIS RUFFIN A 44 HEN B
DAVIS RUFUS A 39 DAV B
DAVIS RUFUS W A 19 BE1 W

DAVIS S D A 26 BLA W
DAVIS S J A 32 CLE W
DAVIS SAML T A 28 01A B
DAVIS SAMUEL A 19 BE1 B
DAVIS SAMUEL A 19 SMY B
DAVIS SAMUEL A 37 ROC B
DAVIS SAMUEL C A 19 DAV W
DAVIS SAMUEL D A 53 BUR W
DAVIS SAMUEL L A 53 BUR W
DAVIS SAMUEL S A 46 GRE W
DAVIS SAMUEL W A 19 BE1 W
DAVIS SAMUEL W A 19 SMY W
DAVIS SANDY A 40 STO B
DAVIS SETH A 35 ALB W
DAVIS SHADE A 35 ALB B
DAVIS SHEPHARD A 39 SPE B
DAVIS SHEPPARD A 19 BE1 B
DAVIS SIDNEY A 39 DAV B
DAVIS SIMEON A 19 BE1 B
DAVIS SIMON A 28 15T B
DAVIS SOLOMAN A 39 DAV B
DAVIS SOLOMON A 32 BRO W
DAVIS SOLOMON A 46 GRE B
DAVIS SQUARE A 44 YXR B
DAVIS STEPHEN A 29 MON W
DAVIS STEPHEN A 44 LED B
DAVIS SUTTON H A 19 DAV B
DAVIS T C A 19 MOR W
DAVIS T D A 32 LOF W
DAVIS T W A 39 DAV W
DAVIS TENNER A 53 GER B
DAVIS THOMAS A 26 WAR W
DAVIS THOMAS A 32 CLE B
DAVIS THOMAS A 32 JAC W
DAVIS THOMAS A 35 LIM W
DAVIS THOMAS E A 35 LIM W
DAVIS THOMAS H A 19 DAV B
DAVIS THOMAS JR A 26 WAR W
DAVIS THOMAS M A 53 LA1 W
DAVIS THOMAS P A 19 SMY W
DAVIS THOS C A 19 SMY W
DAVIS TIMO A 28 04A B
DAVIS TOM A 39 DAV B
DAVIS TONEY A 19 BE1 B
DAVIS TRAVIS A 32 LOF W
DAVIS UMPHRY A 39 FRA B
DAVIS V J A 44 KIT W
DAVIS VAN A 37 PEN B
DAVIS W C A 46 HIG W
DAVIS W G A 29 GRA W
DAVIS W J A 26 MOO W
DAVIS W R A 39 DAV W
DAVIS WALLACE A 19 DAV W
DAVIS WALLACE W A 19 DAV W
DAVIS WALLICE A 39 JOR B
DAVIS WASHINGTON A 24 EDE B
DAVIS WASHINGTON A 44 HEN B
DAVIS WILLAIM F A 19 BE2 W
DAVIS WILLAIM H A 19 BE2 W
DAVIS WILLIAM A 19 BE1 B
DAVIS WILLIAM A 24 EDE B
DAVIS WILLIAM A 28 04A B
DAVIS WILLIAM A 28 7TH B
DAVIS WILLIAM A 29 CED W
DAVIS WILLIAM A 30 MOY B
8-MONTH-RESIDENCE
DAVIS WILLIAM A 32 BRO W
DAVIS WILLIAM A 32 TYR B
DAVIS WILLIAM A 35 ISL W
DAVIS WILLIAM A 39 LOU B
DAVIS WILLIAM B A 30 ROA B
DAVIS WILLIAM B A 53 GER W
DAVIS WILLIAM H A 32 CLE W

DAVIS WILLIAM H A 39 HAY W
DAVIS WILLIAM M A 25 HAY W
DAVIS WILLIAM W A 53 GER W
DAVIS WILLIE A 44 HEN B
DAVIS WILLIS A 39 LOU B
DAVIS WILLIS G A 19 BE1 W
CERT GIVEN RESIDES AT
SMYRNA REGISTRATION
DAVIS WILSON A 29 QUW W
DAVIS WILSON A 32 COT W
DAVIS WILSON A 32 SHE B
DAVIS WM A 24 EDE W
DAVIS WM A 28 03A B
DAVIS WM A 44 SAS W
DAVIS WM B A 19 DAV W
DAVIS WM H A 29 FA1 B
DAVIS WM J A 29 CAR W
DAVIS WM T A 19 BE1 W
DAVIS WM T A 39 JOR W
DAVIS WYATT A 32 JAC W
DAVIS YORK A 32 CLE W
DAVIS YORK A 35 ALB B
DAVIS ZACK A 44 HEN B
DAVISON JOSIAH A 53 LA1 W
DAVISON SYLVESTER A 53 GER W
DAW JESSE H A 28 16T W
DAW NATHAN A 28 13T W
DAW NELSON A 28 14T W
DAW WILEY A A 28 13T W
DAW ZACHERIAH M A 28 13T W
DAWNS MOSES A 26 PEE B
DAWNS R R A 26 PEE W
DAWNS ROBERT A 26 PEE W
DAWNY WILLIAM A 30 KNO B
DAWS ALBERT A 44 OXF B
DAWS CHARLES A 37 SHA B
DAWS HILLIARD A 37 SHA W
DAWS JOHN A 37 SHA W
DAWS MILES A 37 SHA W
DAWS RUBEN A 37 SHA B
DAWS THOMS A 37 SHA B
DAWSON ABRAHAM A 28 8TH B
DAWSON CAESAR A 28 02N B
DAWSON DANL A 28 03A W
DAWSON GABRIEL A 28 9TH B
DAWSON HUBBARD A 28 05A B
DAWSON ISAAC A 28 04A B
DAWSON JOHN A 28 02N B
DAWSON JOHN A 46 GRE B
DAWSON MOSES A 28 6TH B
DAWSON OLIVER A 28 11T B
DAWSON RICHD A 28 02N B
DAWSON ROBERT A 28 01A B
DAWSON ROBT A 44 ISL B
DAWSON SOUTHEY A 28 03A B
DAWSON THOS A 44 SAS B
DAWSON WILLIAM A 28 16T B
DAY ACIL A 25 SHO W
DAY ADOLPHUS A 44 LED B
DAY BENJ A 44 BRA B
DAY BENJAMIN A 19 BE1 W
DAY DAVID A 44 YXS B
DAY DOCTOR A 44 BRA B
DAY GEO W A 19 CED W
DAY GEORGE A 39 HAY B
DAY HAYWOOD A 44 TAR B
DAY ISAAC N A 44 TAR W
DAY JACKSON A 53 LA1 B
DAY JAMES A 44 OXF B
DAY JAMES A 44 YXS B
DAY JAMES W A 19 CED W
DAY JNO C A 44 YXS W
DAY JOHN A 19 CED W
DAY JOHN A 28 01A B
DAY JOHN A 44 BRA B
DAY JOHN A 44 LED W
DAY JOHN A 44 OXF B
DAY JOHN W A 19 BE1 W
DAY JOSEPH W A 19 CED W
DAY KINDERL A 44 KNA B
DAY NACY A 28 10T W
DAY PREASTLY A 44 BRA B
DAY ROBT A 44 LED B
DAY ROBT A 44 OXF B
DAY ROBT J A 44 YXS W
DAY RUFUS A 25 HAY W
DAY SAMUEL A 44 BRA B
DAY SIMEON A 19 CED W
DAY THOMAS A 44 BRA B
DAY VINCENT A 44 FOR B
DAY WASHINGTON A 44 LED B
DAY WILLIAM A 39 SPE B
DAY WILLIAM A 44 KNA B
DAY WILLIAM A 44 SAS B
DE BOSE ANTHONY A 35 MAG W
CERT 11 APRIL 1868
DEADERICK E L A 44 SAS W
DEADMAN H A 26 SHE W
DEADMAN JESSE A 26 SHE W
DEAL A J A 29 FA1 W
DEAL ABEL A 29 ROC W
DEAL ARNETT A 29 FA1 W
DEAL HENRY A 24 MID W
DEAL JAS R A 29 FA1 B
DEAL JNO B A 24 MID W
DEAL JNO H A 29 FA1 B
DEAL JOHN A 35 CYP W
DEAL KINNON A 29 FA1 W
DEAL RUBEN A 37 ROB W
DEAL WILLIAM 1ST A 35 CYP W
DEAL WILLIAM 2ND A 35 CYP W
DEAL WILLIAM B A 24 MID W
DEAL WM H A 29 FA1 W
DEALE ISAAC A 24 EDE B
DEAN BARTLETT Y A 46 GRE W
DEAN G W A 44 TAR W
DEAN GEORGE A 44 LED B
DEAN J R A 44 TAR W
DEAN JAMES A 46 GRE B
DEAN JESSE A 44 TAR W
DEAN JOHN A 39 DAV B
DEAN L D A 44 TAR W
DEAN MOSES C A 44 TAR W
DEAN THOMAS A 39 DAV W
DEAN W J A 44 TAR W
DEAN WM A 44 TAR W
DEAN WM H A 46 GRE W
DEANES J C A 46 JAM W
DEANES JACOB A 46 JAM W
DEANES THOMAS A 24 UPP W
DEANS ALFRED A 19 BE1 B
DEANS JESSEE T A 44 TAR W
DEANS JOHN H A 19 BE1 B
DEANS JORDAN A 37 ROC B
DEANS JOSIAH A 29 FA1 W
DEANS SIMPSON A 44 TAR W
DEANS THOMPSON A 28 7TH B
DEANS WM A A 19 MOR W
DEAVER THOMAS A 35 SMI W
DEAVEREAUX HARKNESS A 37 EDW B
DEAVEREAUX JAMES A 37 PEN B
DEAVEREAUX WILIKIN R 37 EDW B
CONVICTED OF LARCENY
DEAVIS JAMES A 26 WAR W
DEBNAM DR THOS C A 44 HEN W
DEBNAM HENRY A 39 SPE B
DEBNAM J B A 39 LOU W
TRNS BY AFF FROM
HENDERSON OF GRANVILLE
DEBNAM J B JR A 44 HEN W
DEBNAM J R A 44 BRA W
DEBNAM JACOB R A 39 LOU W
TRNS FROM WILSON
GRANVILLE CO BY AFF
DEBNAM JAMES A A 39 SPE W
DEBNAM JAS R A 39 LOU W
DEBNAM JOHN A 39 FRA B
DEBNAM OLIVER A 39 FRE B
DEBNAM PETER F A 39 PUG W
DEBNAM R B A 44 BRA W
DEBNAM SIMON A 39 LOU B
DEBNAM W R JR A 39 PUG W
DEBNAM WILLIAM A 39 HAY B
DEBNUM W R SR A 39 FRA W
DEBOE JOSEPH A 46 SUM W
DEBRO BOSEN A 28 05A B
DEBRUHL C J A 28 03B W
DEBRUHLE JOEL A 28 6TH W
DECK EUSEBIUS A 40 DA1 W
DECK JONAS R 40 DA2 W
NAME LINED OUT
CHALLENGED
JUSTICE OF THE PEACE
BEFORE THE WAR GAVE AID
AND COMFORT TO THE ENEMY
NOT QUALIFIED. REJECTED
DECK PETER A 40 DEC W
DECKER JESSEE A 29 FA1 W
DECKER JOSEPH A 29 FA1 W
DECKERSON WM T A 39 LOU W
DECKERSON WM T A 39 LOU W
TO LOUISBURG
IN FRANKLIN CO
DEEMS WILLIAM A 37 HIG W
DEEN DANIEL A 32 DAV B
DEENS DANIEL A 19 BE1 B
DEES GEORGE A 28 16T W
DEESE ALBERT A 39 FRA W
DEEVER JNO JR A 29 ROC W
DEEVER JOHN SR A 29 ROC W
DEFORE JOHN N A 35 ISL B
DEGRANT WILLIAM A 32 JAC B
DEKEAZER ARCHY A 29 FA1 B
DEKESEY HENRY A 29 FA1 B
DELAMAR JAMES F A 19 BE1 W
DELAMAR KILLIS J A 28 02N B
DELAMAR STEPHEN A 28 16T W
DELAMAR WM J A 28 02N B
DELANCY ALFRED A 46 GRE B
DELANCY W P A 46 MON W
DELAP ALEXANDER A 32 POS W
DELAP AMOS A 32 POS W
DELAP JERRY A 32 SHE B
DELAP JESSE A 32 YAD B
DELAP JOHN A 32 THO B
DELAP JOHN S A 32 YAD W
DELAP LEVI A 32 POS B
DELAP SAMUEL A A 32 POS W
DELAP WESLEY A 32 POS B
DELEMAR
CHRISTOPHER F A 19 BE1 W
DELK JOHN A 28 03A B
DELLENBACK C A 44 FOR W
DELLINGER ALFRED A 40 BLA W
DELLINGER ANDREW A 40 BLA W
DELLINGER DANIEL A 40 BLA W
DELLINGER DAVID A 26 SHE W
DELLINGER F M A 26 WAR W
DELLINGER FREDERIC LA 40 BLA W

DELLINGER GEORGE A 40 BLA W
DELLINGER J R A 40 CAN W
DELLINGER JACOB A 26 SHE W
DELLINGER JOHN A 40 BLA W
DELLINGER M C A 40 CAN W
DELLINGER M P A 26 SHE W
DELLINGER MICHAEL A 40 BLA W
DELLINGER PHILLIP A 40 BLA W
DELLINGER SAMUEL S A 40 BLA W
DELLINGHAM JOSHUA A 26 GOF W
DELLINGNER F W A 26 CAR W
DELLINGNER H K A 26 CAR W
DELLINGNER JAMES A 26 CAR W
DELMAR ASA A 28 01A B
DELMAR BENJAMIN A 28 10T B
DEMENT C H A 44 BEA W
DEMENT FENDAL A 44 BRA W
DEMENT H B A 44 OXF W
DEMENT P J A 39 PUG W
DEMENT S E A 44 BRA W
DEMENT S T A 39 PUG W
DEMENT THOS J A 44 OXF W
DEMENT W W A 44 FIS W
DEMENT WILLIS A 44 FIS W
DEMENT WM A 44 FIS W
DEMMENT HENDERSON A 44 FIS W
DEMPEY AUGUST. A 30 POW W
DEMPSEY GEORGE F A 35 ISL W
DEMPSEY HOSEA A 35 ROC W
DEMPSEY KINCHIN H A 35 ROC W
DEMPSEY PATRICK C A 35 ROC W
DEMPSY J W A 46 MON W
DEMSEY WILLIAM A 24 EDE B
DENARD WM A 28 14T B
DENIS WM N A 72 SWA W
DENISTON RICHD A 39 HAR B
DENNIN WM A 28 03B B
DENNING JOSIAH A 29 CAR W
DENNING M D A 29 FLE W
DENNIS A H R 19 NEW W
DENNIS ABRAHAM A 19 HAD B
DENNIS ALEX H A 19 HAD W
DENNIS ALEXANDER A 46 FRI B
DENNIS ALFRED A 19 POR W
DENNIS ANTHONEY W A 19 POR W
DENNIS BRYAN A 28 9TH B
DENNIS CAESAR A 28 05A B
DENNIS CHARLES A 19 BE1 B
DENNIS DANIEL A 46 SUM W
DENNIS GEO A 19 NEW W
DENNIS ISAIAH C A 28 9TH W
DENNIS J L A 19 NEW W
DENNIS JAMES A 37 TA1 B
DENNIS JAMES A 46 SUM W
DENNIS JOHN A 46 SUM W
DENNIS JOHN HENRY A 46 GRE B
DENNIS NELSON A 28 04B B
DENNIS OWEN A 28 8TH B
DENNIS ROBERT A 46 SUM W
DENNIS SIMON A 19 HAD B
DENNIS W D A 46 SUM W
DENNIS W N A 19 MOR W
DENNISON A R A 28 01A W
DENNY ALBERT A 46 GRE B
DENNY ALEXANDER C A 46 MCL W
DENNY ALFRED A 46 MCL W
DENNY ELI A 46 HIG W
DENNY GEORGE A A 46 GRE W
DENNY JAMES A 28 11T W
DENNY JAMES M A 46 MCL W
DENNY JAMES P A 46 MCL W
DENNY JOHN A 46 GRE W
TO GRAHAM ALAMANCE
DENNY JOHN C A 46 MON W
DENNY JOSEPH A 46 MCL W
DENNY R K A 46 MON W
DENNY ROBT W A 46 GRE W
DENNY SAMUEL A 46 GRE W
DENNY SAMUEL H A 46 MCL W
DENNY THOMAS
89 YEARS OLD A 46 GRE W
DENNY THOMAS D A 46 GRE W
DENNY W C A 46 HIG W
DENSEY HENRY A 24 EDE B
DENSTON PURINGTON A 39 HAR B
DENT A T A 44 BRA W
DENT FRANCIS A 44 FOR W
DENT GILBERT A 39 LOU B
DENT JAMES A 39 LOU W
DENT L W A 44 FOR W
DENT NELSON A 39 FRA B
DENT RUBEN A 39 DAV B
DENT SEZAR A 39 LOU B
DENT WM T A 39 HAR W
DENTON FENNER A 39 GRI W
DENTON FRANKLIN A 37 ROB W
DENTON JAMES A 37 EDW W
DENTON LEVI A 37 ROB W
DENTON WESLEY A 39 HAR W
DERHAM JNO A 29 FA1 B
DERR A J A 40 CAN W
DERR J H A 40 RHY W
DERR JUNIUS A 40 RHY B
DERR NULIS A 40 RHY B
DESILOW W B A 37 ROC W
DETMAN ROBERT A 37 PEN B
DETTMARING FEDRICK A 46 FRI W
DEVANE MILTON K A 35 MAG W
DEVANE T W A 29 FLE W
DEVANE TONEY A 35 MAG B
DEVANE WILLIAM A 35 ROC B
DEVAUGHN ACKMAN A 29 GRA B
DEVAUGHN DAVID A 29 GRA B
DEVAUGHN HAYWOOD A 29 GRA B
DEVAUGHN HENRY A 29 GRA B
DEVAUGHN LEWIS A 29 GRA B
DEVAUGHN PEYTON A 29 GRA B
DEVAUGHN TONY A 29 GRA B
DEVAUGHN WM A 29 GRA B
DEVAULT DAVID A 46 MCL B
DEVENPORT J G A 25 SHO W
DEVENPORT JOHN A 40 RHY B
DEVENPORT M L A 25 SHO W
DEVERS R J A 44 YXR W
DEVINE JAMES A 39 FRA W
DEVINE WILLIAM T A 40 MAU W
DEVINGHN WARREN A 19 MOR B
DEVINNY ELBERT A 46 RAG W
DEVINNY GEORGE W A 46 RAG W
DEW FRANKLIN A 37 HIG B
DEW LIM A 37 ROC B
DEWES REDIN B A 37 SHA W
DEWEY ISAAC A 28 02N B
DEWEY RICHD A 28 03A B
DEWEY ROBERT A 28 14T B
DEWEY S N A 28 01A W
DEWITT FRANCES A 19 HAD W
DEWS ALBERT G A 37 SHA W
DEY A O A 30 CUR W
DEY ABNER A 30 IND B
DEY J W A 28 02N W
DEY SPENCER A 30 IND B
DIAMOND JAMES A 28 05A B
DICK AMOS A 46 GIB B
DICK ANDERSON A 46 GRE B
DICK AUGUSTUS A 46 GRE B
DICK BRUNSICK A 46 GRE B
DICK CAIN A 46 MCL B
DICK FRANKLIN A 46 MCL W
DICK HENRY A 46 GRE B
DICK HIRAM C A 46 MCL W
DICK JAMES A 46 MON B
DICK JAMES H A 46 MCL W
DICK JOHN S A 46 MCL W
DICK JULIUS M A 46 MCL W
DICK LAWSON A 46 GRE B
DICK PRESTON P A 46 MCL W
DICK RALPH A 46 MCL W
DICK REUBEN A 46 MCL B
DICK ROBERT C A 46 MCL W
DICK SHEDRICK A 46 GRE B
DICK THOMAS A 46 MCL W
DICK WILSON A 46 GRE B
DICKEN J M A 39 FRA W
DICKEN JOURDON A 37 EDW B
DICKEN O A 39 FRA W
DICKEN P F A 39 FRA W
DICKENS ADISON A 37 EDW B
DICKENS ANTHONY A 37 TA1 B
DICKENS BENJAMIN A 37 PEN B
DICKENS BLAKE A 37 EDW B
DICKENS CALVIN A 37 EDW B
DICKENS CAPTAIN A 37 EDW B
DICKENS CAREY A 37 EDW B
DICKENS DALLIE A 37 EDW B
DICKENS DAVID A 37 EDW B
DICKENS DAVID A 38 FRE B
DICKENS ELIAS A 37 EDW B
DICKENS GEORGE A 37 EDW B
DICKENS GEORGE A 37 EDW W
DICKENS GILBERT A 39 FRE B
DICKENS GRANVILLE A 37 EDW B
DICKENS GRANVILLE A 37 PIN B
DICKENS HARDY H A 37 EDW W
DICKENS HENRY A 37 EDW B
DICKENS IRVING A 37 EDW B
DICKENS ISAAC A 37 EDW B
DICKENS ISAM A 37 TA1 B
DICKENS ISASOM A 37 PEN B
DICKENS ISHMIAL A 37 EDW B
DICKENS JACOB A 37 EDW B
DICKENS JAMES A 37 EDW B
DICKENS JNO A 39 FRE B
DICKENS JOHN A 32 LOF W
DICKENS JOHN A 37 EDW B
DICKENS JOSEPH A 37 EDW B
DICKENS JOSEPH A 39 HAR B
DICKENS KELLEY H A 37 EDW W
DICKENS LIAS A 37 ROB B
DICKENS LUKE A 37 TA1 B
DICKENS MARTIN A 37 EDW B
DICKENS MILES A 37 EDW B
DICKENS NORFLEET A 37 EDW B
DICKENS PETER A 37 EDW B
DICKENS READICK A 37 EDW B
DICKENS REUBEN A 37 EDW B
DICKENS ROBERT A 37 EDW B
DICKENS SOLOMON A 37 EDW B
DICKENS TRANK A 37 EDW B
DICKENS WILLIAM A 37 EDW B
DICKENSON GEORGE A 39 PUG W
DICKENSON JAMES A 39 SPE W
DICKENSON M A 39 FRA W
DICKENSON PLEASANT A 39 HAY W
DICKENSON SIDNEY A 39 SPE W
DICKENSON W A A 39 PUG W
DICKENSON WILLIAM A 39 PUG W
DICKENSON ZACHARIAH A 39 SPE W
DICKERSON ANDREW A 24 EDE B

DICKERSON ANDREW A 44 BEA W
DICKERSON D B A 19 HAR W
DICKERSON D O A 19 HAR W
DICKERSON DAVID C A 19 BE1 W
DICKERSON E W A 44 FOR W
DICKERSON EDMOND A 37 ROC B
DICKERSON EDWIN A 44 OXF W
DICKERSON JAMES A 44 HEN W
DICKERSON JAMES A 44 KIT W
DICKERSON JNO A 44 BEA W
DICKERSON JOEL A 44 FIS W
DICKERSON JOHN A 44 OXF W
DICKERSON MARTIN A 39 HAR W
DICKERSON NARRIS M A 19 BE1 W
DICKERSON PARAM P A 19 BE1 W
DICKERSON S P A 44 OXF W
DICKERSON S W A 44 FIS W
DICKERSON W A 44 SAS W
DICKERSON WALLACE A 19 HAR W
DICKERSON WILLIS A 19 BE1 B
DICKERSON WM H A 19 HAR W
DICKEY ALEXANDER A 40 DEC W
DICKEY HENDERSON A 46 GRE B
DICKEY HENRY A 46 GRE B
DICKEY JACK A 40 DA1 B
DICKINS ARDEN A 37 TA1 B
DICKINS HENRY A 37 PIN B
DICKINS HOSEY A 37 HIC B
DICKINS JAMES A 37 TA1 B
DICKINS JOSEPH A 37 TA1 B
DICKINS JUDGE A 37 ROB B
DICKINS NATHAN A 37 HIG B
DICKINS TURNER A 37 HIC B
DICKINS WILLIS A 37 MAN B
DICKINSON ARTHUR A 28 10T W
DICKINSON D V A 28 10T W
DICKINSON G W A 28 10T W
DICKINSON J B A 28 01A W
DICKINSON JOHN B A 19 BE1 W
DICKINSON JOHNSON A 39 PUG W
DICKINSON ROBT A 39 HAR W
DICKINSON WILLIAM G A 28 10T W
DICKSON A C A 40 SAN W
DICKSON AARON A 35 KEN B
DICKSON ABRAM A 35 KEN B
DICKSON ALFRED A 35 ISL B
DICKSON ANDERSON A 35 MAG B
DICKSON ANDREW A 35 KEN B
DICKSON ANDREW CHAL A 26 CAR B
ACCUSED OF THEFT
NOT SUSTAINED
DICKSON B F A 26 GOF W
DICKSON BEN A 26 BOR B
DICKSON BENAJAH A 35 ISL W
DICKSON DALLAS A 35 MAG B
DICKSON E D A 26 GRI W
DICKSON EDMON A 44 HEN W
DICKSON FRANKLIN A 26 SHE B
DICKSON GILBRETH R 26 SHE W
WAS MEMBER OF THE
LEGISLATURE PRIOR TO
THE WAR & ENGAGED IN
THE REBELLION
DICKSON HENRY A 35 MAG B
DICKSON HOWARD A 35 ISL B
DICKSON ISAAC A 26 GRI B
DICKSON J A 26 BOR B
DICKSON J F A 26 GOF W
DICKSON J G JR A 35 FAI W
DICKSON J G SR A 35 FAI W
DECEASED
DICKSON J T A 40 SAN W
DICKSON JAMES A 35 ISL W
DICKSON JAMES A 29 SEV B
FELONY D C MUNROE
CHARGE NOT SUSTAINED
DICKSON JAMES A 35 KEN B
DICKSON JAMES A A 26 GOF W
DICKSON L J A 26 GOF W
DICKSON LEWIS A 26 SHE B
DICKSON LEWIS A 35 KEN B
DICKSON PENNY A 44 BRA W
DICKSON ROBERT A 26 SHE W
DICKSON ROBERT S A 35 ISL W
DICKSON SAMEUL A 35 KEN B
DICKSON SAMUEL A 35 ISL B
DICKSON T J A 26 GRI W
DICKSON T M A 26 GRI W
DICKSON THOS A 26 SHE W
DICKSON VIRGEL A 35 MAG B
DICKSON W A A 40 STO W
DICKSON W W A 26 GOF W
DICKSON WILLIAM A 26 GOF W
DICKSON WILLIAM A 26 GRI B
DICKSON WINGATE A 26 SHE B
DICKSON WM S A 40 SAN W
DICKY ALFRED V A 46 GRE B
DICKY CHARLES A 46 GRE B
DIGGINS JAMES A 30 IND B
DIGH A P A 26 PEE W
DIGH WHITSON A 26 PEE W
DIKON ALFRED J A 19 MOR W
DIKSON JESSE A 37 SHA W
DILAMAR JOHN A A 28 15T W
DILL DAVID W A 19 BE1 W
DILL EDWARD H A 19 BE1 W
DILL GEO W A 19 MOR W
DILL JOSEPH R A 19 BE1 W
DILL JOSEPH R JR A 19 BE2 W
DILL S L JR A 19 MOR W
DILL SAMUEL L A 19 BE1 W
DILL WM F A 19 BE1 W
DILLAHUNT HILLIARD A 28 03A B
DILLAHUNT MOSES A 28 04A B
DILLAHUNT SIMON A 28 04A B
DILLARD ALFORD A 44 FOR W
DILLARD BARNET A 46 GRE B
DILLARD BARNETT A 46 GRE B
DILLARD BENJAMIN A 24 UPP B
DILLARD H P A 44 FOR W
DILLARD OREN A 37 ROC W
DILLARD TAYLOR A 46 GRE B
DILLARD WILLIS A 24 MID B
DILLEN J B A 40 SAN W
DILLEN WILLIAM A 40 SAN W
DILLENGER JAMES A 40 RHY B
DILLIAN JOHN E A 32 POS W
DILLIARD DAVID D A 37 ROC W
DILLIARD EDWIN A 37 SHA W
DILLIARD H C A 44 FOR W
DILLIARD J T A 44 FOR W
DILLIARD JAMES A 37 SHA W
DILLIARD LEVI A 37 SHA B
DILLIARD P H A 39 LOU W
DILLING FRENO A 40 FER W
DILLING HARVEY A 40 DA1 W
DILLINGHAM JOHN P A 28 02N W
DILLINGHAM L A 26 BOR B
DILLON A A A 46 HIG W
DILLON JESSE A 46 GRE W
DILLON JOHN A 46 GRE W
DILLON JONATHAN A 46 GRE W
DILWORTH WM M A 46 MON W
DINKINS EDMOND A 28 11T W
DINKINS FRANKLIN A 28 11T W
DINKINS JOHN A 26 WAR B
DISHELL HENRY A 32 SHE W
DISHER EPHRAIM A 32 SHE W
DISHER L J A 32 SHE W
DISMAL KANE A 37 PEN B
DITMORE H M A 25 PIN W
DITMORE VINCENT G A 25 PIN W
DIVERS DEMPSEY A 30 ROA B
DIVINNY J G A 26 PEE W
DIVINNY JENKINS A 26 PEE W
DIVINNY W G A 26 PEE W
DIXON ALLEN A 28 12T B
DIXON ANDREW A 53 LA1 B
SWAN QUARTER
DIXON CALVIN A 35 MAG W
DIXON CHARLES S A 28 16T W
DIXON DAVID F A 28 13T W
DIXON DUKE W A 37 HIG W
DIXON EDWARD A 35 FAI B
DIXON ELIJAH A 19 HAD W
DIXON ELIJAH A 28 15T W
DIXON F M A 44 YXS W
DIXON FRANCIS C A 19 POR W
DIXON GEORGE A 28 13T W
DIXON GOR F A 46 RAG W
DIXON HARDEE A 28 14T W
DIXON HASTON A 28 14T W
DIXON HENRY A 30 IND B
DIXON HENRY A 37 EDW B
DIXON HENRY A 37 MAN B
DIXON HENRY A 44 TOW B
DIXON JAMES A 28 04A B
DIXON JAMES A 28 05A B
DIXON JAMES A 37 SHA B
DIXON JESSE P A 37 SHA W
DIXON JNO A 44 SAS W
DIXON JOHN A 19 HAD W
DIXON JOHN A 28 02N B
DIXON JOHN A 32 POS B
DIXON JOHN D A 28 16T W
DIXON JOHN W A 28 14T W
DIXON JOSEPH A 19 HAD W
DIXON JOSEPH H A 28 11T W
DIXON LEWIS A 28 04A B
DIXON LEWIS D A 28 11T W
DIXON LUCUS J A 28 14T W
DIXON M C A 46 GRE W
DIXON MAJOR A 28 8TH B
DIXON MILES A 28 04A B
DIXON NELSON A 35 MAG B
DIXON NICHOLAS A 28 04A B
DIXON ORIN D A 37 ROB W
DIXON ORIN D A 37 ROB W
DIXON PHILIP H A 28 10T W
DIXON ROBERT JOHN A 37 ROC W
DIXON S J A 19 HAD W
DIXON SOLOMAN H R 46 RAG W
LEFT HOME TO KEEP OUT OF WAR
RETURNED IN THE 1 MO 1867
DIXON STEPHEN H A 19 BE1 W
DIXON T G A 28 01B W
DIXON THOMAS A 19 HAD W
DIXON VINCENT A 28 14T W
DIXON WILLIAM A 37 ROC W
DIXON WILLIAM T A 37 MAN B
DIXON WM A 28 16T W
DIXSON BARCLAY B A 72 SWA W
DIXSON BENJ R A 19 POR W
DIXSON ELIJAH G A 19 POR W
DIXSON GEO S A 19 POR W
DIXSON SOLOMON A 19 POR W
DIXSON SYLVESTER A 19 POR W
DIXSON WM A 44 SAS W
DIXSON WM T A 19 POR W

DOAK ALLEN A 46 GRE B
DOAK ELIJA A 46 GRE B
DOAK GREENE A 46 GRE B
DOAK JAMES W A 46 GRE W
DOANE H P A 28 03A W
DOBBIN ALEX A 29 FA1 B
DOBBIN JAS C A 29 FA1 W
DOBINS D P A 26 MOO W
DOBLE FRANCIS M A 28 01A W
DOBSON ALLEN A 35 KEN B
DOBSON AMOS A 35 KEN B
DOBSON BALAAM A 35 KEN B
DOBSON BENN A 35 FAI W
CERTIF. GIVEN. REMOVED TO ISLAND CREEK
DOBSON CLEM A 35 KEN B
DOBSON GEORGE A 35 KEN B
DOBSON HENRY A 53 GER B
DOBSON JACOB A 35 KEN B
DOBSON JAMES M A 46 RAG W
DOBSON JOHN A 35 KEN W
DOBSON P H A 35 FAI W
DOBSON R S A 32 DAV W
DOBSON THOMAS G A 35 KEN W
DOBY ALLEN A 32 JAC W
DOBY CALVIN A 32 LOF W
DOBY J P A 32 JAC W
DOBY JOHN A 32 JAC W
DODD D C A 26 SHE W
DODD G H A 39 GRI W
DODD ISAAC JR A 29 FA1 W
DODD ISAAC SR A 29 FA1 W
DODD JAS A 29 FA1 W
DODD JAS W A 29 FA1 W
DODD R T A 39 GRI W
DODD RANSOM A 39 GRI W
DODD THEOPHULUS A 39 GRI W
DODD WM M A 29 FA1 W
DODGE C W A 24 EDE W
DODGE DANILE A 37 MAN B
DODGE GRAY A 19 HAR B
DODGEN J W A 25 SHO W
DODGIN A J A 25 SHO W
DODGIN WILLIAM A 25 SHO W
DODSON ABRAM F A 46 GRE W
DODSON BRISTO A 44 YXR B
DODSON DANIEL A 46 GRE B
DODSON EDWARD G A 40 FER W
DODSON G P A 32 THO W
DODSON J T A 46 GRE W
DODSON JEREMIAH J A 46 GRE W
DODSON RICHARD A 46 GRE W
DODSON RUBIN A 44 YXR B
DODSON SAMUEL A 46 MON B
DOE MUNROE A 53 LA2 B
DOGGET M W A 26 SHE W
DOGGETT JAMES W A 46 MON W
DOGGETT JOHN A 46 GIB W
DOGGETT LINDSAY A 46 MCL B
DOGGETT ROBERT A 46 MON B
DOGGETT WILLIAM A 37 TA1 B
DOGGETT WILLIAM A 46 MON B
DOLBY ADOLPHUS A 44 FOR B
DOLLEY MOSES A 30 KNO B
DONAHUE WM A 28 01A W
4TH PRECINCT CERTIFICATE GIVEN
DONELL ALFRED M A 53 FAI B
DONELL BENJAMIN A 53 LA1 B
CERT RES SWAN QUARTER
DONELL FRANCIS A 53 FAI B
DONELL JOHN A 53 LA1 B
DONELL ROBT C A 46 GRE W
DONELL THOMAS A 53 LA1 B
DONER HENRY A 26 SHE B
DONION WILLIAM A 32 DAV W
DONKINS BECTON A 28 04A B
DONNEL HARPER A 46 GRE W
DONNEL MANGUM A 46 ROS B
DONNEL MORRISON A 46 RAG W
DONNEL REUBEN A 46 MCL W
DONNEL SAMUEL A 46 FRI W
DONNEL W O A 46 KIN W
DONNELL ALVUS A 46 RAG B
DONNELL CALVIN A 46 GRE B
DONNELL DANIEL T A 46 GRE W
DONNELL DANL A 46 GRE B
DONNELL DANL C A 46 GRE W
DONNELL ERVEN A 46 MCL W
DONNELL GEORGE A 46 GRE W
DONNELL HAMILTON A 46 GRE B
DONNELL HENRY A 46 GRE B
DONNELL HENRY A 46 GRE B
DONNELL JAMES M A 46 GRE W
DONNELL JOHN A 46 GRE B
DONNELL JOHN A 46 GRE B
DONNELL JOHN A 46 MCL W
DONNELL JOHN D A 46 GRE W
DONNELL JOSEPH A 46 GRE B
DONNELL LATHAM A 46 MON W
DONNELL LEE A 46 GRE B
DONNELL LINDSAY A 46 MON B
DONNELL MADISON A 46 GRE B
DONNELL NATHAN A 46 GRE W
DONNELL RALPH A 46 RAG B
DONNELL REUBEN A 46 GRE B
DONNELL STEPHEN A 28 7TH B
DONNELL THOMAS B A 46 MCL W
DONNELL VENIBLE B A 46 RAG W
DONNELL WARREN A 46 GRE B
DONNELL WILSON A 46 MCL B
DONNELL WM H A 46 MCL W
DONNELL YANCY A 46 GRE B
DONNERSON ANDREW J A 28 7TH W
DONNNEL BENJAMIN A 19 BE1 B
DORCEY ARCHD A 39 JOR W
DORCEY EPHRAIM A 39 JOR W
DORITY JAMES A 46 GRE W
DORMAN GEORGE H A 53 FAI B
DORMAN JAMES E A 37 EDW W
DORMAN LOVET A 35 ALB W
DORRELL A A 39 GRI W
DORSER PETER R 28 11T B
ENTITLED TO A VOTE AFTER JUNE 1, 1868. HAS BEEN IN THE STATE ONLY 3 MONTHS AUG 27, 1869
DORSETT J M A 32 LEE W
DORSETT JOHN A 32 LEE W
DORSETT W W A 32 LEE W
DORSEY HOWARD A 44 OXF W
DORSON TOM A 39 JOR B
DORTCH WASHINGTON A 37 SHA B
DORUM DANIEL A 38 FRE B
DOSSEY HENRY A 46 GRE B
DOSSEY WM A 46 GRE B
DOTY BENJAMIN A 32 CLE W
DOTY JACOB C A 32 CLE W
DOTY JAMES A 46 GRE W
DOUB WILLIAM H A 32 CLE W
DOUGH CHESTER J A 30 ROA W
DOUGH JAMES W A 30 ROA W
DOUGH JESSE E A 30 ROA W
APRIL 16, 1868
DOUGH LEWIS A 30 POP B
DOUGH NATHAN E A 30 ROA W
DOUGH OTIS M A 30 ROA W
DOUGH THOMAS A A 30 ROA W
DOUGH WALTER T A 30 ROA W
DOUGH WARREN A A 30 ROA W
DOUGH WILLIAM A 30 ROA B
DOUGHERTY CULLEN W A 28 8TH W
DOUGHERTY GEORGE W A 28 8TH W
DOUGHERTY H P A 28 8TH W
DOUGHERTY HARDY A 28 8TH W
DOUGHERTY JOHN H A 28 8TH W
DOUGHERTY MAC A 28 10T B
DOUGHERTY RICHARD A 28 8TH W
DOUGHERTY WM W A 28 8TH W
DOUGHIT JOHN A 32 CLE W
DOUGHTY JAMES A 19 NEW W
DOUGHTY JOHN E A 28 04A B
DOUGHTY NAPOLEON B A 19 BE1 W
DOUGHTY THOMAS A 28 15T W
DOUGHTY WILLIAM H A 37 TA1 W
DOUGLAS PETER A 19 MOR B
DOUGLAS WILLIAM H A 53 LA1 W
DOUGLASS JAS A 29 FA1 B
DOUGLASS LAYFAYETT A 53 CHI W
DOUGLESS JOSEPH A A 24 EDE W
DOUSENBERY AUSTIN A 32 DAV B
DOUSENBERY JOHN A 32 DAV B
DOUSENBERY JOSEPH A 32 DAV B
DOUSENBERY SAMUEL A 32 DAV B
DOUSENBERY SIMON A 32 DAV B
DOUTHIT GEORGE A 32 CLE W
DOUTHIT NELSON A 32 CLE B
DOUTHIT WILLIAM A 32 TYR W
DOVE ARNET A 28 9TH B
DOVE DOCTOR A 29 FA1 B
DOVE ISAAC A 28 10T B
DOVE JACOB 2ND A 28 9TH B
DOVE JACOB 3RD A 28 9TH B
DOVE JAMES A 28 03A B
DOVE JOHN P A 28 04A B
DOVE LEMUEL A 28 04A B
DOVE SAMUEL A 28 9TH B
DOVE WILLIAM A 28 10T B
DOVE WILLIAM A 28 9TH W
DOVE WILLIS A 35 KEN B
DOVER ASA G A 40 DEC W
DOVER J A A 25 HAY W
DOVER SHEDRACK A 26 SHE W
DOWD DEMPSEY A 37 TA2 B
DOWD HENRY A A 37 TA1 W
DOWD HILLIARD A 37 TA1 B
DOWDEE J W A 28 03A W
DOWDEE R A 28 03A W
DOWDY CALEB A 30 COI W
DOWDY CALEB D A 30 POW W
DOWDY DANIEL L A 30 POW W
DOWDY DONALDSON S A 30 POW W
DOWDY EAMOND A 30 POP W
DOWDY GEORGE W A 30 POP W
DOWDY HARMON A 28 16T W
DOWDY IVY A 30 NOR W
DOWDY JOHN A 30 ROA W
DOWDY MAJOR A 30 POP W
DOWDY OLIVER A 30 CUR W
DOWDY REDDING A 28 17T W
DOWDY SAMUEL A 30 POW W
DOWDY SAMUEL SR A 30 POP W
DOWDY THOMAS A 30 NOR B
DOWDY THOMAS A 30 POP W
DOWDY WILLIAM A 30 POP W
DOWDY WM A 29 CAR W
DOWDY WM B A 28 17T W
CERT GIVEN 16TH ELEC PRECINCT CRAVEN CO

DOWNES L S A 26 PEE W
DOWNEY DAVID A 44 YXR B
DOWNEY DUDLEY A 44 SAS B
DOWNEY GEORGE A 44 KIT B
DOWNEY HENDERSON A 44 OXF B
DOWNEY HENRY A 44 YXS B
DOWNEY ISAIAH A 44 ISL B
DOWNEY JAMES A 44 YXR B
DOWNEY JOSHUA A 44 HEN B
DOWNEY LARY A 44 YXS B
DOWNEY MORRIS A 44 OXF B
DOWNEY MOSES A 44 YXR B
DOWNEY RUBIN A 44 OXF B
DOWNEY SAML A 44 YXR B
DOWNEY SANDY A 44 YXR B
DOWNEY STEPHEN A 44 YXR B
DOWNEY W J A 44 SAS W
DOWNEY WASHINGTON A 44 YXR B
DOWNING BRINKLY A 37 EDW B
DOWNING ENRY A 37 MAN W
DOWNING FAYETT A 37 HIC B
DOWNING G A A 29 CED W
REMOVE TO BLADEN
DOWNING JAMES H A 37 HIC A
DOWNING JNO A 29 CED W
DOWNING JOS A 29 CED W
DOWNING JOSEPH A 37 HIC A
DOWNING M S R 28 04A W
CONSTABLE PRIOR TO WAR
DOWNING MACK A 37 HIC B
DOWNING MILES A 28 12T B
DOWNING MOSES A 29 CED B
DOWNING SANDY A 37 HIC B
DOWNING VOLN A 29 CED W
DOWNS EDWD A 28 04A B
DOWNS M R A 32 CLE W
DOWNS OLIVER A 28 04B B
DOWTY JAMES B A 28 15T W
DOXEY AARON A 30 IND B
DOXEY ALEXANDER A A 30 NAR W
DOXEY DEMPSEY A 30 IND W
DOXEY HAYWOOD A 30 CUR W
DOXEY ISAAC A 30 CUR W
DOXEY JAMES B A 30 CUR W
DOXEY JEFFERSON A 30 CUR B
DOXEY JESSEE L A 30 POP W
REMOVED TO CURRITUCK CH
DOXEY JOHN A 30 CUR W
DOXEY JOHN A 30 TUL W
DOXEY MATT A 30 CUR B
DOXEY SANFORD E A 30 POP W
DOXEY THOMAS E A 30 CUR W
DOXEY YORK A 30 IND B
DOXEY ZACHANAH M A 30 POP W
DOYLE JOSEPH A 26 PEE W
DOZIER A A A 30 IND W
DOZIER ANDREW A 30 IND B
DOZIER AUSTIN A 37 TA1 B
DOZIER CHESTERFIELD A 37 TA2 B
DOZIER CLEMENT F A 30 POW W
DOZIER DAVID A 37 TA1 B
DOZIER DEMPSEY CHAL A 30 TUL B
NON RESIDENCE
DOZIER G F A 30 TUL W
DOZIER JACOB A 30 IND W
DOZIER JAMES A 37 PEN B
DOZIER JAMES H A 37 TA2 W
DOZIER JOHN A 30 IND B
DOZIER JOHN H A 30 CUR W
DOZIER JOSEPH H A 30 IND W
DOZIER LUKE A 37 MAN B
DOZIER NOAH A 37 TA1 B
DOZIER OFFEY A 37 PIN B

DOZIER PETER A 30 GIB W
DOZIER PHILLIP A 30 TUL W
DOZIER PHILLIP A 37 TA1 B
DOZIER S H A 30 TUL W
DOZIER SAML A 30 IND B
DOZIER THOMAS O A 28 16T W
DOZIER THOS B A 30 IND W
DOZIER TURNER A 37 TA1 B
DOZIER WARREN A 37 TA1 B
DOZIER WILLIAM A 30 CUR B
DOZIER WILLIAM A 30 IND B
7-MOS-RESIDENCE
DOZIER WILLIAM A 30 IND W
DOZIER WILLIAM E A 30 IND W
DOZIER WILLIAM L A 37 TA2 W
DOZIER WILLIS A 19 MOR B
DOZIER WILSON A 30 CUR B
DRAKE CAMILAS A 37 TA1 B
DRAKE CHARLES A 37 MAN B
DRAKE GEORGE A 37 SPA W
DRAKE LEVI A 37 ROC W
DRAKE MILTON A 35 MAG B
DRAKE NICHOLAS Y A 37 ROC W
DRAKE RICHARD A 37 SPA B
DRAKE THOS A 29 FA1 B
DRAKE WARREN A 29 FA1 B
DRANE THOMAS A 32 THO W
CERTIF
DRANEY F M A 28 02N W
DRANEY PETER A 28 01B W
DRAPER HENRY J A 37 ROB W
DRASON WELLS A 37 ROB W
DRAUGHE JAMES A 37 ROB W
DRAUGHN J C A 26 BUR W
DRAUGHON E T A 29 CAR W
DRAUGHON HANDY A 29 CAR B
DRAUGHON RANSOM A 29 CAR B
DRAUGHON W A 29 FA1 W
BRIG GENL MILLITIA
AFTER ENG IN REBELLION
COMMANDED REBS WHO
TOOK U.S. ARSENAL AT
FAYETTEVILLE 1861 WAS
COUNTY ASSESSOR 1859
DRAUGHON W G A 29 CAR W
DRAUGHON WM F A 37 ROB W
DRAWN EMANUEL A 32 POS W
DRAWN HYMAN A 37 EDW B
DRAWN ISAAC A 32 POS W
DRAWN ISUM A 37 ROB B
DRAWNS JEREMIAH A 37 ROB B
DRESSER ROBERT A 37 ROB B
DREW FRANK A 44 HEN B
DREW JOHN M A 35 MAG W
DREW WILLIAM A 24 EDE B
DREW WILLIAM M A 35 MAG W
DREWER ROBERT A 37 ROB B
DRIGGS BENJN A 28 04A B
DRINKWATER EDWARD A 30 ROA W
DRIVEN H JNO A 29 FA1 W
DRIVER ADAM A 44 KIT B
DRIVER CALVIN A 39 GRI W
DRIVER CHAS A 39 GRI W
DRIVER JOHN A 39 DAV W
DRIVER RICHARDSON A 39 GRI W
DRIVER SHAW A 39 GRI W
DRIVER WM A 29 FA1 W
DROWNS RICHARD A 37 ROB B
DRUMENGO ABILARDO A 40 CAN W
DUDLEY ABRAM A 28 04A B
DUDLEY ANDREW A 28 03A B
DUDLEY AUGUSTUS A 19 POR W
DUDLEY BENJAMIN A 19 MOR B

DUDLEY BRISTOE A 28 03A B
DUDLEY BRYAN A 28 04A B
DUDLEY CAESAR A 28 03A B
DUDLEY DANIEL A 28 16T B
DUDLEY EDW R A 28 04A B
DUDLEY G M A 19 MOR W
DUDLEY GEORGE A 28 04A B
DUDLEY GEORGE A 28 8TH B
DUDLEY HAYWOOD D A 53 FAI B
DUDLEY HENDERSON A 28 04A B
DUDLEY HENRY A 19 BE1 W
DUDLEY HENRY A 19 MOR B
DUDLEY ISAAC A 19 HAD W
DUDLEY J R 28 11T W
DID NOT TAKE THE OATH
WAS A PATROLLER AND
AFTERWWARDS TOOK PART
IN THE WAR
DUDLEY J D A 28 04A B
DUDLEY J D A 30 MOY W
DUDLEY J S A 19 HAD W
DUDLEY JACHONIAH A 19 BE1 W
DUDLEY JACOB A 28 04A B
DUDLEY JACOB A 28 8TH B
DUDLEY JAMES A 28 01A B
DUDLEY JOHN A 19 BE1 W
DUDLEY JOHN A 19 HAD W
DUDLEY JOHN W A 35 KEN W
DUDLEY JOSEPH A 30 IND W
DUDLEY MILES A 19 MOR B
DUDLEY MOSES A 19 NEW B
DUDLEY OLIVER A 28 03A B
DUDLEY SAML A 28 03A B
DUDLEY SAML A 28 05A B
DUDLEY SAMUEL A 19 POR W
DUDLEY SAMUEL A 28 11T W
DUDLEY SIM A 28 10T B
DUDLEY STEPHEN A 19 BE1 W
DUDLEY STEPHEN A 19 HAD W
DUDLEY THOMAS A 19 HAD W
DUDLEY WILLIAM A 30 GIB W
DUDLEY WM H A 28 11T W
DUE HARRISON A 28 02N B
DUFF RILEY A 35 LIM W
DUFF WILLIAM A 35 ROC W
DUFFY F S A 28 02N W
DUFFY GEORGE T A 72 SWA W
DUFFY ISAAC A 28 10T B
DUFFY PATRICK F A 46 GRE W
DUFFY R N A 28 02N W
DUFFY S S A 28 01A W
DUFFY WALTER A 28 02N W
DUGAN MAJOR A 28 16T B
DUGAN TIMOTHY A 37 WHI B
DUGGAN WILLIAM S A 53 GER W
DUGGEN JOHN S A 37 PEN W
DUGGEN WILLIAM A A 37 PEN W
DUGGINS HENRY A 28 05A B
DUGLAS SMITH A 30 IND W
DUGLAS WILLIAM W A 53 LA2 W
DUGLIS MARK A 30 CUR W
DUGUID E M A 28 01B W
DUKE D M A 44 HEN W
CERT TO VOTE OUT COUNTY
DUKE HENRY C A 39 HAY W
DUKE JAMES B A 39 PUG W
DUKE JEREMIAH A 30 COI W
DUKE JOHN A 30 COI W
DUKE JOHN A 39 LOU B
DUKE M G A 39 HAY W
DUKE NOAH A 44 LED W
DUKE P B A 44 FIS W
DUKE R L A 39 PUG W

DUKE S H A 44 LED W
DUKE T K K A 19 MOR W
DUKE THOS V A 44 SAS W
DUKE W C A 39 HAY W
DUKE W K A 39 HAY W
REG BRASSFIELD
DUKE W R A 44 FOR W
DUKE WM D A 44 SAS W
DUKE Z M A 44 FIS W
DUMAS JOHNSON A 35 MAG B
DUNBAR CORNELIUS A 35 WOL B
DUNBAR NELSON A 28 05A B
DUNBAR THOMAS J A 53 GER W
DUNCAN ADDISON A 28 05A B
DUNCAN ALEXANDER A 30 IND W
DUNCAN CHARLES A 44 YXS W
DUNCAN CHARLES H A 44 YXS W
DUNCAN DAVID A 44 TAR W
DUNCAN DEMPSEY A 30 IND W
DUNCAN G W A 44 LED W
DUNCAN HENRY A 37 PEN B
DUNCAN HOWELL A 44 YXR W
DUNCAN ISAAC A 44 TAR W
DUNCAN J H A 44 TAR W
DUNCAN J W R 25 HAY W
NAME LINED OUT
FOR NOT ACQUIRING
A RESIDENCE OF 12 MONTHS
IN STATE IS NOT ENTITLED
DUNCAN JAMES A 28 7TH W
DUNCAN JAMES A A 46 MON W
DUNCAN JESSE A 26 GOF W
DUNCAN JOHN W A 35 GLI W
DUNCAN LOUSHEY A 28 7TH B
DUNCAN MEDICUS A 19 MOR B
DUNCAN S D A 44 TAR W
DUNCAN S H A 44 LED W
DUNCAN S H A 44 TAR W
DUNCAN THOS A 19 BE1 W
DUNCAN THOS L A 19 BE1 W
DUNCAN WILLIAM A 30 IND W
DUNCON JOSEPH H A 19 BE1 W
DUNGAN THOMAS A 46 KIN B
DUNGY JOHN B A 46 GRE B
DUNKIN JACOB A 40 RHY B
DUNLAP JOS P A 32 THO W
DUNN ALBERT A 28 8TH B
DUNN ARCHER A 37 ROB B
DUNN CHARLES A 37 PEN B
DUNN DAVID D A 28 12T W
DUNN EDWARD A 28 04A B
DUNN EDWARD A 28 6TH B
DUNN GEORGE A 37 SPA B
DUNN GEORGE W A 35 KEN W
DUNN GREEN A 39 FRE B
DUNN HENDERSON A 28 04B B
DUNN HENRY A 38 FRE B
DUNN HENRY A 39 GRI B
DUNN HENRY T A 28 13T W
DUNN HEYWOOD A 28 10T B
DUNN J J A 40 CAN W
DUNN JAMES A 39 GRI B
DUNN JAMES E A 44 HEN W
CERT TO VOTE OUT COUNTY
DUNN JEREMIAH A 37 TA1 B
DUNN JOHN A 28 6TH B
DUNN JOHN A 28 7TH W
DUNN JOHN A 37 ROB B
DUNN JOHN A 39 GRI B
DUNN JOS D A 37 ROC W
DUNN LEWIS A 29 FA1 B
DUNN LEWIS A 37 ROC B
DUNN MATHEW A 37 PIN B
DUNN NELSON A 37 HOL B
DUNN REDDING A 37 TA2 W
SPARTA
DUNN ROBT A 29 FA1 B
DUNN RUFUS A 37 ROC W
DUNN SAMUEL A 37 HOL B
DUNN SHADRICK A 19 NEW W
DUNN WILLIAM A 37 ROB B
DUNN WILLIE A 37 SPA W
DUNN WILLIS A 28 13T W
DUNN WM C A 40 STO W
DUNN WM J A 28 13T W
DUNN WYATT A 39 GRI B
DUNNIGAN CHARLES A 37 WHI B
DUNSTON ABRAHAM A 39 LOU B
DUNSTON ALEX A 39 FRA B
DUNSTON ALFORD A 39 LOU B
DUNSTON BILLY A 39 FRE B
DUNSTON CHARLES A 39 HAY B
DUNSTON DUKE A 39 FRA B
DUNSTON EDWIN A 39 LOU B
DUNSTON HARRY A 39 LOU B
DUNSTON HENDERSON A 39 FRA B
DUNSTON HENDERSON A 39 LOU B
DUNSTON HENRY A 30 COI B
DUNSTON HENRY A 39 FRA B
DUNSTON HENRY A 39 PUG B
DUNSTON HENRY A 44 HEN B
DUNSTON HILIARD A 39 FRA B
DUNSTON HILRY A 39 FRA B
DUNSTON JAMES A 39 HAY B
DUNSTON JAMES A 39 LOU B
DUNSTON JAMES H A 39 LOU B
DUNSTON JNO A 44 HEN B
DUNSTON MARTIN A 38 FRE B
DUNSTON NELSON A 39 LOU B
DUNSTON NORPHLET A 39 LOU B
TRNS FROM WILSON CO
TO FRANKLIN CO BY AFF
DUNSTON OSBORN A 39 FRE B
DUNSTON PAUL A 38 FRE B
DUNSTON PAYTON A 44 KIT B
DUNSTON PEYTON A 39 LOU B
TRNS FROM WILSON CTY TO
FRANKLIN CO BY AFF
DUNSTON RICHARD A 39 LOU B
CEDAR CREEK
DUNSTON RICHARD A 44 HEN B
DUNSTON RICHARD B A 39 LOU B
DUNSTON RICHARD T A 39 LOU B
DUNSTON ROBT A 24 EDE B
DUNSTON ROBT A 39 PUG B
DUNSTON SAMUEL A 39 LOU B
DUNSTON SIMON A 39 HAR B
DUNSTON SYLVESTER A 24 EDE B
DUNSTON SYLVESTER A 24 UPP B
DUNSTON THOMAS A 39 PUG B
DUNSTON TURNER A 39 DAV B
DUNSTON WILLIAM A 39 PUG B
DUNSTON WILSON A 39 FRA B
DUNSTON WILSON A 39 HAR B
DUNSTON WM A 29 FA1 B
DUNTON ALEXANDER B A 30 NAR W
DUNTON ISHMAEL A 30 COI B
DUNTON JOHN J D A 30 NAR W
DUNTON JOSEPH S A 30 COI W
DUNTON SANFORD D A 30 NAR W
DUNTON SPENCE A 30 CUR B
DUPREE ADAMS A 99 BUS B
DUPREE ALLEN F A 37 PIN W
DUPREE ALVIN A 99 BUS W
DUPREE BURTON A 99 BUS W
DUPREE DILEY A 37 HIC B
DUPREE ELI A 99 BUS W
DUPREE GEORGE A 37 SPA B
DUPREE HALEY A 99 BUS W
DUPREE JAMES A 99 BUS W
DUPREE JOHN G A 99 BUS W
DUPREE LEWIS A 99 BUS W
DUPREE NELSON A 37 SPA B
DUPREE ORANGE A 37 PIN B
DUPREE PATRICK A 37 PIN B
DUPREE RICHMOND R A 37 SPA W
DUPREE ROBERT A 37 PIN B
DUPREE SHAFER A 37 SPA B
DUPREE SOLOMON A 37 SPA B
DUPREE THOMAS A 99 BUS B
DUPREE WILLIAM A 37 SPA W
DURDEN GUY A 28 05A B
DURDEN PETER A 28 05A B
DURDEN SIMON A 28 05A B
DURDEN WHITE A 28 05A B
DURDON DUNCAN J A 29 FA1 W
DURHAM ABE A 26 SHE B
DURHAM D N A 26 SHE W
DURHAM EDMON A 26 MOU W
DURHAM ISHAM A 44 HEN B
DURHAM JOSEPH A 26 SHE B
DURHAM JOSEPHUS A 26 GOF B
DURHAM L N A 26 SHE W
DURHAM M M A 46 KIN W
DURHAM MONROE A 44 HEN B
DURHAM P A 26 SHE W
DURHAM R J A 26 SHE W
DURHAM R M A 46 KIN W
DURHAM RICHARD A 46 KIN W
DURHAM WESLEY A 44 HEN B
DURHAM WILLIAM A 32 POS W
DURHAM WM S A 46 GIB W
DURTON CHAS A 28 03A B
DUSENBERY PETER A 19 BEI B
DUTTON CHAS K A 28 01A W
DUTY GEO L A 44 HEN W
DUTY J K P A 44 HEN W
DUTY SANDY A 44 HEN B
DWAYS JERRY A 37 SHA B
DWIGGEN J B A 46 KIN W
DWIGGINS J R A 46 KIN W
DYE ROBERT A 19 DAV W
DYSON EDMOND A 46 KIN B
DYSON THOMAS A 46 KIN B
DYSON WILLIAM A 46 SUM B

\- E -

EACKES EXUM A 24 EDE B
EAGLE BENJAMIN A 37 SPA W
EAKER CHRISTIAN 40 MAU W
NAME LINED OUT
JUSTICE OF THE PEACE
BEFORE THE REBELLION
AND GAVE AID AND COMFORT
TO THE ENEMY.
DID NOT QUALIFY REJ
EAKER CHRISTIAN R 40 MAU W
NAME LINED OUT
JUSTICE OF THE PEACE
BEFORE THE REBELLION &
GAVE AID & COMFORT TO
THE ENEMY. NOT QUALIFIED
EAKER CHRISTY JR A 40 BLA W
EAKER DANIEL A 40 MAU B
EAKER DANIEL E A 40 BLA W
EAKER DANIEL SEN A 40 BLA W
EAKER DAVID A 40 DEC W
EAKER HIRAM A 40 DEC W
EAKER J C A 26 WAR W
EAKER JACOB A 40 BLA W

EAKER JAMES A 40 DEC W
EAKER JESSE A 26 WAR W
EAKER JOHN SEN A 40 BLA W
EAKER MILES R A 40 DEC W
EAKER PETER A 26 WAR W
EAKER PETER JR A 40 BLA W
EAKER PETER SEN A 40 BLA W
EAKES ALBERT A 44 YXS W
EAKES IVERSON H A 44 YXR W
EAKES ROBT S A 44 YXS W
EAKES WM S A 44 YXS W
EAKES WOODSON A 44 YXS W
EAKES WOODSON T A 44 YXS W
EAKLE CLINTON A 46 HIG B
EAKS JNO S A 44 YXR W
EAKS MADISON A 44 YXR W
EAKS WM S A 44 YXS W
EAKS ZACARIAH A 44 SAS W
EAMES JAMES L A 24 UPP W
EARES ABLE A 26 SWA W
MILITIA OFFICER &
ENGAGED IN REBELLION
EARL W D A 39 DAV W
EARL Z A 26 GOF W
EARLS ISAAC A 26 SWA W
EARLS J N A 26 SWA W
EARLS JOHN A 28 05A B
EARLS LEGRAN A 26 SWA W
EARNHARDT RICHARD A 32 DAV W
EARNHART ALEXANDER A 32 JAC B
EARNHART W M A 32 DAV W
EASLEY JOS A 46 GRE B
EASLEY MOSES A 19 POR W
EASOM JAMES A 29 CAR W
EASOM JAMES A 29 FA1 W
EASOM WM A 29 FA1 W
EASON HARMON A 53 FAI W
EASON HAYWOOD A 24 UPP W
EASON HAYWOOD A 28 03B B
EASON JAMES A 37 WEB W
EASON JOHN A 24 EDE B
EASON JOHN F A 30 TUL W
EASON SOLM A 28 6TH B
EASON WM H A 28 03A B
EASTER HENRY A 32 DAV W
EASTER HENRY A 32 LEE W
EASTER LEVI A 32 DAV W
EASTER MICHAEL A 32 LEE W
EASTON DAVID A 19 HAD B
EASTON GEORGE A 24 UPP W
EASTOR MICHAEL A 32 YAD W
EASTWOOD C T A 44 LED W
EASTWOOD D B A 44 YXS W
EASTWOOD DAVID A 53 LA1 W
EASTWOOD GEO W A 44 YXR W
EASTWOOD JNO A 44 SAS W
EASTWOOD JOHN A 53 LA1 W
EASTWOOD LEWIS A 53 LA1 W
EASTWOOD WILLIAM B A 53 LA1 W
EASTWOOD WILLIAM D A 53 LA1 W
EATON AARON A 44 HEN B
EATON ALLEN P A 44 HEN B
EATON AUSTIN A 44 TOW B
EATON BAKER A 44 HEN B
EATON BEN A 44 HEN B
EATON CHARLES A 44 TOW B
EATON DAVID A 44 KIT B
EATON ESSEX A 44 TOW B
EATON GREEN A 44 TOW B
EATON GREEN A 44 OXF B
EATON HALIFAX A 44 HEN B
EATON JAMES A 44 FIS B
EATON JAMES A 44 KIT B
EATON JAMES A 46 JAM W
EATON MOSES A 37 TA1 B
EATON NED A 44 HEN B
EATON RICHD A 44 TOW B
EATON RICHD A 44 OXF B
EATON ROBT A 44 HEN B
EATON SAML K A 28 01A W
EATON STEPHEN CHAL A 44 TOW B
EATON THOMAS A 44 TOW B
EATON THOMAS A 44 HEN B
EATON TONEY A 44 HEN B
EATON WARREN A 44 TOW B
EATON WELDON A 44 OXF B
EATON WILLIAM A 46 KIN W
EATON WM A 44 TOW B
EATON WM A 44 HEN B
EATON WM A A 39 LOU W
EAVANS GRIFFIN A 44 HEN B
EAVES ANDREW A 26 PEE B
EAVES BALAAM A 28 04A B
EAVES BENJAMIN A 39 PUG W
EAVES J H A 39 PUG W
EAVES LOSSEN A 26 PEE W
EAVINS ORSBORN A 32 TYR B
EBEREN MOSES A 28 03A B
EBORN BENJ A 28 05A B
EBORN DENNIS A 28 05A B
EBORN EBORN A 28 05A B
EBORN GIDEON A 28 05A B
EBORN JAMES A 28 10T B
EBORN JOHN A 28 05A B
EBORN SHADRACH A 28 04A B
EBORN STANLEY A 28 05A B
EBORN WILLIAM A 53 GER B
EBORN WILLIAM R A 28 9TH W
EBSON JOHN A 19 BE1 B
ECCLES TONY A 29 FA1 B
ECCLES VIRGIL A 29 SEV B
ECCLOS U M A 32 CLE W
ECHENWALDER ANTHONY A 28 01A W
ECHLER ANDERSON A 32 CLE B
ECHOLS W E A 25 HAY W
ECKLE GEORGE A 46 GRE B
ECTOR JOS T A 46 GRE W
EDDINGER JAMES A 32 THO W
EDDINGER JOSEPH A 32 THO W
EDDINGER WM M A 32 THO W
EDDY SIMEON A 19 BE1 B
EDGE JAMES A 37 PEN W
EDGERTON BEN A 39 DAV B
EDGERTON C J A 39 LOU W
TRNS FROM FRANKLINTON
TO LOUISBURG
EDGERTON JOHN A 39 LOU W
EDGERTON LEUIS A 39 DAV B
EDINGS JOHN Q A 26 SHE W
EDLEMON D F A 40 CAN W
EDLEMON DANIEL A 40 CAN B
EDMONDS ISIAH A 28 05A B
EDMONDS J M H A 44 ISL W
EDMONDSON DREWRY A 46 HIG B
EDMONDSON SOLM A 28 01B B
EDMONSON J Q A 25 SHO W
EDMONSON WM J A 46 GRE W
EDMUNDSON HENDERSON A 37 TA1 W
EDMUNDSON MACK G A 37 HIC A
EDMUNDSON POLLARD A 37 PIN W
EDMUNDSON WILEY A 37 PIN W
EDMUNDSON WILLIAM H A 37 HIC A
EDMUNDSON WILLIAM M A 37 PIN W
EDNY ANDREW A 24 MID B
EDWARD ALFORD A 46 FRI W
EDWARD CHARLES A 44 KIT B
EDWARD FRANK A 44 OXF B
EDWARD HENRY A 37 WEB B
EDWARD HENRY A 44 KIT B
EDWARD JAMES A 37 SPA W
EDWARD JOSEPH H A 39 LOU W
EDWARD LEE A 44 OXF B
EDWARD MAC A 44 OXF B
EDWARD WM A 44 KIT W
EDWARD Z W A 44 KIT W
EDWARDS ALBERT A 26 SHE B
EDWARDS ALBERT A 37 TA1 B
EDWARDS ALEXR A 29 CED B
EDWARDS ALFRED LEE A 46 GRE W
EDWARDS AMOS A 26 WAR W
EDWARDS ANDREW A 40 FER B
EDWARDS ANDREW J A 37 TA2 W
SPARTA
EDWARDS ANNEL A 46 GRE W
EDWARDS ASA A 28 11T W
EDWARDS ASA J A 28 10T W
EDWARDS AZARIAH A 28 10T W
EDWARDS BILLIE A 37 WHI W
EDWARDS BLUNT A 28 04A B
EDWARDS BRISTER R 19 MOR B
CONVICTED OF FELONY BY A
COMPETENT JURISDICTION
EDWARDS BUCK A 44 OXF B
EDWARDS CALVIN A 19 BE1 B
EDWARDS CALVIN A 37 SHA B
EDWARDS CASWELL A 28 10T W
EDWARDS CASWELL H A 28 10T W
EDWARDS CHARLES A 39 HAY B
1ST REG BOARD
GRANVILLE CO
EDWARDS CHARLES M A 28 10T W
EDWARDS CHURCHILL A 28 11T B
EDWARDS COL SAM A 44 HEN W
EDWARDS D A A 39 PUG W
EDWARDS DOCTOR A 26 BLA B
EDWARDS E J A 29 CED W
EDWARDS ELBERT A 37 WEB W
EDWARDS EPINETUS A 37 SPA W
EDWARDS FELIX A 35 LIM W
EDWARDS FOSTER A 37 SHA B
EDWARDS G S A 29 CED W
EDWARDS GEORGE A 28 02N B
EDWARDS GEORGE A 37 SHA B
EDWARDS HARDY A 37 HIG W
EDWARDS HAYWOOD A 39 HAY B
EDWARDS HENRY A 35 LIM W
EDWARDS HENRY A 37 SPA B
EDWARDS HENRY A 46 JAM W
EDWARDS ISAAC A 35 CYP W
EDWARDS ISRAEL A 35 LIM B
EDWARDS J L B A 39 HAY W
EDWARDS J T A 46 HIG W
EDWARDS J Z A 29 CED W
EDWARDS JACOB A 28 15T W
EDWARDS JACOB J A 35 MAG W
EDWARDS JAMES A 28 11T B
EDWARDS JAMES A 35 LIM W
EDWARDS JAMES A 39 DAV W
EDWARDS JAMES A 44 FOR B
EDWARDS JAMES A 46 FRI W
EDWARDS JAMES W A 37 WEB W
EDWARDS JAS B A 46 GRE W
EDWARDS JESSE A 39 PUG B
EDWARDS JNO A 29 GRA B
EDWARDS JOEL A 37 WEB W
EDWARDS JOHN A 35 LIM W
EDWARDS JOHN A 37 WHI B
EDWARDS JOHN A 39 HAR W
EDWARDS JOHN A 46 JAM W

EDWARDS JOHN A A 39 JOR W
EDWARDS JOHN C A 28 10T W
EDWARDS JOHN H A 37 EDW W
EDWARDS JOHN H A 37 ROC B
EDWARDS JOHN J A 35 LIM W
EDWARDS JONATHAN A 46 JAM W
EDWARDS KINCHIN A 37 SHA W
EDWARDS L L A 39 PUG W
EDWARDS L R A 44 HEN W
EDWARDS LITTLE B A 37 EDW W
EDWARDS M D A 44 HEN W
EDWARDS MICAJAH P A 37 EDW W
EDWARDS MILES A 37 WHI B
EDWARDS MYERS A 28 10T B
EDWARDS ORDER A 46 GRE B
EDWARDS OSCAR A 46 GRE W
EDWARDS PARIS H A 46 GRE W
EDWARDS PETER A 19 NEW B
EDWARDS R D A 44 KIT W
EDWARDS R T A 39 PUG W
EDWARDS R V A 39 HAY W
EDWARDS REUBEN A 39 HAY B
EDWARDS RICHARD A 28 9TH B
EDWARDS SAML A 29 GRA B
EDWARDS SAMPSON A 37 WEB B
EDWARDS SAMUEL L A 46 HIG W
EDWARDS SILAS M A 37 WEB W
EDWARDS SNOWD A 28 11T B
EDWARDS STEPHEN A 28 11T B
EDWARDS THOMAS A 28 11T B
EDWARDS THOMAS A 46 GRE W
EDWARDS TITUS A 28 01A B
EDWARDS TONY A 29 CED B
EDWARDS W H A 39 PUG W
EDWARDS W L A 40 CAN W
EDWARDS WILLIAM A 26 BUR W
EDWARDS WILLIAM A 28 7TH B
EDWARDS WILLIAM A 29 CED B
EDWARDS WILLIAM A 39 HAR W
EDWARDS WILLIAM B A 37 SPA W
EDWARDS WILLIAM E A 37 WEB W
EDWARDS WILLIAM J A 37 EDW W
EDWARDS WILLIAM L A 37 EDW W
EDWARDS WILLIAM R A 35 ROC W
EDWARDS WILLIAM W A 37 WEB W
EDWARDS WINDSOR A 28 11T B
EDWARDS WM A 28 03A B
EDWARDS WM A 28 16T W
EDWARDS WM A 46 GRE W
EDWARDS WM E A 46 GRE W
EDWARDS WM H A 39 HAR W
EDWARDS WM L A 46 GRE W
EDWARDS Z W A 39 HAY W
EDWARDS ZEDAKIAH A 39 PUG W
EDWARDSON JOSEPH A 37 HOL W
EDWELL SAMUEL A 46 GRE B
EFLAND JOHN G A 46 GRE W
EGERTON ALEX A 39 HAR B
EGERTON C J A 39 FRA W
EGERTON GEORGE A 39 DAV B
EGERTON HARRY A 39 LOU B
TRNS FROM SPEED'S STORE
EGERTON HARRY A 39 SPE B
EGERTON HENDERSON A 39 DAV B
EGERTON HENRY A 39 HAR B
EGERTON ISHAM A 39 HAR B
EGERTON JOHN A 39 DAV B
EGERTON JOHN A 39 LOU B
TRNS FROM DAAVIS X ROAD
EGERTON RICHD A 38 FRE B
EGERTON RICHD SR A 39 FRE B
EGERTON SAM A 39 DAV B
EGERTON SIMON A 39 DAV B

EGGERT GEORGE C A 46 GRE W
EGGLESTON WM A 24 EDE B
EGULES WILLIAM H A 53 BUR W
ELAM A S A 26 GRI W
ELAM GEO A 44 OXF B
ELAM HORRIS A 44 YXS B
ELAM J D A 44 SAS W
ELAM P R A 26 SHE W
ELAM R T A 44 SAS W
ELAM S W A 26 GRI W
ELDRIDGE J HOWARD A 28 01A W
ELDRIDGE PETER A 28 05A B
ELENOR LAWRENCE J A 37 ROB W
ELENOR WM T A 37 ROB W
ELINGTON HENRY A 39 PUG B
ELINGTON RUBAN A 40 STO W
ELIOT HENRY A 29 FLE B
ELIOTT ELIJAH A 46 HIG W
ELIOTT THOS W A 26 SHE W
ELIXSON BURTON A 44 YXS B
ELIXSON J J A 44 YXS W
ELLEM JOSEPH C A 19 BE1 W
ELLEN S F A 32 POS W
ELLER G W A 32 POS W
ELLER GEORGE A 32 POS W
ELLER HENRY A 32 POS W
ELLER J A A 32 POS W
ELLER JACK A 32 POS B
ELLER L D A 32 POS W
ELLER WM A 25 SHO W
ELLERSON JAMES A 19 BE1 B
ELLET SAML A 29 FA2 B
ELLICK WILLIAM A 28 05A B
ELLINGER JAMES M A 40 CAN B
ELLINGTON ARCHD A 44 KIT W
ELLINGTON B J A 44 LED W
ELLINGTON CHAS A 44 OXF W
ELLINGTON FRANK A 44 FIS B
ELLINGTON GEO W A 44 HEN W
ELLINGTON H T A 44 LED W
ELLINGTON HENRY A 39 HAY B
2ND REG BOARD
FRANKLIN CO
ELLINGTON HORACE H A 44 RAG W
ELLINGTON J M A 44 HEN W
ELLINGTON JOHN M A 44 OXF W
ELLINGTON MERIDETH A 44 HEN W
ELLINGTON PATRICK A 44 HEN W
ELLINGTON RICHD A 44 TOW W
ELLINGTON SAML J A 44 HEN W
ELLINGTON SOLOMON A 44 HEN B
ELLINGTON W B A 39 HAY W
ELLINGTON WM L A 44 ISL W
ELLINGTON WM N A 44 OXF W
ELLINOR J D A 32 YAD W
ELLINOR WILLIAM A 37 TA1 B
ELLIOT WM H A 24 UPP W
ELLIOTT A J A 26 BLA W
ELLIOTT AARON A 46 JAM W
ELLIOTT ABRM A 29 CAR B
ELLIOTT ABRM A 29 FA1 B
ELLIOTT ADAM A 26 BLA W
ELLIOTT ANDERSON A 24 EDE B
ELLIOTT BALEM 1 A 29 FLE B
ELLIOTT BALEM 2 A 29 FLE B
ELLIOTT BEN A C A 29 FA1 B
ELLIOTT BENJ A 29 CAR B
ELLIOTT BENJAMIN A 24 UPP B
ELLIOTT BRITTON A 29 FLE B
ELLIOTT BRUM A 26 BLA B
ELLIOTT CANCER A 24 UPP B
ELLIOTT CHARLES A 46 HIG W
ELLIOTT DANIEL A 29 FLE B

ELLIOTT DAVID A 26 BLA B
ELLIOTT DAVID A 29 CAR B
ELLIOTT E D A 26 PEE W
ELLIOTT EDWARD A 29 FLE B
ELLIOTT EDWARD A 29 FLE B
ELLIOTT EDWD A 29 CAR B
ELLIOTT ELI S A 19 HAD W
ELLIOTT ELIAS S A 46 FRI W
ELLIOTT EVANDER A 29 FA1 B
ELLIOTT FRANK A 29 FLE B
ELLIOTT G J A 26 BLA B
ELLIOTT GEO A 29 FA1 B
ELLIOTT GEO A 29 FA1 W
ELLIOTT HARRY A 29 FA1 B
ELLIOTT HECTOR A 29 FA1 B
ELLIOTT HENRY A 19 NEW B
ELLIOTT HIRAM A 29 FLE B
ELLIOTT ISAAC A 35 WAR B
ELLIOTT ISHAM A 29 FA1 B
ELLIOTT ISHAM A 29 FLE B
ELLIOTT J C A 26 BLA W
ELLIOTT JABEL A 29 CAR B
ELLIOTT JACOB A 29 FLE B
ELLIOTT JAMES A 24 UPP B
ELLIOTT JAMES A 29 FA2 B
ELLIOTT JAS M A 44 YXR W
ELLIOTT JOHN A 26 BLA B
ELLIOTT JOHN A 29 CAR B
ELLIOTT JOHN E A 46 COB W
ELLIOTT JORDAN A 29 CAR B
ELLIOTT L F A 44 YXR W
ELLIOTT LAREY A 29 FLE B
ELLIOTT LEROY S A 44 YXR W
ELLIOTT LEWIS A 26 BLA B
ELLIOTT LEWIS JR A 29 CAR B
ELLIOTT LEWIS SR A 29 CAR B
ELLIOTT MILES W A 24 UPP W
ELLIOTT N W A 32 LOF W
ELLIOTT NATHAN A 29 FA1 B
ELLIOTT NATT A 29 FA1 B
REMOVED TO BLADEN CO
ELLIOTT NEEDAM A 29 FA1 B
ELLIOTT NEEDHAM A 29 FA1 B
ELLIOTT O S A 32 JAC W
ELLIOTT OWEN A 29 FLE B
ELLIOTT POMPY A 46 GRE B
ELLIOTT REUBEN A 46 COB W
ELLIOTT ROBERT A 29 FLE B
ELLIOTT ROBERT A 37 PEN B
ELLIOTT ROBT A 24 UPP B
ELLIOTT ROBT A 44 YXR W
ELLIOTT S H A 26 SHE W
ELLIOTT SAML A 29 CAR B
ELLIOTT SAMUEL A 32 POS W
ELLIOTT SPENCER D A 46 GRE W
ELLIOTT STEPHEN A 29 CAR B
ELLIOTT STEPHEN R 28 16T W
WAS PRIVATE IN C.S.A.
AND WAS PATROLE
ELLIOTT T B A 32 JAC W
ELLIOTT T F A 26 SHE W
ELLIOTT T M A 26 BLA B
ELLIOTT THOMAS A 26 SHE W
ELLIOTT THOS A 29 CAR B
ELLIOTT V H A 26 BOR W
ELLIOTT WESLEY A A 46 GRE W
ELLIOTT WILEY A 29 FLE B
ELLIOTT WILLIAM A 30 IND W
ELLIOTT WILLIS A 28 05A B
ELLIOTT WILLIS A 28 05A B
ELLIOTT WM A 29 FA1 B
ELLIOTT WM H A 29 FA2 W
ELLIOTT Z A 26 BOR B

ELLIS A D A 39 FRA W
ELLIS A F A 26 MOU W
ELLIS A H A 32 CLE W
ELLIS A J A 44 RAG W
ELLIS ALONZO Z A 26 SWA W
ELLIS AMERICUS A 26 BUR B
ELLIS ANONYMOUS A 26 SWA B
ELLIS ANTNER A 32 DAV B
ELLIS AUTHER A 32 COT B
ELLIS B F A 26 BUR W
ELLIS BENJ JR A 26 BUR W
ELLIS BENJ SR A 26 BUR W
ELLIS BENJAMINE R 26 BUR W
ELLIS BENJM A 28 01B B
ELLIS BENJM A 46 GIB B
ELLIS C H A 26 SWA W
ELLIS CASTEELES A 26 SHE B
ELLIS CHARLES A 32 DAV B
ELLIS CHAS A 28 01A B
ELLIS CHAS D A 24 EDE W
ELLIS CUDGO A 32 DAV B
ELLIS DANIEL A 26 GOF B
ELLIS DANIEL A 29 ROC W
ELLIS DAVID C A 19 STR W
ELLIS E A 28 01A W
ELLIS E R A 26 BUR W
ELLIS E W A 28 01A W
ELLIS ELIJAH A 19 HUN W
ELLIS FENWICK A 44 LED W
ELLIS FRANKLIN A 32 TYR B
ELLIS GEO W A 28 02N W
DEAD
ELLIS GEORGE A 32 DAV B
ELLIS GEORGE W A 32 BRO B
ELLIS H J A 29 SEV W
ELLIS HAZZELL A 26 SWA B
ELLIS HICKMAN A 37 WEB W
ELLIS J F A 19 NEW W
ELLIS J A A 39 FRA W
ELLIS J H A 29 FA1 W
ELLIS J P A 26 MOU W
ELLIS J R A 26 BUR W
ELLIS J R A 32 CLE W
ELLIS JAMES A 26 BUR B
ELLIS JAMES A 28 01B B
ELLIS JAMES A 28 02N W
ELLIS JAMES W A 28 02N W
ELLIS JERIMIAH A 24 MID W
ELLIS JESSE A 29 SEV W
ELLIS JIM A 39 LOU B
ELLIS JNO C A 29 GRA W
ELLIS JNO S A 44 RAG W
ELLIS JOHN A 29 SEV W
ELLIS JOHN A 39 DAV W
TRNS FROM WARREN CO
WARRENTON PRE.
ELLIS L H A 26 GOF W
ELLIS M L A 25 SHO W
ELLIS MARCUS A 26 SWA W
ELLIS MOSES A 44 LED W
ELLIS NATHAN A 26 SWA B
ELLIS R J M A 24 EDE W
ELLIS R S A 26 BUR W
ELLIS REWBIN A 26 GOF B
ELLIS RHEUBEN A 44 DUT B
ELLIS RICHARD A 32 CLE W
ELLIS ROBT T A 29 FA1 W
ELLIS RUFES A 32 DAV B
ELLIS S F A 39 FRA W
ELLIS SAMUEL A 32 DAV B
ELLIS SAMUEL A 32 TYR B
ELLIS SOLOMON A 26 MOU W
ELLIS THOMAS A 46 HIG B
ELLIS THORNTON A 26 BUR B
ELLIS W H A 44 RAG W
ELLIS WESLEY A 24 EDE W
ELLIS WESLEY A 32 CLE B
ELLIS WILLIAM A 26 GOF B
ELLIS WILLIAM A 28 12T B
CERTIF GIVEN LIVES
NOW AT CEDAR GROVE
ELLIS WILLIS A 24 MID W
ELLIS WILLIS A 26 MOU W
ELLIS WM W A 44 KIT W
ELLISON CAESAR A 28 03A B
ELLISON CORNELIUS A 28 03A B
ELLISON EDWARD A 28 11T B
ELLISON FRANKLIN R A 19 BE2 B
ELLISON FRED A 28 01B B
ELLISON HOYT A 26 GOF B
ELLISON ISAAC A 28 03A B
ELLISON J A A 46 HIG W
ELLISON JAMES R A 19 BE1 B
ELLISON MATTHEW A 28 03A B
ELLISON MOSES A 28 01A B
ELLISON ROBERT L A 19 BE1 B
ELLISON STEPHEN A 19 BE1 B
ELLITT DANIEL A 29 LOC B
ELLIXSON JAS S A 44 OXF W
ELLSWORTH A A A 28 03A W
ELLSWORTH WILLIAM N A 35 ISL W
ELLWOOD JOHN A 40 DA1 W
ELMON MICHAEL A 40 BLA W
ELMORE CHARLES B A 35 MAG W
CERT GIVEN 9 AP. 1868
ELMORE H R A 40 STO W
ELMORE JAMES A 26 WAR W
ELMORE JAMES A 29 SEV W
ELROD CHRISTOPHER A 32 CLE W
ELVERSON GEORGE A 32 DAV W
ELVERSON JOHN A 32 TYR W
ELVINTER ABRAM A 28 04A B
EMBLAR H A 32 THO W
EMERSON TENY A 29 FLE B
EMERY GEORGE W A 19 CED W
EMERY J A A 44 DUT W
EMERY JAMES H A 53 SWA W
EMERY JOHN A 53 SWA W
EMERY SORROWFULL A 28 17T W
EMERY STEPHEN B A 53 LA1 W
EMERY W G A 44 DUT W
EMERY ZACHARIAH A 28 17T W
EMORY JOHN A 44 FOR W
EMRY ZACHARIAH A 53 LA1 W
ENGLEBRIGHT B F A 44 YXR W
ENGLISH CHARLES A 35 ISL W
ENGLISH ENOCH D A 53 SWA W
ENGLISH GEORGE W A 35 ISL W
ENGLISH JAMES A 19 POR W
ENGLISH JAMES W A 35 ISL W
ENGLISH MONROE A 35 ISL W
ENGLISH STEPHEN A 35 ISL W
ENLOE CURRY A 40 DA1 B
ENLOW JAMES A 40 DA1 W
ENNIS JAMES J A 35 ROC W
ENNIS JOHN B A 35 ROC W
ENNIS WILLIAM B A 35 ROC W
ENNIS WM B A 29 QUW W
ENSLEY ANDERSON A 32 THO W
ENSLEY BENNERS A A 53 LA1 W
ENSLEY EDWARD A 53 FAI B
ENSLEY MARTIN A 46 HIG W
ENSLEY ROBERT A 53 LA1 W
ENSLEY WM A 28 14T W
EPP Z A 32 JAC W
EPPES ALFRED A 44 TOW B
EPPS B R A 32 DAV W
EPPS GALES B A 32 SHE W
EPPS HENRY A 46 HIG B
EPPS ROBT A 44 TOW B
EPPS WM A 44 TOW B
EPSE WILLIAM A 32 DAV W
ERAMBERT H A 29 FA1 W
SYMPHATHIZED WITH REB
BY H PORTER U S SOLDIER
ERAMBERT H JR A 29 FA1 W
ERAMBERT J M A 29 FA1 W
ERNULL ISAAC A 28 11T B
ERNULL J B A 28 12T W
ERNULL JAMES A A 28 12T W
ERVIN W N A 25 HAY W
ERWIN JOHN F A 46 RAG W
ERWIN WYATT A 46 RAG W
ESHON SAMUEL A 24 EDE W
ESKINSON REUBEN A 28 05A B
ESKIT ANTHONY A 28 05A B
ESKRIDGE AB A 26 BLA B
ESKRIDGE ALEXANDER A 26 BUR B
ESKRIDGE ELIGA A 26 SHE W
ESKRIDGE G M A 26 BLA W
ESKRIDGE H A 26 SHE W
ESKRIDGE J G A 26 BLA W
ESKRIDGE J L A 26 SHE W
ESKRIDGE J W A 26 BLA W
ESKRIDGE LEVIS A 26 HOL B
ESKRIDGE R C A 26 BLA W
ESKRIDGE S T A 26 BLA W
ESKRIDGE W H A 26 BLA W
ESKRIDGE W L A 26 BLA W
ESOM JNO E A 29 CAR W
ESSECK NOAH A 32 DAV W
ESSICK DANIEL A 32 POS W
ESSICK DAVID A 32 CLE W
ESSICK JACOB A 32 CLE W
ESSICK JACOB A 32 SHE W
ESSICK JOHN A 32 DAV W
ESSICK L A 32 SHE W
ESSICK MATHIAS A 32 SHE W
ESSICK RANSOM A 32 SHE W
ESSICK ROBERT A 32 SHE W
ESSICK THOMAS A 32 SHE W
ESSICK VALENTINE A 32 THO W
CERTIF
ESSICK WILLIAM A 32 DAV W
ESSICK WM R A 32 CLE W
ESTES C L A 28 01A W
ESTES GEORGE W G A 46 GRE W
ESTES H B A 44 TOW W
ESTES NELSON A 39 HAR B
ESTES W M A 39 LOU W
TRNS BY AFF FROM
GRANVILLE BRASSFIELDS
TO FRANKLIN CO
ESTES W T A 44 TOW W
ESTIS ALFORD A 44 BEA B
ESTIS JEREMMIAH A 44 FOR W
ESTIS KIT A 46 GRE B
ESTIS W M A 44 FOR W
ESTOR J G R 46 FRI W
WAS NOT A RESIDENT
OF STATE 12 MONTHS
STRICKEN APRIL 11 1868
ETHEREDGE EMANUEL A 30 NOR B
ETHEREDGE HENRY A 39 HAR W
ETHEREDGE TRUXTON S A 30 NOR W
ETHEREDGE WILLIAM E A 30 NOR W
ETHERIDGE AARON A 30 IND B
ETHERIDGE ADAM D A 30 ROA W
ETHERIDGE ALFRED A 28 05A B

ETHERIDGE ALONZO M A 30 ROA W
ETHERIDGE AMOS R A 30 ROA W
ETHERIDGE AMOS R A 53 LA1 W
ETHERIDGE ANDREW J A 30 POW W
ETHERIDGE BENJ A 28 03A W
ETHERIDGE BENJAMIN DA 30 ROA W
ETHERIDGE CALEB A 30 GIB W
ETHERIDGE CALEB A 30 MOY W
ETHERIDGE CAREY A 30 MOY W
ETHERIDGE CHARLES S A 30 ROA W
ETHERIDGE D D A 30 IND W
ETHERIDGE D T A 24 MID W
ETHERIDGE DANIEL M A 30 ROA W
ETHERIDGE DAVIS A 30 MOY W
ETHERIDGE DENNIS A 30 IND W
ETHERIDGE EDMOND A 30 IND B
ETHERIDGE EDWARD A 30 POW W
ETHERIDGE ELDRED A 30 COI W
ETHERIDGE ELIAS A 30 IND W
ETHERIDGE HUMPHRY A 30 IND B
ETHERIDGE ISIAH A 30 GIB W
ETHERIDGE JAMES A 37 ROB W
ETHERIDGE JEFFERSON A 30 MOY W
ETHERIDGE JNO A 30 IND W
ETHERIDGE JOHN A 30 MOY W
ETHERIDGE JOHN A A 30 ROA W
ETHERIDGE JOHN T A 30 NAR W
ETHERIDGE JOSEPH W A 30 ROA W
ETHERIDGE LAMUEL L A 30 POW W
ETHERIDGE LEVI N A 30 IND W
ETHERIDGE LITTLEJOHNA 30 ROA W
ETHERIDGE NATHAN A 30 POP W
ETHERIDGE NATHAN A 30 ROA W
ETHERIDGE Q H A 30 MOY W
ETHERIDGE RICHARD A 30 ROA B
ETHERIDGE SAMUEL A 30 ROA B
ETHERIDGE SPENCER A 30 ROA W
ETHERIDGE TART A 30 ROA W
CHALLENGED
MAGISTRATE PRIOR
TO THE WAR
ETHERIDGE THOS F A 30 GIB W
ETHERIDGE VAN BUREN A 30 ROA W
ETHERIDGE W F A 30 MOY W
ETHERIDGE WILLIAM A 30 TUL W
ETHERIDGE WILLIAM JRA 30 TUL W
ETHERIDGE WILLOUGHBYA 30 TUL W
ETHERIDGE WILLS A 30 MOY W
ETHERIDGE WM A 28 04A B
ETHERIDGE WM F A 30 GIB W
ETHERIDGE WM J A 37 ROB W
ETHERIDGE YORK A 30 ROA B
ETTERS ANDREW A 26 GOF W
ETTERS HENRY A 26 SWA W
ETTERS JOSEPH A 26 GOF W
ETTERS SAMUEL A 26 SWA W
ETTERS T F A 26 GOF W
EUBANK ALLEN G R 28 02N W
CONSTABLE PRIOR TO WAR
EUBANKS REDDING A 28 04B W
EUBANKS REDDING JR A 28 6TH W
EUBANKS THOS A 28 6TH W
EUBANKS WILLIAM A 28 6TH W
EUDY JOHN A 46 GRE W
CERT TO DAVIDSON
EUDY M J A 40 CAN W
EUINS BALEM A 29 CED B
EULESS ELI S A 46 COB W
EULISS ALEX M A 46 COB W
EULISS MICHAEL A A 46 COB W
EULISS WM A A 46 COB W
EURLES ABRAL A 37 MAN B
EUSTON NOAH A 37 SPA B

EVAN ISAAC A 37 ROC B
EVANS ABRAHAM A 44 TAR W
EVANS ADAM A 29 LOC B
EVANS ADEN A 35 CYP W
EVANS ALEX A 44 FOR W
EVANS ALEXANDER A 32 DAV W
EVANS ALEXR A 28 04A B
EVANS BENJAMIN L A 24 MID W
EVANS BRYANT A 35 MAG W
EVANS BURRELL A 29 FA1 B
EVANS C B A 29 ROC B
TRANSFERRED FROM
FAYETTEVILLE BOOK
EVANS C P A 29 FA1 B
TRANSFERRED TO ROCKFISH
EVANS CHRISTAIN A 32 CLE W
EVANS CHS A 29 LOC B
EVANS CLINTON A 29 FA1 B
EVANS DAIRE A 29 ROC W
EVANS DANIEL A 32 SHE W
EVANS DANIEL A 44 HEN B
EVANS DAVID A 26 SHE W
EVANS DAVID A 44 RAG B
EVANS E H R 29 GRA W
COUNTY ASSESSOR 1859
AIDED REBELLION
EVANS EDWARD A 26 SHE B
EVANS ELIJAH A 30 POP W
EVANS FRANK A 28 04B B
EVANS GEO A 39 GRI B
EVANS GEO W A 29 LOC B
EVANS GEORGE A 28 05A B
EVANS GEORGE A 28 6TH B
EVANS HENRY A 24 UPP W
EVANS HENRY A 28 04A B
EVANS HENRY A 29 FA1 B
EVANS HENRY A 30 POP W
EVANS HORATIO A 28 04A B
EVANS ISAAC A 29 FA1 B
EVANS ISAAC A 35 CYP B
EVANS J G A 46 SUM W
EVANS J P R 25 HAY W
NAME LINED OUT
FOR NOT ACQUIRING
A RESIDENCE OF 12 MONTHS
IN STATE IS NOT ENTITLED
EVANS JAMES A 30 IND W
EVANS JAMES A 30 POW W
EVANS JAMES A 32 SHE W
EVANS JAMES G A 26 SHE W
EVANS JAMES JR A 29 LOC W
EVANS JAMES W A 28 03A B
EVANS JAS M A 44 TAR W
EVANS JESSEE A 30 POP W
EVANS JESSEE B A 29 FA2 W
EVANS JNO A 29 GRA B
EVANS JNO A 29 GRA B
EVANS JNO A 29 LOC B
EVANS JNO JR A 29 LOC B
EVANS JOHN A 24 UPP W
EVANS JOHN A 44 LED B
EVANS JOHN D A 35 MAG W
EVANS JOHN S A 25 HAY W
COPPIED FROM ABOVE
NAME LINED OUT
FOR NOT ACQUIRING
A RESIDENCE OF 12 MONTHS
IN STATE IS NOT ENTITLED
EVANS JOHN W A 30 POW W
EVANS JOHNATHAN A 29 LOC W
EVANS JOS A 39 GRI B
EVANS JOSIAH A 24 MID W
EVANS LEWIS A 26 GRI W

EVANS LEWIS A 29 FA1 B
EVANS LEWIS A 44 OXF B
EVANS MACK A 29 GRA B
EVANS MADISON A 39 LOU W
TRNS FROM PUGHES HILL
EVANS MAJOR A 44 KNA B
EVANS MARSELLIS A 44 OXF B
EVANS MICHAEL A 32 SHE W
EVANS MONROE A 44 OXF B
EVANS MOSES A 29 FA1 B
EVANS MOSES A 32 BRO W
EVANS NELSON A 46 GRE B
EVANS OWEN H A 28 03A W
EVANS PATRICK A 29 FA2 B
SEE C P EVANS TRANSFER
TO ROCKFISH BOOKS
EVANS PETER A 29 GRA B
EVANS PETER A 29 LOC B
EVANS PHIL A 39 GRI B
EVANS PHILLIP A 29 GRA B
EVANS PRESTON S A 24 MID W
EVANS RICHARD A 29 FA2 B
EVANS RICHD A 29 LOC B
EVANS RICHD A A 44 HEN W
EVANS ROBERT A 25 HAY W
COPIED FROM ABOVE
NAME LINED OUT
FOR NOT ACQUIRING
A RESIDENCE OF 12 MONTHS
IN STATE IS NOT ENTITLED
EVANS ROBT A 29 FA1 B
EVANS SAMEUL B A 35 MAG W
EVANS SAMUEL A 28 9TH B
EVANS SIPP A 29 LOC B
EVANS SOL A 29 FA1 B
EVANS SPENCER A 30 IND W
EVANS STARKEY B A 24 UPP W
EVANS THEOPH A 29 FA2 W
EVANS THOMAS A 29 FA2 B
EVANS THOMAS A 29 GRA B
EVANS THOS A 29 FA1 B
EVANS THOS R 24 EDE W
REJ BY THE BOARD
CAUSE WAS MAGISTRATE
BEFORE THE WAR AND
DURING THE WAR ALSO
DID NOT TAKE THE OATH
EVANS WESLY A 29 FA2 B
EVANS WILLIAM A 29 LOC B
EVANS WILLIAM A 44 OXF B
EVANS WILLIAM A A 30 POW W
EVANS WILLIAM B A 30 IND W
EVANS WILLIAM M A 35 MAG W
EVANS WILLIS A 24 MID W
EVEARD PARSON A 28 05A B
EVELYN EDWARD A 29 ROC W
EVENS BILLY A 39 DAV B
EVENS ISAAC A 29 LOC B
EVENS J S A 29 LOC W
EVENS JACOB A 39 LOU B
EVENS JOHN A 39 JOR B
EVENS JOHN A 39 PUG W
EVENS PERRY A 39 LOU B
EVENS SAMUEL A 39 PUG W
EVENS THOMAS A 72 SWA B
EVENS W H A 39 SPE W
EVERET WILLIAM A 44 BRA B
EVERETT AARON A 28 8TH B
EVERETT AUSTIN A 37 PIN B
EVERETT BENJAMIN A 37 PIN B
EVERETT EATON A 37 SPA W
EVERETT EDWARD A 46 GRE B
EVERETT ELISHA A 99 BUS B

EVERETT G S A 29 LOC W
EVERETT G W A 29 CED W
EVERETT HENRY A 29 CED W
EVERETT JAMES A 29 LOC W
EVERETT JAMES C A 37 WEB W
EVERETT JAS W A 29 LOC W
EVERETT JNO A 29 CED W
EVERETT JOE A 37 TA2 B
EVERETT JOHN A 28 05A B
EVERETT JOHN A 28 6TH B
EVERETT JOHN A 29 GRA B
EVERETT NATHAN B A 37 SPA W
EVERETT NATHANIEL A 28 8TH B
EVERETT PRINCE A 28 05A B
EVERETT R H A 29 LOC W
EVERETT THOMAS A 19 MOR B
EVERETT WHITMOND A 37 PIN B
EVERETTS PETER A 28 05A B
EVERHART ANDREW A 32 DAV W
EVERHART ANDREW A 32 DAV W
EVERHART ANDREW A 32 DAV W
EVERHART BRITIN A 32 DAV W
EVERHART CHRISTIAN A 32 DAV W
EVERHART DAVID A 32 DAV W
EVERHART EMANUEL A 32 DAV W
EVERHART GEORGE A 32 DAV W
EVERHART H W A 32 DAV W
EVERHART JACOB A 32 DAV W
EVERHART JACOB A 32 DAV W
EVERHART JERRY A 32 COT B
EVERHART JOHN A 32 DAV W
EVERHART LOUIS A 32 DAV W
EVERHART MATHIAS A 32 DAV W
EVERHART MICHAEL A 32 DAV W
EVERHART MICHAEL JR A 32 DAV W
EVERHART NELON A 32 DAV W
EVERHART PHELIX A 32 DAV W
EVERHART VOLANTINE A 32 DAV W
EVERHART WM A 32 DAV W
EVERHEART ALEX. A 32 SHE W
EVERHEART ALFERD A 32 THO W
EVERHEART ANDREW A 32 POS W
EVERHEART CHRISTIAN A 32 POS W
EVERHEART FRANKLIN A 32 POS W
EVERHEART HAMILTON A 32 POS W
EVERHEART JOHN A 32 POS W
EVERHEART WILLIAM A 32 POS W
EVERIT CALVIN A 53 GER B
EVERITE THOMAS A 19 BE1 B
NAME LINED THROUGH
TRANS TO 9TH E. P.
EVERSON GEORGE A 28 01B W
EVERTON CALEB A 30 NAR W
EVERTON MAJOR A 30 POP W
EVERTON THOMAS T A 30 COI W
EVINS BURT M A 44 ISL B
EVINS EDWARD A 29 LOC B
EVINS JERRIMIAH A 24 MID W
EVINS MADISON A 39 PUG W
TRANS TO LOUISBURG
EVINS W J A 39 HAY W
EVRINGTON DAVID A 28 13T W
EVRINGTON JESSE A 28 13T W
EVRINGTON JOHN E A 28 13T W
EVRIT R H NO 2 A 29 LOC W
EVRIT R M A 29 LOC W
EVVINS TURNER A 44 OXF B
EWELL JAMES A 28 11T W
EWELL JOSHUA A 28 11T W
EWELL WILEY A A 28 11T W
EWING H F A 40 STO W
EWING HUGH A 40 STO W
EWING JOHN A 40 STO B
EWING S B A 40 STO W
EWING S L A 40 STO W
EWING W T H A 32 POS W
EZELL BRIDGER A 44 HEN B
EZELL L C A 26 SHE W
EZZELL BENJAMIN S A 35 WAR W
EZZELL CULLEN A 35 WAR W
EZZELL CURTIS H A 35 WAR W
EZZELL FLEETWOOD A 35 WAR W
EZZELL HARRY A 35 WAR B
EZZELL HENRY A 35 MAG W
EZZELL JOHN A 35 WAR W
EZZELL JOSEPH C A 35 WAR W
EZZELL LAMB J A 35 MAG W
EZZELL LEONARD A 35 KEN B
EZZELL LEWIS W A 35 MAG W
EZZELL LOVE J A 35 MAG W
EZZELL SALATHIEL A 35 MAG W
EZZELL STEPHEN A 35 WAR W
EZZELL WILLIAM W A 35 WAR W
EZZELL ZACHARIAH A 35 WAR W

- F -

FACEN GEORGE A 37 HOL B
FACEN ISAAC A 37 MAN B
FACEN OWEN A 19 BE1 B
FACEN VALENTINE A 19 BE1 B
FAIN ALFRED A 44 HEN B
FAIN BURWELL A 44 TOW B
FAIN GRANDISON A 44 HEN B
FAIN HARRY A 44 ISL B
FAIN KENT A 44 ISL B
FAIN SAMUEL A 44 RAG B
FAIN SIMON A 44 ISL B
FAIN WILLIAM A 44 SAS B
FAIR CEASER A 19 BE1 B
FAIR LUKE A 19 NEW B
FAIR SAMUEL A 19 BE1 B
FAIR WILLIAM A 19 NEW B
FAIR WILLIAM A 72 SWA B
FAIRCLOTH A E A 29 FA2 W
FAIRCLOTH BLUFORD A 29 CED W
FAIRCLOTH DANIEL A 29 LOC W
FAIRCLOTH F F A 29 LOC W
FAIRCLOTH G A 29 LOC W
FAIRCLOTH HINTON A 29 CED W
FAIRCLOTH JAMES O A 29 CED W
FAIRCLOTH L B A 29 FAI W
FAIRCLOTH MARK A 29 LOC W
FAIRCLOTH MOSES A 37 SPA B
FAIRCLOTH RAFORD A 29 CED W
FAIRCLOTH THOS A 29 CED W
FAIRCLOTH WM A 29 CED W
FAIRCLOTH WM A 29 LOC W
FAIRCLOTH WM A 29 ROC W
FAIRLY DAVID A 29 FA1 W
FAIRYER THOMAS A 28 15T B
FAIRYON JOHN A 28 04A B
FAISON AARON A 35 WAR B
FAISON ABRAM M A 35 WAR W
FAISON ALEXANDER A 35 MAG B
FAISON ANDREW A 35 WAR B
FAISON ARY A 35 FAI B
FAISON BAKER A 35 WAR B
FAISON BERNARD A 35 WAR B
FAISON BRYANT A 35 FAI B
FAISON DANIEL A 35 KEN B
FAISON DANIEL A 35 ROC B
FAISON DANIEL NO 1 A 35 FAI B
FAISON DANIEL NO 2 A 35 FAI B
FAISON DAVID NO 1 A 35 FAI B
FAISON DAVID NO 2 A 35 FAI B
FAISON E J A 35 FAI W
FAISON EDWARD A 35 WOL B
FAISON GEORGE A 35 FAI B
FAISON GREENE A 35 FAI B
FAISON H W A 35 FAI W
FAISON HARVEY A 35 WAR B
FAISON HAYWOOD A 35 FAI B
FAISON HENRY A 35 FAI B
FAISON HENRY A 35 WAR B
CERTIFICATE
GIVEN TO GOLDSBORO
FAISON ISAAC A 35 ROC B
FAISON JAMES A 35 WAR B
FAISON JEREMIAH A 35 WAR B
FAISON JOHN A 35 FAI B
FAISON JULIEN P A 35 ROC W
FAISON KADER A 35 FAI B
FAISON KANE A 29 FA1 B
FAISON LEON A 28 6TH B
FAISON LOVELESS A 35 ROC B
FAISON LYNN A 35 FAI B
FAISON MARCUS A 35 FAI B
FAISON MILTON A 35 ROC B
FAISON OLIVER A 35 FAI B
FAISON OSCAR A 44 KIT B
FAISON PETER A 35 FAI B
FAISON PETER A 35 WAR B
FAISON PETER NO 2 A 35 FAI B
FAISON RANDOLF A 35 FAI B
FAISON ROBERT A 35 FAI B
FAISON RUFUS A 35 WAR B
FAISON SAMUEL A 35 FAI B
FAISON SIMON A 35 WAR B
FAISON THOMAS A 35 FAI B
FAISON W W A 35 FAI W
FAISON WASHINGTON A 35 FAI B
FAISON WISDOM A 35 KEN B
FAITHFUL WILLIAM A 37 EDW W
FALK ALFORD A 24 MID B
FALKNER ALEXANDER A 39 LOU W
TRNS FROM HAYESVILLE
FALKNER BENJAMIN A 39 LOU W
TRNS FROM HAYESVILLE
FALKNER CHAMPION A 44 HEN W
FALKNER FRANK A 44 HEN W
FALKNER ISAAC A 39 DAV B
FALKNER J H A 44 HEN W
FALKNER JAMES A 39 FRA W
FALKNER N J A 44 KIT W
FALKNER T N A 44 HEN W
FALKNER WM A 44 HEN W
FALKNER WM A 44 OXF W
FALKNER WM H A 44 HEN W
FALL J C A 26 GOF W
FALLS A JACKSON A 40 FER W
FALLS DANIEL A 26 GOF B
FALLS DAVID L A 26 GOF W
FALLS ELI A 40 FER B
FALLS F M A 26 BOR W
FALLS H F A 40 SAN B
FALLS J B JR A 26 GRI W
FALLS J F A 26 GOF W
FALLS J H A 26 BOR B
FALLS J O A 26 BOR W
FALLS J P A 26 GOF W
FALLS JAMES A 40 DA1 B
FALLS JAMES B A 26 GOF W
FALLS JAMES H A 26 GOF W
FALLS JEFFERSON A 40 FER B
FALLS JOHN A 26 GOF W
FALLS JOHN R A 40 FER W
FALLS PETER A 40 SAN B
FALLS R W A 26 GRI W
FALLS ROBERT A 26 GOF W
FALLS ROBERT A A 40 FER W

FALLS T D A 26 CAR W
FALLS THOMAS A 40 DA1 B
FALLS THOMAS L A 40 FER W
FALLS WILLIAM A 40 FER W
FALLS WILLIAM A A 40 FER W
FALLS YORK A 40 SAN B
FANCELY DANIL A 32 CLE W
FANCLER JOSEPH A 32 CLE W
FANE C L A 25 HAY W
FANNER JOSIAH A 37 ROC W
FANNER RICHARD A 37 ROC W
FANSHAW DAVIS A 30 IND W
FANSHAW JOHN A 30 IND W
FANSHAW JOHN A 30 IND W
FANST ORACHIA A 19 MOR W
FARABEE B L A 32 SHE W
FARABEE J H A 32 THO W
CERTIF
FARABEE JOHN A A 32 CLE W
FARABEE LEWIS A 32 DAV B
FARABEE THOMAS A 32 THO B
FARABEE WM M A 32 POS W
FARABOW D C A 44 LED W
FARABOW W S A 44 LED W
FAREBEE WILLOBY D R 28 16T W
PRIVATE IN C.S.A. PATROL
FAREMAN WM J A 19 STR W
FARER CHARLES A 44 OXF B
FARIBAULT HENDERSON A 24 EDE B
FARIBAULT THOMAS A 24 EDE B
FARIBEAU EMANUEL A 24 EDE B
FARINGTON HARBERT A 46 FRI W
FARINGTON JOHN F A 46 ROS W
FARINGTON JOSEPH A 46 FRI W
FARINGTON JOSIAH A 46 FRI W
FARINGTON MARVIN A 46 FRI W
FARINGTON MILTON A 46 FRI W
FARIS R B W A 40 BLA W
FARLAW WILLIAM A 35 WAR B
FARLEY A D A 28 05A B
FARLOW DAVID W A 35 KEN W
FARLOW J L A 19 BE1 W
FARLOW JOHN A 35 KEN W
FARLOW LEWELL A 46 HIG W
FARLOW LEWIS S A 19 BE1 W
FARLOW PHAROAH A 35 KEN B
FARLOW ROBERT H A 35 KEN W
FARLOW WEST A 35 KEN B
FARMER DANIEL A 46 COB W
FARMER GABRIEL A 29 CAR B
FARMER H A 25 SHO W
FARMER ISAAC W A 37 SHA W
FARMER JOHN A 35 WOL B
FARMER JOHN A 37 SPA B
FARMER NORMAN A 37 WHI B
FARMER RILEY A 46 COB W
FARMIDGE ROBERT A 29 ROC W
FARNER WILSON A 26 CAR B
FARR JOHN JR A 28 01A W
FARRAR AMBROSE A 28 05A B
FARRAR FRANCIS A 44 BEA B
FARRAR OWEN C A 37 TA1 W
FARREBEE JOSEPH A 32 POS W
FARRELL ETHIEL A 37 HIG W
FARRELL GEORGE A 30 IND W
FARRELL JAMES A 37 WHI B
FARRER AARON A 40 CAN B
FARRER JOHN A 40 CAN W
FARRER N P A 40 CAN W
FARRER THOMAS J A 37 TA2 W
FARRIER GEORGE A 35 CYP B
FARRIER GEORGE A 35 KEN W
FARRIER HARRY A 35 KEN B
FARRIER JAMES A 35 CYP B
FARRIER PETER A 35 CYP B
FARRINGTON W L A 46 SUM W
FARRIOR DAVID A 35 KEN W
FARRIOR EDWARD A 35 KEN B
FARRIOR EDWARD W A 35 LIM W
FARRIOR GUILFORD A 35 KEN B
FARRIOR HENRY A 35 KEN B
FARRIOR HUGH A 35 ISL W
FARRIOR ISLAND A 35 KEN B
FARRIOR JACKSON A 35 LIM B
FARRIOR JAMES C A 35 LIM W
FARRIOR JOHN W A 35 KEN W
FARRIOR LEWIS A 35 KEN B
FARRIOR LEWIS A 44 TOW B
FARRIOR NICHOLAS P A 35 KEN W
FARRIOR S D A 35 LIM W
FARRIS BENJAMIN A 40 DA1 B
FARRISH JOSEPH B A 46 GRE W
FARRON RICHARD A 53 LA1 W
FARROW ABRAHAM A 44 HEN B
FARROW ABRAHAM C A 53 HAT W
FARROW CHRISTOPHER PA 53 HAT W
FARROW EDWARD A 53 OCR W
FARROW GEORGE A 53 SWA B
FARROW HARVEY S A 30 ROA B
FARROW HENRY A 53 HAT B
FARROW HEZAKIAH A 53 GER W
FARROW JOHN P A 53 KEN W
FARROW JOSEPH A 53 HAT W
FARROW LORANZA B A 53 HAT W
FARROW NASA A 53 SWA W
FARROW RICHARD Z A 53 KEN W
FARROW RILEY A 53 FAI B
FARROW SAMUEL F A 53 HAT W
FARROW TILMON A 53 OCR W
FARROW WILLIAM T A 53 LA2 W
STRICKEN OUT
APRIL 15TH 1868
REJECTED
FARROW WILSON T A 53 OCR W
FARTHING H A 28 04A W
FASTER MINTON A 37 HIG B
FATHERLY WM J A 28 01A W
SWORN TO BY JAS H POOL
DEAF & DUMB
FATON JOHN A 24 EDE B
FAUCET WM A 28 05A B
FAUCET WM M A 28 6TH W
FAUCETT HENRY A 46 MON W
FAUCETT JNO A 44 SAS W
FAUCETT WM A 44 SAS W
FAUCETT WM H JR A 46 GRE W
FAULK ANTHONY A 29 SEV B
FAULK EDMUND A 37 EDW W
FAULK LEVY A 39 DAV W
FAULK NATHANIEL A 39 DAV W
FAULKNER ALEXANDER A 39 HAY W
FAULKNER BENJAMIN A 39 HAY W
FAULKNER HENRY A 44 ISL W
FAULKNER JOSEPH A 44 FIS W
FAULKNER WILLIAM A 44 YXS B
FAULKS JAS F A 29 FA1 W
FAULKS MALCOM A 29 FA1 W
HELD OFFICE BEFORE WAR
& ENG IN REBELLION
FAY CONRAD A 32 THO B
FAY YORK A 32 THO B
FAYSON DAVID A 28 05A B
FEAGAN THOS K A 24 EDE W
FEAR CLITESS A 37 TA2 B
FEARRAND JOHN A 28 6TH W
FEARRAND JOSEPH B A 28 6TH W
FEATHERSTON C A A 40 SAN W
FEATHERSTONE JAMES BA 40 DA1 W
FEE ROBT A 29 SEV B
FEEZER ALFORD A 32 COT B
FEEZER GEORGE A 32 COT W
FEEZER HENRY A 32 COT W
FEEZER JACOB A 32 COT W
FEEZOR JACOB H A 32 TYR W
FEEZOR W A J A 32 LOF W
FELCE JORDAN A 39 SPE W
FELDCAMP BENJ A 19 MOR W
FELL ROBERT A 28 16T W
FELLOWS HENRY A 29 SEV B
FELLOWS JAMES A 46 KIN W
FELTON AMBROSE A 24 EDE B
CHAL BY J R B HATHAWAY
REASON TOO YOUNG NO
EVIDENCE AGAINST HIM
FELTON DAVID A 19 BE1 B
FELTON EDWARD R 24 MID B
CANNOT VOTE BEING ONLY 9
MONTHS IN THE STATE
FELTON ELISHA A 19 BE1 W
FELTON JOH A 37 WEB W
FELTON JOHN H A 19 BE1 W
FELTON JOSIAH A 24 EDE B
FELTON R R A 24 EDE W
FELTON RICHARD R A 24 EDE B
FELTON WRIGHT A 24 MID B
FENCH EDMOND A 39 DAV B
FENDERSON ALBERT A 28 04A B
FENDERSON ALEXANDER A 19 BE1 B
FENDERSON BENJAMIN A 72 SWA B
FENDERSON BENJN A 28 01B B
FENDERSON BOSTON A 28 05A B
FENDERSON CEASER A 19 MOR B
FENDERSON CORNELIOUSA 19 BE1 B
FENDERSON DAVID M A 19 BE1 B
FENDERSON JACOB A 19 BE1 B
FENDERSON JOHN A 19 BE1 B
FENDERSON JOHN A 28 04A B
FENDERSON JOHN 1ST A 19 NEW B
FENDERSON JOHN 2ND A 19 NEW B
FENDERSON STEPHEN A 72 SWA B
FENDERSON W F A 19 BE1 B
FENDERSON WM A 28 04A B
FENNELL ABRAHAM A 29 FLE B
FENNELL BENJAMIN A 35 ROC B
FENNELL DIAMOND A 35 ROC B
FENNELL JACOB A 29 GRA B
FENNELL JOHN A 35 ROC B
FENNELL LEWIS A 29 FLE B
FENNELL ROBT J A 29 GRA W
FENNELL WASHINGTON A 29 GRA B
FENNER GAINBO A 28 10T B
FENNER JACOB A 28 10T B
FENNER JACOB A 28 9TH B
FENNER JOHN A 28 10T B
FENNER JOSEPH A 28 10T B
FENNER NIAS A 28 10T B
FENNER ROBERT A 19 MOR B
FENNER ROBT A 29 FA1 B
FENNER SAMUEL A 28 10T B
FENNER SILAS A 28 10T B
FENNER THOMAS A 28 10T B
FENNER WATSON A 28 10T B
FENNEY THOMAS A 28 6TH B
FENNISON JOHN A 28 16T B
FENTRESS DAVID A 30 IND W
FENTRESS FREDERICK 46 ROS W
DID NOT TAKE THE OATH
WAS DISCONTINUED AFTER
(continued next page)

ABOUT 18 MOS WHEN AT THE
EARNEST SOLICITATION OF
ABOUT 20 UNION PETITION-
ERS HE AGAIN ACCEPTED IT.
AND WAS REJECTED.
HE WAS A MAGISTRATE AND
POST MASTER FOR 25 YEARS
BEFORE THE WARE AND
CONTINUED TO ACT DURING
THE WARE AS MAGISTRATE
WITHOUT CHANGE OF OATH OR
APPOINTMENT THE P OFFICE
FENTRESS HENRY W A 46 ROS W
FENTRESS JOHN M A 46 ROS W
FENTRESS SIMEON CHAL 30 GIB B
3 MONTHS RESIDENCE
FENTRESS THOMAS B A 30 IND B
FENTRESS WM A 46 ROS W
FERABEE E C A 46 HIG W
FEREBEE ANNANIAS A 30 IND B
FEREBEE BENJAMIN A 30 TUL B
FEREBEE CHARLES CHALA 30 TUL B
NON RESIDENCE
FEREBEE CINCINATUS A 30 MOY B
FEREBEE E D A 30 CUR W
FEREBEE ISAAC A 30 CUR B
FEREBEE JAMES H A 30 IND B
7-MOS-RESIDENCE
FEREBEE JAMES M A 30 IND W
FEREBEE MITCHEL A 30 IND W
FEREBEE MUNROE A 30 IND B
FEREBEE PETER A 30 IND B
FEREBEE SAML 30 IND B
FEREBEE SAML A 30 IND W
FEREBEE WILLIS A 30 IND B
CHAL MINOR-REJECTED
FERGASON R F A 40 STO W
FERGERSSON J T A 39 LOU W
FERGUSON A R A 26 GOF W
FERGUSON ALFRED A 40 FER W
FERGUSON BETHEL A 46 SUM B
FERGUSON COLUMBUS F A 40 DA1 W
FERGUSON E A 28 01A W
FERGUSON HARRY A 40 DA1 B
FERGUSON I H A 28 01A W
FERGUSON JAMES R 40 DEC W
NAME LINED OUT
JUSTICE OF PEACE BEFORE
REBELLION GAVE AID AND
COMFORT TO ENEMY
NOT QUALIFIED REJ
FERGUSON JAMES JR A 40 FER W
FERGUSON JAMES SEN A 40 FER W
FERGUSON JOHN A 28 01B W
FERGUSON JOHN L A 29 QUW W
FERGUSON LEROY B A 40 FER W
FERGUSON MILTON A 40 FER W
FERGUSON ROSS A 28 10T B
FERGUSON SAMUEL A 26 SWA W
FERGUSON SYLVANUS A 40 FER B
FERGUSON THOMAS W A 40 FER W
FERIBEE JOHN A 46 GRE B
FERIBEE WILSON A 46 GRE B
FERIL B A 32 JAC W
FERIL E A 32 JAC W
FERLEY HARRY A 29 GRA B
FERMANDERS ANDREW A 26 MOU B
FERREL S H A 44 DUT W
FERRELL FARGES A 37 WHI B
FERRELL JACOB A 32 YAD B
FERRELL JACOB A 37 HIG W
FERRELL JOHN D A 37 HIG W
FERRIBEE ISAAC A 28 05A B
FERRILL G W A 44 LED W
FERRILL SMAL A 44 LED W
FERRIS ELLIS A 19 HAR B
CERTIFIED TO BY
GILLESPIE LAWSON
FESTERMAN ELIAS A 40 DA1 B
FETHERSTON HENRY A 40 SAN B
FETTER F A A 44 HEN W
FETZER JOS H A 46 GRE W
FFISHER RUFUS A 40 CAN W
FIELD ABSALOM A 46 RAG W
FIELD ALBERT A 28 01A B
FIELD BENJM H A 46 RAG W
FIELD BENTON A 46 ROS W
FIELD BRISON A 46 ROS W
FIELD C FRANKLIN A 46 RAG W
FIELD CHAS M A 28 01A W
FIELD CHESTER A 19 BE1 B
FIELD ELONSAR A 44 TAR B
FIELD JOHN A 46 ROS W
FIELD LAYTON A 46 RAG W
FIELD NATHAN B A 46 GRE W
FIELD RALPH A 46 RAG B
FIELDING SMITH A 44 SAS B
(TRANSPOSED)
FIELDS ABSOLEM A 46 ROS W
FIELDS ALFRED A 46 RAG W
FIELDS CHARLES H A 46 RAG W
FIELDS CHAS M A 28 01B W
FIELDS CHRISTOPHER A 46 ROS W
FIELDS
CHRISTOPHER JR A 46 ROS W
FIELDS ELI A 46 ROS W
FIELDS GRANDISON A 44 OXF B
FIELDS HOWARD A 44 TOW B
FIELDS JAS F A 46 GRE W
FIELDS JEREMIAH A 46 JAM W
FIELDS JNO A 44 TOW B
FIELDS PETER L A 46 ROS W
FIELDS THOMAS A 44 SAS B
FIELDS WELDON R 44 OXF B
RES 7 MONTHS REJ
FIFE WM W A 32 THO W
CERTIF GIVEN
FIFER HENRY A 28 03A B
FILE J N A 32 COT W
FILLMON JAMES H A 28 11T W
FILLYAW JOSHUA A 19 BE1 B
FINCH EATON A 99 BUS B
FINCH ELIJAH A 44 HEN W
FINCH F H A 32 LEE W
FINCH ISHAM A 39 PUG W
FINCH J T A 44 FIS W
FINCH JAMES A 39 LOU W
FINCH JAMES A 44 HEN W
CERT TO VOTE OUT COUNTY
FINCH JERRY A 46 RAG B
FINCH JNO A 44 HEN W
CERT TO VOTE OUT COUNTY
FINCH JOHN A 26 BLA W
FINCH JOHN H A 32 LEE W
FINCH JOHN H A 39 LOU W
FINCH ROBT A 44 BRA B
FINCH T W A 44 FIS W
FINCH WILLIAM A 44 HEN W
FINCH Z M A 32 LEE W
FINDLEY S L A 40 STO W
FINE DANIEL A 32 DAV W
FINE GABRIEL A 32 LEE W
FINE HENDERSON CHAL A 32 LOF W
FOR HOLDING OFFICE OF
MAGISTRATE BEFORE AND
DURING WAR. RECON.
FINE JAMES A 32 LEE W
FINLAYSON MALCOM A 29 QUW W
FINNEGAN ZACHARIAH A 28 12T W
FISHBLATE E A 29 FA1 W
FISHBLATE S H A 29 FA1 W
FISHELL C C A 32 SHE W
FISHELL DANIEL A 32 SHE W
FISHELL FRANCIS A 32 SHE W
FISHELL GEORGE A 32 SHE W
FISHELL JACOB A 32 SHE W
FISHELL JESSE A 32 SHE W
FISHELL JOHNATHAN A 32 SHE W
FISHELL MICHAEL A 32 SHE W
FISHELL NATHANIEL A 32 SHE W
FISHELL S J A 32 SHE W
FISHELL W H A 32 THO W
CERTIF
FISHELL ZAC A 32 SHE W
FISHER A T A 28 05A B
FISHER AARON A 46 MON B
FISHER ABEL A 19 BE1 B
FISHER ABSOLAM A 19 NEW B
FISHER ALBERT A 53 LA1 W
FISHER ANDERSON A 19 BE1 B
FISHER ANDREW A 28 04A B
FISHER B A 28 10T B
FISHER BARTEE A 30 COI W
FISHER BENJAMIN P A 28 9TH W
FISHER BOSTON A 29 GRA B
FISHER CASWELL A 28 02N B
FISHER CHARLES A 28 14T B
FISHER CHURCH A 19 BE1 B
FISHER DANIEL A 29 LOC W
FISHER EBENEZER A 30 COI W
FISHER EDWARD A 28 9TH B
FISHER ELI A 35 ISL B
FISHER ELIJAH A 29 CED W
FISHER ELIJAH A 29 ROC W
FISHER ENOCH A 19 NEW B
FISHER FRANK A 35 KEN B
FISHER GEO A 19 NEW B
FISHER GEO S A 28 03A B
FISHER GEORGE F A 46 HIG W
FISHER H C A 29 CED W
FISHER HANDY A 29 GRA B
FISHER HENRY A 28 16T B
FISHER ISAAC A 28 9TH B
FISHER JACOB A 28 01A B
FISHER JACOB A 28 10T B
FISHER JAMES A 29 ROC W
FISHER JAMES R A 53 LA1 W
FISHER JAMES R A 53 LA1 W
FISHER JEREMIAH A 19 BE1 B
FISHER JOHN A 19 BE1 B
FISHER JOHN A 28 03A B
FISHER JOHN L A 28 9TH W
FISHER JOSEPH A 19 BE1 B
FISHER JOSEPH A 19 BE1 B
FISHER MICHAEL N JR A 28 9TH W
FISHER MICHAEL N SR A 28 9TH W
FISHER MOSES A 19 BE1 B
FISHER MOSES A 28 01A B
FISHER MOSES A 28 10T B
FISHER NATHAN A 28 14T B
FISHER PETER A 28 04A B
FISHER PHILIP A 28 01A B
FISHER R A 29 LOC W
FISHER SAMUEL A 28 14T B
FISHER SAMUEL A 46 HIG W
FISHER SILAS A 29 CED B
FISHER SIMBO A 28 9TH B
FISHER SOLOMON A 28 10T B
FISHER T A 29 GRA W

FISHER THOS A 28 03A B
FISHER TIMOTHY M A 53 LA1 W
FISHER WILLIAM A 30 COI W
FISHER WILLIS C A 37 ROC W
FISHER WM A 28 03A B
FISHER WM A 28 04A B
FISHER WM A 46 GRE B
FISHER WM S A 29 GRA W
FITCHETT D E A 46 JAM W
FITCHETT DANIEL E A 46 JAM W
FITE G S A 40 STO W
FITE J C A 40 CAN W
FITE MACK A 40 DA1 B
FITE PETER A 40 STO W
FITE SOLIMON A 40 STO W
FITE WM J A 40 STO W
FITTES A T A 32 THO W
FITTS HENRY A 44 FIS W
FITTS HENRY A 46 KIN W
FITZGERALD CHARLES A 19 NEW W
FITZGERALD GILES A 32 TYR B
FITZGERALD JOHN B A 32 TYR W
FITZGERALD JOSEPH W A 32 COT W
FITZGERALD PLEASANT A 46 SUM W
FITZGERALD SAMUEL A 32 TYR B
FITZGERALD WATSON A 46 SUM B
FITZGERREL ELLIS B A 46 GRE W
FITZPATRICK MARTIN A 35 WOL B
FLACK ANDREW A 46 MON W
FLACK ELISHA A 46 MON W
FLACK J Y A 46 MON W
FLACK SANDERS A 46 MON W
FLAGG WILLIAM A 44 YXR B
FLANNAGAN WALLACE A 30 KNO W
FLEETWOOD FRED A 24 EDE B
FLEMING BENIAH A 46 MCL W
FLEMING BENJ A 44 LED B
FLEMING BENJAMIN F A 53 FAI W
FLEMING E T A 44 LED W
FLEMING G H A 44 HEN W
FLEMING J C A 44 DUT W
FLEMING J D A 44 HEN W
FLEMING J K A 28 01B W
FLEMING J W A 44 DUT W
FLEMING JACOB A 44 HEN B
FLEMING JAMES E A 28 01A W
FLEMING JOHN A 44 LED W
FLEMING M B A 44 LED W
FLEMING NED A 44 HEN B
FLEMING R H A 44 DUT W
FLEMING ROBT A A 46 GIB W
FLEMING THOMAS A 25 HAY W
FLEMING WILLIAM A 25 HAY W
FLEMING WILLIAM A 37 HIG W
FLEMING WM A 44 OXF W
FLEMMING CHARLES C A 37 PEN W
FLEMMING JAMES A 37 ROC B
FLEMMING RUBIN A 44 RAG W
FLEMMING WILLIS A 37 PEN B
FLENINS JOHN A 28 04A B
FLETCHER CHARLES A 19 NEW B
FLETCHER CHRISTOPHERA 53 LA1 W
FLETCHER JOSEPH A 28 9TH B
FLETCHER SOLN A 28 03A B
FLETCHER STEPHEN A 53 LA1 W
FLEURY THOS D A 24 EDE W
FLINN JOHN A 46 SUM B
FLINN WILLIAM M A 46 SUM W
FLOID H H A 40 SAN W
FLOID J L A 40 SAN W
FLOID SAM A 39 HAY B
FLOOD NEWT R A 37 SHA W
FLOOD RICHARD A 37 SHA W

FLOOD ROBERT A 37 HIG W
CERT RES WILSON NC
FLORA ANTHONY A 30 MOY B
8-MONTH-RESIDENCE
FLORA DENNIS A 30 IND W
FLORA ISAAC A 30 MOY W
FLORA ISAAC A 30 MOY W
FLORA ISAAC H A 30 MOY W
FLORA JNO L A 30 MOY W
FLORA R B A 30 MOY W
FLORA RICHARD A 30 MOY W
FLOWERS ALTIMONE A 37 MAN B
FLOWERS BIRLD A 28 04B B
FLOWERS BRYANT A 37 MAN B
FLOWERS CALVIN A 40 RHY W
FLOWERS CHRISTOPER CA 28 15T W
FLOWERS DANELL A 37 MAN B
FLOWERS DARLING A 40 DA1 W
FLOWERS DASSEY A 37 SHA W
FLOWERS DAVID A 29 FA1 B
FLOWERS EDWARD A 37 SHA W
FLOWERS ELBERT H A 37 ROC W
FLOWERS GASTON A 28 04A B
FLOWERS GREEN A 40 DA1 W
FLOWERS HARDIE A 37 SPA B
FLOWERS HARRIS A 99 BUS W
FLOWERS JAMES A 28 04A B
FLOWERS JAMES A 29 FA2 W
FLOWERS JAMES RODNEYA 28 17T W
FLOWERS JESSE A 35 WOL B
FLOWERS JOSEPH P A 53 SWA W
POLITICAL DISABILITIES
REMOVED
FLOWERS JOSHUA B A 28 17T W
FLOWERS LEWIS A 29 FA2 B
FLOWERS MAJOR A 37 MAN B
FLOWERS R G A 40 RHY W
FLOWERS WILLIAM P A 53 SWA W
ERROR
FLOWERS ZION A 53 SWA W
FLOYD ALEX A 44 BRA B
FLOYD AMERICA A 44 BRA B
FLOYD AMERICA A 44 OXF B
FLOYD ANDERSON A 44 FOR B
FLOYD CHARLES A 44 BRA B
FLOYD CHARLES A 44 KIT B
FLOYD ISAAC A 44 FIS B
FLOYD J B A 44 BRA W
FLOYD J F A 26 BLA W
FLOYD J N A 24 EDE W
FLOYD J T A 44 FIS W
FLOYD JACK A 44 KIT B
FLOYD JAMES A 44 BRA B
FLOYD JOSEPH C A 24 EDE W
FLOYD JUDSON J A 24 EDE W
FLOYD RUFUS A 44 FOR B
FLOYD SAML A 28 04A B
FLOYD SAMUEL A 32 THO W
FLOYD SOLOMON A 44 YXS B
FLOYD THOMAS A 44 BRA B
FLOYD THOMAS A 44 KIT B
FLOYD W J A 44 KIT W
FLOYD WILLIAM A 24 MID W
FLOYD WILLIS A 44 KIT B
FLOYD WM A 44 HEN W
FLOYED BASLE A 32 LOF W
FLOYED BENBERY A 24 MID W
FLOYED J R A 32 LOF W
FLOYED JOHN A 32 SHE W
FLOYED LEVI A 32 LEE W
FLUG SAMUEL A 44 SAS B
FLUZ LUKE A 28 05A B
FLY JOHN A 37 ROC W

FLY THOMAS A 37 PEN W
FLYBOS JOHN A 28 6TH W
FOARD DAVID A 44 YXS W
FOARD THOS A 28 04A B
FOARD WM G A 46 ROS W
FOBES ARTHUR A 37 WEB W
FOBES BENJAMIN A 37 WEB W
FOBES BENJAMIN J A 37 WEB W
FOBS ALBERT A 37 WEB W
FODIEY FULFORD A 19 BE1 W
FODREY ELIJAH A 19 HAR W
FODREY JNO H A 19 MOR W
FODREY THOMAS W A 19 HAR W
FODREY WILLIAM D A 19 HAR W
FOGG BALDY A 39 HAR B
FOGG DOCK A 39 DAV B
FOGG GEORGE A 39 PUG B
FOGG ISAAC A 39 PUG B
FOGG JAMES A 39 PUG B
FOGG JESSE A 44 KIT B
FOGG MADISON A 44 HEN B
FOGG WILLIAM A 39 HAY B
FOGG WM A 39 FRE B
FOGLEMAN GEORGE F A 46 COB W
FOGLEMAN JAMES A 46 COB B
FOGLEMAN JOHN F A 46 GRE W
FOGLEMAN JOHN S A 46 GRE W
FOLK JOHN A 30 MOY B
7-MONTH-RESIDENCE
FOLLMAN CASPER A 28 02N W
FONVEAL THOMAS A 53 SWA B
FONVILLE ALFRED A 35 WAR B
FONVILLE J F A 28 02N W
FORBES ADAM A 30 NOR W
FORBES ANDREW J A 30 POP W
FORBES BAILEY A 30 IND W
FORBES CALEB A 30 POW W
FORBES DAVID A 28 05A B
FORBES GEORGE CHAL A 30 POP B
FOR NOT BEING 21 YRS
FORBES GRANVILLE A 28 05A B
FORBES HARVEY F A 40 FER W
FORBES ISAAC A 28 05A B
FORBES ISAAC A 30 IND W
FORBES ISAAC W A 30 COI W
FORBES JAMES A 37 WEB W
FORBES JOHN A 28 05A B
FORBES JOHN A 37 SPA W
FORBES JOHN H A 40 FER W
FORBES JOHN P A 30 ROA W
FORBES MOSES A 28 10T B
FORBES PETER D A 30 COI W
FORBES SAMUEL T A 30 ROA W
FORBES SOLOMON A 30 POP B
FORBES STEPHEN G A 30 COI W
FORBES WALTER R A 30 IND W
FORBES WATEMAN A 30 POW W
FORBES WILSON A 30 IND W
FORBIS ARTHUR F A 46 MCL W
FORBIS DAVID A 46 GRE W
FORBIS DAVID R A 46 MCL W
FORBIS ELISHA A 46 MCL W
FORBIS EMSLY A 46 MCL W
FORBIS WM W A 46 ROS W
FORBUS DAVID W A 46 GRE W
FORBUS JOHN W R 46 MCL W
WAS OVERSEER OF HIGHWAY
BEFORE THE WARE DURING
THE WAR SERVED AS MILITIA
OFFICER RATHER THAN GO
TO SOUTHERN ARMY. ACCPT
FORD A MAXWELL A 40 DA1 W
FORD ALFORD A 32 DAV W

FORD AMZI A 40 DA1 W
FORD ANDREW A 26 GOF W
FORD ANTHONY A 72 SWA B
FORD BRYAN D A 35 KEN W
FORD CALVIN A 37 ROC B
FORD DAVID A 37 ROC B
FORD DREW A 37 ROC B
FORD ELIJAH A 37 ROB B
FORD GEORGE A 28 7TH B
FORD HARRY A 37 ROC B
FORD HENRY W P A 37 PIN W
FORD HUGH M A 40 FER W
FORD ISOM A 40 SAN W
FORD J M A 40 STO W
FORD J W A 26 GOF W
FORD JAMES A A 26 GOF W
FORD JESSE A 37 ROC W
FORD JOZER ? A 37 ROC B
FORD L A A 40 SAN W
FORD L H A 40 STO W
FORD LAWSON A 40 SAN W
FORD MILTON A 40 SAN W
FORD REDDING A 37 TA2 W
FORD T C CHAL A 32 DAV W
FOR HOLDING OFFICE BEF.
AND DURING WAR. RECON.
FORD THO E A 40 SAN W
FORD W F A 32 DAV W
FORD WM B A 40 SAN W
FORD WM P A 37 EDW W
FORDE WM W A 46 GRE W
FORDEY RICHARD H A 19 BE2 W
FOREHAN WILLIAM T A 24 MID W
FOREHAND CALVIN A 24 UPP W
FOREHAND CORNELUS A 24 MID W
FOREHAND J W A 24 UPP W
FOREHAND JOEL A 24 MID W
FOREHAND THOMAS A 24 UPP W
FOREHAND WILLIAM A 35 GLI W
FOREMAN ABRAHAM A 19 HAR B
FOREMAN ABRAHAM A 37 TA2 B
FOREMAN ALBERT A 28 05A B
FOREMAN ALEX A 19 HAR W
FOREMAN BROMFIELD A 28 05A B
FOREMAN CHARLES A 19 BE1 W
FOREMAN CHARLES G A 19 BE1 W
FOREMAN JAMES M A 19 BE1 W
FOREMAN JAMES P A 19 BE1 W
FOREMAN JAMES S A 19 BE1 W
FOREMAN JOHN HENRY A 37 TA1 B
FOREMAN NED A 37 PEN B
FOREMAN OWEN C A 19 HAR W
FOREMAN WILLIAM A 19 HAR W
FOREMAN WILLIAM A 37 TA2 B
FORESIGHT ALLEC A 37 EDW B
FORESIGHT HENRY A 37 TA2 B
FORESIGHT RICHARD A 37 HIC B
FOREST JAMES A 44 TOW W
FOREST WILSON A 37 ROC B
FORLAW JOHN W A 19 BE2 W
FORLAW THOMAS J A 35 MAG W
CERT GIVEN 10 AP. 1868
FORMAN EPHRAM A 19 HAD W
FORMAN JOSEPH A 28 04B B
FORNES ABRAHAM A 28 11T B
FORNEY LEROY A 40 DA1 B
FORNEY PETER A 40 CAN B
FORNEY PETTER A 26 GOF B
FORNEY THOMAS A 40 DA1 B
FORSHEY PAYTON A 29 FA1 B
FORSMAN JOSHUWAY A 19 MOR W
FORSYTH JOHN A 44 DUT B
FORSYTH PHILIP A 44 DUT W
FORSYTH SAMUEL A 44 DUT W
FORSYTH SMITH A 44 DUT W
FORSYTH WILEY A 44 DUT W
FORSYTHE JOHN A 44 LED W
FORSYTHE LAWSON A 44 LED W
FORSYTHE W P A 44 DUT W
FORT ANDERSON A 99 BUS B
FORT HISON A 29 CED B
FORT ISAAC A 29 LOC B
FORT JOHN A 29 ROC W
FORT M B A 29 CED W
FORT THOMAS A 29 CED W
FORT W A 29 CED W
FORTE HENRY A 99 BUS B
FORTE JOHN A 99 BUS B
FORTE WILLIAM A A 99 BUS W
FORTE WILLIAM L A 99 BUS W
FORTENBURY D A 26 SHE W
FORTENBURY WM A 26 SHE W
FORTINBERRY M M A 26 GRI W
FORTINBERRY R A A 26 BLA W
FORTINBURY ANGUS A 26 GRI W
FORTINBURY H S A 26 GRI W
FORTINBURY WM A 26 GRI W
FORTISCUE ANSON A 53 BUR B
FORTISCUE BENJ A 28 03A W
FORTISCUE DOUBLIN A 53 GER B
FORTISCUE ELLIOTT H A 53 GER W
FORTISCUE H C A 28 01A W
FORTISCUE HENRY A 53 GER B
FORTISCUE HIRAM B A 53 GER W
FORTISCUE JARIMIAH A 53 GER B
FORTISCUE JERRY A 53 GER B
FORTISCUE JOHN E A 53 GER W
FORTISCUE LEWIS A 53 GER B
FORTISCUE LOUIS D A 53 GER W
FORTISCUE LUKE A 53 GER B
FORTISCUE ORMAN A 53 GER B
FORTISCUE SPYRES A 53 GER B
FORTISCUE WILLIAM H A 53 GER W
FORTISCUE ZACHES H CA 53 GER W
FORTON NAT A 44 OXF B
FOSCUE DAVID A 28 05A B
FOSCUE HENRY R 28 01A W
WAS POSTMASTER
FOSCUE JAMES A 28 10T W
FOSGATE M G A 28 01A W
FOSHE IRA A 32 COT W
FOSHE JESS A 32 COT W
FOSHEE C A 32 COT W
FOSHEE GEORGE A 32 COT W
FOSTEER SANFORD S A 53 HAT W
FOSTER A H A 28 01A W
FOSTER ABRAHAM A 39 PUG B
FOSTER ALEXR A 44 YXS B
FOSTER AMBROS A 32 DAV B
FOSTER ANDREW A 32 THO B
FOSTER ASA A 46 COB W
FOSTER BEN A 39 LOU B
FOSTER CHARLES A 32 DAV B
FOSTER CHARLES A 53 HAT W
FOSTER DAVID A 39 PUG B
FOSTER DENNIS A 39 PUG B
FOSTER E S A 39 PUG W
FOSTER EDWARD A 37 SHA B
FOSTER ELLIS A 39 PUG B
FOSTER ESQUIRE A 39 PUG B
FOSTER FRANK A 39 PUG B
FOSTER FREDERICK A 19 BE1 B
FOSTER FRIDAY REJ R 44 OXF B
IN STATE 8 MONTHS
FOSTER GEORGE A 28 02N B
FOSTER GEORGE A 39 PUG B
FOSTER GEORGE A A 46 RAG W
FOSTER H A 19 NEW B
FOSTER HARRY A 39 LOU B
FOSTER HENRY A 39 DAV W
FOSTER HENRY A 39 GRI B
FOSTER HENRY A 39 PUG B
FOSTER ISHAM A 39 PUG B
FOSTER J J A 39 SPE W
FOSTER JACK A 39 LOU B
FOSTER JAMES W A 46 MON W
FOSTER JEREMIAH A 53 HAT W
FOSTER JESSE J A 53 HAT W
FOSTER JIM A 39 PUG B
FOSTER JOHN A 39 SPE W
FOSTER JOHN D A 39 LOU B
FOSTER JOSEPH J A 39 JOR W
FOSTER KIE A 44 HEN B
FOSTER LEWIS A 39 PUG B
FOSTER LOUIS A 32 DAV B
FOSTER LUTHER A 39 LOU B
FOSTER NED A 39 SPE B
FOSTER P L A 39 PUG W
FOSTER PATRICK A 39 PUG B
FOSTER PAYTON A 39 PUG B
FOSTER ROBERT A 32 DAV W
FOSTER SAML A 44 OXF B
FOSTER SAMUEL A 39 HAR B
FOSTER SANDY A 28 8TH B
FOSTER SIMEON A 28 8TH B
FOSTER TOM A 39 PUG B
FOSTER W B A 39 PUG W
FOSTER W E A 39 LOU W
FOSTER W H A 32 THO W
FOSTER WILLIAM A 30 IND W
FOSTER WILLIAM A 39 LOU B
FOSTER WILLIS A 39 LOU B
FOSTER YORK A 39 PUG B
FOUGHN ELICK A 39 PUG B
FOUND JAS A 44 YXR W
FOUNTAIN --- A 37 ROB W
NAME LINED OUT
FOUNTAIN ------ A 37 ROB W
NAME LINED OUT
FOUNTAIN ALSEA E A 35 CYP W
FOUNTAIN COFFIELD A 37 ROB W
FOUNTAIN FRANK A 35 CYP W
FOUNTAIN HOSEA A 35 CYP W
FOUNTAIN JAMES A 37 ROB W
FOUNTAIN JOAB A 35 LIM W
FOUNTAIN JOSEPH A 37 ROB B
FOUNTAIN JOSEPH A 37 ROB W
FOUNTAIN JOSEPH J A 37 ROB W
FOUNTAIN LAWRENCE A 37 ROB W
FOUNTAIN SPEARS W A 37 ROB W
FOUNTAIN SPENCER A 46 HIG W
FOUNTAIN STANLEY A 37 ROB B
FOUNTAIN STEPHEN A 44 OXF B
FOUNTAINE P H A 46 GRE W
FOUSE WILLIAM A 37 PEN B
FOUST ALEXANDER A 46 MCL B
FOUST CAIN A 46 GIB B
FOUST CHRISTOPHER A 46 GIB B
FOUST D M A 32 LOF W
FOUST DANIEL A 32 LOF W
FOUST DANIEL A 46 GIB W
FOUST DANIEL Q A 46 MCL W
FOUST DANL P A 46 GIB W
FOUST EDWARD A 46 GRE B
FOUST ELI A 46 COB B
FOUST EMANUEL C A 46 RAG W
FOUST FRANL R 46 GIB B
(LARCENY) WAS TRIED

(continued next page)

CONVICTED & IMPRISONED
FOR STEALING BBL BRANDY
AT SPRING TERM GUILFORD
SUPR COURT
FOUST GEO W A 46 GIB W
FOUST GEORGE A 46 GRE W
FOUST GIEDON A 46 GIB W
FOUST J CALVIN A 46 RAG B
FOUST JOSEPH A 46 GIB W
FOUST LEMUEL A A 46 COB W
FOUST LEONARD A 46 GIB B
FOUST LEWIS W A 46 GRE W
FOUST MONROE A 46 GIB B
FOUST MOSES H A 46 GRE W
FOUST RANSOM A 46 MCL B
FOUST SOLOMON J A 46 RAG W
FOUST WM A 46 GIB B
FOUST WM EDW A 46 MCL B
FOUST ZIMRIE M A 46 COB W
FOUT ERASTUS A 32 THO W
FOUTS ABSALUM A 32 THO W
FOUTS ADDISON A 32 THO W
FOUTS D W A 32 THO W
CERTIF
FOUTS DAVID A 32 LEE W
FOUTS LEVI A 32 THO W
FOWLCON ABNER A 39 JOR B
FOWLE HENRY A 37 TA1 B
FOWLE JOSEPH A 28 01A B
FOWLER CHARLES A 32 BRO W
FOWLER CHARLES A 32 DAV W
FOWLER CHARLES H A 28 16T W
FOWLER DEWITT C A 28 16T W
FOWLER HILSMAN A 44 DUT W
FOWLER J C DR. A 39 GRI W
FOWLER J R A 44 BEA W
FOWLER JNO W A 29 ROC W
FOWLER JOSEPH S A 28 16T W
FOWLER LEWIS A 28 16T W
FOWLER M A 44 BRA W
FOWLER PATRICK A 32 POS W
FOWLER ROBINSON A 46 GRE W
FOWLER SAML A 44 TAR W
FOWLER STEPHEN H A 28 16T W
FOWLER THOMAS A 32 BRO W
FOWLER THOMAS A 39 LOU W
FOWLER W H A 29 FA1 W
FOWLER W S A 32 TYR W
FOWLER WM L A 46 GRE W
FOWLKNER SIDNEY A 39 SPE W
FOX ADAM A 26 SHE B
FOX ISAAC A 46 ROS B
FOX S A 26 BOR B
FOXALL ALFRED A 37 TA1 B
FOXALL BILL A 37 EDW B
FOXALL DALLUS A 37 TA2 B
FOXALL DREAD A 37 PEN B
FOXALL EDWIN D A 37 TA2 W
FOXALL KINCHON A 37 TA1 B
FOXHALL AUTRIN A 37 PIN B
FOXHALL JERRY A 37 HOL B
FOXHALL LEWIS A 37 PIN B
FOXWELL ALFRED A 24 EDE B
FOY ALEXANDER A 28 16T W
FOY ALFRED A 28 04A B
FOY CASWELL A 28 04B B
FOY ENOCH A 28 9TH B
FOY GREEN A 28 9TH B
FOY JACOB A 28 04A B
FOY JAMES A 40 FER W
FOY JOHN A 28 12T B
FOY JOHN F A 40 DEC W
FOY JONA A 29 GRA B
FOY JOURDAN A 28 05A B
FOY LACE A 46 SUM B
FOY LUKE A 28 05A B
FOY SAML A 28 04A B
FOY SOLOMON E A 40 FER W
FOY THOMAS A 28 04B B
FOY THOMAS A 28 12T W
FOY THOS A 28 04A B
FOY THOS A 28 05A B
FRADA A J A 25 TUS W
FRAILEY JOHN A 32 THO W
FRALEY STEPHEN A 40 DA1 W
FRANCES ELIJAH P A 53 LA1 W
FRANCIS BOB A 37 PEN B
FRANCIS FRANKLIN A 53 FAI W
FRANCIS JOHN A 26 BUR W
FRANCIS REUBIN A 26 HOL B
FRANCIS W M A 26 BUR W
FRANK ALEXANDER A 32 LOF W
FRANK ANDREW A 32 LOF B
FRANK CHRISTAIN A 32 SHE W
FRANK JESSE M A 32 LOF W
FRANK JOHN M A 32 LOF W
FRANK P M A 32 DAV W
FRANK PHILIP A 32 LOF W
FRANK THEOFILUS A 32 DAV W
FRANKLIN AMOS A 19 MOR B
FRANKLIN AMOS A 28 03A B
FRANKLIN BENJ L A 19 MOR W
FRANKLIN BENJA A 53 OCR B
FRANKLIN BENJAMIN A 19 BE1 B
FRANKLIN BENJAMIN A 53 SWA B
FRANKLIN EDWARD A 19 MOR W
FRANKLIN ISREAL A 19 BE1 B
FRANKLIN JOHN A 19 NEW B
FRANKLIN JOHN A A 46 JAM B
FRANKLIN JOHN W A 46 GRE B
FRANKLIN JOSEPH R 19 MOR W
U S POST MASTER
AND AFTER POST MASTER
IN CONFEDERATE SERVICE
FRANKLIN PETER A 28 03A B
FRANKLIN PETER A 28 03B B
FRANKLIN PETER A 53 GER B
FRANKLIN SAMUEL A 19 BE1 B
FRANKLIN SAMUEL A 46 JAM W
FRANKLIN THOS F A 44 YXS W
FRANKLIN WILLIAM A 28 8TH B
FRANKLIN WM A 28 01A B
FRANKS CATO A 28 03A B
FRANKS DANL A 28 03A B
FRANKS DANZY A 19 SMY B
FRANKS ELIJAH A 28 03A B
FRANKS GEORGE A 32 LOF W
FRANKS MARTIN A 28 11T W
FRANKS MILES A 53 LA1 B
SWAN QUARTER CERT RES
FRANKS SQUIRE A 28 05A B
FRANKS THOS A 28 04A B
FRANKS THOS A 28 05A B
FRANKS ZENAS A 28 05A B
FRASER DERRY A 28 11T B
FRASER SILAS A 28 11T B
FRASIER B D A 44 SAS W
FRASIER C H A 44 OXF W
FRASIER CHARLES A 44 YXS B
FRASIER D O A 44 OXF W
FRASIER ELIJAH C A 44 YXS W
FRASIER J H A 44 OXF W
FRASIER JACKSON A 39 HAR W
FRASIER R H A 44 OXF W
FRASIER RUSSELL A 44 OXF B
FRASIER WM P A 44 YXS W
FRASURE GEORGE A 28 10T B
FRASURE JAMES A 28 10T B
FRASURE JOHN A 28 10T B
FRATER BENJ M A 28 04A B
FRAZER DAVID A 46 KIN B
FRAZER N R A 46 FRI W
FRAZER R C A 46 FRI W
FRAZIER A D A 44 TAR W
FRAZIER A J A 46 SUM W
FRAZIER DANIEL A 19 BE1 B
FRAZIER DAVID L A 46 JAM W
FRAZIER E T A 44 OXF W
FRAZIER J D A 44 OXF W
FRAZIER JEFFREY H A 46 JAM W
FRAZIER JOHN A 19 BE1 W
FRAZIER JOHN B A 46 HIG W
FRAZIER NEIDEM A 72 SWA W
FRAZIER R H A 44 YXS W
FRAZIER R P A 44 OXF W
FRAZIER SOLOMON H A 46 HIG W
FRAZIER THOS B A 44 YXS W
FRAZIER WILLIAM W A 46 ROS W
FRAZIER WM A 46 JAM W
FREDERICK ALEXANDER A 35 MAG B
FREDERICK BENJAMIN A 35 MAG B
FREDERICK DAVID A 35 WAR B
FREDERICK GEORGE A 35 KEN B
FREDERICK JAMES A 35 MAG B
FREDERICK JAMES A 35 WAR W
FREDERICK JOHN A 28 03A B
FREDERICK JOHN A 35 WAR W
FREDERICK JOHN C A 35 MAG W
FREDERICK JOHN D A 35 MAG B
FREDERICK LEVI A 35 WAR B
FREDERICK MOSES A 35 KEN B
FREDERICK MOSES A 35 MAG B
FREDERICK NORRIS F A 35 WAR W
FREDERICK PATRICK A 35 WAR W
FREDERICK THOMAS A 35 MAG W
FREDERICK WILLIAM A 35 MAG B
FREDRICK J M A 46 FRI W
FREEDEL WILLIAM F A 32 DAV W
FREEDER WILLIAM A A 32 THO W
FREEDLE LOUIS A 32 DAV W
FREEDLE W H A 32 DAV W
FREELIN EDMON A 46 GRE B
FREELY WM H A 24 EDE B
FREEMAN A 44 BEA W
FREEMAN AARON A 37 HIC B
FREEMAN ALBERT A 39 GRI B
FREEMAN ALEX A 29 FA1 B
FREEMAN ALFRED A 28 04A B
FREEMAN ANDREW A 46 GRE B
FREEMAN ANTHONY A 37 HIC B
FREEMAN ARTHUR A 24 EDE B
CERT GIVEN TO PERQUIMANS
PERQUIMANS COUNTY
FREEMAN AUGUSTUS A 28 9TH B
FREEMAN BENJ H A 39 FRE W
FREEMAN BENTON CHAL A 29 FA1 B
W H PORTER MINOR
FREEMAN BERRY A 37 EDW B
FREEMAN BERRY A 37 ROB B
FREEMAN BERRY A 37 ROC B
FREEMAN BERRY A 37 ROC W
FREEMAN BRIANT A 38 FRE W
FREEMAN DAVID A 28 05A B
FREEMAN DOC A 29 GRA B
FREEMAN E A A 44 OXF W
FREEMAN E E A 44 DUT W
FREEMAN E S A 40 SAN W
FREEMAN EATAN A 38 FRE W
FREEMAN ELISIA W A 72 SWA W

FREEMAN ERVIN A 32 TYR B
FREEMAN HENRY A 37 MAN B
FREEMAN HEYWOOD A 37 PEN B
FREEMAN HILLIARD A 37 HIC B
FREEMAN HUDSON A 32 LOF B
FREEMAN ISAAC A 38 FRE B
FREEMAN J E A 44 BEA W
FREEMAN J G A 44 LED W
FREEMAN J H A 44 BEA W
FREEMAN J W A 46 JAM W
FREEMAN JACOB A 32 THO B
FREEMAN JAMES A 46 GRE W
FREEMAN JNO A 29 FA1 B
FREEMAN JNO C A 39 FRE W
FREEMAN JOHN A 30 ROA B
FREEMAN JOHN A 35 KEN B
FREEMAN JOHN A 37 ROC W
FREEMAN JOHN A 39 FRA B
FREEMAN JOS H A 39 HAR W
FREEMAN JOSIAH A 44 BRA B
FREEMAN LAWRENCE A 37 HIC B
FREEMAN LEWIS A 46 SUM B
FREEMAN M D A 39 GRI W
FREEMAN MARCH A 19 BE1 B
FREEMAN MILES A 37 EDW B
FREEMAN MOODY A 46 GRE B
FREEMAN NATHAN A 53 GER B
FREEMAN NEEDHAM A 53 GER B
FREEMAN NELSON A 37 TA1 B
FREEMAN O W A 32 TYR W
FREEMAN PETER A 46 GRE B
FREEMAN PETER S A 19 MOR B
FREEMAN R C A 39 GRI W
FREEMAN R C A 44 BEA W
FREEMAN REUBEN A 39 FRA B
FREEMAN RICHD A 39 HAR B
FREEMAN RILEY A 37 HOL B
FREEMAN ROBBRT 39 HAY B
REG WAKE CO
FREEMAN ROBT A 39 FRE W
FREEMAN SAUNEY A 37 PEN B
FREEMAN THOMAS A 37 PIN B
FREEMAN THOS A 29 FA1 B
FREEMAN THOS A 29 GRA B
FREEMAN TURNER A 39 FRE B
FREEMAN W F A 44 BEA W
FREEMAN W H A 39 HAR W
FREEMAN W H A 39 LOU W
FREEMAN W J A 39 FRE W
FREEMAN WILLIAM A 26 PEE W
FREEMAN WM A 24 EDE B
FREEMAN WM A 39 FRE W
FREEMAN WM A 39 GRI B
FREESE JIM A 32 CLE B
FREEZE JAMES A 32 THO B
FREEZE NATHAN A 32 THO B
FREEZE THOMPSON A 32 SHE B
FREMON JOHN A 44 SAS B
FREMON WILLIS A 44 SAS B
FRENCH EDMOND A 72 SWA B
FRENCH H E A 28 6TH W
FRENCH J B A 28 7TH W
FRENCH JOHN R A 24 EDE W
FRENCH L H A 28 6TH W
FRENCH THOMAS E A 28 6TH W
FRENCH W C A 28 6TH W
FRENCH W J A 28 6TH W
FRENCH WALKER A 46 GRE B
FREY JNO A 29 GRA W
FRIAR JOHN A 46 MON B
FRIDAY ABRAHAM A 40 DA1 B
FRIDAY ANDREW S A 40 MAU W
FRIDAY CALEB R 40 DA1 B
NAME LINED OUT
CHAL CAUSE CONVICTED
OF FELONY REJECTED
FRIDAY CEBORNE A 40 DA1 B
FRIDAY CHARLES A 40 DA1 B
FRIDAY CLEM A 40 DA1 B
FRIDAY DAVID A 40 MAU W
FRIDAY HENRY A 40 MAU B
FRIDAY J NICHOLAS A 40 DA1 W
FRIDAY JACKSON A 40 DA1 B
FRIDAY JACOB W A 40 DA1 W
FRIDAY JEFFERSON A 40 DA1 B
FRIDAY JOHN C A 40 DA1 W
FRIDAY JONAS W A 40 DA1 W
FRIDAY JOSEPH A 40 DA1 B
FRIDAY MARION D A 40 DA1 W
FRIDAY MICHAEL A 40 DA1 W
FRIDAY MONROE A 40 DA1 B
FRIDAY PINK A 40 DA1 B
FRIDAY ROBERT A 40 DA1 B
FRIDAY RUFUS A 40 DA1 B
FRIDAY SAMUEL A 40 DA1 B
FRIDAY WILLIAM J A 40 DA1 W
FRIDDLE HENRY A 46 GIB W
FRIDDLE LEWIS A 46 MCL W
FRIDDLE OLIVER A 46 COB W
FRIEND VALENTINE A 35 KEN W
FRIER GEORGE W A 35 ROC W
FRIER JAMES A 35 ROC W
FRIES JOHN A 32 DAV W
FRITTS A A A 32 SHE W
FRITTS AMOS A 32 DAV W
FRITTS ANDREW A 32 DAV W
FRITTS ELI A 32 SHE W
FRITTS FRANCIS A 32 SHE W
FRITTS GEORGE A 32 DAV W
FRITTS H C A 32 TYR W
FRITTS H G A 32 TYR W
FRITTS HENDERSON A 32 DAV W
FRITTS J H A 32 DAV W
FRITTS JOHN A 32 DAV W
FRITTS PHELIX A 32 LEE W
FRITTS SMITH A 32 DAV W
FRITTS THEO A 32 SHE W
FRITTS WILLIAM A 32 LEE W
FRITZ FRANK A 32 THO W
FROELICH LOUIS A 35 KEN W
FROMVIEL JACOB A 28 03A B
CERTIFICATE GIVEN TO HYDE CO
FROMVIEL JOHN A 28 02N B
FROMVIEL JOHN A 28 6TH B
FROMVIEL MARTIN A 28 04A B
FROMVIEL NELSON A 28 04A B
FROMVIEL PETER A 28 04A B
FROMVIEL POMPEY A 28 03A B
FROMVIEL SOUTHEY A 28 04A B
FROMVIEL STEPHN A 28 03A B
FROMVIEL STEPHN A 28 6TH B
FROMVIEL THOMAS A 28 6TH B
FROMVILLE JOSEPH A 28 04A B
FROMVILLE OLIVER A 28 04A B
FRONEBARGER A L A 26 SHE W
FRONEBARGER ANDREW A 26 HOL B
FRONEBERGER A A 26 BOR W
FRONEBERGER AMBROSE A 40 DA1 W
FRONEBERGER BEN A 40 DA1 B
FRONEBERGER CHARLES A 40 DA1 B
FRONEBERGER DANIEL R 40 DA2 W
NAME LINED OUT
CONSTABLE BEFORE THE WAR
AND GAVE AID OR COMFORT
TO THE ENEMY REJECTED
FRONEBERGER DAVID A 40 DA1 B
FRONEBERGER FALLS A 40 DEC B
FRONEBERGER
JACOB SEN A 40 DEC W
FRONEBERGER JAMES A 40 DA1 B
FRONEBERGER JOHN A 40 DEC B
FRONEBERGER JOHN A 40 DEC W
FRONEBERGER JOSEPH A 40 FER B
FRONEBERGER PETER R 40 DA1 B
NAME LINED OUT
NOT 21 YEARS OLD
FRONEBERGER PHILLIP A 40 MAU W
FRONEBERGER TITUS A 40 DA1 B
FRONEYBERGER DANIEL A 26 CAR B
FRONEYBERGER P A 26 CAR W
FRONEYBERGER W A 26 BOR W
FROST A P A 30 IND W
FROST JNO R A 30 CUR W
FROST ROBERT A 30 CUR B
FROST V A A 28 02N W
FROST W A A 28 02N W
FROST WILLIAM A 30 GIB W
FRUIT ABRAM A 46 RAG B
FRUIT JACOB A 46 ROS B
FRY FRANKLIN A 32 COT W
FRYAR BOSTON A 46 GIB W
FRYAR GEORGE A 46 GIB B
FRYAR ROBERT A 46 GIB W
FRYER HENRY A 35 WAR B
FULCHER AMBROSE J A 19 BE1 W
FULCHER ANDERSON A 19 BE1 B
FULCHER ARCHIE A 28 17T W
FULCHER BENJAMIN T A 53 HAT W
FULCHER
CHRISTOPHER F A 53 HAT W
FULCHER DAVID F A 53 HAT W
FULCHER E L A 19 MOR W
FULCHER ENOCH A 28 10T B
FULCHER ENOCH A 28 12T W
FULCHER FURNEY R 28 12T W
WAS OFFICER OF PATROL
AND OVERSEER OF ROADS
AND ENGAGED IN REBELLION
FULCHER GEO W A 19 HUN W
FULCHER GEORGE L A 53 HAT W
FULCHER HENRY T A 28 12T W
FULCHER JARVIS L A 19 HUN W
FULCHER JESSE A 19 MOR W
FULCHER JESSE SR A 19 BEI W
FULCHER JOHN A 19 HUN W
FULCHER JOHN A 28 11T W
FULCHER JOHN B A 53 HAT W
FULCHER JOHN B SR A 53 HAT W
FULCHER JOHN M A 19 SHA W
FULCHER JOHN T A 19 BE2 W
FULCHER JOHN W A 19 HUN W
FULCHER JOSEPH A A 28 12T W
FULCHER JOSEPH M A 19 HAD W
FULCHER LEVI C A 19 BE1 W
FULCHER LEWIS H A 19 BE1 W
FULCHER MANSON A 19 DAV W
FULCHER REUBEN A 19 HUN W
FULCHER SILAS A 28 12T W
FULCHER WALLACE A 19 HUN W
FULCHER WALLACE L A 19 HUN W
FULCHER WALLACE P A 19 SMY W
FULCHER WM A A 28 11T W
FULCHER WM H A 19 HUN W
FULCHER WM R A 28 16T W
FULCHER WM T A 19 MOR W
FULENWIDER ANDREW A 40 DA1 B
FULENWIDER LEROY A 40 DA1 B
FULFORD ANDREW A 19 BE1 B

FULFORD ANSON H A 19 STR W
FULFORD B W A 44 OXF W
FULFORD BENJAMIN A 53 LA1 W
FULFORD BONAPART A 19 BE1 B
FULFORD BURTRAN A 30 TUL W
FULFORD DANIEL A 44 OXF B
FULFORD DAVID W A 19 STR W
FULFORD ELIJAH A 19 BE2 W
FULFORD ENOCH A 28 04A B
FULFORD FRANCIS K A 19 STR W
FULFORD GEO W A 30 MOY W
FULFORD GEORGE H A 19 STR W
FULFORD HENRY A 19 BE1 B
FULFORD HENRY A 53 SWA B
FULFORD ISAAC A 19 NEW B
FULFORD J A 28 03A W
FULFORD J W A 28 01A W
FULFORD JAMES A 19 BE1 B
FULFORD JAMES M A 28 15T W
FULFORD JAMES W A 19 BE1 W
FULFORD JAS W A 28 04A W
FULFORD JESPER A 19 BE1 B
FULFORD JNO T A 44 OXF W
FULFORD JOHN H A 19 STR W
FULFORD JOHN J A 53 LA1 W
FULFORD JOSEPH A 28 15T W
FULFORD LEVI A 30 IND W
FULFORD LEWIS A 19 BE1 B
FULFORD MARTIN A 19 STR W
FULFORD MATHIS S A 37 ROC W
FULFORD NAPOLIAN A 37 SPA B
FULFORD OBED A 19 BE1 B
FULFORD OWEN B A 19 STR W
FULFORD PETER A 19 BE1 B
FULFORD PETER A 19 BE1 B
FULFORD POMPY A 19 BE1 B
FULFORD RICHARD A 46 ROS W
FULFORD RICHARD W A 19 STR W
FULFORD S F A 28 02N W
FULFORD SAML A 30 IND W
FULFORD SAMUEL A 19 BE1 B
FULFORD SAMUEL A 19 MOR W
FULFORD T H A 30 MOY W
FULFORD TIMOTHY A 19 BE1 B
FULFORD W B A 28 02N W
FULFORD WILLIAM 30 KNO W
6-MOS-RES
FULFORD WILLIAM A 19 MOR W
FULFORD WILLIAM A 53 FAI B
FULFORD WM D A 28 15T W
FULFORD WM J A 44 OXF W
FULGHUM JESSEE A 39 SPE W
FULKES JAMES A 46 MON B
FULKES JORDON A 46 MON B
FULKES ROBERT A 46 MON B
FULKS CALVIN A 46 GRE B
FULKS FOUNTAIN A 46 GRE B
FULLBRIGHT MILES A 25 SHO W
FULLER A C A 44 FOR W
FULLER A C A 44 SAS W
FULLER ALLEN A 29 FA1 B
FULLER ANDREW A 19 MOR B
FULLER ANDW A 29 FA1 B
FULLER ATLAS A 39 FRA B
FULLER BENJ A 44 BEA W
FULLER BRITTON A 44 KIT B
FULLER CALEB A 28 05A B
FULLER CHRISTOPHER CA 19 BE1 W
FULLER D C A 38 FRE W
FULLER D W A 39 FRA W
FULLER D W A 44 BRA W
NAME LINED OUT
FULLER D W A 44 FOR W

FULLER DANIEL C A 39 LOU W
TRNS FROM FREEMANS X
ROADS TO LOUISBURG
FULLER E A 44 BEA W
FULLER E A A 44 KIT W
FULLER EDMOND A 39 LOU B
FULLER F M A 44 KIT W
FULLER FENNER A 29 FA1 B
FULLER GEORGE A 19 NEW B
FULLER GEORGE A 44 TAR B
FULLER H N A 39 DAV W
TRNS FROM GRANVILLE CO
BY AFF TO KITTRELL PRE.
FULLER HENRY A 39 FRA B
FULLER HENRY A 44 KIT B
FULLER HENRY W A 39 LOU B
FULLER ISAAC A 29 FA1 B
FULLER ISHAM A 44 BEA W
FULLER ISHAM A 44 KIT B
FULLER J H A 39 FRA B
FULLER J H A 44 KIT W
FULLER J L A 44 FOR W
FULLER J M A 46 FRI W
FULLER J N A 44 TAR W
FULLER J R A 44 HEN W
FULLER J W A 44 BRA W
FULLER JAMES A 38 FRE W
FULLER JAMES A 44 FOR W
FULLER JAMES T A 46 FRI W
FULLER JESSEE A 29 FA1 B
FULLER JESSEE A 29 FA1 B
FULLER JESSEE W A 29 FA1 W
FULLER JNO A A 44 HEN W
FULLER JOHN A 44 KIT W
FULLER JONATHAN A 44 FOR W
FULLER JONES A 37 HIC B
FULLER JONES A 39 LOU W
FULLER JOS A 38 FRE W
FULLER JOSEPH A 44 LED W
FULLER JOSHUA A 38 FRE B
FULLER JR A 44 FIS W
FULLER LEWIS A 44 TAR B
FULLER MICAJAH A 44 TAR B
FULLER PARKER A 44 DUT B
FULLER PLUMMER A 39 FRA B
FULLER R M A 44 FIS W
FULLER RICHD A 39 FRA B
FULLER ROBERT A 44 FIS W
FULLER ROBT A 29 FA1 B
FULLER S D A 39 HAY W
FULLER SOLOMON A 46 FRI W
FULLER T S A 46 FRI W
FULLER THOMAS A 46 FRI W
FULLER THOS A 39 FRA W
FULLER W B A 39 HAY W
FULLER W L A 46 FRI W
FULLER W N A 39 LOU W
FULLER W S A 44 FIS W
FULLER W T A 39 FRA W
FULLER W W A 44 TAR W
FULLER WASHINGTON A 44 HEN B
FULLER WESLEY A 44 BEA W
FULLER WILLIAM A 44 OXF B
FULLER WILLIAM P A 39 HAY W
FULLER WILLIS A 44 FOR B
FULSHER FRANCIS A 28 15T W
FULSHIRE BARNY A 28 12T W
FULSHIRE LEWIS R R 28 12T W
WAS AN OERSEER OF ROADS
& TOOK PART IN THE WAR
FULTON H D A 26 GOF W
FULTON THOMAS A 46 MON W
FUNWHEL SANDERS A 19 MOR B

FURGERSON J L A 39 LOU W
FURGERSON ROBERT A 44 SAS B
FURGERSON W H A 39 LOU W
FURGESON H F A 29 FA1 W
FURGUSON G W A 26 GOF W
FURMAN H S A 39 FRA W
FURMAN ROBT M A 44 HEN W
FUSSELL BENJAMIN A 35 ISL W
FUSSELL BENJAMIN A 35 ROC W
FUSSELL JOHN A 35 ROC W
FUSSELL JOHN E A 35 ISL W
FUSSELL JOHN G A 35 ISL W
FUSSELL STEPHEN A 35 MAG W
FUSSELL WILLIAM H A 35 ISL W
FUTON LEWIS A 26 GOF B

GABLE RALEIGH A 19 BE1 B
GABRIEL ANTHONY A 19 BE1 W
GABRIEL GEO R A 19 BE1 W
GABRIEL MARTIN A 19 BE1 W
GADDY GREEN A 28 01B B
GADDY J D A 29 QUW W
GADDY THOMAS A 29 FLE B
GAFNEY ANTHONEY A 26 SHE B
GAGE WILLIAM A 32 TYR W
GAILLARD ISAAC A 53 GER B
GAILLER ANTHONY A 19 BE1 B
GAINES ANDREW A 28 14T B
GAINEY A R 29 BLA W
ACTED AS MAGISTRATE
BEFORE, AND DURING WAR
HUNTED CONSCRIPTORS
GAINS J A 26 PEE W
GAINS LITTLEBERRY A 37 ROC W
GAITHER NATHAN A 37 TA1 W
GAITHER SAMUEL A 37 PEN W
GALAGHER EDWARD R 35 WOL B
NATURALIZED CITIZEN
(IRELAND)
GALBOT LOUIS A 29 QUW B
GALE JAMES A 53 GER B
GALE JNO R A 30 KNO W
GALEMORE JOHN A 32 COT W
GALES MAYSON A 44 KIT B
GALES STEPHEN A 29 FA1 W
GALIMORE A B A 32 JAC W
GALIMORE A H A 32 JAC W
GALIMORE A M A 32 JAC W
GALIMORE B L A 32 LOF W
GALIMORE HARMON A 32 JAC W
GALIMORE J W A 32 COT W
GALIMORE JOHN A A 32 DAV W
GALLAGHER HUGH R 35 WOL B
NATURALIZED CITIZEN
(IRELAND)
GALLAGHER JAMES R 35 WOL B
NATURALIZED CITIZEN
(IRELAND)
GALLANT J A A 40 STO W
GALLAWAY M R A 25 SHO W
GALLAWAY ROBERT A 32 TYR W
GALLEWAY EDWARD A 19 MOR B
GALLIMORE G B A 32 JAC W
GALLIMORE JAMES A 32 LOF W
GALLIMORE JONAS A 32 LOF W
GALLIMORE LEVI A 32 LEE W
GALLIMORE WILLIAM A 32 LOF W
GALLOP BENJAMIN G A 30 POW W
GALLOP G GRAHAM CHALA 30 POW W
MALITIA OFF. PRIOR TO WAR
GALLOP HODGERS CHALR 30 NOR W
MAGISTRATE PRIOR TO WAR
GALLOP MERRICK A 30 NOR B

GALLOP PETER G A 30 ROA W
GALLOP RICHARD A 30 NOR B
GALLOP SAML A 30 IND W
GALLOWAY ANTHONY A 46 SUM B
GALLOWAY ARNOLD A 19 BE1 B
GALLOWAY GEORGE A 46 MON B
GALLOWAY H M A 25 SHO W
GALLOWAY ISAAC A 46 SUM B
GALLOWAY J M A 25 SHO W
GALLOWAY LAZARUS A 28 7TH B
GALLOWAY M H A 25 SHO W
GALLOWAY PETER A 46 SUM B
GALLUP GEORGE A 28 05A B
GAMBLE A J A 26 GOF W
GAMBLE A JACKSON A 40 FER W
GAMBLE ANDERSON A 40 DEC B
GAMBLE J G R 46 SUM W
CAUSE CIVIL OFFICER
BEFORE THE WAR
VOLUNTARILY
AIDED REBELLION REJ
GAMBLE JAMES G A 46 GRE W
GAMBLE JOHN E A 46 JAM W
GAMBLE ROBERT F A 40 FER W
GAMBLE ROBT A A 46 HIG W
GAMBLE W F A 26 SWA W
GAMBOL ALFRED A 40 DA1 B
GAMBOL JOHN W A 40 DA1 W
GAMMON JAMES A 30 MOY W
GAMMON JOSIAH A 30 MOY W
GANAWAY JACOB A 46 HIG B
GANETT HARRY A 37 PIN B
GANEY ABRAM A 29 LOC B
GANEY CHARLES A 29 FA2 B
GANEY ELIAS A 29 LOC W
GANEY HAYWOOD R 29 LOC W
AFTER REGISTERED OPENLY
PROCLAIMED HIMSELF A
SECESHIONIST
GANEY HOLEY A 29 FLE W
GANEY ISHAM A 29 FLE B
GANEY J A A 29 LOC W
GANEY J S A 29 LOC W
GANEY MANSON A 29 FLE B
GANEY NEEDAM A 29 FA1 B
GANEY SILAS A 29 LOC B
GANEY W H A 29 LOC W
GANN C W A 28 01A W
GANNON GEORGE A 46 MCL W
GANNON JAMES G A 46 MCL W
GANNON THOMAS C A 46 MCL W
GANNON WM M A 46 MCL W
GANT ALFRED A 46 MON B
GANT ANDREW J A 40 DEC W
GANT JAMES A 46 MON W
GANT JAMES R 46 MON W
NAME LINED OUT
OFFICE OF MAGISTRATE
REJECTED BY HIS
OWN REQUEST
GANT JAS S A 46 MCL W
GANT JOHN G A 46 MCL W
GANT L L A 46 MON W
GANT WM M A 46 MCL W
GANT WM M A 46 MON W
GANT WM SR A 46 GRE W
GANTT HENRY A 26 WAR W
GANTT JOHN C A 40 MAU W
GANTT M P A 26 BUR W
GANTT PINKNEY A 26 WAR W
GANTT TRYON A 26 WAR W
GARDENER DAVID C A 53 FAI W
GARDENOR J W A 29 FLE W
GARDNER A B A 26 CAR W
GARDNER ABE R 46 JAM W
MAGISTRATE BEFORE THE WAR
AND DURING THE WAR COULD
NOT TAKE THE OATH WITH
THE WORD VOLUNTARY
OMITTED REJECTED
GARDNER ALFORD A 46 JAM W
GARDNER AUSTIN A 28 05A B
GARDNER CALVIN A 37 WEB W
GARDNER DAVID D A 37 TA2 W
GARDNER EDWARD A 37 MAN W
GARDNER GEORGE A 29 FLE B
GARDNER GEORGE A 39 DAV W
TRNS FROM NASH CO
ARRINGTON PRE
GARDNER GUIL A 46 JAM B
GARDNER HENRY A 29 FLE B
GARDNER ISRAEL A 28 01A B
GARDNER JAMES B A 28 11T W
GARDNER JAMES W A 37 PEN W
GARDNER JESSE A 46 JAM W
GARDNER JOHN A 19 BE1 W
GARDNER JOHN A 28 05A B
GARDNER JOHN A 40 MAU W
GARDNER JOHN A 46 JAM W
GARDNER JOHN O A 28 01A W
GARDNER JOSEPH A 28 11T B
GARDNER LOUIS A 26 CAR W
GARDNER M H A 46 FRI W
GARDNER MADISON A 26 GOF B
GARDNER MONROE A 46 JAM B
GARDNER P M A 26 GOF W
GARDNER PETER A 28 03A B
GARDNER R W A 26 GRI W
GARDNER SAMUEL A 46 JAM B
GARDNER SAMUEL S A 40 MAU W
GARDNER SETH A 46 KIN W
GARDNER SOLOMON A 46 KIN W
GARDNER STARKEY A 28 03A W
GARDNER T J A 46 FRI W
GARDNER TAYLER A 37 HIG W
GARDNER THOS A 28 01A B
GARDNER URIAH A 46 FRI W
GARDNER WILEY J A 37 TA2 W
GARDNER WILLIAM E A 46 KIN W
GARDNER WM L A 19 MOR W
GARDNER WM N A 28 03A W
GARDNER WM R A 28 04A B
GAREY MICHAEL A 29 FA1 W
GARGAS J A A 39 FRA W
GARISH JAMES C A 53 OCR W
GARISON JAMES A 25 TUS W
GARLAND F A A 19 MOR W
GARLAND JUNIUS A 44 TOW B
GARLAND WILLIAM A 44 TOW B
GARNDNER A B A 46 FRI W
GARNER D B A 19 NEW W
GARNER A B A 19 NEW W
GARNER ALEXANDER A 19 BE1 W
GARNER BASIL A 35 GLI W
GARNER CHARLES A 35 WOL B
GARNER COLUMBUS A 44 FOR B
GARNER D W A 19 NEW W
GARNER DANIEL A 44 YXR B
GARNER DAVID J A 19 NEW W
GARNER DEXTER A 19 NEW W
GARNER E C A 19 HAD W
GARNER E M A 19 NEW W
GARNER E S A 19 NEW W
GARNER ELI A 44 SAS B
GARNER ELIJAH A 19 NEW W
GARNER ELZA A 19 BE1 W
GARNER F M A 19 NEW W
GARNER F M A 35 GLI W
GARNER FRANCIS JR A 19 NEW W
GARNER HENRY A 32 LOF W
GARNER HENRY A 35 WOL B
GARNER ISHAM A 35 WOL B
GARNER J B A 19 NEW W
GARNER J L A 32 LOF W
GARNER J T A 19 NEW W
GARNER JAMES D A 19 NEW W
GARNER JEREMIAH A 28 9TH W
GARNER JESSIE A 37 PEN W
GARNER JNO C A 19 NEW W
GARNER JOHN A 19 NEW W
GARNER JOHN A 32 LOF W
GARNER JOHN A 35 GLI B
GARNER JOHN A 35 WOL B
GARNER JOHN A 46 MON B
GARNER JOHN A A 19 MOR W
GARNER JOSEPH A 44 FOR B
GARNER L J A 19 NEW W
GARNER L M A 19 NEW W
GARNER LEM A 44 KIT B
GARNER LEVEN A 19 NEW W
GARNER LYNDSAY A 32 LOF W
GARNER MOSES A 44 DUT W
GARNER NATHAM A 19 NEW W
GARNER NATHAN A 35 WOL B
GARNER P H A 19 NEW W
GARNER R C A 19 NEW W
GARNER R S A 19 NEW W
GARNER RILEY A 35 GLI B
GARNER ROBT A 44 FOR W
GARNER S C A 19 NEW W
GARNER S C JR A 19 NEW W
GARNER SAMUEL J A 28 9TH W
GARNER STEPHAN A 35 WOL B
GARNER STEWART A 35 WOL B
GARNER THOMAS A 44 DUT W
GARNER THOMAS M A 28 9TH W
GARNER W H A 35 GLI W
GARNER WALTER A A 46 RAG W
GARNER WILL A 35 KEN B
GARNER WM P A 19 NEW W
GARNER ZEMERIAH A 19 NEW W
GARNES GEORGE A 28 04B B
GARNES RICHD 2ND A 28 6TH B
GARNES RICHD JR A 28 6TH B
GARNETT ROBT A 29 FA1 W
GARRANT STEPHEN A 46 FRI B
GARREL AARON A 46 SUM B
GARRELL CALVIN A 46 SUM B
GARRENGER ANDY A 46 GIB B
GARRENTON J F A 30 IND W
GARRET W L A 44 LED W
GARRET WM A 28 15T W
GARRETT ABRAM A 46 COB W
GARRETT ADERSON A 46 ROS W
GARRETT ALFRED A 37 PIN W
GARRETT ALFRED A 40 DA1 B
GARRETT CALEB A 30 POW W
GARRETT CHESTER A 37 ROB B
GARRETT DANIEL A 46 ROS W
GARRETT E THOMPSON A 46 GRE W
GARRETT FRANK A 46 GRE B
GARRETT FREDERICK A 37 HIG B
GARRETT FREDERICK A 46 COB W
GARRETT GEORGE A 37 ROB B
GARRETT GERALDUS A 37 HIC A
GARRETT H E A 44 HEN W
GARRETT HANSEL A 44 BRA B
GARRETT HARRY A 37 PEN B
GARRETT HENRY A 37 HIG B

GARRETT HENRY A 46 ROS W
GARRETT HEYWOOD A 37 PEN B
GARRETT ISAAC M A 37 HIG W
GARRETT J W A 44 YXR W
GARRETT JAMES E A 30 MOY W
GARRETT JAMES W A 24 EDE W
GARRETT JEREMIAH A 37 HIG B
GARRETT JNO T A 30 MOY W
GARRETT JNO W A 44 KIT W
GARRETT JOHN A 30 TUL B
GARRETT JOHN A 37 ROB B
GARRETT JOHN A 46 COB W
GARRETT JOHN A 46 GRE B
GARRETT JOHN H A 24 EDE W
GARRETT JOHN H A 32 TYR W
GARRETT JOHN J A 37 TA1 W
GARRETT JOHN Q A 37 SPA W
GARRETT JOSEPH A 37 ROB W
GARRETT JOSEPH A 46 GRE B
GARRETT LEVI A 46 GRE B
GARRETT LYCORGUS A 30 MOY B
GARRETT MATHIAS A 30 MOY W
GARRETT MICHAEL A 46 COB W
GARRETT NEADHUM A 37 ROB B
GARRETT OLIVER A 44 LED B
GARRETT OSBURN A 37 ROB B
GARRETT PETER A 28 05A B
GARRETT PHILLIP A 30 MOY W
GARRETT PHILLIP C A 30 MOY W
GARRETT RICHARD H A 37 HIG W
GARRETT RILEY A 46 RAG W
GARRETT SAML A 37 ROB B
GARRETT SAML S A 30 MOY W
GARRETT VIRGIL A 37 HIG B
GARRETT WILLIAM A 37 ROB B
GARRETT WILLIAM E A 37 PIN W
GARRETT WILLIS A 37 HIG B
GARRETT WILLIS A 37 PEN B
GARRETT WILLIS A 37 WHI B
GARRETT YANCY A 46 GRE B
GARRETT YORK A 28 05A B
GARRETT YORK A 30 CUR B
GARRIL LEMUEL A 24 MID W
GARRIS JOHN B A 35 GLI W
GARRISON ALONZO A 29 FA1 W
GARRISON E N A 25 HAY W
GARRISON H T A 25 TUS W
GARRISON J W A 32 BRO W
GARRISON JOHN M A 40 STO W
CHALLENGED & ACCEPTED
GARRISON JONATHAN T A 30 ROA W
GARRISON PHILIP A 28 11T B
GARRITT JOHN A 32 LEE W
GARROTT EDWARD J A 44 YXR W
GARROTT EDWARD W A 44 TAR W
GARROTT RUFUS A 44 OXF B
GARROTT S O A 44 TAR W
GARROTT SILUS A 44 SAS B
GARUS WILLIAM A 37 TA2 B
GARVES HENRY A 46 GRE W
GARVEY ANDREW J A 37 ROC W
GARVEY JAS T A 37 ROC W
GASH DAVID A 32 POS W
GASKILL AARON A 19 BE1 B
GASKILL ANSON W A 19 STR W
GASKILL BAZEL A 19 HUN W
GASKILL BELCHER H A 19 STR W
GASKILL BENJA A 53 OCR W
GASKILL ELIJAH S A 19 POR W
GASKILL ELIJAH W A 19 STR W
GASKILL ENOCH H A 53 SWA W
GASKILL GEO W A 19 STR W
GASKILL ISAAC A 19 CED B

GASKILL JOHN W A 19 POR W
GASKILL JOHN W A 53 OCR W
GASKILL JOSEPH A 19 CED W
GASKILL JOSEPH A 19 HUN W
GASKILL JOSEPH A 28 9TH W
GASKILL JOSEPH B A 28 01B W
GASKILL JOSEPH E A 19 POR W
GASKILL JOSEPH N A 19 HUN W
GASKILL MARCH A 30 IND B
GASKILL MASON A 19 HUN W
GASKILL MASON A 19 STR W
GASKILL N M A 28 03A W
GASKILL OBED A 19 BE2 B
GASKILL SYLVESTER B A 28 10T B
GASKILL THOMAS A 19 HUN W
GASKILL THOMAS A 19 HUN W
GASKILL THOS S A 19 POR W
GASKILL VALENTINE W A 19 STR W
GASKILL WILLIAM A 19 CED W
GASKILL WILLIAM JR A 19 CED W
GASKILL WILLIS A 19 HUN W
GASKILL WM S A 53 OCR W
GASKILL WM W A 53 HAT W
GASKIN ABRAHAM A 28 10T B
GASKIN DOC A 19 HAD B
GASKIN NELSON A 24 MID B
GASKIN WILLIAM A 28 7TH B
GASKIN WILLIAM A 28 9TH B
GASKINS ALFRED A 28 12T W
GASKINS ARTHUR A 28 13T W
GASKINS ASA A 28 12T W
GASKINS ASA A A 28 13T W
GASKINS BENJA W A 53 OCR W
GASKINS BRYAN A 28 12T W
GASKINS CAESAR A 28 11T B
GASKINS CHARLES A 28 8TH B
GASKINS DAVID A 28 11T W
GASKINS DUNN A 28 13T B
GASKINS E A A 28 12T W
GASKINS F P A 28 12T W
GASKINS GEORGE A 53 FAI B
GASKINS GEORGE W A 53 HAT W
GASKINS GILBERT F A 53 LA1 W
GASKINS HENRY A 28 12T W
GASKINS HENRY A A 28 12T W
GASKINS IRA C A 53 LA1 W
GASKINS JAMES G A 28 16T W
GASKINS JAMES H A 28 16T W
GASKINS JOHN A 28 10T B
GASKINS JOHN A 28 11T W
GASKINS JOHN A 28 12T W
GASKINS JOHN H A 53 SWA W
GASKINS JOHN J R 28 11T W
DID NOT TAKE OATH
WAS A PATROLLER AND
OVERSEER OF ROADS AND
GAVE AID AND COMFORT
GASKINS JOHN S A 28 02N W
GASKINS JOSEPH A 28 12T W
GASKINS JOSEPH W A 53 HAT W
GASKINS KELLY A 28 11T W
GASKINS LEVEN A 28 12T W
GASKINS MAJOR A 28 11T W
GASKINS MANUEL A 28 6TH B
GASKINS MOSES A 19 BE1 B
GASKINS NATHANIEL A 28 12T W
GASKINS NOAH B A 28 13T W
GASKINS RAYMOND R 28 12T W
WAS AN OFFICER OF PATROL
& GAVE AID & COMFORT
GASKINS REDDING A 28 12T W
GASKINS ROBERT A 53 LA1 B
GASKINS ROBERT W A 28 16T W

GASKINS SAMUEL A 46 SUM B
GASKINS SAMUEL T A 53 LA1 W
GASKINS SETH A 53 GER W
CERT RES LAKE LANDING
GASKINS SILAS A 28 11T W
GASKINS T H R 28 12T W
WAS MEMBER OF STATE
LEGISLATURE AND A
CONFEDERATE MAGISTRATE
GASKINS THOMAS E A 28 7TH W
GASKINS THOMAS J A 28 11T W
GASKINS WILLIAM A 53 HAT W
GASKINS WILLIAMS D A 28 12T W
GASKINS WM A 28 04A B
GASKINS WM A A 24 MID W
GASKINS WM S A 28 02N W
GASSOM WM A 29 FA1 B
GASTON H HARRY A 28 04A B
GASTON J R A 40 SAN W
COPIED FROM DUPLICATE
GASTON MANUEL A 40 STO B
GASTON POMPEY A 28 04B B
GASTON R M A 40 STO W
GASTON SIMEON A 28 15T B
GASTON WILLIAM A 37 ROC B
GASWICK JEFFREY A 39 SPE W
GATCH THOS A A 44 KIT W
GATES CHARLES A 46 FRI W
GATES P J A 46 KIN W
GATES SHADE A 28 01B B
GATES SHADRACK A 28 04A B
GATES THOS A 28 01A W
GATES WILLIAM M A 40 BLA W
GATHER MILES A 32 YAD B
GATLAND NOAH A 44 HEN B
GATLAND THOS A 44 HEN B
GATLIN BRYAN B A 37 PEN W
GATLIN CAESAR A 28 03A B
GATLIN CALVIN A 37 PEN W
GATLIN DAVID A 28 14T W
GATLIN DAVID A 28 7TH B
GATLIN FRANCIS C A 28 11T W
GATLIN GEORGE A 28 03B B
GATLIN JACOB A 28 04B B
GATLIN JACOB A 28 12T B
GATLIN JAMES A 19 BE1 B
GATLIN JAMES A 28 03A B
GATLIN JOHN A 28 12T W
CERTIF GIVEN TO VOTE
AT NEW BERN
GATLIN JOSIAH A 28 12T B
GATLIN PATRICK H A 37 PEN W
GATLIN PEARSON A 28 12T W
GATLIN PETER A 28 11T B
GATLIN PHILLIP A 19 BE1 B
GATLIN RICHD A 28 04A B
GATLIN RILEY A 28 6TH W
GATLIN SHADRAC A 28 10T B
GATLIN SIMEON A 19 BE1 B
GATLIN SIMON A 28 03A B
GATLIN THOMAS H A 37 EDW W
GATTIS C L A 40 RHY W
GATTIS NELSON A 26 BLA B
GATTIS THOMAS A 99 BUS W
GATTIS THOS J A 29 LOC W
GAUNT JAMES M A 46 GRE W
GAVIN DAVID A 35 ISL B
GAVIN FRANK A 28 16T B
GAVIN JOHN A 35 KEN B
GAVIN LONSBY A 35 ISL B
GAVIN SAMEUL H A 35 WAR W
GAVIN SAMEUL J A 35 MAG W
GAVIN SAMEUL S A 35 WAR W

GAVIN WILLIAM A A 35 WAR W
GAVIN WILLIAM C A 35 MAG W
GAY A W A 44 LED W
OF GRANVILLE CO
GAY ALBERT A 39 GRI W
GAY ALFRED A 37 ROC W
CERT RES WILMINGTON NC
GAY BENNETT A 37 ROC W
GAY BURRELL A 37 ROC W
GAY C H A 44 KIT W
GAY DAVID B A 37 ROC W
GAY EVIN A 39 DAV B
GAY HARRISON A 37 EDW B
GAY HENRY A 37 WEB W
GAY IRVING A 37 PIN B
GAY JAMES A 37 PIN B
GAY JAMES A 37 WEB W
GAY JOHN A 37 SHA W
GAY JOHN C A 37 ROB W
GAY KINCHIN A 37 ROC W
GAY LEVEN A 37 WEB W
GAY LOUIS G A 35 SMI W
GAY NATHANIEL A 37 SHA W
GAY ROBERT A 28 05A B
GAY SHERWOOD A 39 DAV W
GAY SILAS H A 37 WHI W
GAY THOMAS A 39 DAV W
GAY W H A 39 DAV W
GAY WILEY A 37 TA1 B
GAY WILLIAM A 37 ROC W
GAY WILLIAM A 39 DAV W
GAY WILLIAM T A 37 ROC W
GAY WILSON A 39 DAV W
GAYLIARD ELI A 28 05A B
GAYLIARD NELSON A 28 05A B
GAYLOR ANTHONY A 28 15T B
GAYLOR LEWIS A 35 MAG W
CERT GIVEN 11 APRIL 1868
GAYLORD HARDY A 28 05A B
GAYLORD JAMES A 28 10T B
GAYLORD STEPHEN A 30 ROA W
GAYLUM SILAS A 28 05A B
GAYNEL KADOR A 30 NOR W
GAYNOR JAMES A 28 05A B
GAYNOR SANDERS A 28 05A B
GEAR WALKER A 37 PEN B
GEARIN MADISON A 46 GRE B
GEARY ISAAC A 28 05A B
GEDDIE DANL A 29 LOC W
GEDDU CARY A 29 FLE B
GEDDY D A A 29 FLE W
GEDDY DUGAL A 29 FLE W
GEDDY J C A 29 LOC W
GEDDY J D A 29 FLE W
GEDDY JOHN A 29 FLE W
GEDDY MCDD A 29 FLE W
GEDDY THOMAS NO 2 A 29 FLE B
GEDDY THOS A 29 FLE B
GEDDY W J A 29 FLE W
GEDNEY J C A 26 SHE W
GEDNEY J W A 26 SHE W
GEE JNO A 29 FA1 W
GEGORS MAXEY A 72 SWA B
GEISERT JACOB A 28 01B W
GELDING GRIFIN A 30 POP W
GENTELS R B A 32 YAD W
GEORGE ALLEN A 44 OXF B
GEORGE DANIEL A 37 WHI B
GEORGE EMANUEL A 28 10T B
GEORGE HENRY A 37 ROC B
GEORGE JAMES 1ST A 28 10T B
GEORGE JAMES 2ND A 28 10T B
GEORGE JOHN A 28 03A B
GEORGE MARTIN A 28 10T B
GEORGE SQUIRE A 28 9TH B
GEORGE THEOPHILUS A 28 10T B
GERAM ARON A 37 MAN B
GERINGER ANDREW A 46 MCL W
GERINGER JOHN A 46 GIB W
GERKINS ELI H A 53 SWA W
GERMAN JAMES A 28 16T B
GERMAN MORRIS A 35 SMI B
GERMAN MOSES A 28 6TH B
GERREL JAMES S A 46 MCL W
GERRELL THOMAS S A 46 GRE B
GERRINER HENRY A 46 MCL W
GERRINER JOHN A 46 MCL W
GERRINGER JACOB A 46 GIB W
GERRINGER JEFFERSON A 46 MCL B
GERRINGER JOHN A 46 COB W
GERRINGER LEWIS A 46 MCL B
GERRINGER MARTIN A 46 GIB W
GERRINGER ROBT A A 46 GIB W
GERRINGER WM A 46 GIB W
GESINGLER PETER A 46 MON W
GETTYS WM H A 25 SHO W
GHIRKINS JAMES E A 53 SWA W
GHROOM ISRELL A 37 MAN B
GHROOM THOMAS A 37 MAN B
GIBBINGS WM J A 32 BRO W
GIBBLE B A 19 HAD B
GIBBLE FRANKLIN W A 19 BE1 B
GIBBLE GEO F A 19 BE1 W
GIBBLE JACOB L A 19 BE1 W
GIBBLE SAMUEL S A 19 BE1 W
GIBBLE THOS D A 19 BE1 W
GIBBLE THOS D SR A 19 BE1 W
GIBBONS JACKSON A 26 SWA W
GIBBONS JACOB A 26 SWA W
GIBBONS JESSE A 26 BUR W
GIBBONS WILLIAM E A 19 MOR W
GIBBS AARON A 53 LA1 B
GIBBS ALEXANDER H A 53 LA1 W
GIBBS ALEXANDRIA A 53 LA1 B
GIBBS ALEXANDRIA A 53 LA1 W
GIBBS ANDERSON A 24 EDE B
GIBBS ANSON A 28 05A B
GIBBS ANSON A 53 LA1 B
GIBBS ANSON L A 53 LA1 W
GIBBS ARNAL A 53 LA1 B
GIBBS ARNOLD A 28 04A B
GIBBS AUGUSTUS A 28 04A B
GIBBS BARTLET A 53 LA1 B
GIBBS BARTLETT A 28 04A B
GIBBS BENJAMIN A 53 LA1 B
GIBBS BENJAMIN A 53 LA1 B
GIBBS BENJAMIN S A 53 LA2 W
GIBBS BENJM D A 53 GER W
GIBBS BURAGE L A 53 LA1 W
GIBBS CALEB A 53 LA1 B
GIBBS CARNE A 53 LA1 W
GIBBS CASON A 53 LA1 W
GIBBS CASON J A 28 16T W
GIBBS CHARLES A 53 LA1 B
GIBBS CHARLES A 53 LA1 B
GIBBS CHARLES E P A 53 LA1 W
GIBBS CHARLES W A 53 LA2 W
GIBBS CHRISTOPHER A 53 LA2 W
GIBBS CORNELIOUS S A 53 LA1 W
GIBBS DAVID A 28 05A B
GIBBS DAVID D A 53 LA2 W
GIBBS DAVID S JR A 53 LA1 W
GIBBS DAVID SR A 53 LA1 W
GIBBS DAVID W A 53 LA1 W
GIBBS DURANT H A 53 LA1 W
GIBBS EDWARD A 53 LA1 B
GIBBS FREDERICK S A 53 LA1 W
GIBBS GEORGE A 53 FAI B
GIBBS GEORGE A 53 LA1 B
GIBBS GEORGE W A 53 SWA W
GIBBS HENRY A 53 GER W
GIBBS HENRY R A 53 LA1 W
GIBBS HENRY S A 53 LA1 W
GIBBS HENRY W A 53 SWA W
GIBBS ISAAC A 53 LA1 B
GIBBS ISRAEL A 53 LA2 W
GIBBS ISRAEL W A 53 LA1 W
GIBBS J C A 25 HAY W
GIBBS JABEZ S A 53 LA1 W
GIBBS JACK A 53 LA1 B
GIBBS JAMES A 28 04A B
GIBBS JAMES A 53 LA1 B
GIBBS JAMES A 53 LA1 B
GIBBS JAMES A A 53 LA1 W
GIBBS JAMES M A 53 FAI W
GIBBS JAMES W A 53 LA1 W
GIBBS JESSE A 53 LA1 B
GIBBS JESSE A 53 LA1 W
GIBBS JOHN A 28 04A B
GIBBS JOHN A 30 MOY B
GIBBS JOHN A 53 FAI B
GIBBS JOHN A 53 LA1 B
GIBBS JOHN A 53 LA1 B
GIBBS JOHN S A 53 LA1 B
GIBBS JOHN W A 19 BE1 B
GIBBS JOHN W A 53 LA1 W
GIBBS JONAS A 53 SWA B
GIBBS JONATHAN H A 53 FAI W
GIBBS JOSEPH A 53 LA1 B
GIBBS JOSEPH B A 53 LA1 W
GIBBS JOSEPH B SR A 53 LA1 W
GIBBS LEMUEL A 53 LA1 B
GIBBS LOCKHART R 19 BE1 W
GIBBS LOCKHERT A 19 BE2 W
GIBBS M WILLIAMS A 53 LA2 B
GIBBS MAJOR A 53 FAI B
GIBBS MATTHIAS S A 53 SWA W
GIBBS MILTON S A 53 LA2 W
GIBBS MOSES A 53 LA1 B
GIBBS NATHANIEL A 53 FAI W
GIBBS OLIVER A 53 LA1 W
GIBBS ORMON A 53 SWA B
GIBBS PARKER A 53 LA1 B
GIBBS PELEDGE S A 53 LA1 W
GIBBS PICKET A 53 LA1 B
GIBBS RICHARD A 53 SWA B
GIBBS ROBERT A 53 LA1 B
GIBBS ROBERT A 53 LA1 B
GIBBS ROBERT C A 53 LA1 W
GIBBS ROBINSON A 53 LA1 W
GIBBS ROLENT A 19 BE1 B
GIBBS SAML A 28 04A B
GIBBS SAMUEL A 53 LA1 B
GIBBS SELBY A 53 LA1 W
GIBBS SETH A 28 04A B
GIBBS SETH A 53 FAI B
GIBBS SETH A 53 LA1 W
GIBBS SETH W A 53 LA1 W
GIBBS SMITH A 53 LA1 B
GIBBS STEPHEN A 53 SWA B
GIBBS SYLVESTER A 53 FAI W
GIBBS THOMAS L A 53 LA1 W
GIBBS THOMAS M A 53 LA1 W
GIBBS THOS H B A 53 SWA W
GIBBS TILMON H A 53 SWA W
GIBBS WALLACE A 53 LA1 B
GIBBS WILLIAM A 53 LA1 W
GIBBS WILLIAM A A 53 LA2 B
GIBBS WILLIAM B A 53 FAI W

GIBBS WILLIAM B A 53 LA1 W
GIBBS WILLIAM H A 53 LA1 W
GIBBS WILLIAM H A 53 SWA B
GIBBS WILSON A 53 FAI W
GIBBS ZACHARIAH A 53 GER W
GIBBS ZACHARIAH A 53 LA1 B
CERT SWAN QUARTER
GIBSON ABNER A 30 POW W
GIBSON ALFRED A 46 MCL B
GIBSON CALVIN A 46 GRE B
GIBSON DAVID A 46 GRE B
GIBSON G S A 29 FA1 W
GIBSON GEORGE A 32 LOF W
GIBSON GEORGE A 37 TA1 B
GIBSON GEORGE A 40 DA1 W
GIBSON J W A 46 JAM W
GIBSON JAMES A 30 CUR W
GIBSON JOHN A 30 TUL W
GIBSON JOHN A 32 LOF W
GIBSON JOSEPH A 28 14T B
CERTIFICATE GIVEN
RESIDENCE NEW BERN
CRAVEN CO NC
GIBSON LEWIS B A 46 GRE B
GIBSON LINDSAY A 46 GIB B
GIBSON NATHAN A 46 GIB B
GIBSON O P A 26 BUR W
GIBSON ROBERT A 29 CED B
GIBSON RUFUS B A 46 GRE W
GIBSON SAML A 28 05A B
GIBSON THOMAS A 46 ROS B
GIBSON YANCY A 46 GRE B
GIDNEY BENJ A 26 WAR B
GIDNEY JAMES A 26 WAR B
GIDNEY SAM A 26 BLA B
GIDNEY T J A 26 BLA B
GIFFORD J H A 28 02N W
DEAD
GIFFORD J W A 28 10T W
GIFFORD M D A 24 EDE W
GIGGS J M A 40 RHY W
GIGGS W W A 30 IND W
GILBERT C R A 32 POS W
GILBERT CORNEALIOUS A 29 FLE W
GILBERT D W A 28 10T W
GILBERT GEORGE A 53 GER B
GILBERT JAMES A 28 10T W
GILBERT JAMES A 38 FRE W
GILBERT JOHN A 28 6TH W
GILBERT JOHN A 39 HAR W
GILBERT JOSEPH A 24 EDE B
GILBERT OLIVER F A 24 EDE W
GILBERT WILLIAM A 30 IND W
GILCHRIST BADE ? D A 32 DAV W
GILCHRIST C D A 29 FA1 W
GILCHRIST EMSLY A 46 MON B
GILCHRIST HENRY A 32 DAV B
GILCHRIST J J A 29 FA1 W
GILCHRIST J P A 29 FA1 W
GILCHRIST JAMES D A 46 MON W
GILCHRIST JOHN A 46 MON B
GILCHRIST WM A 32 DAV B
GILCREASE ANDREW A 32 DAV B
GILCREASE BENJ A 28 05A B
GILCREASE HENRY A 28 05A B
GILCREASE JOSEPH A 32 DAV B
GILE E T A 39 FRA W
GILES A A 29 BLA W
GILES ALEX A 29 CAR W
GILES CALVIN A 44 DUT B
GILES JACOB A 29 CAR W
GILES JOHN A 46 JAM B
GILES JOHN S A 32 TYR W
GILES JOSEPH A 19 MOR B
GILES NATHANIEL A 29 CAR W
GILES SAMEL A 44 DUT B
GILES WILLIAM A 29 CAR W
MAGISTRATE DURING THE
WAR DID NOT ENGAGE
IN THE REBELLION
GILESON RYAN A 29 FA1 B
GILFORD CHARLES A 53 SWA B
GILFORD JOHN A 28 04A B
GILGO WILLIAM A 19 POR W
GILIET JACOB A 19 MOR B
GILL A S A 44 FOR W
GILL ALEX A 39 FRA B
GILL AUGUSTUS A 28 01A B
GILL EZRA A 39 FRA W
GILL G G A 39 LOU W
GILL GEORGE A 44 HEN B
GILL H F A 44 SAS W
GILL HENRY A 39 HAY B
GILL J T A 39 JOR W
GILL JACOB A 39 PUG B
GILL JAMES A A 39 HAY W
GILL JAMES JR A 39 LOU B
GILL JAMES S A 39 HAY W
GILL JAMES SR A 39 LOU B
GILL JAS T A 44 KNA W
GILL JNO A 29 FA1 B
GILL JOE A 39 HAY B
GILL JOHN A 39 LOU B
GILL LEVI A 44 TAR B
GILL LEWIS A 39 FRA B
GILL MADISON A 39 HAY B
GILL MARTIAN A 39 FRA B
GILL OSEA A 39 LOU B
GILL PLEASANT A 44 KNA B
GILL R E A 39 FRA W
GILL R F A 39 HAY W
GILL RANSOM A 39 HAY B
GILL ROBERT A 39 HAY W
GILL THOMAS A 44 HEN B
GILL THOS A 29 FA1 W
GILL WILLIAM A 29 FA2 B
GILL WM A 44 BRA B
GILL Y W A 39 FRE W
GILLAM A M A 26 GRI W
GILLAM ALFRIED A 53 LA1 B
GILLAM HARDEY A 30 CUR B
GILLAM HENRY A 39 JOR W
GILLAM JAMES A 39 JOR W
GILLAM JAMES K A 39 SPE W
GILLAM JOHN A 39 JOR W
GILLAM MARCUS A 39 JOR W
GILLAM NATHANIAL A 39 JOR W
GILLAM NELSON A 28 15T B
GILLARD GEORGE A 19 MOR B
GILLASPIE DANL D A 46 GRE W
GILLESPIE ALLEN A 35 MAG B
GILLESPIE CLEM A 35 KEN W
GILLESPIE DANIEL A 35 MAG B
GILLESPIE DERRY A 35 MAG B
GILLESPIE ELIAS A 35 KEN B
GILLESPIE HENRY A 35 KEN B
GILLESPIE J M A 26 GRI W
GILLESPIE LEWIS A 35 KEN B
GILLESPIE LEWIS A 35 MAG B
GILLESPIE RICHARD A 35 KEN B
GILLESPIE THOMAS A 35 KEN B
GILLESPIE TOMLIN A 35 MAG B
GILLESPIE WARRICK A 35 MAG B
GILLESPIE WILLIAM A 26 BLA W
GILLET IVERY A 19 HAD B
GILLIAM ATLAS A 24 EDE B
GILLIAM EDWARD A 44 HEN B
GILLIAM GEORGE A 44 OXF B
GILLIAM HENRY A 44 OXF B
GILLIAM HENRY A A 24 EDE B
GILLIAM JAMES K A 39 JOR W
GILLIAM JEFFERSON M A 44 HEN B
GILLIAM JOHN A 44 OXF B
GILLIAM JOHN E A 53 LA1 B
GILLIAM LESLEY A 44 FOR W
GILLIAM PETER A 44 OXF B
GILLIAM PETERSON A 24 EDE B
GILLIAM Q A 19 MOR B
GILLIAM SABRA A 44 HEN B
GILLIAM THOMPSON A 24 EDE B
GILLIAMS CHAS H A 28 04A B
GILLIKEN ABSOLOM A 19 STR W
GILLIKEN ALPHUS W A 19 STR W
GILLIKEN AMOS A 19 STR W
GILLIKEN ANSON A 19 STR W
GILLIKEN BAKER A 19 STR W
GILLIKEN BENJAMIN A 19 STR W
GILLIKEN ELIJAH A 19 STR W
GILLIKEN GEO D A 19 STR W
GILLIKEN GEO R A 19 STR W
GILLIKEN ISAIAH A 19 STR W
GILLIKEN JAMES A 19 STR W
GILLIKEN JAMES W A 19 STR W
GILLIKEN JESSE A 19 STR W
GILLIKEN JOHN W A 19 BE1 W
GILLIKEN MARTIN R A 19 STR W
GILLIKEN OLIVER C A 19 STR W
GILLIKEN RANSOM S A 19 BE1 W
GILLIKEN SAMUEL C A 19 BE1 W
GILLIKEN STEPHEN F A 19 STR W
GILLIKEN THOS M A 19 STR W
GILLIKEN
WASHINGTON W A 19 STR W
GILLIKEN WILLIAM B A 19 STR W
GILLIKEN WM W A 19 STR W
GILLIKIN BOWEN A 19 BE1 W
GILLIKIN CICERO S A 19 STR W
GILLIKIN GEO A A 19 STR W
GILLIKIN JOHN A 19 MOR W
GILLIS ARCHIBALD A 29 SEV W
GILLIS CATO A 29 SEV B
GILLIS CHAS A 29 ROC B
GILLIS DAVID A 29 ROC W
COUNTY ASSESSOR
GILLIS EVISS A 44 YXS B
GILLIS GEO A 29 ROC B
GILLIS HENERY A 29 ROC B
GILLIS ISAAC A 29 SEV B
GILLIS JAMES A 29 ROC B
GILLIS JOHN A A 29 SEV W
GILLIS JOHN A R 29 QUW W
MAGISTRATE J P BEFORE THE
REBELLION AFTERWARDS EN-
GAGED IN THE REBELLION
OATH NOT TAKEN
GILLIS LAND M A 29 SEV W
GILLIS RODRICK D R 29 QUW W
MAGISTRATE J P BEFORE THE
REBELLION AFTERWARDS GAVE
AID AND COMFORT TO THE
ENEMIES. OATH NOT TAKEN
GILLIS WM A 29 SEV B
GILLISBIE LOGAN A 46 GRE B
GILLISPIE J M A 26 MOO W
GILLISPIE JOHN A 26 MOO W
GILLUM H C A 29 FA2 B
GILLUM JOHN A 72 SWA B
GILLUM JOHN ESAP A 46 KIN B
GILMER ALFRED A 46 FRI B

GILMER BENJ W A 46 RAG B
GILMER CHARLES A 46 GRE B
GILMER FRANK A 46 GRE B
GILMER JOHN A JR A 46 GRE W
GILMER JOHN E A 46 GRE W
GILMER MARSHAL A 46 GRE B
GILMER ROBT A 46 GRE B
GILMER TBIAS A 46 GRE B
GILMER WILLIAM V A 46 RAG W
GILMON WM A 28 03A B
GILMORE ALFRED A 29 FA1 B
GILMORE ALFRED A 29 GRA B
GILMORE ALLEN A 46 ROS B
GILMORE ALVEAS A 46 ROS B
GILMORE CALVIN A 46 GRE B
GILMORE CHELSY A 29 FA1 B
GILMORE DAVID A 29 GRA B
GILMORE GEORGE A 46 GRE B
GILMORE HENRY A 46 GRE B
GILMORE JOHN H A 46 GRE B
GILMORE JOS A 29 FA1 B
GILMORE JOS H A 46 GRE B
GILMORE MADISON A 46 GRE B
GILMORE NATHAN A 29 FA2 B
GILMORE NATHL A 29 GRA B
GILMORE ROBT A 29 GRA B
GILMORE SAML A 29 FA1 B
GILMORE THOS A 29 GRA B
GILMORE WM A 29 FA1 B
GILSSON ROBERT A 35 FAI B
GINGLES BALES A 40 SAN B
GIRESH ALEXANDER E A 32 THO W
GIST EDMON A 26 HOL B
GLACKLEY WM A 44 FOR B
GLADDEN JOHN J A 40 DA1 W
GLADDEN L W A 26 GOF W
GLADDEN LACY A 26 GRI W
GLADDEN NATHAN A 40 SAN B
GLADDEN R C A 26 GOF W
GLADDEN REUBEN A 40 DA1 B
GLADDIN J A A 26 GRI W
GLADSON ALBERT B A 46 GRE B
GLADSON DANIEL S A 46 GRE W
GLADSON MADISON M A 46 GRE W
GLANCEY BOWEN A 72 SWA W
GLANCY HILLIARD A 19 NEW W
GLANCY RUFUS A 19 NEW W
GLANCY WILLIAM A 19 NEW W
GLANCY WILLIAM JR A 19 NEW W
GLASGOE JOHN A 44 KIT B
GLASGOW MARTIN A 44 HEN B
GLASS BRUNSICK A 46 MON B
GLASS ELI A 46 GRE W
GLASS G W A 46 GRE W
GLASS GEORGE M A 46 GRE W
GLASS J B A 46 GRE W
GLASS JOHN A 46 GRE W
GLASS LEVIN A 46 GRE B
GLASSCOCK GILES T A 46 GRE W
GLASSCOCK J C A 32 BRO W
GLASSCOCK TROY A 32 BRO W
GLASSGOW HENRY A 26 GRI W
GLEAN PINK A 26 GRI W
GLEASON RIANT A 28 14T B
GLENN A C A 28 7TH W
GLENN BESLING A 44 KNA B
GLENN ISAAC A 46 RAG B
GLENN J W A 40 SAN W
GLENN JAMES T A 40 SAN W
GLENN JOHN A 40 STO B
GLENN JULIUS A 46 ROS B
GLENN PATRICK A 44 YXS B
GLENN R W A 46 GRE W

GLENN ROBERT J A 40 BLA W
GLENN SAMPSON B A 46 ROS W
GLENN STANHOPE A 40 BLA W
GLENN WILLIAM D A 40 FER W
GLENN WILLIAM H A 37 EDW W
GLEWAR JOHN B A 46 FRI W
GLISSOM HAYWOOD A 35 GLI W
GLISSON BENJAMIN A 35 FAI W
GLISSON H J A 35 FAI W
GLISSON MILLARD A 35 FAI W
GLISSON SAMUEL A 35 WOL B
GLLISSON DANIEL A 35 WOL B
GLOVER A A 26 BOR B
GLOVER ADAM A 26 SHE W
GLOVER ANDREW J A 53 SWA W
GLOVER CALVIN F A 29 CAR W
GLOVER CHAS A 29 FA2 W
GLOVER EDWIN A 29 FA1 W
GLOVER HENRY A 44 TOW B
GLOVER J D A 32 COT W
GLOVER JACOB A 44 TOW B
GLOVER JAMES A 29 LOC B
GLOVER JOSEPH B A 19 HAR W
GLOVER JOSIAH A 40 DA1 B
GLOVER RANDALL A 26 SHE B
GLOVER WALLACE A 44 SAS B
GLOVER WM A 28 6TH W
GLOVER WM A 46 GRE B
GLOVER WM R A 29 CAR W
GOBBLE B C A 32 DAV W
GOBLE A A 40 SAN W
GOBLE ALEXANDER A 32 TYR W
GOBLE ANDERSON A 32 TYR W
GOBLE ANDERSON A 32 TYR W
GOBLE DAVID A 32 TYR W
GOBLE GODFREY A 32 TYR W
GOBLE H C A 32 TYR W
GOBLE HYRAM A 32 TYR W
GOBLE J H A 32 TYR W
GOBLE MANUEL A 32 TYR B
GOBLE R A A 32 TYR W
GOBLE RICHMON A 32 TYR W
GOBLE THOMAS A 32 TYR W
GOBLE WILLIAM A 32 TYR W
GOBY THOMAS A 46 SUM W
GODDARD CHAS R 29 FA1 W
LEVY U.S. SOLDIER HELD
CLERK OF MARKET OFFICE
DURING REBELLION
GODDEN WILLIAM A 19 HAD W
GODDIN ALLEN A 29 FA1 W
GODDIN ISHAM A 29 LOC W
GODETT ANDREW A 28 10T B
GODETT ESAU JR A 28 10T B
GODETT ESAU SR A 28 10T B
GODETT JAMES A 28 10T B
GODETT JEREMIAH A 28 10T B
GODETT JESSE P A 28 10T B
GODETT PETER A 28 03A B
GODETT PETER A 28 10T B
GODETT WILLIAM H A 28 10T B
GODETT
WILLIAM PARKER A 28 10T B
GODFREY RICHARD A 30 MOY B
GODFREY QUILLER A 28 05A B
GODFREY RICHARD A 46 JAM B
GODFREY TAFF A 28 14T B
GODFREY WASHINGTON A 28 14T B
GODFREY WM A 28 04A B
CERTIFICATE GRANTED
JONES CO.
GODING WILEY A 28 04A B
GODLEY ALFRED A 46 GRE B

GODLEY ISAAC A 28 01A B
GODLEY N H A 19 BE2 W
GODLEY TONEY A 19 BE1 B
GODLY MARRIS A 19 BE1 B
GODWIN B A 29 FLE W
GODWIN CARY A A 29 BLA X
GODWIN D J A 29 BLA W
GODWIN E A 29 BLA W
GODWIN ISAAC A 29 CED B
GODWIN JESSEY A 29 LOC W
GODWIN JOSEPH A 28 9TH W
GODWIN L W A 29 BLA W
GODWIN LOFTIN A 29 BLA X
GODWIN SIMON A 29 FA1 W
GODWIN WILLIAM T A 37 PEN W
GOFF HENRY A 28 04A B
GOFF THOMAS A 35 FAI W
GOFORTH ANDREW A 26 GOF W
GOFORTH H W A 26 GOF W
GOFORTH MURRY A 26 GOF B
GOFORTH SAM A 26 BOR W
GOFORTH WILLIAN A 26 HOL B
GOINS A B A 26 SHE W
GOINS DAVID A 29 QUW B
GOINS LEVI A 46 MON B
GOINS THOMAS A 37 ROC W
GOINS TURNER A 29 SEV B
GOLBRETH ROBERT A 32 POS W
GOLD ALEX A 26 BLA W
GOLD B J A 26 MOO W
GOLD J H A 26 BLA W
GOLD MELTON A 26 BLA W
GOLD P G A 26 BLA W
GOLD W F A 26 BLA W
GOLDING EZKIEL A 19 HUN W
GOLDING JOHN H A 19 HUN W
GOLDING JOSEPHUS A 19 SMY W
GOLDING MARTIN A 19 STR W
GOLDING MARTIN T A 19 STR W
GOLDING THOMAS A 19 HUN W
GOLDING TISON A 19 HUN W
GOLDSON NELSON A 37 EDW B
GOOCH A H A 44 LED W
GOOCH ALBERT A 44 HEN B
GOOCH AMIS A 44 TAR W
GOOCH BILLY R 44 ISL B
8 MOS REJ
GOOCH CALVIN A 44 TAR B
GOOCH D T A 44 TAR W
GOOCH DANIEL J A 44 TAR W
GOOCH DAVID A 44 HEN B
GOOCH EMMITT A 44 LED W
GOOCH GEORGE A 44 LED W
GOOCH GEORGE A 44 TAR B
GOOCH H R A 44 LED W
GOOCH H S A 44 LED W
GOOCH HAYWOOD A 44 KNA B
GOOCH HENRY A 44 RAG B
GOOCH J D A 44 TAR W
GOOCH JAMES A 44 BEA B
GOOCH JAMES A 44 HEN B
GOOCH JAMES A 44 HEN W
GOOCH JERRY A 44 OXF B
GOOCH JOSEPH A 44 TAR W
GOOCH MAJOR A 44 HEN B
GOOCH NAPPER A 44 TAR B
GOOCH PETER A 44 OXF B
GOOCH RADFORD A 44 LED W
GOOCH ROBERT A 44 DUT B
GOOCH SCOTT A 39 HAY B
GOOCH SILUS A 44 OXF B
GOOCH W R A 44 LED W
GOOCH W T A 44 LED W

GOOCH WILLIAM	A	44	TAR	W
GOOD BENJN	A	28	03B	B
GOOD EDWARD	A	26	MOO	W
GOOD JOHN R	A	28	04A	B
GOODDEN ROBERT	A	30	CUR	B
GOODDN D A	A	40	CAN	W
GOODE D P	A	26	BOR	W
GOODE J G	A	26	BOR	W
GOODE JOSEPH	A	26	WAR	B
GOODE N A G	A	26	BOR	W
GOODE SAMUEL	A	44	SAS	B
GOODE T F	A	26	BOR	W
GOODE W C	A	26	BOR	W
GOODEN WILLIAM	A	32	LEE	B
GOODIN CALEB	A	30	TUL	W
GOODING ABNER	A	19	HAR	B
GOODING ANDREW	A	28	13T	B
GOODING F C	A	28	7TH	W
GOODING JACOB	A	28	04A	W
GOODING JACOB JR	A	28	04B	W
GOODING JOHN	A	28	7TH	W
GOODING JOHN H	A	19	STR	W
GOODING SILAS	A	32	THO	B
GOODING SIMON	A	32	YAD	B
GOODLOE DAVID	A	37	PIN	B
GOODLOE HARRISON (HARRY)	A	37	TA1	B
GOODLOE JOHN	A	44	KIT	B
GOODLOE LEWIS	A	37	PIN	B
GOODMAN A J	A	29	GRA	W
GOODMAN BENJ	A	29	ROC	B
GOODMAN DAVID A	A	46	GRE	W
GOODMAN HY	A	29	FA1	W
GOODMAN J A	A	29	SEV	W
GOODMAN J C	A	29	FA1	W
GOODMAN WILLIAM	A	30	MOY	W
GOODMAN WM D	A	30	MOY	W
GOODNEY AMBROSE	A	28	03A	B
GOODRIDGE JNO	A	30	IND	W
GOODSON C P	A	39	PUG	W
GOODSON G W	A	35	WOL	B
GOODSON JAMES	A	39	SPE	W
GOODSON JOHN F	A	40	DA1	W
GOODSON WILLIAM	A	39	PUG	W
GOODSPEED C P	A	28	01A	W
GOODWIN ELLSBERY	A	19	BE1	B
GOODWIN EXAM	A	24	MID	W
GOODWIN GABRIEL	A	24	UPP	W
GOODWIN GEO A	A	19	CED	W
GOODWIN HILARY	A	28	9TH	B
GOODWIN JACKSON	A	19	CED	W
GOODWIN JAMES	A	24	MID	W
GOODWIN JESSE	A	19	CED	W
GOODWIN JNO E	A	24	MID	W
GOODWIN JOHN	A	24	MID	W
GOODWIN JOHN A	A	24	MID	W
GOODWIN JOHN E JR	A	24	MID	W
GOODWIN JOHN L	A	19	CED	W
GOODWIN MILES	A	24	EDE	B
GOODWIN MILES	R	24	MID	W
ERASED BY HIS OWN REQUEST HAVING FOUND OUT WAS NOT ENTITLED FINAL REVISION				
GOODWIN PALLY	A	24	UPP	B
GOODWIN RICHARD	A	24	MID	W
GOODWIN SAMUEL	A	29	SEV	B
GOODWIN STEPHEN	A	24	EDE	B
GOODWIN THOS B	A	19	CED	W
GOODWIN WILLIAM	A	24	MID	B
GOORE DAVID	A	35	WAR	W
GOORE DAVID J	A	35	MAG	W
GOORE ISAAC	A	35	KEN	W
GOORE ISAAC J	A	35	WAR	W
GOORE JOHN	A	35	WAR	W
GOORE LINTON	A	35	WAR	W
GOORE MARSHALL H	A	35	WAR	W
GOORE SOLOMON R	A	35	WAR	W
GORAM HENRY	A	37	MAN	W
GORDAN ALBERT	A	30	KNO	W
GORDAN HOWEL	A	44	FIS	W
OXFORD DIST				
GORDAN J R	A	44	FIS	W
GORDAN J W	A	44	FIS	W
WAULNUT GROVE				
GORDAN JOHN	A	30	CUR	B
GORDAN JOSEPH	A	30	CUR	B
GORDAN JOSEPH	A	30	NOR	W
GORDAN NATHAN	A	30	POP	B
GORDAN POMPEY	A	44	FIS	B
GORDAN R M	A	40	STO	W
GORDEN A A	A	46	HIG	W
GORDEN GEORGE	A	40	SAN	B
GORDEN JAMES	A	40	SAN	B
GORDEN JAMES J	A	46	FRI	W
GORDEN JOHN	A	40	SAN	W
GORDEN LENDON	A	19	MOR	B
GORDEN LEVI	A	40	SAN	B
GORDEN THOMAS	A	40	SAN	B
GORDEN WM F	A	28	16T	W
GORDIN ALFORD	A	39	SPE	W
GORDON A T	A	32	LOF	W
GORDON BACCHUS	A	28	04B	B
GORDON BENJ	A	29	GRA	B
GORDON BENJAMIN	A	28	16T	W
GORDON CALVIN	A	44	TAR	W
GORDON D D	A	32	LOF	W
GORDON FRANKLIN	A	44	TAR	W
GORDON HENRY	A	44	HEN	W
GORDON J H	A	44	HEN	W
GORDON J W	A	46	FRI	W
GORDON JAMES	A	32	LOF	W
GORDON JOHN	A	28	16T	W
GORDON JOHN	A	32	LEE	W
GORDON JOHN W	A	46	HIG	W
GORDON JOSEPH	A	32	LOF	W
GORDON JOSEPH	A	32	LOF	W
GORDON L D	A	32	LEE	W
GORDON LEMUEL	A	30	POW	B
GORDON PETER	A	53	HAT	B
GORDON R S	A	32	THO	W
GORDON SHARPER	A	28	9TH	B
GORDON TASWELL	A	39	HAY	B
GORDON THOMAS	A	30	POW	B
GORDON W E	R	32	LOF	W
NAME LINED THROUGH FOR FELONY				
GORDON WILLIAM	A	32	DAV	W
GORDON WILLIAM	A	32	LOF	W
GORDON WM B	A	28	03B	W
GORDON WM M	A	28	02N	W
GORHAM ALBERT	A	28	8TH	B
GORHAM B C	A	29	FA1	W
GORHAM CAESAR	A	28	01A	B
GORHAM JOE	A	28	01A	B
GORHAM RALPH	A	37	PIN	B
GORHAM RICHARD K	A	37	MAN	W
GORHAM SIMON	A	37	PIN	B
GORHAM WILLIAM	A	37	MAN	W
GORHAM WINDSOR	A	28	04A	B
GORHAM WISELEY	A	37	PIN	B
GORRELL ABRAM	A	46	GRE	B
GORRELL CALVIN	A	46	GRE	B
GORRELL ISHAM	A	46	GRE	B
GORRELL JACK	A	46	GRE	B
GORRELL JAMES E	A	46	RAG	W
GORRELL JESSE	A	46	GRE	B
GORRELL NELSON	A	46	GRE	B
GORRELL PARIS	A	46	GRE	B
GORRELL RICHARD	A	46	GRE	B
GORRELL ROBT	A	46	GRE	B
GORRELL WASHINGTON	A	46	GRE	B
GORRELL WM DAVID	A	46	GRE	B
GOSDEN WILLIAM	A	46	MON	W
GOSDIN GREEN	A	46	MON	W
GOSETT DOCTOR	A	32	DAV	B
GOSLIN ALEXANDER	A	28	10T	W
GOSS BENJ	A	19	BE1	B
GOSS CICERO	A	32	DAV	W
GOSS DAVID	A	32	LOF	W
GOSS DAVID	A	44	DUT	B
GOSS ELEXANDER	A	32	DAV	W
GOSS ELIJAH	A	44	LED	W
GOSS JOHN	A	44	LED	W
GOSS LOUIS	A	19	MOR	B
CERT TO HADNOTS CREEK				
GOSS ROLLIN JR	A	44	LED	W
GOSS ROLLIN SR	A	44	LED	W
GOSS SANDY	A	32	TYR	B
GOSS SHEARMAN	A	44	DUT	W
GOSS T N	A	44	DUT	W
GOSS W G	A	44	LED	W
GOSS WILLIAM	A	44	LED	W
GOSSETT ABSOLEM	A	32	THO	B
GOSSETT ALPHEUS	A	46	ROS	B
GOSSETT ANDREW	A	32	THO	B
GOSSETT JESSE	A	32	THO	B
GOSSETT JOSHUA	A	46	ROS	W
GOSSETT NATHAN	A	46	FRI	W
GOSWICK JOHN	A	39	LOU	W
GOSWICK W H	A	39	HAY	W
GOUGH JAMES W	A	35	GLI	W
GOUGH ROBERT W	A	35	GLI	W
GOULD DAVID	A	19	NEW	W
GOULD MICHAEL	A	19	NEW	W
GOULDING SAMUEL J	A	46	GRE	W
GOWER JAMES H	A	53	BUR	W
GOWINS SULINGER	A	46	MCL	B
GOWNS OTIS	A	28	05A	B
GRABON JNO	A	29	FA1	B
GRACE JOHN	A	19	POR	W
GRACIE HENRY S	A	28	6TH	W
GRADDY ISAAC	A	29	FLE	B
GRADDY JAS C	A	29	FA1	W
GRADDY JNO C	A	29	FA1	W
GRADDY KILBY	A	35	KEN	B
GRADDY MARTIN	A	29	FA1	W
GRADDY RILEY	A	35	GLI	B
GRADDY WILLIAM	A	35	CYP	W
GRADRELL WHITMAN	A	19	NEW	B
GRADY AHAZ	A	35	ALB	W
GRADY ALEXANDER	A	35	KEN	W
GRADY ANDREW J	A	35	KEN	W
GRADY BENSON	A	35	ALB	W
GRADY BRYAN W	A	35	ALB	W
GRADY CHARLES	A	35	SMI	B
GRADY EMANUEL	A	35	ALB	B
GRADY FREDERICK	A	35	ALB	W
GRADY JAMES	A	44	TOW	W
GRADY JOHN	A	35	ALB	W
GRADY JOHN H	A	35	GLI	W
GRADY JOHN P	A	35	KEN	W
GRADY JOURDAN	A	28	05A	B
GRADY LOUIS	A	35	GLI	W
GRADY R M	A	35	ALB	W
GRADY SHERWOOD	A	35	ALB	W
GRADY STEPHEN H	A	35	KEN	W
GRADY THOMAS M	A	35	GLI	W
GRADY THOMAS N	A	35	KEN	W
GRADY W H	A	35	ALB	W

GRADY WILLIAM A 35 KEN W
GRADY WILLIAM A 35 SMI B
GRADY WILLIE A 37 ROC B
GRAGHM CUFF A 40 CAN B
GRAHAM A B A 26 SWA W
GRAHAM ALBERT A 35 CYP B
GRAHAM ALEX. C A 29 QUW W
GRAHAM ALEXANDER A 29 QUW W
GRAHAM ALLEN A 35 KEN B
CERTIFICATE TO
WILMINGTON APRIL 13, 68
GRAHAM ARCHD J A 29 SEV W
GRAHAM BENJAMIN A 26 SHE B
GRAHAM BEVERLEY A 44 SAS B
GRAHAM BRYANT J A 35 MAG B
GRAHAM D MCK A 29 FA1 W
GRAHAM DANIEL A 19 NEW B
GRAHAM DAVID A 35 KEN B
GRAHAM DERRY A 35 CYP B
GRAHAM DERRY A 46 GRE B
GRAHAM EMANUEL A 35 CYP B
GRAHAM EMANUEL A 35 WOL B
GRAHAM ESAU A 40 DA1 B
GRAHAM FRANCIS A 29 FA1 B
GRAHAM G W A 29 QUW W
MILITIA OFF TAKEN AN OATH
TO SUPPORT THE CONSTITU-
TION OF THE US AFTERWARDS
ENGAGED IN THE REBELLION
GRAHAM HARRY A 35 CYP B
GRAHAM HENRY A 24 EDE B
GRAHAM HENRY A 35 CYP B
GRAHAM HENRY A 35 CYP B
GRAHAM HUGH A 29 SEV W
GRAHAM ISHAM A 35 MAG B
GRAHAM J C A 29 LOC W
GRAHAM JACK A 29 FA2 B
GRAHAM JACK A 35 CYP B
GRAHAM JACOB A 26 SHE B
GRAHAM JAMES A 19 BE1 W
GRAHAM JAMES A 35 CYP B
GRAHAM JERRY A 28 15T B
GRAHAM JOHN A 35 ROC B
GRAHAM JOHN M A 29 QUW W
MILITIA OFF AFTERWARDS
ENGAGED IN THE REBELLION
TAKEN AN OATH TO SUPPORT
THE CONSTITUTION OF US US
GRAHAM JOHN M A 35 MAG W
GRAHAM JORDAN A 44 RAG B
GRAHAM JOSEPH A 35 MAG B
GRAHAM JOSEPH A 40 CAN W
GRAHAM LOT A 35 MAG B
GRAHAM M J R 29 FA1 W
NATURALIZED CITIZEN
BOUGHT CONFED BONDS
GRAHAM MAJOR A 35 FAI B
GRAHAM MARSELLUS A 44 YXR B
GRAHAM MENGLE A 29 FA2 W
COPIED FROM DUPLICATE
GRAHAM NATHAN A 29 ROC B
GRAHAM NED A 35 CYP B
GRAHAM NEILL A 29 QUW W
GRAHAM NEILL A A 29 ROC W
GRAHAM NEILL C A 29 QUW W
GRAHAM ROBERT A 35 KEN B
GRAHAM ROBT A 29 FA1 B
GRAHAM ROBT A 29 SEV B
GRAHAM SAM A 26 SWA B
GRAHAM SAMEUL A 35 KEN B
GRAHAM SAML L A 44 SAS W
GRAHAM SIMON A 28 9TH B
GRAHAM STEPHEN A 29 FA1 B
GRAHAM THOMAS A 35 CYP B
GRAHAM THOMAS A 35 ROC B
GRAHAM THOMAS A 44 SAS B
GRAHAM THOMAS R 46 KIN W
NAME LINED OUT
U.S. POSTMASTER BEFORE
THE WAR CONFEDERATE P M
DURING REBELLION COULD
NOT TAKE THE OATH WITHOUT
THE WORD VOLUNTARY REJ
GRAHAM W C A 26 SWA W
GRAHAM WILLIAM A 35 MAG B
GRAHAM WM A 28 16T B
GRAHAM WM A 44 ISL B
GRANBERRY GEORGE A 30 CUR W
GRANBURY HARRISON A 24 EDE B
GRANBY JOHN A 24 EDE B
GRANBY ROBERT A 24 MID B
GRAND ANDERSON A 29 FA1 B
GRANDY EDMOND A 44 OXF B
GRANDY EDWARD A 44 OXF B
GRANDY EMANUEL A 44 OXF B
GRANDY JOSEPH B A 30 IND W
GRANDY MILES A 44 OXF B
GRANDY T T A 44 OXF W
GRANDY W S A 44 OXF W
GRANGE GEO A 29 FA1 B
GRANGE GEO W SR A 29 FA1 B
GRANT ALLEN A 37 SPA B
GRANT CANNEY A 37 ROC B
GRANT EDWARD H A 29 FA2 W
GRANT ISAAC A 28 04A B
GRANT LUCAS A 19 BE1 B
GRANT RADFORD A 44 KNA B
GRANT SILAS A 37 ROC B
GRANT STAFFORD A 35 FAI W
GRANT WILLIAM A 28 02N W
GRANVILLE NELSON A 28 05A B
GRAVES ALFRED A 46 GRE B
GRAVES ALLEN A 46 GIB B
GRAVES ALLEN A 46 GRE W
GRAVES DAVID A 46 GRE W
GRAVES EDMOND A 44 OXF B
GRAVES EDWARD P A 30 NAR W
GRAVES JOHN A 30 POW W
GRAVES MADISON A 46 GRE W
GRAVES R H A 44 SAS W
GRAVES SIDNEY A 46 MCL B
GRAY ABNER A 53 KEN W
GRAY ALEXANDER A 46 MCL B
GRAY ALLEN W A 53 CHI W
GRAY ALLEN W A 53 KEN W
GRAY ANDERSON A 53 KEN W
GRAY ARTHUR A 37 ROC B
GRAY AUSTON A 37 ROC B
GRAY BANISTER B A 53 KEN W
GRAY BANISTER M A 53 CHI W
GRAY BENJAMIN A 37 MAN B
GRAY BENTON W A 46 MCL W
GRAY DAMOND M A 53 KEN W
GRAY DANIEL A 32 THO B
GRAY DAVID P A 53 CHI W
GRAY DAVIS A 53 KEN W
GRAY DEMPSEY A 37 PEN B
GRAY DEMPSEY A 37 WHI W
GRAY EDMOND A 28 04A B
GRAY EDMUND A 30 IND B
GRAY EDMUND D A 53 KEN W
GRAY EDWARD A 28 10T B
GRAY ELIJAH A 53 GER B
GRAY ETMORE A 53 GER B
GRAY GEORGE A 37 ROC B
GRAY GEORGE A 46 HIG B
GRAY GEORGE W A 53 LA1 B
GRAY GILES A 46 MCL W
GRAY HARISON A 46 FRI W
GRAY HENNRY A 30 IND B
GRAY HORACE A 37 ROC B
GRAY HYMAN A 37 SHA B
GRAY ITHAMER A 46 FRI W
GRAY J W A 32 THO W
GRAY JACOB A 37 ROC B
GRAY JAMES A 46 MCL W
GRAY JAMES A A 46 JAM W
GRAY JAMES H F A 46 RAG W
GRAY JENKINS A 46 MCL B
GRAY JESSE A 32 BRO W
GRAY JESSE A 37 ROC B
GRAY JESSE A 46 FRI W
GRAY JESSE SR A 53 KEN W
GRAY JOHN A 37 MAN B
GRAY JOHN A A 28 01A W
GRAY JOHN F A 30 IND W
GRAY JOHN F A 46 JAM W
GRAY JOHN FRANKLIN A 46 GRE B
GRAY JOHN H A 53 KEN W
GRAY JOSEPH A 32 THO B
GRAY JOSEPH C A 53 KEN W
GRAY JOSEPH S A 53 CHI W
GRAY JOSHUA A 53 KEN W
GRAY JULIUS A 46 GRE W
GRAY LEWIS A 37 SHA B
GRAY LORENZO A 46 HIG B
GRAY LUKE M A 53 CHI W
GRAY MALLICHI A 53 KEN W
GRAY NATHAN N A 53 KEN W
GRAY NATHEN A 46 FRI W
GRAY NOAH A 30 MOY W
GRAY NORFLEET A 37 ROC B
GRAY OLIVER N A 53 KEN W
GRAY PARKER A 35 SMI W
GRAY PETER A 30 CUR B
GRAY PETER A 37 ROC B
GRAY PRESIDENT A 37 PIN B
GRAY RANDALL A 37 PEN B
GRAY RANDEL A 37 ROC B
GRAY RICHARD A 53 SWA B
GRAY RICHMOND A 37 MAN B
GRAY ROBERT A 32 THO W
GRAY ROBIN A 37 ROC B
GRAY S F A 46 FRI W
GRAY S H A 19 HUN W
GRAY SAMUEL L A 53 GER B
GRAY SANDERSON P A 53 KEN W
GRAY SANDY A 46 HIG B
GRAY SILBY M A 53 KEN W
GRAY SPENCER G A 30 NAR W
GRAY SQUIRE A 46 FRI W
GRAY STEPHEN A 46 HIG B
GRAY THOMAS A 53 KEN W
GRAY THOS C A 30 MOY W
GRAY W P A 46 FRI W
GRAY WALLACE A 53 KEN W
GRAY WALLACE D A 53 CHI W
GRAY WATSON R A 53 KEN W
GRAY WILLIAM A 46 FRI W
GRAY WILLIAM G A 37 ROC W
GRAY WILLIAM T A 37 PEN W
CRAVEN CO
GRAY WILSON A 32 DAV B
GRAY WM A 46 MCL W
GRAY WORKINGTON A 37 MAN B
GREEN A H A 39 FRA W
GREEN AARON A 39 HAY B
GREEN AARON A 44 BRA B
GREEN ABNER A 53 GER W

GREEN ABRAM A 44 LED B
GREEN ABRAM A 46 GIB W
GREEN ADAM A 39 HAR B
GREEN ALBERT A 26 SHE W
MILITIA OFFICER &
ENGAGED IN REBELLION
GREEN ALEX A 39 HAR B
GREEN ALEX A 39 HAY B
GREEN ALEXANDER A 28 7TH B
GREEN ALEXR A A 28 02N B
GREEN ALLEN A 44 LED B
GREEN ALLISON R A 46 COB W
GREEN AMASIAH A 37 TA1 B
GREEN AMBROSE A 28 11T B
GREEN ANDREW A 39 HAY B
GREEN ANDREW J A 25 PIN W
GREEN ANTHONY A 32 BRO B
GREEN ARCHEY A 72 SWA W
GREEN ASA A 26 MOO W
GREEN AUSTIN A 39 FRA B
GREEN AUSTIN A 39 FRE B
GREEN B F A 32 POS W
GREEN B F DR A 39 FRA W
GREEN BARRICK A 28 14T B
GREEN BENJ H A 28 6TH W
GREEN BENJAMIN A 32 DAV W
GREEN BERRY A 26 MOO W
GREEN BRYAN A 28 03A B
GREEN BRYAN A 28 04A B
GREEN BRYANT A 19 NEW B
GREEN BURTON A 39 FRA B
GREEN CALDONY A 39 FRA B
GREEN CALVIN A 39 FRA B
GREEN CALVIN A 44 DUT B
GREEN CHAS C A 28 02N W
GREEN CHRIST A 28 04A B
GREEN CICERO A 28 6TH W
GREEN CLABON A 44 DUT B
GREEN CORNELIAS A 26 SHE W
GREEN D O A 26 HOL B
GREEN DANL A 44 LED B
GREEN DAVID A 26 MOU W
GREEN DAVID A 28 03A B
GREEN DICK A 39 PUG B
GREEN DRURY A 26 MOU W
GREEN DURWARD A 28 11T B
GREEN E A 39 FRA B
GREEN EDWARD A 28 04A B
GREEN EDWD A 39 FRA B
GREEN ELI A 46 COB W
GREEN ELIAS A 26 MOO W
GREEN ELIJA A 26 MOU W
GREEN ELIJAH A 44 TAR B
GREEN ELISHA A 28 02N B
GREEN ELISHA A 28 03B B
GREEN ENNELS A 46 MON B
GREEN ESQUAR A 44 KNA B
GREEN ESQUIRE A 28 6TH B
GREEN ESSEX A 28 01A B
GREEN EWELL A 26 HOL B
GREEN FORNEY A 28 7TH B
GREEN FRANK A 28 10T B
GREEN FRANK A 37 PIN B
GREEN FRANK A 44 YXS B
GREEN FREMAN F A 53 FAI B
GREEN FURNEY A 28 14T W
GREEN FURNEY A 44 OXF B
GREEN G A 44 LED B
GREEN G W A 32 TYR W
GREEN GEO A 39 HAR B
GREEN GEO R A 28 01A B
GREEN GEORGE A 26 MOO W
GREEN GEORGE A 28 04A B
GREEN GEORGE A 39 LOU B
GREEN GUSTON A 39 DAV B
GREEN H A 38 FRE B
GREEN H G A 25 SHO W
GREEN H H A 26 BLA W
GREEN HARRY A 39 PUG B
GREEN HASTY A 28 10T B
GREEN HAWKINS A 39 FRA B
GREEN HAYWOOD A 28 05A B
GREEN HAYWOOD A 44 FOR B
GREEN HENDERSON A 28 04A B
GREEN HENDERSON A 44 BRA B
GREEN HENRY A 28 04B B
GREEN HENRY A 28 9TH B
GREEN HENRY A 39 FRE B
GREEN HENRY A 44 LED B
GREEN ISAAC A 25 SHO B
GREEN ISAAC A 46 MON B
GREEN ISERAL A 39 HAY B
GREEN ISHAM A 39 FRA B
GREEN ISHMAEL A 28 01A B
GREEN IVY A 28 03A B
GREEN IVY A 35 WAR B
GREEN J B A 44 DUT W
GREEN J D DR A 26 MOO W
GREEN J M A 26 MOO W
GREEN J S P A 32 THO W
GREEN JACOB A 28 01B B
GREEN JACOB A 44 BRA B
GREEN JAMES A 26 MOU W
GREEN JAMES A 28 14T W
GREEN JAMES A 28 9TH B
GREEN JAMES A 39 FRE B
GREEN JAMES A 44 BRA B
GREEN JAMES M A 26 MOU W
GREEN JAMES N A 39 FRA W
GREEN JEREMIAH A 30 ROA B
* YOU WILL RECOLLECT THAT
GREEN WAS TRIED AT LAST
SUP. CT. REGISTRARS
GREEN JERRY A 26 BUR B
GREEN JESSE A A 46 MON W
GREEN JNO JR A 38 FRE W
GREEN JNO S A 44 OXF W
GREEN JOHN A 26 MOU W
GREEN JOHN A 28 04A B
GREEN JOHN A 28 05A B
GREEN JOHN A 28 05A B
GREEN JOHN A 28 6TH B
GREEN JOHN A 32 POS W
GREEN JOHN A 35 ISL B
GREEN JOHN A 44 BRA B
GREEN JOHN A 44 DUT B
GREEN JOHN H A 28 03A B
GREEN JOHN JR A 26 MOO W
GREEN JOHN SR A 26 MOO W
GREEN JOHN SR A 39 FRE W
GREEN JOSEPH A 28 04A B
CERTIFICATE GRANTED
JONES CO
GREEN JOSEPH A 32 POS W
GREEN JOSEPH A 32 POS W
GREEN JOSEPH JR A 32 POS W
GREEN JOSIAH A 39 DAV W
GREEN KILLIS A 28 05A B
GREEN L A 32 DAV W
GREEN LEWIS A 28 04B B
GREEN LEWIS A 39 FRA B
GREEN LEWIS A 39 LOU B
GREEN LOGAN A 44 DUT B
GREEN MAJOR A 32 YAD B
GREEN MARTIN A 32 TYR B
GREEN MARTIN A 26 MOO W
GREEN MC A 38 FRE B
GREEN MICHL A 28 03A B
GREEN MILES A 39 PUG B
GREEN MINUS A 44 FOR B
GREEN MOSES A 28 04A B
GREEN N T A 44 LED W
GREEN NELSON A 53 SWA B
GREEN OSBERN A 44 DUT B
GREEN PEYTON A 39 HAR B
GREEN PHINNEY A 99 BUS W
GREEN POMPEY A 44 FOR B
GREEN PRIESTLEY A 44 DUT B
GREEN R F A 39 FRE W
GREEN R H A 26 MOO W
MILITIA OFFICER &
ENGAGED IN REBELLION
GREEN RANSOM A 39 FRA B
GREEN REUBEN A 28 8TH B
CERTIF GIVEN NOW
LIVES AT JAMES CITY
GREEN RICHARD A 28 01A B
GREEN RICHD A 28 6TH B
GREEN ROBBIN A 39 SPE B
GREEN ROBERT A 39 FRE W
GREEN ROBERT A 44 HEN B
GREEN ROBERT L A 32 POS W
GREEN ROBERT S A 32 DAV W
GREEN ROBT T A 44 YXS W
GREEN ROGERS A 44 KNA B
GREEN ROWTON A 44 FOR B
GREEN RUFFIN A 39 FRA B
GREEN RUFFIN A 39 HAR B
GREEN S A A 44 LED W
GREEN SAM A 39 PUG B
GREEN SAML A 28 03A B
GREEN SAML J A 26 BLA W
GREEN SAMUEL A 39 FRA B
GREEN SAMUEL A 44 YXS B
GREEN SIDNEY A 39 LOU B
TRNS TO GRANVILLE CO
APRIL 15TH 1868
GREEN SIDNEY P A 39 PUG W
GREEN SIMON A 28 04A B
GREEN SIMON A 44 LED B
GREEN SIMPSON R A 46 COB W
GREEN SOLOMON A 32 POS W
GREEN SOLOMON A 44 FOR B
GREEN SOLOMON A 44 LED B
GREEN SPENCER A 44 DUT B
GREEN THOMAS A 26 MOU W
GREEN THOMAS A 28 11T B
GREEN THOS A 28 04A B
GREEN THOS A 39 FRA B
GREEN THOS A 44 FOR B
GREEN THOS A 44 LED W
GREEN THOS A A 28 01A W
GREEN THOS F A 26 SHE W
GREEN THOS P A 29 FA1 B
GREEN TONY A 39 FRA B
GREEN VIRGIL A 39 FRA B
GREEN VIRGIN A 44 FOR B
GREEN W D A 39 FRA W
GREEN W D A 39 LOU W
GREEN W H A 44 ISL W
GREEN W W A 39 LOU W
GREEN WALTER A 46 GRE W
GREEN WASHINGTON A 39 LOU B
GREEN WILLIAM A 28 6TH W
GREEN WILLIAM A 28 9TH B
GREEN WILLIAM A 37 ROC B
GREEN WILLIAM A 39 LOU B
GREEN WILLIAM A 44 HEN B
GREEN WILLIAM E A 37 HIG W

GREEN WILLIAM H A 53 SWA B
GREEN WILLIAM M A 26 MOO W
GREEN WILLIS A 26 BUR W
GREEN WILLIS A 44 SAS B
GREEN WM A A 44 OXF W
GREEN WM H A 26 MOO W
MILITIA OFFICER &
ENGAGED IN REBELLION
GREEN WM R A 32 POS W
GREEN WM R A 38 FRE W
GREEN WM R A 46 COB W
GREEN WRIGHT A 28 03A B
GREENFIELD ADAM A 28 10T B
GREENFIELD COUNCIL A 28 10T B
GREENWOOD BENJ A 38 FRE W
GREENWOOD W B A 44 TAR W
GREENWOOD W H A A 25 HAY W
GREER G W A 32 DAV W
GREER JAMES A 37 EDW B
GREER JOHN A 32 LOF W
GREESON DAVID R 46 COB W
WAS CONSTABLE BEFORE THE
WARE AND HAD A CONF
GOVERNMENT CONTRACT
FOR COOPERING TO HAVE
HIS SONS AND HIS
NEIGHBOURS DETALED TO
KEEPE THEM OUT OF ARMY
GREESON DAVID L A 46 MCL W
GREESON ELI A 46 COB W
GREESON GEORGE C A 46 GIB W
GREESON GEORGE W A 46 COB W
GREESON HENRY A 46 COB W
GREESON J ELI A 46 COB B
GREESON JOHN P A 46 GIB W
GREESON JOHNATHAN C A 46 COB W
GREESON L H A 46 COB W
GREESON THOMAS R A 46 RAG W
GREESY W F A 24 EDE W
GREFFIN ELISHA A 30 ROA W
GREGG GEORGE W A 46 COB W
GREGGORY J H K A 29 LOC W
GREGORY A H A 44 ISL W
GREGORY A J A 19 STR W
GREGORY ABRAHAM A 44 YXS B
GREGORY ALFRED A 24 EDE B
CHAL BY J R B HATHAWAY
REASON TOO YOUNG NO EVI
DENCE AGAINST HIM
GREGORY ALFRED A 44 SAS B
GREGORY ARTHUR A 44 YXS B
GREGORY BALAAM A 35 KEN B
GREGORY CALEB E A 30 IND W
GREGORY CEVIN A 44 SAS B
GREGORY CHARLES A 24 EDE B
GREGORY CHARLES A 44 SAS B
GREGORY CHLS A A 44 SAS W
GREGORY DAVID A 44 SAS B
GREGORY ESQUIORE A 44 RAG B
GREGORY F R A 44 SAS W
GREGORY FRED A 44 OXF B
GREGORY GRANDERSON A 44 SAS B
GREGORY HARRY A 24 EDE B
GREGORY HARRY J A 24 EDE B
GREGORY HENRY A 24 EDE W
GREGORY HERBERT A 44 SAS W
GREGORY HIRAM CHAL A 30 POP W
FOR BEING A CONSTABLE
PRIOR TO THE WAR
GREGORY ISAAC A 28 05A B
GREGORY JAMES A 24 EDE B
GREGORY JAMES G A 30 IND W
GREGORY JAS A 44 HEN B
GREGORY JEHU A 28 16T W
GREGORY JERRY A 24 EDE B
GREGORY JOHN JR A 30 TUL W
GREGORY JOHN SR A 30 TUL W
GREGORY JOHNSON A 44 YXR B
GREGORY KENNER A 44 ISL B
GREGORY LEWIS A 44 SAS B
GREGORY M A A 44 SAS W
GREGORY MARJOR A 53 LA2 W
GREGORY MICHAEL A 35 KEN B
GREGORY MOMFORD A 44 SAS B
GREGORY MOSES A 44 HEN B
GREGORY MOSES A 44 SAS B
GREGORY N A A 44 OXF W
GREGORY NED A 44 OXF B
GREGORY NOAH A 44 OXF B
GREGORY PETER A 44 ISL B
GREGORY R A A 44 SAS W
GREGORY RANSOM A 24 EDE B
GREGORY RIAS A 24 EDE B
GREGORY RUBEN A 44 OXF B
GREGORY SANFORD A 19 NEW W
GREGORY SIMON A 28 01B B
GREGORY SOLOMON A 24 EDE B
CHAL BY J R B HATHAWAY
REASON TOO YOUNG NO EVI
DENCE AGAINST HIM
GREGORY SPENCER A 30 IND W
GREGORY STEPHAN A 44 HEN B
GREGORY THOMAS A 24 EDE W
GREGORY THOMAS A 44 OXF B
GREGORY THOS A 30 IND W
GREGORY THOS A 44 OXF B
GREGORY WILEY A 30 CUR W
GREGORY WILLIAM A 44 OXF B
GREGORY WILSON A 24 EDE B
GREGORY WM --- A 44 HEN B
GREGORY WM H A 44 SAS W
GREGSON BURGESS A 46 JAM W
GRESHAM ARCHABAL A A 44 SAS W
GRESHAM G W A 44 SAS W
GRESHAM JAS A 44 ISL W
GRETTER JAMES A 46 GRE B
GRETTER JOHN B A 46 GRE W
GRETTER MICHAEL A 46 GRE W
GRETTER ROBT M A 46 GRE W
GREY CALEB B A 28 16T W
GREY THOMAS A 28 16T W
GRIBBLE JOHN D A 46 JAM W
GRICE AARON A 28 05A B
GRICE ABRAHAM A 28 05A B
GRICE J L A 40 RHY W
GRICE J M A 40 CAN W
GRICE JOHN A 28 7TH B
GRICE LEWIS A 28 7TH B
GRICE NATHAN A 28 03A B
GRICE WILLIAM A 46 SUM B
GRICE WILLIAM HENRY A 39 HAY B
REGSD AT CLINTON
SAMPSON CO
GRICE WILLIS A 28 03A B
GRIER BENJAMIN A 40 DA1 B
GRIER HENRY A 40 DEC B
GRIER J H A 32 LOF W
GRIFFEN --- A 37 WHI B
GRIFFIN ABIAN A 37 HIG B
GRIFFIN ALEXANDER A 24 MID W
GRIFFIN ALEXR A 28 05A B
GRIFFIN ALLEN A 38 FRE B
GRIFFIN B F A 28 03B W
GRIFFIN B F A 39 JOR W
GRIFFIN B J A 39 JOR W
GRIFFIN DENNY A 46 GRE W
GRIFFIN EXUM A 24 MID W
GRIFFIN GEO C A 24 UPP W
GRIFFIN HARDY A 28 11T W
GRIFFIN HENRY H A 37 ROC W
GRIFFIN J D A 39 JOR W
GRIFFIN J R A 39 JOR W
GRIFFIN J R F A 24 UPP W
GRIFFIN J T A 39 FRA W
GRIFFIN JACOB A 28 05A B
GRIFFIN JAMES H A 37 PEN W
GRIFFIN JNO A 39 FRE B
GRIFFIN JNO H A 39 JOR W
GRIFFIN JNO JR A 39 GRI W
GRIFFIN JNO SR A 39 GRI W
GRIFFIN JOACHIM A 28 11T W
GRIFFIN JOSEPH A 53 BUR B
GRIFFIN JOSEPH B A 37 PEN W
GRIFFIN JOSEPH J A 28 16T W
GRIFFIN LEWIS A 44 HEN W
GRIFFIN LUCKY M A 37 HIG W
GRIFFIN MINGO A 37 TA1 B
GRIFFIN NELSON A 53 GER B
GRIFFIN ROBT A 39 GRI W
GRIFFIN RUFFIN A 39 JOR W
GRIFFIN SIMEON A 24 MID W
GRIFFIN SIMEON H A 37 ROC W
GRIFFIN T H A 39 FRA W
GRIFFIN THOMAS H A 37 ROC W
GRIFFIN WM B A 28 8TH W
GRIFFIN ZECHARIAH A 44 HEN W
GRIFFIS JAMES A 28 13T B
GRIFFIS JOHN A 46 GRE B
GRIFFIS NAT A 99 BUS B
GRIFFIS YANCEY A 99 BUS B
GRIFFITH J E A 46 JAM W
GRIFFITH JAMES A 46 JAM W
GRIFFITH WILLIAM M A 35 MAG W
GRIFFITHS BALAAM A 28 04A B
GRIFFITHS J S A 29 FA1 W
GRIGG A R A 26 GRI W
GRIGG ADAM A 26 GRI B
GRIGG B T A 26 GRI W
GRIGG B W A 26 GRI W
GRIGG BANISTER A 26 CAR W
GRIGG BUNELL A 26 GRI W
GRIGG EDWARD A 26 GRI W
GRIGG GEORGE A 26 GRI B
GRIGG J W A 26 GRI W
GRIGG JAMES Y A 26 GRI W
GRIGG P D A 26 GRI W
GRIGG P H A 26 BLA W
GRIGG R A 26 CAR W
GRIGG S M A 26 GRI W
GRIGG T G A 26 BLA W
GRIGG W J A 26 BLA W
GRIGGS DANIEL L A 30 POW W
GRIGGS DUPLIN A 28 17T W
GRIGGS GEORGE A 28 05A B
GRIGGS LAMUL D A 30 POP W
GRIGGS LEMUEL A 30 POP W
GRIMES A A A 32 DAV W
GRIMES A L A 32 THO W
GRIMES AARON A 28 05A B
GRIMES ABNER A 28 02N B
GRIMES ABNER A 28 04A B
GRIMES ABSOLEM A 32 THO W
GRIMES ALEXANDER A 35 WOL B
GRIMES ALEXR A 28 05A B
GRIMES AMOS A 37 HIC B
GRIMES ANTHONY A 39 HAY B
GRIMES AUSTIN A 28 05A B
GRIMES BAKER A 37 HIC B
GRIMES BLOUNT A 37 HIC B

GRIMES C M A 32 SHE W
GRIMES DANL L A 29 ROC W
MILLITIA OFFICER AFTER
ENGAGED IN REBELLION
GRIMES EPHM A 28 05A B
GRIMES FRANK A 37 HIC B
GRIMES GEORGE A 32 POS B
GRIMES H J A 32 DAV W
GRIMES H L A 32 DAV W
GRIMES HENRY A 35 KEN W
GRIMES HENRY A 37 PIN B
GRIMES HULL A 28 05A B
GRIMES J T A 32 THO W
GRIMES JACOB A 28 05B B
GRIMES JACOB A 32 DAV W
GRIMES JAMES A 37 PIN B
GRIMES JERRY A 32 YAD B
GRIMES JOHN A 37 HIC B
GRIMES LEWIS A 28 05A B
GRIMES LYNDSAY A 32 DAV W
GRIMES MOSES A 28 05A B
GRIMES NATHAN M A 37 HIC A
GRIMES PETER A 32 DAV W
GRIMES RUBEN A 32 DAV W
GRIMES SAML A 28 05A B
GRIMES SOUTHEY A 28 03A B
GRIMES THOMAS A 37 HIC A
GRIMES THOMAS F A 32 SHE W
GRIMES WILLIAM A 32 POS W
GRIMES WM W A 29 ROC W
GRIMWAY W H A 44 SAS W
GRINWAY J E A 44 SAS W
GRISE WILLIS A 53 SWA B
GRISHAM ELVIS A 44 KIT W
GRISHAM J W A 44 KIT W
GRISSAM NEWELL S A 44 HEN W
GRISSHAM STEPHEN A 44 RAG W
GRISSOM A B A 44 FOR W
GRISSOM A T A 44 FOR W
GRISSOM BADGER A 44 FOR B
GRISSOM C H A 44 BEA W
GRISSOM C W A 44 FIS W
GRISSOM E A 44 FIS W
GRISSOM E T A 44 FOR W
GRISSOM FRANKLIN J A 40 DA1 W
GRISSOM G A 44 RAG W
GRISSOM HENDER'N A 44 FOR B
GRISSOM ISAAC D A 46 MCL W
GRISSOM J B A 44 FOR W
GRISSOM J D A 44 FOR W
GRISSOM J H A 44 FIS W
GRISSOM J H A 44 HEN W
GRISSOM JAMES HENRY A 44 HEN W
GRISSOM JOHN W A 35 LIM W
GRISSOM LOUIS R A 35 LIM W
GRISSOM R A A 44 BEA W
GRISSOM R D A 44 FIS W
GRISSOM RUFUS A 44 FIS W
GRISSOM SQUIRE A 44 FOR B
GRISSOM THOMAS A 35 LIM W
GRISSOM THOMAS A 44 FIS W
GRISSOM W T A 35 LIM W
GRISSOM WESLEY A 44 HEN W
GRISSOM WILLIS A 44 BRA B
GRISSOM WM M A 46 MCL W
GRISSUM WM A 24 EDE B
GRIST HENRY A 29 FA2 B
GROOM JOSEPH S A 35 MAG W
GROVER AUSTIN A 40 DA1 W
GROVER GEORGE H A 28 10T W
GROVER THOMAS H A 28 10T W
GROVES ANDREW A 25 HAY W
GROVES BONEY W A 35 MAG W
GROVES JAMES L A 40 DA1 W
GROVES JOHN A 40 FER W
GROVES JOHN K A 35 MAG W
GROVES ROBERT A 40 DA1 W
GROVES THOMAS A 26 WAR W
GROVES W B A 29 FA1 B
GROVES W C A 25 HAY W
GROVES WILLIAM E A 35 ISL W
GRUB ADISON A 32 DAV W
GRUB ALEXANDER A 32 DAV W
GRUB ALEXANDER A 32 TYR W
GRUB AMBROS A 32 LOF W
GRUB ANDREW A 32 TYR W
GRUB HENRY A 32 TYR W
GRUB JOHN A 32 LEE W
GRUB JOHN A 32 TYR W
GRUB JOHN A 32 TYR W
GRUB MICHAEL A 32 DAV W
GRUB PETER A 32 DAV W
GRUB RANSOM A 32 DAV W
GRUB WILLIAM A 32 DAV W
GRUBB DAVID A 32 THO W
GRUBBS A A 44 OXF W
GRUBBS W T A 44 OXF W
GRUITT JAS C A 44 HEN W
GRUMELL ELIAS A 37 PEN W
GRUNSTEAD GIDEON A 30 KNO W
GUARD BANISTER J A 30 POW W
GUARD JOHN E A 30 NOR W
GUARD JOSHUA A 30 NOR W
GUESS LUKE A 37 PIN B
GUESS MATHEW A 37 PIN B
GUIE HENRY A 46 FRI B
GUILCHRIEST LEWIS A 46 GRE B
GUILFORD AMOS A 28 9TH B
GUILFORD HENRY A 28 12T B
GUILFORD RICHARD A 37 TA2 B
GUIN A D C A 32 THO W
GUIN ASA A 29 ROC W
GUINS ARTHUR A 29 QUW W
GUINS ARTHUR JR A 29 QUW W
GUION JOHN A 28 02N W
GUION NED A 28 03A B
GUION NED A 28 03A B
GUIRE JOSEPH A 32 POS W
GUIRES BURWELL B A 37 HOL W
GUITON MARTIN A 26 GOF B
GUITON THOMAS W A 29 QUW W
GULLECK J G A 40 STO W
GULLETT EMSLEY A 46 GRE W
GULLETT ROBERT A 46 MCL W
GULLEY LUCIUS J A 99 BUS W
GULLEY NICK A 37 ROB B
GULLIE ANDREW B A 40 SAN B
GULLIE THOMAS A 40 STO B
GUN ANDREW A 37 ROB B
GUNN FREDK A 28 04A B
GUNN J H A 44 ISL W
GUNN WM G A 44 SAS W
GUNTER ISAAC A 29 LOC B
GUNTER NATHAN G A 99 BUS W
GUNTER ROBERT A 37 TA2 B
GUNTER SAML A 29 FA1 B
GUNTHER MURRELL ? A 37 WHI W
GUPTON BENJAMIN A 39 SPE B
GUPTON C A A 39 LOU W
GUPTON COOPER A 39 SPE W
GUPTON EATON A 39 JOR W
GUPTON G W A 39 SPE W
GUPTON GEORGE A 39 JOR W
GUPTON H G A 39 SPE W
GUPTON H S A 39 JOR W
GUPTON HARDY A 39 JOR W
GUPTON ISHAM A 39 JOR B
GUPTON J A A 39 JOR W
GUPTON JACOB A 39 JOR B
GUPTON JAMES P A 39 JOR W
GUPTON JOHN B A 39 JOR W
GUPTON JOHN E A 39 JOR W
GUPTON JOHN H A 39 SPE W
GUPTON JOSEPH P A 39 JOR W
GUPTON JOSHUA R A 39 JOR W
GUPTON JOSIAH A 39 JOR W
GUPTON KINCHIN A 39 FRA B
GUPTON KINDRED A 39 SPE W
GUPTON OMEGA C A 39 SPE W
GUPTON P W A 39 SPE W
GUPTON REDICK A 39 JOR B
GUPTON ROBBERT A 39 SPE W
GUPTON ROBT A 39 JOR B
GUPTON SAM A 39 JOR B
GUPTON SIMON A 39 JOR B
GUPTON STEAVEN A 39 JOR B
GUPTON THOMAS B A 39 JOR W
GUPTON THOMAS J A 39 SPE W
GUPTON THOMAS SR A 39 JOR W
GUPTON W B A 39 JOR W
GUPTON W C C A 39 JOR W
GUPTON W H A 39 SPE W
GUPTON WILLIAM A 39 JOR B
GUPTON WILLIE A 39 JOR W
GURGESS WILLIAM A 25 HAY W
GURLEY JOHN L A 46 HIG W
GURLEY ROBT A 46 HIG W
GURLY DANIEL A 29 ROC W
GURNEY THOMAS A 24 EDE W
GUST WM T A 32 JAC W
GUSTAVUS WILLIAM A 35 WAR B
GUSTIS HENRY A 28 05A B
GUSTIS JONES A 32 DAV B
GUTHERI ELIJAH D A 19 BE1 W
GUTHERIE EDWARD J A 28 01A W
GUTHRIE ABNER P A 19 SHA W
GUTHRIE ABSALOM F A 19 SHA W
GUTHRIE BANISTER A 19 SMY W
GUTHRIE BENJ F A 19 BE1 W
GUTHRIE BENJ F A 19 SHA W
GUTHRIE C H A 19 BE1 W
GUTHRIE
CHRISTOPHER F A 19 BE2 W
GUTHRIE CICERO A 19 SHA W
GUTHRIE DANIEL S A 19 SHA W
GUTHRIE EDMOND C A 28 01B W
GUTHRIE ELSY F A 19 SHA W
GUTHRIE ELZA A 19 SHA W
GUTHRIE GEO W A 19 BE1 W
GUTHRIE GEORGE A 19 BE2 W
GUTHRIE JAMES A 19 SHA W
GUTHRIE JAMES R A 19 SHA W
GUTHRIE JOHN F A 28 01A W
GUTHRIE JOHN W A 19 HAD W
GUTHRIE JOSEPH R A 19 SHA W
GUTHRIE MADISON A 19 SHA W
GUTHRIE MARTIN A A 19 SHA W
GUTHRIE SALMON M A 19 SHA W
GUTHRIE STEPHEN A 19 SHA W
GUTHRIE STEPHEN C A 19 SHA W
GUTHRIE T W A 29 FA2 W
GUTHRIE W O A 19 SHA W
GUTHRIE WALACE A 19 SHA W
GUTHRIE WALAID A 19 SHA W
GUTHRIE WM A A 29 FA1 W
GUTHRIE WM G A 19 BE1 W
GUTHRIE WM H A 19 SHA W
GUY ALEXANDER A 35 FAI W
GUY C T A 29 FLE W

GUY J J A 35 ALB W
GUY JAMES A 29 FLE W
GUY JAMES A 46 GRE B
GUY JOHN A 35 MAG W
GUY JOHN A A 35 WAR W
GUY JOHN H A 35 WAR W
GUY MILES A 44 FIS B
GUY MORRIS A 35 WAR W
GUY OWEN A 35 WAR W
GUY S J A 29 FLE W
GUY THOMAS J A 35 WAR W
GUY W A A 29 FLE W
GUYAN ABRAHAM A 29 ROC W
GUYAN JOSEPH A 29 GRA B
GUYER J M A 46 HIG W
GUYER J W A 46 HIG W
GUYER JACOB A 46 HIG W
GUYER JOSEPH A 46 JAM W
GUYER NATHAN W A 46 JAM W
GUYTON JAS M A 29 ROC W
GWALTNEY JOSEPH F B A 28 11T W
GWALTNEY LAFAYETTE A 28 11T W
GWATNEY WM D A 28 11T W
GYER L V A 46 HIG W

- H -

H--IE GEORGE A 32 BRO B
HACHETT CRISTOPHER A 46 RAG W
HACHETT JAMES J A 46 MCL W
HACHETT JOHN C A 46 RAG W
HACHETT LEVIN A 46 RAG W
HACHETT LEVIN M A 46 RAG W
HACKETT ROBERT C A 46 RAG W
HACKETT S HOLLAND A 24 EDE W
BY J Z PRATT CAUSE WAS
AN OFFICER IN THE FEDERALE
NAVY AND DISMISSED THE
SERVICE DID NOT ENGAGE
IN THE REBELLION
HACKNEY ALFRED A 29 FA1 B
HACKNEY THOMAS A 37 MAN W
HACKNEY WILLIAM H A 37 EDW W
HADDICK TONY A 28 9TH B
HADDICK WILLIS A 28 9TH B
HADDOCK J M A 32 LOF W
HADDUCK BLUNT A 28 05A B
HADEN ABRIHAM A 32 TYR B
HADEN BENJAMIN 32 DAV W
NAME LINED THROUGH
HADEN BENJAMIN A 32 DAV B
HADEN C A A 32 TYR W
HADEN J H A 32 TYR W
HADERS B F A 32 TYR W
HADLEY CHAS A 29 FA2 B
HADLEY LEWIS A 29 FA1 B
HADLEY SAML A 29 FA1 B
HADLY CHAS A 29 FA1 W
HADLY DAVID A 29 FA1 B
HADLY JOSHUA A 29 FA1 B
HADLY THOMAS A 29 FA1 B
HADSON THOMAS A 53 LA2 B
HAGAN BENNETT A 37 WEB W
HAGAN GEORGE A 40 DEC W
HAGAN JESSE K A 37 HIG W
HAGAN SIMEON A 37 HIG W
HAGAN WATSON A 37 TA1 B
HAGAN WILLIE A 37 WHI W
HAGAR JOHN T A 40 MAU W
HAGAR WILLIAM E A 40 DEC W
HAGE JOHN A 32 DAV W
HAGEE CHRISTIAN A 32 SHE W
HAGEE D F A 32 SHE W
HAGEE HENRY A 32 YAD W
HAGEE JACOB A 32 SHE W
HAGEE MATHIAS A 32 YAD W
HAGEE P A A 32 SHE W
HAGEE ROME A 32 YAD B
HAGEE SAMUEL A 32 POS B
HAGEE SOLOMAN A 32 SHE W
HAGEE VOLENTINE A 32 SHE W
HAGEN ANDREW A 29 FA1 B
HAGEN JAS A 29 FA1 B
HAGEN JILES A 40 STO B
HAGENS WILEY A 29 FA1 B
HAGER M S P A 40 CAN W
HAGER WILLIAM A 26 BUR B
HAGEWOOD J S A 46 GRE W
HAGGARD WILLIAM A 24 EDE B
HAGGATY THOMAS A 24 MID W
HAGGINS AMAS A 37 PEN W
HAGGINS BIAS A 37 PEN B
HAGGINS CEASER A 37 EDW B
HAGGINS DANIEL A 37 PEN B
HAGGINS DANIEL A 37 PEN B
HAGGINS RICHARD A 37 EDW B
HAGIN NEVISON A 44 RAG B
HAGOOD W R A 44 TOW W
HAGWOOD ISHAM H A 39 GRI W
HAIGH CHAS A 29 FA1 W
HAIGH CHAS T R 29 FA1 W
NATURALIZED CITIZEN
PURCHASED CONFED BONDS
HAIGH GEO H A 29 FA1 W
NAME LINED OUT
HAIGH GEO P A 29 FA2 W
HAIGH JNO C A 29 FA1 W
HAIGH THOS D A 29 FA1 W
SURGEON IN MILLITIA
AFTERWARDS ENG IN
REBELLION
HAIGH WM H A 29 FA1 W
HAILEY HARMOND A 32 THO W
CERTIF
HAILEY HENRY A 44 BEA W
HAILS J W A 29 CED W
HAINES AMOS A 46 HIG B
HAINES ARCHEY A 29 FA1 B
HAINES BURRELL A 32 POS W
HAINES ELY A 37 MAN B
HAINES HENRY A 37 HIG B
HAINES JACOB A 26 BLA W
HAINES JAMES HENRY A 37 HIC A
HAINES JESSE A 37 HIG W
HAINES JOHN A 37 HIG B
HAINES JOHN O A 26 BLA W
HAINES MINGO A 37 HIG B
HAINES SIMON A 37 MAN B
HAINES STUART A 37 ROC B
HAINES WESLEY A 37 HIG B
HAINES WILLIAM A 26 BLA W
HAINES WILLIAM A 26 MOU W
HAIR DUNCAN A 29 CED W
HAIR J J A 29 BLA W
HAIR JNO B A 29 GRA W
HAIR JOHN A 29 CED W
HAIR MAJOR A 37 SHA B
HAIR S W A 29 CED W
HAIR V B A 29 GRA W
HAIR W C A 29 CED W
HAIR W S A 29 CED W
HAIR WILLIAM A 29 CED W
HAIRGROWS HENRY A 28 16T B
HAIRGROWS JOSEPH A 28 16T B
HAIRSTON JOE A 32 DAV B
HAIRSTON PACK A 32 TYR B
HAIRSTON S A 32 TYR B
HAIRSTON WASH A 32 DAV B
HAISE YORK A 53 GER B
HAIST ABNER A 24 MID W
HAIST ANDREW J A 24 MID W
HAIST MILES D A 24 MID W
HAIST WILLY A 24 MID W
HAITH CESER A L A 39 LOU W
HAITH ROBT F A 46 GRE W
HAITH WALTER F A 46 MCL W
HAITHCOCK E A 44 ISL W
HAITHCOCK N W A 29 FA1 W
HAITHCOCK WILLIAM A 39 HAY B
HAITHCOCK WM H A 29 FA1 B
HAKENS DAVID T A 37 MAN W
HALBERSON JOHN A 19 CED W
HALE HAYS A 29 LOC W
HALE HENDERSON A 39 SPE W
HALE J H A 39 SPE W
HALE J J A 29 ROC W
HALE SCIPIO A 28 9TH B
HALEBROOK HENLY A 46 KIN W
HALEN MYER A 28 01A W
HALES ALONZO A 19 BE1 B
HALES CURTIS A 19 BE1 B
HALES HENRY A 37 HOL W
HALES JOSEPH J A 37 TA1 W
HALES WILLIAM A 37 PEN B
HALEY BEDFORD A 28 02N B
HALEY CHARLES A 32 CLE W
HALEY CORNELEUS A 29 FA2 W
HALEY JOHN A 44 DUT W
HALIDIA THOS F A 19 BE1 W
HALL A F A 29 FLE W
HALL A J A 25 PIN W
HALL A J A 29 CED W
HALL AARON A 30 IND B
HALL ABNER A 30 POW B
APRIL 9, 1868
HALL ALEXANDER A 40 STO B
HALL ALFRED A 35 ROC W
HALL ALX A 29 LOC W
HALL AMERICA A 30 IND B
CHAL MINOR
HALL AUSTIN A 32 CLE B
HALL B F A 35 LIM W
CERTIF GIVEN REMOVED
TO NEW HANOVER CO
HALL BENJAMIN A 53 LA1 W
HALL BENJAMIN B A 53 FAI W
HALL BRIER W A 72 SWA W
HALL CALVIN A 35 ROC B
HALL D K A 29 CED W
HALL DANIEL A 28 04A B
HALL DANIEL A 29 LOC W
HALL DANIEL A 32 JAC W
HALL DAVID A 19 NEW W
HALL DAVID S A 46 ROS W
HALL DENNIS A 35 MAG B
HALL DERRY A 28 10T B
HALL E H A 29 GRA W
HALL EDMUND A 35 CYP B
HALL EDWARD A 35 LIM B
HALL EDWARD A 72 SWA B
HALL EDWARD NO 2 A 35 LIM B
HALL EUGENE A 28 04A B
HALL F X A 28 01A W
HALL FRANCIS X A 53 OCR W
HALL G B A 44 DUT W
HALL G W A 32 JAC W
HALL GEORGE A 28 04B B
HALL GEORGE A 37 ROC B
HALL GEORGE M A 35 LIM W
HALL GRANDISON A 44 OXF B
HALL H L A 29 BLA W

HALL HENRY S A 28 02N W
HALL HENRY W A 30 MOY W
HALL HERRING A 35 MAG W
HALL HOWARD A 35 LIM B
HALL ISAIAH A 35 MAG B
HALL J A A 29 LOC W
HALL J D A 40 STO W
HALL J L A 44 DUT W
HALL J M A 32 DAV W
HALL J T A 28 01A W
HALL JAMES A 19 BE1 B
HALL JAMES A 28 8TH B
HALL JAMES A 29 LOC W
HALL JAMES A 30 IND W
HALL JAMES A 35 LIM B
HALL JAMES A 35 LIM W
HALL JAMES A 35 MAG B
HALL JAMES A 35 ROC B
HALL JAMES K A 46 FRI W
HALL JAS A 29 FA1 B
HALL JERRY A 35 LIM B
HALL JESSE A 28 14T W
HALL JNO H A 29 FA1 W
COUNTY COMM AFTERWARD
ENGAGED IN REBELLION
HALL JOHN A 28 14T W
HALL JOHN A 35 LIM W
HALL JOHN A 35 MAG B
HALL JOHN A 46 FRI B
HALL JOHN A 46 ROS W
HALL JOHN R 24 EDE W
REJECTED BY THE BOARD
WAS MAGISTRATE OF THE
TOWN BEFORE THE WAR &
ENGAGED IN OVERSEER IN
THE REBELLION
HALL JOHN A A 32 LEE W
HALL JOHN G A 29 SEV W
HALL JOHN G A 44 YXR W
HALL JOHN L A 32 LOF W
HALL JOHN Q A A 29 CED W
HALL JOSEPH A 35 ROC B
HALL JOSEPH A 53 LA2 B
HALL JOSHUA A 44 OXF B
HALL L R A 29 GRA W
HALL LEWIS A 29 CED W
HALL MACK A 35 LIM B
HALL MANUEL A 28 04A B
HALL MILLS A 28 04A B
HALL MUMFORD A 32 DAV W
HALL NATHAN JR A 29 ROC W
HALL NATHAN SR A 29 ROC W
HALL NATHANIEL A 29 FA1 B
HALL NELSON A 35 ROC B
HALL NICHOLAS A 35 MAG B
HALL NORRIS A 35 LIM B
HALL OLLIVER A 29 FLE W
REMOVED TO GRAYS CREEK
HALL PETER A 35 LIM B
HALL PETER A 37 TA1 B
HALL PLATO A 35 ISL B
HALL POMPEY A 30 CUR B
HALL RAFORD A 29 ROC W
HALL RALPH A 29 FA1 B
HALL REGAN A 28 05A B
HALL RICHARD S A 19 BE2 W
HALL ROBT A 29 FA1 B
HALL RUBEN A 37 MAN B
HALL RUBIN A 35 LIM B
HALL S A 29 LOC W
HALL S A 29 LOC W
HALL S T A 39 FRE W
HALL SAML L A 29 FA2 W

HALL SAMUEL A 40 RHY B
HALL SAMUEL A 46 GRE B
HALL SAMUEL J A 32 THO W
HALL SHADRICK A 35 ROC B
HALL SMART A 40 RHY B
HALL SOLOMON A 35 LIM W
HALL STEWART A 37 HOL B
HALL T L A 19 MOR W
HALL THOMAS A 28 03A B
HALL THOMAS A 40 RHY B
HALL THOS G A 29 CED W
HALL VIRGIL A 29 FA1 B
HALL W G A 28 01A W
HALL W G A 29 LOC W
HALL W H A 29 LOC W
HALL W J A 29 CED W
HALL WASHINGTON A 29 FA1 B
HALL WASHINGTON A 35 CYP B
HALL WILBER G A 29 FA1 W
HALL WILLIAM A 32 POS W
HALL WILLIAM A 35 KEN B
HALL WILLIAM A 35 LIM W
HALL WILLIAM A 46 FRI W
HALL WILLIAM A 46 ROS W
HALL WILLIAM D A 53 LA2 W
HALL WILLIAM S A 29 SEV W
HALL WILLIAM Y A 53 LA1 W
HALL WM A 28 04A B
HALL WM A 29 LOC W
HALL WM B A 29 FA1 B
HALL WM P A 29 SEV W
HALL WRIGHT A 35 MAG B
HALLMAN AMBROSE A 40 BLA W
HALLMAN ANDREW A 40 BLA W
HALLMAN ANDY A 26 GOF B
HALLMAN D A 26 BOR W
HALLMAN DANIEL A 40 BLA W
HALLMAN JACOB A 26 GOF W
HALLMAN S E A 26 GOF W
HALLMAN W D A 26 SHE W
HALSEY HENRY A 30 CUR B
HALSEY ISAAC A 24 EDE W
HALSEY R S A 24 EDE W
HALSEY WASHINGTON A 24 EDE B
HALSO JAMES G A 35 CYP W
HALSO WILSON W A 35 CYP W
HALSTEAD AFRICA A 30 CUR B
HALSTEAD G N A 30 MOY W
HALSTEAD JAMES R A 30 MOY W
8-MONTH-RESIDENT
HALSTEAD TULLEY A 30 CUR W
HALSY SAMUAL A 24 MID W
HALTOM A C A 32 JAC W
HALTOM E A 32 JAC W
HAM -- A D A 32 THO W
CERTIF
HAM B B A 39 PUG W
HAM BRITTON A 28 04A B
HAM GEORGE A 28 04A B
HAM GILES JR A 29 CAR W
HAM GILES SR A 29 CAR W
HAM ISHAM J A 39 SPE W
HAM J H A 39 SPE W
HAM JAMES A 32 DAV W
HAM JOHN A 26 SHE W
HAM JOHN W A 39 PUG W
HAM L B A 39 JOR W
TRNS TO WARREN CO
APRIL 16 1868
HAM LEWIS A 28 04A B
HAM LORRICK A 28 6TH B
HAM MORTICA A 28 04A B
HAM NATHAN A 28 16T B

HAM ROSS H A 46 GIB B
HAM WM A 28 04A B
HAM WRIGHT A 28 04A B
HAMANS AARON A 28 12T B
HAMBLETON JAMES A 19 BE1 B
HAMBLETON JAS A 44 ISL B
HAMBLETON ROBT A 44 ISL B
HAMBLIN J P A 28 03A W
HAMBRICK JOHN T A 32 THO W
HAMBRIGHT JAMES A 26 GOF W
HAMERICK JACOB E A 40 MAU W
HAMESLEY BENJ A 26 GRI W
HAMILTON ALEX A 44 HEN B
HAMILTON ALLEN A 19 HUN W
HAMILTON BENJAMIN T A 37 MAN W
HAMILTON BOLING A 44 HEN B
HAMILTON CHARLES H A 28 16T W
HAMILTON ELIJAH A A 19 HUN W
HAMILTON FRANKLIN A 19 HUN W
HAMILTON GEORGE A 53 GER W
HAMILTON GILBIRD A 19 HUN W
HAMILTON GORDAN A 53 LA2 W
HAMILTON HENRY A 26 MOO B
HAMILTON HENRY A 53 SWA W
HAMILTON JAMES A 44 HEN B
HAMILTON JAMES A 53 GER W
HAMILTON JAS H A 26 BLA W
HAMILTON JNO D A 29 ROC W
HAMILTON JOHN A 19 HUN W
HAMILTON JOHN A 53 LA1 W
HAMILTON JOHN W A 28 01B W
HAMILTON LOUIS A 28 05A B
HAMILTON MITCHEL A 19 BE1 W
HAMILTON O C A 46 KIN W
HAMILTON SAML A 28 05A B
HAMILTON SAMUEL A 53 LA1 W
HAMILTON SAMUEL C A 32 THO W
HAMILTON SIDNEY A 28 05A B
HAMILTON WALLACE A 19 HUN W
HAMILTON WILLIAM A 19 HUN W
HAMIRCK A W A 26 HOL B
HAMLET W J A 44 DUT W
HAMLETT A N A 39 JOR W
HAMLETT P B A 39 SPE W
HAMLIN CHAS A 44 OXF W
HAMMATT GEO B A 44 HEN W
HAMMELL JOHN A 46 JAM W
HAMMER ISAAC A 32 BRO W
HAMMER ISAAC A 44 FIS B
HAMMIE JNO A A 44 OXF B
HAMMIE JOSEPH A 44 OXF B
HAMMIE NATHAN A 44 HEN B
HAMMIE PHIL A 44 OXF B
HAMMIE R F A 44 OXF W
HAMMIE R H A 44 OXF W
HAMMIE RICHARD A 44 HEN B
HAMMIE SAMUEL A 44 HEN B
HAMMIE WILLIAM A 44 OXF B
HAMMOND ENDERSON A 28 05A B
HAMMOND MAJOR A 28 05A B
HAMMOND ROBERT A 37 ROC B
HAMMOND SAML A 28 03A B
HAMMOND WM A 29 LOC W
HAMMONDS SYLVESTER A 28 9TH B
HAMMONS AARON A 19 BE1 B
HAMNER W B A 32 DAV W
HAMOND WILEY A 37 TA1 B
HAMONS WRIGHT A 28 03A B
HAMPLETON FERNEY A 28 02N B
HAMPTON ANDREW J A 30 NAR W
HAMPTON CHARLES A 53 LA2 B
HAMPTON DAVID A 30 COI W
HAMPTON DAVID A 32 SHE B

HAMPTON GILBERT A 37 EDW B
HAMPTON ISAAC H A 30 NAR W
HAMPTON ISAAC N A 30 NAR W
HAMPTON JOE A 32 CLE B
HAMPTON JOHN A 30 IND W
HAMPTON JOHN A 40 DA1 B
HAMPTON JOHN T A 30 NAR W
HAMPTON NATHANIEL N A 30 NAR W
HAMPTON P E A 44 LED W
HAMPTON ROBERT L A 32 YAD W
HAMPTON S H A 46 FRI W
HAMPTON W B A 30 IND W
HAMPTON W P A 44 LED W
HAMPTON WILLIAM A 30 NAR W
HAMPTON WM S A 46 FRI W
HAMPTON Z H A 44 LED W
HAMRICK A A 26 BUR W
HAMRICK A A 26 CAR W
HAMRICK A H A 26 HOL B
HAMRICK A M A 26 HOL B
HAMRICK A W A 26 SHE W
HAMRICK ABE A 26 SHE B
HAMRICK ABLERT A 26 SHE W
HAMRICK ADAM A 26 HOL B
HAMRICK ARTHUR A 26 BUR B
HAMRICK ASA A 26 HOL B
HAMRICK BERRY A 26 SHE W
HAMRICK C J A 26 HOL B
HAMRICK C S A 26 HOL B
HAMRICK CASWELL A 26 BUR W
HAMRICK CHESLY A 26 MOO W
HAMRICK D A F A 26 MOO W
HAMRICK DAVID A 26 BLA W
HAMRICK DAVID A 26 HOL B
HAMRICK DAVID JR A 26 MOU W
HAMRICK E A 26 CAR W
HAMRICK E O A 26 SHE W
HAMRICK ELIJA A 26 HOL B
HAMRICK G A A 26 HOL B
HAMRICK G R A 26 HOL B
HAMRICK H G A 26 MOU W
HAMRICK HENRY A 26 MOO B
HAMRICK J L A 26 HOL B
HAMRICK J M A 26 MOU W
HAMRICK JABES A 26 HOL B
HAMRICK JAMES A 26 BLA W
HAMRICK JAMES A 26 MOO W
HAMRICK JAMES SR A 26 MOO W
HAMRICK JOHNATHAN A 26 HOL B
HAMRICK L D A 26 BUR W
HAMRICK M N A 26 HOL B
HAMRICK MILES A 26 SHE W
HAMRICK MOSES A 26 HOL B
HAMRICK NATHAN A 26 BUR W
HAMRICK P W A 26 HOL B
HAMRICK PRICE A 26 SHE W
HAMRICK REUBIN A 26 HOL B
HAMRICK SAM A 26 GRI B
HAMRICK T T A 26 SHE W
HAMRICK THOS A 26 BUR W
HAMRICK W A A 26 HOL B
HAMRICK W A A 26 SHE W
HAMRICK W A J A 26 SHE W
HAMRICK W R A 26 SHE W
HAMRICK WILLIAM A 26 GRI B
HAMRICK WILLIAM A 26 HOL B
HAMRICK WILLIAM CHAR 26 BUR W
MILITIA OFFICER &
ENGAGED IN REBELLION
HANA S J A 40 SAN W
HANA W R A 40 SAN W
HANBERRY HENRY A 53 FAI W
HANCE DANIEL A 26 GOF W
HANCE T W A 26 GOF W
HANCE WILLIAM A 26 GOF W
HANCHEY EPHRAM A 35 ISL W
HANCHEY JOHN W A 35 ISL W
HANCHEY OWEN A 35 ISL W
HANCOCK DENARD A 28 01B W
HANCOCK ELIJAH A 19 SHA W
HANCOCK ELIJAH A 19 SMY W
HANCOCK JAMES A 28 04B W
HANCOCK JAMES F A 19 SMY W
HANCOCK JAMES W A 28 01B W
HANCOCK JERREMIAH A 25 HAY W
HANCOCK JOHN W A 19 SMY W
HANCOCK JOHN W A 28 01B W
HANCOCK LENO A 72 SWA B
HANCOCK MICHIAL A 19 SHA W
HANCOCK R D A 28 02N W
HANCOCK RICHARD B A 25 HAY W
HANCOCK ROBT JR A 28 02N W
HANCOCK ROBT SR A 28 02N W
HANCOCK RUMULUS B A 72 SWA W
HANCOCK SAMUEL W A 19 SMY W
HANCOCK THOMAS A 28 04B W
HANCOCK THOS C A 19 SHA W
HANCOCK THOS J A 44 HEN W
HANCOCK WILLIAM A 19 SHA W
HANCOCK WILLIAM A 19 SMY W
HANCOCK WM B A 19 STR W
HAND A J A 40 CAN W
HAND BENJAMIN A 40 STO B
HAND GEORGE A 40 STO B
HAND JESSE A 26 BOR W
HAND JOSEPH A 40 STO B
HAND R H A 40 STO W
HAND THOMAS A 28 16T B
HAND W L A 40 STO W
HANDCOCK HORATIO A 28 03A W
HANDCOCK J A 19 HAD W
HANDEMAN J W A 40 SAN W
HANDEN ISAAC A 29 SEV B
HANDEN PETER A 29 SEV B
HANDING HENRY A 29 FA1 B
HANDING WELCOME A 29 FA2 B
HANDLE CHARLES A 24 EDE B
HANDON JAMES A 29 FA1 B
HANDY (DUMB) A 28 04A B
HANER JACKSON A 32 TYR B
HANES H F A 32 SHE W
HANES JAMES A 32 SHE W
HANES JOHN CHAL FORA 32 DAV W
HOLDING OFFICE OF REGIS-
TER AND DEP CLERK BEFORE
AND DURING THE WAR. RECON
HANES YLEY A 32 TYR B
HANEY SOLOMON A 25 HAY W
HANFF JOHN F A 28 03B W
HANK JOHN A 32 POS W
HANK JOHN SR A 32 POS W
HANK METHIAS A 32 POS W
HANKERSON SANCHO A 35 KEN B
HANKINS JAMES A 39 SPE B
HANKS ALBANY A 40 CAN B
HANKS ELLSWORTH A 28 6TH W
HANKS G W A 40 STO W
HANKS JACOB A 44 TOW B
HANKS JAMES B A 28 03A W
HANKS JAS A 44 TOW B
HANKS LARKIN A 40 STO B
HANNA F S A 40 SAN W
HANNA J M A 40 SAN W
COPIED FROM DUPICATE
HANNA S B A 40 SAN W
HANNA T M A 40 SAN W
HANNA W D A 40 SAN W
HANNAFORD WILLIAM T A 35 MAG W
HANNAH SOLOMON A 46 JAM W
HANNAR MADISON A 46 GRE B
HANNER ALLEN A A 46 GRE W
HANNER AMOS A 46 RAG W
HANNER CHARLES A 46 ROS B
HANNER ERVIN A 46 RAG W
HANNER JAMES A A 46 GRE W
HANNER JEREMIAH A A 46 RAG W
HANNER JOHN R A 46 GRE W
HANNER JOSEPH W A 46 MCL W
HANNER NATHAN A A 46 RAG W
HANNER ORPHEUS S A 46 GRE W
HANNER RANSOM A 46 RAG B
HANNER ROBERT A 46 RAG W
HANNER ROBERT T A 46 ROS W
HANNER RODEY T A 46 GRE W
HANNER RODY A 46 RAG W
HANNER THOMAS V A 46 ROS W
HANNER WM C A 46 GRE W
HANNOR C A 19 NEW W
HANSEL J P A 40 RHY W
HANY T S A 46 HIG W
HARALD FRANK A 37 PIN B
HARALD HANNEN A 37 PIN B
HARALD WILLIS A 37 PIN B
HARD J Y A 26 BOR W
HARD JERRY A 26 GRI B
HARD T J A 26 GRI W
HARDEE ISERAEL A 28 16T B
HARDEN ALFRED A 28 05A B
HARDEN CHARLES H A 46 ROS W
HARDEN GEORGE A 40 RHY B
HARDEN JAS II A 29 FA1 W
HARDEN JESSEE A 44 KIT B
HARDEN JOHN A A 46 RAG W
HARDEN LEWIS A 29 ROC B
HARDEN ZACHERIAH A 46 RAG W
HARDESON JAMES H A 35 SMI W
HARDESON WILLIAM A 35 GLI W
HARDESTON L A 35 GLI W
HARDESTY B M A 19 HAR W
HARDESTY BENJAMIN A 19 HAR W
HARDESTY JOSEPH A 19 HAR W
HARDESTY MICAJAH A 19 NEW W
HARDESTY MICAJAH R 19 NEW W
NAME LINED THROUGH
HARDESTY WASHINGTON A 19 HAR W
HARDESTY WILLIAM A 19 HAR W
HARDIE HENRY A 40 DA1 B
HARDIN A B A 26 SHE W
HARDIN CHARLES A 46 ROS W
HARDIN CHISTOPHER V A 46 RAG W
HARDIN D J A 26 SWA W
HARDIN E A A 26 SHE W
HARDIN E S A 26 MOO W
HARDIN GEORGE A 26 BLA W
HARDIN J H A 26 HOL B
HARDIN JAMES A 26 BUR B
HARDIN JOHN A 46 ROS W
HARDIN JOHN L A 26 GOF W
HARDIN JOSEPH R 26 SHE W
NAME LINED OUT
STRICKEN OUT
APR 9 1868
HARDIN LEVIN R A 46 ROS W
HARDIN PETER F A 46 RAG W
HARDIN ROBERT A 40 FER W
HARDIN W H A 26 SHE W
HARDIN W L A 26 SWA W
HARDIN W R A 26 SHE W
HARDIN WM A 44 KNA B

HARDIN WM D A 46 ROS W
HARDING SOLOMON A 44 KNA B
HARDING W R A 39 LOU W
HARDISDY AARON A 28 9TH B
HARDISDY DANIEL A 28 9TH B
HARDISON ALEXR A 28 6TH W
HARDISON CHARLES W A 28 9TH W
HARDISON FREDRICK A 28 14T W
HARDISON GABRIEL A 28 9TH W
HARDISON GEO W A 28 9TH W
HARDISON ISAM B A 28 6TH W
HARDISON JAMES A 28 14T W
HARDISON JASPER A 28 14T W
HARDISON JOHN A 28 14T W
HARDISON JOSEPH A 28 05A B
HARDISON JOSIAH A 28 14T W
HARDISON LEVEN A 28 14T W
HARDISON LEVI A 28 14T W
HARDISON ROBERT B A 28 14T W
HARDISON RUFUS W A 28 14T W
HARDISON THOMAS A 35 WOL W
HARDMOND ALLEN A 32 SHE B
HARDY ALEXANDRIA A 53 FAI B
HARDY ANDREW J A 35 ALB W
HARDY CHARLES A 53 SWA B
HARDY DAVID A 28 04A B
HARDY EDWARD A 28 03A B
HARDY GEORGE A 37 PEN B
HARDY HENRY AUGUSTUSA 28 10T B
HARDY ISAAC A 28 10T B
HARDY JAMES A 35 ALB W
HARDY JAMES J A 37 PIN W
HARDY JOHN A 28 03A B
HARDY JOHN A 37 PIN W
HARDY JOSEPH A 28 04A B
HARDY LAML A 39 FRA W
HARDY LEWIS A 28 8TH W
HARDY LUNNEN A 28 04A B
HARDY NOAH A 28 6TH W
HARDY REUBEN A 28 10T B
HARDY ROBERT A 53 SWA B
HARDY ROBT W A 29 FA1 W
HARDY SIMON A 53 LA1 B
HARDY W C A 44 ISL W
HARDY W T A 44 ISL W
HARDY WILLIAM A 37 PIN B
HARE BRYANT A 29 CAR W
HARE DUNCAN J A 29 CAR W
HARE HENRY A 29 GRA B
HARE JAMES A 26 MOO B
HARE JAS A 29 CAR W
HARE JNO W A 29 CAR B
HARE JOHN A 29 GRA B
AFFADAVIT TO "HOLLOW"
BLADEN CO
HARE JOSEPH A 29 GRA B
HARE ORAN A 37 WHI B
HARE REUBEN A 29 GRA W
HARE THOS A 28 05A B
HARELD JOHN A 46 FRI B
HARGATE HAMILTON A 28 8TH B
HARGATE MONROE A 28 15T B
HARGESS ISRIAL A 37 TA1 B
HARGET ALFRED A 28 03A B
HARGET AUSTIN A 28 05A B
HARGET BENJ A 28 04A B
HARGET DUMMER A 19 MOR B
HARGET FRANK A 28 04A B
HARGET GEORGE A 28 6TH B
HARGET JOHN A 28 03A B
HARGET JOHN M A 28 03A W
HARGET JOSEPH A 28 04A B
HARGET SILAS A 28 03A B

HARGETT CEZAR A 72 SWA B
HARGETT DANIEL A A 72 SWA W
HARGETT ENOCH A 19 NEW B
HARGETT ENOCH 2ND A 19 NEW B
HARGETT JOHN A 19 NEW B
HARGETT SILAS A 19 NEW B
HARGETT STEPHEN A 72 SWA B
HARGRAV W M A 32 DAV B
HARGRAVE ANDY A 32 DAV B
HARGRAVE ANTHONY A 32 DAV B
HARGRAVE EDMOND A 32 THO B
HARGRAVE JAMES A 32 THO B
HARGRAVE JESSE A 32 COT W
HARGRAVE ROBERT A 32 DAV B
HARGRAVE WILLIAM A 32 DAV B
HARGRAVE WM A 29 FA1 B
HARGRAVE YLEY A 32 COT B
HARGRAVES JOSEPH A 99 BUS B
HARGROVE SIMON A 32 DAV B
HARGROVE ALBERT A 32 DAV B
HARGROVE ALEXANDER A 32 BRO W
HARGROVE ALFORD A 32 DAV B
HARGROVE ALFORD A 32 DAV B
HARGROVE ALLEN A 44 TOW B
HARGROVE ANTNA A 32 DAV B
HARGROVE ARMSTED A 32 DAV B
HARGROVE B R A 29 CAR W
HARGROVE BEN A 37 TA2 B
HARGROVE BURWELL A 44 TOW B
GUILTY OF LARCENY
ACC UNDER LAST ORDER
HARGROVE CAPT A 32 COT B
HARGROVE CESAR A 32 DAV B
HARGROVE CHARLES A 32 DAV B
HARGROVE CHARLES M A 44 TOW W
HARGROVE DAVID A 32 COT B
HARGROVE DAVID A 32 DAV B
HARGROVE DAVID A 44 TOW B
HARGROVE EDMON A 32 DAV B
HARGROVE EDWARD A 37 HIG W
HARGROVE EDWARD A 44 HEN B
HARGROVE EPHRAIM A 44 TOW B
HARGROVE FOSTER A 32 DAV B
HARGROVE FRANKLIN A 32 COT B
HARGROVE FRANKLIN A 32 LOF B
HARGROVE FREDRICK A 32 DAV B
HARGROVE GEO A 44 TOW B
HARGROVE GEO A 44 TOW B
HARGROVE GEORGE A 37 EDW B
HARGROVE GIDEON A 44 TOW B
HARGROVE GRANDERSON A 44 TOW B
HARGROVE GRAY L A 37 TA1 W
HARGROVE H H A 44 FIS W
HARGROVE HAMILTON A 32 COT B
HARGROVE HARY A 32 DAV B
HARGROVE HENRY A 32 COT B
HARGROVE HENRY A 32 DAV B
HARGROVE HENRY A 44 TOW B
HARGROVE HENRY A 44 TOW B
HARGROVE J H JR A 32 DAV W
HARGROVE JACK A 37 EDW B
HARGROVE JACK A 44 TOW B
HARGROVE JACOB A 29 FLE B
HARGROVE JAMES A 32 COT B
HARGROVE JAMES A 32 DAV B
HARGROVE JAMES A 32 TYR B
HARGROVE JAMES A 37 HOL B
HARGROVE JAY A 37 ROC B
HARGROVE JESSIE A 32 DAV B
HARGROVE JESSIE A 32 DAV B
HARGROVE JIM A 44 TOW B
HARGROVE JNO A 44 TOW B
HARGROVE JNO A 44 TOW B

HARGROVE JOHN A 32 COT B
HARGROVE JOHN A 32 DAV B
HARGROVE JOHN A 32 DAV B
HARGROVE JOHN A 32 DAV B
HARGROVE JOHN A 32 DAV B
HARGROVE JOHN A 37 EDW B
HARGROVE JOHN A 44 TOW W
HARGROVE JOHN L A 32 DAV B
HARGROVE JOSHUA A 32 COT B
HARGROVE JULIUS A 32 DAV B
HARGROVE KELLEY A 32 DAV B
HARGROVE LAWSON A 44 TOW B
HARGROVE LEONARD A 37 TA2 B
HARGROVE LEWIS A 44 TOW B
HARGROVE LOUIS A 32 COT B
HARGROVE LOUIS A 32 DAV B
HARGROVE LYNDSAY A 32 DAV B
HARGROVE MC A 32 COT B
HARGROVE MC A 44 TOW B
HARGROVE MERREDITH A 44 TOW B
HARGROVE MUMFORD A 32 DAV B
HARGROVE NATHAN A 32 DAV B
HARGROVE OBADIAH A 32 COT B
HARGROVE ORANGE A 32 DAV B
HARGROVE OTTOWAY A 44 TOW B
HARGROVE PEARSON A 32 DAV B
HARGROVE PETER A 32 COT B
HARGROVE PETER A 32 DAV B
HARGROVE PHIL A 44 TOW B
HARGROVE RANSOM A 44 TOW B
HARGROVE RICHMOND A 44 TOW B
HARGROVE ROBERT A 32 DAV B
HARGROVE SAMUEL H A 37 ROC W
HARGROVE SHADRICK A 32 DAV B
HARGROVE SIMEON A 32 DAV B
HARGROVE T A 32 COT B
HARGROVE THOMAS A 32 DAV B
HARGROVE THOS A 44 TOW B
HARGROVE W L A 44 KIT W
HARGROVE WASHINGTON A 32 DAV B
HARGROVE WILSON A 32 DAV B
HARGROVE WINSTON A 32 DAV B
HARGROVES ARTAWAY A 44 FIS B
HARGROVES HENRY A 35 WAR B
HARGROVES HILLIARD A 37 ROC B
HARGROVES ROBT A 44 FIS B
HARGROVES RUFUS A 44 FIS B
HARGROVES WASHINGTONA 44 FIS B
HARGROVES WILLIAM A 44 FIS B
HARILL N S A 26 MOO W
HARIS J A A 40 CAN W
HARISON RICHMOND A 37 PEN B
HARISON SAMUEL A 30 CUR W
HARISTON WM A 46 GRE B
HARKER GEO A A 19 BE1 W
HARKER HASTY A 19 BE1 B
HARKER JACOB A 19 BE1 B
HARKER JAMES W A 19 BE1 W
HARKER JOHN A 19 SMY W
HARKER MARANDA A 19 BE1 B
HARKER SAMUEL A 19 STR W
HARKER WILLIAM A 24 EDE B
HARKER WM M A 19 BE1 W
HARKLEY GEORGE A 28 10T B
HARKLEY TONY A 28 10T B
HARMAN H V A 32 POS W
HARMAN HENRY A 40 DEC W
HARMAN JOHN L A 40 DEC W
HARMAN PETER A 29 FA1 B
HARMAN VOLENTINE A 32 POS W
HARMON A N A 26 GOF W
HARMON HAYWOOD A 26 GOF W
HARMON HENRY A 32 POS W

HARMON J J A 26 BOR W
HARMON JACOB A 26 GOF W
HARMON JESSE M A 46 COB W
HARMON JOHN A 26 BOR W
HARMON JOHN G A 26 GOF W
HARMON JOHN W A 26 GOF W
HARMON P B A 26 BOR W
HARMON PETER A 32 POS W
HARMON PETER SR A 26 GOF W
HARMON R C A 26 BOR W
HARMON T W A 26 SHE W
HARMON WILLIAM H A 26 GOF W
HARMOND ALFRED A 29 FA1 B
HARN AMOS A 26 GRI B
HARN ANTHONY A 37 TA1 B
HARN FRANKLIN A 19 BE1 B
HARNEY LEWIS A 29 FA1 B
HARNEY PARIS A 32 BRO W
HARNEY THOMAS S A 30 NAR W
HARNEY WM A A 46 GRE W
HAROLD DAVID A 37 PIN W
HAROLD HENRY A 37 PIN B
HAROLD JOSEPH C A 37 PIN W
HAROLD LEWELLING A 37 PIN W
HARP BENJAMIN A 39 HAY W
HARP HARRY A 39 FRA B
HARP HARRY A 39 FRA B
HARP THOMSON A 44 FOR W
HARP WM JR A 44 FOR W
HARP WM SR A 44 FOR W
HARPE WILLIS A 39 LOU B
HARPER ADDISON A 44 YXS B
HARPER ALLEN A 37 HIC A
HARPER ALVIN A 39 FRA B
HARPER ANDREW A 29 FA1 B
HARPER BERRY A 32 CLE B
HARPER BRYAN A 28 11T B
HARPER CHANKS A 28 04A B
HARPER CHARLES A 28 15T W
HARPER ELI A 37 PEN B
HARPER F M A 28 02N W
HARPER G T A 39 LOU W
HARPER GEO W A 29 FA1 B
HARPER J J A 39 LOU W
HARPER JACK A 46 GRE B
HARPER JAMES K A 37 TA1 W
HARPER JEDDIAH A 28 16T W
HARPER JOSEPH A 39 JOR W
HARPER JOSEPH J A 37 SPA W
HARPER LEROY A 28 16T W
HARPER MACK A 37 PEN W
HARPER RICHD A 39 HAR W
HARPER RILEY A A 28 14T W
HARPER SPENCER H A 37 TA1 W
HARPER STEPHEN A 37 HIG W
HARPER WATSON A 28 04A B
HARPER WILLIAM A 28 10T B
HARPER WILLIAM A 28 9TH B
HARPER WILLIAM B A 37 HIC A
HARPER WILLIAM B A 37 SPA W
HARRAL SIMON A 24 EDE B
HARRALL THOMAS A 32 THO B
HARRALSON JAMES F A 40 BLA W
HARRALSON W O CHAL R 40 BLA W
  NAME LINED OUT
  JUSTICE OF PEACE
  VOLUNTEERED WAS CAPTAIN
  IN CONFEDERATE ARMY
  NOT QUALIFIED REJ.
HARRALSON WILLIAM A 40 BLA W
HARRASON JAMES A 35 KEN B
HARREL AMOUS A 37 WHI W
HARREL DAVID A 24 EDE W
HARREL JAMES A A 24 EDE W
HARREL JOSIAH A 24 EDE W
HARRELL AMOS A 37 WHI B
HARRELL BENJAMIN A 37 WEB B
HARRELL ELISHA A 37 WEB W
HARRELL ENOS A 37 WHI W
HARRELL JACOB A 35 ISL W
HARRELL JAMES F A 46 GRE W
HARRELL JESSE A 37 WEB W
HARRELL JOHN A 37 WEB W
HARRELL JOHN H A 37 TA2 W
HARRELL JONES A 37 WHI B
HARRELL JOSEPH H A 35 WAR W
HARRELL LEVEN A 37 WEB W
HARRELL PETER A 37 WEB W
HARRELL STREET A 26 SHE W
HARRELL WASHINGTON A 37 ROC W
HARRELL WATSON A 37 WEB W
HARRELL WILLIAM A 37 TA2 W
HARRELL WILLIAM A 37 WEB W
HARRIE J J A 26 HOL B
HARRILL A G A 26 MOO W
HARRILL E N A 26 MOO W
HARRILL HOSEA A 26 SHE W
HARRILL HOUSEIN A 26 MOO W
HARRILL JAMES A A 26 BUR W
HARRILL JOHN H CHALA 26 BUR W
  MILITIA OFFICER &
  ENGAGED IN REBELLION
HARRILL JOHN T A 26 MOO W
  MILITIA OFFICER
HARRILL R E A 26 SHE W
HARRILL WM M A 26 MOO W
HARRING ISAAC SR A 35 GLI B
HARRINGTON DANL A 37 ROB B
HARRINGTON HECTOR A 29 FA1 B
HARRINGTON J W A 29 FA1 B
HARRINGTON ORVIN A 29 FA1 B
HARRINGTON W C A 19 NEW W
HARRINGTON WILLIAM A 37 PEN B
HARRIS A J A 44 HEN W
HARRIS A J P A 39 HAR W
HARRIS A S A 39 DAV W
HARRIS ABNER A 39 PUG B
HARRIS ABRAHAM A 44 HEN B
HARRIS ABRAM A 44 FOR B
HARRIS ABSALUM A 44 FOR W
HARRIS ALBERT A 44 LED B
HARRIS ALEX A 44 FIS W
HARRIS ALEX A 44 LED B
HARRIS ALEX A 44 OXF B
HARRIS ALEX C A 44 HEN W
HARRIS ALEXANDER A 30 NAR W
HARRIS ALEXR A 28 04B B
HARRIS ALFORD A 37 PIN B
HARRIS ALFORD A 39 LOU B
HARRIS ALFRED A 44 OXF B
HARRIS ALISON A 39 HAR B
HARRIS ALISON B A 53 LA1 W
HARRIS ALLEN A 29 FA1 B
HARRIS ALLEN A 39 SPE W
HARRIS ALONZO A 28 9TH B
HARRIS ALSEY A 38 FRE B
HARRIS AMASA M A 53 FAI W
HARRIS AMOS A 44 OXF B
HARRIS ANDERSON A 44 DUT B
HARRIS ANDERSON A 44 LED B
HARRIS ANDERSON G A 44 HEN W
HARRIS ANDREW A 28 03A B
HARRIS ANDREW J A 28 7TH W
HARRIS ANDY A 24 EDE B
HARRIS ANNIASE A 53 LA1 B
HARRIS ANTHONEY A 44 TAR B
HARRIS ANTHONY A 28 04A B
HARRIS ARMESTEAD A 44 RAG B
HARRIS AUSTEN A 32 LOF B
HARRIS B A 44 LED W
HARRIS B B A 26 MOO W
HARRIS B Y A 44 FIS W
HARRIS BALEM A 44 KNA B
HARRIS BEN A 39 LOU B
HARRIS BENJAMIN A 28 9TH B
HARRIS BENJAMIN A 39 DAV B
HARRIS BENJAMIN A 39 SPE W
HARRIS BENJAMIN A 44 HEN B
HARRIS BENJAMIN A 53 SWA W
HARRIS BERTON A 44 OXF B
HARRIS BLUNT A 39 DAV B
HARRIS BOB A 39 DAV B
HARRIS BRISTOE A 28 04A B
HARRIS BRISTOW A 28 7TH B
HARRIS BRONSON A 46 JAM W
HARRIS BRYANT A 39 GRI B
HARRIS BUCK A 44 HEN B
HARRIS C C A 39 DAV W
HARRIS C H A 46 FRI W
HARRIS CALVIN A 32 TYR B
HARRIS CHARLES A 28 7TH B
HARRIS CHARLES A 32 THO B
HARRIS CHARLES A 44 LED B
HARRIS CHARLES A 44 LED W
HARRIS CHARLES A 44 SAS B
HARRIS CHARLTON A 24 EDE W
HARRIS CICERO R A 29 FA2 B
HARRIS CLARKE A 44 RAG B
HARRIS CYRUS A 39 DAV W
HARRIS DANCY A 28 04A B
HARRIS DANIEL A 35 MAG B
HARRIS DANIEL A 39 DAV B
HARRIS DANL A 28 02N B
HARRIS DANL H A 28 04A B
HARRIS DAVID A 32 SHE W
HARRIS DAVID A 44 OXF B
HARRIS DAVID A 44 YXR W
HARRIS DAVID A 53 FAI W
HARRIS DAVID D A 37 ROB W
HARRIS DAVID W A 37 TA1 B
HARRIS DENNIS A 24 EDE B
HARRIS DENNIS A 44 OXF B
HARRIS DICK A 44 HEN B
HARRIS DOC A 44 HEN B
HARRIS DOCTOR A 44 BRA B
HARRIS DOLPHIN A 39 DAV B
HARRIS DOLPHIN A 44 OXF B
HARRIS DONAM A 28 7TH B
HARRIS DONNAHU A 44 FIS B
HARRIS DRURY A A 39 JOR W
HARRIS DUKE A 44 BRA B
HARRIS E H A 28 04A B
HARRIS E L A 37 ROB W
HARRIS E P A 38 FRE W
HARRIS EDMOND A 19 CED W
HARRIS EDWARD A 28 11T B
HARRIS EDWD A 28 04A B
HARRIS EHNRY A 37 TA1 B
HARRIS ELI A 28 7TH B
HARRIS ELI H A 19 CED W
HARRIS ELLICK A 44 RAG B
HARRIS ENOCH A 28 10T B
HARRIS F A 44 LED W
HARRIS F A A 32 CLE W
HARRIS FIELDING A 44 OXF B
HARRIS FRED A 44 HEN B
HARRIS FREDERICK A 28 7TH B
HARRIS FREEMAN A 28 11T B
HARRIS G A A 44 LED W

HARRIS G W A 32 LOF W
HARRIS G W A 39 HAR B
HARRIS GEO A 39 HAR W
HARRIS GEO A A 19 SMY W
HARRIS GEO A A 44 HEN W
HARRIS GEO R A 44 HEN W
HARRIS GEORGE A 28 11T W
HARRIS GEORGE A 39 DAV B
HARRIS GEORGE R A 53 LA1 W
HARRIS GEORGE W A 37 PIN W
HARRIS GEORGE W R 39 DAV W
HARRIS GILLIAM A 38 FRE B
HARRIS GRANDERSON A 44 BRA B
HARRIS GRANDISON A 44 HEN B
HARRIS H H A 39 HAR W
HARRIS H W A 32 CLE W
HARRIS H W A 44 FIS W
HARRIS HANDY A 39 FRE B
HARRIS HANDY A 39 HAR B
HARRIS HANSON A 44 BRA W
HARRIS HARDY A 29 FA1 B
HARRIS HARDY A 44 HEN W
HARRIS HARRIL R 39 LOU W
STRICKED FOR BEING A
JUSTICE OF THE PEACE
BEFORE THE WAR AND DUR-
ING THE WAR AS OFFICER
OF THE HOME GUARD
HARRIS HARVEY A 44 FIS W
HARRIS HAYWOOD A 39 FRA B
HARRIS HAYWOOD G A 28 10T W
HARRIS HENDERSON A 39 DAV B
HARRIS HENDERSON A 44 FOR B
HARRIS HENRY A 24 EDE W
HARRIS HENRY A 29 FA1 B
HARRIS HENRY A 32 JAC B
HARRIS HENRY A 44 FOR W
HARRIS HENRY A 44 HEN B
HARRIS HENRY A 44 HEN B
HARRIS HENRY A 44 LED B
HARRIS HENRY A 44 OXF B
HARRIS HENRY H A 39 LOU W
TRNS BY AFF FROM
BRASSFIELD GRANVILLE
HARRIS HINTON A 44 HEN B
HARRIS HORACE A 44 OXF B
HARRIS HUBBARD A 46 SUM B
HARRIS HUBORN A 44 YXR W
HARRIS IASIAH A 32 THO W
HARRIS IRVIN A 37 SPA W
HARRIS IRVIN A A 24 EDE W
HARRIS ISAAC A 39 DAV B
HARRIS ISAAC A 39 FRE B
HARRIS ISAAC A 44 FIS B
HARRIS ISAAC A 44 HEN B
HARRIS ISAH A 44 OXF B
HARRIS ISAH A 44 OXF B
HARRIS ISHAM A 39 DAV B
HARRIS ISRAEL A 28 04A B
HARRIS IVEY A 44 HEN W
HARRIS J D A 44 FIS B
HARRIS J E A 32 JAC W
HARRIS J F A 26 SHE W
HARRIS J H A 39 FRA W
HARRIS J J A 39 GRI W
HARRIS J M A 46 SUM W
HARRIS J R A 39 DAV W
HARRIS J R A 44 FIS W
HARRIS J R JR A 39 JOR W
HARRIS J ROBERT A 39 HAR W
HARRIS J T A 44 FIS W
HARRIS J T A 44 HEN W
HARRIS JABEZ K A 53 SWA W

HARRIS JACKSON A 44 OXF B
HARRIS JACOB A 53 LA1 B
HARRIS JAMES A 28 10T B
CERTIF GIVEN NOW LIVES
AT NEW BERN
HARRIS JAMES A 28 7TH B
HARRIS JAMES A 29 QUW B
HARRIS JAMES A 32 JAC W
HARRIS JAMES A 37 PIN W
HARRIS JAMES A 39 GRI B
HARRIS JAMES A 39 GRI B
HARRIS JAMES A 39 HAR B
HARRIS JAMES A 44 OXF B
HARRIS JAMES A 46 SUM B
HARRIS JAMES A 46 SUM W
HARRIS JAMES A 53 GER B
HARRIS JAMES H A 37 PIN W
HARRIS JAMES H A 44 YXS W
HARRIS JAMES H A 53 LA1 W
HARRIS JAMES M H A 37 PIN W
HARRIS JAMES N A 44 TOW W
HARRIS JAMES SR A 38 FRE W
HARRIS JAS A 29 FA1 W
HARRIS JAS A 39 FRA W
HARRIS JAS A 44 ISL B
HARRIS JAS E A 28 04A B
HARRIS JESSE A 39 DAV B
HARRIS JESSE A 39 GRI B
HARRIS JIRDON A 39 DAV B
HARRIS JNO A A 44 HEN W
HARRIS JNO J A 44 HEN W
HARRIS JNO L A 44 OXF B
HARRIS JNO P A 44 TOW W
HARRIS JOEL A A 46 SUM W
HARRIS JOHN A 28 04A B
HARRIS JOHN A 28 11T B
HARRIS JOHN A 37 PEN B
HARRIS JOHN A 37 TA1 W
HARRIS JOHN A 44 FOR W
HARRIS JOHN A 44 TAR B
HARRIS JOHN A 53 LA1 B
HARRIS JOHN A A 28 05A B
HARRIS JOHN G A 44 OXF W
HARRIS JOHN G A 53 FAI W
HARRIS JOHNSON A 44 FOR B
HARRIS JONATHAN S A 53 SWA W
HARRIS JONATHEN A 46 FRI W
HARRIS JONT T A 39 FRE W
HARRIS JORDAN M A 53 SWA W
HARRIS JOS A 39 GRI B
HARRIS JOSEPH A 37 HOL W
HARRIS JOSEPH A 44 DUT W
HARRIS JOSEPH A 46 SUM W
HARRIS JOSEPH N A 28 14T W
HARRIS JOSEPH R A 46 JAM W
HARRIS JOSIAH A 24 EDE W
HARRIS JOURDAN A 28 10T B
HARRIS KENNEY A 37 EDW W
HARRIS KING A 37 PEN B
HARRIS KITCHEN A 99 BUS W
HARRIS L J A 46 SUM W
HARRIS LAZERUS A 32 THO B
HARRIS LEVI A 37 SPA W
HARRIS LEWIS A 28 04A B
HARRIS LEWIS H A 37 ROB W
HARRIS M J A 39 GRI W
HARRIS M T A 44 LED W
HARRIS MAGER A A 30 NOR W
APRIL 8, 1868
HARRIS MAJA A 46 KIN W
HARRIS MALACHI A 28 11T B
HARRIS MARTIN A 19 CED W
HARRIS MICAGA T A 53 GER W

HARRIS MINGO A 28 10T B
HARRIS MINGO A 39 DAV B
HARRIS MINTER A 32 JAC B
HARRIS MORGAN J A 53 FAI W
HARRIS MOSES A 44 LED B
HARRIS N H A 32 CLE B
HARRIS NAT T A 39 LOU B
REGISTRAR
HARRIS NATHANIEL A 39 HAR B
HARRIS NED A 39 DAV B
HARRIS NELSON A 39 DAV B
HARRIS NORFLET A 39 HAR B
HARRIS P H A 46 SUM W
HARRIS PARKER A 29 FA1 B
HARRIS PASON A 44 OXF B
HARRIS PELEDGE A 53 FAI W
HARRIS PETER A 32 LOF B
HARRIS PETER A 44 HEN B
HARRIS PETER A 46 GRE W
HARRIS PINA A 39 FRA B
HARRIS PLUMMER A 44 RAG B
HARRIS R C A 46 SUM W
HARRIS R D A 44 SAS W
HARRIS R R A 39 LOU W
HARRIS RANSOM A 39 PUG B
HARRIS RANSOM A 44 HEN B
HARRIS REMOUS A 39 SPE B
HARRIS RICHARD A 24 UPP B
HARRIS RICHARD A 44 HEN B
HARRIS RICHD A 44 TAR B
HARRIS ROBERT A 29 FA2 B
HARRIS ROBERT A 32 SHE B
HARRIS ROBERT A 44 HEN W
HARRIS ROBERT D A 53 SWA W
HARRIS ROBERT H A 37 HIC A
HARRIS ROBERT H JR A 53 SWA W
HARRIS ROBERT H SR A 53 SWA W
HARRIS ROBT A 29 FA1 B
HARRIS ROBT A 44 OXF W
HARRIS RUBEN A 44 HEN B
HARRIS RUFFIN A 39 DAV B
HARRIS RUFFIN SR A 39 DAV B
HARRIS S H A 32 JAC W
HARRIS S P J A 44 HEN W
HARRIS S R A 32 THO W
HARRIS SAM A 44 HEN B
HARRIS SAM A 44 OXF B
HARRIS SAML A 44 DUT W
HARRIS SAML A 44 FOR W
HARRIS SAMUEL A 28 7TH B
HARRIS SAMUEL A 44 KIT B
HARRIS SAMUEL A 44 SAS B
HARRIS SANDY A 44 FOR B
HARRIS SETH B JR A 53 FAI W
HARRIS SILAS A 28 04A B
HARRIS SILAS A 39 HAR B
HARRIS SILLUS A 39 DAV B
HARRIS SOL A 39 DAV B
TRNS FROM NASH CO
NASHVILLE PRE.
HARRIS SOLOMAN A 39 JOR W
HARRIS STARK A 30 NOR W
HARRIS STEPHEN A 28 16T W
HARRIS STEPHEN A 29 QUW B
HARRIS STEPHEN F A 28 16T W
HARRIS SYLVANUS A 30 NOR W
HARRIS SYLVESTER A 53 FAI B
HARRIS T A A 44 BEA W
HARRIS T C A 44 FIS W
HARRIS T M A 32 LOF W
HARRIS THOMAS A 28 11T B
HARRIS THOMAS A 28 16T W
HARRIS THOMAS A 30 NOR W

HARRIS THOMAS A 38 FRE W
HARRIS THOMAS A 53 FAI W
HARRIS THOMAS D A 53 SWA W
HARRIS THOMAS E A 19 CED W
HARRIS THOMAS E A 53 SWA W
HARRIS THOMAS W A 53 SWA W
HARRIS THOS A 28 03A B
HARRIS THOS A 39 FRA B
HARRIS THOS A 44 BRA W
HARRIS THOS C A 19 SMY W
HARRIS THOS H A 28 04A B
HARRIS THOS M A 24 EDE W
HARRIS TIMOTHY A 37 SPA W
HARRIS TONEY A 35 KEN B
HARRIS TONEY A 39 DAV B
HARRIS TURNER A 32 LOF W
HARRIS URIAH A 53 FAI W
HARRIS VIRGIL A 28 9TH B
HARRIS W D A 39 LOU W
HARRIS W H A 39 FRA W
HARRIS W H A 44 HEN W
HARRIS W H A A 39 DAV W
HARRIS W J A 32 LOF W
HARRIS W N A 44 BRA W
HARRIS W T A 44 BEA W
HARRIS WAIN A 39 LOU W
HARRIS WALLER C A 44 HEN W
HARRIS WARREN A 44 HEN B
HARRIS WASHINGTON A 44 YXR B
HARRIS WASHINGTON 39 DAV W
FOR THE OATH BEFORE THE
REBELION AS MEMBER OF
THE LEGISLATURE AND
DURING THE REBELION
VOTED TO CLOTHE THE
N CAROLINA SOLDIERS
STRICKEN OUT
APRIL 10TH 1868
HARRIS WATSON A 24 EDE B
HARRIS WESLEY A 44 OXF B
HARRIS WILLIAM A 19 BE1 B
HARRIS WILLIAM A 32 JAC W
HARRIS WILLIAM A 37 PIN B
HARRIS WILLIAM A 37 WHI B
HARRIS WILLIAM A 46 JAM W
HARRIS WILLIAM R A 53 FAI W
HARRIS WILLIAM R A 53 SWA W
HARRIS WILLIAM S A 53 SWA W
HARRIS WILLIAM T A 53 SWA W
HARRIS WILLIAM V A 19 SMY W
HARRIS WILLIE A 44 HEN B
HARRIS WILLIS A 30 KNO B
8-MOS-RES
HARRIS WILLIS A 44 HEN B
HARRIS WILLIS A 44 OXF B
HARRIS WILLIS H A 37 MAN B
HARRIS WM A 39 LOU B
HARRIS WM A 44 FOR B
HARRIS WM A 44 HEN B
HARRIS WM A 44 HEN B
HARRIS WM A 44 ISL B
HARRIS WM A 46 GRE B
HARRIS WM A A 44 HEN W
HARRIS WM H A 28 04B B
HARRIS WM N A 24 EDE W
HARRIS WM S A 28 14T W
HARRIS WOODLY A 39 HAR B
HARRIS WOODSON A 40 DEC B
HARRIS WOODSON A 40 DEC B
6 MOS RESIDENCE
1ST SEPT 1867
HARRIS WYLEY O A 40 DEC W
HARRIS YOUNG A 39 PUG W

HARRISON ALFORD A 37 PIN B
HARRISON ANDREW A 37 PEN B
HARRISON ANTINY A 37 MAN B
HARRISON ANTY A 37 MAN B
HARRISON BENJ A 28 05A B
HARRISON BENJ S A 30 POW W
HARRISON BENJN A 28 04A B
HARRISON CHARLES A 37 PEN B
HARRISON COFFIELD A 37 PEN B
HARRISON DAULPHIN A 37 EDW B
HARRISON DAVID A 30 ROA B
HARRISON DAVID A 37 EDW B
HARRISON DICK A 37 PEN B
HARRISON EDWARD A 30 POP B
HARRISON ELIJAH A 37 EDW B
HARRISON G W A 44 FIS W
HARRISON GEORGE A 30 ROA B
HARRISON GEORGE A 37 MAN B
HARRISON GEORGE A 37 PEN B
HARRISON GEORGE W A 30 POW W
HARRISON H A 32 JAC W
HARRISON HENRY A 32 JAC W
HARRISON HENRY A 39 HAY B
HARRISON HENRY A 39 LOU B
HARRISON HENRY H A 30 POW W
HARRISON ISAAC A 28 6TH W
HARRISON J C A 32 JAC W
HARRISON J H C A 32 JAC W
HARRISON JACOB A 37 MAN B
HARRISON JAS C A 28 03A W
HARRISON JESSE A 28 03A W
HARRISON JOHN A 32 JAC W
HARRISON JOHN A 40 STO W
HARRISON JOHN S A 30 CUR W
HARRISON JOSEPH A 30 IND B
HARRISON JOSHUA A 30 POW W
HARRISON JOSHUA A 37 HIC B
HARRISON LEWIS A 37 TA1 B
HARRISON MARTIN A 30 POP B
HARRISON N B A 32 JAC W
HARRISON NEDD A 37 MAN B
HARRISON ORPHY A 37 EDW B
HARRISON PETER A 44 KIT B
HARRISON PETER C A 30 IND W
HARRISON PEYTON M A 38 FRE W
HARRISON PRESTON A 37 PEN B
HARRISON R J A 29 FLE W
HARRISON RANSOM A 39 HAR B
HARRISON RICHD A 39 JOR B
HARRISON ROBERT A 37 ROC B
HARRISON SAMUEL A 32 JAC B
HARRISON SAMUEL A 37 ROC B
HARRISON SIMON A 28 04A B
HARRISON SIMON A 28 04A B
HARRISON SIMON A 37 PEN B
HARRISON SLATE A 37 ROC B
HARRISON THOS B A 30 POW W
HARRISON THOS Y A 44 YXR W
HARRISON TURNER A 37 EDW B
HARRISON TURNER A 37 TA1 B
HARRISON W C A 30 IND W
CERTIFICATE TO
E CITY PASQUOTANK
HARRISON WALTER S A 30 POW W
HARRISON WILEY A 37 PEN B
HARRISON WILLIAM A 28 03B B
HARRISON WILLIE A 39 JOR B
HARRISON WILSON A 37 PEN B
HARRISON WM H A 28 04A W
HARRISS CALVIN G A 32 JAC W
HARRISS DENNIS A 44 YXS B
HARRISS JAMES A 44 YXS B
HARRISS NED A 44 YXS B

HARRISS OSBORN A 44 YXS B
HARRISS OXFORD A 44 YXS B
HARRISS RHODEN A 37 PIN B
HARRISS RICHARD A 44 YXS B
HARRISS SCOTT A 44 YXS B
HARRISS STERLING A 44 YXS B
HARROL ANDERSON A 24 EDE B
HARROL ELIJAH A 24 EDE W
HARROL ELISHA A 24 EDE W
HARROL GILBERT A 24 EDE W
HARROL HARVY A 24 EDE W
HARROL THOS A A 24 EDE W
HARROLL GEORGE W A 46 GRE W
HARROLL JOHN A 24 UPP W
HARROW SPENCER A 19 MOR B
HARRY J W M A 26 GOF W
HARRY LABAN A 40 CAN B
HARRY WILLIAM A 37 ROC B
HARSEL ASA A 37 WEB W
HARSTEN FRANK A 32 DAV B
HARSTEN WILLIAM A 32 DAV B
HARSTON ALEXANDER A 32 TYR B
HARSTON AUSTON A 32 TYR B
HARSTON B A 32 TYR B
HARSTON BRYUS A 32 TYR B
HARSTON BUCK A 32 TYR B
HARSTON GEORGE A 46 GRE B
HARSTON JAMES A 32 TYR B
HARSTON PETER A 32 TYR B
HARSTON R A 32 TYR B
HARSTON SAMUEL A 32 TYR B
HARSTON W A 46 GRE B
HART AMOS A 37 HOL B
HART C A A 28 01B W
HART C C A 28 05A W
HART CHARLES A 37 TA1 B
HART DANIEL A 37 PEN B
HART DAVID A 29 FA1 B
HART FRANK A 37 ROB B
HART FRANK A 44 RAG B
HART FRANKLIN A 37 TA1 W
HART G W A 44 OXF W
HART GEO W A 28 05A W
HART GIDEON 46 GIB W
CHAL FOR FELONY
HART GRAY A 37 EDW B
HART HENRY A 37 PIN B
HART HENRY A 37 ROB B
HART ISAAC A 37 PIN B
HART ISHAM ? T A 28 11T W
DEAD
HART J F A 44 OXF W
HART JAS R A 44 OXF W
HART JESSIE A 37 TA1 B
HART JNO L A 44 YXR W
HART JOSEPH A 37 MAN B
HART JOSEPH A 44 YXR W
HART LEWIS A 32 CLE B
HART LEWIS A 44 SAS B
HART MIKE A 44 RAG B
HART MORGAN A 37 HIG B
HART NATHAN A 37 HOL B
HART R D A 44 OXF W
HART RICHMOND A 37 PEN B
HART SHEPHARD A 44 SAS B
HART SPENCER L A 37 TA1 W
HART THOS A A 44 YXS W
HART W C A 39 FRA W
HART WALTER A 37 PEN B
HART WILLIAM A 37 EDW B
HART WILLIAM L A 37 ROC W
HART WILLIE A 37 HOL B
HART WM H A 44 RAG W

HART WM W A 44 YXS W
HART WOODSON A 44 RAG B
HARTGROVE DUNCAN A 37 HIG W
HARTKILL POMPEY A 28 10T B
HARTLETT MICHAEL A 32 SHE W
HARTLEY ANDREW A 28 8TH B
HARTLEY DANIEL A 32 YAD W
HARTLEY JAMES R A 32 DAV W
HARTLEY JOHN A 28 12T W
HARTLEY LENON A 28 8TH B
HARTLEY MOSES A 28 8TH B
HARTLEY T M A 32 YAD W
HARTLEY WILLIAM A 32 CLE W
HARTLEY WM F A 28 13T W
HARTLY HYRAM H A 32 TYR W
HARTLY J F A 32 TYR W
HARTLY NATHAN H A 32 TYR W
HARTMAN CHRISTAIN A 32 SHE W
HARTMAN J H A 26 GRI W
HARTMAN JESSE A 32 SHE W
HARTMAN THOMAS A 32 DAV B
HARTMAN WARREN A 37 TA1 B
HARTMAN WILEY A 26 GRI W
HARTNER JOHN A A 32 POS W
HARTON ALLEN A 46 GRE B
HARTSELL JACKSON M A 35 MAG W
HARVEL JOSEPH J A 35 ROC W
HARVEL THOMAS H A 35 ROC W
HARVEL WILLIAM H A 35 ROC W
HARVEY ALEXD DEAD 28 01A W
HARVEY BEN A 44 OXF B
HARVEY DENNIS A 28 6TH B
HARVEY EDWARD A 28 01A B
HARVEY H H A 28 03A B
HARVEY HENRY A 28 03A B
HARVEY JACOB A 24 EDE B
HARVEY JAMES A 40 BLA W
HARVEY JOHN A 19 BE1 B
HARVEY PALL A 39 DAV B
HARVEY RICHARD A 24 EDE B
HARVEY SAML A 28 01A B
HARVEY SAML A 28 05A B
HARVEY THOS E A 24 EDE W
HARVEY THOS H A 28 6TH W
HARVEY WILLIAM A 19 BE1 B
HARVEY WM JR A 19 BE1 B
HARVY ISAC J A 46 FRI W
HARVY JNO A 44 OXF B
HARVY JOHN F A 46 GRE W
HARVY SAML A 46 GRE W
HASE GEORGE W A 24 MID W
HASKEL VERGIE A 37 WHI B
HASKELL WILLIAM S A 28 10T W
HASKET THOMAS A 24 EDE W
HASKETT DAVID A 28 14T W
HASKILL WM H A 28 16T W
HASKIN ELESHA A 37 WHI B
HASKIN JOHN A 37 WHI B
HASKIN STEPHEN A 24 EDE B
HASKIN THOMAS A 32 THO W
CERTIF
HASKIN THOMAS A 37 WHI B
HASKINS ALLEN A 44 TOW B
HASKINS AMERICA A 24 EDE B
HASKINS CHARS A 46 GRE B
HASKINS CREED A 44 TOW B
HASKINS ELISHA A 44 DUT B
HASKINS FRANK A 37 PIN B
HASKINS GEORGE O A 46 SUM W
HASKINS ISAAC A 44 LED W
HASKINS JACK A 24 EDE B
HASKINS JASPER A 44 SAS B
HASKINS JNO M A 44 YXS W
HASKINS LEON A 37 PIN B
HASKINS PLEASANT A 44 LED B
HASKINS STEPHEN A 44 LED B
HASKINS TALTON A 44 LED B
HASKINS THOMAS A 24 EDE B
HASKINS THOMAS F A 46 FRI W
HASKINS W W A 24 EDE W
HASKINS WELLINGTON A 44 DUT B
HASKITT DANIEL P A 19 BE1 W
HASKITT DAVID D A 19 BE2 W
HASKITT JOHN P A 19 BE1 W
HASKITT WILLIAM A 28 10T W
MOVED AWAY
HASKY LAWRENCE A 28 03A B
HASLER JAS A 29 FA1 B
HASLIN HENRY A 28 03A B
HASSALL WM A 28 14T W
HASSEL W W A 24 EDE W
HASSELL BENJAMIN A 46 FRI W
HASSELL DURAND A 28 01B W
HASSELL JOHN L A 28 01A W
HASSELL SAML A 28 05A B
HASSER JACOB A 46 COB B
HASSON PHILIP A 32 YAD B
HASTE JOHN H A 19 BE2 B
HASTING H C A 26 GRI W
HASTING H F A 26 GRI W
HASTING S A 26 GRI W
HASTING WILLIAM A 26 GRI W
HASTON ALEXANDER A 46 FRI B
HASTON BURRELL A 37 PIN B
HASWELL ED A 44 FOR W
HASWELL T N A 44 FOR W
HASWELL W A A 44 FOR W
HATCH ALFRED A 28 04A B
HATCH AMOS A 28 03A B
HATCH CALVIN A 28 04A B
HATCH F A A 39 FRE W
HATCH FRANK A 28 05A B
HATCH GEORGE A 28 04A B
HATCH ISAAC A 28 04A B
HATCH JAMES A 28 04A B
HATCH JESSE A 28 04A B
HATCH JOHN A 28 02N B
HATCH JOHN C A 28 04B B
HATCH JOSEPH A 28 04A B
HATCH NATHAN A 28 16T B
HATCHELL ISAAC A 19 HAD B
HATCHER HOWEL A 29 FLE B
HATCHER WM A 29 FLE B
HATH J WASHINGTON A 46 GRE W
HATHAWAY ANTHONY A 24 EDE B
HATHAWAY DAVID A A 53 FAI W
HATHAWAY J R B A 24 EDE W
HATHAWAY JOSEPH F A 24 EDE B
HATHAWAY MACK A 24 EDE B
HATHAWAY NATHAN A 24 EDE W
HATHAWAY NELSON A 24 EDE B
HATHAWAY PETER A 24 EDE B
HATHAWAY RICHARD A 24 EDE B
HATHAWAY RICHARD A 37 WHI W
HATHWAY BENJAMIN A 37 SPA W
HATSEL GEO A A 19 BE1 W
HATSEL WM F A 19 BE1 W
HATSELL BRYAN A 72 SWA W
HATTAWAY JAS A 29 FA1 B
HATWOOD JAMES A 29 FA1 B
HAUGHTON ALEX A 24 EDE B
HAUGHTON ANDREW A 24 EDE B
HAUGHTON EDWARD B A 53 FAI W
HAUGHTON EMANUEL A 24 EDE B
HAUGHTON GANSEY A 24 EDE B
HAUGHTON JAMES A 24 EDE B
HAUGHTON JAMES H A 24 EDE B
HAUGHTON JEFFERSON A 24 EDE B
HAUGHTON JOHN A 28 04A B
HAUGHTON LUKE A 24 EDE B
HAUGHTON RICHARD A 24 EDE B
HAUGHTON RICHARD A 24 EDE B
HAUGHTON RICHARD JR A 24 EDE B
HAUGHTON SOLOMON A 24 EDE B
HAUGHTON THOMAS A 24 EDE B
HAUGHTON WM R A 24 EDE W
HAULSEY HENRY A 53 LA1 B
HAUSER JOSEPH A 26 CAR W
HAVELL S A 26 BOR B
HAVENS EDWARD A 28 02N B
HAVENS GANSEY A 28 02N B
HAVENS HENRY A 28 05A B
HAVENS RICHD A 28 05A B
HAVNER MICHAEL A 26 GOF W
HAVNER PHILIP A 26 GOF W
HAVRELL J J A 26 BOR W
HAWARD EDWARD A 32 POS B
HAWCKING R N A 26 HOL B
HAWCKINS W A A 26 SHE W
HAWES ASAHEL W A 35 ROC W
HAWES REUBEN J T A 35 ROC W
HAWES WILLIAM B A 35 ROC W
HAWKINS ADAM A 39 HAY B
HAWKINS ALLEN A 39 HAY B
HAWKINS ALLEN J A 28 8TH W
HAWKINS ANTHONY A 72 SWA B
HAWKINS ANTHONY A 72 SWA B
HAWKINS ASA A 28 8TH W
HAWKINS B G A 39 LOU W
HAWKINS BAALAM A 19 HAD B
HAWKINS BEN A 39 FRA B
HAWKINS BRYANT J A 28 8TH W
HAWKINS CHARLES S A 26 MOO W
HAWKINS CHRIS A 28 03A B
HAWKINS D A A 26 MOO W
MILITIA OFFICER
HAWKINS DAVID A 44 BRA B
HAWKINS DAVID A 44 HEN B
HAWKINS EDMOND A 19 STR B
HAWKINS EDMUND A 44 HEN B
HAWKINS EDWARD A 26 MOO W
HAWKINS EDWARD A 28 01A B
HAWKINS ELITIA A 40 CAN W
HAWKINS ENOS A 44 HEN B
HAWKINS FRANK A 72 SWA B
HAWKINS FREDK A 28 6TH W
HAWKINS FREDRICK A 37 HOL W
HAWKINS FURNEY A 28 8TH W
CERTIFICATE GIVEN
EXPECTS TO VOTE AT
RUSSELL'S
HAWKINS G M A 26 BLA W
HAWKINS GEORGE A 39 HAY B
HAWKINS GLASTI A 39 HAY B
HAWKINS HARRY A 39 PUG B
HAWKINS HENRY A 44 HEN B
HAWKINS HENRY T A 28 8TH W
HAWKINS HOPEWELL A 44 HEN B
HAWKINS J R A 26 MOO W
HAWKINS JAMES A A 40 CAN W
HAWKINS JAMES B A 26 MOO W
HAWKINS JAMES F A 28 8TH W
HAWKINS JNO A 44 TOW B
HAWKINS JOHN A 28 8TH W
HAWKINS JOHN A 37 HOL W
HAWKINS JOHN A 39 PUG B
HAWKINS JOHN A 40 STO W
HAWKINS LEONADAS A 44 RAG B
HAWKINS LEWIS A 39 HAY B

HAWKINS LEWIS H A 44 RAG B
HAWKINS MARK G A 37 HOL W
HAWKINS MILES A 28 8TH W
HAWKINS MINGO A 39 HAY B
HAWKINS N M A 39 LOU W
HAWKINS NAPOLEON B A 39 LOU B
HAWKINS NAT A 44 HEN B
HAWKINS NATHAN A 44 HEN B
HAWKINS NED A 39 LOU B
HAWKINS NELSON A 39 LOU B
HAWKINS PETER A 28 15T B
HAWKINS PITT A 19 BE1 B
HAWKINS RICHARD C A 28 8TH W
HAWKINS ROBERT A 44 HEN B
HAWKINS ROBT A 39 FRA B
HAWKINS S J A 40 CAN W
HAWKINS SAML A 28 03A B
HAWKINS SAMPSON A 44 HEN B
HAWKINS SAMUEL A 19 BE1 B
HAWKINS SQUARE A 44 HEN B
HAWKINS STEPHEN A 44 HEN B
HAWKINS THOS A 26 MOO W
HAWKINS TOM A 39 HAY B
HAWKINS TUMER A 44 SAS B
HAWKINS UMPHRY A 39 HAY B
HAWKINS W P A 44 HEN W
HAWKINS WASHINGTON A 39 HAY B
HAWKINS WILLIAM A 26 MOU W
HAWKINS WILLIAM A 39 LOU B
HAWKINS WILLIAM A A 26 MOO W
HAWKINS WILLIAM H A 72 SWA W
HAWKINS WM J A 26 MOO W
MILITIA OFFICER
HAWKINS WM T A 28 8TH W
HAWKINS WOODLEY A 39 PUG B
HAWKINS WOODLY A 40 SAN W
HAWLEY F O A 29 FA1 W
HAWLEY J B A 29 FA1 W
HAWLEY MILLS A 24 EDE B
HAWLEY NATHAN A 44 TAR B
HAWLEY S T A 29 FA1 W
COUNTY ASSESSOR AFTER
AIDED REBELLION
HAWLEY THOMAS A 44 OXF B
HAWLEY WM A 44 BRA B
HAWN CORNELIUS A 32 DAV W
HAWN NOAH A 32 DAV W
HAY CALVIN A 19 HAD W
HAY GEO W A 19 HAD W
HAY HENRY A 46 GRE B
HAY R S A 28 03A W
HAYES ALEXANDER A 35 MAG B
HAYES ALIC A 37 HIC B
HAYES ALVAN A 44 LED B
HAYES BENJ A 44 BRA B
HAYES CHARLES A 39 HAY B
HAYES D H A 44 KIT W
HAYES DANIEL A 44 KIT B
HAYES G W A 39 LOU W
HAYES GEO W A 44 YXR W
HAYES GEORGE A 28 03A B
HAYES GEORGE A 30 ROA B
HAYES GEORGE A 39 HAY B
HAYES H S A 39 HAY W
HAYES HENRY A 35 ROC B
HAYES HYE A 39 HAY B
HAYES ISAAC A 44 LED B
HAYES ISAH A 44 KIT B
HAYES J G A 44 OXF W
HAYES J J A 39 PUG W
HAYES J M A 44 OXF W
HAYES J S A 44 BEA W
HAYES J M S A 39 LOU W
TRNS FROM WAKE CO
BY AFF TO FRANKLIN CO
HAYES JACK A 39 PUG B
HAYES JAMES A 28 03A B
HAYES JAMES A 35 ROC B
HAYES JAMES A 44 HEN B
HAYES JAMES A 44 YXS B
HAYES JOHN A 28 6TH B
HAYES JOHN A 35 WAR B
HAYES JOHN A 44 TAR B
HAYES JOHN CHAL R 35 ROC B
CONVICTED OF STEALING
HAYES JORDAN A 39 HAY B
HAYES JOS A A 44 HEN W
CERT TO VOTE OUT COUNTY
HAYES LEON A 37 PIN B
HAYES LEWIS A 28 10T B
HAYES LEWIS A 44 FOR B
HAYES NEIL A 29 FA2 B
HAYES NELSON A 44 HEN B
HAYES PETER A 44 FIS W
OXFORD DIST
HAYES S G A 44 KIT W
HAYES WELDON A 44 BEA W
HAYES WILLIAM A 30 ROA W
HAYES WILLIAM A 44 OXF B
HAYES WILLIAM M A 30 ROA W
HAYES WM A A 44 HEN W
CERT TO VOTE OUT OF COUNTY
HAYLE ADNREW A 26 GRI B
HAYLE B M A 26 WAR W
HAYLE D A A 26 WAR W
HAYLE D D A 26 PEE W
HAYLE D R A 26 WAR W
HAYLE DAVID A 26 WAR W
HAYLE HENRY SR A 26 WAR W
HAYLE J C A 26 CAR W
HAYLE JACOB A 26 PEE W
HAYLE JOEL A 26 PEE W
HAYLE JOHN A 26 WAR W
HAYLE JOHN SR A 26 WAR W
HAYLE M H A 26 WAR W
HAYLE MANUEL A 26 GRI B
HAYLE MARTIN A 26 CAR W
HAYLE NICHOLAS A 26 WAR W
HAYLE NOAH A 26 WAR W
HAYLE PETER A 26 WAR W
HAYLE ROBERT A 26 WAR W
HAYLE SOLOMON A 26 WAR W
HAYMAN DANIEL A 30 NOR W
HAYMAN MATTHIAS A 30 ROA W
HAYNES EDEN A 37 HIC A
HAYNES FRANKLIN A 32 POS B
HAYNES JONATHAN A 32 DAV W
HAYNES N N A 26 SHE W
HAYNES TURNER A 28 04A B
HAYS CHARLES A 40 CAN B
HAYS DAVID A 29 FA1 B
HAYS DOCTOR A 39 FRA B
HAYS DUDLEY A 44 SAS B
HAYS FURNEY A 28 13T B
HAYS HARRY A 38 FRE B
HAYS HARRY A 39 FRA B
HAYS JACOB A 39 FRE B
HAYS JACOB A 39 HAR B
HAYS JAMES W A 53 SWA W
HAYS JOHN A 26 GOF W
HAYS JOHN H A 40 DA1 W
HAYS JONATHAN J A 40 MAU W
HAYS STEPHEN A 19 HAR B
HAYS THOMAS A 44 SAS B
HAYS THOMAS S A 46 GRE W
HAYS WILLIAM A 44 SAS B
HAYS WILLIAM L A 40 DA2 W
CERT ISSUED TO
FERGUSON'S PRECINCT
APRIL 10 1868
HAYWARD JAMES A 28 01A W
CERT GRANTED
JONES COUNTY
HAYWOOD ALX A 29 LOC W
HAYWOOD BENJ A 19 BE1 B
HAYWOOD CHARLES F A 30 ROA W
HAYWOOD DAIRY A 28 03A B
HAYWOOD DAVD A 29 LOC W
HAYWOOD HENDERSON A 38 FRE B
HAYWOOD JOSEPH A 24 MID B
HAYWOOD LEVI A 99 BUS B
HAYWOOD POMPEY A 26 BLA B
HAYWOOD THOMAS A 99 BUS B
HAYWORTH ALFRED A 32 BRO W
HAYWORTH ANDREW A 32 BRO W
HAYWORTH ELI A 46 HIG W
HAYWORTH G F A 32 BRO W
HAYWORTH J A A 32 BRO W
HAYWORTH J A A 46 HIG W
HAYWORTH JAMES A 46 HIG W
HAYWORTH JAMES SR A 46 HIG W
HAYWORTH JOHN A 32 BRO W
HAYWORTH LINDSAY A 46 JAM W
HAYWORTH N G R 46 JAM W
NAME LINED OUT
CONSTABLE AND MAGISTRATE
BEFORE THE WAR AIDED
IN REBELLION COULD NOT
TAKE THE OATH WITH THE
WORD VOLUNTARY OMITTED
IS REJECTED
HAYWORTH S S A 32 BRO W
HAYWORTH T B F A 46 JAM W
HAYWORTH W A A 32 BRO W
HAYWORTH W M A 46 HIG W
HAYWORTH W M SR A 46 HIG W
HAYWORTH WILLIAM W A 46 HIG W
HAYZLEWOOD FERRY A 39 FRA B
HAYZLEWOOD HENDSON A 39 FRA B
HAZE GABRIEL A 46 SUM B
HAZE JACOB A 46 KIN B
HAZE RICHARD A 40 SAN B
HAZE SAMUEL A 46 HIG B
HAZEL HENRY A 28 11T B
HAZELL WM A 28 04A B
HAZLE GARRISON A 19 BE1 B
HAZLEWOOD MARCUS A 39 FRA B
HAZLEWOOD MATTHEW A 39 LOU B
HAZLEWOOD SID A 39 FRA B
HEADIN ORRIN A 46 GRE B
HEADING BULAKIE A 44 YXR W
HEADING CALEB A 29 FA1 B
HEADY HAMILTON D A 72 SWA W
HEARN JOHN T A 40 DA1 W
HEART ARTHER A 37 HOL B
HEART JOHN A 37 HOL B
HEART LAWSON A 44 BRA B
HEARTMAN AUTHER D A 19 BE1 W
HEARTSFIELD WM A 39 FRE B
HEATERS JAMES A 28 01A W
HEATH ALFRED L A 28 9TH W
HEATH ARTHUR A 30 IND W
HEATH AUGUSTUS S A 46 GRE W
HEATH BENJAMIN J A 28 7TH W
HEATH BRYAN A 28 9TH W
CERT GIVEN NOW LIVES
AT BIG SWIFT CREEK
HEATH BRYAN M A 28 9TH W

HEATH BRYANT A 28 12T B
HEATH DANCY H A 28 03A B
HEATH EDMUND A 28 8TH W
HEATH ERVIN A 46 GRE W
HEATH G M A 46 SUM W
HEATH HENRY A 35 ALB W
HEATH HENRY A 35 MAG B
HEATH J H A 28 03A B
HEATH J H A 39 LOU W
HEATH JACOB A 35 MAG W
HEATH JAMES A 28 11T W
HEATH JAMES A 28 8TH B
HEATH JAMES DENNIS A 28 8TH B
HEATH JESSE A 28 8TH W
HEATH JOHN A 28 15T B
HEATH JOHN C A 46 MCL W
HEATH JOHN S A 28 6TH W
ROADMASTER
HEATH JOHN W A 46 ROS W
HEATH JOSEPH A 44 YXS B
HEATH JOSEPH C A 46 GRE W
HEATH KINYON A 28 7TH W
HEATH NATHAN A 28 8TH B
HEATH RIGDON R A 28 8TH W
HEATH SAMUEL A 28 7TH B
HEATH SAMUEL S A 46 MCL W
HEATH SILAS S A 28 6TH W
HEATH SMITH A 46 MCL W
HEATH THOMAS B A 35 MAG W
HEATH WILLIAM A A 35 MAG W
HEATH WILLIAM T A 35 MAG W
HEATH WM T A 28 8TH W
HEATHCOCK ALSEY A 46 JAM B
HEATHCOCK DANL A 44 BRA W
HEATHCOCK JOSHUA A 46 JAM B
HEATHCOCK K A 44 DUT W
HEATON DAVID A 28 01A W
HEAVLIN R A A 44 SAS W
HEAVNE JOHN A 28 11T W
HEDDEN A J A 25 HAY W
HEDDEN JOHN B A 25 HAY W
HEDERICK WILLIAM A 32 DAV W
HEDGCOCK DAVID M A 46 HIG W
HEDGCOCK J G A 46 HIG W
HEDGCOCK J T A 46 HIG W
HEDGCOCK JAMES A 46 HIG W
HEDGCOCK JOHN JR A 46 HIG W
HEDGCOCK JOHN P A 46 HIG W
HEDGECOCK BARNET A 32 BRO W
HEDGECOCK DANIEL A 32 BRO W
HEDGECOCK E A 32 BRO W
HEDGECOCK E T A 32 BRO W
HEDGECOCK G S A 32 BRO W
HEDGECOCK J W A 32 BRO W
HEDGECOCK WILLIAM A 32 BRO W
HEDGEPETH J H A 44 OXF W
HEDGEPETH JIM A 39 SPE B
HEDGEPETH JOSEPH A 37 ROB W
HEDGEPITH A P A 39 SPE W
HEDGEPITH A P A 39 SPE W
HEDGPETH GASTON A 44 LED B
HEDGPETH J E A 39 HAY W
HEDGPETH JESSE A 44 LED B
HEDGPETH JOHN F A 39 HAY W
HEDRICK ADAM A 32 DAV W
HEDRICK ADAM A 32 DAV W
HEDRICK ALFORD A 32 COT W
HEDRICK B F A 32 LOF W
HEDRICK BENJAMIN A 32 LOF W
HEDRICK CASPER A 32 LOF W
HEDRICK CASPER A 32 TYR W
HEDRICK CORMADORE D A 32 LOF W
HEDRICK DANIEL A 32 DAV W

HEDRICK DANIEL R A 32 DAV W
HEDRICK DAVID A 32 DAV W
HEDRICK DAVID A 32 YAD B
HEDRICK EPHRAYM A 32 LOF B
HEDRICK G S A 32 LOF W
HEDRICK G W A 32 LOF W
HEDRICK GEORGE A 32 COT W
HEDRICK GEORGE F A 32 DAV W
HEDRICK GEORGE SR A 32 LOF W
HEDRICK H CHAL A 32 LEE W
FOR HOLDING OFFICE OF
MAGISTRATE BEFORE AND
DURING THE WAR. RECON.
HEDRICK HENRY A 32 DAV W
HEDRICK J F A 32 DAV W
HEDRICK JACOB A 32 LOF W
HEDRICK JACOB B A 32 DAV W
HEDRICK JEFERSON A 32 LOF W
HEDRICK JNO OF GEO A 32 DAV W
HEDRICK JOHN A 32 DAV W
HEDRICK JOHN A A 19 BE1 W
HEDRICK JOHN P A 32 DAV W
HEDRICK JOSEPH A 32 DAV W
HEDRICK JOSEPH A 32 DAV W
HEDRICK JOSEPH L A 32 DAV W
HEDRICK M L A 32 LOF W
HEDRICK MICHAEL A 32 LOF W
HEDRICK NOAH A 32 DAV W
HEDRICK P E A 32 LOF W
HEDRICK PETER A 32 DAV B
HEDRICK PETER A 32 JAC W
HEDRICK PHILIP A 32 LOF W
HEDRICK RICHARD S A 24 EDE W
HEDRICK SAMUEL A 32 LOF B
HEDRICK THOMAS A 32 LOF B
HEDRICK WILEY A 32 DAV W
HEDRICK WILLIAM A 32 THO W
HEDRICK WM S A 24 EDE W
HEDSPETH WM A 44 FIS W
HEESNER DAVID A 32 JAC W
HEFLIN H H A 44 BRA W
HEFLIN LEWIS A 44 BRA W
HEFNER J RUFUS A 40 MAU W
HEFNER JACOB A 40 BLA W
HEFNER MARTIN A 40 BLA W
HEFNER PETER A 40 BLA W
HEGE A C CHAL A 32 DAV W
FOR HOLDING OFFICE OF
POSTMASTER BEFORE AND
DURING THE WAR.
HEGE ALEXANDER A 32 DAV W
HEGE G W A 32 YAD W
HEGGIE C A 44 SAS W
HEGGIE J M A 44 SAS W
HEGINS JESSIE A 32 DAV B
HEGPETH MOSES A 44 DUT B
HEIDE R E R 29 FA1 W
NATURALIZED FOREIGNER
AIDED REBELLION
HEIDELBURG HENRY A 28 05A B
HEITMAN C B A 32 SHE W
HEITMAN JNO A A 32 DAV W
HELAT ENOCH A 35 ISL W
HELAT WILLIAM H A 35 ISL W
HELLEN J A A 28 01A W
HELMS JACOB A 40 BLA W
HELMS JOHN A 26 BOR W
HELMSTITER HANADLE A 32 DAV W
HELMSTITER JOHN A 32 DAV W
HELTON E J A 26 MOU W
HELTON J W A 32 THO W
HELTON JOHN A 46 SUM B
HELTON JOHN E A 32 THO W

HELTON JOSEPHUS A 32 THO W
HELTON LORENZO A 32 THO W
HELTON MILTON B A 40 DA1 W
HELTON THOMAS E A 32 THO W
HELTON W W A 40 STO W
HEMES ANTHONY A 32 YAD B
HEMMINGS ELIHU W A 28 16T W
HEMMINGS ROBT L A 28 16T W
HEMPHILL CLINTON A 46 ROS W
HEMPHILL JOHN A 46 RAG W
HEMPHILL MILTON A 46 ROS W
HEMPHILL ROBT A 46 RAG W
HEMPHILL SIMPSON A 46 ROS W
HENDERSON HEZEKIAH A 35 CYP W
HENDERSON A B A 46 HIG W
HENDERSON A E A 44 ISL W
HENDERSON A L A 40 SAN W
COPIED FROM DUPLICATE
HENDERSON A R A 40 CAN W
HENDERSON AB J A 29 FA1 B
HENDERSON ABRAHAM A 29 FA1 B
HENDERSON ALEXANDER A 28 10T B
HENDERSON ALFRED A 44 TOW B
HENDERSON AUGUSTUS LA 40 DA2 W
CERT ISSUED TO
1ST REG PRECINCT
APR 10 1868
HENDERSON AVEL A 44 SAS B
HENDERSON CEPHUS A 32 DAV B
HENDERSON D L A 29 GRA W
HENDERSON DANIEL A 35 CYP W
HENDERSON DAVID A 46 HIG W
HENDERSON DEMPSY A 37 PIN B
HENDERSON DOCTOR A 44 HEN B
HENDERSON DR W F A 44 HEN W
HENDERSON E H A 28 03A W
HENDERSON EDWD A 28 04A B
HENDERSON ELIJAH A 35 CYP W
HENDERSON ELIJAH A 35 MAG W
HENDERSON FREDERICK A 44 TOW B
HENDERSON GEORGE A 29 FA1 B
HENDERSON HARRY A 44 HEN B
HENDERSON ISAAC A 37 ROB B
HENDERSON ISHAM A 44 OXF B
HENDERSON J A A 44 LED W
OF BRASSFIELDS
HENDERSON J A CHAL R 40 CAN W
REJ WAS A JUSTICE OF THE
PEACE AND AFTERWARDS WAS
ENGAGED IN INSURRECTION
AND REBELLION AGAINST
THE UNITED STATES
BY ENCOURAGING THE REBE-
LION AND HUNTING
CONSCRIPS AND DESERTERS
HENDERSON JAMES 40 DA1 B
STRICKEN OUT APR 10 1868
HENDERSON JAMES A 25 TUS W
HENDERSON JAMES A 44 HEN B
HENDERSON JAMES M A 35 CYP W
HENDERSON JEREMIAH A 35 MAG W
HENDERSON JESSIE A 37 ROB B
HENDERSON JNO A 44 ISL B
HENDERSON JOHN A 37 ROB B
HENDERSON JOHN A 37 ROB B
HENDERSON JOHN A 40 MAU B
HENDERSON JONES S A 53 LA1 W
HENDERSON JORDON A 32 POS B
HENDERSON JOSEPH A 44 TOW B
HENDERSON KITT A 44 HEN B
HENDERSON LEAPOLD A 44 HEN W
HENDERSON LEWIS A 44 TOW B
HENDERSON M A A 40 CAN W

HENDERSON MARK A 46 GRE B
HENDERSON NELSON A 29 FA1 B
HENDERSON NELSON A 44 SAS B
HENDERSON NICKSON A 35 CYP W
HENDERSON OLIVER A 19 BE1 B
HENDERSON OWEN A 72 SWA W
HENDERSON PETER A 44 TOW B
HENDERSON RALPH A 44 HEN B
HENDERSON ROBERT A 44 HEN B
HENDERSON ROBERT A 44 HEN B
HENDERSON ROBERT F A 40 FER W
HENDERSON ROBT R 44 OXF B
RES 7 MOS REJ
HENDERSON S C A 46 HIG W
HENDERSON S W A 35 CYP W
HENDERSON SHADRACK A 28 05A B
HENDERSON SIMON A 19 BE1 B
HENDERSON STEPHEN A 44 HEN B
HENDERSON STERLING A 44 HEN B
HENDERSON THOMAS A 35 CYP W
HENDERSON THOMAS A 44 HEN B
HENDERSON THOS B A 28 01A W
HENDERSON WALTER A 37 ROC W
HENDERSON WILLIAM A 32 DAV W
CHAL FOR HOLDING OFFICE
OF MAGISTRATE BEFORE AND
DURING THE WAR. RECON.
HENDERSON WILLIAM A 37 ROB B
HENDERSON WM A 28 04A B
HENDERSON WM A 40 CAN B
HENDLY J A A 39 FRA W
HENDRICK B A 26 GRI W
HENDRICK C A 26 CAR W
HENDRICK EUSEBUOUS A 26 SHE W
HENDRICK GEORGE K A 46 ROS W
HENDRICK J A A 26 SHE W
HENDRICK JAMES A 26 GRI W
HENDRICK W D A 26 SHE W
HENDRICK WM H A 19 BE1 W
HENDRICKS E A A 29 FA1 W
HENDRICKS J T S A 32 THO W
HENDRICKS NATHANIEL A 24 MID B
HENDRICKS THOS A A 29 FA1 W
HENDRICKS WM T A 24 MID W
HENDRIX ALFRED M A 46 GRE W
HENDRIX ANDREW A 46 GRE B
HENDRIX JOHN T A 46 GRE W
HENDRIX MILTON C A 46 ROS W
HENDRIX THOMAS F A 46 ROS W
HENDRIX TOBIAS A 32 THO W
HENGSON HENRY A 37 ROC W
HENING LOFTEN A 29 FLE B
HENLEY BURRIL A 44 FOR W
HENLEY CAREY A 44 FOR W
HENLEY DAVID V A 46 JAM W
HENLEY HENRY JR A 44 FOR W
HENLEY HENRY SR A 44 FOR W
HENLEY WILLIAM A 44 FOR W
HENLEY WM A 44 FOR W
HENLY ALEXANDER A 32 TYR B
HENLY DANUL A 32 TYR B
HENNY CHARLES A 32 THO W
HENREYS HENRY W A 28 16T W
HENREYS JOSEPH N A 28 16T W
HENREYS LEWIS D A 28 16T W
HENRIES SAMUEL A 53 FAI W
HENRY BENJ A 28 05A B
HENRY CHARLES A 24 EDE B
HENRY CHARLES H A 19 BE1 B
HENRY CHAS A 28 03A B
HENRY CULBERT A 19 BE1 B
HENRY DANIEL A 19 BE1 B
HENRY DANIEL A 19 MOR B

HENRY F L A 40 STO B
HENRY FRANK A 29 FA1 B
HENRY J B A 28 03A W
HENRY J W A 39 JOR W
HENRY J W A 40 SAN W
HENRY JERRY A 37 ROC B
HENRY JOEL A 28 03A W
HENRY JOHN A 19 BE1 B
HENRY JOHN A 28 10T B
HENRY JOHN A 39 GRI W
HENRY JOHN E A 19 BE1 B
HENRY JOHN W A 19 BE1 B
HENRY JOHN W A 19 BE1 B
HENRY LEVI A 40 DA1 B
HENRY OLIVER N A 19 BE1 B
HENRY PERO A 19 BE1 B
HENRY R M A 24 MID W
HENRY R N A 40 STO W
HENRY REDICK A 37 ROC B
HENRY RICHARDS A 44 SAS B
HENRY SAMUEL A 25 HAY B
HENRY SAMUEL A 39 JOR W
HENRY THOS A A 28 01A W
HENRY WILLIAM A 19 NEW B
HENSDEL WM B A 24 MID W
HENSHAW GEORGE A 46 JAM B
HENSHAW J J A 19 MOR W
HENSON EDWARD A 25 SHO W
HENSON GEORGE A 25 PIN W
HENSON PHILIP A 37 ROC B
HENSON THOMAS A 25 SHO W
HENTER MILTON A 40 CAN B
HEOVINER PETER A 26 GRI W
HEPLAR JOSEPH A 32 THO W
HEPLAR R P A 32 THO W
HEPLAR SAMUL JONES A 32 THO W
HEPLAR SOLOMAN A 32 THO W
HEPLER D H A 32 LEE W
HEPLER GEORGE A 32 LEE W
HEPLER JOHN A 32 BRO W
HEPLER JOHN A 32 LEE W
HEPLER S L A 32 LEE W
HEPLER THOMAS A 32 LEE W
HERBERT BEN A 25 HAY B
HERBERT D S R 25 HAY W
FOR HOLDING OFFICE IN
TIME OF WAR TO KEEP OUT
OF WAR
HERBERT LONDON A 25 HAY B
HERBIN AARON R 46 MON B
CAUSE PUNISHED
FOR STEALING
HERBIN ROBT A 46 MON W
HERINGTON G M A 26 SHE W
HERINGTON J P A 26 SHE W
HERITAGE ADAM JR A 28 03A B
HERITAGE ADAM SR A 28 03A B
HERITAGE JOHN L A 28 03A W
HERITAGE WM W A 46 MCL W
HERNDON BUCK A 44 OXF B
HERNDON CHARLES A 44 OXF B
HERNDON D C A 44 OXF W
HERNDON H C A 44 OXF W
HERNDON JAMES A 44 LED B
HERNDON NAT A 44 OXF B
HERNDON PASON A 44 OXF B
HERNDON PETER A 44 OXF B
HERNDON RUFUS A 44 OXF B
HERNDON SANDY A 44 KIT B
HERNDON SHACK A 44 HEN B
HERNDON WILLIAM A 26 GOF W
HERNDON WM H A 26 GOF W
HERRELL HENRY A 19 HAR W

HERRING AARON A 28 7TH B
HERRING ALEXANDER A 35 GLI W
HERRING ALFRED A 37 TA1 B
HERRING ANDREW A 35 ISL B
HERRING ANDREW A 35 ROC B
HERRING BENJAMIN A 35 ROC B
HERRING BRYANT A 29 GRA B
HERRING CALVIN A 35 GLI W
HERRING CESAR A 35 MAG B
HERRING DANIEL A 35 MAG B
HERRING DANIEL A 35 MAG B
HERRING DAVID A 35 GLI B
HERRING E B A 35 GLI W
HERRING ENOCH A 29 FA1 W
HERRING EVERETT A 35 KEN W
HERRING GEORGE A 35 KEN B
HERRING HARDY A 35 MAG B
HERRING ISAAC A 35 ROC B
HERRING ISAAC JR A 35 GLI B
HERRING J F A 35 GLI W
HERRING J S A 29 CED W
HERRING J W A 35 ALB W
HERRING JAMES SCOTT A 35 MAG B
HERRING JOSEPH A 28 04A B
HERRING JOSEPH A 35 ISL B
HERRING LEWIS A 28 6TH B
HERRING LEWIS H A 35 KEN W
HERRING LOUIS A 35 GLI W
HERRING MOSES A 28 6TH B
HERRING NEEDHAM A 35 KEN W
HERRING OWEN A 29 GRA B
HERRING QUINNY A 28 04A B
HERRING RICHARD A 35 KEN B
HERRING RICHARD A 35 ROC B
HERRING RICHD A 28 04A B
HERRING ROBERT A 35 MAG B
HERRING STEPHEN A 35 KEN W
HERRING STEPHEN A 35 ROC W
HERRING THOMAS J A 35 MAG W
CERT TO
WHITEVILLE 16 AP. 1868
HERRING URIAH A 35 GLI W
HERRING VALENTINE A 35 KEN B
HERRING WILLIAM A 35 GLI B
HERRING WILLIAM A 35 GLI W
HERRING WILLIAM SR A 35 GLI W
HERRINGTON BENSON R A 53 SWA W
HERSEY J R A A 29 FA1 W
HERSSHINER WASH A 29 FLE B
HERTMAN A M A 32 DAV W
HERTMAN H N CHAL A 32 DAV W
FOR HOLDING OFFICE OF SU-
PERIOR COURT CLERK BEFORE
AND DURING WAR. RECON.
HERTMAN WILLIAM A A 32 DAV W
HESTER ABRAHAM A 44 OXF B
HESTER ALEX A 44 OXF B
HESTER ALFRED G A 44 YXR W
HESTER ALLEN A 44 OXF B
HESTER ANDERSON A 44 OXF B
HESTER B B A 44 BEA W
HESTER B F A 44 OXF W
HESTER BENJAMIN A 19 MOR B
HESTER BURWELL A 44 OXF B
HESTER CALVIN A 44 DUT B
HESTER CHARLES A 44 YXR B
HESTER DANIEL A 44 OXF B
HESTER DANL A 44 BEA B
HESTER DANL A 44 BEA B
HESTER DR C J H W A 44 HEN W
HESTER ELIC A 44 OXF B
HESTER F A 44 YXR W
HESTER F B A 44 OXF W

HESTER F G A 44 OXF W
HESTER F K A 44 OXF W
HESTER GEO W A 44 TOW W
HESTER GEORGE A 44 LED B
HESTER GEORGE A 44 SAS W
HESTER GREEN A 44 OXF B
HESTER GREEN A 44 YXS B
HESTER HAYWOOD A 44 DUT B
HESTER HENRY A 44 OXF B
HESTER HENRY A 44 YXS B
HESTER HENRY J A 44 YXR W
HESTER ISAAC A 44 RAG B
HESTER J P A 44 BEA W
HESTER J W A 44 DUT W
HESTER JAMES A 44 OXF B
HESTER JERRY A 44 DUT B
HESTER JOHN A 44 OXF B
HESTER JOHN H A 44 TOW W
HESTER JORDEN A 44 DUT B
HESTER JOSEPH A 44 OXF B
HESTER M H A 44 OXF W
HESTER MATHEW A 44 SAS W
HESTER MERION H A 44 OXF W
HESTER MOSES A 44 OXF B
HESTER MOSES M A 39 FRA B
HESTER NAPPER A 44 OXF B
HESTER RICHARD JR A 44 OXF B
HESTER RICHD A 44 OXF B
HESTER ROBT A 44 OXF B
HESTER SHADRICK A 44 OXF B
HESTER SILAS A 44 BRA B
HESTER SOLOMON A 44 SAS B
HESTER STARLIN A 44 OXF B
HESTER T D A 44 HEN W
HESTER W H JR A 39 FRA W
HESTER W H M A 39 FRE W
HESTER W S A 44 YXS W
HESTER WILLIAM A 44 OXF B
HESTER WM H A 44 OXF B
HESTER WM S A 44 OXF W
HESTER WOODFIN A 44 OXF B
HETFIELD JACOB A 30 POP B
HEUGHS ALSON A 32 LEE W
HEUGHS J R A 32 LOF W
HEUGHS JAMES A 32 DAV W
HEUGHS JAMES A 32 LOF W
HEUGHS JOHN W A 32 LEE W
HEUGHS PHILIP A 32 DAV W
HEUGHS WILLIAM A 32 DAV W
HEWELL JACOB A 28 01A B
HEWELL JACOB A 30 ROA B
HEWELL THOS A 29 FA2 W
HEYMEN HENRY A 37 ROC B
HEYWOOD A H A 28 01A W
HEYWOOD JOHN D A 28 01A W
HEYWOOD SANDY A 37 EDW B
HIATT ABRAM A 46 GRE B
HIATT ALLEN A 46 HIG W
HIATT BARTLETT Y A 46 HIG W
HIATT FOUNTAIN A 46 GRE B
HIATT J E A 46 FRI W
HIATT JESSE A 46 FRI W
HIATT JOB A 46 HIG W
HIATT JOHN A 32 SHE W
HIATT JOSEPH A 32 POS W
HIATT MARTIN J A 46 GRE B
HIATT PHILANDER F A 46 GRE W
HIATT RICHARD A 46 GRE B
HIATT W A 46 GRE B
HIATT WESLEY A 32 DAV W
HIATT WILEY A 32 POS W
HIATT WILLIAM A 46 HIG W
HIATT WILLIS A 32 DAV W
HIATT WILSON A 46 HIG W
HIATT ZEBULON A 46 HIG W
HIBBARD CHAS A 28 03A W
HIBBS H W A 19 NEW W
HICKMAN HENRY P A 28 03A B
HICKMAN JAMES A 28 9TH B
HICKMAN ROBERT A 32 TYR B
HICKS A R JR A 35 FAI W
HICKS ABRAHAM A 44 OXF B
HICKS ALFRED A 35 FAI B
HICKS ALFRED A 44 RAG B
HICKS ANDREW A 29 FAI B
HICKS ARMSTEAD A 44 RAG B
HICKS B W A 44 OXF W
HICKS BEN A 39 SPE B
HICKS BURTON A 25 HAY W
COPIED FROM DUPLICATE
HICKS C G A 26 MOO W
HICKS CHARLES A 35 FAI B
HICKS CHARLES A 44 OXF B
HICKS CORNELIUS A 46 JAM B
HICKS DANIEL A 26 SHE W
HICKS DAVID A 44 BRA B
HICKS EDMOND A 44 OXF B
HICKS EDMUND A 28 05A B
HICKS EDWARD A 28 01B B
HICKS ELLIS A 28 9TH B
HICKS ELY A 35 FAI B
HICKS EMANUEL A 44 YXS B
HICKS EVERETT A 28 03A B
HICKS F Y A 26 GRI W
HICKS GEO N A 44 OXF W
HICKS GEORGE A 35 WOL B
HICKS H C A 44 OXF W
HICKS H N A 44 BRA W
HICKS HARTLESS A 44 SAS B
HICKS HENRY A 35 FAI B
HICKS HENRY A 44 OXF B
HICKS HENRY A 44 TAR B
HICKS HILLIARD A 19 BE1 B
HICKS HOWELL A 44 OXF B
HICKS ISAAC A 44 HEN B
HICKS J M A 25 TUS W
HICKS JAMES A 28 04A B
HICKS JAMES A 44 HEN B
HICKS JAMES A 44 OXF B
HICKS JAMES L A 39 HAR W
HICKS JEFF A 44 RAG B
HICKS JNO A 44 SAS B
HICKS JNO W A 44 ISL W
HICKS JOHN B A 44 RAG W
HICKS JOHN P A 25 SHO W
HICKS JORDAN A 44 HEN B
HICKS JOSEPH C A 37 PIN W
HICKS JUDSON A 44 FOR B
HICKS L H A 44 BRA W
HICKS LEVY A 35 FAI B
HICKS LEWIS A 29 FA1 B
HICKS LEWIS A 39 HAY B
HICKS LEWIS A 44 OXF B
HICKS LUKE A 28 03A B
HICKS MACY A 39 LOU W
FROM R A SPEED'S
HICKS MACY A 39 SPE W
HICKS MILES A 44 HEN B
HICKS PETE A 39 HAY B
HICKS PETER A 28 03A B
HICKS PRINCE A 37 PEN B
FASON DEPOT
HICKS R A A 39 FRE W
HICKS RICHARD A 44 SAS B
HICKS RICHIE A 37 HOL W
HICKS ROBT J A 44 HEN W
HICKS RUSSELL A 39 HAY B
HICKS SILAS A 39 HAY B
HICKS SIMON A 44 RAG B
HICKS SQUIRE A 44 SAS B
HICKS STEPHEN A 25 TUS W
HICKS THOMAS A 39 SPE B
HICKS THOS W A 44 RAG W
HICKS TOMSON A 37 ROC W
HICKS W A A 25 TUS W
HICKS WILLIAM A 26 GOF W
HICKS WILLIAM A 99 BUS W
HICKS WILLIAM CHAL A 44 SAS B
HICKS WILLIAM H A 99 BUS W
HICKS WILLIS A 26 MOO W
HICKS WM A 28 03A B
HICKS WM A 28 05A B
HICKS WM A 44 OXF B
HICKS WM H A 44 TAR W
HIDE JAMES T A 37 EDW W
HIDLEBERG JACOB A 28 9TH B
HIGGINS EDWARD B A 46 ROS W
HIGGINS HILLIARD A 37 PIN B
HIGGINS JOHN A 24 EDE W
HIGGINS JOSEPH A 72 SWA B
HIGGINS JOSIAH A 37 PIN B
HIGGINS W T A 25 TUS W
HIGGINS WILEY F A 28 01A W
HIGGS ALLEN A 44 FIS B
HIGGS JORDAN A 44 KIT B
HIGGS MERRYMAN A 44 HEN B
HIGHFILL HENRY A 46 SUM W
HIGHFILL HEZEKIAH A 46 SUM W
HIGHFILL JAMES A 46 MON W
HIGHFILL JEREMIAH A 46 SUM W
CAUSE MILITIA OFFICER
BEFORE WAS REJ BY HIS
OWN REQUEST
HIGHFILL JOHN A 46 SUM W
HIGHFILL W F A 46 SUM W
HIGHFILL WM A 46 FRI W
HIGHSMITH CURTIS A 35 ROC B
HIGHSMITH JERE A 35 ROC B
HIGHSMITH JEREMIAH A 35 MAG B
HIGHSMITH PETER A 35 ROC B
HIGHSMITH SAMEUL A 35 ROC B
HIGHSMITH SYLVESTER A 35 ROC B
HIGHT BENJA A 44 KIT B
HIGHT EDWARD A 44 KIT B
HIGHT H A 44 KIT W
HIGHT H H A 39 HAY W
HIGHT H H A 44 FIS W
HIGHT H T A 39 HAY W
HIGHT HENDERSON A 39 HAY B
HIGHT ISHAM A 44 KIT B
HIGHT J H A 39 PUG W
HIGHT J R A 38 FRE W
HIGHT REDDIC A 44 KIT W
HIGHT REDDING A 44 KIT W
HIGHT ROBT A 39 FRA W
HIGHT SANDY A 39 LOU B
HIGHT T D A 44 HEN W
HIGHT THOS G A 39 FRA W
HIGHT WM M A 44 KIT W
HIGSON GEORGE A 53 FAI B
HIGSON JOHN A 53 FAI W
HIGSON SAMUEL A 53 FAI B
HILDERSHEMER JOS A 46 GRE W
HILDRITH A F A 19 BE1 W
HILL A A A 32 DAV W
HILL AARON A 35 WAR B
HILL AARON A 44 KIT B
HILL ABNER A 35 FAI B
HILL ABRAHAM A 28 11T B

HILL ABRAM A 24 EDE B
HILL ADAM A 35 WAR B
HILL ALEXANDER A 32 POS W
HILL ALEXANDER A 35 FAI B
HILL ALLEN A 35 FAI B
HILL ALVIN A 28 04A B
HILL ANDERSON A 28 6TH B
HILL ASA A 37 ROC W
HILL ASBERRY A 37 WHI B
HILL ASBURY A 37 HIG W
HILL ATLAS A 29 FA1 W
HILL BENJAMIN A 37 MAN B
HILL BENJAMIN A 46 HIG B
HILL BENJAMIN H A 53 LA1 B
HILL BOLIVAR A 40 FER B
HILL BRYANT A 28 03A B
HILL BURL A 37 ROC B
HILL C W A 19 HAD W
HILL CAESAR A 28 04A B
HILL CALHOUN A 35 WOL W
HILL CALVIN A 28 6TH B
HILL CAREY A 37 PEN B
HILL CEAZER A 19 NEW B
HILL CHARLES A 28 04A B
HILL CHARLES A 30 NOR W
HILL CHARLES A 37 MAN B
HILL CHAS A 28 04A B
HILL CHRISTDORE A 28 05A B
HILL CLARKE A 44 YXS B
HILL CLEM A 35 FAI B
HILL COY A 35 LIM B
HILL D W A 32 LOF W
HILL DANIEL S R 39 LOU W
STRICKEN OUT APRIL 10TH
1868 CHAL FOR BEING A
JUSTICE OF PEACE FROM
1841 TO COMMENCEMENT
OF THE WAR AND A J P
AGAIN UNTIL 1867
HILL DANILE A 37 MAN B
HILL DAVID A 39 HAY B
HILL DAVY A 72 SWA B
HILL DICK A 37 PEN B
HILL DOLPHUS A 39 PUG B
HILL DONAM A 19 NEW B
HILL ED H JR A 28 04A B
HILL EDEN A 28 04A B
HILL EDMON A 46 GRE B
HILL EDMOND A 28 04A B
HILL EDMOND A 46 FRI B
HILL EDMOND A 53 FAI B
HILL EDMUND A 28 05A B
HILL EDWARD A 28 01B W
HILL EDWARD A 28 10T B
HILL EDWARD A 35 KEN B
HILL EDWARD H A 28 7TH B
HILL EDWARD M A 19 SMY W
HILL ELIJAH A 25 HAY W
HILL ENOCH A 35 FAI B
HILL ESSEX A 35 WAR B
HILL FRANK A 28 04A B
HILL FRIDAY A 35 FAI B
HILL GEO W A 28 6TH W
HILL GEORGE A 28 05A B
HILL GEORGE A 28 05B B
HILL GEORGE A 35 FAI B
HILL GEORGE A 39 JOR B
HILL GEORGE W A 32 SHE W
HILL GREEN A 28 04A B
HILL GREENE A 37 SHA W
HILL H B A 19 NEW W
HILL H G A 29 FA2 W
HILL H H A 32 SHE W

HILL HARDY A 37 ROC W
HILL HARMON A 19 HUN W
HILL HARVEY A 46 SUM B
HILL HENRY A 28 01A B
HILL HENRY A 28 03A B
HILL HENRY A 28 9TH B
HILL HENRY A 32 JAC W
HILL HENRY A 32 SHE W
HILL HENRY A 35 FAI B
HILL HENRY A 39 HAR B
HILL HORACE A 35 FAI B
HILL ISAAC A 30 TUL B
HILL ISAAC A 32 SHE W
HILL ISAAC A 35 FAI B
HILL ISAAC A 37 HIG W
HILL ISAAC A 44 DUT B
HILL ISAAC S A 19 NEW W
HILL ISAM A A 53 GER W
HILL ISHAM J A 44 OXF B
HILL IVY A 35 FAI B
HILL J L A 28 11T W
HILL JACKSON A 28 04A B
HILL JACKSON A 32 SHE W
HILL JACOB A 37 MAN B
HILL JAMES A 28 10T W
HILL JAMES A 35 WAR B
HILL JAMES A 39 HAR B
HILL JAMES B A 37 HIG W
HILL JAMES R A 37 WHI B
HILL JEFFERSON A 35 FAI B
HILL JERREMIAH A 25 HAY W
HILL JESSE A 32 DAV W
HILL JESSEE A 29 GRA B
HILL JOE A 28 04A B
HILL JOE 2ND A 28 04A B
HILL JOHN A 19 POR W
HILL JOHN A 30 NOR W
HILL JOHN A 32 CLE W
HILL JOHN A 32 SHE W
HILL JOHN A 35 WAR B
HILL JOHN A 53 LA2 B
HILL JOHN B A 19 SMY W
HILL JOHN B A 35 WAR B
HILL JOHN D A 32 LOF W
HILL JOHN J A 19 HAD B
HILL JOHN W A 19 BE1 B
HILL JOHN W JR A 19 POR W
HILL JOHN W SR A 19 POR W
HILL JONARS A 19 NEW B
HILL JOSEPH A 28 11T W
HILL JOSEPH A 35 LIM B
HILL JOSEPH A 37 ROC B
HILL JOSEPH R 44 SAS B
8 MOTHS REJ
HILL JOSEPH A A 19 POR W
HILL JOSHUA A 30 NOR W
HILL JOSIAH A 35 WAR B
HILL KALEN A 32 SHE W
HILL LARRY S A 28 04A B
HILL LAZERUS A 32 THO W
CERTIF
HILL LEANDER A 40 DA1 B
HILL LEVI A 32 JAC W
HILL MARCUS A 37 SHA W
HILL MARSHALL A 28 11T W
HILL MARTIN A 39 LOU B
HILL MELBA A 32 JAC W
HILL MOSES A 19 MOR B
HILL MOSES A 35 FAI B
HILL MOSES A 72 SWA B
HILL MOSES D A 28 04A B
CERTIFICATE GRANTED
IVES PR

HILL NATHAN A 29 LOC B
HILL NATHANIEL A 37 SHA W
HILL OWEN A 35 WOL B
HILL PETER A 19 BE1 B
HILL PETER A 28 05A B
HILL PHILLIP A 46 SUM B
HILL PRINCE A 37 MAN B
HILL R R A 28 01A W
HILL RANSOM A 35 FAI B
HILL RANSOM A 39 HAY B
HILL RICHD A 28 05A B
HILL ROBT A 29 FA1 B
HILL ROBT A 46 GRE B
HILL ROYAL A 35 FAI B
HILL RUFUS A 28 6TH B
HILL RUFUS A A 46 GIB W
HILL SAMUEL A 19 HAD B
HILL SAMUEL A 19 NEW B
HILL SAMUEL A 28 05A B
HILL SAMUEL A 32 JAC W
HILL SAMUEL A 35 FAI B
HILL SAMUEL A 53 GER B
HILL SILVESTER A 30 TUL W
HILL SMAUEL A 40 FER B
HILL SOLN A 28 04A B
HILL SPAIGHT A 35 WOL B
HILL SQUIRE A 28 04A B
HILL SQUIRE A 35 FAI B
HILL STEPHEN A 28 03A B
HILL THOMAS A 19 NEW W
HILL THOMAS A 30 ROA B
HILL THOMAS A 35 KEN W
HILL TUNSTALL A 39 LOU B
HILL VIRGIL A 35 WAR B
HILL VOLENTINE A 32 SHE W
HILL W A A 26 MOU W
HILL W D A 39 FRA W
HILL W H A 39 LOU W
TRANS FROM WAKE CO
FORESVILLE PRE BY AFF
HILL WADE A 26 BOR W
HILL WESLEY A 39 FRA W
HILL WILLIAM A 19 BE1 B
HILL WILLIAM A 19 HUN W
HILL WILLIAM A 19 MOR B
HILL WILLIAM A 28 11T B
HILL WILLIAM A 28 11T W
HILL WILLIAM A 32 JAC W
HILL WILLIAM A 32 SHE W
HILL WILLIAM A 35 FAI B
HILL WILLIAM A 40 DEC B
HILL WILLIAM F A 53 FAI B
HILL WILLIAM H A 72 SWA W
HILL WILLIS A 37 MAN B
HILL WM A 19 NEW W
HILL WM H A 19 POR W
HILL WM W A 44 YXS W
HILL WRIGHT A 35 FAI B
HILL YORK A 28 04A B
HILL ZACKARIAH A 53 GER B
HILLARD JACOB A 37 MAN B
HILLARD JACOB A 37 MAN B
HILLIAMS EDMUND A 28 05A B
HILLIARD B F A 32 DAV W
HILLIARD FRANCIS W A 24 EDE W
HILLIARD GEO W A 29 ROC W
HILLIARD RICHMOND A 39 SPE B
HILLIARD S R A 44 HEN W
CERT GRANTED TO
VOTE OUT OF COUNTY
HILLIARD THOMAS A 37 HIG B
HILLIARD WILLIAM A 37 PEN B
HILLIARD WM A 39 FRA B

HILLRED THOMAS A 37 MAN B
HILMON SMITH A 44 SAS B
HILTON CYRUS A 32 THO W
HILTON J B A 28 01A W
HILTON JAMES A 32 THO W
HILTON JAMES F A 32 THO W
HILTON JAMES M A 46 SUM W
HILTON JOHN W A 28 01A W
HILTON LEMUEL A 46 JAM W
HILTON R H A 28 01A W
HILTON RANDALL A 32 THO W
HILTON TRUMAN A 32 THO W
HILTON ZEBELON A 32 THO W
HIMMON WILLIAM A 25 TUS W
HIMSEY J A 25 HAY W
HINCHA HARRISON A 28 04A B
HINCLE DAVID A 32 DAV W
HINE ANDREW A 32 POS W
HINER JOHN A 32 THO W
HINES A D A 39 DAV W
HINES ABRAHAM A 28 15T B
HINES ABRAM A 37 HIG B
HINES ALLAN A 37 HIG B
HINES ANDREW A 46 MON B
HINES ASHLEY A 28 15T B
HINES AUSTIN A 28 04A B
HINES AUTRY A 37 HIG B
HINES BENJAMIN A 37 EDW B
HINES BLUNT A 37 HIG B
HINES BRYANT A 28 9TH B
HINES CHARLES A 28 11T B
HINES CHARLES A 37 HIG B
HINES CHARLES A 37 WHI B
HINES CHARLES C A 35 ALB W
HINES DANIEL S A 40 MAU W
HINES DANILE A 37 MAN B
HINES DOLPHIS A 37 HIG B
HINES E D A 46 MON W
HINES EDWARD A 44 SAS W
HINES ELIAS A 28 03A B
HINES G W A 39 DAV W
HINES GEORGE A 40 MAU W
HINES GUILBERT A 37 HIG B
HINES GUILBERT A 37 SPA B
HINES H A A 39 DAV W
HINES HARDY A 37 PEN B
HINES HAYWOOD A 37 HIG B
HINES HENDERSON A 37 PIN B
HINES HENRY A 37 TA1 B
HINES HILLIARD R 37 TA1 B
CONVICTED OF LARCENY
HINES ISAAC A 35 CYP W
HINES ISAAC A 37 HIG B
HINES J C A 44 FIS W
HINES J J A 39 DAV W
HINES JAMES A 37 WHI B
HINES JERRY A 37 HIG B
HINES JOHN A 28 8TH B
HINES JOHN A 37 ROC B
HINES JOHN A 37 ROC W
HINES JOHN A 44 YXS B
HINES JOHN R A 46 GRE W
HINES JOSHUA A 37 HIG B
HINES LEWIS A 37 EDW B
HINES LOT A 28 03A B
HINES MOSES A 28 04A B
HINES MOSES A 28 04B B
HINES MOSES M A 40 DEC W
HINES NEPTON A 37 PIN B
HINES REDDIN A 39 FRA W
HINES SIMON A 28 6TH B
HINES THOS C A 44 KIT W
HINES W G A 46 MON W
HINES WILLIAM A 37 SPA B
HINES WILLIAM A 39 DAV B
HINES WILLIAM A 46 MON W
HINES WILLIS A 37 ROC B
HINES WRIGHT A 28 04A B
HINEY WILLIS A 39 DAV B
HINKEL OSBURN A 40 CAN W
HINKLE CHRISTIAN A 32 DAV W
HINKLE EMANUEL A 32 DAV W
HINKLE MATTHIAS A 32 DAV W
HINKLE MATTHIAS A 32 DAV W
HINKLE RANSOM A 32 DAV W
HINNANT W R A 39 HAR W
HINNIE W J A 29 FLE W
HINSDALE JNO W A 29 FA1 W
HINSDALE S J A 29 FA1 W
HINSHAW A B A 46 JAM W
HINSON JOHN A 37 HOL B
HINTON ABRAHAM A 44 OXF B
HINTON ALONZO A A 46 GRE W
HINTON CALVIN A 24 EDE B
HINTON CASWELL A 99 BUS B
HINTON DAVID A 24 EDE B
HINTON EDMOND A 26 GOF B
HINTON GEORGE A 37 MAN B
HINTON JAMES H A 37 HIG W
HINTON JOHN A 37 HOL B
HINTON JOHN A 99 BUS B
HINTON JOSHUA T A 24 EDE B
HINTON MARK A 37 HOL B
HINTON MICHL A 28 05A B
HINTON NEAL A 37 HOL B
HINTON PRIME A 37 HOL B
HINTON RICHARD A 37 PEN B
HINTON ROBT A 39 FRA B
HINTON RUFFUS A 39 LOU B
HINTON SOLOMON A 37 HOL B
HINTON W J A 44 HEN W
HINTON WM A 44 TOW B
HIPP THOMAS A 40 STO W
HISKINS EDMOND A 19 BE1 B
HITCHCOCK ALFRED A A 46 HIG W
HITCHCOCK H H A 28 01A W
HITCHCOCK JOSHUA A 32 BRO W
HIX JORDAN A 32 TYR B
HIX W W A 32 COT W
HOAK BENJAMIN A 40 RHY B
HOARD JOHN A 40 DA1 B
HOARD WILLIAM F A 37 HIC A
HOBB C A A 26 SHE W
HOBBES DANIEL A 32 THO B
HOBBS AARON A 28 05A B
HOBBS ALFRED F A 29 FA1 W
HOBBS G L A 46 RAG W
HOBBS GEORGE W A 30 POW W
HOBBS HALSEY A 24 UPP W
HOBBS HAMBLETON A 24 UPP W
HOBBS HENRY C A 24 UPP W
HOBBS HENRY H A 24 UPP W
HOBBS JAMES R A 30 NOR W
HOBBS M V A 46 SUM W
HOBBS MOSES A 24 EDE W
HOBBS ROBIN A 28 03A B
HOBBS THOS M A 24 MID W
HOBBY HENRY P A 99 BUS W
HOBBY SIMEON A 99 BUS W
HOBGOOD AARON A 44 DUT B
HOBGOOD ABRAHAM A 44 TAR B
HOBGOOD ALFRED A 44 OXF W
HOBGOOD B E A 44 OXF W
HOBGOOD BARNITT A 44 TAR W
HOBGOOD D J A 44 YXS W
HOBGOOD FRANKLIN A 44 HEN W
HOBGOOD GEO W A 44 TAR W
HOBGOOD HENRY A 44 OXF B
HOBGOOD HENRY A 44 OXF W
HOBGOOD J B A 44 OXF W
HOBGOOD J L A 44 OXF W
HOBGOOD J N A 44 TAR W
HOBGOOD J S A 44 OXF W
HOBGOOD JAMES A 44 TAR B
HOBGOOD JNO Y A 44 TAR W
HOBGOOD JOSEPH A 44 OXF W
HOBGOOD L A 44 OXF W
HOBGOOD LEGAN A 44 OXF W
HOBGOOD MOSES A 44 YXS B
HOBGOOD OSBORN A 44 TAR B
HOBGOOD P B A 44 TAR W
HOBGOOD R B A 44 TAR W
HOBGOOD R H A 44 DUT W
HOBGOOD R W A 44 OXF W
HOBGOOD RUBIN A 44 OXF B
HOBGOOD SAMUEL A 44 TAR W
HOBGOOD THOMAS A 44 OXF W
HOBGOOD THOMAS A 44 YXS B
HOBGOOD THOS A 44 OXF W
HOBGOOD THOS A 44 OXF W
HOBGOOD WM A 44 LED W
HOBNAM HAMILTON A 46 GRE B
HOBS JAMES A 32 TYR W
HOBSON ANDERSON A 32 TYR B
HOBSON L H A 29 FLE W
HOBSON WM A 29 CAR B
HOCKADAY JAS M A 44 FOR W
HOCKADAY WM A 44 FOR W
HOCKADY ALBERT A 44 FOR B
HOCKADY JOS A 44 BEA B
HOCKADY SQUIRE A 44 FOR B
HOCKADY THOS A 44 FOR B
HOCKEDY EDWARD A 39 LOU B
HOCKENS F A A 40 CAN W
HOCKETT J M A 46 HIG W
HOCKETT JAMES A 46 ROS W
HOCKETT JOHN A 46 ROS W
HOCKETT JOSEPH A 46 HIG W
HOCKETT MILTON A 46 ROS W
HOCKETT SETH B A 46 ROS W
HOCKETT WM A 46 ROS W
HOCKETT WM B A 46 ROS W
HODGE C C A 39 HAR W
HODGE CAESAR A 28 03A B
HODGE CASWELL A 44 HEN B
HODGE FRANK A 44 YXR B
HODGE GEORGE A 28 16T B
HODGE H C A 39 HAR W
HODGE HENRY A 44 HEN B
HODGE JERAMIAH A 19 HAR B
HODGE JOHN A 28 01A B
HODGE M C A 99 BUS W
HODGE NEALAND A 40 DA1 W
HODGE OLIVER A 39 HAR B
HODGE RUFUS A 44 HEN B
HODGE SIMON A 39 HAY B
HODGE SWAN A 28 14T B
HODGE TONEY A 99 BUS B
HODGE WILLIAM A 44 HEN B
HODGES ALEX A 29 FA1 B
HODGES CHARLES A 28 04B B
HODGES DANIEL A 35 MAG B
HODGES ISHAM A 29 BLA X
HODGES JAMES A 37 PEN W
HODGES JOS A 29 FA1 B
HODGES JOSEPH A 53 LA1 W
HODGES LINN A 35 WAR B
HODGES MATHEW J A 53 GER W
HODGES ROBERT A 53 GER W

HODGES SILAS A 35 WAR B
HODGES SIMON A 28 6TH B
CERT GIVEN 1ST PRECINCT
HODGES THOS W A 30 MOY W
HODGES WILLIAM A 53 FAI W
HODGES WILLIS A 28 17T W
HODGES WILSON A 53 GER B
HODGES WM J A 28 17T W
HODGES WYLY A 53 GER B
HODGGARD H C A 44 TOW W
HODGIN ABSALEM A 46 ROS W
HODGIN ASA M A 46 ROS W
HODGIN DAVID A 46 ROS W
HODGIN DAVID JR A 46 ROS W
HODGIN DAVID S A 46 ROS W
HODGIN DICKS A 46 ROS W
HODGIN ELLIS A 46 GRE W
HODGIN GEORGE A 46 ROS W
HODGIN HENRY A 46 GRE W
HODGIN HENRY A 46 ROS W
HODGIN JABEZ A 46 ROS W
HODGIN JAMES A A 46 ROS W
HODGIN MICAJAH C A 46 ROS W
HODGIN NELSON A 46 GRE W
HODGIN PLEASANT A 46 ROS W
HODGIN SIMEON A 46 ROS W
HODGIN STEPHEN P A 46 ROS W
HODGIN ZIMRI A 46 ROS W
HODKINSON HENY A 29 FA1 B
HODSON P H A 32 THO W
HOELL ALPHONSA A 28 11T W
HOELL FRANKLIN JR A 28 11T W
HOELL FRANKLIN SR A 28 11T W
HOEY JOHN E A 26 SHE W
HOEY S A A 26 GOF W
HOFF EDWARD A 19 HAD W
HOFFMAN A M A 40 STO W
HOFFMAN ADAM A 32 SHE W
HOFFMAN BENJAMIN A 40 DA1 B
HOFFMAN CALEB A 40 DA1 W
HOFFMAN D J A 32 SHE W
HOFFMAN DAVID A 32 SHE W
HOFFMAN DAVID A 40 DA1 W
HOFFMAN F L A 40 SAN W
COPIED FROM DUPLICATE
HOFFMAN ISAAC A 40 DA1 B
HOFFMAN JACOB A 32 SHE W
HOFFMAN JACOB A 40 SAN W
HOFFMAN JAMES A 40 DA1 B
HOFFMAN JC A 40 SAN W
HOFFMAN JOHN M A 40 DA1 W
HOFFMAN JOHN S A 32 SHE W
HOFFMAN JONAS A 40 DA1 W
HOFFMAN JOSEPH A 40 SAN B
HOFFMAN JOSEPH JR A 40 SAN B
HOFFMAN L M A 40 DA2 W
HOFFMAN LEVI A 40 SAN W
HOFFMAN MILES A 40 DA1 W
HOFFMAN P A A 32 SHE W
HOFFMAN S E A 40 SAN W
COPIED FROM DUPICATE
HOFFMAN S J A 32 SHE W
HOFFMAN SOLOMON H A 40 DA1 W
HOFFMAN WILLIAM H A 40 DA2 W
HOFFSTETLER
HARLEY B R 40 DEC W
NAME LINED OUT
JUSTICE OF THE PEACE
BEFORE THE WAR AND
GAVE AID OR COMFORT
TO THE ENEMY. REJ
HOGAN ALLEN A 39 SPE B
HOGAN JAMES A 32 THO W
HOGAN ROB A 40 STO B
HOGANS D A 29 FA1 B
HOGG ALFRED A 39 HAR B
HOGG THOMAS G A 37 HOL W
HOGGARD ABNER L A 24 EDE W
HOGIN ARMSTED A 32 DAV B
HOGIN CIDNEY A 32 DAV B
HOGIN SANDY A 32 DAV B
HOGSED G W A 25 SHO W
HOGSED JAMES A 25 SHO W
HOGSED W H A 25 SHO W
HOGUE BRISON A 26 SHE B
HOGUE HENRY A 26 SHE B
HOGUE ISAM A 26 SHE B
HOGUE JACOB A 26 SHE W
HOGUE JESSE A 26 SHE W
HOGUE PETER A 26 SHE B
HOGUE RICHARD A 26 SHE B
HOGUE ROBERT A 26 SHE B
HOGUE W A 26 SHE B
HOGUET HENRY A 40 STO W
HOGWOOD JAMES A 39 PUG B
HOGWOOD JOE A 39 PUG B
HOGWOOD JOHN A 46 GRE W
HOGWOOD JOHN H A 39 PUG B
HOGWOOD JOHN S A 39 PUG B
HOGWOOD TURNER A 39 PUG B
HOGWOOD WILLIE A 39 PUG B
HOHRS F J A 39 LOU W
HOKE LEROY A 40 DA1 B
HOKE P P A 26 SHE W
MILITIA OFFICER &
ENGAGED IN REBELLION
HOLAWAY GREEN A 44 FIS B
HOLAWAY SAM A 44 FOR B
HOLBROOK GEORGE A 46 FRI W
HOLBROOK LEWIS A 46 SUM W
HOLBROOKE ROBERT S DA 30 ROA W
HOLDEN A J A 25 SHO W
HOLDEN A L A 44 DUT W
HOLDEN ALSEY A 39 FRE B
HOLDEN BENJ A 39 FRE W
HOLDEN CALVIN A 38 FRE B
HOLDEN CLEBURG A 38 FRE B
HOLDEN DAVID A 38 FRE B
HOLDEN FREDICK A 44 DUT W
HOLDEN GEO A 38 FRE B
HOLDEN GILBERT A 39 FRA B
HOLDEN H F A 39 FRA W
HOLDEN JOE A 39 FRA B
HOLDEN PATRICK A 38 FRE B
HOLDEN RICHARD A 25 SHO W
HOLDEN RICHARD A 39 FRE W
HOLDEN RICHD A 38 FRE B
HOLDEN RICHD A 39 FRE B
HOLDEN SIM A 37 HIG W
HOLDEN SOLOMAN A 39 FRE B
HOLDEN SOLOMON D A 46 GRE W
HOLDEN SQUIRE A 39 FRE B
HOLDEN STEPHEN A 39 FRA B
HOLDEN WILLIAM A 25 SHO W
HOLDEN Z M A 38 FRE W
HOLDER ALBERT A 32 CLE W
HOLDER ALEXANDER A 37 PEN B
HOLDER HENRY L A 46 GRE W
HOLDER JAMES A 99 BUS B
HOLDER JAMES W A 46 COB W
HOLDER JOHN A 32 SHE W
HOLDER JOHN A 46 JAM W
HOLDER NELSON A 32 CLE W
HOLDER RICHARD A 99 BUS B
HOLDER SOWELL A 32 CLE W
HOLDER W M A 44 DUT W
HOLDERER JOHN A 46 JAM W
HOLDIN RICH JR A 39 FRA W
HOLDING DOC A 38 FRE B
HOLDING SOLOMON A 39 FRE B
HOLEDIA JONATHAN H A 19 BE1 W
HOLEMAN ABNER A 44 LED B
HOLEMAN H T A 44 LED W
HOLEMAN LEVI A 32 BRO B
HOLEMAN RICHD A 44 LED W
HOLEWAY EDWARD A 37 ROC B
HOLIDAY SIMON A 53 FAI B
HOLLAND AMZI A 40 DA1 B
HOLLAND BENJ A 37 PIN W
HOLLAND C W A 26 MOO W
HOLLAND CEPHAS A 40 FER B
HOLLAND DR E B A 40 DA1 W
HOLLAND E P A 28 10T W
CERTIFICATE GIVEN LIVES
NOW AT NEW BERN
HOLLAND EDWARD A 40 SAN B
HOLLAND ELI A 40 DA1 B
HOLLAND F A 26 BOR B
HOLLAND FRANKLIN A 40 DA1 W
HOLLAND GEORGE A 40 DA1 B
HOLLAND GREEN A 40 DA1 B
HOLLAND J B A 19 HAD W
HOLLAND JAMES A 40 DA1 B
HOLLAND JAMES D A 72 SWA W
HOLLAND JAMES Q A 40 DA2 W
HOLLAND JOHN A A 72 SWA W
HOLLAND JOHN L A 35 ALB W
HOLLAND JOHN P A 28 9TH B
HOLLAND JOSEPH A 35 ALB W
HOLLAND JOSEPH W A 28 9TH B
HOLLAND JULIUS A A 40 DA1 W
HOLLAND JULIUS SEN A 40 DEC W
HOLLAND KENNETH A 37 EDW W
HOLLAND M D L A 26 MOU W
HOLLAND MERIT A 99 BUS W
HOLLAND O W R 26 HOL B
MILITIA OFFICER &
ENGAGED IN REBELLION
HOLLAND PHILEMON A 28 01A W
HOLLAND PORTER A 40 DA1 B
HOLLAND PRINCE A 40 DA1 B
HOLLAND ROBERT A 40 DA1 W
HOLLAND ROBERT JR A 40 DEC W
HOLLAND STEPH D A 28 03A W
CERTIFICATE GRANTED
TO RALEIGH
HOLLAND THOMAS A 40 DA1 B
HOLLAND THOS J A 26 HOL B
HOLLAND W R R 40 SAN W
CHALLENGED REJ
WAS A CORRONER
BEFORE THE WAR
HOLLAND WILLIAM A 37 EDW W
HOLLAND WILLIAM R R 40 DA2 W
NAME LINED OUT
CORONER AND GAVE AID OR
COMFORT TO THE ENEMY
HOLLAND WILLIS J A 35 WAR W
HOLLAND WM H A 29 FA1 W
HOLLAWAY G F A 44 DUT W
HOLLAWAY JNO T A 29 FA1 W
HOLLAWAY JONAS A 44 FOR B
HOLLEN HOSEA A 28 05A B
HOLLESTER WM A 28 01A W
HOLLEY ELIAS A 24 MID B
HOLLEY GEORGE A 24 UPP B
HOLLEY PRIMAS A 24 MID B
HOLLEY SAMUEL A 24 MID B
HOLLEY WILLIAM A 35 MAG W

HOLLIDAY ABEL A 29 FA1 B
HOLLIDAY ADAM A 29 FA1 B
HOLLIDAY GEO A 29 FA1 B
HOLLIDAY WM B A 29 QUW W
HOLLINGSWORTH A J A 29 LOC W
HOLLINGSWORTH
ALFRED A 35 MAG W
HOLLINGSWORTH B F A 29 FA1 W
HOLLINGSWORTH B G A 29 FA1 W
HOLLINGSWORTH E J A 29 CED W
HOLLINGSWORTH
GEORGE A 35 MAG B
HOLLINGSWORTH H A 29 FA2 W
SEE GREYS CK BOOK
HOLLINGSWORTH H J A 29 GRA W
HOLLINGSWORTH HARRY A 35 MAG B
HOLLINGSWORTH HENRY A 29 SEV B
HOLLINGSWORTH HENRY A 35 MAG W
HOLLINGSWORTH ISAAC A 29 FA1 W
HOLLINGSWORTH J JR A 29 GRA W
HOLLINGSWORTH J W A 29 FA1 W
HOLLINGSWORTH JAMES A 35 MAG W
HOLLINGSWORTH JOS A 29 FA1 W
HOLLINGSWORTH KIBBY A 35 MAG W
HOLLINGSWORTH
MARSHALL A 35 WAR W
HOLLINGSWORTH S C A 39 JOR W
HOLLINGSWORTH SIMON A 29 SEV B
HOLLINGSWORTH W A 29 FA1 B
HOLLINGSWORTH W J A 29 GRA W
AFFIDAVIT FAYETTEVILLE
MARKED ERROR
HOLLINGSWORTH WM A 29 GRA W
HOLLIS ARTHUR A 28 02N B
HOLLIS DAVID A 28 03B W
HOLLIS JAMES A A 32 THO B
HOLLIS JAMES H A 28 9TH B
HOLLIS THOMAS A 28 9TH B
HOLLIS WILLIAM R A 28 10T B
HOLLISTER ALFRED A 28 03A B
HOLLODAY SIMONS A 53 FAI B
HOLLOWAY ALFRED A 28 03A B
HOLLOWAY DAVID A 28 03A B
HOLLOWAY FRANCISCO A 32 DAV W
HOLLOWAY GEO T A 44 FOR W
HOLLOWAY ISOM A 44 YXS B
HOLLOWAY JOHN A 44 DUT B
HOLLOWAY NATHAN A 28 6TH B
HOLLOWAY SAML A 28 04A B
HOLLOWAY W A A 46 HIG W
HOLLOWAY W S A 44 YXS W
HOLLOWELL ANTONY A 53 SWA B
HOLLOWELL FRANK A 53 SWA B
HOLLOWELL J B A 24 UPP W
HOLLOWELL JOHN A 24 UPP W
HOLLOWELL JOSEPH A 28 15T B
HOLLOWELL JOURDAN A 24 UPP W
HOLLOWELL NATHANIEL A 53 SWA B
HOLLOWELL NOAH A 24 UPP W
HOLLOWELL PETER A 28 15T B
HOLLOWELL QUINTON A 24 UPP W
HOLLOWELL REDDING A 53 SWA B
HOLLOWELL ROGER W A 53 GER W
HOLLOWELL SAMUEL H A 53 SWA B
HOLLOWELL THOMAS F A 24 UPP W
HOLLOWELL ZADOCK A 28 15T W
HOLLY ABRAM A 24 EDE B
CERT GIVEN TO BERTIE
HOLLY ABRAM A 28 02N B
HOLLY ALBERT A 28 01A B
HOLLY ALFRED A 46 JAM B
HOLLY ARTHUR A 24 EDE B
HOLLY BENJAMIN A 24 MID B
HOLLY CHARLES A 24 MID B
HOLLY DAVID A 24 EDE B
HOLLY DAVID A 24 MID B
HOLLY DAVID A R 24 MID W
REJECTED BY THE BOARD BE
CAUSE HE HELD THE OFFICE
OF INSPECTOR BEFORE THE
WAR AND DURING THE WAR
FURNISHED THE CONFEDERA
TION WITH SERVICE DEALT
IN CONFEDERATE BONDS &C,
DID NOT TAKE THE OATH
HOLLY DEVREAUX A 24 MID B
HOLLY DILWORTH A 24 MID B
HOLLY EPHRAM A 24 MID B
HOLLY FRED A 24 EDE B
HOLLY GEORGE A 37 PEN B
HOLLY HARDY A 24 MID B
HOLLY HARRY A 24 MID B
HOLLY ISAAC A 24 MID B
HOLLY ISOM A 24 MID B
HOLLY ISOM JR A 24 MID B
HOLLY JOHN A 24 EDE B
HOLLY JOHN A 28 01A B
HOLLY JOURDAN A 24 EDE B
HOLLY MILES A 24 EDE B
HOLLY MILES A 28 04A B
HOLLY NORFLEET A 24 MID B
HOLLY OSBON A 29 FLE W
HOLLY PRINCE A 28 01A B
HOLLY RALPH A 28 03A B
HOLLY STEPHEN A 46 JAM B
HOLLY THOMAS A 24 UPP B
HOLLY W N A 24 EDE W
HOLLY WILLIS A 24 MID B
HOLMER WM A 44 FOR W
HOLMES A A 29 FLE W
HOLMES AARON A 35 MAG B
HOLMES ADAM A 53 LA1 B
HOLMES ALEX A 39 FRA W
HOLMES ANTHONY A 35 WAR B
HOLMES C C A 28 01B W
HOLMES C K A 32 JAC W
HOLMES CABIN A 32 COT B
HOLMES CALVIN A 32 COT B
HOLMES CHARLES A 29 LOC B
HOLMES CHARLES A 35 ALB B
HOLMES CHAS A 28 04A B
HOLMES GABL A 29 FLE B
HOLMES GARDNER A 29 FA1 W
HOLMES GEO JR A 29 FLE W
HOLMES GEO SR A 29 FLE W
HOLMES H A 44 FOR W
HOLMES H B A 39 FRA W
HOLMES HAMPTON A 28 05A B
HOLMES HENRY A 29 FA1 B
HOLMES HENRY A 29 LOC B
HOLMES HENRY A 46 GRE B
HOLMES JACK A 37 HIG B
HOLMES JAMES A 29 FLE W
HOLMES JAMES B A 46 ROS W
HOLMES JESSE A 32 LOF B
HOLMES JESSIE A 32 COT B
HOLMES JOHN A 28 05A B
HOLMES JOHN A 29 FLE W
HOLMES JOURDAN A 28 05A B
HOLMES M D A 44 FOR W
HOLMES MARCH A 28 03A B
HOLMES MARCILLUS A 39 LOU W
HOLMES MCGUFFIE A 37 ROC B
HOLMES MOSES A 29 FLE B
HOLMES NATHAN A 35 GLI W
HOLMES PHILIP A 44 ISL B
HOLMES R A 32 COT B
HOLMES R R A 44 FOR W
HOLMES REV WM A 44 HEN W
HOLMES RICHARD A 32 COT B
HOLMES ROBERT A 32 COT B
HOLMES SAMUEL A 29 FLE B
HOLMES STEPHEN A 35 GLI W
HOLMES THOS A 29 FLE B
HOLMES W H A 29 ROC W
HOLMES WILLIE A 39 FRA W
HOLMS WILSON A 46 GRE B
HOLOWAY CHARLES A 44 DUT B
HOLT ABRIHAM A 32 DAV B
HOLT CASUEL A 32 DAV B
HOLT CASUEL A 32 DAV B
HOLT CASUELL A 32 DAV B
HOLT E W A 30 MOY W
HOLT JAMES A 29 SEV W
HOLT JOHN A 46 RAG W
HOLT JOHN F A 46 SUM W
HOLT JOHN S A 32 DAV B
HOLT JORDAN A 32 DAV B
HOLT JORDON A 32 COT B
HOLT LEWIS A 46 MCL W
HOLT MANUEL A 32 DAV B
HOLT MARTIN A 32 DAV B
HOLT MICHAEL A A 46 GRE W
HOLT MICHAEL B A 46 MCL W
HOLT MONRO A 32 DAV B
HOLT MOSES A 19 HAD B
HOLT NATHAN A 32 TYR B
HOLT NICHOLAS A 46 GRE W
HOLT PETER A 32 DAV B
HOLT RICHD A 29 GRA W
HOLT RICHD B A 29 SEV W
HOLT S THOMAS A 46 SUM W
HOLT SAML A 28 04A B
HOLT SANDIS A 32 DAV B
HOLT SANDY A 46 COB B
HOLT THOMAS A 24 EDE B
HOLT THOMAS A 32 DAV B
HOLT THOS J A 30 MOY W
HOLT W C A 30 MOY W
HOLT WILLIAM A 19 NEW B
HOLT WILLIS A 32 DAV B
HOLTE WM A A 46 GRE W
HOLTON A L A 46 JAM W
HOLTON ALONZA J A 28 13T W
HOLTON ANSON A 46 JAM W
HOLTON BARZELLIE A 28 13T W
HOLTON DANIEL P A 28 14T W
HOLTON ELIAS A 28 16T W
HOLTON ISAAC P A 28 13T W
HOLTON J F A 46 JAM W
HOLTON JEHU A 46 HIG W
HOLTON JEPTHA B A 28 13T W
HOLTON JESSE H A 28 16T W
HOLTON JESSE W P A 28 14T W
HOLTON M C A 46 JAM W
HOLTON MATTHEW A 28 16T W
HOLTON REV Q A 46 JAM W
HOLTON S R A 46 HIG W
HOLTON SIMEON L A 28 14T W
HOLTON THOMAS A 28 16T W
HOLTON WM A 28 16T W
HOLTON WM H A 28 13T W
HOMAN BENJAMIN A 37 HIG B
HOMER JOHN A 28 05A B
HOMESLY AMOS B A 40 BLA W
HOMESLY EDWARD A 26 SHE B
HOMESLY WRIGHT A 26 SHE B
HONEYCUTT
WASHINGTON A 99 BUS B

HOOD ABRAM A 46 MCL W
HOOD CHARLES E A 46 JAM B
HOOD JACOB A 25 HAY W
HOOD JAS W A 29 FA1 B
HOOD SAMUEL A 28 7TH B
HOODS WM A 44 LED W
HOOKER DANIEL D A 28 16T W
HOOKER EDMOND 2ND A 28 9TH B
HOOKER EDMOND S A 28 9TH B
HOOKER HARDIN R A 28 16T W
HOOKER HAYWOOD A 28 9TH B
HOOKER JOHN A 28 03B W
HOOKER JOHN J A 28 10T W
CERTIF GIVEN NOW LIVES
AT BIG SWIFT CREEK
HOOKER NATHAN A 28 9TH B
HOOKER NATHAN A 30 ROA W
HOOKER PETER A 37 PIN B
HOOKER SAMUEL D A 30 ROA W
HOOKER SPENCER A 30 ROA W
HOOKER THOMAS A 28 03B W
HOOKER WM R A 28 16T W
HOOKS ISAAC A 28 9TH B
CERT GIVEN NOW
LIVES AT NEW BERN
HOOPER ABRAM F A 53 CHI W
HOOPER CYRUS A 53 CHI W
HOOPER CYRUS K A 53 KEN W
HOOPER DANL A 29 FA1 B
HOOPER EDWARD O A 53 CHI W
HOOPER EDWARD R A 53 CHI W
HOOPER EZEKIEL A 53 CHI W
HOOPER ISAAC H A 53 KEN W
HOOPER JAMES A 40 SAN W
COPIED FROM DUPLICATE
HOOPER JAMES P A 40 STO W
HOOPER JOS C A 29 FA1 B
HOOPER LORENZO D A 53 CHI W
HOOPER RICHARD G A 53 CHI W
HOOPER S T A 39 SPE W
HOOPER WILLIAM A 53 HAT W
HOOPER WM W A 53 CHI W
HOOSER EMANUEL A 32 CLE W
HOOTEN BRYANT A A 53 GER W
HOOTEN JOHN T A 53 GER W
HOOVE JACOB A 40 RHY W
HOOVER A S A 46 JAM W
HOOVER ANDREW A 32 DAV B
HOOVER B A 32 LOF B
HOOVER CHARLES A 32 THO W
HOOVER F A 32 POS B
HOOVER HENRY A 32 POS B
HOOVER JOHN A 32 POS B
HOOVER JOSEPH A 28 10T B
HOOVER JOSEPH A 28 14T W
HOOVER M T A 32 THO W
HOOVER P A A 32 POS W
CERTIF GIVEN
HOOVER PETER A 32 SHE W
HOOVER S A 32 POS B
HOOVER SAMUEL J A 28 14T W
HOOVER SOLN A 28 04A W
HOOVER SOLOMON A 32 COT B
HOOVER THOMAS A 40 RHY W
HOOVER VOLENTINE A 32 THO W
HOOZER JOHN A 32 CLE W
HOPE CHRISTFER A 40 STO W
HOPE HENRY A 40 DA1 W
HOPE J M A 44 HEN W
HOPE M N A 44 ISL W
HOPE WILLIAM A 40 MAU W
HOPKENS JOSEPH A 37 MAN B
HOPKINS A H A 39 GRI W
HOPKINS ANDERSON A 32 JAC W
HOPKINS BENJAMIN A 53 FAI W
HOPKINS CANNON A 44 LED W
HOPKINS CHAS A 39 GRI B
HOPKINS COLEMAN A 39 GRI B
HOPKINS D A A 39 GRI W
HOPKINS DANIEL A 39 GRI B
HOPKINS DAVID A 53 LA1 W
HOPKINS DEMPSEY A 39 GRI B
HOPKINS EXUM A 37 EDW B
HOPKINS GEORGE A 37 PIN B
HOPKINS GEORGE A 37 PIN B
HOPKINS HAMPTON A 37 PIN B
HOPKINS HENRY A 37 HOL W
HOPKINS J H A 19 NEW W
HOPKINS JAMES A 32 THO W
HOPKINS JAMES A 37 PIN B
HOPKINS JAMES A 37 TA1 B
HOPKINS JEREMIAH A 37 PIN B
HOPKINS JERRY A 39 GRI B
HOPKINS JNO W A 29 FA1 W
HOPKINS JOHN A 37 PIN B
HOPKINS JOHN HENRY A 37 PIN B
HOPKINS JOHN S A 37 EDW B
HOPKINS JORDAN A 37 PIN B
HOPKINS JOSEPH A 37 PEN B
HOPKINS JOSEPH A 37 PIN B
HOPKINS JOSEPH A 37 PIN B
HOPKINS N B A 39 GRI W
HOPKINS NATHAN A 37 PIN B
HOPKINS RANDALL A 37 PIN B
HOPKINS RICHARD A 37 PIN B
HOPKINS SAMUEL A 32 JAC W
HOPKINS SAMUEL A 37 PIN B
HOPKINS THOMAS A 37 PEN B
HOPKINS WADE A 44 LED W
HOPKINS WALTER A 46 SUM W
HOPPER ANDREW A 26 BUR B
HOPPER BENJAMIN A 26 MOO B
HOPPER C C A 26 BUR W
HOPPER J M D A 26 SHE W
HOPPER J N A 26 SHE W
HOPPER J T A 26 BUR W
HOPPER JOHN A A 26 SHE W
HOPPER JOHN S A 26 BUR W
HOPPER L M A 26 BUR W
HOPPER R M S A 26 SHE W
HOPPER W O A 46 SUM W
HOPPER WILLIS A 26 MOO B
HOPPER Z A 26 BUR W
HOPSON PETER A 37 TA1 B
HOPSON WM A 26 SHE B
HOPTON WILLIAM A 28 03B B
HORD A S A 26 GRI W
HORD ETHEL A 26 GRI B
HORD F M A 26 BLA W
HORD R M A 26 BLA W
HORD R T A 26 BLA W
HORD RICHARD A 26 GRI B
HORN AMOS A 37 HIG B
HORN AUSTON A 37 HIG B
HORN AUTHOR A 29 LOC W
HORN D T A 29 LOC W
HORN DAIEL A 29 LOC W
HORN DEMPY A 37 ROC B
HORN EPHRIM A 37 HIG B
HORN FRANCIS A 37 ROC B
HORN GEORGE A 37 HIG B
HORN IRVIN A 37 HIG B
HORN ISOM A 26 BLA W
HORN J B A 29 LOC W
HORN JNO JR A 29 LOC W
HORN JNO SR A 29 LOC W
HORN JOHN A 19 BE1 B
HORN JOHN A 26 MOO W
HORN JOHN A 37 HIG W
HORN JOSHUA L A 37 HIG W
HORN M A 29 LOC W
HORN ORAN A 37 HIG B
HORN R D A 29 LOC W
HORN ROBERT A 37 TA1 B
HORN SAMUEL A 37 HIG B
HORN SAMUEL A 37 HIG B
(LITTLE SAM HORN)
HORN SIMON A 37 WHI B
HORN SIMON A 37 WHI W
HORN SION A 29 LOC W
HORN THOMAS A 37 HIG B
HORN VIRGEL A 37 WHI B
HORN W D A 29 LOC W
HORN W W A 26 BLA W
HORN WILEY A 29 LOC W
HORNBUCKLE AARON A 46 MON B
HORNE DREW A 37 PEN B
HORNE GEORGE A 37 PIN B
HORNE H R A 29 FA1 W
HORNE H W A 29 FA1 W
HORNE HOWELL A 35 CYP W
HORNE JAMES R A 37 TA2 W
HORNE JNO M A 44 HEN W
HORNE ORPHEY A 37 PEN B
HORNE POMPEY A 37 PEN B
HORNE THOMAS A 35 CYP W
HORNER CHARLES A 44 LED B
HORNER GREEN A 44 YXR B
HORNER HARRIS A 44 BEA B
HORNER J H A 44 OXF W
HORNER J T A 44 BRA W
HORNER JAMES A 44 BRA B
HORNER NORMAN A 44 LED B
HORNER R D A 44 BRA W
HORNER T J A 44 LED W
HORNEY C F A 46 HIG W
HORNEY CHARLES P A 46 JAM W
HORNEY E P A 46 HIG W
HORNEY H M A 46 HIG W
HORNEY J C A 46 HIG W
HORNEY S B A 46 HIG W
HORNEY S G A 46 HIG W
HORNIBLOW JOHN B A 28 01B W
HORNRINE GEO R A 29 FA1 W
HORNRINE J B A 29 LOC W
HORNY HAMPTON A 32 DAV W
HORSHAM ELISH A 25 TUS B
HORSLEY A R A 40 STO W
HORSLEY R R A 40 SAN W
HORTON A C A 32 CLE W
HORTON ACREEL A 37 PIN B
HORTON BENJN A 28 02N B
HORTON CEASER A 19 MOR B
HORTON D B A 44 BEA W
HORTON DANL A 44 FOR W
HORTON HARDIE A 44 BEA W
HORTON J F A 39 GRI W
HORTON JOHN A 32 CLE B
HORTON JOHN W A 28 03B W
HORTON LEWIS A 32 CLE B
HORTON MERICK A 39 HAR W
HORTON MOSES A 37 HOL B
HORTON NOAH A 37 TA1 B
HORTON RICHARD A 40 RHY W
HORTON SAMUEL A 37 HOL B
HORTON SIDNEY A 39 HAR W
HORTON T C A 39 LOU W
HOSKEN WASHINGTON A 29 FA1 B
FLEA HILL

HOSKING H J A 46 JAM W
HOSKINS E J A 46 SUM W
HOSKINS E N A 46 GRE W
HOSKINS J A A 46 SUM W
HOSKINS JOHN A 53 LA1 B
HOSKINS W H A 46 SUM W
HOSKINS WILLIAM A 37 TA1 B
HOUGH A G A 32 THO W
HOUGHF JESSIE A 32 DAV B
TO GREENSBORO N C
HOULAND HENRY A 19 HAD B
HOUSE AARON A 32 TYR B
HOUSE ALFRED A 39 FRA B
HOUSE CORNELIUS A 28 03A B
HOUSE EDMOND A 39 DAV W
HOUSE GEORGE A 28 03A B
HOUSE HAMTEN A 19 HAR B
HOUSE JESSY A 37 MAN W
HOUSE JOSEPH A 44 OXF W
HOUSE JOSEPH J A 37 MAN W
HOUSE PETER A 19 BE1 B
HOUSER L C A 26 SHE W
HOUSER WILLIAM A 40 DA1 B
HOUSTED LARRY A 28 03A B
HOUSTON ALFRED A 35 KEN W
HOUSTON ALLEN A 35 SMI B
HOUSTON BRINKLEY A 35 LIM W
HOUSTON BUCK A 35 KEN B
HOUSTON CAPTAIN D A 35 KEN B
HOUSTON CLAYBORN A 35 SMI B
HOUSTON DERRY A 28 7TH B
HOUSTON EDWARD A 35 KEN W
HOUSTON EDWARD A A 35 KEN W
HOUSTON EDWARD S A 35 KEN W
HOUSTON EDWARD W A 35 SMI W
HOUSTON EMANUEL A 35 CYP B
HOUSTON GEORGE A 35 SMI B
HOUSTON GEORGE E A 35 KEN W
HOUSTON HIRAM V A 35 KEN W
HOUSTON J T A 29 FA1 W
HOUSTON JACKSON A 35 ISL B
HOUSTON JESSE A 46 MCL B
HOUSTON JOSEPH A 35 SMI B
HOUSTON JUPITER A 35 SMI B
HOUSTON LEVI A 46 GRE W
HOUSTON LINDSAY A 46 GRE B
HOUSTON MADISON A 46 GRE B
HOUSTON O A 29 FA1 W
HOUSTON ROBERT C A 35 KEN W
HOUSTON ROBERT J A 35 KEN W
HOUSTON STEPHAN M A 35 SMI W
HOUSTON THOMAS A 35 KEN B
HOUSTON WILLIAM A 35 LIM W
HOVER STEVEN A 40 SAN B
HOVIS A A 40 RHY W
HOVIS ADAM A 40 RHY W
HOVIS DAVID A 40 CAN W
HOVIS GEORGE A 40 DEC W
HOVIS JACOB D A 40 DEC W
HOVIS JOHN A 40 RHY W
HOVIS M A 40 RHY W
HOVIS MARTIN V A 40 DEC W
HOVIS MONROW A 40 CAN W
HOVIS MOSES A 40 STO W
HOW PORTER A 29 FA1 B
HOW SAMUEL A 26 MOO W
HOWARD A B A 53 OCR W
HOWARD AMBROS J A 53 SWA W
HOWARD AMON A 53 OCR W
HOWARD BENJA C A 53 OCR W
HOWARD BENJAMIN A 37 WHI B
HOWARD CHARLES A 19 BE1 B
HOWARD CHARLES A 44 OXF B
HOWARD CLINTON A 53 GER B
HOWARD CORNELIOUS A 53 GER W
HOWARD CYRUS A 44 YXS B
HOWARD DANIEL C A 53 SWA W
HOWARD DICK A 37 HIC B
HOWARD DR JOHN A 35 SMI W
DECEASED
HOWARD EDEN A 37 HIC B
HOWARD EDWARD A 28 9TH B
HOWARD ELIJAH A 44 HEN B
HOWARD ENOCH C A 53 OCR W
HOWARD FRED A 44 OXF B
HOWARD GEO W A 28 01A W
HOWARD GEORGE W A 37 HIC A
HOWARD HARRIS A 35 MAG W
HOWARD HARRY A 37 EDW B
HOWARD HENRY A 44 KNA B
HOWARD HIMAN A 35 MAG W
HOWARD JAMES A 30 ROA W
HOWARD JAMES J A 28 01A W
HOWARD JAMES T A 37 HIC A
HOWARD JAMES W A 53 OCR W
HOWARD JAS A 44 HEN B
HOWARD JAS A 44 YXR B
HOWARD JAS A A 44 TAR W
HOWARD JAS H A 44 YXR W
HOWARD JERRY A 37 HIC B
HOWARD JOHN A 19 BE2 B
HOWARD JOHN A 28 01A W
HOWARD JOHN T A 35 MAG W
HOWARD JOSEPH SR A 44 TAR W
HOWARD L P A 44 YXS W
HOWARD LEWIS A 44 YXS B
HOWARD LITTLETON A 37 EDW B
HOWARD LORENZO A 35 MAG W
HOWARD MASON A 29 FA1 W
HOWARD MIKE A 37 HIC B
HOWARD MIKE A 44 TAR B
HOWARD MOSES A 19 HAD B
HOWARD PERRY C A 53 OCR W
HOWARD PETER A 35 SMI B
HOWARD PETER A 44 YXS B
HOWARD POMPEY A 37 HIC B
HOWARD RICHARD A 53 SWA W
HOWARD RICHARD W A 53 OCR W
HOWARD ROBERT A 37 HIC A
HOWARD ROBT A 44 TAR W
HOWARD S L A 44 LED W
HOWARD S W A 28 03A W
HOWARD SAML A 44 TAR B
HOWARD SIMON B A 53 OCR W
HOWARD SOLOMAN A 44 OXF W
HOWARD SQUIRE A 53 LA1 B
HOWARD SYVANUS A A 46 GRE W
HOWARD THOMAS A 37 HIC A
HOWARD THOMAS G A 53 SWA W
HOWARD THOS S A 28 01B W
HOWARD WALLACE A 53 OCR W
HOWARD WATT A 44 TAR B
HOWARD WILEY A 37 TA2 B
HOWARD WILLIAM A 37 TA2 W
HOWARD WILLIAM A 72 SWA B
HOWARD WM A 29 FA1 W
HOWE R O A 40 SAN W
HOWE WILLIAM T A 99 BUS W
HOWEL ISAAC A 46 GRE B
HOWELL ALEX A 44 FIS B
HOWELL AMOS A 29 FA1 W
HOWELL BRINKLEY G A 37 HIC A
HOWELL BYTHAL A 37 EDW W
HOWELL D DR A 26 GOF W
HOWELL D H A 29 LOC W
HOWELL DANIEL A 26 SWA B
HOWELL ELI A 37 EDW W
HOWELL ELIJAH A 44 OXF B
HOWELL ESIC A 37 HIC B
HOWELL F R A 44 OXF B
HOWELL FRANK A 37 EDW B
HOWELL HARVEY A 44 OXF B
HOWELL HENRY A 29 FA1 B
HOWELL ISAAC A 29 GRA B
HOWELL J M A 44 FIS W
HOWELL J T A 44 FIS W
HOWELL J W A 29 FA1 W
HOWELL JAMES A 44 OXF B
HOWELL JAMES E A 44 OXF B
HOWELL JAMES M A 37 EDW W
HOWELL JOHN A 37 HOL B
HOWELL JOHN H A 37 HIC A
HOWELL JOHN H A 37 TA1 W
HOWELL JORDAN A 44 ISL B
HOWELL JOSEPH A 37 EDW B
HOWELL MOSES A 29 FLE B
HOWELL MOSES A 37 EDW B
HOWELL REUBEN A 37 PIN B
HOWELL ROBERT A 37 TA1 B
HOWELL SAMUEL A 29 FA2 B
HOWELL THOMAS A 29 FLE B
HOWELL WILLIAM A 37 EDW B
HOWELL WILLIAM A 37 TA2 W
HOWELL WILLIS A 44 ISL B
HOWELL WILLIS 1ST A 37 EDW B
HOWELL WILLIS 2ND A 37 EDW B
HOWELL WM R A 37 EDW W
HOWELL WM S A 19 BE1 W
HOWERENTON JOHN A 46 KIN W
HOWERTON JAMES A 32 DAV W
HOWERTON N C A 32 DAV W
HOWERTON S W A 32 THO W
HOWERTON T A 46 SUM W
HOWINGTON PATRICK A 39 PUG B
HOWKINS JAMES A 37 HOL W
HOWLAND B T A 19 SMY W
HOWLAND DAVID W A 28 10T W
HOWLAND GEO W A 19 SMY W
HOWLAND J S A 28 04B W
HOWLAND JAMES E A 19 BE1 W
HOWLAND JAMES M A 19 MOR W
HOWLAND JOHN A 19 BE1 B
HOWLAND LEVI C A 19 BE1 W
HOWLAND WILLIAM H A 35 WAR W
HOWLAND WM J A 19 NEW W
HOWLAND ZEPHANIAH J A 19 BE2 W
HOWLETT GEORGE W A 46 GRE W
HOWLETT HARBERT A 46 GRE W
HOWLETT JAMES M A 46 GRE W
HOWLETT JONATHAN W A 46 GRE W
HOWSER A M A 26 SHE W
HOWSER PETER A 40 SAN W
COPIED FROM DUPLICATE
HOWSER WM A 28 16T W
HOYL ALEXANDER A 40 DA1 B
HOYL BENJAMIN A 40 DA1 B
HOYL CALEB W A 40 DA1 W
HOYL DANIEL A 40 DA1 B
HOYL JOHN A 40 DA1 B
HOYL NELSON A 40 DA1 B
HOYL RUFUS A 40 DA2 B
HOYL SAMUEL A 40 DA1 B
HOYL WILLIAM 40 DA1 B
STRICKEN OUT APR 15 1868
HOYLE HENRY A 26 PEE W
HOYLE W B A 26 BLA W
HOYME CHARLES A 46 GRE W
HOYT PIERSON A 28 04B B

HUBANKS GASKINS A 19 SMY B
CERT TO BEAUFORT
HUBBARD D M A 46 MCL W
HUBBARD E K A 28 01B W
HUBBARD JAMES A 28 05A B
HUBBARD JAMES A A 46 FRI W
HUBBARD JNO H A 29 FA2 W
HUBBARD JOHN A 28 7TH B
HUBBARD JOHN A 46 COB B
HUBBARD MALACHI J A 30 ROA W
HUBBARD MARK C A 28 10T W
HUBBS ETHELBERT A 28 03A W
HUBBS ORLANDO A 28 03A W
HUDDLESTON J H A 28 03A W
HUDDLESTON
WILLIAM C A 40 BLA W
HUDGGINS J C A 44 LED W
HUDGINGS WM A 24 EDE B
HUDLER MOSES A 28 04A B
HUDNAL STANLY A 53 FAI B
HUDNALL R R A 39 FRA W
HUDSON A J A 38 FRE W
HUDSON C E A 46 MON W
HUDSON C W A 44 OXF W
HUDSON CALVIN A 46 MCL W
HUDSON CEPHAS A 44 OXF W
HUDSON DAVID A 53 SWA B
HUDSON EJIJAH P A 53 SWA W
HUDSON FAYETT A 37 TA2 B
HUDSON GARRISON F A 53 SWA B
HUDSON HARDISON E A 53 GER W
HUDSON HEZAKIAH A 53 SWA B
HUDSON JESSIE A 37 TA2 B
HUDSON JNO A 44 YXR W
HUDSON JOSEPH A 24 MID W
HUDSON L H A 29 LOC W
HUDSON LEWIS A 28 16T W
HUDSON LUIS A 44 FIS B
NOT 21 YEARS OLD
HUDSON MARCUS A 32 DAV W
HUDSON T S A 29 CED W
HUDSON THE A 44 LED W
HUDSON WILLIAM A 24 MID W
HUDSON WILLIAM A 53 SWA W
HUDSON WM A 39 FRE W
HUDSON WM R A 28 04A W
HUE HENRY A 37 WHI B
HUE SAMUEL A 37 WHI B
HUES BENJAMIN A 32 THO W
HUEY JERRY A 46 RAG B
HUFF ANSON A 19 HUN W
HUFF ANTHONY A 28 10T W
HUFF HEYWOOD A 28 10T W
HUFF J D A 44 HEN W
HUFF J G A 44 HEN W
HUFF N M A 44 KIT W
HUFF OBEDIAH A 32 DAV W
HUFFHINES DAVID A 46 FRI W
HUFFINES ABEL A 46 GIB W
HUFFINES DAVID A 46 GIB W
HUFFINES HENRY A 46 GIB W
HUFFINES JACOB A 46 GIB W
HUFFINES JOHN A 46 GIB W
HUFFINES JOHN A 46 MON W
HUFFINES PETER A 46 GIB W
HUFFINES SAML A 46 GIB W
HUFFMAN ALEX A 46 GIB B
HUFFMAN C C A 46 GRE W
HUFFMAN HENRY R A 46 GIB W
HUFFMAN JOHN R A 46 GIB W
HUFFMAN JOSEPH A 46 GIB B
HUFFMAN MONROE A 46 GIB B
HUFFSTETLER A C A 26 BOR W

HUFFSTETLER
EPHRAIM M A 40 BLA W
HUFFSTETLER JACOB A 40 DA1 W
HUFFSTETLER JOHN A 40 DEC W
HUFFSTETLER JOHN P A 40 DEC W
HUFFSTETLER L C A 26 BOR W
HUFFSTUTLER DANIEL A 26 SHE W
HUFFSTUTLER J M A 40 SAN W
HUFHAM JOHN A 35 ROC B
HUFHAM JOHN A 35 ROC W
HUFHAM PETER JR A 35 ROC B
HUFHAM PETER SR A 35 ROC B
HUFSTITLER D R A 26 SHE W
HUGGINS ALLEN A 35 MAG B
HUGGINS BROOK A 19 NEW B
HUGGINS EDWARD A 72 SWA B
HUGGINS MICHAEL A 40 DA1 W
HUGGINS NATHAN A 19 HAR B
HUGGINS SAMUEL A 28 9TH B
HUGGINS SETH H A 72 SWA W
HUGGINS WARREN A 35 WAR B
HUGHES ANTHONEY A 44 HEN B
HUGHES GEO B A 44 HEN W
HUGHES GRIDLEY A 44 HEN B
HUGHES HENRY A 44 HEN B
HUGHES ISAAC W A 28 01A W
HUGHES J B A 28 02N W
HUGHES JOHN A 28 01A W
HUGHES MILES H A 24 EDE W
HUGHES PETER A 46 GIB W
HUGHES R P A 44 OXF W
HUGHES REDDIC A 44 HEN B
HUGHES STEPHEN A A 44 SAS W
HUGHES THOS C A 44 HEN W
HUGHES WM A 26 SHE W
HUGHES WM A 29 FA1 B
HUGHINS BAILEY A 30 MOY W
HUGHS BENJAMIN A 46 MCL B
HUGHS CHAS A 30 TUL W
HUGHS GEO M A 44 YXS W
HUGHS ISREL A 40 CAN W
HUGHS J E A 26 MOO W
HUGHS J M A 46 GRE W
HUGHS JAMES A 26 MOO W
HUGHS RICHARD D A 26 HOL B
HUGHS S R A 44 ISL W
HUGHS SAML B A 30 CUR W
HUGHS W P A 46 GRE W
HUGHS WILLIAM A 35 GLI W
HUGHS WM B A 26 HOL B
HUKINS EDWARD A 28 9TH B
HUKINS HENRY A 28 9TH B
HULL BENJ A 26 PEE W
HULL HENRY A 44 SAS B
HULLENDER C A 26 BOR W
HULLENDER WILLIAM A 26 SWA W
HULLET CALEB A 40 BLA W
HULLET JOHN A 26 BOR W
HULLET PETER A 40 BLA W
HUMBLE ALFRED A 46 COB W
HUMBLE DAVID A 46 COB W
HUMBLE LEVI A 46 COB W
HUMBLE PETER O A 46 COB W
HUMBLE WILLIAM A A 46 COB W
HUME JOHN A 28 02N W
HUMFRUS WILLIAM A 40 STO B
HUMPHINS SAML A 30 MOY W
HUMPHRES MORRIS A 28 14T B
HUMPHREY CHARLES A 28 16T B
HUMPHREY DANIEL E A 72 SWA W
HUMPHREY DAVID A 19 NEW B
HUMPHREY HIRAM A 28 7TH W
HUMPHREY JAMES A 53 LA1 B

HUMPHREY JOHN A 28 7TH W
HUMPHREY R H A 32 DAV W
HUMPHREY ROBERT W A 72 SWA W
HUMPHREYS JAM G A 40 SAN W
HUMPHRIES ALFRED A 30 IND W
HUMPHRIES B R A 44 YXS W
HUMPHRIES DANIEL A 26 MOU W
HUMPHRIES G M A 30 IND W
HUMPHRIES JNO B A 30 TUL W
HUMPHRIES JOHN A 26 MOU B
HUMPHRIES JOHN A 26 MOU W
HUMPHRIES JOHN A 30 TUL W
HUMPHRIES L A 26 MOO W
HUMPHRIES L L A 26 MOU W
HUMPHRIES LAWSON A 26 MOO W
HUMPHRIES LEWIS A 26 MOU W
HUMPHRIES MOSES A 30 IND B
HUMPHRIES OLIVER A 26 MOU W
HUMPHRIES P G A 26 MOO W
HUMPHRIES PHILIP A 30 CUR W
HUMPHRIES S H A 26 MOU W
HUMPHRIES S R A 26 MOU W
HUMPHRIES THOMAS C R 30 IND W
CHALLENGED
HUMPHRIES WILLIAM A 26 MOU W
HUMPHRIES WILLIAM B A 26 MOU W
HUMPHRIES WILLIAM F A 30 IND W
HUMPHRIES WILLIS R 26 MOU W
MILITIA OFFICER &
ENGAGED IN REBELLION
HUMPHRY JOHN N A 32 DAV W
HUND JACKSON A 46 FRI B
HUNDLEY J A A 44 FIS W
KITTRELLS DISt
HUNICUTT ARCHY A 29 GRA W
HUNICUTT B A 29 GRA W
HUNICUTT G W A 29 GRA W
HUNNICUTT ALBERT D A 99 BUS W
HUNNICUTT DAVID A 99 BUS W
HUNNICUTT RUFUS A 99 BUS W
HUNT A A 26 PEE B
HUNT A A A 39 PUG W
HUNT A P A 29 FA2 W
HUNT A W A 32 LEE W
HUNT ABASLEM A 44 HEN B
HUNT ALEX A 44 TOW B
HUNT ALEX A 44 OXF B
HUNT ALEX A 44 OXF B
HUNT ANDERSON A 44 OXF B
HUNT ANDERSON A 44 TAR B
HUNT ANDREW A 32 DAV B
HUNT ARMSTRONG A 44 OXF B
HUNT B M A 32 LOF W
HUNT BARTLET A 32 DAV W
HUNT BENJN A 44 TOW B
HUNT BIRD A 44 OXF B
HUNT BOOKER A 39 PUG B
HUNT BRAXTON A 44 KIT B
HUNT CHARLES A 44 OXF B
HUNT COLLINS A 44 OXF B
HUNT CYRUS A 44 HEN B
HUNT D A A 44 OXF W
HUNT D Y A 44 OXF W
HUNT DAVID A 32 DAV W
HUNT DAVID A 32 DAV W
HUNT DAVID A 32 DAV W
HUNT DAVID A 44 OXF B
HUNT DAVID W A 32 LEE W
HUNT DICK A 44 TOW B
HUNT E M A 44 FIS W
HUNT ELIJAH A 44 OXF B
HUNT ELIJAH A 44 YXS B
HUNT ENOCH A 44 TOW B

HUNT ESLY A 29 FA2 W
HUNT FIELDING A 44 OXF B
HUNT FRANK A 44 TOW B
HUNT FREDRICK A 46 FRI B
HUNT G W A 44 OXF W
HUNT GEORGE A 44 TOW B
HUNT GILBERT A 46 FRI W
HUNT GRANVILL A 44 OXF B
HUNT HARRISON A 44 OXF B
HUNT HENDERSON A 44 OXF B
HUNT HILMON A 44 TOW B
HUNT ISAAC A 44 KIT B
HUNT ITHAMER A 46 FRI W
HUNT J D A 46 FRI W
HUNT J M B A 44 TOW W
HUNT J P H A 44 BRA W
HUNT JACOB A 39 FRA B
HUNT JACOB A 44 OXF B
HUNT JACOB A 44 SAS B
HUNT JAMES A 44 TOW B
HUNT JAMES A 44 HEN B
HUNT JAMES A 44 HEN W
HUNT JAMES A 44 KIT B
HUNT JAMES A 44 OXF B
HUNT JAMES H A 44 HEN W
HUNT JAS M A 44 KIT W
HUNT JAS P A 44 KIT W
HUNT JAS T A 44 OXF W
HUNT JESSE A 26 PEE B
HUNT JESSE A 46 FRI W
HUNT JNO L A 44 KIT W
HUNT JNO W A 44 YXR W
HUNT JOHN A 26 PEE W
HUNT JOS P A 44 RAG W
HUNT JOSEPH A 44 ISL B
HUNT JOSEPH A 44 KIT B
HUNT JOSEPH S A 39 HAY W
HUNT LEONADOR A 44 SAS B
HUNT LEWIS A 44 OXF B
HUNT M J A 44 FOR W
HUNT MADISON A 39 HAY B
HUNT MANUEL A 26 PEE B
HUNT MARK A 44 TOW B
HUNT MERICA A 44 HEN B
HUNT MOSES A 44 OXF B
HUNT MOSES A 44 YXS B
HUNT NAPPER A 44 OXF B
HUNT NELSON A 44 HEN B
HUNT NOVEL A 44 SAS B
HUNT OLIVER A 29 FA2 B
HUNT ORSBORN A 32 LOF W
HUNT OSBORN A 44 SAS B
HUNT OWEN A 44 HEN B
HUNT PETER A 44 OXF B
HUNT PRIMUS A 26 PEE B
HUNT PRIMUS A 44 TOW B
HUNT R H A 44 HEN W
HUNT R L A 44 OXF W
HUNT RICHARD A 44 HEN B
HUNT ROBBIN A 44 HEN B
HUNT ROBERT A 44 SAS B
HUNT ROBT A 39 PUG B
HUNT ROBT A 44 ISL B
HUNT ROBT A 44 KIT B
HUNT ROBT A 44 OXF B
HUNT SAML A 44 KIT B
HUNT SAML A A 44 OXF W
HUNT SAML R A 44 KIT W
HUNT SAMUEL A 44 OXF W
HUNT SAMUEL A 46 HIG W
HUNT SQUARE A 44 OXF B
HUNT STEPHEN JR A 46 FRI W
HUNT STPHEN SR A 46 FRI W

HUNT THOMAS A 44 KIT B
HUNT THOS A 44 SAS B
HUNT THOS H A 44 RAG W
HUNT W H A 32 DAV W
HUNT W T A 44 LED W
HUNT WALTER A 26 PEE B
HUNT WILLIAM A 44 SAS B
HUNT WILLIAM JR A 30 POW B
HUNT WILLIAM SR A 30 POW B
HUNT WILLIS A 44 TOW B
HUNT WM A 44 OXF B
HUNT WM J A 44 KIT W
HUNT WOODSON A 44 TAR B
HUNTER ALBERT A 37 HOL B
HUNTER ALEXANDER A 37 ROB B
HUNTER ALISON A 40 CAN B
HUNTER AUSTON A 37 MAN B
HUNTER BENJAMIN F A 24 EDE W
HUNTER C R A 35 CYP W
HUNTER CALVIN A 29 FA1 B
HUNTER CHARLES A 46 RAG W
HUNTER DANILE A 37 MAN B
HUNTER DAVID A 44 OXF B
HUNTER DAVID H A 46 RAG W
HUNTER FRANK A 28 10T B
HUNTER FRANK A 44 FIS B
NOT 21 YEARS OLD
HUNTER HENRY A 40 CAN B
HUNTER HOGAN A 35 CYP W
HUNTER HOSEA A 35 LIM W
HUNTER J Z A 24 UPP W
HUNTER JACK A 44 HEN B
HUNTER JAMES A 28 05A B
HUNTER JAMES A 37 HOL B
HUNTER JAMES A 37 ROC B
HUNTER JAMES H A 28 9TH W
HUNTER JOB A 28 04A B
HUNTER JOHN A 26 SHE B
HUNTER JOHN C A 46 RAG W
HUNTER JORDEN A 37 MAN B
HUNTER JOSEPH A 40 CAN B
HUNTER LODEN A 37 MAN B
HUNTER M A 35 CYP W
HUNTER MADISON A 44 KIT B
HUNTER MANUEL A 28 05A B
HUNTER MEREDITH A 44 KIT B
HUNTER MOSES A 29 FA1 B
HUNTER NICHOLAS A 35 ISL W
HUNTER PETER A 37 PEN B
HUNTER R W A 40 CAN B
HUNTER RICHARD A 37 MAN B
HUNTER RICHARD A 37 ROC B
HUNTER ROBERT A 30 IND B
HUNTER SAM A 26 BOR B
HUNTER SAML J A 28 02N W
HUNTER SAMUEL H A 46 RAG W
HUNTER SOUTHEY A 28 05A B
HUNTER STEPHEN A 39 PUG B
HUNTER WILLIAM A 44 OXF W
HUNTER WM A 28 04A B
HUNTER YOUNG A 37 ROC B
HURDLE LEMUEL A 24 UPP W
HURDLE QUINTON R A 24 UPP W
HURDLE REDDICK A 24 UPP W
HURDLE RICHARD A 24 UPP W
HURDLE ROBT A 24 UPP W
HURDLE WILLIAM A 24 UPP W
HURST BENJAMIN A 35 WAR B
HURST G W A 28 01B W
HURST JACOB A 35 WAR B
HURST JAMES R A 35 WAR W
HURST JOHN A 35 KEN B
HURST ROBERT A 35 KEN B

HURTT D W A 28 01A W
HURTT ISAAC A 72 SWA W
HUSBAND ENOS A 46 COB B
HUSK J C A 29 FA2 W
HUSK JAS A 29 GRA B
HUSK JERRY A 29 FA1 B
HUSK JERRY A 29 FA1 B
HUSK JORDAN A 29 ROC B
HUSK L H A 29 FA1 W
HUSK MILBON A 29 FA1 B
HUSK R H A 29 FA2 W
HUSK THOS A 29 FA1 B
HUSK WM A 29 FA1 W
MILLITIA OFFICER AFTER-
WARDS ENG IN REBELLION
HUSK WRIGHT A 29 FA1 W
NOTARY PUBLIC MILITIA
OFFICER AFTER AIDED
IN REBELLION
HUSKEY HENDERSON A 44 FOR B
HUSKEY JOSEPH A 26 MOU W
HUSKINS JOHN A 26 BUR B
HUSKY BENJ A 44 BEA B
HUSSEY DAVID A 35 KEN B
HUSSEY JAMES A 35 ISL B
HUSSEY JESSIE J A 37 TA1 W
HUSSEY JOHN A 28 04A B
HUSSEY JOHN B A 35 KEN W
HUSSEY LEWIS A 37 TA1 B
HUSSEY MARSELLUS L A 37 TA1 W
HUSSEY ORREN A 35 KEN B
HUSSEY RICHARD A 35 KEN B
HUSSEY ROBT A 28 05A B
HUSSEY SAMEUL A 35 KEN B
HUSSEY THADDEUS A 37 TA1 W
HUSSEY THOMAS C A 37 TA1 W
HUSSEY THOMAS W A 37 TA1 W
HUSSEY TONEY A 35 ISL B
HUSSY DANL A 29 FA1 W
HUSSY JOHN E A 35 SMI W
HUST ROBERT A 44 DUT B
HUSTED GEORGE A 37 PIN B
HUSTELLER M A H A 26 GRI W
HUSTON HICKS A 37 ROC W
HUSTON JOHN A 37 HIC B
HUTCHINS ALBERT J A 99 BUS W
HUTCHINS COSTEN A 30 MOY W
HUTCHINS J W A 99 BUS W
HUTCHINS JOHN H A 99 BUS B
HUTCHINS SMITH A 46 KIN W
HUTCHINS W T A 46 KIN W
HUTCHINS WILLIAM A 30 IND W
HUTCHINSON ALFERD A 32 THO B
HUTCHINSON JOHN A 28 01A W
HUTCHINSON WILLIAM A 35 ROC W
HUTCHINSON WRIGHT A 35 ROC W
HUTCHISON C L A 40 RHY W
HUTSON EDMAND A 46 FRI B
HUTSON HENRY A 46 JAM W
HUTSON HENRY M A 46 COB W
HUTSON JOHN A 46 JAM B
HUTSON JOHN B A 32 THO W
HUTSON SETH A 29 LOC W
HUTSON W A 46 GRE W
HUTSON WILLIAM A 46 COB W
HUTTON JAMES A 46 COB W
HUTTS B E A 24 EDE W
HUX J K A 26 CAR W
HUZA STEPHEN A 46 FRI W
HUZZEY HARDY A 29 FA1 W
HYAT LARKINS A 32 THO W
HYATT JAMES A 25 HAY B
HYBURT WM M A 29 FA2 W

HYMAN ABRAHAM	A	28	9TH	B
HYMAN ABRAHAM H	A	28	9TH	B
HYMAN ABRAHAM JR	A	28	9TH	B
HYMAN ABRAHAM T	A	28	9TH	B
HYMAN ADAM	A	28	9TH	B
HYMAN ADAM	A	37	HIC	B
HYMAN AFRICA	A	28	9TH	B
HYMAN ALBERT	A	37	EDW	B
HYMAN ARDEN	A	37	PEN	B
HYMAN ARDEN	A	37	PIN	B
HYMAN ARTHUR B	A	37	HIC	A
HYMAN ATHICA	A	28	04A	B
HYMAN AUSTIN	A	37	HIC	B
HYMAN BENJAMIN	A	37	TA2	B
HYMAN FRANK	A	37	PIN	B
HYMAN GEORGE	A	28	04A	B
HYMAN GRANVILLE	A	37	TA1	B
HYMAN HAMAN	A	28	9TH	B
HYMAN HENRY	A	37	PEN	B
HYMAN HUNTER	A	37	PEN	B
HYMAN JEFFRY	A	37	EDW	B
HYMAN NATHAN	A	37	EDW	B
HYMAN NATHAN	A	37	HIC	A
HYMAN OPIKY	A	37	PEN	B
HYMAN PAUL	A	37	PEN	B
HYMAN PETER	A	28	9TH	B
HYMAN RICHARD	A	28	01A	B
HYMAN RUFFIN	A	37	PEN	B
HYMAN SAML	A	28	05A	B
HYMAN STEPHEN	A	28	9TH	B
HYMAN TURNER	A	37	TA1	B
HYMAN WILLIAM	A	28	9TH	B
HYMAN ZION	A	37	PIN	B

- I -

IAMS JOHN	A	32	POS	W
IDDINGS JNO H	A	46	GRE	W
IDDINGS WM	A	46	GRE	W
IDINGS JOS M	A	46	GRE	W
IDLE A S	A	46	FRI	W
IDLE BURNET M	A	46	FRI	W
IDLE THOMAS	A	46	FRI	B
IDLET SAML	A	28	05A	B
IDLEY HENRY	A	24	EDE	B
IDOL B D K	A	32	BRO	W
IDOL DAVID	A	32	CLE	W
IDOL DAVID H	A	32	BRO	W
IDOL H N	A	32	CLE	W
IDOL J W	A	32	DAV	W
IDOL JACOB	A	32	BRO	W
IDOL JEHU	A	32	BRO	W
IDOL JOHN N	A	32	BRO	W
IESELY DR	A	46	MCL	B
ILES JAMES	A	37	MAN	B
IMBLER DAVID	A	32	LEE	W
IMBLER DAVID SR	A	32	LEE	W
IMBLER DUGAIN	A	32	THO	W
IMBLER EPHRAM	A	32	DAV	W
IMBLER JACOB	A	32	LEE	W
IMBLER ROBERT	A	32	LEE	W
IMBLER STEVAN	A	32	LEE	W
IMBLER WESLEY	A	32	LEE	W
INGLE ALBERT	A	46	GIB	W
INGLE ANTHONY	A	46	MCL	W
INGLE DAVID	A	46	GIB	W
INGLE JESSE	A	46	MCL	B
INGLE JOHN	A	26	GRI	W
INGLE JONES	A	46	MCL	B
INGLE MEBANE	A	46	GIB	W
INGLE MOSES	A	46	GIB	B
INGLE ROBT	A	46	GIB	B
INGLE RUFUS W	A	46	GIB	W
INGOLD ALFRED	A	46	GRE	W
INGOLD ALPHONSO W	A	46	GRE	W
INGOLD DANIEL	A	46	COB	W
INGOLD DAVID	A	46	COB	W
INGOLD F N	A	46	GRE	W
INGOLD GEORGE	A	46	COB	W
INGOLD SOLOMON	A	46	RAG	W
INGRAHAM HENRY	A	29	FA1	W
INGRAHAM MARK	A	29	FA1	B
INGRAHAM RICHARD	A	29	FA2	B
INGRAHAM THOS	A	29	FA1	B
INGRAHAM WM	A	28	02N	B
INGRAM H C	A	32	JAC	W
INGRAM JAMES	A	32	DAV	W
INGRAM JOE	A	39	HAY	B
INGRAM JOHN	A	32	JAC	B
INGRAM JONES B	A	39	SPE	W
INGRAM SAM	R	39	SPE	B
NAME LINED OUT UNDER 21 YEARS OLD				
INGRAM URIAH	A	32	THO	W
INGRAM W S	A	32	JAC	W
INGRAM WILLIS P	A	39	SPE	W
INMAN JACKSON	A	29	GRA	B
INSCO DANIEL	A	39	SPE	W
INSCO DANIEL SR	A	39	PUG	W
INSCO GRAY	A	39	JOR	B
INSCO JAMES	A	39	SPE	W
INSCO JOHN	A	39	LOU	W
INSCO NORFHLET	A	39	PUG	W
INSCO PLEASANT W	A	39	LOU	W
INSCO W H	A	39	SPE	W
INSCO WILLIAM	A	39	JOR	W
INSCORE ABNER	A	44	BRA	W
INSCORE JOSEPH	A	44	FOR	W
INSSCORE A P	A	44	DUT	W
IPOCH BRYAN H	A	28	16T	W
IPOCK BRICE	A	28	6TH	W
IPOCK BURTON	A	28	11T	W
IPOCK CHARLES	A	28	11T	W
IPOCK FREDERICK	A	28	8TH	W
IPOCK FREDERICK G	A	28	8TH	W
IPOCK GEORGE	A	28	8TH	W
IPOCK HARDY	A	28	11T	W
IPOCK HENRY	A	28	16T	W
IPOCK JOHN	A	28	8TH	W
IPOCK JOHN A	A	28	12T	W
IPOCK JOHN P	A	28	11T	W
IPOCK LEVI B	A	28	13T	W
IPOCK LEWIS	A	28	11T	W
IPOCK MORGAN	A	28	13T	W
IPOCK NOAH	A	28	12T	W
IPOCK OLIVER	A	28	11T	W
IPOCK SAML	A	28	6TH	W
IPOCK SAMUEL	A	28	8TH	W
IPOCK STEPH B	A	28	04A	W
IPOCK STEPHEN	A	28	11T	W
IPOCK WILLIAM H	A	28	11T	W
IPOCK WM	A	28	13T	W
IRDLAND EDWD	A	19	POR	W
IRELAND DAVID D	A	53	SWA	W
IRELAND JOHN	A	28	03A	B
IRELAND JOHN	A	35	WAR	B
IRELAND JOHN B	A	28	15T	W
IRELAND JOHN D	A	28	15T	W
IRELAND JOHN W	A	28	16T	W
IRELAND PETER	A	35	FAI	B
IRELAND THOMAS	A	28	15T	W
IRELAND THOMAS E	A	28	10T	W
IRILAND ARCHEBALD A	A	28	15T	W
IRVIN B H	A	19	HAD	W
IRVIN JAMES M	A	46	JAM	W
IRVIN SAMUEL	A	35	SMI	B
IRVING A C	A	26	BLA	W
IRVING A J	A	26	BLA	W
IRVING PETER	A	26	BLA	B
IRVINGS JUNE	A	72	SWA	B
IRWIN DAVID	A	46	GIB	W
IRWIN IRA	A	26	CAR	W
IRWIN J W	A	26	SWA	W
IRWIN JAMES G	A	26	SHE	W
IRWIN MARK	A	46	MON	B
ISCO HENRY	A	39	JOR	W
ISELY LEWIS N	A	46	MCL	W
ISELY RICHARD	A	46	COB	B
ISLER CESAR	A	32	TYR	B
ISLEY CHRISTIAN	A	46	GIB	W
ISLEY ELI	A	46	GIB	W
ISLEY GEORGE	A	46	GIB	W
ISLEY GEORGE K	A	46	RAG	W
ISLEY JOHN C	A	46	GRE	W
ISLEY PETER R	A	46	GIB	W
ISRAEL ABRAHAM	A	25	PIN	W
IVES COLONIAN	A	30	IND	W
IVES FREEMAN E	A	28	16T	W
IVES GIDEON	A	28	15T	W
IVES HASTY	A	28	10T	B
IVES JAMES	A	46	ROS	B
IVES JOHN	A	28	15T	W
IVES JOHN F	A	53	SWA	W
IVES JOHN P	A	28	9TH	W
IVES NELSON N	A	30	IND	W
IVES SOLOMON C	A	28	17T	W
IVES WILLIAM H	A	28	9TH	W
IVESTER A P	A	26	WAR	W
IVESTER ISAAC	A	26	WAR	W
IVESTER JOHN	A	26	WAR	W
IVEY RICHARD	A	29	FA1	W
IVEY STINCEN	A	99	BUS	W
IVY ANDREW	A	46	ROS	W
IVY CASWELL	A	28	04A	B
IVY CASWELL	A	28	04B	B
IVY JOHN P	A	37	ROC	W
JACKSON A	A	29	LOC	B
JACKSON A R	A	46	HIG	W
JACKSON A W	A	37	ROC	W
JACKSON A W	A	39	DAV	W
JACKSON AARON	A	40	DEC	W
JACKSON ABE	A	26	SWA	B
JACKSON ADAM CHAL		40	SAN	B
NAME LINED OUT				
JACKSON ALEX	A	28	8TH	B
JACKSON ALEX	A	29	FA1	B
JACKSON ALFRED	A	28	01A	B
JACKSON ALFRED	A	29	FA1	B
JACKSON ALFRED	A	37	TA1	B
JACKSON AMOS	A	37	ROC	B
JACKSON ANDREW	A	28	01A	B
JACKSON ANDREW	A	28	03A	B
JACKSON ANDREW	A	28	04A	B
JACKSON ANDREW	A	29	GRA	B
JACKSON ANDREW	A	53	OCR	W
JACKSON ANDREWS	A	39	HAR	W
JACKSON ANTHONY	A	37	PEN	B
JACKSON ARCHY	A	29	FA1	B
JACKSON BENJ	A	19	BEI	B
JACKSON BENJN	A	29	LOC	B
JACKSON BRISTOW	A	28	8TH	B
JACKSON BRYAN	A	28	04A	B
JACKSON CHARLES H	A	39	HAY	W
JACKSON DAVID	A	28	11T	W
JACKSON DAVID	A	29	FA1	B
JACKSON DAVID	R	28	11T	W
DID NOT TAKE THE OATH WAS OVERSEER OF ROADS & PATROL AND GAVE AID & COMFORT TO REBEL SOLDIERS				
JACKSON E	A	28	05A	B

JACKSON E J A 39 LOU W
JACKSON EDMUND A 28 8TH B
JACKSON EDWARD A 28 04A B
JACKSON EDWARD A 37 WHI W
JACKSON ELBERT A 37 ROC W
JACKSON ELI A 28 02N B
JACKSON FRANCIS A 29 GRA B
JACKSON FREDK A 29 FA1 B
JACKSON FURNEY A 28 11T W
JACKSON GEORGE W A 53 OCR W
JACKSON H C A 19 HAR W
JACKSON HENRY A 29 FA1 B
JACKSON HENRY A 29 GRA B
JACKSON HENRY A 39 SPE B
JACKSON HENRY A 46 FRI B
JACKSON HENRY H A 46 GRE B
JACKSON HERBERT A 44 SAS B
JACKSON HILLIARD A 28 04B B
JACKSON ISAAC A 28 05A B
JACKSON ISAAC A 29 FA1 B
JACKSON ISAAC A 29 GRA B
JACKSON J C A 29 CED W
JACKSON J D A 29 FA1 W
JACKSON J E A 29 FLE W
JACKSON J J A 39 LOU W
JACKSON J M A 26 BOR W
JACKSON J W A 39 JOR W
JACKSON JAMES A 28 10T W
JACKSON JAMES A 28 8TH B
JACKSON JAMES A 40 CAN B
JACKSON JAMES A 46 SUM W
JACKSON JAMES B A 32 THO W
JACKSON JAMES E A 53 LA1 W
JACKSON JAMES H M A 37 TA1 B
JACKSON JAMES S A 24 EDE W
JACKSON JAS A 29 GRA B
JACKSON JILES A 39 DAV B
JACKSON JIM A 39 DAV B
JACKSON JOE A 28 03A B
JACKSON JOHN A 24 EDE B
JACKSON JOHN A 28 04A B
JACKSON JOHN A 37 ROC W
JACKSON JOHN A 44 FOR B
JACKSON JOHN A 46 JAM W
JACKSON JOHN A A 28 11T W
JACKSON JOHN W A 28 13T W
JACKSON JOSEPH A 28 04A B
JACKSON JOSHUA A 29 FA2 B
JACKSON KESSIA A 37 SHA W
JACKSON L R A 29 CED W
JACKSON LAZARUS A 28 11T B
JACKSON LONDON A 29 FA1 B
JACKSON LORENZO A 35 LIM W
JACKSON M A A 24 MID W
JACKSON M J A 39 PUG W
JACKSON MAJOR A 28 11T B
JACKSON MAJOR A 32 THO B
JACKSON MOSES A 35 WAR B
JACKSON NATHAN A 28 03A B
JACKSON NATHAN A 28 04A B
JACKSON NOAH A 19 BE1 B
JACKSON NOAH A 28 11T W
JACKSON OREN S A 37 ROC W
JACKSON P G A 44 DUT W
JACKSON P M A 29 FA1 W
JACKSON R W A 29 CED W
JACKSON RICHARD A 28 10T B
JACKSON RICHARD A 30 CUR B
JACKSON SAML A 28 04A B
JACKSON SAML SR A 29 FA1 B
JACKSON SAMUEL A 25 SHO W
JACKSON SAMUEL A 37 PEN B
JACKSON SAMUEL A 46 JAM W

JACKSON SETH A 28 05A B
JACKSON SIMON A 37 PIN B
JACKSON SIMON A 44 HEN B
JACKSON SINGULAR A 30 MOY B
JACKSON SOL A 29 FA1 B
JACKSON SQUARE A A 44 OXF B
JACKSON THOMAS A 37 ROC W
JACKSON THOMAS A 53 OCR W
JACKSON W D A 39 DAV W
JACKSON W W A 29 LOC W
JACKSON WASHINGTON A 44 FOR B
JACKSON WILLIAM A 32 DAV B
JACKSON WILLIAM A 37 ROC W
JACKSON WILLIAM H A 28 10T W
JACKSON WILLIS A 46 JAM W
JACKSON WM A 28 15T W
JACOB ALLEN A 37 ROC B
JACOB WM A A 19 BE1 B
JACOBS ALEXANDER E A 30 ROA W
JACOBS BENJM A 28 01A W
JACOBS GABL A 29 BLA X
JACOBS GEORGE A 37 ROC B
JACOBS ISAAC A 29 BLA X
JACOBS JNO A 29 BLA X
JACOBS STEPHN A 28 04A B
JACOBS WILLIAM A 29 FLE W
JAMES ALBERT A 28 04A B
JAMES ANDREW A 32 SHE W
JAMES ANTHONY A 28 04B B
JAMES C C A 35 WOL W
JAMES DANIEL A 19 BE1 B
JAMES DAVID A 32 SHE W
JAMES DAVID A 35 CYP W
JAMES DAVID H A 35 ROC W
JAMES ELIJAH A 28 05A B
JAMES HENRY A 24 EDE B
JAMES HENRY A 37 HOL W
JAMES HEZEKIAH A 37 SHA W
JAMES J H A 29 FA1 W
JAMES JACOB A 35 CYP W
JAMES JOHN A 26 GOF B
JAMES JOHN A 32 SHE W
JAMES JOHN A 99 BUS B
JAMES JOHN E A 35 ROC W
JAMES JOHN W A 35 ROC W
JAMES JOS THOS A 29 FA1 W
JAMES OLLIN A 35 MAG B
JAMES PRIMUS A 35 KEN B
JAMES T B A 28 02N W
JAMES THOMAS A 28 14T B
JAMES WILLIAM A 37 HOL B
JAMES WM F A 28 03A B
JANNEY FRANCIS A 28 01B W
JARARD THOMAS A 30 NAR W
JARD JASPER A 30 TUL W
JARMAN ANDREW A 35 LIM B
JARMAN HENRY A 35 KEN B
JARMAN LUNNUN A 28 03A B
JARMAN WILLIAM A 35 KEN B
JARMON BENJ A 28 6TH B
JARMON ELIE A 19 BE1 B
JARMON EVAN A 28 03A B
JARMON GILES A 28 03A B
JARMON ISAAC A 35 KEN B
JARMON MATTHIAS A 28 6TH B
JARRAT A W A 32 COT W
JARRELL ABSALEM A 46 ROS W
JARRELL JNO A 46 HIG W
JARRET J M A 26 SHE W
JARRETT BENJAMIN D A 37 TA2 W
JARRETT CHARLES F A 40 DA2 W
JARRETT DANIL A 32 THO W
JARRETT GEORGE A 37 HIG W

JARROTT WM P A 32 COT W
JARVIS ABEL A 30 POW W
JARVIS ABRAHAM A 53 SWA B
JARVIS ALEXANDER V A 30 COI W
JARVIS CORNELIUS A 30 POP B
JARVIS DAVID A 53 SWA W
JARVIS DAVID S A 53 SWA W
JARVIS GEORGE A 53 SWA W
JARVIS GEORGE JR A 53 GER W
JARVIS GEORGE N A 30 POP W
JARVIS HENRY A 32 LOF B
JARVIS JACOB A 53 SWA B
JARVIS JAMES N A 53 SWA W
JARVIS JESSE A 28 04A B
JARVIS JESSE M A 53 SWA W
JARVIS JOHN A 30 COI W
JARVIS JOHN B A 30 NAR W
JARVIS JOHN C A 53 SWA W
JARVIS JOHN H A 19 BE1 W
JARVIS JOHN H A 53 GER W
JARVIS JOHN W A 53 GER W
JARVIS JONATHAN A 53 SWA W
JARVIS JOSEPH A 53 SWA W
JARVIS LAMUL A 30 POP W
JARVIS LEWIS A 32 CLE B
JARVIS LODAWICK C A 53 SWA W
JARVIS MAJOR A 30 POP B
JARVIS MAJOR CHAL A 30 IND B
PROVED TO BE 22 YEARS
JARVIS MOSES A 28 9TH B
CERTIFICATE GIVEN WORKS
NOW DOWN THE RIVER
JARVIS NATHANIEL A 53 SWA W
JARVIS OLIVER A 53 FAI W
JARVIS PLYMOUTH A 30 COI B
JARVIS RICHARD A 30 POP W
JARVIS RICHARD A 30 POW W
JARVIS SAMUEL A 53 FAI W
JARVIS SAMUEL B R 30 ROA W
CHALLENGED
MEMBER OF LEGISLATURE
PRIOR TO 1861
JARVIS THOMAS A 53 FAI W
JARVIS THOMAS R A 53 GER W
JARVIS THOS B A 30 POP W
JARVIS TILMON F A 53 SWA W
JARVIS WILLIAM A 19 BE1 B
JARVIS WILLIAM A 30 CUR B
JARVIS WILLIAM A A 30 POP W
JARVIS WILLIAM R A 53 SWA W
JARVIS WILLIS B A 53 SWA W
JASPER GEORGE A 28 01A B
JASPER H N A 39 LOU W
TRNS TO WILMINGTON NC
JAYCOX JOHN A 28 05A B
JAYCOX ROSCOE A 28 02N B
JEAMS WM A 46 GRE B
JEAN DORSEY A 39 GRI W
JEFFERS JOHN A 46 SUM B
JEFFERS WILLIAM A 46 SUM B
JEFFERS WILLIS A 46 FRI B
JEFFERSON DAVID A 29 FA1 B
JEFFERSON GEORGE A 44 HEN B
JEFFERSON HENERY A 29 FA1 B
JEFFERSON JNO A 44 OXF B
JEFFERSON JOHN A 46 GIB B
JEFFERSON NED A 44 TOW B
JEFFREYS ALLEN A 39 HAR B
JEFFREYS C E A 44 BEA W
JEFFREYS GEO A 39 FRE B
JEFFREYS H G A 44 BRA W
JEFFREYS HAYWOOD A 39 HAR B
JEFFREYS JNO A 38 FRE B

JEFFREYS JNO A 39 GRI W
JEFFREYS JOHN A 26 WAR W
JEFFREYS LAZARUS A 39 HAR B
JEFFREYS LITTLETON A 44 BRA W
JEFFREYS MACK A 39 JOR B
JEFFREYS MINGO A 39 HAR B
JEFFREYS NOFFLET A 39 HAR B
JEFFREYS OFFEY A 39 HAR B
JEFFREYS ROMULUS A 39 HAR B
JEFFREYS SAM A 38 FRE B
JEFFREYS SANDAFORD A 39 FRE B
JEFFREYS SOLOMON A 26 GOF B
JEFFREYS TURNER A 39 HAR B
JEFFREYS W B A 44 BEA W
JEFFREYS WILLIAM A 44 SAS B
JEFFREYS WILLIE A 39 GRI W
JEFFREYS WM A 44 BRA W
JEFFRIES HUNTER A 37 PIN B
JENKINS A BERRY A 40 DA1 W
JENKINS A JACKSON A 40 DA1 W
JENKINS A L A 44 BRA W
JENKINS A T A 44 BEA W
JENKINS AARON A 40 CAN W
JENKINS AARON A 40 DA1 W
JENKINS AARON D A 40 DA2 W
JENKINS ABE A 26 HOL B
JENKINS ADAM A 40 FER B
JENKINS ADAM R 40 FER B
6 MOS RESIDENCE
1ST SEPT 1867
JENKINS ADAMS A 37 HIG B
JENKINS AMOS A 37 PEN B
JENKINS ANTHONY A 37 PEN B
JENKINS AUGUSTUS A 28 14T B
JENKINS B F A 44 OXF W
JENKINS BENJ A 28 03A B
JENKINS BENJAMIN A 37 PEN B
JENKINS BENJAMIN A 37 ROC B
JENKINS BENNETT A 37 HIG W
JENKINS BERRYMAN A 40 DA2 W
JENKINS BRINKLEY A 29 FA1 B
JENKINS BYRON A 37 PIN B
JENKINS CHARLES H A 37 PIN W
SPARTA
JENKINS CHRISTY A 40 DA1 W
JENKINS COOPER A 40 SAN B
JENKINS D A 26 BOR W
JENKINS D A A 32 THO W
JENKINS DAVID A 29 FA1 B
JENKINS DAVID A 40 DA1 W
JENKINS DAVID A A 40 DA1 W
JENKINS E J A 44 BRA W
JENKINS E S A 44 BRA W
JENKINS EDMUND A 37 TA1 B
JENKINS EDWARD A 26 HOL B
JENKINS EDWARD A 40 DA1 W
JENKINS ELI A A 40 DA1 W
JENKINS ELIJAH A 28 16T B
JENKINS EPHRAIM A 37 HIG B
JENKINS EPHRAIM A 37 HIG B
JENKINS EPHRAM A 37 WHI B
JENKINS EVERETT A 37 HIG B
JENKINS FRANK A 44 HEN B
JENKINS FREDRICK A 37 HIG B
JENKINS GARDNER A 37 TA1 B
JENKINS GEO A 29 FA1 B
JENKINS GEORGE A 37 PEN B
JENKINS GEORGE A 44 FOR B
JENKINS GRAY A 37 HIG B
JENKINS HARRISON A 40 DA1 W
JENKINS HARRY H A 28 03A B
JENKINS HENDERSON A 44 OXF B
JENKINS HORACE A 28 16T B

JENKINS ISAAC A 26 HOL B
JENKINS ISAAC A 37 EDW B
JENKINS J A 44 BRA W
JENKINS J H R 26 HOL B
MILITIA OFFICER &
ENGAGED IN REBELLION
JENKINS J R A 32 CLE W
JENKINS J W A 44 SAS W
JENKINS JACK A 37 PIN B
JENKINS JACOB A 37 PEN B
JENKINS JACOB A 37 PIN B
JENKINS JACOB A 40 DA1 W
JENKINS JAMES A 29 FA1 W
JENKINS JAMES A 46 ROS B
JENKINS JAMES F A 37 HIG W
JENKINS JAMES L A 37 HIG W
JENKINS JAMES P A 37 HIG W
JENKINS JAS L A 44 SAS W
JENKINS JESSEE A 39 SPE W
JENKINS JESSIE A 37 TA1 B
JENKINS JNO A 44 ISL B
JENKINS JNO MCL A 29 FA1 W
JENKINS JNO T A 44 OXF W
JENKINS JOAB A 37 SPA W
JENKINS JOHN A 37 HIG W
JENKINS JOHN A 44 RAG W
JENKINS JOHN M A 37 PIN W
JENKINS JONAS A 40 DA1 W
JENKINS JONATHAN SR A 44 BRA W
JENKINS JOSEPH A 26 HOL B
JENKINS JOSEPH A 40 DA1 W
JENKINS JOURDAN A 28 05A B
JENKINS KINCHEN A 37 HIG B
JENKINS KING A 44 HEN B
JENKINS L G R 26 HOL B
MILITIA OFFICER &
ENGAGED IN REBELLION
JENKINS LEWIS A 37 HIG B
JENKINS M W A 44 BRA W
JENKINS MICHAEL A 37 HIG B
JENKINS MOSES A 37 SPA B
JENKINS NED A 44 OXF B
JENKINS PARMER A 44 SAS B
JENKINS PAUL A 39 HAY B
NAME LINED OUT
1ST REG BOARD EPPING
FOREST IN GRANVILLE
JENKINS PAUL A 44 KIT W
JENKINS R A A 32 THO W
JENKINS R A A 44 TOW W
JENKINS RICHARD A 24 EDE B
JENKINS RICHD A 44 OXF B
JENKINS ROBERT A 37 PIN B
JENKINS RUFUS A 44 SAS B
JENKINS RUFUS M A 40 DA1 W
JENKINS S D A 44 BRA W
JENKINS SAMUEL A 40 CAN W
JENKINS SAMUEL F A 37 HIG W
JENKINS SAMUEL P A 37 HIG W
JENKINS SHADRACH O A 40 DA1 W
JENKINS SMITH A 40 DA1 W
JENKINS T S A 44 LED W
JENKINS THOMAS A 37 HIG B
JENKINS THOS A 29 FA1 B
JENKINS TILMON A 40 DA1 W
JENKINS W G A 44 SAS W
JENKINS W H A 44 LED W
JENKINS W K A 44 OXF W
JENKINS WILEY A 53 SWA B
JENKINS WILLIAM A 40 DA1 W
JENKINS WILLIAM A 44 LED W
JENKINS WILLIS A 37 EDW B
JENNETT BENJAMIN F A 53 LA1 W

JENNETT BURKET A 53 LA1 B
JENNETT EDWARD A 30 IND B
JENNETT HENRY A 53 LA1 W
JENNETT J THOMAS A 53 BUR W
JENNETT JESSE JR A 53 GER W
JENNETT JESSE SR A 53 GER W
JENNETT JOHN A 53 LA1 B
CERT APRIL 18 1868
JENNETT JOHN A 53 SWA B
JENNETT JOSEPH E A 53 HAT W
JENNETT RICHARD A 53 LA1 B
JENNETT SETH CHAL A 30 IND B
JENNETT WALLNER R A 53 HAT W
JENNINGS ALBERT A 26 SHE B
JENNINGS ALLAN A 40 FER B
JENNINGS HILSY A 26 CAR B
JENNINGS JOHN R A 28 05A B
JENNINGS MARSHALL A 30 IND W
JENNINS EVENS A 28 16T B
JENSEN NELSON A 28 15T W
JERKINS BENJ A 19 BE1 B
JERKINS GEO W A 19 BE1 B
JERKINS MICHAEL A 19 MOR B
JERMIN JACOB A 46 HIG B
JERNAGEN CHAS A 29 FA1 B
JERNIGAN ADAM A 35 WOL W
JERNIGAN LOUIS A 35 WOL W
JERNIGAN STEPHAN B A 35 GLI W
JESPER WM A 19 BE1 B
JESPERS JABIN A 28 04A B
JESSOP C Y A 46 FRI W
JESSOP JOHN A 46 FRI W
JESSOP THOMAS A 46 FRI W
JESSUP AMOS A 29 FA1 W
JESSUP FORTUNE A 29 CED B
JESSUP J MCD A 29 CED W
JESSUP JESSEE A 29 FA1 B
JESSUP JOHN HENRY A 29 GRA B
JESSUP JONATHAN A 29 FA1 W
JESSUP WM S A 29 FA2 W
JESTER HENRY A 53 SWA W
JESTER J B A 46 JAM W
JESTER P J A 46 JAM W
JESTOR WM A 46 JAM W
JESUP B F A 29 CED W
JEULL REDWELL A 37 ROC B
JEWEL THOMAS E A 28 15T W
JEWELL BENJA H A 99 BUS W
JEWELL JAMES R A 28 16T W
JEWELL JOHN W A 99 BUS W
JEWELL JOSIAH A 28 16T W
JEWELL WILLIS A 99 BUS B
JEWETT WILLIAM H A 99 BUS B
JIGGITTS ANDERSON A 44 TOW B
JINEY ANDREW T A 37 MAN W
JINKINS BENJN A 28 03A B
JINKINS W H A 39 LOU B
TRNS BY AFF FROM
WARRENTON PRE
TO LOUISBURG
JIRKINS WILLIAM A 19 HAR B
JOBE JOHN W A 46 RAG W
JOBE JOSIAH G A 46 RAG W
JOBE MICHAEL H A 46 RAG W
JOBE SAMUEL W A 46 RAG W
JOBE THOMAS R A 46 RAG W
JOBE WASHINGTON A A 46 RAG W
JOCK MANUEL A 29 LOC B
JOHN ARTHUR A 19 HAD W
JOHNES SIVIA A 24 MID B
JOHNIGAN SQUIRE A 28 11T B
JOHNNICAN WM A 39 PUG W
JOHNS ALLEN A 99 BUS B

JOHNS CHARLES T	A	99	BUS	W
JOHNS HENRY	A	99	BUS	B
JOHNS JACKSON	A	99	BUS	B
JOHNS JOHN S	A	99	BUS	W
JOHNS THOMAS	A	99	BUS	W
JOHNS WASHINGTON	A	99	BUS	B
JOHNSEN ANTHONY	A	37	HOL	B
JOHNSEN BEN	A	37	HOL	B
JOHNSON A	A	26	BOR	B
JOHNSON A A	A	29	MON	W
DIST CONST. BEFORE THE REBELLION AFTERWARDS ENGAGED IN THE REBELLION CONSCRIPTS				
JOHNSON AARON	A	53	LA2	B
JOHNSON ALBERT	A	28	05A	B
JOHNSON ALEXANDER	A	29	FA2	W
JOHNSON ALEXANDER	A	29	SEV	B
JOHNSON ALF M	A	29	FA2	W
JOHNSON ALFORD	A	39	LOU	B
JOHNSON ALFRED	A	24	EDE	B
JOHNSON ALFRED	A	28	16T	B
JOHNSON ALLEN	A	24	EDE	B
JOHNSON ALLEN	A	39	HAY	B
JOHNSON ALSEY	A	99	BUS	W
JOHNSON AMOS	A	35	ROC	B
JOHNSON AMOS	A	35	WAR	W
JOHNSON AMPY	A	44	OXF	B
JOHNSON ANDERSON	A	44	OXF	B
JOHNSON ANDREW	A	26	SHE	B
JOHNSON ANDREW	A	28	01A	B
JOHNSON ANDREW	A	35	ROC	B
JOHNSON ANDY	A	29	CED	B
JOHNSON ANTHONEY	A	19	HAD	B
JOHNSON ANTHONEY	A	24	EDE	B
JOHNSON ANTHONEY	A	37	EDW	B
JOHNSON AUG	A	29	FA1	B
JOHNSON B	A	29	FA1	W
JOHNSON B D	A	46	SUM	W
JOHNSON B W	A	46	SUM	W
JOHNSON BARNABAS	A	99	BUS	W
JOHNSON BEN	A	39	HAY	B
JOHNSON BENJ	A	44	FOR	B
JOHNSON BENJ	A	46	GRE	B
JOHNSON BENJN	A	28	03A	B
JOHNSON BOSTON	A	28	04A	B
JOHNSON BRYLEM	A	39	GRI	W
JOHNSON C	A	26	BOR	B
JOHNSON C K	A	29	LOC	W
REMOVED TO FLEA HILL				
JOHNSON CALVIN	A	37	HIC	B
JOHNSON CALVIN	A	39	HAY	B
JOHNSON CARIDON	A	39	HAY	B
JOHNSON CASWELL	A	39	LOU	B
JOHNSON CHARLES	A	25	TUS	B
JOHNSON CHARLES	A	37	TA1	B
JOHNSON CHARLES	A	39	LOU	B
JOHNSON CHARLES	A	44	OXF	B
JOHNSON CHAS	A	28	04A	B
JOHNSON CLEM	A	37	ROB	B
JOHNSON CLINTON	A	19	BE1	B
JOHNSON D B	A	44	LED	W
JOHNSON D J	A	29	LOC	W
REMOVED TO FLEA HILL				
JOHNSON D W C	A	32	THO	W
JOHNSON DANIEL	A	24	EDE	B
JOHNSON DANIEL	A	39	LOU	B
JOHNSON DANIEL	A	46	HIG	W
JOHNSON DAVID	A	24	EDE	B
JOHNSON DAVID	A	28	03B	B
JOHNSON DAVID	A	28	11T	W
JOHNSON DAVID	A	29	GRA	W
JOHNSON DAVID	A	29	SEV	W
JOHNSON DRED	A	37	ROB	B
JOHNSON DUNCAN	A	29	FA1	W
JOHNSON DUNDEE	A	24	EDE	B
JOHNSON EDMOND	A	26	PEE	W
JOHNSON EDWARD	A	28	11T	B
JOHNSON EDWARD	A	53	FAI	B
JOHNSON ELI	A	28	02N	B
JOHNSON EMANUELL	A	39	HAY	B
JOHNSON ENSEBIUS S	A	35	ROC	W
JOHNSON EVERETT	A	28	05A	B
JOHNSON F H	A	32	DAV	W
JOHNSON FLEET	A	28	03A	B
JOHNSON FRANK	A	28	6TH	B
JOHNSON FRANK	A	37	ROB	W
JOHNSON FRANKLIN	A	39	HAY	B
JOHNSON G W	A	39	HAY	W
NAME LINED OUT MILTON PRECIT CASWELL CO NC				
JOHNSON GABRIEL	A	24	EDE	B
JOHNSON GABRIEL	A	24	EDE	W
JOHNSON GEO	A	19	HAR	B
JOHNSON GEO	A	29	GRA	B
JOHNSON GEO L	A	29	FA1	W
JOHNSON GEORGE	A	19	BE1	B
JOHNSON GEORGE	A	28	01A	B
JOHNSON GEORGE	A	28	02N	B
JOHNSON GEORGE	A	37	SPA	B
JOHNSON GEORGE	A	53	SWA	B
JOHNSON GREEN B	A	46	GRE	W
JOHNSON GREEN L	A	46	HIG	W
JOHNSON H J J	A	29	FLE	B
JOHNSON HAMILTON	A	24	EDE	B
JOHNSON HANDY	A	99	BUS	B
JOHNSON HARRY	A	29	FA1	B
JOHNSON HARRY	A	39	LOU	B
JOHNSON HENDERSON	A	28	7TH	B
JOHNSON HENRY	A	19	BE1	B
JOHNSON HENRY	A	19	BE1	B
JOHNSON HENRY	A	24	EDE	B
JOHNSON HENRY	A	39	HAY	B
JOHNSON HENRY	A	99	BUS	W
JOHNSON HENRY L	A	46	HIG	W
JOHNSON HENRY M	A	35	ISL	B
JOHNSON HENRY MILTON	A	39	HAY	B
JOHNSON HEZEKIAH	A	46	JAM	W
JOHNSON HOLLY	A	29	FA1	W
JOHNSON HORACE	A	28	6TH	B
JOHNSON HOWARD	A	37	WEB	B
JOHNSON HUMPHREY	A	37	PIN	B
JOHNSON IRA G	A	35	ROC	W
JOHNSON IRVIN	A	29	LOC	W
JOHNSON ISA	A	46	HIG	W
JOHNSON ISAAC	A	37	SPA	B
JOHNSON ISAAC	A	37	TA1	B
JOHNSON ISAIAH	A	28	04A	B
JOHNSON ISHAM	A	39	LOU	B
JOHNSON J C	A	46	HIG	W
JOHNSON J H	A	25	TUS	W
JOHNSON J W	A	25	TUS	W
JOHNSON JACKSON	A	19	HAR	B
JOHNSON JAMES	A	28	6TH	B
JOHNSON JAMES	A	28	8TH	B
JOHNSON JAMES	A	29	CED	W
JOHNSON JAMES	A	30	CUR	B
JOHNSON JAMES	A	30	POW	W
JOHNSON JAMES C	A	19	SHA	W
JOHNSON JAMES W	A	37	ROB	W
JOHNSON JAMS R	A	53	HAT	W
JOHNSON JERDON	A	29	FLE	B
JOHNSON JEREMIAH	A	29	FA1	W
JOHNSON JESSE	A	28	13T	W
JOHNSON JESSE	A	29	SEV	W
JOHNSON JESSE	A	37	ROB	B
JOHNSON JESSE	A	46	JAM	W
JOHNSON JESSIE JR	A	29	FA2	W
JOHNSON JNO	A	29	FA1	B
JOHNSON JNO	A	29	GRA	B
JOHNSON JNO	A	29	LOC	W
JOHNSON JNO A	A	30	TUL	W
JOHNSON JNO B	A	29	FA1	W
JOHNSON JNO H	A	19	HAR	B
JOHNSON JNO P	A	29	FA1	W
JOHNSON JOHN	A	19	BE1	W
JOHNSON JOHN	A	26	SHE	B
JOHNSON JOHN	A	28	01B	W
JOHNSON JOHN	A	28	04A	B
JOHNSON JOHN	A	28	05A	B
JOHNSON JOHN	A	28	9TH	B
JOHNSON JOHN	A	37	ROB	B
JOHNSON JOHN	A	37	WEB	B
JOHNSON JOHN	A	39	HAY	B
JOHNSON JOHN	A	44	TAR	B
JOHNSON JOHN	A	46	MON	B
JOHNSON JOHN	A	46	SUM	W
JOHNSON JOHN A	A	29	MON	W
JOHNSON JOHN B	A	53	HAT	W
JOHNSON JOHN W	A	37	HOL	W
JOHNSON JOHN WM	A	29	SEV	W
JOHNSON JORDAN W	A	37	ROB	W
JOHNSON JOSEPH	A	26	PEE	W
JOHNSON JOSEPH	A	28	03A	B
JOHNSON JOSEPH	A	28	11T	B
JOHNSON JOSEPH	A	46	HIG	W
JOHNSON JOSHUA	A	28	04A	B
JOHNSON JOSHUA	A	30	ROA	W
JOHNSON JOSHUA	A	46	HIG	W
JOHNSON L	A	39	LOU	W
JOHNSON L E	A	32	DAV	W
JOHNSON L S	A	40	SAN	B
JOHNSON LAFAYETT	A	37	TA2	W
JOHNSON LAWRENCE	A	37	ROB	W
JOHNSON LEMUEL	A	37	WEB	W
JOHNSON LEONIDAS	A	30	ROA	B
JOHNSON LEVEN	A	28	04A	B
JOHNSON LEVI	A	37	EDW	B
JOHNSON LEVY	A	29	FA2	W
JOHNSON LEVY	A	39	PUG	B
JOHNSON LEWIS	A	24	EDE	B
JOHNSON LEWIS	A	37	ROB	B
JOHNSON LEWIS	A	39	HAY	B
JOHNSON LINSEY	A	28	04B	B
JOHNSON LITTLETON B	A	99	BUS	W
JOHNSON LUNFORD	A	29	FA1	W
JOHNSON M C	A	32	CLE	W
JOHNSON MACK	A	24	EDE	B
JOHNSON MACK	A	28	04A	B
JOHNSON MADDISON	A	35	ROC	B
JOHNSON MADISON	A	39	HAY	B
JOHNSON MAJOR O	A	35	MAG	W
JOHNSON MASON	A	37	HIG	B
JOHNSON MAT	A	37	PEN	B
JOHNSON MATHEW	A	29	FA1	W
JOHNSON MATHEW	A	29	GRA	W
JOHNSON MICHAEL	A	28	11T	B
JOHNSON MICHL	A	28	02N	B
JOHNSON MILES	A	24	MID	B
JOHNSON MOSES	A	38	FRE	B
JOHNSON N F	A	46	HIG	W
JOHNSON N M	A	44	LED	W
JOHNSON NATHAN	A	29	FA1	W
JOHNSON NATHAN	A	44	HEN	B
JOHNSON NATHAN	A	46	HIG	W
JOHNSON NED	A	29	FA1	B
JOHNSON NEILL A	A	29	FA1	W

JOHNSON NICHS F A 29 ROC W
JOHNSON NIXON A 28 04A B
JOHNSON OFFICE A 37 ROB B
JOHNSON ORSBURN P A 32 JAC W
JOHNSON OSBORN A 39 PUG B
JOHNSON OWEN D R 46 MON W
OFFICER BEFORE WAR REJECT
BY HIS OWN REQUEST.
JOHNSON PETER A 28 05A B
CERTIFICATE GRANTED
WASHINGTON NC
JOHNSON PETER A 32 DAV W
JOHNSON PETER P A 29 FA1 W
JOHNSON PRIMUS A 24 EDE B
JOHNSON R W A 29 CED W
JOHNSON REDDING A 28 16T B
JOHNSON REDICK A 39 LOU B
JOHNSON REUBEN A 29 FA2 W
JOHNSON RICHARD A 25 TUS B
JOHNSON RICHARD A 37 HOL B
JOHNSON RICHARD A 37 ROB B
JOHNSON RICHARD A 37 WEB W
JOHNSON RICHARD M A 35 ROC W
JOHNSON RICHARD M A 37 TA1 B
JOHNSON RIGDON A 99 BUS W
JOHNSON ROBERT A 28 9TH B
JOHNSON ROBERT A A 37 ROB W
JOHNSON ROBERT C A 35 ROC W
JOHNSON ROBT A 29 FA1 B
JOHNSON ROBT A 29 FA1 W
JOHNSON ROBT A 44 KIT B
JOHNSON ROMEO A 28 02N B
JOHNSON S N A 28 03A B
JOHNSON SAM A 39 HAY B
JOHNSON SAM A 39 LOU B
JOHNSON SAM A 39 SPE B
JOHNSON SAMEUL A 35 ROC B
JOHNSON SAML A 28 05A B
JOHNSON SAMUEL A 44 SAS B
JOHNSON SANDY A 37 EDW B
JOHNSON SHEPPARD A 19 NEW B
JOHNSON SOLOMON A 28 9TH B
JOHNSON SPENCER A 25 TUS B
JOHNSON SQUIRE A 46 GRE B
JOHNSON STEPH A 28 05A B
JOHNSON STEPHEN A 24 EDE B
JOHNSON STEPHEN H A 29 GRA W
JOHNSON STEPHN A 28 04A B
JOHNSON T C A 29 FA2 W
JOHNSON T J A 25 TUS W
JOHNSON T J A 29 FA1 W
JOHNSON T J A 44 RAG W
JOHNSON T L A 46 SUM W
JOHNSON TALTON A 44 LED W
JOHNSON TAYLOR A 29 ROC W
JOHNSON THOMAS A 28 02N B
JOHNSON THOMAS A 28 16T B
JOHNSON THOMAS A 28 8TH B
JOHNSON THOMAS A 29 SEV B
JOHNSON THOMAS A 39 HAY B
JOHNSON THORNAL A 29 FA2 B
JOHNSON THOS L A 24 EDE W
JOHNSON TONY A 37 ROB B
JOHNSON TURNER A 35 ROC B
JOHNSON UMSTEAD S A 46 COB W
JOHNSON VALENTINE A 35 WAR B
JOHNSON VAN A 37 TA2 B
JOHNSON VERGIL A 44 HEN B
JOHNSON W G A 44 LED W
JOHNSON W H A 25 TUS W
JOHNSON W H A 28 03A B
CERTIFICATE GRANTED
TO LATHAM'S

JOHNSON W H A 29 FA1 B
JOHNSON W J A 29 BLA W
JOHNSON W J A 39 JOR W
JOHNSON WALTER A 30 COI B
JOHNSON WASHINGTON A 39 LOU B
IDIOT
JOHNSON WASHINGTON A 53 GER B
JOHNSON WASHN A 28 04A B
JOHNSON WELLS A 24 EDE B
JOHNSON WILEY A 28 10T B
JOHNSON WILEY A 28 11T B
JOHNSON WILEY A 35 MAG W
JOHNSON WILLIAM A 19 BE1 B
JOHNSON WILLIAM A 29 FA1 B
JOHNSON WILLIAM A 29 GRA W
JOHNSON WILLIAM A 29 QUW W
JOHNSON WILLIAM A 35 ROC B
JOHNSON WILLIAM A 37 TA1 B
JOHNSON WILLIAM A 46 SUM B
JOHNSON WILLIAM A 53 HAT W
JOHNSON WILLIAM R A 30 POW W
JOHNSON WILLIAM T A 35 LIM W
JOHNSON WILLIE A 44 KIT B
JOHNSON WILLIS A 39 SPE B
JOHNSON WM A 28 04A B
JOHNSON WM A 28 04A B
JOHNSON WM A 29 FA1 B
JOHNSON WM A 29 FA1 B
JOHNSON WM A 29 FLE B
JOHNSON WM A 29 GRA B
JOHNSON WM C A 28 04A B
JOHNSON WM J JR A 29 ROC W
JOHNSON WM J SR A 29 ROC W
JOHNSON WM K A 44 RAG W
JOHNSON WM R A 28 04A B
JOHNSON WM S A 30 POW W
JOHNSON ZACHARIAH A 28 12T B
JOHNSTON ALFRED A 40 CAN B
JOHNSTON ALFRED M A 46 GIB W
JOHNSTON ALFRED S A 40 CAN B
JOHNSTON ALLEN J C A 37 SPA W
JOHNSTON ANDREW A 40 CAN B
MOVED TO LINCON
JOHNSTON ANDY A 39 LOU B
JOHNSTON BANDON A 24 MID B
JOHNSTON BENJAMIN A 40 RHY B
JOHNSTON CLEM A 40 DEC B
JOHNSTON COLMON A 40 CAN B
JOHNSTON ELIAS A 40 CAN B
JOHNSTON G W A 40 SAN W
JOHNSTON GREEN A 40 DEC B
JOHNSTON HAWOOD A 19 BE1 B
JOHNSTON HAYWOOD A 39 GRI B
JOHNSTON HENRY A 40 FER W
JOHNSTON HENRY A 46 GRE B
JOHNSTON ISAAC A 40 STO B
JOHNSTON J M A 40 CAN W
JOHNSTON J R A 40 CAN W
JOHNSTON JACOB A 39 LOU B
JOHNSTON JACOB A 40 CAN B
JOHNSTON JACOB A A 40 SAN W
JOHNSTON JAMES C A 24 EDE W
JOHNSTON JAMES F A 19 SMY W
JOHNSTON JOHN A 24 EDE W
JOHNSTON JOHN A 25 HAY W
JOHNSTON JOHN A 29 ROC W
JOHNSTON JOHN A 40 CAN B
JOHNSTON JOSEPH J A 37 ROB W
JOHNSTON LABAN A 40 FER B
JOHNSTON LARKEN R 25 HAY W
REJECTED FOR NOT
ACQUIRING RESIDENCE
NAME LINED OUT

JOHNSTON LARKEN A 25 HAY W
COPIED FROM ABOVE
JOHNSTON LEWIS A 39 LOU B
JOHNSTON LONDON A 24 EDE B
JOHNSTON LYMON A 39 LOU B
JOHNSTON M A A 32 CLE W
JOHNSTON MANUEL A 40 CAN B
JOHNSTON MATTHEW A 39 LOU B
JOHNSTON MOSES A 40 DA1 B
JOHNSTON PATRICK A 37 MAN W
JOHNSTON RUFUS A 29 ROC W
JOHNSTON S C A 40 STO W
JOHNSTON S D A 40 SAN W
JOHNSTON S S A 40 CAN W
JOHNSTON SAMUEL A 40 CAN W
JOHNSTON SPINCER A 39 LOU B
JOHNSTON THOMAS H A 40 FER W
JOHNSTON THOS C A 40 STO W
JOHNSTON W H R 40 STO W
CHALLENGED AND
REJECTED ACTED AS
CONSTABLE 20 YEARS SENCE
JOHNSTON WM H A 40 SAN W
JOHNSTONE G W A 32 YAD W
JOHNSTONE SOLOMON A 32 THO B
JOINER ALFRED A 37 PEN B
JOINER ALLEN A 37 EDW B
JOINER ASTIN A 44 TOW B
JOINER BRITTON A 53 GER B
JOINER HILLIARD A 37 PEN B
JOINER ISAIAH A 19 BE1 B
JOINER JACKSON A 19 HAR B
JOINER JAVID A 28 03A B
JOINER LEWIS A 37 PEN B
JOINER LOUIS V A 28 01A B
JOINER MARTIN A 19 HAR B
JOINER NATHANIEL A 53 GER B
JOINER NORFLEET A 37 PEN B
JOINER ORRIS A 37 EDW B
JOINER PETER A 19 BE1 B
JOINER PETER A 44 TOW B
JOINER THOMAS J A 35 MAG W
JOINER TILMAN A 28 01A B
JOINER WESLEY A 44 TOW B
JOLLY A H A 26 MOU W
JOLLY C D L A 26 SHE W
JOLLY CALEB A 46 ROS W
JOLLY G W A 26 MOU W
JOLLY GEORGE A 26 SHE B
JOLLY HENRY A 28 05A B
JOLLY J T A 38 FRE W
JOLLY JESSE A 26 MOO W
JOLLY LEWIS A 19 NEW B
JOLLY MILFORD A 19 HAD W
JOLLY SAMUEL A 26 MOU B
JOLLY T J A 26 MOU W
JOLLY THOMAS A 26 MOU W
JOLLY W P A 26 MOU W
JONAS AMOS A 19 NEW B
JONES A C A 46 HIG W
JONES A S A 46 MON W
JONES A W A 30 TUL W
JONES AARON A 28 02N B
JONES AARON A 28 7TH B
JONES ABNER A 19 HAR B
JONES ABNER A 28 7TH B
JONES ABNER A 35 WOL W
JONES ABNER A 46 RAG W
JONES ABRAHAM A 28 16T B
JONES ABRAM A 28 04A B
JONES ABRAM B A 53 LA1 W
JONES ADAM A 39 SPE B
JONES ADAM A 44 HEN B

JONES ALBERT G A 24 EDE W
JONES ALEX A 44 FIS B
JONES ALEXANDER A 24 EDE B
JONES ALEXANDER A 46 SUM B
JONES ALEXR A 44 YXS B
JONES ALFRED A 28 05A B
JONES ALFRED A 46 RAG W
JONES ALFUS A 44 OXF B
JONES ALLEN A 28 7TH W
JONES ALLEN A 28 7TH W
JONES ALLEN A 29 FA1 W
JONES ALLEN A 37 EDW B
JONES ALLEN A 37 ROC W
JONES ALLEN A 46 GRE B
JONES ALSON A 46 ROS W
JONES AMBROSE A 19 SMY W
JONES AMERICA A 24 EDE B
JONES AMIS A 24 EDE W
JONES AMOS A 28 03A B
JONES AMOS A 28 03A B
JONES AMOS A 29 SEV B
JONES AMOS A 35 ALB W
JONES AMOS A 44 DUT B
JONES AMOS J A 35 KEN B
JONES ANDERSON W A 46 GRE W
JONES ANDREW A 28 05A B
JONES ANDREW A 28 11T B
JONES ANDREW A 32 JAC B
JONES ANDREW A 35 WOL B
JONES ANDREW J A 46 GRE B
JONES ANTHONY A 39 HAY B
JONES ANTHONY A 39 PUG B
JONES ANTHONY A 44 TOW B
JONES ANTHONY 2ND A 37 PIN B
JONES ANTHONY 1ST A 37 PIN B
JONES AQUILLA A 32 THO W
JONES ARCHER A 39 PUG B
JONES ARCHID A 39 HAY B
NAME LINED OUT
1ST REGIS BOARD
FRANKLINTON
JONES ARDEN A 37 HIC B
JONES ARETUS A 35 ALB W
JONES ASA A 28 03A W
JONES ASA A 28 04B B
JONES ATHEN A 28 03A B
JONES ATLAS A 39 GRI W
JONES AUSTON A 37 ROC B
JONES B D A 46 JAM W
JONES BADGER A 39 PUG B
JONES BADGER A 99 BUS B
JONES BARN A 32 POS W
JONES BEN A 39 HAY B
JONES BENJ A 28 04A B
JONES BENJ A 28 05A B
JONES BENJ L A 19 BE1 W
JONES BENJAMIN A 24 EDE W
JONES BENJAMIN A 28 15T B
JONES BENJAMIN A 29 FA1 B
JONES BENJAMIN A 37 HIC B
JONES BENJAMIN A 99 BUS B
JONES BENJAMIN T A 24 EDE W
JONES BERRY A 37 HIC B
JONES BERRY A 46 GRE B
JONES BERRY 1ST A 37 HIC B
JONES BIAS A 28 04A B
JONES BLUNT A 37 HIG B
JONES BRATCHER A 35 MAG W
JONES BRISTOL A 28 6TH B
JONES BRYAN W A 35 WOL W
JONES BUCK A 39 SPE B
JONES BUCK YOUNG A 37 ROC B
JONES BUCKNER A 28 6TH W
JONES BURIL A 44 LED B
JONES BURRELL A 28 11T B
JONES C A 19 HAD B
JONES C B A 28 03A W
JONES CAESAR A 28 05A B
JONES CALVIN A 19 MOR B
JONES CALVIN A 37 HIC A
JONES CALVIN A 37 SHA W
JONES CALVIN A 46 COB B
JONES CALVIN A 46 GRE B
JONES CALVIN G A 39 DAV W
JONES CALVIN M A 46 COB W
JONES CANE A 32 JAC B
JONES CANTINE A 28 01A W
JONES CASON A 53 FAI W
JONES CASON W A 53 LA1 W
JONES CATO A 44 LED B
JONES CEASER A 19 MOR B
JONES CEAZER A 19 NEW B
JONES CESAR A 28 16T B
JONES CHARLES A 28 01A B
JONES CHARLES A 28 01A B
JONES CHARLES A 32 DAV B
JONES CHARLES A 35 MAG B
JONES CHARLES A 39 HAY B
JONES CHARLES A 53 LA1 B
JONES CHARLES A 99 BUS B
JONES CHAS B A 29 FA1 W
JONES CHESTER A 39 GRI B
JONES CICERO A 28 03A B
JONES COLUMBUS A 37 PEN W
JONES CONRED A 39 SPE B
JONES CORNELIAS A 39 JOR B
JONES CORNELIUS A 30 KNO W
JONES D L A 26 MOO W
JONES D S R 19 MOR W
JONES DALLIS A 46 GRE B
JONES DANIEL A 19 MOR B
JONES DANIEL A 44 KNA B
JONES DANIEL A 46 JAM B
JONES DANIEL A 99 BUS B
JONES DANL A 28 04A B
JONES DANL S A 28 03A W
JONES DASSON A 32 BRO W
JONES DAVID A 26 BLA W
JONES DAVID A 29 FA1 B
JONES DAVID A 29 FA1 B
JONES DAVID A 29 FA1 W
JONES DAVID A 72 SWA W
JONES DAVID 1ST A 37 PIN B
JONES DAVID 2ND A 37 PIN B
JONES DAVID F A 35 WAR W
JONES DAVID H A 32 POS W
JONES DAVID M A 19 BE1 W
JONES DAVID S A 19 MOR W
JONES DAVID SR A 53 LA2 W
JONES DAVIS A 19 BE1 B
JONES DERREY A 37 PIN B
JONES DICK A 39 DAV B
JONES DRURY A 26 MOU W
JONES DUNCAN A 24 EDE B
JONES E D A 28 03A W
JONES E M A 32 CLE W
JONES E T A 39 LOU W
JONES ED H A 44 KNA W
JONES EDMAND A 30 KNO W
JONES EDMOND A 44 OXF B
JONES EDMUND A 37 HIC B
JONES EDMUND A 46 SUM B
JONES EDWARD A 19 STR W
JONES EDWARD A 24 EDE W
JONES EDWARD A 28 6TH B
JONES EDWARD A 28 8TH W
JONES EDWARD A 37 PIN B
JONES EDWARD A 37 SPA B
JONES EDWARD A 44 LED B
JONES EDWARD A 44 OXF B
JONES EDWARD A 53 GER B
JONES EDWARD A 53 OCR W
JONES EDWARD A 53 SWA W
JONES EDWARD H A 53 SWA W
JONES EDWARD M A 72 SWA W
INDICATION THAT THIS
MAN MAY BE BLACK
AND IN THE WRONG COLUMN
JONES ELI A 28 04A B
JONES ELIAS A 72 SWA B
JONES ELIGA A 46 GRE B
JONES ELIJAH A 28 17T W
JONES EMANUEL A 35 WOL B
JONES ENOCH A 39 PUG B
JONES ENOCH A 46 FRI B
JONES EPHRAIM A 39 SPE B
JONES EVERETT A 28 7TH W
JONES EZEKIEL P A 46 GRE W
WAS AN OVERSEER OF A
HIGHWAY BEFORE THE WARE
DURING THE WAR GAVE
VOLUNTARY ADE REJ.
JONES F H A 46 SUM W
JONES FED A 44 LED B
JONES FRANK A 28 6TH B
JONES FRANK A 99 BUS B
JONES FRANKLIN A 30 POP B
JONES FRDK A 29 FA2 W
JONES FREDERICK A 28 7TH W
JONES FREDERICK 2ND A 28 7TH W
JONES FREDK A A 28 03A W
JONES FURNEY A 28 17T B
JONES GASTON A 37 PIN B
JONES GASTON A 99 BUS B
JONES GASTON A 99 BUS W
JONES GEO A 44 OXF B
JONES GEO W A 28 03A W
JONES GEORGE A 19 BE2 B
JONES GEORGE A 28 03A B
JONES GEORGE A 28 05A B
JONES GEORGE A 28 13T B
JONES GEORGE A 28 16T B
JONES GEORGE A 29 FA1 B
JONES GEORGE A 35 GLI B
JONES GEORGE A 37 PIN B
JONES GEORGE A 37 ROC B
JONES GEORGE A 39 SPE B
JONES GEORGE A 44 HEN B
JONES GEORGE W A 39 HAY W
JONES GIDEON A 28 17T W
JONES GILBERT A 44 OXF B
JONES GOODWIN A 39 HAR W
JONES GRAHAM A 99 BUS B
JONES GRANVILLE A 37 HIC B
JONES GRAY J A 39 HAR W
JONES GRAYHAM A 53 LA1 B
JONES GRIFFIN A 30 IND W
JONES GRIFFIN A 35 GLI W
JONES GUILFORD A 37 HIC B
JONES H F A 26 SHE W
JONES H W A 28 02N W
JONES H W A 44 LED W
JONES HAMILTON A 46 FRI B
JONES HARDY A 28 9TH B
JONES HARDY A 44 LED B
JONES HARRY A 28 02N B
JONES HARY A 29 LOC W
JONES HASCHAWAY A 19 NEW B
JONES HASKELL A 28 03A B

JONES HASKELL A 28 03A B
JONES HAYS A 29 LOC W
JONES HAYWOOD A 28 02N B
JONES HENDERSON A 24 EDE W
JONES HENDERSON A 53 LA1 B
JONES HENNIS A 46 GRE W
JONES HENRY A 19 BE1 B
JONES HENRY A 28 04A B
JONES HENRY A 28 04A B
JONES HENRY A 28 04A B
JONES HENRY A 28 04A B
JONES HENRY A 28 16T B
JONES HENRY A 37 MAN B
JONES HENRY A 37 TA1 B
JONES HENRY A 39 HAR B
JONES HENRY A 44 BRA B
JONES HENRY A 44 LED B
JONES HENRY A 46 SUM B
JONES HENRY A 53 SWA W
JONES HENRY 2 ND A 28 04A B
JONES HENRY A A 28 04A B
JONES HENRY C A 19 BE1 B
JONES HENRY D A 28 02N B
JONES HENRY J A 28 05A B
JONES HEZEKIAH A 24 MID W
JONES HILLIARD A 28 03A B
JONES HILLIARD A 37 PIN B
JONES HINSON A 35 WOL W
JONES HIRAM A 28 8TH B
JONES HORACE A 19 MOR W
JONES HUGH A 29 LOC W
JONES IRA A 53 LA1 B
JONES IRVING A 37 HIC B
JONES ISAAC A 19 NEW B
JONES ISAAC A 28 04A B
JONES ISAAC A 29 ROC W
JONES ISAAC A 30 MOY B
JONES ISAAC A 37 HIC B
JONES ISAAC A 39 GRI B
JONES ISAAC A 99 BUS B
JONES ISHAM A 29 LOC W
JONES ISIAH A 53 SWA B
JONES J A A 44 BRA B
JONES J G A 44 OXF W
JONES J J JR A 39 LOU W
TRNS TO SPEEDS STORE
JONES J J W A 44 FOR W
JONES J M A 26 GRI W
JONES J N A 19 NEW W
JONES J O A 46 JAM W
JONES J R A 29 ROC W
JONES J R A 44 FOR W
JONES J R A 46 FRI W
JONES J T A 39 FRA W
JONES J T A 44 TOW W
JONES J T A 44 LED W
JONES J V A 29 FLE W
JONES J W A 32 THO W
JONES J W A 44 FOR W
JONES J W A 99 BUS W
JONES JACK A 28 03A B
JONES JACK A 28 11T B
JONES JACKSON A 29 FA1 W
JONES JACKSON A 37 PIN B
JONES JACKSON A 44 BRA B
JONES JACKSON A 53 LA1 B
JONES JACOB A 26 SHE B
JONES JACOB A 28 6TH B
JONES JACOB A 37 HIC B
JONES JACOB A 44 LED B
JONES JACQUELINE A 35 WOL W
JONES JAMES A 19 HAR B
JONES JAMES A 19 MOR B

JONES JAMES A 28 10T B
JONES JAMES A 29 FA1 W
JONES JAMES A 29 FA1 W
JONES JAMES A 35 GLI W
JONES JAMES A 35 WOL B
JONES JAMES A 37 EDW W
JONES JAMES A 37 PIN B
JONES JAMES A 37 ROB B
JONES JAMES A 37 WHI W
JONES JAMES A 39 FRA B
JONES JAMES A 39 FRE W
JONES JAMES A 44 FIS B
JONES JAMES A 44 KNA B
JONES JAMES A 44 OXF B
JONES JAMES A 46 GRE B
JONES JAMES A 53 SWA B
JONES JAMES A A 35 WOL W
JONES JAMES E A 37 EDW W
JONES JAMES H A 28 03A W
JONES JAMES H A 37 ROC W
JONES JAMES JR A 30 KNO B
JONES JAMES L A 28 17T W
JONES JAMES M A 46 GRE W
JONES JAMES P A 28 04A B
JONES JAMES P A 46 GRE W
JONES JAMES SR 30 KNO B
JONES JAMES T A 28 15T W
JONES JAMES T A 35 GLI W
JONES JAS A A 44 YXR W
JONES JAS B F A 46 GRE W
JONES JEFFERSON A 28 03A B
JONES JEFFREY A 44 DUT B
JONES JEREMIAH A 24 EDE W
JONES JEREMIAH A 44 LED W
JONES JERRY A 44 KNA B
JONES JESSE A 32 POS W
JONES JESSE JR A 28 7TH W
JONES JESSE S A 32 POS W
JONES JESSE SR A 28 7TH W
JONES JESSEE A 30 POW B
JONES JNO A 29 FA1 B
JONES JNO B A 30 IND W
JONES JNO H A 44 HEN W
JONES JNO V A 44 YXS W
JONES JNO W A 30 MOY W
JONES JOBE A 44 YXS B
JONES JOEL A 29 CED W
JONES JOHN A 19 BE2 B
JONES JOHN A 19 MOR W
JONES JOHN A 28 03A B
JONES JOHN A 28 16T B
JONES JOHN A 28 6TH B
JONES JOHN A 28 7TH B
JONES JOHN A 28 9TH B
JONES JOHN A 29 FA1 B
JONES JOHN A 29 FA1 B
JONES JOHN A 32 POS W
JONES JOHN A 35 LIM B
JONES JOHN A 37 EDW B
JONES JOHN A 37 HOL W
JONES JOHN A 37 ROC B
JONES JOHN A 37 ROC W
JONES JOHN A 37 ROC W
JONES JOHN A 37 TA1 B
JONES JOHN A 44 HEN B
JONES JOHN A 46 JAM B
JONES JOHN R 72 SWA B
NO EXPLANATION
JONES JOHN A A 19 HAR W
JONES JOHN A A 28 04A B
JONES JOHN A A 32 POS W
JONES JOHN B A 28 8TH W
JONES JOHN H A 24 EDE W

JONES JOHN J A 28 03A B
JONES JOHN J A 35 ISL W
JONES JOHN M A 28 8TH W
JONES JOHN M A 46 GIB W
JONES JOHN M A 99 BUS B
JONES JOHN M JR A 24 EDE W
JONES JOHN M
OF WILLIAM A 24 EDE W
JONES JOHN Q A 28 17T W
JONES JOHN R A 19 BE1 W
JONES JOHN REID R 19 MOR W
JONES JOHN W A 37 TA1 W
JONES JOHN Y A 39 LOU W
JONES JOHNSON A 37 WHI W
JONES JONAS A 35 KEN W
JONES JORDAN A 37 MAN B
JONES JORDAN A 39 SPE B
JONES JORDEN A 44 DUT B
JONES JOSEPH A 19 HAD W
JONES JOSEPH A 29 GRA B
JONES JOSEPH A 37 PIN B
JONES JOSEPH A 37 PIN B
JONES JOSEPH A 37 PIN B
JONES JOSEPH A 39 HAY B
JONES JOSEPH A 46 FRI B
JONES JOSEPH A 46 GRE B
JONES JOSEPH E A 24 EDE B
TRANS TO MIDDLE GROUND AS
INSPECTOR OF ELECTIONS
AND WILL VOTE AT THAT
PRECINCT AS HE CANNOT
VOTE IN EDENTON
JONES JOSEPH W A 28 01B W
JONES JOSEPHUS A 28 16T B
JONES JOSHUA A 28 17T W
JONES JOSIAH A 28 17T W
JONES JOSIAH H A 24 MID W
JONES JOSIAH H A 35 MAG W
JONES JOURDAN A 28 9TH B
JONES KILBEY D A 19 SMY W
JONES KILLES A 28 05A B
JONES KING A 37 HIC B
JONES KINSEY A 35 WOL W
JONES L C A 29 FAI W
JONES L H A 26 MOU W
JONES L H A 39 DAV W
JONES LAWRENCE A 37 PIN B
JONES LEALLEN A 25 HAY W
JONES LEMUEL A 30 POP W
JONES LEVI A 72 SWA W
JONES LEWELLEN A 37 PEN W
BEAUFORT CO
JONES LEWIS A 26 MOU W
JONES LEWIS A 28 04A B
JONES LEWIS A 28 04A W
JONES LEWIS A 28 16T B
JONES LEWIS A 29 FA1 B
JONES LEWIS A 39 SPE B
JONES LEWIS A 99 BUS B
JONES LIMON A 37 ROB B
JONES LINNES A 37 PEN B
JONES LIVI A 46 JAM W
JONES LONDONN A 28 17T B
JONES LOT A 28 04A B
JONES LOUIS A 29 SEV B
JONES LOUIS A 35 WOL B
JONES LOUIS R A 35 ALB W
JONES LOVE A 29 GRA W
JONES LUCAS A 19 BE1 B
JONES LUKE A 28 05A B
JONES LUMBARD A 46 GRE B
JONES M A 32 JAC B
JONES M B A 35 WOL W

JONES M B A 44 OXF W
JONES M C A 32 CLE W
JONES M H A 44 KNA W
JONES M L A 44 KNA W
JONES MACK A 28 04A B
JONES MACK G A 37 HIC A
JONES MACLESON A 44 OXF B
JONES MADISON J A 32 DAV W
JONES MAINUS A 28 16T B
JONES MAJOR A 19 NEW B
JONES MANUEL A 19 MOR B
JONES MARCUS A 99 BUS B
JONES MARTIN A 28 8TH W
JONES MARTIN A 29 FA1 B
JONES MARTIN A 44 LED W
JONES MATTHEW A 28 05A B
JONES MATTHEW M A 35 KEN W
JONES MICHAEL A 24 EDE B
JONES MILES A 28 01B B
JONES MILLS A 37 HIC B
JONES MINGO A 28 05A B
JONES MINGO 2ND A 28 05A B
JONES MOSES A 28 03A B
JONES MOSES A 28 7TH B
JONES MOSES A 37 HIC B
JONES MOSES A 39 DAV B
JONES NATHAN A 28 03A B
JONES NATHAN A 28 05A B
JONES NATHAN H A 29 GRA W
JONES NATHANIEL A 39 HAR W
JONES NED A 39 DAV B
JONES NELSON A 28 03A B
JONES NOAH A 30 IND W
REMOVED TO
E CITY PASQUOTANK
JONES NOAH A 53 FAI B
JONES NORPHLET H A 39 LOU B
JONES OCREE A 28 15T B
JONES OLIVER A 19 MOR B
JONES OWEN A 28 04A B
JONES P E A A 44 HEN W
JONES PARY A 25 SHO B
JONES PASS A 44 LED B
JONES PELIGE A 53 GER W
JONES PERRY A 28 16T B
JONES PETER A 28 04A B
JONES PETER A 29 ROC B
JONES PETER A 30 NAR B
JONES PETER A 39 PUG B
JONES PETER A 44 OXF B
JONES PETER K A 24 EDE B
JONES PETER T A 24 EDE B
JONES PETTER K A 24 MID B
JONES PHARO A 35 WOL B
JONES PHILIP A 28 01A B
JONES PHILIP H A 46 GRE W
JONES PHILIP H P A 46 GRE B
JONES PHILLIP A 37 HIC B
JONES PINKNEY A 46 GRE B
JONES POMPEY A 19 BE1 B
JONES PRESCOTT A 19 BE1 B
JONES PRIMUS A 28 17T B
JONES R A A 44 FOR W
JONES R A A 44 LED W
JONES R B A 32 JAC W
JONES REDDEN A 19 HAD B
JONES REDDIC H A 35 KEN W
JONES RETUS A 29 CED W
JONES REUBEN A 29 FA2 W
JONES REUBEN A 46 RAG W
JONES REV HENRY W A 28 03A B
JONES RICHARD A 28 15T B
JONES RICHARD A 28 7TH B
JONES RICHARD A 46 FRI B
JONES RICHARD A 46 MCL B
JONES RICHD D A 44 YXS W
JONES RICHMOND A 37 PIN B
JONES RICHMOND A 99 BUS B
JONES RIGDON A 28 6TH B
JONES RILEY A 25 SHO W
JONES RILEY A 35 CYP W
JONES RILEY A 37 TA1 B
JONES RILEY A 53 LA1 B
JONES ROBBERT A 39 DAV B
JONES ROBBIN A 37 EDW B
JONES ROBERSON D A 35 KEN W
JONES ROBERT A 26 BLA W
JONES ROBERT A 30 MOY B
JONES ROBERT A 32 DAV B
JONES ROBERT A 37 PIN B
JONES ROBERT A 37 TA2 W
SPARTA
JONES ROBERT A 46 HIG B
JONES ROBERT A 46 KIN W
JONES ROBT A 28 03A B
CERTIFICATE GRANTED
BIG SWIFT CREEK
JONES ROBT A 28 05A B
JONES ROBT A 28 6TH B
JONES ROBT A 39 FRE B
JONES ROBT H A 28 03A B
JONES RODEN A 19 MOR B
JONES ROGER A 44 OXF B
JONES ROMEO A 29 LOC B
JONES ROSCOE A 28 04A B
JONES RUFFUS A 39 FRA B
JONES RUFUS A 24 EDE B
JONES S A 28 04A B
JONES S A A 39 HAR W
JONES S S A 32 SHE W
JONES S W A 28 03A W
JONES SALEM A 29 FA1 W
JONES SAM A 39 PUG B
JONES SAML A 28 04A B
JONES SAML 2ND A 28 04A B
JONES SAML T A 28 01A W
JONES SAMUEL A 24 MID B
JONES SAMUEL A 29 SEV B
JONES SAMUEL A 32 POS W
JONES SAMUEL A 35 WOL B
JONES SANDERS A 28 03A B
JONES SANDY A 29 FA1 B
JONES SCOTT A 29 CED B
JONES SEYBRON A 46 GRE B
JONES SHADRACK A 28 04A B
JONES SHEPARD A 28 7TH W
JONES SILAS A 28 16T B
JONES SIMON A 28 10T B
JONES SIMON A 37 HIC B
JONES SIMON A 53 LA1 B
JONES SIMON T W A 37 TA1 W
JONES SIMPSON A 37 MAN B
JONES SMITH A 28 10T B
JONES SOLM A 28 05A B
JONES SOLOMON A 30 MOY W
JONES SOMERSET A 28 02N B
JONES SQUIRE A 35 WAR B
JONES STEPHEN A 19 BE1 B
JONES STEPHEN A 19 NEW B
JONES STEPHEN S A 35 KEN W
JONES STEPHENS A 37 ROB B
JONES STERLIN A 44 FIS B
JONES STERLING A 37 TA1 B
JONES SUTTON A 28 16T B
JONES SYLVANUS A 35 SMI W
JONES SYLVESTER A 28 05A B
JONES T H A 44 LED W
JONES T M A 39 LOU W
JONES T Y A 44 LED W
JONES TAFFY A 28 16T B
JONES TEMPLES A 37 PIN B
JONES THADDEUS A 35 WOL W
JONES THOMAS A 28 01B W
JONES THOMAS A 28 14T B
JONES THOMAS A 29 CAR B
JONES THOMAS A 37 PEN B
JONES THOMAS A 44 KIT B
JONES THOMAS A 44 YXR W
JONES THOMAS A 46 GRE W
JONES THOMAS A 46 RAG W
JONES THOMAS CHAL A 30 CUR B
8-MOS RESIDENCE
JONES THOMAS A A 32 THO W
JONES THOMAS G A 35 MAG W
JONES THOMAS M A 53 SWA W
JONES THOMPSON A 32 BRO W
JONES THOMPSON A 46 GRE B
JONES THOS A 29 LOC B
JONES THOS A 30 IND W
JONES THOS C A 19 POR W
JONES TOM A 39 PUG B
JONES VIRGIN A 28 05A B
JONES W D A 39 JOR W
JONES W D A 44 FOR W
JONES W E A 32 THO W
JONES W H A 28 01A W
JONES W H JR A 44 LED W
JONES W H SR A 44 LED W
JONES W O A 46 HIG W
JONES WALKER A 44 OXF B
JONES WARREN A 37 TA1 B
JONES WARRENTON A 28 03A B
JONES WATT A 39 SPE B
JONES WENDALL A 28 03A B
JONES WESLEY Y A 44 OXF W
JONES WESTERN A 39 GRI B
JONES WILEY A 19 BE1 B
JONES WILEY A 37 PEN B
JONES WILEY A 37 ROC B
JONES WILEY A 37 SHA B
JONES WILEY A 99 BUS W
JONES WILEY W A 28 17T W
JONES WILLIAM A 19 BE1 B
JONES WILLIAM A 28 01B W
JONES WILLIAM A 28 04B B
JONES WILLIAM A 28 10T B
JONES WILLIAM A 28 9TH B
JONES WILLIAM A 29 CED B
JONES WILLIAM A 35 KEN W
JONES WILLIAM A 37 ROC B
JONES WILLIAM A 37 ROC W
JONES WILLIAM A 39 SPE B
JONES WILLIAM A 44 KIT B
JONES WILLIAM A 46 FRI B
JONES WILLIAM A 99 BUS B
JONES WILLIAM A A 26 MOO W
JONES WILLIAM A A 37 TA2 W
JONES WILLIAM G A 37 HIC A
JONES WILLIAM H A 72 SWA W
JONES WILLIAM J A 26 MOO W
JONES WILLIAM W A 35 MAG W
JONES WILLIAMS A 28 01B B
JONES WILLIE D A 39 HAR W
JONES WILLIS A 28 03A B
JONES WILLIS A 28 14T B
JONES WILLIS M A 26 MOO W
JONES WILSON A 37 HIC B
JONES WILSON A 44 TOW B
JONES WM A 29 FLE W

JONES WM A 44 KNA B
JONES WM 24 EDE B
CHAL BY J R B
HATHAWAY CONVICTED OF
FELONY COUTY SHOWS IT
CONVICTED BEFORE HE HAD
THE RIGHT OF SUFFRAGE
THEREFORE COULD NOT LOSE
WHAT HE NEVER HAD FINAL
DECISION HE IS ACCEPTED
JONES WM A 44 KNA W
JONES WM A 46 GRE B
JONES WM C A 19 MOR W
JONES WM E A 29 ROC W
JONES WM F A 28 15T W
JONES WM H A 24 EDE W
JONES WM JR A 44 YXR W
JONES WM P A 24 MID W
JONES WM P A 28 17T W
JONES WM T A 37 HIC A
JONES WM W A 44 HEN W
JONES YOUNG A 44 LED W
JONES ZACHARIAH A 28 7TH W
JONES ZEDICK A 72 SWA W
INDICATION THAT THIS
MAN MAY BE BLACK
AND IN THE WRONG COLUMN
JONHSON EVANS A 46 FRI W
JONSON GEORGE A 30 CUR B
JORDAIN SAMPSON A 19 BE1 B
JORDAIN SAMUEL A A 19 BE1 B
JORDAN ALFRED A 44 OXF B
JORDAN BENJ F A 46 GRE W
JORDAN CHARLES A 37 ROC B
JORDAN FRANKLIN A 46 JAM W
JORDAN GRANVILLE A 44 OXF B
JORDAN GREY A 28 16T W
JORDAN HANNIBAL A 46 MON B
JORDAN HARRISON A 44 HEN B
JORDAN HENRY B A 99 BUS W
JORDAN J V A 28 02N W
JORDAN JAMES A 37 SHA W
JORDAN JAMES A 46 JAM W
JORDAN JOHN 30 IND B
JORDAN LAWRENCE A 37 ROB B
JORDAN LEROY A 99 BUS W
JORDAN MATHEW A 29 FA1 W
JORDAN MATHEW A 44 OXF B
JORDAN MOSES A 44 OXF B
JORDAN OVID A 44 LED B
JORDAN PHILLIP A 19 BE1 B
JORDAN PLUTO A 53 GER B
JORDAN SAMUEL A 46 HIG W
JORDAN THOMAS A 46 GRE B
JORDAN THOS J A 29 FA1 W
JORDAN W H A 29 FA1 W
JORDAN W H A 29 LOC W
JORDAN WADDY A 99 BUS B
JORDAN WILLIAM V A 53 GER W
JORDAN WILLIS A 44 OXF B
JORDEN BENJAMIN A 19 BE1 B
JORDEN DANIL A 37 MAN W
JORDEN FRANK A 46 GRE B
JORDEN MOSE A 19 NEW B
JORDEN WILLIAM A 19 NEW B
JORDIN ELIUS JR A 37 SHA W
JORDON A G A 32 THO W
JORDON ALEX A 29 FA2 W
JORDON CEASER A 24 MID B
JORDON EDWARD S A 53 FAI W
JORDON J M A 32 THO W
JORDON JAMES SR A 24 MID W
JORDON JOHN A 24 MID W
JORDON MICKAL A 24 MID W
JORDON NORFLET A 24 MID W
JORMAN WILEY A 28 12T B
JOSEPH JOHNSON A 39 DAV W
JOUNIGAN JAMES A 39 HAY W
JOURDAN CASWELL A 28 04A B
JOURDAN COLUMBUS A 24 EDE B
JOURDAN DANIEL T A 24 EDE W
JOURDAN ELIJAH A 24 EDE B
JOURDAN FRANK A 28 05A B
JOURDAN GEO W A 24 UPP W
JOURDAN HANCE A 24 MID W
JOURDAN JACOB A 24 UPP W
JOURDAN JAMES A 28 9TH B
JOURDAN JAMES JR A 24 MID W
JOURDAN JOHN R A 24 EDE W
JOURDAN LAMB A 28 8TH B
JOURDAN MILES A 28 03A B
JOURDAN SALEM A 28 03A B
JOURDAN SALEM R 28 01A B
JOURDAN THOMAS A 24 EDE W
JOURDAN WESLEY A 24 EDE B
JOURDAN WILLIS A 24 EDE W
JOURDAN WILLIS A 24 UPP B
JOURDAN WILLIS H A 24 EDE W
JOURDAN WILLIS K A 24 EDE W
JOURDAN WM A 24 EDE W
JOURDAN WM H A 24 UPP W
JOURNER ISAAC A 28 04A B
JOURNER JOSEPH A 28 03A B
JOY COLUMBUS A 37 ROC B
JOY JAMES A 40 CAN W
JOYCE WILLIAM A 46 SUM B
JOYCOX HAYWOOD A 28 04A B
JOYNER - - - - A 28 11T W
JOYNER A P A 39 SPE W
JOYNER ABE A 39 FRA B
JOYNER ALFORD A 39 SPE W
JOYNER AUGUSTUS A 37 SPA B
JOYNER BOLEKY A 37 SHA B
JOYNER DANIEL A 44 FIS B
JOYNER DAVID A 37 ROC B
JOYNER EDWARD A 37 SHA B
JOYNER ELI A 37 SHA W
JOYNER EVERETT A 35 WOL W
JOYNER G H A 39 LOU W
JOYNER GEORGE A 39 HAY B
JOYNER GUSTUS A 39 FRA B
JOYNER HENDERSON A 37 ROC B
JOYNER HENRY A 37 HIG B
JOYNER HENRY A 37 WHI B
JOYNER HENRY A 39 JOR W
JOYNER J S A 39 FRA W
JOYNER JAS D A 39 FRA W
JOYNER JOHN A 39 SPE W
JOYNER JOHN E A 39 LOU W
JOYNER JOSEPH A 37 ROC B
JOYNER KINCHON A 37 MAN B
JOYNER L W A 39 FRA W
JOYNER L W A 39 FRA W
JOYNER M B A 39 LOU W
JOYNER M E A 39 DAV W
JOYNER MARCELLUS A 39 FRA B
JOYNER NED A 39 HAR B
JOYNER NOAH A 39 LOU W
JOYNER PAUL A 39 FRA B
JOYNER PETER A 37 ROC B
JOYNER REDIN A 37 HIG B
JOYNER RICHARD A 39 JOR W
JOYNER RUBEN A 37 ROC B
JOYNER RUBIN A 37 WHI B
JOYNER S C A 39 SPE W
JOYNER SAMUEL A 28 11T B
JOYNER SAMUEL A 39 JOR W
JOYNER SIDNEY A 39 LOU W
JOYNER SOLOMON A 39 FRA B
JOYNER STEPHEN A 37 ROC B
JOYNER STEWART A 37 EDW B
JOYNER THOMPKIN ? A 37 ROC B
JOYNER TURNER A 28 11T B
JOYNER W B A 39 DAV W
JOYNER W H A 39 FRA W
JOYNER WILLIAM A 39 LOU W
JOYNER WILLIE A 39 SPE W
JUDGE ANDREW A 35 LIM B
JUDGE ISRAEL H A 35 KEN W
JUDGE J E A 35 LIM W
JUDGE JACOB A 35 CYP B
JUDGE JAMES B A 35 LIM W
JUDGE S M A 35 LIM W
JUENS BAILEM A 29 CED B
SAME AS EUINS BALEM?
JULIAN WESLEY A 46 RAG W
JUNIOR JOHN A 19 MOR W
JUSTICE ALEX A 28 02N W
JUSTICE B T A 28 02N W
JUSTICE BENJAMINE A 26 SHE W
JUSTICE BILL A 37 TA2 B
JUSTICE DAVID A 37 PIN B
JUSTICE DICKSON A 26 SHE W
JUSTICE J T A 26 SHE W
JUSTICE JOHN A 26 SHE W
JUSTICE JOHN JR A 26 SHE W
JUSTICE LEWIS A 26 BLA W
JUSTICE PIHRAM A 35 FAI W
JUSTICE PRESTON A 37 TA1 B
JUSTICE SOLOMON A 37 PIN B
JUSTIN ROBERT A 37 PIN B
KAHOE WILEY A 28 04A B
KAIN O JOHN A 28 05A B
KAINE DUNCAN A 37 HIG B
KALE ABRAM A 24 EDE B
KALE JOHN A 24 EDE B
KANADA CHARLES A 28 11T B
KANADA WILLIAM J A 28 11T B
KANE ANDREW A 28 05A B
KANE DAVID A 29 FA1 B
KANE HENRY A 37 HIC B
KANE ISAM A 28 05A B
CERTIFICATE GRANTED
WASHINGTON NC
KANE JAMES A 29 FA1 B
KANE JNO A 29 FA1 B
KANE MIKE A 29 FA1 B
KANE RICHD A 29 FA1 B
KANNADA HOGAN A 28 9TH B
KANNADA MORRIS A 28 9TH B
KANNADA SQUIRE A 28 9TH B
KAPOT AUSTIN A 28 03A B
KEA HARRY A 37 EDW B
KEA JAMES E A 35 MAG W
KEA JOHN A 37 EDW W
KEACH DANIEL A 19 HUN W
KEAR BENJAMIN A 37 SPA W
KEAR MANUEL A 37 SPA B
KEAR NAT A 37 SPA B
KEARNEY DOCTOR A 39 PUG B
KEARNEY G D A 39 FRA W
KEARNEY GEORGE W A 39 HAY W
KEARNEY HENRY A 44 BRA W
KEARNEY ISAAC A 37 PIN B
KEARNEY JACK A 37 EDW B
KEARNEY JAMES A 39 LOU B
TRNS FROM GRANVILLE CO
BRASSFIELDS
TO LOUISBURG FRANK. CO

KEARNEY LOGAN A 37 SPA B
KEARNEY LUKE A 37 PIN B
KEARNEY MACGILBERT A 37 PIN B
KEARNEY OSBERN A 39 JOR B
CERT SHOCCO WARREN CO
KEARNEY PETER A 37 PIN B
KEARNEY RICHARD A 39 LOU B
KEARNEY S F A 44 BRA W
KEARNEY WASHINGTON A 37 PIN B
KEARNEY WILLIAM A 37 SPA B
KEARNY ALFORD A 39 FRA B
KEARNY B S A 39 FRA W
KEARNY BARTLETT A 39 FRA B
KEARNY DANIEL A 39 FRE B
KEARNY DENNIS A 39 FRA B
KEARNY FRANK A 39 FRA B
KEARNY H C A 39 FRA W
KEARNY HENRY JR A 39 FRA B
KEARNY HENRY SR A 39 FRA B
KEARNY ISHAM A 38 FRE B
KEARNY ISHAM A 39 FRA B
KEARNY NELSON A 39 FRE B
KEARNY NORTEN A 39 FRA B
KEARNY RICHD A 39 FRA B
KEARNY RICHD JR A 39 FRA B
KEARNY RUFFUS A 39 FRA B
KEARNY RUFUS A 39 FRE B
KEARNY S H A 39 FRA W
KEARNY SAMUEL A 39 HAR B
KEARNY SANDERS A 39 FRA B
KEARNY SQUIRE A 39 FRA B
KEARSON RICHMOND A 37 HIC B
KEATON JERRY A 28 04A B
KECK ANDREW A 46 COB W
KEECH BRYAN J A 37 TA1 W
KEECH JACB A A 53 GER W
KEEL BARTHOLAMEW A 28 14T W
KEEL BENJAMIN H A 28 16T W
KEEL GEORGE A 28 16T W
KEEL JOHN A 37 TA1 B
KEEL JOHN R A 28 16T W
KEELER CHAS B A 28 02N W
KEELER TIMOTHY A 28 04A W
KEELING C B A 24 EDE W
KEELING JOHN L A 46 GRE W
KEEN JOHN H A 46 MON B
KEESE LACEY A 28 05B B
KEHOE PETER A 44 TOW W
KEHOE ROBT C A 28 02N W
KEITH JOHN A 29 FA2 W
KELLAM GEO A 29 FA1 B
KELLAM JAMES A 28 03A W
KELLETT WILLIAM A 28 01A W
KELLEY ADAM A 44 RAG B
KELLEY ALLEN A 32 DAV B
KELLEY ALLEN A 35 FAI B
KELLEY ANDREW A 44 RAG B
KELLEY ANDW A 29 FA1 B
KELLEY BOSS A 44 HEN B
KELLEY BRYAN A 28 04A B
KELLEY CALVIN H A 99 BUS W
KELLEY CHELSON A 29 FA1 B
KELLEY DAVID A 35 ISL B
KELLEY ELLIC A 44 HEN B
KELLEY GASTON A 35 WOL W
KELLEY GEO B A 29 FA1 B
KELLEY HENRY A 32 DAV B
KELLEY JNO A 29 FA1 B
KELLEY JNO A 29 FA1 B
KELLEY JOHN A 26 WAR B
KELLEY JOSEPH A 44 HEN B
KELLEY LIBEERTY A 35 ISL B
KELLEY MINGO A 39 LOU B
KELLEY P C A 32 BRO W
KELLEY SAML A 29 FA1 B
KELLEY SIMON A 35 KEN B
KELLEY THOMAS A 99 BUS W
KELLEY TOM A 39 DAV B
KELLEY W L A 35 WOL W
KELLEY WASHINGTON A 39 LOU B
KELLEY WESLEY W A 99 BUS W
KELLOGG HENRY A 46 GRE W
KELLUM ANSLEM A 46 KIN W
KELLUM CHARLES A 46 SUM W
KELLUM JOHN H A 46 SUM W
KELLUM MARTIN R A 46 MCL W
KELLUM NATHANIEL A 46 MCL W
KELLY ABRAHAM A 39 FRA B
KELLY ARCHIBALD A 29 MON B
KELLY BENJAMIN A 19 BE1 B
KELLY DANL A 29 FA1 W
KELLY DAVID J A 28 8TH W
CERTIF GIVEN TO VOTE
AT BACHELOR'S CREEK
KELLY EDWARD A 46 ROS B
KELLY HAYWOOD A 39 SPE B
KELLY HENRY A 44 SAS B
KELLY IRVIN A 29 FA2 B
KELLY J H A 46 MON B
KELLY JAMES A 29 LOC B
KELLY JAMES A 29 MON B
KELLY JAMES JR A 29 MON B
KELLY JOE A 28 03A B
KELLY JOHN A 29 QUW B
KELLY JOHN A 99 BUS W
KELLY LUSTER A 29 MON B
KELLY NORPHLETT A 39 LOU B
KELLY REUBEN A 99 BUS W
KELLY THOS A 28 04A B
KELLY WILLIAM A 30 IND B
KEMP J W A 44 BEA W
KEMP SAMUEL A 30 CUR W
KEMPER CLEMENCE S A 37 TA1 B
KEMPT WILLIAM A 30 CUR W
KENAN ALEXANDER A 35 MAG B
KENAN BRYANT A 35 MAG B
KENAN CHARLES A 35 CYP B
KENAN GEORGE A 35 CYP B
KENAN JAMES G A 35 KEN W
KENAN LOT A 35 KEN B
KENAN THOMAS A 35 CYP B
KENDALL HENRY A 32 THO B
KENDALL JACOB A 32 THO B
KENDRICK J W A 40 SAN W
KENDRICK JOHN A 26 BOR W
KENDRICK JOHN A 26 SHE W
KENDRICK THOMAS A 26 SHE W
WAS CAPT OF A B?
COMPANY & AIDED
IN THE REBELION
KENDRICK THOS A 26 SHE W
KENEDY ALEX A 26 WAR W
KENEDY DUGALD A 29 SEV W
KENEDY J J A 40 SAN W
KENLEY JAMES A 32 LOF W
KENLY JNO W A 30 CUR W
KENNEDAY A J A 32 THO W
KENNEDAY A L A 32 THO W
KENNEDAY BURRELL A 32 THO W
KENNEDAY DANIEL A 32 THO W
KENNEDAY DANIEL A 32 THO W
KENNEDAY E A 32 THO W
KENNEDAY F B A 32 THO W
KENNEDAY ISAIAH A 32 THO W
KENNEDAY J C A 32 THO W
KENNEDAY JAMES A 32 THO W
KENNEDAY JAMES A 32 THO W
KENNEDAY JAMES A 32 THO W
KENNEDAY JOHN A 32 THO W
KENNEDAY LEWIS A 32 THO W
KENNEDAY SHERWOOD A 32 THO W
KENNEDAY THOMAS A 32 DAV W
CHAL. FOR BEING OUT OF
PRECINCT AND HOLDING
OFFICE. RECON.
KENNEDAY W C A 32 THO W
KENNEDAY WILLIAM A 32 POS W
KENNEDAY WILSON A 32 THO W
KENNEDY A W A 46 HIG W
KENNEDY AUGUSTUS A 28 02N B
KENNEDY BRYANT A 35 SMI W
KENNEDY CHAS A 29 FA1 W
KENNEDY CORNELIOUS A 19 NEW W
KENNEDY HENRY A 28 03A B
KENNEDY HENRY A 28 05A W
KENNEDY HENRY A 35 LIM W
KENNEDY HENRY R 28 01A B
MARKED THRU
REMOVED TO 2ND PRE
KENNEDY J D A 35 SMI W
KENNEDY J T A 35 SMI W
KENNEDY J W A 35 SMI W
KENNEDY JAMES E A 35 GLI W
KENNEDY JAS A 29 GRA W
KENNEDY JNO A 29 FA1 W
KENNEDY JOHN A 46 HIG W
KENNEDY JOHN B A 35 SMI W
KENNEDY JOHN W A 35 SMI W
KENNEDY JOSEPH A 46 JAM W
KENNEDY JOSEPH W A 28 8TH W
KENNEDY KELLIS J A 40 DA1 W
KENNEDY LABAN A 40 DA1 W
KENNEDY LEVI T A 35 MAG W
KENNEDY MOSES P A 28 02N B
KENNEDY PETER A 28 01A B
KENNEDY ROBERT A 35 LIM W
KENNEDY THOMAS A 35 KEN W
KENNEDY W H A 35 LIM W
KENNEDY WILLIAM C A 46 JAM W
KENNEDY WILLIAM M A 35 MAG W
KENNETT JOHN T R 46 ROS W
NAME LINED OUT
DID NOT TAKE THE OATH.
WAS OVERSEER OF HIGHWAY
BEFORE THE WARE, WAS
MECHANIC AND WORKED
IN GOVERNMENT SHOPS
BECAUS OF THE ONLY
CHANCE TO GET WAGES
TO SUBSIST ON
KENNEY A D A 32 JAC W
KENNY WILLIAM A 46 COB W
KENORY LEWIS A 32 THO B
KENOY DAVID A 32 THO W
KENOY F W A 32 POS W
KENOY PHILLIP 32 THO W
KENOY SAMUEL A 32 POS W
KENT STEPHEN A 28 6TH B
KENYAN WARREN A 28 04A B
KEOGH THOMAS B A 46 GRE W
KEOUGH RICHARD R 24 EDE W
REJ BY THE BOARD FOR THE
REASON HE RECEIVED A PAROLE
FROM THE "SO CALLED" CONFED.
STATES ARMY" IN APR 1865
AT THE SURRENDER OF
JOHNSTON TO GEN SHERMAN
FINAL REVISIONS
SEE HIS OATH

KEOUGH RICHARD 2 R 24 EDE W
REJ BY THE BOARD ON THE GROUNDS THAT HE IS A NATURALIZED CITIZEN AND VOL. TOOK UP ARMS AGAINST THE U.S. GOV. IN THE CONFEDERATE STATES. FINAL
FINAL REVISION REJECTED
KEPLAR PETER A 32 THO B
KEPLEY GEORGE A 32 DAV W
KEPLEY JAMES A 32 DAV W
KEPLEY JOHN A 32 LEE W
KEPLEY MATHIAS A 32 LEE W
KEPLY DAVID A 32 DAV W
KEPLY GEORGE A 32 LEE W
KEPLY LENARD A 32 DAV W
KEPLY P A A 32 DAV W
KER LOUIS A 32 TYR B
KERBY A L A 25 SHO W
KERBY J K A 25 SHO W
KERBY JESSEE A 25 SHO W
KERBY WILLIAM A 25 HAY W
AFF TO SHOOTING CREEK
KERKMAN LEWIS A 46 GRE W
KERMAN MICHEL A 53 GER W
KERNER ALEXANDER A 46 FRI B
KERNER CALVIN A 46 KIN B
KERNER CORNELIOUS A 46 KIN W
KERNERY BERRY A 46 COB W
KERNEY HENDERSON A 44 FOR B
KERNEY JAMES A 44 FOR B
KERNEY SAML A 44 FOR B
KERNODLE GEORGE R A 46 GIB W
KERNODLE JOHN R A 46 GIB W
KERNODLE LOVIC L A 46 GIB W
KERNODLE R B A 46 MON W
KERNODLE RUFUS W A 46 GIB W
KERNS ALEXANDER A 32 LEE W
KERNS H N A 32 JAC B
KERNS JOHN A 32 JAC B
KERNS JOHN A 32 JAC W
KERNS MILLER A 32 COT B
KERR SAMUEL A 32 TYR B
KERRNY JOSEPH A 39 FRA W
KERSEY CLARKSON A 46 GRE W
KERSEY DAVID A 46 GRE W
KERSEY E L A 46 JAM W
KERSEY E N A 46 JAM W
KERSEY JASPER A 46 JAM W
KERSEY JOHN A 44 TOW B
KERSEY JOHN P A 46 JAM W
KERSEY STEPHEN A 46 JAM W
KERSEY WM J A 44 OXF B
KERSHAW ROBT A 28 02N W
KERSSY BALDY A 44 OXF B
KESELER ALFORD A 32 TYR W
KESLER ROBERT A 32 TYR W
KESTER HARVEY A 40 FER W
KETCHUM CHRISTOPHER A 35 WAR W
KETCHUM JOHNATHAN A 35 WAR W
KETER PARKER R A 37 ROB W
KETHLEY ARCHIE A 35 GLI W
KETHLEY MARK A 35 GLI W
KETRON REUBEN G A 25 HAY W
KEY CHARLES A 37 EDW B
KEY CHARLES A 37 EDW B
KEY HILLIARD A 37 EDW B
KEY ISAAC A 28 7TH W
KEY ISAM A 37 EDW B
KEY JOSEPH A 37 ROB B
KEY LEM A 37 EDW B
KEY SPEAR A 37 PIN B
KEYS ALLEN A 28 04A B
KEYS DANIEL A 28 10T B
KEYS JOHN A 28 04A B
KEYS JOHN A 28 10T B
CERTIF GIVEN LIVES NOW AT LITTLE SWIFT CREEK
KEYS WM A 28 03A B
KEYS ZACHARIAS A 28 9TH B
KIGHT DEMPSEY A 30 IND W
KIGHT NOAH A 30 CUR W
KILABREW JOSEPH A 37 HIC B
KILABREW RICHARD A 37 TA1 B
KILBORN HARMON A 46 GRE W
KILBURN D N A 28 01A W
KILBURN J M A 28 01A W
KILBY MICHAEL A 25 PIN W
KILEBREW CHARLES L A 37 HIG W
KILEBREW JERALD A 37 HIG W
KILEBREW JOHN J A 37 HIG W
KILLABREW ISAM A 37 PEN B
KILLABREW NED A 37 PEN B
KILLAM NELSON A 46 MCL W
KILLBAN JOHN A 37 WHI B
KILLEBREW COLLINS A 37 MAN B
KILLEBREW JOHN A 37 HIG B
KILLEBREW NATHAN A 37 SPA B
KILLEBREW THOMAS A 37 HIG B
KILLET JOHN T A 35 FAI W
KILLET PRIMES A 72 SWA B
KILLIAN J L A 25 SHO W
KILPATRICK AMOS A 35 KEN W
KILPATRICK FRANCIS A 28 7TH W
KILPATRICK HENRY A 37 PIN B
KILPATRICK JAMES A 28 7TH W
KILPATRICK THOMAS A 35 KEN W
KILPATRICK WM F A 35 KEN W
KIMBALL GEO R A 28 01A W
KIMBALL JEFF A 44 LED B
KIMBALL PASS A 44 LED B
KIMBALL W D A 44 LED W
KIMBELL DANIEL A 32 SHE W
KIMBELL NOAH A 32 SHE W
KIMBLE MIKE A 37 ROB B
KIMBLES ISAAC A 32 CLE B
KIMBRAL JOHN A 39 JOR B
KIMBUL D J A 44 ISL W
KIME HENRY A 46 COB W
KIME J M A 46 COB W
KIME WM M A 46 COB W
KIMEL D C A 32 SHE W
KIMMEL CONRAD A 72 SWA W
KIMMEY ABRAM A 35 WOL B
KIMMEY AUSTIN A 35 WOL B
KIMMONS MILES A 28 8TH B
KIMSEY WILLIAM S A 25 HAY W
KINCEY SOLOMON A 53 HAT W
KINCY STEVEN A 19 HAD W
KINDRICK J G A 26 BOR W
KINDRICK J L A 26 BOR W
KINDRICK L H A 26 BOR W
KINDRICK L S A 26 BOR W
KINDRICK T L A 26 BOR W
KINEY MOSES A 28 04A B
KING ALFRED A 39 HAR B
KING ALFRED A 46 MON W
KING ALLEN A 37 ROB B
KING AMOS A 19 BE1 B
KING AMOS A 28 03A B
KING ANDERSON A 46 FRI W
KING B J A 39 FRA W
KING BRAY A 39 LOU B
TRNS BY AFF FROM BLADEN CO, BLADERSBOROUGH TO LOUISBURG FRANK CO
KING BLOUNT A 37 EDW B
KING BURRWELL A 39 JOR W
KING CEZER A 39 LOU B
KING CHARLES A 37 ROB B
KING COFFIELD A 37 TA1 W
KING COLIN A 39 HAR B
KING DANL A 29 CAR B
KING DEMPSY A 37 HOL B
KING DICK A 39 LOU B
KING DR E B A 46 HIG W
KING DREAD A 37 EDW B
KING EDMOND A 38 FRE B
KING EDWD B A 29 GRA W
KING ELI A 37 ROB B
KING ELI A 37 TA1 B
KING EZEKIL M A 29 FLE W
KING FRANCIS L A 19 BE2 W
KING GENERAL A 37 TA1 B
KING GEO A 29 CAR B
KING GEORGE A 26 GOF W
KING GEORGE A 35 ALB B
KING GILBERT A 39 FRE B
KING GILMON E A 44 SAS W
KING HENRY A 39 FRE B
KING HENRY R A 29 CAR W
KING ISAAC A 37 TA1 B
KING J G A 39 LOU W
KING JAMES A 28 04B W
KING JAMES A 46 FRI W
KING JAMES E A 53 GER B
KING JAS A 29 CAR B
KING JAS A A 29 FA1 W
KING JEREMIAH A 44 LED W
KING JNO A 39 FRE B
KING JNO A 44 SAS W
KING JNO D A 44 SAS W
KING JOB A 28 05A B
KING JOE A 39 DAV B
KING JOEL G A 39 LOU W
KING JOHN A 24 EDE B
KING JOHN A 37 TA1 B
KING JOHN A 46 JAM B
KING JOHN E A 35 ISL W
KING JOHN F A 19 BE1 W
KING JOHN H A 46 MCL W
KING JOSEPH A 44 OXF B
KING LEONIDAS A 46 GRE W
KING LITTLETON A 28 04A B
CERTIFICATE GRANTED WASHINGTON N C
KING LIUIS A 37 MAN B
CERT RES MAGNOLIA NC
KING M W A 29 CAR W
KING MINGO A 39 LOU B
KING N G A 29 CAR W
KING NATHAN A 38 FRE B
KING PETER A 24 EDE B
KING PLEASANT A 39 HAR B
KING RICHARD A 37 ROB B
KING RICHARD A 37 TA1 W
KING RICHD A 28 02N B
KING ROBERT A 37 ROB W
KING ROBT A 29 CAR B
KING ROBT A 39 HAR B
KING ROSWEL SR CHALA 32 DAV W
FOR HOLDING OFFICE OF MAGISTRATE BEFORE AND DURING THE WAR. RECON.
KING SAML A 29 CAR B
KING SAML A 39 DAV B
KING SAML JR A 29 CAR B
KING SANDERS A 72 SWA B
KING SANDY A 29 FLE B

KING SIMON A 53 LA1 B
KING SLADE A 28 05A B
KING SMIDRICK A 29 FA1 W
KING SOLOAN S A 46 GRE W
KING SPENCER A 44 YXS B
KING THOMAS A 35 FAI B
KING THOS A 29 CAR B
KING W A A 29 CED W
KING W R A 39 LOU W
KING WASHINGTON A 38 FRE B
KING WILLIAM A 53 GER B
KING WILLIAM C A 19 BE1 W
KING WILLIAM J A 35 ROC W
KING WILLIAM J A 39 LOU W
TRNS BY AFF FROM NASH
CO GRIFFINS PRE
KING WM A 38 FRE B
KING WM A 44 SAS W
KING WM B A 29 CAR B
KING WM R A 29 CAR W
KINGSBERRY DAN'L A 44 FIS B
KINGSBERRY JOHN A 44 OXF B
KINGSBURRY R H A 44 OXF W
KINGSBURY C F A 44 OXF W
KINGSBURY GEORGE A 28 02N W
KINLAW ELI A 29 CED W
KINLAW R W A 29 FA1 W
KINLEY CALEP A 32 TYR B
KINLEY KING A 32 TYR B
KINLEY W R A 32 LOF W
KINLY EDWARD A 32 LEE W
KINLY FRANKLIN A 32 LEE W
KINLY JESSE A 32 LOF W
KINLY MADISON A 32 LEE W
KINNEAIR ABRAM A 35 WAR B
KINNEAIR THOMAS H A 35 WAR W
KINNEAIR THOMAS J A 35 WAR W
KINNEY D F A 32 DAV W
KINNEY E A 32 LOF W
KINNEY EDWIN A 46 COB W
KINNEY J C A 32 LOF W
KINNEY MARK A 28 05A B
KINNEY PETER A 46 COB W
KINNIN RICHARD M A 28 11T W
KINNION ALI A 19 NEW B
KINNION HARDY A 19 NEW B
KINNION PETER A 19 NEW B
KINNION SAMUEL A 19 NEW B
KINNION WILLIAM A 19 NEW B
KINNY GEORGE A 32 DAV W
KINNY ISAAC A 32 DAV W
KINS JOHN A 28 03A W
KINSALL GEORGE W A 28 11T W
KINSEY AB A 19 HAD W
KINSEY EZEKIL B A 53 HAT W
KINSEY J L A 28 03B W
KINSEY JAMES M A 30 CUR W
KINSEY JOEL A 28 7TH W
KINSEY JULIUS A 28 05A B
KINSEY SAML A 28 02N B
KINSEY SAML A 30 CUR W
KINSEY SANDERS A 19 NEW B
KINSEY STEPHN A 28 03A B
KINSEY W H A 30 CUR W
KINSEY WILLIAM A 30 COI W
KINTON J R A 44 OXF W
KINTON JOHN A 44 OXF W
KINTON L A 44 OXF W
KINTON THOMAS A 44 SAS B
KINTON WM L A 44 OXF W
KIRBY J L A 25 SHO W
KIRBY J P A 25 SHO W
KIRK CHAS A 29 FA1 B
KIRK JACKSON J A 46 FRI W
KIRKENDALL HENRY A 26 WAR B
KIRKENDALL JESSE A 26 WAR B
KIRKLAND JOHN A 44 KNA W
KIRKMAN A E A 46 JAM W
KIRKMAN A G A 46 FRI W
KIRKMAN A W A 46 JAM W
KIRKMAN ANDREW M A 46 GRE W
KIRKMAN AVERY C A 46 GRE W
KIRKMAN CALVIN A 28 11T W
KIRKMAN CYRUS S A 46 GRE W
KIRKMAN DANIEL M A 46 GRE W
KIRKMAN DANL W A 46 RAG W
KIRKMAN EDWARD A 46 RAG W
KIRKMAN ELISHA W A 46 JAM W
KIRKMAN FRANKLIN M A 46 GRE W
KIRKMAN GEORGE A 46 GRE W
KIRKMAN GEORGE A A 46 GRE W
KIRKMAN GEORGE H A 46 JAM W
KIRKMAN GEORGE W A 46 ROS W
KIRKMAN JAMES A 46 GRE W
KIRKMAN JAMES L A 46 GRE W
KIRKMAN JESSE A 46 JAM W
KIRKMAN JNO N A 46 GRE W
KIRKMAN JOHN A 28 11T W
DEAD
KIRKMAN JOHN A A 46 GRE W
KIRKMAN JOHN D A 46 JAM W
KIRKMAN JOHN W A 46 GRE W
KIRKMAN JOSEPH A 46 GRE W
KIRKMAN JOSEPH A 46 ROS W
NAME LINED OUT
TRNS TO RAGANS
KIRKMAN JULIAN A A 46 GRE W
KIRKMAN JULIAS A A 46 RAG W
KIRKMAN LAFAYETTE A 28 11T W
KIRKMAN LAVIN B A 46 GRE W
KIRKMAN LEVIN A 46 FRI W
KIRKMAN PETER A 46 GRE W
KIRKMAN ROBERT A 46 ROS W
KIRKMAN ROBT A 46 GRE W
KIRKMAN SAMUEL C A 46 ROS W
NAME LINED OUT
TRNS TO RAGANS
KIRKMAN SAMUEL E A 46 GRE W
KIRKMAN WILLIAM A 28 11T W
KIRKMAN WM R 46 GRE W
WAS A MAGISTRATE BEFORE
AND DURING THE REBELLION
WE HAVE EVIDENCE THAT HE
GAVE AID ALSO THAT HE
GAVE MONE VOLUNTARILY
REJECTED
KIRKMAN WM JR A 46 GRE W
KIRKMAN WM M A 46 GRE W
KIRKMAN WM O A 46 GRE W
KIRKPATRICK BRANSON A 46 GRE B
KIRKPATRICK
DANIEL N A 46 GRE W
KIRKPATRICK ISAAC A 29 ROC B
KIRKPATRICK ISAAC A 46 GRE B
KIRKPATRICK JACK A 29 GRA B
KIRKPATRICK JNO A 29 GRA B
KIRKPATRICK JNO A 29 GRA W
KIRKPATRICK JOHN A 46 HIG W
KIRKPATRICK LEWIS A 29 GRA B
KIRKPATRICK NEILL A 29 FA1 B
KIRKPATRICK NEILL A 29 GRA B
KIRKPATRICK PARIS A 46 GRE B
KIRKPATRICK RUFUS A 46 HIG W
KIRKPATRICK
THOMAS J A 46 FRI W
KIRMAN HENRY A A 53 GER W
KISER DAVID S A 40 MAU W
KISER HENRY A 40 MAU W
KISER HIRAM A 40 MAU W
KISER JACOB SEN A 40 BLA W
KISER JOHN A 40 MAU W
KISER LARKIN M A 40 MAU
KISER LEVI A 26 BOR W
KISER LEVI A 40 MAU W
KISER MICHAEL A 40 MAU W
KISER PHILLIP A 40 MAU W
KISSELBURG W H A 25 SHO W
KISSNER HENRY A 35 ROC W
KISTLER DANIEL A 26 WAR W
KISTLER J J A 26 WAR W
KISTLER PAUL A 28 16T W
KITCHENS DAVID A 25 SHO W
KITCHENS JASON A 25 SHO W
KITCHENS STEPHIN A 25 SHO W
KITCHIN JACK A 37 EDW B
KITCHINS EPHRAIM A 25 SHO W
KITE BURTON A 28 11T W
KITE DEMPSEY A 30 MOY W
KITE EDMUND A 30 GIB W
KITE ENOCH A 30 IND W
KITE SAMUEL A 28 11T W
KITRELL ESEX A 39 HAY B
KITTLE J M A 44 BRA W
KITTLE L H A 44 HEN W
KITTLE LEVI A 44 SAS B
KITTRELL B F A 44 KIT W
KITTRELL CHARLES A 44 KIT B
KITTRELL E H A 44 HEN W
KITTRELL E P A 44 ISL W
KITTRELL EPHRAM A 44 KIT B
KITTRELL ESSIC A 44 KIT B
KITTRELL GEO A 44 HEN B
KITTRELL GEO E A 44 HEN B
KITTRELL GEO W A 44 KIT W
KITTRELL GEORGE A 44 KIT B
KITTRELL GILES A 44 KIT B
KITTRELL H C A 44 HEN W
KITTRELL HENRY A 44 FIS B
KITTRELL ISAAC A 44 KIT B
KITTRELL J W A 44 HEN W
KITTRELL JARAMIAH A 44 KIT B
KITTRELL JAS P A 44 KIT B
KITTRELL JNO W A 44 KIT W
KITTRELL JOHN A 44 KIT B
KITTRELL KINDRICK A 53 GER W
KITTRELL NORVILLE A 44 OXF B
KITTRELL ROBT A 44 HEN B
KITTRELL S W A 44 HEN W
KITTRELL THOS G A 44 KIT W
KIVETT DAVID A 29 FA1 W
KIVIT WM Y A 29 ROC W
KIZER HARRY A 40 MAU B
KIZER ROBERT A 26 BUR W
KLINE JACOB D A 46 GRE W
KLOUS JOSEPH A 46 KIN W
KLUTTS GEORGE A A 46 GRE W
KNABEN HENRY A 19 BE1 W
KNAPP T J A 24 MID W
KNIGHT GEORGE A 37 HIG W
(BLACK IN PENCIL)
KNIGHT ALBERT A 37 ROB B
KNIGHT ALBERT A 37 TA1 B
KNIGHT ALBERT A 37 WHI B
KNIGHT ALFRED A 37 HIG B
KNIGHT ALFRED A 37 HIG B
KNIGHT ALLEN A 37 HIG B
KNIGHT ANDREW A 37 PIN B
KNIGHT ANDREW A 37 TA1 B
KNIGHT ARNOLD A 37 EDW B

KNIGHT ARRIC	A	37	PIN	B
KNIGHT ASA	A	46	FRI	W
KNIGHT BAT	A	37	HIG	B
KNIGHT BENJ	A	44	BEA	W
KNIGHT BENJAMIN	A	37	EDW	B
KNIGHT BERRY	A	37	PIN	B
KNIGHT CADE	A	37	PIN	B
KNIGHT CALVIN	A	37	EDW	B
KNIGHT CHARLES W	A	37	HIG	W
KNIGHT COFIELD C	A	37	ROB	W
KNIGHT E S	A	46	FRI	W
KNIGHT EDWARD	A	37	HIG	B
KNIGHT EDWARD E	A	37	PIN	W
KNIGHT ELISHA C	A	37	PIN	W
KNIGHT EMANUEL	A	37	HIC	B
KNIGHT FRANCIS H	A	37	HIG	W
KNIGHT GEORGE	A	28	04A	B
KNIGHT GEORGE	A	37	PIN	B
KNIGHT GLASGO	A	37	WHI	B
KNIGHT GUILFORD	A	28	04A	B
KNIGHT HENRY	A	37	EDW	B
KNIGHT HENRY	A	37	EDW	B
KNIGHT HENRY	A	37	HIG	B
KNIGHT HENRY	A	37	PEN	B
KNIGHT HENRY	A	37	PIN	B
KNIGHT HILLIARD	A	37	EDW	B
KNIGHT HILLIARD	A	37	PIN	B
KNIGHT ISAAC	A	37	HIG	B
KNIGHT ISAAC	A	37	WHI	B
KNIGHT J H	A	46	FRI	W
KNIGHT J R	A	44	BEA	W
KNIGHT JACOB	A	37	EDW	B
KNIGHT JACOB	A	37	HIC	B
KNIGHT JAMES	A	37	EDW	B
KNIGHT JAMES	A	37	HIC	B
KNIGHT JAMES	A	46	GRE	B
KNIGHT JAMES W	A	37	EDW	W
KNIGHT JAS W	A	29	FA1	W
KNIGHT JEREMIAH	A	37	TA1	B
KNIGHT JERRY	A	37	PEN	B
KNIGHT JOAB	A	46	FRI	W
KNIGHT JOHN	A	37	HIG	B
KNIGHT JOHN	A	37	TA1	B
KNIGHT JOHN NO 2	A	37	HIG	B
KNIGHT JOHN F	A	37	HIG	W
KNIGHT JOHN H	A	37	EDW	W
KNIGHT JOHN P	A	37	EDW	W
KNIGHT JOSEPH	A	37	HIG	B
KNIGHT JOSEPH	A	37	WHI	B
KNIGHT JOSEPH L	A	37	TA2	W
KNIGHT JOSIAH	A	37	HIG	B
KNIGHT JOSIAH	A	37	PEN	B
KNIGHT JOURDAN	A	37	PIN	W
KNIGHT KING	A	37	EDW	B
KNIGHT L A	A	40	SAN	W
KNIGHT LEWIS	A	37	PIN	B
KNIGHT LONDON	A	37	EDW	B
KNIGHT LOUIS B	A	37	EDW	W
KNIGHT MOSCO	A	37	HIG	B
KNIGHT N M	A	46	FRI	W
KNIGHT NATHAN	A	37	EDW	B
KNIGHT NATHAN	A	37	PIN	B
KNIGHT NATHAN 2ND	A	37	PIN	B
KNIGHT NATHANIEL	A	37	PIN	B
KNIGHT RALPH	A	37	EDW	B
KNIGHT RICHARD	A	37	PEN	B
KNIGHT RICHARD	A	37	PEN	B
KNIGHT ROBERT	A	37	EDW	B
KNIGHT ROBERT	A	37	HIG	B
KNIGHT ROBERT A	A	37	PIN	W
KNIGHT SANDY	A	37	PIN	B
KNIGHT SAUNY	A	37	EDW	B
KNIGHT SOLOMAN	A	37	PEN	B
KNIGHT TONY	A	37	HIG	B
KNIGHT VERGEL	A	37	ROC	B
KNIGHT WESTON	A	37	EDW	B
KNIGHT WILLIS B	A	37	PIN	W
KNIGHT WRIGHT	A	28	6TH	B
KNOTT ALLEN	A	44	SAS	B
KNOTT BARTLETT	A	44	SAS	W
KNOTT CALEB	A	44	OXF	W
KNOTT F	A	44	OXF	W
KNOTT G W	A	44	ISL	W
KNOTT G W B	A	46	KIN	B
KNOTT GEO F	A	44	SAS	W
KNOTT GEORGE	A	44	RAG	B
KNOTT J R	A	44	RAG	W
KNOTT J W	A	44	SAS	W
KNOTT JNO	A	44	SAS	W
KNOTT LAWSON	A	44	OXF	W
KNOTT R W	A	44	ISL	W
KNOTT ROBT	A	44	SAS	W
KNOTT S G	A	44	ISL	W
KNOTT THOS	A	44	SAS	W
KNOTT THOS H	A	44	SAS	W
KNOTT WILEY	A	46	KIN	W
KNOTT WM	A	29	SEV	W
KNOUND JESSE	A	32	SHE	W
KNOUND JOHN S	A	32	SHE	W
KNOWLES GEORGE W	A	35	ROC	W
KNOWLES JOHN	A	35	ROC	W
KNOWLES STEPHEN	A	35	ROC	W
KNOWLES WILLIAM	A	35	ROC	W
KNOX JACK	A	24	EDE	B
KOBB JAMES K	A	37	HIG	W
KOONCE AMOS	A	28	03A	B
KOONCE BENJN	A	28	03A	B
KOONCE G W	A	19	HAD	W
KOONCE JAMES	A	28	8TH	B
KOONCE KIT	A	28	03B	B
KOONCE MIKE	A	32	DAV	W
KOONCE PHILIP H	A	32	DAV	W
KOONCE PHILLIP	A	19	HAD	W
KOONES ALEXANDER	A	32	THO	B
KOONES HARRISON	A	32	POS	W
COLORD WRITTEN BESIDE NAME				
KOONTS HENRY F	A	32	TYR	W
KOONZ BRYAN	A	28	9TH	B
KORNBAW DANL	A	29	FA1	W
KORNEGA RICHARD	A	46	HIG	B
KORNEGAY A	R	35	GLI	W
FOR BEING INSANE				
KORNEGAY A G	A	35	ALB	W
KORNEGAY BENJAMIN F	A	35	GLI	W
KORNEGAY BRYANT	A	35	KEN	W
KORNEGAY BUCK	A	35	FAI	B
KORNEGAY CURTIS	A	35	FAI	B
KORNEGAY D K	A	35	WOL	W
KORNEGAY DANIEL	A	35	GLI	W
KORNEGAY DAVID	A	35	WOL	B
KORNEGAY DAVID C	A	35	GLI	W
KORNEGAY EVERET	A	35	GLI	B
KORNEGAY G T	A	35	WOL	W
KORNEGAY H C	A	35	WOL	W
KORNEGAY HARDY	A	35	GLI	B
KORNEGAY HARDY	A	35	WOL	B
KORNEGAY HARGET JR	A	35	GLI	W
KORNEGAY HENRY	A	35	GLI	B
KORNEGAY IMANUEL	A	35	ALB	W
KORNEGAY ISAAC	A	35	GLI	W
KORNEGAY J E	A	35	WOL	W
KORNEGAY JAMES	A	35	GLI	B
KORNEGAY JAMES	A	35	WOL	B
KORNEGAY JAMES H	A	35	KEN	W
KORNEGAY JOHN	A	35	WOL	B
KORNEGAY JOHN	A	35	WOL	B
KORNEGAY JOHN W	A	35	GLI	W
KORNEGAY KIT	A	35	WOL	B
KORNEGAY PETER	A	35	GLI	B
KORNEGAY PETER	A	35	WOL	B
KORNEGAY POMPEY	A	35	ALB	B
KORNEGAY S A	A	35	WOL	W
KORNEGAY SIMMONS	A	35	GLI	W
KORNEGAY SIMON	A	35	WOL	B
KORNEGAY STEP	A	35	WOL	B
KORNEGAY STEPHEN H	A	35	ALB	W
KORNEGAY WEBB	A	35	CYP	B
KORNEGAY WILL	A	35	GLI	B
KORNEGAY WILLIAM	A	35	GLI	W
KOUNTS ARCH	A	32	DAV	B
KOUNTS AUSTIN	A	32	TYR	B
KOUNTS DAVID	A	32	DAV	W
KOUNTS DAVID	A	32	DAV	W
KOUNTS DAVID	A	32	DAV	W
KOUNTS DAVID J	A	32	DAV	B
KOUNTS E S	A	32	TYR	W
KOUNTS GEORGE	A	32	DAV	W
KOUNTS GEORGE	A	32	DAV	W
KOUNTS H Z	A	32	DAV	W
KOUNTS HYRAM	A	32	TYR	W
KOUNTS J H	A	32	DAV	W
KOUNTS JACOB H	A	32	DAV	W
KOUNTS JOEL	A	32	TYR	W
KOUNTS JOHN W	A	32	TYR	W
KOUNTS JOSEPH	A	32	TYR	B
KOUNTS SAMUEL	A	32	TYR	W
KOUNTS WILLIAM A	A	32	TYR	W
KOUNTS WILLIAM F	A	32	DAV	W
KRENOY JACOB	A	32	THO	W
KROOM JAMES	A	35	WOL	B
KUNTZ JAMES	A	28	16T	B
KYLE AARON	A	44	OXF	B
KYLE DERRY	A	29	FA1	B
KYLE HARVEY	A	44	OXF	B
KYLE JESSEE K	A	29	FA1	W
KYLE NEVISON	A	44	OXF	B
KYLE THEOFFILUS	A	44	OXF	B
KYLE WM E JR	A	29	FA1	W
- L -				
LA ROQUE J D	A	28	6TH	W
LACKEY DICKSON	A	26	GOF	W
LACKEY EDWARD	A	26	GOF	W
LACKEY EDWARD	A	40	DEC	W
LACKEY GEORGE	A	40	DEC	W
LACKEY JACOB	A	26	GRI	W
LACKEY JAMES	A	26	GRI	W
LACKEY JOHN M	A	40	DEC	W
LACKEY ROBERT	A	26	GRI	W
LADD JOHN	A	28	8TH	W
LAGEL JACOB	A	32	CLE	W
LAGLE WILLIAM	A	32	DAV	W
LAHMAN P T	A	32	CLE	W
LAINE HENRY	A	37	MAN	B
LAMAY PATRICK	A	44	BRA	B
LAMB ANDERSON	A	46	JAM	W
LAMB ANTHONY	A	35	ROC	B
LAMB BENJAMIN	A	24	EDE	B
LAMB CHRISTOPHER	A	19	MOR	W
LAMB DAVID	A	46	JAM	W
LAMB GARRISON	A	24	EDE	B
LAMB GEORGE	A	19	MOR	W
LAMB GEORGE A	A	19	HAR	W
NAME LINED OUT				
LAMB GRIFFIN	A	24	EDE	B
LAMB H C	A	46	JAM	W
LAMB H C	A	46	JAM	W
LAMB H W	A	46	JAM	W
LAMB JAMES	A	35	ROC	B

LAMB JOHN A 24 EDE B
LAMB JOSEPH A 24 EDE B
LAMB MEBAN A 46 GRE W
LAMB MOSES A 32 TYR W
LAMB ORLANDO A 46 JAM W
LAMB ROBERT A 46 ROS W
LAMB ROBT A 24 EDE B
LAMB THOMAS A 30 MOY B
LAMB THOMAS A 46 ROS W
LAMB THOS A 30 IND B
LAMB U H A 46 JAM W
LAMB W H A 38 FRE W
LAMB WILLIAM A 46 JAM W
CAUSE CAPTAIN MILITIA
BEFORE THE REBELLION
AIDED VOLUNTARILY IN
REBELLION
IS ACCEPTED
LAMB ZEMRI A 35 WAR W
LAMBERT D H A 35 FAI W
LAMBERT J H A 46 MON W
LAMBERT J W A 29 FA1 B
LAMBERT JOAB A 46 ROS W
LAMBERT W H A 35 GLI W
LAMBERT W S A 30 KNO W
LAMBERTH JOHN A 32 LEE W
LAMBERTH JOSEPH A 32 LEE W
LAMBERTH LOUIS A 32 LEE W
LAMBERTH N G A 32 LEE W
LAMBERTH SAMUEL S A 32 LEE W
LAMBETH B C A 32 THO W
LAMBETH B F A 32 THO W
LAMBETH BENJN A 46 GIB B
LAMBETH CHARLES A 46 JAM B
LAMBETH D H A 32 DAV W
LAMBETH DAVID SR A 32 THO W
LAMBETH E T A 46 MON W
LAMBETH F T A 32 THO W
LAMBETH GREEN A 32 THO B
LAMBETH ISAAC A 46 SUM B
LAMBETH J H A 32 THO W
LAMBETH J HARRISON A 32 THO W
LAMBETH JOHN A 32 DAV W
LAMBETH JOHN A A 46 SUM W
LAMBETH JOHN J A 46 MON W
LAMBETH JOSEPH A 46 GIB B
LAMBETH L D A 32 POS W
LAMBETH L H A 46 SUM W
LAMBETH R D A 46 SUM W
LAMBETH S J A 32 THO W
LAMBETH SILAS A 32 THO W
LAMBETH Z A 32 DAV W
LAMOND JAS F A A 44 HEN W
LAMONDS ROBERT A 46 MON W
LAMONT M C A 29 SEV W
LANAIR ALEXANDER A 40 DA2 W
LANCASTER ----- M A 28 11T W
BADLY STAINED
LANCASTER ABRAM A 44 TOW W
LANCASTER ALFORD A 39 JOR W
LANCASTER BERRY J A 37 HIG W
LANCASTER BLOUNT A 37 PIN B
LANCASTER BUND A 37 HIG W
LANCASTER
CHRISTOFER C A 46 GRE W
LANCASTER DAVID W A 37 HIG W
LANCASTER G F A 28 11T W
LANCASTER GEORGE A 28 11T B
LANCASTER GID A 39 JOR B
LANCASTER HARRY A 39 JOR B
LANCASTER J A A 39 JOR W
LANCASTER J R A 39 JOR W
LANCASTER JACOB H A 28 11T W
LANCASTER JAMES A 44 TOW W
LANCASTER JESSE A 28 11T W
LANCASTER JESSE A 37 HIG W
LANCASTER JOHN A 37 HIG W
LANCASTER JOHN A 44 HEN W
LANCASTER L H A 39 JOR W
LANCASTER LACY JR A 28 11T W
LANCASTER LACY SR A 28 11T W
LANCASTER LACY V A 28 11T W
LANCASTER LAWRENCE A 37 ROB W
LANCASTER LEVI L A 37 SHA W
LANCASTER LITTLETON A 39 JOR B
LANCASTER M V A 39 JOR W
LANCASTER MICAJAH A 39 PUG W
LANCASTER R W A 39 LOU W
LANCASTER ROSCOE A 28 11T W
LANCASTER SINCLAIR A 28 11T W
LANCASTER ST CLAIR A 28 11T W
LANCASTER STEPHEN A 28 11T W
LANCASTER THOMAS A 37 HIG B
LANCASTER WARREN A 37 HIG B
LANCASTER WASHINGTONA 44 HEN W
LANCASTER WILLIAM A 28 11T W
LANCASTER WILLIAM F A 28 11T W
LANCASTER WILLIE A 39 JOR W
LAND BRAXTON A 44 YXS W
LAND CHAMBERS E A 40 DA1 W
LAND CHARLES L A 37 SHA W
LAND ISAAC A 25 HAY W
LAND JAMES K A 28 14T W
LAND JAMES M A 28 14T W
LAND JEREMIAH W A 28 14T W
LAND JERREMIAH A 25 HAY W
LAND JERRY A 37 ROC B
LAND MYSANDIA A 46 SUM W
LAND THOMAS A 40 CAN B
LAND W M A 30 IND W
LANDAS DANNEL A 44 DUT B
LANDAS ENOCH A 44 DUT B
LANDAS IVERSON A 44 DUT B
LANDAS WILEY A 44 DUT B
LANDEN LUCIUS C A 37 TA1 W
LANDER MOSES A 19 BE1 B
LANDIN JAS Y A 44 OXF W
LANDIS A JR A 44 OXF W
LANDIS C E A 44 OXF W
LANDIS EDWARD A 44 BEA B
LANDIS GEO W A 44 OXF W
LANDIS WILLIS A 44 OXF B
LANDON LEMUAL L A 37 TA1 W
LANDON O C A 26 WAR W
LANDON WILL A 37 HIG W
LANDREATH MCKINLEY DA 46 GRE W
LANE A C A 19 MOR W
LANE ALFRED A 28 7TH W
LANE AMOS A 28 04A B
LANE B B A 28 02N W
LANE BRYANT A 46 MON B
LANE CHARS CHAL R 19 MOR B
DOUBTFUL AS TO AGE
LANE DANIEL A 28 11T W
LANE DAVID A 37 HIG W
LANE E H A 28 7TH W
LANE EVERETT A 35 FAI B
LANE FRANK D A 28 02N B
LANE FREDK A 28 04A B
LANE GEORGE A 32 COT W
LANE GEORGE D A 46 GRE W
LANE GRAHAM D A 28 04A B
LANE H B A 28 02N W
LANE HENRY A 28 04A B
LANE HENRY A 37 PEN B
LANE ISAAC B A 28 7TH W
LANE J B A 28 02N W
LANE JACOB A 28 03A B
LANE JAMES A 28 7TH B
LANE JAMES A 32 COT W
LANE JESSE A 32 JAC W
LANE JEWIS A 39 HAY B
LANE JOHN A 19 BE1 B
LANE JOHN W A 46 GRE W
LANE JOSEPH A 37 EDW B
LANE JOSHUA A 37 HOL W
LANE LEMON A 99 BUS B
LANE LEVI A 46 GRE W
LANE M A 26 BOR W
LANE MACK A 28 16T B
LANE MOSES A 28 11T B
LANE MOSES D A 30 NOR W
APRIL 17, 1868
LANE NOAH S A 28 13T W
LANE PATRICK A 37 ROB W
LANE PATRICK A 37 ROB W
LANE RICHARD A 19 BE1 B
LANE ROBERT A 99 BUS B
LANE SAMUEL A 24 UPP W
LANE SAMUEL A 32 THO W
LANE SHADRACK A 28 04A B
LANE STEPHAN A 35 FAI B
LANE STEPHEN A 19 BE1 B
LANE THEOPHILUS A 37 PIN W
LANE THOMAS A 46 GRE W
LANE WILLIAM A 35 WOL W
LANE WILLIAM A 37 HOL W
LANE WILLIAM B A 28 7TH W
LANE WILLIAM H A 37 EDW W
LANE WILLIAM P A 28 7TH W
LANE WILLIAM P A 30 IND W
LANE WM A 28 04A W
LANE WM A 28 6TH B
LANE WM A 29 FA1 B
LANE WM A 29 FA1 B
LANE WM H A 46 GRE W
LANEY DAVID W A 40 MAU W
LANG HENRY A 44 SAS B
LANG N J A 26 CAR W
LANG P R A 26 BOR W
LANG R A 26 BOR W
LANGDALE J N A 19 BE1 W
LANGLEY FRANKLIN A 37 WEB W
LANGLEY HILLERY A 37 WEB W
LANGLEY JAMES A 37 WEB W
LANGLEY LEVI A 28 15T W
LANGLEY WILLIAM A 28 11T W
LANGLEY WILLIAM A 37 WEB W
LANGMAID HENRY A 19 HAR B
LANGSTON ALBERT A 44 SAS B
LANGSTON DAVID SR A 37 WHI B
LANGSTON FENNIAL A 35 ALB W
LANGSTON JESSE E A 99 BUS W
LANGSTON JOHN W A 35 ALB W
LANGSTON PRINCE A 28 05A B
LANIER ALLEN A 35 CYP W
LANIER ALLIN A 39 PUG B
LANIER AMOS A 35 CYP W
LANIER B W A 35 CYP W
LANIER BRANTLEY A 35 CYP W
LANIER BRYANT A 35 MAG W
LANIER BYRD A 35 WAR W
LANIER C A 32 LOF W
LANIER DAVID E A 35 CYP W
LANIER DENNIS A 35 CYP W
LANIER EDMOND A 32 YAD W
LANIER GIBSON A 35 CYP W
LANIER H F A 35 CYP W
LANIER H G A 35 CYP W

LANIER HOLDEN A 35 CYP W
LANIER HOSEA G A 35 CYP W
LANIER IVY A 35 LIM W
LANIER IVY A 35 LIM W
LANIER J A A 35 CYP W
LANIER J T A 35 LIM W
LANIER J W A 35 CYP W
LANIER JACOB A 35 CYP W
LANIER JACOB S A 35 CYP W
LANIER JAMES F A 46 GRE W
LANIER JAMES T A 35 ROC W
LANIER JESSE A 32 DAV W
LANIER JESSE A 35 KEN W
LANIER JOHN A 32 LOF W
LANIER JOSEPH J A 35 KEN W
LANIER M V A 44 OXF W
LANIER OWEN S A 35 CYP W
LANIER OWEN W A 35 CYP W
LANIER PHILIP A 32 JAC W
LANIER RHAFORD A 35 CYP W
LANIER SPIOUS A 35 CYP W
LANIER STEPHEN A 35 MAG W
LANIER STEPHEN S A 35 CYP W
LANIER THOMAS A 35 CYP W
LANIER THOMAS F A 32 LOF W
LANIER W J A 32 LOF W
LANIER WILLIAM A 32 JAC W
LANIER WILLIAM A 32 LOF W
LANIER WILLIAM H A 35 KEN W
LANIER WILSON W A 35 CYP W
LANIER ZEBULON A 35 CYP W
LANING GEO W A 32 SHE W
LANING JOHN A 32 TYR W
LANKFORD ABERT A 39 LOU B
TRNS FROM DAVIS X ROADS
LANKFORD ALBERT A 39 DAV B
TRNS TO LOUISBURG
LANKFORD ALFORD A 39 DAV B
LANKFORD BLUNT A 39 LOU B
LANKFORD ELBEREY A 26 PEE W
LANKFORD HARDY A 39 DAV B
LANKFORD L E A 26 SHE W
LANKFORD ROBERT A 26 PEE W
LANKFORD W C A 39 DAV W
NAME LINED OUT
TRNS FROM LOUISBURG
TO DAVIS
LANKFORD W C A 39 LOU W
TRNS TO DAVIS PREC
FROM LOUISBURG
LANKSON ALBERT A 44 SAS B
LANNING DAVID A 32 DAV W
LANNING ELICK A 32 DAV W
LANNING HENDERSON A 32 DAV W
LANNING JAMES A 32 DAV W
LANNING JOSEPH A 32 DAV W
LANNING THOMAS F A 32 TYR W
LANSDAL J J A 44 DUT W
LAPISH D H A 46 GRE W
LAPP ALEX. A 32 THO B
LAPP GEORGE A 32 DAV B
LAPP HUBBARD A 32 DAV B
LAPP JACOB A 32 DAV W
LAPP JOHN A 32 DAV B
LAPP JULIUS A 32 DAV B
LAPP LEWIS A 32 DAV B
LAPP MACK A 32 DAV B
LAPP MATHIAS A 32 DAV W
LAPP PETER A 32 DAV W
LAPP PHILIP A 32 DAV W
LARKIN JAMES A 46 GRE B
LARKINS ALEXR A 28 04A B
LARRENCE GALTON A 44 DUT B

LARYMOORE RUSSEL A 32 SHE W
LASH ISAAC A 46 SUM B
LASH WILLIS A 32 CLE B
LASHMET FRANKLIN A 32 SHE W
LASITER J G A 39 PUG W
LASLIE JOHN W A 29 QUW W
LASLIE PETER A 29 QUW B
LASLIE THOMAS A A 29 QUW W
LASSATER S W A 39 HAR W
LASSATER WM A 39 HAR W
LASSELL WM H R 30 MOY W
CHALLENGED
LASSELL WM H R 30 MOY W
OATH TO THE REBBEL
STATE REJECTED
LASSETER JAMES H A 30 TUL W
LASSITER ABRAM A 46 GRE B
LASSITER ALEX A 44 OXF B
LASSITER DAVID A 44 OXF B
LASSITER ESAU A 44 OXF B
LASSITER EZEKIEL A 44 HEN B
LASSITER GEORGE W A 35 WAR W
LASSITER GRANDERSON A 44 YXS B
LASSITER HOWELL C A 44 OXF B
LASSITER JAS H A 44 HEN W
LASSITER JOSEPH A 44 OXF B
LASSITER LEONARD A 99 BUS W
LASSITER MOSIS A 44 HEN B
LASSITER PETER A 44 YXS B
LASSITER R W A 44 OXF W
LASSITER THOMAS A 30 CUR B
LASSITER W C A 44 HEN W
LASSITER WARREN A 37 WHI B
LASSITER WARREN A 44 OXF B
LASTEIN ELI A 37 SPA B
LASTER DOLPHIN A 28 6TH B
LASUE JERRY A 37 WHI B
LATAN NORFLET A 39 FRA W
LATCHCO JOHN A 46 GRE W
LATEN ABNER A 39 LOU W
TRNS FROM HORN'S X
ROADS TO LOUISBURG
LATHAM ADAM A 28 9TH B
LATHAM AUSTIN A 28 04A B
LATHAM BOSSON A 28 9TH B
LATHAM BOSTON A 28 13T B
LATHAM BRAXTON A 28 05B B
LATHAM BRISTOL A 28 03A B
LATHAM C H A 28 02N W
LATHAM CAESAR A 28 9TH B
LATHAM CORNELIUS A 28 03A B
LATHAM GEO A A 28 01A W
LATHAM HARDY A 28 05A B
LATHAM HI A 28 05A B
LATHAM JARVIS A 28 04A B
LATHAM JESSE A 28 05A B
LATHAM JESSE A 28 05B B
LATHAM JESSIE A 37 TA1 B
LATHAM JOB A 28 13T B
LATHAM JOHN A 28 03A B
LATHAM JOHN A 28 05A B
LATHAM LYMAN A 44 OXF W
LATHAM MOSES A 28 03B B
LATHAM OTTER A 37 TA1 B
LATHAM REED A 28 05A B
LATHAM SAMUEL W A 28 13T W
LATHAM THOS J A 28 02N W
LATHAM W P A 44 OXF W
LATHAM WILLIAM A 28 9TH B
LATHAN HENRY A 28 16T B
LATHAN WM A 19 BE1 B
LATHINGHOUSE W M A 28 11T W
LATHMON D A 26 GRI B

LATON ABNER A 39 HAR W
LATON ALFRED A 24 MID W
LATTA HENDERSON A 44 LED W
LATTA ISAAC A 44 TAR B
LATTA NEVISON A 44 TAR B
LATTA ROBERT A 44 LED W
LATTA THOS A 44 TAR W
LATTEY HENDERSON A 37 PIN B
LATTIMORE A M A 26 BLA W
LATTIMORE D D A 26 BLA W
LATTIMORE D D A 26 GRI W
LATTIMORE FRANKLIN A 26 BLA W
LATTIMORE ISAAC A 26 BLA B
LATTIMORE J C A 26 BLA B
LATTIMORE J C JR A 26 BLA B
LATTIMORE J C JR A 26 BLA W
LATTIMORE J H A 26 BLA W
LATTIMORE J L A 26 BLA W
LATTIMORE JAMES A 26 PEE B
LATTIMORE JESSE A 26 BLA B
LATTIMORE JESSE A 26 GRI B
LATTIMORE JOHN A 26 BLA W
LATTIMORE OLIVER A 26 PEE B
LATTIMORE S A 26 GRI W
LATTIMORE SAMPSON A 26 BLA B
LATTIMORE W C A 26 BLA W
LAUDER GEO A 29 FA1 W
LAUGHFINHOUSE RILEY A 28 03A W
LAUGHINGHOUSE BRYAN A 28 11T W
LAUGHINGHOUSE JOHN A 28 11T W
LAUGHINGHOUSE THOMASA 28 11T W
LAUGHTON GEO A 19 MOR W
LAUGHTON THOS E A 30 POP W
LAUR THOMAS A 32 CLE B
LAURENCE ABRAHAM A 44 FOR W
LAURENCE B F A 44 FOR W
LAURENCE J J A 44 FOR W
LAURENCE J P A 44 FOR W
LAURENCE J W A 44 FOR W
LAURENCE MERTIN A 26 BLA B
LAURENCE PETER A 29 LOC B
LAURENCE SQUIRE A 44 FOR B
LAVEIC BRISTOR A 19 HAR B
LAVENDER ELLIS A 28 04A B
LAVENDER ISARIEL A 19 BE1 B
LAWARNCE CANELUM A 19 STR W
LAWES BENJAMIN A 37 HIC B
LAWING JAMES J A 40 DA1 W
LAWN HENRY A 28 04A B
LAWRANCE HANDY A 37 SHA B
LAWRANCE SOLOMON A 37 SHA B
LAWRENCE ADAM R 37 TA2 B
NOT OF AGE
LAWRENCE ALFRED A 37 TA2 B
LAWRENCE ALFRED A 40 FER B
LAWRENCE ANDREW A 37 HIC B
LAWRENCE ANSON A 19 STR W
LAWRENCE ANTHONY D A 19 STR W
LAWRENCE ARDEN A 37 HIC B
LAWRENCE AUGUSTUS A 37 TA1 B
LAWRENCE BENJ A 19 POR W
LAWRENCE BLOUNT A 37 EDW B
LAWRENCE C A A 46 SUM W
LAWRENCE CANY A 28 05A B
LAWRENCE CHARLES A 37 EDW B
LAWRENCE COLLINS A 37 HIC B
LAWRENCE DAVID W A 19 STR W
LAWRENCE DEMPSEY A 37 TA1 B
LAWRENCE DREAD A 37 EDW B
LAWRENCE E B A 44 BEA W
LAWRENCE EDWARD A 46 ROS B
LAWRENCE HARRY A 37 EDW B
LAWRENCE HENRY A 28 14T B

LAWRENCE JACOB A 37 PIN B
LAWRENCE JAMES A 19 STR W
LAWRENCE JAMES A 37 HIC B
LAWRENCE JAMES J A 37 PIN W
LAWRENCE JAMES K A 37 MAN W
LAWRENCE JERRY A 37 EDW B
LAWRENCE JOHN A 19 STR W
LAWRENCE JOHN B A 19 STR W
LAWRENCE JOHN H A 24 MID W
LAWRENCE JOHN J A 37 HIC A
LAWRENCE JOHN L A 37 PIN W
LAWRENCE JOHN W A 37 TA1 B
LAWRENCE JOHN W A 99 BUS W
LAWRENCE JONES A 44 BEA W
LAWRENCE JOSEPH A 19 STR W
LAWRENCE JOSEPH A 37 EDW B
LAWRENCE JOSIAH A 37 TA1 W
LAWRENCE LEWIS A 37 HIC A
LAWRENCE NATHAN M A 37 TA1 W
LAWRENCE OLIVER C A 19 STR W
LAWRENCE PARK A 28 04A B
LAWRENCE PETER A 37 EDW B
LAWRENCE PETER A 37 TA2 B
LAWRENCE PETER A 40 FER B
LAWRENCE PHILLIP A 37 PIN B
LAWRENCE POMPEY A 37 PIN B
LAWRENCE PRESTON A 37 EDW B
LAWRENCE RHODEN A 37 TA1 B
LAWRENCE RICHMOND A 37 TA1 B
LAWRENCE ROBERT A 37 EDW B
LAWRENCE ROMEO A 37 EDW B
LAWRENCE RUFFIN A 37 EDW B
LAWRENCE SAMUEL A 37 PIN B
LAWRENCE SHARPER A 37 PIN B
LAWRENCE STEPHEN A 30 CUR B
LAWRENCE STEWART A 37 EDW B
LAWRENCE T C A 19 NEW W
LAWRENCE THOMAS A 24 EDE B
LAWRENCE THOMAS A 26 GRI B
LAWRENCE THOS D A 24 MID B
LAWRENCE VINYARD A 37 EDW B
LAWRENCE WARREN A 37 EDW B
LAWRENCE WATSON W A 28 14T W
LAWRENCE WHIT A 37 EDW B
LAWRENCE WILLIAM A 99 BUS W
LAWRENCE WILLIAM J A 37 EDW W
LAWRENCE WM H A 19 STR W
LAWRENCE WM W A 28 01A B
LAWRENCE Y S A 46 SUM W
LAWS ELIAS A 37 EDW B
LAWS G T A 28 02N W
LAWS GEO R A 44 LED W
LAWS HENRY A 37 HIC B
LAWS PHILLIP A 44 FOR B
LAWSON CHARLES A 44 YXS B
LAWSON CHRISTOPHER A 35 SMI W
LAWSON COLUMBUS A 19 HAR B
LAWSON DAVID A 19 HAR B
LAWSON DAVID A 44 TAR W
LAWSON EDMOND A 19 BE1 B
LAWSON GILLESPIE A 19 HAR B
LAWSON ISAM A 28 8TH B
LAWSON MARTIN A 19 HAR B
LAWSON T G A 44 KNA W
LAWSON T T A 44 KNA W
LAWSON WM P A 44 KNA W
LAY ALFRED L A 40 DA1 W
LAY COURTSWORTH H A 40 DA1 W
LAY J A A 40 SAN W
LAY JESSE A 40 DA1 W
LAY JOHN A 40 DA1 W
LAY JOHN W A 40 DA1 W
LAY WILLIAM B A 40 DA1 W
LAY WILLIAM J A 40 DA1 W
LAY WM A 40 SAN W
LAYTON CHARLES A 46 RAG W
LAYTON DANIEL A 46 COB W
LAYTON DAVID S A 46 COB W
LAYTON JAMES E A 46 GRE W
LAYTON JOHN A 46 COB W
LEACH ALEXANDER A 29 SEV W
LEACH ALEXANDER A 32 DAV B
LEACH EMSLEY A 32 DAV B
LEACH FERNEY A 28 01A B
LEACH GEORGE A 32 THO B
LEACH HORACE A 99 BUS B
LEACH J T A 99 BUS W
LEACH JACK A 32 BRO B
LEACH PARKER A 99 BUS B
LEACH RULAND A 37 ROC B
LEACHFIELD JACOB A 30 GIB W
LEADBETTER ERASTUS A 46 JAM W
LEADBETTER J F A 46 JAM W
LEADBETTER JNO R A 29 FA1 W
LEADFORD E E A 26 CAR W
LEADFORD GEORGE A 46 GRE W
LEADFORD J L A 26 CAR W
LEADFORD MARTIN A 26 CAR W
LEADWELL THOS A 46 JAM W
LEAF ISAAC A 28 04A B
LEAK D F A 32 THO W
LEAK KELLY A 32 THO B
LEANIER GRAY A 39 DAV B
LEARY A A 28 05A B
LEARY ASA J A 28 15T W
LEARY EPHRAIM A 24 EDE B
LEARY HARDY A 28 17T W
LEARY HARRY A 24 EDE B
CHALLENGED BY J R B HATHAWAY
REASON TOO YOUNG
NO EVIDENCE AGAINST HIM
LEARY HARSTON A 19 BE1 B
LEARY JERRY A 24 EDE B
LEARY JNO S A 29 FA1 B
LEARY JOHN S A 24 EDE W
LEARY JOHN S JR A 24 EDE W
LEARY JOSEPH A 28 17T W
LEARY M N JR A 29 FA1 B
LEARY M N SR A 29 FA1 B
LEARY MARTIN A 28 05A B
LEARY NELSON A 28 05A B
LEARY QUINTON T A 24 MID W
CERT TO PERQUIMANS CO
LEARY ROBT A 24 EDE B
LEARY SIMON A 28 04A B
LEARY SPENSER A 24 EDE B
LEARY STEPHEN S A 24 EDE W
LEARY SYLVESTER A 28 04A B
LEARY THOMAS A 24 EDE B
LEARY THOMAS J A 19 HAR W
LEARY THOMPSON A 24 EDE B
LEARY WASHINGTON A 24 EDE B
LEARY WEST R A 24 MID W
LEARY WEST THE ELDERR 24 MID W
REJ BY BOARD FOR THE REA
SON HE HELD THE OFFICE OF
MAGISTRATE BEFORE THE WAR
ALSO CONSTABLE & DURING
THE WAR HE PERSUADED
PEOPLE TO GO INTO THE
CONFEDERATE SERVICE
DEALT IN CONFEDERATE
BONDS & DID NOT TAKE OATH
LEARY WILSON A 28 10T B
LEARY WM A 24 EDE B
LEARY WM H A 24 EDE W
LEARY WM H A 24 MID W
LEASON JACOB A 24 EDE B
LEATH JOHN A 53 BUR B
LEATH MATTHEW A 53 GER B
LEATH STEPHEN A 19 BE1 B
LEATHERMAN WM A 32 DAV W
LEATHERWOOD REUBEN A 25 TUS W
LEATHERWOOD WILLIAM A 25 TUS W
LEAVISTER BRISON A 44 FOR B
LEAVISTER G D A 44 BRA W
LEAVISTER G T A 44 BRA W
LEAVISTER JOS A 44 FOR B
LEAVISTER WM A 44 FOR B
LEDBETTER C E A 46 FRI W
LEDBETTER HENRY A 26 HOL B
LEDBETTER HENRY A 46 JAM W
LEDBETTER THOS W A 46 SUM W
LEDBETTER Z J A 46 JAM W
LEDFORD A C A 25 HAY W
LEDFORD A J A 25 HAY W
LEDFORD A R A 25 SHO W
LEDFORD AMOS A 25 SHO W
LEDFORD CENTER A 25 SHO W
LEDFORD CURTIS A 25 SHO W
LEDFORD D A A 25 HAY W
LEDFORD D J A 25 SHO W
LEDFORD E C A 25 HAY W
LEDFORD E MC CHAL R 25 SHO W
FOR HOLDING THE OFFICE OF
CONSTABLE BEFORE THE RE-
BELLION AND BEING FOARCED
INTO THE WAR UNDER THE
CONSCRIPT LAW
LEDFORD E W A 25 SHO W
LEDFORD F A 26 BLA W
LEDFORD F A 26 PEE W
LEDFORD H C A 25 HAY W
LEDFORD HENLY A 25 SHO W
LEDFORD ISAIAH A 25 SHO W
LEDFORD J A A 25 SHO W
LEDFORD J B A 25 HAY W
LEDFORD J H A 25 SHO W
LEDFORD J K A 25 SHO W
LEDFORD J M A 25 SHO W
LEDFORD J M A 25 TUS W
LEDFORD J R A 26 GRI W
LEDFORD JASON D A 25 SHO W
LEDFORD JOEL A 26 WAR W
LEDFORD JOHN A 25 SHO W
LEDFORD JOHN A 26 PEE W
LEDFORD L M A 26 GRI W
LEDFORD L S A 25 SHO W
LEDFORD M D A 25 SHO W
LEDFORD PRESTON L A 32 POS W
LEDFORD ROBERT A 25 HAY W
LEDFORD ROBERT A 26 BLA W
LEDFORD S B A 25 SHO W
LEDFORD S H A 25 HAY W
LEDFORD S H JR A 25 HAY W
LEDFORD S J A 25 SHO W
LEDFORD S M A 25 SHO W
LEDFORD SAMUEL A 25 SHO W
LEDFORD THOMAS A 25 TUS W
LEDFORD THOMAS S A 25 HAY W
LEDFORD W C A 25 SHO W
LEDFORD W R A 25 SHO W
LEDFORD WILBURN A 25 SHO W
LEDFORD WILLIAM A 25 HAY W
LEDFORD WILLIAM A 26 PEE W
LEDWELL JAMES A 46 JAM W
LEE A J A 46 KIN W
LEE ABNER A 28 16T W
LEE ABRAHAM A 28 14T W

LEE ABRAM	A	35	ROC	W
LEE ALISON	A	39	DAV	W
LEE ANTHONY	A	46	MON	B
LEE ASA	A	28	16T	W
LEE B L	A	46	SUM	W
LEE BENJAMIN	A	28	13T	W
LEE BURTON	A	46	HIG	B
LEE D W	A	30	IND	W
LEE DANIEL	A	28	13T	W
LEE DAVID J	A	30	TUL	W
LEE DENNIS	A	28	8TH	B
CERTIF GIVEN NOW				
LIVES AT JAMES CITY				
LEE DUN	A	37	PIN	B
LEE EDWARD	A	37	HIC	B
LEE ELIAS	A	28	13T	W
LEE ELIAS	A	30	TUL	W
LEE FRANCIS M	A	37	PIN	W
LEE GEORGE	A	26	BLA	W
LEE H D	A	26	SHE	W
LEE HENRY	A	29	FA2	W
LEE HENRY W	A	46	SUM	W
LEE ISAAC	A	26	MOO	B
LEE ISAAC	A	37	PIN	B
LEE J B	A	26	HOL	B
LEE J C	A	29	FLE	B
LEE J H	A	26	HOL	B
LEE J M JR	A	46	SUM	W
LEE J W	A	30	TUL	W
LEE JACK	A	28	04A	B
LEE JAMES E	A	30	TUL	W
LEE JAMES M	R	46	SUM	W
CAUSE MILITIA				
OFFICER BEFORE REBELLION				
REJ BY HIS REQUEST				
LEE JAS M	A	29	FA1	W
LEE JAS R	A	29	FA1	W
LEE JEROME B	A	30	TUL	W
LEE JIM	A	39	DAV	B
LEE JOHN	A	24	EDE	B
LEE JOHN	A	26	BOR	W
LEE JOHN A	A	53	LA1	W
LEE JOHN J	A	30	IND	W
LEE JOHN L	A	28	16T	W
LEE JOHN L	A	32	THO	W
LEE JOSEPH	A	28	14T	W
LEE JOURDAN	A	37	PIN	B
LEE LEVI	A	37	PIN	W
LEE LUNDY	A	35	GLI	W
LEE MADISON	A	30	TUL	W
LEE NEEDHAM	A	29	LOC	B
LEE PHILIP J	A	28	05A	B
LEE RALEIGH	A	37	EDW	B
LEE RANSOM	A	29	BLA	W
LEE RICHARD	A	28	14T	W
LEE RILEY	A	28	16T	W
LEE ROBERT	A	28	14T	W
LEE SAMEUL	A	35	MAG	B
LEE SAMUEL	A	28	03A	B
LEE SHADRICK	A	28	14T	W
LEE W C	A	26	SHE	W
LEE W E W	A	46	KIN	W
LEE W W	A	26	HOL	B
LEE WASHN	A	28	03A	B
LEE WESTERN	A	28	6TH	B
LEE WILEY	A	28	05A	B
LEE WILLIAM	A	30	CUR	B
LEE WILLIAM C	A	26	HOL	B
LEE WILLIAM S	A	46	KIN	W
LEE WILSON	A	30	POP	W
LEE WM	A	28	16T	W
LEE WM	A	29	FA1	B
LEE Y G	A	26	HOL	B
LEE ZOREL	A	28	13T	W
LEECRAFT DAVID	A	19	BE1	B
LEECRAFT N F	A	19	BE2	W
LEEMIER HANS	A	28	9TH	B
LEEMIER NOAH	A	28	9TH	B
LEEPER ANDREW	A	40	STO	W
LEEPER ANDREWS A	A	40	STO	W
LEEPER BONY	A	40	STO	B
LEEPER F W	A	40	STO	W
LEEPER GREEN W	A	40	STO	B
LEEPER JACOB	A	40	SAN	B
LEEPER JAMES	A	40	STO	W
LEEPER ROBT B	A	40	STO	B
LEEPER STANHOPE	A	40	STO	B
LEES GREEN	A	53	SWA	B
LEFFERS GEORGE	A	19	STR	W
LEFFERS ISAIAH	A	19	STR	W
LEFFERS RICHARD	A	19	STR	W
LEFFERS SAMUEL	A	19	STR	W
LEFFINGHOUSE AJAX	A	28	9TH	B
LEGGET DAVID A	A	37	ROB	W
LEGGET GEORGE	A	28	16T	B
LEGGET HENRY	A	37	HOL	W
LEGGETT J G	A	29	GRA	W
LEGGETT MARK	A	37	ROB	W
LEGGETT WILLIAM	A	24	EDE	W
LEGGETT WILLIAM H	A	37	ROB	W
LEGGINS JOHN	A	28	05A	B
LEGO WM F	A	28	8TH	W
LEHMAN R F	A	28	01A	W
LEICESTER GEORGE	A	24	UPP	W
LEIGH JOHN	A	37	HIG	W
LEIGH JOHN H	A	37	HIG	W
LEITD JAMES C	A	37	PIN	W
LEITH FRANK	A	28	15T	B
LEMAY ANTHONEY	A	44	RAG	B
LEMAY RATLER	A	44	RAG	B
LEMBOCH R G	A	32	SHE	W
LEMMONS L C	A	26	MOU	W
LEMMONS WILLIAM	A	26	BUR	W
LEMONS G W	A	46	MON	W
LENANCE BRANTLEY	A	46	COB	W
LENAND RILEY	A	32	DAV	W
LENARD A	A	32	TYR	W
LENARD ALEXANDER	A	32	DAV	B
LENARD ALFORD	A	32	DAV	W
LENARD ANDERSON	A	32	DAV	B
LENARD B	A	32	LOF	W
LENARD DANIEL	A	32	POS	W
LENARD DANIEL HON	A	32	DAV	W
LENARD DAVID	A	32	DAV	W
LENARD DAVID	A	32	DAV	W
LENARD DAVID	A	32	DAV	W
LENARD DAVID	A	32	DAV	W
LENARD ELICK	A	32	DAV	B
LENARD F W	A	32	DAV	W
LENARD G W	A	32	THO	W
LENARD GEORGE	A	32	DAV	W
LENARD HENRY	A	32	DAV	B
LENARD HENRY	A	32	DAV	W
LENARD HENRY N	A	32	DAV	W
LENARD JACOB	A	32	DAV	W
LENARD JACOB	A	32	DAV	W
LENARD JESSE	A	32	DAV	W
LENARD JOHN	A	32	DAV	W
LENARD JOHN A	A	32	DAV	W
LENARD JOSEPH	A	32	COT	W
LENARD JOSEPH A	A	32	DAV	W
LENARD MATHIAS	A	32	DAV	W
LENARD MICHAEL	A	32	DAV	W
LENARD PARKER	A	39	JOR	W
LENARD SAMUEL	A	32	DAV	W
LENARD SOLOMON	A	32	DAV	W
LENARD VOLANTINE	A	32	DAV	W
LENARD VOLANTINE	A	32	TYR	W
LENARD WILLIAM C B	A	32	DAV	W
LENARD WILLIAM M	A	39	JOR	W
LENARD WM	A	39	HAR	B
LEND HENRY G	A	30	POP	W
LENDEKE WILHELM	A	28	05A	W
LENEAR ELBERT	A	46	JAM	B
LENING ROBERT	A	32	DAV	W
LENIUS SAMUEL	A	46	COB	W
LENORD SOLOMON	A	32	THO	B
LENYEAR MCLANE	A	53	SWA	B
LEONARD A C	A	39	JOR	W
LEONARD A L	A	39	JOR	W
LEONARD ABRAHAM	A	39	JOR	B
LEONARD ALEX.	A	32	DAV	W
LEONARD ALEX. SR	A	32	DAV	W
LEONARD ALFORD	A	32	SHE	W
LEONARD ALFRED	A	29	FA1	B
LEONARD ALFRED	A	46	ROS	W
LEONARD B H	A	39	JOR	W
LEONARD BERRY	A	39	JOR	B
LEONARD CASPER	A	32	DAV	W
LEONARD CHARLES	A	46	SUM	W
GIVEN A CERT TO				
FRIENDSHIP PRECINCT				
LEONARD CHARLES S	A	46	ROS	W
LEONARD D S	A	39	JOR	W
LEONARD DANIEL	A	32	SHE	W
LEONARD DAVID	A	32	DAV	W
LEONARD DAVID	A	46	JAM	W
LEONARD DAVID D	A	32	DAV	W
LEONARD DAVID S	A	32	DAV	W
LEONARD EATON	A	39	JOR	W
LEONARD ELI	A	46	HIG	W
LEONARD FRANK	A	39	JOR	B
LEONARD GILFORD	A	39	JOR	B
LEONARD GREEN	A	32	POS	W
LEONARD HENDERSON	A	32	DAV	W
LEONARD HENRY E	A	32	POS	W
LEONARD J B	A	46	HIG	W
LEONARD J F	A	32	DAV	W
LEONARD J F	A	39	SPE	W
LEONARD JAMES	A	39	JOR	W
LEONARD JAMES	A	39	LOU	B
LEONARD JAMES	A	46	JAM	W
LEONARD JAMES H	A	46	GRE	W
LEONARD JNO G	A	39	SPE	W
LEONARD JOAB	A	46	GRE	W
LEONARD JOAB	A	46	JAM	W
LEONARD JOB W	A	46	ROS	W
LEONARD JOHN	A	37	ROC	W
LEONARD JONATHAN	A	46	GRE	W
LEONARD JONATHAN	A	46	ROS	W
HERE 5 MO				
LEONARD JONATHAN	R	46	GRE	W
NAME LINED OUT				
HERE 5 MOS				
LEONARD JOSEPH	A	37	ROC	W
LEONARD JOSEPH	A	46	GRE	W
LEONARD JOSEPH Z	A	32	POS	W
LEONARD LARKER	A	39	JOR	W
LEONARD PHILIP W	A	32	POS	W
LEONARD R F	A	39	JOR	W
LEONARD ROBERT	A	46	GRE	W
LEONARD THOMAS	A	39	JOR	B
LEONARD W L	A	46	JAM	W
LEONARD WILLIAM	A	32	SHE	W
LEONARD WM H	A	39	JOR	W
LEONARD-DAVID	A	39	JOR	B
UNDER-21-YEARS				
HIS FORMER SAYS				
HE IS 21 YEARS OLD				

Name	Status	Age	Area	Race
LEONHOUSER J HENRY	A	30	ROA	W
LEOPOLD PHILLIP	A	37	SHA	W
LEPPER P	A	19	MOR	W
LESESNE CHS	A	29	CED	W
LESTER ANDREW W	A	39	SPE	W
LESTER WILLIAM H	A	72	SWA	W
LETHCO HENRY	A	32	TYR	W
LETHERWOOD A N	A	25	HAY	W
LETHERWOOD R N	A	25	HAY	W
LETHERWOOD SAMUEL	A	25	HAY	W
LETHERWOOD SAMUEL	A	25	HAY	W
LETT J W	A	29	FA1	W
LEUS JOSEPH	A	40	RHY	B
LEVENS WM D	A	46	MCL	W
LEVESTER FENNER	A	39	FRA	B
LEVESTER HENRY	A	39	FRA	B
LEVI ISHAM	A	44	SAS	B
LEVICK WM	A	29	FA1	W
LEVIN JAMES	A	46	ROS	W
LEVIN RICHARD	A	46	MCL	W
LEVIS MOSES	A	29	FA1	W
LEVISTER G W	A	39	LOU	W
LEVISTER J J	A	39	HAY	W
LEVISTER JAMES	A	39	FRE	W
LEVISTER JORDAN	A	38	FRE	B
LEVISTER RICHARD	A	38	FRE	W
LEVY L W	A	29	FA1	B
LEVY LEWIS W	A	29	ROC	B
LEVY ROBT	A	29	FA1	B
LEWEY WM R	A	46	GIB	W
LEWIE JOHN	A	46	GIB	W
LEWIE ROSWELL	A	32	DAV	W
LEWING MEDDLINTON	A	40	RHY	W
LEWIS AARON	A	28	05A	B
LEWIS ABNER	A	44	SAS	B
LEWIS ABRAHAM	A	19	SHA	W
LEWIS ALFRED	A	26	BLA	W
LEWIS ALLEN	A	37	PIN	B
LEWIS ALLIE	A	37	PEN	B
LEWIS AMOS	A	28	03A	B
LEWIS ANDREW	A	44	OXF	B
LEWIS ANSON	A	19	BE1	W
LEWIS ARNOLD	A	39	DAV	W
LEWIS ARTHER	A	37	ROC	B
LEWIS B M	A	46	SUM	W
LEWIS BRYAN W	A	28	14T	W
LEWIS C A	A	46	MON	W
LEWIS C P	A	26	GRI	W
LEWIS CAESAR	A	28	04A	B
LEWIS CASHWIN	A	29	FLE	W
LEWIS CASWELL	A	46	MON	B
LEWIS CESAR	A	28	14T	B
LEWIS CHARLES	A	28	9TH	B
LEWIS CHARLES	A	44	HEN	B
LEWIS CHARLES	A	44	OXF	B
LEWIS CHARLES	R	19	MOR	B
CONVICTED OF FELONY BY A COURT OF COMPETENT JURISDICTION				
LEWIS CHLS K	A	44	SAS	W
LEWIS CHRISTOPHER	A	28	16T	B
LEWIS DANIEL	A	37	ROB	B
LEWIS DANIEL	A	39	LOU	B
LEWIS DAVID	A	19	HUN	W
LEWIS DAVID	A	24	EDE	B
LEWIS DAVID H	A	19	STR	W
LEWIS DERASTUS	A	46	GRE	W
LEWIS DICK	A	44	HEN	B
LEWIS DRED	A	37	TA1	B
LEWIS E F M	A	26	GRI	W
LEWIS EDWARD	A	28	01B	W
LEWIS EDWARD	A	44	HEN	B
LEWIS ELIJAH	A	19	MOR	W
LEWIS ELIJAH	A	28	16T	W
LEWIS ELIJAH H	A	19	BE1	W
LEWIS FRANK	A	28	05A	B
LEWIS FRANK	A	37	ROB	B
LEWIS FRANK	A	44	OXF	B
LEWIS FREEMAN	A	19	HUN	W
LEWIS FULFORD B	A	19	BE1	W
LEWIS GARRISON	A	19	HUN	W
LEWIS GARRISON	A	19	STR	W
LEWIS GEO	A	44	ISL	B
LEWIS GEO P	A	28	6TH	W
LEWIS GEORGE	A	24	UPP	B
LEWIS GEORGE	A	44	TOW	B
LEWIS GEORGE A	A	19	SMY	W
LEWIS GEORGE M	A	28	16T	W
LEWIS GEORGE R	A	28	14T	W
LEWIS GLOSTER	A	44	SAS	B
LEWIS GRANDISON	A	44	OXF	B
LEWIS GRANVILLE	A	44	TOW	B
LEWIS GREEN	A	44	HEN	B
LEWIS GRIM	A	44	TOW	B
LEWIS H	A	28	05A	B
LEWIS HANDY	A	37	PEN	B
LEWIS HARRY	A	37	HOL	B
LEWIS HAYWOOD	A	28	16T	W
LEWIS HENRY	A	39	FRE	B
LEWIS HENRY	A	44	OXF	B
LEWIS HENRY CHAL	R	44	SAS	B
NAME LINED OUT				
LARCENY GUILTY REJ				
LEWIS HENRY L	A	46	JAM	W
LEWIS HILLARD	A	37	ROC	B
LEWIS HOPSON	A	37	ROC	B
LEWIS IRA	A	46	GRE	W
LEWIS ISAAC	A	28	01A	W
LEWIS ISAAC	A	37	EDW	B
LEWIS ISAAC	A	37	WHI	B
LEWIS ISAAC W	A	19	BE2	W
LEWIS ISAAC W	A	19	STR	W
LEWIS J J	A	40	SAN	W
LEWIS J M	A	19	HAD	W
LEWIS J W	A	32	THO	W
LEWIS JACINTH	A	37	MAN	B
LEWIS JACK	A	44	OXF	B
LEWIS JACKSON	A	44	TOW	B
LEWIS JACOB	A	28	10T	B
LEWIS JACOB	A	37	ROB	B
LEWIS JACOB	A	39	LOU	B
LEWIS JACOB JR	A	37	ROB	B
LEWIS JAMES	A	19	HUN	W
LEWIS JAMES	A	19	MOR	W
LEWIS JAMES	A	19	SHA	W
LEWIS JAMES	A	28	04A	B
LEWIS JAMES	A	37	WEB	W
LEWIS JAMES	A	40	STO	B
LEWIS JAMES	A	40	STO	W
LEWIS JAMES	A	44	TOW	B
LEWIS JAMES	A	44	KIT	B
LEWIS JAMES R	A	19	BE1	W
LEWIS JAMES R	A	19	SHA	W
LEWIS JAMES T	A	28	01B	W
LEWIS JAMES W	A	37	EDW	W
LEWIS JAS	A	44	TOW	B
LEWIS JIM	A	39	LOU	B
LEWIS JNO J	A	37	WHI	W
LEWIS JOHN	A	19	BE1	B
LEWIS JOHN	A	26	GRI	W
LEWIS JOHN	A	28	04A	B
LEWIS JOHN	A	28	05A	B
LEWIS JOHN	A	28	16T	W
LEWIS JOHN	A	37	ROB	B
LEWIS JOHN	A	37	SPA	B
LEWIS JOHN	A	44	HEN	B
LEWIS JOHN	A	44	OXF	B
LEWIS JOHN D	A	53	SWA	W
LEWIS JOHN L	A	19	HUN	W
LEWIS JOHN M	A	19	SMY	W
LEWIS JOHN S	A	19	HUN	W
LEWIS JOHN W	A	19	SHA	W
LEWIS JOHN W	A	19	SMY	W
LEWIS JOHNSTON	A	37	ROC	B
LEWIS JOSEPH B	A	37	ROB	B
LEWIS JOSEPHUS	A	19	HUN	W
LEWIS JOSHUA	A	37	ROB	B
LEWIS JOSIAH	A	44	FOR	B
LEWIS JUBA	A	44	SAS	B
LEWIS JULIUS	A	28	02N	W
LEWIS KINCHIN O	A	37	WEB	W
LEWIS KING	A	44	TOW	B
LEWIS KIT	A	44	SAS	B
LEWIS LEVI	A	46	GRE	W
LEWIS LEWIS	A	39	LOU	B
LEWIS LINSEY	A	32	DAV	W
LEWIS M M	A	25	HAY	W
LEWIS MAGOR	A	44	OXF	B
LEWIS MARCUS A	A	53	GER	W
LEWIS MARTIN	A	19	MOR	W
LEWIS MATTHEW L	A	28	03A	B
LEWIS MONGOMERY	A	44	SAS	B
LEWIS MORRIS	A	19	HUN	W
LEWIS MOSSES	A	44	OXF	B
LEWIS NEMIAH	A	19	SHA	W
LEWIS NORFLETE	A	28	05A	B
LEWIS OLIVER	A	44	ISL	B
LEWIS ORANGE	A	44	TOW	B
LEWIS OTTAWAY	A	44	OXF	B
LEWIS PETER	A	26	GRI	W
LEWIS PINK	A	40	DA1	B
LEWIS QUINNEY	A	35	FAI	B
LEWIS RALEY	A	19	BE1	W
LEWIS RATIS	A	44	SAS	B
LEWIS REDDICK	A	38	FRE	B
LEWIS REDIN J	A	37	WEB	W
LEWIS REDIN S	A	37	WHI	W
LEWIS RICHARD	A	37	PEN	B
LEWIS RICHARD	A	44	OXF	B
LEWIS ROBERT	A	28	16T	W
LEWIS ROBERT	A	44	SAS	B
LEWIS SAM	A	44	TOW	B
LEWIS SAML	A	28	03A	B
LEWIS SAML	A	44	BRA	B
LEWIS SIMBER	A	28	02N	B
LEWIS STEPHEN	A	44	OXF	B
LEWIS T EDWARD	A	37	TA2	W
LEWIS T S	A	26	GRI	B
LEWIS THOMAS	A	37	ROB	B
LEWIS THOMAS	A	37	WEB	W
LEWIS THOMAS	A	46	GRE	W
LEWIS THOMAS C	A	19	BE2	W
LEWIS THOS	A	28	05A	B
LEWIS THOS	A	44	TOW	B
LEWIS THOS C	A	19	SHA	W
LEWIS VALENTINE	A	19	HUN	W
LEWIS W GASTON	A	37	PIN	W
LEWIS WALLACE	A	19	BE1	W
LEWIS WALLACE W	A	19	BE2	W
LEWIS WESLEY	A	44	TOW	B
LEWIS WILLIAM	A	37	HIG	W
LEWIS WILLIAM	A	44	SAS	B
LEWIS WILLIAM H	A	37	PEN	W
LEWIS WILLIAM M	A	37	PEN	W
LEWIS WILLIS	A	37	ROB	B
LEWIS WILLIS M	A	28	03A	B
LEWIS WM	A	28	03A	B
LEWIS WM	A	29	FA1	W
LEWIS WM	A	44	TOW	B

LEWIS WM A A 46 MCL W
CERT TO ROCKING CTY
LEWIS WM B A 32 THO W
WITHDRAWN AT HIS OWN
REQUEST APRIL 8, 1868
LEWIS WM C A 19 BE1 W
LEWIS WM H A 28 04A B
LEWIS WM H A 28 15T W
LEWIS WM H A 28 16T W
LEWIS ZORABALED A 19 HUN W
LICKFIELD GOERGE A A 53 LA1 W
LIDMAN JOHN A 37 PIN B
LIEBERGER WILLIAM C A 40 DA2 W
LIGHTFOOT ALEX A 29 FA1 B
LIGON CHARLES A 44 SAS W
LIGON H C A 28 7TH W
PATROLER
CERTIF GIVEN LIVES NOW
IN FORESTVILLE NC
LILES JAMES A 46 GRE W
LILES WM A 46 GRE W
LILEY MCROLAND A 19 MOR B
LILLEY E J A 29 FA1 W
LILLEY GEORGE L A 37 EDW W
LILLEY HENRY D A 37 EDW W
LILLY ANDREW A 29 GRA B
LILLY HENRY A 29 FA1 W
LILLY MOSES A 35 WAR W
LIMMAN MATTHEW A 28 03A B
LINANS MARTIN V A 46 GRE W
LINBARGER ANDREW N A 40 SAN B
LINBARGER ANTHONY A 40 SAN B
LINBARGER BERY A 40 SAN B
LINBARGER J W A 26 SHE W
LINBERGER MOSES A 40 CAN B
LINBERRY BEVLY A 46 ROS W
LINCOLN BARNEY A 28 17T W
LINCOLN BRIGHTMAN A 28 17T W
LINCOLN GEORGE A 28 12T B
LINCOLN HEPNEY A 19 MOR B
LINCOLN JOHN C A 28 16T W
LINCOLN RICHARD A 28 17T W
LIND ADAM A 26 BOR W
LIND SAM M A 26 BOR W
LIND T H A 26 BOR W
LINDER JESSE H A 37 HIG W
LINDER LEWIS A A 37 HIG W
LINDLEY JOHN V A 46 FRI W
LINDLY JOSHUA A 46 FRI W
LINDSAY A B A 29 SEV W
LINDSAY ABRAM A 32 POS B
LINDSAY ALBERT A 32 POS B
LINDSAY ALFORD A 32 POS B
LINDSAY ALFRED A 46 SUM B
LINDSAY ANDREW A 32 POS W
LINDSAY ANDREW D A 46 GRE W
LINDSAY ARCHD A 29 SEV W
LINDSAY AUGUSTIN A 46 SUM B
LINDSAY BILLY A 46 GRE B
LINDSAY BROCK A 32 THO B
LINDSAY CARY A 46 SUM B
LINDSAY CEZAR A 46 GRE B
LINDSAY DAVID A 32 POS B
LINDSAY E D A 46 HIG W
LINDSAY ELI A 46 FRI B
LINDSAY ELIJAH A 46 SUM B
LINDSAY ENOCH A 46 GIB B
LINDSAY ERNIST A 46 GRE W
LINDSAY FRANKLIN A 46 HIG B
LINDSAY GREEN A 46 SUM B
LINDSAY HENRY A 46 GRE B
LINDSAY HENRY A 46 MCL B
LINDSAY HIRAM A 46 GRE B
LINDSAY HUGH A 32 BRO W
LINDSAY J A A 32 POS W
LINDSAY J F A 46 HIG B
LINDSAY J H A 26 CAR W
LINDSAY JACOB A 32 THO B
LINDSAY JESSE A 46 GRE B
LINDSAY JIM A 32 POS B
LINDSAY JOHN A 29 SEV W
LINDSAY JOHN A A 46 GRE W
CERT TO HIGH POINT
LINDSAY JOSHUA A 46 FRI B
LINDSAY LEWIS A 46 SUM B
LINDSAY NEILL A 29 SEV W
LINDSAY NORMAN A 32 THO B
LINDSAY PETER A 32 POS B
LINDSAY PETER A 46 FRI B
LINDSAY PINKNEY A 46 GRE B
LINDSAY R W A 32 POS W
LINDSAY ROBERT G A 46 GRE W
LINDSAY ROBT A 46 GRE B
LINDSAY SOLOMON A 32 POS B
LINDSAY SPENCER A 46 JAM B
LINDSAY THOMAS S A 46 GRE W
LINDSAY THOS W A 19 BE1 W
LINDSAY WESLEY A 46 GRE B
LINDSAY WESLEY A 46 HIG B
LINDSAY WHIT A 32 POS B
LINDSAY WILLIAM A 26 PEE W
LINDSAY WILLIAM A 46 JAM B
LINDSAY WM A 46 GRE B
LINDSAY WM A A 32 THO W
CERTIFICATE
LINDSAYE
G HARPER JR A 46 GRE W
LINDSAYE JESSE A 46 RAG B
LINDSAYE OLIVER A 46 GRE B
LINDSAYE ROBERT J A 46 GRE W
CERT TO HIGH POINT
LINDSEY D MCD CHAL A 30 CUR W
LINDSEY DANIEL B A 30 COI W
LINDSEY DANIEL C A 30 NAR W
LINDSEY DAVID A 30 COI W
LINDSEY DAVID A 30 ROA B
LINDSEY DUNCAN A 29 ROC W
LINDSEY EDWARDS A 19 HAR B
LINDSEY EVERETT A 28 03A B
LINDSEY H M A 29 FA1 W
LINDSEY HANNIBAL A 30 CUR B
IS A MINOR
LINDSEY JOHN A 28 10T B
LINDSEY JOHN H A 28 10T B
LINDSEY SAM A 26 GRI W
LINDSEY WILLIAM A 30 IND W
LINDSEY WILLIS A 30 COI B
LINDSEY WM A 28 14T W
LINDSLEY MILES A 37 TA1 B
LINEBARGER JACOB A 40 SAN W
LINEBARGER L M A 40 STO W
LINEBERGER BATTY A 40 DA1 B
LINEBERGER CALEB A 40 DA1 W
(L'S SON)
LINEBERGER CALEB J A 40 DA1 W
LINEBERGER CEPHAS A 40 DA1 B
LINEBERGER DAVID A 40 DA1 B
LINEBERGER DAVID A A 40 DA1 W
LINEBERGER ISAAC A 40 DA1 B
LINEBERGER J LABAN A 40 DA1 W
LINEBERGER
J MELANCTHON A 40 DA1 W
LINEBERGER JAMES A 40 DA1 B
LINEBERGER JOHN D A 40 DA2 W
LINEBERGER JOHN F A 40 DA1 W
LINEBERGER JONAS R A 40 DA1 W
LINEBERGER JONAS R R 40 DA1 W
NAME LINED OUT
MILITIA OFFICER BEFORE
THE REBELLION AND GAVE
AID AND COMFORT TO THE
ENEMY REJECTED
LINEBERGER L JONAS A 40 DA1 W
(L'S SON)
LINEBERGER LEWIS A 40 DA1 W
(L'S SON)
LINEBERGER LEWIS M A 40 DA1 W
LINEBERGER MARCUS A A 40 DA2 B
LINEBERGER MONROE M A 40 MAU W
LINEBERGER PINCKNEY A 40 DA1 W
LINEBERGER PINK A 40 DA1 B
LINEBERGER S JONAS A 40 DA1 W
(M'S SON)
LINEBERGER WILLIAM CA 40 DA1 W
LINEBERGER WILLIAM DA 40 DA1 W
LINEBERGER WILLIAM SA 40 DA1 W
LINEBERRY DANL A 46 COB W
LINEBERRY ELWOOD A 46 GRE W
LINEBERRY ORLAND W A 46 GRE W
LINEBERRY WM A A 46 GRE W
LINEBERY A D A 32 DAV W
LINEBERY SAMUEL A 46 GRE W
LINEBURY AQUILLA A 46 COB W
LINES C M A 32 THO W
LINES ELIJAH A 44 HEN B
LINES GEORGE A 32 THO W
LINES JOSEPH A 44 SAS B
LINES R J A 32 THO W
LINES WILLIAM A 44 SAS B
LINGUISH GEORGE A 19 SMY W
LINK DAVIDSON A 32 SHE W
LINK JACOB A 32 SHE W
LINK JOSEPH A 32 SHE W
LINK WILLIAM A 32 SHE W
LINNEUS ISAAC A 46 COB W
LINSAY HERBERT A 44 ISL W
LINSDAY DANIEL A 46 FRI B
LINSDAY JAMES M A 32 POS W
LINSEY EDWARD A 44 BRA B
LINSEY HENRY A 37 SHA B
LINSLEY ALFRED A 28 05A B
LINSLEY JESSE A 28 16T B
LINSLEY JOHNSON A 28 14T B
LINTHICUM ZACHEUS A 46 HIG W
LINTON DAVID A 53 LA1 W
LINTON GEORGE A 35 MAG W
LINTON ISAAC A 30 IND W
LINTON JOHN G A 28 15T W
LINTON JOHN M A 30 IND W
LINTON JOHN W A 35 MAG W
LINTON KILRY A 53 LA1 W
LINTON MICHAEL A 28 17T W
LINTON PLEASANT A 35 MAG B
LINTON WELLS A 35 MAG W
LINTON WILLIAM A 30 IND W
LINTON ZACHEUS A 28 16T W
LINVILL W F A 46 KIN W
LINY DAVID A 32 TYR B
LIONS HARRY R 44 OXF B
RES 10 MON REJ
LIPSCOMB JOHN W A 37 TA2 W
LIPSCOMB SAMUEL A 37 TA2 B
LIPSCOMBE GEORGE B A 37 TA1 W
LISBON OLIVER K A 28 01A B
LISBON ROBT H A 28 01A B
LITCHFIELD EDMUND A 30 KNO W
LITCHFIELD EZEKIEL A 30 KNO W
LITCHFIELD JAMES A A 30 KNO W
LITCHFIELD JEREMIAH A 30 NAR W

LITCHFIELD JOHN	A	30	KNO	W
LITCHFIELD JOHN	A	30	KNO	W
LITCHFIELD SPENCER	DA	30	NAR	W
LITCHFUL THOS B	A	30	POP	W
LITTLE ALEXANDER	A	40	CAN	B
LITTLE BENJ	A	28	03A	B
LITTLE BRIGHT	A	28	11T	B
LITTLE CALEB	A	40	MAU	B
LITTLE DAVID	A	28	9TH	B
LITTLE DOC	A	28	05A	B
LITTLE FREDK	A	28	05A	B
LITTLE GEORGE A	A	37	PIN	W
LITTLE H R	A	46	FRI	W
LITTLE HAMBLETON	A	24	EDE	B
LITTLE HARRISON	A	24	EDE	B
LITTLE HENRY	A	37	ROB	B
LITTLE HENRY	A	46	GRE	W
LITTLE HENRY D	A	37	WHI	W
LITTLE HUGH	A	46	JAM	W
LITTLE J O R	A	46	FRI	W
LITTLE JAMES	A	28	05A	B
LITTLE JAMES E	A	37	PIN	W
LITTLE JESSE C	A	28	16T	W
LITTLE JESSIE	A	37	TA1	W
LITTLE JOHN	A	39	LOU	B
LITTLE JOHN A	A	37	TA2	W
LITTLE JOHN G	A	40	MAU	W
LITTLE JOHN O	A	53	SWA	B
LITTLE JOURDAN	A	24	EDE	B
LITTLE KINCHEN	A	37	PIN	B
LITTLE LEONIDAS	A	37	PIN	W
LITTLE MOSES	A	28	05A	B
LITTLE MOSES	A	28	05A	B
LITTLE PHILLIP	A	24	EDE	B
LITTLE ROBERT	A	46	JAM	W
LITTLE SANDY	A	37	PIN	B
LITTLE THOMAS	A	37	PIN	B
LITTLE WILLIAM	A	72	SWA	W
LITTLEJOHN ALLEN	A	44	OXF	B
LITTLEJOHN HANSE	A	24	EDE	B
LITTLEJOHN HARRY	A	39	SPE	B
LITTLEJOHN HENRY	A	39	LOU	B
LITTLEJOHN JOE	A	39	PUG	B
LITTLEJOHN JOHN	A	39	SPE	B
LITTLEJOHN KINCHEN	A	39	LOU	B
LITTLEJOHN LOUIS	A	39	GRI	B
LITTLEJOHN PETER	A	39	LOU	B
LITTLEJOHN PRIMAS	A	39	PUG	B
LITTLEJOHN RUFFIN	A	39	PUG	B
LITTLEJOHN SANDY	A	39	LOU	B
LITTLEJOHN SIDNEY	A	39	SPE	B
LITTLEJOHN THOMAS	A	39	LOU	B
LITTLETON GEORGE T	A	28	04A	B
LITTLETON THOMAS S	A	72	SWA	W
LITTON J W	A	40	CAN	W
LIVANGOOD DAVID	A	32	DAV	W
LIVENGOOD ANDREW	A	32	POS	W
LIVENGOOD JOHN	A	32	POS	W
LIVENGOOD LEWIS	A	32	POS	W
LIVENGOOD PETER	A	32	POS	W
LIVENGOOD S L	A	32	POS	W
LIVENGOOD WILLIAM	A	32	DAV	W
LIVERMAN BENJAMIN F	A	28	16T	W
LIVERMAN WILLIAM	A	53	FAI	W
LIVINGSTON GEORGE H	A	46	GRE	W
LLOY STUART	A	37	SPA	B
LLOYD AARON	A	37	TA1	B
LLOYD BARTLETT Y	A	46	GRE	W
LLOYD BOB	A	37	TA2	B
LLOYD DAVID	A	46	FRI	W
LLOYD EDWARD	A	37	TA1	B
LLOYD GEORGE	A	37	TA1	B
LLOYD GILBERT	A	37	TA1	B
LLOYD HARDY 2ND	A	37	TA1	B
LLOYD HARDY 1ST	A	37	TA1	B
LLOYD ISAM	A	28	03A	B
LLOYD J S	A	46	SUM	W
LLOYD JACKSON	A	37	PEN	B
LLOYD JAMES	A	37	PIN	B
LLOYD JAMES	A	37	SPA	B
LLOYD JEREMIAH	A	37	TA1	B
LLOYD JESSE	A	46	SUM	W
LLOYD JESSIE	R	37	PIN	B
CONVICTED OF LARCENY				
LLOYD JOHN	A	37	ROC	W
LLOYD JOSEPH	A	46	FRI	W
LLOYD JOSEPH W	A	37	TA1	W
LLOYD MACK	A	37	TA1	B
LLOYD MILTON	A	46	SUM	W
LLOYD NOAH	A	37	TA1	B
LLOYD ROBERT	A	37	TA1	B
LLOYD ROBERT	A	37	TA1	B
LLOYD THOMAS	A	39	DAV	W
LLOYD THOMAS	A	46	FRI	W
LLOYD THOMAS C	A	72	SWA	W
LLOYD WHITMOND P	A	37	PIN	W
LLOYD WILLIAM	A	37	TA1	B
LLOYD WILLIAM	A	46	FRI	W
LLOYD WM H	A	46	FRI	W
LLOYD ZEALOUS	A	37	TA1	B
LLOYD-GASTON	R	37	TA1	B
NAME LINED OUT				
LOCETT WILLIAM	A	37	ROB	B
LOCK J H	A	29	LOC	B
LOCK JNO II	A	29	LOC	B
LOCK MINGAL		29	LOC	B
LOCKAMY JOSEPH	A	29	ROC	W
LOCKEMY DANIEL J	A	29	SEV	W
LOCKEMY HENDERSON	A	29	FA1	W
CHAL BY W H PORTER				
LOCKER SAMPSON	A	53	SWA	B
LOCKERT W M	A	40	SAN	W
LOCKLAYER HENRY	A	46	GRE	B
LOCKLEAR MAJOR	A	46	SUM	B
LOCUST OFFEY	A	39	GRI	B
LOCUST SIMON	A	39	HAR	B
LOCUST THOS	A	39	GRI	B
LOCUST WESLEY	A	39	GRI	B
LODGE CHARLES	A	28	04B	B
LOFLEN STEMSON (?)	A	32	JAC	W
LOFLIN ALEXANDER A	A	32	LOF	W
LOFLIN B T	A	32	JAC	W
LOFLIN CLARKSON	A	32	JAC	W
LOFLIN H L	A	32	POS	W
LOFLIN ISAAC	A	32	JAC	W
LOFLIN JOHN	A	32	JAC	W
LOFLIN JOHN	A	32	JAC	W
LOFLIN M	A	32	JAC	B
LOFLIN T C	A	32	LOF	W
LOFLIN WILEY J	A	32	LOF	W
LOFLIN WILLIAM	A	32	LOF	W
LOFTEN JON	A	32	JAC	W
LOFTEN WILLIAM	A	32	JAC	W
LOFTIN BRYANT	A	28	05A	B
LOFTIN BUCK	A	32	JAC	B
LOFTIN CHARLES	A	35	WOL	W
LOFTIN D	A	32	THO	W
LOFTIN GEORGE	A	28	8TH	B
LOFTIN ISAAC	A	44	YXS	B
LOFTIN J C	A	32	JAC	W
LOFTIN JAMES	A	28	04A	B
LOFTIN JAMES	A	46	JAM	W
LOFTIN JOHN	A	32	JAC	W
LOFTIN LEWIS	A	46	GRE	B
LOFTIN M G	A	32	LOF	W
LOFTIN NEEDHAM	A	28	11T	W
LOFTIN SAMPSON	A	35	WOL	B
LOFTIN SIMON	A	35	WOL	B
LOFTIN SOLOMON	A	35	FAI	B
LOFTIN T G	A	32	JAC	W
LOFTIN THOMAS	A	32	JAC	W
LOFTIN WM	A	28	04A	B
LOFTIN WM	A	32	JAC	W
LOFTIS JOHN	A	44	YXS	B
LOFTIS MAJOR	A	44	SAS	B
LOFTIS PHIL	A	44	YXS	B
LOFTIS W D	A	44	YXR	W
LOFTON G T	A	35	WOL	W
LOFTON ILA C M	A	35	KEN	W
CERT TO MT OLIVE				
13 APRIL 1868				
LOFTON JAMES	A	35	MAG	B
LOFTON JOEL	A	35	WOL	W
LOFTON OAKLEY	A	35	CYP	B
LOFTON RANSOM	A	35	WAR	B
LOGAN B F		26	SHE	W
WAS ASSISTANT PM				
PRIOR TO WAR &				
ENGAGED IN REBELLION				
LOGAN H G	A	26	SHE	W
LOGAN J C	A	26	MOO	B
LOGAN J W	A	26	MOO	W
LOGAN JOHN	A	28	9TH	B
LOGAN JOHN E	A	46	GRE	W
LOGAN JOSEPH	A	26	MOO	B
LOGAN L M	A	26	GOF	W
LOGAN PARKER	A	46	GRE	B
LOGAN R P	A	26	SHE	W
LOGAN T S	A	26	SHE	W
LOMAN ADAM	A	46	MON	W
LOMAN ANDREW	A	46	MON	W
LOMAN FRANKLIN	A	32	SHE	W
LOMAN JNO H	A	37	ROB	W
LOMAN JOHN	A	46	MON	W
LOMAX DAVID	A	29	FA1	B
LOMAX H K	A	32	TYR	W
LOMAX IRA	A	32	JAC	W
LOMAX J F	A	32	TYR	W
LOMAX JOHN	A	32	JAC	W
LOMAX JOSEPH	A	29	SEV	B
LOMAX THOS H	A	29	FA1	B
LOMAX WILLIAM	A	32	JAC	W
LOMAX WILLIAM	A	32	TYR	W
LOMON JOHN	A	32	SHE	W
LONDERGAN PAUL	A	40	STO	B
LONDON A J JR	A	26	GRI	W
LONDON A J SR	A	26	GRI	W
LONDON C L	A	26	GRI	W
LONDON CHANDLER	A	26	BLA	W
LONDON D D	A	26	GRI	W
LONDON EDWARD	A	26	GOF	W
LONDON ISHAM	A	46	COB	B
LONDON J W	A	26	GRI	W
LONDON JAMES	A	26	GRI	B
LONDON JAMES	A	26	GRI	W
LONDON JOHN	A	26	GRI	W
LONDON MICHAEL	A	19	STR	B
LONDON NELSON	A	26	SHE	B
LONG A L	A	46	FRI	W
LONG A V	A	44	FOR	W
LONG ADAM	A	32	DAV	B
LONG ANDREW	A	40	DA1	W
LONG ANDREW G	A	32	POS	W
LONG ANTHONEY	A	37	EDW	B
LONG ARDEN	A	37	EDW	B
LONG BENJN	A	28	04A	B
LONG BURTON	A	32	DAV	B
LONG CHARLES	A	32	DAV	W
LONG CHARLES	A	37	TA2	B

LONG DANIEL	A	32	POS	W
LONG DAVID	A	32	POS	W
LONG DREW	A	37	HIC	B
LONG DREWRY	A	46	FRI	W
LONG E J	A	39	FRA	W
LONG EDWARD	A	37	ROC	B
LONG FRANK	A	44	DUT	B
LONG FREDRICK	A	53	LA1	B
LONG GEORGE	A	28	7TH	W
LONG GEORGE	A	32	DAV	B
LONG GEORGE	A	37	EDW	B
LONG GEORGE	A	44	BRA	B
LONG GEORGE W	A	32	DAV	W
LONG GREEN	A	32	DAV	B
LONG HENRY	A	32	CLE	W
LONG HENRY	A	37	HIC	B
LONG HENRY	A	37	MAN	B
LONG HENRY	A	39	HAR	B
LONG ISRUL	A	32	POS	W
LONG J A	A	32	POS	W
LONG J C	A	39	FRA	W
LONG J R	A	40	STO	W
LONG J S	A	28	04B	W
LONG J W	A	32	POS	W
LONG JACOB F	A	40	DA1	W
LONG JAMES F	A	39	GRI	W
LONG JAMES S	A	37	HIC	A
LONG JESSE	A	32	POS	W
LONG JNO	A	39	FRA	W
LONG JOHN	A	24	EDE	B
LONG JOHN	A	24	EDE	W
LONG JOHN	A	32	COT	W
LONG JOHN	A	37	WHI	B
LONG JOHN	A	39	FRA	B
LONG JOHN	A	46	GRE	W
LONG JOHN A	A	32	THO	W
LONG JOHN P	A	32	POS	W
LONG JOHN R	A	40	SAN	W
LONG JOSEPH	A	37	ROC	W
LONG JOSEPH	A	40	DEC	W
LONG LAFAYETT	A	37	ROC	B
LONG MARTIN	A	37	ROC	W
LONG MATHIAS	A	32	COT	W
LONG NATHANIEL	A	46	COB	B
LONG NELSON	A	32	COT	B
LONG NEWSON	A	37	ROC	W
LONG NORMAN	A	44	FOR	W
LONG P A	A	32	POS	W
LONG P T	A	39	FRA	W
LONG PETER	A	37	EDW	B
LONG POMPEY	A	37	EDW	B
LONG RAFE	A	28	05A	B
LONG RICHARD	A	26	GOF	W
LONG RICHARD D	A	37	ROC	W
LONG ROBERT	A	44	FOR	B
LONG ROBT	A	28	05A	B
LONG S L	A	39	FRA	B
LONG SAML	A	28	02N	B
LONG SAML	A	28	04A	B
LONG SAMUEL	A	24	UPP	W
LONG SANFORT A	A	53	LA1	W
LONG SOLOMON	A	32	POS	W
LONG SOLOMON	A	32	POS	W
LONG SPENCER M	A	32	THO	B
LONG STANFORD	A	44	FIS	W
LONG STEPNEY	A	28	04A	B
LONG THOMAS	A	25	SHO	W
LONG THOMAS	A	32	POS	W
LONG THOMAS	A	44	FIS	B
LONG THOS	A	28	05A	B
LONG VALENTINE	A	28	7TH	B
LONG VATHAN	A	37	MAN	B
LONG WILEY	A	37	PEN	W

LONG WILLIAM	A	32	POS	W
LONG WILLIAM	A	40	BLA	W
LONG WILLIAM B	A	37	ROC	W
LONG WILLIAM J	A	53	BUR	W
LONG WILLIAM R	A	37	EDW	W
LONG WILSON	A	28	10T	B
LONG WM D	A	32	COT	W
LONG WM F	A	32	POS	W
LONGEST ABRAHAM	A	53	LA1	B
LONGEST BENJ W	A	19	BE1	W
LONGEST DAVID	A	19	BE2	W
LONGEST ELIJAH J	A	19	BE1	W
LONGEST ELIJAH W	A	19	BE1	W
LONGEST JAMES	A	19	BE1	W
LONGEST JONES S	A	19	BE1	W
LONGEST JOSHUA F	A	19	BE1	W
LONGEST WILLIAM H	A	53	SWA	W
LONGMILES A R	A	46	JAM	W
LONGMIRE BURWELL	A	44	ISL	B
LONGMIRE IVERSON	A	44	BRA	W
LONGMIRE J Y	A	44	BRA	W
LONGMIRE R R	A	44	LED	W
LONGMIRE S H	A	44	BRA	W
LONGMIRE SANDY	A	44	OXF	B
LONSDON WM MCK	A	29	FA1	W
TOWN GUARD ENG IN REB				
LOOKABIL JACOB	A	32	DAV	W
LOOKANBILL JOHN W	A	32	LOF	W
LOOKENBA J L F	A	32	DAV	W
LORANCE MARTIN C	A	40	FER	W
LORANCE MARTIN C	R	40	FER	W
NAME LINED OUT				
CAPTAIN OF MILITIA BEFORE				
THE REBELLION AND GAVE				
AID & COMFORT TO THE ENEMY				
DID NOT QUALIFY				
LORANCE ZACHARIAH	A	37	MAN	B
LORCH E P	A	28	03A	W
LORCH WM	A	28	03A	W
LORD JAS	A	29	FA1	B
LORD LEWIS	A	29	FA1	B
LORD PLEASANT	A	46	GRE	B
LORD SARGENT	A	29	FA1	B
LORY CHAS	A	28	04A	B
LOUCH SIMON	A	28	05A	B
LOUGHLIN JAMES	A	28	01A	W
LOUIS HENRY	A	39	FRA	W
LOUIS HENRY	A	39	LOU	B
TRNS FROM FREEMANS X				
ROADS TO LOUISBURG				
LOUIS JOSEPH T	A	53	GER	W
LOUIS JOSPH	A	24	MID	B
LOUIS RICHARD	A	19	MOR	B
LOUIS SAMUEL	A	39	HAR	B
LOUIS THOS F	A	29	FA1	W
LOUTHER ANTHONY	A	24	EDE	B
LOUTHER BAKER	A	24	EDE	B
LOUTHER CHAS	A	24	EDE	B
LOUTHER HENRY	A	24	EDE	B
LOUTHER ISAAC	A	24	EDE	B
LOUTHER JAMES	A	24	EDE	B
LOUTHER NELSON	A	24	EDE	B
LOUTHER NELSON JR	A	24	EDE	B
LOUTHER RANSOM	A	24	EDE	B
LOUTHER SCIPIO	A	24	EDE	B
LOUTHER WILLIAM	A	24	EDE	B
LOUTHER WM JR	A	24	EDE	B
LOVE A JACKSON	A	40	FER	W
LOVE C G		26	SHE	W
WAS COL OF MILITIA				
PRIOR TO REB &				
GAVE VOLUNTARY AID TO				
THE REBELION				

LOVE ALEN	A	46	KIN	W
LOVE E W	A	32	DAV	W
LOVE JAMES	A	26	SHE	W
LOVE JNO W	A	32	DAV	W
LOVE JOHN C	A	46	KIN	W
LOVE MOSES	A	40	DA1	B
LOVE NATHAN	A	46	HIG	W
LOVE NEAD	A	37	MAN	B
LOVE NEILL A	A	29	FA1	W
LOVE PETER	A	40	DA1	B
LOVE R C GRIER	A	40	DA1	W
LOVE T W	A	26	SHE	W
LOVE THOMAS	A	29	QUW	B
LOVE TONY	A	32	POS	B
LOVE W J	A	46	KIN	W
LOVE W P	R	26	MOU	W
LOVE WILLIAM	A	29	QUW	W
LOVE WM	A	46	GRE	W
LOVE WM R	A	29	FA1	W
LOVELACE ASA	A	26	MOO	W
LOVELACE B A	A	26	MOO	W
LOVELACE BENJAMINE	A	26	MOU	W
LOVELACE J L	A	26	MOO	W
LOVELACE JAMES	A	26	MOO	W
LOVELACE THOMAS	A	26	MOO	W
LOVELESS NATHAN	A	26	BLA	W
LOVELL A J	A	25	HAY	W
COPIED FROM ABOVE				
LOVELL A J	R	25	HAY	W
FOR NOT ACQUIRING A				
RESIDENCE NOT ENTITLED				
LOVEN JOHN	A	25	HAY	W
LOVET SCOTT	A	53	LA1	B
CERT RES SWAN QUARTER				
LOVETT CHESTER	A	29	SEV	W
LOVETT HORATIO	A	28	04A	B
LOVETT ISAAC	A	46	KIN	W
LOVETT RICHD	A	29	SEV	B
LOVETT WADE	A	46	GRE	B
LOVICK ALONZO	A	28	04A	B
LOVICK BENJN	A	28	03A	B
LOVICK CICERO	A	28	04A	B
LOVICK DANCY	A	28	04A	B
LOVICK DANL	A	28	04A	B
LOVICK GEORGE	A	28	8TH	B
LOVICK H J	A	28	9TH	W
LOVICK JAMES	A	28	11T	B
LOVICK MARTIN	A	28	14T	B
LOVICK NELSON	A	28	9TH	B
LOVICK WM	A	28	01B	B
LOVING GEO	A	29	FA1	B
LOVIT YORK	A	53	SWA	B
LOW BARNEY F	A	46	GIB	W
LOW DANL R	A	46	GIB	W
LOW GEORGE	A	32	TYR	B
LOW HESEKIAH	A	46	COB	W
LOW J W (?)	A	32	DAV	W
NAME LINED THROUGH				
LOW JEREMIAH	A	46	SUM	B
LOW JOHN	A	46	COB	W
LOW JULIUS	A	28	6TH	B
LOW WILLIAM	A	46	COB	W
LOW WILSON M	A	46	COB	W
LOWE AARON	A	40	DEC	W
LOWE ALEXANDER	A	32	DAV	B
LOWE JAMES	A	32	DAV	B
LOWE JOHN	A	40	DEC	W
LOWE THOMAS	A	37	EDW	B
LOWE WILLIAM	A	26	GRI	W
LOWE WILLIAM	A	37	TA1	B
LOWENBERG BENJ	A	19	BE1	W
LOWENBERG CHARLES	A	19	BE1	W
LOWERRY SANDERFORD	A	39	FRA	W

LOWERY ALLEN A 46 KIN W
LOWERY HOWEL A 25 TUS W
LOWERY JAMES A A 46 KIN W
LOWERY LUKE A 46 KIN B
LOWERY R P A 25 TUS W
LOWERY WM A 26 SWA W
LOWES ELIJAH A 28 10T B
LOWES GID A 32 DAV B
LOWES S B A 32 DAV W
LOWRENCE J L A 26 GRI W
LOWRENCE J Z A 26 GRI W
LOWREY J G A 26 MOU W
LOWRY DAVID A 46 SUM B
LOWRY HARRY A 40 DA1 B
LOWRY JUBITER A 29 FA1 B
LOWRY MEYERS A 19 NEW B
LOWRY THOS A 26 SWA W
LOWRY WILEY H A 28 9TH B
LOWRY WM A 29 FA1 W
LOY HARDY A 46 MON W
LOY JACOB A 46 GIB W
LOYD A J A 25 TUS W
LOYD CAESER A 29 FA1 B
LOYD DAVID A 44 RAG W
LOYD EDWIN A 44 YXR W
LOYD GEO W A 44 FOR W
LOYD HENRY A 29 FA1 B
LOYD J M A 44 FOR W
LOYD J S A 44 FOR W
LOYD JAMES JR A 44 YXR W
LOYD JAMES M A 53 SWA W
LOYD JOHN W A 46 GRE W
LOYD JOS A 29 GRA B
LOYD JOSEPH SR A 44 YXR W
LOYD LEWIS H A 44 RAG W
CERT TO VOTE
OUT OF COUNTY
LOYD LUNSFORD A 44 HEN W
LOYD RICHARD A A 44 YXR W
LOYD T J A 44 FOR W
LOYD W Y A 44 FOR W
LOYD WILLIAM A 25 TUS W
LOYD WILSON A 44 YXR W
LUCAS ANDREW A 37 ROC B
LUCAS ANSON A 53 SWA B
LUCAS AUGUSTUS A 37 TA1 B
LUCAS BERRY A 37 ROC B
LUCAS DAVID A 29 FA1 B
LUCAS EDWARD A 29 CED B
LUCAS EDWARD A 29 FA2 B
LUCAS HENRY A 26 WAR W
LUCAS HENRY A 53 LA1 W
LUCAS J S A 28 01B W
LUCAS JAMES A 28 01A B
LUCAS JAMES A 28 03A B
LUCAS JESSIE A 37 PEN W
LUCAS JNO A 29 FA1 B
LUCAS JOEL A 39 JOR W
LUCAS JOHN A 26 WAR W
LUCAS JOHN H A 46 GRE W
LUCAS OMON A A 28 01B B
LUCAS P J A 26 BLA W
LUCAS PETER A 26 BLA W
LUCAS R W A 46 MON W
LUCAS SETH A 28 9TH B
LUCAS THOS A 29 FA1 B
LUCAS WRIGHT A 37 TA1 B
LUCEY WILLIAM H A 37 PEN B
LUCUS AARON A 19 HAR B
LUCUS GENERAL A 19 BE2 B
LUCUS GEORGE A 46 FRI B
LUCUS JOHN A 44 OXF B
LUCUS WILSON A 19 HAR B

LUCUS WILSON H A 53 LA1 W
LUDLOW JNO A 29 FA2 B
LUMKIN JOHN A 44 RAG W
LUMM THOS A 29 FA1 B
LUMPKINS J R T A 44 RAG W
LUNCE HENRY A 39 DAV B
LUNCFORD PHILLIP A 37 ROC B
LUNDY ANTHONY A 37 TA2 B
LUNSFORD ADAM A 44 TAR B
LUNSFORD MACON A 39 HAR B
LUNSFORD W A A 44 LED W
LUNTS CHARLES A 39 HAY B
LUPER JAMES A 37 SHA W
LUPTON ANDREW G A 53 GER W
LUPTON CHRISTOPHER A 19 CED W
LUPTON
CHRISTOPHER J A 53 LA1 W
LUPTON D G A 28 15T W
LUPTON FRANCIS M A 19 CED W
LUPTON HARRIS J A 19 CED W
LUPTON JAMES H A 53 GER W
LUPTON JAMES J A 19 CED W
LUPTON JOHN A A 28 16T W
LUPTON JOHN J A 19 CED W
LUPTON JOHN W A 19 HUN W
LUPTON JOHN W A 53 GER W
LUPTON JOSEPH W A 19 BE1 W
LUPTON REDDING J A 53 GER W
LUPTON ROBINSON A 53 GER W
LUPTON SILAS A 19 BE1 W
LUPTON SILAS S A 19 CED W
LUPTON WILSON A 19 CED W
LUPTON WM H A 19 CED W
LUTHAR ISAM A 32 LOF W
LUTHERLOH
WASHINGTON A 46 COB B
LUTHEROW ANTHONY A 46 RAG B
LUTON ANDERSON A 24 EDE B
LUTON ENOCH A 28 7TH B
LUTTERLOAH JULIUS A 29 FA1 B
LUTTERLOH JACOB A 29 FA1 B
LUTZ J W A 26 WAR W
LUTZ LEANDER A 26 WAR B
LUTZ LUTHER A 26 WAR W
LUTZ SOLOMON A 26 WAR B
LYNAM C W A 44 FOR W
LYNAM M A A 44 FOR W
LYNAM WM A 44 FOR W
LYNCH DANIEL A 19 BE1 W
LYNCH HENRY A 28 04A B
LYNCH JOHN A 19 BE1 W
LYNCH JOSEPH P A 40 DA2 W
LYNCH RUFUS N A 99 BUS W
LYNDSAY DAVID A 32 LEE B
LYNDSAY WILLIAM D A 32 DAV W
LYNK MOSES A 44 YXS B
LYNUM G W A 44 FOR W
LYON A O A 25 HAY W
CHAL FOR HOLDING OFFICE
LYON ALFRED A 37 ROB B
LYON AYERS A 37 ROB B
LYON BENNETT T A 37 ROB W
LYON CHARLES A 37 ROB B
LYON DANL A 44 LED B
LYON DAVID A 37 ROB B
LYON DAVID A 44 LED B
LYON E E A 44 DUT W
LYON E H A 44 DUT W
LYON EMERSON A 44 DUT B
LYON FOSEPH A 44 DUT B
LYON FRANK A 37 ROB B
LYON HAYWOOD A 44 DUT B
LYON HENRY A 44 LED B

LYON HILLMAN A 44 LED B
OF DUTCHVILLE
LYON HOWARD A 44 DUT B
LYON HOWARD A 44 DUT B
LYON J H A 44 BEA W
LYON J W A 44 DUT W
LYON J W A 44 DUT W
LYON JACKSON A 44 DUT B
LYON JAS T A 44 TAR W
LYON JOHN A 37 ROB B
LYON JOSHUA L A 37 TA2 W
LYON JULIUS A 44 YXS B
LYON KIMBRO SR A 37 ROB B
LYON KINCHINS JR A 37 ROB B
LYON LANDIS A 37 ROB B
LYON LEWIS A 37 ROB B
LYON LEWIS A 44 DUT B
LYON MOSES A 44 DUT B
LYON N C A 44 DUT W
LYON NORFLEET A 37 ROB B
LYON P A A 44 DUT W
LYON PETER A 44 DUT B
LYON PETER A 44 LED B
LYON RALPH R 44 TOW B
CHAL NOT OF AGE
LYON RICHARD A 44 DUT B
LYON RICHARD A 44 DUT B
LYON RILEY A 37 ROB B
LYON SAMUEL A 44 DUT B
LYON THOMAS A 44 DUT B
LYON W M A 44 DUT W
LYON W S A 44 TAR W
LYON W W A 44 DUT W
LYON WASHINGTON A 37 ROB B
LYON WILLIAM A 44 DUT B
LYON WILLIE A 44 DUT B
LYON WILSON A 37 ROB B
LYON WM A 44 LED B
LYON YOUNG A 44 DUT B
LYON Z E A 44 BEA W
LYONS ALFRID A 37 ROB B
LYONS ALVIN A 44 TOW B
LYONS ANTHONY A 44 TOW B
LYONS BENJAMIN A 37 MAN B
LYONS DRED A 37 ROB B
LYONS EDWARD A 37 ROB B
LYONS ELIAS A 37 ROB B
LYONS HENRY A 37 ROB B
LYONS HENRY A 37 ROB W
LYONS KIT A 37 EDW B
LYONS MOSES A 37 ROB B
LYONS NEMIAH A 37 ROC B
LYONS PATRICK M A 37 ROB W
LYONS WILLIAM A 37 ROB B
LYONS WILSON A 37 MAN B

- M -

MABRAY ALFRED 1ST A 37 EDW B
MABRAY ALFRED 2ND A 37 EDW B
MABRAY ALLEN A 37 EDW B
MABRAY BYTHAL A 37 EDW W
MABRAY CHARLES A 37 HIC B
MABRAY ELI A 37 EDW B
MABRAY FARMAN A 37 PEN B
MABRAY JACOB A 37 EDW B
MABRAY JERRY A 37 EDW B
MABRAY JOHN A 37 EDW B
MABRY FRANKLIN A 32 DAV B
MABRY HARDY A 37 EDW B
MABRY J H A 32 DAV W
MABRY J P A 32 DAV W
MACCOLLOM ISAAC A 46 SUM B
MACDARMON JAMES A 19 SMY W
MACE FRANCIS A 28 9TH W

MACE HENRY A 46 GRE W
MACE THOMAS A 46 GRE W
MACE THOMAS E A 53 SWA W
MACE THOS E A 19 BE1 W
MACHLAMORE ARCH A 29 FA2 W
MACINTIRE JAMES A 46 MON W
MACK BENJ A 28 04A B
MACK HAMILTON A 32 DAV B
MACK MADISON A 28 04A B
MACK PHILIP A 32 DAV B
MACK SIMON A 28 04A B
MACKAY ISHMON A 30 IND B
MACKELWAIN REDDING A 53 LA1 B
MACKENTOUCH W A 40 CAN W
MACKEY ARNALD A 53 FAI B
MACKEY BENJAMIN A 53 FAI B
MACKEY CAMBELL A 53 GER B
MACKEY GEORGE A 53 GER B
MACKEY HENDERSON A 19 BE1 B
MACKEY HENRY A 53 FAI B
MACKEY JAMES R A 53 FAI B
MACKEY JESPER A 53 GER B
MACKEY JOHN A 53 LA1 B
MACKEY JORDAN A 53 FAI B
MACKEY MILES A 53 FAI B
MACKEY SAML A 29 FA1 B
MACKEY SHADRACK A 53 LA1 B
MACKEY SYLVESTER A 28 04A B
MACKEY WM A 28 16T B
MACKLIN SAMUEL A 37 ROC B
MACNAIR ALTIMOORE A 37 TA1 B
MACNAIR ANTHONY A 37 TA1 B
MACNAIR AUGUSTUS H A 37 TA1 W
MACNAIR AUSTIN A 37 PEN B
MACNAIR CHRISTOPHER A 37 TA1 B
MACNAIR COLIN A 37 PEN W
MACNAIR DAVID A 37 PEN B
MACNAIR EDWARD A 37 TA1 B
MACNAIR HUGH A 37 TA2 W
MACNAIR JACOB A 37 PEN B
MACNAIR JOHN A 37 TA1 B
MACNAIR JOHN A 37 TA1 B
MACNAIR JOSEPH A 37 EDW B
MACNAIR NED A 37 PEN B
MACNAIR POLLDO A 37 PEN B
MACNAIR RUFUS A 37 PEN B
MACON BOB A 39 PUG B
MACON GEORGE W A 39 PUG W
MACON LEUIS A 39 PUG B
MACON N T A 39 HAY W
MACON P L A 39 PUG W
MACON REDICK A 39 LOU B
MACON SEBASTIAN A 39 PUG W
MACON SOLOMAN A 39 PUG B
MACON YOUNG A 39 PUG B
MACY DAVID A 46 ROS W
MACY FREDERICK H A 46 ROS W
MACY HENRY A 46 ROS W
MACY STEPHEN A 46 FRI W
MACY URIAH A 46 FRI W
MADDOX ALFRED A 19 HAD B
MADDOX LUKE A 19 HAD B
MADDOX MOSES A 19 HAR B
MADE DECIMA A 26 BLA W
MADE J C A 26 BLA W
MADE SAMUEL A 26 GRI W
MADISON JAMES A 28 05A B
MADISON JEFFERSON A 37 HIG B
MADISON JEFFERSON A 37 WHI B
MADISON WASH A 37 WHI B
MADRIE JOSEPH A 24 EDE W
MADRIS SAMPSON A 24 EDE B
MAGALLANE TOBY A 46 GRE B
MAGDAHAM WILLIAM A 37 SPA B
MAGEE WASHINGTON A 32 TYR B
MAGHEE ZACHARIAH A 44 FOR W
MAGHY DAVID A 44 YXS B
MAGILLIS MOSES A 37 TA1 B
MAGLEEN JAMES A 28 02N W
MAGNESS RICHARD A 26 MOO B
MAGNESS S P A 26 BLA W
MAGNESS SAMUEL A 26 MOO W
MAGOR WASHINGTON A 32 DAV B
MAHALEY JOHN A 32 COT W
MAIDS JOHN A 19 BE1 W
MAIDS WM J A 19 BE1 W
MAINER REDIN A 29 BLA X
MAINOR HARRISON A 29 LOC B
REMOVED TO FLEA HILL
MAINOR HIRAM A 29 FLE B
MAINOR ROBT A 29 FLE B
MAINOR STEPHEN A 29 FLE B
MAISE GRANDERSON A 44 YXS B
MAJOR JERRY A 37 ROB B
MAJOR KICKSON A 37 ROB B
MALER FREDK WM A 28 01A W
MALEY J H A 32 COT W
MALEY PETER J A 32 COT W
MALEY SAMUEL A 32 DAV B
MALHEND JOHN C A 35 CYP W
MALLARD ALFRED A 35 ROC W
MALLARD ASA B A 35 ISL W
MALLARD DICKSON A 35 KEN W
MALLARD JACK A 35 MAG B
CERT 16 APR 1868
TO KENANSVILLE
MALLARD JOHN W A 35 ISL W
MALLARD WILLIAM W A 35 MAG W
MALLARY EDWARD A 44 LED B
MALLARY WILLIE A 44 OXF B
MALLEN PLATO A 28 03A B
MALLERD ROBERT A 32 THO W
MALLETT C G A 29 FA1 W
MALLETT C P JR A 29 FA1 W
MALLEY COOPER A 29 LOC B
MALLISON BENJAMIN K A 28 16T W
MALLISON
FRANCIS D JR A 28 14T W
MALLISON
FRANCIS D SR A 28 14T W
CERTIF GIVEN RESIDENCE
16TH ELECT. PRE.
CRAVEN CO
MALLISON T H A 28 9TH W
MALLORY ADAM A 37 ROB B
MALLORY ALFRED A 44 OXF B
MALLORY GEORGE A 44 OXF B
MALLORY HARRISON A 44 OXF B
MALLORY HENRY A 44 OXF B
MALLORY J R A 44 LED W
MALLORY J R A 44 OXF W
MALLORY S C A 44 OXF W
MALLORY W C A 44 OXF W
MALLORY WILLIAM S A 37 TA2 W
MALLORY WILLIS A 44 OXF B
MALLORY WM A 29 LOC B
MALLORY WM A 44 OXF B
MALLORY WM J A 44 OXF W
MALOG AARON A 19 BE1 B
MALONE C D A 39 LOU W
MALONE CHARLES A 39 LOU B
MALONE FEDRICK A 44 FIS B
MALONE HENRY A 39 LOU B
MALONE HILLIARD A 39 LOU B
MALONE JAMES A 39 LOU B
MALONE JAS A 44 TOW B
MALONE JOHN A 39 LOU B
MALONE KIMP A 39 LOU B
MALONE LEWIS A 39 LOU B
MALONE OLIS A 39 LOU W
MALONE SAML A 44 OXF B
MALONE WILLIE A 39 PUG B
MALONE WYATT A 39 LOU B
MALONE YANCEY A 44 TAR B
MALORY ROBERT G A 37 ROC W
MALOY MALCOM A 29 BLA W
DISMAL SAMPSON CO
MALPASS JOHN A 35 ALB W
MALRY UMPHREY A 44 BEA B
MALSON CHARLES A 53 SWA B
MALTSBY DAVID S A 29 FA1 W
MALVIN SIMPKINS A 19 BE1 W
MALY DAVID A 28 03B B
MAN THOMAS A 28 16T W
MANARD WILLIAM R 19 NEW B
MANER AUSTIN A 37 MAN B
MANER GILES A 37 MAN B
MANER JAMES A 37 MAN B
MANER LIUIS A 37 MAN B
MANER LIUIS A 37 MAN B
MANEY J M A 25 SHO W
MANEY JAMES A 25 SHO W
MANEY M R A 25 SHO W
MANEY S B A 25 SHO W
MANGAM SIMON A 37 ROC B
MANGESS ROBERT A 26 MOO W
MANGUM A J A 44 FIS W
MANGUM ANDW A 44 FOR B
MANGUM C T A 44 FOR W
MANGUM CALVIN A 44 FOR B
MANGUM D L A 44 DUT W
MANGUM DAVID A 44 FOR B
MANGUM ESSET A 44 FIS B
MANGUM FIELDING A 46 MCL W
MANGUM G A A 44 FIS W
MANGUM GEORGE A 44 FOR B
MANGUM H T A 44 FOR W
MANGUM HARVEY A 44 FOR B
MANGUM J G A 44 FIS W
TABBS CREEK DIST
MANGUM J G A 44 OXF W
MANGUM J Y A 44 FOR W
MANGUM JERRY A 44 FOR B
MANGUM O P A 44 DUT W
MANGUM PETER A 44 OXF W
MANGUM SAM'L A 44 FIS W
MANGUM SILAS A 44 TAR B
MANGUM T P A 44 FOR W
MANGUM W A 44 LED W
MANGUM W C A 44 KNA W
MANGUM W J A 44 BEA W
MANGUM W P A 44 FIS W
MANGUM W P A 44 FOR W
MANGUM W P A 44 LED W
MANGUM WILEY A 44 DUT W
MANGUM WILLIAM A 44 KIT B
MANGUM WILLIE A 44 HEN W
CERT TO VOTE OUT COUNTY
MANGUM WM A 44 OXF B
MANGUM WOODY A 44 OXF B
MANIN JAMES A 19 BE1 B
MANING LARKINS A 19 BE2 B
MANING MICHEL A 53 GER W
MANING NATHAN A 37 MAN W
MANIX JOHN S A 28 01A W
MANLEY COFFIELD A 37 ROC B
MANLEY DAVIS A 19 BE1 B
MANLEY JOSEPH A 39 LOU B
MANLY DAVID A 28 03A B

MANLY DAVID	A	28	11T	B
MANLY GEORGE	A	28	03A	B
MANLY J M	A	28	04A	B
MANLY JO	A	28	03B	B
MANLY JOSEPH	A	44	HEN	B
MANLY LEWIS	A	19	MOR	B
MANLY N D	A	28	04B	W
MANLY WM H	A	28	04B	W
MANN ALEXANDRIA	A	53	LA1	B
MANN ALFRED	A	53	LA1	B
MANN BENJAMIN	A	30	ROA	B
MANN BENJAMIN D	A	30	ROA	B
MANN C C	A	19	NEW	W
MANN CALEER	A	39	DAV	B
MANN CASWELL	A	53	LA1	B
MANN CHARLES	A	53	FAI	B
MANN CHARLES M	A	53	FAI	B
MANN D F	A	19	NEW	W
MANN DALLAS	A	39	DAV	B
MANN DAVID JR	A	39	DAV	B
MANN DAVID SR	A	39	DAV	B
MANN DOCK	A	39	PUG	B
MANN EDWIN	A	53	FAI	W
MANN ELZE	A	19	NEW	W
MANN FREDRICK	A	53	FAI	B
MANN GEORGE	A	44	HEN	B
MANN GRAY	A	39	DAV	B
MANN INGE	A	39	DAV	B
MANN ISHAM	A	44	HEN	B
MANN J B	A	19	NEW	W
MANN JABEZ	A	19	NEW	W
MANN JACOB	A	53	LA1	B
MANN JAMES	A	53	FAI	B
MANN JAMES	A	53	LA1	B
MANN JAMES SR	A	53	LA1	B
MANN JOEL	A	53	FAI	B
MANN JOHN	A	19	NEW	W
MANN JOHN	A	53	LA1	B
MANN JOHN H	A	19	NEW	W
MANN JOHN J	A	30	NOR	W
MANN JOHN M	A	53	FAI	W
MANN JONAS	A	39	GRI	B
MANN JOSEPH	A	28	15T	B
MANN JOSEPH	A	53	FAI	W
MANN JOSEPH S	A	53	LA1	W
MANN LEWIS S	A	30	ROA	W
MANN NATHANIEL	A	44	KIT	B
MANN P P	A	19	NEW	W
MANN RICHARD	A	19	NEW	W
MANN S H	A	39	HAR	W
MANN SAMUEL	A	53	FAI	W
MANN SAMUEL	A	53	LA1	B
MANN SAMUEL SR	A	53	LA1	B
MANN STEPHEN	A	30	ROA	B
MANN THOMAS	A	53	FAI	B
MANN THOMAS	A	53	FAI	W
MANN THOS S	A	19	NEW	W
MANN WESLEY	A	39	HAR	B
MANN WILLIAM	A	53	LA2	B
MANN WM	A	19	NEW	W
MANN WM A	A	29	FA1	W
MANNEGO JOSEPH	A	28	02N	B
MANNERY JAMES L	A	19	BE1	W
MANNING GERSHOM	A	28	12T	W
MANNING JOHN	A	37	ROB	W
MANNING MOSES M	A	24	EDE	B
MANNING SOLOMAN	A	37	HIC	B
MANNING THOMAS	A	37	HIG	W
MANNING THOMAS	A	37	WHI	B
MANNING WILLIAM P	A	24	MID	W
MANNVILL JONES	A	19	MOR	B
MANNY FESTUS A	A	40	SAN	B
MANOR DAVID	A	35	MAG	B
MANOR HARDY	A	35	KEN	B
MANSFIELD CIDNEY	A	46	GRE	W
MANSFIELD HENRY M	A	30	MOY	W
MANSFIELD JESSEE JR	A	30	GIB	W
MANSFIELD JESSEE SR	A	30	GIB	W
MANSFIELD JOHN	A	46	MON	W
MANSON CEASER	A	19	BE1	B
MANSON DAVID H	A	19	BE2	W
MANSON H C	A	28	01A	W
MANSON JOHN C	A	19	BE1	W
MANSON WM	A	44	TOW	B
MANUEL DANL	A	29	FA1	B
MANUEL EDW	A	29	FLE	B
MANUEL ISAAC	A	29	FA1	B
MANUEL JACOB	A	29	LOC	B
MANUEL JAMES	A	46	JAM	B
MANUEL JESSEE	A	29	FA1	B
MANUEL LEMUEL	A	29	CAR	B
MANUEL MASHRACK	A	29	FA1	B
MANUEL P K	A	29	FA1	B
MANUEL STARKEY	A	29	SEV	B
MANUELL JAMES	A	28	01A	W
MARABLE ARMSTEAD	A	44	OXF	B
MARABLE DANIEL	A	44	FIS	B
MARABLE GRANDISON	A	44	OXF	B
MARABLE JEFFERSON	A	44	OXF	B
MARABLE MASON	A	44	OXF	B
MARABLE OLIVE	A	44	RAG	B
MARABLE OSBORN	A	44	OXF	B
MARABLE ROBT	A	44	OXF	B
MARABLE SAM	A	44	OXF	B
MARABLE WILLIAM	A	44	OXF	B
MARADDY OLIN	A	35	CYP	W
MARCH ANDERSON	A	32	DAV	B
MARCH DAVID	A	26	PEE	B
MARCH GEORGE	A	32	TYR	B
MARCH HENDERSON	A	32	DAV	W
MARCH SILAS	A	26	GRI	B
MARCHANT JOHNSON	A	30	CUR	W
MARDRE MOSES	A	30	CUR	B
MARDREN THOS	A	30	IND	W
MARIS WM OF FRIENDSHIP	A	46	GRE	W
MARIZ JOHN	A	46	JAM	W
MARKELL JOSEPH D	A	35	KEN	W
MARKET FRED	A	19	HAD	W
MARKET W E	A	19	NEW	W
MARKLAND W W	A	32	CLE	W
MARKS LUCIEN H	A	99	BUS	W
MARLEY VIRGIL	A	35	ROC	B
MARLOW JAMES	A	46	FRI	W
MARMON SAMUEL	A	26	GOF	W
MARPER GREEN	A	28	04A	B
MARPLEY JOHN	A	37	SPA	B
MARR W C	A	32	DAV	W
MARR W J	A	25	SHO	W
MARRABLE PETER	A	44	OXF	B
MARRADDY GEORGE	A	35	CYP	W
MARRICK PRESTON	A	24	EDE	B
MARRIL BRIAN	A	19	BE1	B
MARRINER WILLIAM C	A	37	PEN	W
MARRIS JOHN	A	19	BE1	B
MARRIS JOSIAH	A	26	BLA	W
MARROW ABRAM	A	44	SAS	B
MARROW ALBERT	A	44	TOW	B
MARROW ALEXANDER	A	44	SAS	B
MARROW ALEXANDER	A	44	SAS	B
MARROW ANDERSON	A	44	TOW	B
MARROW ANTHONY	A	44	ISL	B
MARROW ARON	A	44	SAS	B
MARROW ARON	A	44	SAS	B
MARROW BURWELL	A	44	SAS	B
MARROW CEZAR	A	44	SAS	B
MARROW CYRUS	A	44	HEN	B
MARROW D J	A	44	ISL	W
MARROW D S	A	44	TOW	W
MARROW EDMOND	A	44	SAS	B
MARROW ELI	A	44	ISL	B
MARROW GODFREE	A	44	SAS	B
MARROW HARROD	A	44	ISL	B
MARROW HENRY	A	44	TOW	B
MARROW HENRY	A	44	HEN	B
MARROW HENRY	A	44	SAS	B
MARROW HERRIN	A	44	SAS	B
MARROW ISAAC	A	44	HEN	B
MARROW ISAAC	A	44	SAS	B
MARROW JACK	A	44	TOW	B
MARROW JAMES SR	A	44	RAG	B
MARROW JAS A	A	44	TOW	W
MARROW JAS JR	A	44	ISL	B
MARROW JNO	A	44	SAS	B
MARROW JOHN	A	44	KIT	B
MARROW LEVI	A	44	SAS	B
MARROW LOVELIS	A	44	SAS	B
MARROW NED	A	44	OXF	B
MARROW PHIL	A	44	SAS	B
MARROW PHILEMON MISTAKE	A	44	SAS	B
MARROW POMPY	A	44	TOW	B
MARROW ROBERT	A	44	TOW	B
MARROW STERLING	A	44	HEN	B
MARROW THOMAS H	A	44	TOW	W
MARROW W D	A	44	SAS	W
MARROW WM	A	44	HEN	B
MARROW WM	A	44	SAS	B
MARS WILEY	A	37	HIG	W
MARSH ABSOLEM	A	29	GRA	W
MARSH AZORD	A	29	GRA	W
MARSH DAVID	A	28	05A	B
MARSH HENERY J	A	29	FA1	W
MARSH ISAIAH	A	46	HIG	W
MARSH J S	A	46	HIG	W
MARSH JACK	A	29	FLE	B
MARSH JAMES M	A	46	GRE	W
MARSH ROBERT	A	37	ROB	B
MARSH THOMAS	A	46	JAM	W
MARSH THOS	A	29	GRA	W
MARSH YORK	A	28	03A	B
MARSHAL HAILEY	A	44	ISL	B
MARSHAL JOHN	A	19	NEW	B
MARSHAL SUTTON	A	19	NEW	B
MARSHALL ALFRED	A	72	SWA	B
MARSHALL BEN	A	44	OXF	B
MARSHALL HANDY	A	19	MOR	B
MARSHALL ISAAC	A	28	05A	B
MARSHALL JAMES H	A	19	BE1	W
MARSHALL JNO	A	29	CAR	B
MARSHALL JOHN	A	28	14T	B
MARSHALL JOHN	A	29	FA1	B
MARSHALL JOHN B	A	19	BE1	W
MARSHALL JOHN O	A	19	BE1	W
MARSHALL JOSEPH	A	72	SWA	B
MARSHALL MARTIN	A	28	05A	B
MARSHALL SOLOMAN	A	38	FRE	W
MARSHALL THOMAS J	A	19	BE2	W
MARSHALL THOS E	A	19	BE1	W
MARSHEL OSKER	A	19	HAR	B
MARSHEL THOMAS	A	53	LA1	W
MARSTER ELIAS	A	32	DAV	W
MARTEN ALEXANDER	A	46	FRI	W
MARTEN B M	A	46	FRI	W
MARTIN A C	A	25	HAY	W
MARTIN A J	A	25	HAY	W
MARTIN A J	A	40	STO	W
MARTIN A M	A	26	SHE	W
MARTIN ALX	A	46	GRE	W

MARTIN ANDREW A 26 SHE W
MARTIN ARTHUR A 35 FAI W
MARTIN BATES A 37 EDW B
MARTIN BEN A 28 11T B
MARTIN BENJAMIN A 28 10T B
MARTIN BENJAMIN H A 28 14T W
MARTIN BROWN A 38 FRE B
MARTIN BRYANT A 39 GRI W
MARTIN C A 19 NEW W
MARTIN CALVIN A 29 QUW B
MARTIN CHARLES A 30 KNO W
MARTIN CHRISTOPHER A 26 GRI B
MARTIN DANIEL A 26 MOO W
MARTIN DAVID A 28 14T W
MARTIN EDMOND R 46 GRE B
WAS CONVICTED
AND WHIPED AS A FELON
MARTIN ELIJAH A 28 14T W
MARTIN FREDK A 28 05A B
MARTIN G W A 40 SAN W
MARTIN GEORGE T A 28 14T W
MARTIN H K A 25 TUS W
MARTIN HAYWOOD A 38 FRE B
MARTIN HENRY A 25 HAY W
MARTIN HENRY A 30 ROA B
REMOVED TO ELIZABETH
CITY, PASQUOTANK Co.
MARTIN HENRY C A 35 KEN W
MARTIN J A 26 BOR W
MARTIN J O A 26 BLA W
MARTIN J S A 25 HAY W
MARTIN JACKSON A 39 FRE B
MARTIN JACOB A 28 04A B
MARTIN JAMES A 25 HAY W
MARTIN JAMES A 26 SHE W
MARTIN JAMES A 28 14T W
MARTIN JAMES A 29 FA1 B
MARTIN JAMES A 44 SAS B
MARTIN JAMES A 53 SWA B
MARTIN JAMES C A 28 14T W
MARTIN JAMES C A 28 16T W
MARTIN JEFFERSON A 40 SAN W
MARTIN JNO M A 29 FA1 W
MARTIN JNO T A 29 FA1 W
MARTIN JOHN A 28 10T B
MARTIN JOHN A 28 16T W
MARTIN JOHN A 35 WAR B
MARTIN JOHN A 40 DA1 B
MARTIN JOHN B A 28 14T W
MARTIN JOHN D A 26 GRI W
MARTIN JOHN H A 46 FRI W
MARTIN JOHN S A 28 15T W
MARTIN JONES A 19 MOR W
MARTIN JOSEPHUS A 28 15T W
MARTIN L M C A 25 HAY W
MARTIN L W A 19 BE1 W
MARTIN LUKE P A 28 04A B
MARTIN M A A 25 HAY W
MARTIN MARION A 26 MOO B
MARTIN NATHAN A 26 BUR B
MARTIN ORRIN D A 46 GRE W
MARTIN PETER A 19 NEW B
MARTIN R H A 26 SHE W
MARTIN REUBEN A 30 POW B
MARTIN RICHARD A 26 MOO W
MARTIN RICHARD A 35 FAI W
MARTIN ROBERT A 25 HAY W
MARTIN ROBERT H R 25 HAY W
WAS CHALLENGED FOR
HOLDING OFFICE IN THE
MILITIA AS LIEUT OF A
COMPANY BEFORE THE WAR
(continued)
SAYING HE HAD NOT HEARD
THE OATH RED BEFORE IT .
WAS ADMINISSTERED DESIRES
HIS NAME STRICKEN OFF THE
LISTING
NAME LINED OUT
MARTIN SAMUEL A 28 10T B
MARTIN SAMUEL A 53 GER B
MARTIN STEPHEN A 28 10T B
MARTIN T J A 25 HAY W
MARTIN THOMAS A 72 SWA W
MARTIN TITUS A 32 POS B
MARTIN W A G A 26 SHE W
MARTIN W J A 25 HAY W
MARTIN W K JR A 39 FRE W
MARTIN W R A 40 SAN W
MARTIN WESLEY A 29 FA2 B
MARTIN WILLIAM A 26 GRI W
MARTIN WILLIAM A 28 03B B
MARTIN WILLIAM A 28 10T B
MARTIN WILLIAM R A 25 HAY W
MARTIN WILLIS A 29 FA1 B
MARTIN WM A 28 04A B
MARTIN WM H A 46 GRE B
MARTIN YORK A 26 SHE B
MARTINDAIL JAMES A 35 SMI W
MARTINE THEO A 29 FA1 W
MARTINS HENRY A 37 ROC B
MARTON CHARLES A 37 PEN B
MARVIN DANIEL A 37 ROC B
MARVIN J B A 28 01A W
MARYLAND JOHN A 37 ROC B
MASHBURN HALSEY A 35 CYP W
MASHBURN JAMES M A 35 ROC W
MASHBURNE RICHARD A 46 JAM B
MASON ABNER N A 28 10T W
MASON ALEX A 29 CAR W
TRANSFERRED TO
FAYETTEVILLE APRIL 68
MASON ALEX A 29 FA2 W
MASON ALEXANDER A 53 GER W
MASON ALLEN A 44 TOW B
MASON ANDREW S A 53 LA1 W
MASON ARCHBD A 19 HUN W
MASON ASA A 28 03A B
MASON BENJ JR A 19 HUN W
MASON BENJ SR A 19 HUN W
MASON BENJAMIN A 53 SWA W
MASON CALEB A 40 DA1 W
MASON CALVIN L A 53 SWA W
MASON CEASER A 32 THO B
MASON CICERO A 28 02N B
MASON COFIELD A 37 MAN W
MASON DAVID A 19 HUN W
MASON DAVID J A 19 HUN W
MASON DAVID J A 53 SWA W
MASON DAVID JR A 19 HUN W
MASON DOCTOR A 39 HAY B
MASON DORSET A 53 SWA W
MASON DURK W A 37 MAN W
MASON EDWIN A 25 HAY W
MASON EMANUEL A 53 LA1 B
MASON FOSTER A 29 CAR W
MASON FOSTER A 53 SWA W
MASON FRANCIS A 19 HUN W
MASON FRANCIS A A 28 10T W
MASON GILES A 40 DA1 B
MASON HAZEKIAH A 19 HUN W
MASON HENRY A 37 TA2 B
MASON HENRY T A 19 BE1 W
MASON HEZZEKIAH A 19 BE1 W
MASON HUGH A 29 CAR W
MASON ICHABOD A 19 BE1 W
MASON ISAIAH A 19 HUN W
MASON ISOM L A 46 FRI W
MASON ISRAEL A 53 SWA W
MASON J D A 29 CAR W
MASON J H A 28 10T W
MASON J W A 32 LOF W
MASON JAMES A 19 POR W
MASON JAMES A 53 SWA W
MASON JAMES A A 53 LA1 W
MASON JAS B A 28 02N B
MASON JESSE A 53 SWA W
MASON JESSE T A 53 SWA W
MASON JOHN A 19 HUN W
MASON JOHN A 28 04B B
MASON JOHN A 39 HAY B
MASON JOHN A 53 GER B
MASON JOHN W A 19 HUN W
MASON JOHN W A 53 LA1 W
MASON JOSEPH A 28 02N W
MASON JOSEPH A 37 ROB B
MASON LAWSON A A 40 DA1 W
MASON LITTLETON A 28 10T W
MASON LUKE A 28 02N B
MASON M LAFAYETTE A 40 DA1 W
MASON MANAIN W A 19 SMY W
MASON MARCUS A 19 POR W
MASON MILTON A 37 MAN B
MASON OSBON F A 53 LA1 W
MASON SAML A 44 FOR W
MASON SAMUEL A 19 HAD B
MASON SYLVESTER J A 19 BE1 W
MASON THOMAS S A 19 HUN W
MASON THOMAS T A 37 MAN W
MASON THOS C A 19 HUN W
MASON W CEPHAS A 40 DA1 W
MASON WALTER A 37 TA2 B
MASON WASHINGTON A 19 HUN W
MASON WILLIAM A 19 HUN W
MASON WILLIAM H A 53 LA1 W
MASON ZACHARIAH A 53 SWA W
MASS CHAS A 29 FA1 B
MASSA L J A 39 GRI W
MASSENBURG ABRAHAM A 39 LOU B
MASSENBURG COLUMBUS A 39 LOU B
MASSENBURG GARRICK A 39 SPE B
MASSENBURG JAS P A 39 FRA W
MASSENBURG OSCAR A 39 LOU B
CHAL FOR BE UNDER AGE
DISSABILITY REMOVED
MASSENBURG TOM A 39 LOU B
MASSEY A B A 99 BUS W
MASSEY ELIJAH A 46 SUM B
MASSEY JAMES A 46 GRE W
MASSEY JOHN A 26 SHE B
MASSEY THOS H A 29 FA1 W
MASSINBURG CHARLES A 39 LOU B
MASSINGILL JAMES A 39 HAR W
MASSY W FRENO A 40 FER W
MASTERS ALEXANDRIA A 53 LA1 B
MASTERS MARTIN A 28 8TH B
MASTERS SAML A 28 02N W
MASTERS SAML JR A 28 02N W
MASTON MARK A 32 THO B
MASY THOMAS A 46 FRI W
MATEER JEMY A 46 MON B
MATEER YANCY A 46 SUM B
MATHENY JOHN A 26 MOO W
MATHERS JAMES A 28 8TH B
MATHES HENRY A 99 BUS B
MATHESON E D A 25 HAY W
MATHESON ELISHA A 25 HAY W
MATHESON J A A 25 HAY W
MATHESON J A A 25 HAY W

MATHESON JOHN A 25 HAY W
MATHESON L W A 25 HAY W
MATHESON WILLIAM A 25 HAY W
MATHEWS BENJAMIN A 35 ROC B
MATHEWS BENJAMIN W A 35 ROC W
MATHEWS CORK A 35 ROC B
MATHEWS DANL A 29 LOC W
MATHEWS FORTUNE A 35 ROC B
MATHEWS HARMAN A 35 ROC W
MATHEWS HENRY A 44 SAS W
MATHEWS JAMES J A 44 TOW W
MATHEWS JAMES JR A 44 OXF W
MATHEWS JAMES SR A 44 OXF W
MATHEWS JAMES T A 35 ROC W
MATHEWS JNO W A 29 FA1 W
MATHEWS OLIVER M A 35 ROC W
MATHEWS SATHER R A 35 ROC W
MATHEWSON CAREY A 37 TA1 B
MATHEWSON GEORGE A 37 TA1 B
MATHEWSON JAMES A 37 TA1 B
MATHEWSON MACK A 37 TA1 B
MATHEWSON NATHAN A 37 TA2 W
MATHEWSON SAMUEL A 37 TA1 B
MATHIAS ANARSON A 24 MID B
MATHIAS B C A 30 CUR W
MATHIAS B F A 30 TUL W
MATHIAS C B A 30 CUR W
MATHIAS WILEY A 30 CUR W
MATHIS BRYANT A 35 MAG W
MATHIS DANIEL A 35 MAG B
MATHIS DAVIS B A 35 MAG B
MATHIS EDWARD A 35 MAG B
MATHIS EDWARD A 35 MAG W
MATHIS ESSEX A 35 MAG B
MATHIS HARRY A 35 MAG B
MATHIS JACOB A 35 MAG B
MATHIS JAMES K P A 35 MAG W
MATHIS JAMES T A 35 WAR W
MATHIS JEREMIAH A 35 MAG B
MATHIS JOHN W A 35 MAG W
MATHIS JOSEPH A 35 WAR B
MATHIS LEONARD A 35 MAG B
MATHIS LEWIS A 35 MAG W
MATHIS LEWIS A 35 WAR B
MATHIS NICHOLAS P A 35 MAG W
MATHIS PEYTON P A 35 MAG W
MATHIS WARRICK A 35 MAG B
MATHIS WELLS A 35 MAG W
MATHUS HENION A 37 MAN B
MATIER WESLEY A 46 GRE B
MATTHEW JAMES T A 28 03A W
CITY CLERK AND MALITIA
OFFICER BEFORE WAR
MATTHEW JOHN A A 28 15T B
MATTHEWS BURRELL A 35 ROC B
MATTHEWS D A 29 LOC W
MATTHEWS FREDERICK A 35 ROC B
MATTHEWS GIBSON A 35 ROC B
MATTHEWS JOEL A 29 FLE W
MATTHEWS JOHN E A 28 03A W
MATTHEWS JOHN P A 40 SAN W
MATTHEWS R A 29 LOC W
MATTHEWS R E A 29 LOC W
MATTHEWS R H A 39 LOU W
MATTHEWS S J A 44 BRA W
MATTHEWS THOMAS A 35 CYP B
MATTHIAS JNO A A 30 TUL W
MATTICKS AMOS A 53 GER B
MATTOCK EDWARD W A 72 SWA W
MATTOCKS C J A 19 HAD W
MATTOCKS MASTIN A 72 SWA B
MAULTSBY JNO S A 29 FA2 W
MAULTSBY JNO W A 29 FA2 W

MAUN ASA A 19 HAD W
MAUNEY A A A 40 MAU W
MAUNEY ALLEN A 40 MAU B
MAUNEY CALEB A 40 DEC W
MAUNEY ELI A 40 DEC W
MAUNEY EMANUEL A 40 DEC W
MAUNEY J R A 26 SHE W
MAUNEY LAWSON A 26 GOF W
MAUNEY LAWSON A 40 BLA W
MAUNEY M M A 26 SHE W
CERT GIVEN RESID.
SHELBY APR 9 1868
MAUNEY MICHAEL A 40 BLA W
MAUNEY MWYLEY A 40 DEC W
MAUNEY NOAH A 40 BLA W
MAUNEY PINK A 40 MAU B
MAUNEY RUFUS A 40 MAU B
MAUNEY SAMUEL A 40 BLA W
MAUNEY SAMUEL JR A 40 MAU B
MAUNEY SAMUEL SEN A 40 MAU B
MAUNEY SAMUEL
(LITTLE SAM) A 40 BLA B
MAUNEY WILLIAM A 40 BLA W
MAXFIELD ISAAC A 32 THO B
MAXWELL A A 29 LOC W
MAXWELL ARCHIBALD A 35 KEN W
MAXWELL CHAS A 29 FA1 B
MAXWELL DAVID C A 35 KEN W
MAXWELL DAVID W A 35 KEN W
MAXWELL GEO A 29 FA1 B
MAXWELL JAMES A 35 KEN W
MAXWELL JESSY A 29 FLE B
MAXWELL SAML A 29 LOC B
MAXWELL SAMUEL D A 40 FER W
MAXWELL WILEY A 29 ROC B
MAXWELL WILLIAM A 46 MON W
MAXWILL ALEX A 29 LOC B
MAY ABRAHAM A 39 HAR B
MAY ANTHONY A 39 FRE B
MAY ANTHONY A 39 LOU W
MAY AUSTIN A 37 HIC B
MAY AUSTIN A 39 FRE B
MAY B C A 44 FOR W
MAY BENJAMIN A 37 PIN B
MAY BENJAMIN A 39 FRE B
MAY BENJAMIN R 39 FRE B
NOT 21 YEARS OLD
MAY C LEMUEL A 46 RAG W
MAY CALVIN A 46 MCL W
MAY CHARLES A 39 LOU B
MAY E ANTHONY A 46 GIB B
MAY EATON A 39 FRE B
MAY EDWARD A 46 GIB W
MAY ELI A 46 RAG W
MAY HAWKINS A 38 FRE B
MAY HENRY A 37 HIC B
MAY HENRY C A 39 LOU W
MAY J A A 39 DAV W
MAY J E A 28 6TH W
MAY J J A 39 JOR W
MAY J W A 39 LOU W
MAY J Y A 39 JOR W
MAY JAMES A 46 MCL W
MAY JAMES M A 46 MCL W
MAY JAS A A 39 HAR W
MAY JESSE L A 46 COB W
MAY JOHN A A 46 MON W
MAY JONATHAN A 46 GIB W
MAY JOSEPH A 37 EDW B
MAY JOSEPH A 46 SUM B
MAY JOSHUA A 46 MCL W
MAY JOSIAH A 46 COB W
MAY KINCHEN A 39 LOU B

MAY KING A 38 FRE B
MAY LEVI A 46 COB W
MAY N D D A 39 LOU W
MAY NATHAN A 39 FRA W
MAY PAUL A 39 LOU B
MAY PHIL A 39 HAR B
MAY PRIOR R 25 PIN W
NAME LINED OUT
NOT ALLOWED CITIZENSHIP
FROM NOT BEING IN STATE
12 MONTHS
MAY R C A 32 THO W
MAY RICHARD A 19 MOR B
MAY ROBERT A 44 FOR W
MAY ROBERT R A 46 GRE W
MAY RUEBEN A 32 THO W
MAY S K A 39 LOU W
MAY SAMUEL A 32 LOF B
MAY T C A 39 DAV W
TRNS TO NASH CO
APRIL 10 1868
MAY T H A 44 FOR W
MAY THOMAS A 39 JOR W
MAY THOMAS H A 39 LOU W
MAY THOS A 39 GRI W
MAY TURNER A 28 6TH W
MAY TURNER J A 28 6TH W
MAY W C A 39 FRA W
MAY W G A 44 BRA W
MAY W H A 28 6TH W
MAY W H A 39 DAV W
MAY WASH A 38 FRE B
MAY WILLIAM A 39 LOU W
MAY WILLIE A 39 FRE B
MAY WILLIE A 39 HAR B
MAY WM A 44 BRA W
MAY WM D A 39 LOU W
MAY WM H A 46 RAG W
MAY WRIGHT A 37 HIC B
MAYBERRY ISAAC A 28 05A B
MAYBRAY JAMES A 37 PIN B
MAYDON COFIELD A 37 ROB B
MAYES W W A 44 OXF W
MAYFIELD ADAM A 44 HEN B
MAYFIELD CROFFORD A 44 HEN B
MAYFIELD CUFFEY A 44 HEN B
MAYFIELD EDWARD A 44 HEN B
MAYFIELD ELLIC A 44 HEN B
MAYFIELD G M A 26 GOF W
MAYFIELD J P A 26 GOF W
MAYFIELD JOHN A 44 HEN B
MAYFIELD LOUIS A 39 FRA B
MAYFIELD MILES A 39 FRE B
MAYFIELD RICHARD A 44 HEN B
MAYFIELD ROBERT N A 40 DEC W
MAYFIELD WASHINGTON A 44 HEN B
MAYFIELD WESLEY A 44 HEN B
MAYHOE RICHD A 39 GRI B
MAYHUE DAVID A 26 SHE W
MAYHUE JACOB A 26 SHE W
MAYMEN BENNETT F A 53 LA1 W
MAYNARD ALFRED A 46 MON B
MAYNARD BOSS A 44 KIT B
MAYNARD J P A 44 HEN W
MAYNARD JACOB A 46 HIG W
MAYNARD JAS R A 29 FA1 B
MAYNARD JERRY A 46 MON B
MAYNARD JOHN E A 46 GRE W
MAYNARD RICHARD A 46 MON B
MAYNARD ROBT A 46 MON W
MAYNOR JESSEE A 29 CAR B
MAYNOR JNO A 29 CAR B
MAYNOR JOHN A 35 KEN W

MAYNORD ARCHIBALD H A 28 16T W
CERT GIVEN RESIDENCE
15TH ELECTION PRECINCT
MAYO ABRAM A 37 HIC B
MAYO ALFRED A 37 ROC B
MAYO AMOS A 37 EDW B
MAYO ARDEN A 37 HIC B
MAYO BENJ A 37 PEN W
MAYO EDWARD A 19 POR W
MAYO EDWARD A 24 EDE B
MAYO ELDRIGE A 44 DUT B
MAYO GEO R A 19 POR W
MAYO HENRY A 28 04A B
MAYO JAMES A 19 POR W
MAYO JAMES A 37 EDW B
MAYO JAMES A 37 PIN W
MAYO JOHN A 28 03A B
MAYO JOHN A 28 04A B
MAYO JOHN 2ND A 28 04A B
MAYO KING A 37 PIN B
MAYO LORENZA A 44 FOR B
MAYO LUKE A 37 EDW B
MAYO ONSLOW M A 37 HIC A
MAYO ORANGE A 37 HIC B
MAYO RALPH A 37 PIN W
MAYO REUBEN A 37 HIC A
MAYO SANDY A 37 HIC B
MAYO THOMAS L A 37 HIC A
MAYO WILLIAM H A 37 HIC A
MAYO WILLIAM H A 37 PIN W
MAYR JAMES M A 37 ROB W
MAYS BOOKER A 44 OXF B
MAYS CHAS A 44 OXF B
MAYS CUFFEY A 44 OXF B
MAYS ELIJAH A 44 OXF B
MAYS GEORGE A 37 HIC B
MAYS HARMON A 37 ROB B
MAYS HILLMAN A 44 KIT B
MAYS PRESLEY H A 39 PUG B
MAZE JAMES A 24 EDE B
MAZELLE ROWLAND A 40 BLA B
MAZINGLE EWD A 29 FA1 W
MAZINGO GREENE A 35 WOL W
MAZINGO W A 29 LOC W
MAZINGO WILEY A 29 BLA X
MCADAMS J R A 46 JAM W
MCADAMS RICHARD A 46 JAM W
MCADAMS WILLIAM A 46 HIG W
MCADAMS WM A 28 04B B
MCADDEN ADISON A 44 OXF B
MCADOO ALBERT M A 46 GRE W
MCADOO ALFRED A 46 GRE B
MCADOO BOSTON A 46 GRE B
MCADOO CALVIN A 46 GRE W
MCADOO CARTER A 46 SUM B
MCADOO GABRIEL A 46 GRE B
MCADOO HENRY A 46 GRE B
MCADOO JAMES A 46 GRE B
MCADOO JOHN A 46 GRE W
MCADOO JOHN L A 46 GRE W
MCADOO JOHN W A 46 GRE B
MCADOO KING A 46 GRE B
MCADOO MADISON A 46 GRE B
MCADOO MILTON A 46 GRE B
MCADOO MONROE A 46 GRE B
MCADOO ORPHEUS A 46 GRE B
MCADOO PLEASANT A 46 GRE W
MCADOO ROBT A 46 GRE B
MCADOO TATE A 46 GRE B
MCADOO VIC C A 46 GRE W
MCADOO WALTER D A 46 GRE W
MCADOO WEBSTER A 46 GRE B
MCADOO WM DAVIS A 46 GRE B

MCAFEE A A A 26 SHE W
MCAFEE LEE M A 26 SHE W
MCAIN ALBERT A 40 RHY B
MCALESTER W H A 29 FLE B
MCALISTER ELISHA A 40 DA1 W
MCALISTER GEORGE W R 40 DA1 W
NAME LINED OUT
CHAL CAUSES: JUSTICE OF
THE PEACE BEFORE THE
REBELLION & ENGAGED IN
INSURRECTION OR REBELLIONN
OR GAVE AID OR COMFORT
TO THE ENEMY. REJECTED
MCALISTER HERVEY C A 40 DA1 W
CERT ISSUED APRIL 11
1867 TO CABARRUS CO NC
MCALISTER JAS A 29 FA1 W
FLEA HILL
MCALISTER LEE A A 26 SHE W
MCALLESTER C A 29 FLE W
MCALLESTER GUSS A 29 FLE B
MCALLESTER HECTOR A 29 FLE W
MCALLESTER HENRY A 29 FLE B
MCALLESTER J A A 29 FLE W
REMOVED TO ROBESON
MCALLESTER JAMES A 29 FLE W
MCALLESTER RAFORD A 29 FLE B
MCALLESTER SOL A 29 FA2 B
COPIED FROM DUPLICATE
MCALLESTER W B A 29 FLE W
MCALLESTER WILLIS A 29 FLE B
MCALLESTER WM A 29 FLE B
MCALLISTER AMOS A 29 FA1 B
MCALLISTER CHAS A 29 FA1 B
MCALLISTER HENRY A 29 FA1 B
MCALLISTER ISAAC A 29 GRA B
MCALLISTER JAS A 29 FA1 B
MCALLISTER JAS SR A 29 FA1 B
MCALLISTER JESSEE A 29 FA1 B
MCALLISTER JNO A 29 FA1 B
MCALLISTER JOHN A 29 FA2 B
MCALLISTER NATHAN A 29 FA1 B
MCALLISTER RICHD A 29 FA2 B
MCALLISTER VIRGIL A 29 FA2 B
MCALLISTER WM H A 29 FA1 B
MCALLUM C H A 46 FRI W
MCALPIN M A 29 LOC W
MCARTHUR A W A 29 FA1 W
MCARTHUR ALEX A 29 GRA W
MCARTHUR ALEX A 29 ROC W
MCARTHUR BURTON A 29 FA1 B
MCARTHUR CALVIN A 35 LIM B
MCARTHUR DONALD A 29 FA1 W
MCARTHUR DUNCAN A 29 SEV W
MCARTHUR GEO A 29 FA1 B
MCARTHUR J A A 29 FA1 W
MCARTHUR JACOB A 29 FA1 B
MCARTHUR JASPER A 29 FA2 W
MCARTHUR JNO A 29 ROC W
MCARTHUR JNO D A 29 ROC W
DEP SHERIFF ALSO ACTED
AS SHERIFF SYMPATHIZED
WITH REBELS
MCARTHUR JOHN A A 35 KEN W
MCARTHUR JOHN F A 29 SEV W
MCARTHUR MALCOM A 29 CAR W
MCARTHUR NEILL A 29 ROC W
MCARTHUR PATRICK A 29 ROC W
MCARTHUR SIMON A 29 FA1 B
MCARTHUR SIMON A 29 FA2 B
MCAULLEY ANGUS M A 32 THO W
MCBRAYER A H A 26 MOO W
MCBRAYER CALVIN A 26 CAR B

MCBRAYER D B A 26 MOO W
MCBRAYER D O A 26 SHE W
MCBRAYER E A 26 SHE W
MILITIA OFFICER &
ENGAGED IN REBELLION
MCBRAYER R B A 26 MOO W
MCBRAYER R H A 26 SHE W
MILITIA OFFICER &
ENGAGED IN REBELLION
MCBRAYER ROBERT A 26 MOO W
MCBRAYER SAMUEL A 26 BUR W
MCBRAYER TOLIVER A 26 MOO B
MCBRAYRE EDWARD A 26 SHE B
MCBRIDE ANDREW A 32 TYR W
MCBRIDE JOSEPH C A 29 FA1 B
MCBRIDE ROBT A 29 SEV B
MCBRIDE THOMAS P A 32 TYR W
MCBRIDE WILLIAM A 32 TYR W
MCBRIDE WILLOUGHBY A 30 TUL W
MCBRYDE D D A 29 CAR W
MCCABE ALEXANDER A 37 TA1 W
MCCABE JAMES A 19 NEW W
MCCABE JNO B A 19 HAD W
MCCABE THOMAS A 19 NEW W
MCCABE WILLIAM A 53 SWA B
MCCADDEN JOSEPH A 44 YXS B
MCCAFFERTY JOHN A 28 11T W
MCCAFFERTY SOUTHY A 28 11T W
MCCAFFERTY THOMAS A 28 11T W
MCCALL A M A 40 CAN W
MCCALL ARCHIBALD A 29 SEV W
MCCALL D A 29 LOC W
MCCALL D JR A 29 LOC W
MCCALL DANIEL A 29 QUW W
MCCALL DUNCAN A 29 QUW W
DEAD
MCCALL HUGH A 29 ROC W
MCCALL HUGH A 29 SEV W
MCCALL JOHN A 29 SEV W
MCCALL JOHN D A 29 QUW W
MCCALL JOHN R A 29 ROC W
MCCALL WM B A 26 SHE W
MCCALL WM F A 26 SHE W
MCCALLAR JOHN H A 37 HIG W
MCCAMBS HENDERSON A 26 BLA B
MCCANE DAVID R 19 NEW W
MCCANE LEWIS A 19 NEW W
MCCANELLESS M J A 46 JAM W
MCCANN J B A 35 CYP W
MCCARTER C R A 40 SAN W
MCCARTER GREEN A 28 02N B
MCCARTER J A A 26 CAR W
MCCARVER FRANKLIN H A 40 DA1 W
MCCARVER HERVEY P A 40 DA1 W
MCCARVER J E A 40 SAN W
MCCASKILL DANIEL A 29 SEV W
MCCASKILL NORMAN A 29 SEV W
MCCASKILL W P A 29 SEV W
MCCAUCHADALE D A 29 BLA W
MCCAUCHADALE D A A 29 BLA W
MCCAUCHADALE J A 29 BLA W
MCCAUCHADALE JNO A 29 BLA W
MCCAUCHADALE JOEL A 29 BLA W
MCCAUSLY ABRAHAM A 19 HAD W
MCCEURY LOUIS A 26 PEE B
MCCHESNEY HENRY A 28 04A B
MCCHOLER GEORGE A 19 NEW B
MCCHURD JOHN A 26 WAR W
MCCHURD WADE A 26 WAR W
MCCITHAN SAML A 29 FLE B
MCCITHAN VIRGIL A 29 FLE B
MCCITHAN WILSON A 29 FLE B
MCCLAIN GEO A 29 LOC B

MCCLAIN HIRAM A 25 TUS W
MCCLAMB JNO A 29 FLE W
MCCLANAN BENJAMIN A 37 HIC A
MCCLANEN WM B A 30 CUR W
MCCLAREN ALEX A 29 FLE B
MCCLAREN D JR A 29 FLE W
MCCLAREN D SR A 29 FLE W
MCCLAREN DUNCAN JR A 29 FLE W
MCCLAREN JNO A 29 FLE B
MCCLARIN A A 29 LOC B
MCCLARIN H A 29 LOC B
MCCLARIN RICHD A 29 LOC B
MCCLARINE THOS A 29 LOC B
MCCLEASE JAMES A 30 IND B
MCCLEASE JOHN A 28 16T B
MCCLEESE EVERETT A 28 04A B
MCCLEESE HERMON A 30 ROA B
MCCLEESE JACOB A 28 03A B
MCCLEESE LEWIS A 28 05A B
MCCLEESE MARK A 28 04A B
MCCLEESE SILAS A 28 05A B
MCCLENAHAN S L R 44 KIT W
RES OF ST 8 MOS
MCCLENAN ARCH A 29 BLA W
MCCLENNDY J R A 24 EDE W
MCCLENTOCK GEORGE W A 46 GRE W
MCCLINNING KADER A 24 EDE W
MCCLINTOCK ABSALOM A 46 JAM B
MCCLINTOCK WM A 46 GRE W
MCCLORD ALEXANDER A 37 SHA B
MCCLOUD HIRAM G A 53 LA1 W
MCCLOUD J E A 29 LOC W
MCCLOUD JACKSON A 29 FA1 B
MCCLOUD JAMES C A 53 LA1 W
MCCLOUD JNO F A 29 ROC W
MCCLOUD M L A 29 LOC W
MCCLOUD T A 29 LOC W
MCCLUNG CHARLES R A 35 ROC W
MCCLURE ANDREW A 25 SHO W
MCCLURE BERMUDER A 40 STO W
MCCLURE HENRY A 28 9TH B
MCCLURE ISAAC B A 19 HAD B
MCCLURE J D A 25 SHO W
MCCLURE J J A 25 SHO W
MCCLURE J S A 25 SHO W
MCCLURE JACOB A 40 RHY B
MCCLURE JAMES M A 40 FER W
MCCLURE WILLIAM A 25 SHO W
MCCLURE WILLIAM C D A 40 FER W
MCCLURE WM A 40 STO W
MCCOLISTER A L A 40 SAN W
MCCOLLOUGH
CHRISTOPHER A 35 MAG B
MCCOMBER J W A 35 CYP W
MCCOMBS ANDREW A 26 SHE W
MCCOMBS GOVAN A 26 SWA B
MCCONNEL ANDY A 46 RAG B
MCCONNEL WM A 46 RAG B
MCCONNELL D N A 25 HAY W
MCCONNELL GEORGE W A 25 HAY W
MCCONNELL MILAS A 25 HAY W
MCCONNELL W J R A 25 PIN W
MCCONNELL W R A 25 HAY W
MCCONNELL WILLIAM A 25 HAY W
MCCORMICK DUNCAN A 29 CAR W
MCCORMICK HUGH A 29 CAR W
MCCOSLEY WILLIAM A 19 HAD W
MCCOTTER BENJAMIN A 28 16T W
MCCOTTER BIAS M A 28 15T B
MCCOTTER GEORGE A 28 15T B
MCCOTTER HEZEKIAH A 28 15T W
MCCOTTER JOHN R A 28 16T W
MCCOTTER JOSEPH A 28 15T W

MCCOTTER JOSEPH SR A 28 15T W
MCCOTTER RICHARD D A 28 15T W
MCCOTTER SAMUEL A 28 16T B
MCCOTTER THOMAS Y A 28 15T W
MCCOTTOR SAMUEL W A 28 16T B
MCCOY BENJAMIN A 28 8TH B
MCCOY C W A 28 8TH W
MCCOY FREDK A 28 03A W
MCCOY FREDRICK A 30 GIB W
MCCOY GAMBER A 29 FLE B
MCCOY GEO L A 29 FLE W
MCCOY ISAAC A 28 8TH B
MCCOY JAMES A 24 EDE W
MCCOY JOE A 28 8TH B
MCCOY JOHN A 28 8TH B
MCCOY JOHN W S A 28 6TH W
MCCOY JOS A 29 FLE B
MCCOY WRIGHT A 28 8TH B
MCCRACKEN P L A 25 SHO W
MCCRACKEN RICHD A 29 FA1 B
MCCRACKING THOMAS A 46 GRE W
MCCRANEY MALCOM A 29 MON W
MCCRANEY NEIL R A 29 MON W
MCCRANEY NEILL A 29 FA1 W
MCCRANEY WM J A 29 MON W
MCCRAW A B A 26 MOU W
MCCRAW ARMSTEAD A 44 FOR B
MCCRAW C A A 26 MOU W
MCCRAW CHESLY A 26 MOU W
MCCRAW FRANCIS A 44 HEN W
MCCRAW HENRY A 26 MOU B
MCCRAW J C A 26 MOU W
MCCRAW JOSIAH A 26 MOU W
MCCRAW ROBERT A 26 MOU W
MCCRAW W T A 44 HEN W
MCCRAY CHRISTOPHER A 28 04A B
MCCRAY THOS A 28 04A B
MCCREA ROBT A 29 FA1 B
MCCREARY ALEXANDER A 32 THO W
MCCREARY JOHN C A 32 POS W
MCCREEDY JAMES A 40 FER W
MCCREEDY JOHN A 40 FER W
MCCROSSON HUGH A 28 01A W
MCCRUM WILLIAM A 40 RHY B
MCCUISTAN JOHN F A 46 KIN W
MCCUISTAN W JAMES A 46 SUM W
MCCULLEM E A 29 FA2 W
MCCULLERS ABRAHAM A 99 BUS B
MCCULLERS MANGUM A 99 BUS B
MCCULLOCH MOSES A 28 04A B
MCCULLOCK CALVIN A 46 ROS W
MCCULLOCK DAVID H A 46 ROS W
MCCULLOCK HENRY A 37 WHI B
MCCULLOCK JOSEPH A 46 ROS W
MCCULLOM WILLIAM A 28 8TH B
MCCULLOUGH ALEX A 35 LIM B
MCCULLOUGH HUGH A 35 SMI B
MCCULLOUGH JOHN A 37 WHI B
MCCULLOUGH LOT A 35 FAI B
MCCURSTON W R A 32 COT W
MCCUTCHEON E H A 32 THO W
MCCUTCHIN JOSEPH A 37 ROB W
MCDAIRMID A A 29 FA2 W
MCDANIEL A A 29 LOC B
MCDANIEL AARON A 29 FA1 B
MCDANIEL ALEX A 29 FA1 B
MCDANIEL ALEXANDER A 29 SEV B
MCDANIEL AMAS A 29 LOC B
MCDANIEL BENJ A 29 FA1 B
MCDANIEL BENJAMIN A 29 FA1 B
MCDANIEL CUPID A 29 FA1 B
MCDANIEL DAVE A 29 LOC B
MCDANIEL DAVID A 37 ROC B

MCDANIEL DR A P A 46 MCL W
MCDANIEL ELISHA B A 40 FER W
MCDANIEL ISAAC A 29 SEV B
MCDANIEL ISHAM A 29 GRA B
MCDANIEL JAS A 29 FLE B
MCDANIEL JERRY A 29 LOC B
MCDANIEL JOSEPH A 40 SAN W
MCDANIEL L JR A 29 LOC W
MCDANIEL L SR A 29 LOC W
MCDANIEL M A 29 LOC B
MCDANIEL PETER A 29 FLE B
MCDANIEL PETER A 99 BUS B
MCDANIEL R A 44 HEN W
CERT TO VOTE IN COUNTY
MCDANIEL RICHD A 29 FA1 B
MCDANIEL ROBT A 29 LOC B
MCDANIEL ROBT 2ND A 29 LOC B
MCDANIEL THOS A 29 GRA B
MCDANIEL WALLIS A 40 SAN W
MCDANIEL WASN A 29 LOC B
MCDANIEL WILLIAM A 26 MOO W
MCDANIEL WILLIS A 29 GRA B
MCDANIEL WM A 29 FA1 B
MCDANIEL WM A 29 LOC B
MCDANIEL WM A 44 ISL W
MCDANIEL WM C A 29 FA2 W
MCDANIELS E F A 29 FA2 W
MCDERMITT DANL R 29 FA1 W
DID NOT TAKE THE OATH OF REGISTRATION HELD THE FOLLOWING OFFICES BEFORE THE WAR VIZ-MEMBER OF LEGISLATURE, MAGISTRATE, CLERK OF COUNTY COURT, MILLITIA OFFICER, & AFTERWARDS GAVE AID AND COMFORT TO THE REBELLION & AFTERWARDS WAS PARDONED BY HIS EXCELLENCY ANDREW JOHNSON UNDER THE $20,000 ACT--DESIRES HIS NAME ON BOOKS IS REJECTED
MCDERMOT WM A 28 02N W
MCDERMOTT A A 29 ROC W
MCDERMOTT ARCHY A 29 FA1 W
MCDIARMID D A A 29 SEV B
MCDONALD A C A 29 FA1 W
MCDONALD A J A 29 GRA W
MCDONALD D A 29 BLA W
MCDONALD D J A 29 SEV W
MCDONALD DANL M A 29 FA1 W
MCDONALD EDWD H A 29 ROC W
MCDONALD FRANK A 39 LOU W
MCDONALD GEO W A 29 FA1 W
MCDONALD ISAAC A 24 EDE B
CHALLENGED BY J R B HATHAWAY
REASON LARCENY
NO EVIDENCE AGAINST HIM
MCDONALD J R A 29 FA1 W
MILLITIA OFFICER AFTER-WARDS ENG IN REBELLION
MCDONALD J W A 29 FA1 W
MCDONALD JAMES A 29 SEV B
MCDONALD JAS A A 29 ROC W
MCDONALD JAS G A 29 ROC W
MCDONALD JERRY A 28 05B B
MCDONALD JERRY A 29 ROC B
MCDONALD JNO A 29 ROC W
MCDONALD JNO H A 29 ROC W
COPIED FROM DUPLICATE
MCDONALD JNO T A 29 ROC W
MCDONALD JOSEPH A 28 04A B
MCDONALD MALCOM A 29 SEV W

MCDONALD MUSTOPHER A 24 EDE B
MCDONALD N M A 29 ROC W
MCDONALD NEILL A 29 ROC W
MCDONALD PHILLIP A 24 EDE B
MCDONALD ROBT A 29 FA1 B
MCDONALD SMICK A 29 FA1 W
MCDONALD THOS A 29 FA1 W
MCDONALD THOS A 29 FA1 W
MCDONALD THOS A 46 GRE W
MCDONALD W J A 29 FA1 W
MCDONALD WILLIAM A 32 SHE W
MCDONALD WM A 29 CED B
MCDONALD WM A 29 FA1 B
MCDONALD WM O A 29 GRA W
MCDONOLD GIFFORD A 29 FLE B
MCDONOLD J A 29 LOC W
MCDONOLD JAS A 29 LOC W
MCDONOLD JNO A 29 LOC W
MCDONOLD L JR A 29 LOC W
MCDOO RUFUS A 28 01A B
MCDOUGAL ABRM A 29 CAR B
MCDOUGAL ALEX A 29 FA1 B
MCDOUGAL ANTHONY A 29 FA1 B
MCDOUGAL SALTER A 28 01A B
MCDOUGALD ALLEN A 29 QUW W
MCDOUGLAD ALEXANDER A 29 SEV W
MCDOWEL DANIEL A 40 RHY B
MCDOWELL ABRAM A 40 CAN B
MCDOWELL DRED A 37 TA1 B
MCDOWELL EDWIN A 37 HIG B
MCDOWELL HARRY A 40 CAN B
MCDOWELL HENDERSON R 40 CAN B
CHALLENGED REJ
NOT 21 YEARS OF AGE
MCDOWELL JERRY A 37 EDW B
MCDOWELL JNO B R 24 EDE W
REJECTED BY THE BOARD
ON REVISION BECAUSE
HE WAS CONSTABLE BE-
FORE THE WAR AND ENGAGED
IN THE REBELLION. FINAL
REVISION
MCDOWELL JOHN A 37 ROB B
MCDOWELL NED A 37 EDW B
MCDOWELL STEPHEN A 37 EDW B
MCDOWELL WILLIAM A 37 HOL W
MCDUFFIE ALEXANDER A 29 QUW W
MCDUFFIE ALEXANDER A 29 SEV W
MCDUFFIE ARCHD A 29 SEV W
MCDUFFIE ARCHIBALD A 29 SEV W
MCDUFFIE DANID G A 29 SEV W
MCDUFFIE DAVID A 29 FA1 W
MCDUFFIE DOUGALD A 29 SEV W
MCDUFFIE DUNCAN K A 29 QUW W
MCDUFFIE GILBERT A 29 SEV W
MCDUFFIE JAMES R A 29 SEV W
MCDUFFIE JNO A 29 FA2 B
MCDUFFIE MORRIS A 29 FA1 B
MCDUFFIE PETER A A 29 SEV W
MCDUFFIE W C A 29 FA1 W
MCDUGAL WM A 29 FLE W
MCDUGALD HUGH A 29 SEV W
MCDUGALD J Q A 29 SEV W
MCDUGALD NEILL R 29 FLE W
MILITIA OFFICER BEFORE
WAR DISTRICT ASSESSOR
BEFORE & DURING THE
WAR HUNTED DESERTERS
MCELVAIN DAVID A 53 LA2 B
MCENTIRE B A 26 SHE W
MCENTIRE C W A 25 SHO W
MCENTIRE HILLRY A 26 SHE B
MCENTIRE J J A 26 SHE W
MCENTIRE M M A 26 BUR W
MCENTIRE M O A 26 BUR W
MCENTIRE PATRICK A 40 STO W
MCENTIRE WILLIAM A 26 BUR W
MCENTOUCH ISAAC A 40 CAN W
MCFADDEN ABRM A 29 FA1 B
MCFADDEN JOHN A A 29 FA1 W
MCFADDEN R M A 29 FA1 B
MCFADYEN ARCHY A 29 ROC W
MCFAIL ARNOLD A 29 FLE B
MCFAIL STEPHEN A 29 FLE B
MCFAIL WM C A 29 FLE W
MCFALLS N M A 25 TUS W
MCFARLAND ROBERT A 28 02N B
MCFARLAND ROBT A 28 05B B
MCFARLAND WILLIAM A 35 CYP B
MCFARLAND YANCY A 46 FRI W
MCFARLANE JOHN A 46 FRI W
MCFARLING WM A 32 THO W
MCFAYDEN D A 29 SEV W
MCFAYDEN NEILL A 29 ROC W
MCFERSON ANDREW A 30 MOY W
MCGEE BALAAM A 35 KEN B
MCGEE BENJ A 28 03A B
MCGEE BURRIS A 35 KEN B
MCGEE CHARLES A 35 KEN B
MCGEE FRANKLIN A 44 OXF B
MCGEE GEORGE A 46 JAM W
MCGEE HENRY A 46 ROS B
MCGEE JAMES A 25 HAY W
MCGEE JAMES A 37 ROC B
MCGEE JAMES A 40 RHY B
MCGEE JAMES W A 35 MAG W
MCGEE JOSEPH B A 40 DA1 W
MCGEE RICHARD A 35 KEN B
MCGEE ROBERT A 35 KEN B
MCGEE SILAS A 35 KEN B
MCGEE THOMAS A 35 KEN B
MCGEE THOMAS H A 35 KEN W
MCGEEHEE
G WASHINGTON A 44 KNA W
MCGEEHEE THOS A 39 DAV W
TRNS FROM GRANVILLE CO
BRASSFIELD PRE
MCGEHEE J Y A 44 FOR W
MCGEHEE JAMES A 44 BRA B
MCGEHEE JAMES A 46 JAM W
MCGEHEE JOSEPH A 44 BRA W
MCGEHEE MILES A 46 JAM W
MCGEHEE OLIVER A 44 BRA B
MCGHEE J B A 44 FOR W
MCGHEE J C A 39 FRA W
MCGHEE L P A 44 FOR W
MCGHEE N W A 46 HIG W
MCGHEE OZIAS A 46 JAM W
MCGHEE SHEM A 44 FOR W
MCGHEE THOMAS A 44 FOR W
MCGHEE W H A 39 FRA W
MCGHEEHE NATHAN A 44 FOR W
MCGHEHEE BANKS A 44 LED W
MCGHEHEE JOSIAH A 44 LED W
MCGHEHEE ZACHARIAH A 44 LED W
MCGIBANY ANDREW A 46 MON B
MCGIBANY CARTER A 46 MON B
MCGIBANY JOSEPH A 46 MON B
MCGILL A D A 29 SEV W
MCGILL ALEXANDER A 40 RHY B
MCGILL DANIEL A 29 MON W
MCGILL DANIEL K A 29 SEV W
MCGILL DUNCAN A 29 SEV W
MCGILL HENRY A 29 MON B
MCGILL J A 26 BOR W
MCGILL NATHAN A 40 DA1 B
MCGILL NEILL A 29 SEV W
MCGILL THOMAS J A 40 DEC W
MCGILL TONY A 26 BOR B
MCGILL WILLIAM A 28 04B B
MCGILL WILSON A 29 FA2 B
MCGILVERY JNO H A 29 FA1 W
MCGILVRY JAMES A 29 FA1 W
MCGINES J W A 26 MOU W
MCGINIS JAMES A 26 MOU W
MCGINIS O J A 26 MOU W
MCGINIS RICHARD A 26 MOO W
MCGINNAS FRANK S A 40 DEC W
MCGINNAS FRANKLING A 40 RHY B
MCGINNAS JOHN J A 40 BLA W
MCGINNAS JOHN M A 40 BLA W
MCGINNAS NATHAN A 40 BLA W
MCGINNIS CHARLES C A 40 DEC W
MCGINNUS B C A 40 STO W
MCGLAMMERY ANDREW A 26 PEE W
MCGOUGAN AMOS A 29 FA1 B
MCGOUGAN D R A 29 QUW W
MCGOWAN ALEXANDER D A 35 KEN W
MCGOWAN BENJAMIN F A 35 KEN B
MCGOWAN DAVID C A 35 KEN W
MCGOWAN FOSTER J A 53 LA1 W
MCGOWAN GEORGE A 35 KEN B
MCGOWAN GEORGE A 35 KEN W
MCGOWAN JAMES W A 53 LA2 W
MCGOWAN JOHN A 35 KEN B
MCGOWAN JOHN J A 53 SWA W
MCGOWAN LEVI A 53 SWA W
MCGOWAN SYLVESTER A 53 SWA W
POLITICAL DISABILITIES
REMOVED
MCGOWAN THOMAS A 35 KEN B
MCGOWAN THOMAS A 35 KEN B
MCGOWAN WILLIAM A 35 KEN W
MCGOWAN WILLIAM W A 35 KEN W
MCGOWAN WILLIAM Y A 53 SWA W
MCGOWEN HENRY A 35 WAR B
MCGOWEN JAMES H A 35 KEN W
MCGOWEN JOHN Q A 35 KEN W
MCGOWEN MILO A 35 KEN B
MCGOWEN ROBERT A 35 KEN B
MCGREGOR JAMES A 28 02N W
MCGREGOR NATHAN A 29 SEV B
MCGRIDER HENRY A 40 DA1 B
MCGRIGOR A B A 39 FRE W
MCGUGAN JOHN C A 29 SEV W
MCGUGAN NEILL A 29 QUW W
MCGUGAN ROBT A 29 FA1 B
MCGUIRE D A 29 FA1 W
MCGUIRE FRANK A 29 FA1 B
MCGUIRE JAMES A 29 GRA B
MCGUIRE JOHN A 24 EDE W
MCGUIRE STEPHEN A 29 GRA B
MCHEAR WILLIAM T A 37 HIG W
MCHORNEY EDMUND A 30 COI W
MCHORNEY JAMES A 30 CUR W
MCHORNEY SAMUEL A 30 COI W
MCHORNEY THOMAS A 30 NAR W
MCHORNY MANLOFF A 30 POP W
MCHORNY NOAH A 30 POP W
MCILWAIN JNO S A 29 ROC W
MCILWAINE JACOB A 28 01B B
MCILWEAN FRANCIS J A 28 6TH W
MCINNES MALCOM A 29 ROC W
MCINNIS DANIEL A 29 SEV W
MCINNY DEMPSEY A 46 SUM W
MCINTIRE D A 29 FLE W
MCINTIRE DAVID M A 35 KEN W
MCINTIRE JOHN A 28 10T B
MCINTIRE R A 26 BLA W

MCINTIRE WILLIAM A 26 BLA W
MCINTOSH C R A 30 IND W
MCINTOSH CALVIN A 28 13T W
MCINTOSH FURNEY A 28 12T W
MCINTOSH HENRY A 28 6TH W
MCINTOSH ISAAC A 29 FA1 B
MCINTOSH J R A 29 FA1 W
MCINTOSH MONROE A 29 FA1 B
MCINTOSH R H A 30 IND W
MCINTRYE HENRY A 29 FA1 B
MCINTRYE SOL A 29 FA1 B
MCINTYRE D A 29 BLA W
MCINTYRE GASTON C A 35 KEN W
MCINTYRE HENRY A 29 SEV B
MCINTYRE MALCOM A 29 BLA W
MCINTYRE MALCOM A 29 QUW W
MCINTYRE WM A 29 FA1 W
MCIVA ISHAM A 29 FA1 B
MCIVEN BENJ A 29 FA1 B
MCIVER HENRY A 35 KEN B
MCIVER KING A 46 GRE B
MCIVOR YANCEY A 46 HIG B
MCKABE JACOB A 28 10T B
MCKABE SCIPIO A 28 10T B
MCKALL NEILL A 29 SEV W
MCKANE OSCAR A 37 TA1 B
MCKARNE A A 32 LOF W
MCKARNE ALEXANDER A 32 COT W
MCKARNE G W A 32 COT W
MCKARNE MICHAEL A 32 COT W
MCKARNS JOHN U A 32 COT W
MCKASKILL DANIEL A 29 QUW W
MCKAUGHAN A G A 46 HIG W
MCKAY ALEXANDER A 29 FA1 B
MCKAY ANDREW A 29 SEV B
MCKAY ARCHY A 29 FA1 W
MCKAY BENJAMIN A 29 SEV B
MCKAY BUFF A 29 FA1 B
MCKAY C W A 29 FA1 W
MCKAY CHAS A 29 FA1 B
MCKAY DANIEL A 29 FA1 B
MCKAY EDWD A 29 FA1 B
MCKAY G A A 26 GOF W
MCKAY GEO A A 29 CAR W
MCKAY GILBERT A 29 SEV W
MCKAY HECTOR A 29 FA1 B
MCKAY JAMES A 29 ROC B
MCKAY JAMES A 29 SEV B
MCKAY JAMES A 29 SEV B
MCKAY JAS A 29 FA1 B
MCKAY JNO A 29 FA1 B
MCKAY JNO ALEX A 29 FA1 W
MCKAY JNO M A 29 FA1 W
MCKAY JNO T A 29 FA1 W
MILLITIA OFFICER AFTER-
WARDS ENG IN REBELLION
MCKAY JOHN A 29 FA1 B
MCKAY JOHN A 29 SEV B
MCKAY JULIOUS A 53 FAI B
MCKAY NATHANIEL A 29 SEV B
MCKAY PETER A 29 SEV B
MCKAY ROBT A 29 SEV B
MCKAY ROBT A A 29 SEV B
MCKAY SOL A 29 FA1 B
MCKAY THOMAS A 29 SEV B
MCKAY THOMAS A 29 SEV B
MCKAY WM A 29 FA1 B
MCKAY WM H A 29 ROC W
MCKAY WM M A 29 FA1 W
MCKEE G O A 40 SAN W
MCKEE G W A 40 STO W
MCKEE JAMES E A 40 DEC W
MCKEE L L A 40 STO W
MCKEE P C A 26 SHE W
MCKEE W S A 40 STO W
MCKEE WILLIAM A 40 STO W
MCKEE WILLIAM D A 40 DA1 B
MCKEEL ABSALOM A 46 GIB W
MCKEEVER EDWARD M A 35 KEN B
MCKEEVER JAMES A 35 KEN B
MCKEEVER JOHN A 35 KEN B
MCKEEVER JOHN A 44 OXF B
MCKEEVER SOLOMAN R 44 OXF B
RES 8 MOS REJ
MCKEITHEN DAVID A 28 11T W
MCKELLAM JOHN A 29 SEV W
MCKELLER EDWARD A 29 ROC B
MCKELLER ISAAC A 29 GRA B
MCKELLER NED A 29 GRA B
MCKELLER STEPHEN A 29 GRA B
MCKELLER STEWARD A 29 FA2 B
MCKELLER THOMAS A 29 FA1 B
MCKENZIE ELIJAH A 46 SUM B
MCKENZIE HENRY A 29 SEV B
MCKENZIE LOFTON A 29 FA1 B
MCKETHAN A A R 29 FA1 W
SUPT OF MILLITIA AFTER-
WARDS AIDED REBELLION
COUNTY ASSESSOR 1859
MCKETHAN A A JR A 29 FA2 W
MCKETHAN ALEX A 29 FA1 W
OF 71ST DIST
WAS DEPT SHERIFF 1850
D C MUNROE
MCKETHAN D B A 29 MON W
MCKETHAN DANIEL J A 35 KEN W
MCKETHAN E F A 29 FA1 W
MCKETHAN ELIJAH A 29 MON B
MCKETHAN H A 29 FA1 W
MCKETHAN HECTOR A 29 FA1 W
MCKETHAN JOHN G A 29 SEV W
MCKETHAN JOSEPH A 29 SEV B
MCKETHAN PETER A 29 QUW B
MCKETHEN DAVID A 29 BLA X
MCKETHEN PHILLIP A 29 FA1 B
MCKETHIN ALLEN A 29 BLA X
MCKEVER JORDAN A 44 OXF B
MCKIMEY THOMAS A 30 NOR W
MCKIMMEY JAMES A 35 WOL W
MCKIMMON DUNCAN A 29 FA1 W
MCKIMMON SAMUAL A 29 MON B
MCKINEY BENJAMIN A 53 FAI W
MCKINEY JESSE A 53 FAI W
MCKINEY NATHANIEL M A 53 FAI W
MCKINEY ROBERT A 53 FAI W
MCKINEY THOMAS A 53 LA1 W
MCKINNEY GEORGE R A 53 FAI W
MCKINNEY JAMES A 26 MOO W
MCKINNEY W B A 26 CAR W
MCKINNEY WILLIAM B A 53 LA1 W
MCKINNON DANL A 29 CAR W
MCKINNON HECTOR A 29 GRA B
MCKINNON HECTOR A 29 ROC B
MCKINNON JERIMIAH A 29 SEV B
MCKINNON MURDOC A 29 FA1 W
TOWN COMMISSIONER AFTER-
WARDS AIDED REBELLION
MCKINNON WM H A 29 FA1 W
MCKINSEY EDWARD A 46 GRE B
MCKINSEY ROBERT A 28 16T B
MCKINZIE WALKER A 35 CYP B
MCKITHAN JNO W R 29 FLE W
POSTMASTER BEFORE THE
WAR ENGAGED IN REBELION
(WORD EROR APPEARS, ALL
OTHER WORDS STRUCK THROUGH)
MCKNIGHT ALFRED G A 46 GRE B
MCKNIGHT BIAS A 39 FRA B
MCKNIGHT DAVID A 46 GRE W
WAS OVERSEER OF HIGHWAY
BEFORE WARE AFTERWARD
SOLD HORSES TO CON. OF-
FICERS, WHICH HE THINKS
WAS AID
MCKNIGHT EDWARD A 39 FRA B
MCKNIGHT
GENERAL TAYLOR A 39 LOU B
MCKNIGHT H A 39 FRA B
MCKNIGHT H C A 39 FRA B
MCKNIGHT HENRY A 39 FRA B
MCKNIGHT ISHAM A 39 FRA B
MCKNIGHT J M A 40 STO W
MCKNIGHT JERRY A 39 FRA B
MCKNIGHT JOHN A 39 FRA B
MCKNIGHT JOHN A 46 GRE W
MCKNIGHT JOS A 39 FRA B
MCKNIGHT JULY A 39 FRA B
MCKNIGHT LEWIS HENRYA 39 LOU B
MCKNIGHT MAT A 39 FRA B
MCKNIGHT REUBEN A 39 FRA B
MCKNIGHT ROBT A 39 FRA B
MCKNIGHT SAMUEL A 39 FRA B
MCKNIGHT SOL A 39 FRA B
MCKOY GEORGE A 29 FA2 B
MCKOY JAMES A 29 FA2 W
MCL PATTERSON A ? A 29 ROC W
MCLACHLIN ALEX A 28 02N W
MCLAIN ARCHD A 29 ROC W
MILLITIE OFFICER HELPED
TO TAKE FAYETTE ARSENAL
IN 1861
MCLAIN ARCHIBALD R 29 FA1 W
DID NOT TAKE OATH OF
REGISTRATION HELD THE
FOLLOWING OFFICES BEFORE
THE WAR CLERK OF COURT,
TOWN COMMISSIONER, MIL-
LITIA OFFICER, MAYOR OF
TOWN &C &C AFTERWARDS
AIDED AND COMFORTED THE
REBELLION DESIRES HIS
NAME PLACED ON THE BOOKS
MCLAIN CUPID A 29 FA1 B
MCLAIN D M A 29 FA1 W
REMOVED TO RANDOLPH CO
MCLAIN GEO A 29 CAR B
MCLAIN GEO A 29 FA1 B
MCLAIN HENERY A 29 FA1 B
MCLAIN HENRY A 29 FA1 B
MCLAIN HENRY A 29 FA1 B
MCLAIN JACK A 29 FA1 B
MCLAIN JACOB A 29 FA1 B
MCLAIN JAMES A 29 FA1 B
MCLAIN JEFFERSON A 29 FA1 B
MCLAIN JNO A 29 CAR B
MCLAIN JNO A A 29 FA1 W
MCLAIN OWEN A 29 FA1 B
MCLAIN WILSON A 29 FA1 B
MCLAIN WILSON A 29 FA1 B
MCLAMB WILEY A 29 FLE W
MCLAMORE REDON A 29 ROC W
MCLANAHAN ALEX A 44 OXF B
MCLANAHAN
ALEXANDER J A 40 MAU W
MCLANE CHARLES A 99 BUS B
MCLANE DOCTOR A 99 BUS B
MCLANE JARET A 99 BUS B
MCLANE W R A 40 STO W
MCLAUCHLEIN A N A 29 GRA W

MCLAUCHLIN DAVID A 29 ROC B
MCLAUCHLIN DUGALD A 29 MON W
MILITIA OFF BEFORE
THE REBELLION
MCLAUCHLIN ISAAC A 29 GRA B
MCLAUCHLIN J W A 29 CAR W
MCLAUGHIN ROBERT J A 40 DA1 W
MCLAUGHLEN JOE A 29 FA1 B
MCLAUGHLIN ALEX A 29 FA1 B
MCLAUGHLIN ALEX A 29 FA1 W
MCLAUGHLIN ALEX A 29 GRA B
MCLAUGHLIN ARCHY 29 FA1 W
MCLAUGHLIN HANDY A 29 FA1 B
MCLAUGHLIN ISAAC A 29 FA1 B
MCLAUGHLIN JA A 29 FA1 W
MILLITIA OFFICER AFTER-
WARDS ENG IN REBELLION
MCLAUGHLIN M MCR A 29 SEV W
REMOVED TO HARNETT CO
STUART CREEK
CERTIFICATE GIVEN
MCLAUGHLIN NEILL A 29 FA1 W
MCLAUGHLIN W C A 29 CAR W
MCLAUGHLIN WM A 29 SEV W
MCLAUREN D A 29 LOC W
MCLAUREN GEO A 29 FA1 B
MCLAUREN JNO A A 29 FLE W
MCLAURIN DUNCAN A 29 FA1 W
MILLITIA OFFICER AFTER-
WARDS ENG IN REBELLION
MCLAURIN GEO A 29 FA1 B
MCLAURIN J W A 29 FLE W
MCLAURIN MOSES A 29 FA1 B
MCLEAN ALFRED A 28 7TH B
MCLEAN ANDERSON A 46 GRE B
MCLEAN ANGS A 29 ROC W
MCLEAN ANTHONY A 40 SAN B
MCLEAN ANTHONY A 40 STO B
MCLEAN BEDFORD A 46 GRE B
MCLEAN C W A 28 01B W
MCLEAN D H A 29 FA2 W
MCLEAN DANIEL A 29 SEV B
MCLEAN ESSICK A 46 MCL B
MCLEAN FOUNTAIN B A 46 MCL W
MCLEAN G W A 26 GOF B
MCLEAN GEORG WM A 46 MCL B
MCLEAN GUSTUS A 40 SAN B
MCLEAN ISAAC A 29 SEV B
MCLEAN ISAAC HENRY A 46 MCL B
MCLEAN J C A 29 QUW W
COUNTY ASSESSOR
MCLEAN J D A 40 STO W
MCLEAN J J A 25 TUS W
MCLEAN J L A 40 STO W
MCLEAN JAMES A 46 MCL W
MCLEAN JAMES H A 29 ROC B
MCLEAN JAMES H A 29 SEV B
MCLEAN JESSE R A 46 GRE W
MCLEAN JOHN A 46 GRE B
MCLEAN JOHN R 46 MCL W
WAS A MAGISTRATE BEFORE
THE WARE AND DURING THE
REBELLION ACTED AS A MAG
ISTRATE THO HE SAID HE
GAVE NO AID. TWO OF HIS
NEIGHBOURS QUALIFIED,
STATED THEY DO NOT KNOW
OF HIS HAVING AIDED THE
REBELLION ONE STATED HE
SWORE IN SOULDIERS. REJ
MCLEAN JOHN C A 40 STO W
MCLEAN JOHN D JUNIORA 40 STO W
MCLEAN JOHN M A 46 MCL W

MCLEAN JOSEPH A A 46 MCL W
MCLEAN JOSEPH M A 46 MCL W
MCLEAN JULES G A 40 STO B
MCLEAN KUMOS A 29 MON B
MCLEAN LOGAN J A 40 DA1 W
CERTIFICATE ISSUED
APRIL 10 1868 TO 1ST REG
PRECINCT GASTON CO NC
MCLEAN MILES A 40 STO B
MCLEAN R G A 40 STO W
MCLEAN ROBERT S A 72 SWA W
MCLEAN ROBT B A 46 GRE W
MCLEAN SAMUEL D A 46 MCL W
MCLEAN SANDY A 29 FA2 B
MCLEAN SIMON A 29 SEV B
MCLEAN STANHOPE A 40 CAN B
MCLEAN THOMAS G A 46 MCL W
MCLEAN THOS A 29 MON B
MCLEAN THOS H A 29 FA2 W
MCLEAN WM A A 29 ROC W
MCLEAN WM R R 40 STO W
CHALLENGED AND REJECTED
WAS A MALITIA OFFICIER
BEFORE THE WAR
MCLEARY WILSON A 40 DA1 B
MCLELLERAN C C A 29 BLA W
MCLENAHAN RICHMOND A 44 OXF B
MCLENAN GEORGE A 29 MON B
MCLENEY BANJAMIN A 39 LOU B
MCLENLEN ARCHD A 29 BLA W
MCLEOD A D A 29 QUW W
MCLEOD ARCHD A 29 QUW W
MCLEOD HENRY A 29 SEV B
MCLEOD JOHN A 29 FA2 W
SEE QUIWHIFFLE BOOK
MCLEOD JOHN O A 29 QUW W
MCLEOD KENNEY A 29 QUW B
MCLEOD LAUCHLIN A 29 QUW W
MCLEOD NEILL A 29 QUW W
MCLEOD NELSON A 29 SEV B
MCLEON ARCHY A 29 ROC W
MCLESSE FREDRICK A 53 LA1 B
MCLIN HENRY A 28 02N W
MCLIN JOHN A 30 MOY W
8-MONTH-RESIDENT
MCLOUD ALFRED A 29 FA2 B
MCLOUD MATTHIAS A 53 LA1 B
MCLURD R L A 40 RHY W
MCLURE J M A 25 HAY W
MCLURE JASON A 25 TUS W
MCLURE JV A 25 HAY W
MCLURE L H A 25 HAY W
MCLURE W H A 25 HAY W
MCLURE W S A 25 TUS W
MCLVAIN FREDRICK A 53 SWA B
MCMANIE PETER F A 44 HEN W
MCMARY JAMES G W A 46 GRE W
MCMASTERS ALLEN A 46 ROS B
MCMASTERS JNO E A 29 FA1 W
MCMASTERS WILEY A 46 RAG B
MCMELEON ROBERT A 29 ROC B
COPIED FROM DUPLICATE
MCMICHAEL ARCHIBALD A 46 SUM W
MCMICHAEL GREEN A 46 GRE B
MCMICHAEL JESSE A 46 SUM W
MCMICHAEL OBADIAH A 46 SUM W
MCMILLAN AARON A 35 ISL B
MCMILLAN ABERDEEN A 28 9TH B
MCMILLAN ABRAM A 35 ISL B
MCMILLAN ALEXANDER A 29 SEV B
MCMILLAN ALFRED A 29 GRA B
MCMILLAN ARCHD A 29 QUW W
MCMILLAN BASS A 29 FLE B

MCMILLAN BLUNT A 29 GRA B
MCMILLAN BRYANT A 35 ISL B
CERTIF GIVEN APRIL 16,
1868 TO NEW HANOVER CO
MCMILLAN DANIEL T A 35 MAG W
MCMILLAN DEAN A 29 FA1 B
MCMILLAN FRANCIS D A 29 GRA W
MCMILLAN FRANK A 35 ROC B
MCMILLAN GEO A 29 GRA B
MCMILLAN H A 29 FA1 W
MCMILLAN HAMILTON A 29 FA2 W
MCMILLAN JAMES A 35 ISL B
MCMILLAN JOHN A 35 ISL B
MCMILLAN JOHN A A 29 MON W
MCMILLAN JOHN C A 35 ISL W
MCMILLAN JOHN H A 35 ISL W
MCMILLAN LEWIS A 29 FA1 B
MCMILLAN M A 29 LOC W
MCMILLAN MORRIS A 35 ISL B
MCMILLAN OWEN A 35 ISL B
MCMILLAN PETER A 29 FA1 B
MCMILLAN SALTER A 35 ISL B
MCMILLAN THOS A 29 LOC B
MCMILLAN TONEY A 35 ISL B
MCMILLEN C B A 29 FA2 W
MCMILLEN CHAS A A 29 FA2 W
MCMILLEN D A A 29 FLE W
MCMILLEN GEO A 29 ROC B
MCMILLEN ISAAC A 29 GRA B
MCMILLEN ISAIAH A 19 BE2 B
MCMILLEN LEWIS A 29 LOC B
MCMILLEN LOUIS A 29 FA2 B
MCMILLEN MILES A 29 GRA B
MCMILLEN N A 29 FLE W
MCMILLEN S N A 29 FLE W
MCMILLIAN DANL A 29 FLE W
MCMILLIAN EDGAR L A 35 ISL B
MCMILLIN D A 29 LOC W
MCMILLIN PETER A 29 CED B
MCMULIN CARRIE A 19 NEW B
CERT TO HADNOT CREEK
MCMURRAY B Y A 26 GRI W
MCMURRAY GEORGE A 46 GRE B
MCMURRAY ISAAC A 46 GRE B
MCMURRAY J W A 26 GRI W
MCMURRY J G A 46 GRE W
MCMURRY J W A 46 GRE W
MCMURRY JOHN W A 26 SHE W
MCMURRY WM A 46 SUM W
MCNAIR AMZI A 40 DA1 B
MCNAIR JAMES A 40 FER W
MCNAIR MARK A 29 GRA B
MCNAIR NEIL A 29 GRA B
MCNAIR TIMON A 29 GRA B
MCNAIR TURNER A 29 GRA B
MCNAIR WM A 29 ROC B
MCNAIRY WASHINGTON A 46 HIG B
MCNAIRY WYATT H A 46 RAG W
MCNAMARA MARTIN J A 28 01A W
MCNATT WM A 29 CED W
MCNEAL ALEX R 29 BLA W
AFTER REGISTERING, OPENLY
PROCLAIMS HIMSELF SECES-
SIONISH WITNESSES ARE
RANDERSON SIMMONS
AND JAS MURPHY
MCNEAL DUBLIN A 29 FLE B
MCNEAL JOHN A 19 NEW B
MCNEAL LOTT A 29 CED B
MCNEAL N A 29 CED B
MCNEAL STEPHEN A 29 FLE B
MCNEAL THOS A 28 04A B
MCNEED JESSIE A 37 HIC B

MCNEED OTTER A 37 HIC B
MCNEEL ALEXANDER A 29 SEV B
MCNEELEY HENRY A 46 GRE B
MCNEIL ALEXANDER A 29 MON B
MCNEIL GIBBS A 29 SEV B
MCNEIL JOHN D A 29 SEV W
MCNEIL RICHARD A 29 FA1 B
MCNEIL SANDY A 29 FA1 B
MCNEIL STEPHEN A 29 MON B
MCNEILL AARON A 29 ROC B
MCNEILL ADAM A 29 FA1 B
MCNEILL ALLEN A 29 GRA B
MCNEILL ALX A 29 ROC W
MCNEILL ALX B A 29 ROC W
MCNEILL AUGUSTA A 29 QUW B
MCNEILL CALVIN A 29 FA1 B
MCNEILL CATO A 29 CAR B
MCNEILL D J A 29 ROC W
MCNEILL DAVID A 29 CAR B
MCNEILL DAVID A 29 FA1 B
MCNEILL DUBLIN A 29 CAR B
MCNEILL FRANK A 29 CAR B
MCNEILL GEO A 29 CAR B
MCNEILL H C A 29 FA1 B
MCNEILL JAMES A 29 MON B
MCNEILL JAS R A 29 FA1 B
MCNEILL JNO A 29 FA1 B
MCNEILL JOHN A 29 ROC W
MCNEILL JOS A 29 FA1 B
MCNEILL LONDON A 29 QUW B
MCNEILL LOUIE A 29 QUW B
MCNEILL MACK A 29 GRA B
MCNEILL NEILL A 29 ROC W
MCNEILL RANDALL A 29 CAR B
MCNEILL RICHD A 29 CAR B
MCNEILL ROBERT A 29 ROC B
MCNEILL RUPERT A 29 FA1 B
MCNEILL SAML A 29 CAR B
MCNEILL VIRGIL A 29 ROC B
MCNEILLY A D A 26 PEE W
MCNEILLY J A 26 PEE W
MCNEILLY R W A 26 PEE W
MCNEILLY THOMAS A 26 PEE W
MCNEILLY W D A 26 PEE W
MCNEILY THOMAS A 46 GRE W
MCNIAL QUINCE A 29 FLE B
MCNICKLE ARMOR R 46 GRE W
WAS IN THE STATE SINCE
7TH 1 MO 1867
MCNILLIS CHARLES A 35 ISL W
MCOIN FAIRSTER A 46 FRI W
MCOIN J H A 46 FRI W
MCOLLUM SANDY A 29 FA1 B
MCPHAIL ALEXANDER A 29 SEV B
MCPHAIL CALEB A 29 FA1 B
MCPHAIL D A 29 BLA W
MCPHAIL D J A 29 FA1 W
MCPHAIL JOHN A 29 FLE W
MCPHAIL JOHN A 29 ROC W
MCPHAIL PHILLIP A 29 FA1 B
MCPHAIL W J A 29 FLE W
MCPHAIL WM C A 29 FA1 W
FLEA HILL
MCPHEARSON AMOS A 29 GRA B
MCPHERSON ADAM A 29 SEV B
MCPHERSON ALEX A 29 FA1 B
MCPHERSON ALEX A 46 RAG W
MCPHERSON ALEX SR A 29 FA1 W
MCPHERSON ALLEN A 29 ROC B
MCPHERSON BALTIMORE A 29 FA1 B
MCPHERSON DANIEL A 29 FA1 B
MCPHERSON DAVID A 29 FA1 B
MCPHERSON DAVID A 29 SEV B
MCPHERSON EDMUND A 29 FA1 B
MCPHERSON GOULD A 29 FA1 B
MCPHERSON GULLET A 29 FA1 B
MCPHERSON HENRY A 29 FA1 B
MCPHERSON HIRAM A 29 FA1 B
MCPHERSON HUGH A 29 FA1 W
MCPHERSON ISAAC A 29 FA1 B
MCPHERSON J A 29 FA1 B
MCPHERSON J A A 29 FA1 W
MCPHERSON J H A 29 FA1 W
MCPHERSON JACOB A 29 FA1 B
MCPHERSON JAMES A 29 SEV B
MCPHERSON JAMES D A 29 QUW W
MCPHERSON JNO A 29 FA1 B
MCPHERSON JNO Q A 29 FA1 W
MCPHERSON JOSEPH A 29 SEV B
MCPHERSON MILES A 30 MOY W
MCPHERSON MURDOCH A 29 QUW W
MCPHERSON P M A 29 FA1 B
MCPHERSON SANDY A 29 FA1 B
MCPHERSON TOBIAS A 29 FA1 B
MCPHERSON WILLIS A 29 FA1 B
MCPHERSON WM H A 29 FA1 W
MCQUEEN MARTIN A 29 QUW B
MCQUEEN NEILL A 29 FA1 W
MCQUEEN NEILL A 29 ROC W
MCQUEEN NEILL 2ND A 29 ROC W
MCQUEEN ROBT A 29 SEV B
MCQUEEN WM A 29 ROC W
MCRAE BENJAMIN A 29 SEV B
MCRAE COLIN A 29 SEV W
MCRAE FORTUNE A 29 ROC B
MCRAE GEO A 29 FA1 B
MCRAE JAMES C A 29 FA1 W
MCRAE JOHN A 29 QUW W
MCRAE LEWIS A 29 ROC B
MCRAE OLIVER A 29 QUW B
MCRAE PHILLIP A 29 QUW W
MCRAE RANDALL A 29 GRA B
MCRAE REUBEN A 28 9TH B
MCRAE TURNER A 28 9TH B
MCRAE TURTLE A 29 QUW B
MCRARY JOHN A 32 DAV W
MCRARY JOHN A 32 DAV W
MCRARY LEVI A 32 DAV W
MCRARY WILLIAM A 32 DAV W
MCRARY WILLIAM F A 32 DAV W
MCRAY RODRICK A 29 ROC B
MCREA JNO A 29 FA1 W
MCRIMMON RICHARD A 29 QUW B
MCROY ASA A 28 11T W
MCROY JOHN A 28 11T W
MCSWAIN A A A 26 MOO W
MCSWAIN ALFRED M A 29 FA1 B
MCSWAIN B B A 26 BUR W
MCSWAIN B F A 26 MOO W
MCSWAIN BERRYMAN A 26 MOO W
MCSWAIN BERRYMAN JR A 26 MOO W
MCSWAIN DAVID A 26 MOO W
MCSWAIN ELIJA A 26 MOO W
MCSWAIN GEORGE A 26 BUR W
MCSWAIN GEORGE A 26 MOO W
MCSWAIN GEORGE G A 26 MOO W
MCSWAIN H A A 29 FA1 W
TOWN COMMISSIONER AFTER-
WARDS ENG IN REBELLION
MCSWAIN H K A 26 BUR W
MCSWAIN J D A 26 MOO W
MCSWAIN JAMES A 26 MOU W
MCSWAIN JOHN A 26 BUR W
MCSWAIN JOHN A 26 MOO W
MCSWAIN MADISON A 26 BUR B
MCSWAIN RICHARD A 26 BUR W
MCSWAIN T J A 26 MOO W
MCSWAIN THOS A 26 BUR W
MCSWAIN THOS A 26 BUR W
MCSWAIN THOS A 26 MOO W
MCSWAIN W B A 26 BUR W
MCSWAIN WILLIAM A 26 MOO W
MCSWAIN WILLIAM A 26 SHE W
MCSWAIN WM A 29 FA1 B
BLADEN STA BLADEN CO
MCUISTAN JAMES A 46 SUM W
MCWILLIAMS JOHN S A 53 OCR W
MEABUN HIMEN A 46 FRI B
MEABUN ISAC A 46 FRI B
MEACHAM H T A 29 LOC W
MEACHAM
WASHINGTON D A 32 DAV W
MEAD JOSEPH R 26 PEE W
NAME LINED THROUGH
CHALLENGED FOR HAVING
BEEN AN OFFICER OF THE
U S ARMY IN CAMPAIGN
AGAINST MEXICO AND FOR
AIDING THE REBELLION.
REJECTED FROM DUPLICATE
MEAD WM C A 28 02N W
MEADER EZARER M A 46 FRI W
MEADERIS JOHN W A 46 KIN W
MEADLEY ABSOLEM A 32 THO B
MEADOW ELIJAH A 44 LED W
MEADOWS BRODIE A 44 KNA W
MEADOWS CISCERO A 19 HAD W
MEADOWS DOCTOR A 44 LED B
MEADOWS ED H A 28 02N W
MEADOWS ELDRIDGE A 44 TAR B
MEADOWS ENOCH A 44 LED B
MEADOWS ENOCK A 19 HAD B
MEADOWS H M A 44 LED W
MEADOWS HENDERSON A 44 TAR W
MEADOWS J A 44 KNA W
MEADOWS J J A 44 KNA W
MEADOWS J S A 44 LED W
MEADOWS JAMES A 44 LED W
MEADOWS JAS A 44 LED B
MEADOWS JERRY A 44 LED B
MEADOWS JESSE SR A 44 TAR W
MEADOWS JESSEE A 44 LED W
MEADOWS LEWIS A 19 HAD B
MEADOWS LEWIS A 28 16T B
MEADOWS PINKNEY A 44 TAR W
MEADOWS SETH A 44 LED W
MEADOWS T M A 44 LED W
MEADOWS W L A 44 LED W
MEADOWS WILLIAM T A 19 HAD W
MEADOWS WILLIS A 44 LED W
MEADOWS WM A 44 KNA B
MEADOWS WM A 44 LED B
MEARIT HAYWOD A 37 MAN B
MEARS JESSE A 37 ROC W
MEARS KEEL A 37 ROC W
VOTED AS REDIN
MEARS REDMOND A 37 ROC W
MEARS STEPHEN B A 37 ROC W
MEARS W B A 32 DAV W
MEASON G W A 19 HAD W
MEBAN ALBERT A 46 GRE B
MEBAN JOSEPH A 46 GRE B
MEBAN RICHARD A 46 GRE B
MEBAN ROBERT A 46 GRE B
MEBAN WILLIS A 46 GRE B
MEDDLING GARY A 53 LA1 B
MEDDOWS ZEDDICK A 19 HAD W
MEDFORD JOSEPH R A 37 PEN W
MEDLEY HENRY A 32 DAV W

MEDLEY NATHAN A 32 DAV W
MEDLIN BRITTON A 39 LOU W
MEDLIN CHRISTOFER A 39 LOU W
MEDLIN HARTLY A 39 GRI W
MEDLIN J R A 39 FRE W
MEDLIN NATHAN A 32 DAV W
MEDLIN RIAL A 39 GRI W
MEDLIN THOS A 39 GRI W
MEDLIN TURNER A 39 FRE W
MEDLIN WILLIS A 39 HAR W
MEDLIN WM A 38 FRE W
MEDLIN WM HENRY A 29 FA1 W
MEDLING CULLEN A 28 02N B
MEDOWS ISAAC W A 72 SWA W
MEDOWS JAMES A A 72 SWA W
MEDOWS WILLIAM A 72 SWA W
MEEDE WILSON A 37 ROC B
MEEKINS DANIEL S A 30 ROA W
MEEKINS DANIEL W A 30 ROA W
MEEKINS EPHRAIM M A 30 ROA W
CHALLENGED
ASSIST LT HOUSE KEEPER
PRIOR TO THE WAR
MEEKINS FIELDS A 53 KEN W
MEEKINS FRANCIS A A 30 ROA W
MEEKINS ISAAC C R 30 ROA W
CHALLENGED
CONSTABLE PRIOR TO WAR
MEEKINS JAMES A 53 CHI W
MEEKINS JOHN A 30 ROA B
MEEKINS JOHN A 53 LA1 W
MEEKINS JOHN W A 30 ROA W
MEEKINS MADISON M A 28 17T W
MEEKINS SILBY A 53 KEN W
MEEKINS SILBY A 53 KEN W
MEEKINS WILLIAM A 28 01B W
MEEKINS WM H A 53 CHI W
MEEKINS ZION F A 53 GER W
MEEKS FREDERICK A 37 HIG B
MEEKS JOSHUA A 37 HOL W
MEEKS SOLOMON A 37 HIC B
MEES JOHN A 32 TYR W
MEGAHA JEFFERSON A 25 PIN W
MEGHEE LINDSAY A 46 HIG W
MEHAGAN JAMES A 37 TA1 W
MEINY GORDENTIA H A 46 KIN W
MEIRS LAYER A 19 MOR B
MELLING WILLIAM A 40 DA1 W
MELLING WILLIAM A 40 FER W
MELLON G W A 40 SAN W
MELONE NELSON A 29 LOC B
MELSON GABRIEL A 28 04A B
MELSON JOHN A 30 POW W
MELTION C B A 25 TUS W
MELTON B B A 26 MOO W
MELTON SCOTT A 28 05A B
MELVILLE LEVI A 72 SWA W
MELVILLE SUTTON A 28 9TH B
MELVIN A W A 29 CED W
MELVIN ANDREW A 29 CED B
MELVIN ELIAS A 46 MON W
MELVIN FORTY A 29 ROC B
MELVIN HARDY A 29 CED B
MELVIN HARDY A 46 MON W
MELVIN HENRY A 29 CED W
MELVIN ISAAC A 29 CED B
MELVIN ISAAC A 29 LOC B
MELVIN J C A 29 CED W
MELVIN JNO A A 29 CED W
MELVIN LEWIS A 29 CED B
MELVIN M H A 29 CED W
MELVIN SAM A 29 CED B
MELVIN VIRGIL A 29 CED B

MELVIN W H A 29 LOC W
MELVINE FORTUNE A 29 FA1 B
MEMORY G W A 29 GRA W
MEMORY LOTT A 29 GRA W
MENDENHALL A 46 GRE B
MENDENHALL A L A 46 HIG W
MENDENHALL AARON A 46 GRE B
MENDENHALL ADAM A 32 THO B
MENDENHALL ALBERT A 46 JAM B
MENDENHALL ALFRED A 46 GRE B
MENDENHALL BENJAMIN A 32 POS W
MENDENHALL BERRILL A 46 GRE B
MENDENHALL
CHARLES H A 46 HIG W
MENDENHALL
CLEMMONS M A 46 COB W
MENDENHALL E A 46 HIG W
MENDENHALL E E A 46 HIG W
MENDENHALL EDMOND A 46 JAM B
MENDENHALL ELI A 40 FER W
MENDENHALL ELI R 40 FER W
NAME LINED OUT
CAPTAIN OF MILITIA BEFORE
THE REBELLION AND GAVE
AID & COMFORT TO THE
ENEMY. DID NOT QUALIFY
MENDENHALL J L A 32 THO W
MENDENHALL J M A 46 HIG W
MENDENHALL J R A 32 DAV W
MENDENHALL J W A 46 HIG W
MENDENHALL JAS A 46 GRE B
MENDENHALL JASON A 32 THO W
MENDENHALL JOHN J A 32 THO W
MENDENHALL JOHN J A 40 DA2 B
MENDENHALL LEWIS A 46 GRE B
MENDENHALL M A 46 HIG W
MENDENHALL M H A 46 HIG W
MENDENHALL NATHAN A 40 FER W
MENDENHALL NEREUS A 46 JAM W
MENDENHALL S H A 46 HIG W
MENDENHALL STANTON A 46 HIG W
MENDENHALL WM A 46 GRE B
MENETREE J J A 39 LOU W
MENHALL CLAVIN A 28 04A B
MENILLIS JOHN A 35 ISL W
MENNINGER F J A 28 05A W
MENNINGER H J A 28 02N W
MENNINGHALL SMITH A 28 04A B
MEPHAUL W J A 25 HAY W
MERCEL DAVID O A 37 SPA W
MERCER ALBERT A 37 WHI B
MERCER ALEXANDER A 28 16T B
MERCER ALPHONSO A 30 MOY W
MERCER ANDREW A 37 HIG B
MERCER BENJIMAN F A 30 NOR W
MERCER DEMPSEY A 37 HIG B
MERCER DEMSY A 37 WHI B
MERCER EDMUND A 30 MOY B
MERCER GEORGE A 30 CUR B
MERCER GEORGE A 37 HIG B
MERCER GEORGE A 37 HIG B
MERCER GREEN A 37 HIG B
MERCER HARRY A 30 MOY B
MERCER HILLIARD A 37 HIG B
MERCER ISAM A 37 HIG B
MERCER ISOM A 37 HIG B
MERCER JACOB A 37 SHA B
MERCER JACOB J A 37 WEB W
MERCER JERRY A 37 HIG B
MERCER JESSE A 37 HIG W
MERCER JESSE M A 30 COI W
MERCER JESSE SR A 30 COI W
MERCER JESSY A 37 WHI B

MERCER JOHN A 30 POP W
MERCER JOHN A 35 SMI W
MERCER JOHN R A 37 WHI W
MERCER JOHN W A 35 LIM W
MERCER JOSEPH A 30 MOY W
MERCER JOSEPH H A 35 SMI W
MERCER KINCHIN A 37 WEB W
MERCER LEWIS A 28 05A B
MERCER LOUIS B A 35 SMI W
MERCER MAJOR A 30 COI W
MERCER MILES A 30 MOY B
MERCER REID A 37 WHI B
MERCER RICHARD A 37 HIG B
MERCER RILEY A 37 HIG B
MERCER SAML A 30 CUR W
MERCER SIMON A 37 SPA B
MERCER SMITH A 37 HIG B
MERCER THESA ? A 37 WHI B
MERCER THOMAS A 37 HIG B
MERCER THOMAS A 37 WHI B
MERCER WILLIAM A 35 SMI W
MERCER WILLIAM A 37 HIG B
MERCER WILLIAM C A 30 MOY W
MERCER WILLIAM D A 37 HIG W
MERCER WILLIAM T A 37 HIG W
MERCER WILSON A 37 SHA B
MEREDITH J H A 46 KIN W
MERETT ABNER A 35 MAG W
MERETT EDWARD A 35 MAG W
MERETT KENAN A 35 WAR W
MERETT RUNATHAN A 35 ROC B
MERETT TIMOTHY W A 35 MAG W
MERIDETH A M A 46 HIG W
MERIDETH E S A 46 HIG W
MERIDETH J M A 46 HIG W
MERIDETH J W A 46 HIG W
MERIDETH JAMES A A 46 HIG W
MERIDETH MORRIS A 46 HIG W
MERIDTH A M A 46 KIN W
MERILL M T A 40 CAN W
MERIT LEWIS A 28 01A B
MERJORAM THOMAS H A 37 ROC W
MERRELL AARON A 19 MOR W
MERRELL ARTHUR A 19 HAR W
MERRELL BENJ F A 19 BE1 W
MERRELL PETER A 19 NEW B
MERRELL WILLIAM A 19 HAR W
MERRET SAM A 39 HAY B
MERRETT ALEXANDRE A 19 HAR W
MERRETT CULLEN A 35 WAR W
MERRETT GEORGE W A 35 WAR W
MERRETT JAMES M A 35 WAR W
MERRETT JAMES T A 35 WAR W
MERRETT JOSIAH A 35 ROC W
MERRETT LEWIS W A 35 MAG W
MERRETT MAJOR A 35 WAR W
MERRETT MORDECAI A 35 WAR W
MERRETT NEEDHAM E A 35 WAR W
MERRETT RICHARD A 35 WAR W
MERRETT SHADRICK A 35 WAR W
MERRETT THOMAS W A 35 WAR W
MERRICK EDWD A 29 FA1 B
MERRICK EDWD A 29 FA1 B
MERRICK EZEKIEL A 29 FA1 W
MERRICK GABE A 53 SWA B
MERRICK HARRY A 53 SWA B
MERRICK JNO A 29 FA1 B
MERRICK JOHN A 28 04A B
MERRICK KIMBRO A 53 SWA B
MERRICK LARRY A 53 SWA B
MERRICK RICHD A 28 04A B
MERRICK RILEY A 53 SWA B
MERRICK SCIPIO A 28 04A B

MERRICK WM A 29 FA1 B
MERRIET JAMES A 44 FOR W
MERRIETT THOS A 44 FIS B
MERRIL E A 32 COT W
MERRIL SAMUEL A 37 TA1 W
MERRILL HILL A 28 6TH B
MERRILL ISAAC A 40 DA2 W
MERRIMAN ALFRED A 35 MAG B
MERRIMAN LEONARD A R 35 MAG W
NOT TAKEN THE OATH. POST MASTER BEFORE THE WAR, GAVE SOME AID TO FRIENDS IN THE CONFEDERATE ARMY.
MERRIOTT GEO H A 44 KIT W
MERRIOTT H G A 39 LOU W
MERRIOTT THOS C A 44 KIT W
MERRIS GEORGE A 46 FRI W
MERRIT BENJAMIN A 35 LIM W
MERRIT HENRY C A 46 FRI W
MERRIT THOMAS F A 46 FRI W
MERRITT BRADLEY A 35 MAG W
MERRITT CICERO A 28 6TH B
MERRITT DANIEL A 28 10T W
MERRITT DAVID J A 35 MAG W
MERRITT HALEY A 35 MAG W
MERRITT HARDY A 37 HIC B
MERRITT ISAAC W A 35 MAG W
MERRITT ISRAIL A 37 PEN B
MERRITT JAMES A A 35 MAG W
MERRITT JOHN W A 46 JAM W
MERRITT LEWIS A 37 TA1 B
MERRITT MARION A 35 WAR W
MERRITT MORRIS A 39 PUG W
MERRITT
SOLONIUS HAYWOOD A 28 04B B
MERRITT W H A 39 FRA W
MERRY CHAS A 28 04A B
MERRYMAN EDWARD A 44 HEN B
MERRYMAN HENRY A 44 HEN B
MERRYMAN HORICE A 44 HEN B
MERRYMAN JOHN A 44 HEN B
MERRYMAN P R A 44 HEN W
MERRYMAN SAML A 44 HEN B
MERRYMAN WM A 44 HEN B
MERVIN PHINEAS A 28 01A W
MESLEY R D A 46 JAM W
MESSIC SHADRACK A 28 17T W
MESSIC WM C A 28 15T W
METALGART SAMUEL A 25 HAY W
METON JOHN A 46 FRI B
METTERS JAMES A 32 LOF W
METTS THOMAS A 28 01A B
METTS WM P A 28 01B W
MEWKIRK FENNELL A 35 MAG B
MEWS AARON A 24 EDE B
MEWS JACOB A 24 EDE B
MEZELL REUBEN A 28 6TH B
MIASELS JACK A 37 HIC B
MICCULLOUS JAMES A 39 HAY B
MICHAEL AMOS A 32 DAV B
MICHAEL CAMRON A 44 SAS B
MICHAEL D L A 32 THO W
CERTIF
MICHAEL DANIEL A 32 DAV B
MICHAEL HENRY A 32 DAV W
MICHAEL J W A 32 DAV W
MICHAEL JACOB A 32 DAV W
MICHAEL JACOB A 32 YAD W
MICHAEL JOHN A 32 CLE W
MICHAEL JOHN A 46 MON W
MICHAEL JONAS A 32 DAV B
MICHAEL NATHANIEL A 32 SHE W
MICHAEL PETER A 32 JAC B
MICHAEL PHILIP A 32 DAV W
MICHAEL VOLANTINE A 32 TYR W
MICHAEL VOLENTINE A 32 SHE W
MICHAEL W R A 32 DAV W
MICHAEL WILLIAM A 44 SAS B
MICHAEL ZACRIAH A 44 SAS B
MICHAUX D M A 46 SUM W
MICHEAL GEORGE A 53 SWA B
MICHEL MILTON A 46 GRE B
MICHENER NEEDHAM A 39 FRA B
MIDDLETON ABRAM A 35 KEN B
MIDDLETON BAZIL A 35 ISL B
MIDDLETON CAESAR A 28 04A B
MIDDLETON CALVIN A 35 WAR B
MIDDLETON DAVID J A 35 KEN W
MIDDLETON EDWARD A 35 KEN B
MIDDLETON FRANK A 35 KEN B
MIDDLETON GEORGE W A 35 WAR W
MIDDLETON J A A 46 SUM W
MIDDLETON JAMES G A 35 CYP W
MIDDLETON JAMES M A 35 MAG W
MIDDLETON JEREMIAH A 35 KEN B
MIDDLETON JERRY A 35 KEN B
MIDDLETON JOSEPH A 24 EDE B
TRNS TO BANKS OF MIDDLE PRECINCT AS HE IS ONE OF THE INSPECTORS OF POLLS FOR THAT PRECINCT
MIDDLETON JOSEPH A 24 MID B
MIDDLETON KADER A 35 KEN B
MIDDLETON LEVI A 35 KEN B
MIDDLETON LEWIS A 28 05A B
MIDDLETON LOT A 35 KEN B
MIDDLETON MARSHALL A 35 CYP B
MIDDLETON MINGLE A 35 KEN B
MIDDLETON PETER A 35 KEN B
MIDDLETON RANSOM M A 35 WAR W
MIDDLETON SANDERS A 35 KEN B
MIDDLETON SQUIRE A 35 KEN B
MIDDLETON STEPHEN A 35 WAR B
MIDDLETON THOMAS A 35 KEN B
MIDDLETON TONEY A 35 KEN B
MIDDLETON WILLIAM A 35 MAG B
MIDDLETON WILLIAM A 35 WAR B
MIDDLETON WILLIAM B A 35 KEN W
MIDGET JOHN A 28 15T B
MIDGETT BENJAMIN A 30 ROA B
MIDGETT EDWARD B CHR 30 COI W
COMMISSIONER OF WRECKS PRIOR TO WAR
MIDGETT HENRY A 28 10T B
MIDGETT JAMES A 53 SWA B
MIDGETT JOHN A 53 SWA W
MIDGETT JOSEPH A 19 NEW W
MIDGETT LEVI A 19 NEW W
MIDGETT ROBT A 19 NEW W
MIDGETT WILLIAM R A 53 KEN W
MIDGETT WILLIS A 53 SWA B
MIDGETT ZACHARIAS R A 53 SWA W
MIDLING REDNEK A 37 ROB W
MIDYETT BANNITER A 53 LA1 W
MIDYETT BELSHAZER A 53 LA1 W
MIDYETT BENAJMIN A 53 LA1 W
CERT RES GERMANTON
MIDYETT BENJAMIN D A 30 ROA B
MIDYETT BENJAMIN H A 53 LA2 W
MIDYETT BENJAMIN J A 53 LA1 W
MIDYETT DAMORN G A 53 CHI W
MIDYETT DANIEL A 53 HAT W
MIDYETT DANIEL A 53 LA1 W
MIDYETT DAVID A 53 CHI W
MIDYETT DAVID A 53 LA1 B
MIDYETT DAVID A 53 LA1 B
MIDYETT EBENEZER A 53 CHI W
MIDYETT EBENEZER A 53 LA1 B
MIDYETT EDMOND A 53 LA1 W
MIDYETT EDMOND D A 53 HAT W
MIDYETT EDWARD S A 53 HAT W
MIDYETT EZEKIEL A 53 CHI W
MIDYETT EZEKIEL A 53 CHI W
MIDYETT FIELDS A 30 ROA B
MIDYETT GEO W A 53 CHI W
MIDYETT GEORGE A 53 LA1 B
MIDYETT GEORGE R A 30 ROA B
MIDYETT GEORGE R A 53 LA1 B
MIDYETT IRA A 53 CHI W
MIDYETT IRA SR A 53 CHI W
MIDYETT JACOB A 53 HAT W
MIDYETT JAMES A 53 LA1 B
MIDYETT JAMES D A 30 ROA B
MIDYETT JOHN A 53 GER W
MIDYETT JOHN A 53 LA1 B
MIDYETT JOHN A A 53 CHI W
MIDYETT JOHN H A 53 KEN W
MIDYETT JOHN S A 53 GER W
MIDYETT JOHN W A 30 ROA W
MIDYETT JOHN W A 53 LA1 W
MIDYETT JOSHUA A 53 LA1 B
MIDYETT L N A 53 CHI W
MIDYETT LITTLE B A 53 CHI W
MIDYETT LITTLE S A 53 LA1 W
MIDYETT
LITTLEJOHN T A 53 LA1 W
MIDYETT MANN A 30 ROA W
MIDYETT MAURICE M A 30 ROA W
MIDYETT NATHAN O A 53 CHI W
MIDYETT RICHARD A 53 CHI W
MIDYETT RICHARD W A 53 HAT W
MIDYETT RILEY A 53 LA1 B
MIDYETT ROBERT P A 30 ROA W
MIDYETT SAMUEL A 30 ROA B
MIDYETT SAMUEL A 53 LA1 B
MIDYETT SAMUEL A 53 LA1 W
MIDYETT SAMUEL N A 30 ROA W
MIDYETT SAMUEL P A 53 LA1 W
MIDYETT THOMAS G A 53 FAI W
MIDYETT TIMOTHY A 53 HAT W
MIDYETT WARREN S A 53 LA1 W
MIDYETT WATSON L A 53 CHI W
MIDYETT WILLIAM B A 53 LA2 W
MIDYETT WILLIAM F A 53 FAI W
MIDYETT WILLIAM R A 30 ROA B
MIDYETT WILLIAM W A 53 LA1 W
MIFONG ALEXANDER A 32 POS W
MILDRUM JOHN A 28 02N W
MILES AMAS A 19 BE1 B
MILES E A 46 SUM W
MILES HENRY A 29 CED B
MILES JAMES A 46 SUM W
MILES MORSE A 30 CUR B
MILES WYATT A 99 BUS B
MILLAR JOHN A 40 RHY W
MILLARD B J A 35 FAI W
MILLARD CHARLES A 35 FAI W
MILLARD LARKIN A 35 FAI B
MILLARD RICHARD W A 35 KEN W
MILLEN ROBERT A A 40 FER W
MILLER ABBERT A 26 CAR B
MILLER ADAM A 30 ROA B
MILLER ADAM A 35 KEN B
MILLER ALBT M A 29 GRA B
MILLER ALEX A 29 FA1 W
MILLER ALEXANDER A 32 JAC B
MILLER ALEXR A 28 04A W
MILLER ALEXR JR A 28 01A W
MILLER ALFORD A 32 DAV B

MILLER ALFRED A 35 SMI B
MILLER ALLEN A 30 IND B
MILLER ALLEN A 35 KEN B
MILLER AMOS A 35 KEN B
MILLER ANDREW A 35 SMI W
MILLER AUGUSTUS A 24 EDE W
MILLER BASETT A 30 MOY W
MILLER BATMAN P A 53 KEN W
MILLER BENJ C A 24 EDE W
MILLER BENJAMIN A 32 COT W
MILLER C W A 35 SMI W
MILLER CALVIN A 35 KEN B
MILLER CHARLES A 26 CAR B
MILLER CHARLES A 32 DAV B
MILLER CHARLES A A 28 16T W
MILLER CHAS A A 29 FA1 W
MILLER
CHRISTOPHER C A 53 KEN W
MILLER CHURCH W A 28 16T W
MILLER CONSTANTINE A 28 14T W
MILLER CURTIS A 35 WAR W
MILLER CYRUS A 35 KEN B
MILLER D W A 26 BOR W
MILLER DANIEL A 35 KEN B
MILLER DANIEL A 46 MCL B
MILLER DANIEL P A 28 14T W
MILLER DAVIS A 37 ROC B
MILLER DEED A 30 MOY B
MILLER EDWIN A 26 HOL B
MILLER ELIAS A 32 SHE W
MILLER FABIUS D A 28 16T W
MILLER FESTUS A 28 16T W
MILLER FRANK A 28 04A B
MILLER FRANK A 35 KEN B
MILLER FRANK JR A 35 SMI B
MILLER FRANK SR A 35 SMI B
MILLER FRANKLIN A 32 DAV B
MILLER FRANKLIN A 32 DAV W
MILLER FREDERICK B A 28 16T W
MILLER G M A 32 LEE W
MILLER G W A 35 SMI W
MILLER GATLIN A 35 KEN B
MILLER GEO A 29 FA1 B
MILLER GEORGE A 35 KEN B
MILLER GEORGE A 35 KEN W
MILLER GEORGE A 44 SAS B
MILLER H V A 32 COT W
MILLER HENDERSON A 26 CAR B
MILLER HENRY A 24 EDE B
MILLER HENRY A 28 04A B
MILLER HENRY A 28 04B W
MILLER HENRY A 28 10T B
MILLER HENRY A 32 DAV B
MILLER HENRY A 32 DAV B
MILLER HENRY A 35 KEN B
MILLER HEZEKIAH A 35 WAR W
MILLER ISAAC A 32 DAV B
MILLER ISAAC B A 32 COT W
MILLER ISAM A 32 DAV B
MILLER J H A 32 COT W
MILLER JACK A 35 KEN B
MILLER JACOB A 32 COT W
MILLER JACOB D A 28 16T W
MILLER JAMES A 24 EDE W
MILLER JAMES A 28 10T B
MILLER JAMES A 32 DAV B
MILLER JAMES A 32 DAV B
MILLER JAMES A 46 SUM B
MILLER JAMES JR A 46 SUM B
MILLER JAMES P A 32 DAV W
MILLER JEFFERSON A 35 KEN B
MILLER JEFFERSON A 46 FRI B
MILLER JEFREY A 32 COT B

MILLER JESSE A 32 SHE W
MILLER JESSEE A 30 IND W
MILLER JNO C A 29 FA1 W
MILLER JOHN A 30 MOY W
MILLER JOHN A 32 CLE W
MILLER JOHN A 32 COT W
MILLER JOHN A 32 LOF W
MILLER JOHN A 32 THO W
CERTIF
MILLER JOHN B A 28 14T W
MILLER JOHN BW [?] A 32 COT W
MILLER JOHN C A 28 16T W
MILLER JOHN R A 28 16T W
MILLER JOHN S A 28 14T W
MILLER JOHN SR A 28 14T W
MILLER JOHN T A 28 16T W
MILLER JOSEPH A 32 COT B
MILLER JOSEPH A 32 POS W
MILLER JOSEPH H A 32 SHE W
MILLER JOSEPHUS A 28 14T W
MILLER JOSIAH A 32 SHE W
MILLER L A 28 01A W
MILLER L F A 32 YAD W
MILLER LAWRENCE A 28 16T W
MILLER LEE A 44 OXF B
MILLER LEVI A 32 CLE W
MILLER LEWIS W A 32 POS W
MILLER MACK A 35 KEN B
MILLER MARTIN A 32 SHE W
MILLER MASON A 24 EDE W
MILLER MASSA A 32 TYR B
MILLER MICHAEL A A 32 POS W
MILLER MILES A 28 03A B
MILLER MILTON A 46 GRE B
MILLER N A 32 SHE W
MILLER NICHELS A 40 CAN W
MILLER OBA A 32 COT W
MILLER P P A 19 HAD W
MILLER PETER A 35 KEN B
MILLER PETER A 44 OXF B
MILLER PRINCE A 26 CAR B
MILLER RANDLE A 26 SHE B
MILLER REDIS A 28 6TH B
MILLER REUBEN A 24 EDE W
MILLER RICHARD A 32 LEE W
MILLER RICHARD E A 35 KEN W
MILLER RICHD A 29 FA1 B
MILLER ROBERT A 28 10T B
MILLER ROBERT A 28 9TH B
MILLER SAMPSON A 30 POW B
MILLER SAMUEL A 26 SHE B
MILLER SAMUEL A 32 DAV B
MILLER SAMUEL A 53 GER B
MILLER SCIPIO A 35 KEN B
MILLER SILAS A 24 EDE B
MILLER SIMON A 44 SAS B
MILLER SIMON A 44 SAS W
MILLER SOLOMAN W A 30 KNO W
MILLER SOLOMON A 24 EDE W
MILLER SOLOMON A 35 GLI B
MILLER STEP A 26 HOL B
MILLER THOMAS A 29 GRA B
MILLER THOMAS J A 32 COT W
MILLER THOS A 28 01A W
MILLER TILMON F A 53 KEN W
MILLER W F A 32 COT W
MILLER W H A 26 HOL B
MILLER WASHINGTON A 28 03B B
MILLER WASHINGTON A 46 FRI B
MILLER WASHINGTON A 46 GRE B
MILLER WILEY A 32 CLE W
MILLER WILEY A 46 GRE W
MILLER WILLIAM J A 35 KEN W

MILLER WISDOM A 32 LEE W
MILLER WM A 28 01B B
MILLER WM C A 30 KNO W
MILLER WM H A 35 SMI W
MILLET B G A 29 FA1 B
MILLETT CHAS A 29 FA1 B
MILLETT R J A 29 FA1 W
MILLETT VIRGIL A 29 FA1 B
MILLETT VIRGO A 29 FA1 W
MILLINDER WILEY A 29 CAR B
MILLING JOHN A 40 FER W
MILLIS HIRUM A 46 FRI W
MILLIS ISAAC A 46 JAM B
MILLIS JAMES A 46 JAM W
MILLIS JAMES JR A 46 JAM W
MILLIS WM F A 46 FRI W
MILLS ALEX A 19 NEW W
MILLS ANDREW A 35 ROC B
MILLS DAVID A 28 05A B
MILLS FREDK A 28 05A B
MILLS JAMES O A 53 GER W
MILLS JIM A 39 JOR B
CERT NASH CO
MILLS JOHN A 39 PUG B
MILLS JOHN A 44 KIT B
MILLS ROBBERT A 39 JOR B
CERT NASH CO
MILLS ROSWELL A 28 02N W
MILLS TIMOTHY W A 35 ROC W
MILLS WM A 44 HEN B
MILLS WM H A 28 15T W
MILONE GEORGE A 39 HAY B
MILSTEAD SHAFFER A 37 SPA B
MILTON HENRY A 46 MON B
MILTON P HOSANNA A 46 MCL B
MILTON PEYTON A 46 GRE B
MILTON SILAS A 28 03A B
MILTON SIMPSON A 46 MON B
MILUM PLUMMER A 39 PUG B
MINCEY MOSES A 40 DA1 W
MINCY W A 40 STO W
MINER CORNELIUS A 46 MON W
MINER G W A 44 OXF W
MINER JAMES A 46 GRE W
MINER JNO A 44 SAS W
MINER JOSEPH A 46 ROS B
MINES WM ABLE A 46 GRE B
MINGA ANTHONY A 39 GRI B
MINGA H W A 39 GRI W
MINGA HARTWELL A 39 HAR W
MINGA ROBT A 39 GRI B
MINGA W T A 39 GRI W
MINGO EDWARD A 37 MAN B
MINIS CHARLES A 44 FOR B
MINNIS JOHN A 28 01A B
MINNIS Y A A 39 FRA W
MINOR ABRAM A 44 LED B
MINOR DAVID A 44 OXF W
MINOR ERASMUS A 44 OXF B
MINOR J J 29 ROC W
REGISTER & SUPT OF
ELECTION CHAL
MINOR J J A 29 FA1 W
SUPT AT GREYS CREEK
MINOR J J A 29 GRA W
SUPT AT ROCK FISH
MINOR JOSIPH A 44 OXF W
MINOR PATRICK A 44 KNA B
MINOR R V A 44 LED W
MINOR ROBT A 44 OXF B
MINOR SAM A 44 OXF B
MINOR W H A 44 LED W
MINSEY JESSE A 35 GLI W

MINSON JOHN A 35 WOL W
MINTER JAMES HENRY A 30 GIB B
7-MONTHS-RESIDENCE
MINZESHEIMER DAVID A 28 02N W
MIRECK J H A 32 TYR W
MIRICK WILLIAM A 37 MAN B
MISE GEORGE A 32 SHE W
MISE HENRY A 32 SHE W
MITCHAL RICHARD A 24 MID W
MITCHAL TIMOTHY A 24 MID W
MITCHAM R J A 26 GOF W
MITCHEAM BERRY A 26 CAR W
MITCHEAM HENRY A 26 PEE W
MITCHEAM L A 26 CAR W
MITCHEAM PINK A 26 CAR W
MITCHEAM THOMAS A 26 GRI W
MITCHEL CASWELL A 46 KIN B
MITCHEL DROMET F A 19 BE1 B
MITCHEL ELLIS A 46 FRI B
MITCHEL GABREL A 39 PUG B
MITCHEL H C D A 39 LOU W
MITCHEL HAWEL A 46 FRI B
MITCHEL HAYWOOD A 39 DAV B
MITCHEL HENDERSON A 39 DAV B
MITCHEL HENDERSON A 39 LOU B
MITCHEL HENRY A 46 GRE B
MITCHEL JIM A 32 CLE B
MITCHEL JIRDAN A 39 DAV B
MITCHEL JOE JR A 39 PUG B
MITCHEL JOE SR A 39 PUG B
MITCHEL JOHN C A 44 DUT B
MITCHEL JOHN JR A 44 DUT B
MITCHEL JOHN T A 39 DAV W
MITCHEL MAJ SR A 29 ROC W
MITCHEL O H P A 39 DAV W
MITCHEL PETER A 44 BRA B
MITCHEL ROSS A 39 DAV B
MITCHEL RUFUS A 46 FRI B
MITCHEL SAMUEL A 37 MAN B
MITCHEL SIDNEY A 39 DAV B
MITCHEL SOLOMAN A 39 DAV B
MITCHEL THOMAS A 46 FRI B
MITCHEL W A A 44 DUT W
MITCHEL W S A 39 DAV W
MITCHEL WASH A 39 DAV B
MITCHEL WASHINGTON A 39 DAV B
MITCHEL WILLIAM A 46 KIN B
MITCHEL WILLIAM JR A 39 PUG B
MITCHEL WM P A 46 GRE W
MITCHEL ZIPH A 46 GRE B
MITCHELL A C A 38 FRE W
MITCHELL ABRAHAM A 39 FRA B
MITCHELL ABRAM A 44 FOR B
MITCHELL ABSALOM A 28 10T B
MITCHELL ALBERT A 24 EDE B
MITCHELL ALEX A 44 FOR B
MITCHELL ALEXANDER A 46 SUM B
MITCHELL ALEXR A 28 02N W
MITCHELL ANDERSON A 39 FRA B
MITCHELL B B A 44 FOR W
MITCHELL BALDY A 39 FRE W
MITCHELL BILL A 39 DAV B
MITCHELL CLAYBORN A 44 FOR B
MITCHELL DANIEL A 38 FRE B
MITCHELL DANIEL A 44 OXF B
MITCHELL DAVID A 29 FA1 B
MITCHELL DAVID A 44 FOR B
MITCHELL EDMOND A 28 7TH B
MITCHELL EDWARD A 37 ROB B
MITCHELL EDWARD A 44 KIT B
MITCHELL ELIAS A 28 04A B
MITCHELL H A 39 FRA B
MITCHELL H B A 39 FRA W
MITCHELL H W A 44 LED W
MITCHELL HAMILTON A 39 HAY B
MITCHELL HARRY A 37 EDW B
MITCHELL HAYWOOD A 44 FOR B
MITCHELL HENRY A 29 FA1 B
MITCHELL HENRY A 39 FRE B
MITCHELL HENRY A 44 KIT B
MITCHELL HERY A 44 BRA B
MITCHELL HUNLEY A 37 TA1 B
MITCHELL ISAIAH A 39 HAY B
MAVOS NAT 1ST BOARD
OF REGIS APP INFOR
MITCHELL ISHMIEL A 44 FOR B
MITCHELL J E A 44 LED W
MITCHELL J L A 44 BRA W
MITCHELL JACKSON A 37 SHA W
MITCHELL JACOB A 39 HAR B
MITCHELL JAMES A 28 03A W
MITCHELL JAMES A 28 11T W
MITCHELL JAMES A 35 ISL W
MITCHELL JAMES A 44 FIS W
MITCHELL JAMES S A 28 16T W
CERT GIVEN. RESIDENCE
LENOIR CO., NC
MITCHELL JAS A 29 FA1 B
MITCHELL JEFF A 39 DAV B
MITCHELL JESSE A 44 FOR B
MITCHELL JNO W A 44 BRA W
MITCHELL JOEL H A 37 ROB B
MITCHELL JOHN A 24 EDE W
MITCHELL JOHN A 24 MID W
MITCHELL JOHN A 28 03A B
MITCHELL JOHN A 28 05A B
MITCHELL JOHN A 35 KEN W
MITCHELL JOHN A 37 ROB B
MITCHELL JOHN A 39 FRA B
MITCHELL JOSEPH A 28 04A B
MITCHELL JOSEPH A 46 GRE B
MITCHELL JULIUS A 39 FRA B
MITCHELL LEMUEL A 44 BRA W
MITCHELL LEWIS A 44 FOR B
MITCHELL LUKE A 46 KIN B
MITCHELL MAJOR JR A 29 ROC W
MITCHELL MORDICA A 28 16T B
MITCHELL NAT A 39 FRA B
MITCHELL NAZARETH A 35 KEN W
MITCHELL NELSON A 28 04A B
MITCHELL NEWTON A 46 JAM W
MITCHELL PHIL A 39 FRA B
MITCHELL R A 29 LOC B
MITCHELL R D A 44 FOR B
MITCHELL R G A 24 EDE W
MITCHELL RICHARD A 37 MAN B
MITCHELL RICHD A 39 HAR W
MITCHELL ROBERT J A 29 FA2 W
MITCHELL ROBT A 44 BRA B
MITCHELL ROBT A 44 BRA B
MITCHELL ROBT A 44 FOR B
MITCHELL RUFFUS A 38 FRE B
MITCHELL RUFUS A 44 LED B
MITCHELL SAML A 39 HAR B
MITCHELL SAMUEL A 24 EDE B
MITCHELL SANFORD A 46 SUM B
MITCHELL SIM A 39 FRE B
MITCHELL SOWELL A 44 BEA B
MITCHELL THOMAS A 24 UPP B
MITCHELL THOMAS A 28 10T B
MITCHELL THOMPSON A 19 BE1 B
MITCHELL THOMPSON A 19 HAD B
MITCHELL THOS A 44 FOR B
MITCHELL THOS J A 28 02N W
MITCHELL W B A 44 BEA W
MITCHELL W H A 44 FIS B
MITCHELL W J A 35 ALB W
MITCHELL W J A 44 BRA W
MITCHELL W L A 44 BEA W
MITCHELL WILEY A 37 PEN B
MITCHELL WILEY A 46 JAM B
MITCHELL WILLIAM A 37 TA1 B
MITCHELL WILLIAM A 39 HAY B
MITCHELL
WILLIAM HENRY A 28 9TH B
CERT GIVEN APL 20
NOW LIVES IN NEW BERN
MITCHELL WILLIE A 39 HAR W
MITCHELL WILLIE JR A 44 FOR W
MITCHELL WILLIE SR A 44 FOR W
MITCHELL WILLIS A 39 FRE B
MITCHELL WISDOM A 39 FRE B
MITCHELL WM A 39 FRA B
MITCHELL WM A 39 FRA W
MITCHELL WM R 29 FA1 W
CONSTABLE BEFORE WAR
ENCOURAGED ENLISTMENTS
DURING WAR, CHALLENGED
BY J C COLLAHAN
TESTIMONY OF FRANK
GRAHAM TAKEN UNDER OATH
MITCHELL WM A A 39 HAR W
MITCHELL WM F A 39 FRE B
MITCHELL WM T A 44 TAR B
MITCHEM WILLIAM A 40 DEC W
MITCHENER F A 39 FRA W
MITCHENER GEORGE A 99 BUS W
MITCHENER JOHN A 99 BUS W
MITCHENER PHILO A 99 BUS W
MITCHENER R S A 39 LOU W
MITCHENER RICHARD A 99 BUS B
MITCHENER S J A 99 BUS W
MITCHENER SIMON A 99 BUS B
MITCHENOR LOUIS A 39 FRA B
MITCHENOR VIRGIL A 39 FRA B
MITTAG W K A 26 SHE W
MIXEN WM A 24 EDE B
MIXON ARTHUR A 24 EDE B
MIXON HARDY A 24 EDE B
MIXON J A A 24 EDE W
MIZE ALEX A 44 TAR W
MIZE JAMES P A 44 TAR W
MOBELLY STANLEY A 19 HAD W
MOBLEY BIGUS A 35 CYP W
MOBLEY GEORGE S A 35 CYP W
MOBLEY ISEA A 19 HAD W
MOBLEY OBED A 35 CYP W
MOBLEY RILEY A 35 CYP W
MOBLEY W C A 46 SUM W
MOBLY ANSON A 35 LIM W
MOCK A B A 32 SHE W
MOCK A L A 32 CLE W
MOCK ENOCH A 32 SHE B
MOCK JOHN A A 32 POS W
MOCK JOHN A A 32 THO W
MOCK L N A 32 SHE W
MOCK LEWIS A 32 POS B
MOCK P W A 32 SHE W
MOCK PETER A 32 CLE W
MOCK PIERSON A 32 THO B
MOCK S A A 32 THO W
MOCK SAMUEL A 32 SHE B
MOCK WILSON A 32 SHE B
MODE JAMES A 26 SHE W
MODEN DOCTOR A 28 11T B
MODICA ABRAHAM A 37 HIG B
MODICA CAMERON A 37 ROC B
MODLIN B N A 46 JAM W
MODLIN EDMOND A 46 JAM W

MODLIN F H A 46 JAM W
MODLIN FRANCIS A 24 UPP W
MODLIN H C A 46 JAM W
MOFFITT DAVID V A 32 DAV W
MOFFITT M A A 32 THO W
MOHAB JERRY A 32 THO W
MOIZE DURETTE A 44 TAR W
MOIZE WM A 44 TAR W
MONAGAN SAMPSON A 29 FA2 B
MONAGHAN B A 29 FA1 W
MONAGHAN E A 29 FA1 W
MONAGHAN JOS H A 29 FA1 W
MONDAY MIDYETT A 53 LA1 B
MONDS JAMES A 24 MID W
MONDS JOHN J A 24 UPP W
MONDS LEMUEL A 24 MID W
MONDS THOMAS A 24 EDE W
MONDS WILLIAM A 24 MID W
MONETT
CHRISTOPHER F A 46 RAG W
MONGUMERY W R A 29 FLE W
MONK DUDLEY A 35 KEN B
MONK JACOB D A 35 KEN B
MONK JAS M A 29 FA2 W
MONRO JAMES A 19 BE2 B
MONROE A J A 29 MON W
MONROE ADAM A 29 FA1 B
MONROE ALEXANDER A 29 QUW B
MONROE BARRY A 29 FA1 B
MONROE COOLEY A 29 FA1 B
MONROE DANIEL A 29 FA2 W
MONROE DAVID A 19 NEW B
MONROE HARRY A 29 FA1 B
MONROE HASSET A 28 04A B
MONROE HENRY A 29 FA1 B
MONROE HENRY A 29 MON B
MONROE ISHMAEL A 29 MON B
MONROE J A 29 FA1 W
MONROE J B A 29 ROC W
MONROE JAS A 29 FA1 B
MONROE JAS A 29 FA1 W
MONROE JAS A A 29 FA1 W
MONROE JOHN A 29 FA1 B
MONROE JOHN A 29 FA2 B
MONROE JOS A 29 FA1 B
MONROE JUDGE RUFFIN A 37 ROC B
MONROE MACK A 29 FA2 B
MONROE MALCOM A 29 QUW W
MONROE MALCOM M A 29 FA1 W
MONROE MINGO A 29 FA1 B
MONROE NEILL C A 29 ROC W
MONROE PATRCK M C A 24 MID W
MONROE PETER A 29 FA2 B
MONROE PETER A 29 MON W
MONROE PETER A 29 SEV B
MONROE WILLIAM A 29 SEV B
MONTAGUE A W A 44 LED W
MONTAGUE ALBERT A 44 OXF B
MONTAGUE ALEX B A 44 FIS W
MONTAGUE E C A 44 OXF W
MONTAGUE E J A 44 LED W
MONTAGUE J P A 44 LED W
MONTAGUE JOHN A 44 OXF W
MONTAGUE JORDEN A 44 OXF B
MONTAGUE LATNEY A 44 LED W
MONTAGUE LEWIS A 44 OXF W
MONTAGUE MOSES A 39 SPE B
MONTAGUE NATHAN A 44 OXF B
MONTAGUE P G A 44 LED W
MONTAGUE ROBT A 44 OXF B
MONTAGUE SAML A 44 LED W
MONTAGUE UMPHREY A 44 OXF B
MONTAGUE WILLIAM L A 30 ROA W

MONTGOMERY ELIGH W A 46 MCL W
MONTGOMERY JESSE A 46 MCL W
MONTGOMERY JOHN W A 46 MCL W
MONTGOMERY JOS P A 46 MCL W
MONTGOMERY JOSEPH A 46 COB B
MONTGOMERY ROBERT A 32 DAV B
MONTGOMERY W T A 39 FRA W
MONTGUMMERY G A 29 FLE B
MONTIGEW Y M A 44 YXR W
MOODY J Q A 39 HAR W
MOODY J W A 35 ALB W
MOODY JOHN A 28 04A B
MOODY JOHN A 40 RHY W
MOODY JOS A 38 FRE B
MOODY NICHOLAS A 46 GRE B
MOODY ROBERT L A 46 KIN W
MOODY W C A 35 ALB W
MOON ALLEN A 35 MAG B
MOON BRISTO A 37 HIG B
MOON C L A 46 JAM W
MOON CHARLES R 24 EDE B
CHAL BY J R B HATHAWAY
CAUSE CONVICTED OF LARCENY
BY THE MILITARY & PUNISHED
BY THEM ? OATH CONVICTED
BEFORE HE HAD THE RIGHT
OF SUFFRAGE THEREFORE
COULD NOT LOSE WHAT HE
NEVER HAD FINAL REVISION
MOON ECULBERT A 37 HIG B
MOON ISAAC A 37 HIG B
MOON JOHN A A 46 JAM W
MOON L J A 28 02N W
MOONEE ISAAC A 32 JAC B
MOONEN DIAMOND A 28 10T B
MOONEN SLADE A 28 11T B
MOONEY A A 26 BOR W
MOONEY D A 26 BOR W
MOONEY DAVID A 26 BOR W
MOONEY HUAK A 53 FAI W
MOONEY ISAAC A 26 WAR W
MOONEY JOHN A 26 SHE W
MOONEY JONATHAN A 26 SHE W
MOONEY PETER A 26 GRI W
MOONEY STEWARD A 26 BOR B
MOONEY W A A 26 BOR W
MOONING SANDY A 37 EDW B
MOONY J M A 46 KIN W
MOONY URIAS A 46 KIN W
MOOR DANIEL A 39 DAV B
MOOR DAVID A 37 SHA W
MOOR DAVID D A 37 HIG W
MOOR DOCTOR R A A 37 SHA W
MOOR EXUM L A 37 SPA W
MOOR GUILFORD A 37 HIG W
MOOR HENRY A 37 ROB B
MOOR ISAAC C A 37 HIG W
MOOR JACKSON L A 37 ROC B
MOOR JACOB A 37 SHA W
MOOR JAMES A 37 ROC W
MOOR MOSES A 37 SPA W
MOOR NATHAN A 37 WEB W
MOOR NEWELL A 32 DAV B
MOOR SPAR D A 37 HIG W
MOOR THEOPOLIS A 37 SHA W
MOOR YORK A 37 ROC B
MOORE A A 29 FA1 W
MOORE A F A 39 HAY W
MOORE A L A 46 KIN W
MOORE A M A 32 THO W
MOORE A S A 39 FRA W
MOORE A S A 39 HAR W
MOORE A S A 46 MON W

MOORE AARON A 35 MAG B
MOORE AARON A 37 TA1 B
MOORE ABRAHAM A 28 15T B
MOORE ABRAM A 40 DA1 B
MOORE ADAM A 40 DA1 B
MOORE ADDISON H A 46 GRE W
MOORE ALDIN A 19 SHA W
MOORE ALEXANDER C A 72 SWA W
MOORE ALEXANDRIA A 53 GER B
MOORE ALFORD A 44 LED B
MOORE ALFRED A 28 02N B
MOORE ALFRED A 28 03A B
MOORE ALFRED A 29 LOC B
MOORE ALFRED A 35 WAR W
MOORE ALLEN A 35 WAR B
MOORE AMARIAH A 28 9TH B
MOORE AMOS A 26 SHE B
MOORE AMOS A 28 05A B
MOORE AMOS A 39 DAV B
MOORE ANDREW A 29 FA1 B
MOORE ANGUS A 28 05A B
MOORE ANTHONY W A 29 FA1 B
MOORE AP A 35 WAR B
MOORE ASA W A 72 SWA W
MOORE AUGUSTUS M A 24 EDE W
MOORE AUSTIN A 28 05A B
MOORE B A 29 CAR W
MOORE B W A 25 HAY W
MOORE BAKER A 28 12T B
MOORE BANNON A 28 9TH B
MOORE BENJ A 44 LED B
MOORE BENJAMIN A 19 HAR B
MOORE BENTON A 29 FA1 B
MOORE BIAS A 28 01A B
MOORE BUCK A 37 HIC B
MOORE CAESAR A 28 05A B
MOORE CHARLES A 25 SHO B
MOORE CHARLES A 26 SWA B
MOORE CHARLES A 28 16T B
MOORE CHARLES A 39 DAV B
MOORE CHARLES A 72 SWA W
MOORE CHARLES H A 35 MAG B
MOORE CHAS F A 29 FA1 B
MOORE CHURCHWELL A 28 01B B
MOORE CICERO A 28 12T B
MOORE COLLINS A 28 05A B
MOORE CORNELIUS A 28 05A B
MOORE D O H P A 26 BUR W
MOORE DANIEL A 28 16T B
MOORE DANIEL A 28 16T B
MOORE DANIEL W A 35 WAR W
MOORE DAVID A 28 01A B
MOORE DAVID A 28 12T B
MOORE DAVID A 37 PIN B
MOORE DENNIS A 19 NEW B
MOORE DIXON B A 53 GER W
MOORE E L A 29 GRA W
MOORE EDWARD G A 53 LA1 B
MOORE EDWIN G A 19 BE1 W
MOORE ELI A 37 HIC B
MOORE ELI A 46 HIG W
MOORE ELIJAH A 32 BRO W
MOORE ELIZAH F A 29 FA1 W
MOORE EMANUEL A 28 10T B
MOORE FERNEY A 28 04A B
MOORE FRANCIS A 26 MOU W
MOORE G L A 26 SWA W
MOORE G M A 26 HOL B
MOORE GEORGE A 28 04A B
MOORE GEORGE A 28 05A B
MOORE GEORGE A 35 CYP B
MOORE GEORGE A 35 GLI B
MOORE GEORGE A 37 PIN B

MOORE GEORGE M R 26 MOO W
MILITIA OFFICER
MOORE GILES A 28 03A B
MOORE GRANISON A 37 MAN B
MOORE GREENE A 53 GER B
MOORE GRIEF A 40 DA1 B
MOORE H T A 44 LED W
MOORE HAMMOND A 28 03A B
MOORE HANS A 28 11T B
MOORE HARBERT C A 46 SUM W
MOORE HARRY A 35 KEN B
MOORE HENRY A 28 03A B
MOORE HENRY A 28 11T W
MOORE HENRY A 28 16T B
MOORE HENRY A 53 FAI B
MOORE HENRY C A 35 KEN W
MOORE HIRAM A 72 SWA W
MOORE ISAAC A 29 GRA B
MOORE ISAAC A 39 DAV B
MOORE J A A 25 TUS W
MOORE J C A 25 HAY W
MOORE J C A 28 04A B
MOORE J C A 39 DAV W
MOORE J F W A 46 SUM W
MOORE J H A 40 SAN W
MOORE J J A 44 FOR W
MOORE J L A 26 SHE W
MOORE J M A 40 CAN W
MOORE J O A 26 MOU W
MOORE JACOB A 28 04A B
MOORE JACOB A 28 04A B
MOORE JACOB A 28 9TH B
MOORE JACOB A 40 RHY B
MOORE JAMES A 26 MOO W
MILITIA OFFICER &
ENGAGED IN REBELLION
MOORE JAMES A 28 01A W
MOORE JAMES A 28 17T B
MOORE JAMES A 28 7TH B
MOORE JAMES A 29 FA1 B
MOORE JAMES A 35 ISL W
MOORE JAMES A 37 PIN B
MOORE JAMES A 37 ROB B
MOORE JAMES A 40 BLA W
MOORE JAMES A 53 LA1 B
MOORE JAMES E A 19 SHA W
MOORE JAMES H A 28 03A B
MOORE JAMES H A 28 16T B
MOORE JAMES P A 37 MAN B
MOORE JAMES W A 37 MAN B
MOORE JAMES W A 40 SAN W
MOORE JE A 39 FRA W
MOORE JESSE A 40 DA1 B
MOORE JESSE A 46 HIG W
MOORE JESSE R 40 DA1 B
9 MOS RESIDENCE
15 AUGUST 1867
MOORE JESSEE B A 29 CAR W
MOORE JNO T A 29 FA1 W
MOORE JOHN A 24 EDE B
MOORE JOHN A 28 03A B
MOORE JOHN A 28 04A B
MOORE JOHN A 35 GLI B
MOORE JOHN A 44 LED W
MOORE JOHN A 46 GRE B
MOORE JOHN A A 24 EDE W
MOORE JOHN ADAM A 28 03A B
MOORE JOHN E A 28 03A B
MOORE JOHN E A 28 12T B
MOORE JOHN R A 28 02N W
CERT GRANTED WILSON CO
MOORE JOHN W A 35 WAR W
MOORE JORDAN A 39 DAV B
MOORE JOSEPH A 28 05A B
MOORE JOSEPH A 35 MAG B
MOORE JOSEPH C A 37 ROB W
MOORE JOSEPH JR A 28 05A B
MOORE LEONARD A 35 MAG B
MOORE LEVI A 35 MAG W
MOORE LEWIS A 32 JAC W
MOORE LEWIS A 53 GER B
MOORE LOUIS A 19 MOR B
MOORE MACLIN A 28 03A B
MOORE MAJOR A 46 GRE W
MOORE MANUEL A 53 GER B
MOORE MARCUS A 35 CYP B
MOORE MARSHALL A 37 TA1 B
MOORE MARTEN A 53 GER B
MOORE MARTIN A 28 15T W
MOORE MATTHEW A 35 WAR W
MOORE MICHAL A 53 LA1 B
MOORE MOSES A 44 TAR B
MOORE NAT A 44 FOR W
MOORE NATHAN A 28 12T B
MOORE NATHAN A 46 HIG W
MOORE NEEDHAM A 39 FRA W
MOORE NEWTON A 28 7TH W
MOORE NOAH A 28 10T B
MOORE OLIVER A 28 03A B
MOORE OLIVER A 28 05A B
MOORE OTIS A 37 HIC B
MOORE P H A 39 HAY W
MOORE PETER A 24 EDE B
MOORE PETER A 25 SHO B
MOORE R G A 39 LOU W
MOORE R G A 44 HEN W
MOORE RILEY A 28 05A B
MOORE RILEY A 53 GER B
MOORE ROBERT A 35 MAG B
MOORE ROBERT A 53 GER B
MOORE ROBERT CHAL A 32 TYR W
FOR HOLDING OFFICE OF
MAGISTRATE BEFORE AND
DURING THE WAR. RECON.
MOORE ROBERT A A 39 DAV W
MOORE ROBT A 28 05A B
MOORE ROGER W A 53 GER W
MOORE S H A 39 FRA W
MOORE S T A 26 BOR W
MOORE SAMEUL A 35 MAG B
MOORE SAML A 44 LED B
MOORE SAMUEL A 19 SHA W
MOORE SAMUEL A 28 11T B
MOORE SAMUEL A 28 11T W
MOORE SAMUEL L A 37 TA1 W
MOORE SAMUEL R A 37 SPA W
MOORE SILAS A 28 03A B
MOORE SOLOMON A 30 NOR W
MOORE STEPHEN A 28 04A B
MOORE STEPHEN A 28 9TH B
MOORE STEPHEN A 37 MAN B
MOORE STYRON S A 53 LA1 W
MOORE THOMAS A 28 11T W
MOORE THOMAS A 28 7TH B
MOORE THOMAS A 28 9TH B
MOORE THOMAS A 35 KEN B
MOORE THOMAS A 35 MAG B
MOORE THOMAS A 46 MON W
MOORE THOMAS M A 35 KEN W
MOORE THOS A 26 HOL B
MOORE THOS A 46 JAM W
MOORE TIREY A 72 SWA W
MOORE TONEY A 35 MAG B
MOORE TURNER A 28 11T B
MOORE TYREE A 19 SHA W
MOORE W E A 29 FA1 W
MOORE W H A 26 GRI W
MOORE W P A 46 GRE W
MOORE W R A 44 FOR W
MOORE W T A 32 THO W
MOORE WILLIAM A 28 7TH W
MOORE WILLIAM A 32 BRO W
MOORE WILLIAM A 35 MAG B
MOORE WILLIAM A 37 PIN B
MOORE WILLIAM A 39 JOR W
MOORE WILLIAM A 53 GER B
MOORE WILLIAM A A 37 TA1 W
MOORE WILLIAM D A 46 GRE W
MOORE WILLIAM HENRY A 28 12T B
MOORE WILLIAM J A 28 9TH B
MOORE WILLIAM JOHN A 37 TA1 B
MOORE WILLIAM M A 53 GER W
MOORE WILLIAM P A 32 TYR W
MOORE WILLIAM Y A 37 TA2 W
SPARTA
MOORE WILLIS A 28 03A B
MOORE WILSON A 24 EDE B
MOORE WM A 28 04A B
MOORE WM A 28 04A B
MOORE WM A 28 05A B
MOORE WM A 44 LED B
MOORE WM A A 19 BE1 W
MOORE WM C A 29 FA1 W
MOORE WM G A 46 GRE W
MOORE WM H A 28 04A B
MOORE WM H A 44 FOR W
MOORE WM J A 19 BE1 B
CERT REMOVED TO NEWPORT
MOORE WM P A 28 02N W
MOORE WM S A 46 GRE W
MOORE WM T A 28 6TH W
MOORE WRIGHT A 28 7TH W
MOORE YORK A 53 SWA B
MOORE ZACHARIAH A 28 9TH B
MOORE
(MUNN?) ANDREW A 24 EDE B
MOOREFIELD
WASHINGTON A 32 SHE W
MOORING GUILFORD A 37 HIC B
MOORING JOHN A 37 HIC B
MOORING NOAH A 37 HIC B
MOORING RICHMOND A 37 TA1 B
MOORING SPENCER A 37 HIC B
MORAN JOSEPH A 24 EDE W
MORBLY JOHN A 19 HAD W
MORDACAI WESLEY A 44 DUT B
MORDECAI ISAIAH A 28 04A B
MORDECAI JOHN A 28 04A B
MORDECAI JOHN A 28 05A B
MORDECAI THOS A 28 04A B
MORDICA HENDERSON A 37 SPA B
MORDICAI ANTNA A 32 DAV B
MORDICIA SAML A 39 LOU B
MORE GILBERT A 19 HAR B
MORE JAMES A 19 BE2 B
MORE MACK A 19 BE1 B
MORE RUFERS A 19 BE1 B
MORE SILAS A 19 HAR B
MORE W B A 29 LOC B
MOREHEAD C A A 46 GRE B
MOREHEAD CHARLES A 46 SUM B
MOREHEAD CURBY A 46 GRE B
MOREHEAD DRAPER A 46 SUM B
MOREHEAD E J A 26 HOL B
MOREHEAD ELLIS A 46 GRE B
MOREHEAD FRANK A 46 GRE B
MOREHEAD GEORGE A 46 GRE B
MOREHEAD GRAVES A 46 GRE B
MOREHEAD HENRY A 46 GRE B

MOREHEAD HORACE A 46 SUM B
MOREHEAD JAMES A 46 SUM B
MOREHEAD JAMES C A 46 GRE B
MOREHEAD JAMES JR A 46 SUM B
MOREHEAD JAMES SR A 46 SUM B
MOREHEAD JAMES T A 46 GRE W
MOREHEAD JOHN A 46 SUM B
MOREHEAD JOSEPH M A 46 GRE W
MOREHEAD PINKNEY A 46 GRE B
MOREHEAD R L A 46 SUM W
MOREHEAD RICHARD A 46 SUM B
MOREHEAD ROBT A 46 SUM B
MOREHEAD SANDY A 46 SUM B
MOREHEAD SIDNEY A 46 SUM B
MOREHEAD THOMAS A 46 GRE B
MOREHEAD THOMAS M A 46 SUM B
MOREHEAD TININ A 46 GRE B
MOREHEAD TYLER A 46 GRE B
MOREHEAD WASHINGTON A 46 GRE B
MOREHEAD WILLIAM A 46 SUM B
MOREHEAD WM A 46 GRE B
MOREHEAD WM JR A 46 GRE B
MOREHEAD WM Y A 46 GRE B
MORES THOMAS A 37 ROB W
MORGAN A S A 30 IND W
REMOVED TO E CITY
PASQUOTANK CO
MORGAN ALEXANDER A 32 CLE B
MORGAN ALLEN A 44 FOR B
MORGAN ANDREW A 46 FRI W
MORGAN BENJ A 44 BRA B
MORGAN CALVIN R 46 GRE W
NAME LINED OUT
WAS AN OVERSEER OF A
HIGHWAY BEFORE THE WARE
AND AFTERWARD VOLUNTEERED
IN THE CONFEDERATE ARMY
BECAUS OF BEING DRAFTED
HAS NOT QUALIFIED.
MORGAN CHARLES A 37 TA2 B
MORGAN COLLUMBUS A 26 BUR B
MORGAN ELWOOD A 46 FRI W
MORGAN EPHRAIM A 32 SHE B
MORGAN GRAFTON W A 46 FRI W
MORGAN H G A 44 FOR B
MORGAN HENRY A 24 MID W
ERAST FROM MIDDEL AND
PLASTE ON EDENTON PRE
CINCT FOR EDENTON
MORGAN HENRY A 28 01B B
MORGAN HENRY A 29 FA1 B
MORGAN HEZEKIAH A 37 ROB W
MORGAN HILLARY A 37 ROB W
MORGAN HILLIARD A 28 9TH B
MORGAN J B CHAL R 30 IND W
MORGAN J S A 44 SAS W
MORGAN JNO A 29 FA1 W
MORGAN JNO B A 37 ROB W
MORGAN JOHN A 37 TA1 B
MORGAN JOHN E A 24 MID W
MORGAN JONAS A 28 11T B
CERTIFICATE GIVEN LIVES
NOW AT ELIZABETH CITY
MORGAN JOSIAH A 99 BUS B
MORGAN KADER A 99 BUS B
MORGAN LEWIS A 37 TA1 B
MORGAN LONEY A 28 05A B
MORGAN MARK A 29 ROC W
MILLITIA OFFICER HELPED
TO TAKE ARSENAL AT FAY-
ETTEVILLE IN 61
MORGAN MARTIN A 37 PEN B
MORGAN MATHEW A 29 FA1 B
MORGAN MOSSE A 39 GRI W
MORGAN N M A 46 KIN W
MORGAN NATHAN A 29 FA1 B
MORGAN NATHAN A 38 FRE B
MORGAN O P A 26 GOF W
MORGAN P H A 30 IND W
MORGAN R B A 44 ISL W
MORGAN REDIN A A 37 ROB W
MORGAN RUFUS A 28 01A W
MORGAN SAM A 39 PUG B
MORGAN STEPHEN A 37 HIG B
MORGAN WIAT A 44 DUT B
MORGAN WILLIAM A 39 LOU B
MORGAN WILLIAM A 46 FRI W
MORGAN WILLIAM F A 28 10T B
MORGAN WILLIAMSON A 37 ROB W
MORGAN WILLIE A 37 ROC B
MORGAN WM J A 19 HAR W
CERT TO BEAUFORT
MORGIN HILLSMAN A 39 GRI B
MORGIN WILLIAM A 32 DAV W
MORGON GABRAL A 32 DAV B
MORISETT ASA A 30 IND W
MORISETT PETER A 30 IND W
MORISEY DANIEL A 35 WAR B
MORISEY DAVID J A 35 WAR W
MORISEY GEORGE A 35 WAR W
MORISEY HARRY A 35 WAR B
MORISEY HAYWOOD A 35 WAR B
MORISEY SAMUEL A 35 WAR B
MORISEY THOMAS A 35 MAG B
MORISON JOHN A 40 BLA W
MORISON LEVI A 40 BLA W
MORISON MAXVILL A 40 BLA W
MORISON NELSON A 29 SEV B
MORISON WILLIAM A 40 BLA W
MORRELL OSBORN A 28 9TH B
MORRIL WM H A 44 SAS W
MORRIS A G A 32 JAC W
MORRIS ADAM A 46 KIN B
MORRIS ALEXR A 28 6TH B
MORRIS AMOS A A 40 DA1 W
CERT ISSUED TO LINCOLN
CO NC APRIL 13 1868
MORRIS ASA A 44 OXF W
MORRIS ATHEN A 53 GER B
MORRIS AXAM A 35 FAI W
MORRIS B H A 19 HAD W
MORRIS B W A 28 03A B
MORRIS BENJAMIN A 53 FAI B
MORRIS BENJAMIN W A 28 15T W
MORRIS BENNETT A 24 EDE B
MORRIS CALVIN J A 28 16T W
MORRIS CHRIS. A 32 JAC W
MORRIS DAVID A 24 EDE B
MORRIS DAVID A 44 OXF B
MORRIS DURAN A 53 LA1 B
MORRIS E K A 32 THO W
MORRIS FED A 39 PUG B
MORRIS FREDRICH A 32 JAC W
MORRIS FREDRICK A 32 JAC W
MORRIS GARRY A 37 HIG W
MORRIS HENDERSON A 28 01A B
MORRIS HENRY A 32 JAC W
MORRIS HENRY A 44 KNA W
MORRIS HENRY J A 28 11T W
MORRIS HENRY W A 32 POS W
MORRIS HEZAKIAH A 53 LA1 B
MORRIS J A A 44 OXF W
MORRIS J H A 44 FOR W
MORRIS J M A 26 BLA W
MORRIS J W A 32 JAC W
MORRIS JACOB A 44 RAG B
MORRIS JAMES H A 28 14T W
MORRIS JAMES R A 19 HUN W
MORRIS JAS L A 24 EDE W
MORRIS JESSE A 28 10T B
MORRIS JESSE A 32 JAC W
MORRIS JESSE A 32 THO W
MORRIS JOHN A 28 16T W
MORRIS JOHN A 28 8TH B
MORRIS JOHN A 32 JAC W
MORRIS JOHN A 32 JAC W
MORRIS JOHN A 53 FAI B
MORRIS JOHN A A 28 13T W
MORRIS JOHN W A 28 15T W
MORRIS JOSEPH A 28 11T W
MORRIS JOSEPH A 28 8TH B
MORRIS JOSEPH A 44 KNA W
MORRIS JOSEPH A 53 LA1 B
MORRIS JOSEPH H A 44 TAR W
MORRIS JOTHAN A 32 JAC W
MORRIS LEONARD A 28 8TH B
MORRIS LYNDSAY A 32 JAC W
MORRIS PRESTON A 37 SHA B
MORRIS R F A 32 JAC W
MORRIS R T A 26 SHE W
MORRIS RICHARD A 53 GER B
MORRIS RICHARD A 53 LA1 B
MORRIS ROBERT A 37 ROC B
MORRIS RUFUS A 28 04A B
MORRIS S G A 32 THO W
MORRIS SHEPHERD A 32 THO W
MORRIS STEPH A 28 6TH B
MORRIS STEPHEN A A 28 12T W
MORRIS SYLVESTER A 53 BUR W
MORRIS THOMAS A 28 03A B
MORRIS THOMAS A 32 JAC W
MORRIS W L A 32 THO W
MORRIS W N A 32 JAC W
MORRIS W W OF JAMES A 24 EDE W
MORRIS WILLIAM A 28 11T W
MORRIS WILLIAM A 32 JAC W
MORRIS WILLIAM A 32 LOF W
MORRIS
WILLIAM AUGUSTUS A 28 12T W
MORRIS WILLIAM G A 40 DA1 W
MORRIS WILLIAM JR A 53 BUR W
MORRIS WILLIAM SR A 53 BUR W
MORRIS WILLIE P A 44 OXF W
MORRIS WILLIS A 44 RAG B
MORRIS WM A A 24 EDE W
MORRIS WM B A 28 11T W
MORRIS WM T A 28 15T W
MORRIS WM W A 24 EDE W
MORRIS ZACHARIAH A 53 FAI B
MORRISETT CASON A 30 COI W
MORRISETT JOHN A 30 GIB W
MORRISETT NATHAN A 30 POP W
MORRISEY ALBT A 29 LOC B
MORRISON DUNCAN A 29 MON W
MORRISON FINDLY A 29 MON W
MORRISON HUCE A 40 CAN B
MORRISON JACOB A 40 CAN B
MORRISON JNO H A 44 KNA W
MORRISON JOHN A 40 CAN B
MORRISON LEWIS A 40 CAN B
MORRISON MALCOM A 29 ROC W
MORRISON ROBT A 29 QUW B
MORRISON THOMAS A 40 BLA W
MORRISSERY JUBATER A 19 HAD B
MORRISSON D A 26 BOR W
MORRISSON D J A 26 CAR W
MORRISSON J A 26 BOR W
MORRISSON WM A 26 CAR W
MORROW ASTIN A 44 SAS B

MORROW JOHN A A 40 DA1 W
MORROW MORISON A 46 GRE B
MORROW ROBERT A 26 GOF W
MORROW SIFUS A 44 SAS B
MORROW WM H A 29 FA1 W
MORSE DAVID W A 19 BE1 W
MORSE DAVIS B A 30 TUL W
MORSE ELIJAH A 30 IND W
MORSE HILLARY A 30 CUR W
MORSE J F A 19 HAD W
MORSE J J A 30 MOY W
MORSE JACOB A 19 BE2 W
MORSE JAMES A 30 TUL W
MORSE JAMES A 30 MOY W
MORSE SIMEON A 30 POP B
MORSE SOLAMON A 30 CUR B
MORSE THOMAS A 19 MOR B
MORSE WILLIAM J A 30 NOR W
MORSE WILLIS A 30 IND W
MORSE WILLSON H A 19 BE1 W
MORSE ZACH B A 30 POW W
MORTEN ABNER A 19 NEW B
MORTON B G A 39 FRA W
MORTON BENJAMINE A 72 SWA W
MORTON C E A 30 CUR W
MORTON C R A 44 TOW W
MORTON CAESAR A 28 05A B
MORTON CLIM A 44 SAS B
MORTON D A A 19 HAD W
MORTON E CHAL R 30 CUR W
GIVING AID & ASST
MORTON ELISHA A 19 NEW W
MORTON EZEKEL H A 72 SWA W
MORTON FRANCE A 19 NEW W
MORTON GEO A 19 NEW W
MORTON GEO W A 39 FRA W
MORTON GEORGE A 44 TOW B
MORTON ISHAM A 44 SAS B
MORTON JAMES A 37 MAN B
MORTON JAS A 44 SAS B
MORTON JNO A 44 TOW B
MORTON JOHN A 19 NEW W
MORTON KITT A 44 HEN B
MORTON LENORD A 19 NEW W
MORTON LEWIS A 72 SWA W
MORTON LUCY A 44 SAS B
MORTON MOMFORD A 44 SAS B
MORTON N D A 44 YXS W
MORTON PHIL A 44 YXS B
MORTON ROBERT A 44 HEN B
MORTON ROBERT A 44 SAS B
MORTON SAML C A 44 TOW W
MORTON SPOTSWOOD A 44 YXR B
MORTON T W A 19 HAR W
MORTON THOMAS A 72 SWA W
MORTON W H A 39 FRA W
MORTON WESLEY E A 72 SWA W
MORTON WILLIAM A 44 YXS B
MORTON WILSON A 44 SAS B
MORTON YORK A 44 SAS B
MOSELEY AMERICA A 28 03A B
MOSELEY CHARLES A 28 6TH B
MOSELEY CRAVEN A 28 9TH B
MOSELEY FREDK A 28 6TH B
MOSELEY HENRY A 28 7TH B
MOSELEY JOHN A 28 6TH B
MOSELEY NICHOLAS A 28 6TH B
MOSELEY ROBIN A 28 03A B
MOSELEY ROBT G A 28 03A B
MOSELEY WM A 28 03A B
MOSELEY WM A 28 6TH B
MOSELY HANDY A 19 NEW B
MOSES AARON T A 99 BUS W
MOSES ELI A 24 EDE W
MOSES L H A 39 DAV W
MOSES WILLIAM THOMASA 39 DAV W
MOSLEY JAMES A 37 SHA W
MOSLEY JAMES A 39 PUG W
TRANS TO LOUISBURG
MOSLEY ROBERT A 37 MAN B
MOSS A H A 26 CAR W
MOSS ABRAM A 44 BEA B
MOSS ANDREW A 40 SAN W
MOSS B Y A 44 LED W
MOSS BENJAMIN L A 39 JOR W
MOSS C J A 39 HAY W
NAME LINED OUT
1ST BORD OF REGIS
APP IN FOR PRECT.
MOSS C W A 32 CLE W
MOSS CEZAR A 44 BRA B
MOSS CHAS A 44 KIT W
MOSS CION A 40 SAN W
MOSS DANNEL A 44 DUT B
MOSS EMOND A 44 OXF B
MOSS H M A 25 HAY W
MOSS HOWEL A 25 TUS W
MOSS J C A 44 BRA W
MOSS J D A 44 BRA W
MOSS J F DR A 39 FRA W
MOSS J J A 44 ISL W
MOSS J M A 25 TUS W
MOSS J R A 39 HAY W
MOSS J W A 25 SHO W
MOSS J Y A 44 BRA W
MOSS JAMES A 26 CAR W
MOSS JERRY A 44 OXF B
MOSS JOHN D A 44 BRA W
MOSS L H A 44 BRA W
MOSS M G A 39 HAR W
MOSS MARTIN A 26 CAR W
MOSS MELTON A 25 SHO W
MOSS MELTON A 26 PEE W
MOSS NED A 32 CLE B
MOSS NEWTON A 44 BRA B
MOSS PETER A 19 MOR W
MOSS RICHARD A 44 FOR W
MOSS S H A 44 BRA W
MOSS SAML A 44 BRA W
MOSS THOMAS A 44 KIT W
MOSS VIRGIL A 44 BRA B
MOSS W F A 44 BEA W
MOSS WALTER W A 44 SAS B
MOSS WILLIAM A 44 KIT W
MOSS WM A 26 CAR W
MOSS WM A 44 BRA B
MOSTILLER G W A 25 TUS W
MOSTILLER PETER CHALA 25 TUS W
FOR VOTING AGAINST THE
RATIFICATION OF CONSTI-
TUTION
MOSTILLER VARDE A 25 TUS W
MOTEN ANDREW A 44 FOR W
MOTLEY JOHN M A 46 GRE W
MOTLEY WM D A 46 GRE W
MOTON ANDREW R A 40 DA1 W
MOTON G F A 44 BRA W
MOTON LUKE A 28 7TH B
MOTON RICHARD A 32 JAC B
MOTSINGER A H A 32 POS W
MOTSINGER ANDREW A 32 POS W
MOTSINGER D P A 32 BRO W
MOTSINGER GEORGE L A 32 POS W
MOTSINGER HENRY A 32 POS W
MOTSINGER JACOB A 32 POS W
MOTSINGER JAMES W A 32 BRO W
MOTSINGER JOSEPH A 32 POS W
MOTSINGER M M A 46 HIG W
MOTSINGER P N A 32 BRO W
MOTTOCKS ANTHONY A 72 SWA B
MOTZ ALFRED A 40 DA1 B
MOTZ YORK A 26 GRI B
MOULTON DAVID A 28 03A B
MOUNGER PETER A 39 PUG W
MOUNTAIN HENRY A 28 04A B
MOURNING JACOB A 19 BE1 B
MOUSON KENNETH M A 32 DAV W
MOWERS S H A 28 01A W
MOYE GARRETT G A 28 05A B
MOYE GILBERT A 28 10T B
MOYE JOS A 39 GRI W
MOYE LINSEY A 39 GRI W
MOYE THOMAS A 39 GRI W
MOYE THOMAS H A 37 TA2 W
MOYE WM A 39 GRI W
MOYE WM B A 28 11T W
MOYNING ALFRED A 28 05A B
MOYNING MUSTAPHA A 28 04A B
MOYNING WM A 28 02N B
MOYNING WM A 28 05A B
MOZINGO JAMES A 28 15T W
MOZINGO THOMAS A A 28 16T W
MUDDYMORE MITCHELL A 28 9TH B
MULCHI G W A 44 YXR W
MULCHI WILLIAM A 44 YXR W
MULENO P S A 26 SHE W
MULL JULIUS A A 26 WAR W
MULL WILLIAM A 26 WAR W
MULLEN CHADWICK A 28 04A B
MULLEN HENRY A 24 EDE B
MULLEN HENRY A 28 05A B
MULLEN JAMES K A 37 ROC W
MULLEN LEVI A 28 03A B
MULLEN THOS A 28 05A B
MULLENAX HENRY M A 40 DA2 W
MULLENAX WILLIAM T A 40 DA2 W
MULLETT WM A A 44 YXR W
MULLICAN E W A 32 CLE W
MULLICAN L C A 32 CLE W
MULLICAN L S A 32 CLE W
MULLIGAN JAMES A 40 CAN W
MULLIN ADAM A 29 FA1 B
MULLIN JNO T A 29 FA1 W
MULLINAX T H A 26 CAR W
MULLINS BERRY A 39 GRI W
MULLINS BURGESS A 39 GRI W
MULLINS J C A 39 GRI W
MULLINS W A A 39 GRI W
MULLY WESTLY A 29 ROC B
MUMFORD ALFRED A 28 04A B
MUMFORD BERRI A 19 NEW B
MUMFORD DANL A 28 04A B
MUMFORD EZEKEL A 72 SWA B
MUMFORD JOSEPH A 28 04A B
MUMFORD MOSSIS A 19 BE1 B
MUMFORD PETER A 28 03A B
MUMFORD WARRICK A 28 03A B
MUNDEN THOS G A 30 CUR W
MUNDS HINTIN A 29 BLA W
MUNDS W W A 29 BLA W
MUNDS WILLIAM A 24 MID W
MUNET LUCIUS A 39 PUG W
MUNJOHN JAMES A 28 01A B
MUNN ALEXANDER A 44 ISL W
MUNN DUNCAN JR A 29 CAR W
MUNN WHEELER A 44 RAG W
MUNN WM A 29 CAR W
MUNROE CALVIN A 29 SEV B
MUNROE CHRISTOPHER A 29 SEV W

MUNROE DANIEL R 29 MON B
UNDER AGE NO OATH
MUNROE DANIEL C A 29 SEV W
MUNROE DUNCAN J A 29 SEV W
MUNROE DUNCAN L A 29 SEV W
MUNROE ELISHA A 29 SEV W
MILITIA OFF TAKEN AN OATH TO SUPPORT THE CONSTITUTION OF THE U.S. BEFORE THE REBELLIION AFTERWARDS ENGAGED IN THE REBELLION
MUNROE GILBERT A 29 SEV W
MUNROE H N A 29 SEV W
MUNROE HASTY A 19 BE1 B
MUNROE J A A 29 SEV W
MUNROE JOHN A 19 BE1 B
MUNROE JOHN A 29 SEV W
MUNROE NEILL L A 29 SEV W
MUNROE P D P A 29 SEV W
MUNROE STEPNEY A 29 SEV B
MUNROE THOMAS A 29 SEV W
MUNROE WHITNEY A 29 SEV B
MURCER STEVEN A 30 IND W
MURCHASEN BUCK A 29 FA1 B
MURCHASEN JACK A 29 FA1 B
MURCHASEN SAML A 29 FA1 B
MURCHASIN ISAAC A 29 FA1 B
MURCHASIN KATO A 29 FA1 B
MURCHASIN PATK A 29 CAR B
MURCHASIN WM A 29 FA1 B
MURCHASON CHARLES A 29 MON B
MURCHASON HECTOR A 29 MON B
MURCHISEN ISAAC A 29 FA1 B
MURCHISON ALEX A 29 FLE B
MURDAUGH DAVID A 24 EDE B
MURDAUGH MILLS A 24 EDE B
MURDEN CHAS M A 24 EDE W
MURDEN SOLOMAN A 53 FAI B
MURDOCK HUGH A 19 MOR W
MURPHEY ANDERSON P A 46 ROS W
MURPHEY BIRD A 39 JOR W
MURPHEY C A A 39 JOR W
MURPHEY D F A 39 LOU W
MURPHEY GRAY B A 39 JOR W
MURPHEY J J A 39 JOR W
MURPHEY J M A 39 JOR W
MURPHEY JESSE A 53 HAT W
MURPHEY JOHN W A 39 JOR W
MURPHEY JOSEPH JR A 39 LOU W
MURPHEY PARKER A 39 JOR W
MURPHEY PLEASANT A 32 POS W
MURPHREY JEHU A 32 THO W
MURPHREY ROBERT A 32 THO W
MURPHY ABNER A 28 03A B
MURPHY ALEX A 29 FA1 B
MURPHY ALEX A 29 FLE B
MURPHY ALFRED A 53 HAT W
MURPHY ALSON A 46 GRE W
MURPHY AMOS A 28 11T B
MURPHY ANTHONY A 28 03A B
MURPHY ANTHONY A 28 03A B
MURPHY ARNOLD A 19 BE1 B
MURPHY BLUNT A 28 05A B
MURPHY CHARLES A 35 ROC B
MURPHY CHAS A 29 GRA B
MURPHY DANIEL A 29 FLE B
MURPHY DANL A 29 FA1 B
MURPHY DANL A 29 GRA B
MURPHY EPH A 29 FLE B
MURPHY FREDK A 29 FA1 B
MURPHY GABRIEL A 35 MAG B
MURPHY GEO A 29 FA1 B
MURPHY GEO A 29 GRA B
MURPHY GRAY SR A 39 JOR W
MURPHY HENRY A 28 11T B
MURPHY HENRY A 29 FA1 B
MURPHY HENRY JR A 35 MAG B
MURPHY ISAAC A 29 FLE B
MURPHY J FRANKLIN A 40 DA1 W
MURPHY J J A 39 LOU W
MURPHY JACOB A 29 FLE B
MURPHY JACOB A 35 ISL B
MURPHY JAMES A 29 FLE B
MURPHY JAMES L A 28 11T W
MURPHY JNO A 29 FLE W
MURPHY JOHN A 28 7TH W
MURPHY JOHN E DR A 40 DEC W
MURPHY JONATHAN JR A 46 GRE W
MURPHY JONATHAN SR A 46 GRE W
MURPHY JOS A 29 FLE B
MURPHY KILLIS A 24 EDE B
MURPHY KINCHEN A 35 ROC B
MURPHY LEWIS A 44 YXR B
MURPHY MILTON A 46 GRE W
MURPHY MOSES A 37 ROB B
MURPHY ORMAND A 40 DA1 B
MURPHY PERMENUS A 29 ROC B
MURPHY PETER A 29 GRA B
MURPHY POINDEXTER D A 19 DAV W
MURPHY RICHD A 29 GRA B
MURPHY RILEY A 35 MAG B
MURPHY SAMEUL A 35 ROC B
MURPHY SIRUS A 29 FLE W
MURPHY TIMOTHY C A 35 ISL W
MURPHY WASHINGTON A 35 MAG B
MURPHY WILLIAM A 29 FLE B
MURPHY WM A 29 FA1 B
MURPHY WM A 29 FA1 W
MURPHY WM A 29 FLE W
MURPHY WM A 29 GRA B
MURRAY BENJ A 39 GRI W
MURRAY BENJAMIN A 35 ISL B
MURRAY COGDON A 28 9TH B
MURRAY DANIEL H A 35 ISL W
MURRAY DAVID A 35 ISL W
MURRAY GEORGE A 35 CYP B
MURRAY GUILFORD S A 35 KEN W
MURRAY HARVEY A 35 ISL B
MURRAY HILRY A 35 ISL B
MURRAY HILRY A 35 ROC B
MURRAY HIRAM A 35 ISL W
MURRAY HOSEA R A 35 MAG W
MURRAY ISAAC A 35 ISL B
MURRAY J J A 39 DAV W
MURRAY JAMES C A 35 ISL W
MURRAY JNO T A 44 TAR W
MURRAY JOHN A 35 ISL B
MURRAY JOHNATHAN A 35 ISL W
MURRAY JONATHAN W A 46 COB W
MURRAY JOSEPH A 35 ROC B
MURRAY KINYON A 28 9TH B
MURRAY LUCION H A 46 COB W
MURRAY M G A 39 LOU W
MURRAY MORGAN M A 53 LA2 W
MURRAY MORRIS A 35 ISL B
MURRAY NATHAN A 35 ISL W
MURRAY OBED W A 35 ISL W
MURRAY PATRICK A 35 ISL B
MURRAY PETER A 35 ISL B
MURRAY PRESLEY A 39 DAV W
MURRAY RICHD A 38 FRE B
MURRAY ROBERT F A 35 ISL W
MURRAY S M A 39 PUG W
MURRAY THOMAS A 19 BE1 W
MURRAY THOMAS A 35 CYP B
MURRAY THOMAS D A 53 SWA W
MURRAY THOMAS M A 35 ISL W
MURRAY WILLIAM H A 35 KEN W
MURRAY WILLIAM H A 35 MAG W
MURRAY WRIGHT A 35 CYP B
MURRAY WRIGHT A 35 ISL B
MURRELL HENRY A 32 TYR B
MURRELL JAMES A 30 POP W
MURRELL JOHN A 30 POW W
APRIL 17, 1868
MURRELL LEVI A 30 POW W
MURRILL PINK A 40 DA1 B
MURRY ABRAHAM A 53 LA1 B
MURRY ANDREW G R 46 ROS W
NAME LINED OUT A POSTMASTER BEFORE WAR BUT THE OFFICE WAS SOON REMOVED BECAUS OF HIS UNION CENTAMENTS. WAS APT MAGISTRATE BY THE UNION ELEMENT DURING THE WARE. WAS NOT QUALIFIED.
MURRY BENJAMIN A 53 LA1 B
MURRY DAVID A 53 LA1 B
MURRY DAVID A 53 LA1 W
MURRY JAMES A 24 MID B
MURRY JAMES A 53 FAI B
MURRY MARKANTHONY A 53 FAI B
MURRY MOSES A 53 SWA B
MURRY R J A 46 SUM W
MURRY RICHARD A 53 LA1 B
MURRY W R A 46 GRE W
MURRY WILLIAM D A 53 FAI W
MURRY WILLIAM G 53 FAI W
NAME LINED OUT WAS STRUCK FROM THE BOOK BECAUSE HE WAS CONVICTED OF MANSLAUGHTER THE THIRD DEGREE NOT KNOWN IT COME UNDER THE HEAD OF A FELONY AND HE WISHES US TO STRICK HIS NAME FROM THE BOOK WHICH WE DID
MUSE HENRY H A 28 16T W
MUSE LEWIS A 28 15T W
MUSE SETH A 28 16T W
MUSE STEPHEN A A 29 FA1 W
MUSGRAVE C A 32 DAV W
MUSGRAVE CALVIN A 35 FAI W
MUSGROVE GEORGE A 32 DAV W
MUSSELWHITE JNO A 29 ROC W
MUSSELWHITE NEILL W A 29 ROC W
MUSTON ROBERT A 46 KIN W
MUSTON WILLIAM A 46 KIN W
MYATT J B A 99 BUS W
MYDGETT S D A 30 IND W
MYERS A L A 32 DAV W
MYERS A L A 32 THO W
MYERS ALEXANDER W A 24 EDE W
MYERS ALFERD M A 32 THO W
MYERS AMBROSE A 32 THO W
MYERS ANDREW A 32 THO W
MYERS ANDREW A 32 YAD W
MYERS CAANAN A 32 THO W
MYERS DANIEL A 32 THO W
MYERS DAVID A 28 05A B
MYERS DAVID A 32 THO W
MYERS DAVID SR A 32 THO W
MYERS GEORGE A 32 THO W
MYERS GREEN A 32 THO B
MYERS H F A 32 THO W
MYERS HENRY A 35 WAR W
MYERS ISAAC A 28 04A B

MYERS J A A 32 YAD W
MYERS J C A 32 THO W
MYERS JACKSON A 32 THO W
MYERS JOHN A 28 05B W
MYERS JOHN A 32 YAD W
MYERS M M A 32 THO W
MYERS MADISON A 32 THO B
MYERS MARK A 35 KEN W
MYERS MERIT A A 32 SHE W
MYERS PETER A 32 THO W
MYERS R B A 32 DAV W
MYERS ROBT A 32 DAV W
MYERS SAMUEL L A 32 THO W
MYERS W A A 32 THO W
MYERS W J A 32 THO W
MYERS WM H A 32 THO W
MYNER J W A 28 01A W
MYRES BENJAMIN A 32 DAV W
MYRES DAVID A 32 LEE W
MYRES HALY A 32 LEE W
MYRES HENRY A 32 TYR W
MYRES JESSE A 32 LEE W
MYRES PHILIP A 32 COT W
MYRES THOMAS A 32 THO W
MYRES VOLANTINE A 32 DAV W
MYRES WILLIAM A 32 TYR W
MYRES WILLIAM A A 32 LEE W
MYRICK JOHN G A 39 SPE W
MYRICK O F JR A 39 SPE W
MYRICK O F SR A 39 SPE W
MYRICK SASER A 32 TYR W
MYROVER H L A 29 FA1 W
MYROVER J H A 29 FA1 W
MYROVER THOS A 29 FA1 B
MYROVER W J A 29 FA1 W
LUMBERTON ROBESON CO
CERTIFICATE APL 9TH 68

- N -

NAILING EATON A 44 BRA B
NANCE CLAYBOURNE A 40 DA1 W
NANCE EDWARD A 40 CAN B
NANCE HARISON A 32 JAC W
NANCE JOHN A 40 DA1 W
NANCE JOHN A 44 LED W
NANCE L P A 32 JAC W
NANCE LAWSON A 40 CAN W
NANCE LAWSON A 40 DA1 W
NANCE MARTIAL A 32 JAC W
NANCE VINCENT A 26 GOF W
NANCE WM J A 29 FA1 W
NANCE ZAC H A 32 THO W
NANTHANIELS JACOB A 19 BE1 B
NANTZ RICHARD C A 40 DA1 W
NAPPER JOSEPH A 46 MON B
NARRIS JNO A 44 OXF B
NASH ANDREW A 29 FA1 B
NASH JAMES E A 28 03B W
NASH LAFAYETTE A 28 03A B
NASH LEVI A 29 FA1 B
NASH WILLIAM A 29 FA1 B
NASH WILLIS A 29 FA1 B
NASON GEO W JR A 28 01A W
NATCH GEORGE A 28 8TH B
NATHANIEL ISAAC A 19 HAR B
NATHANIEL JOHN A 19 BE1 B
NATHANIELS BENJ A 19 BE1 B
NATT MILTON A 46 SUM W
NCCALL JOHN A 29 ROC W
NEAGLE FRANKLING A 40 STO B
NEAGLE ISAAC A 40 STO B
NEAL ABRAHAM A 39 HAR B
NEAL ABRAHAM A 39 SPE B
NEAL ALEXANDER A 39 SPE B
NEAL ALEXANDER A 40 STO B
NEAL ANDREW A 39 HAR B
NEAL AUSTIN A 39 LOU B
NEAL BENJAMIN A 39 SPE B
NEAL BENJAMIN F A 53 LA1 W
NEAL BENJAMIN O A 53 LA1 W
NEAL BENJAMIN R A 53 FAI W
NEAL BOB A 39 LOU B
TRNS FROM HARRIS X
ROADS TO LOUISBURG
NEAL CALVIN A 39 LOU B
NEAL CHARLES E A 37 TA1 W
NEAL DANIEL A 53 LA1 W
NEAL DAVID A 37 TA1 W
NEAL DAVID A 53 GER B
NEAL DAVID M A 53 SWA W
NEAL DAVID SR A 53 LA2 B
NEAL GEO W A 39 FRA W
NEAL GEORGE JR A 37 ROB W
NEAL HENRY A 53 LA1 B
NEAL HEZAKIAH H A 53 LA1 W
NEAL ISHAM A 39 SPE B
NEAL ISIAH S O A 53 GER W
NEAL J W A 26 BOR W
NEAL JACKSON A 53 LA1 B
NEAL JACOB A 26 GRI B
NEAL JACOB A 39 LOU B
NEAL JACOB A 39 SPE B
NEAL JAMES A 28 01A B
NEAL JAMES A 39 DAV B
NEAL JERRY A 39 PUG B
NEAL JOBE A 39 SPE B
NEAL JOHN B A 28 02N W
NEAL JOHN H A 53 LA1 W
NEAL JONATHAN A 53 SWA W
NEAL JOS A 46 GRE B
NEAL JOSEPH S A 53 FAI W
NEAL LEWIS A 39 SPE B
NEAL LEWIS A 53 SWA B
NEAL MATHEW A 39 FRA B
NEAL MINGO A 39 FRE B
NEAL MOSES A 28 04A B
NEAL MOSES A 39 LOU B
NEAL NEHEMIAH B A 53 FAI W
NEAL NOAH A 53 GER B
NEAL OLIVER O A 53 SWA W
NEAL PARKER A 53 GER B
NEAL PELIDGE A 53 GER B
NEAL PETER A 28 05A B
NEAL PETER A 53 GER B
NEAL REDIN A 39 DAV B
NEAL ROBERT A 39 LOU B
NEAL ROBT A 39 HAR B
NEAL SAMUEL A 39 LOU B
NEAL SIDNEY A 39 SPE B
NEAL SILAS A 28 03A B
NEAL SIMMONS O A 30 COI W
NEAL SIMON A 39 LOU B
NEAL SOLOMAN A 38 FRE B
NEAL STEVEN A 40 STO B
NEAL SYLVESTER A 53 SWA B
NEAL SYLVESTER O A 53 SWA B
NEAL T C A 39 FRA W
NEAL THOMAS A 39 DAV B
NEAL THOMAS O A 30 COI W
NEAL THOMAS O A 30 POW W
NEAL TOM A 39 DAV B
NEAL VERNAL A 53 SWA W
NEAL W R A 44 YXS W
NEAL WILLIAM O A 30 COI W
NEAL WM D A 26 CAR W
NEAL YANCEY A 44 YXS B
NEATHERY JAMES A 38 FRE W
NEELEY DANL G A 46 ROS W
NEELEY MARK A 46 ROS B
NEELY ANSON A 40 SAN B
NEELY SIPA A 40 SAN B
NEELY WILLIAM A 40 SAN B
NEEMAN DENNIS P A 44 FOR W
NEES DANIEL M A 46 COB W
NEES DAVID A 46 COB W
NEES J CHRISTIA A 46 COB W
NEES JAMES A 46 COB W
NEES JAMES P A 46 COB W
NEES JAMES R A 46 COB W
NEESE JOAB A 46 COB W
NEESE JORDAN A DR A 46 GIB W
NEESE SOLOMON A 46 GIB W
NEIL BENJAMIN A 28 10T B
NEIL DRURY A 26 SWA W
NEIL LEWIS A 28 10T B
NEIL LUKE A 28 15T B
NEIL PLEASANT A 29 FA1 W
NEIL SAMUEL A 28 10T B
NEIL YORK A 30 IND B
NEILL GEN MARION A 40 DEC W
NEILL JOHN C A 40 DEC W
NEILL JOS A 29 FA1 B
NEILL PETER A 40 DEC W
NEISBIT WM A 26 BOR B
NELMS JAMES N A 39 JOR W
NELSON A M A 46 GRE W
NELSON AARON A 28 9TH B
NELSON ABNER A 28 11T W
NELSON ALEC A 37 HIC B
NELSON ANSON H A 19 STR W
NELSON ARNET A 28 10T B
NELSON ASA A 28 04B B
NELSON AUGUSTUS W A 28 11T W
NELSON BERRY A 28 11T W
NELSON CALVIN A 32 SHE B
NELSON CHARLES A 19 BE1 B
NELSON CHARLES A 28 14T B
NELSON CHARLES A 28 6TH B
NELSON CHARLES A 46 JAM B
NELSON CHAS A A 28 01A W
NELSON E H A 28 10T W
NELSON EDNEY A 24 MID B
NELSON ELISHA A 28 05B B
NELSON EMANUAL M A 32 THO B
NELSON FRANCIS A 28 10T B
NELSON FRANCIS A 28 10T B
NELSON FRANK A 28 03B B
NELSON FRANK A 28 05A B
NELSON FRANK A 29 FA1 B
NELSON GEDDION A 32 SHE B
NELSON GEORGE A 28 04A B
NELSON GEORGE A 28 9TH B
NELSON GEORGE A 46 MCL B
NELSON GEORGE A 46 SUM B
NELSON GEORGE 2ND A 28 04A B
NELSON GILBERT A 44 HEN B
NELSON HARDY A 28 01A B
NELSON HENRY A 28 01A B
NELSON HENRY A 28 10T B
NELSON HILLIARD A 28 04A B
NELSON ISRAEL P A 28 04A W
NELSON ITHAMER A 46 SUM W
NELSON J S A 28 01B W
NELSON J S A 46 KIN W
NELSON JACKSON A 99 BUS B
NELSON JACOB A 44 YXS B
NELSON JAMES S A 19 STR W
NELSON JAMES A 25 SHO W
NELSON JAMES A 28 11T B
NELSON JAMES A 46 KIN W

NELSON JAMES F CHAL R 28 10T W
WAS OVERSEER OF ROADS
HIRED OUT TWO HANDS TO
WORK ON BLOCKADE AND
GUNBOAT AT NEW BERN
NELSON JOHN A 19 BE1 B
NELSON JOHN A 19 HUN W
NELSON JOHN A 19 MOR B
NELSON JOHN A 19 STR W
NELSON JOHN A 46 MCL B
NELSON JOHN H CHAL R 28 10T W
WAS A MAGISTRATE & CHAIR
MAN OF A REBEL VIGILENCE
COMMITTEE
NELSON JOHN P A 32 SHE W
NELSON JOHN T A 28 10T W
NELSON JOHN W A 37 HIC A
NELSON JONES A 28 03B B
NELSON JOSEPH A 28 01A W
NELSON JOSEPH A 28 9TH B
NELSON JOSEPH A 46 KIN W
NELSON JOSIAH B A 19 BE1 W
NELSON KANE A 28 05A B
NELSON M H A 28 04A B
NELSON MALORY A 19 STR W
NELSON MICAJAH F A 19 STR W
NELSON MONROE A 46 MCL B
NELSON OBED B A 19 BE1 B
NELSON PETER A 32 THO B
NELSON RANDAL A 28 02N B
NELSON RICHARD P A 28 11T W
NELSON ROBERT A 28 10T B
NELSON ROBERT A 28 9TH B
NELSON ROBT A 29 FA1 B
NELSON SAML A 28 01A B
NELSON SMITH A 28 9TH B
NELSON SOUTHEY J A 19 BE1 W
NELSON SPENCER A 28 9TH B
NELSON THOS A 28 04A B
NELSON THOS S A 44 KNA W
NELSON VIRGIL A 28 04A B
NELSON WILLIAM A 19 HUN W
NELSON WILLIAM A 28 10T B
NELSON WILLIAM A 32 TYR B
NELSON WM B A 28 14T W
NESBET HARISON A 32 TYR B
NETHERCUT JAMES A 35 LIM W
NETHERCUT JESSE A 35 LIM W
NETHERCUT JOHN A 35 LIM W
NETHERLAND JOSEPH A 53 BUR W
NETHERLEY G D A 44 YXR W
NETHERLEY HENRY H A 44 YXR W
NETTLE
BENJAMIN THOMAS A 37 PEN B
NETTLE GEORGE A 37 SPA B
NETTLE ISAAC A 37 SPA B
NETTLE ROBERT A 37 PEN B
NETTLE TIM A 37 PEN B
NETTLE WILLIS A 37 SPA B
NEVELLS J T A 44 DUT W
NEVILLS DAVY A 28 01A B
NEW HENERY A 29 FA1 W
NEWBERN BENJAMIN A 24 EDE B
NEWBERN J C A 24 EDE B
NEWBERN JOHN CHAL A 30 POW W
WAS CONSTABLE PRIOR TO
THE WAR REMOVED TO POPLAR
BRANCH ACCEPTED AT THE
REVISION OF APRIL 1868.
NEWBERN THOMAS A 24 EDE B
NEWBERN THOS E A 30 POP W
NEWBERN WALTER S A 30 POW W
NEWBERN WM A 24 EDE B
NEWBERN WM T A 30 TUL W
SEE FORM AT END OF
THIS SECTION.
NEWBERRIE BRYANT A 28 16T B
NEWBERRY J B A 29 FA1 W
LUMBERTON ROBESON CO
CERT APRIL 11 '68
NEWBERRY S H A 19 NEW W
NEWBERRY W H A 29 FA1 W
LUMBERTON ROBESON CO
CERT APRIL 11 '67
NEWBOLD LEVI A 72 SWA W
NEWBURN MILES A 24 EDE B
NEWBURY FRANKLIN A A 35 MAG W
NEWBURY KING E A 35 MAG W
NEWBY ALLEN A 53 SWA B
NEWBY D T A 29 FA1 W
NEWBY H W A 32 THO W
NEWBY J B A 29 FA2 W
NEWBY JOHN A 19 BE1 W
NEWBY TAYLOR A 28 03B B
NEWBY THOMAS A 53 SWA W
NEWBY W H A 44 HEN W
NEWBY WASHN A 28 04A B
NEWCOMB JAMES A 29 CAR B
NEWEL JOHN A 46 SUM W
NEWEL THOMAS A 46 SUM W
NEWELL ARCHY P A 29 FA1 W
NEWELL GEO A 29 FA1 B
NEWELL GEO W A 29 FA1 W
NEWELL GEORGE A A 35 KEN W
NEWELL HIRAM A 35 KEN W
NEWKIRK ABRAM A 35 MAG B
NEWKIRK ALEXANDER A 35 LIM W
NEWKIRK ANDREW A 35 MAG B
NEWKIRK ARTHUR A 35 ROC B
NEWKIRK BENJAMIN R A 35 ROC W
NEWKIRK BRISTER A 35 ROC B
NEWKIRK DANIEL A 35 ROC B
NEWKIRK EDMUND A 35 MAG B
NEWKIRK ESSEX A 35 ROC B
NEWKIRK FRANK A 35 ROC B
NEWKIRK GEORGE A 35 ROC B
NEWKIRK HAYES A 35 ROC B
NEWKIRK JAMES O A 35 ROC B
NEWKIRK JAMES S A 35 ROC W
NEWKIRK JEREMIAH A 35 MAG B
NEWKIRK JOSEPH A 35 ROC B
NEWKIRK MANSFIELD A A 35 ROC B
NEWKIRK RICHARD A 35 ROC B
NEWKIRK SWAN HILL A 35 MAG B
NEWKIRK THOMAS J A 35 ROC B
NEWKIRK TIMOTHY A 35 ROC B
NEWKIRK TIMOTHY H R A 35 MAG W
NEWKIRK VIRGIL A 35 ROC B
NEWKIRK WILLIAM A 35 ROC B
NEWKIRK WILLIAM H A 35 ROC B
NEWLIN A L A 46 HIG W
NEWLIN J F A 46 HIG W
NEWLON JAMES T A 19 POR W
NEWLON THOMAS A 44 HEN W
NEWLUN RICHARD A 30 IND W
NEWMAN JEROME A 30 CUR B
NEWMAN JOSEPH A 46 ROS W
NEWMAN MICHAEL A 24 EDE W
NEWMAN PETER A 30 KNO W
NEWMAN RICHARD G A 24 EDE W
NEWMAN WILEY J A 44 TOW W
NEWMON L H A 44 TOW W
NEWMON WM A A 44 SAS W
NEWSOM A G A 32 JAC W
NEWSOM ABRAM A 28 6TH B
NEWSOM ABRAM A 32 LOF W
NEWSOM ALLEN A 32 JAC W
NEWSOM CLABON A 32 JAC W
NEWSOM DAVID A A 37 EDW W
NEWSOM JESSE A 32 JAC W
NEWSOM N H A 32 JAC W
NEWSOM SAMSON A 32 JAC W
NEWSOM WILLIAM T A 37 EDW W
NEWTON A S A 44 YXR W
NEWTON ABRAM A 28 05A B
NEWTON ALFRED A 26 WAR W
NEWTON B B A 26 WAR W
NEWTON B O A 26 WAR W
NEWTON CASWELL A 35 WAR B
NEWTON D B A 35 FAI W
NEWTON E A A 40 RHY W
NEWTON EBENEZER A 26 WAR W
NEWTON ELI A 26 WAR W
NEWTON G W A 44 YXR W
NEWTON GEORGE A 26 PEE W
NEWTON GEORGE A 29 SEV W
NEWTON ISAAC J A 29 SEV W
MILITIA OFF TAKEN AN OATH
TO SUPPORT THE CONSTITU-
TION OF THE U.S. BEFORE
THE REBELLIION AFTERWARDS
ENGAGED IN THE REBELLION
NEWTON J B A 46 HIG W
NEWTON J O A 26 WAR W
NEWTON J W A 44 ISL W
NEWTON JAMES A 44 YXR W
NEWTON JNO M A 44 ISL W
NEWTON JOHN J A 35 KEN W
NEWTON L J A 32 THO W
NEWTON LEVING A 53 LA1 B
NEWTON LEWIS A 35 ROC B
NEWTON MARS A 28 10T B
NEWTON OWEN A 35 ROC B
NEWTON PETER A 40 RHY W
NEWTON R H A 44 ISL W
NEWTON R L A 44 TAR W
NEWTON SAMEUL A 35 ROC W
NEWTON SAMEUL B A 35 MAG W
NEWTON T B A 28 01A W
NEWTON THOMAS A 37 TA1 B
NEWTON TIMOTHY A 19 NEW B
NEWTON WILLIAM A 46 KIN W
NEWTON WILLIAM S A 26 WAR W
NEWTON WM A 44 ISL B
NEWTON WM P A 46 GRE W
NEWTON WM R A 26 WAR W
NICHOLS DOLPHIN A 28 04A B
NICHOLS E J A 46 HIG W
NICHOLS EDWARD A 28 05A B
NICHOLS HENRY A 24 EDE B
NICHOLS JAMES A 37 EDW B
NICHOLS JOHN A 37 PIN B
NICHOLS MARK A 28 05A B
NICHOLS PAUL A 29 GRA W
NICHOLS WILLIS A 39 LOU B
NICHOLS WM A 39 FRA B
NICHOLSON ALFRED A 35 KEN B
NICHOLSON CALEB A 30 CUR W
NICHOLSON CALEB A 39 FRA B
NICHOLSON DENNIS A 40 DEC B
NICHOLSON J C A 39 FRA W
NICHOLSON JACKSON A 39 FRA B
NICHOLSON JOHN A 35 KEN B
NICHOLSON JOHN A 39 LOU B
NICHOLSON LEE A 38 FRE B
NICHOLSON MACKLIN A 39 FRA B
NICHOLSON NAT A 39 FRA B
NICHOLSON NATHAN A 35 KEN B
NICHOLSON PETER A 35 MAG B

NICHOLSON ROBERT S	A	35	MAG	B
NICHOLSON W A	A	25	TUS	W
NICHOLSON WESLEY	A	35	MAG	B
NICHOLSON WILLIAM E	A	35	MAG	W
NICKEL ALLEN B	A	37	HIG	W
NICKENS HENRY	A	29	FA1	W
NICKERSON HENRY	A	37	PEN	B
NICKINS RICHD	A	29	FA1	W
NICKLOS WM A	A	40	SAN	W
NICKOLS ISAAC	A	24	MID	B
NICKOLS JOHN H	A	28	16T	W
NIFONG ANDREW	A	32	POS	W
NIFONG ROBERT	A	32	POS	W
NIFONG WILEY	A	32	POS	W
NIGHT HUGH	A	40	SAN	W
NIKENS SHERIDAN	A	35	SMI	W
NIMS BERRY	A	40	CAN	B
NIMS BRUM	A	40	CAN	B
NISCOM EDWIN	A	24	EDE	B
NISCOM HARRY	A	24	EDE	B
NISCOM JOHN	A	24	EDE	B
NITCHELL HENRY	A	39	GRI	B
NITCHELL JNO	A	38	FRE	W
NIXEN BENJAMIN	A	24	EDE	B
NIXEN CHAS P	A	24	EDE	B
NIXEN JAMES A	A	24	EDE	B
NIXEN JOHN	A	24	EDE	B
NIXEN ROBERT	A	24	MID	W
NIXEN SQUIRE	A	24	EDE	B
NIXEN THOMAS	A	24	EDE	B
NIXEN WILLIAM L	A	24	MID	W
NIXON EDWARD	A	28	04B	B
NIXON ELIJAH	A	28	03A	B
NIXON ISRAEL	A	28	9TH	B
NIXON JAMES	A	24	EDE	W
NIXON JAS L	A	29	FA2	W
NIXON JOHN N	A	53	LA1	W
NIXON L A	A	29	FA2	W
NIXON MILLS	A	28	03B	B
NIXSON HENRY	A	40	CAN	B
NOAH JOSEPH	A	32	JAC	B
NOBLE BAKER E	A	53	LA1	W
NOBLE DANIEL	A	37	HIG	B
NOBLE DAVID	A	37	HIG	B
NOBLE JOE	A	39	SPE	B
NOBLE LUKE	A	37	HIG	B
NOBLE LUKE	A	39	LOU	B
NOBLE MALVERN	A	39	LOU	B
NOBLE RICHD	A	39	LOU	W
NOBLE WILLIAM	A	39	LOU	B
NOBLES ISAAC K	A	28	11T	W
NOBLES WM M	A	28	13T	W
NOBLIN ALEXANDER	A	44	YXR	W
NOBLIN J H	A	44	YXS	W
NODING WILLIAM	A	32	POS	W
NOE DAVID H	A	19	BE1	W
NOE ISAAC H	A	19	BE1	W
NOE ISAIAH B	A	19	BE1	W
NOE JOHN B	A	19	BE1	W
NOE JOHN W	A	19	BE1	W
NOE SIMEON M	A	30	MOY	W
NOE THOMAS D	A	19	BE1	W
NOGGLE SILVANNUS	A	26	SHE	W
NOLAND W W DR	A	40	DA1	W
NOLAND WM M	A	40	SAN	W
NORCUM MILES	A	28	04A	B
NORCUM STEPHEN	A	28	01A	B
NORCUT JOHN	A	28	05A	B
NOREL KINCHIN	A	37	WEB	B
NOREL THOMAS	A	37	SPA	B
NORFLEET ABNER	A	37	PEN	B
NORFLEET ARTER	A	37	PEN	B
NORFLEET ASA	A	37	PEN	B
NORFLEET BENJAMIN	A	37	PEN	B
NORFLEET BENJAMIN	A	37	TA1	W
NORFLEET BLOUNT	A	37	TA1	B
NORFLEET DEMSEY	A	37	PEN	B
NORFLEET DOWD	A	37	PEN	B
NORFLEET ELI	A	37	TA1	B
NORFLEET GION	A	37	TA1	B
NORFLEET HORTON	A	37	TA1	B
NORFLEET HORTON	A	37	TA2	B
NORFLEET JOHN B	A	37	TA1	B
NORFLEET LUKE	A	37	EDW	B
NORFLEET MELVEN	A	37	PEN	B
NORFLEET OTTEN		37	PEN	B
NORFLEET RANDALL	A	37	PEN	B
NORFLEET READING	A	37	PEN	B
NORFLEET SILAS	A	37	SPA	B
NORFLEET SIMON	A	37	TA1	B
NORFLEET SOLOMON	A	37	TA1	B
NORFLEET WM J	A	24	EDE	W
NORFLETE HARDY	A	28	04A	B
NORFLETE ROBT	A	28	03A	B
NORIS HENRY	A	72	SWA	W
NORMAN COLIER	A	44	OXF	B
NORMAN GRANDISON	A	44	OXF	B
NORMAN HENRY	A	26	WAR	W
NORMAN J M	A	44	OXF	B
NORMAN JAMES	A	26	WAR	W
NORMAN JOHN S	A	19	SMY	W
NORMAN LEVI	A	46	RAG	B
NORMAN OLIVER	A	44	OXF	B
NORMAN PROVIDENCE	A	40	FER	B
NORMAN R H	A	26	WAR	W
NORMAN RICHD	A	44	OXF	B
NORMAN TURNER	A	28	03A	B
NORMAN WM	A	44	OXF	B
NORRIS EDMUN	A	37	MAN	B
NORRIS FREDRICK	A	37	SPA	B
NORRIS GEORGE	A	28	10T	B
NORRIS HENRY A	A	37	PIN	W
NORRIS ISHAM	A	35	ISL	W
NORRIS JESSE	A	37	ROC	W
NORRIS JOHN A	A	19	BE1	W
NORRIS JOSEPH	A	35	ISL	W
NORRIS PATRICK	A	28	11T	W
NORRIS RHEUBEN	A	35	ISL	W
NORRIS TIMOTHY	A	35	ISL	W
NORRIS WILLIAM	A	35	ISL	W
NORRIS WILLIAM G	R	40	DA1	W
NAME LINED OUT MILITIA OFFICER BEFORE THE REBELLION ENGAGED IN IN INSURRECTION AND REBELLION REJECTED				
NORRIS WILLIAM W	A	35	ISL	W
NORROW ALONSO	A	44	SAS	B
NORTH J W	A	26	SHE	W
NORTHAN JOHN	A	53	BUR	B
NORTHAN SOLOMAN	A	53	GER	W
NORTHER HENRY	A	37	TA2	W
NORTON G W	A	25	TUS	W
NORTON WILLIAM	A	40	DA1	B
NORVELL ALEXR	A	28	05B	B
NORVILL HYMAN	A	37	SPA	W
NORVILL LESLIE	A	37	SPA	B
NORVILL OLIVER	A	37	SPA	B
NORVILL PETER	A	37	SPA	B
NORWOOD A J	A	44	TOW	W
NORWOOD ANTHONEY	A	44	YXR	B
NORWOOD F C JNO	A	44	ISL	W
NORWOOD HENRY	A	44	YXS	B
NORWOOD ISAAC	A	19	BE1	B
NORWOOD JAMES G	A	44	YXS	W
NORWOOD JAS	A	44	OXF	B
NORWOOD JAS S	A	44	ISL	W
NORWOOD JESSIE	A	44	HEN	B
NORWOOD JNO	A	44	ISL	B
NORWOOD JNO E	A	44	ISL	W
NORWOOD JOHN	A	44	OXF	B
NORWOOD JOHN A	A	19	BE1	B
NORWOOD JOS A	A	44	YXS	W
NORWOOD JOSEPH L	A	44	ISL	W
NORWOOD LAWSON	A	44	TOW	B
NAME LINED OUT GUILTY OF LARCENY ACCEPT UNDER LAST ORDER				
NORWOOD N M	A	44	YXS	W
NORWOOD NORVELL	A	44	YXS	B
NORWOOD P H	A	44	ISL	W
NORWOOD PARKER	A	44	YXS	B
NORWOOD R G	A	44	SAS	W
NORWOOD ROBERT	A	44	YXS	B
NORWOOD SIDNEY	A	44	YXS	B
NORWOOD SUMNER	A	44	YXS	B
NORWOOD WILLIAM	A	25	HAY	W
NORWOOD WILLIAM E	A	19	BE1	W
NORWOOD WM E	A	44	ISL	W
NOTHINGTON WARREN	A	37	SPA	B
NOTT HARDY	A	29	FA1	B
NOTT JAMES D	A	29	SEV	W
NOVEL HARDING	A	37	SPA	W
NOWAL GREEN	A	37	PIN	B
NOWEL J P	A	26	SHE	W
MILITIA OFFICER & ENGAGED IN REBELLION				
NOWEL THOMAS	A	24	UPP	B
NOWELL JONETHAN	A	32	THO	W
NOWELL JOSEPH W	A	24	UPP	W
NOWELL LUKE	A	28	04A	B
NOWELL W C	A	39	GRI	W
NOWLIN A	A	26	GRI	W
NOWLIN HENRY	A	32	POS	B
NOWLIN J G	A	26	GRI	W
NOWLIN NELSON	A	26	BLA	W
NUCKELS W H	A	44	HEN	W
NUGENT LEWIS	A	46	FRI	W
NUNN JOSHUA	A	39	LOU	W
NUNNARY WILLIAM	A	37	ROB	W
NUNNERY ALXR	A	29	CED	W
NUNNERY AND	A	29	CED	W
NUNNERY G W	A	29	CED	W
NUNNERY H	A	29	LOC	W
NUNNERY HENRY	A	29	CED	W
NUNNERY J S	A	29	CED	W
NURRILL CAIN	A	19	BE1	B
NUSCOM CORNELIUS	A	24	EDE	B
NUTALL C A	A	39	HAY	W
NUTT B J	A	46	HIG	W
- O -				
O'DANIEL ANDREW	A	40	DA1	B
OAKLEY ADOLPHUS	A	44	LED	W
OAKLEY BARNETT	A	44	TAR	W
OAKLEY BARTLET	A	44	LED	W
OAKLEY DAVID	A	46	GRE	W
OAKLEY DAVID	A	46	JAM	W
OAKLEY DUNCAN	A	44	LED	W
OAKLEY HAYWOOD	A	44	TAR	W
OAKLEY HINTON	A	44	LED	W
OAKLEY JAS D	A	44	TAR	B
OAKLEY JAS W	A	44	TAR	W
OAKLEY JESSEE	A	44	LED	W
OAKLEY JOHN	A	46	JAM	W
OAKLEY TINGLEY	A	44	DUT	W
OAKLEY W J	A	44	LED	W
OAKLEY W L	A	44	TAR	W
OAKLEY WILLIAM N	A	44	FOR	W
OAKLEY WM	A	44	TAR	W

OAKLEY WM R A 44 TAR W
OAKLY ADDISON A 44 LED W
OAKS ELLIOTT H A 46 SUM W
OAKS ISAAC A 46 SUM W
OAKS JAS E A 46 SUM W
OAKS RANSOM A 32 THO B
OATES DANL A 28 04A B
OATES GEORGE P A 46 JAM W
OATES HENRY R 40 DEC B
NAME LINED OUT
CAUSE: CONVICTED OF
FELONY CHARGE SUSTAINED
OATES J A 26 BOR B
OATES J C A 26 BOR W
OATES J H A 26 BOR W
OATES J K A 26 BOR W
OATES J REID A 40 DEC W
OATES J S A 26 BOR W
OATES JAMES B A 40 DA1 W
OATES JAMES P A 40 DA1 W
OATES JETHRO A 28 7TH B
OATES PATRICK C A 35 MAG W
OATES R A 26 BOR B
OATES RANDAL A 26 BOR B
OATES S W A 26 BOR W
OATES SAMUEL A 40 DA1 B
OATES SAMUEL R A 40 FER W
OATES THOMAS M A 40 DEC W
OATES WILLIAM A 40 FER W
OATS ALBERT A 37 WHI B
OATS CHARLES A 28 11T B
OATS JESSE A 37 WHI B
OATS SCOTLAND A 53 GER B
OATS T M A A 26 SHE W
OBERMAN AARON A 28 04A B
OBERRY GREEN A 37 TA1 W
OBERRY THOMAS A 37 TA1 W
OBERTON RICHD A 28 05A B
OBRIAN RICHARD N A 37 ROB B
OBRIANT HENRY A 44 FOR W
OBRIANT JOHN A 44 DUT W
OBRIANT M A 44 YXS W
OBRIANT THOMAS A 44 DUT W
OBRIANT THOMAS A 44 LED W
OBRIANT WILLIAM A 46 COB W
OBRIANT Z H A 44 LED W
OBRIANT ZACHARIAH A 44 LED W
OBRIEN A D A 44 TAR W
OBRIEN A P A 44 OXF W
OBRIEN DENNIS A 44 TAR W
OBRIEN GARDNER A 44 OXF W
OBRIEN PATRICK H A 28 01A W
OBRIEN S R A 44 KNA W
OBRIEN THOS A 29 FA1 W
OBRYAN TOM A 39 HAY B
OBRYEN JOHN A 39 HAY W
OCHILTREE HENRY A 19 MOR W
OCHLETREE CHAS A 29 FA1 B
OCONNOR JOHN A 28 01A W
ODAM ARNOLD A 29 CED W
ODAM WILLIAM A 72 SWA W
ODANIEL J L A 40 STO W
ODAY BILLY A 39 JOR B
ODAY FRANCIS A 39 JOR W
ODEN ALLEN G A 28 03A B
ODEN ASA A 28 05A B
ODEN EDWD STANLEY A 28 04A B
ODEN JAMES P A 72 SWA W
ODEN OWENS A 28 05A B
ODEN STARKEY A 28 05A B
ODEN STARKEY JR A 28 05A B
ODEN THOMAS T A 53 FAI B
ODEN WM A 28 14T B

ODENHEIMER J E A 44 OXF W
ODIN CHARLES H A 53 HAT W
ODOM ELIAS A 37 MAN B
ODOM EZEKIEL A 28 7TH B
ODOM HENRY A 37 HOL B
ODOM HENRY D A 37 MAN W
ODOM JAMES M A 39 GRI W
ODOM JAMES R A 37 MAN W
ODOM JAMES R A 37 MAN W
ODOM MADICK A 37 MAN W
ODOM WILLIAM A 37 ROB B
ODOM WILLIAMS H A 37 MAN W
ODON COLLINS A 19 BE1 B
ODON HARMON A 19 BE1 B
ODON MARTIN A 28 10T B
ODON THOMAS A 28 10T B
ODON WILEY A 28 10T B
ODONNELL PATRICK A 28 04B W
ODUM ELISIA A 72 SWA W
ODUM THOMAS A 28 9TH B
OGBURN GEORGE A 46 SUM B
OGBURN JNO L A 46 SUM W
OGESLESBY ELIJAH A 19 NEW W
OGESLESBY ISAAC M A 19 NEW W
OGESLESBY KILBY A 19 NEW W
OGESLESBY L A A 19 NEW W
OGESLESBY L L A 19 NEW W
OGESLESBY
ZEMERIAH JR A 19 NEW W
OGESLESBY
ZEMERIAH SR A 19 NEW W
OGLESBY CHARLES M A 35 CYP W
OGLESBY F N A 28 9TH W
OGLESBY G N A 28 9TH W
CERT GIVEN LIVES
NOW IN JONES CO.
OGLESBY SAMUEL A 40 DA1 W
OGLESBY W V A 28 03B W
OKEY ALISON G A 46 GRE W
OLDS HARROD A 30 MOY B
7-MONTH-RESIDENCE
OLDS SPENCER A 30 POP B
OLDS WILLOUGHBY A 30 POP W
OLISON RICHARD A 53 GER B
OLIVE ANDERSON A 99 BUS W
OLIVER ABNER A 19 NEW B
OLIVER ALEXANDER A 32 CLE B
OLIVER ALLEN A 46 SUM B
OLIVER GLASCOE A 35 KEN B
OLIVER HENRY A 37 PEN B
OLIVER JAMES D A 28 01A W
OLIVER JISAEL A 32 CLE B
OLIVER JOHN R A 35 FAI W
OLIVER JOHN W A 32 DAV B
OLIVER JOSEPH H A 30 ROA W
OLIVER P A 19 NEW B
OLIVER PHARO A 35 WOL W
OLIVER ROBT A A 46 SUM W
OLIVER VIRGIL A 35 MAG B
OLIVER WILLIAM A 40 DA1 W
OLIVER WM H A 28 01A W
CITY COMMISSIONER
OLLIFORD F M A 29 CED W
OLLIVER ABEL A 35 FAI B
OLLIVER ALFRED A 35 FAI B
OLLIVER ARTHUR A 35 FAI B
OLLIVER JOSEPH B A 35 FAI W
OLLIVER LEWIS A 35 FAI B
OLLIVER SAWNEY A 35 FAI B
OLMS ISAAC A 32 DAV B
OLSTON MILTON A 44 SAS B
OMARY JOHN A 44 LED W
OMERRY THOS A 44 OXF W

OMERRY WM A 46 GRE W
ONEAL AMASA A 53 OCR W
ONEAL BERRY A 28 6TH B
ONEAL CHRISTOPHER A 53 GER W
ONEAL CHRISTOPHER A 53 OCR W
ONEAL EDWARD S A 53 FAI W
ONEAL EVAN A 30 ROA W
APRIL 16, 1868
ONEAL FARROW A 30 NOR W
ONEAL HENRY W A 53 LA1 W
ONEAL HOWARD A 53 SWA W
ONEAL HUEY G A 53 LA2 W
ONEAL ISAAC A 30 NOR W
ONEAL JAMES A 37 SHA W
ONEAL JAMES A 53 GER W
ONEAL JOHN B A 53 HAT W
ONEAL JOHN B A 53 HAT W
ONEAL JOHN F A 53 HAT W
ONEAL JOSEPH A 53 OCR W
ONEAL JOSEPH A 53 SWA W
ONEAL JOSEPH A 53 SWA W
ONEAL LEVI A 53 LA1 W
ONEAL MARCUS A 28 04A B
ONEAL MILES A 30 POP B
ONEAL NATHAN A 30 NOR W
ONEAL NATHAN B A 53 LA1 W
ONEAL OLIVER A 30 NOR W
ONEAL OLIVER A 53 LA2 W
ONEAL OLIVER JR A 53 LA1 W
ONEAL TILMON A 53 HAT W
ONEAL WARREN A 53 KEN W
ONEAL WILLIAM B A 53 HAT W
ONEAL WILLIAM B A 53 OCR W
ONEAL WILLIAM C A 53 LA1 W
ONEAL YORK A 30 NAR B
ONEIL B A 28 11T W
ONEIL J B A 28 11T W
ONEIL J W A 19 MOR W
ONEIL JOHN A 19 NEW B
ONEIL W A 30 IND W
ONEILL BENJN A 28 01A W
ONEILL OWEN A 28 16T W
ONELL JOS A A 29 FA2 W
ONIEL HARDIE A 37 ROB W
ONIEL NATHAN A 30 CUR W
ONIEL WYAT A 37 ROB W
ONLY WM D A 24 EDE W
ONSLOW JACOB A 28 15T B
OOTEN ROBERT A 28 9TH B
ORANGE JOHN A 24 EDE B
ORANGE JOHNSON A 24 EDE B
ORANGE KINCHON A 28 7TH B
ORGURN HARMON A 46 GRE B
ORMAND BENJ M A 40 DEC W
ORMAND ROBERT D A 40 DEC W
ORMAND ZENAS S A 40 DEC W
ORMSBEE WM W A 28 04B W
ORR ROBERT A 28 01A W
ORRELL DANIEL B A 32 BRO W
ORRELL DANL W A 46 GRE W
ORRELL J N A 44 HEN W
ORRELL LORANZO D A 46 GRE W
ORRELL N B A 32 BRO W
ORRELL WASHINGTON C A 46 GRE W
OSBORN D S A 44 OXF W
OSBORN DR A F A 44 OXF W
OSBORN JOHN A 46 ROS W
OSBORN JOHNATHAN A 44 OXF W
OSBORN JOSEPH A 44 OXF B
OSBORN NATHAN A 46 GRE W
OSBORN ROBERT A 32 POS W
OSBORN S A 32 POS W
OSBORNE DANIEL SR A 46 JAM W

OSBORNE DAVID A 46 JAM W
OSBORNE JESSE A 32 BRO W
OSBORNE JESSE H A 46 JAM W
OSBORNE LORENZO A 46 JAM W
OSBURN ANDREW A 40 CAN B
OSBURNE J R A 46 JAM W
OSBURNE JOHN A A 46 JAM W
OSBURNE WM F A 46 JAM W
OSGOOD JAMES A 28 03A W
OSGOOD JOHN A 28 03A W
OSMENT CHARLES M A 46 HIG W
OSMENT MARTIN A 46 JAM W
OSULIVAN JOHN A 46 GRE W
OTTERBERG JOS A 29 FA1 W
OTWELL JAMES A 46 GRE W
OULDS DANIEL A 30 COI W
OULDS YOUNG A 30 POP W
OUTEN FRANKLIN A 32 JAC B
OUTEN FREDRICK A 32 COT B
OUTEN HANDY A 32 DAV B
OUTLAW ABSALAM A 35 SMI B
OUTLAW C J A 39 FRA B
OUTLAW CALEP A 35 ALB B
OUTLAW CLEVELAND A 28 7TH B
OUTLAW DAVID A 24 MID W
OUTLAW DAVID A 35 WOL W
OUTLAW EDWARD JR A 35 ALB W
OUTLAW ELIAS A 53 HAT W
OUTLAW FREDERICK A 35 WOL W
OUTLAW FREDRICK A 35 ALB W
OUTLAW GEORGE A 35 ALB W
OUTLAW GRADY A 35 ALB W
OUTLAW ISAAC A 28 8TH B
OUTLAW ISAAC H A 35 WOL W
OUTLAW J K A 35 ALB W
OUTLAW JACOB T A 53 HAT W
OUTLAW JAMES A 35 WOL W
OUTLAW JAMES B A 35 ALB W
OUTLAW JOHN E A 35 ALB W
OUTLAW JOSEPH A 28 05A B
OUTLAW JULIUS A 35 WOL W
OUTLAW KING A 28 7TH B
OUTLAW LEMUEL A 24 UPP B
OUTLAW LOUIS A 35 ALB W
SON OF JOHN
OUTLAW N B A 35 ALB W
OUTLAW STEPHAN A 35 ALB B
OUTLAW T E A 28 6TH W
OUTLAW THOMAS A 39 FRA B
OUTLAW WILLIAM A 35 WOL W
OUTLAW WILLIAM JR A 35 ALB W
OUTLAW WILLIAM SR A 35 ALB W
OUTLAW WM B A 30 IND W
OVERBAUGH AMBROSE A 29 FA1 W
OVERBEY DAVID JR A 44 YXR W
OVERBEY GEORGE A 44 YXS B
OVERBEY HENRY A 44 YXS B
OVERBEY JNO A 44 SAS B
OVERBEY JNO A 44 SAS B
OVERBEY JNO B A 44 TOW W
OVERBEY JNO S A 44 YXR W
OVERBEY JORDAN A 44 SAS B
OVERBEY MARK A 44 SAS B
OVERBY DAVID SR A 44 YXR W
OVERBY FRANK A 44 YXR B
OVERBY JACK A 44 YXR B
OVERBY JAMES Y A 44 TOW W
OVERBY JAS M A 44 YXR W
OVERBY L K A 44 HEN W
OVERBY L W A 44 HEN W
OVERBY LEX A 44 KIT B
OVERBY OBADIAH A 44 TOW W
OVERBY RICHD A 44 YXR B
OVERBY ROBERT A 44 TOW W
OVERBY SAML A 44 YXR B
OVERBY STEPHEN A 44 YXR B
OVERBY THOMAS A 44 HEN B
OVERBY THOS J A 44 YXR W
OVERBY WILLIAM A 44 HEN B
OVERBY WM A 29 FA1 W
OVERBY WM A 44 YXR B
OVERBY WM B A 29 FA1 W
OVERMAN DAVID A 46 COB W
OVERMAN N G A 30 MOY W
OVERMAN WM A 46 COB W
OVERTON A A 29 FA1 W
OVERTON A A A 44 BRA W
FISHING CREEK
OVERTON AURELIOUS A 44 FOR W
OVERTON DAVID A 30 ROA B
OVERTON GEO A 44 BRA W
FISHING CREEK
OVERTON JACKSON A 29 FA1 W
OVERTON JOHN A 29 FA2 W
OVERTON JOHN A 39 HAY W
OVERTON JOHN A 39 LOU W
OVERTON JOHN R A 37 TA1 W
OVERTON MARTIN A 29 FA2 W
OVERTON MOSES S A 39 HAY W
OVERTON NATHAN A 24 EDE B
OVERTON R P A 44 KIT W
OVERTON R T A 44 KIT W
OVERTON W T A 44 BRA W
FISHING CREEK
OVERTON WM R A 30 IND W
OVERTON WM T A 39 HAY W
OWANS JNO M A 19 MOR W
OWEN A J CHAL A 32 DAV W
FOR HOLDING OFFICE OF
MAGISTRATE BEFORE AND
DURING WAR. RECON.
OWEN ALEXANDER A 32 DAV B
OWEN ALFORD A 32 COT B
OWEN ALFORD A 32 DAV W
OWEN AMBROS A 32 DAV B
OWEN AMOS A 32 DAV B
OWEN ANDERSON A 32 COT W
OWEN BABE A 44 OXF B
OWEN D A A 44 TAR W
OWEN DAVID A 32 DAV B
OWEN DAVID A 32 LOF W
OWEN DAVID A 44 TAR W
OWEN DAVID S A 32 DAV W
OWEN DEMPEY A 37 WEB W
OWEN DENY L A 32 COT W
OWEN E W A 44 OXF W
OWEN EDWARD A 32 COT B
OWEN EDWARD A 32 JAC B
OWEN FREDRICK A 32 DAV B
OWEN FRIDAY A 44 HEN B
OWEN HENRY A 32 COT W
OWEN HENRY A 32 DAV B
OWEN J S A 44 OXF W
OWEN JACOB A 32 DAV B
OWEN JACOB A 32 LOF W
OWEN JAMES A 28 16T W
OWEN JAMES A 32 DAV B
OWEN JAMES A 32 JAC W
OWEN JAMES A 37 TA1 W
OWEN JAMES A 46 GRE W
OWEN JAMES F A 37 WEB W
OWEN JAMES H A 32 DAV B
OWEN JESSE A 32 DAV B
OWEN JESSE A 32 TYR W
OWEN JESSIE H A 32 DAV W
OWEN JOHN A 32 DAV B
OWEN JOHN A 37 TA1 W
OWEN LISBON A 35 WAR B
OWEN LUKE A 32 DAV B
OWEN MICHAEL A 32 LOF W
OWEN MOSSES A 44 OXF B
OWEN RALPH A 32 LOF W
OWEN ROBERT A 32 DAV B
OWEN ROBERT A 32 DAV B
OWEN THOMAS M A 46 GRE W
OWEN THOMAS R A 37 PEN W
OWEN THOS J A 29 FA1 W
MILLITIA OFFICER AFTER-
WARDS ENG IN REBELLION
OWEN WALLACE A 44 TOW B
OWEN WILLIAM R A 37 WEB W
OWEN WM F A 46 GRE W
OWEN WOODSON A 44 SAS B
OWEN YORK A 32 DAV B
OWENBY JOEL A 40 MAU W
OWENS A E A 46 SUM W
OWENS ALEXANDER A 30 POW W
OWENS ASHLEE A 30 TUL W
OWENS BENJAMIN S A 53 SWA W
OWENS CLARK A 24 EDE B
OWENS DAVID A 30 ROA B
OWENS EDWARD A 30 POP W
OWENS FORTUNE A 29 CED B
OWENS GEO A 29 FA1 B
OWENS HENRY A 46 JAM B
OWENS HEZAKIAS A 30 POW W
OWENS HEZEKIAH JR A 30 POW W
OWENS HODGES G CHALA 30 POW W
TAKING OATH OF ALLEG-
ENCE AND VIOLATE IT
OWENS ISAAC A 30 NAR W
OWENS ISAAC JR A 24 EDE B
OWENS ISAM A 26 MOO W
OWENS J R A 37 WHI W
OWENS JAMES A 30 IND W
OWENS JAMES A 30 POP W
OWENS JAMES F A 30 TUL W
OWENS JOHN A 28 05A B
OWENS JONATHAN L A 30 POW W
APRIL 17, 1868
OWENS JORDAN A 30 POP B
OWENS JORDAN A 30 POP W
OWENS JOSEPH B A 30 NOR W
OWENS JOSEPH C A 53 GER W
OWENS MATTHIAS CHAL R 30 POW W
WAS CONSTABLE
PRIOR TO THE WAR
OWENS MONREO J A 30 POP W
OWENS NOAH JR A 30 POW W
OWENS NORRIS A 30 POP W
OWENS OWEN A 37 EDW B
OWENS PATRICK H A 30 POW W
OWENS PETER A 29 SEV B
OWENS PHARO A 29 GRA B
OWENS POMPY A 30 POP B
OWENS PRICE A 29 FLE B
OWENS SAML A 28 05A B
OWENS SAMUEL A 29 LOC B
OWENS SAMUEL A 30 POP W
OWENS SAMUEL A 30 ROA B
OWENS THOMAS A 37 WEB W
OWENS THOS S A 30 TUL W
OWENS THOS W A 19 BEI W
OWENS WILLIS A 30 POP W
OWENS WILLOUGHBY A 30 POP W
OWENS WILSON A 30 POW W
OWNBEY G W A 25 SHO W
OWNBEY H P A 25 SHO W
OWNBEY J M A 25 SHO W

OWNBEY P M A 25 SHO W
OWNE JAMES A 46 GRE W
OZBORNE GEORGE A 28 6TH W
OZMENT CALVIN A 46 GRE W
OZMENT CALVIN A 46 SUM W
OZMENT ELI A 46 GRE W
OZMENT JONATHAN A 46 GRE W
OZMENT JONATHAN A 46 HIG W
OZMENT RISE A 46 GRE W
OZMENT ROBERT C A 46 GRE W

- P -

PACE J A A 44 FIS W
PACE JAMES M A 99 BUS W
PACE WM A 39 GRI W
PACK DAVID A 32 CLE W
PADGET JACOB A 35 WAR W
PADGET JAMES A 35 WAR W
PADGET MOSES A 35 MAG W
PADGET REASON A A 35 ROC W
PADGETT E A 26 BLA W
PADGETT E B A 25 HAY W
PADGETT HAMPTON A 40 STO W
PADGETT JOHN A 25 HAY W
PADGETT WILLIAM A 26 BLA W
PADRICK NATHANIEL A 53 SWA W
PAGE ALLEN A 35 CYP B
PAGE BENJAMIN A 24 EDE B
PAGE CHARLES A 35 ROC W
PAGE CHESHIRE A 24 EDE B
PAGE DANIEL N A 35 ROC W
PAGE DAVID A 35 ROC B
PAGE DEMPSEY A 37 SPA W
PAGE EPHRAIM A 29 FA1 W
PAGE GEORGE W A 46 GRE W
PAGE HARKLESS A 24 EDE B
PAGE HIRAM J A 35 ROC W
PAGE JOHN A 29 BLA W
PAGE JOHN E A 35 ROC W
PAGE JOHN R A 24 EDE B
PAGE JOHNSON A 37 SPA W
PAGE JOSEPH A 37 WHI W
PAGE L A A 29 FLE W
PAGE LEWIS A 35 ROC B
PAGE LOGAN C A 46 GRE W
PAGE LONDON A 24 EDE B
PAGE MATHEW A 46 KIN B
PAGE NATHAN A 24 EDE B
PAGE PEYTON A 35 ROC W
PAGE SIMONS A 24 EDE B
PAGE SION A 29 BLA W
PAGE STEPHEN A 19 BE2 W
PAGE W T A 46 SUM W
PAGE WELLS A 24 EDE B
PAGE WILLIAM A 29 BLA W
PAGE WILLIAM L A 46 SUM W
PAGE WINSOR A 37 HIC B
PAGET W L A 26 MOO W
PAGET WILLIAM A 26 MOO W
PAGETT HAMTON A 40 SAN W
COPIED FROM DUPLICATE
PAGGET EPHRAM A 26 SHE W
PAIN ALBERT A 44 ISL B
PAIN SPARROW M A 53 LA2 W
PAIN THOS E S A 53 LA2 W
PAINE HAGGAR A 40 DA1 W
PAINE JOHN A A 40 DA1 W
PAINE JOSEPH D A 40 DA2 W
PAINE MALACA A 28 16T W
PAINE ROBERT A 40 DEC W
PAINE THOMAS A 40 DA1 W
PAINTER HIRAM A 32 CLE W
PAISLEY BAXTER A 46 MCL B
PAISLEY GEORGE A 46 MCL B
PAISLEY JAMES A 46 MCL W
NAME LINED OUT
WAS AN OVERSEER OF HIGHWAY
BEFORE THE WARE AND DURING
THE WAR AS AGENT FOR QUAR-
TERMASTER GATHERED BLANKET
AND BEDDING FOR THE
SOULDIERS. NOT QUALIFIED
PAISLEY JAMES P A 46 MCL W
PAISLEY WM A A 46 MCL W
PAKE JOHN A 19 SMY W
PAKE WM T A 19 SMY W
PALAMOUNTAIN ISAAC R 37 TA2 W
VOTED WRITTEN IN
PALAMOUNTAIN
ISAAC B R 37 TA1 W
NAME LINED OUT
PALMER AARON A 26 GRI B
PALMER ALLEN A 46 SUM B
PALMER D P CHAL R 26 BUR W
MILITIA OFFICER &
ENGAGED IN REBELLION
PALMER DAVID A 30 COI W
PALMER GEORGE A 32 DAV B
PALMER H J A 32 COT W
PALMER HENRY A 32 COT W
PALMER JAMES A 46 GRE W
PALMER JAMES B A 32 COT W
PALMER JESSE A 26 MOU B
PALMER JOHN A 28 05A B
PALMER JOHN A 29 QUW B
PALMER JOHN A 46 FRI B
PALMER JOHN A 46 GRE B
PALMER LOUIS A 32 COT B
PALMER SAM A 26 BOR B
PALMER THOMAS CHAL R 26 MOU W
EXERCISED TO OFF.
CONS. STRICKEN OUT
PALMER WALTEN A 46 JAM W
PALMER WM L A 28 01A W
PAMELY HARMON A 28 05A B
PANE SOLOMON E A 30 CUR W
PANEL MARTIN A 26 MOO W
PANNELL H S A 26 MOO W
PANTON W CATLETT A 46 SUM W
PANTON WILLIAM A 46 SUM W
PARDEU J D A 39 HAY W
PARDUE A T A 44 KIT W
PARDUE S O A 44 HEN W
PAREN OTWAY A 32 SHE B
PARHAM S J A 44 HEN W
PARHAM A C A 44 HEN W
PARHAM AARON JR A 44 OXF B
PARHAM AARON SR A 44 OXF B
PARHAM ALBERT C A 44 OXF W
PARHAM ARCHER A 39 PUG B
PARHAM ARON A 44 TOW B
PARHAM ASA A 44 OXF W
PARHAM C W A 44 OXF W
PARHAM CHARLES A 44 OXF B
PARHAM CYRUS A 44 OXF B
PARHAM DANIEL A 44 OXF B
PARHAM HARRY A 44 FIS B
PARHAM ISAAC A 44 FIS B
PARHAM JAS A A 44 OXF W
PARHAM JAS D A 44 HEN W
PARHAM JOHN A 39 HAY B
PARHAM JOHN A 39 PUG B
PARHAM JOHN A 44 FIS B
PARHAM JORDAN A 44 RAG B
PARHAM JUNIUS A 44 OXF B
PARHAM KENNON A 44 OXF W
PARHAM LEWIS W A 44 SAS W
PARHAM MARK A 44 OXF B
PARHAM MILES A 44 OXF B
PARHAM MOSES A 44 OXF B
PARHAM NATHAN A 44 HEN B
PARHAM PETER A 44 HEN B
PARHAM PHIL A 44 OXF B
PARHAM RICHD A 44 OXF B
PARHAM ROBT A 44 OXF B
PARHAM SAML A A 44 OXF W
PARHAM SAML R A 44 SAS W
PARHAM SANDY A 44 OXF B
PARHAM STEPHEN A 44 OXF B
PARHAM THOS A 44 OXF B
PARHAM THOS B A 44 HEN W
PARHAM W A A 44 FIS W
PARHAM WILLIE A 44 OXF W
PARHAM WM A 44 FIS W
PARIS DANIEL A 37 ROB B
PARIS EDWARD A 28 03A B
PARIS JAMES S A 29 MON W
PARIS ZADOC A 28 15T W
PARISH ALFORD A 46 KIN W
PARISH C H A 44 OXF W
PARISH C T A 44 FIS W
PARISH H A 46 KIN W
PARISH HENRY A 35 WAR B
PARISH HENRY A 46 GRE W
PARISH HENRY C A 28 13T W
PARISH J S A 32 CLE W
PARISH J W A 44 FIS W
PARISH JUSTUS A 99 BUS W
PARISH KITCHEN Q A 99 BUS W
PARISH NATHAN A 99 BUS W
PARISH PASCHAL A 99 BUS W
PARISH PINKNEY A 99 BUS W
PARISH PUTNEY A 99 BUS W
PARISH RICHARD A 35 MAG B
PARISH ROLLEN A 46 KIN W
PARISH S L A 44 RAG W
PARISH W G A 46 KIN W
PARISH WESTLY A 46 KIN W
PARISH WILLIAM A 99 BUS W
PARISH WILLIAM M 40 FER W
PARISH WILLIS A 32 CLE W
PARISH WOODSON A 39 GRI W
PARK ALBERT N A 32 DAV W
PARK J A CHAL A 32 DAV W
FOR HOLDING OFFICE OF
DPD SHERIFF BEFORE AND
DURING WAR. RECON.
PARKER A C A 26 BOR W
PARKER ABNER H A 35 KEN W
PARKER ABRAHAM A 37 ROB B
PARKER ALEXANDER A 19 BE1 B
PARKER AMOS A 29 FA1 B
PARKER ANDERSON A 30 KNO W
PARKER ANDREW J A 30 NAR W
PARKER ARTHUR A 37 PEN B
PARKER BENJ A 28 03A B
PARKER BENJ A 46 GRE B
PARKER BENJAMIN A 24 EDE B
PARKER BENJAMIN A 37 HIG B
PARKER BRYANT A 29 CED W
PARKER BUNION A 44 FIS B
PARKER C A 46 KIN W
PARKER C A A 26 SWA W
PARKER CALEB A 29 CAR W
MILLITIA OFFICER AFTER-
WARDS ENG IN REBELLION
PARKER CALEB A 30 POW W
PARKER CESSER JR A 19 BE1 B
PARKER COUNCIL C A 35 CYP W
PARKER DANIEL A 24 UPP B

PARKER DANIEL	A 37 HIG B
PARKER DAVID	A 24 EDE B
PARKER DAVID	A 40 RHY W
PARKER DAVID	A 44 FOR B
PARKER DAVID W	A 19 BE1 B
PARKER DUDLEY	A 37 HIC B
PARKER ELISHA	A 44 LED B
PARKER ELIZAH	A 29 CAR W
PARKER ENOCH	A 26 WAR W
PARKER GATES	A 24 UPP B
PARKER GEO	A 28 04A B
PARKER GEORGE	A 24 UPP B
PARKER GEORGE H	A 46 GRE W
PARKER HAINES	A 37 ROC B
PARKER HARRY	A 28 04A B
PARKER HARRY	A 37 EDW W
PARKER HARRY	A 37 HIG B
PARKER HENRY	A 29 FA1 B
PARKER HENRY	A 44 FIS B
PARKER HILLIARD	A 37 HIG B
CONFESSED TO CRIME	
PARKER ISAAC	A 24 UPP B
PARKER ISAAC	A 37 TA1 B
PARKER ISAAC	A 99 BUS B
PARKER J M	A 40 RHY W
PARKER J W	A 29 CAR W
PARKER J W S	A 46 GRE W
PARKER JACK	A 28 03A B
PARKER JACOB	A 24 MID B
PARKER JAMES	A 19 NEW B
PARKER JAMES	A 28 04A B
PARKER JAMES	A 37 ROC B
PARKER JAMES A	A 44 TOW W
PARKER JAMES E	A 19 POR W
PARKER JAMES H	A 35 LIM W
PARKER JAMES W	A 30 COI W
PARKER JAS	A 29 GRA W
PARKER JESSE M	A 25 HAY W
PARKER JESSEE	A 29 FA2 B
PARKER JILES	A 44 KIT B
PARKER JNO	A 29 FLE W
PARKER JNO	A 44 ISL W
PARKER JNO T	A 30 IND W
PARKER JOHN	A 24 MID B
PARKER JOHN	A 24 UPP B
PARKER JOHN	A 37 WHI B
PARKER JOHN	A 44 KIT B
PARKER JOHN	A 46 GRE W
PARKER JOHN H	A 40 FER W
PARKER JOHN W	A 40 FER B
PARKER JOHNATHAN	A 30 POW W
PARKER JONATHAN	A 35 LIM W
PARKER JORDAN	A 30 POW W
PARKER JOSEPH	A 26 PEE W
PARKER JOSEPH J	A 37 EDW W
PARKER JUDITH ?	A 37 HIG B
PARKER LEWIS	A 37 HIG B
PARKER LIBERTY	A 37 EDW B
PARKER LISBON	A 29 FLE B
PARKER MAITIN	A 37 MAN W
PARKER MAJOR	A 30 NAR W
PARKER MARK	A 26 BLA W
PARKER MARK	A 37 EDW W
PARKER MASON W	A 30 NAR W
PARKER MATTHEW	A 28 04A B
PARKER MOSES	A 24 EDE B
PARKER NAT	A 37 ROC B
PARKER NELSON	A 37 ROC B
PARKER OLLIE	A 37 EDW W
PARKER OSCAR	A 19 BE2 B
PARKER OWENS	A 32 JAC B
PARKER PETER	A 30 CUR W
PARKER PETER	A 30 NAR W
PARKER PETER	A 37 HIG B
PARKER REILY	A 29 FA2 B
PARKER RICHARD	A 37 HIG B
PARKER ROBERT	A 37 ROC B
PARKER ROBT	A 29 LOC B
PARKER S L	A 26 GOF W
PARKER S R	A 29 CED W
PARKER S W N	A 24 MID W
PARKER SAMUEL	A 26 GOF W
PARKER SAMUEL	A 29 FLE B
PARKER SIMM	A 29 CED W
PARKER SOLOMON	A 46 GRE B
PARKER T B	A 24 MID W
PARKER T R	A 29 CED W
PARKER THACK	A 44 BEA B
PARKER THOS	A 26 CAR W
PARKER TONEY	A 37 SHA B
PARKER W A	A 30 CUR W
PARKER W M	A 40 RHY W
PARKER W T	A 35 WOL W
PARKER WADE	A 28 03A B
PARKER WEEKS B	A 37 ROC W
TRANSFERD TO HIGH LEVEL	
PARKER WEEKS R	A 37 HIG W
PARKER WILEY	A 24 UPP B
PARKER WILEY	A 35 WOL W
PARKER WILEY	A 35 WOL W
PARKER WILLIAM	A 24 MID B
PARKER WILLIAM	A 26 SHE W
PARKER WILLIAM	A 26 WAR W
PARKER WILLIAM	A 44 KIT B
PARKER WILLIAM	A 46 KIN W
PARKER WILLIAM K	A 37 TA1 W
PARKER WILLIAM S	A 35 MAG W
PARKER WILLIAM W	A 37 EDW W
PARKER WILLIAMS	A 35 ISL W
PARKER WILLIS	A 24 MID W
PARKER WM	A 29 FA1 B
PARKER WM B	A 46 SUM W
PARKES JOHN	A 39 LOU W
PARKES JOHN	A 39 LOU W
NAME LINED OUT	
PARKES JOHN	A 46 GRE W
PARKES NATHANIEL	A 39 LOU W
PARKS AMOS	A 46 GRE W
PARKS ELI	A 32 YAD B
PARKS ELISHA	A 24 UPP W
PARKS J A	A 32 DAV W
PARKS JOHN	A 32 COT W
PARKS THOMAS	A 32 JAC W
PARKS THOS	A 39 GRI B
PARKS WM E	A 46 GRE W
PARMER ABRAHAM	A 40 DA1 B
PARMER GEORGE	A 32 DAV W
PARMER JOSEPH	A 32 DAV B
PARNELL WILLIAM	A 37 ROC B
PARNELL WM	A 44 TAR W
PARNER CHRISTIAN	A 32 SHE W
PARR B F	A 46 JAM W
PARR L S	A 46 JAM W
PARR M V	A 46 JAM W
PARR WILSON	A 30 MOY W
PARRISH ALFRED	A 44 HEN B
PARRISH AMOS	A 44 BRA B
PARRISH ANSEL	A 32 LOF W
PARRISH AUGUSTUS F	A 24 UPP W
PARRISH B L	R 44 KIT W
RES SINCE 27TH NOV 66 IS REJECTED	
PARRISH BENJAMIN JR	A 46 SUM W
PARRISH BENJAMIN SR	A 46 SUM W
PARRISH EDMON	A 24 MID W
PARRISH ELI	A 44 HEN B
PARRISH EZEKIEL	A 46 SUM W
PARRISH G G	A 46 FRI W
PARRISH GEO W	A 24 EDE W
PARRISH H C	A 32 LEE W
PARRISH H J	A 44 FIS W
PARRISH HARBORD	A 46 SUM W
PARRISH HENDERSON	A 24 MID W
PARRISH J J	A 24 MID W
PARRISH JAMES	A 24 UPP W
PARRISH JAMES H	A 32 LEE W
PARRISH JNO M	A 44 HEN W
PARRISH JOHN	A 44 BRA B
PARRISH JOHN	A 46 SUM W
PARRISH JOHN D	A 24 EDE W
PARRISH JOHN S	A 32 LOF W
PARRISH LINDSAY	A 46 SUM W
PARRISH PLEASANT	A 46 SUM W
PARRISH R G	A 24 MID W
PARRISH R M	A 39 PUG W
PARRISH T M T	A 32 LEE W
PARRISH THOS	A 46 SUM W
PARRISH W	A 32 LEE W
PARRISH WM J	A 29 MON W
PARROTT H T	A 44 LED W
PARROTT JAMES P	A 44 OXF W
PARROTT M E	A 44 FIS W
PARROTT SAML	A 28 01A W
PARS WILLIAM	A 37 ROB W
PARSON GEORGE	A 37 ROB B
PARSON J S	A 32 JAC W
PARSON JAMES	A 53 SWA W
PARSON MADISON	A 39 HAY B
PARSONS J T	A 30 TUL W
PARSONS JOHN C	A 46 HIG W
PARSONS JOHN N	A 19 BE1 W
PARSONS JOHN N	A 28 10T W
PARSONS JOSEPH	A 19 POR W
PARSONS JOSEPH W	A 32 THO W
PARSONS SAML	A 28 03A B
PARSONS SAMUEL	A 46 HIG W
PARSONS THOS	A 28 02N W
PARTON J P	A 46 FRI W
PARTON THOMAS	A 46 FRI W
PARTRIDGE JOHN W	A 30 COI W
PASCAL ELISHA	A 46 FRI W
PASCHAL W T	A 44 FOR W
PASCHALL CHARLES	A 44 OXF B
PASCHALL D A	A 44 OXF W
PASCHALL EDMOND	A 44 OXF B
PASCHALL GEORGE	A 44 OXF B
PASCHALL HENDERSON	A 44 LED B
PASCHALL JOHN	A 44 OXF B
PASCHALL JOSEPH	A 44 BRA B
PASCHALL NED	A 44 OXF B
PASCHALL NEVISON	A 44 OXF B
PASCHALL POTTER	A 39 FRA B
PASCHALL R H M	A 44 TOW W
PASCHALL R H M	A 44 TOW W
DEBT SHFF NOT SWORN	
PASCHALL WASHINGTON	A 44 OXF B
PASCHALL WM	A 44 BEA W
PASCHALL Z M	A 44 OXF W
PASKELL W T	A 39 LOU W
FROM BRASSFIELDS GRANVILLE CO BY AFF	
PASOUR ADAM M	A 40 MAU W
PASOUR CALEB JR	A 40 DA1 W
PASOUR D RUFUS	A 40 DA1 W
PASOUR DAVID	A 40 DA1 B
PASOUR ELI	A 40 DA1 W
PASOUR ELI F	A 40 DA1 W
PASOUR FELIX	A 40 MAU W
PASOUR GEORGE J JR	A 40 DA1 W

PASOUR GEORGE J SEN A 40 MAU W
PASOUR JACOB A 40 DA1 W
PASOUR JACOB A A 40 DA1 W
PASOUR JAMES M A 40 DA1 W
PASOUR JOSEPH A 40 DA1 W
PASOUR MARTIN A 40 DA1 B
PASOUR MENASSEH A 40 DA1 W
PASOUR MOSES E A 40 MAU W
PASOUR PHILLIP H A 40 DA1 W
PASOUR SAMUEL A 40 MAU W
PASOUR SIMON P A 40 DA1 W
PASS GREEN A 46 SUM B
PASS PETER A 46 SUM B
PASS RICHARD A 25 HAY W
PASSMORE CALAWAY A 25 TUS W
PASSMORE ELIJAH A 25 HAY W
PASSMORE ENOCH A 25 HAY W
PASSMORE JOHN A 25 TUS W
PASSMORE WARREN A 25 TUS W
PASSMORE WM F SR A 25 HAY W
PASSMORE
WM FRANCIS JR A 25 HAY W
PASTON ARMISTED A 26 BLA B
PASTON ARTHUR A 26 GRI B
PASTON BENJAMIN A 26 GRI B
PASTON ROBERT A 26 BLA W
PASTOR GEORGE A 28 9TH B
PATE ALEX A 29 GRA W
PATE FREDERICK A 28 7TH W
PATE GEORGE A 28 10T W
PATE JOS A 29 GRA W
PATE JOSEPH A 28 03A B
PATE LAWSON A 28 7TH W
PATE REDDIN A 28 6TH W
PATE WILLIAM A 28 11T W
PATE WILLIAM R A 35 WOL W
PATE WYATT A 28 03A B
PATILLO GEORGE A 44 ISL B
PATRICK A WILSON A 53 BUR W
PATRICK ALLEN A 28 6TH B
PATRICK CORNELUS H A 53 OCR W
PATRICK G A A 40 SAN W
COPIED FROM DUPLICATE
PATRICK GEORGE A 28 04A B
PATRICK JOHN A 24 EDE B
PATRICK JOHN A 28 16T W
PATRICK SPENCER A 46 MON B
PATRICK WALKER A 40 STO B
PATRICK WM A 28 03A B
PATRIDGE GEORGE A 30 IND W
PATRIDGE JESSE A 30 NOR W
PATRIDGE WILLIS G A 30 NOR W
PATTERSAL ALX A 29 ROC W
PATTERSAL BAXTER A 29 ROC W
PATTERSON ALLEN A 26 SHE B
PATTERSON ARCHIBALD A 29 MON W
PATTERSON AUTHUR A 26 GOF W
PATTERSON B A 39 PUG W
PATTERSON BRYANT A 37 ROC B
PATTERSON C G A 44 HEN W
PATTERSON C H A 26 SHE W
PATTERSON C W A 28 03A W
PATTERSON D A A 26 GOF W
PATTERSON D M A 44 TOW W
PATTERSON DANL H A 29 ROC W
MILLITIA OFFICER AFTER
ENGAGED IN REBELLION
PATTERSON DAVID A 29 GRA B
PATTERSON DUNCAN J A 29 QUW W
PATTERSON E A 39 PUG W
PATTERSON ELI A A 26 GOF W
PATTERSON F A A 26 BOR W
PATTERSON F T A 26 GOF W

PATTERSON FENDOL A 26 SHE W
PATTERSON FRED A 39 FRA B
PATTERSON GEORGE A 39 PUG W
PATTERSON H C A 39 FRA W
PATTERSON HENRY A 46 GRE B
PATTERSON ISAAC A 26 GOF B
PATTERSON ISAAC A 28 01A W
PATTERSON J B A 26 GOF W
PATTERSON J L A 25 SHO W
PATTERSON J W A 26 GOF W
PATTERSON JACOB A 53 LA1 B
PATTERSON JAMES A 39 LOU W
PATTERSON JHON A 25 SHO W
PATTERSON JNO H A 44 RAG W
PATTERSON JOHN A 26 SHE W
PATTERSON JOHN A 28 01A W
PATTERSON JOHN M A 26 GOF W
PATTERSON JOHN O A 35 WAR W
PATTERSON MCL. ANGS A 29 ROC W
PATTERSON MOSES A 28 01A W
PATTERSON NED A 39 FRA B
PATTERSON NEIL A 29 MON W
PATTERSON NEILL A 29 QUW W
PATTERSON NICHOLAS A 39 PUG W
PATTERSON P D A 26 GOF W
PATTERSON PETER A 29 FA1 B
PATTERSON PETER A 29 QUW W
PATTERSON R D A 29 BLA W
PATTERSON R L A 26 GOF W
PATTERSON R U A 26 GOF W
PATTERSON ROBERT A 46 RAG W
PATTERSON ROBT H A 46 GRE W
PATTERSON SAMUEL A 25 SHO W
PATTERSON T C A 26 GOF W
PATTERSON THOMAS A 44 HEN W
PATTERSON W D A 29 QUW W
PATTERSON W G A 26 SHE W
PATTERSON W T A 29 QUW W
PATTERSON WESTAR A 25 SHO W
PATTERSON WILLIAM A 29 QUW B
PATTERSON WILLIAM A 37 ROC B
PATTERSON WILLIAM A 39 PUG W
PATTERSON WILLIAM A 40 FER W
PATTERSON WILLIAM J A 35 WAR W
PATTERSON WM W A 46 GRE W
PATTILLO JAS E A 44 RAG W
PATTOM W N A 44 FIS W
PATTON (?) KINSON A 32 THO W
PATTON ALFRED B A 25 HAY W
PATTON ALLEN A 40 STO B
PATTRICK JOHN H A 53 LAI W
PATTS M L A 25 HAY W
PAUL ALEXANDER M A 28 14T W
PAUL ALLEN A 28 05A B
PAUL AQUILLA T A 53 BUR W
PAUL CHARLES A 28 04B B
CERTIFICATE GRANTED
WASHINGTON NC
PAUL DAVID J A 28 14T W
PAUL GEORGE H A 28 15T W
PAUL JESSE A 28 16T W
PAUL JOHN F A 28 14T W
PAUL RAYMOND L A 19 DAV W
PAUL SOLOMON N A 28 10T W
PAUL STEPHEN A 28 13T W
PAUL VALENTINE W A 28 10T W
PAUL WM T A 28 14T W
PAUL ZACHEUS A 28 14T W
PAULETT J M A 44 HEN W
PAVIE EDWD M A 28 01A W
PAXTEN WILSON A 28 05A B
PAXTER THOMAS A 19 BE1 B
PAXTON ABRAHAM JR A 24 EDE B

PAXTON ABRAHAM SR A 24 EDE B
PAXTON CHARLES A 24 EDE B
PAXTON CRAVEN A 24 EDE B
PAXTON DAVID A 24 EDE B
PAXTON HENRY A 24 EDE B
PAXTON ISAAC A 24 EDE B
PAXTON JAMES A 24 EDE B
PAXTON JOB A 24 EDE B
PAXTON JOHN A 24 EDE B
PAXTON JOHN A 24 EDE B
PAXTON NAT A 24 EDE B
PAXTON NATHANIEL A 24 EDE B
PAXTON ROBT A 24 EDE B
PAXTON SAMUEL A 24 EDE B
PAXTON WALTER A 24 EDE B
PAYLOR GEORGE W A 46 GRE W
PAYLOR J D A 32 THO W
PAYLOR JOHN W A 46 GIB W
PAYNE ABEL A 29 FA1 B
PAYNE ABEL JR A 29 FA1 B
PAYNE ALFERD A 32 THO W
PAYNE B A A 32 BRO W
PAYNE CHARLES A 32 BRO W
PAYNE CHARLES M A 32 DAV W
PAYNE CORNELIUS A 53 CHI W
PAYNE DR R L A 32 DAV W
PAYNE EDWARD A 53 CHI W
PAYNE FRANCIS M A 53 CHI W
PAYNE GEORGE A 32 DAV B
PAYNE HIRAM A A 32 SHE W
PAYNE HUGHES A 29 FA1 B
PAYNE JAMES A 32 DAV B
PAYNE JAMES A 46 GRE B
PAYNE JAMES A A 32 SHE W
PAYNE JOHN A 32 DAV B
PAYNE JOHN A 32 SHE W
PAYNE JOHN W A 46 GRE W
PAYNE JOSEPH A 32 BRO W
PAYNE LEWIS A 30 POP B
PAYNE LEWIS A 32 DAV B
PAYNE NATHAN O A 53 CHI W
PAYNE SANDERSON A 53 CHI W
PAYNE SANDERSON JR A 53 CHI W
PAYNE SOLOMON A 32 THO W
PAYNE THOMAS A 30 KNO W
PAYNE WARREN L A 32 DAV B
PAYNE WARREN SR A 32 DAV B
PAYNE WILLIAM A 32 DAV B
PAYNE WILLIAM E A 32 POS W
PAYNE WM A 53 CHI W
PAYTON ALEXANDER A 28 12T B
PAYTON ELIAS A 28 04A B
PAYTON HENRY A 28 04A B
PAYTON JAMES W A 28 04A B
PAYTON JESSE A 37 SPA B
PAYTON JOHN A 28 04A B
PAYTON JONAS A 28 04A B
PAYTON LEWIS A 28 04A B
PAYTON PHILIP A 28 04A B
PEACE A D A 44 BEA W
PEACE A S A 44 BEA W
PEACE ANDREW A 44 FIS B
PEACE C C A 44 FIS W
PEACE CHARLES A 44 HEN B
PEACE CHARLES JR A 44 KIT B
PEACE DOCTOR A 44 YXR B
PEACE EDWARD A 44 HEN B
PEACE G T A 44 BEA W
PEACE HARRY A 44 FIS B
PEACE HENRY A 44 KIT B
PEACE J L A 44 FIS B
PEACE JAMES H A 32 THO W
PEACE JOHN A 44 YXR B

PEACE JOHN C A 44 OXF W
PEACE JOSEPH W A 32 THO W
PEACE L E A 32 THO W
PEACE MACKLIN A 44 BRA B
PEACE MADISON A 44 HEN B
PEACE P P A 44 FIS W
PEACE PETER A 44 BRA B
PEACE PHIL A 44 YXR B
PEACE RALPH A 44 BRA B
PEACE SAML A 44 BRA B
PEACE SILAS A 46 HIG W
PEACE W J A 44 BEA W
PEACE W K A 44 BEA W
PEACE W L A 44 FIS W
PEACE WILLIE A 44 BRA B
PEACE WM A 44 YXR B
PEACOCK ALEXANDER A 35 MAG B
PEACOCK J A 32 JAC W
PEACOCK MADISON A 37 ROC W
PEACOCK WILLIAM A 32 JAC W
PEACOCK WM R A 32 JAC W
PEADE JESSE A 28 10T B
PEADE JOHN A 28 10T B
PEAGRAM ISAIH A 46 KIN W
RES 2 MOS
PEAGRAM J F A 46 FRI W
PEAGRAM J W A 46 FRI W
PEAGRAM JESSE E A 46 KIN W
PEAK JAMES A 46 KIN W
PEAK P R A 19 NEW W
PEAL AUSTIN A 24 EDE B
PEAL JOHN A 44 SAS B
PEAL JOSEPH A 37 PEN W
PEAL WILLIAM A 37 PEN W
PEALE JOSEPH J A 24 EDE W
PEARCE A W JR A 39 JOR W
PEARCE A W SR A 39 JOR W
PEARCE ABRAHAM A 39 JOR B
PEARCE ALEXANDER C A 24 EDE W
PEARCE ALFRED A 37 EDW B
PEARCE HENRY A 39 FRA W
PEARCE ISAAC A 30 IND B
PEARCE J J A 39 JOR W
PEARCE J T A 39 DAV W
PEARCE JAMES R A 46 GRE W
PEARCE JOHN A 39 JOR B
CERT NASH CO
PEARCE JOSEPH A 28 01A B
PEARCE JOSEPH A 37 HIG B
PEARCE KERNEY A 39 GRI W
PEARCE LEE A 39 GRI W
PEARCE LEWIS A 39 JOR B
PEARCE PETER A 39 JOR B
PEARCE PHIL A 37 EDW B
PEARCE R M A 39 JOR W
PEARCE RICKS A 39 JOR B
PEARCE S M A 39 GRI W
PEARCE W C A 28 01B W
PEARCE W H A 28 01A W
PEARCE WILLIAM A 35 FAI B
PEARCE WILLIE A 39 JOR B
PEARCE WILLIS A 39 LOU W
PEARCE YOUNG A 39 JOR B
PEARDEU WM E A 39 HAY W
PEARSALL ARTHUR A 35 KEN B
PEARSALL BEDFORD A 35 KEN B
PEARSALL BENJAMIN F A 35 KEN W
PEARSALL CALVIN A 35 ISL B
PEARSALL DAVID A 35 ALB B
PEARSALL DAVID A 35 KEN B
PEARSALL DAVID M A 35 KEN W
PEARSALL EDWARD A 35 KEN W
PEARSALL ESSEX A 35 KEN B
PEARSALL HAMLET A 35 GLI B
PEARSALL HAYWOOD A 35 KEN B
PEARSALL HENRY A 35 KEN B
PEARSALL HENRY A 35 KEN B
PEARSALL HORACE A 35 KEN B
PEARSALL HORACE A 35 KEN B
PEARSALL JACKSON A 35 KEN B
PEARSALL JERRY A 35 LIM B
PEARSALL JOHN H A 35 KEN W
PEARSALL JOHN W A 35 KEN W
PEARSALL JOSEPH A 35 KEN W
PEARSALL MARSHALL A 35 KEN B
PEARSALL MOSES A 35 KEN B
PEARSALL NEEDHAM A 35 KEN B
PEARSALL NICKSON A 35 KEN B
PEARSALL RICHARD A 35 KEN B
PEARSALL SANDAL A 35 KEN B
PEARSALL SHADE A 35 FAI B
PEARSALL SQUIRE A 35 KEN B
PEARSALL STEPHEN A 35 GLI B
PEARSALL STILLA A 35 SMI B
PEARSALL VIRGIL A 35 KEN B
PEARSALL W D A 35 ALB W
PEARSALL W F A 35 FAI W
PEARSALL WILLIAM A 35 KEN B
PEARSOL ESSIEX A 28 15T B
PEARSON CLINTON D A 28 03A B
PEARSON J W A 28 02N B
PEARSON JAS W A 28 03A B
PEARSON JNO G A 46 SUM W
PEARSON JOHN A 46 SUM W
PEARSON PASKILL A 39 SPE W
PEARSON RICHD A 28 05A B
PEARSON WILLIAM A 40 DA1 W
PEARSON WILLIAM A A 40 FER W
PEARTREE ISAAC A 19 BE1 W
PEARTREE SAMUEL A 53 GER B
PEARTREE STEPHEN A 28 9TH W
PECAR JACOB A 28 05A B
PECK GEO P A 37 TA2 W
PECK REASON A 32 CLE W
PEDRICK LEVI A 28 6TH B
PEED JOHN A 44 LED W
PEED RICHARD A 44 LED W
PEED SHERMAN A 44 LED W
PEED W C A 44 LED W
PEED W H A 44 LED W
PEEL BARNY F A 53 HAT W
PEEL CHRISTOPHER W A 53 HAT W
PEEL IVA A 53 KEN W
PEEL JOHN A 37 ROC W
PEEL JOHN T A 53 HAT W
PEEL LENARD A 37 HIG W
PEEL TURNER A 37 ROC W
PEEL WILLIAM A 35 ALB W
PEEL WM E A 53 HAT W
PEEL WM E A 53 KEN W
PEELER A G A 26 WAR W
PEELER ABRAM A 26 WAR B
PEELER CALEB A 32 SHE W
PEELER D C A 26 GRI W
PEELER D H A 26 WAR W
PEELER DAVID A 26 GRI W
PEELER DAVID JR A 26 GRI W
PEELER J H JR A 26 GRI W
PEELER JAMES A 26 GRI W
PEELER JOHN JR A 26 GRI W
PEELOR THEOFILUS A 32 DAV B
PEEPLES JAMES H A 46 KIN W
PEEPLES PLUMMER A 39 SPE W
PEER HAYMAN A 37 SPA B
PEGG JESSE A 46 FRI W
PEGG M H A 46 FRI W
PEGG OLIVER L A 46 FRI W
PEGG PRESTON A 46 FRI W
PEGG R A A 46 FRI W
PEGG WILLIAM A 46 FRI W
PEGRAM A W A 46 SUM W
PEGRAM ALLEN W A 46 KIN W
PEGRAM AMZI A 40 DA1 B
PEGRAM ANTHONY A 40 STO B
PEGRAM BAKER A 46 KIN W
PEGRAM DANIEL A 46 KIN B
PEGRAM E M A 46 KIN W
PEGRAM EDWARD L 40 DA2 W
CERT ISSUED APRIL 7
1868 TO 1ST REG PRE
GASTON CO NC
PEGRAM F S A 46 KIN W
PEGRAM HENRY J A 46 KIN W
PEGRAM J F A 46 KIN W
PEGRAM J H A 46 KIN W
PEGRAM JAMES A A 53 GER W
PEGRAM JAMES H A 46 KIN W
PEGRAM JESSE A 46 KIN W
PEGRAM SAMUEL A 53 BUR W
PEGRAM
SINGLETON G W A 53 GER W
PEGRAM T H A 32 SHE W
PEGRAM WILLIAM A A 46 KIN W
PEGRAM WM C A 46 SUM W
PEIRCE DANIEL A 30 COI B
PEIRCE JOHN W A 39 JOR W
PEIRCE SAMPSON A 35 KEN W
PELHAM EPHRAIM A 28 05A B
PELHAM HENRY A 28 05A B
PELITIER ED W A 19 HAD W
PELITIER JER J A 19 HAD W
PELITIER LEVI A 19 MOR W
PELL A J A 30 IND W
PELLETIER GEORGE A 19 HAD B
PELLITIER JNO W A 19 MOR W
PELLIUM ALNER A 44 TAR B
PEMBERTON ALLEN A 29 FA1 B
PEMBERTON E L A 29 FA1 W
PEMBERTON JNO A A 29 FA1 W
MILLITIA OFFICER AFTER-
WARDS ENG IN REBELLION
PEMBERTON SMITH A 44 OXF B
PEMBLETON SYLVESTER A 28 03A B
PENDER ALLEN A 37 TA1 B
PENDER BLOUNT A 37 PIN B
PENDER GEORGE A 37 PEN B
PENDER JAMES A 37 HIG B
PENDER JARYD J A 37 SHA W
PENDER JOHN A 19 BE1 B
PENDER JOHN A 28 05A B
PENDER JOHN A 37 PEN W
PENDER JOHN A 37 ROB B
PENDER JOHN A 37 TA1 B
PENDER JOSEPH A 37 EDW B
PENDER JOSEPH A 37 TA1 B
PENDER JOSEPH A 37 TA1 W
PENDER JOSHUA A 37 PEN W
PENDER LITTLETON A 37 HIG W
PENDER MADISON A 28 04A B
PENDER POMPEY A 37 EDW B
PENDER RUFUS A 37 ROB B
PENDER SOLOMON M A 37 HIC A
PENDER WILLIAM A 37 TA1 B
PENDERGRAST JOHN A 40 SAN W
COPIED FROM DUPLICATE
PENDLETON K R A 24 EDE W
PENELETON BINSTEAD A 19 NEW B
PENIX J K A 32 POS W
PENLAND C M A 25 SHO W

PENLAND H M A 25 HAY W
PENN JOHN A 46 GRE B
PENN ROBERT A 46 GRE W
PENNELL LEWIS A 39 SPE B
PENNELL M R A 44 BRA W
PENNEY BOSTON A 99 BUS B
PENNICK MOSES A 46 ROS B
PENNINGTON DANIEL A 40 FER W
PENNIX M A A 32 POS W
PENNY ASBURY A 99 BUS B
PENNY DALLAS A 99 BUS B
PENNY JOSEPH J A 99 BUS W
PENNY LEONIDAS H A 99 BUS W
PENNY MICHAEL A 99 BUS W
PENNY NED A 32 DAV B
PENNY SETH A 44 LED W
PENNY WILLIAM H A 99 BUS W
PENNY WILSON A 99 BUS B
PENNY YOUNG A 99 BUS W
PENRY JONAS A 32 DAV B
PEOPLES ABRAM A 28 05A B
PEOPLES ASHLEY A A 29 FA2 W
PEOPLES H W A 46 KIN W
PEOPLES MUMFORD A 37 EDW B
PEOPLES ROBERT G A 46 KIN W
PEOPLES W H H A 28 03A B
PEPINS RAIF A 37 HIG W
PEPPERS WILSON A 29 FA1 B
PERCE EDWARD A 24 MID W
PERCY WILLIAM A 28 01B W
PERDEW EDMOND A 46 FRI B
PERDEW JOHN A 46 GRE W
PERDUE J L A 39 HAY W
PERDUE JAMES A 32 LOF W
PERDUE WASHINGTON A 39 FRE B
PERDY GEORGE A 46 KIN W
PERDY THOMAS A 37 HIG B
PERGERSON J T A 44 BRA W
PERGRAM D J A 46 KIN W
PERIMON WILLIAM A 32 POS W
PERIN GUST A 37 ROC B
PERKINS BENJAMIN J A 28 14T W
PERKINS CASIN M A 40 DA1 W
PERKINS CHARLES A 30 CUR B
PERKINS DENNIS A 28 6TH B
PERKINS EDWARD A 30 IND B
PERKINS ELIAS A 46 FRI W
PERKINS HENRY A 19 NEW B
PERKINS ISAAC A 24 EDE B
PERKINS ISAAC A 40 DA1 W
PERKINS J J A 40 SAN W
PERKINS JEREMIAH A 30 TUL W
PERKINS JOHN A 30 CUR B
PERKINS JOHN A 30 MOY W
PERKINS JOSEPH A 28 04A B
PERKINS JOSEPH A 28 6TH B
PERKINS JULIUS A 30 ROA B
PERKINS KING A 28 05A B
PERKINS MAJOR A 24 EDE B
PERKINS NATHAN S A 24 EDE W
PERKINS OBIA A 29 FA1 B
PERKINS P L A 19 NEW W
PERKINS POMPY A 32 DAV B
PERKINS R B A 24 EDE W
PERKINS SAML A 28 6TH B
PERKINS SAMUEL A 28 10T B
PERKINS WILLIAM A 28 10T B
PERKINS WM B A 24 EDE W
PERKINSON HENRY A 44 KIT W
PERKINSON RANSOM A 44 KIT W
PERMAR PLESANT A 46 GRE W
PERMAR WM A 46 GRE W
PERPEEWELL THOMAS A 53 LA1 W

PERREN FRANK A 72 SWA B
PERRILL D C A 32 DAV W
PERRIMAN C M A 32 DAV W
PERRIMAN JOHN F A 32 POS W
PERRIMAN SAMUEL A 32 POS W
PERRSON M P A 39 HAY W
PERRY A K A 39 DAV W
PERRY A S A 39 HAR W
PERRY A S A 39 LOU W
PERRY AARON A 39 LOU B
TRNS FROM PUGHE'S HILL
TO LOUISBURG
PERRY AARON A 39 PUG B
TRANS TO LOUISBURG
PERRY ABRAHAM A 44 KIT B
PERRY ABRAM A 28 05A B
PERRY ADAM A 39 JOR B
PERRY ADAMS A 39 HAR B
PERRY ALEXANDER A 39 HAR B
PERRY ALFORD A 39 LOU W
TRNS FROM HARRIS X
ROADS TO LOUISBURG
PERRY ALFRED A 39 HAR W
PERRY ALLEN A 39 HAY B
PERRY AMAS A 24 MID W
PERRY AMOS A 39 FRE B
PERRY ANDERSON A 39 SPE B
PERRY ANDERSON S A 24 UPP W
PERRY ANDREW A 39 HAY B
PERRY ANTHONY A 39 PUG B
PERRY ASA A 24 UPP W
PERRY AUGUSTUS A A 24 MID W
PERRY AUSTER A 44 BRA B
PERRY B B A 39 LOU W
PERRY BATTLE A 39 HAR B
PERRY BEB A 39 DAV B
PERRY BENJ A 38 FRE B
PERRY BENJAMIN 39 LOU B
PERRY BERKLEY A 39 HAR W
PERRY BRYANT A 24 MID B
PERRY BUCK A 44 KIT B
PERRY BURWELL A A 39 HAR W
PERRY BUTTON A A 30 POW W
PERRY C H A 39 FRA W
PERRY C H A 39 LOU W
TRNS FROM FRANKLINTON
PERRY CALAWAY A 26 SHE W
PERRY CALEB G A 24 MID W
PERRY CALVIN A 28 03A W
PERRY CALVIN A 39 LOU B
PERRY CALVIN A 39 PUG B
PERRY CASWELL A 39 LOU B
PERRY CEZAR A 44 FOR B
PERRY CHARLES A 39 HAY W
PERRY CHARLES A 39 SPE B
PERRY CHARLES A 44 KIT B
PERRY CHAS A 39 FRA B
PERRY CILAS A 39 HAY B
PERRY COLLIER A 39 DAV B
PERRY CUFFEE A 39 LOU B
PERRY DALLAS A 29 FA1 B
PERRY DANIEL A 44 BRA B
PERRY DANIEL E A 39 LOU B
PERRY DAVID A 39 JOR B
PERRY DEMPSEY A 30 NOR W
PERRY DEMPSY A 39 HAR B
PERRY DICK A 39 LOU B
PERRY DOCTOR A 39 PUG B
PERRY E M A 44 DUT W
PERRY EAPHRAM A 39 DAV B
PERRY EATON A 39 DAV B
PERRY EDMOND A 39 FRA B
PERRY EDMOND A 39 SPE B

PERRY EDWD A 29 FA1 B
PERRY ELIJA A 39 HAY B
2ND BOARD REG
PINE HILL FRANKLIN CO
PERRY ELIJAH A 39 PUG B
PERRY EVERETT A 39 FRE B
PERRY FRANK A 39 HAY B
PERRY FRENCH A 39 FRA B
PERRY G W A 28 9TH W
PERRY GEO A 39 FRE B
PERRY GEO A 39 HAR B
PERRY GID A 39 JOR B
PERRY GREEF A 39 FRE B
PERRY GUY A 39 HAR B
PERRY HANDYPERSON H A 39 FRA B
PERRY HARRY A 24 MID W
PERRY HARRY A 39 FRA B
PERRY HARRY A 39 FRA B
PERRY HARRY A 39 SPE B
PERRY HARRY 1 A 39 FRA B
PERRY HARTSFIELD A 39 JOR W
PERRY HENRY A 32 DAV B
PERRY HENRY A 39 GRI B
PERRY HENRY A 39 LOU B
PERRY HENRY A 53 GER B
PERRY HIRAM A 28 9TH B
PERRY HOWEL W A 39 LOU W
TRNS BY AFF FROM CHOWAN
PERRY HOWELL A 28 02N W
PERRY ISAAC A 39 FRA B
PERRY ISAAC A 39 FRA W
PERRY ISAAC A 39 HAR B
PERRY ISAAC A 39 JOR B
PERRY ISAIAH A 28 01B B
PERRY ISAIAH A 28 02N B
PERRY ISHAM A 39 HAR B
PERRY ISHAM A 39 JOR B
PERRY ISRAEL A 30 NOR W
PERRY ISREAL A 39 HAR B
PERRY J M A 32 THO W
PERRY J R A 39 LOU W
PERRY J W A 44 DUT W
PERRY JACK A 39 DAV B
PERRY JACKSON A 39 JOR B
PERRY JACOB A 39 FRA B
PERRY JACOB A 44 FOR B
PERRY JACOB B A 24 EDE W
PERRY JACOB JR A 39 HAR B
PERRY JACOB SR A 39 HAR B
PERRY JAMES JR A 39 FRA B
PERRY JAMES M A 19 BE1 W
PERRY JASPER A 39 FRA B
PERRY JERRY A 39 DAV W
PERRY JERRY A 39 JOR B
CERT WARREN CO
PERRY JERRY M A 39 JOR B
PERRY JESSE A 39 JOR B
PERRY JESSEE A 39 HAR W
PERRY JIM A 39 DAV B
PERRY JIM A 39 DAV B
PERRY JIM A 39 HAY B
PERRY JNO A 38 FRE B
PERRY JNO A C A 29 ROC W
PERRY JNO L A 29 FA2 W
PERRY JNO W A 39 GRI W
PERRY JOE A 39 DAV B
PERRY JOE S A 39 DAV B
PERRY JOHN M A 19 BE1 W
STRICKEN OUT APR 11 1868
PERRY JOHN A 24 EDE W
PERRY JOHN A 39 FRA W
PERRY JOHN A 39 JOR B
PERRY JOHN A 39 SPE B

PERRY JOHN A 44 DUT W
PERRY JORDAN A 39 FRA B
PERRY JORDAN A 39 HAY B
PERRY JOS A 38 FRE W
PERRY JOSEPH A 29 FA2 B
PERRY JOSEPH A 39 LOU B
PERRY JOSEPH A 39 LOU W
PERRY JOSEPH B A 39 LOU B
PERRY JOSHUA A 38 FRE B
PERRY JOSHUA A 39 SPE W
PERRY JOSIAH D A 30 POW W
PERRY KEARNY A 39 GRI W
PERRY KEINSS A 39 FRE W
PERRY LEUIS A 39 PUG B
TRANS TO LOUISBURG
PERRY LEVIN A 39 JOR B
PERRY LEWIS 39 LOU B
PERRY LEWIS A 39 DAV B
PERRY LEWIS JR A 39 JOR B
PERRY LEWIS SR A 39 JOR B
PERRY LISTER A 39 JOR B
PERRY LOUIS A 39 FRE B
PERRY LUKE A 39 FRE B
PERRY LUNNEN A 39 DAV B
TRNS TO LOUISBURG
PERRY M L A 39 FRA W
PERRY MARTIN A 24 MID B
PERRY MASON A 39 FRE B
PERRY MICAJAH A 39 LOU W
PERRY MILES A 24 MID B
PERRY MILES A 39 HAY B
PERRY MINGER A 44 FOR B
PERRY MINGO A 39 PUG B
PERRY MOSES A 39 JOR B
PERRY NATHAN A 39 FRA W
PERRY NORPHLET A 39 PUG B
PERRY ORRAN JR A 39 PUG B
TRANS TO DAVIS' X ROADS
PERRY ORRANGE A 39 SPE B
PERRY OSBORN A 39 LOU B
PERRY OSCAR A 39 PUG B
PERRY PETER A 39 DAV B
PERRY PETER A 39 PUG B
PERRY PEYTON A 39 DAV B
TRNS TO BLADEN CO
PERRY POWEL A 39 LOU B
PERRY PRESSLY A 39 FRA B
PERRY RATCLIFF A 29 FA1 B
PERRY REDAFORD A 39 GRI W
PERRY REDICK A 39 DAV B
PERRY RICHARD A 39 HAR B
PERRY RICHD A 28 05A B
PERRY RICHD A 39 FRA B
PERRY RICHD JR A 39 FRE B
PERRY RICHD SR A 38 FRE B
PERRY ROBERT A 28 05B B
PERRY ROBT A 38 FRE B
PERRY ROBT A 39 FRA B
PERRY ROBT A 39 PUG B
PERRY RODIN A 39 HAY B
PERRY S A 46 HIG W
PERRY S H A 44 DUT W
PERRY S W A 39 JOR W
PERRY SAMUEL A 39 GRI W
PERRY SAMUEL A 39 SPE W
PERRY SIMION A 38 FRE B
PERRY SIMON JR A 38 FRE B
PERRY SIMON SR A 38 FRE B
PERRY SOLOMAN A 39 LOU B
PERRY SOLOMON A 39 FRA B
PERRY STARKEY A 24 EDE W
PERRY STEPHEN A 39 DAV B
PERRY STEPHEN A 39 GRI W
PERRY STEPHEN A 39 LOU B
PERRY T H A 44 DUT W
PERRY T P A 39 FRA B
PERRY TAYLOR A 24 EDE B
PERRY THEOFFILOUS A 39 LOU W
PERRY THOMAS A 30 NOR W
PERRY THOMAS D A 30 NOR W
PERRY THOS A 39 GRI B
PERRY TILER A 39 HAR B
PERRY TOM A 39 HAY B
PERRY W D A 44 DUT W
PERRY W H A 24 MID W
PERRY W H A 39 HAR W
PERRY W H A 44 DUT W
PERRY W P JR A 39 FRA W
PERRY W P SR A 39 FRA W
PERRY W T A 39 LOU W
PERRY WARREN A 39 GRI B
PERRY WARREN A 44 HEN B
PERRY WASH A 39 DAV B
PERRY WASH A 39 FRA B
PERRY WASHINGTON A 39 HAR B
PERRY WASHINGTON A 39 HAY B
PERRY WASHINGTON A 39 JOR B
PERRY WASHINGTON A 44 BRA B
PERRY WESLY A 39 FRA B
PERRY WILCE A 39 DAV B
PERRY WILLIAM A 24 EDE W
PERRY WILLIAM A 30 NOR W
PERRY WILLIAM A 39 JOR B
PERRY WILLIAM A 39 LOU B
PERRY WILLIS A 39 FRA B
PERRY WILLIS A 39 LOU W
PERRY WISTON A 39 LOU W
PERRY WM A 39 GRI W
PERRY WM A 39 JOR B
PERRY WM A 44 BRA B
PERRY WM F A 28 02N W
PERRY YORK A 39 FRE B
PERRYMAN ANDREW A 32 THO W
PERRYMAN CHARLES A 32 SHE W
PERRYMAN FRANKLIN A 32 SHE W
PERRYMAN HAMILTON A 32 SHE W
PERRYMAN JESSE A 32 SHE W
PERRYMAN JOHN A 32 CLE W
PERSAN B F A 44 OXF W
PERSLEY ANDREW A 40 CAN W
PERSLEY D M A 40 SAN W
PERSON A J A 39 LOU W
TRNS TO SPEEDS STORE
PERSON ABRAHAM A 39 PUG B
PERSON ALFRED A 39 FRA B
PERSON ALLEN A 39 SPE B
PERSON ANTHONY A A 39 SPE W
PERSON BEN A 39 HAY B
PERSON BENJ JR A 39 FRA B
CHAL FOR NOT
BEING 21 YEARS OLD
PERSON BENJAMIN A 39 FRA B
PERSON BIRD A 39 FRA B
PERSON BURWELL A 39 HAY B
PERSON CALVIN A 39 FRA B
PERSON CROOK A 39 FRA B
PERSON DANIEL A 44 HEN B
PERSON ELLICK A 39 SPE B
PERSON FRANK A 39 FRA B
PERSON FRANK A 39 LOU B
PERSON GILBERT A 44 BRA B
PERSON HENDERSON A 39 FRA B
PERSON ISAAC A 39 SPE B
PERSON JAMES A 39 FRA B
PERSON JESSE A 39 HAY W
PERSON JOE 39 LOU B
PERSON JORDAN A 39 FRA B
PERSON JOS A A 44 FOR W
PERSON LEWIS A 39 FRA B
PERSON NELSON A 39 FRA B
PERSON P C A 39 FRA W
PERSON PETER A 39 FRA B
PERSON PLUMMER A 39 HAY B
PERSON ROBT A 39 FRA B
PERSON ROGER A 39 FRA B
PERSON ROGER A 39 SPE B
PERSON SOLOMAN A 39 SPE B
PERSON THOMAS A 44 BRA B
PERSON W N A 39 FRA W
PERSON WESLEY A 44 KIT B
PERSONS WESLY A 39 HAY B
2ND BORD REGIS
EPPING FOREST
PERVIS DICK A 37 HIC B
PERVIS JESSIE A 37 HIC B
PERVIS JOHN A A 37 HIC
PERVIS JOHN A A 37 HIC
PERVIS LOUIS K A 37 HIC
PERVIS NED A 37 PIN B
PERVIS WRIGHT A 37 HIC B
PERVISS MEMBRAY A 37 TA2 B
PERY J L A 25 TUS W
PERY P C A 25 TUS W
PERYEAR BENJ A 46 GRE B
PERYEAR JOHN A 46 GRE B
PETAFORD H C A 44 FOR B
PETAFORD MAYNARD A 44 FOR B
PETAFORD N O A 44 FIS B
PETAFORD REUBEN A 44 FOR B
PETAFORD SILUS A 44 FOR B
PETAFORD T Y A 44 FIS B
PETAFORD WILLIAM A 46 FRI B
PETAFORD WILLIE A 44 FOR B
PETAFORD WM A 44 FIS B
PETAWAY ISAAC A 19 BE1 B
PETAWAY MACEAJIAH A 37 HOL B
PETERS BENJAMIN P A 37 ROB W
PETERS WILLIAM A 37 SHA W
PETERSON ALLEN A 35 ROC W
PETERSON E A 35 FAI W
PETERSON ELIJAH A 53 LA1 B
PETERSON HARRY A 53 SWA B
PETERSON HENRY A 28 01A B
PETERSON JOHN A 28 9TH B
PETERSON JOHN J A 37 TA1 W
PETERSON JOHN W A 35 ROC W
PETERSON KILBY A 35 ROC W
PETERSON LARRIE A 19 NEW B
PETERSON LARY A 53 SWA B
PETERSON LEWIS A 35 ROC W
PETERSON NATHAN A A 28 04A B
PETERSON REV J R A 40 DA1 W
PETERSON THOMAS A 53 LA1 B
PETEWAY JAMES A 37 HOL B
PETFORD THOMAS A 44 BRA B
PETNER AUSTIN A 37 HIG B
PETON ALFRED A 28 9TH B
PETTAGRU CRISTESPER A 44 DUT B
PETTAGRU S H A 44 DUT W
PETTAWAY CORNEALOUS A 37 PIN B
PETTAWAY DANIEL A 37 PIN B
PETTAWAY GEDEON A 37 EDW B
PETTAWAY WILLIAM L A 37 EDW W
PETTEFORD SOLOMAN A 44 HEN B
PETTEPHER WM H A 19 BE1 B
PETTERSON JOHN A 29 QUW W
PETTERSON W D A 25 SHO W
PETTEWAY DANIEL A 32 DAV B
PETTEWAY KADER A 37 TA1 B

PETTIFOOT CHAS A 29 FA1 B
PETTIFOOT JERRY A 44 ISL B
PETTIFORD ALVEN A 46 JAM B
PETTIFORD BRYAN A 28 12T B
PETTIFORD DEMSEY A 44 SAS B
PETTIFORD FRANCIS A 28 12T B
PETTIFORD FRANKLIN A 46 JAM B
PETTIFORD GEORGE A 39 HAR B
PETTIFORD HENDERSON A 46 JAM B
PETTIFORD ISRAEL A 28 12T B
PETTIFORD RANSOM A 46 JAM B
PETTIFORD RICHARD A 28 12T B
PETTIFORD THOMAS A 46 HIG B
PETTIFORD WILLIAM A 44 SAS B
PETTIFORD WILLIS A 28 12T B
PETTIFORD WRIGHT L A 28 12T B
PETTIGREW HAYWOOD A 24 EDE B
ALTHOUGH HE CLAIMS THIS AS HIS RESIDENCE THE BOARD ARE OF THE OPINION THAT HE LOST IT HAVING BEEN GONE SO LONG AND ONLY 4 MONTHS RETURNED
PETTIGREW SMITH A 28 04A B
PETTIGREW THOMAS A 46 GRE B
PETTIS M A 40 RHY W
PETTIS S T A 40 SAN W
PETTIT SILAS A 28 6TH B
PETTIT WILEY A 28 03A B
PETTWAY BLOUNT A 37 ROC B
PETTWAY CARY A 37 HIG B
PETTWAY THOMAS A 37 HIG B
PETTY CHARLES Q R 40 FER W
NAME LINED OUT CAPTAIN OF MILITIA BEFORE THE REBELLION & GAVE AID AND COMFORT TO THE ENEMY DID NOT QUALIFY * IS REJECTED
PETTY CHARLES Q * R 40 FER W
PETTY DAVID M A 46 HIG W
PETTY GEORGE A 46 ROS W
PETTY LEWIS A 40 FER B
PETTY PINKNEY A 26 WAR W
PETTY W S A 29 FA1 W
PETTY WILLIAM A 46 ROS W
PETWAY PRESTON S A 37 SHA W
PETWAY REDIN S A 37 ROC W
PEW ANDERSON A 28 8TH B
PEW JEFFERSON A 28 11T B
PEYDON WILLIAM A 46 FRI W
PEYTON ALEXR A 28 01B B
PEYTON HENRY A 46 FRI W
PEYTON JOHN A 46 FRI W
PEYTON TROY A 46 SUM W
PHARE BENJAMIN A 29 QUW B
PHARIS ALEX A 29 CAR W
PHARIS HENRY A 29 CAR W
PHAROAH BRIAN A 19 BE1 B
PHELPS ALVIN A 32 CLE W
PHELPS BENJ A 28 04A B
PHELPS EPHRAIM A 32 SHE B
PHELPS GEORGE A 32 CLE W
PHELPS JACOB A 32 CLE W
PHELPS JOHN A 32 DAV W
PHELPS M C A 19 BE1 W
PHELPS MOSES A 28 01A B
PHELPS PETER A 30 ROA B
PHELPS SAMUEL A 32 CLE W
PHELPS SAMUEL A 32 SHE W
PHELPS SANDY A 32 SHE B
PHELPSH A B A 39 PUG W
PHIBBS JAMES A 46 MON W
PHIBBS WILLIAM A 46 MON W
PHIFER GEORGE A 40 DA1 B
PHIFER GEORGE R 40 DA1 B
7 MOS RESIDENCE 15 AUG 1867 SEE BELOW
PHIFER JACCOB A 26 SHE B
PHIFER JOHN M A 26 GOF W
PHIILLIPS RICHARD A 19 BE1 W
PHILBECK A H A 26 BLA W
PHILBECK J P A 26 BLA W
PHILBECK JAMES A 26 SHE W
PHILBECK JOHN A 26 BLA W
PHILBECK JOHN P A 26 BLA W
PHILBECK RICHARD A 26 BLA W
PHILBECK T F A 26 BLA W
PHILIP MANUEL A 37 MAN B
PHILIPIC CHRISTIAN A 46 COB W
PHILIPIC WILLIAM M A 46 COB W
PHILIPPS LOSSEN A 26 GRI W
PHILIPS ALBERT A 25 HAY W
PHILIPS ALBERT A 37 MAN B
PHILIPS AMOS A 46 GRE B
PHILIPS AUSTON A 37 MAN B
PHILIPS CAIMBRIGE A 37 MAN B
PHILIPS EMPEROR A 28 04A B
PHILIPS HENDERSON A 37 MAN B
CERT RES TARBORO
PHILIPS JESSY A 37 MAN B
PHILIPS JOHN S A 32 YAD W
PHILIPS LEWIS A 37 MAN B
PHILIPS MORTON A 37 MAN B
PHILIPS PETER A 37 MAN B
PHILIPS SAMUEL A 37 MAN B
CERT RES NASH CO
PHILIPS TURNER A 37 MAN B
PHILIPS WASHINGTON A 37 MAN B
PHILLIP VAN BURIN A 72 SWA W
PHILLIPIC ALFRED A A 46 COB W
PHILLIPPS ABSALOM A 35 WAR W
PHILLIPPS JOHN A 35 KEN B
PHILLIPPS JOSEPH 35 WAR B
CONVICTED OF STEALING
PHILLIPPS THOMAS A 35 KEN W
PHILLIPPS THOMAS A 35 KEN W
PHILLIPS A J A 19 MOR W
PHILLIPS AARON A 72 SWA W
PHILLIPS ALEXANDER A 32 SHE W
PHILLIPS ALLEN A 72 SWA W
PHILLIPS BARNEY A 72 SWA W
PHILLIPS BARNHAM A 32 CLE W
PHILLIPS BENJ C A 46 GRE W
PHILLIPS BRICE A 72 SWA W
PHILLIPS C H A 46 ROS W
PHILLIPS D B A 29 FA1 W
PHILLIPS E A 28 11T W
PHILLIPS EATMAN A 37 ROB W
PHILLIPS EATUS A 37 ROB W
PHILLIPS EDWARD H A 72 SWA W
PHILLIPS FREDRICK A 37 TA1 W
PHILLIPS GIDEON A 39 GRI W
PHILLIPS HARRESON A 29 FA1 B
PHILLIPS HENRY A 32 THO B
PHILLIPS HILLIARD A 37 MAN B
PHILLIPS J W A 29 FA1 W
PHILLIPS JACKSON A 40 BLA B
PHILLIPS JACOB A 37 ROB W
PHILLIPS JAMES A 28 04A B
PHILLIPS JAMES A 29 FA2 W
PHILLIPS JAMES A 37 MAN B
PHILLIPS JNO C A 29 ROC W
PHILLIPS JNO D A 19 MOR W
PHILLIPS JOAB H A 37 ROB W
PHILLIPS JOHN A 28 04A B
PHILLIPS JOHN A 35 KEN B
PHILLIPS JOHN A 37 MAN B
PHILLIPS JOHN A 39 GRI W
PHILLIPS JOHN B A 37 SPA W
PHILLIPS JOHN H A 24 EDE W
CERT TO RALEIGH NC
PHILLIPS JOHN T A 46 FRI W
PHILLIPS JORDAN A 37 ROB W
PHILLIPS JOSEPH A 35 WAR B
PHILLIPS K A 29 FA1 W
PHILLIPS KINYON A 28 7TH B
PHILLIPS L B A 39 GRI W
PHILLIPS LACEY A 28 01A W
PHILLIPS LEVEN A 39 GRI W
PHILLIPS LINCEY A 28 05A B
PHILLIPS M J A 35 ALB W
PHILLIPS MOSES A 37 ROB B
PHILLIPS MOSES A 37 ROB B
PHILLIPS NED A 37 MAN B
PHILLIPS NELSON A 37 HOL B
PHILLIPS NOAH A 37 TA1 B
PHILLIPS PETER H A 37 TA2 W
PHILLIPS PHILIP A 37 MAN B
PHILLIPS PRIMUS A 28 7TH B
PHILLIPS RICHARD A 37 WEB W
PHILLIPS S H A 35 ALB W
PHILLIPS SILAS A 28 8TH W
PHILLIPS SOLOMON C A 19 MOR W
PHILLIPS SPENCER A 28 8TH W
PHILLIPS W A A 32 YAD W
PHILLIPS W K A 39 GRI W
PHILLIPS W S A 28 04A W
PHILLIPS WILLIAM A 19 MOR W
PHILLIPS WILLIAM A 28 7TH W
PHILLIPS WILLIAM A 30 MOY B
PHILLIPS WILLIAM A 37 MAN B
PHILLIPS WILLIAM A 46 JAM W
PHILLIPS WILLIAM A 72 SWA W
PHILLIPS WILLIAM H A 72 SWA W
PHILLIPS WILLIAM J A 37 WEB W
PHILLIPS WILLIS A 37 MAN B
PHILLIPS WILLIS E A 37 WHI W
PHILPOTT ANTHONEY A 44 OXF B
PHILPOTT CHARLES A 44 LED B
PHILPOTT EDWARD A 44 YXR B
PHILPOTT HOWELL A 44 OXF B
PHILPOTT JAMES A 44 TAR W
PHILPOTT R S A 44 OXF W
PHILPOTT RICHD A 44 OXF B
PHIPP RANSOM S A 46 MCL W
PHIPPS GEORGE W JR A 46 RAG W
PHIPPS GEORGE W SR A 46 RAG W
PHIPPS JOSEPH J A 44 TOW W
PHIPPS LEMUEL A A 46 RAG W
PHIPPS LEVI D A 46 RAG W
PHIPPS ROBERT S A 46 MCL W
PHIPPS SAMUEL R A 46 RAG W
PHIPPS SAMUEL W A 46 RAG W
PHIPPS THEOPHOLUS A 35 KEN W
PHIPPS WILLIAM A 35 WAR W
PHIPPS WM H A 46 RAG W
PHYSICK GEORGE A 28 04A B
PHYSIOC WM B A 19 BE1 W
PICKARD W W A 32 BRO W
PICKARD WILLIAM A 32 BRO W
PICKENS CHRISTLEY A 37 ROB W
PICKENS HENRY A 29 FA1 B
PICKENS SAMUEL T A 46 JAM W
PICKET CHRISTIAN D A 32 SHE W
PICKET F A A 32 SHE W
PICKET JOSEPH A 32 SHE W
PICKET SANDY (DEAD) A 19 HAD B
PICKETT ALFORD F A 32 DAV W

PICKETT BENJAMIN A 19 NEW B
PICKETT FREDERICK A 35 CYP W
PICKETT FRIDAY A 35 LIM B
PICKETT GEORGE W A 32 DAV W
PICKETT J J A 29 FA1 W
PICKETT J Q A 35 LIM W
PICKETT JAMES A 35 CYP B
PICKETT JERRY A 19 HAD B
PICKETT JOHN S JR A 35 CYP W
PICKETT JOHN S SR A 35 CYP W
PICKETT JOS A 46 GRE B
PICKETT OLIVER A 35 CYP B
PICKETT PETER A 35 CYP B
PICKETT PHILLIP A 29 FA1 B
PICKETT PHILLIP A 29 FA1 B
PICKETT RALPH A 32 SHE W
PICKETT STEPHEN A 35 CYP B
PICKETT THEO A 32 SHE W
PICKETT THOMAS A 32 SHE W
PICKETT W D A 35 CYP W
PICKETT WILLIAM R A 35 MAG W
PICKETT WILLIS A 35 LIM W
PIELER ANDREW A 26 BOR W
PIERCE A J A 25 HAY W
PIERCE AKREL A 39 GRI W
PIERCE ALLEN A 28 04A B
PIERCE B F A 29 FA1 W
MILLITIA OFFICER AFTER-
WARDS ENG IN REBELLION
PIERCE BENJ A 39 GRI W
PIERCE BERRY A 38 FRE B
PIERCE BERRY A 39 HAR W
PIERCE
CHRISTOPHER C A 19 BE1 W
PIERCE ENSEL A 39 FRA W
PIERCE FURNIE A 39 GRI W
PIERCE GEORGE A 35 WAR B
PIERCE J C A 24 EDE W
PIERCE J C A 39 GRI W
PIERCE J D A 39 GRI W
PIERCE JAMES A 39 GRI W
PIERCE JAS F A 46 GRE W
PIERCE JOS A 39 FRA W
PIERCE JOSEPH A A 19 BE1 B
PIERCE NICKSON A 35 CYP W
PIERCE O P A 29 FA1 W
PIERCE PETER A 39 GRI B
PIERCE RICHD A 39 GRI B
PIERCE ROBT A 38 FRE B
PIERCE SIMON A 39 GRI W
PIERCE SOLOMON A 28 11T B
PIERCE THOS R A 19 BE1 W
PIERCE WM A 39 FRA W
PIERSON ALEX A 35 CYP B
PIFER GEORGE A 24 EDE W
PIGATT GEORGE A 19 STR B
PIGATT SANDY A 19 STR B
PIGETT DAVID P A 19 SMY W
PIGFORD EDWARD T A 35 ISL W
PIGFORD JAMES L A 35 ISL W
PIGGOETT W D A 32 THO W
CERTIF
PIGGOTT W J A 46 HIG W
PIGOTT BATEMON A 19 BE1 B
PIGOTT BAZEL A 19 SMY B
PIGOTT BENJAMIN A 19 BE2 B
PIGOTT CUFF A 19 BE1 B
PIGOTT CULL A 53 KEN W
PIGOTT DAVID A 19 STR W
PIGOTT DEMSEY A 19 MOR B
PIGOTT E S A 30 IND W
PIGOTT FRANCIS A 19 BE1 B
PIGOTT FRANKLIN A 19 BE1 B
PIGOTT ISIAH A 19 BE1 B
PIGOTT JAMES A 19 BE1 B
PIGOTT JAMES A 19 STR W
PIGOTT JAMES P A 19 STR W
PIGOTT JENNINGS W A 19 STR W
PIGOTT JERRY A 19 BE2 B
PIGOTT JERRY A 19 STR B
NAME LINED THROUGH
TO BEAUFORT APR 18 1868
PIGOTT JOCHONIAH A 19 BE1 W
PIGOTT JOSEPH SR A 19 STR W
PIGOTT MICAJA A 19 BE2 W
PIGOTT RALPH A 19 STR W
PIGOTT RICHARD A 19 STR B
PIGOTT SILAS A 19 BE1 B
PIGOTT TIMOTHY A 19 BE2 B
PIKE DAVID A 46 COB B
PIKE JEFFRE A 19 BE1 B
PIKE JOEL A 46 COB W
PIKE JOHN H A 46 GRE W
PIKE SAML R A 46 GRE W
PILE JOHN A 46 KIN W
PILES SHEDRICK A 46 GRE B
PILKINTON ANDREW A 46 MON W
PILLARD T J A 44 SAS W
PINCKSTON AUGUSTUS A 37 TA1 B
PINER A W A 19 MOR W
PINER BANISTER M A 19 SMY W
PINER CALEB W A 19 SMY W
PINER DANIAL W A 19 SMY W
PINER EDWARD A 19 MOR W
PINER GEORGE W A 19 SMY W
PINER JAMES M A 19 SMY W
PINER JAS A 29 FA1 W
PINER JOHN W A 19 NEW W
PINER JOHN W A 28 10T W
PINER JOS A 29 CAR W
PINER JOSEPHUS A 19 SMY W
PINER WALLACE W A 19 SMY W
PINER WILLIAM A 19 SMY W
PINER WILLIAM H A 19 SMY W
PINER WM R A 19 HAD W
PINES L J A 19 NEW W
PINKLETON LINDSAY A 46 MON W
PINKNEY SOLOMON A 29 FA1 B
PINKSTON ADISON A 32 DAV B
PINKSTON JACKSON A 32 TYR B
PINKSTON NELSON A 32 TYR B
PINKSTON ROBERT A 32 TYR B
PINKSTON SIMON A 32 DAV B
PINNELL A W A 39 SPE W
PINNELL G R A 39 SPE W
PINNER WILSON N A 53 GER W
PINNIX EDMOND A 32 POS B
PINNIX HENRY A 32 POS B
PINNIX WESLEY A 32 BRO B
PINSON GILBERT A 26 MOO W
PINSON J M A 26 MOO W
PIPER GEORGE A 28 9TH W
PIPKIN ISAAC H A 28 14T W
PIPKIN JOHN W A 28 14T W
PIPKIN LEVI A 28 01B W
PIPKIN SAML A 28 04A B
PIPPEN WESLEY A 39 GRI W
PIPPIN CALVIN A 39 GRI W
PIPPIN FRANK A 37 PIN B
PIPPIN HENRY A 37 PIN B
PIPPIN ISAAC A 37 PIN B
PIPPIN JAMES S A 37 TA1 W
PIPPIN JEFFRY A 37 PIN B
PIPPIN JOHN W A 37 HIC A
PIPPIN JOSEPH H A 37 ROB W
PIPPIN JOSEPH J A 37 EDW W
PIPPIN LUKE A 37 TA1 B
PIPPIN NATHAN K A 37 PIN W
PIPPIN OTTER A 37 HIC B
PIPPIN REDMAND A 37 PIN B
PIPPIN WASHINGTON A 37 PIN B
PIPPING EXAM A 37 PIN B
PIPPING JACOB A 37 PIN B
PIPPING SAMUEL A 37 PIN B
PITCHARD HUBBERD A 46 GRE W
PITCHFORD ANTHONEY A 44 OXF B
PITCHFORD BRANCH C A 46 MON W
PITCHFORD J O A 44 OXF W
PITCHFORD JAMES L A 46 GRE W
PITCHFORD SHEPHERD A 46 SUM W
PITCHFORD W J A 44 YXS W
PITKIN CHARLES S A 28 13T W
PITMAN A H A 39 LOU W
TRANS TO DAVIS X ROADS
PITMAN ALLEN A 37 ROB B
PITMAN BENJ A 37 ROB B
PITMAN CICERO F A 37 ROB W
PITMAN DAVID J A 35 MAG W
PITMAN GUILBERT R 37 MAN B
SWORN TO BE 21 BUT WAS
PROVED TO BE FALSE
PITMAN HENRY A 37 ROB B
PITMAN HERMAN A 37 ROB B
PITMAN J A A 39 FRA W
PITMAN JAMES A 37 ROB B
PITMAN JOHN D A 28 9TH W
PITMAN JOHN H A 35 MAG W
PITMAN JOSEPH H A 35 MAG W
PITMAN LEMUEL A 37 ROB B
PITMAN MERRITT A 39 JOR W
PITMAN RANDOLPH A 37 ROB W
PITMAN SAMUEL A 37 ROB B
PITMAN SHAD A 37 ROB B
PITMAN SPEER A 37 MAN B
PITMAN WESLEY A 37 ROB W
PITMAN WM A 37 ROB B
PITT ABRAM A 37 HIG B
PITT BENJAMIN 37 PEN B
PITT BRYAN A 37 PEN W
PITT FRANKLIN A 37 SPA W
PITT GARRY A 37 HIG B
PITT GRAY A 37 PIN B
PITT HARDY A 37 EDW B
PITT HARRY A 37 HIG B
PITT HENDERSON A 37 SPA B
PITT HENRY A 37 PEN B
PITT HUGHES A 37 PIN B
PITT ISAAC A 37 PIN B
PITT JAMES A A 37 PIN W
SPARTA
PITT JAMES W A 37 SHA W
PITT JESSE A 37 WHI W
PITT JOHN A 37 WHI B
PITT JOHN A 37 WHI B
PITT LEWIS A 37 HIG B
PITT LEWIS A 37 SPA B
PITT MARK B SPARTA A 37 TA1 W
PITT NATHAN A 37 WHI B
PITT RICHARD A 37 EDW B
PITT THEOPHILUS A 37 PIN W
SPARTA
PITTARD GEO W A 44 YXR W
PITTARD J W A 44 OXF W
PITTARD JACOB A 44 OXF B
PITTARD JAMES A 44 YXS B
PITTMAN A J A 28 01B W
PITTMAN ABRAM A 37 PIN B
PITTMAN ABRAM A 37 ROB B
PITTMAN BEVERLY T A 37 TA2 W

PITTMAN DEMSEY A 37 ROB B
PITTMAN DREAD A 37 PEN B
PITTMAN EDWIN A 37 ROB B
PITTMAN GEO E A 28 01B W
PITTMAN GEO W A 28 01A W
PITTMAN HANSOM A 37 ROB B
PITTMAN HARRY A 37 ROB B
PITTMAN J W A 37 MAN W
PITTMAN JACOB A 37 TA1 B
PITTMAN JAMES A A 72 SWA W
PITTMAN MEREDITH A 28 10T W
DID NOT VOTE
PITTMAN NATHANIEL A 37 ROB B
PITTMAN NEWSOM J A 37 TA1 W
PITTMAN OFFIE A 37 ROB B
PITTMAN OSCAR A 37 EDW B
PITTMAN PETER A 37 MAN B
PITTMAN RALPH A 37 EDW B
PITTMAN RANDOLPH A 37 ROB B
PITTMAN RICHARD A 37 ROB B
PITTMAN ROBERT A 37 ROB B
PITTMAN ROBERT E A 37 ROB W
PITTMAN ROBIN A 37 PEN B
PITTMAN SAMUEL A 37 ROB B
PITTMAN SPEAR A 37 EDW B
PITTMAN SPIER A 37 ROB B
PITTMAN WEST A 37 ROB B
PITTMAN WILEY A 37 ROB B
PITTMAN WILLIAM A 37 ROB B
PITTMAN WILLIAM A 37 ROB W
PITTS ADAM A 37 MAN B
PITTS AUGUSTUS R A 30 CUR W
PITTS E S (?) A 32 BRO W
PITTS GEO W A 30 CUR W
PITTS HANDY A 37 MAN B
PITTS J Q A 46 HIG W
PITTS JAMES A 28 04A B
PITTS JOHN W A 46 HIG W
PITTS JOSEPH A 32 BRO W
PITTS LEVI A 46 HIG W
PITTS MAJOR A 46 HIG B
PITTS SAMUEL R 46 FRI W
PITTS SAMUEL R 46 FRI W
CAUSE-MILITIA
OFFICER-BEFORE-THE
REBELLION-REJECTED
PIVER ALLEN A 19 STR W
PIVER ASA A 19 MOR W
PIVER DAVID A 19 BE1 W
PIVER EDWARD M A 28 9TH W
PIVER ELIAS A 19 BE1 W
PIVER ELIJAH W A 19 SMY W
PIVER FRANCIS J A 28 03A W
PIVER HENRY A 19 BE1 W
PIVER ISAAC L A 19 BE1 W
PIVER JAMES A 19 MOR B
PIVER JAMES A 28 03A W
PIVER JESSE C A 19 BE2 W
PIVER WILSON F A 19 POR W
PIVER WM F A 19 BE1 W
PIVER WM H JR A 19 BE1 W
PIVER WM J A 19 BE1 W
PLACE RUFUS A 39 FRE W
PLANK DAVID A 40 BLA W
PLANK JACOB R 40 DA1 W
NAME LINED OUT
CHAL
CAUSE: JUSTICE OF THE
PEACE BEFORE THE
REBELLION AND GAVE AID
OR COMFORT TO THE ENEMY
REJECTED
PLAUG ANDREW A 26 PEE W

PLEASANT J L A 46 HIG W
PLEASANT SCIDMORE A 39 SPE W
PLEASANTS H M A 39 LOU W
PLEASANTS HARDY A 46 GRE B
PLEASANTS J W A 39 HAY W
PLEASANTS J W A 39 JOR W
PLEASANTS J W JR A 39 HAY W
2ND BRD REG TO COOK'S
PRECINCT, FRANKLIN CO
PLEASANTS JAMES A 44 FIS W
TABBS CREEK DIST
PLEASANTS MATHIAS A 46 GRE B
PLEASANTS RICHARD A 39 HAY W
PLEASANTS T T A 44 FIS W
PLEASANTS WM A 44 FIS W
PLEDGER JAMES P A 53 FAI W
PLEDGER SAMUEL A 53 FAI W
PLEGER JOSEPH A 53 FAI W
LAKE LANDING
PLONK FREDERIC A 40 DA1 B
PLONK JACOB F A 40 DA1 W
PLOTT W F A 25 HAY W
PLUMBER JAS A 29 GRA W
PLUMER PHILEMON A 32 LEE W
PLUMMER BERNARD A 29 FA1 W
PLUMMER FRANK A 44 TOW B
PLUMMER LEWIS A 39 SPE B
PLUMMER Z A 29 LOC W
PLUNK J J A 26 BOR W
PLUNKETT GEORGE W A 46 GRE W
PLUNKETT JOHN A 46 GRE W
POASMORE MARION A 25 TUS W
POE ABRAHAM A 29 FA1 B
POE ABRM A 29 FA1 B
POE HARPER A 46 FRI W
POE JAMES S A 46 FRI W
POE JOHN T A 46 FRI W
POE MARCUS A 32 DAV B
POE REV E A A 40 DA1 W
POINER THOMAS A 30 CUR W
POINTER AARON A 28 05A B
POINTER SHADRICK A 44 TAR B
POLLARD ----- A 28 11T B
BADLY STAINED
POLLARD CHARLES A 28 01A B
POLLARD ELIJAH E A 37 TA1 W
POLLARD FURNEY A 28 11T B
POLLARD JOHN A 26 BOR B
POLLARD JOSHUA A 44 HEN W
POLLARD PETER A 28 01A B
POLLARD TURNER A 28 11T W
POLLOCK ALFRED C A 35 WAR W
POLLOCK ALFRED W A 35 MAG W
POLLOCK GIBBLE A 19 HAD B
POLLOCK JOHN C A 35 WAR W
POLLOCK WARRICK A 35 WAR B
POLLOCK WRIGHT A 35 WAR W
POLLOK SAML A 28 04A B
POLLOK SCIPIO A 28 03A B
POLLS JAMES E A 37 WEB W
PONDER W D A 28 03A W
PONDS ROBERT A 37 PEN W
POOL A W A 44 FIS W
POOL ABE A 26 SHE B
POOL ALBERT J A 99 BUS W
POOL ALFRED A 99 BUS W
POOL ALFRED A A 28 02N B
POOL ALLEN A 99 BUS B
POOL BENJ A 28 05A B
POOL CAESAR A 99 BUS B
POOL CALVIN A 99 BUS W
POOL ETHEL A 99 BUS W
POOL G T A 44 FIS W

POOL GEORGE JR A 99 BUS W
POOL GEORGE SR A 99 BUS W
POOL HANSEL A 99 BUS W
POOL HARDY A 99 BUS W
POOL HARDY SR A 99 BUS W
POOL HENRY A 99 BUS W
POOL HENRY C A 28 01A W
POOL HOWARD A 99 BUS W
POOL J D C A 44 FIS W
POOL J H A 44 FIS W
POOL J T A 26 GRI W
POOL JACOB A 28 03A B
POOL JACOB A 44 YXR B
POOL JAMES A 99 BUS W
POOL JAMES A A 99 BUS W
POOL JAMES K A 99 BUS W
POOL JAS H A 28 01A W
POOL JEFFERSON A 99 BUS B
POOL JOHN A 99 BUS W
POOL JOHN L A 99 BUS W
POOL JOHN M A 99 BUS W
POOL JOHN R A 99 BUS W
POOL JONATHAN A 99 BUS W
POOL LAWRENCE E A 99 BUS W
POOL LEVI A 44 OXF B
POOL LEWIS A 99 BUS W
POOL LOOK A 30 CUR W
POOL M A A 26 SHE W
POOL MADISON A 99 BUS W
POOL MILES A 26 GRI W
POOL NATHAN A A 44 YXS W
POOL P P A 99 BUS W
POOL PETER A 99 BUS W
POOL RALPH A 44 YXS B
POOL RANSOM (B) A 99 BUS W
POOL RANSOM JR A 99 BUS W
POOL RANSON R A 99 BUS W
POOL RUFUS A 99 BUS W
POOL S C A 99 BUS W
POOL S D A 37 MAN W
POOL SAMUEL A 28 7TH B
POOL SETH P A 44 YXS W
POOL SIDNEY A 99 BUS W
POOL T W A 44 OXF W
POOL THOMAS R A 99 BUS W
POOL WESLEY A 99 BUS W
POOL WILLIAM J A 99 BUS W
POOL WM A 39 FRA W
POPE ABRAHAM A 26 GOF B
POPE ALFRED R 37 EDW B
CONVICTED OF LARCENY
POPE ASHBURN A 35 MAG W
POPE CARTER A 37 MAN W
POPE F S A 32 POS W
POPE HARRIS A 37 TA2 W
POPE HENRY A 29 CED W
POPE HENRY A 37 PIN B
POPE ISAAC A 37 MAN B
CERT RES NASH CO
POPE ISAAC A 37 MAN W
POPE ISON A 37 MAN B
POPE J D A 29 LOC W
POPE JESSE A 46 KIN W
POPE JOHN A 40 DEC B
POPE JOHN T A 35 MAG W
POPE KENIEL C A 37 ROC W
POPE KNRED C A 37 MAN W
POPE LEWIS A 28 03A B
POPE MARTEN T A 37 MAN W
POPE NATHAN A 37 MAN B
POPE NED A 37 MAN B
CERT RES NASH CO
POPE PETER A 37 MAN B

POPE REDDICK A 28 05A B
POPE SPENCER A 32 THO W
POPE THOMAS A 32 THO W
POPE W H A 29 BLA W
POPE W J A 29 BLA W
POPE W P A 29 FLE W
POPE WESTLY A 29 LOC W
POPE WILLIAM A 46 HIG W
POPE WILLIAM B A 32 LEE W
POPHELSTON JOHN A 24 EDE B
POPPERWELL ISAAC A 28 01B W
PORE JEREMIAH A 46 JAM W
PORTELL CHAS T A 37 ROB B
PORTER A A 29 CAR W
ERROR REGISTEED
IN HARNETT CO
PORTER A S A 46 GRE W
PORTER CHARLES A 32 DAV B
PORTER COOPER A 28 05A B
PORTER D W A 19 MOR W
PORTER GEORGE A 37 EDW B
PORTER ISAAC A 37 ROC W
PORTER ISRAEL B A 53 SWA W
PORTER JAS H A 28 02N W
PORTER JNO A 29 LOC W
PORTER JOHN A 19 MOR W
PORTER JOHN A 37 PIN B
PORTER JOHN A 37 TA1 B
PORTER JOHN H A 37 SHA W
PORTER JOHN S A 32 DAV B
PORTER JOSHUA A 37 PIN B
PORTER LAWRENCE A 37 PIN B
PORTER READING A 37 PEN B
PORTER THOS P A 28 04A B
PORTER W B A 29 CAR W
PORTER W C A 46 GRE W
PORTER WHIT A 37 ROC B
PORTER WILEY A 29 BLA W
PORTER WILLIAM A 53 SWA W
PORTER WM A 19 MOR W
PORTER WM H A 29 FA1 W
PORTER YANCEY A 28 11T B
PORTIS HEYWOOD A 37 PEN B
PORTIS LEWIS A 37 PEN B
PORTIS RALPH A 37 PEN B
PORTIS STARLING A 39 DAV B
PORTIS WILLIE A 39 LOU B
POSTON ABLE A 26 SHE W
POSTON DANIEL A 26 SHE W
POSTON GEORGE A 26 SHE B
POSTON JAMES A 26 SHE W
POSTON ROBERT A 26 HOL B
POSTON SAMUEL R 26 SHE W
WAS CONS PRIOR TO REB &
VOTED FOR CONVENTION
IN 1861
POSTON SILVESTER A 26 SHE B
POTSLE THOMAS A 25 HAY W
POTTER ALLEN A 35 ALB W
POTTER BURNEY A 19 BE1 B
POTTER CHARLES A 46 HIG W
POTTER DANIEL A 35 ALB W
POTTER FREDRICK A 35 LIM B
POTTER GEORGE H A 28 9TH W
POTTER HIRAM JR A 28 03B W
POTTER J W A 28 9TH W
POTTER JACKSON A 35 ALB W
POTTER JAMES A 35 WOL W
POTTER JESSE A 35 ALB W
POTTER JORDAN A 44 OXF B
POTTER JORDEN A 35 ALB W
POTTER L A A 19 BE1 W
POTTER LEDAM A 28 03A B

POTTS GEO A 29 FA1 B
POTTS JOHN A 46 GRE B
POTTS ROBT E A 46 GRE W
POTTS S T A 28 01A W
POTTS WILLIAM A 32 TYR B
POULAND H H A 37 ROC W
POWEL ENOCH A 39 HAY W
POWEL EPHESUS A 37 MAN B
POWEL JAMES A 28 16T B
POWEL JOHN A 26 HOL B
POWEL WILLIAM A 39 HAY W
POWELL A B A 28 01A W
POWELL A J A 44 FOR W
POWELL ALAN A 37 MAN B
POWELL ARTHUR A 35 ROC B
POWELL B S A 29 GRA W
POWELL BENJAMIN A 37 MAN B
POWELL CABOT A 99 BUS W
POWELL CASWELL A 99 BUS W
POWELL CHARLES A 37 PEN B
POWELL CHARLES D A 30 MOY W
POWELL D J S A 26 PEE W
POWELL DAVID A 29 FA1 W
POWELL DAVID R A 35 CYP W
POWELL DAVID S A 35 KEN W
POWELL E L A 39 HAR W
POWELL EDMUND A 37 PIN B
POWELL EDWARD A 37 MAN B
POWELL EDWD A 29 FA1 B
POWELL ERASTUS A 44 KIT W
POWELL EVERETT A 35 KEN W
POWELL FURNIFOLD A 28 11T W
POWELL GEO W A 39 HAR W
POWELL GEORGE A 28 11T W
POWELL GEORGE W A 26 PEE W
POWELL GILFORD A 37 MAN B
POWELL GRANT A 37 MAN B
POWELL GUILFORD W A 35 MAG W
POWELL H H A 26 BLA W
POWELL HENRY A 28 11T W
POWELL HENRY A 37 MAN B
POWELL HENRY A 44 KIT W
POWELL HILLIARD A 37 ROB B
POWELL ISAAC A 26 BLA W
POWELL ISAAC A 29 FA1 B
POWELL J W A 26 BLA W
POWELL J W A 37 MAN W
POWELL JAMES A 26 BLA W
POWELL JAMES A 35 ROC B
POWELL JAMES A 37 ROC B
POWELL JAMES SR A 26 PEE W
POWELL JESSE H A 37 MAN W
POWELL JOHN A 35 KEN W
POWELL JOHN A 37 PEN B
POWELL JOHN A 39 JOR B
POWELL JOHN A 44 FIS W
POWELL K S A 39 LOU W
TRNS FROM FREEMANS X
ROADS TO LOUISBURG
POWELL KADER J A 99 BUS W
POWELL LAWRENCE A 99 BUS W
POWELL LEE A 99 BUS W
POWELL LEWIS A 35 WAR W
POWELL LEWIS A 37 PIN B
POWELL LOUIS A 35 LIM W
POWELL LUTHER A 37 MAN B
POWELL MIKE A 37 PEN B
POWELL MORRIS A 29 SEV W
POWELL NATHAN A 37 MAN B
POWELL NOAH A 28 03A B
POWELL OLIVER A 37 ROB B
POWELL PETER A 37 EDW B
POWELL RANDALL A 35 ROC W

POWELL REUBEN A 37 PEN B
POWELL RICHARD A 37 EDW B
POWELL RICHARD A 99 BUS B
POWELL RICHMOND A 37 EDW B
POWELL ROBERT A 37 PEN B
POWELL SAMUEL A 37 PEN B
POWELL SAMUEL A 37 TA1 B
POWELL SILAS A 39 PUG W
POWELL SIMON A 37 MAN B
POWELL SPEAR A 37 HIG B
POWELL STEPN A 28 04A B
POWELL THOMAS C A 37 HIC A
POWELL THOMAS C A 37 ROC W
POWELL TONEY A 37 PIN B
POWELL W H A 44 KIT W
POWELL WILEY A 35 MAG W
POWELL WILLIAM A 37 MAN B
POWELL WILLIAM A 37 PEN B
POWELL WILLIAM A 37 ROC W
POWELL WILLIAM H A 37 ROB W
POWELL WILLIAM J A 26 GRI W
POWELL WILLIAM S A 99 BUS W
POWELL WM A 29 FA1 W
POWELS JOHN A 28 04A B
POWER EDWARD A 39 PUG W
POWER JOHN A 28 11T W
POWERES JOHN A 39 SPE W
POWERS A P A 28 05A B
POWERS BENJAMIN A 28 14T W
POWERS CORNELIUS A 30 MOY W
POWERS E P A 29 FA1 W
POWERS EDWD A 29 FA1 B
POWERS GEO W A 30 MOY W
POWERS HARDY C A 28 15T W
POWERS ISIAH A 53 FAI W
POWERS J E A 29 FA2 W
POWERS J W R 29 FA1 W
CONSTABLE BEFORE WAR
AFTER AIDED REBELLION
POWERS JOHN A 30 MOY W
POWERS LEVIN A 28 04A B
POWERS M A 29 FA1 W
POWERS MATTHEW A A 28 15T W
POWERS MECHRISTA A 30 MOY W
POWERS MILES A 28 14T W
POWERS R J A 30 MOY W
POWERS S A A 30 MOY W
POWERS SAMUEL A 19 HAR B
POWERS THOMAS A 35 ROC B
POWERS THOS #1 A 28 01A W
POWERS VALENTINE A 35 ISL B
POWERS W B A 29 FLE W
POWERS W W A 30 MOY W
POWERS W W A 30 MOY W
POWERS WILLIAM A A 30 MOY W
POWERS WILLIAM M A 30 MOY W
POWERS WILLIS A 30 MOY W
POWERS WM H A 30 MOY W
POWERS WM J A 30 MOY W
POYNE JACOB A 30 CUR B
POYNER AANIAS A 30 MOY B
POYNER CHARLES A 30 COI B
POYNER DANL A 30 CUR B
POYNER EDMUND D A 30 NAR W
POYNER JACOB JR A 30 MOY B
POYNER JACOB SR A 30 MOY B
POYNER JOHN A 30 IND B
POYNER JOHN S A 30 COI W
POYNER JORDAN A 30 POP W
POYNER NATHAN JR A 30 POP W
POYNER NATHAN S SR A 30 POP W
POYNER NELSON A 30 CUR W
POYNER PETER A 30 NAR W

POYNER R W A 30 MOY W
POYNER THOMAS A 30 POP B
POYNER THOS J A 30 POP W
POYNER WILLIAM A 30 POP B
POYTHRESS J S A 39 LOU W
PRAG MOSES A 28 01A W
PRATCHER AARON A 44 HEN B
PRATER ISAAC A 25 HAY W
PRATER JULIUS A 25 HAY B
PRATER JULIUS A 25 HAY B
PRESENT RESIDENCE MACON
CO N C, FRANKLIN
11 APR 1868
PRATHER J J A 40 CAN W
PRATHER JOHN N A 46 GRE W
PRATHER ROBT P A 46 GRE W
PRATT ALEXANDRA A 37 MAN B
PRATT EDMOND A 37 MAN B
PRATT JOHN A 44 FOR B
PRATT JOSEPH Z A 24 EDE W
PREDDY ALEX A 44 FOR W
PREDDY HAYWOOD A 46 SUM W
PREDDY HENRY A 44 FOR B
PREDDY ISAAC A 44 FOR B
PREDDY JOSEPH A 44 BRA W
PREDDY ROBT A 44 FOR B
PREDDY WM A 38 FRE W
PREDDY WM A 44 FOR B
PRESCOTT CHARLES R A 28 16T W
PRESCOTT JAS R A 28 6TH W
PRESCOTT JOHN A A 28 6TH W
PRESCOTT RICHD A 28 6TH W
PRESCOTT WILEBY A 19 HAD W
PREVITT RICHD A 44 TOW W
DEEF & DUM
CAN READ & RITE
PREW GEO A 44 HEN B
PRICE ABNER A 28 14T W
PRICE ALEXANDER A 28 13T W
PRICE AMOUS A 37 MAN W
PRICE ANDREW A 40 STO B
PRICE BATMAN Z A 53 KEN W
PRICE BENJAMIN A 99 BUS W
PRICE CHARLES A 37 ROC B
PRICE CHARLES A 37 ROC B
PRICE D G A 26 BUR W
PRICE E A A 26 GOF W
PRICE F M A 29 FA1 W
PRICE FRENCHMAN A 37 PEN B
PRICE GASTON A 19 BE1 W
PRICE GEORGE W A 28 16T W
PRICE GREGORY A 35 ALB W
PRICE ISAAC N A 40 DEC W
PRICE J T A 26 PEE W
PRICE JACKSON A 37 PEN B
PRICE JAMES A 24 EDE B
PRICE JAMES A 28 13T W
PRICE JAMES A 37 ROB B
PRICE JAMES A 37 ROB W
PRICE JAMES D A 37 ROC B
PRICE JERRY A 19 BE1 B
PRICE JNO C A 29 LOC W
MILITIA OFFICER BEFORE
THE WAR CONSCRIPTED 6
MONTHS BEFORE THE SUR-
RENDER
PRICE JOEL A 37 MAN W
PRICE JOHN A 28 8TH B
PRICE JOHN A 35 WOL W
PRICE JOHN H A 37 MAN W
PRICE JOHN J A 40 DEC W
PRICE JOSEPH A 24 EDE B
PRICE JOSEPH A 37 TA1 B
PRICE JOSEPH H A 37 ROC W
PRICE MAJOR A 32 DAV B
PRICE PETER A 37 ROC B
PRICE R A 29 FLE W
PRICE R B A 26 SWA W
PRICE SYLVESTER A 28 05A B
PRICE THOMAS A 37 HIG B
PRICE THOMAS H A 28 12T W
PRICE WILLIAM A 37 ROC W
PRICE WM H A 28 14T W
PRICHARD ALFRED A 26 MOU W
PRICHARD JOSHUA A 26 SHE W
PRICHARD WILLIAM A 32 DAV W
PRICHETT WM A 46 MON W
PRIDE J C A 26 MOO W
PRIDE WILY A 26 MOO W
PRIDGEN DAVID A 37 ROB W
PRIDGEN GASTON A 35 WAR B
PRIDGEN GEORGE W A 35 WAR W
PRIDGEN ROBERT G A 35 KEN W
PRIEST CORNELIUS A 29 QUW W
PRIEST GILBERT A 29 MON W
COPIED FROM DUPLICATE
PRIEST JOHN A 29 MON W
PRIEST NEILL A 29 QUW W
PRIESTLEY STEPHEN A 28 10T B
PRIGDEN L A 29 FLE W
PRIGGIN WILLIAM A 37 TA1 B
PRIM JOHN JR A 46 JAM W
PRIME GEORGE A 28 02N W
PRIME JOHN A 28 02N W
PRINCE ABE A 28 01A W
PRINCE MILLS A 24 EDE B
PRINCE MINGO A 24 EDE B
PRINCE PHILIP A 37 MAN B
PRINCE ROBERT A 40 DA1 B
PRINCE TURNER A 37 TA1 B
PRINGLE ELIJAH S A 19 HAD W
PRINGLE HENRY A 19 HAD W
PRINGLE K F A 19 HAD W
PRINGLE STEPHEN A 19 HAD W
PRIOR R P A 26 BLA W
PRIOR W A A 26 BLA W
PRIOR WILLIAM A 40 DEC W
PRITCHARD JAMES R A 28 10T B
PRITCHARD MOSES A 28 10T B
PRITCHET CHARLES A 19 HAD B
PRITCHET NATHAN A 28 04A B
PRITCHETT AARON A 46 MON B
PRITCHETT ALLEN A 46 MON B
PRITCHETT BENJAMIN A 28 10T B
PRITCHETT DAVID A 46 MON B
PRITCHETT ELIAS A 46 RAG W
PRITCHETT FRANKLIN A 46 MON B
PRITCHETT JACOB A 28 10T B
PRITCHETT JAMES A 46 MON B
PRITCHETT JAMES C A 28 10T B
PRITCHETT JOHN A 28 05A B
PRITCHETT JOHN A 46 FRI B
PRITCHETT JOHN A A 46 GRE W
PRITCHETT JOHN A A 46 RAG W
PRITCHETT JOHN C A 46 MON W
PRITCHETT JOHN R A 46 RAG W
PRITCHETT MARTIN A 46 MON B
PRITCHETT WEBB A 46 MON W
PRIVET J R A 24 MID W
PRIVET THEOPLAS A 24 MID B
PRIVET WILLIAM A 24 MID W
PRIVET WILLIS A 24 MID B
PRIVET WM T A 24 MID W
PRIVETT JOHN C A 28 03A W
PRIVETT STEPHEN A 24 MID B
PRIVETT TERRELL A 39 GRI B
PRIVETT WILLIS R R 39 HAR W
FOR BEING CONSTABLE
BEFORE THE WAR AND
THEN IN THE WAR
PRIVETT WM JR A 39 GRI W
PRIVETT WM SR A 39 GRI W
PRIVOTT JOHN M A 24 MID W
PRIVOTT THOS H A 24 MID W
PROCTER JOSHUA A 37 PEN W
PROCTER TERRY A 37 ROC B
PROCTER WILLIAM H A 37 EDW W
PROCTOR SAMUEL D A 37 PEN W
PROCTOR A G A 26 BLA W
PROCTOR AARON A 37 SHA B
PROCTOR ABSOLAM A 37 ROC W
PROCTOR ANDREW A 32 POS W
PROCTOR BENJAMINE A 26 SHE B
PROCTOR DAVID A 28 03A B
PROCTOR EDWARD A 37 SHA B
PROCTOR FREDERICK A 37 ROC W
PROCTOR HARDY W A 37 ROC W
PROCTOR HENDERSON A 32 THO W
PROCTOR HENRY A 26 CAR B
PROCTOR HENRY A 37 HIG W
PROCTOR HENRY A 53 FAI B
PROCTOR HINES B A 37 SHA W
PROCTOR JACKSON A 44 YXR W
PROCTOR JAMES J A 37 HIG W
PROCTOR JOHN A 26 SHE B
PROCTOR JOHN A 37 ROC W
PROCTOR JOHN A A 32 POS W
PROCTOR JOSEPH A 37 ROC W
APRIL 10, 1868
PROCTOR NATHANIEL A 37 HIG W
PROCTOR S A A 26 PEE W
PROCTOR S M A 26 WAR W
PROCTOR WILLIAM A 37 ROC W
PROCTOR WILLIAM G A 37 ROC W
PROCTOR YOUNG A 37 SHA W
PROSCHE EDWARD A 28 01B W
PROVOW BENJAMIN D A 72 SWA W
PROVOW GEORGE D A 72 SWA W
PROVOW JOHN L R 72 SWA W
REJECTED WAS ROAD MASTER
BEFORE THE WAR AND AFTER
WARDS, PARTICIPATED IN
THE REBELLION.
PRUDEN RANSOM A 24 EDE B
PRUDENT DORSEY A 28 04B B
PRUET THOMAS A 26 MOU W
PRUETT CHARLES A 44 TOW W
DEEF & DUM
CANNOT R & RITE
PRUETT ROBERT A 44 YXS W
PRUETT W H A 44 HEN W
PRUIT ELISHA A 44 FOR W
PRUIT NEWBERRY A 26 PEE W
PRUIT W C A 26 SHE W
PRUITT JAMES A 44 TOW W
DEEF & DUM
CANNOT R & RITE
PRYON WILEY A 40 CAN W
PRYOR ALSON A 46 MCL W
PRYOR WARREN A 29 FA1 W
PUCKETT JESSE A 44 YXS W
PUCKETT S A A 44 YXS W
PUCKETT STEPHEN R A 44 YXS W
PUCKETT THOS C A 44 YXS W
PUCKETT WILLIAM A 44 YXS W
PUGH ABEL F A 28 04A B
PUGH ABRAM A 28 03B B
PUGH ARMISTEAD A 28 05A B
PUGH CROATAN A 53 LA1 B

PUGH DANIEL S A 53 LA1 W
PUGH HOSEA A 30 COI B
PUGH ISAAC A 28 01B B
PUGH JAMES A 30 NOR W
PUGH JAMES E A 32 DAV W
PUGH JAS A A 32 DAV W
PUGH JOHN A 28 04A B
PUGH JOHN A 53 LA1 W
PUGH JOHN J A 53 LA2 W
PUGH JOHN P A 53 CHI W
PUGH JOHN W A 46 GIB W
PUGH LITTLEJOHN A 30 ROA W
PUGH MERIDA S A 53 HAT B
PUGH OSCAR A 44 HEN B
PUGH SPARROW M A 53 CHI W
PUGH TILLMAN F A 53 CHI W
PUGH TONY A 44 FOR B
PUGH W P A 46 HIG W
PUGH WILLIAM H A 53 LA1 W
PUGH WM M A 30 IND W
PUGHE ALEXD A 44 KIT B
PULLIUM ANDERSON A 44 YXR B
PULLY DAN'L A 44 FIS W
PULLY DEMPSY A 39 FRA B
PULLY FREDERIC A 39 GRI B
PULLY J P A 44 FIS W
PULLY JOHN A 39 GRI B
PULLY MADISON A 39 FRA B
PULLY THOS M A 44 FIS W
PULLY WM G A 39 HAR B
PURCELL CHAS A 29 QUW B
PURCELL JAS J A 26 BLA W
PURCIN REUBEN A 19 STR B
PURDY EDWARD A 28 05A B
PUREFOY JNO K A 39 FRE W
PURGERSON J R A 44 FOR W
PURGERSON W J A 44 FOR W
PURIFY ARRINGTON A 28 13T W
PURIFY DAVID A 28 13T W
PURIFY THOMAS A 28 13T W
PURSER DAVID A 28 11T W
PURSER JOSHUA A 28 11T W
PURSON DANIEL A 46 SUM B
PURVIS HENRY A 19 BE1 B
PURYEAR AMBROSE A 44 YXS B
PURYEAR ELLIS A 44 YXR B
PURYEAR FLEM A 44 YXR B
PURYEAR GEO W A 44 YXR W
PURYEAR GEORGE A 44 YXS B
PURYEAR GRANDESON F A 44 YXR W
PURYEAR H L A 44 YXR W
PURYEAR HENRY A 44 YXS B
PURYEAR HENRY Y A 44 YXS W
PURYEAR J A A 44 YXR W
PURYEAR J D A 44 YXS W
PURYEAR JACOB A 44 YXS B
PURYEAR JAMES A 44 YXS W
PURYEAR JEFF A 44 YXS B
PURYEAR JNO Y A 44 YXR W
PURYEAR JOSEPH R A 44 YXS W
PURYEAR MAJOR JR A 44 YXS B
PURYEAR MAJOR SR A 44 YXS B
PURYEAR PAUL A 44 OXF B
PURYEAR PAUL A 44 SAS B
PURYEAR PETER A 44 YXR B
PURYEAR PEYTON A 44 YXS W
PURYEAR STEPHEN L A 44 YXS W
PURYEAR WASHINGTON A 44 YXR B
PURYEAR WM G A 44 YXS B
PURYER HARMON R 44 YXR B
9 MOS RES REJ
PURYER MAT A 44 OXF B
PUTMAN D C A 26 SHE W
PUTMAN
CHRISTOPHER G A 46 GRE W
PUTMAN E L A 26 SHE W
PUTMAN HAMBY W A 40 BLA W
PUTMAN L D A 26 SHE W
PUTMAN M L A 26 SHE W
PUTMAN MARTIN V A 35 MAG W
PUTMAN ROBERT R 26 SHE W
WAS CONS PRIOR TO REB &
VOTED FOR CONVENTION
IN 1861
PUTMAN ROBERTS A 26 SHE W
PUTMAN RUFUS A 26 SHE W
PUTMAN S G A 26 SHE W
PUTMAN SIMMION A 26 SHE W
PUTMAN T J A 26 SHE W
PUTMAN W A A 26 SHE W
PUTMAN WILLIAM A 26 SHE W
PUTNAM B A 26 BOR W
PUTNAM D A 26 BOR W
PUTNAM D A 46 FRI W
PUTNAM D A A 26 GRI W
PUTNAM JEREMIAH A 46 GRE W
PUTNAM P G A 26 BOR W
PUTNAM SAMIL A 26 BLA W
PYNES R H A 44 ISL W
PYRUM MAC A 37 PEN B

- Q -

QUALLS ADKIN A 44 FOR B
QUALLS CHESLEY A 44 BRA W
QUALLS JAMES A 44 BRA W
QUALLS W C A 44 BRA B
QUATE ABNER M A 46 ROS W
QUATE HARMON A 46 GRE W
QUATE RICHARD A 46 GRE W
QUATE WM A 46 GRE W
QUEEN ISAAC A 26 PEE W
QUEEN JOSEPH A 26 PEE W
QUEEN L A 26 WAR W
QUIDLEY ASBRY A 53 HAT W
QUIDLEY REDDING A 28 01B W
QUIDLEY REDDING R A 53 HAT W
QUIDLEY REUBEN R A 53 HAT W
QUIDLY JAMES T A 53 KEN W
QUIN JAMES A 32 DAV W
QUIN W O A 29 CED W
REMOVED TO BLADEN
QUINCE CHARLES A 28 11T B
QUINN A W R 26 SHE W
MILITIA OFFICER &
ENGAGED IN REBELION
QUINN AMOS A 35 WAR W
QUINN BRANTLEY D A 35 SMI W
QUINN DAVID S A 19 NEW W
QUINN DAVID S JR A 19 NEW W
QUINN GEORGE A 35 ALB W
QUINN GEORGE A 40 DA1 B
QUINN J B A 35 WOL W
QUINN JAMES A 35 ALB W
QUINN JAMES A 35 MAG W
QUINN JAMES L A 40 DA1 W
QUINN JOHN R R 40 DA1 W
MILITIA OFFICER & GAVE AID
OR COMFORT REJECTED
QUINN JOHN R * A 40 DA1 W
QUINN JOHN T A 35 MAG W
QUINN JOHN W A 40 BLA W
QUINN PETER A 35 KEN B
QUINN ROBT K A 19 NEW W
QUINN W F A 35 WOL W
QUINN WARREN A 40 DA1 B
QUNETCHE JOHN A 37 TA2 B

- R -

RABBERS THOS A A 19 BE1 W
RABUN H M A 25 SHO W
RABUN JOHN M A 25 HAY W
RACHEL ALEXANDER A 32 JAC W
RACKLEY HARRY A 35 ROC B
RACKLEY HENRY A 35 ROC B
RACKLEY JAMES S A 35 ROC W
RACKLEY JOSEPH C A 35 ROC W
RACKLEY JOSEPH R A 35 ROC W
RACKLEY JOSHUA A 35 ROC W
RACKLEY WILLIAM A 35 MAG W
RADCLIFFE SAML A 28 02N W
RADFORD JOSEPH A 44 KIT B
RAE ISAAC A 29 FA1 B
RAE SANDY A 29 FA1 B
RAFORD B B A 28 02N W
RAFORD BERRY B A 53 LA1 W
RAFTER P A 40 CAN W
RAGAN DANIEL F CHAL R 40 DA2 W
NAME LINED OUT
JUSTICE OF THE PEACE
BEFORE THE WAR. MEMBER TO
LEGISLATURE GAVE AID AND
COMFORT TO THE ENEMY.
NOT QUALIFIED REJ
RAGAN G W A 40 STO W
RAGAN JACOB A 46 RAG B
RAGAN MARK A 46 KIN W
RAGAN THOMAS 46 RAG W
WAS A CIVIL OFFICER BEFORE
THE WARE AND FUNDED CONFED
MONEY DURING THE WAR WHICH
HE FEARS WAS AIDING THE
GOVERNMENT, DID NOT TAKE
THE OATH ON THAT ACCOUNT
THE MONEY FUNDED BELONGED
TO ORFENT CHILDREN AND
DONE AT THE REQUEST OF
THERE FRIENDS. REJECTED
RAGIN E A 44 TAR W
RAGIN J T A 44 TAR W
RAGIN SAML A 44 TAR W
RAGLAND ANDERSON A 44 YXS B
RAGLAND J W A 44 RAG W
RAGLAND LEWIS C A 44 TAR W
RAGLAND LITTLETON A 44 YXS W
RAGLAND ROBT A 44 OXF B
RAGLAND STEPH S A 44 OXF W
RAGLAND WILLIS A 44 RAG B
RAGNER BENJ A 28 04A B
RAGSDALE GREEN A 46 KIN B
RAGSDALE J R A 46 FRI W
RAGSDALE J S A 46 JAM W
RAGSDALE SMITH Y A 44 YXR W
RAGSDALE WIATT W R 46 KIN W
MAGISRATE & CO TRUSTEE
BEFORE & DURING THE WAR
RAIFORD JOHN Y A 37 ROC W
RAILLY WM A 29 CED W
RAIN W Z A 44 FIS W
RAINES IZAIR A 39 HAR W
RAINES J H A 39 HAR W
RAINES JNO W A 39 HAR W
RAINEY LEWIS A 44 SAS B
RAINEY ROBT A 44 TOW B
RAINOR R A 29 LOC W
RAINY PETER A 30 MOY B
7-MONTH-RESIDENCE
RAKER DANIEL A 32 SHE W
RALLEIGH HENRY A 46 FRI B
RAMSAY DAVID A 40 DA2 W
RAMSAY JACOB A 40 DEC W

RAMSAY WILLIAM H A 40 DA1 W
RAMSEUR J L A 26 GRI B
RAMSEUR P S A 26 SHE W
RAMSEY A A 26 WAR W
RAMSEY DAVID S J A 19 BE1 W
RAMSEY FLETCHER Y A 37 ROC W
RAMSEY ISAAC E A 19 BE1 W
RAMSEY J M A 44 SAS W
RAMSEY JOSEPH A 26 BOR W
RAMSEY TALCOTT W A 19 BE2 B
RAMSOUR CALEB A 40 DA1 B
RAMSOUR F S A 26 BUR W
RAMSOUR THOMAS A 40 DA1 B
RAN PETER A 44 DUT B
RANCHER WM A 29 FA1 B
RAND ALBERT A 99 BUS B
RAND BURT A 99 BUS B
RAND CALVIN A 99 BUS W
RAND CHARLES A 99 BUS B
RAND DALLAS A 99 BUS W
RAND DANIEL A 99 BUS B
RAND DAVID A 99 BUS B
RAND EDMOND A 99 BUS B
RAND JEFFERS A 99 BUS B
RAND JOHN R A 99 BUS W
RAND PARKER A 99 BUS W
RAND STEPHEN A 99 BUS B
RAND W H A 99 BUS W
RAND WILLIAM A 99 BUS B
RAND WILLIAM A 99 BUS W
RANDALL DAVID A 26 WAR W
RANDALL HENRY A 28 14T B
RANDALL J H A 26 MOO W
RANDALL JACOB A 26 BUR W
RANDALL JAMES W A 26 BUR W
RANDALL JOHN A 26 BUR W
RANDALL JOHN A 26 WAR W
RANDALL M H A 26 BUR W
RANDALL MARTIN A 26 BUR W
RANDALL R S A 26 BUR W
RANDALL S C A 26 BUR W
RANDALL S D CHAL R 26 BUR W
MILITIA OFFICER &
ENGAGED IN REBELLION
RANDALL SIMON A 37 PEN B
OF PIT CO
RANDALL WILLIAM A 26 GRI W
RANDEL AUGUSTINE A 37 SPA B
RANDEL CHARLES A 37 SPA B
RANDEL WILLIAM A 37 SPA B
RANDOLPH H T A 28 03A B
RANDOLPH JOHN JR A 28 03A B
RANDOLPH JOHN SR A 28 03A B
RANDOLPH LOUIS S A 28 03A B
RANEY AUSTIN A 39 PUG B
RANEY C W A 44 KIT W
RANKIN A M A 40 RHY W
RANKIN AARON A 46 GRE B
RANKIN ADAM R A 46 ROS B
RANKIN ALBERT A 46 GRE W
RANKIN CEBORNE A 40 DA1 B
RANKIN COLLUMBUS A 40 CAN B
RANKIN DAVID A 40 DA1 B
RANKIN DERRY A 46 GRE B
RANKIN HIRAM A 40 CAN B
RANKIN ISAAC A 40 DA1 B
RANKIN J A 40 RHY W
RANKIN J C A 40 RHY W
RANKIN J D A 40 CAN W
RANKIN JAMES A 46 GRE W
RANKIN JERRY A 46 GRE B
RANKIN JOHN A 46 GRE B
RANKIN JOHN A 46 ROS B
RANKIN JOHN C A 46 HIG W
RANKIN JOHN C A 46 MCL W
RANKIN JOHN H A 46 GRE W
RANKIN JOHN H A 46 MCL W
RANKIN JONES A 40 RHY B
RANKIN JOSEPH M A 40 RHY W
RANKIN LINDSAY A 46 MON B
RANKIN MACK A 40 RHY B
RANKIN MOSES A 40 CAN B
RANKIN MOSES A 46 GRE W
RANKIN NATHANIEL A 46 MCL W
RANKIN PERSIS A 46 MCL W
RANKIN ROBERT A 46 RAG W
RANKIN ROBERT C A 46 MCL W
RANKIN S C A 46 MON W
RANKIN SAMUEL A 46 MCL W
RANKIN SAMUEL A 46 MON B
RANKIN SIDNEY 40 DA2 W
CERT ISSUED APR 10 68
TO RHYNES BOX 1ST REG
PRE GASTON CO
RANKIN SOLOMON A 46 ROS B
RANKIN THOMAS A 40 RHY B
RANKIN THOMAS A 46 MCL W
RANKIN THOMAS R 46 MCL W
NAME LINED OUT
WAS AN OVERSEER OF HIGHWAY
BEFORE THE WARE AND DURING
THE WARE SERVED AS ONE OF
A COMMITTEE TO DECIDE WHO
MIGHT STAY AT HOME DURING
THE WAR HE SAID HE ACCEP-
TED THE OFFICE RATHER
THAN TO GO THE ARMY ONE
OF WHICH HE HAD TO DO.
HAS NOT QUALIFIED
RANKIN THOMAS A A 46 MCL W
RANKIN THOMAS A R 46 MCL W
NAME LINED OUT
WAS AN OVERSEER OF HIGHWAY
BEFORE THE WARE.
HE WAS A MILITIA OFFICER
DURING THE WARE WHICH IS
THE CAUS OF HIS NOT
TAKEING THE OATH.
HAS NOT QUALIFIED.
RANKIN THOMAS G A 46 MCL B
RANKIN W D A 40 CAN W
RANKIN W G A 40 STO W
RANKIN W R A 40 STO W
RANKIN W S A 46 GRE W
RANKIN W W A 40 RHY W
RANKIN WILL T A 46 HIG W
RANKIN WILLIAM W A 46 MON W
RANKIN WM C A 46 MCL W
RANKIN WM H A 46 MCL W
RANKIN WM N A 46 RAG W
RANSDALL SILVESTER A 39 HAR W
RANSDELL E W A 39 DAV W
RANSDELL G W A 39 PUG W
RANSOM W H A 39 FRA B
RANSON PEARCE A 28 04A B
RANSY ALFED A 40 SAN W
RANY HENRY A 44 FIS B
RANY T H A 44 FIS W
RAPER ELISHA A 32 DAV W
RAPER HIRAM A 32 BRO B
RAPER JAMES A 32 BRO B
RAPER
JESSE ANDERSON A 32 BRO B
RAPER M D A 32 SHE W
RAPER M D A 32 THO W
RAPER MANLON R A 46 HIG W
RAPER ROBERT A 46 FRI W
RAPER WASHINGTON A 32 BRO B
RAPER WILLIAM A 32 THO W
RAPHOD EDWD A 29 FA1 B
RAPHOD FREDK A 29 FA1 B
RAPHOD MOSES A 29 FA1 B
RASBERRY WHITE A 19 NEW B
RASBY CHAS A 28 05A B
RASCOE JOHN K A 53 GER W
RASER COLIN A A 37 HOL W
RASPBERRY ALFRED A 37 ROC B
RASPBERRY ALLEN A 35 ISL W
RASPBERRY ERWIN A 28 11T B
RASPBERRY HANDY A 19 HAR B
RASPBERRY WM A 29 FA1 W
RATCHFORD JAMES A 40 STO B
RATCHFORD JOHN A 40 STO W
RATCHFORD JOHN A A 40 DA1 W
RATCHFORD JOSEPH A 40 STO W
RATCHFORD R B A 40 STO W
RATCHFORD ROBERTSON A 40 DA1 B
RATCHFORD WESLEY A 40 STO B
RATCLIFF GRAHAM J A 53 BUR W
RATCLIFF WILLIAM J A 53 BUR W
RATHRUP WILLIAM A 32 POS W
RATLIFF EMSLEY A 46 ROS B
RATLIFF SAMUEL A 46 GRE B
RATLY JESSEE A 39 FRA B
RATLY JULUS A 39 FRA B
RATTS HENDERSON A 32 TYR B
RATTS OBADIAH A 32 TYR W
RATTS THOMAS A 32 TYR W
RATTS VOLANTINE A 32 TYR W
RAVANDER THOMAS A 37 PIN B
RAVIS TREDRICK A 44 HEN B
RAWLES HENRY A 39 LOU W
TRNS FROM FREEMAN'S
X ROADS TO LOUISBURG
RAWLINGS JESSE A 37 MAN W
RAWLINGS REV WILLIAMA 40 DA1 W
8 MOS RESIDENCE
1ST SEPT 1867
REJECTED SEE BELOW
RAWLS ALFRED D A 28 14T W
RAWLS ELIJAH A 37 TA2 W
RAWLS HENRY A 38 FRE W
RAWLS WM H A 28 16T W
RAWLS WM Q A 37 ROB W
RAY A G A 29 QUW W
RAY A W A 29 FA1 W
RAY ALEXANDER A 29 MON B
RAY ALFRED A 29 SEV B
RAY ALLEN A 29 SEV W
RAY AND C A 29 ROC W
RAY ANDERSON A 39 FRA B
RAY ANDERSON A 46 MCL B
RAY ANGUS A 29 QUW W
RAY ANGUS A 29 SEV W
RAY ARCHD A 29 SEV W
RAY ARCHD S A 29 QUW W
RAY AUBY A 29 CAR B
RAY CALVIN A 29 QUW B
RAY D H A 29 FA2 W
RAY D J A 29 QUW W
RAY D MCNEILL A 29 SEV W
RAY DAVID A 29 FA1 B
RAY DAVID A 29 SEV B
RAY DAVID A A 29 FA1 W
RAY DUNCAN A 29 SEV W
RAY DUNCAN K A 29 SEV W
RAY EDMOND A 28 04A B
RAY EVANDER A 29 SEV B
RAY G B A 29 SEV W

RAY GEORGE D A 29 SEV W
RAY HANDY A 29 SEV B
RAY HARSTON A 37 ROB B
RAY J S A 46 JAM W
RAY JACOB A 29 SEV B
RAY JAMES A 29 SEV B
RAY JAMES R 29 QUW W
MILITIA OFF BEFORE THE REBELLION. REFUSE TO TAKE THE OATH. TAKEN THE OATH AFTER APRIL 9-----
RAY JOHN A 29 FA1 B
RAY JOHN A 29 SEV W
OF PUPPY CREEK
RAY JOHN A 46 RAG B
RAY JOHN (TAILOR) A 29 SEV W
RAY JOHN D A 29 SEV W
RAY JOHN K A 29 SEV W
MILITIA OFF TAKEN AN OATH TO SUPPORT THE CONSTITU- TION OF THE U.S. BEFORE THE REBELLIION AFTERWARDS ENGAGED IN THE REBELLION
RAY JOHN R A 29 SEV W
RAY JOHNSON A 37 TA1 B
RAY MALCOM C A 29 SEV W
RAY NEIL L A 29 MON W
RAY NEILL A 29 SEV B
RAY NEILL (TAILOR) A 29 SEV W
RAY NEILL A A 29 SEV W
RAY NEILL JR A 29 SEV W
MILITIA OFF BEFORE THE REBELLION TAKEN AN OATH TO SUPT THE CONST. OF THE U.S. AFTERWARDS GAVE AID AND COMFORT TO THE ENEMIES
RAY NEILL SR A 29 SEV W
RAY NELSON A 29 CAR B
RAY NEPTUNE A 29 CAR B
RAY NICKLE A 29 QUW B
RAY PETER L A 46 GRE W
RAY RICHARD A 29 MON B
RAY ROBT A 29 FA1 B
RAY ROBT A 29 FLE B
RAY SAML A 29 FA1 B
RAY SANDY A 29 CAR B
RAY SOLOMON A 29 SEV B
RAY STEPHEN A 29 FLE B
RAY STEPHEN A 29 MON B
RAY WM A 46 GRE W
RAY WM D A 29 SEV W
RAY WM G A 29 SEV W
RAYBOLD JNO A 29 FA1 W
RAYBURN WILLIAM J A 53 LA1 W
RAYFIELD FRANKLIN M A 40 MAU W
RAYFIELD ROBERT M A 40 MAU W
RAYL A C A 46 FRI W
RAYL LINCH A 46 FRI W
RAYL THORNBURG A 46 FRI W
RAYNER ELRYEE M A 35 CYP W
RAYNER GUILFORD A 35 CYP W
RAYNER ISUM R 24 MID B
CANNOT VOTE BEING 10 MONS IN STATE
RAYNER JASON A 35 CYP W
RAYNER JOHN C A 35 CYP W
RAYNER JOHN S A 35 CYP W
RAYNER JOHN S A 35 CYP W
RAYNER PRINCE A 24 EDE B
RAYNOR JNO S A 29 FA1 W
RAYNOR STEPHEN R A 29 FA1 W
READ ARTHUR A 37 WHI B
READ EDWARD A 44 YXR B
READ J C A 40 STO W
READ JOS E A 30 GIB W
READ JOSEPH A 37 WHI B
READ JOSEPH A 39 HAY B
READ R H A 44 TOW W
DBT P. M.
READ ROYAL A 44 SAS B
READ W H A 28 9TH W
READ WILLIAM A 37 WHI B
READ WM F A 46 FRI W
READDICK JOHN W A 32 POS W
READY JOE A 28 9TH B
READY SOLOMON A 28 9TH B
CERTIF GIVEN LIVES NOW IN NEW BERN
REAMES ALEX A 44 KIT W
REAMS C F A 44 FOR W
OXFORD DIST
REAMS D C A 44 FOR W
REAMS G W A 44 FIS W
RAGLAND DIST
REAMS J M A 44 FIS W
REAMS STEPHEN A 29 FLE W
REAMS W H A 44 FIS W
REAMS W H A 44 LED W
REARDON J W A 29 FA1 W
REASONS JOSEPH F A 35 MAG W
REAVES ADAM A 35 WOL W
REAVES CHARLES A 35 FAI W
REAVES DAVID A 35 WOL W
REAVES JOHN R A 35 WOL W
REAVES LEVI W A 37 SPA W
REAVES ROBERT A 35 FAI W
REAVES TIMOTHY A 35 WOL W
REAVIS ABRAHAM A 44 HEN B
REAVIS ALFRED A 44 HEN B
REAVIS CARY A 44 HEN B
REAVIS CHARLES A 44 HEN B
REAVIS GEO B A 44 OXF W
REAVIS GRANDISON A 44 OXF B
REAVIS GREEN A 44 KIT B
REAVIS HARBRT A 44 HEN B
REAVIS HENRY A 44 HEN B
REAVIS HILMAN A 44 HEN B
REAVIS JACK A 44 HEN B
REAVIS JAMES A 44 HEN B
REAVIS JORDAN A 44 HEN B
REAVIS LEWIS A 44 HEN W
REAVIS RICHARD A 44 HEN B
REAVIS RUFUS A 44 HEN B
REAVIS SAML A 44 HEN B
REAVIS SAML W A 44 HEN W
REAVIS THOS A 44 HEN W
REAVIS WM A A 44 HEN W
REAVIS WM H A 44 HEN B
REAVIS WOODSON A 44 OXF B
REAVIS ZAN A 44 HEN B
RECARD WM A 28 04A B
REDD A F A 44 OXF W
REDDEN FRANKLIN A 46 FRI B
REDDIC JOSEPH A 53 SWA B
REDDICK ALFRED A 28 01A B
REDDICK BEMOS A 28 7TH B
REDDICK CORNELIUS A 28 02N B
REDDICK DAVID A 28 10T B
REDDICK HENRY A 28 02N B
REDDICK JAMES A 37 PIN W
REDDICK JOURDAN A 28 04A B
REDDICK MICHL A 28 04A B
REDDICK MILES A 28 05A B
REDDICK MINGO A 28 05A B
REDDICK PIERCE A 28 05A B
REDDICK RANSOM A 28 7TH B
REDDICK RANSOM A 53 GER B
REDDICK RHODEN A 28 10T B
REDDICK SAML A 28 05A B
REDDICK SOLM A 28 04A B
REDDICK SOLOMON A 28 03A B
REDDICK WILLIAM A 28 16T B
REDDICK WM HENRY A 28 01A B
REDDICK WM R A 30 POW B
REDDING GEORGE A 28 05A B
REDDING JOHN P A 28 16T W
REDDITT DAVID F A 37 TA1 W
REDDOCK ISAAC A 29 FA1 B
REDDON JACK A 29 FA1 B
REDINGHOUR ADAM A 32 TYR W
REDLEY WILLIAM 39 LOU B
REDMOND BENJAMIN A 37 EDW B
REDMOND HARRISON A 37 TA1 B
REDMOND KILLET A 19 BE1 B
REDWINE JACOB A 32 COT W
REDWINE JAMES A 32 JAC B
REDWINE M A 32 JAC W
REDWINE W P CHAL A 32 DAV W
FOR HOLDING OFFICE OF MAGISTRATE BEFORE AND DURING WAR. RECON.
REDWINE W S A 32 JAC W
REDWINE WILLIAM A 32 JAC W
REECE ALFORD A 46 FRI W
REECE ANDREW W A 32 POS W
REECE DANIEL J A 32 POS W
REECE DAVID A 46 MCL W
REECE HENRY A 46 FRI W
REECE JACOB A 46 MON W
REECE JACOB R A 32 POS W
REECE JOHN M A 46 HIG W
REECE JOHN W A 32 POS W
REECE L S A 46 JAM W
REECE SAMUEL B A 46 GRE W
REECE WILLIAM E A 32 POS W
REECE WM A 46 GRE W
REECE WM F A 46 MCL W
REED AARON A 28 04A B
REED ALFRED A 28 01A B
REED ALFRED A 37 TA1 B
REED AUGUSTUS A 28 04A B
REED B W A 46 GRE W
REED DAVID H A 32 DAV W
REED DAVIS A 28 03A B
REED GEO W A 32 DAV W
REED GEORGE A 19 NEW B
REED GEORGE A 28 04A B
REED H C A 32 SHE W
REED JACOB A 44 FOR B
REED JACOB A 46 MON B
REED JAMES A 72 SWA W
REED JAMES M A 46 GRE W
REED JAMES R A 37 MAN W
REED JASON C A 25 HAY W
REED JOHN A 28 6TH B
REED JOHN W A 46 SUM W
REED JOS C A 39 HAY W
REED JOSEPH A 37 TA1 B
REED RIAL A 24 EDE B
REED ROBERT A 26 SHE W
REED ROBT A 24 EDE B
REED ROBT A 28 05A B
REED SAMPSON A 28 05A B
REED WIATT A 46 SUM B
REED YANCEY A 46 SUM B
REEDE H A 32 DAV W
REEDE H W A 32 JAC W
REEDE HAM A 32 JAC B

REEDE HARY	A	32	COT	B
REEDE JAMES	A	32	TYR	B
REEDE JERRY	A	32	JAC	B
REEDE JERY	A	32	TYR	B
REEDE PETER	A	32	JAC	B
REEDE SAMUEL	A	32	JAC	B
REEL FREDERICK	A	28	10T	B
REEL GEORGE CHAL	A	28	12T	W
FOR AIDING THE REBELLION, AFTER BEING A MAGISTRATE & U.S. MARSHALL				
REEL JAMES M	A	28	12T	W
REEL JOHN	A	28	12T	W
REEL JOHN B	A	28	16T	W
REEL MCDUFFY	A	28	12T	W
CERTIF GIVEN LIVES NOW IN CARTERET CO				
REESE CHARLES	A	24	EDE	B
REESE DAVID	A	44	SAS	W
REESE JOHN C	A	46	GRE	W
REESE JOHN T	A	46	GRE	W
REEVES EDWARD	A	37	HIC	B
REEVES EPHERIAM	A	37	PIN	B
REEVES FRANK	A	28	02N	B
REEVES FRANK A	A	40	MAU	W
REEVES J C	A	32	JAC	W
REEVES J C	A	32	JAC	W
REEVES NIXON	A	28	01A	B
REEVES TIMOTHY	A	29	FA1	B
REEVES WILLIAM C	A	35	MAG	W
REEVIS HARRISON	A	24	EDE	B
REGAN J T	A	44	TAR	W
REGANS ISAAC	A	29	SEV	B
REGISTER DANL	A	29	GRA	W
REGISTER DIXON S	A	35	ROC	W
REGISTER FRANK E	A	35	MAG	W
REGISTER J J	A	29	FA1	W
REGISTER JOHN R	A	35	ISL	W
REGISTER JOHN R	A	35	ISL	W
REGISTER JOHN S	A	35	ISL	W
REGISTER KING D	A	35	ISL	W
REGISTER LEWIS	A	35	MAG	W
REGISTER NEWTON F	A	35	ROC	W
REGISTER RICE P	A	35	ISL	W
REGISTER SAMEUL C	A	35	ROC	W
REGISTER WM C	A	29	GRA	W
REHM FREDRICK	A	24	MID	W
REHM JAMES	A	28	03A	B
REICHARD WILLIAM	A	32	DAV	W
REID A H	A	44	FOR	W
REID ABRAHAM	A	40	DA1	B
REID ANTHONY		39	LOU	B
REID C A	A	32	THO	W
CERTIF				
REID H K	A	44	HEN	W
REID HAL	A	44	HEN	B
REID JACOB	R	40	STO	B
CHALLENGED AND REJ CONVICTED OF FELONY SINCE HE WAS FREE				
REID JAMES	A	39	SPE	W
REID JAMES	A	39	SPE	W
REID JAS W	A	40	SAN	W
REID JESSE	A	46	FRI	W
REID JESSEE	A	39	SPE	B
REID MAJOR	A	46	GRE	B
REID N F	A	32	THO	W
REID THOMAS	A	39	HAR	B
REID WM A	A	46	GRE	W
REIGER HENRY	A	19	BE1	W
REILLEY JNO	A	29	LOC	W
REILLY JNO	A	29	FA1	W
REITZEL H C	A	46	COB	W
REITZEL MICHAEL M	A	46	COB	W
REITZELL FREDERICK	AA	46	COB	W
REIVES RICHARD E	A	37	MAN	W
REIVS J G	A	37	MAN	W
REMLY E F	A	46	KIN	W
RENALEY JOHN	A	24	EDE	B
RENN G P	A	39	HAY	W
RENN GREEN C	A	44	HEN	W
RENN J H	A	39	HAY	W
RENN LEWIS	A	44	HEN	W
RENN THOMAS M	A	39	LOU	W
RENYOLDS J B	A	25	SHO	W
RESPASS ALLEN	A	28	05A	B
RESPASS CHAUNCEY	A	28	04A	B
RESPASS HENRY W	A	28	05A	B
RESPASS MARCELLUS	A	28	10T	B
RESPESS OWEN	A	19	BE1	B
REVELLS DAVID	A	46	FRI	B
REVELS ALLAN	A	40	FER	B
REVELS GABRIEL	A	40	FER	B
REVELS JOHN	A	46	FRI	B
REVELS ROBERT	A	26	HOL	B
REVELS WASHINGTON	A	29	FA1	B
REVES EPHRAIM	A	19	NEW	B
REVILLS EDMOND	A	46	FRI	B
REVILS ELIAS	A	46	GRE	B
REVIS JACK	A	37	PIN	B
REVIS PETER	A	37	PIN	B
REVIS REDDING	A	37	PIN	B
REVIS WASHINGTON	A	37	PIN	B
REY JAMES	A	24	EDE	B
REY WM D	A	24	EDE	W
REYNALDS PETER	A	46	GRE	B
REYNOLDS FELIX	A	29	FA1	W
REYNOLDS J P	A	29	FA1	W
REYNOLDS JOASH	A	46	HIG	W
REYNOLDS JOHN	A	26	SHE	W
REYNOLDS JOSHUA	A	46	ROS	W
REYNOLDS LEWIS	A	46	ROS	W
REYNOLDS MARTIN	A	46	GRE	B
REYNOLDS THOMAS	A	28	7TH	B
RHEA A B	A	26	GOF	W
RHEA J C	A	26	GOF	W
RHEA R A	A	26	GOF	W
RHEIM EDWARD H	A	28	7TH	W
RHEM BENJAMIN	A	28	8TH	B
RHEM CURTIS	A	28	7TH	W
RHEM ELIAS	A	28	7TH	B
RHEM GEORGE	A	28	8TH	B
RHEM HARKLESS	A	28	8TH	B
RHEM J E	A	28	7TH	W
RHEM J W	A	28	8TH	W
RHEM JOHN	A	28	7TH	B
RHEM JOS L	A	28	03A	W
RHEW ADAM	A	39	FRA	B
RHINE ABSOLEM	A	19	HAD	W
RHOADES EDWARD	A	28	16T	B
RHOADS ALEXANDER	A	46	FRI	B
RHOADS DAVID	A	35	LIM	B
RHOADS EMANUEL	A	35	LIM	B
RHOADS G E	A	35	SMI	W
RHOADS JAMES	A	35	SMI	W
RHOADS THOS	A	29	FA1	W
RHOADS W T	A	29	FA1	W
RHODERICK MOSES	A	28	10T	B
RHODES A E	A	19	MOR	W
CERT TO NEWPORT IN CARTERET CO				
RHODES ALBERT	A	35	MAG	B
RHODES ALFRED	A	28	05A	B
RHODES BENJN	A	28	04A	B
RHODES CLEM	A	40	DA1	B
RHODES DANIEL	A	24	EDE	B
RHODES GLASGOW	A	28	8TH	B
RHODES GREEN	A	46	GRE	B
RHODES H C	A	28	02N	W
RHODES HILLIARD	A	28	01A	B
RHODES HOSEA	A	40	DA1	W
RHODES ISAAC	A	32	DAV	W
RHODES ISAAC	A	40	DA1	B
RHODES J W	A	44	OXF	W
RHODES JORDAN	A	37	HIG	B
RHODES JOSEPH	A	35	ISL	B
RHODES JOSEPH	A	40	DA1	B
RHODES JOSEPH	A	40	DA1	W
RHODES THOS	A	28	6TH	B
RHODES WARREN	A	37	HIG	B
RHODES WILLIAM	A	19	MOR	B
RHODES WILLIS	A	28	03A	B
RHOLER ISAIAH	A	19	BE1	B
RHUE ANSON	A	19	HAD	W
RHUE EDWARD	A	19	HAD	W
RHUE RUBAN	A	19	HAD	W
RHY M J	A	40	STO	W
RHYNE A	A	40	RHY	W
RHYNE A M	A	32	DAV	W
RHYNE A MILLER	A	40	DA1	W
RHYNE A P	A	40	CAN	W
RHYNE ABEL B	A	40	DA1	W
(JONATHAN'S SON)				
RHYNE ADAM	A	40	CAN	B
RHYNE ADAM A JR	A	40	DA1	W
RHYNE ALEXANDER A SEN	A	40	DA1	W
RHYNE AMBROSE	A	40	DA1	W
RHYNE AMZI	A	40	DA1	B
RHYNE ANDREW	A	40	DA1	B
RHYNE BENJAMIN F	A	40	DA1	B
RHYNE CHRISTY	A	40	DA1	W
RHYNE CLAEB	A	40	DA1	W
RHYNE D R	A	40	RHY	W
RHYNE DANIEL	A	40	DA1	W
RHYNE DANIL	A	40	RHY	W
RHYNE DAVID	A	40	RHY	B
RHYNE DAVID JR	A	40	DA1	W
RHYNE EMANUEL	A	40	DA1	W
RHYNE ESLI	A	40	DA1	W
RHYNE EZEKIEL	A	40	DA1	B
RHYNE G C	A	40	RHY	W
RHYNE GEORGE M	A	40	DA2	W
RHYNE HENRY	A	40	STO	W
RHYNE HENRY M	A	40	DA1	W
RHYNE HERVEY L	A	40	DA1	W
RHYNE ISAAC	A	40	DA1	B
RHYNE J BUNYAN	A	40	DA2	W
RHYNE JACOB A	A	40	DA1	W
RHYNE JACOB E	A	40	DA1	W
RHYNE JACOB H	A	40	DA1	W
RHYNE JACOB K	A	40	DA1	W
RHYNE JAMES	A	40	SAN	B
RHYNE JEFFERSON	A	40	DA1	B
RHYNE JESSEY	A	40	SAN	B
RHYNE JOHN	A	40	DA1	B
RHYNE JOHN L	A	40	DA1	W
RHYNE JONATHAN	A	40	DA1	W
RHYNE JOSEPH K	A	40	DA1	W
NAME LINED OUT MILITIA OFFICER BEFORE THE REBELLION & GAVE AID OR COMFORT TO THE ENEMY DID NOT QUALIFY				
RHYNE MARCUS	A	40	DA1	W
RHYNE MIKEL	A	40	RHY	W
RHYNE MILES	A	40	DA1	B
RHYNE MILES A	A	40	DA1	W
RHYNE PATEN S	A	40	RHY	W

RHYNE PHILLIP A 40 DA1 B
RHYNE PHILLIP S A 40 DA1 B
RHYNE PINCKNEY J A 40 DA1 W
RHYNE R D A 40 RHY W
REMOVED TO
MECKLENBURG CO
IS FURNISHED WITH
CERTIFICATE
RHYNE WILLIAM A 40 CAN B
RICE BENJAMIN A 28 16T W
RICE BENJAMIN F A 28 13T W
RICE DEMSEY A 28 15T W
RICE EDWARD A 44 ISL B
RICE EMERY A 28 14T W
RICE ENOCH B A 28 13T W
RICE FREDERICK L A 28 14T W
RICE G W A 46 GRE W
RICE GIDEON B A 28 15T W
RICE ISAAC A 37 WEB W
RICE J W A 44 TOW W
RICE JAMES A 28 13T W
RICE JESSE A 28 01A W
RICE JOAB A 28 16T W
RICE JOHN H A 28 14T W
RICE NOAH A 28 16T W
RICE P B A 28 01A W
RICE PATRICK A 46 GIB B
RICE RICHARD A 19 BE2 B
RICE ROBT L A 44 TOW W
RICE S W A 32 DAV W
RICE STEPHEN A 44 TOW B
RICE THOS A 44 RAG W
RICE W F A 32 DAV W
RICE WILLIAM A 44 FIS B
RICE ZADOC A 44 RAG W
RICH ALFRED A 35 SMI B
RICH ALFRED A 46 JAM W
RICH CLAIBORN A 35 MAG B
RICH GEORGE A 46 GRE W
RICH JAMES A 35 MAG B
RICH JOHN A 46 GRE B
RICH PINKNEY CERT A 35 MAG W
GIVEN 11 APR 1868
RICH ROBERT A 35 MAG B
RICH SAMUEL A 46 JAM W
RICH THOMAS A 46 GRE W
RICH WM A A 46 GRE W
RICH ZAZA A 46 GRE W
RICHALD E G A 32 JAC W
RICHARDS ALEXANDER A 40 DA1 W
RICHARDS BENJ A 44 FOR W
RICHARDS ELIJAH A 28 9TH B
RICHARDS GRAHAM A 53 SWA W
RICHARDS H R A 26 PEE W
RICHARDS HANDY A 37 EDW B
NAME LINED OUT
RICHARDS J A 26 CAR W
RICHARDS J M A 26 WAR W
RICHARDS J W A 26 WAR W
RICHARDS JAMES A 28 10T B
RICHARDS JOHN A 39 HAR W
RICHARDS MARCUS J A 40 DA2 B
RICHARDS ROBERT A 40 FER B
RICHARDS SID A 39 HAR W
RICHARDS SILAS A 28 10T B
RICHARDS WILLIAM A 28 10T B
RICHARDS WM A 40 RHY W
RICHARDS WYATT A 28 7TH B
RICHARDSON ALEXANDERA 40 CAN B
RICHARDSON BALDWIN A 29 ROC W
RICHARDSON BENJ A 44 OXF B
RICHARDSON BEVELY A 39 HAY B
RICHARDSON CHAMPION A 39 GRI B
RICHARDSON DANCY A 28 05A B
RICHARDSON E A A 28 02N B
RICHARDSON EDWARD A 46 SUM W
RICHARDSON G A A 28 8TH W
RICHARDSON G A H A 28 04A B
RICHARDSON GEO A 29 FA1 B
RICHARDSON GEO A 44 FOR B
RICHARDSON GEORGE A 28 04B B
RICHARDSON GEORGE A 44 SAS B
RICHARDSON GEORGE W A 28 01A W
RICHARDSON H CLAY A 28 01A W
RICHARDSON H H A 28 03B B
RICHARDSON H V A 28 04A W
RICHARDSON HANDY A 37 EDW B
RICHARDSON HENRY A 28 04A B
RICHARDSON HEZKH A 28 03A B
RICHARDSON ISAAC R A 28 02N B
RICHARDSON J A A 28 01A W
RICHARDSON JAMES A 29 FA2 B
RICHARDSON JAMES A 44 KIT B
RICHARDSON M A 39 GRI B
RICHARDSON M C A 28 6TH W
RICHARDSON MILES A 28 04A B
RICHARDSON NATHAN A 28 8TH B
RICHARDSON PETER A 28 03A B
RICHARDSON SAML A 44 FOR B
RICHARDSON SAML A 44 OXF B
RICHARDSON THOMAS A 29 FA2 B
RICHARDSON W B A 46 JAM W
RICHARDSON W H A 28 04A B
RICHARDSON W T A 44 FOR B
RICHARDSON WM A 28 15T W
RICHARDSON WM HENRY A 28 04A B
RICHARSON JOSHUA A 24 MID B
RICHIE JOHN A 32 COT W
RICHIE WILLIAM A 32 DAV B
RICHMOND ALFRED A 46 ROS B
RICHMOND BRUCE A 37 ROC B
RICHMOND BURRELL A 46 ROS B
RICHMOND MADISON A 44 OXF B
RICHMOND PETER A 44 TAR B
RICHMOND WILLIAM A 37 HIG W
RICK BENJAMIN A 53 FAI B
RICKARD GEORGE A 32 COT W
RICKARD JACOB A 32 COT W
RICKARD JESSE A 32 COT W
RICKARD LENARD A 32 COT W
RICKARD PETER A 32 COT W
RICKETTS WM A 46 MON W
RICKS ABSALOM A 37 ROC B
RICKS ABSOLOM A 37 ROC B
RICKS ALFRED A 37 ROC B
RICKS BLUNT A 37 ROC B
RICKS BRITTEN A 37 ROC B
RICKS DEMPSY A 37 ROC B
RICKS HEYWOOD A 37 PEN B
RICKS HILLIARD A 37 ROC B
RICKS ISAAC A 37 TA1 B
RICKS JACOB A 37 ROC B
RICKS JAMES W A 46 GRE W
RICKS JOHN A 46 JAM W
RICKS JOLLY A 37 ROC B
RICKS JOYNER A 37 ROC B
RICKS KINCHIN A 37 ROC B
RICKS MILTON A 46 JAM W
RICKS NATHAN A 37 ROC B
RICKS ROBERT A 37 ROC B
(WHITE VOTER)
RICKS ROBERT A 37 TA1 B
RICKS SAUL A 37 ROC B
RICKS W M A 46 SUM W
RICKS WILEY B A 37 ROC W
RICKS WILLIAM G A 37 PEN W
RICKS WILLIE A 37 ROC W
RIDDICK C B A 44 KIT W
RIDDICK GILES A 26 GRI B
RIDDICK H A 44 KIT W
RIDDICK HENRY A 30 IND B
RIDDICK JERRY A 24 MID B
RIDDICK JOBE A 24 MID W
RIDDICK JOS H A 44 KIT W
RIDDLE J B F A 40 SAN W
RIDDLE J L A 26 SHE W
RIDDLE JAMES A A 29 FA1 W
RIDDLE MAJOR A 28 10T B
RIDLEY BEN A 44 OXF B
RIDLEY BRUMFIELD A 44 YXS B
RIDLEY DOLPHIN A 44 OXF B
RIDLEY FRANK A 44 OXF B
RIDLEY HENRY A 44 OXF B
RIDLEY JACOB A 44 OXF B
RIDLEY JASPER A 44 OXF B
RIDLEY JUDA A 44 YXR B
RIDLEY RICHD A 44 OXF B
RIDLEY RICHD A 44 OXF B
RIDLEY ROBT A 44 OXF B
RIECHARD J J E A 32 THO W
RIEKARD ALEXANDER A 32 DAV W
RIEKARD J A A 32 DAV W
RIELEY WILLIAM A 30 ROA B
RIEVS SAMUEL A 37 MAN B
RIGDON GEORGE W A 28 9TH W
RIGGAINS J J A 32 BRO W
RIGGAN LITTLETON E A 99 BUS W
RIGGINS ARCHIBALD A 28 9TH B
RIGGINS ISOM A 32 THO W
RIGGINS JACOB J A 44 TOW W
RIGGINS JAMES A 44 TOW W
RIGGINS M G A 44 SAS W
RIGGS ABRAHAM A 28 16T B
RIGGS ALEXANDER A 30 TUL W
RIGGS ASA A 72 SWA W
RIGGS BAZZIL N A 72 SWA W
RIGGS CORNELIUS A 30 IND W
RIGGS EVERETT L A 72 SWA W
RIGGS G W A 44 LED W
RIGGS HAYWOOD A 28 6TH W
RIGGS ISAAC A 72 SWA W
RIGGS JESSE A 28 17T W
RIGGS JOHN A A 28 15T W
RIGGS JOHN D A 28 17T W
RIGGS JOHN R A 28 17T W
RIGGS JOHN S A 28 16T W
RIGGS MICHEAL R A 72 SWA W
RIGGS NELSON A 28 04A W
RIGGS WILSON A 30 IND W
RIGGS WM D A 28 15T W
RIGHT W R A 40 SAN W
RIGONS ALEXANDER A 32 DAV W
RILES D W A 29 FLE W
RILEY DUDLEY A 37 PEN W
RILEY GEORGE A 30 IND B
RILEY GEORGE E-- A 32 DAV W
CHAL FOR HOLDING OFFICE
OF MAGISTRATE BEFORE AND
DURING WAR. RECON.
RILEY HENRY A 46 GRE W
RILEY JAMES A 19 HAD W
RILEY JAMES A 32 JAC W
RILEY PETER A 32 JAC W
RILEY PETER A 32 THO W
RILEY PLEASANT A 46 GRE W
RILEY WILLIAM A 35 SMI B
RILEY WM L A 99 BUS W
RILY C A 32 JAC W
RILY HENRY C A 32 JAC W

RILY JOHN L A 32 JAC W
RILY RODIAS A 32 JAC W
RIMBLEY SAMUEL D A 19 BE1 W
RINE MOSES H A 40 STO W
RINGDON BENJAMIN A 19 HAD W
RINGO WILLIAM A 28 7TH B
RINNLEY JAMES A 19 BE1 W
RINNLEY WARTON A 19 BE1 B
RINSLEY BRIAN H A 19 BE1 W
RIPPEY CALVIN A 26 BUR W
RIPPEY E M A 26 SWA W
RIPPEY E R A 26 SWA W
RIPPEY GREEN A 26 SWA B
RIPPEY HOWARD A 26 BUR B
RIPPEY ISAAC A 26 BUR B
RIPPEY JAMES A 26 BUR W
RIPPEY JAMES A 26 SWA W
RIPPEY JERRY A 26 SHE B
RIPPEY MASTIN A 26 SWA W
RIPPEY S H A 26 SWA W
RIPPEY W C A 26 BUR W
RIPPEY WILLIAM A 26 BUR W
RIPPLE CHRISTIAN A 32 SHE W
RIPPLE PHILIP A 32 SHE W
RIPPLE WILLIAM A 32 YAD B
RISPRESS ISIAH A 19 BE1 B
RITCH JOHN F A 28 10T W
RITTER BENJ A 30 MOY W
RITTER JAMES T A 29 SEV W
RITTER JOHN T A 29 SEV W
RITTER JOSEPH A 30 MOY W
RIVENBARK BENJAMIN A 35 MAG W
RIVENBARK DANIEL J A 35 WAR W
RIVENBARK DAVID A 35 ROC W
RIVENBARK GEORGE A 35 ISL W
CERTIF GIVEN
APRIL 9, 1868
RIVENBARK HENRY A 35 WAR W
RIVENBARK JAMES T A 35 ROC W
RIVENBARK JOHN A 35 ISL W
RIVENBARK JONIS A 35 WAR W
RIVENBARK SAMEUL D A 35 ROC W
CERT GIVEN
APRIL 10, 1868
RIVENBARK TEACHEY A 35 ROC W
RIVENBARK WILLIAM T A 35 MAG W
RIVENBARK WILLIAM W A 35 ROC W
RIVENBARK WRIGHT A 35 ROC W
RIVERS AARON B A 28 8TH B
RIXFORD GEO C A 28 01A W
ROACH ABRAM A 28 03A B
ROACH C M A 28 11T W
ROACH JAMES A 28 11T W
ROACH JAMES A 32 THO W
ROACH JOHN A 32 COT W
ROACH JOSEPH A 32 COT W
ROACH NELSON A 46 SUM B
ROACH SAMUEL A 28 11T B
ROACH SLADE A 28 11T B
ROACH W L A 28 11T W
ROAN ALLEN A 46 MCL B
ROAN GEORGE A 46 MCL B
ROAN JNO A 29 LOC B
ROAN JOSHY A 29 LOC B
ROAN JOSHY A 29 LOC B
ROAN WILLIAM A 37 SHA W
ROANOKE JOHN A 44 SAS B
ROARK RAN A 26 BOR B
ROBARD JOSEPH A 44 RAG B
ROBARDS ALEX A 44 OXF B
ROBARDS DAVID A 44 KIT W
ROBARDS HENRY A 44 OXF B
ROBARDS J W A 44 OXF W

ROBARDS JAS W A 44 HEN W
ROBARDS NORVILL A 44 OXF B
ROBARDS SILUS A 44 ISL B
ROBARDS W J A 44 HEN W
ROBARDS W L A 44 FIS W
ROBBARDS SANDY A 39 SPE B
ROBBERSON PATRICK A 39 SPE B
ROBBERTS DANIEL A 39 SPE B
ROBBERTS DIMENT A 39 SPE B
ROBBINS CEASER A 46 JAM B
ROBBINS CHRISTOPHER A 32 THO W
ROBBINS DAVID A 28 04A B
ROBBINS ENOCH A 28 05A B
ROBBINS FRED W A 28 01A W
CERT GIVEN
2ND PRECINCT
ROBBINS HILL A 32 THO B
ROBBINS JOHN A 29 LOC B
ROBBINS JOHN JR A 25 HAY W
ROBBINS JOHN SR A 25 HAY W
ROBBINS KELLEY A 46 JAM B
ROBBINS NEWTON A 25 HAY W
ROBBINS RICHARD A 46 JAM W
ROBBINS STEPHEN A 46 JAM B
ROBBINS T A A 28 04A W
ROBBINS TOM A 28 04A B
ROBBISON WIELY A 32 POS B
ROBENSON S A 40 CAN W
ROBERSON A C A 32 DAV W
ROBERSON ANDERSON A 28 9TH B
ROBERSON ARNOLD A 28 11T B
ROBERSON BANISTER A 44 OXF W
ROBERSON CHARLES A 28 9TH B
ROBERSON D D A 26 BLA W
ROBERSON EURIAH A 19 HUN W
ROBERSON FRANK A 28 04A W
ROBERSON GEORGE A 44 HEN W
ROBERSON H P A 46 SUM W
ROBERSON HILMAN A 44 RAG W
ROBERSON J D A 26 MOU W
ROBERSON JACK A 44 OXF B
ROBERSON JACOB A 28 10T B
ROBERSON JERRY A 28 03B B
CERTIFICATE GRANTED
TO RALEIGH
ROBERSON JOHN A 28 9TH B
ROBERSON JOHN A 44 FIS W
ROBERSON JOSEPHUS A 19 HUN W
ROBERSON LENNOR A 19 BE1 B
ROBERSON LEVI A 30 CUR B
ROBERSON LEWIS JR A 44 HEN W
ROBERSON LEWIS SR A 44 HEN W
ROBERSON MAJOR A 44 FOR W
ROBERSON MASON A 19 HUN W
ROBERSON PETER JR A 44 HEN W
ROBERSON PETER SR A 44 HEN W
ROBERSON ROBERT A 44 HEN W
ROBERSON THOMAS A 19 HUN W
ROBERSON VALENTINE A 19 HUN W
ROBERSON W J A 46 SUM W
ROBERSON WALLACE A 19 HUN W
ROBERSON WASHINGTON A 44 HEN B
ROBERSON WILLIAM A 53 FAI B
ROBERSON WILLIE A 44 HEN W
ROBERSON WM A 44 TAR W
ROBERT RUDISILL A 40 DEC B
ROBERTS A A 26 BOR B
ROBERTS A A 26 BOR B
ROBERTS A L A 32 COT W
ROBERTS ABRAHAM A 40 FER B
ROBERTS ARTHUR A 40 MAU B
ROBERTS ASWELL A 37 TA1 W
ROBERTS B A 26 BOR B

ROBERTS BENJ A 29 FA1 B
ROBERTS BENJAMIN A 30 CUR W
ROBERTS BENJAMIN A 46 SUM B
ROBERTS C A 26 BOR B
ROBERTS CAESAR A 28 04A B
ROBERTS CALEB A 40 DEC B
ROBERTS CHARLES A 32 CLE B
ROBERTS CHARLES A 37 TA1 B
ROBERTS CHAS E A 29 FA1 W
ROBERTS CUFF A 32 TYR B
ROBERTS D M A 19 NEW W
ROBERTS D M A 44 LED W
ROBERTS ED B A 28 02N W
ROBERTS ELI A 40 CAN B
ROBERTS ELIS A 26 SHE B
ROBERTS FILETUS A 26 SHE B
ROBERTS FRED L A 24 EDE W
ROBERTS FREELAND A 37 TA1 B
ROBERTS GAINY A 44 SAS B
ROBERTS GEO W A 19 POR W
ROBERTS GEO W JR A 19 POR W
ROBERTS GEORGE A 26 GOF B
ROBERTS GEORGE A 40 FER B
ROBERTS GLASCOW A 24 EDE B
ROBERTS GRANVILLE A 24 MID B
ROBERTS H A 26 BOR B
ROBERTS HENDERSON A 26 SHE W
ROBERTS HENRY A 44 LED B
ROBERTS HILLIARD A 28 04A B
ROBERTS ISAAC A 32 DAV B
ROBERTS J A 26 BOR B
ROBERTS J B A 35 WOL W
ROBERTS J E A 26 SHE W
ROBERTS J M A 26 BUR W
ROBERTS J T A 35 WOL W
ROBERTS J V A 44 LED W
ROBERTS J W A 26 SHE W
ROBERTS J W A 32 COT W
ROBERTS JACK A 24 EDE B
ROBERTS JACK JR A 24 EDE B
ROBERTS JACOB A 28 05A B
ROBERTS JACOB A 32 DAV B
ROBERTS JAMES B A 28 01A W
ROBERTS JOHN A 25 SHO W
NAME MARKED OUT
CHALLENGED FOR HOLDING THE OFFICE OF JUSTICE OF THE PEACE BEFORE THE REBELLION & HOLDING SAID OFFICE DURING THE WAR FOR THE PURPOZ OF SAVING MYSELF FROM BEING CONSCRIPTED INTO THE WAR
ROBERTS JOHN A 24 EDE W
ROBERTS JOHN A 37 PEN W
ROBERTS JOHN B A 19 POR W
ROBERTS JOHN G A 19 STR W
ROBERTS JOHN P A 24 EDE W
ROBERTS JOHN SR A 26 SHE W
ROBERTS JOSEPH A 19 POR W
ROBERTS JOSEPH R 46 GIB B
(LARCENY) INDICTED FOR PETTY LARCENY & COMPROMISED UPON HIS PAYING THE COSTS
ROBERTS JULIUS A 32 TYR B
ROBERTS M A 26 BOR B
ROBERTS M H D A 26 SHE W
ROBERTS M P A 44 LED W
ROBERTS MATHIAS A 32 DAV B
ROBERTS MICHAEL A 40 MAU W
ROBERTS MORRIS A 26 SHE W
ROBERTS N A 26 BOR B
ROBERTS OXNER A 26 SHE B

ROBERTS P M A 26 SHE W
ROBERTS R S A 32 TYR W
ROBERTS RICHARD A 30 CUR W
ROBERTS RICHARD A 37 HIG B
ROBERTS RICHARD JR A 19 NEW W
ROBERTS RICHARD SR A 19 NEW W
ROBERTS ROBERT A 26 GOF B
ROBERTS SAMUEL A 32 TYR B
ROBERTS SEFUS A 37 PIN B
ROBERTS STEPHEN A 28 05A B
ROBERTS STEPHEN A 35 KEN B
ROBERTS STEPHEN G A 19 POR W
ROBERTS STEPHEN W A 24 EDE W
ROBERTS THOMAS A 28 04B B
ROBERTS THOMAS A 44 LED W
ROBERTS THOMAS M A 40 BLA W
ROBERTS THOS A 24 EDE B
ROBERTS W R A 26 MOU W
ROBERTS W W A 46 KIN W
ROBERTS WASHINGTON A 32 TYR B
ROBERTS WESTERN A 39 SPE B
ROBERTS WILLIAM A 24 MID W
ROBERTS WILLIAM A 26 MOU W
ROBERTS WILLIAM A 37 PIN B
ROBERTS WILLIS A 28 05A B
ROBERTS WM F A 28 01B W
ROBERTS WM J A 19 POR W
ROBERTS WYATT A 44 SAS B
ROBERTSON DALLAS A 99 BUS B
ROBERTSON GABREL A A 53 GER W
ROBERTSON GEORGE A 28 10T B
ROBERTSON GEORGE A 37 ROB B
ROBERTSON J K A 29 LOC W
ROBERTSON JAMES A 37 ROB B
ROBERTSON JAMES A 46 JAM W
ROBERTSON JEREMIAH A 30 TUL W
ROBERTSON JOHN J A 37 ROB W
ROBERTSON L H A 44 TOW W
ROBERTSON MARCUS W A 37 ROB W
ROBERTSON N Y A 44 TOW W
ROBERTSON THOMAS A 44 TOW W
ROBERTSON TILMON A 19 SMY W
ROBERTSON W G A 30 IND W
ROBESON AMOS A 29 FA2 B
ROBESON CHAS A 29 GRA B
ROBESON CHAS A 29 GRA W
ROBESON GEORGE A 46 GRE B
ROBESON THOMAS A 25 HAY W
ROBIN F C A 32 DAV W
ROBINS CICERO A 28 03A B
ROBINS ISAAC A 37 SHA W
ROBINS J L A 46 FRI W
ROBINS JOHN B A 37 SHA W
ROBINS JOHN C A 37 SHA W
ROBINS JOHN W A 37 SHA W
ROBINS TONEY A 37 SHA B
ROBINS WILLIAM B A 37 SHA W
ROBINSON ABNER A 35 MAG W
ROBINSON ALEXANDER A 19 POR W
ROBINSON ALFRED A 29 FA1 B
ROBINSON ALFRED A 46 MON W
ROBINSON ALLEN A 37 PIN B
ROBINSON ALLEN A 46 MON W
ROBINSON ALX A 29 ROC B
ROBINSON ANDW A 29 FA1 B
ROBINSON B W A 29 FA1 W
ROBINSON BENJ L A 19 BE1 W
ROBINSON BENJ L A 19 BE1 W
ROBINSON BENJAMIN A 29 FA2 W
ROBINSON BENJAMIN A 37 TA1 B
ROBINSON BENJAMIN T A 53 HAT W
ROBINSON CHRISTOPHERA 53 HAT W

ROBINSON CHAS E R 24 EDE W
REJECTED BY THE BOARD
WAS A CONSTABLE BEFORE
THE WAR & ENGAGED
IN THE REBELLION
FINAL REVISION
ROBINSON DANIEL A 35 ROC B
ROBINSON DANL A 29 FA1 B
ROBINSON DAVID A 29 FA1 B
ROBINSON E J A 40 SAN W
ROBINSON E JASPER A 40 DA2 W
ROBINSON ELHANAN W A 40 DEC W
ROBINSON FDRK A 29 FA1 B
ROBINSON GEO A 29 GRA B
ROBINSON GEO S A 53 HAT W
ROBINSON HANDY A 35 MAG B
ROBINSON HAZARD A 28 04A B
ROBINSON HENRY A 29 GRA B
ROBINSON ISAAC A 19 HAR B
ROBINSON ISAAC A 46 GRE B
ROBINSON ISAAC W A 40 DA1 W
ROBINSON JACK A 29 FA1 B
ROBINSON JACK A 29 GRA B
ROBINSON JAMES A 28 16T W
ROBINSON JAMES A 29 BLA X
FLEA HILL CERTIFICATE
ROBINSON JAMES A 37 EDW B
ROBINSON JAMES A 46 GRE B
ROBINSON JAMES D A 29 FLE B
REMOBED TO BLK RIVER
ROBINSON JAMES H A 46 COB W
ROBINSON JAMES L A 19 MOR W
ROBINSON JAMES R A 40 DA2 W
ROBINSON JEFFRY A 29 FA1 B
ROBINSON JERRY A 24 EDE B
ROBINSON JESSE P A 53 HAT W
ROBINSON JNO H A 29 FA1 W
WILMINGTON, NC
CERT APRIL 10, 68
ROBINSON JOHN A 46 JAM W
ROBINSON JOHN C A 40 DA2 W
ROBINSON JOHN M A 29 GRA W
AFF CLINTON SAMPSON CO
ROBINSON JOHN W A 53 HAT W
ROBINSON JOSEPH A 19 NEW B
ROBINSON JOSEPH A 28 16T W
ROBINSON JOSEPH L A 19 BE1 W
ROBINSON JOSEPH P A 19 BE1 W
ROBINSON JOSHUA A 37 ROC W
STRICKEN OFF
ROBINSON LEWIS A 35 ISL B
ROBINSON LUCIEN W A 35 MAG W
ROBINSON MAURICE E A 40 DA2 B
NAME LINED OUT
HAD REGISTERED LAST YEAR
ROBINSON MORRIS E A 40 DA1 B
ROBINSON N A 30 IND W
ROBINSON ODEN A 28 05A B
ROBINSON PHILIP A 46 GRE B
ROBINSON R R A 29 BLA W
ROBINSON RANSOM A 28 05A B
ROBINSON RICE A 46 MON W
ROBINSON ROBERT A 19 HUN W
ROBINSON ROBERT A 35 ROC B
ROBINSON ROBERT A 53 HAT W
ROBINSON S L A 40 SAN W
ROBINSON SHADRACK A 39 HAR B
ROBINSON SILVESTER A 53 HAT W
ROBINSON THOMAS A 19 POR W
ROBINSON THOMPSON A 40 MAU W
ROBINSON THOS A 28 03A B
ROBINSON TONY A 72 SWA B
ROBINSON VALENTINE A 19 POR W

ROBINSON VALENTINE R 19 POR W
NAME MARKED THROUGH
ROBINSON WHITTINGTONA 19 CED W
ROBINSON WILEY A 29 FA1 B
ROBINSON WILLIAM A 19 MOR W
ROBINSON WILLIAM A 30 MOY B
ROBINSON WILLIAM A 35 MAG B
ROBINSON WILLIAM A 46 JAM W
ROBINSON WILLIAM A 53 GER W
ROBINSON WILLIAM E A 40 DEC W
ROBINSON WM A 19 BE1 B
ROBINSON WM A 19 POR W
ROBINSON WM H A 24 MID W
ROBINSON WM P A 28 01A W
ROBINSON WM S A 19 BE1 W
ROBISON AARON A 32 POS B
ROBISON B A 32 POS B
ROBISON ELAM A 40 SAN W
ROBISON GEORGE A 40 SAN B
ROBISON J A A 40 SAN W
ROBISON J F A 46 KIN W
ROBISON JOHN A 37 WEB W
ROBISON JOHN A 46 FRI W
ROBISON JOHN A 46 MON W
ROBISON KALEB C A 46 FRI W
ROBISON ZIMRI A 40 SAN W
ROCHELL BENJAMIN A 35 MAG W
ROCHELLE EDWARD G A 35 KEN W
ROCHELLE JOHN T A 35 KEN W
CERT TO KENANSVILLE
ROCHESTER JOHN A 37 PIN B
ROCHIEL GREEN A 44 FOR B
ROCK ROBERT A 32 DAV B
RODDY WILLIAMS A 30 IND W
RODEN JAMES R A 37 MAN W
RODEN JOHN A 53 SWA B
RODERICK JOHN A 28 10T B
RODGERS ABSALOM A 39 GRI W
RODGERS AGREABLE A 30 COI W
RODGERS BUCKNER A 37 TA1 W
RODGERS CHARLES A 35 FAI W
RODGERS CIP A 37 PIN B
RODGERS DANIL A 44 KIT B
RODGERS DURANT A 30 POW W
RODGERS EDWARD P A 30 NOR W
RODGERS FRANK A 39 PUG B
RODGERS GEORGE A 37 TAI B
RODGERS JAMES S A 30 POW W
RODGERS JOHN A 35 WOL W
RODGERS JOHN A 35 WOL W
RODGERS JOHN A 37 EDW W
RODGERS JOHN B F A 30 COI W
RODGERS JOSEPH H A 30 COI W
RODGERS JOSEPH H A 30 NOR W
RODGERS MAJOR JR A 30 NOR W
RODGERS MAJOR SR A 30 NOR W
RODGERS STEPHEN A 35 WOL W
RODGERS WARREN A 46 GRE B
RODGERS WM A 44 HEN B
RODMAN ALFRED A 28 01A B
RODMAN LEWIS A 28 05A B
RODMAN WM A 28 05A B
RODWELL ARTHER A 39 PUG B
RODWELL EVERIT A 39 PUG B
RODWELL ROBT A 39 PUG W
RODWELL WILLIAM A 39 PUG B
ROE ALEXANDER A 28 14T W
ROE BARNEY H A 28 8TH W
ROE BRYCE A 28 13T W
ROE CALVEN H A 39 LOU W
ROE EARLY A 28 05B B
ROE GEORGE A 53 FAI W
ROE JOSEPH A 28 05A B

ROE WILLIAM A 39 LOU W
ROE WILLIAM JR A 39 LOU W
ROE WINFIELD S A 39 LOU W
ROE WM A 28 13T W
ROGER EDMUND A 35 MAG B
ROGER W H A 44 BEA B
ROGERS ALFORD A 44 FIS B
ROGERS ARCHABLE A 25 SHO W
ROGERS AUGUSTINE A 37 ROC B
ROGERS BRYCE A 37 SPA B
ROGERS CALVIN R A 35 WAR W
ROGERS CHESLEY A 99 BUS W
ROGERS DANIEL S R 72 SWA W
MILITIA OFFICER BEFORE
THE WAR AND AFTERWARDS
PARTICIPATED IN REBELLION
ROGERS DAVID A 28 05A B
ROGERS DAVID J A 35 MAG W
ROGERS ELBERT S A 25 HAY W
ROGERS ESSEE A 44 HEN B
ROGERS FRANK A 44 HEN B
ROGERS G W A 44 BEA W
ROGERS G W A 44 BRA B
ROGERS GEORGE A 44 LED B
ROGERS GEORGE A 44 OXF B
ROGERS HARVEY A 44 FIS B
ROGERS HENRY A 39 HAY B
ROGERS HENRY W A 35 WAR W
ROGERS HORACE A 44 LED B
ROGERS HUGH A 25 HAY W
ROGERS ISAAC A 44 LED B
ROGERS ISHAM A 44 DUT B
ROGERS J B A 44 BEA B
ROGERS J C A 44 BEA W
ROGERS J H A 25 SHO W
ROGERS JAMES A 44 HEN B
ROGERS JAMES C A 35 ROC W
ROGERS JESSEE A 44 BEA B
ROGERS JOHN T A 39 LOU W
ROGERS JOSEPH A 26 GRI W
ROGERS LEWIS A 46 SUM B
ROGERS LEWIS A 99 BUS B
ROGERS MATHIS A 35 MAG W
ROGERS MITCHELL A 44 BEA B
ROGERS NED A 44 OXF B
ROGERS NICHOLAS A 26 GRI W
ROGERS PETER A 39 FRA B
ROGERS RANDEL A 44 DUT B
ROGERS REUBEN A 39 GRI W
ROGERS ROBT R D A 28 04A B
ROGERS RUFUS A 28 8TH B
ROGERS SAML A 44 FOR B
ROGERS T J A 44 BEA W
ROGERS THOMAS A 28 10T B
ROGERS THOMAS A 35 MAG W
ROGERS THOMAS A 35 WAR W
ROGERS WILLIAM A 37 ROB B
ROGERS WILLIAM A 44 OXF B
ROGERS WILLIE A 44 BEA W
ROGERS WILLIS A 44 FIS W
ROGERS WM A 39 GRI W
ROGERSON J W R 24 EDE W
REJECTED BY THE BOARD
ON REVISION
WAS CONSTABLE BEFORE THE
WAR & ENGAGED IN REBEL-
LION. FINAL REVISION
ROGERSON MATHEW A 24 EDE W
ROGERSON WM H A 19 BE1 W
ROGGERS ALLEN A 32 JAC W
ROGGERS ELETIA A 32 JAC W
ROHM DAVID A 40 DEC W
ROLING FRANKLING A 53 GER B

ROLLAND M A 39 JOR W
ROLLENS ERASMOS A 44 ISL B
ROLLINGS MARK A 30 IND B
ROLLINS D D R 26 MOO W
MILITIA OFFICER
ROLLINS D O A 26 MOO W
ROLLINS JOHN P A 26 MOO W
ROLLINS L R A 26 MOO W
ROLLINS R A 26 BOR W
ROLLINS WILLIAM A A 53 LA1 W
ROLLS ANDREW A 53 SWA B
ROMAINE JOHN A 28 01A W
ROMAINE WM H A 28 01A W
ROME JOHN A 28 02N B
ROMINGER ELI C A 32 CLE W
ROMINGER SANDY A 32 CLE B
ROMMGER ANDREW A 32 THO W
CERTIF
ROMMIGER J E A 32 SHE W
ROMMIGER JORDON A 32 SHE W
ROMMIGER PAUL A 32 SHE W
ROMMIGER PHILLIP A 32 SHE W
ROOK A L A 46 HIG W
ROOKS DEMPSEY A 28 03A B
ROOKS JAMES A 30 POP W
ROPER FREDRICK S A 53 LA1 W
ROPER JOHN A 53 LA1 B
ROPER P H A 40 CAN W
ROPER SAMUEL A 53 LA1 B
ROPER WILLIAM F A 53 LA2 W
ROSE ALEXANDER A 53 LA1 W
ROSE AMDECK A 53 LA1 W
ROSE BEVERLY A 29 FA1 W
TOWN COMMISSIONER AFTER-
WARDS AIDED REBELLION
ROSE DUKE A 37 ROB W
ROSE F R A 29 FA1 W
ROSE GEO M A 29 FA1 W
ROSE GEORGE A 19 POR W
ROSE JAMES A 19 HUN W
ROSE JNO M A 29 FA2 W
ROSE JOHN A 19 HUN W
ROSE JOHN B A 99 BUS W
ROSE JOHN E A 44 TOW W
ROSE JOSEPH A 19 SHA W
ROSE JULIUCCESOR A 53 LA1 B
ROSE KILBEY A 19 HUN W
ROSE MATHEW A 37 ROC W
ROSE MELTON A 29 FA1 W
ROSE NATHAN A 37 ROC B
ROSE ROBERT H A 53 SWA W
ROSE RUBIN A 53 LA1 W
ROSE SAMUEL A 44 HEN B
ROSE SYMONS A 19 MOR B
ROSE TILLMAN F A 19 HUN W
ROSE WILLIAM D A 53 LA1 W
ROSE ZION A 53 LA1 W
ROSEL JOHN A 40 CAN B
ROSEL ROBERT A 40 RHY B
ROSEL SANDY A 40 RHY B
ROSS ADDISON S A 46 ROS W
ROSS CHARLES A 44 FOR W
ROSS COLEMAN A 26 BUR B
ROSS DANIEL J A 29 ROC B
ROSS FRANCIS A 37 PIN B
ROSS HARRISSON A 26 CAR B
ROSS HENRY A 38 FRE B
ROSS HENRY B A 53 GER W
ROSS J P A 44 FOR W
ROSS J W A 44 FOR W
ROSS JAMES A 26 BOR B
ROSS JAMES A 26 SHE W
ROSS JAMES A 28 05A B

ROSS JOHN A 44 FOR W
ROSS JOSEPH A 26 GRI W
ROSS LEMUEL L A 53 GER W
ROSS LEVIN G A 46 ROS W
ROSS M A 44 FOR W
ROSS MADISON A 44 OXF B
ROSS MATTHEW A 26 PEE W
ROSS MOSES A 26 SHE W
ROSS N W A 26 SHE W
ROSS PARKER A 26 MOU B
ROSS SANDY A 29 ROC B
ROSS THOMAS A 46 GRE B
ROSS THORNTON A 37 TA1 B
ROSS VINCEN A 46 SUM B
ROSS WILLIAM A 37 EDW B
ROSS WILLIAM D A 46 ROS W
ROSS YANCY A 46 GRE W
ROSS ZELUS A 44 OXF B
ROSSER ANTHONY A 37 ROB B
ROSSETER JOHN A 28 01A W
ROTHROCK A A A 32 POS W
ROTHROCK HENRY T A 32 POS W
ROTHROCK JOSEPH A 32 BRO W
ROTHROCKS JONATHAN A 32 LEE W
CHAL. FOR HOLDING OFFCE
OF MAGISTRATE BEFORE AND
AFTER REBELLION
ROTHROK J M A 32 POS W
ROTROCK JOSEPH A 32 POS W
ROUGET JAMES A 28 03A W
ROUGHTON MCALLESTER A 28 16T W
ROUNDTREE BENJAMIN A 28 14T B
ROUNDTREE GEO T A 24 UPP W
ROUNDTREE LEWIS A 24 UPP B
ROUNDTREE THOMAS A 28 16T B
ROUNTREE DEMUS A 44 KIT B
ROUNTREE HENRY A 28 05A B
ROUNTREE LOUIS A 28 11T B
ROUNTREE MONROE A 28 6TH B
ROUNTREE RILEY A 28 01A B
ROUSE ALEXANDER A 35 FAI W
ROUSE ALLEN A 28 6TH B
ROUSE ANDREW A 28 05A B
ROUSE BENJAMIN A 35 ISL B
ROUSE DANL A 28 03A B
ROUSE DAVID A 35 KEN W
ROUSE DAVID W A 35 ISL W
ROUSE EMPEROR A 28 7TH B
ROUSE HARVEY A 28 8TH B
ROUSE ISRAEL A 28 16T B
ROUSE JACOB A 35 ISL W
ROUSE JAMES A 28 8TH B
ROUSE JOHN W A 28 8TH W
ROUSE LOUIS A 28 8TH B
ROUSE OWEN W A 35 ISL W
ROUSE ROBERT A 35 MAG W
ROUSE T B A 28 8TH W
ROUTON W B A 44 OXF W
ROUTZAHN L H A 46 GRE W
ROW WILLIS A 44 BRA W
ROWE DAVID A 28 10T W
ROWE DAVID A 28 12T W
ROWE GEORGE H A 28 9TH W
ROWE ISREAL A 19 HAR B
ROWE JOHN A 19 HAR B
ROWE ROBERT H A 37 TA1 W
ROWE SQUIRE A 28 7TH B
ROWE THOMAS A 28 9TH W
ROWE WILEY A 28 10T B
ROWE WILEY A 28 10T W
ROWE WILLIAM A 28 9TH W
ROWE WILLIAM T A 28 10T W
ROWIN HANDY A 29 LOC B

ROWLAND A W A 44 HEN W
ROWLAND B W A 44 HEN W
ROWLAND BENJ A 44 OXF B
ROWLAND D T A 39 JOR W
ROWLAND DANIEL A 44 HEN B
ROWLAND DICK A 44 HEN B
ROWLAND G J A 44 LED W
ROWLAND J H A 44 LED W
ROWLAND JAMES H A 44 HEN W
ROWLAND JNO H A 44 KIT W
ROWLAND ROBERT A 44 TOW W
ROWLAND SAM A 44 TOW B
ROWLAND STEPHEN A 44 HEN B
ROWLAND T T A 39 JOR W
ROWLAND THOMAS A 44 TOW W
ROYAL A A 29 BLA W
ROYAL H G A 46 SUM W
ROYAL J C A 29 FLE W
ROYAL JAMES A A 46 GRE W
ROYAL JAMES F A 46 GRE W
ROYAL JOHN R A 19 SHA W
ROYAL JOSEPH A 19 SHA W
ROYAL MARTIN A 19 SHA W
ROYAL ROBT A 29 FLE W
ROYCROFT B T A 44 DUT W
ROYCROFT K T A 44 DUT W
ROYCROFT THOMAS A 44 DUT W
ROYE ISRAEL A 28 02N B
ROYL CALEB A 46 SUM W
ROYL ELAM A 46 SUM W
ROYL H L A 46 SUM W
ROYL JABEZ A 46 SUM W
ROYL LEWIS A 46 SUM W
ROYSTER ABRAM A 44 SAS B
ROYSTER ADDERSON A 44 SAS B
ROYSTER ALFRED A 44 SAS B
ROYSTER BALAM A 44 YXS B
ROYSTER BANISTER A 44 SAS W
ROYSTER BEN B A 44 OXF B
ROYSTER BENJAMIN A 44 YXS B
ROYSTER BERRY A 44 OXF B
ROYSTER CHARLES A 26 GRI W
ROYSTER CHARLES A 44 YXS B
ROYSTER CHARLES L A 44 YXS B
ROYSTER CLARK A 44 ISL W
ROYSTER CLARKE A 44 YXS B
ROYSTER CYRUS A 44 HEN B
ROYSTER DANDRED A 44 SAS B
ROYSTER DAVID A 39 PUG B
ROYSTER DENNIS A 44 YXR B
ROYSTER EDMOND A 44 OXF B
ROYSTER EDMOND A 44 YXR B
ROYSTER EDWARD A 44 YXS W
ROYSTER ELLIE A 44 HEN B
ROYSTER F A A 44 YXR W
ROYSTER FRANKLIN A 44 SAS B
ROYSTER FREDRICK A 44 YXR B
ROYSTER G D A 44 SAS W
ROYSTER G JR A 44 YXR W
ROYSTER G W A 44 SAS W
ROYSTER GEORGE A 44 HEN B
ROYSTER H T A 44 HEN W
ROYSTER HENDERSON A 44 YXS B
ROYSTER HENRY A 44 HEN B
ROYSTER HENRY A 44 OXF B
ROYSTER HENRY A 44 SAS B
ROYSTER HENRY A 44 YXS B
ROYSTER HENRY A 44 YXS B
ROYSTER HENRY A 44 YXS B
ROYSTER ISAAC A 44 KIT B
ROYSTER JACOB A 44 YXR B
ROYSTER JAMES A 44 SAS B
ROYSTER JAMES A 44 SAS B

ROYSTER JAMES A 44 YXS B
ROYSTER JAMES A 44 YXS B
ROYSTER JEFFERSON A 44 YXS B
ROYSTER JERREMIAH A 44 HEN B
ROYSTER JNO H A 44 SAS W
ROYSTER JOHN A 44 YXR B
ROYSTER LEO A 44 HEN B
ROYSTER LEVI A 44 YXS B
ROYSTER LEWIS A 44 OXF B
ROYSTER LEWIS A 44 YXR B
ROYSTER LEWIS A 44 YXS B
ROYSTER MADISON A 44 OXF B
ROYSTER MAURICE A 44 YXS B
ROYSTER MOSES A 44 SAS B
ROYSTER MOSSES A 44 SAS B
ROYSTER PETER A 44 OXF B
ROYSTER PETER A 44 YXS B
ROYSTER PLEASANT A 44 YXR B
ROYSTER R L A 44 OXF W
ROYSTER RALEIGH A 44 SAS B
ROYSTER RALPH A 44 HEN B
ROYSTER RASSMUS A 44 TOW B
ROYSTER ROBERT D A 37 EDW W
ROYSTER ROBT CHAL A 44 YXR B
ROYSTER RUFUS A 44 YXR B
ROYSTER SETH JR A 44 YXS B
ROYSTER SETH SR A 44 YXS B
ROYSTER THOMAS A 44 HEN B
ROYSTER TYLER A 44 YXR B
ROYSTER W B A 28 03A W
ROYSTER W D A 44 HEN W
ROYSTER WASHINGTON A 44 YXS B
ROYSTER WATKINS A 44 HEN B
ROYSTER WILLIAM A 44 YXS B
ROYSTER WILLIS A 44 ISL B
ROYSTER WILLIS A A 44 OXF W
ROYSTER WM A 44 TOW B
ROYSTER WM B A 44 SAS W
ROYSTER WM E A 44 YXR W
ROYSTER WM H A 44 HEN B
ROYSTER WM L A 44 SAS W
ROZZELL JACOB A 40 DA2 B
RUARK SOLOMON A 19 POR W
RUDD WM L A 39 PUG W
RUDDISILL JOSEPH A 44 YXR W
RUDICEL ALEXANDER A 26 SWA B
RUDICIL M E A 26 SHE W
RUDISILL AARON A 40 DA1 W
RUDISILL ELI J A 40 MAU W
RUDISILL EMANUEL A A 40 BLA W
RUDISILL JACOB A 40 DEC W
RUDISILL JACOB W A 40 MAU B
RUDISILL JONAS A 40 BLA W
RUDISILL JONAS P A 40 MAU W
RUDISILL WYLEY A 40 BLA W
RUDISILL WYLEY M A 40 BLA W
RUE ISAAC A 28 02N B
RUE JAMES B A 28 01A B
RUE JAMES R A 28 01A B
RUE JOHN A 53 GER B
RUE JOHN G A 53 GER W
RUE JOHN H A 28 04A B
RUE JOSHUA A 28 10T B
RUE OSCAR F A 19 POR W
RUE WILLIAM P A 53 FAI W
RUE WM A 28 04A B
RUE WM L A 28 04B B
RUFFIN DANIEL A 39 LOU B
RUFFIN DAVID A 39 HAR B
RUFFIN DAVID C A 37 ROC W
RUFFIN DICKERSON A 37 HOL W
RUFFIN ELIAS A 39 LOU B
RUFFIN GREEN A 39 LOU B

RUFFIN HARRY A 39 LOU B
TRNS FROM GREEN CO
AT SPATES BRIDGE TO
FRANKLIN CO LOUISBURG
RUFFIN ISAAC A 39 LOU B
RUFFIN JAMES A 37 HIG W
RUFFIN JAMES A 37 PIN B
RUFFIN JAMES A 37 WHI B
RUFFIN JERRY A 24 EDE B
RUFFIN JOHN R A 37 HIG W
RUFFIN JOURDAN A 28 05A B
RUFFIN LEWIS JR A 39 FRE B
RUFFIN PETER A 39 HAR B
RUFFIN RICHARD A 37 WHI B
RUFFIN RICHMOND A 37 HIG B
RUFFIN ROBT A 39 LOU B
RUFFIN RUFUS ? A 39 HAR B
RUFFIN THOMAS A 37 HIG W
RUFFIN THOMAS C A 37 ROC W
RUFFIN WASHINGTON 39 LOU B
RUFFIN WYATTE A 39 LOU B
RUFUS STEPHEN A 19 NEW B
RUIK DANIEL A 37 ROB B
RULIFSON J M A 28 03A W
RUMBEAU ABRAM A 24 EDE B
RUMBEAU JOHN A 24 EDE B
RUMBEAU MATTHAIUS A 24 EDE B
RUMFELT H W A 40 STO W
RUMFELT ISSAC A 40 DA1 W
RUMFELT JOHN F A 40 DA1 W
RUMFELT JOHN G A 40 STO W
RUMFELT MARTIN L A 40 DA1 W
RUMFELT ROBERT A 40 CAN W
RUMFELT W H A 40 CAN W
RUMLEY ISRAEL A 46 MCL W
RUMLY MARSHILL A 46 MCL W
RUMLY THOMAS A 46 MON W
RUNELLS ANDREW A 46 JAM B
RUNFORD JOSEPH A 37 ROC B
RUNION BRITTON A 28 03A B
RUNNELS JOHN A 40 BLA W
RUNNELS LAWSON A 40 DA2 W
RUNNELS MARTIN A 40 BLA W
RUNNELS MATTHEW A 40 BLA W
RUNYAN A D A 26 SHE W
RUNYAN JACOB A 26 BUR W
RUNYAN JAMES A 26 SWA W
RUNYAN R H CHAL A 26 BUR W
MILITIA OFFICER &
ENGAGED IN REBELLION
RUSH BENJ A 29 FA1 W
RUSH ISAAC A 32 COT B
RUSH ISAAC A 32 JAC B
RUSH J M A 32 JAC W
RUSHMAN PETER A 37 ROB B
RUSS ANDREW A 26 BUR W
RUSS CHARLES A 53 BUR W
RUSS P R A 26 BUR W
RUSSE DANIEL A 26 MOU W
RUSSE SAMUEL A 26 MOU W
RUSSE T M A 26 MOU W
RUSSEL ALEXANDER A 32 LOF W
RUSSEL DANIEL A 32 JAC W
RUSSEL DAVID A 19 HAD W
RUSSEL EDWARD A 19 HAD W
RUSSEL J W A 46 FRI W
RUSSEL JAMES A 25 PIN W
RUSSEL JAMES A 32 JAC W
RUSSEL JOHN A 53 LA1 B
RUSSEL JONATHAN A 46 JAM W
RUSSEL R G A 44 LED W
RUSSEL ROLLIN A 44 FOR B
RUSSEL SPRIGG A 44 LED B

RUSSEL THOMAS A 19 HAD B
RUSSEL Z A 32 JAC W
RUSSELL A B A 29 FA1 W
RUSSELL CHARLES A 28 05A B
RUSSELL CYRUS A 44 OXF B
RUSSELL DANIEL W R 72 SWA W
ROADMASTER BEFORE THE
WAR & AFTERWARDS.
HE ALSO PARTICIPATED
IN THE REBELLION
RUSSELL DAVID W A 19 BE1 W
RUSSELL E D A 19 HAD W
RUSSELL EDMOND A 72 SWA W
RUSSELL GEORGE A 28 7TH B
RUSSELL GRANDISON A 44 OXF B
RUSSELL H C A 28 01B W
RUSSELL H C A 44 TAR W
RUSSELL HABAKUK A 19 HAD W
RUSSELL HENRY A 19 BE1 W
RUSSELL ISAAC A 44 OXF B
RUSSELL JACOB A 44 OXF B
RUSSELL JAMES A 28 05A B
RUSSELL JNO C A 44 OXF W
RUSSELL JOHN A 28 16T B
RUSSELL JOHN A 37 TA1 B
RUSSELL JOSEPH A 44 YXR B
RUSSELL MANSFIELD A 72 SWA B
RUSSELL NEVILLE A 19 HAD W
RUSSELL P M A 19 HAD W
RUSSELL RICHARD A 44 HEN B
RUSSELL S E A 29 FA1 W
RUSSELL SMITH J A 53 GER W
RUSSELL THOMAS A 19 BE1 W
RUSSELL W A A 46 HIG W
RUSSELL WILIAM A 19 BE1 W
RUSSELL WILLIAM A 37 TA2 B
RUSSELL WM F A 29 FA1 W
RUSSELL WM H A 44 TAR W
RUSSELL WM J A 29 FA1 W
RUSSELL YORK A 53 GER B
RUSSELLS GEO A 72 SWA B
RUSSLE GEORGE L A 32 THO W
RUSSOM ABIJAH A 46 ROS B
RUSSOM ELIHU A 46 GRE W
RUSSOM JAMES A A 46 GRE W
RUST HENRY A 46 GRE W
RUSTELL JOHN A 19 BE1 W
RUTLEDG MILES A 40 SAN B
RUTLEDGE A R A 40 RHY W
RUTLEDGE JAMES A 40 RHY W
RUTLEDGE JEREMIAH A 37 TA1 B
RUTLEDGE ROBERT A 40 DA1 W
RUTLEDGE ROBERTUS G A 40 DA1 W
CERTIFICATE GRANTED
TO LINCOLN CO NC
APL 18 1868
RUTLEDGE W G A 40 RHY W
RUTTER WILLIAM H A 37 ROC W
RYAL WM TITUS A 28 02N B
RYAL WRIGHT A 28 02N B
RYALS ALFORD A 29 LOC B
RYALS D W A 28 04B W
RYAN ADRION A 46 GRE W
RYAN BENJAMIN A 30 ROA B
RYAN JAMES A 28 04A B
CERTIFICATE GRANTED
TO CROATAN
RYAN JAMES M A 46 GRE W
RYAN STEPHEN A 29 FLE W
RYAN THADDEUS A 24 EDE B
RYAN WATSON A 28 04A B
RYBROWN ANDREW A 40 CAN W
RYBURN W E A 26 SHE W
RYLES JNO A 29 FA1 B
RYOUST CHARLES A 19 BE1 B

\- S -

SABISTON DAVID O A 19 BE2 W
SABISTON ELIJAH A 19 MOR W
SABISTON GEO W A 19 BE1 W
SABISTON JAMES A 19 BE1 W
SABISTON JOHN A 19 MOR W
SABISTON JOHN A 19 NEW W
SABISTON JOHN T A 19 BE1 W
SABISTON JOSEPH W A 19 BE1 W
SABISTON MANASSAH A 19 BE1 W
SABISTON WILLIAM A 19 BE1 W
SABISTON WM B A 19 HAR W
SABRIE STOKERY A 19 BE1 B
SADBERRY LEWIS A 19 BE1 B
SADDLER ALFRED A 53 SWA W
SADDLER JAMES B A 53 SWA W
SADDLER JOHN G A 53 SWA W
SADDLER WILLIAM J A 53 SWA W
SADDLER WM E A 28 16T W
SADLER BENJAMIN A 53 FAI W
SADLER BENNET A 53 GER W
SADLER CALVIN G A 53 GER W
SADLER GREEN A 53 LA1 W
SADLER HENRY A 40 RHY W
SADLER ISIAH S A 53 FAI W
SADLER MERRICK A 53 LA1 B
SWAN QUARTER CERT RES
SADLER MILTON A 53 LA1 W
SADLER NOAH S A 53 FAI W
SADLER RICHARD A 53 LA1 W
SADLER RICHARD T A 53 LA1 W
SADLER RILEY B A 53 FAI W
SADLER ROBERT A 53 LA1 B
SADLER SAMUEL A 53 GER W
SADLER SAMUEL R A 53 LA1 W
SADLER SHADICK A 53 LA2 W
SADLER SHADRACK M A 53 FAI W
SADLERSON LEWIS A 53 FAI B
SADUCE WILLIAM A 19 SMY W
SAFERIGHT ABNER A 46 GRE W
SAFERIGHT CALVIN A 46 ROS W
SAFERIGHT HENRY A 46 GRE W
SAFERIGHT HENRY A 46 ROS W
SAFERIGHT JEREMIAH A 46 ROS W
SAFERIGHT JESSE A 46 ROS W
SAFERIGHT JOHN A 46 GRE W
SAINTSING WILEY A 32 DAV W
SALEM PETER A 28 04A B
SALISBURY MOSES A 37 HIC B
SALMON BRYANT A 29 FA1 W
SALMON KILBY A 35 ROC W
SALMON R A 29 LOC W
SALMON RANDALL A 29 FA1 W
SALTEN JOHN A 37 MAN B
SALTER CHRISTOPHER A 19 POR W
SALTER DAVID W A 28 16T W
SALTER EDWARD A 28 9TH W
SALTER ELIJAH B A 19 SHA W
SALTER HARMON A 19 HUN W
SALTER HENRY A 19 HUN W
SALTER JAMES A 19 HUN W
SALTER JAMES A 19 HUN W
SALTER JAMES A 28 05A B
SALTER JAMES MONROE A 28 03B B
SALTER JOHN A 19 HUN W
SALTER JOHN A A 19 DAV W
SALTER JOHN B A 19 DAV W
SALTER JOHN H A 19 BE1 W
SALTER JOS A 46 GRE B
SALTER JOSEPH A 19 BE1 W
SALTER JOSEPHUS A 19 HUN W
SALTER OLIVER A 19 HUN W
SALTER OWEN A 19 HUN W
SALTER PERHAM A 19 HUN W
SALTER RILEY L A 19 SHA W
SALTER SAMUEL W A 19 HUN W
SALTER T H A 28 9TH W
SALTER TISON A 19 HUN W
SALTER WALLACE A 19 HUN W
SALTER WARREN A 28 10T W
SALTER WILLIAM A 19 HUN W
SALTER WILLIAM A 28 02N W
SALTER WILLIS A 19 HUN W
SALTER WILSON SR A 19 HUN W
SALTER WM E A 19 HUN W
SALTER WM L A 19 HUN W
SALTER WM W A 19 POR W
SALYER SAML A 28 01B W
SAM WILLIAM A 28 9TH B
SAMPLE JAMES A 19 BE1 W
SAMPSON DEMPSEY A 19 BE1 B
SAMPSON JOHN A 30 CUR B
SAMPSON LUCUS A 19 BE2 B
SAMPSON SIMMONS A 30 CUR B
SAMSON WM A 19 NEW B
SAMUEL DAVID D A 19 BE1 W
SANDELING CALEB A 30 COI W
SANDERFER GREEN A 44 BEA W
SANDERFER W N A 44 BEA W
SANDERFUL JOEL A 99 BUS W
SANDERLIN J W A 30 IND W
SANDERLIN JORDAN A 30 IND B
SANDERLIN THOMAS A 30 MOY W
SANDERLIN WILSON A 30 IND W
SANDERS ABRAHAM A 28 7TH B
SANDERS ALEXR A 28 04A B
SANDERS ALFRED A 72 SWA B
SANDERS ANTHONY A 28 04A B
SANDERS BENJAMIN A 53 FAI W
SANDERS CALVIN A 24 MID W
SANDERS D C A 26 SHE W
SANDERS DANL A 29 FA1 B
SANDERS DAVID A 40 CAN B
SANDERS DAVID A 46 MON W
SANDERS DAVID S A 19 BE1 W
SANDERS DICK A 35 CYP B
SANDERS EDWARD A 72 SWA B
SANDERS ELI W A 19 MOR W
SANDERS ELIAS A 28 04A B
SANDERS G S A 26 BOR W
SANDERS HARMON A 28 16T B
SANDERS HARRY A 29 FA1 B
SANDERS HASTY A 72 SWA B
SANDERS HOLIDAY A 72 SWA B
COPIED FROM DUPLICATE
SANDERS ISAAC C A 40 CAN W
SANDERS ISOM A 32 JAC B
SANDERS J J A 46 KIN W
SANDERS J W A 19 HAD W
SANDERS JAMES A 28 04B B
SANDERS JEFFREY A 26 SHE W
SANDERS JOHN A 28 05A B
SANDERS JOHN A 28 15T W
SANDERS JOHN A 37 ROB B
SANDERS JOSUA A 26 SHE W
SANDERS K P A 39 SPE W
SANDERS LAMB A 24 EDE B
SANDERS M W A 26 SHE W
SANDERS MANUEL A 46 SUM B
SANDERS MICHAEL A 24 EDE B
SANDERS MINOR A 28 04A B
SANDERS NELSON A 28 9TH B
SANDERS P H A 19 NEW W

SANDERS PETER A 53 SWA B
SANDERS POMPEY A 28 12T B
SANDERS POMPEY A 28 9TH B
SANDERS R R A 46 KIN W
SANDERS STEPHEN A 24 MID W
SANDERS WILLIAM F A 72 SWA B
SANDERS WILSON A 28 03B B
SANDERSON AARON A 53 LA1 B
SANDERSON ALBERT A 53 LA1 B
SANDERSON ANDREW A 53 LA1 B
SANDERSON BURAGE A 53 LA1 B
SANDERSON DANIEL A 30 NAR W
SANDERSON DEMPSEY A 53 LA1 B
SANDERSON ELI A 53 FAI B
SANDERSON ERASMUS A 53 LA2 W
SANDERSON EVINS A 53 FAI B
SANDERSON GEORGE A 53 LA1 B
SANDERSON GEORGE H A 35 SMI W
SANDERSON GEORGE JR A 53 FAI B
SANDERSON GEORGE SR A 53 FAI B
SANDERSON GEORGE W A 53 FAI B
SANDERSON GREGORY A 72 SWA W
SANDERSON HAMAN A 53 FAI B
SANDERSON ISAAC A 35 LIM W
SANDERSON IVY A 35 SMI W
SANDERSON JOHN A 30 IND W
SANDERSON JOHN A 35 LIM W
SANDERSON LEVY A 35 LIM W
SANDERSON LOUIS A 35 LIM W
SANDERSON MERRICK A 53 LA1 B
SANDERSON NATHAN A 53 FAI B
SANDERSON RILEY A 53 FAI B
SANDERSON RUBIN A 53 FAI B
SANDERSON SAMUEL A 53 FAI B
SANDERSON SAMUEL H A 53 LA1 W
SANDERSON STEWART A 53 FAI B
SANDERSON SYLVESTER A 53 FAI B
SANDERSON THOMAS H A 30 COI W
SANDFORD ABB A 44 YXS B
SANDFORD ALEXR A 44 YXS B
SANDFORD ANDERSON A 44 YXS B
SANDFORD CHARLES A 44 YXS B
SANDFORD CHRISTOPHERA 44 YXS B
SANDFORD EPPS A 44 YXS B
SANDFORD JAMES A 44 YXS B
SANDFORD JAMES A 44 YXS W
SANDFORD JAS R A 44 YXS W
SANDFORD JOSEPH A 44 YXS B
SANDFORD R F A 44 YXS W
SANDFORD THOS H A 44 YXS W
SANDFORD WILLIAM A 30 MOY W
SANDLIN ALSA A 35 LIM W
SANDLIN DANIEL A 35 LIM W
SANDLIN FREDK A 28 05A B
SANDLIN GEORGE A 37 WEB W
SANDLIN HIRAM L A 35 LIM W
SANDLIN JAMES A 35 KEN B
SANDLIN JERRY A 35 LIM W
SANDLIN JESSE A 35 LIM W
SANDLIN JOHN A 28 15T W
SANDLIN KILLIS A 28 05A B
SANDLIN NICODEMUS A 35 LIM W
SANDLIN ROBERT A 35 LIM W
SANDLIN ROBERT SR A 35 LIM W
SANDLIN WAXEL A 35 LIM W
SANDLIN WILLIAM A 35 LIM W
SANDLIN WILLIAM J A 35 LIM W
SANDLING ARTHUR A 39 FRA W
SANDLING C H A 44 BRA W
SANDLING H K A 44 BRA W
SANDLING JACKSON A 30 NOR W
SANDON HENRY A 28 05A B
SANDRIDGE THOMAS J A 46 GRE W

SANDSBURY CHAS H A 24 EDE W
SANDY JOHN A 29 ROC W
SANDY JOHN A A 29 SEV W
SANDY WM J A 29 ROC W
SANE NATHAN A 32 DAV W
SANFORD DANIEL A 37 ROC B
SANFORD J W A 29 FA1 W
SANFORD JACOB A 44 TAR B
SANFORD JILES A 44 BEA W
SANFORD MOSES A 40 CAN W
SANFORD THOMAS A 40 BLA W
SANFORD W T A 44 BEA W
SANPLE H B A 40 CAN W
SANSING P A 26 CAR W
SAPENFIELD ALFORD A 32 TYR W
SAPP A J A 46 HIG W
SAPP ANDERSON A 46 JAM B
SAPP J A A 46 KIN W
SAPP JESSE W A 46 FRI W
SARRATT COLLUMBUS A 26 MOU B
SARRATT FELO A 26 BUR B
SARRATT GOODMAN A 26 MOU B
SARRATT GRIFFIN A 26 BUR B
SARRATT JOSEPH A 26 MOU B
SARRATT N J A 26 MOU W
SARRATT O C A 26 BUR W
SARRATT RANSUM A 26 BUR B
SARRATT UGINIUS A 26 MOU W
SARVICE FRANKLIN A A 40 DA2 W
SARVICE JOHN R A 40 DEC W
SARVICE SAMUEL T A 40 DA1 W
SARVIS ALEXANDER E A 26 GOF W
SARVIS THOMAS A 26 GOF W
SASMER JERRY A 37 HIG B
SASNETT JOSHUA T A 28 15T W
SASNETT REDDING B A 28 15T W
SASSER BENJ A 28 04A B
SASSER W B A 35 WOL W
SASSNUT ROBERT A 37 PEN B
SATATHIGHT BENJ A 19 BE1 B
SATCHELL JOB A 53 FAI B
SATCHELL SETH A 28 9TH B
CERTIF GIVEN LIVES
NOW AT NEW BERN
SATEFIELD J B A 24 MID W
SATERTHWAITE MAJOR JA 37 HIC A
SATTERFIELD BANNER A 46 KIN B
SATTERFIELD ISAAC A 24 EDE B
SATTERFIELD JEREMIAHA 24 EDE B
SATTERFIELD JOHN A 24 EDE B
SATTERFIELD JOHN A 46 KIN W
SATTERFIELD TRADWELLA 24 EDE B
SATTERFIELD WM A 24 EDE B
SATTERTHWAITE
ELIAS S A 53 LA2 W
SATTERTHWAITE
GEORGE H A 53 BUR W
SATTERTHWAITE
JAMES F A 53 BUR W
SATTERTHWAITE L E A 28 11T W
SATTERTHWAITE POMPEYA 28 05A B
SATTERTHWAITE
WILLIAM N A 53 BUR W
SATTERWHITE A A 44 SAS W
SATTERWHITE ADAM A 44 HEN B
SATTERWHITE ADAM A 44 YXR B
SATTERWHITE BOOKER A 44 HEN B
SATTERWHITE D W A 44 RAG W
SATTERWHITE DAVID A 44 YXS B
SATTERWHITE ELI A 44 HEN B
SATTERWHITE HARRY A 44 YXS B
SATTERWHITE HENRY A 44 ISL B
SATTERWHITE HENRY A 44 YXR B

SATTERWHITE HOWELL A 44 RAG W
SATTERWHITE ISOM A 44 YXS B
SATTERWHITE J E A 44 ISL W
SATTERWHITE J F A 44 RAG W
SATTERWHITE J P A 44 FIS W
EPPING FORREST DIST
SATTERWHITE JAS M A 44 ISL W
SATTERWHITE JOHN A 44 ISL W
SATTERWHITE LEWIS A 44 SAS B
SATTERWHITE M H A 44 RAG W
SATTERWHITE MAT A 44 HEN B
SATTERWHITE OWEN A 44 BRA B
SATTERWHITE PETER A 44 TOW B
SATTERWHITE ROBT A 44 HEN B
SATTERWHITE ROBT A 44 RAG W
SATTERWHITE SOLOMON A 44 YXR W
SATTERWHITE SQUIRE A 44 YXS B
SATTERWHITE STEPHEN A 44 ISL W
SATTERWHITE THOS A 44 SAS W
SATTERWHITE TIM A 44 YXS B
SATTERWHITE W H A 44 ISL W
SATTERWHITE W L A 44 RAG W
SATTERWHITE WM A 44 YXS B
SATTERWITE CHARLES A 44 DUT W
SATTEWHITE JNO A 44 BRA B
SAUNDERS ABE A 40 DA1 B
SAUNDERS J G A 44 HEN W
SAUNDERS JESSEE A 30 POP W
SAUNDERS JOHN A 30 CUR W
SAUNDERS KERNEY A 44 KNA W
SAUNDERS PETER A 28 01A B
SAUNDERS ROBT A 28 05A B
SAUNDERS THOMAS A 30 NAR W
SAUNDERS THOMAS A 30 POW B
SAUNDERS THOMAS L A 40 DA1 W
SAUNDERS W H A 29 FA1 W
SAUNDERSON ELI A 25 HAY W
SAUNDERSON G W A 25 HAY W
SAUNDERSON J PERRY A 25 HAY W
SAUNDERSON JESSEE A 30 CUR W
SAUNDERSON LATIMORE A 30 IND W
SAUNDERSON LEWIS A 30 MOY B
SAUNDERSON ROBERT A 30 CUR B
SAUNDERSON W T A 30 IND W
CHANGED TO MOYOCK
SAVAG LEWIS A 37 MAN W
SAVAGE A J A 28 01A W
SAVAGE ABRAM A 37 TA1 B
SAVAGE ALLEN A 37 HIC A
SAVAGE ARCHY B A 35 SMI B
SAVAGE AUGUSTUS A 37 EDW W
SAVAGE BERRY A 37 PEN B
SAVAGE BUCK A 37 TA1 B
SAVAGE BUKRELL A 37 PEN W
SAVAGE BYTHAL A 37 EDW W
SAVAGE CALVIN A 37 EDW W
SAVAGE CHARLES W A 35 ROC W
CERTIFICATE GIVEN
APRIL 11, 1868
SAVAGE DEMPSEY A 37 EDW B
SAVAGE ELI A 37 EDW B
SAVAGE FRANCIS A 35 ISL W
SAVAGE FRANK A 19 NEW B
SAVAGE FRANK A 37 EDW B
SAVAGE FREDERICK A 35 ISL W
SAVAGE GEORGE A 37 TA1 B
SAVAGE HENRY A 37 PEN B
SAVAGE HENRY T A 35 ISL W
SAVAGE HENRY T A 37 HIC A
SAVAGE JACK A 37 PEN B
SAVAGE JACOB A 37 EDW B
SAVAGE JAMES A 37 EDW B
SAVAGE JAMES A 37 HOL W

SAVAGE JAMES M A 35 ROC W
SAVAGE JESSIE T A 37 EDW W
SAVAGE JOHN A 28 05A B
SAVAGE JOHN A 35 ISL W
SAVAGE JOHN A 37 EDW B
SAVAGE JOHN A 37 HIG W
SAVAGE JOHN A 37 TA1 B
SAVAGE JOHN FENTON A 37 EDW B
SAVAGE JOHN H A 37 EDW W
SAVAGE JOHN L A 37 MAN W
SAVAGE JOHN R A 24 MID W
SAVAGE JOSEPH A 37 EDW B
SAVAGE JOSEPH A 39 DAV W
SAVAGE JOSEPH B A 37 EDW W
HALIFAX CO
SAVAGE JOSEPH B A 37 EDW W
SAVAGE KENDALL A 37 TA1 B
SAVAGE LAYFAYETT A 37 HIC A
SAVAGE LEWIS R 37 EDW B
CONVICTED OF LARCENY
SAVAGE MARK A 37 HIC B
SAVAGE MATHEW A 37 TA1 B
SAVAGE MICHAEL A 35 ROC W
SAVAGE OLLE A 37 EDW B
SAVAGE QUENY A 37 EDW B
SAVAGE RAYMOND A 37 EDW B
SAVAGE REUBEN A 37 EDW B
SAVAGE RICHARD A A 37 EDW W
SAVAGE ROBERT A 37 EDW B
SAVAGE ROBERT A 37 EDW B
SAVAGE SAMUEL A 37 TA1 B
SAVAGE SMITH A 37 TA1 B
SAVAGE TAYLOR A 35 ROC W
SAVAGE WILLIAM C A 35 ROC W
SAVAGE WILLIAM R A 37 EDW W
SAVAGE WILLIAM W A 37 PIN W
SAWYER ASA A 30 IND W
SAWYER BENJAMIN A 53 FAI W
SAWYER BENJAMIN R A 53 FAI W
SAWYER CALEB T JR A 30 POW W
APRIL 8, 1868
SAWYER CHARLES A 28 04A B
SAWYER CHARLES A 53 SWA W
SAWYER CHARLES H A 35 KEN W
SAWYER CORNELIUS A 19 BE1 B
SAWYER COSEY A 30 TUL W
SAWYER DANIEL H A 53 GER W
SAWYER DAVID D A 30 IND W
SAWYER DEMPSEY A 53 GER W
SAWYER EDWD J A 29 FA1 B
SAWYER FRE'D A 29 FA1 B
SAWYER FREDERICK A 28 16T W
SAWYER GEO W A 30 IND W
SAWYER GILBERT H A 53 GER W
SAWYER HANEABLE A 53 GER B
SAWYER HARDY G A 53 GER W
SAWYER HARDY W A 53 GER W
SAWYER HARVEY A 35 KEN W
SAWYER HENRY A 28 05A B
SAWYER HENRY H A 28 16T W
SAWYER HIRAM A A 35 KEN W
SAWYER ISAAC A 19 BE1 B
SAWYER ISAAC S A 53 FAI W
SAWYER JAMES A 30 COI W
SAWYER JAMES B A 30 POW W
SAWYER JEROME B JR A 28 16T W
SAWYER JEROME B SR A 28 16T W
SAWYER JESSE A 28 16T W
SAWYER JESSE L A 28 16T W
SAWYER JNO L F A 30 IND W
SAWYER JOHN A 24 EDE B
SAWYER JOHN A 28 03A B
SAWYER JOHN A 28 05A B

SAWYER JOHN A 28 15T W
SAWYER JOHN A 46 SUM B
SAWYER JOHN A 53 FAI W
SAWYER JOHN B A 53 FAI W
SAWYER JOHN JR A 24 EDE B
SAWYER JORDAN A 28 15T W
SAWYER K R A 30 IND W
SAWYER L G A 30 IND W
SAWYER LAMUEL B A 53 GER W
SAWYER LEVIN B A 37 PEN W
SAWYER MACK A 24 EDE B
SAWYER MARK A 28 17T W
SAWYER MARTIN A 28 16T W
SAWYER MICAGA A 28 16T W
SAWYER MICAJAH A 53 FAI W
SAWYER MILES A 30 CUR W
SAWYER MITCHELL A 28 16T W
SAWYER N GRANDY A 28 15T W
SAWYER NELSON A 30 GIB W
SAWYER RICHD A 28 02N B
SAWYER SETH A 53 SWA W
SAWYER SHELDON A 28 16T W
SAWYER SILIE A 28 16T W
SAWYER SPENCER A 30 TUL W
SAWYER SQUIRE A 28 03A B
SAWYER THOMAS J A 28 16T W
SAWYER W A A 30 CUR W
SAWYER WARNER A 30 POW W
SAWYER WILLBY A 26 BOR B
SAWYER WILLIAM A 30 IND W
SAWYER WM A 28 16T B
SAWYER WM B A 28 16T W
SAWYER WM H A 28 16T W
SAWYER WM R A 28 16T W
SAWYER ZACHRIAH A 53 GER W
SAYDAN J V N A 19 BE1 W
SCABORO ISHAM A 29 FA1 B
SCALES HAYWOOD A 44 HEN B
SCALES JACOB A 46 GRE W
SCANLIN R T A 29 FA1 W
SCARBO JAMES A 37 SHA B
SCARBORO LOUIS A 38 FRE B
SCARBOROUG HENDRED A 53 KEN W
SCARBOROUG HENRY B A 53 HAT W
SCARBOROUGH ARNOLD HA 53 KEN W
SCARBOROUGH ELI O A 35 MAG W
SCARBOROUGH EZEKEL HA 53 KEN W
SCARBOROUGH GEO W JRA 30 NOR W
SCARBOROUGH GEO W SRA 30 NOR W
SCARBOROUGH
IGNATIOUS A 53 KEN W
SCARBOROUGH JOHN A A 53 KEN W
SCARBOROUGH JOSEPH A 53 KEN W
SCARBOROUGH MANCIL A 53 KEN W
SCARBOROUGH MARK A 53 HAT B
SCARBOROUGH PHAROH A 53 KEN W
SCARBOROUGH
THADIUS C A 53 OCR W
SCARBOROUGH THOMAS A 53 KEN W
SCARBOROUGH TIM F A 53 KEN W
SCARBOROUGH WILLIAM A 53 KEN W
SCARBOROUGH
WILLIAM N A 53 KEN W
SCARBOUR JESSY A 37 WHI B
SCARBREW EDWARD A 37 HIG B
SCARLETT SAMUEL A 37 ROC W
SCARLOTT WM H A 46 GRE W
SCEWELL THOMAS A 37 MAN B
SCHENCK HENRY A 26 GRI W
SCHENCK RICH A 26 GRI B
SCHENCK THOMAS A 26 GRI B
SCHENCK WILLIAM A 26 GRI B
SCHENCK WILLIAM A 40 DA1 B

SCHOOLER JNO A 44 SAS B
SCHOOLFIELD D G A 46 MON W
SCHRADER JACK A 37 ROC B
SCIPPER LENSEY A 44 SAS B
8 MOS REJ
SCISM PETER A 26 CAR W
SCOGGINS L M A 26 MOO W
SCOT MANUEL O A 39 HAR B
SCOTT MARTIN A 46 MON B
SCOTT A B A 46 JAM W
SCOTT A WALKER A 46 GRE W
SCOTT ABRAM A 40 RHY W
SCOTT ALLEN H A 46 GRE W
SCOTT ANDREW A 40 DA1 B
SCOTT ANDY A 46 GRE B
SCOTT BENJ A 46 GRE W
SCOTT BENJAMIN H A 28 16T W
SCOTT C A A 28 04B B
SCOTT CALVIN A 46 FRI B
SCOTT CHAS A 28 03A B
SCOTT CORNELIUS A 28 05A B
SCOTT DANIEL A 28 14T W
SCOTT DANIEL A 46 FRI B
SCOTT DAVEY A 44 OXF B
SCOTT DAVID A 46 GRE W
SCOTT DAVID A 46 MON W
SCOTT DAVID W A 72 SWA W
SCOTT DENNARD A 28 14T W
SCOTT DONNELL A 46 GRE W
SCOTT E N A 40 SAN W
SCOTT EDWARD A 44 HEN B
SCOTT EDWARD A 44 OXF B
SCOTT ELLINGTON A 39 JOR B
SCOTT FRANCIS M A 46 GRE W
SCOTT FRANKLIN A 32 SHE W
SCOTT FREDK A 29 FA1 B
SCOTT G W A 19 HAR W
SCOTT H O A 39 FRA W
SCOTT HENDERSON A 44 HEN B
SCOTT HENDERSON H A 28 14T W
SCOTT HENRY A 30 MOY W
SCOTT ISAAC A 44 TOW B
SCOTT J W A 44 BRA W
SCOTT JACK A 46 GRE B
SCOTT JAMES A 40 DA1 B
SCOTT JAMES A 44 FIS B
SCOTT JESSIE A 29 FA1 B
SCOTT JNO A 29 FA1 B
SCOTT JOHN A 28 14T W
SCOTT JOHN A 28 7TH B
CERTIFICATE GIVEN LIVES
AT POLLOCKSVILLE NC
SCOTT JOHN A 44 HEN B
SCOTT JOHN A 46 FRI W
SCOTT JOHN D A 46 GRE W
SCOTT JOHN E A 29 ROC B
SCOTT JOHN W A 46 GRE W
SCOTT JORDAN A 35 CYP W
SCOTT JORDON A 29 ROC B
SCOTT JOS L A 46 GRE W
SCOTT JOSEPH A 30 MOY W
SCOTT JOSEPH A 37 HIG B
SCOTT JOSEPH A 46 SUM B
SCOTT JOSHUA A 28 16T W
SCOTT JUNIUS A 28 11T B
SCOTT LEROY A 28 16T W
SCOTT LEWIS A 37 WHI B
SCOTT LEWIS A 46 SUM B
SCOTT LINDSAY A 46 GRE B
SCOTT MAJOR A 24 EDE B
SCOTT NEWTON A 46 GRE B
SCOTT OLIVER A 46 GRE B
SCOTT PETER A 19 HAD B

SCOTT PETER A 39 JOR B
SCOTT R M A 46 FRI W
SCOTT RILEY A 28 17T W
SCOTT RUFUS A 46 GRE W
SCOTT SAMUEL A 30 POP W
SCOTT SPENCER A 29 FA1 B
SCOTT STEPHEN A 28 04A B
SCOTT T B A 46 JAM W
SCOTT T H DR A 39 DAV W
SCOTT TILMON A 40 DA1 B
SCOTT WALTER A 35 LIM W
SCOTT WILLIAM A 28 14T W
SCOTT WILLIAM A 46 SUM W
SCOTT WILLIAM M A 30 COI W
APRIL 10, 1868
SCOTT WM A A 19 SMY W
SCOTT WM H A 29 FA1 B
SCOTT WM L A 46 GRE W
SCROGGINS GILES A 29 FA1 B
SCROGS DAVID A 25 HAY W
SCROGS ENOS A 25 HAY W
SCROGS J C A 25 HAY W
SCROGS JOSEPH E A 25 HAY W
SCRUGGS J M A 26 MOU W
SCRUGGS JOHN A 26 MOU W
SCRUGGS L B A 26 MOU W
SCRUGGS T D A 26 MOU W
SCRUGGS WALTOR A 26 WAR W
SEAL CHARLES A 37 TA1 B
SEAPAUGH EDWARD A 26 MOU B
SEAPAUGH HENRY A 26 BUR W
SEAPAUGH J P A 26 BUR W
SEAPAUGH PHILIP A 26 BUR W
SEAPAUGH THOS A 26 SHE B
SEARLES ISBOND R 28 16T W
DOUBTFUL AS TO AGE
SEARLES PETER A 28 03A B
SEARS A 30 IND B
CHARLES/JAMES
SEARS ALEXR A 28 01A B
SEARS B A 44 OXF W
SEARS CALEB T A 30 IND W
SEARS FRANK A 30 IND B
SEARS HENRY B A 53 GER W
SEARS JACK A 30 IND B
SEARS JNO D A 30 IND W
SEARS JOHN A 28 04B B
SEARS JOHN A 30 IND W
SEARS JOSEPH A 30 IND B
SEARS LONDON A 30 IND B
SEARS REUBEN A 37 PEN B
SEARS THOS A 30 IND W
SEARS WILLIAM J A 53 GER W
SEARS WILLIAM R A 30 MOY W
SEAT L C A 46 SUM W
SEAWELL ASA A 99 BUS W
SEBERRY ROLLAN A 29 CAR B
SECARES THOMAS A 37 ROB B
SECHREAST PAUL A 32 SHE W
BY CERTIFICATE
SECHREST J N A 46 HIG W
SECHREST M S A 46 HIG W
SECHREST T A A 46 HIG W
SECHRIST A L A 32 DAV W
SECHRIST ANDREW A 32 LEE W
SECHRIST ANDREW J A 32 THO W
SECHRIST DANIEL A 32 LEE W
SECHRIST FELIX A 32 THO W
SECHRIST FRANKLIN A 32 DAV W
SECHRIST HENRY A 32 THO W
SECHRIST JACOB A 32 DAV W
SECHRIST JESSE S A 32 LEE W
SECHRIST JOHN A 32 DAV W
SECHRIST LAWRENCE A 32 DAV W
SECHRIST S W A 46 FRI W
SEDBERRY B E A 29 FA1 W
SEDBERRY H O A 29 FA1 W
SEDMON THOMAS A 24 EDE B
SEGROVES JOEL A 37 ROC W
SEIB HENRY A 28 01A W
SEIDEL CHARLES F W R 28 8TH W
LIVING OUT OF PRECINCT
SEIDEL WILLIAM A 28 01B W
SELBY BENJAMIN R A 53 LA2 W
SELBY CASWELL A 53 LA1 B
SELBY HOLLAND A 53 LA1 B
SELBY JOHN A 53 LA1 B
SELBY JOHN A 53 LA1 W
SELBY ROBERTS A 53 LA2 B
SELBY WILLIAM B A 53 LA1 W
SELBY WILLIAM F A 53 LA1 B
SELBY WILLIAM P A 53 LA1 W
SELD JOHN A 32 BRO W
SELF ALVIS L A 46 KIN W
SELF B D A 26 GRI W
SELF BENJAMIN A 46 KIN W
SELF J V A 26 WAR W
SELF J W A 26 PEE W
SELF JOHN C A 46 KIN W
SELF LEMUAL A 26 WAR W
SELF RUFUS A 26 WAR W
SELF WILLIAM A 26 PEE W
SELF WILLIAM A 46 KIN W
SELLAR JOHN A 35 MAG B
SELLARS DAVID G A 35 WAR W
SELLARS GEORGE W A 35 WAR W
CERTIFICATE TO
COLUMBUS CO. WHITEVILLE
APRIL 13TH 1868
SELLARS JAS W A 29 FA1 W
SELLARS JOSEPH A 35 MAG W
SELLARS THOMAS A 35 ISL W
SELLECK ROBERT L A 19 BE1 W
SELLERS ALFRED A 40 BLA W
SELLERS E A 26 BOR W
SELLERS F A 26 BOR W
SELLERS F H A 25 SHO W
SELLERS GEORGE A 26 GOF W
SELLERS IRVIN A 29 LOC B
SELLERS J T A 29 FA1 W
SELLERS LEVI J A 35 WAR W
SELLERS N A 26 BOR W
SELLERS P A 26 BOR W
SELLS TELMA A 32 JAC W
SELVY JOSEPH A 40 SAN W
SELVY WM A 40 SAN W
SEMMONS BRYANT A 29 FA2 B
SEMORE SILAS A 30 IND W
SERMON ELIJAH A 53 SWA W
SERMONS WILLIAM W A 53 LA2 W
SERVER FELIX A 32 THO W
CERTIF
SESOM JOHN J A 37 HIG W
SESSION MILTON A 37 ROC B
SESSOM RICHARD H A 37 HIG W
SESSOMS ALEX A 29 LOC W
SESSOMS DAVID A 29 LOC W
SESSOMS HENRY A 29 CED W
SESSOMS HENRY A 29 FA1 W
SESSOMS HENRY S A 37 MAN W
SESSOMS NEAL A 29 LOC W
SESSOMS T L A 29 FLE W
SESSOMS THOS A 29 LOC W
SESSOMS W J A 29 FLE W
SESSOMS WILLIAM W A 37 MAN W
SESSOMS WM A 29 FLE W
SETSER THOMAS R A 25 HAY W
SETTLE MOSES A 46 MON B
SETTLEMIRE A J A 26 MOU W
SETZER CAIN A 40 DA1 B
SETZER HENRY A 40 DA1 W
SEUMORE MATTHEW A 44 FOR W
SEURAT SPENCER A 32 DAV W
SEWELL ELISHA A 53 LA1 W
SEWELL FABIUS A 37 HOL W
SEWELL JOHN A 29 FA1 W
SEWELL THOS B A 19 BE1 W
SEWELL W C A 25 HAY W
SEXTON CORNELIUS A 32 JAC W
SEXTON DANIEL A 32 JAC W
SEXTON E A 25 HAY W
SEXTON JAMES A 32 LOF W
SEXTON WILLIAM A 32 JAC W
SEYMOUR AUG S A 28 01A W
SEYMOUR RIGDON A 28 02N B
SHACKLEFOOT WILLIAM A 37 ROC B
SHACKLEFORD ALLEN A 39 FRE B
SHACKLEFORD JOS A 39 FRA B
SHAD DANIEL A 32 JAC B
SHAD JAMES A 32 JAC B
SHADD TINDALL A 32 SHE B
SHADRACK D J A 44 BRA W
SHADWICK JOHN A 32 BRO W
SHAEFFER E A A 29 FA1 W
SHALER ANDREW A 32 THO W
SHALER JOHN A 32 THO W
SHALLINGTON DANL A 28 01A B
SHALLINGTON ISAC A 37 ROB B
SHANIEHOUSE NATHAN A 39 PUG B
SHANKLIN WILLIAM A 53 LA1 W
SHANKS ALEX A 44 ISL B
SHANKS BUTLER A 44 SAS B
SHANNINGHOUSE
ASBERRY A 28 05A B
SHANNINGHOUSE
JOSHUA A 28 04A B
SHANNON J R A 40 SAN W
SHANNON JAMES A 40 SAN W
SHANNON NATHANIEL A 30 ROA W
SHANNONHOUSE ALFRED A 24 EDE B
SHANNONHOUSE NELSON A 30 CUR B
SHARK ALEX A 29 FA1 B
SHARP A CALDWELL DR A 24 EDE B
SHARP ABEL A 37 PEN B
SHARP ABRAM A 37 HIG B
SHARP ALEXANDER A 32 TYR W
SHARP ALFRED A 46 GIB W
SHARP ARTHUR A 37 HIG B
SHARP AUGUSTINE A 37 HOL B
SHARP BENJAMIN A 37 ROC B
SHARP DAVID A 19 NEW W
SHARP DAVIEL A 37 EDW B
SHARP EDMOND A 37 HIG B
SHARP EDWARD P A 37 SPA W
SHARP EDWIN T A 46 RAG W
SHARP H P A 32 DAV W
SHARP HARDY A 24 MID B
SHARP HENRY A 37 WHI B
SHARP HENRY A A 46 GRE W
SHARP HENRY JR A 46 GIB W
SHARP HORATIO J A 24 MID B
SHARP J W A 24 EDE B
SHARP JAMES B A 37 EDW W
SHARP JENKINS A 24 MID B
SHARP JOHN A 37 ROB B
SHARP JOHN A 37 SPA B
SHARP JOHN A 46 GIB W
SHARP JOHN J A 37 SHA W
SHARP JOHNATHAN A 19 NEW W

SHARP MATHIAS A 32 TYR W
SHARP MOSES A 37 SPA B
SHARP NELSON A 37 EDW B
SHARP R L A 32 TYR W
SHARP R P A 32 TYR W
SHARP R S A 32 TYR W
SHARP SOLOMON A 46 COB W
SHARP STARKY A 24 MID W
SHARP WILLIAM A 19 NEW W
SHARP WILLIS A 32 TYR W
SHAVER MILAS A 28 05A B
SHAW A Y A 46 FRI W
SHAW ALBERT A 30 IND B
SHAW ALEXANDER A 29 SEV B
SHAW AMOS A 29 FA1 B
SHAW ANDERSON T A 39 LOU B
SHAW AUSTIN A 53 LA1 B
SHAW BEN A 39 LOU B
SHAW CHARLES A 29 SEV B
SHAW CHARLES A 37 ROC B
SHAW CHAS A 29 FA1 B
SHAW COBBIN A 39 LOU B
SHAW DANIEL CHAL A 29 QUW B
NO REASON GIVEN
SHAW DANL A 29 GRA W
AFF ST PAULS ROBESON CO
SHAW DAVID A 29 FA1 B
SHAW FINLEY W A 46 COB W
SHAW HANDY A 35 WAR B
SHAW HENRY A 28 05A B
SHAW HENRY A 29 MON B
SHAW HENRY A 32 TYR W
SHAW HUGH A 29 SEV B
SHAW ISAIAH A 39 LOU B
SHAW J H A 32 DAV W
SHAW J K A 39 PUG W
TRANS TO LOUISBURG
SHAW JACK A 39 LOU B
SHAW JAMES A 29 FA1 B
SHAW JAMES A 29 SEV B
SHAW JAMES E A 46 RAG W
SHAW JAMES M A 46 COB W
SHAW JESSIE A 32 DAV W
SHAW JNO A 29 FA1 B
SHAW JNO A 29 FA1 W
SHAW JNO S A 29 FA1 W
SHAW JOHN A 35 WAR W
SHAW JOHN A 44 DUT B
SHAW JOHN F A 46 RAG W
SHAW JOHN K A 39 LOU W
FROM PUGHES HILL
SHAW JOSEPH A 30 POP B
SHAW MATTHEW A 39 LOU B
SHAW MOSES A 44 LED B
SHAW NED A 39 FRA B
SHAW NEILL A 29 ROC W
SHAW OBEDIAH A 32 DAV W
SHAW PHILLIP A 44 FOR B
SHAW ROBT P A 46 RAG W
SHAW SYLVESTER A 53 LA1 B
SHAW THOMAS A 19 BE1 B
SHAW TRADER A 37 ROC B
SHAW WILLIAM R 29 SEV W
COUNTY TRUSTEE AFTERWARDS
TITLE AGENT FOR REBS
SHAW WILLIAM B A 30 IND W
SHAW WILLIS A 53 LA1 B
SHAW WILLIS P A 46 MCL W
SHAW WM H A 46 RAG W
SHAW WM M A 46 RAG W
SHEARER J W A 25 TUS W
SHEARER S J A 25 TUS W
SHEARIN J H A 39 JOR W
SHEARMAN SAMUEL A 25 SHO W
SHEARRAN AARON A 44 DUT W
SHEARRAN J W A 44 DUT W
SHEARRON J B A 44 FOR W
SHEARRON J W A 44 DUT W
SHEARS DAVID A 32 TYR B
SHEETS J W A 32 THO W
CERTIF
SHEETS SILAS A 29 FA1 W
SHEETS SIMION A 32 JAC W
SHEETS WILLIAM A 32 CLE W
SHEFFIELD ISHAM A 35 MAG W
SHEILDS A H A 46 FRI W
SHEILDS W W A 46 FRI W
SHELBY DAVID A 46 ROS W
SHELDON DAVID A 53 SWA B
SHELDON JAMES A 28 8TH B
SHELDON O F A 28 01A W
SHELLEY R W A 32 THO W
IS DEAD
SHELLEY WM W A 32 THO W
SHELLY JOHN A 46 GRE W
SHELTON J H DR A 32 SHE W
SHELTON JACKSON A 25 SHO W
SHELTON L S A 25 TUS W
SHELTON RUFUS A 37 PIN W
SHELTON SQUIRE A 46 FRI B
SHEMWELL O M A 32 TYR W
SHEPARD BENJ A 28 03A B
SHEPARD BENJAMIN A 72 SWA B
SHEPARD BOSTON A 35 CYP B
SHEPARD ENOCH A 28 01A B
SHEPARD GILBERT A 32 DAV B
SHEPARD GREEN A 28 05A B
SHEPARD HENRY A 28 05A B
SHEPARD JAMES A 28 03A B
SHEPARD JAMES A 28 04A B
SHEPARD JAS A 29 FLE W
REMOVED TO
GRAYS CREEK
SHEPARD JAS A 29 GRA W
CERTIFICATE FLEA HILL
SHEPARD JEREH A 28 03A B
SHEPARD JERIMIAH A 28 02N B
SHEPARD JOHN A 28 05A B
SHEPARD MILES A 28 04A B
SHEPARD THOMAS E A 35 MAG W
SHEPARD WILLIAM A 28 02N B
SHEPARD WILLIAM A 99 BUS B
SHEPARD WM B A 24 EDE W
SHEPHERD ABRAM A 46 COB W
SHEPHERD ALEXANDER A 46 GIB W
SHEPHERD ANDY A 46 COB B
SHEPHERD BIRD A 46 KIN W
SHEPHERD DANIEL A 46 COB W
SHEPHERD DAVID JR A 46 COB W
SHEPHERD DAVID SR A 46 COB W
SHEPHERD ELIZA A 29 FA1 W
SHEPHERD G W A 46 JAM W
SHEPHERD GEORGE A 46 GIB W
SHEPHERD GILES A 29 FA1 B
SHEPHERD H C A 39 LOU W
SHEPHERD HENRY A 46 COB W
SHEPHERD HENRY A 46 MCL W
SHEPHERD JACOB A 46 COB W
SHEPHERD JACOB P A 46 COB W
SHEPHERD JAMES M A 46 MCL W
SHEPHERD JAS A 29 CAR B
SHEPHERD JOSHUA A 46 GIB W
SHEPHERD LEWIS A 46 MCL W
SHEPHERD MARTIN A 46 COB W
SHEPHERD REUBEN R A 46 GIB W
SHEPHERD SIMON A 29 FA1 B
SHEPHERD SIMON A 46 COB W
SHEPHERD SOLOMAN A 46 COB W
SHEPHERD THADEUS A 46 GIB W
SHEPHERD W W A 29 FA1 W
SHEPHERD WILY A 46 GRE B
SHEPHERD WM R A 46 MCL W
SHEPPARD CATO A 19 HAR B
SHEPPARD CEZAR A 19 NEW B
SHEPPARD CHADWICK A 19 NEW B
SHEPPARD CHAS A 19 NEW B
SHEPPARD EDWIN A 19 BE1 B
SHEPPARD JOHN A 19 NEW B
SHEPPARD JOHN A 37 HOL B
SHEPPARD MOSES A 19 HAD B
SHEPPARD PETER A 19 MOR B
SHEPPARD SAMUEL A 19 NEW B
SHEPPARD THOMAS A 19 NEW B
SHEPPARD THOS 2ND A 19 NEW B
SHEPPERD W R A 26 GOF W
SHEPPHARD PETER A 19 HAD B
SHEPPHERD ELIJAH A 29 ROC W
SHEPTON GEORGE A 32 LOF W
SHERER ALLEN A 25 HAY W
SHERMAN ALFORD A 44 LED W
SHERMAN J W A 25 TUS W
SHERMAN JOHN A 44 TAR W
SHEROD IRA A 37 HIC B
SHERRID JEMIRAH A 37 MAN B
SHERRIDAN WRIGHT A 37 HIG B
SHERROD A S A 39 FRA W
SHERROD HILLIARD A 37 EDW B
SHERROD HILLIARD A 37 TA2 B
SHERROD JOHN A 39 FRA W
SHERROD LUCIAN A 39 FRA W
SHERROD READING A 37 PEN W
SHERROD RICHD A 39 FRA B
SHERROD SAML A 39 HAR B
SHERRON B R A 44 LED W
SHERRY GIFFORD A 28 03A B
SHERWOOD COL M S A 46 GRE W
SHERWOOD GEORGE A 46 GRE B
SHERWOOD ISHAM A 46 GRE B
SHERWOOD J M A 29 FA1 W
SHERWOOD JOHN A 19 NEW W
SHIELDS BENJAMIN A 32 BRO W
SHIELDS CALEB A 37 TA1 B
SHIELDS DAVID D A 25 HAY W
SHIELDS J M A 32 BRO W
SHIELDS J W A 40 CAN W
SHIELDS JAMES C A 40 CAN W
SHIELDS JOSEPH A 37 HIC B
SHIELDS O M A 32 BRO W
SHIELDS WILLIAM A 32 BRO W
SHILBURN W A 44 OXF W
SHINE J F A 35 FAI W
SHINE JOHN A 35 FAI W
SHINE JOSEPH A A 35 WOL W
SHINE JOSEPH B A 28 14T W
SHINE WM A 28 14T W
SHINE YORK A 35 WOL W
SHINES DANIEL A 35 FAI B
SHINES LUKE A 35 FAI B
SHINES SHADE A 35 FAI B
SHINGLETON ARCTUS A 35 WOL W
SHIP HENDERSON A 44 BEA B
SHIPP JOHN T A 28 02N W
SHIPP WILSON A 40 RHY B
SHIRLEY BURTON A 37 TA1 B
SHIRLEY EDGER A 37 EDW B
SHIRLEY GEORGE A 37 TA1 B
SHIRLEY HENRY A A 37 TA1 W
SPARTA
SHIRLEY JAMES A 37 PIN B

SHIRLEY PETER A 28 16T B
SHIRLEY SOLOMON A 37 EDW B
SHIRLEY WILLIAM A 37 PIN B
SHITLE HENRY A 26 GRI W
SHIVA TULES A 25 PIN W
SHIVER JOHN H A 28 04A B
SHIVER JOHN H A 28 04B B
SHIVER RILEY A 28 03A B
SHOAF ADISON A 32 DAV W
SHOAF ALFORD A 32 DAV W
SHOAF ANDREW A 32 DAV B
SHOAF ARCH A 32 TYR B
SHOAF H W A 32 POS W
SHOAF HENDERSON A 32 TYR W
SHOAF HENRY A 32 DAV W
SHOAF HENRY A 32 TYR W
SHOAF HENRY A 32 TYR W
SHOAF J T A 32 TYR W
SHOAF MANERING A 32 DAV W
SHOAF S R A 32 POS W
SHOE DAVID W A 46 COB W
SHOE HENRY A 46 COB W
SHOE PETER A 46 COB W
SHOE PETER A 46 COB W
SHOEERAY SIMEON A 46 FRI B
SHOFF JOHN A 32 DAV W
SHOFFNER ANDY A 46 COB B
SHOFFNER DAVID A 46 COB B
SHOFFNER FREDERICK A 46 COB W
SHOFFNER GEAR A 46 COB W
SHOFFNER
HENRY BOLDEN A 46 RAG W
SHOFFNER JACOB A 46 COB W
SHOFFNER JOHN A 46 GRE W
SHOFFNER JOHN A 46 ROS B
SHOFFNER MONROE A 46 COB B
SHOFFNER SEYMORE A 46 COB W
SHOLER RILEY A 35 CYP W
SHOLLINGTON DAVID P A 53 GER W
SHORT ALBERT A 44 SAS B
SHORT CESOR A 44 SAS B
SHORT DANIEL A 26 PEE W
SHORT DOUBLIN A 37 ROC B
SHORT ED M A 44 ISL W
SHORT EDWARD A 44 SAS B
SHORT J C A 44 ISL W
SHORT J T A 44 HEN W
SHORT JASPER V A 46 GRE W
SHORT JNO R A 44 OXF B
SHORT JOHN F A 44 ISL W
SHORT MARTIN A A 46 GRE W
SHORT ROBERT A 26 SHE W
SHORT W H A 26 PEE W
SHORT W H A 44 HEN W
SHORT WINSTON A 46 GRE W
SHOTWELL J A A 44 TAR W
SHOTWELL JAS H A 44 TAR W
SHOTWELL THOS L A 44 SAS W
SHOULAR DAVID A 35 CYP W
SHOULAR JAMES H A 35 CYP W
SHOULAR JAMES R A 35 CYP W
SHOULAR WILLIAM A 35 CYP W
SHOVE H L A 29 FA1 W
SHRUM JOHN A A 40 MAU W
SHRUM MICHAEL A 40 DA1 W
SHUFFIELD FARRIOR A 35 KEN B
SHUFFIELD JOHN B A 35 CYP W
SHUFORD E P A 26 HOL B
SHUFORD EPHRAIM A 26 WAR W
SHUFORD JACOB A 26 SWA W
SHUFORD LAWSON A A 40 MAU W
SHUFORD MARTIN H A 40 MAU W
SHUFORD WESLEY A 26 GRI B

SHULAR ADAM A 32 THO W
SHULAR NICHLAS A 32 DAV W
SHULER EMSLEY F A 46 GRE W
SHULER JAMES A 32 THO W
SHULER JOHN A 32 DAV W
SHULEY JOSEPH A 37 PEN B
SHULEY SAMPSON A 37 PEN B
SHURROD ALBERT A 37 EDW B
SHURROD BOB A 37 EDW B
SHURROD DAVID A 37 EDW B
SHURROD H H A 39 FRA W
SHURROD HARDY A 37 EDW B
SHURROD JACK A 37 EDW B
SHURROD JAMES A 37 EDW B
SHURROD JAMES A 37 EDW B
SHURROD KAY A 37 EDW B
SHURROD NED A 37 EDW B
SHURROD REUBEN A 37 EDW B
SHURROD WILSON A 37 EDW W
SHUTE JESSE A 28 9TH B
SHUTE WILLIAM A 28 04B B
SHUTTS SOLOMON A 32 THO W
CERTIF
SIBBERNE ELIJAH A 30 NOR W
SICELOFF ALEXANDER A 32 POS W
SICLOFF PHILLIP A 32 POS W
SIESLOFF AHARD A 32 POS W
SIGMAN BARNETT A 26 WAR W
SIGMAN C C A 39 FRA W
SIKES A W A 44 FOR W
SIKES EMSLY M A 46 MCL W
SIKES HENRY A 44 FOR W
SIKES HOLLOWELL A 35 FAI W
SIKES P A 29 LOC W
SIKES PETER A 46 GRE B
SIKES WILLIAM N A 46 MCL W
SILLIMAN JOHN A 46 GRE W
SILLIVAN JAMES A 46 ROS W
SILLS HARRY A 39 DAV B
SILLS HENRY A 39 LOU B
SILLS HILLIARD A 39 JOR B
SILLS THOMAS A 24 EDE B
SILLS TONEY A 39 JOR B
CERT TO NASH
SILLS W H A 32 JAC W
SILVA SYLVESTER A 28 05A B
SILVAY BENDERSE A 53 SWA B
SILVAY GEORGE A 53 SWA B
SILVAY THOMAS A 53 SWA B
SILVAY WALLIS A 53 SWA B
SILVERTHORN A B A 28 04B W
SILVERTHORN AZOR B A 53 BUR W
SILVERTHORN
CLONDIOUS J A 53 GER W
SILVERTHORN DAMON A 53 BUR W
SILVERTHORN DANEL A 53 GER B
SILVERTHORN
ROBERT R A 53 BUR W
SILVERTHORN SAMUEL A 53 BUR W
SILVERTHORN
STEPHEN D A 53 GER W
SILVERTHORN
WILLIAM C A 53 BUR W
SILVESTER ALEXANDER A 39 HAR B
SIMERSON JAMES E A 37 TA1 B
SIMESON ROBERT A 32 TYR W
SIMESON W H A 32 TYR W
SIMISON SAMUEL E A 32 TYR W
SIMMES BENJ A 29 GRA W
SIMMES JNO W A 29 GRA W
SIMMON J D A 26 MOU W
SIMMON P H A 28 04A B
SIMMONDS RANDERSON A 29 FLE B

SIMMONDS SAM A 28 11T B
SIMMONS A W A 35 ALB W
SIMMONS ABRAM A 28 04A B
SIMMONS ALEXANDER A 30 COI B
SIMMONS ALLEN A 19 NEW W
SIMMONS ALLEN A 99 BUS B
SIMMONS AMOS A 28 04A B
SIMMONS ANTHONY A 19 NEW B
SIMMONS B H A 26 MOU W
SIMMONS BENJ A 28 04A B
SIMMONS BRITTON A 35 ALB B
SIMMONS C C A 26 MOU W
SIMMONS CAESAR A 28 04A B
SIMMONS CAESAR A 28 04A B
SIMMONS CHARLES A 26 MOU W
SIMMONS CLARK A 28 01B W
SIMMONS D H A 35 ALB W
SIMMONS DANIEL S A 30 COI W
SIMMONS DANL A 28 05A B
SIMMONS DAVID A 19 BE1 B
SIMMONS DAVID A 28 01A B
SIMMONS DAVID A 28 03A B
SIMMONS DAVID A 28 05A B
SIMMONS E B A 30 GIB W
SIMMONS EDMUND A 30 CUR B
SIMMONS EDMUND CHAL R 30 CUR W
GIVING AID & ASST
SIMMONS FRANCIS A 30 ROA B
SIMMONS FREDERICK A 28 8TH B
SIMMONS GEO D A 29 FA1 B
SIMMONS GEO L A 30 GIB W
SIMMONS GEORGE A 28 03A B
SIMMONS H E A 30 GIB W
SIMMONS H H A 28 04A B
SIMMONS H H A 30 GIB W
SIMMONS HENRY A 30 CUR B
SIMMONS HENRY A 35 WOL W
SIMMONS HERBERT A 30 MOY B
SIMMONS ISAIAH A 28 9TH B
SIMMONS ISRAEL A 28 04A B
SIMMONS JACKSON A 28 04A B
SIMMONS JACKSON A 28 7TH B
SIMMONS JACOB A 28 10T B
SIMMONS JACOB A 37 PEN B
SIMMONS JAMES A 28 02N B
SIMMONS JAMES A 28 10T B
SIMMONS JAMES E A 37 TA1 W
SIMMONS JAMES E A 37 TA2 W
SIMMONS JEROME A 30 CUR W
SIMMONS JESSE A 30 KNO B
SIMMONS JESSE A 30 ROA B
SIMMONS JOHN A 19 NEW W
SIMMONS JOHN A 26 CAR B
SIMMONS JOHN A 30 CUR W
SIMMONS JOHN A 30 KNO W
SIMMONS JOHN ALLEN A 28 01A B
SIMMONS JOHN R A 28 13T W
SIMMONS JOHN ROBERT A 28 05B B
SIMMONS JOSEPH A 28 04A B
SIMMONS JOSEPH A 30 COI B
SIMMONS JOURDAN A 28 04A B
SIMMONS LAFAYETTE A 30 COI B
SIMMONS LEWIS A 28 04A B
SIMMONS LEWIS A 28 7TH B
SIMMONS LOUIS N A 30 COI W
REMOVED TO NORTH BANKS
SIMMONS M W A 30 CUR W
SIMMONS MAJOR A 35 WOL W
SIMMONS MATHEW A 28 03A B
SIMMONS NOAH A 28 9TH B
SIMMONS OLIVER A 28 05A B
SIMMONS OSTEN A 28 03A B
SIMMONS PETER A 28 04A B

Name		Age	Place	Race
SIMMONS PETER	A	28	05A	B
SIMMONS PETER	A	46	GRE	B
SIMMONS PRIMUS	A	28	04A	B
SIMMONS REUBEN	A	46	ROS	B
SIMMONS ROBERT	A	30	ROA	B
SIMMONS ROBT H	A	29	FA1	B
SIMMONS S	A	29	CED	W
SIMMONS S H	A	35	ALB	W
SIMMONS SAML	A	29	FA1	B
SIMMONS SAMUEL	A	28	10T	B
SIMMONS SETH	A	53	SWA	B
SIMMONS SHEPARD	A	30	CUR	B
SIMMONS SIMON	A	28	04A	B
SIMMONS SOUTHEY	A	28	9TH	B
CERTIF GIVEN NOW LIVES AT NEW BERN				
SIMMONS SYLVESTER	A	28	7TH	B
SIMMONS THOS	A	29	FA1	B
SIMMONS TONEY	A	28	04A	B
SIMMONS WM	A	28	04A	B
SIMMONS WM P	A	19	NEW	W
SIMMS JOHN A	A	26	GOF	W
SIMMSON TONY	A	37	SHA	B
SIMONDS ALEX	A	28	05A	B
SIMONDS WILLIAM	A	37	EDW	B
SIMONS BENJAMIN	A	32	DAV	B
SIMONS DANIEL	A	46	HIG	B
SIMONS EBENEZER	A	28	13T	W
SIMONS GEORGE	A	29	QUW	B
SIMONS GEORGE	A	32	DAV	B
SIMONS ISRAEL	A	32	TYR	B
SIMONS JAMES H	A	53	FAI	W
SIMONS JAMES V	A	32	COT	W
SIMONS JOH E	A	53	GER	W
SIMONS JOSEPH D	A	53	FAI	W
SIMONS PADRICK H	A	53	FAI	W
SIMONS TONEY	A	28	03A	B
SIMONS WILLIAM R	A	53	BUR	W
SIMPKIN SAMUEL	A	24	EDE	B
SIMPKINS JOHN	A	19	BE1	W
SIMPKINS JOHN JR	A	19	BE1	W
SIMPKINS REDDING	A	19	BE1	W
SIMPLER OWEN G	A	28	03A	W
SIMPSON ABERT J	A	30	KNO	W
SIMPSON ALFRED	A	46	GRE	B
SIMPSON ALLEN	A	28	6TH	W
SIMPSON ALPHUS W	A	53	HAT	W
SIMPSON ARTHUR	A	24	EDE	B
SIMPSON BRYOM H	A	19	BE1	W
SIMPSON CALVIN	A	46	GRE	B
SIMPSON CHARLES	A	46	MON	B
SIMPSON CLIFFORD	A	28	9TH	W
SIMPSON CLIFFORD F	A	28	9TH	W
SIMPSON DAVID R	A	46	GRE	W
SIMPSON DENNIS	A	46	MON	B
SIMPSON E	A	46	GRE	B
SIMPSON E D	A	30	KNO	W
SIMPSON EDWARD	A	19	HAD	W
SIMPSON EPHRAIM	A	28	11T	W
SIMPSON FRANK P	A	24	UPP	B
SIMPSON FREDERICK	A	24	MID	W
SIMPSON GEO W	A	19	BE1	W
SIMPSON GEORGE	A	46	MON	B
SIMPSON H CAUSEY REVA		46	RAG	W
SIMPSON H H	A	30	KNO	W
SIMPSON HAUGHTER B	A	24	EDE	B
SIMPSON HENDERSON	R	24	MID	W
NAME MARKED OUT REJ BY THE BOARD FOR THE REASON THAT HE WAS MAGIS TRATE BEFORE THE WAR & DURING THE WAR DEALT IN (continued) CONFEDERATE BONDS & PER SUADED PEOPLE TO GO INTO THE CONFEDERATE SERVICE DID NOT TAKE THE OATH				
SIMPSON HILLIARD	A	19	BE1	W
SIMPSON J A	A	28	04A	W
SIMPSON J R	A	24	EDE	W
SIMPSON JAMES	A	29	LOC	B
SIMPSON JAMES D	A	28	15T	W
SIMPSON JOHN	A	29	LOC	B
SIMPSON JOHN D	A	19	BE1	W
SIMPSON JOHN R	A	28	14T	W
SIMPSON JOSEPH	A	24	EDE	B
SIMPSON JOSEPH F	A	28	14T	W
SIMPSON JOSIAH	A	30	POP	W
SIMPSON JOSIAH	A	46	SUM	W
SIMPSON LEWIS	A	46	GIB	B
SIMPSON M B	A	24	MID	W
SIMPSON N A	A	24	EDE	W
SIMPSON NATHAN	A	46	GRE	B
SIMPSON NATHANIEL	A	46	GRE	W
SIMPSON PETER	A	28	14T	W
SIMPSON PETER	A	28	6TH	B
SIMPSON PHILLIP	A	72	SWA	W
SIMPSON RICHARD	A	24	EDE	B
SIMPSON ROSS	A	19	BE1	W
SIMPSON S M	A	46	MON	W
SIMPSON S T	A	24	EDE	W
SIMPSON SAML	A	28	04A	B
CERTIFICATE GRANTED BIG SWIFT CREEK				
SIMPSON SAML	A	44	HEN	W
SIMPSON SAMUEL	A	46	MON	B
SIMPSON SANDY ALLEN	A	19	NEW	B
SIMPSON THOMAS	A	29	FA2	B
SIMPSON THOMPSON	A	46	MON	B
SIMPSON W J	A	53	OCR	W
SIMPSON WALLACE W	A	53	OCR	W
SIMPSON WILSON	A	28	05A	B
SIMPSON WM	A	24	MID	W
SIMPSON WM	A	28	14T	W
SIMPSON WM F	A	19	BE1	W
SIMPSON WM J	A	30	KNO	W
SIMPSON WM R	A	30	POP	W
SIMS AARON	A	29	GRA	W
SIMS AARON	A	46	GRE	B
SIMS B L	A	44	KIT	W
SIMS B Y	A	44	KIT	W
SIMS J C	A	44	KIT	W
SIMS JAS	A	29	GRA	W
SIMS JAS G	A	44	KIT	W
SIMS WM	A	28	04A	B
SIMSON J P	A	39	FRA	W
SINCLAIR AARON	A	29	QUW	B
SINCLAIR CALVERT	A	46	ROS	W
SINCLAIR DUNCAN	A	29	ROC	W
SINCLAIR JACOB	A	29	MON	B
SINCLAIR JOHN C	A	29	SEV	W
SINCLAIR JOHN T	A	29	QUW	W
SINCLAIR THOMAS	A	29	QUW	B
SINCLARE IVIN	A	29	FLE	W
SINGLETON HARDY	A	28	10T	B
SINGLETON JEFFERSON	A	46	GRE	B
SINGLETON JOHN	A	35	MAG	B
SINGLETON JOSEPH	A	28	10T	B
SINGLETON WM HENRY	A	28	01A	B
SINGSING ELI	A	32	THO	W
SINGSING T W	A	32	THO	W
SINK A H	A	32	DAV	W
SINK A R	A	32	TYR	W
SINK ADAM	A	32	DAV	W
SINK ANDREW	A	32	DAV	W
SINK ANDREW	A	32	POS	W
SINK COLUMBUS	A	32	DAV	B
SINK D P	A	32	THO	W
SINK DANIEL	A	32	POS	W
SINK DANIEL	A	32	THO	W
SINK DAVID	A	32	DAV	W
SINK EDMOND	A	32	SHE	W
SINK EDMOND	A	32	SHE	W
SINK HENRY	A	32	TYR	W
SINK HENRY	A	32	TYR	W
SINK HENRY L	A	32	DAV	W
SINK J A	A	32	BRO	W
SINK J L	A	32	DAV	W
SINK JACOB	A	32	SHE	W
SINK JOSEPH	A	32	DAV	W
SINK MATHIAS	A	32	DAV	W
SINK MICHAEL	A	32	DAV	W
SINK NOAH	A	32	DAV	W
SINK OBADIAH	A	32	COT	W
SINK PETER	A	32	TYR	W
SINK PHILLIP	A	32	POS	W
SINK PHILLIP	A	32	SHE	W
SINK ROBERT	A	32	DAV	B
SINK WILLIAM	A	32	DAV	W
SISELOFF JOSEPH B	A	32	POS	W
SISLOFF D S	A	32	POS	W
SISSON WM	A	28	01A	W
SISSONS D	A	28	6TH	B
SITTON THOMAS	A	25	PIN	W
SITZIN JOHN F	A	24	EDE	W
SIVILS ETHELBERT	A	30	IND	W
SIVILS JOHN	A	30	MOY	B
8-MONTH-RESIDENCE				
SIVILS LEMUEL	A	30	IND	W
SIVILS LUKE	A	30	MOY	B
SIVILS MALACHI	A	30	IND	W
SIVILS SAML J	A	30	IND	W
SIZER ROBERT A	A	37	TA1	W
SKARREN JOHN H	A	19	BE1	W
SKARREN WM E	A	19	BE2	W
SKATES MATTHEW	A	40	DA2	W
SKEEN CLARKSON	A	32	LOF	B
SKEEN J C CHAL	A	32	JAC	W
FOR HOLDING OFFICE OF MAGISTRATE BEFORE AND DURING THE WAR. RECON				
SKEEN J L	A	32	JAC	W
SKEEN MARTIN	A	32	JAC	W
SKEEN N	A	32	LOF	W
SKEEN ORSBURN	A	32	JAC	W
SKELLY JOHN M	A	32	THO	W
SKENE HENRY	A	46	GIB	W
SKENE JAMES	A	46	GIB	W
SKENES JOHN Y	A	46	GIB	W
SKIDMON JAMES T	A	40	DA2	W
SKIDMORE FERRY	A	44	OXF	B
SKIDMORE IREDELL	A	32	THO	W
SKIDMORE JAS	A	44	OXF	B
SKIDMORE WILLIAM	A	40	DA1	W
SKILES WASHINGTON	A	44	HEN	B
SKINNER ALLEN	A	24	EDE	B
SKINNER ANDREW	A	24	EDE	B
SKINNER ANTHONY	A	24	EDE	B
SKINNER ARNOLD	A	24	EDE	B
SKINNER AUGUSTUS	A	24	EDE	B
SKINNER AXUM	A	28	7TH	B
SKINNER B F	A	24	UPP	W
SKINNER BENJAMIN	A	37	WHI	B
SKINNER BRUTUS	A	28	05A	B
SKINNER C C	A	30	MOY	B
SKINNER CAESAR O	A	28	04A	B
SKINNER CHARLES E	A	40	DA1	W
SKINNER CHAS	A	24	EDE	B
SKINNER CHAS W	A	24	EDE	W

SKINNER DANIEL A 24 EDE B
SKINNER DAVID A 24 EDE B
SKINNER FRANCIS A 24 EDE B
SKINNER FREDERICK A 24 EDE B
SKINNER GEORGE A 24 EDE B
SKINNER GEORGE A 24 EDE B
SKINNER HENRY A 24 EDE B
SKINNER HENRY A 28 10T B
SKINNER HENRY A 30 NOR B
SKINNER J R A 24 EDE W
SKINNER JACOB R 24 EDE B
CHALLENGED BY J R B HATHAWAY REASON TOO YOUNG NO EVIDENCE AGAINST HIM AFTER BEING CHALLENGED HE REQUESTED HIS NAME BE ERASED
SKINNER JAS A 24 EDE B
SKINNER JOE A 28 05A B
SKINNER JOHN A 24 EDE B
SKINNER JOHN A 37 WHI W
SKINNER JOHN SR A 24 EDE B
SKINNER JOSEPH A 37 TA1 W
SKINNER LEVI A 28 01A B
SKINNER LONDON A 24 UPP B
SKINNER MOSES A 24 EDE B
SKINNER NELSON A 24 EDE B
SKINNER PETER A 24 EDE B
SKINNER PETER A 28 03A B
SKINNER R J A 24 EDE B
SKINNER RANSOM A 28 05A B
SKINNER RICHARD A 24 EDE B
SKINNER RICHARD A 37 TA1 W
SKINNER S W A 29 FA1 W
SKINNER SETH A 37 ROC B
SKINNER SIMON A 24 EDE B
SKINNER T G A 24 MID W
SKINNER THOMAS A 24 EDE B
SKINNER TIMOTHY A 37 TA1 W
SKINNER W S A 44 OXF W
SKINNER W W A 29 FA2 W
SKINNER WILLIAM A 24 EDE B
SKINNER WILLIAM A 24 MID W
SKINNER WILLIS A 24 EDE B
SKINNER WM H A 24 EDE B
SKINNER WM R R 24 EDE W
REJECTED BY THE BOARD CAUSE HELD THE OFFICE OF CLERK OF COURT. BEFORE THE WAR AND DURING THE WAR & ADVISED MEN TO ENLIST IN CONFED-ERATE SERVICE DID NOT TAKE THE OATH
SKIPPER FEDERRICK A 44 SAS B
SKIPPER J H E A 44 SAS B
SKIPPER JNO W A 29 FA1 W
SKIPPER ROBERT A 44 SAS B
SKIPPERETH HUME CHAL 44 SAS B
SKYLARK AARON A 29 FA1 B
SKYLARK CORNELIUS A 29 FA1 B
SKYLARK E A 29 FA1 B
SKYLARK ROBT A 29 FA1 B
SLACHTER FRED D A 28 01A W
SLACK JOSIAH A 30 MOY W
SLADE ABNER D A 28 15T W
SLADE BRYAN A 28 9TH B
SLADE CHAS A 28 05A B
SLADE DANL A 53 GER B
SLADE EDWARD A 28 04A B
SLADE ELIJAH A 53 GER B
SLADE ESSEX A 28 05A B
SLADE GEORGE A 28 01A B
SLADE GEORGE A 28 04B B
SLADE HARDY A 28 04A B
SLADE HENRY A 53 FAI B
SLADE J G A 28 03B B
SLADE JOSEPH A 28 01A B
SLADE LAWRENCE A 28 05A B
SLADE MILES A 28 05A B
SLADE MORGAN A 53 SWA B
SLADE OLIVER A 28 01A B
SLADE PETER A 46 MCL B
SLADE PRIMUS A 28 05A B
SLADE QUASH W A 28 04A B
SLADE REUBEN A 28 03A B
SLADE SAMUEL A 53 BUR B
SLADE SANDY A 19 NEW B
SLADE SIGH A 46 GRE B
SLADE SIMON A 19 HAD B
SLADE STEPHN A 28 03A B
SLADE WASHN A 28 03A B
SLADE WEAVER A 28 03A B
SLADE WHTNEY A 53 LA1 B
SLADE WILEY A 28 9TH B
SLADE WILLIAM A 53 GER B
SLADE WM A 28 03A B
SLADE ZACCHEUS A 28 04B W
SLATE MOSES A 19 NEW B
SLATE WILSON A 37 HOL B
SLATEN WEST A 37 SPA B
SLATER JOSEPH A 37 HIG B
SLATER RODE A 37 HIG B
SLATON ISAAC A 28 04B B
SLAUGHTER ABRAHAM A 44 TAR W
SLAUGHTER BRYAN A 28 05A B
SLAUGHTER DAVID A 44 TAR B
SLAUGHTER DAVID A 44 TAR W
SLAUGHTER RICHD A 44 TAR W
SLAUGHTER T D A 44 TAR W
SLAUGHTER T S A 44 TAR W
SLAUGHTER W P S A 44 TAR W
SLAUGHTER WM P A 44 TAR W
SLEDGE ALFORD A 39 DAV W
SLEDGE BENJAMIN A 32 THO W
SLEDGE ERASTUS A 39 FRA B
SLEDGE JAMES H A 39 LOU W
SLEDGE MOSES S A 32 DAV W
SLEDGE SHERRAD A 39 LOU W
SLIDGE JOHN A 39 DAV B
SLOAN ADAM A 40 MAU B
SLOAN CALVIN A 46 GRE B
SLOAN CLAIBORN A 35 MAG B
SLOAN EPHRAM A 35 MAG B
SLOAN FORTUNE A 35 MAG B
SLOAN G RANDALL A 46 GRE B
SLOAN HORACE A 46 GRE B
SLOAN ISAAC A 46 GRE B
SLOAN JERRY A 46 GRE B
SLOAN LEWIS A 35 MAG B
SLOAN NELSON A 35 KEN B
SLOAN PRIMUS A 35 ISL B
SLOAN ROBERT A 35 WAR W
SLOAN ROBERT M A 46 GRE W
SLOAN SILAS A 35 MAG B
SLOAN THOMAS W A 35 ISL W
SLOAN THOS A 29 FA1 B
REMOVED TO MOORE CO
SLOAN WILLIS A 35 MAG B
SLOAN WILSON A 46 GRE B
SLOAN WM A 46 GRE B
SLOCOMB A H A 29 FA1 W
SLONE ROBERT A 46 GRE W
SLONE THOMAS J A 46 GRE W
SLOVER CHAS A 28 02N W
SLOVER GEORGE A 28 02N W
SLOWN ALFRED A 46 GRE B
SLOWN JOHN A 46 GRE W
SMALL ABRAM A 28 05A B
SMALL ALFRED A 28 05A B
SMALL ALONZO F A 24 EDE W
SMALL B B A 19 HAR W
SMALL BENJAMIN P A 28 15T W
SMALL CHARLES A 37 TA1 W
SMALL EDWARD A 53 GER B
SMALL FRANKLIN A 28 05A B
SMALL HENRY A 28 7TH B
SMALL HENRY H A 32 THO W
SMALL JAMES A 24 MID W
SMALL JAMES A 28 05A B
SMALL JOHN A 30 MOY B
SMALL JOHN G A 24 EDE W
SMALL JOSHUWAY A 19 HAR W
SMALL M A 32 LOF W
SMALL MUSTIFER A 32 THO B
SMALL REDMOND A 28 05A B
SMALL SAMUEL A 46 MON W
SMALL STEPHEN A 37 PEN B
SMALL THOS A 24 MID W
SMALL THOS M A 24 EDE W
SMALL WINDSOR A 19 MOR B
SMALL WM A 19 NEW W
SMALLWOOD ASA A 28 01A B
SMALLWOOD C W A 28 03A B
SMALLWOOD EDW F A 28 02N W
SMALLWOOD EDWARD A 28 04A B
SMALLWOOD GEO A 28 04A B
SMALLWOOD JACOB A 53 LA1 B
SMAW BENJAMIN A 28 01A B
SMAW D G A 28 02N W
SMIDDICK SANDERS A 28 05B B
SMIDDICK STANLEY A 28 05A B
SMILEY A J A 39 LOU W
SMILEY THEODORE B A 37 ROC W
SMITH A A 29 BLA X
SMITH A A 39 HAR B
SMITH A B A 46 HIG W
SMITH A H A 32 TYR W
SMITH AARON A 44 KIT B
SMITH ABRAHAM BEN A 35 SMI B
SMITH ABRAM A 28 03A B
SMITH ADAM A 32 POS B
SMITH ADAM A 44 SAS B
SMITH ADDSON A 37 ROB B
SMITH ALBERT A 28 6TH B
SMITH ALBERT A 46 GRE B
SMITH ALEX A 29 LOC B
SMITH ALEX A 44 LED W
SMITH ALEXANDER A 29 MON W
SMITH ALEXANDER A 32 DAV B
SMITH ALEXANDER A 32 DAV B
SMITH ALEXANDER A 32 DAV W
SMITH ALFERD A 32 POS B
SMITH ALFORD A 32 DAV B
SMITH ALFORD A 32 JAC W
SMITH ALFORD A 32 JAC W
SMITH ALFORD A 32 THO W
SMITH ALFORD A 32 TYR W
SMITH ALFRED A 28 03A B
SMITH ALFRED A 29 FA1 B
SMITH ALLEN A 28 7TH B
SMITH ALLEN A 99 BUS B
SMITH AMOS A 28 8TH B
SMITH AMOS A 32 DAV B
SMITH ANDERSON A 39 DAV B
SMITH ANDERSON A 44 KNA B
SMITH ANDREW A 19 BE1 B
SMITH ANDREW A 19 MOR B

SMITH ANDREW A 32 JAC W
SMITH ANDREW A 37 TA2 B
SMITH ANDREW A 40 DA1 W
SMITH ANDREW F 40 DA1 W
REMOVED TO LINCOLN CO
CERT GRANTED APR 4 1868
SMITH ANDW A 29 FA1 B
SMITH ANSON A 53 GER B
SMITH ANTHONY A 29 FA1 B
SMITH ANTHONY A 35 SMI B
SMITH ANTHONY A 46 ROS B
SMITH ANTNY A 37 ROC B
SMITH ARCH B A 29 FA1 W
SMITH ARCHIBALD A 19 HAD W
SMITH ARNOLD A 28 05A B
SMITH ARNOLD A 53 SWA B
SMITH ARRINGTON A 46 COB W
SMITH ASA A 37 ROC B
SMITH ASA A 72 SWA W
SMITH ASA J A 53 GER W
SMITH AUGUSTUS A 28 6TH B
SMITH B D A 44 HEN W
SMITH B F A 35 ALB W
SMITH B M A 29 CED W
SMITH B W A 29 CAR W
SMITH BAKER A 24 UPP W
SMITH BALTHROP A 44 OXF W
SMITH BALTIMORE A 29 FA1 B
SMITH BARTLETT A 44 TAR B
SMITH BEN A 28 9TH B
SMITH BENJ A 28 05A B
SMITH BENJ A 29 FA1 B
SMITH BENJ A 29 FA1 B
SMITH BENJ A 29 FA1 B
SMITH BENJ A 29 FA1 B
SMITH BENJAMIN A 32 DAV W
SMITH BENJAMIN A 35 WAR B
SMITH BENJAMIN A 39 HAY W
SMITH BERRY A 37 ROC B
SMITH BIJAH A 53 FAI W
SMITH BILLY A 44 YXR B
SMITH BOURBON A 44 OXF W
SMITH BRANCH A 46 GRE W
SMITH BRANSOR A 32 JAC W
SMITH BRIGHT A 29 CAR B
SMITH BROWN A 44 TAR B
SMITH BRYANT A 35 SMI W
SMITH BRYANT A 37 WHI B
SMITH BURNS A 72 SWA W
SMITH BURTON E A 99 BUS W
SMITH C A 29 BLA W
SMITH C A 29 GRA W
SMITH C C N A 26 HOL B
SMITH CAINBRIDGE A 24 EDE B
SMITH CAJOR A 44 YXS B
SMITH CALVERT A 46 ROS W
SMITH CALVIN A 35 ALB W
SMITH CALVIN A 44 SAS B
SMITH CALVIN D A 46 ROS W
SMITH CANNON A 28 6TH W
SMITH CASPER M A 32 DAV W
SMITH CATLET A 25 HAY W
SMITH CEIZAR A 44 TAR B
SMITH CHARLES A 28 11T B
SMITH CHARLES A 28 12T B
SMITH CHARLES A 28 7TH B
SMITH CHARLES A 32 COT W
SMITH CHARLES A 32 COT W
SMITH CHAUNCY A 35 SMI W
SMITH COLLINS A 44 OXF B
SMITH COLONEL A 44 YXR B
SMITH CONSTANTINE P A 46 RAG W
SMITH D B A 40 STO W
SMITH D H A 26 BLA W
SMITH D L A 29 CED W
SMITH D M A 26 MOO W
SMITH D W A 29 FA1 W
SMITH DANIAL A 37 TA1 B
SMITH DANIEL A 24 EDE B
SMITH DANIEL A 32 DAV B
SMITH DANIEL A 44 OXF B
SMITH DANIEL A 46 MON W
SMITH DANIEL A 46 ROS B
SMITH DANIEL A 46 ROS W
SMITH DANL A 29 FA1 B
SMITH DANL A 29 GRA W
SMITH DANL A 46 COB W
SMITH DAVID A 29 GRA B
SMITH DAVID A 29 ROC W
SMITH DAVID A 32 DAV W
SMITH DAVID A 32 JAC W
SMITH DAVID A 35 SMI W
SMITH DAVID A 40 BLA W
SMITH DAVID A 44 YXS B
SMITH DAVID A 46 FRI W
SMITH DAVID F A 28 01B W
SMITH DAVID W A 72 SWA W
SMITH DEMPSEY A 30 MOY W
SMITH DENNIS A 30 MOY B
SMITH DOCTOR A 35 LIM B
SMITH DOCTOR A 46 ROS B
SMITH DR W A 28 11T W
SMITH DREW A 37 MAN B
SMITH DUNCAN A 29 LOC B
SMITH DUNCAN G A 29 QUW W
SMITH E G CHAL A 25 HAY W
FOR HOLDING OFFICE AS A
CLERK IN TIME OF WAR
TAKING NO PART IN THE WAR
SMITH E H A 25 SHO W
SMITH E M A 25 HAY W
SMITH E W A 32 COT W
SMITH EDGAR A 29 GRA B
SMITH EDMOND A 53 GER B
SMITH EDWARD A 28 05A B
SMITH EDWARD A 29 QUW B
SMITH EDWARD A 35 ALB W
SMITH EDWD A 29 FA1 B
SMITH EDWIN A A 99 BUS W
SMITH ELI A 32 JAC B
SMITH ELIGH A 40 SAN W
SMITH ELIJAH A 24 EDE W
SMITH ELIJAH A 44 HEN B
SMITH ELIJAH A 44 TAR B
SMITH ELIJAH A 53 GER B
SMITH ELIJAH A A 19 DAV W
SMITH ELISHA A 46 MON W
SMITH ELISHA L A 46 GIB W
SMITH ELSY A 19 HAD W
SMITH EPP A 39 GRI B
SMITH EUGENE D A 37 TA1 W
SMITH FAROD A 29 CAR W
SMITH FIELDING A 44 SAS B
SMITH FRANCES M A 32 DAV W
SMITH FRANCIS A 24 UPP W
SMITH FREDERICK A 46 MON W
SMITH FREDK A 29 GRA B
SMITH G F A 32 DAV W
SMITH G J A 46 SUM W
SMITH G M A 32 DAV W
SMITH G R A 46 MON W
SMITH G W A 24 EDE W
SMITH G W A 46 SUM W
SMITH GABRIEL A 44 TOW B
SMITH GENERAL A 35 SMI B
SMITH GEO A 29 FA1 B
SMITH GEO A 29 FA1 B
SMITH GEO S A 19 POR W
SMITH GEO S A 28 03A W
SMITH GEO W L A 24 EDE W
SMITH GEORGE A 19 MOR B
SMITH GEORGE A 28 03A B
SMITH GEORGE A 28 04B B
SMITH GEORGE A 28 7TH W
SMITH GEORGE A 32 JAC W
SMITH GEORGE A 40 DA1 B
SMITH GEORGE A 46 GIB B
SMITH GEORGE A 46 GIB B
SMITH GEORGE A 46 ROS W
SMITH GEORGE A 53 BUR B
SMITH GEORGE CHAL A 32 JAC W
FOR HOLDING OFFICE OF
MAGISTRATE BEFORE AND
DURING THE WAR. RECON.
SMITH GEORGE L A 35 LIM W
SMITH GEORGE W A 19 STR W
SMITH GEORGE W A 37 ROC W
SMITH GEORGE W A 46 ROS W
SMITH GODFREY A 29 FA1 B
SMITH GREEN A 32 DAV B
SMITH GREEN A 32 DAV W
SMITH H E A 29 CAR W
REMOVED TO NEW HANOVER
SMITH H H A 29 CED W
SMITH HAMPTEN A 39 JOR B
SMITH HANDLEY A 53 GER B
SMITH HARDY A 28 04A B
SMITH HARMON A 28 16T B
SMITH HARRACE A 19 BE1 B
SMITH HARRISON A 24 EDE B
SMITH HARRY A 37 EDW B
SMITH HARVEY A 35 WAR W
SMITH HAWKINS A 44 BRA B
SMITH HENRY A 19 BE1 W
SMITH HENRY A 29 FA1 B
SMITH HENRY A 29 FA1 B
SMITH HENRY A 32 DAV B
SMITH HENRY A 32 DAV W
SMITH HENRY A 40 DA1 W
SMITH HENRY A 44 BEA W
SMITH HENRY A 44 TAR B
SMITH HENRY A 46 FRI B
SMITH HENRY A 46 MON W
SMITH HENRY A 99 BUS B
SMITH HENRY E A 35 ALB W
SMITH HENRY M A 29 FA1 B
SMITH HILL A 35 SMI B
SMITH HOLLOWELL A 53 FAI W
SMITH HUBARD A 32 TYR B
SMITH HUMPHRY A 32 DAV B
SMITH ISAAC A 19 NEW B
SMITH ISAAC A 24 EDE W
SMITH ISAAC A 28 8TH B
SMITH ISAAC A 29 FA1 B
SMITH ISAAC A 29 FLE B
SMITH ISAAC A 29 FLE B
SMITH ISAAC A 35 FAI B
SMITH ISAAC A 40 DA1 B
SMITH ISAAC A 40 FER W
SMITH ISAAC A 46 GRE B
SMITH ISHUM A 44 YXS B
SMITH IVY A 30 KNO W
SMITH IVY A 35 SMI W
SMITH J A 19 HAD W
SMITH J A 26 BOR W
SMITH J A A 25 TUS W
SMITH J B A 40 RHY W
SMITH J B A 40 STO W
SMITH J C A 29 BLA W

SMITH J C A 32 JAC W
SMITH J F A 32 THO W
SMITH J G A 29 CED W
SMITH J H A 32 DAV W
SMITH J H A 39 FRE B
SMITH J H A 44 BEA W
SMITH J H A 46 GRE W
SMITH J J A 29 FA1 W
SMITH J L A 46 HIG W
SMITH J M A 28 02N W
SMITH J M A 28 03A B
SMITH J M A 39 HAY W
SMITH J N A 25 TUS W
SMITH J T A 44 BEA W
SMITH J W A 19 HAD W
SMITH J W A 28 01B W
SMITH J W A 40 SAN W
SMITH J Y A 44 BRA W
SMITH JACK A 32 DAV B
SMITH JACK A 35 SMI B
SMITH JACK 1 A 29 FLE B
SMITH JACK 2 A 29 FLE B
SMITH JACKSON A 35 ALB W
SMITH JACOB A 28 04A B
SMITH JACOB A 28 05A B
SMITH JACOB A 28 05A B
SMITH JACOB A 28 9TH B
SMITH JACOB A 32 COT W
SMITH JACOB A 46 MON W
SMITH JACOB B A 19 BE1 W
SMITH JACOB J A 35 SMI W
SMITH JACOB JR A 35 SMI W
SMITH JACOB SR A 35 SMI W
SMITH JAMES A 19 BE1 B
SMITH JAMES A 28 7TH B
SMITH JAMES A 29 FA2 B
SMITH JAMES A 29 GRA W
SMITH JAMES A 32 COT B
SMITH JAMES A 32 DAV W
SMITH JAMES A 32 SHE W
SMITH JAMES A 37 SPA B
SMITH JAMES A 37 TA1 B
SMITH JAMES A 38 FRE W
SMITH JAMES A 39 FRA B
SMITH JAMES A 40 STO W
SMITH JAMES A 44 BEA W
SMITH JAMES A 44 HEN B
SMITH JAMES A 44 OXF B
SMITH JAMES A 44 YXS B
SMITH JAMES A 46 GRE B
SMITH JAMES A 99 BUS W
SMITH JAMES C A 29 FA2 B
SMITH JAMES H A 28 03A W
SMITH JAMES H A 28 10T W
SMITH JAMES K A 35 KEN W
SMITH JAMES L A 32 POS W
SMITH JAMES L A 35 SMI W
SMITH JAMES M A 19 STR W
SMITH JAMES M A 46 GIB W
SMITH JAMES M J A 29 FA2 W
SMITH JAS A A 44 YXS W
SMITH JAS B A 29 FA1 W
SMITH JAS N A 29 FA1 W
SMITH JEFFERSON A 99 BUS W
SMITH JERRY A 44 YXS B
SMITH JESSE A 24 EDE W
SMITH JESSE A 46 FRI B
SMITH JESSE JR A 24 EDE W
SMITH JNO A 29 FA1 B
SMITH JNO A 29 FA1 W
SMITH JNO A 29 GRA W
SMITH JNO M A 29 GRA W
SMITH JNO MCLAIN A 29 ROC W
SMITH JNO W A 44 YXS B
SMITH JOE A 28 03A B
SMITH JOHN A 19 BE1 W
SMITH JOHN A 24 EDE W
SMITH JOHN A 25 HAY W
SMITH JOHN A 28 04A B
SMITH JOHN A 28 04A B
SMITH JOHN A 28 11T B
SMITH JOHN A 28 9TH B
SMITH JOHN A 29 FA2 B
SMITH JOHN A 29 MON W
SMITH JOHN A 30 KNO W
SMITH JOHN A 32 BRO W
SMITH JOHN A 32 COT W
SMITH JOHN A 32 DAV W
SMITH JOHN A 32 DAV W
SMITH JOHN A 35 FAI W
SMITH JOHN A 35 MAG B
SMITH JOHN A 37 TA1 B
SMITH JOHN A 37 TA1 W
SMITH JOHN A 40 STO W
NAME LINED OUT
SMITH JOHN A 44 BRA W
SMITH JOHN A 44 FOR B
SMITH JOHN A 44 HEN W
SMITH JOHN A 44 YXS B
SMITH JOHN A 44 YXS B
SMITH JOHN A 46 COB B
SMITH JOHN A 46 GIB B
SMITH JOHN A 46 GRE W
SMITH JOHN A 46 MON W
SMITH JOHN A 46 SUM W
SMITH JOHN A 46 SUM W
SMITH JOHN A A 28 03A W
SMITH JOHN A A 46 MON W
SMITH JOHN B A 39 PUG W
SMITH JOHN D A 40 SAN W
SMITH JOHN D A 46 GRE W
SMITH JOHN E A 35 SMI W
SMITH JOHN G A 28 6TH W
SMITH JOHN G A 29 QUW W
SMITH JOHN G A 53 FAI W
SMITH JOHN H A 28 10T B
SMITH JOHN H A 28 11T W
SMITH JOHN H A 32 DAV W
SMITH JOHN J A 46 SUM W
SMITH JOHN JR A 35 SMI W
SMITH JOHN L A 28 02N W
SMITH JOHN L A 40 SAN W
SMITH JOHN M A 24 UPP W
SMITH JOHN M A 40 DEC W
SMITH JOHN M A 53 GER W
SMITH JOHN R A 24 UPP W
SMITH JOHN S A 19 SMY W
SMITH JOHN SR A 35 ALB W
SMITH JOHN SR A 35 SMI W
SMITH JOHN W A 46 ROS W
SMITH JONAS A 35 ALB W
SMITH JONES A 35 SMI W
SMITH JOSEPH A 19 HAD W
SMITH JOSEPH A 28 16T B
SMITH JOSEPH A 29 ROC W
SMITH JOSEPH A 35 LIM B
SMITH JOSEPH A 35 MAG B
SMITH JOSEPH A 35 SMI B
SMITH JOSEPH A 40 MAU W
SMITH JOSEPH A 44 FOR B
SMITH JOSEPH A 72 SWA B
SMITH JOSEPH A 99 BUS W
SMITH JOSEPH T A 46 GRE W
SMITH JOSEPH W A 19 HAD W
SMITH JOSEPH W A 19 HAD W
SMITH JOSEPH W A 19 HUN W
SMITH JOSEPHUS A 19 HUN W
SMITH JOSHUA A 37 TA1 B
SMITH JUNIUS A 28 9TH B
SMITH KIA A 40 SAN B
SMITH L C A 44 YXS W
SMITH L J A 46 MON W
SMITH L L A 26 HOL B
MILITIA OFFICER &
ENGAGED IN REBELLION
SMITH LAFAYETTE A 28 05A B
SMITH LAFAYETTE A 35 ALB W
SMITH LARKIN A 24 EDE B
SMITH LEANDER A 40 SAN B
SMITH LERVY A 53 LA1 W
SMITH LEVANDER A 29 FA2 B
SMITH LEVI A A 40 DA1 W
SMITH LEWIS A 28 7TH B
SMITH LEWIS A 28 7TH W
SMITH LEWIS A 29 BLA X
SMITH LEWIS A 29 FA1 B
SMITH LEWIS A 29 GRA B
SMITH LEWIS A 46 GIB B
SMITH LOTT A 29 FA1 B
SMITH LOVELESS A 44 YXS B
SMITH LUANDER A 40 RHY W
SMITH LUCIUS A 99 BUS W
SMITH LUKE A 28 03A B
SMITH LUKE A 53 GER B
SMITH LUNNUN A 28 04A B
SMITH M A 28 02N B
SMITH M B A 19 SMY W
SMITH M H A 40 STO W
SMITH M L A 25 HAY W
SMITH MAASEY A 19 HUN W
SMITH MACK A 35 SMI B
SMITH MAJOR J A 53 BUR W
SMITH MALECHI A 30 TUL W
SMITH MARSHALL A 28 04A B
SMITH MARTIN R A 19 SMY W
SMITH MATHEW A 29 GRA W
SMITH MCLUNY C R 40 FER W
11 MOS RESIDENCE
24TH SEPT 1867
SMITH MEMBER A 44 TAR B
SMITH MERRIT A 44 YXS B
SMITH MICHAEL A 19 HAD W
SMITH MICHAEL A 32 JAC W
SMITH MILLS A 28 05A B
SMITH MITCHEL A 19 HAD W
SMITH MORRIS A 35 SMI B
SMITH MORRIS A 53 LA1 W
SMITH MORRISON A 46 MCL B
SMITH MOSES A 32 BRO W
SMITH MOSES A 99 BUS B
SMITH N G A 29 BLA W
SMITH NATHAN A 29 FA1 W
SMITH NEILL A 29 FA1 W
SMITH NELSON A 19 MOR B
SMITH NOAH A 28 9TH B
SMITH NOAH A 40 DA1 W
SMITH NOTT A 29 FA1 B
SMITH O A 26 BOR W
SMITH ORANGE C A 53 SWA W
SMITH ORREN A 99 BUS W
SMITH OSWELL A A 99 BUS W
SMITH P H A 39 LOU W
SMITH P J A 28 10T W
SMITH PARKER W A 28 03A B
SMITH PETER A 28 7TH B
SMITH PETER A 32 DAV B
SMITH PETER A 32 DAV W
SMITH PETER A 35 MAG B
SMITH PETER A 37 PEN B
ROCKY MOUNT

SMITH PETER A 44 YXS B
SMITH PETER A 46 GRE B
SMITH PETER A 46 JAM B
SMITH PETER M A 32 TYR W
SMITH PHIL A 44 YXS B
SMITH PINKNEY R A 46 MON W
SMITH PINNAL A 72 SWA W
SMITH PLEASANT A 32 DAV B
SMITH PREASTLY A 44 FOR B
SMITH R A 26 BOR W
SMITH R G A 19 MOR W
SMITH R H A 25 SHO W
SMITH R L A 26 SHE W
SMITH R O A 44 RAG W
SMITH R T A 40 STO W
SMITH RANDAL A 29 MON B
SMITH RANDEL A 37 SPA B
SMITH RANSOM A 35 FAI B
SMITH RANSOM A A 99 BUS W
SMITH RAPHOD A 29 GRA W
SMITH REDDICK A 29 FA1 B
SMITH RICHARD A 19 HAD W
SMITH RICHARD A 29 MON B
SMITH RICHARD A 37 WHI B
SMITH RICHARD A 72 SWA W
SMITH RICHARD CHALA 30 GIB B
NON-RESID-8-MONTHS
SMITH RICHARD H A 46 MCL W
SMITH RICHARD S A 46 GRE W
SMITH RICHD A 29 FA1 B
SMITH RICHD A 29 FA1 B
SMITH RICHD A 44 YXR B
SMITH RILEY J A 40 BLA W
SMITH ROBERT A 29 FLE B
SMITH ROBERT A 32 DAV B
SMITH ROBERT A 32 DAV B
SMITH ROBERT A 40 BLA W
SMITH ROBERT A 44 YXS B
SMITH ROBT A 24 EDE B
SMITH ROBT A 28 03A B
SMITH ROBT A A 46 COB W
SMITH RUFFIN A 44 YXS B
SMITH RUFUS A 28 03B W
SMITH RUFUS A A 99 BUS W
SMITH RUFUS W A 46 MCL W
SMITH S A A 40 STO W
SMITH S F A 32 DAV W
SMITH S H A 32 THO W
SMITH SAM A 39 HAY B
SMITH SAMEUL J A 35 WAR B
SMITH SAML A 28 01A B
SMITH SAML A 28 05A B
SMITH SAML W A 44 TAR W
SMITH SAMUEL A 28 11T W
SMITH SAMUEL A 28 15T B
SMITH SAMUEL A 29 FLE B
SMITH SAMUEL A 37 MAN B
SMITH SAMUEL A 53 FAI W
SMITH SAMUEL B A 72 SWA W
SMITH SAMUEL E A 19 SMY W
SMITH SAMUEL R A 46 GRE W
SMITH SAMUEL W A 46 ROS W
SMITH SAMUEL W H A 46 GRE W
SMITH SANDERSON A 53 FAI W
SMITH SANDY A 29 BLA X
SMITH SANDY R A 46 MCL B
SMITH SETH A 53 GER B
SMITH SETH D A 35 SMI W
SMITH SEYMOUR A 28 04A B
SMITH SHARPER A 29 FLE B
SMITH SHEROD A 28 11T W
CERT TO VOTE IN NEW BERN
GIVEN APRIL 22, 1868

SMITH SHEROD T R 28 11T W
DID NOT TAKE THE OATH
WAS AN OVERSEER OF
ROADS AND AFTERWARDS
ENGAGED IN WAR
SMITH SHORT A 32 COT B
SMITH SILAS A 28 03A B
SMITH SIMEON A 30 TUL W
SMITH SIMON A 29 BLA X
SMITH SIMON A 29 CAR B
SMITH SIP A 35 MAG B
SMITH SIP CHAL R 35 MAG B
NOT BEING IN THE STATE
MORE THAN 5 MOS.
SMITH SIRAS A 32 DAV B
SMITH SOLN A 28 04A B
SMITH SQUIRE A 44 YXS B
SMITH STEPHEN A 24 UPP W
SMITH STEPHEN A 29 BLA X
SMITH STEPHEN A 29 CAR B
SMITH STEPHEN A 29 FA1 B
SMITH STEPHEN A 44 YXS B
SMITH T A A 29 BLA X
SMITH T A A 29 BLA X
SMITH T G A 99 BUS W
SMITH T L D A 39 HAY W
SMITH T R A 29 BLA W
SMITH T W A 44 ISL W
SMITH THOM T A 46 GRE W
SMITH THOMAS A 19 MOR B
SMITH THOMAS A 24 EDE W
SMITH THOMAS A 24 EDE W
SMITH THOMAS A 26 CAR W
SMITH THOMAS A 28 14T W
SMITH THOMAS A 29 LOC B
SMITH THOMAS A 32 JAC W
SMITH THOMAS A 35 WAR B
SMITH THOMAS A 37 MAN B
SMITH THOMAS A 37 PIN W
SMITH THOMAS A 39 GRI B
SMITH THOMAS A 44 SAS B
SMITH THOMAS A 46 MON W
SMITH THOMAS C A 99 BUS W
SMITH THOMAS H A 28 9TH W
SMITH THOMPSON A 32 THO W
SMITH THOS A 28 04A B
SMITH THOS A 29 FA1 B
SMITH TOBY A 29 BLA X
SMITH TOBY A 29 FA1 B
SMITH TONEY A 28 05A B
SMITH VINCENT A 44 TAR B
SMITH W C A 44 BEA W
SMITH W D A 29 FA1 W
SMITH W D A 46 SUM W
SMITH W E A 32 POS W
SMITH W H A 35 CYP W
SMITH W J A 29 GRA W
SMITH W P A 44 FOR W
SMITH W S A 25 HAY W
SMITH WALLACE A 53 HAT W
SMITH WASHINGTON A 28 11T B
SMITH WESLEY A 29 FA1 W
SMITH WESLEY A A 99 BUS W
SMITH WESLY A 29 FA2 B
SMITH WILEY A 29 FA1 B
SMITH WILEY A 35 SMI W
SMITH WILLIAM A 24 EDE W
SMITH WILLIAM A 29 BLA X
SMITH WILLIAM A 29 FA2 B
SMITH WILLIAM A 29 MON W
SMITH WILLIAM A 32 BRO W
SMITH WILLIAM A 32 TYR W
SMITH WILLIAM A 35 SMI B

SMITH WILLIAM A 37 ROC B
SMITH WILLIAM A 39 HAY W
SMITH WILLIAM A 40 FER B
SMITH WILLIAM A 44 YXR B
SMITH WILLIAM A 46 HIG W
SMITH WILLIAM A 46 MON W
SMITH WILLIAM R 46 COB W
BRANDED FOR MANSLAUGHTER
IN ORANGE CO NEAR 20
YEARS AGO. REJECTED
SMITH WILLIAM SR A 46 FRI W
SMITH WILLIAM A A 53 HAT W
SMITH WILLIAM A A 99 BUS W
SMITH WILLIAM B A 53 GER W
SMITH WILLIAM F A 99 BUS W
SMITH WILLIAM G A 72 SWA W
SMITH WILLIAM J A 53 GER W
SMITH WILLIAM JR A 46 COB W
SMITH WILLIAM SR A 28 9TH B
CERTIF GIVEN LIVES
NOW AT BAIRD'S CREEK
SMITH WILLIAM W A 19 DAV W
SMITH WILLIS A 24 UPP W
SMITH WM A 19 NEW B
SMITH WM A 28 04A B
SMITH WM A 29 BLA X
SMITH WM A 29 CAR B
SMITH WM A 29 FA1 B
SMITH WM A 29 FA1 B
SMITH WM A 29 FA1 B
BLK RIVER
SMITH WM A 29 GRA B
SMITH WM A 29 ROC W
SMITH WM A 32 COT B
SMITH WM A 40 STO B
SMITH WM A 44 FOR B
SMITH WM A 44 HEN W
SMITH WM R 29 LOC W
SMITH WM A A 24 EDE W
SMITH WM B A 19 HUN W
SMITH WM E A 46 FRI W
SMITH WM F A 19 BE1 W
SMITH WM J A 19 BE1 W
SMITH WM J A 29 MON W
SMITH WM J A 29 ROC W
DEPT SHERIFF BEFORE THE
WAR WAS CONSCRIPT SOLDIER
SMITH WM J A 39 PUG W
SMITH WM M A 28 04A W
SMITH WM M A 46 JAM W
SMITH WM R A 46 GRE W
SMITH WM S A 19 HUN W
SMITH WM W A 19 DAV W
SMITH YANCEY L A 99 BUS W
SMITH YLEY A 32 DAV B
SMITHERMAN RUSSELL A 46 SUM B
SMITHICK BENJAMIN A 46 RAG B
SMITHSON AMASA A 53 HAT W
SMITHSON GEORGE W A 37 EDW W
SMITHWICK MADISON A 44 HEN B
SMITICK STANLEY A 28 14T W
SMOTHERS ALFRED A 46 GRE W
SMOTHERS PINKNEY A 46 GRE W
SMOTHERS ROBT A 46 GRE W
SMOTHERS W G A 46 MON W
SMOTHES SEYBORN A 46 GRE W
SMYER FRANK A 40 BLA B
SNDEN GEORGE A 30 IND W
SNDEN ISAAC A 30 IND W
SNEED ALEX A 44 TOW B
SNEED ALFRED A 99 BUS W
SNEED BENJAMIN A 44 TOW B
SNEED CHARLES A 44 FIS B

SNEED GEORGE A 44 HEN B
SNEED GILES A 44 HEN B
SNEED HAMPTON A 44 HEN B
SNEED HORACE A 44 HEN B
SNEED JOHN A 44 HEN B
SNEED JORDAN A 44 FOR B
SNEED LEWIS A 44 HEN B
SNEED MOSSES A 44 ISL B
SNEED PETER A 44 HEN B
SNEED PETER B A 44 SAS W
SNEED POPLAR CHAL A 44 ISL B
GUILTY NOW IN JAIL UNDER
LAST ORDER ACCEPTED
SNEED RICHARD G A 44 TOW W
SNEED ROBERT A 44 HEN B
SNEED ROBT A 44 ISL B
SNEED SAMUEL A 44 FIS B
SNEED THOMAS A 39 PUG B
SNEED W B G A 44 HEN W
SNEED W M JR A 44 TOW W
SNEED WALTER A 44 HEN B
SNEED WM A 44 FIS B
SNELL HOLSA A 53 GER W
SNELL SAMUEL L A 53 GER W
SNELL THOMAS A 28 16T B
SNELLING WILLIAM N A 99 BUS W
SNIDER D H A 32 TYR W
SNIDER G W A 32 YAD W
SNIDER H A 32 LOF W
SNIDER J L A 32 TYR W
SNIDER JOHN A 32 LOF W
SNIDER K D A 32 SHE W
SNIDER PHILIP A 32 JAC W
SNIDER PINKNEY A 32 POS W
SNIDER SOLOMON A 32 DAV W
SNIDER SOLOMON A 32 LOF W
SNIDER WILLIAM D A 32 TYR W
SNIDER WILLIAM G A 32 LOF W
SNIDER WILLIAM L A 32 TYR W
SNIPES EDMOND A 44 TAR B
SNIPES JAMES A 44 TAR W
SNIPES JAMES P A 44 TAR W
SNIPES RUSSELL A 37 HIG B
SNIPES THOMAS A 46 SUM W
SNIPES THOS F A 44 TAR W
SNODEN AMERICA A 30 IND B
SNODEN BENJ A 30 IND B
CHAL
MINOR-REJECTED
SNODEN DANIEL A 30 IND B
SNODEN J B A 30 IND W
SNODEN MARK A 30 IND B
SNODEN SILAS A 30 CUR B
SNODEN WILLIAM A 30 CUR W
SNOTHERLY J A 32 JAC W
SNOTHERLY WILLIAM A 32 JAC W
SNOW JORDAN E A 30 POW W
SNOWDEN BENJAMIN A 30 ROA B
SNOWDEN ISAAC A 24 EDE B
SNOWDEN SAMPSON A 30 ROA B
SNOWDEN WM E A 19 BE1 W
SNOWDON CARROLL A 28 05A B
SNOWDON JOHN A 37 EDW B
SNOWTON POMPY A 19 BE1 B
SOCKWELL BENJN A 46 GIB B
SOCKWELL DAVID A 46 GIB W
SOCKWELL DAVID R A 46 MCL W
SOCKWELL DICK A 46 GRE B
SOCKWELL ROBT A 46 GIB W
SOCKWELL SAMUEL A 46 GIB B
SOCKWELL THOS A 46 GIB W
SOLACE BOSTWICK A 35 WOL W
SOLACE MOSES A 35 WOL W
SOLACE NEEDHAM A 35 WOL W
SOLLOMAN JORDAN A 44 KIT W
SOLOMAN LEWIS A 39 PUG B
SOLOMON BLUNT A 39 PUG B
SOLOMON JOSEPH A 46 MON W
SOLOMON RANTSOM A 39 HAY B
SOLOMON WM A 28 05A B
SOMERS ALFRED A 46 GRE W
SOMERS JACOB A 46 GIB B
SOMERS PETER H A 46 GIB W
SOMERVILLE OTTOWAY A 38 FRE B
SOMMERVILLE OSCAR A 44 HEN B
SOMREAUX FRED A 37 PEN B
SOREY JOSIAH A 37 PEN B
SORG ANDREW A 37 TA1 W
SORRELL BENJAMIN A 37 PEN B
SORRELL EMANUEL A 37 TA1 B
SORREY DENNIS A 37 MAN W
SOSSAMON H M A 32 TYR W
CERTIFICATE GIVEN TO
SALISBURY HIS RESIDENCE
SOSSEGOOD JOHN H A 32 TYR W
SOUELL THOS P A 24 UPP W
SOURES FELIX A 32 SHE W
SOURES MICHAEL A 32 POS W
SOURES ROBERT A 32 THO B
SOURS CHRISTIAN A 32 DAV W
SOURS CHRISTIAN A 32 DAV W
SOURS J A A 32 DAV W
SOURS JACOB A 32 DAV W
SOURS JESSE A 32 TYR W
SOURS JOSEPH S A 32 DAV W
SOURS PHILIP A 32 TYR W
SOURS ROBERT A 32 SHE W
SOURS SAMUEL A 32 DAV W
SOUTHALL GEORGE A A 35 KEN W
SOUTHERD WILLIAM A 46 KIN W
SOUTHERLAN
WILLIAM B A 35 LIM W
SOUTHERLAND ABRAM A 35 MAG W
SOUTHERLAND
ALEXANDER A 35 MAG W
SOUTHERLAND BRYANT A 35 KEN B
SOUTHERLAND BRYANT A 35 KEN W
SOUTHERLAND
CHRISTOPHER A 35 KEN B
SOUTHERLAND DANIEL A 35 ISL B
SOUTHERLAND DANIEL A 35 MAG W
SOUTHERLAND DAVID A 35 KEN W
SOUTHERLAND GEORGE A 35 KEN B
SOUTHERLAND HARRY A 39 PUG B
SOUTHERLAND HIRAM A 35 MAG W
SOUTHERLAND HUGH A 35 KEN W
SOUTHERLAND ISAAC A 35 MAG B
SOUTHERLAND ISHAM A 35 WAR W
SOUTHERLAND ISHAM A 35 WOL W
SOUTHERLAND J R A 35 LIM W
SOUTHERLAND JAMES A 32 DAV B
SOUTHERLAND JAMES A 35 ISL W
SOUTHERLAND JAMES A 35 KEN B
SOUTHERLAND JAMES A 35 KEN W
SOUTHERLAND JERRY A 35 LIM W
SOUTHERLAND JESSE B A 35 KEN W
SOUTHERLAND JOHN A 35 KEN B
SOUTHERLAND JOHN A 35 WOL W
SOUTHERLAND JOHN H A 35 LIM W
SOUTHERLAND JOHN H A 35 WAR W
SOUTHERLAND JOHN JR A 35 LIM W
SOUTHERLAND JOHN N A 35 KEN W
SOUTHERLAND JOHN SR A 35 LIM W
SOUTHERLAND LONDON A 35 KEN B
SOUTHERLAND MARTIN A 35 MAG B
SOUTHERLAND NEEDHAM A 35 WOL W
SOUTHERLAND PETER A 39 PUG B
SOUTHERLAND
ROBERT J A 35 KEN W
SOUTHERLAND SAMUEL A 35 ISL W
SOUTHERLAND THOMAS A 35 ISL B
SOUTHERLAND
THOMAS J A 35 KEN W
SOUTHERLAND
THOMAS JR A 35 KEN B
SOUTHERLAND
THOMAS SR A 35 KEN B
SOUTHERLAND
WILLIAM J A 35 KEN W
SOUTHERLIN HOWARD A 44 BRA B
SOWELL JAMES A 29 BLA W
SOWERS GEORGE A 32 DAV W
SOWERS W A A 32 DAV W
SPACK J H A 26 MOU W
SPADE RUFUS A 28 03A B
SPAFFORD L A 32 DAV W
SPAIGHT JAMES A 37 TA1 B
SPAIGHT JOSEPH A 37 WHI B
SPAIN GREEN A 46 GRE W
SPAIN H D A 19 HAR W
SPAIN WM F A 46 GRE W
SPAKE ADAM A 26 SHE W
SPAKE ALEX A 26 CAR W
SPAKE PHILIP A 26 SHE W
SPAKE SAM A 26 CAR W
SPAKE SAMUEL A 40 BLA W
SPAKE W M A 26 CAR W
SPANGLER A B A 26 SHE W
SPANGLER J A 26 BLA W
SPANGLER J W A 26 SHE W
SPANN CALEB CHAL A 30 GIB W
8-MONTHS-RESIDENCE
SPAR AARON A 28 17T B
SPARK JAMES F A 37 ROB W
SPARKMAN HARRIS A 37 TA1 B
SPARKMEN WILLIAM A 37 WHI B
SPARKS ALPHA A 26 SHE W
SPARKS B W A 26 GRI W
SPARKS BONNETT A 26 GRI W
SPARKS CAROLINA A 29 FA1 B
SPARKS GEORGE A 19 BE1 B
SPARKS JACKSON A 37 EDW W
SPARKS JOSHUA A 26 GRI W
SPARKS THOS A 26 SHE W
SPARROW ALFRED JR A 19 BE1 B
SPARROW ALFRED P A 19 BE1 B
SPARROW ALONZA T J A 53 FAI W
SPARROW ASA A 19 HAD B
SPARROW CHAS H A 28 04A B
SPARROW DAVID A 19 BE1 B
SPARROW DAVID A 28 05A B
SPARROW DAVID A 28 10T B
SPARROW DOLPHIN A 28 04A B
SPARROW H W A 26 BOR W
SPARROW HENRY A 37 TA1 B
SPARROW JAMES A 19 BE1 B
SPARROW JAMES A 28 01B B
SPARROW JAMES A 28 03A B
SPARROW JAMES A 28 05A B
SPARROW JAMES H A 28 03A B
SPARROW JASPER A 28 01A B
SPARROW JERRY A 28 04A B
CERTIFICATE GIVEN
BIG SWIFT CREEK
SPARROW PETER A 28 03A B
SPARROW RICHD A 28 04A B
SPARROW SIMEON A 19 BE1 B
SPARROW SPENCER A 28 05A B
SPARROW STEPHEN A 37 TA1 B

SPARROW STEPHEN P A 53 LA1 W
SPARROW THOS G A 28 02N W
SPARROW VIRGIL A 28 03B B
SPARROW WILLIAM H A 40 DEC W
SPARROW WINDSOR A 28 05A B
SPARS OLIVER A 28 03A B
SPATE FAYETT A 37 ROB B
SPATE RUFUS A 37 ROB B
SPATE WILLIS A 37 ROB B
SPAUGH CHRISTIAN A 32 SHE W
SPAUGH DANIEL A 32 SHE W
SPAUGH E J A 32 SHE W
SPAUGH GUTLIP A 32 CLE W
SPAUGH JOHN A 32 SHE W
SPAUGH ROBERT A 32 YAD B
SPAUGH SAMEL. A 32 DAV W
SPAUGH SAMUEL A 32 SHE W
SPAUGH T T A 32 SHE W
SPAUGH TIMOTHY A 32 SHE W
SPAYN B Y A 32 JAC W
SPEAR J B A 28 11T W
SPEAR WILLIAM A 28 11T W
SPEARMAN ALEXANDER A 35 ROC B
SPEARMAN ELIJAH A 35 KEN B
SPEARMAN HENRY A 28 15T B
SPEARMAN ISAAC A 29 GRA B
SPEARMAN WALLACE A 29 GRA B
SPEED CUFFEY A 44 YXR B
SPEED DAVID S A 44 HEN W
SPEED G H A 39 FRA W
SPEED JAMES A 44 SAS B
SPEED JOHN A 37 ROC B
SPEED LEWIS A 37 TA2 B
SPEED ROBERT A 44 SAS B
SPEED ROBT A 44 TAR B
SPEED SANDY A 44 YXR B
SPEED THEO A 44 TAR B
SPEED THOMAS A 53 FAI B
SPEED THOS A 39 FRA W
SPEED TOHMAS A 44 TAR B
SPEED WILLIAM A 44 OXF B
SPEIGHT ESSEX A 37 HIG B
SPEIGHT JOHN F A 37 ROB W
SPEIGHT JOSEPH F A 24 MID W
SPEIGHT RICHARD H A 37 TA2 W
SPELL ABRAHAM A 19 BE1 B
SPELL J J R 29 FLE W
RESIDENT OF SAMPSON
SPELLMAN DAMON A 24 EDE B
SPELLMAN DAVID A 28 10T B
CERTIF GIVEN TO LIVES
NOW AT BROAD CREEK
SPELLMAN MOSES A 28 10T B
SPELLMAN RICHARD A 30 IND B
SPELLMAN SILAS A 30 MOY B
SPELMAN ALLEN A 28 05A B
SPELMAN ANTHONY A 28 05A B
SPELMAN JOHN R 28 01A W
STATE PRINTER PREVIOUS
TO AND DURING THE WAR
SPENCE BENJAMIN A A 99 BUS W
SPENCE CAREY A 30 MOY W
SPENCE GEORGE A 30 MOY W
SPENCE GEORGE CHAL A 30 CUR B
MINORITY ABSCENCE
OF PROOF
SPENCE MARK B A 24 MID W
SPENCE THOMAS R A 28 16T W
SPENCE WILLIAM A 30 MOY W
SPENCE WILLIAM A 35 ALB W
SPENCE WM H A 30 MOY W
SPENCER A F A 44 OXF W
SPENCER AFRICA A 28 04B B

SPENCER ALLEN A 53 LA1 B
SPENCER BENJ A 28 04A B
SPENCER BENJ A 28 05A B
SPENCER BENJAMIN A 46 JAM W
SPENCER BENJAMIN B A 53 LA1 W
SPENCER BENJAMIN F A 53 LA1 W
SPENCER CHARLES A 53 FAI B
SPENCER CHARLES A 53 LA1 B
SPENCER CHARLES A 53 LA1 B
SPENCER CHRISTOPHER A 53 FAI W
SPENCER CLARK A 53 LA1 B
SPENCER D A A 44 OXF B
SPENCER DAVID A 53 LA1 B
SPENCER DAVID A 53 LA1 W
SPENCER ENOCK A 53 LA1 B
SPENCER ESSEX A 53 GER B
SPENCER FRANK A 53 SWA B
SPENCER FYRMAN A 28 10T W
SPENCER GEORGE A 53 LA1 B
SPENCER GIB A 28 03A B
SPENCER HARDY A 29 FLE B
SPENCER HASTY A 53 LA1 B
SPENCER HENRY A 53 FAI B
SPENCER HENRY B A 53 LA1 W
SPENCER HENRY S A 53 SWA W
SPENCER HERSEY A 28 05A B
SPENCER HILLIARD A 28 01A B
SPENCER ISRAEL A 53 LA1 B
SPENCER J K A 38 FRE W
SPENCER JACK SR A 53 LA1 B
SPENCER JACOB A 28 04A B
SPENCER JAMES A 28 04A B
SPENCER JAMES P A 53 FAI B
SPENCER JEFFREY A 53 LA1 B
SPENCER JESSE N A 28 16T W
SPENCER JESSIE A 32 COT W
SPENCER JOE A 28 04A B
SPENCER JOHN A 28 05A B
SPENCER JOHN A 53 LA1 B
SPENCER JOHN A 53 LA1 B
SPENCER JOHN A 53 SWA W
SPENCER JOHN J A 53 LA1 W
SPENCER JOHN T A 40 FER W
SPENCER JOHN W A 53 LA1 W
SPENCER JOHN W A 53 LA1 W
SPENCER JONES A 53 LA1 W
SPENCER JOSEPH A 53 LA1 W
SPENCER JOSEPH A 53 LA2 W
SPENCER LAFAYETTE A 53 LA1 B
SPENCER LEVI A 29 FLE B
SPENCER LEWIS A 53 LA1 B
SPENCER MACK A 53 LA1 B
SPENCER MOSES A 28 05A B
SPENCER MOSES A 53 LA1 B
SPENCER NATHAN A 53 FAI W
SPENCER NEEDHAM A 28 04B B
SPENCER PETERS P A 53 LA1 W
SPENCER RICHARD A 53 GER B
SPENCER ROBERT A 53 FAI B
SPENCER ROBT A 44 OXF B
SPENCER SAMUEL A 28 16T W
SPENCER SAMUEL A 53 LA1 B
SPENCER SAMUEL G A 53 OCR W
SPENCER SAMUEL H A 53 LA1 W
SPENCER SELBY A 53 LA1 W
SPENCER SETH A 53 LA1 B
SPENCER SHELDON A 53 FAI B
SPENCER SOLOMAN A 53 LA1 B
SPENCER SUTTON A 53 GER B
SPENCER VIRGIL A 28 04A B
SPENCER WILLIAM A 39 LOU B
SPENCER WILLIAM A 40 DA1 W
SPENCER WILLIAM A 53 OCR W

SPENCER WILLIAM B A 53 LA1 W
SPENCER WILLIAM S A 53 LA2 W
SPENCER WILLIAM T A 53 LA1 W
SPENSE JACK A 24 EDE B
SPENSER BENJM E A 53 GER W
SPENSER CALEB F A 53 GER W
SPENSER FREDRICK F A 53 GER W
SPENSER REZAR A 53 GER B
SPENSER SOLOMAN A 53 GER B
SPENSER WILLIAM W A 53 GER W
SPERGEON J S A 32 BRO W
SPERLIN WM A 26 SHE W
SPERLING ISAAC A 26 BLA W
SPERLING J J A 26 BLA W
SPICER ANDERSON A 37 SHA B
SPICER CHRISTOPHER A 35 KEN B
SPICER DOLYIER A 37 ROC B
SPICER JAMES A 37 ROC B
SPICER JASON A 37 PEN B
SPICER JORDAN A 37 SPA B
SPICER OLIVER A 35 KEN B
SPICER ROBERT A 35 CYP B
CERT. TO KENANSVILLE
13 APR 1868
SPICER RUFUS A 37 SHA B
SPICER SCIPIO A 28 05A B
SPICER SHADRICK L A 37 ROC W
SPICER SOLOMON J A 37 ROC W
SPICER WETHERINGTON A 28 05B B
SPICER WHITTINGTON A 28 05A B
SPIGHT J W A 35 SMI W
SPIGHT MILES A 37 ROB B
SPIKE WASHN A 28 6TH B
SPIKES DANL A 28 04A B
SPIKES NED A 37 PEN B
SPIKES P B A 32 TYR B
SPIKES THOS A 26 MOO B
SPIVEY ALLEN A 24 UPP W
SPIVEY BOB A 39 DAV B
SPIVEY HILLIARD A 39 HAR B
SPIVEY ISHAM A 39 DAV B
SPIVEY JACOB A 24 UPP W
SPIVEY JAMES A 39 HAR B
SPIVEY JOSEPH A 39 HAR B
SPIVEY MAJOR A 39 DAV B
SPIVEY NORPHLET A 39 DAV B
SPIVEY ROBT A 28 05A B
SPIVEY TOM A 39 DAV B
SPIVEY WASHINGTON A 24 UPP W
SPIVEY WASHN A 28 05A B
SPIVEY WILLIAM A 24 UPP W
SPIVIA A W A 25 SHO W
SPIVIA ANDREW A 25 SHO B
SPIVIA J M A 25 SHO W
SPIVIA WILLIAM A 25 SHO W
SPIVY SAMUEL A 25 SHO W
SPOOLMAN CHARLES A 32 THO W
SPOOLMAN EPHRAIM A 32 THO W
SPOOLMAN J R A 32 BRO W
SPOON ABRAHAM A 46 JAM W
SPRADLEY LIMON A 37 ROB B
SPRAGGINS JAMES M A 37 TA1 W
SPRATT JACKSON A 30 KNO W
SPREUEL HENRY A 53 GER B
SPREWEL HENRY A 30 IND B
SPREWEL ISHMAN A 30 IND B
SPREWEL JESSEE A 30 IND B
SPREWEL ZEPHENIAH A 46 GRE W
SPRIGGS THOS A 28 03A B
SPRIGHT JOHN R A 28 13T W
SPRIGHT JOHN W A 28 13T W
SPRINGLE ELIJAH A 19 BE1 W
SPRINGLE GEO W A 19 BE1 W

SPRINGLE JAMES A 19 BE1 W
SPRINGLE RICHARD A 19 BE1 W
SPRINGLE WILLAIM A 19 BE2 W
SPRINGLE WM P A 19 BE1 W
SPRINGS EZEKIEL A 29 GRA W
SPRINGS FRANKLING A 40 CAN B
SPRINGS MURAT A 40 DA1 B
SPRINGS THOS A 29 GRA W
SPRUEL AARON A 28 03A B
SPRUEL BANKUM A 28 05A B
SPRUEL EMPEROR A 28 05A B
SPRUEL GILBERT A 28 05A B
SPRUEL HARKLIS A 28 05B B
SPRUEL JAMES A 28 04A B
SPRUEL JEROME A 28 05A B
SPRUEL JOSEPH A 28 04A B
SPRUEL MILES A 28 03A B
SPRUEL MONROE A 28 04A B
SPRUEL MOSES A 28 15T B
SPRUEL THOMAS A 28 03B B
SPRUELL BENJAMIN A 37 EDW B
SPRUELL DAVID A 28 8TH B
CERTIF GIVEN LIVES
NOW AT NEW BERN
SPRUELL MAC A 28 10T B
SPRUILL ALBERT R A 28 16T W
SPRUILL DANIEL N A 28 16T W
SPRUILL GEO W A 24 EDE W
SPRUILL MINGO A 30 ROA B
SPRUILL SAML E A 24 EDE W
SPRUILL T C A 24 EDE W
SPRUILL TULLY A 28 16T W
SPRUILL WM C A 24 EDE W
SPRUL PEMBROOK A 19 NEW B
SPRUNT JAMES M A 35 KEN W
SPRY EDMUND A 30 COI W
SPRY JAMES A 30 CUR W
SPRY JESSE J A 30 COI W
SPRY SAMUEL A 30 IND W
SPURGEON A R A 32 THO W
SPURGEON JOHN A 32 BRO W
SPURGEON WM B A 32 POS W
SQUIRES ABRAHAM A 28 17T B
SQUIRES AMOS A 28 16T W
SQUIRES BENJAMIN T A 28 17T W
SQUIRES JOHN F A 28 17T W
SQUIRES JOSEPH A 28 13T W
SQUIRES SAML G A 30 IND W
STACK A J A 46 FRI W
STACK CORNELIUS A 46 GRE W
STACK DAVID A 46 FRI W
STACK DAVID T A 46 GRE W
STACK ELIJA A 46 GRE W
STACK J M A 46 FRI W
STACK J P A 32 BRO W
STACK L T A 46 FRI W
STACK SAMUEL A 46 JAM W
STACK W B A 32 BRO W
STACY JOSHUA T A 24 EDE W
STADEN MOSES A 28 04A B
STADEN RANDOLPH A 28 03A B
STADEN WILLIS A 28 04A B
STAFFORD ANDERSON A 32 BRO B
STAFFORD CHAS A 28 01A B
STAFFORD D S A 46 SUM W
STAFFORD G W A 32 JAC W
STAFFORD JAS B A 46 GRE W
STAFFORD JOURDAN A 28 05A B
STAFFORD LEWIS A 46 JAM B
STAFFORD M T A 46 SUM W
STAFFORD SIMON A 32 JAC B
STAFFORD THOMAS A 46 COB W
STAFFORD W P A 32 JAC W
STAFFORD WM A 24 UPP W
STAINBACK B F A 39 PUG W
STAINBACK JAS H A 39 PUG W
STAINBACK JOHN F A 39 PUG W
STAINBACK N H A 39 PUG W
STAINBACK R C A 39 SPE W
STALEY ALSON G A 46 COB W
STALEY CHRISTAIN A 46 COB W
STALEY HENRY A 32 COT W
STALEY HENRY L A 46 COB W
STALEY OLIVER A 46 COB W
STALLENS CALEB A 28 7TH B
STALLIN OLIVER A 19 HAD B
STALLING BAKER A 37 ROC W
STALLING HENRY A 37 ROC B
STALLING JACK A 37 SPA B
STALLING JAMES R A 37 PEN W
STALLING JOSEPH J A 37 PEN W
STALLINGS A J R 39 GRI W
A JUDICIAL OFFICER
PRIOR TO THE WARE
AND VOLUNTEERED
IN JUNE OF 1861
REJECTED
STALLINGS ABNER A 39 DAV W
STALLINGS ALEXANDER A 39 JOR W
STALLINGS ALFRED A 35 ISL W
STALLINGS BENJAMINE A 35 ISL B
STALLINGS BENNETT A 37 ROC W
STALLINGS BENNITT A 39 LOU W
STALLINGS BERRY A 39 JOR B
STALLINGS C J A 39 DAV W
STALLINGS CALEB A 99 BUS B
STALLINGS EDMOND A 37 SPA W
STALLINGS EDWIN A 39 DAV W
STALLINGS EMANUEL A 35 ISL B
STALLINGS GEORGE A 39 DAV W
STALLINGS HIGH A 35 ISL W
STALLINGS JOHNSON A 37 SPA B
STALLINGS KADER A 24 UPP B
STALLINGS KINCHEN A 39 DAV B
STALLINGS MARSHALL A 35 ISL W
STALLINGS NAT A 39 LOU B
STALLINGS OLIVER A 35 ISL B
STALLINGS R W A 39 LOU W
STALLINGS RHUBBIN A 39 DAV W
STALLINGS SAMUEL A 35 SMI B
STALLINGS SAMUEL P A 37 SPA W
STALLINGS W B A 39 DAV W
STALLINGS W E A 39 JOR W
STALLINGS WILLIAM A 39 SPE B
STALLINGS WILLIE P A 53 LA1 W
STALLINGS WILLIS A 39 DAV B
STALLINS SAML A 28 05A B
STALLION JOHN A 99 BUS B
STALLIONS GILBERT A 99 BUS B
STALY JOSEPH A 32 COT W
STAMEY JOHN A 25 TUS W
STAMEY LEANDER A 25 TUS W
STAMP DOC A 28 05A B
STAMP GEORGE A 28 05A B
STAMPER ADAM A 44 HEN B
STAMPER FRANK A 44 HEN B
STAMPER GEO (W COTY) A 44 HEN B
STAMPER GILBERT A 44 HEN B
STAMPER HENRY A 44 HEN B
STAMPER JAMES A 44 HEN W
STAMPER JOHN A 39 PUG B
STAMPER KITT A 44 HEN B
STAMPER M D A 39 JOR W
STAMPER MOSSES A 44 RAG B
STAMPER RANDELL A 44 HEN B
STAMPERS ROBBINS A 39 JOR B
STAMY E A A 25 SHO W
STAMY E S A 25 HAY W
STAMY ELIGH A 25 SHO W
STANCER JOHN A 37 SPA B
STANCIL CASWELL J H A 37 PIN W
STANCIL GEORGE M A 37 PIN W
STANCIL JESSE A 28 03A B
STANCIL JOURDAN A 37 PIN B
STANCIL WILLIS A 37 PIN B
STANCILL JESSIE A 37 PIN W
STANDIN W H A 24 EDE W
STANDLEY CHARLES A 46 GRE W
STANDLY BENJAMIN A 30 TUL W
STANFIELD EDMOND A 46 ROS B
STANFORD DAVID A 35 KEN B
STANFORD GEORGE A 35 KEN B
STANFORD JOHN 1ST A 35 KEN B
STANFORD JOHN 2ND A 35 KEN B
STANFORD LEONIDAS A 35 KEN W
STANFORD OWEN A 35 KEN B
STANFORD WASHINGTON A 35 KEN B
STANFORD WILLIAM A 35 WAR B
STANHOPE THOMAS A 46 GRE B
STANIFUR DENNIS A 39 FRA B
STEALING AND CHARGES
NOW PENDING IN COURT
(NOTE: LET HIM VOTE
HAS BEEN AQUITTED)
STANLEY AMOS A 28 03A B
STANLEY CLARENCE A 28 02N B
STANLEY DANIEL A 28 8TH B
STANLEY DAVID E A 28 05A B
STANLEY E A 44 DUT W
STANLEY FREDK A 28 03A B
STANLEY GEO W A 19 BE1 B
STANLEY ISAAC H A 46 ROS W
STANLEY JACK A 35 SMI B
STANLEY JOHN A 37 HOL B
STANLEY JOHN A 46 HIG W
STANLEY JOHN B A 72 SWA W
STANLEY MILTON M A 46 GRE W
STANLEY MOSES A 28 04A B
STANLEY OWEN A 28 04A B
STANLEY ROBT A 44 FIS B
STANLEY SHADRACK A 28 02N B
STANLEY SIMM A 72 SWA B
STANLEY THOS A 28 01B W
STANLEY WILLIAM A 19 BE1 B
STANLEY WILLIAM F A 28 01A W
CERT GIVEN TO LENOIR CO
STANLEY WM A 28 05A B
STANLEY WRIGHT A 19 BE1 B
STANLEY WRIGHT A 28 04B B
STANLOE G G A 39 HAY B
NAME LINED OUT
STANLY C F A 46 FRI W
STANLY EDWARD A 53 LA1 B
STANLY EDWARD A 53 LA1 B
STANLY ELWOOD A 46 FRI W
STANLY G F A 46 FRI W
STANLY J D A 46 FRI W
STANLY JACOB A 46 FRI W
STANLY JESSE H A 46 FRI W
STANLY JOHN A 19 BE1 B
STANLY JOHN T A 46 FRI W
STANLY K T A 46 FRI W
STANLY LOUIS A 53 FAI B
STANLY PRESTON A 46 FRI W
STANLY THOMAS A 46 FRI W
STANLY W A A 46 FRI W
STANTON B FRANKLIN A 46 GRE W
STANTON DAVID A 19 BE1 W
STANTON G G A 44 KIT W

STANTON H B A 29 FA2 W
STANTON HEYWOOD A 37 SPA B
STANTON I G A 39 FRA W
STANTON J R A 39 HAY W
STANTON JOHN W A 19 BE1 W
STANTON JONATHAN A 19 BE1 W
STANTON WILLIAM P R 28 10T W
WAS AN OFFICER OF THE
MILITIA AND A PATROLLER
TOOK A COMPANY OF
MILITIA TO NEW BERN TO
AID IN DEFENCE OF
NEWBERN
STANTON WM H A 44 HEN W
STAPLEFORD OZIAS C A 28 13T W
STAPLEFORD WM D A 28 13T W
STAPLES GEORGE A 46 GRE B
STAPLES H H A 46 GRE W
STAPLES JOHN M A 46 GRE W
STAPLES JOSEPH A 46 GRE B
STAR GEORGE F A 32 DAV W
STAR J D A 32 COT W
STAR SOLOMON A 32 COT W
STARBUCK ELIHU A 46 FRI W
STARBUCK LEWIS A 46 FRI W
STARBUCK M H A 46 FRI W
STARBUCK RUBEN A 46 FRI W
STARBUCK T C A 46 FRI W
STARBUCK THOMAS A 46 FRI W
STARK CHARLES A 44 HEN B
STARK JAS T JR A 44 OXF W
STARK JAS T SR A 44 OXF W
STARK R W A 44 OXF W
STARKE JNO W A 30 IND W
CHAL
8-MOS-RESIDENCE
STARKES RUFUS A 44 LED W
STARKEY ABRAHAM A 28 01A B
STARKEY BENJ A 28 05A B
STARKEY BENJN A 28 04A B
STARKEY EDWD A 28 04A B
STARKEY HENRY A A 28 04A B
STARKEY HUMPHREY A 28 02N B
STARKEY JAMES A 28 04A B
STARKEY JERRY A 28 03A B
STARKEY LOVELESS A 28 04A B
STARKEY MARCUS A 28 9TH B
STARKEY PRIMUS A 28 04A B
STARKEY SAML A 28 04A B
STARKEY THOS A 28 04A B
STARKS ALFRED A 44 HEN B
STARKS HENRY A 19 NEW B
STARKS K J A 44 OXF W
STARKS NELSON A 29 FA1 B
STARKS THOS A 39 FRA B
STARLING ISAAC A 29 FLE W
STARLING ROBT W A 29 CED B
STARLING SIMON A 29 BLA W
STARNS MONTGOMARY A 26 SWA W
STARNS R P A 26 SWA W
STARR DANIEL M A 46 MCL W
STARR GEORG C A 46 COB W
STARR NELSON A 29 FA1 B
STARR SMART A 29 CAR B
STARRETT JAMES D A 46 GRE W
STASTON RICHMOND A 37 MAN B
STATEN AARON A 37 PIN B
STATEN ALLEN A 37 EDW B
STATEN ANTHONY A 37 PEN B
STATEN ANTHONY A 37 PIN B
STATEN BARRY A 37 HIC B
STATEN BENJAMIN A 37 TA1 B
STATEN COOPER A 37 HIC B
STATEN DAVID A 37 PIN B
STATEN DORSON A 37 HIC B
STATEN EDMUND A 37 HIC B
STATEN EDMUND A 37 PIN B
STATEN ELI A 37 EDW B
STATEN ELI A 37 PIN B
STATEN FERDENANDE B A 37 HIC A
STATEN FRAZIER A 37 TA1 B
STATEN GEORGE A 37 HIC B
STATEN GEORGE A 37 TA1 B
STATEN HILLIARD A 37 HIC B
STATEN HOWELL A 37 PIN B
STATEN JAMES B A 37 HIC A
STATEN JANET A 37 EDW B
STATEN JOSEPH A 37 TA1 B
STATEN JOSIAH A 37 TA1 B
STATEN JOURDAN A 37 HIC B
STATEN JUDGE A 53 FAI B
STATEN LAZARUS A 37 EDW B
STATEN MOSES A 37 HIC B
STATEN NATHAN A 37 EDW B
STATEN NOLVIN A 37 PEN B
STATEN NORWOOD A 37 TA1 B
STATEN RALPH A 37 EDW B
STATEN RODGER A 37 TA1 B
STATEN SIMON 2ND A 37 TA1 B
STATEN SOLOMON A 37 PEN B
STATEN SPENCER A 37 HIC B
STATEN THOMAS A 37 HIC B
STATEN WESTON A 37 PIN B
STATEN WILLIAM A 37 PEN B
STATEN WILLIS A 37 EDW B
STATEN WILLIS A 37 PIN B
STATEN WILSON A 37 PIN B
STATEN WINSOR A 37 EDW B
STATIN FRANK A 37 PIN B
STATON ANTHONY A 19 BE1 B
STATON FRANK A 19 BE1 B
STATON HOYT A 37 TA1 B
STATON JACK A 37 EDW B
STATON SIMON 1ST A 37 TA1 B
STATON SIMON S A 28 04A B
STATON WHITFORD A 37 MAN B
STAUNTON R T A 44 BRA W
STAYLOR THOS A 30 MOY W
STEADMAN ANDW A 29 FA1 B
STEADMAN H A 29 FA1 W
REMOVED TO WILMINGTON
CERT APRIL 10, 68
STEAPLETON W S A 46 SUM W
STEARNES JAMES W A 24 MID W
STEARNS JOHN A 24 MID W
STEAVENS ALFRED A 19 HAD B
STEDMAN R W A 29 FA2 W
STEED FRANK A 44 HEN B
STEED LAWSON A 44 HEN B
STEED S F A 32 JAC W
STEEL A W A 29 FA1 W
STEEL JOHN A 24 EDE W
STEEL PETER A 46 GRE W
STEEL S H A 29 FA1 W
STEEL SEYMORE R 46 GRE W
NAME LINED OUT
WAS A CONSTABLE BEFORE THE
WARE DURING THE WARE HE
HIRED A SUBSTITUTE THEN
TOOK A CONTRACT TO MAKE
HORS SHOES AND USED EVERY
MEANS THAT PROMISED RELIEF
FROM THE ARMY.
HAS NOT QUALIFIED. REJ
STEEL STEPEN A 46 GRE W
STEGALL JAS T A 44 OXF W
STEGALL LEONARD A 44 TOW W
STEGALL ROBERT A 44 TOW W
STEGALL S J A 44 OXF W
STEIFF HENRY A 37 EDW B
STEM G C A 44 LED W
STEM R J A 44 LED W
STEM W T A 44 LED W
STEPHANS JOHNSON A 35 FAI B
STEPHEN HAYWARD A 19 HAR B
STEPHEN JACKSON A 29 LOC B
STEPHEN MARTIN A 29 FA1 B
STEPHEN WILLIS A 37 SPA B
STEPHENS ANDERSON A 44 HEN B
STEPHENS BENJ A 26 SHE B
STEPHENS DANIEL A 39 LOU B
STEPHENS HARRY A 28 03A B
STEPHENS JOHN A 37 TA1 B
STEPHENS JOHN F A 26 SHE W
STEPHENS LEWWIS A 19 BE1 B
STEPHENS SANDY A 29 FA1 B
STEPHENS WILLIAM H A 37 TA1 B
STEPHENS WM A 19 BE1 B
STEPHENSON B N A 46 FRI W
STEPHENSON JOHN A 53 GER B
STEPHENSON ROBT A 46 JAM W
STEPLETON S B A 46 SUM W
STERLING CHS A 29 CED W
STERLING RICHARD A 46 GRE W
STERLING RICHARD O A 46 GRE W
STERLING THOS A 29 CED W
STERLING W S A 29 CED W
STEVENS AMUSA W A 28 16T W
STEVENS EMANUEL A 37 TA1 B
STEVENS GEORGE A 30 MOY W
STEVENS JOHN A 35 FAI B
STEVENS JOHN O A 46 GRE W
STEVENS WILLOUGHBY A 29 GRA W
CERTIFICATE GIVEN
STEVENSON GEO S A 28 01B W
STEVENSON HENRY B A 46 GRE W
STEVENSON M D W A 28 02N W
STEVENSON PETER A 28 01A B
STEVENSON PETER A 28 03A B
STEVENSON ROBERT A 46 GRE W
STEVENSON ROBT F A 28 6TH W
STEVENSON ROBT H A 46 GRE W
STEVENSON SIBERT W A 46 ROS W
STEVENSON W W A 28 02N W
STEVINS WILLIAMS A 35 KEN B
STEVINSON JOHN A 46 ROS W
STEVONS M H A 32 LOF W
STEWARD DUCY A 24 EDE B
STEWARD ISAIAH A 24 EDE B
STEWARD JOHN A 28 6TH W
STEWARD JOHN C A 28 6TH W
STEWARD JOHN P A 37 MAN W
STEWARD JOHN T A 37 MAN W
STEWARD N T A 26 BOR W
STEWARD RICHARD W A 19 STR W
STEWARD STANFIELD A 44 DUT B
STEWARD WM R A 28 6TH W
STEWART ABNER A 46 MCL B
STEWART ALBERD A 46 FRI B
STEWART ALEXANDER A 19 STR W
STEWART BACKERS A 19 STR B
STEWART ELISHA A 29 FA1 B
STEWART GABRIEL A 46 MCL B
STEWART JAMES A 28 7TH W
STEWART JAMES A 46 FRI B
STEWART JAMES W A 19 STR W
STEWART JAS H A 28 6TH W
STEWART JAS S A 29 FA1 W
STEWART JNO A 29 FA1 B

STEWART JOHN A 28 16T B
STEWART JOHN A 32 THO W
STEWART JOHN A 39 PUG B
STEWART JOHN W A 46 RAG W
STEWART JOHNATHAN A 32 POS W
STEWART JOSEPH A 29 BLA X
STEWART LEWIS T A 32 POS W
STEWART MARCUS A 19 BE1 B
STEWART RICHARD A 46 FRI B
STEWART ROBERT A 46 MCL W
STEWART SIMON A 29 BLA X
STEWART THOMAS A 28 10T B
STEWART THOMAS J A 37 TA1 W
STEWART WILLIAM A 46 FRI B
STEWARTS OLIVER A 19 STR W
STICKNEY MOSES A 28 02N B
STIGALL E L A 39 LOU W
STILLER GEORGE A 40 MAU W
STILLEY FREEMAN A 28 13T W
STILLEY JOHN W R 28 16T W
CAPT OF MILITIA DURING
THE WAR CONSTABLE
AND DEP SHEFF AFTER
STILLEY ROBERT F A 28 13T W
STILLEY WILLIAM J A 28 12T W
STILLS WASHINGTON A 39 LOU B
STILLWELL JOHN A 25 TUS W
STIMSON DANIEL A 19 MOR W
STIMSON E D A 32 DAV W
STIMSON J H A 32 DAV W
STIMSON STEVENS A 32 DAV B
STINER WM W A 46 GRE W
STITH J G A 35 FAI W
STITH N Q A 32 THO W
STITH ROBERT B A 35 FAI W
STITH WILLIS A 37 PEN B
STOCKINGER MATHIAS A 32 DAV W
STOCKINGER MATTHIAS A 32 DAV W
STOCKS ABEL A 28 05A B
STOCKS GEO A 29 GRA B
STOCKS WM A 29 GRA B
STOCKTON F M A 26 BLA W
STOCKTON GEORGE A 26 BLA W
STOCKTON J W A 26 MOO W
STOCKTON THOMAS A 46 KIN B
STOCKTON WM A F A 30 POP W
STOKES ADAM A 32 JAC B
STOKES AVERY A 35 MAG B
STOKES BRYANT A 35 MAG B
STOKES CALVIN A 35 CYP B
STOKES CARY A 39 DAV B
STOKES CHARLES A 39 JOR B
STOKES DAVID A 35 CYP B
STOKES DAVID S A 35 MAG B
STOKES G W A 39 JOR W
STOKES GEORGE A A 35 WAR W
STOKES GRAY A 44 KIT B
STOKES HOWARD A 35 MAG B
STOKES JACK A 32 JAC B
STOKES JACK A 35 MAG B
STOKES JACOB A 35 CYP B
STOKES JACOB A 35 MAG B
STOKES JAMES G A 35 MAG W
STOKES JAMES W A 35 KEN W
STOKES JEREMIAH A 35 ISL B
STOKES JEREMIAH A 35 MAG B
STOKES JERRY A 39 DAV B
STOKES JOHN A 35 MAG B
STOKES JOHN A 37 PIN B
STOKES JOHN W A 35 MAG W
STOKES JORDON A 35 MAG B
STOKES JOSEPH A 35 MAG B
STOKES KINCHEN A 32 JAC W
STOKES MICHAEL A 35 ISL B
STOKES NATHAN A 39 DAV B
STOKES PATRICK A 35 MAG B
STOKES R A 32 JAC B
STOKES ROBERT J A 35 KEN W
STOKES SCOTT A 35 CYP B
STOKES SPENCER A 37 TA1 W
STOKES T B A 32 JAC W
STOKES THOMAS JR A 39 JOR W
STOKES W B A 37 ROC W
STOKES WARRICK A 35 MAG B
STOKES WILLIAM A 32 JAC W
STOKES WILLIAM J A 35 KEN W
STONE A R A 32 SHE W
STONE ANTHONY J A 37 TA1 W
STONE B F A 39 DAV W
STONE BLOOM F A 32 THO W
STONE D A A 44 FIS W
STONE D B A 44 OXF W
STONE DANIEL A 44 OXF W
STONE DAVID A 39 HAY W
STONE EMANUEL A 39 JOR B
STONE F M A 39 FRA W
STONE ISAIAH A 32 THO W
STONE ISAIAH A 39 HAY B
STONE J A A 39 FRA W
STONE J J A 39 HAY W
STONE JEHU A 32 THO W
STONE JOHN A 32 THO W
STONE JOHN A 39 HAY B
STONE JOHN A 39 LOU B
STONE JOHN A 44 HEN B
STONE JOHN A 53 LA2 B
STONE JOHN T A 40 STO W
STONE JOSEPH A 32 THO W
STONE LEWIS A 44 TOW B
STONE LEWIS A 44 OXF B
STONE M H A 39 HAY W
STONE ROBERT A 44 HEN B
STONE ROBT A 39 HAY B
STONE S M A 39 FRE W
STONE THOS A A 44 ISL W
STONE W H A 44 HEN W
STONE WILLIAM A 30 KNO W
STONE WILLIAM A 39 DAV W
STONE WILLIAM A 39 HAY B
STONE WILLIAM E A 30 COI W
STONER HENRY C A 32 POS W
STONER LEVI A 32 POS W
STONER W F A 32 COT W
STORY WM R A 46 MCL W
STOTESBERRY GEORGE BA 53 SWA W
STOTESBERRY JAMES B A 53 SWA W
STOTESBERRY THOMAS MA 53 SWA W
STOTESBURY ANSON A 53 LA1 B
STOTESBURY RILEY B A 53 SWA W
STOTESBURY TILMON F A 53 SWA W
STOURS GEORGE A 32 DAV B
STOUT SAMUEL A 32 THO W
STOVALL ELIJAH A 44 YXS B
STOVALL H A 44 OXF W
STOVALL JAS D A 44 YXS W
STOVALL MOSES A 44 SAS B
STOVALL SHARPER A 44 SAS B
STOVALL W A 44 SAS W
STOW CALEB B A 53 HAT W
STOW DAVID B A 53 HAT W
STOW EDMUND D A 53 HAT W
STOW WALLACE A 53 HAT W
STOWE ABRAM A 40 SAN W
STOWE ABRAM SEN A 40 SAN W
STOWE C T A 40 STO W
STOWE EPHRAM A 40 SAN B
STOWE GERDON A 40 STO B
STOWE GERDON SEN A 40 STO B
STOWE ISOM A 40 STO B
STOWE J G A 40 SAN W
COPIED FROM DUPLICATE
STOWE J L A 40 SAN W
STOWE J P A 40 SAN W
COPIED FROM DUPLICATE
STOWE JABEZ (JARVIS)A 40 DA1 B
STOWE JAMES L A 40 STO B
STOWE JOHN W A 40 STO B
STOWE JOSEPH A 40 STO B
STOWE LEROY A 40 DA1 B
STOWE MONROE A 40 DA1 B
STOWE NEIL A 40 STO B
STOWE R B A 40 STO W
STOWE ROBT S A 40 STO B
STOWE SEROY P A 40 DA1 W
STOWE THOMAS A 40 STO B
STOWE W J A 40 SAN W
STOWE WM R A 40 STO B
STOWE ZIMRI A 40 SAN B
STRADER JONATHAN A 46 SUM W
STRADLEY J A A 44 OXF W
STRANGE FRENCH A 29 FA1 W
STRANGE JAMES A 39 LOU W
STRANGE W A A 25 PIN W
STRANGE WILLIAM J A A 25 PIN W
STRATFORD CHRIS W A 46 MCL W
STRATFORD EMSLEY W A 46 MCL W
STRATFORD HENRY B A 46 MCL W
STRATFORD ROBERT A A 46 MCL W
STRATTON ALEX A 29 FA1 W
STRAUGH L C A 29 FA1 W
STRAUGHN GEORGE W A 99 BUS W
STRAYHORN C G A 44 FOR W
STREAK MYNER A 19 HAD B
STREET CHAS A 28 01B B
STREET GEORGE A 44 YXS B
STREET JOHN J A 46 GRE W
STREET S E A 28 6TH W
ROADMASTER
STRICKLAND ABRAHAM A 39 LOU B
STRICKLAND ARCH A 39 GRI W
STRICKLAND BUNN A 39 GRI W
STRICKLAND CALVIN A 35 MAG W
STRICKLAND CHARLES A 28 7TH B
STRICKLAND DAVIS A 37 EDW W
STRICKLAND DUNCAN A 29 ROC W
STRICKLAND EPHRAM A 35 WAR W
STRICKLAND G W A 39 HAR W
STRICKLAND H A 29 FA1 W
STRICKLAND HARDY A 35 MAG W
STRICKLAND HENRY A 39 FRE B
STRICKLAND ISAAC J A 35 MAG W
STRICKLAND JAMES A 35 MAG W
STRICKLAND JAMES T A 37 EDW W
STRICKLAND JEREMIAH A 35 MAG W
STRICKLAND
JEREMIAH SR A 35 MAG W
STRICKLAND JESSE A 35 MAG W
STRICKLAND JNO A 29 GRA W
STRICKLAND JOHN W A 35 MAG W
STRICKLAND KENNITH A 29 ROC W
COPIED FROM DUPLICATE
STRICKLAND M JR A 29 ROC W
STRICKLAND MATH SR A 29 ROC W
STRICKLAND N J A 39 HAY W
STRICKLAND
NATHANIEL A 39 HAY W
STRICKLAND
RICHARD JR A 35 MAG W
STRICKLAND ROBERT A 37 EDW W

STRICKLAND STEPHEN A 35 MAG W
STRICKLAND THOMAS A 37 EDW W
STRICKLAND TIMOTHY A 35 MAG W
STRICKLAND W R A 29 FA1 W
STRICKLAND W S A 39 FRA W
STRICKLAND WILLIAM DA 37 HOL W
STRICKLAND WILLIAM HA 35 MAG W
STRICKLAND WILSON A 39 GRI W
STRICKLEN ABINGTON A 46 FRI B
STRICKLIN A S A 39 HAR W
STRICKLIN DAVE A 29 LOC W
STRICKLIN G S A 39 LOU W
STRICKLIN HAYWOOD A 29 FLE W
STRICKLIN HECTOR A 29 LOC W
STRICKLIN ISAAC A 29 BLA W
STRICKLIN J H A 39 HAR W
STRICKLIN J R A 46 FRI W
STRICKLIN J R R 29 FLE W
NOT OF AGE
STRICKLIN R A 29 LOC W
STRICKLIN R F A 29 LOC W
MILITIA OFFICER BEFORE
THE WAR VOLUNTEERED IN
THE REBELLION
STRICKLIN RICHD A 29 LOC W
STRICKLIN SN A 29 BLA W
STRICKLIN WILLIAM O A 46 SUM W
STRICTLAND GEORGE W A 37 EDW W
STROMER HENRY A 28 01A W
STRONG EDMOND A 44 SAS B
STRONG ESSEX A 44 SAS B
STRONG JAMES A 44 SAS B
STRONG SHACK A 44 SAS B
STROTHER A S A 39 LOU W
STROTHER HENRY A 39 LOU B
STROTHER J P A 39 FRA W
STROTHER J P A 39 FRA W
STROTHER JOHN A 39 FRA B
STROTHER KEMP A 39 LOU B
STROTHER L A 39 FRA B
STROTHER MAJOR A 39 FRA B
STROTHER W H A 39 LOU W
STROUD CALVIN A 26 CAR B
STROUD CROOM A 35 ALB W
STROUD EDWARD A 26 MOO B
STROUD GEO A 44 BRA W
STROUD J M A 44 LED W
STROUD JOHN A 44 LED W
STROUD MAJOR A 26 CAR B
STROUD MONTGOMERY A 39 FRE W
STROUD OWEN A 35 ALB W
STROUD R F A 38 FRE W
STROUD RANSOM A 44 OXF W
STROUD SAMUEL A 26 GOF B
STROUD THOS A 26 MOO W
STROUD W C A 44 LED W
STROUD WILLIAM A 35 ALB W
STROUP A W A 26 CAR W
STROUP ABNER A 40 BLA W
STROUP ANDREW J 40 DA2 W
CERT ISSUED TO 1ST REG
PRE GASTON CO
APRIL 9 1868
STROUP BNJAMIN A 40 DA1 W
STROUP COLUMBUS A 40 DEC W
STROUP DAVID C A 40 DA1 W
STROUP ISRAEL R A 40 DA1 W
STROUP JASON J A 40 BLA W
STROUP JASPER S A 40 BLA W
STROUP MILES A A 40 BLA W
STROUP MOSES JR A 40 DEC W
STROUP MOSES SR A 40 DEC W
STROUP SEPHUS A 40 SAN W

STROUP W W A 40 SAN W
STROUP WESLEY A 40 DA1 W
STRUDIN GEORGE A 24 EDE B
STRUM A T A 44 FIS W
STRUM T B A 39 PUG W
STRUM W H A 44 TOW W
STRUNK SHELBY A 46 GRE W
STRUTS BONEY W A 35 ISL W
STRUTS JAMES A 35 ISL W
STUART D S A 26 SHE W
STUART DAVID C 46 RAG W
STUART E J A 46 HIG W
STUART JAMES A 46 FRI B
STUART JAMES A A 46 RAG W
STUART JAMES A A 46 RAG W
STUART JERRY A 46 RAG B
STUART JESSEE A 44 HEN B
STUART JOHN A 46 MCL W
STUART M M A 32 POS W
STUART MANSON A 44 OXF B
STUART MARTIN A 46 RAG B
STUART RICHARD A 46 RAG B
STUART SAMPSON R A 46 MCL W
STUART SAMUEL F A 46 RAG W
STUART T A A 46 HIG W
STUART W C A 44 HEN W
STUART WM H A 46 RAG W
STUBBS PRINCE A 24 EDE B
STURDIVANT ALBERT J A 99 BUS W
STURDIVANT ALLEN A 99 BUS W
STURDIVANT BURRILL A 99 BUS B
STURDIVANT CASWELL A 99 BUS W
STURDIVANT FABIUS A 99 BUS W
STURDIVANT HENDERSONA 99 BUS B
STURDIVANT JESSE W A 39 JOR W
STURDIVANT JETHRO A 99 BUS B
STURDIVANT NATHANIELA 99 BUS B
STURDIVANT RUFUS A 99 BUS B
STURDIVANT THOMAS H A 99 BUS W
STURDIVANT WESLEY A 99 BUS B
STURDIVANT WILLIAM AA 99 BUS W
STYATEN EPHRIHAM A 37 PEN B
STYREN GEORGE A 28 02N B
STYRES ABRIHAM A 32 COT W
STYRES M A 32 JAC W
STYRON ABISHA N A 19 CED W
STYRON AMBROSE A 19 POR W
STYRON BENJ G A 19 POR W
STYRON BENJA G A 53 OCR W
STYRON DAVID C A 28 15T W
STYRON DAVID V R 72 SWA W
NO EXPLANATION GIVEN
STYRON EMANUEL A 19 BE1 W
STYRON GEO W A 19 BE1 W
STYRON GEO W A 19 BE1 W
STYRON HAMER W A 53 HAT W
STYRON HENRY T A 19 CED W
STYRON HEZEKIAH A 19 CED W
STYRON ISAIAH A 19 SMY W
STYRON J R A 28 05B W
STYRON JAMES A 53 OCR W
STYRON JOHN A A 19 HUN W
STYRON JOHN E A 19 STR W
STYRON JOHN W A 19 DAV W
STYRON JOHN W A 28 16T W
STYRON JOHN W A 72 SWA W
STYRON JOSEPH A 19 BE1 W
STYRON JOSEPH F A 53 FAI W
STYRON KILBY A 19 DAV W
STYRON L H A 19 STR W
STYRON LARENZO W A 19 DAV W
STYRON RICHARD B A 19 CED W
STYRON ROBERT A 53 HAT W

STYRON SIMON A 19 CED W
STYRON STEPHEN R A 53 HAT W
STYRON THOS W A 19 STR W
STYRON W S A 28 01A W
STYRON WALLACE A 19 POR W
STYRON WALLACE D A 19 HUN W
STYRON WALLACE H A 19 HUN W
STYRON WALLACE K A 19 POR W
STYRON WALLACE S A 19 HUN W
STYRON WHITFORD SR A 19 DAV W
STYRON WILLIAM A 53 SWA W
STYRON WILSON W A 53 HAT W
STYRON ZACHARIAH A 19 POR W
STYRON ZACHARIAH A 28 10T W
SUGG PHESANTON S A 37 TA2 W
SPARTA
SUGG REDDING S A 37 TA1 W
SPARTA
SUGGS ALEXANDER A 40 SAN B
SUGGS ALLEN A 37 SPA B
SUGGS GRANVILLE A 37 SPA B
SUGGS HARRY A 40 SAN B
SUGGS HENRY A 37 SPA B
SUGGS JACK A 37 PIN B
SUGGS JOHN A 19 NEW B
SUGGS JOHN A 28 8TH B
SUGGS JOHN T A 40 DA1 W
SUGGS LEROY L A 40 DA1 W
SUGGS LEWIS A 37 EDW B
SUGGS MINGS A 19 NEW B
SUGGS OSCAR A 37 WHI B
SUGGS WARREN A 37 ROB B
SUGGS WILLIAM A 37 SPA B
SUGGS WILLIAM A 72 SWA W
SUGGS WILLIS A 37 HIC B
SUGS ROBERT A 19 HAD B
SUIT E F A 44 DUT W
SUIT J G A 44 DUT B
SUIT J R A 44 LED W
SUIT M H A 44 LED W
SUIT MARCUS A 44 DUT B
SUIT R S A 44 LED W
SUIT R T A 44 DUT W
SUIT RICHMOND A 44 DUT B
SUIT WM R A 44 LED W
SUITS ADAM A 46 GRE W
SUITS FREDERICK B A 46 COB W
SUITS HENRY A 46 ROS W
SUITS J C A 46 HIG W
SUITS JOHN A 46 GRE W
SUITS SAMUEL A 46 RAG W
SUITS ZEBULON A 46 GRE W
SUITZ WM A 46 HIG W
SULEVAN J W A 26 SHE W
SULIVAN J G A 32 THO W
SULIVAN JESSE A 26 SHE B
SULLIVAN B F A 46 HIG W
SULLIVAN B J A 35 GLI W
SULLIVAN CICERO C A 35 GLI W
SULLIVAN DANIEL A 28 02N W
SULLIVAN ELISHA A 35 KEN W
SULLIVAN HARRY A 32 THO W
SULLIVAN HENRY A 35 WOL W
SULLIVAN INSIL A 35 GLI W
SULLIVAN J J A 32 THO W
SULLIVAN J L A 46 JAM W
SULLIVAN JAMES C A 32 THO W
SULLIVAN JAMES G A 46 GRE W
SULLIVAN JERRY A 35 WOL W
SULLIVAN JOSHUA A 35 GLI W
SULLIVAN SAMUEL A 35 WOL W
SULLIVAN SOLOMAN A 46 JAM W
SULLIVAN SOLOMON A 46 JAM W

SULLIVAN W A A 32 DAV W
SULLIVAN WILLIS A 46 GRE W
SUMERLIN D J A 35 FAI W
SUMERLIN J W A 35 FAI W
SUMERLIN WILLIAM A 37 HIG W
SUMERLING DANIEL A 37 WHI B
SUMMER GEORGE A 37 ROC B
SUMMER WM A 46 MCL W
SUMMERLIN BENJAMIN A 35 WAR W
SUMMERLIN D C A 35 GLI W
SUMMERLIN DENNIS A 29 CAR W
SUMMERLIN ISAAC A 35 KEN W
SUMMERLIN J D A 35 WOL W
SUMMERLIN JACOB A 35 WAR W
SUMMERLIN LEVY A 35 WOL W
SUMMERLIN WILLIAM A 37 ROC W
SUMMEROW HENRY A 40 BLA W
SUMMERS ALFRED A 46 MCL B
SUMMERS ANDERSON A 46 GIB W
SUMMERS ARCHIBALD A 46 GIB W
SUMMERS CHAS A 46 GIB B
SUMMERS FELTY A 46 GIB W
SUMMERS FRANK A 24 EDE B
SUMMERS HENRY A 46 GIB B
SUMMERS ISAAC A 46 GIB W
SUMMERS ISAAH A 46 GIB W
SUMMERS JAMES S SR A 46 GRE W
SUMMERS JOHN A 46 GIB B
SUMMERS JOHN A 46 MCL W
SUMMERS LUDWICK A 46 GIB W
HE TOOK THE OATH THAT HE
DID NOT VOLUNTARILY AID
THOUGH HE WAS A MAGIS-
TRATE BEFORE DURING AND
SINCE THE WAR AND WAS
ACCEPTED BY A MAJORITY
VOTE, & LATER REJECTED.
SUMMERS LUDWICK JR A 46 GIB W
SUMMERS MASEHIME A 46 MON W
SUMMERS NATHAN M A 46 GRE W
SUMMERS NELSON A 46 MCL B
SUMMERS ROBT A 46 GIB B
SUMMERS SAUNDERS A 46 GIB W
SUMMERVILLE ANDERSONA 44 SAS B
MISPLACED
SUMMERVILLE JOSEPH A 44 OXF B
SUMMEY DAVID A A 40 DA1 W
SUMMEY JACOB M E A 40 DA1 W
SUMMEY JOHN B A 40 MAU W
SUMMEY JONAS A 40 DA1 W
SUMMEY LEVI A 40 DA1 B
SUMMEY MICHAEL R 40 DA1 W
NAME LINED OUT
CHAL CAUSE: COUNTERFEITING
& CONVICTED BY STATE
COURT BEFORE THE WAR
REJECTED
SUMMEY MICHAEL JR A 40 DA1 W
SUMMEY WILLIAM A 40 DA1 W
SUMMIT HENRY A 40 BLA W
SUMMIT LAWSON M A 40 DA1 W
SUMMY ANDREW A 32 DAV W
SUMMY JUDIAH A 32 LEE W
SUMNER ALLEN A 53 LA1 B
SUMNER ASA A 35 SMI W
SUMNER GEORGE A 32 TYR B
SUMNER HENRY A 32 COT B
SUMNER J E A 32 COT W
SUMNER MARTIN A 35 SMI W
SUMNER SAMUEL A 35 SMI W
SUMRELL M W H A 28 01A W
SUNMER THOMAS A 37 ROC B
SURAT ALLEN A 32 JAC W

SURATT B A 32 JAC W
SURATT DAVID A 32 JAC W
SURATT GEORGE A 32 JAC W
SURATT JAMES A 32 JAC W
SURATT LOUIS A 32 JAC W
SURATT WM A 32 JAC W
SURATT WM M A 32 JAC W
SURLES ALLEN A 29 CAR B
SURLES CALVIN B A 29 CAR W
REMOVED TO HARNETT CO
SURLES HENRY A 29 CAR B
SURLES ISHAM A 29 CAR B
SURLES L M A 29 CAR W
SURLES SAML R A 29 CAR W
SURLES WM A 29 CAR B
SURRATT ALISON A 32 JAC W
SURRATT RICHARD A 40 BLA B
SURRELLS ISAAC A 29 FA1 B
SURRELS DANIEL A 29 CAR B
SUTHERLAND JORDEN A 44 DUT B
SUTTLE C B A 26 SHE W
SUTTLES D B F A 26 BLA W
SUTTLES D D A 26 BLA W
SUTTON ALFRED A 28 03A B
SUTTON ALFRED A 28 8TH W
SUTTON ANDREWS A 46 GIB W
SUTTON BENJAMIN A 30 POW B
SUTTON CHARLES A 28 11T W
SUTTON FRANK A 28 03A B
SUTTON FRANK A 28 15T B
SUTTON GILES A 35 GLI W
SUTTON HENRY A 28 03A B
SUTTON ISAAC A 28 6TH B
SUTTON ISAAC A 28 7TH B
SUTTON J D A 35 FAI W
SUTTON JEREMIAH W A 28 14T W
SUTTON JOHN A 28 05A B
SUTTON JOHN A 28 11T W
SUTTON JOHN G A 28 02N B
SUTTON LOYED H A 29 LOC W
SUTTON MIKIEL A 30 IND B
SUTTON PATTERSON F A 46 GIB W
SUTTON PROVIDENCE A 37 ROC B
SUTTON RANSOM A 24 EDE B
SUTTON ROBERT A 28 01A B
SUTTON ROBT A 46 MCL B
SUTTON RODEN A 28 03A B
SUTTON S S A 24 EDE W
SUTTON SAMUEL A 28 11T W
SUTTON STEPHEN A 28 8TH W
SUTTON THOMAS A 35 WOL W
SUTTON WILSON R CHALA 30 ROA W
MAGISTRATE PRIOR TO 1861
SUTTON WM A 46 SUM W
SWAIM A A 46 HIG W
SWAIM HENRY A 46 GRE B
SWAIM WILLIAM A 26 BUR B
SWAIN DAVID A 32 DAV W
SWAIN E V A 32 POS W
SWAIN J F A 32 POS W
SWAIN PAUL A 46 GRE W
SWAIN POMPEY A 19 MOR B
SWAIN R C A 46 GRE W
SWAIN RHODEN A 37 HIC B
SWAIN SALATHIAL A 46 ROS W
SWAIN SANDFORD A 46 JAM W
SWAN NIXEN W A 24 EDE B
SWAN R W A 28 04B W
SWAN SIDNEY A 37 TA1 B
SWAN THOMAS A 24 EDE B
SWAN WM C A 46 GRE W
SWANE COLUMBUS F A 32 BRO W
SWANE P H A 32 SHE W

SWANN MORRIS A 29 FA1 B
SWANN SAML A 29 FA1 B
SWANNEE HILLIARD A 37 EDW B
SWANSON J G A 39 JOR W
TRNS TO WARREN CO
APRIL 10, 1868
SWANSON W C A 39 JOR W
SWANSON W E A 39 SPE W
SWANSON W H A 39 SPE W
SWANSY ALFRED A 35 KEN W
SWANSY JAMES A 35 KEN W
SWEAT ISHAM A 29 FA1 B
SWEET C L A 44 HEN W
SWEET J L A 44 HEN W
CERT TO VOTE OUT COUNTY
SWEET W H S A 28 04A W
SWEETZER WM A A 19 BE2 W
SWEITZER WM H A 19 BE1 W
SWEPSON CALVAN A 37 MAN B
SWERT BERNHARD A 28 02N W
SWET J A 40 SAN W
SWICEGOOD GEORGE A 32 TYR W
SWICEGOOD H H A 32 TYR W
SWICEGOOD HENRY F A 32 TYR W
SWICEGOOD J A A 32 TYR W
SWICEGOOD JAMES H A 32 TYR W
SWICEGOOD JESSIE S A 32 TYR W
SWICEGOOD PHILIP A 32 TYR W
SWIFT CALVIN A 46 GRE B
SWIFT LEVIN A 46 FRI W
SWIFT RUSSEL A 46 GRE B
SWIFT SHEPHERD A 46 GRE B
SWIGGETT GEORGE H A 46 JAM W
SWINDEL ANSON M A 53 SWA W
SWINDELL AARON A 53 LA1 B
SWINDELL ALBIN B A 53 SWA W
SWINDELL ALEXANDRIA A 53 GER W
SWINDELL ANDERSON A 53 LA1 B
SWINDELL
BARTHOLMEW J A 53 SWA W
SWINDELL CASON E A 53 LA2 W
SWINDELL CHARLES A 53 LA1 B
SWINDELL CHARLES A 53 LA1 B
SWINDELL CHAS H A 28 16T W
SWINDELL CORNELIOUS A 53 LA1 W
SWINDELL DAVID D A 53 LA1 W
SWINDELL DAVID W A 53 LA1 W
SWINDELL DIXSON A 53 LA1 W
SWINDELL FRANCIS M A 53 LA1 W
SWINDELL FRANCIS W A 53 FAI W
SWINDELL GEORGE W A 53 SWA W
SWINDELL HARDY A 53 LA1 W
SWINDELL ISAAC A 28 16T W
SWINDELL ISAAC G A 53 LA1 W
SWINDELL ISAAC S A 53 FAI W
SWINDELL JAMES A 28 16T W
SWINDELL JAMES D A 53 FAI W
SWINDELL JOSHUWA V A 53 LA1 W
SWINDELL LEWIS L A 53 FAI W
SWINDELL PERRY A 53 SWA B
SWINDELL POMPY A 53 SWA B
SWINDELL
SILVERTER G A 53 FAI W
SWINDELL SOLOMAN F A 53 LA1 W
SWINDELL THOMAS D A 28 16T W
SWINDELL THOMAS M A 53 LA2 W
SWINDELL WAIDE A 53 SWA W
SWINDLE DAVID A 28 05A B
SWINDLE DAVID A 28 15T W
SWINDLE DAVID A 53 GER B
SWINDLE GAMALIEL A 53 SWA W
SWINDLE JOEL A 19 BE1 W
SWINDLE LYNDON E A 53 SWA W

SWINDLE THOMAS D A 53 SWA W
SWINDLE WILLIAM M A 53 SWA B
SWING ABRIHAM A 32 DAV W
SWING ALFORD A 32 DAV W
SWING DANIEL B A 32 COT W
SWING DAVID A 32 DAV W
SWING DAVID A 32 DAV W
SWING HENRY A 32 DAV W
SWING HENRY A 46 COB W
SWING HENRY E A 46 COB W
SWING J H A 32 COT W
SWING J H A 32 LOF W
SWING J J A 32 DAV W
SWING JAMES F A 32 DAV W
SWING JEFFERSON A 32 DAV W
SWING JOHN D A 32 DAV W
SWING JOHN J A 46 COB W
SWING OBIDIAH A 32 DAV W
SWING WILLIAM A 32 DAV B
SWING WILLIAM A 32 DAV W
SWINK A W A 32 COT W
SWINSON A T A 35 FAI W
SWINSON A W A 35 FAI W
SWINSON ANDREW A 35 MAG B
SWINSON CALVIN A 35 MAG B
SWINSON D H A 35 WOL W
SWINSON EDMUND A 35 MAG B
SWINSON ELIJAH A 35 SMI W
SWINSON FARIN A 35 FAI B
SWINSON GEORGE L A 35 SMI W
SWINSON JACK A 35 WAR B
SWINSON JACOB A 35 WOL W
SWINSON JAMES W A 35 MAG W
SWINSON JESSE A 35 WAR W
SWINSON JOHN W A 35 MAG W
SWINSON JOSEPH A 35 WAR B
SWINSON MACON A 35 WOL W
SWINSON MORDECAI A 35 MAG W
SWINSON NAPOLEON A 35 WAR B
SWINSON R J A 35 FAI W
SWINSON R W A 35 WOL W
SWINSON SAMEUL A 35 WAR B
SWINSON SAMUEL CHAL R 35 WOL W
UNDER AGE
SWINSON SPEIGHT A 35 WAR B
SWINSON TONEY A 35 KEN B
SWINSON WILEY A 35 MAG B
SWINSON WILLIAM 1ST A 35 WAR B
SWINSON WILLIAM 2ND A 35 WAR B
SWISEGOOD D J A 32 THO W
SWISEGOOD JOHN A 32 BRO W
SWISON LOUIS A 35 FAI B
SWOFFARD WILLIAM A 26 WAR W
SYDNER BEVELLY A 44 HEN B
SYDNER LONDON A 44 HEN B
SYKES ANTHONY A 28 9TH B
SYKES ASHLY A 30 POP W
SYKES BENJAMIN A 28 9TH B
SYKES CALEB A 30 TUL W
SYKES DAVID A 30 POW B
SYKES DAVID A 35 WAR B
SYKES EDMOND A 39 DAV W
SYKES EDWD A 29 FA1 W
SYKES ENNIS A 28 9TH B
SYKES HENRY E A 29 FA1 W
SYKES ISAAC A 28 01A B
SYKES JERRY A 28 10T B
SYKES JIM A 39 DAV B
SYKES JNO A A 29 FA1 W
SYKES LEWIS A 28 9TH B
SYKES MINGO A 28 04A B
SYKES PHILIP A 29 GRA B
SYKES RILEY A 28 9TH B
SYKES S S A 29 FA1 W
SYKES SAMUEL A 28 9TH B
SYKES SIMON A 28 9TH B
SYKES THOMAS A 30 NAR W
SYKES TRIMAGAN A 30 IND W
SYKES WILLIAM A 30 TUL W
SYKS WILLIAM A 30 CUR W
SYMES D E A 29 CED W

\- T -

TABERN AVERY A 44 OXF B
TABERN HARRISON A 44 OXF B
TABON JOHN A 44 LED B
TABON THOS A 44 LED B
TABOR F ISAIAH A 28 03A W
TABORN ANDERSON A 44 SAS B
TABORN ARTHUR A 44 BRA B
TABORN LITTLETON A 44 OXF B
TABORN MONROE A 46 GRE B
TABORN ROBT A 44 TAR B
TABORN WILLIAM A 44 OXF B
TABOUT THOS A 29 CED W
TABUN ORANGE A 39 GRI B
TAKE WILLIAM HENRY A 37 ROC B
TALBERT JNO A 29 FLE W
TALLEY LONDON A 37 HIC B
TALLEY WILLIAM A 37 HOL W
TALLY HENRY M A 44 SAS W
TALLY ROBT A 44 FIS B
TALSTON WILLIAM H A 37 PEN W
TALTON AARON L A 37 SHA W
TANKARD SAML A 28 01A B
TANKARD WM A 28 05A B
TANNER C P A 40 RHY W
TANNER DUNCAN A 29 CAR B
TANNER JAMES A 37 ROB W
TANNER WM M A 44 SAS W
TANNERHILL LEWIS A 37 HOL B
TANNERHILL LUKE A 37 PEN B
TANT RICHARD A 39 LOU W
TAPER DANL A 28 01B B
TARNER EBENEZER A 37 ROC B
TARPLEY JERRY H A 46 GRE W
TARPLEY WATSON A 46 GRE B
TARRENDEN ISAAC A 28 05A B
TARRENDEN MILES A 28 05A B
TART JEREMIAH F A 53 LA1 W
TATAM AUGS A 29 LOC W
TATE ALLEN B A 46 GIB W
TATE BRADFORD A 40 CAN B
TATE DANIEL A 40 CAN B
TATE ELI A 35 MAG B
TATE GEORGE A 40 CAN B
TATE GEORGE A 44 DUT B
TATE HARVEY A 29 GRA B
TATE HENRY H A 46 GRE W
TATE JAMES W A 35 MAG B
TATE JOHN A A 46 MCL W
TATE JOSEPH A 39 FRA B
TATE K Y A 26 HOL B
TATE LEWIS A 39 FRA B
TATE R W E A 39 HAY W
TATE R W E A 39 LOU W
TRNS FROM HAYESVILL
TATE ROBT H A 46 GRE B
TATE THOMAS A 40 CAN B
TATE THOMAS A A 40 CAN W
TATE THOMAS R A 40 CAN W
TATE W D A 30 IND W
TATE WESLEY A 46 JAM B
TATE WILLIS A 44 DUT B
TATE WM J A 46 RAG W
TATEM CALEB H A 30 IND W
TATEM DAVID A 30 CUR W
TATEM GIDEON A 30 CUR W
TATEM H W A 30 KNO W
TATEM JEHUE A 30 CUR W
TATEM P L A 30 CUR W
TATEM S H A 30 CUR W
TATEM THADEUS C A 30 CUR W
TATEM W B A 30 CUR W
TATEM WILLIAM C A 30 CUR W
TATOM W V A 46 KIN W
TATTER ALEC A 37 PEN B
TATTER NOAH A 37 PEN B
TATUM JAMES A 46 SUM B
TATUM JOHN A 30 TUL W
TATUM JOHN H A 46 GRE W
TATUM JOHN J A 30 TUL W
TATUM JOHNSON A 37 PIN B
TATUM LOGAN A 46 SUM B
TATUM M J A 46 GRE W
TATUM RALEIGH A 46 SUM B
TATUM THOMAS A 46 SUM B
TATUM WILIFORD A 29 CED W
TAUNT CORDY A 39 GRI W
TAUNT DAVID A 39 GRI W
TAUNT JAMES A 39 GRI W
TAUNT JNO A 39 GRI W
TAUNT KINNEL A 39 GRI W
TAUNT KINSMAN A 39 GRI W
TAUNT LEE A 39 GRI W
TAWRY JOHN A 26 WAR W
TAYBURN SAMUEL A 37 PEN B
TAYLER FRANKLIN A 32 JAC B
TAYLOR A G A 19 HAD W
TAYLOR A G A 29 BLA W
TAYLOR ALBERT A 28 02N B
TAYLOR ALEX A 44 TOW B
TAYLOR ALEX A 44 LED B
TAYLOR ALEXANDER A 19 HAR W
TAYLOR ALEXANDER A 28 8TH B
TAYLOR ALEXR A 28 04A W
TAYLOR ALFORD A 39 JOR B
CERT WARREN CO
TAYLOR ALLEN A 35 MAG B
TAYLOR ALLEN A 37 HIG B
TAYLOR ALLEN A 46 SUM B
TAYLOR ANTHONEY A 44 OXF B
TAYLOR ARCHD A 39 JOR W
TAYLOR
ARNOLD WASHINGTON A 46 ROS B
TAYLOR AUTRY A 37 ROC B
TAYLOR B F A 19 HAD W
TAYLOR BENJ A 29 FA1 B
TAYLOR BENJ A 44 OXF B
TAYLOR BENJ F A 30 POP W
TAYLOR BENJ R A 29 FA1 W
TAYLOR BENJAMIN A 30 CUR W
TAYLOR BENJAMIN A 30 POP B
TAYLOR BENJAMIN A 44 FIS B
TAYLOR BERRY A 28 01A B
TAYLOR BERRY A 46 FRI B
TAYLOR BOWSER A 44 OXF B
TAYLOR BRYANT A 32 JAC B
TAYLOR BURRELL S A 37 WHI W
TAYLOR BURTON H A 37 HIC A
TAYLOR BUTLER A 32 JAC W
TAYLOR C C A 19 HAD W
TAYLOR C C A 19 NEW W
TAYLOR CAESAR A 28 04A B
TAYLOR CALLINS A 39 HAY B
TAYLOR CALVIN A 32 THO B
TAYLOR CALVIN A 37 HIC A
TAYLOR CALVIN G A 46 FRI W
TAYLOR CEASER A 37 PIN B

TAYLOR CEZER A 37 MAN B
TAYLOR CHARLES A 35 MAG B
TAYLOR CHARLES A 44 FIS B
TAYLOR CHARLES A 44 HEN B
TAYLOR CHAS A 28 03A B
TAYLOR CHAS H A 28 01A W
TAYLOR D J A 29 FLE W
FROM DUPLICATE COPY
TAYLOR D W A 28 9TH W
TAYLOR DANBY A 39 JOR B
TAYLOR DAVID A 37 EDW B
TAYLOR DAVID A 44 RAG B
TAYLOR DAWSON A 37 HIC A
TAYLOR DEMPSEY A 35 MAG W
TAYLOR DIVOR A 24 EDE B
TAYLOR DOCTOR A 37 MAN B
TAYLOR DREAD A 37 EDW B
TAYLOR DREW A 37 HIC B
TAYLOR DUDLEY A 30 CUR B
TAYLOR DURANT A 19 HAD W
TAYLOR EDMOND A 44 FIS B
TAYLOR EDWARD A 19 HAD W
TAYLOR ELIJAH A 19 HUN W
TAYLOR ELIJAH A 72 SWA W
TAYLOR ELIJAH R 28 10T W
TAYLOR EMSLY A 32 JAC W
TAYLOR ENOCH A 44 TOW B
TAYLOR EPHRIUM A 44 TOW B
TAYLOR F R A 29 FLE W
TAYLOR FEDRICK A 39 PUG B
TAYLOR FELIX W A 35 MAG W
TAYLOR FRANKLIN A 40 BLA W
TAYLOR FYRMAN A 28 10T W
TAYLOR G N A 25 TUS W
TAYLOR G W A 46 FRI B
TAYLOR GABRIEL A 44 HEN B
TAYLOR GEO A 44 OXF B
TAYLOR GEO H A 28 01A W
TAYLOR GEO W A 19 BE1 W
TAYLOR GEO W A 19 HAR W
TAYLOR GEORGE A 28 6TH W
TAYLOR GEORGE A 30 POP B
TAYLOR GEORGE A 44 YXS B
TAYLOR GREEN A 37 WHI B
TAYLOR GUY A 39 JOR B
CERT WAREN CO
TAYLOR H A A 29 FLE W
TAYLOR H A A 44 OXF W
TAYLOR HARBERT A 44 RAG B
TAYLOR HENRY A 28 03A B
TAYLOR HENRY A 37 SHA W
TAYLOR HENRY A 39 PUG B
TAYLOR HENRY A 44 BEA B
TAYLOR HENRY A 44 ISL B
TAYLOR HENRY A 44 OXF B
TAYLOR HENRY A 46 GRE B
TAYLOR HILLIARD S A 37 SHA W
TAYLOR HORACE A 44 OXF B
TAYLOR IRVING A 35 MAG B
TAYLOR ISAAC A 19 BE1 B
TAYLOR ISAAC A 19 HAD W
TAYLOR ISAAC A 28 10T W
TAYLOR ISHAM A 39 JOR B
TAYLOR IVY A 28 6TH W
TAYLOR J B A 28 02N W
TAYLOR J E A 28 10T W
TAYLOR J H A 44 ISL W
TAYLOR J R A 29 BLA W
TAYLOR J W C A 28 10T W
TAYLOR JABEZ A 28 9TH W
TAYLOR JACOB A 19 HAR W
TAYLOR JACOB A 24 UPP B
TAYLOR JACOB A 29 FA1 B

TAYLOR JACOB A 28 11T B
CERTIFICATE TO
VOTE AT NEW BERN
TAYLOR JACOB A 35 MAG W
TAYLOR JACOB A 44 TOW B
TAYLOR JACOB A 53 GER B
TAYLOR JAKE A 37 ROB B
TAYLOR JAMES A 19 MOR B
TAYLOR JAMES A 28 6TH W
TAYLOR JAMES A 40 BLA W
TAYLOR JAMES A 40 RHY W
TAYLOR JAMES A 44 OXF B
TAYLOR JAMES A 44 SAS B
TAYLOR JAMES R A 35 ALB W
TAYLOR JAMES W A 37 MAN W
TAYLOR JAMES Z A 37 TA2 W
TAYLOR JERRY A 44 TOW B
TAYLOR JESOP A 44 OXF B
TAYLOR JESSEE A 44 OXF B
TAYLOR JIM A 39 JOR B
TAYLOR JOBE A 44 OXF B
TAYLOR JOHN A 28 16T B
TAYLOR JOHN A 28 6TH W
TAYLOR JOHN A 29 FA1 B
TAYLOR JOHN A 37 MAN W
TAYLOR JOHN A 44 BEA B
TAYLOR JOHN A 44 OXF B
TAYLOR JOHN A A 19 HUN W
TAYLOR JOHN A A 28 10T W
TAYLOR JOHN B A 37 ROC W
TAYLOR JOHN B A 46 ROS W
TAYLOR JOHN E A 28 6TH W
TAYLOR JOHN F A 35 MAG W
TAYLOR JOHN F A 37 MAN W
TAYLOR JOHN M A 35 ALB W
TAYLOR JOHN N A 37 ROC W
TAYLOR JOHN P A 29 FA1 W
BLACK RIVER
TAYLOR JOHN SR A 44 OXF B
TAYLOR JOHN T A 19 HAD W
TAYLOR JONITHAN A 35 GLI W
TAYLOR JOSEPH A 19 HUN W
TAYLOR JOSEPH A 30 COI W
TAYLOR JOSEPH A 44 OXF B
TAYLOR JOSEPH H H A 37 TA1 B
TAYLOR JOSH G A 29 FLE W
TAYLOR JOSHUA A 28 10T W
TAYLOR JOSHUA L CHAL 28 10T W
TAYLOR JOSIAH A 28 6TH W
TAYLOR KENAN A 35 WOL W
TAYLOR KILLIS A 44 YXS B
TAYLOR L C A 39 FRA B
TAYLOR L C A 44 OXF W
TAYLOR LEMUEL A 46 SUM W
TAYLOR LEW A 39 JOR B
TAYLOR LEWIS A 28 6TH W
TAYLOR LEWIS A 53 GER B
TAYLOR LEWIS G A 28 6TH W
TAYLOR LEWIS JR A 44 OXF W
TAYLOR LONDON A 44 FIS B
TAYLOR LOUIS H A 35 ALB W
TAYLOR LUCK A 39 JOR B
TAYLOR LUNSFORD A 44 OXF B
TAYLOR M B A 26 SHE W
TAYLOR MACKLIN A 44 YXS B
TAYLOR MAJOR A 35 MAG W
TAYLOR MALACHI C A 30 COI W
TAYLOR MALICHI A 44 OXF B
TAYLOR MARBLE N A 29 QUW W
TAYLOR MAT A 44 OXF B
TAYLOR MATHEW A 44 OXF B
TAYLOR MILES A 44 OXF B
TAYLOR MINOR A 44 SAS B

TAYLOR MITCHELL A 35 WOL W
TAYLOR MOSES A 37 HIG B
TAYLOR MOSES A 37 ROB B
TAYLOR NATHANIEL A 24 UPP W
TAYLOR NED A 39 JOR B
TAYLOR NED C A 44 OXF B
TAYLOR NELSON A 44 OXF B
TAYLOR NOAH A 37 HIC B
TAYLOR NOEL A 44 YXS B
TAYLOR ORANGE A 37 HIC B
TAYLOR OWEN A 37 TA2 B
TAYLOR P B A 46 HIG W
TAYLOR PATRICK C A 37 ROC W
TAYLOR PETER A 28 8TH W
CERTIF GIVEN LIVES
NEAR WIGGINS CR.
TAYLOR R P A 44 OXF W
TAYLOR REDDIN A 28 6TH W
TAYLOR REDMAN H A 37 ROC W
TAYLOR REDMOND R 37 HIC B
CONVIC(T)ED OF LARCENY
TAYLOR RICHARD A 28 11T W
TAYLOR RICHD A 44 OXF B
TAYLOR RICHD JR A 44 OXF B
TAYLOR ROBERT L A 28 9TH W
TAYLOR ROBT A 44 KIT B
TAYLOR RUFUS D A 72 SWA W
TAYLOR S M A 44 RAG W
TAYLOR SAM A 39 JOR B
TAYLOR SAM A 44 OXF B
TAYLOR SAML A 28 04B B
TAYLOR SAMUEL A 24 EDE W
TAYLOR SAMUEL A 28 10T B
TAYLOR SAMUEL A 46 SUM W
TAYLOR SAMUEL F A 46 ROS W
TAYLOR SANDY A 44 TOW B
TAYLOR SEZAR A 40 STO B
TAYLOR SMITH A 44 SAS B
TAYLOR SOLOMON A 28 8TH W
TAYLOR SOLOMON A 44 LED B
TAYLOR STEPHEN A 53 LA2 W
TAYLOR T W A 44 RAG W
TAYLOR THOMAS A 32 JAC W
TAYLOR THOMAS A 37 PIN B
TAYLOR THOMAS A 37 ROC B
TAYLOR THOMAS B A 37 HIC A
TAYLOR THOMAS M A 37 HIC A
TAYLOR THOMAS W A 19 HAD W
TAYLOR THOMAS W A 46 ROS W
TAYLOR THOS A 29 FA1 B
TAYLOR THOS P A 44 TAR W
TAYLOR TILMON A 19 HUN W
TAYLOR TIMOTHY G A 19 NEW W
TAYLOR TONEY A 35 WAR B
TAYLOR W F A 29 FA1 W
TAYLOR W J A 29 BLA W
TAYLOR W J A 29 LOC W
TAYLOR WALLACE A 19 HUN W
TAYLOR WASHINGTON A 37 MAN B
TAYLOR WILLIAM A 19 HAD W
TAYLOR WILLIAM A 19 HAR B
TAYLOR WILLIAM A 35 WOL W
TAYLOR WILLIAM A 37 MAN B
TAYLOR WILLIAM A 37 PEN B
TAYLOR WILLIAM J A 30 COI W
TAYLOR WILLIAM J A 37 WHI W
TAYLOR WILLIS A 19 BE2 B
TAYLOR WILLIS A 44 TOW B
TAYLOR WILSON A 32 DAV W
TAYLOR WILSON A 44 TOW B
TAYLOR WM A 26 SHE W
TAYLOR WM A 28 05A B
TAYLOR WM A 28 6TH W

TAYLOR WM A 29 FA1 W
TAYLOR WM A 44 TOW B
TAYLOR WM F A 29 FA1 B
TAYLOR WM H A 28 01A W
TAYLOR WM J A 28 6TH W
TAYLOR WM S A 29 FA1 B
TAYLOR WM W A 46 GRE W
TAYLOR WRIGHT S A 19 HAD W
TAYLOR ZACHARIAH A 28 04B B
TEACHEY ALFRED A 35 ISL W
TEACHEY ANDREW J A 35 KEN B
TEACHEY ATLAS A 35 ISL W
TEACHEY CHARLES A 35 ROC B
TEACHEY DANIEL A 35 ISL W
TEACHEY DANIEL JR A 35 ISL W
TEACHEY DANIEL T A 35 ISL W
TEACHEY DANIEL W A 35 ISL W
TEACHEY ENOCH W A 35 ISL W
TEACHEY FELIX A 35 ISL B
TEACHEY ISAAC A 35 ISL W
TEACHEY JACOB T A 35 ISL W
TEACHEY JOHN A 35 KEN W
TEACHEY JOSEPH A 35 ISL B
TEACHEY KETTER A 35 ISL B
TEACHEY MATT 1ST A 35 ISL B
TEACHEY MATT 2ND A 35 ISL B
TEACHEY OWEN A 35 ISL W
TEACHEY PEOLY A 35 ROC B
TEACHEY ROBERT A 35 ISL W
TEACHEY ROGER A 35 ROC B
TEACHEY STEPHEN B A 35 KEN W
TEACHEY THADDEUS A 35 ISL W
TEACHEY WILEY A 35 ISL W
TEACHEY WILEY B A 35 ISL W
TEACHEY WILEY W A 35 ISL W
TEACHEY WILLIAMS A 35 ISL W
TEAGUE A J A 32 BRO W
TEAGUE A O P A 32 BRO W
TEAGUE AUSTIN A 32 THO W
TEAGUE JACOB R A 32 POS W
TEAGUE JOHN A 32 BRO W
TEAGUE JOHN A 32 BRO W
TEAGUE MOSE JR A 32 BRO W
TEAGUE MOSES A 32 BRO W
TEAGUE R Q A A 32 BRO W
TEAGUE ROBT F A 46 ROS W
TEAGUE WM J A 46 ROS W
TEASLEY GROVES A 44 FOR B
TEASLY HAYWOOD A 19 NEW W
TEBEAULT DANIEL CHAA 30 GIB W
8-MONTH-RESIDENCE
TEEL HENRY D A 37 TA1 W
TEER WM A 28 13T W
TELFAIR DANIEL A 37 PIN B
TELFAIR HARRY A 37 PIN B
TELFAIR HORACE A 39 FRE B
TELFAIR JOHN A 37 TA1 B
TELLEY WILLIAM A 19 BE1 B
TEMPLE NEEDOM A 32 SHE W
TEMPLE WILLIAM A 28 10T W
TEMPLE WILLIAM G A 28 10T W
TEMPLE WILLIAM G A 53 SWA W
TEMPLES JOHN B A 46 GRE W
TENENT BENJAMINE A 26 MOU W
TENNEY HORACE F A 19 BE1 W
TENNIN THOS D A 28 01A W
TERREL GREEN A 39 DAV B
TRNS TO NASH CO
APRIL 17 1868
TERREL MATHEW A 39 JOR B
TERREL NED A 39 PUG B
TERRELL A A 39 FRA B
TERRELL AGGY A 39 SPE B
TERRELL AUSTIN A 39 PUG B
TERRELL BENJAMIN A 39 PUG B
TERRELL GEORGE A 37 TA2 W
TERRELL GEORGE A 39 LOU B
TERRELL GEORGE B A 39 PUG B
TERRELL JAMES M A 39 PUG W
TERRELL LOUIS C A 37 TA1 W
TERRELL NATHANIAL M A 37 TA1 W
TERRELL RAIF A 37 ROC B
TERRILL HELLAND A 39 SPE B
TRANS TO BLADEN CO
TERRILL HILLIARD A 37 PIN B
TERRILL LEWIS A 39 DAV B
TERRILL RICHMOND A 39 LOU B
TERRY AVIL A 44 TOW B
TERRY BENJ A 44 OXF W
TERRY BENJ F A 44 KNA W
TERRY BENJ JR A 44 KNA W
TERRY DAVID A 44 TOW B
TERRY GEORGE A 37 MAN B
TERRY J C A 44 TAR W
TERRY JAMES H A 35 WAR B
TERRY JEHU A 46 GRE B
TERRY JIM A 44 TOW B
TERRY JOHN F A 46 GRE W
TERRY JOS A 29 FA1 B
TERRY JOSEPH E A 46 SUM W
TERRY NEUSOM A 29 LOC B
TERRY ROGISTER A 44 KIT B
TERRY SAMUEL A 44 ISL B
TERRY SIMEON R 44 ISL B
8 MOS REJ
TERRY SOL A 29 FA1 B
TERRY STEPHEN A 44 TAR W
TERRY WESTERN A 44 ISL B
TERRY WILLIAM A 44 TAR W
TERRY WILLIAM A A 46 SUM W
TERRY WM A 29 FA1 B
TERRY WM A 44 TOW B
TESH CHARLES A 32 SHE W
TESH GEORGE A 32 SHE W
TESH GEORGE A 32 SHE W
TESH J M A 32 BRO W
TESH JACOB ADAM A 32 SHE W
TESH JOHN A 32 SHE W
TESH LEVEN A 32 POS W
TESH LEVI A 32 BRO W
TESH LEVI A 32 POS W
TESH R B A 32 POS W
TESH SAMUEL A 32 SHE W
TETTERDON FREDK A 28 03A B
TEW A J A 29 CED W
TEW BEDFORD A 29 BLA W
TEW J L A 35 FAI W
TEW J R A 29 BLA W
MINGO SAMPSON CO
TEW L B A 29 BLA W
TEW LOUDIN A 29 BLA W
TEW PHILLIP A 37 PIN B
TEW T L A 29 CED W
TEW W H A 29 BLA W
TEW WM A 29 LOC B
THACKER ANDERSON A 46 MON B
THACKER HARDY A 46 MON B
THACKER HENRY A 46 MON B
THACKER ISAAC A 46 MON B
THACKER JACOB A 46 MON B
THACKER JAMES A 46 MON B
THACKER JOSEPH A 46 MON B
THACKER NATHANIEL A 46 MON B
THACKER ROBERT A 46 MON B
THACKER THOMAS A 46 MON B
THACKER SAMUEL R 46 MON B
NAME LINED OUT
LIVING IN ROCKINGHAM
EXCUSED FOR IGNORANCE
THAGGARD ALX A 29 CED W
THAGGARD G F A 29 CED W
THAGGARD G R A 29 CED W
THAGGARD POMPY A 29 CED B
THAGGARD W M A 29 CED W
THAMES C A 29 GRA W
THAMES JAS A 29 GRA W
THAMES JOS A 29 GRA W
THARINGTON J E A 39 FRE W
THARP ABEL A 37 EDW B
THARP J E A 46 FRI W
THARP JOSIAH A 37 PEN B
THARP LETTUS A 37 PEN B
THARP NEWMAN A 39 LOU B
THARRINGTON A P A 39 PUG W
THARRINGTON ALFRED A 39 FRA B
THARRINGTON D C A 39 FRA W
THARRINGTON ENOCH A 39 SPE W
THARRINGTON FENNE 39 FRA W
A MAGISTRATE BEFORE THE
WAR BUT DID NOT GIVE
AID AND COMFORT HE SAYS
THARRINGTON HARBORD A 39 PUG W
THARRINGTON JNO A 39 FRA B
THARRINGTON P H A 38 FRE W
THARRINGTON RUFFIN A 44 FOR W
THARRINGTON S H A 44 FOR W
THARRINGTON T M A 44 FOR W
THARRINGTON THOS A 44 FOR W
THARRINGTON W W A 44 FOR W
THARRINGTON WILLIS A 39 FRA W
THARRINGTON WILLIS A 39 PUG W
THARRINGTON WM A 39 FRA W
THARRINGTON
WM HENDERSON A 39 SPE W
THAYER J H A 32 JAC W
THAYER JOHN A 28 11T W
THAYRE JAMES A 32 JAC W
THICKE WILLIAM A 19 BE1 B
THIGPEN ALFRED A 37 TA2 B
THIGPEN ALLEN A 35 CYP W
THIGPEN ALLEN A 37 HIC B
THIGPEN AMOSE A 37 EDW B
THIGPEN ARCHY A 37 EDW B
THIGPEN ARETUS A 35 LIM W
THIGPEN ASHLEY A 37 TA1 B
THIGPEN BITHEL A 35 LIM W
THIGPEN DANIEL A 37 PEN B
THIGPEN DAVID A 37 PIN B
THIGPEN DICK A 37 EDW B
THIGPEN DREW A 35 LIM W
THIGPEN EDWARD S A 37 WHI W
THIGPEN ELLICK A 37 PIN B
THIGPEN FRANK L A 37 TA1 W
THIGPEN GRAY A 37 PIN B
THIGPEN HARDY A 37 PIN B
THIGPEN HENRY A 37 PIN B
THIGPEN JAMES A 37 PIN W
THIGPEN JAMES R A 37 PIN W
THIGPEN JESSE G A 35 LIM W
THIGPEN JOB JR A 35 LIM W
THIGPEN JOB SR A 35 LIM W
THIGPEN JOHN A 35 LIM W
THIGPEN JOHN A 37 EDW B
THIGPEN JOHN JR A 35 LIM W
THIGPEN STEPHAN M A 35 LIM W
THIGPEN THOMAS A 35 LIM W
THIGPEN THOMAS D A 37 PIN W
THIGPEN WILLIAM A A 37 PIN W

THOM CALVIN A 46 RAG B
THOM JAMES A 46 RAG W
THOM JOEL D A 46 ROS W
THOM JOHN B A 46 GRE W
THOM JOHN M A 46 RAG W
THOM JOHN W A 46 RAG W
THOM ROBERT A 46 GRE B
THOM ROBERT D A 46 GRE W
THOM WM F A 46 RAG W
THOMAS AARON A 30 POP B
THOMAS ADAM A 32 THO B
THOMAS ALEXANDER A 39 DAV W
THOMAS ALFORD A 39 SPE B
THOMAS ALFRID A 44 HEN B
THOMAS ALLEN A 39 DAV B
THOMAS ANDREW A 32 POS B
THOMAS ANDREW A 46 MCL W
THOMAS ANTHONY A 37 SPA B
THOMAS ASHLEY A 32 THO W
THOMAS B F A 39 DAV W
TRNS FROM NASH CO
NASHVILLE PRE
THOMAS BENJAMIN A 29 SEV B
THOMAS BENJAMINE A 35 ALB B
THOMAS BROOKER A 39 HAY B
THOMAS C A A 39 DAV W
THOMAS C G A 35 LIM W
THOMAS C H A 39 LOU W
THOMAS CALVIN A 35 LIM W
THOMAS CHARLES A 19 BE1 B
THOMAS CHARLES A 37 TA2 W
THOMAS D F A 35 LIM W
THOMAS DANIEL A 24 EDE B
THOMAS DANIEL A 53 LA1 B
THOMAS DAVID A 32 THO B
THOMAS DEDRICK A 39 SPE B
THOMAS DENNIS A 35 SMI B
THOMAS DOVER A 35 LIM B
THOMAS EDWARD A 39 JOR B
THOMAS EDWARD A 46 GRE W
THOMAS ELISHA A 37 ROC B
THOMAS ELLIC A 44 HEN B
THOMAS FRANK A 32 THO W
THOMAS FRANK A 35 MAG B
THOMAS FRANK A 39 LOU B
THOMAS FRANK A 44 YXS B
THOMAS FURNY A 44 BRA B
THOMAS GEORGE A 28 02N B
THOMAS GEORGE A 28 16T W
THOMAS GEORGE A 39 JOR B
THOMAS GEORGE W A 37 ROC W
THOMAS GREGORY A 35 LIM W
THOMAS H H A 39 LOU W
THOMAS HAYWOOD A 44 BRA B
THOMAS HAYWOOD A 44 TOW B
THOMAS HENRY A 28 9TH B
THOMAS HENRY A 30 IND B
THOMAS HENRY A 37 ROC W
THOMAS HENRY A 39 SPE B
THOMAS HENRY A 40 STO W
THOMAS HENRY A 44 TAR B
THOMAS HENRY C A 32 THO W
THOMAS ISAAC A 37 HIG B
THOMAS ISAIAH A 37 PEN W
THOMAS ISRAEL A 46 MCL W
THOMAS J J A 39 DAV W
THOMAS J J SR A 39 FRA W
THOMAS J R A 19 HAD W
THOMAS JACK A 39 LOU B
THOMAS JACK A 46 GIB B
THOMAS JACKSON A 35 LIM B
THOMAS JACOB A 32 THO B
THOMAS JAMES A 30 POW B

THOMAS JAMES A 44 TOW B
THOMAS JAMES A 46 MCL B
THOMAS JAMES R 44 YXS B
GUILTY OF LARCENY ACT
SINCE LAST ORDER
NAME LINED OUT
THOMAS JAMES (--?) A 32 DAV W
THOMAS JAMES D A 46 GRE W
THOMAS JAMES G A 39 LOU W
THOMAS JEREMIAH A 30 POW B
THOMAS JERRY A 28 01A B
THOMAS JERRY A 32 THO B
THOMAS JERRY JR A 32 THO B
THOMAS JESSE A 46 SUM W
THOMAS JESSE E A 53 FAI W
THOMAS JNO A 44 TOW B
THOMAS JOEL A 39 LOU W
THOMAS JOHN A 32 THO B
THOMAS JOHN A 37 MAN B
THOMAS JOHN A 39 LOU B
TRNS FROM SPEEDS STORE
TO LOUISBURG
THOMAS JOHN A 39 SPE B
THOMAS JOHN A 40 DEC W
THOMAS JOHN NO. 1. A 30 ROA B
THOMAS JOHN NO. 2. A 30 ROA B
THOMAS JOHN C A 32 POS W
THOMAS JOHN C A 46 MON W
THOMAS JOHN E A 39 LOU W
THOMAS JOHN H A 37 EDW W
THOMAS JOHN J A 28 16T W
THOMAS JOHN P A 19 BE1 W
THOMAS JOHN R A 37 EDW B
THOMAS JOHN T A 44 TOW W
THOMAS JOHN W A 46 GIB W
THOMAS JOHN WESLEY A 32 THO W
THOMAS JORDAN A 44 BRA B
THOMAS JOSEPH A 32 POS B
THOMAS JOSEPH A 32 THO W
THOMAS JOSEPH A A 39 DAV W
THOMAS JOSIAH A 37 ROC W
THOMAS KNIBB A 39 SPE B
THOMAS LEN A 39 SPE B
THOMAS LEWIS A 19 NEW B
THOMAS LEWIS A 28 04A B
THOMAS LEWIS A 32 THO B
THOMAS LEWIS A 44 OXF B
THOMAS LEWIS R 44 OXF B
RES SINCE 15 MAR REJ
THOMAS LEWIS G A 19 HAD W
THOMAS LEWIS L A 32 THO W
THOMAS LOVELESS A 44 YXS B
THOMAS LUKE A 35 ALB B
THOMAS MATHEW A 39 DAV B
THOMAS MATTHEW A 39 LOU B
THOMAS MORRIS S A 44 YXR W
THOMAS MOSES A 44 HEN B
THOMAS NATHAN A 32 THO B
THOMAS NEHEMIAH A 46 KIN W
THOMAS OSSEY A 39 JOR B
THOMAS PETER A 44 YXS B
THOMAS PHILIP A 28 11T W
THOMAS PHILIP A 32 POS B
THOMAS PHILLIPS A 46 GRE W
THOMAS R S A 39 DAV W
THOMAS RED W A 37 ROC W
THOMAS REDDICK A 28 03A B
THOMAS RICHARD A 44 YXS B
THOMAS ROBERT A 28 05A B
THOMAS RUFUS A 39 LOU B
THOMAS S J A 39 DAV W
THOMAS SALISBURY A 44 TOW B
THOMAS SAMPSON A 32 THO B

THOMAS SAMUEL A 19 BE2 W
THOMAS SAMUEL A 35 SMI B
THOMAS SAMUEL A 40 DEC W
THOMAS SOLOMAN A 32 THO B
THOMAS STEPHEN A 29 FA1 B
THOMAS STEPHEN A 44 YXS B
THOMAS THEOPHILUS A 37 ROB W
THOMAS THOMAS A 19 BE1 W
THOMAS THOMAS A 30 POW B
THOMAS THOMAS K A 39 LOU W
THOMAS TIPP A 39 SPE B
THOMAS TOM A 39 LOU B
THOMAS TONEY A 44 YXS B
THOMAS TONY A 44 FIS B
THOMAS TURNER A 39 LOU B
THOMAS VINE ALLEN A 28 13T W
THOMAS W D A 32 THO W
THOMAS W H JR A 44 YXS W
THOMAS W N A 32 POS W
THOMAS WILLIAM A 32 DAV W
THOMAS WILLIAM A 35 LIM W
THOMAS WILLIAM A 40 DEC W
THOMAS WILLIAM A 44 TOW B
THOMAS WILLIAM H A 37 ROC W
THOMAS WILLIAM H A 39 SPE B
THOMAS WILLIAM JR A 35 LIM W
THOMAS WM G A 30 POW B
THOMAS WM G A 44 YXS W
THOMAS YOUNG A 39 DAV B
THOMASON AMOS A 32 DAV B
THOMASON G A A 32 DAV W
THOMASON GEORGE A 32 SHE W
THOMASON JESSEE A 32 DAV W
THOMASON P D A 32 DAV W
THOMASS BRYAN A 35 LIM W
THOMASSON BIRT A 32 DAV B
THOMASSON D W CHALL 40 STO W
REJ NOT BEN IN THE
STATE TWELVE MONTHS
THOMASSON F A 46 KIN W
THOMASSON HEUGH A 32 DAV W
THOMASSON SAMUEL A 32 DAV B
THOMASSON W J A 44 ISL W
THOMERSON BENJ A 44 LED W
THOMERSON C R A 44 LED W
THOMERSON F T A 44 FIS W
THOMERSON GEO B A 44 FIS W
OXFORD DIST
THOMERSON J G A 44 BRA W
THOMERSON J H A 44 LED W
THOMERSON J M A 44 LED W
THOMERSON J U A 44 LED W
THOMERSON S A 44 KNA W
THOMERSON W A A 44 BRA W
THOMERSON W H A 44 LED W
THOMERSON WILLIAM A 44 DUT B
THOMERSON WM A 44 KNA W
THOMPKEN BRYAN A 37 WHI B
THOMPSON A B A 25 HAY W
THOMPSON AARON A 28 04A B
THOMPSON ABRAM A 35 ISL B
THOMPSON ALLEN A 44 OXF W
THOMPSON ANDERSON A 46 GRE B
THOMPSON ANDREW A 32 JAC W
THOMPSON ANTHONY A 35 FAI B
THOMPSON AUGUSTUS A 37 TA1 W
THOMPSON BASOM A 37 EDW B
THOMPSON BENJAMIN A 37 HIG B
THOMPSON C M A 32 TYR W
THOMPSON CALVIN A 46 COB B
THOMPSON CHAS A 29 FA1 B
THOMPSON DANIEL A 32 TYR B
THOMPSON DAVID A 29 CED B

THOMPSON DENNIS A 28 8TH B
THOMPSON E A 32 THO W
THOMPSON EDEN A 28 15T B
THOMPSON EDMOND A 30 POP W
THOMPSON ERASMUS A 37 ROC B
THOMPSON F W A 40 DA1 W
THOMPSON FRANKLIN A 32 TYR B
THOMPSON G A A 29 FA1 W
THOMPSON GEO A 19 HAD B
THOMPSON H A 29 FA1 W
THOMPSON H H A 28 01A W
THOMPSON HARRY A 46 GRE B
THOMPSON HUMFREY A 26 GRI B
THOMPSON HYMON A 19 BE1 B
THOMPSON IRVIN A 28 02N B
THOMPSON JAMES A 37 PEN B
THOMPSON JAMES E A 28 04B W
THOMPSON JASON R 46 KIN W
CONSTABLE BEFORE WAR
AIDED THE REBELION REJ
THOMPSON JERRY A 28 03A B
THOMPSON JERRY A 46 SUM B
THOMPSON JIM A 32 YAD B
THOMPSON JNO M A 28 01A W
THOMPSON JOE A 39 HAY B
THOMPSON JOHN A 19 BE1 B
THOMPSON JOHN A 24 EDE W
THOMPSON JOHN A 28 05A B
THOMPSON JOHN A 35 ALB W
THOMPSON JOHN A 37 ROC B
THOMPSON JOSEPH A 24 EDE B
THOMPSON JOSEPH H A 32 DAV W
THOMPSON JOSHUA A 24 EDE B
THOMPSON LAWRENCE A 35 WAR B
THOMPSON LEMUEL A 32 THO W
THOMPSON LORENZO A 32 THO W
THOMPSON LUKE A 28 10T B
THOMPSON MILES A 24 EDE B
THOMPSON NELSON A 32 TYR B
THOMPSON PETER A 44 TAR B
THOMPSON PHILIP A 32 YAD B
THOMPSON R B A 25 HAY W
THOMPSON RICHARD A 30 IND W
THOMPSON RICHD A 28 03A B
THOMPSON SANDY A 32 YAD B
THOMPSON THOMAS A 32 YAD B
THOMPSON THOMAS A 53 SWA B
THOMPSON THOS A 24 EDE W
THOMPSON W H A 46 SUM W
THOMPSON W L A 32 DAV W
THOMPSON W P A 28 7TH W
THOMPSON WILEY A 19 HAD B
THOMPSON WILLIAM A 29 MON W
THOMPSON WILLIAM A 37 ROC B
THOMPSON WM A 32 JAC W
THOMPSON WM A 46 GRE B
THOMPSON WM M A 46 COB W
THOMSON D A A 35 WOL W
THOMSON GASTON A 35 WOL W
THOMSON SAWNEY A 35 WOL W
THOMSON YORK A 35 WOL W
THORN DEMPSEY A 37 PEN W
THORN GEORGE A 37 ROC B
THORN JOEL A 37 TA1 B
THORN JOSEPH A 37 ROB B
THORN ROBERT A 37 SPA B
THORNBERG M M A 40 SAN W
THORNBURG A LEMUEL A 40 DA2 W
THORNBURG DANIEL R 40 MAU W
NAME LINED OUT MILITIA
OFFICER BEFORE WAR GAVE
AID AND COMFORT TO THE
ENEMY * REJECTED
THORNBURG DANIEL * A 40 MAU W
THORNBURG DAVID B A 40 MAU W
THORNBURG JOSEPH A 40 MAU W
THORNBURG JOSEPH A 46 FRI W
THORNBURG LARKIN A A 40 DA1 W
THORNBURG MOSES A 40 DA1 W
THORNBURG ROBT A 32 DAV W
THORNBURG WILLIAM A 40 DA1 W
THORNE GEORGE A 53 GER B
THORNE JACOB A 37 TA2 B
THORNTON A G R 29 FA1 W
HELD OFFICE OF CONSTABLE
BEFORE & DURING WAR WAS
COMMISSIONER
THORNTON A W A 46 JAM W
THORNTON ADAM A 28 11T B
THORNTON ARTHUR A 37 HIG B
THORNTON E S A 46 JAM W
THORNTON G M A 29 BLA W
AVERSBORO
THORNTON HORACE A 44 OXF B
THORNTON J L A 29 FA2 W
THORNTON J W A 29 FA1 W
THORNTON JUDGE A 44 YXS B
THORNTON PRESLEY A 44 OXF B
THORNTON R W A 29 FA1 W
THORNTON SAMUEL A 44 YXR B
THORNTON THOMAS J A 35 WAR W
THORNTON THOS H A 29 BLA W
AVESBORO
THORNTON WILLIAM A 44 YXS B
THORP ALLEN A 44 YXS B
THORP ANDERSON A 44 OXF B
THORP ASBERRY A 44 TAR B
THORP B P JR A 44 YXS W
THORP BENJ P SR A 44 YXS W
THORP BENJAMIN A 44 YXS B
THORP BILLY A 44 OXF B
THORP BIRD A 44 YXS B
THORP BROOMFIELD A 44 OXF B
THORP EDMUND A 44 YXS B
THORP EPHRAM A 44 TAR B
THORP FREDERICK A 44 YXS B
THORP GEORGE A 44 TAR B
THORP GEORGE A 44 YXS B
THORP GIDEON A 44 YXS B
THORP GILBERT A 44 OXF B
THORP GREEN JR A 44 YXS B
THORP GREEN SR A 44 YXS B
THORP HARRY A 44 OXF B
THORP HARRY A 44 SAS B
THORP HAYWOOD A 44 YXS B
THORP HENRY A 44 TAR B
THORP HENRY A 44 YXS B
THORP HILLARD A 37 ROC B
THORP HIRAM A 46 SUM W
THORP ISAAC A 44 OXF B
THORP J F A 46 SUM W
THORP JAMES A 44 OXF B
THORP JAMES A 44 SAS B
THORP JAMES A 44 YXS B
THORP JAMES A 44 YXS B
THORP JAMES A 46 SUM W
THORP JESSE A 44 HEN B
THORP JOHN A 44 SAS B
THORP JOHN A 44 TAR B
THORP JOHN A 44 YXR B
THORP JOHN W A 46 SUM W
THORP JONAS A 37 ROC B
THORP JORDAN A 44 TAR B
THORP JOSEPH A 44 OXF B
THORP JOSEPH SR A 44 OXF B
THORP JUBEN A 44 YXS B
THORP LEWIS A 44 TAR W
THORP LEWIS A 44 YXS B
THORP LEWIS A 44 YXS B
THORP LUCIOUS A 44 TAR B
THORP MARTIN A 44 TAR B
THORP MICAJAH A 44 TAR B
THORP MICAJOR A 44 OXF B
THORP NATHAN A 37 ROC B
THORP PETER A 44 TAR B
THORP PETERSON JR A 44 OXF W
THORP RICHARD A 44 YXS W
THORP ROBERT A 37 ROC B
THORP SAMUEL A 44 YXS B
THORP SIMON A 44 SAS B
THORP THOS A 44 TAR B
THORP WESLEY A 44 TAR B
THORP WILLIAM A 44 TAR B
THORP WM A 44 OXF B
THORP WM DR A 44 YXS W
THORPE FRANK A 37 HOL B
THORPE HENRY L A 37 ROC B
THORPE JOHN M A 28 9TH W
THOS WASH H A 44 YXS W
THRIFT ALLEN A 26 SHE W
THRIFT G F A 46 JAM W
THURMAN GEORGE W A 46 GRE W
THURMAN THOMAS L A 46 GRE W
THUTEH JOSHUA A 24 EDE B
TICESING JOHN A 32 COT W
TIDBALL WILLIAM B A 46 RAG W
TIDWELL T P A 25 TUS W
TIDWELL W B A 25 TUS W
TIGUE KERBY A 40 SAN W
TIGUE WM A 40 SAN W
TIGUE WM SEN A 40 SAN W
TILERY LIMON JR A 37 ROB B
TILERY LIMON SR A 37 ROB B
TILFAIR WESTON A 37 PIN B
TILGHMAN CHARLES A 46 HIG B
TILLERY FRANK A 37 ROC B
TILLERY JOHN J A 37 ROC W
TILLERY RICHARD C A 37 ROC W
TILLERY STARKEY A 19 MOR B
TILLETT CHARLES A 30 IND B
TILLETT JAS W A 44 OXF W
TILLETT JOHN A 44 OXF W
TILLETT JOHN B A 30 IND W
TILLEY DENNIS A 44 LED W
TILLEY F J A 44 LED W
TILLEY HENRY A 44 LED W
TILLEY J D A 44 LED W
TILLEY LEWIS A 37 PIN B
TILLEY MARCUS A 44 LED B
TILLEY RICHARD A 44 LED B
TILLINGHAST W N A 29 FA1 W
TILLITT ALFRED H A 30 POW W
TILLITT BENJIMAN D A 30 NOR W
TILLITT EDWARD A 30 POW W
TILLITT FRANCIS A 30 ROA B
TILLITT ISAAC JR A 30 NOR W
TILLITT ISAAC SR A 30 NOR W
TILLITT JOHN A 30 NOR W
TILLITT JOHN F A 30 ROA B
TILLITT JOSEPH A 30 ROA B
TILLITT JOSIAH H A 30 NOR W
TILLITT LEVI A 30 ROA B
TILLITT MILES F A 30 ROA B
TILLITT POMPEY A 30 NOR B
TILLITT SAMUEL A A 30 NOR W
TILLITT SAMUEL A A 30 NOR W
TILLITT SAMUEL B A 30 NOR W
TILLITT SAMUEL JR A 30 NOR W
TILLITT THOMAS A 30 ROA W

TILLITT WILLIAM A 30 NOR W
TILLITT WILLIS A 30 NOR W
TILLITT WILLIS A 30 ROA W
TILLOTSON HENRY A 44 YXR W
TILLOTSON WM R A 44 YXR W
TILMAN BRISTOE A 28 03A B
TILMAN CAESAR A 28 04A B
TIMBERLAKE ISHAM A 39 HAR B
TIMBERLAKE J P A 38 FRE W
TIMBERLAKE JAMES A 38 FRE B
PERHAPS PUT IN
HARRIS X ROADS BOOK
TIMBERLAKE JAMES A 39 FRA B
TIMBERLAKE JNO A 38 FRE B
TIMBERLAKE JOSEPH A 39 FRE W
TIMBERLAKE R H DR A 39 FRE W
TIMBERLAKE W B A 39 FRE W
TIMBERLAKE W H A 39 FRA B
TIMBERLAKE WILLIE A 38 FRE B
TIMBERLAKE WM T A 28 15T W
TIMBERLICK PETER A 44 LED B
TIMS PETER A 29 FA1 B
TINDAL JAMES A 29 ROC W
TINDAL JESSE A 35 ALB W
TINDEL ARRINGTON K A 28 16T W
TINDEL JOHN A 28 16T W
TINGEN S H A 44 TAR W
TINGEN W W A 44 LED W
OF BEAVER DAM
TINGLE ANDREW J A 28 16T W
TINGLE BURNEY S A 28 16T W
TINGLE DANIEL A 28 16T W
TINGLE EDMUND J A 28 14T W
TINGLE GEORGE A 28 16T B
TINGLE JOHN A 28 16T W
TINGLE JOHN D A 28 16T W
TINGLE JOHN W A 28 14T W
TINGLE JOSIAH JR A 28 16T W
TINGLE JOSIAH SR A 28 16T W
TINGLE LEVI W A 28 16T W
TINGLE RICHARD H A 28 16T W
TINGLE RICHARD W A 28 14T W
TINGLE WM P A 28 13T W
TINKER GEO E A 28 01A W
TINNIN GILES A 46 COB B
TINNIN JOHN A 46 MCL B
TINSBLOOM J C W A 44 FIS W
TINSLEY ALFRED JR A 44 OXF B
TIPETT TRAVIS A 32 JAC W
TIPPET M N A 39 HAR W
TIPPETT ABNER A 28 9TH W
TIPPETT F A 28 9TH W
TIPPETT J H A 44 FIS W
TIPPETT JOHN H A 39 HAY W
TIPPETT JONATHAN A 44 FIS W
TIPPETT SIMEON A 44 FIS W
TIPPITT JOTHANHAM A 39 HAY W
TIPTON JACOB A 25 TUS W
TIPTON WILLIAM A 25 TUS W
TIRE WILLIAM A 28 11T W
TISDAL ISACK A 39 FRA B
TISDALE GEO F A 28 01B W
TISDALE JACK A 99 BUS B
TISDALE LAFAYETTE A 26 GRI W
TISDALE NATHAN A 28 01A W
TISE HAMILTON A 32 POS W
TISE JACOB A 32 POS W
TISE PETER M A 32 BRO W
TISINGER M A 32 JAC W
TISSINGER HENRY A 32 COT W
TISSINGER ROBERT A 32 JAC W
TISSINGER THOMAS A 32 JAC W
TITMAN A B A 40 SAN W

TITMAN ANTHONY A 40 RHY W
TITMAN GRANVEL A 40 SAN B
TITUS HENRY A 37 MAN B
TODD BRYANT A 99 BUS W
TODD H H A 39 GRI W
TODD J H A 39 DAV W
TOFFELMIN WM A A 25 SHO W
TOLAR HIRAM A 29 GRA W
TOLAR JAS A 29 GRA B
TOLAR JNO R A 29 GRA W
TOLAR NEEDAM S A 29 GRA W
TOLAR SIMON A 29 ROC W
TOLAR THOMAS A 35 FAI B
TOLAR THOS J A 29 ROC W
TOLAR WILLIAM H A 35 WOL W
TOLBERT JOHN F A 37 ROB W
TOLBERT JOHN R A 37 ROB W
TOLER AMARIAH A 28 12T W
TOLER AMARIAH 2ND A 28 12T W
TOLER CHARLES A 28 12T W
TOLER HARDY A 29 FA1 B
TOLER ISAIAH W A 28 12T W
TOLER JAMES A 28 12T W
TOLER JAMES JR A 28 12T W
INSPECTOR EL
TOLER JASPER CHAL A 30 NOR W
MALITIA OFFICER
PRIOR TO WAR
TOLER MATTHIAS A 28 13T W
TOLER STEPHEN A 28 12T W
TOLER THOMAS A 28 13T W
TOLER THOMAS T A 30 ROA W
TOLER THOMAS W A 37 TA2 W
TOLER W D A 28 12T W
TOLER WILLIAM A 28 12T W
TOLER WILLIAM A 53 OCR W
TOLER ZACHARIAH A 28 13T W
TOLSON C C A 19 NEW W
TOLSON GEO W A 53 HAT W
TOLSON GIDEON A 19 POR W
TOLSON J A 19 NEW W
TOLSON J H A 28 9TH W
CERTIF GIVEN NOW
LIVES IN CARTERET CO.
TOLSON JOHN W A 28 01B W
TOLSON KILBY A 19 NEW W
TOLSON KILBY J P A 19 NEW W
TOLSON SANUEL A 19 POR W
TOLSON THOMAS A 19 POR W
TOLSON THOMAS J A 28 9TH W
TOLSON V A A 28 9TH W
TOLSON V W A 28 01B W
TOLSON WILLIAM S A 53 OCR W
TOLSON WM N A 19 NEW W
TOM WILLIS A 37 ROC B
TOMASSON HENRY A 32 DAV B
TOMB SAMUEL A 19 HAD B
TOMES SAM A 29 GRA B
AFFA FAYETTEVILLE
TOMLINSON ENGLISH A 32 THO W
TOMLINSON ENSOR A 32 THO W
TOMLINSON GASTON A 99 BUS B
TOMLINSON J S A 32 THO W
TOMLINSON JOHN A 99 BUS B
TOMLINSON RANSOM A 99 BUS B
TOMLINSON SAMUEL A 32 THO W
TOMLINSON W H A 29 FA1 W
TOMLINSON WM G A 32 THO W
TOMLINSON Z J A 32 THO W
TOMMA PETER A 29 LOC B
TOMPKINS BLOUNT A 46 JAM B
TOMPSON CHRISTOPHER A 30 CUR W
TOMPSON SAMUEL A 30 CUR W

TOMSON JAMES A 37 MAN B
TOMWELL HENRY G A 37 SHA W
TOMWELL MARTIN V A 37 SHA W
TONEY MORDECAI A 44 HEN B
TONEY WILLIAM A 19 STR B
TOODLE WILLIAM A 30 ROA B
TOOKER CHAS A 28 04A W
TOOLE NATHAN A 37 TA1 B
TOOLEY JOHN C A 53 GER W
TOOLEY MORACE A 53 GER W
TOOLY ANDREW J A 53 GER W
TOOLY HENRY O A 53 GER W
TOOLY JOHN B A 53 GER W
TOOLY LUKE A 53 GER B
TOOLY THOMAS A 30 MOY W
TOOLY WILLIAM B 53 SWA W
CHALLENGED
NAME LINED OUT
WILLIAM B TOOLY SAYS THAT
UPON REFLECTION HE THINKS
HE MAY HAVE DONE SOMETHING
THAT AMOUNTS TO AID &
COMFORT, HE THEREFORE
REQUEST US TO STRIKE OUT
HIS NAME.
WHICH WE HAVE DONE
TOOLY WILLIAM B JR A 53 GER W
TOOLY WILLIAM B.. A 53 SWA W
POLITICAL DISABILITIES
REMOVED
TOOMER G C A 28 04B W
TOOMER SAML A 29 FA1 B
TOOMES WM F SR A 46 ROS W
TOOMS ALPHEUS L A 46 ROS W
TOOMS J A 46 ROS W
WATER STAINED
TOPPIN SAMUEL A 24 MID W
TOPPING JAMES A 53 SWA B
TOPPING REED A 53 SWA B
TOPPING THOMAS W A 53 SWA W
TORNEY DAVID A 37 TA1 B
TORRANS THOMAS K JR A 35 MAG W
TORRANS THOMAS K SR A 35 MAG W
TORRENCE ABRAM A 40 STO B
TORRENCE CLISBY E A 40 FER W
TORRENCE E B A 26 PEE W
TORRENCE EPHRAM A 40 STO B
TORRENCE HARRISON A A 40 DA2 W
TORRENCE HUGH A A 40 DEC W
TORRENCE J C A 40 SAN W
TORRENCE J N A 40 SAN W
TORRENCE JAMES D A 40 FER W
TORRENCE JOHN A A 40 DEC W
TORRENCE R S A 40 SAN W
TORRENCE ROBERT A 40 SAN W
TORRENCE SAMUEL A A 40 DEC W
CHAL: CAUSE
POSTMASTER BEFOR THE WAR
AND GAVE AID AND COMFORT
CHARGE NOT SUSTAINED
TORRENCE STEPHEN A 26 PEE B
TORRENCE WILLIAM J A 40 FER W
TORRENCE WILLIAM W A 40 FER W
TOSTOR JOSEPH R 28 10T W
FOREIGNER NOT A NATURAL-
IZED CITIZEN AND REBEL
SOLDIER 4 YRS
TOTTER BLUNT A 37 HIG B
TOURGEE ALBION W A 46 GRE W
TOW MARTIN A 32 TYR W
TOWER ELIJAH A 28 03A B
TOWLES DANIEL T A 37 ROC W
TOWNES ALBERT A 44 TOW B

TOWNES ALFRED A 44 TOW B
TOWNES CHONNER A 44 TOW B
TOWNES GEORGE R 44 TOW B
NAME LINED OUT
10 MONTHS IN STATE
NOT SWORN REJ
TOWNES HARRY A 44 TOW B
TOWNES ISAAC A 44 TOW B
TOWNES JAMES E A 44 TOW W
TOWNES JOSEPH A 44 TOW W
TOWNES MAJOR A 44 TOW B
TOWNES SHEPHARD A 44 TOW B
TOWNES SIDNEY A 44 TOW B
TOWNES THOMAS A 44 TOW B
TOWNS ALBERT A 44 HEN B
TOWNS BRANDON A 44 SAS B
TOWNS DICK A 44 SAS B
TOWNS GEORGE A 44 TOW B
TOWNS MINTUS A 44 TOW B
TOWNS THOMAS A 44 TAR B
TOWNS WESLEY A 44 TAR B
TOWNSEN LAWRENCE W A 46 GRE W
TOWNSEND DEBERRY A 29 ROC W
TOWNSEND DEMPS A 44 YXS B
TOWNSEND JNO T A 29 ROC W
TOWNSEND JNO T JR A 29 ROC W
TOWNSHEN ELI A 46 GRE W
TOWNSON EDMON A 19 BE1 B
TOWNY J H A 26 BLA W
TOWRY GEORGE A 26 PEE W
TOWRY GEORGE S A 26 PEE W
TOWRY JOHN A 26 PEE W
TOXEY JOSEPH A 30 GIB W
TOYLOR LEWIS A 35 MAG W
TRACEY ENSLY A 26 GOF B
TRACEY J W R 26 GOF W
TRACY MILES A 26 GOF B
TRADWELL DAVID A 24 EDE B
TRADWELL FRANK A 24 EDE B
TRAHN SAMUEL A 37 HIG W
TRAINUM THOMAS A 37 PEN B
TRAMMELL L A 26 BOR W
TRAMMELL R B A 26 CAR W
TRAMMELL THOS A 26 SHE W
TRANTHAM A J A 32 DAV W
TRANTHAM ALLEN A 32 DAV B
TRANTHAM BRANAN A 32 DAV B
TRANTHAM H A A 32 DAV W
TRAVATHAN BENJAMIN A 37 HIG W
TRAVATHAN MARTIN G A 37 HIG W
TRAVIS BENJAMIN A 44 HEN W
TRAVIS MILLS A 30 MOY B
TRAYAHAM J P A 32 BRO W
TRAYLER C L A 44 OXF W
TRAYNHAM MOSES A 32 BRO B
TREADWELL CEASER A 30 MOY B
TREADWELL JOS A 28 04A B
TREMBLE S H A 35 CYP W
TRENT PETER W A 32 DAV W
TRENTHAM THOMAS A 32 DAV B
TRENTHAN ALBERT A 32 DAV B
TRENWITH P A 28 01A W
TREVAN JORDON A 44 FOR B
TREVAN MONTGOMERY A 44 BRA B
TREVATHAN LEWIS A 37 ROC B
TREVATHAN PETER A 37 ROC B
TREVATHAN ROBERT H A 37 MAN W
TREVATHAN WILLIAM C A 37 PIN W
TREVATHEN DEMPSEY A 37 MAN W
TREVATHIAN MERDY A 37 SHA W
TREXLER DAVID A 32 DAV W
TREXLER JOSEPH A 32 COT W
TREXLER R A A 32 TYR W

TRIMBLE JAS H A 46 GRE W
TRIP JOSEPH A 37 TA1 B
TRIP ROBERT A 28 04B B
TRIPP AARON A 28 04A B
TRIPP ALFRED A 28 01B B
TRIPP OLIVER A 28 04A B
TRIPP ROBT A 24 EDE B
TRIPP SAML A 28 05A B
TRIPP SIMON A 28 05A B
TRIPTLET WARREN A 25 TUS W
TRITATON JAMES A 28 14T B
TRITATON NATHAN A 28 16T W
TROGDEN SOLOMON A 32 THO W
TROLER JAMES A 44 SAS B
TROLER ROBERT A 44 SAS B
TROLER WILLIAM A 44 SAS B
TRON GEORGE W A 46 GRE B
TROTMAN AMOS A 30 MOY W
TROTMAN MAJOR A 30 IND B
TROTMAN MATHEW A 30 TUL B
TROTTER JAS J A 46 GRE W
TROTTER STEPHEN A 46 GRE W
TROTTER W D A 46 GRE W
TROUT NTH A 25 HAY W
TROUTMAN ALLEN A 28 16T B
TROXLER ALFRED A 46 MON B
TROXLER G R A 46 MON W
TROXLER J R A 46 MON W
TROY JNO B A 29 FA1 W
TROY PHILLIP A 46 ROS B
TROY ROB P A 46 GRE W
TROY W C A 29 FA1 W
TROY WM A 46 ROS B
TRUBLUD JESSE A 46 FRI W
TRUEBLOOD ROWAN A 32 DAV B
TRUETT CHARLES A 25 HAY W
TRUIL WM A 28 14T W
TRUITT J W A 46 MON W
TRUSTEE ALEXANDER A 37 MAN B
TRUVETT GEORGE F A 28 10T W
TRYE COUNCIL A 46 GRE W
73 YRS OLD
TRYFORD JESSE A 30 NOR W
TRYYELL DAVID ED A 28 02N W
TUBWELL WILLIAM L A 37 SPA W
TUCK WM A A 44 YXS W
TUCKER A G A 46 HIG W
TUCKER A M A 40 STO W
TUCKER ALFRED S A 19 BE2 B
TUCKER B T A 44 HEN W
TUCKER B T A 44 OXF W
TUCKER CALVIN M A 46 ROS W
TUCKER CATO A 26 SHE B
TUCKER CHAS A 28 04A B
TUCKER CONRAD A A 46 ROS W
TUCKER DAVID A 35 WAR W
TUCKER EDD E A 28 03A B
TUCKER FRANCIS A 53 SWA B
TUCKER FRANK A 28 04A B
TUCKER HENRY A 24 EDE B
TUCKER HENRY A 28 7TH W
TUCKER J B A 39 SPE W
TUCKER J B A 44 OXF W
TUCKER J P A 19 NEW W
TUCKER JACOB A 28 04A B
TUCKER JAMES P A 35 KEN W
TUCKER JAS A 29 FA1 B
TUCKER JOHN A 19 NEW W
TUCKER JOHN A 28 15T B
TUCKER JOHN A 40 STO W
TUCKER JOHN M A 26 BLA W
TUCKER JOHN R A 46 GRE W
TUCKER JOHN W A 35 KEN W

TUCKER JOHN W A 46 GRE W
TUCKER JOS A 46 GRE B
TUCKER JOSEPH A 35 KEN W
TUCKER JUPITER A 28 01A B
TUCKER LUKE A 35 WAR W
TUCKER R G A 44 TOW W
TUCKER RICHARD A 28 01A B
TUCKER RUFFIN A 99 BUS B
TUCKER THOMAS A 39 SPE W
TUCKER WILLAIM A 19 BE2 W
TUCKER WILLEY A 37 TA2 B
TUCKER WILLIAM A 29 FLE B
TUCKER WILLIAM A 35 WAR W
TUCKER WM A 39 JOR W
TRNS TO WARREN CO
APRIL 10 1868
TUCKER WM G A 19 BE2 W
TUCKER WM G A 46 ROS W
TUCKER WM R A 44 HEN W
TUCKER ZADOCK A 46 ROS W
TUDAL WILSON A 19 NEW B
TULEY FOY A 28 05A B
TULIN YORK A 19 BE1 B
TUMER BENJ A 44 SAS B
TUMER LEWIS A 44 SAS B
TUMNER JOHN A 26 BLA W
TUNE BARNEY A 28 8TH B
TUNIS E C A 28 02N W
TUNNEL MISHACK A 19 BE1 B
TUNNEL WM A 28 15T W
TUNSIL ALFRED A 28 12T W
TUNSTALL GEORGE R 39 LOU W
FOR BEING A JUSTICE OF
THE PEACE BEFORE THE WAR
AND DURING THE WAR WAS
WAIGH MASTER OF PROVINDER
STRICKEN APRIL 10 1868
TUNSTALL J B A 44 FIS W
TUNSTALL L C A 39 SPE W
TUNSTALL P A A 44 BRA W
TUNSTALL PAYTON R A 28 12T W
TUNSTALL R A A 44 BRA W
TUPPENCE EDWARD A 44 OXF B
TURBEFILL JAMES A 26 SHE W
TURNAGE BRYANT A 35 FAI W
TURNAGE J E A 28 8TH W
TURNER A J A 24 MID W
TURNER A N A 26 HOL B
TURNER AARON A 30 ROA B
REMOVED TO ELIZABETH
CITY PASQUOTANK Co.
TURNER ADOLPHUS A A 37 EDW B
TURNER ALLEN A 37 TA1 B
TURNER ALMOND A 99 BUS W
TURNER ARETUS A 35 LIM W
TURNER B F A 26 SWA W
TURNER C F A 44 BRA W
TURNER CURTIS A 44 HEN B
TURNER D R A 44 OXF W
TURNER DAVID A 26 SHE B
TURNER DAVID W A 35 ROC W
TURNER DENNY A 46 ROS W
TURNER DEXTER B A 35 LIM W
TURNER DR V E A 44 HEN W
TURNER EDWARD A 26 BUR W
TURNER ELI A 32 JAC W
TURNER ELIJA A 26 SWA W
TURNER ELLIC A 44 HEN B
TURNER ENOCH S A 46 GRE W
TURNER FRANCIS A 30 ROA B
REMOVED TO ELIZABETH
CITY PASQUOTANK Co.
TURNER GASTON A 99 BUS W

TURNER GEORGE A 35 ALB W
TURNER GEORGE A 44 KIT B
TURNER GEORGE A 99 BUS B
TURNER GEORGE A A 99 BUS W
TURNER HENRY A 44 BRA W
TURNER HENRY A 99 BUS B
TURNER HENRY A 99 BUS W
TURNER HESEZEKIAH A 37 ROB W
TURNER ISAAC A 44 HEN B
TURNER IVY B A 35 WAR W
TURNER J E A 44 FOR W
TURNER J J A 46 SUM W
TURNER J P A 26 SWA W
TURNER J W A 99 BUS W
TURNER JACK A 44 HEN B
TURNER JACOB A 35 LIM W
TURNER JACOB A 37 SHA W
TURNER JACOB A 37 TA2 B
TURNER JAMES A 28 05A B
TURNER JAMES B A 35 KEN W
TURNER JAMES H A 35 KEN W
TURNER JOHN A 19 BE1 B
TURNER JOHN A 35 LIM W
TURNER JOHN A 44 OXF B
TURNER JOHN C A 46 MCL W
TURNER JOHN W A 35 KEN W
TURNER JOSEPH J A 24 MID W
TURNER L T A 44 FOR W
TURNER LASANDRUS A 44 FOR W
TURNER LEONADES A 26 BUR W
TURNER LEVI A 46 ROS W
TURNER LEWIS A 44 HEN B
TURNER LOWELL A 99 BUS B
TURNER M D A 44 SAS W
TURNER M V A 26 GRI W
TURNER MATHIAS A 26 SWA W
TURNER NELSON A 26 HOL B
TURNER PAUL A 32 COT W
TURNER PETER A 28 6TH B
TURNER PETER A 29 FA1 B
TURNER R A A 44 FOR W
TURNER ROBERT A 37 ROC B
TURNER S S A 99 BUS W
TURNER SAML A 28 6TH B
TURNER SAML E A 29 FA1 W
TURNER SIMMEON A 35 LIM W
TURNER SOLOMON A 35 ROC W
TURNER STARLING A 26 PEE W
TURNER STEPHEN A 19 BE1 B
TURNER THOMAS A 46 ROS W
TURNER THOS A 29 FA1 B
TURNER W G A 28 03A B
TURNER W H A 26 HOL B
TURNER W R A 26 SWA W
TURNER WASH A 39 FRE B
TURNER WILEY A 26 PEE W
TURNER WILLIAM A 32 JAC W
TURNER WILLIAM C A 35 ALB W
TURNER WILLIAM D A 99 BUS W
TURNER WILLIAM G A 37 HIC A
TURNER WILLIAM S A 99 BUS W
TURNER WILLIAM W A 35 LIM W
TURNER WM H A 32 COT W
TURNER YORK A 99 BUS B
TURNETT OCTAVIUS A 29 FA1 B
TURPENCE ANDERSON A 44 OXF B
TURRENTINE W H A 28 02N W
TUSSEY HENRY A 46 HIG B
TUSSEY JAMES A 32 DAV W
TUSSEY JOHN A 32 DAV W
TUSSEY JOHN A 32 DAV W
TUSSEY JOSEPH A 46 HIG B
TUSSEY Z B A 32 DAV W
TUTHEROW GEORGE W A 40 DA1 W
TUTTLE SIDNEY A 28 01A W
TUTTLE THOMAS A 32 POS B
TUTTLE WM A 28 16T W
TWIFORD TRUXON A 30 IND W
TWIN ALFRED N A 24 UPP W
TWIN E D A 24 MID W
TWIN ELISHA A 24 UPP W
TWIN ROBT A 24 UPP B
TWIN SAMUEL A 24 UPP B
TWIN WILLIAM A 24 UPP W
TWINE ABRAHAM JR A 30 ROA W
TWINE BENJAMINE A 37 ROB B
TYER JOHN E PITT COA 37 TA1 W
TYER WM P A 46 GRE W
TYLER BARTLETT A 29 FA1 B
TYLER EDWARD A 29 SEV B
TYLER JAMES Y D A 37 ROB W
TYLER JOHN A 28 01A B
TYLER JOHN A 29 FA1 B
TYLER JUNIUS A 44 OXF B
TYLER M R A 32 THO W
TYLER THOMAS K A 37 EDW W
TYLER WARREN A 24 EDE B
TYLER WILLIAM A 44 OXF B
TYLER WILLIAM A 44 OXF B
TYSINGER ALEXANDER A 32 LOF W
TYSINGER ALEXANDER A 32 THO W
CERTIF
TYSINGER P N A 32 DAV W
TYSON AARON A 29 GRA W
TYSON C B A 29 GRA W
TYSON DANIEL A 29 GRA W
TYSON JOHN O A 53 GER W

\- U -

UCERY GRANDISON A 44 KIT B
ULLRICHS F A 28 01A W
ULTZ W W A 28 01A W
UMPHREYS CHARLES A 40 DA1 B
UMPHREYS CHARLES R 40 DA1 B
7 MOS RESIDENCE
16 AUGUST 1867
UMPHRIS JOSEPH A 32 DAV B
UMSTED T W A 44 LED W
UNDERHILL HENRY A 35 WOL W
UNDERHILL JOSEPH S A 19 STR W
UNDERHILL NELSON A 28 16T B
UNDERWOOD ASA A 32 THO W
UNDERWOOD BALT A 29 FLE B
UNDERWOOD CADER A 29 FLE B
UNDERWOOD D J A 29 CED W
UNDERWOOD DANIEL A 29 CED B
UNDERWOOD DANL A 29 FLE B
UNDERWOOD DAVID A 40 CAN W
UNDERWOOD J B A 29 FA1 W
UNDERWOOD J D A 40 SAN W
UNDERWOOD J O A 40 CAN W
UNDERWOOD J W A 40 CAN W
UNDERWOOD JACOB A 40 CAN W
UNDERWOOD JAMES A 46 GIB W
UNDERWOOD RUBAN A 40 CAN W
UNDERWOOD SANDY A 29 FLE B
UNDERWOOD SIDNEY J A 32 THO W
UNDERWOOD SILAS A 29 FLE B
UNDERWOOD THOS A 46 GIB W
UNDERWOOD W A 29 CED W
UNDERWOOD W A 40 CAN W
UNTHANK HARMON A 46 GRE B
UNTHANK JASPER A 46 GRE B
UNTHANK JOHN A 46 FRI W
UPCHURCH AMBROSE A 39 GRI W
UPCHURCH BENJ A 39 DAV B
UPCHURCH BERRY A 39 GRI W
UPCHURCH CHAS G A 28 01B W
UPCHURCH ELIJHA A 39 GRI B
UPCHURCH J C A 39 SPE W
UPCHURCH LYON M A 39 DAV W
UPCHURCH RICHMOND A 39 DAV W
UPCHURCH SAMUEL A 39 GRI B
UPCHURCH W M A 39 DAV W
UPCHURCH WM A 39 DAV B
UPPERMAN J H A 39 LOU W
URKET JAMES A 53 GER B
URKET JESSE A 53 GER B
URKET THOMAS A 53 GER B
USERY HENERY A 29 FA1 W
USHER E G A 29 CED W
USHER HENRY A 35 MAG B
USHER JOSEPH A 35 ROC B
USRY D W A 44 LED W
USRY HAMPTON A 26 GOF W
USRY J C A 44 BRA W
USRY J F A 44 LED W
USRY S W A 44 BRA W
USRY WILLIAM A 44 LED W
UTLEY CASWELL A 99 BUS B
UTLEY HENRY A 29 FA1 B
UTLEY HENRY A 99 BUS B
UTLEY HENRY A 99 BUS W
UTLEY JACOB A 19 BE1 W
UTLY M A 29 FA1 W
UZZELL GEORGE A 28 7TH B
UZZELL ISAIAH A 28 7TH B
UZZLE JAMES N A 39 LOU W
REGISTRAR
UZZLE W B A 39 DAV W
TRNS TO LOUISBURG
UZZLE WILLIAM B A 39 LOU W
TRNS FROM
DAVISES X ROADS

\- V -

VAIL THOS A 28 05A B
VALENTINE JOSEPH A 28 04A B
VALENTINE POMFREY A 44 OXF B
VAN GEORGE A 44 FOR B
VAN JAMES M A 29 FA1 W
VAN MAYNARD A 35 GLI B
VAN VIEL ANTHONY A 28 11T B
VAN VIEL PETER A 28 11T B
VANBUREN MATIN A 53 LA1 B
VANDERBRIGH HENRY A 28 03B W
VANDERFORD W B A 46 SUM W
VANDIKE JOSHUA A 26 GOF W
VANDRICK EDWARD W A 28 14T W
VANDRICK JOHN A 28 14T W
VANDYKE J A A 26 BOR W
VANDYKE L S A 26 BOR W
VANE ABRAHAM A 46 JAM B
VANE JOHN A 46 MON B
VANGOR ABRAM A 30 MOY B
VANN ISAAC A 19 BE1 B
VANN JOHN R A 35 ROC W
VANN LEWIS A 44 KIT B
VANN MOSES A 35 KEN B
VANN SAMEUL A 35 ROC B
VANN STEPHEN A 35 MAG W
VANSLYCK GEORGE S A 30 POP W
VANSTORY CAESAR A 46 GRE B
VANSTORY JOHN A 46 GRE W
VANSTORY JOHN H A 46 MON W
VANSTORY PETER A 46 MON B
VANSTORY ROBERT A 46 MON B
VANSTORY WM A 46 GRE W

VARNELL BOLEN A 37 TA2 W
SPARTA
VARNER E C A 32 JAC W
VARNER JESSE A 32 LEE W
VARNER JOHN A 32 THO W
VARNER MATHEW A 32 JAC W
VARNER P T A 32 JAC W
VARNER WILLIAM E A 32 LEE W
VARSER JOHN P A 30 ROA W
IS DEAD
VARSER JOHN P A 30 ROA W
(COPIED FROM DUPLICATE)
VARSER WILLIAM H A 30 ROA W
VASS CRUDUP A 53 FAI B
VASS DENNIS A 44 YXS B
VASS JOHN A 44 YXS W
VASS L C A 28 02N W
VASS MOSES A 44 YXS B
VASS ROBERT H A 44 SAS W
VAUGHAN A J A 44 DUT W
VAUGHAN AUTHOR A 44 HEN B
VAUGHAN D A 44 DUT W
VAUGHAN DAVID A 35 ISL W
VAUGHAN FIELDING A 44 HEN W
VAUGHAN GEORGE A 39 HAY B
VAUGHAN HENRY A 39 HAY B
VAUGHAN HENRY J R 44 TOW W
NAME LINED OUT
8 MOS IN STATE
NOT SWORN
VAUGHAN J J A 44 FOR W
VAUGHAN JAMES A 44 FOR W
VAUGHAN JNO W A 44 HEN W
VAUGHAN JONAS A 24 EDE B
VAUGHAN LEWIS A 44 HEN B
VAUGHAN M H A 44 OXF W
VAUGHAN SILAS A 44 ISL W
VAUGHAN SOLON A 44 HEN B
VAUGHAN W E A 44 FOR W
VAUGHAN W L A 44 BRA W
VAUGHN ADOLPHUS A 28 01B W
VAUGHN JOHN A 37 ROC B
VAUGHN JOHN W A 28 01A W
VAUGHN JOSEPH A 35 KEN B
VAUGHN SPENSER A 26 GRI W
VAUGHN STEPHEN A 29 FA1 W
VAUGN H A 29 FA1 W
VAUGN RUFFIN A 29 FA1 W
VAUS JOSEPHUS A 46 RAG B
VEACH E S A 32 THO W
VEACH J R P A 32 THO W
VEACH JOSEPH A 32 THO W
VEACH SALAI A 32 THO W
VEACH SAMUL J A 32 THO W
VEACH W O (?) A 32 THO W
VEACH Z M A 32 THO W
VEALE BRITTON A 24 EDE B
VEAZEY ABNER A 44 LED W
VEAZEY J E A 44 DUT W
VEAZEY J H A 44 DUT W
VEAZEY JOHN A 44 DUT B
VEAZEY M W B A 44 DUT W
VEAZEY W E A 44 DUT W
VEITCH THOS E A 26 BOR W
VENABLE ABRAHAM A 44 YXR B
VENABLE T B A 44 OXF W
VENERABLE HARRY A 44 SAS B
VENERABLE WILLIAM A 44 SAS B
VENTER SPICER A 28 11T W
VENTERS FREDK A 28 04A B
VENTERS JOHN A 28 03A B
VENTERS JOHN E A 28 15T W
VERNON ROBT L A 46 GRE W

VICK --- A 37 WHI B
VICK AUTHUR A 37 WHI B
VICK BENJ H A 37 ROC W
VICK CHESTER A 37 ROB B
VICK DAVIS A 37 SHA B
VICK EXUM A 37 MAN W
VICK EXUM L A 37 MAN W
VICK HILLARD A 37 ROC B
VICK JAMES A 37 HIC A
VICK JAMES J A 37 MAN W
VICK JAMES R A 37 MAN W
VICK PAYTON A 37 HIG B
VICK READING A A 37 EDW W
VICK ROBERT A 37 HIG W
VICK ROBERT E A 35 MAG W
VICK SAMUEL A 37 ROC W
VICK SAMUEL A 37 SHA B
VICK W B A 37 ROC W
VICK WALLUS A 37 ROC B
VICK WILLIAM B A 37 MAN W
VICK WILLIAM H A 37 ROB W
VICKERS HIRAM A 29 FA1 W
VICKERS HIRAM R 19 MOR W
CONSTABLE AFTERWARDS
ENGAGED IN REBELLION
VICKES JOHN A 28 01A W
VICKORY WM B A 28 15T W
VICKS SUTNEY A 37 HIG B
VICORY ABIATHER A 46 JAM W
VICORY J S A 46 JAM W
VINCE WATSON A 37 SPA B
VINCENT BEN A 39 DAV B
VINCENT YOUNG A 29 FA1 B
VINES BENJAMIN A 37 SPA B
VINES CHARLES A 37 SPA W
VINES DENNIS A 37 SPA B
VINES HARDE A 37 SPA B
VINES HOWELL A 37 SPA B
VINES HOWELL A 37 WHI B
VINES JAMES T A 28 16T W
VINES JORDAN A 37 SPA B
VINES JOSEPH A 37 SPA B
VINES KETTER A 37 SPA B
VINES LEVI A 37 SPA B
VINES SAMUEL A 37 HIG W
VINSON JOSEPH H A 46 HIG W
VINSTEAD GEORGE W A 37 SHA W
VITIETOE ISAAC A 46 MON W
VOLANTINE EDWARD A 32 TYR B
VOLANTINE ELI A 32 TYR B
VOLIVA ASA JR A 53 FAI W
VOLIVA ASA SR A 53 FAI W
VOLIVA HINES A 53 FAI W
VOLIVA ISAAC A 53 GER W
VOLIVA JOSEPH A 53 FAI W
VOLIVA WILLIAM A 53 FAI W
VOLK WM J A 28 01A W

- W -

WACESTER JOHN A 40 BLA W
WADDELL E M A 29 FA1 W
WADDELL ISAAC A 39 PUG B
WADDELL JAMES A 29 FA1 B
WADDELL JNO H A 29 FA1 B
WADDELL JOHN A 29 FA1 B
WADDELL T D A 28 01A W
WADDILL JNO A 29 FA1 B
WADDILL WM A 29 FA1 B
WADDLE THOMAS A 29 FLE B
WADDLETON OLIVER A 46 MON B
WADE A D A 19 MOR W
WADE A L A 46 JAM W
WADE ALPHEUS A 19 SMY W

WADE ARETUS J A 35 LIM W
WADE BENJAMIN A 19 SMY W
WADE C M A 35 SMI W
WADE CHAS A 29 BLA W
WADE DANIEL A 19 MOR W
WADE ERASMUS A 35 LIM B
WADE FREEMAN A 19 MOR W
WADE GEORGE A 19 BE1 W
WADE H A 19 MOR W
WADE HENRY A 19 DAV W
WADE HENRY A A 35 WAR W
WADE J A A 29 BLA W
WADE J B A 19 MOR W
WADE J F A 19 STR W
WADE JAMES O A 19 STR W
WADE KEMP A 19 NEW W
WADE LEMEUL A A 35 WAR W
WADE M L A 29 BLA W
WADE MITCHEL A 19 SMY W
WADE NEVIL C A 53 HAT W
WADE ROBBERT A 35 LIM W
WADE ROBERT A 19 MOR W
WADE S F A 46 JAM W
WADE W H A 29 BLA W
WADE W H A 44 FIS W
WADE WILLIAM A 19 BE1 W
WADE WILLSON A 19 SMY W
WADELL F F JR A 39 FRA W
WADFORD S C CHAL A 32 LEE W
FOR HOLDING OFFICE OF
CONSTABLE BEFORE AND
DURING THE WAR.
WADFORD WM A 44 FOR W
WADKINS BRYANT A 28 6TH B
WADKINS HESEKIAH A 46 FRI B
WADKINS J H A 44 FOR W
WADKINS J J A 26 SHE W
WADKINS JESSE F A 35 KEN W
WADKINS JOHN A 32 TYR W
WADKINS JOHN A 46 KIN B
WADKINS RIAL A 35 WAR B
WADKINS SIM A 37 ROC W
WADKINS WILLIAM A 35 ISL W
WADLE ALEXANDER A 40 SAN W
WADLETON REMUS A 46 MON B
WADLETON SAMUEL A 46 MON B
WADLETON TAYLOR A 46 MON B
WADLINTON RUFUS A 46 GRE B
WADRIP LEMUEL A 39 SPE B
WADSON A L CHAL A 32 DAV W
FOR HOLDING OFFICE
OF MAGISTRATE BEFORE
AND DURING WAR. RECON.
WADSON H P A 32 DAV W
WADSWORTH DANIEL A 28 8TH B
WADSWORTH DOMAN A 28 01A B
WADSWORTH ENOCH A 28 7TH W
WADSWORTH G S A 28 01A W
WADSWORTH ISAAC A 28 10T B
WADSWORTH JOHN A 28 03B B
CERTIFICATE GRANTED
TO BEAUFORT
RESIDES IN SALISBURY
CERTIFICATE GIVEN.
WAFF GEORGE A 24 EDE B
WAFF T J R 24 EDE W
REJECTED BY THE BOARD
BECAUSE WAS MAGISTRATE
BEFORE AND DURING
THE WAR & SOLD PROVISIONS
TO THE CONFEDERATES
WAFF THOMPSON A 24 EDE B
WAFF WM W A 24 EDE W

WAGGONER DAVID A 32 POS B
WAGGONER EDWARD A 32 POS B
WAGGONER GEORGE A 32 POS B
WAGGONER GEORGE A 32 POS W
WAGGONER HENRY A 28 04A B
WAGGONER HENRY A 32 POS W
WAGGONER J P A 32 SHE W
WAGGONER JACOB A 46 GRE W
WAGGONER MORRIS A 32 POS B
WAGNER G J A 46 MON W
WAGONER A A 46 MON W
WAGONER ANTNA A 32 DAV B
WAGONER DALIEL W A 32 DAV W
CHAL FOR HOLDING OFFICE
OF CONSTABLE BEFORE AND
DURING THE WAR ---
THEN TO THE ARMY
WAGONER DANIEL A 32 DAV B
WAGONER DAVID A 32 DAV B
WAGONER EDWARD A 32 THO B
WAGONER JACOB A 32 DAV W
WAGONER JOHN A 46 GIB W
WAGONER JONAS A 32 DAV B
WAGONER MOSES A 32 DAV B
WAGONER R L A 32 DAV B
WAGONER RANKIN A 46 MON B
WAGONER SIMEON A 46 GIB W
WAGONER WM A 46 MCL W
WAGSTAFF J F A 40 SAN W
WAGSTAFF J S A 44 BEA W
WAGSTAFF JAMES R A 40 DA1 W
WAHAB DALLIS A 53 GER W
WAHAB HENRY W A 53 OCR W
WAHAB JAMES H A 53 GER W
WAHAB JAMES H A 53 OCR W
WAHAB ROBERT P A 53 GER W
WAHAB URIAH M A 53 GER W
WAIL HARDY A 28 05A B
WAILLIAMS LAMB A 35 CYP W
WAILS FRANCIS A 28 02N B
WAINWRIGHT CHARLES A 44 OXF B
WAINWRIGHT JACKSON A 19 DAV W
WAINWRIGHT K H A 44 OXF W
WAITMAN DAVID A 32 DAV W
WAITMAN JACOB A 32 DAV W
WAITMAN JACOB L A 32 DAV W
WALDEN MATTHEW A 28 04A B
WALDEN W H A 28 01A W
WALDEN W S A 29 FA1 W
WALES BURTON A 37 ROB W
WALES S M A 32 BRO W
WALFORD JOSIAH A 39 HAR W
WALK J J A 32 SHE W
WALKER A A 46 SUM W
WALKER A W A 32 CLE W
WALKER ABE A 28 04B B
WALKER ABSALOM A 46 FRI B
WALKER ADAM A 28 05A B
WALKER ADAM J C A 28 05A B
WALKER ALEX A 29 CAR W
WALKER ALEX A 44 DUT B
WALKER ALFRED A 28 04B B
WALKER ALFRED A 28 05A B
WALKER ANDERSON A 44 DUT B
WALKER ANTHONY A 44 YXS B
WALKER AUGUSTUS A 30 CUR W
WALKER B H A 35 WOL W
WALKER BASLEY J A 46 GRE W
WALKER BENJ A 29 FLE B
WALKER BENJ C A 30 TUL W
WALKER BENJAMIN S A 30 COI W
WALKER BENNET A 39 DAV W
WALKER BERNICE A 44 BRA W
WALKER BROWN A 32 TYR W
WALKER C J A 39 DAV W
WALKER CAREY W A 44 YXS W
WALKER CHARLES A 35 ISL B
WALKER CHAS A 29 CAR B
WALKER DANIEL A 32 JAC W
WALKER DANIEL C A 46 RAG W
WALKER DAVID A 29 CAR B
WALKER DAVID A 29 FA1 B
WALKER DAVID A 30 TUL B
WALKER DAVID A 44 YXS W
WALKER DAVID C A 46 GRE W
WALKER DAVID M A 40 FER W
WALKER DEMPSEY A 30 CUR W
WALKER DENNES A 44 DUT B
WALKER DUDLEY A 44 DUT W
WALKER EDGAR A 28 04A B
WALKER EDWARD H A 30 COI W
WALKER EDWARD S A 28 02N B
WALKER ELI A 28 05A B
WALKER ELIJAH A 28 05A B
WALKER ELLIS A 44 DUT W
WALKER ENOCH A 19 NEW B
WALKER ENOCH A 30 CUR W
WALKER FOSTER J A 30 COI W
WALKER FRANK A 29 FA1 B
WALKER FRANK A 37 HIG B
WALKER G B A 30 TUL W
WALKER G WILLIAM A 46 RAG W
WALKER GEO A 19 BE1 W
WALKER GEORGE A 32 TYR B
WALKER GEORGE A 37 WHI B
WALKER GEORGE A 46 JAM W
WALKER GEORGE M A 37 ROC W
WALKER H A 32 TYR B
WALKER HARDY A 19 BE1 B
WALKER HARRISON A 37 EDW B
WALKER HARRY A 30 IND B
WALKER HARTEN A 46 FRI W
WALKER HARTWELL A 37 ROB B
WALKER HARTWELL A 37 ROB W
WALKER HENRY A 28 05A B
WALKER HENRY A 28 05A B
WALKER HENRY A 37 TA2 B
WALKER HENRY A 46 SUM B
WALKER HIRAM R A 40 DA1 W
WALKER ISAAC A 28 05A B
WALKER J J A 44 DUT W
WALKER J W A 32 CLE W
WALKER J W A 44 BRA W
WALKER JACK A 32 TYR B
WALKER JACOB A 28 05A B
WALKER JARRET A 44 DUT W
WALKER JAS A A 24 UPP W
WALKER JASPER A 30 CUR W
WALKER JEFF A 28 04A B
WALKER JEREMIAH A 37 ROC B
WALKER JOHN A 19 BE1 W
WALKER JOHN A 26 MOO W
WALKER JOHN A 28 05A B
WALKER JOHN A 32 TYR B
WALKER JOHN A 46 FRI W
WALKER JOHN A A 32 CLE W
WALKER JOHN H A 30 COI W
WALKER JOHN P A 44 DUT W
WALKER JORDAN A 46 SUM B
WALKER JOSHUA A 44 DUT B
WALKER LAWRANCE A 53 GER W
WALKER LEWIS A 29 CAR B
WALKER LORENZA A 44 DUT W
WALKER LOUIS A 28 05A B
WALKER MARCH A 30 POP B
WALKER MATHEW A 39 DAV W
WALKER MATHEW A 39 FRE B
WALKER MOSES A 44 TOW B
WALKER MOSES A 44 TOW B
WALKER N B A 39 LOU W
WALKER NATHAN B A 30 COI W
WALKER NELSON A 28 05A B
WALKER NORIS A 30 CUR W
WALKER NORRIS A 35 ISL W
WALKER P G W A 46 SUM W
WALKER P PELAGE A 30 CUR W
WALKER PETER A 29 SEV B
WALKER PHILIP A 44 DUT B
WALKER POMPEY A 30 COI B
WALKER R A A 32 CLE W
WALKER REV WYATT A 44 HEN B
WALKER RICHARD A 24 EDE B
WALKER RICHARD A 44 DUT B
WALKER ROBERT E A 19 BE1 W
WALKER ROBT A 29 FA1 B
WALKER S K A 46 SUM W
WALKER SAMPSON A 30 CUR B
WALKER SANDER A 46 HIG W
WALKER SANDY A 29 CAR B
WALKER SNOWED B A 53 FAI W
WALKER STEPHEN A 30 COI B
WALKER STEPHN A 28 03A B
WALKER T D A 30 TUL W
WALKER THOMAS A 44 DUT B
WALKER THOMAS A A 53 KEN W
WALKER W O A 30 TUL W
WALKER W R A 25 SHO W
WALKER WESLEY A 44 DUT B
WALKER WILLIAM A 29 GRA B
WALKER WILLIAM A 30 IND B
WALKER WILLIAM A 46 FRI W
WALKER WILLIAM J A 30 COI W
WALKER WILLIAM L A 30 CUR W
WALKER WILLIS A 44 DUT W
WALKER WILLIS S A 44 LED W
WALKER WILLSON A 30 CUR W
WALKER WM H A 53 FAI B
WALKER WM R A 19 BE1 W
WALKER YOUNG A 46 FRI W
WALL A M A 26 PEE W
WALL ALLEN D A 46 JAM W
WALL G P A 32 LEE W
WALL J B A 26 MOO W
WALL J S A 26 PEE W
WALL J W R 26 SHE W
WAS A CONSTABLE &
ENGAGED IN REBELION
SWORN. STRICKEN OUT
APRIL 9 1867
WALL JESSE A 99 BUS W
WALL JOHN A 32 COT W
WALL MILES S A 44 YXS W
WALL NELSON A 29 LOC W
WALL NELSON A 46 ROS W
WALL REUBEN A 39 GRI W
WALL SAML A 44 FOR B
WALL SAMUEL A 44 ISL B
WALL SOLOMON M A 46 ROS W
WALL W A A 32 LEE W
WALLAC CHRISTOPHER A 53 LA1 B
CERT RES SWAN QUARTER
WALLACE ABRAHAM A 28 15T B
WALLACE ALEXANDER A 35 ISL B
WALLACE BENJ A 28 04A B
WALLACE BLAND A 35 ISL W
WALLACE CLINTON A 19 BE1 B
WALLACE D S A 40 STO W
WALLACE DANL A A 29 GRA W
WALLACE DAVID A 26 CAR W

WALLACE EDMUND A 28 8TH B
WALLACE FRANK A 28 03A B
WALLACE G W A 35 FAI W
WALLACE GEORGE A 35 KEN B
WALLACE HASTY A 19 NEW B
WALLACE HENRY D A 28 9TH W
WALLACE J B A 28 01A W
WALLACE J L A 40 RHY W
WALLACE J N A 40 SAN W
WALLACE JACKSON A 28 8TH B
WALLACE JAMES H A 32 BRO B
WALLACE JOHN A 28 05A B
WALLACE JOHN O A 19 SMY W
WALLACE JOHN W A 35 ROC W
WALLACE JOSEPH F A 35 CYP W
WALLACE JOSEPHUS H A 28 10T W
WALLACE JOSHUA A 37 TA1 B
WALLACE LONDON A 35 KEN B
WALLACE MICHAEL A 35 ISL B
WALLACE PERRY DEAD 28 10T B
WALLACE PETER A 53 FAI B
WALLACE PRIMROSE A 28 10T B
WALLACE ROBERT A 19 POR W
WALLACE ROBERT A 28 10T B
WALLACE ROBERT A 35 CYP W
WALLACE STEPHEN A 19 MOR B
WALLACE STEPHEN A 28 04B B
WALLACE T C A 32 THO W
WALLACE T J A 40 STO W
WALLACE THOMAS A 35 KEN W
WALLACE THOMAS F A 35 GLI W
WALLACE W D A 28 01B W
WALLACE WILLIAM A 19 MOR B
WALLACE WM E A 29 GRA W
WALLACK G W A 28 01A W
WALLAS THOMAS A 40 SAN W
WALLER AMIS A 44 KNA B
WALLER CALVIN A 44 LED W
WALLER DUNCAN A 44 LED B
OF DUTCHVILLE
WALLER EDWARD A 44 BRA B
WALLER EDWARD A 44 LED B
WALLER HENRY A 44 LED B
WALLER JAMES A 37 PEN W
WALLER JOB A 44 DUT B
WALLER JOHN A 44 DUT B
WALLER JOHN A A 44 LED W
WALLER JOHN SR A 44 DUT W
WALLER N A A 44 DUT W
WALLER OLIVER A 37 EDW B
WALLER SAMUEL A 44 DUT B
WALLER STARLING A 37 TA2 W
WALLER STEPHEN A 37 TA2 B
WALLER T D A 44 LED W
WALLER TORRY A 44 DUT B
WALLER WARREN A 44 HEN B
WALLIS ARNOLD A 53 FAI B
WALLIS CALVIN A 40 SAN W
WALLIS HENRY J A 35 GLI W
WALLS WILLIS A 44 FIS B
WALSER ALBERT A 32 YAD W
WALSER GAITHER A 32 DAV W
WALSER GILES A 32 YAD W
WALSER H C A 32 YAD W
WALSER HENDERSON A 32 YAD W
WALSER JOHN A 32 YAD W
WALSER JOHN H A 32 YAD W
WALSER LOUIS A 32 TYR B
WALSER ROLAND A 32 SHE W
WALSER WILLIAM A 32 YAD W
WALSER WILLIAM A 32 YAD W
WALSON ANTHONY A 28 05A B
WALSTON EPHRIAM A 37 HOL B
WALSTON FESTHUR A 37 WHI W
WALSTON JAMES A 37 TA2 B
WALSTON JOHN A 37 PIN W
WALSTON LESTOR A 37 HIG W
WALSTON LITTLETON A 37 EDW W
WALSTON MAURICE B A 37 HOL B
WALSTON NOAH A 37 PIN B
WALSTON REUBEN A 37 PIN B
WALSTON WILEY A 37 TA1 W
WALSTON WILLIAM R A 37 EDW W
WALSTON WILSON A 37 WHI W
WALSTON WILSON A 37 WHI W
WALTER SQUIRE A 44 FOR B
WALTERS ANDREW J A 44 TAR W
WALTERS BANISTER A 44 BRA B
WALTERS E P A 44 LED W
WALTERS EDWARD A 19 MOR B
WALTERS J G A 44 TAR W
WALTERS R D A 44 FOR W
WALTON BENJAMIN F A 99 BUS W
WALTON FRANKLIN A 37 WHI W
WALTON JNO A 44 HEN B
WALTON JOSEPH A A 99 BUS W
WALTON RICHARD H A 24 UPP W
WALTON SAMUEL A 37 MAN B
WALTON SAMUEL J A 37 ROC W
WALTON SCOTT A 44 HEN B
WAMACK G A 26 PEE W
WAMACK WM A 26 PEE W
WAMDLE W G A 24 MID W
WAMMICK CALEB A 40 BLA B
WAMMOTH LOCH A 32 THO W
WAMOCK LEONARD A 29 FA1 B
WAMOCK MATT A 29 FA1 B
WAMOTH RICHD C A 39 LOU W
WARBITTEN CHARLES A 37 HIG W
WARBITTEN SIMEON A 37 HIG W
WARD A J A 24 UPP W
WARD ALFRED A 28 04A B
WARD ALFRED A 35 ROC W
WARD ALFRED C A 35 ROC W
WARD ALLEN C A 24 UPP W
WARD ALONZO A 28 9TH B
WARD ANDERSON S A 24 UPP W
WARD ANDREW A 19 NEW B
WARD ANDREW A 24 UPP W
WARD ARNOLD A 19 NEW B
WARD AUGUSTUS A 24 UPP W
WARD BENJ A 28 05A B
WARD BRISTER A 35 ROC B
WARD BRISTER A 35 ROC B
WARD BUTLER A 39 HAY B
WARD C H A 19 NEW W
WARD C O A 46 FRI W
WARD CEASER A 19 BE1 B
WARD CEASER A 19 MOR B
WARD CHARLES A 37 MAN B
WARD CHAS A 28 03A B
WARD D S A 19 HAD W
WARD DANIEL A 19 BE1 B
WARD DANIEL A 19 HAD B
WARD DANIEL A 19 NEW B
WARD DANIEL CHAL 32 LOF W
FOR HOLDING OFFICE OF
MAGISTRATE BEFORE AND
DURING THE WAR.
WARD DANL A 28 04A B
WARD DAVID A 29 CED W
WARD DORCEY C A 24 UPP W
WARD EDWARD A 19 NEW B
WARD EDWARD A 30 KNO W
WARD ELISHA A 24 UPP W
WARD FRANKLIN A 19 BE1 B
WARD GEORGE A 32 DAV W
WARD GEORGE A 35 FAI B
WARD GEORGE W A 72 SWA W
WARD HARDY A 24 UPP W
WARD HENRY A 28 04A B
WARD HENRY A 35 WOL W
WARD HENRY A 37 MAN B
WARD HIRAM A 46 GRE W
WARD HUGH A 46 JAM W
WARD HUMPHREY A 24 UPP W
WARD HUMPHREY N A 24 UPP W
WARD HYRAM CHAL A 32 JAC W
FOR HOLDING OFFICE OF
MAGISTRATE BEFORE AND
DURING THE WAR. RECON.
WARD J A A 28 11T W
WARD J D A 24 UPP W
WARD JAMES A 28 03A B
WARD JAMES A 37 TA1 B
WARD JAMES M A 46 GRE W
WARD JEPTHA A A 24 UPP W
WARD JOHN A 19 BE1 B
WARD JOHN A 28 03A B
WARD JOHN A 28 03A B
WARD JOHN A 29 CED W
WARD JOHN A 32 COT W
WARD JOHN A 53 FAI B
WARD JOHN F A 37 TA1 W
WARD JOHN H A 37 SHA B
WARD JOHN H A 53 LA1 W
WARD JOSEPH A 19 HAD B
WARD JOSEPH A 24 UPP W
WARD JOSEPH A 53 LA1 W
WARD JOSEPH H A 37 PIN W
WARD JOSEPH M A 35 ROC W
WARD KENETH F A 24 UPP W
WARD KINNION A 19 NEW B
WARD LAWRENCE A 37 TA1 B
WARD LOUIS A 19 BE1 B
WARD LUIS A 19 BE1 B
WARD LUKE A 19 HAD B
WARD MITCHELL A 46 ROS W
WARD NAERO A 19 BE1 B
WARD NATHAN A 28 9TH B
WARD NOAH A 24 UPP W
WARD PETER A 19 BE1 B
WARD PETER A 19 MOR B
WARD QUINTON H A 24 UPP W
WARD R W A 19 HAR W
WARD RICHD A 28 05A B
WARD ROBERT A 28 01A B
WARD S H A 46 JAM W
WARD SAMPSON A 19 BE1 B
WARD SAMUEL A 19 BE1 B
WARD SAMUEL A 37 ROC B
WARD SETH A 39 FRA W
WARD SETH W A 32 DAV W
WARD SOLOMON A 19 BE1 B
WARD SQUIRE A 28 03A B
WARD STEPHEN A 29 CED W
WARD THOMAS A 19 MOR B
WARD THOS N A 24 UPP W
WARD TIMOTHY A 24 UPP W
WARD TOWNSEND E A 24 UPP W
WARD W W A 32 LOF W
WARD W W A 46 GRE W
WARD WILEY A 28 05A B
WARD WILLIAM A 19 BE1 B
WARD WILLIAM A 19 BE1 B
WARD WILLIAM A 19 NEW B
WARD WILLIAM A 37 EDW B
WARD WILLIAM H A 28 11T W
WARD WILLIAM M A 24 UPP W

WARD WM G A 24 UPP W
WARD WM G JR A 24 UPP W
WARD WM W A 19 NEW W
WARD WRIGHT A 19 NEW B
WARD WRIGHTEN A 24 UPP W
WARDEN J T A 29 FA1 W
WARDEN WM A 29 FA1 W
TOWN COMMISSIONER AFTER-
WARDS ENG IN REBELLION
WARDS ALFRED A 46 GRE B
WARE A B A 26 GOF W
WARE A F A 26 GOF W
WARE HENRY A 46 GIB B
WARE J A A 26 GOF W
WARE JAMES A A 26 GOF W
WARE JOHN A 46 JAM W
WARE JOHN F A 26 GOF W
WARE MARTIN A 26 GRI W
WARE THOS G A 44 YXR W
WARE WILLIAM A 26 GOF W
WARE WILLIAM A 26 GRI W
WAREN LEWIS A 46 KIN B
WARFF FRANK A 28 05A B
WARFORD NOAH A 32 COT W
WARFORD SAMUEL A 32 COT W
WARLICK A 1 A 26 WAR W
WARLICK A 2 A 26 WAR W
WARLICK ABSOLOM A 26 GRI W
WARLICK LAWSON A 40 BLA W
WARLICK N B A 26 WAR W
WARLICK PINCKNEY H A 40 BLA W
WARLICK SIMPSON A 40 BLA W
WARLICK W A A 26 WAR W
WARNER BRITTIAN A 32 THO W
WARNER CRANE A 53 HAT B
WARNER GEORGE A A 53 HAT B
WARNER HUBARD A 32 LEE W
WARNER ISHM A 37 HIG B
WARNER LEWIS A 32 YAD W
WARNER VINCENT A 32 SHE W
WARNER WILLIAM A 32 YAD W
WARNER WILLIAM A 37 TA2 W
WARNER WILLIAM SR A 32 YAD W
WARNNING WILLIAM A 32 THO W
WARREN A E A 26 BUR W
WARREN AARON H A 46 KIN B
WARREN ALFRED A 37 HOL W
WARREN BRUNSON A 29 FA1 B
WARREN EGBERT A 44 SAS B
WARREN FORNEY H A 40 DA1 W
WARREN FULFORD A 28 11T W
WARREN GASTON A 99 BUS W
WARREN GEORGE R A 40 SAN W
WARREN H M A 26 SWA W
WARREN HENRY O A 37 EDW W
WARREN J R A 40 STO W
WARREN J T A 40 SAN W
WARREN JACKSON A 46 KIN B
WARREN JAHANY A 46 KIN W
WARREN JAMES A 24 EDE B
WARREN JAMES C A 24 EDE W
WARREN JAMES L A 28 11T W
WARREN JAMES R A 37 PIN W
WARREN JOHN A 28 03A B
WARREN JOHN A 30 GIB W
WARREN JOHN A 37 MAN B
WARREN JOHN A 37 PIN W
WARREN JOHN A 46 GRE B
WARREN L P A 24 EDE W
WARREN LEWIS A 28 11T W
WARREN MAJOR A 28 6TH B
WARREN MUNROE A 37 EDW B
WARREN OLEN A 37 PIN W
PITT CO
WARREN PETER M A 24 EDE W
WARREN RUFUS A 46 KIN B
WARREN SAMSON A 40 SAN B
WARREN SOLOMON A 46 SUM W
WARREN THOS D JR A 24 EDE W
WARREN W B A 29 FA1 W
WARREN W G A 40 SAN W
WARREN W P C A 40 DA2 W
WARREN WILLIAM H A 53 GER W
WARREN WM A 40 STO W
WARRICK WM A 29 FA1 W
WASHBURN ABNER A 26 SHE W
WASHBURN JOHN A 46 MON B
WASHBURN JOSEPH A 46 GRE W
WASHINGTON BENJAMIN A 37 ROB B
WASHINGTON DAVID A 44 OXF B
WASHINGTON EDWARD A 28 04B B
WASHINGTON EDWD A 28 04A B
WASHINGTON ELI A 30 MOY B
WASHINGTON GENERAL A 44 TAR B
WASHINGTON GEO A 19 BE1 B
WASHINGTON GEO A 29 FA1 B
WASHINGTON GEORGE A 19 BE1 B
WASHINGTON GEORGE A 19 BE1 B
WASHINGTON GEORGE A 28 04A B
WASHINGTON GEORGE A 28 11T B
WASHINGTON GEORGE A 28 16T B
WASHINGTON GEORGE A 35 WOL W
WASHINGTON GEORGE A 37 HIG B
WASHINGTON GEORGE A 37 PEN B
WASHINGTON GEORGE A 37 ROB B
WASHINGTON HENRY A 32 DAV B
WASHINGTON HORICE A 44 LED B
WASHINGTON J P A 44 LED W
WASHINGTON JAMES A 28 9TH B
WASHINGTON JEREMIAH A 19 BE1 B
WASHINGTON JOHN A 19 BE1 B
WASHINGTON JOHN A 37 MAN B
WASHINGTON LISIOUS A 28 03A B
WASHINGTON M C A 44 LED W
WASHINGTON S R A 28 11T W
WASHINGTON WM A 44 SAS B
WASHINGTON WOODS A 44 DUT W
WASHINGTON WOODSIN A 44 DUT W
WASTON MILES A 28 16T B
WATERFIELD ALEXANDERA 30 KNO W
WATERFIELD CALEB J A 30 KNO W
WATERFIELD DAVID A 30 KNO W
WATERFIELD H K A 30 KNO W
WATERFIELD HENRY J A 30 KNO W
WATERFIELD J C A 30 KNO W
WATERFIELD JAMES 30 KNO W
8-MOS-RES
WATERFIELD JOHNSON WA 30 KNO W
WATERFIELD KNOLLY A 30 KNO W
WATERFIELD M J A 30 KNO W
WATERFIELD MALICHI A 30 KNO W
WATERFIELD NELSON A 30 KNO W
WATERFIELD R R A 30 KNO W
WATERFIELD R S A 30 KNO W
WATERFIELD REUBIN A 30 KNO W
WATERFIELD S D A 30 KNO W
WATERFIELD S S A 30 KNO W
WATERFIELD SAML J A 30 KNO W
WATERFIELD TAYLOR A 30 GIB W
WATERFIELD W C A 30 KNO W
WATERFIELD WATEMAN A 30 KNO W
WATERFIELD WILLIAM A 30 KNO W
WATERMAN A A 30 KNO W
WATERMAN GODFREY A 53 LA1 W
WATERS ALLEN W A 19 BE1 B
WATERS BENAJAH A 35 MAG W
WATERS E S A 46 MON W
WATERS GREEN A 28 05A B
WATERS HENRY A 19 BE1 W
WATERS HENRY C A 53 LA1 W
WATERS JOHN D A 35 MAG W
WATERS JOHN F A 35 CYP B
WATERS JOHN H A 35 WAR W
WATERS MATHEW A 35 FAI W
WATERS MORRIS A 28 03A B
WATERS NATHAN A 35 MAG W
WATERS O T A 35 GLI W
WATERS REUBEN A 28 04A B
WATERS SETH A 28 9TH B
WATERS WILLIAM R A 35 WAR W
WATHAM KITT A 37 TA2 B
WATHINGTON
GRANDERSON A 46 MON B
WATHINGTON WILLIAM A 46 MON W
WATKINS A S A 32 CLE W
WATKINS ADAM A 44 YXS B
WATKINS ALEX A 44 YXR B
WATKINS ALVIN A 46 SUM B
WATKINS ANDREWS A 44 HEN B
WATKINS BENJA A 44 SAS B
WATKINS BURWELL A 44 SAS B
WATKINS DANCEY A 44 HEN W
WATKINS GEO W A 44 YXR W
WATKINS H T A 44 HEN W
WATKINS HARPER A 46 KIN B
WATKINS HARRY A 28 03A B
WATKINS HENRY A 46 FRI B
WATKINS HENRY A 46 KIN B
WATKINS ISAAC A 37 PEN W
WATKINS ISAAC A 44 SAS B
WATKINS J H A 46 KIN B
WATKINS JNO A A 44 YXR W
WATKINS JOHN A 44 SAS B
WATKINS JOHN S A 28 01A W
WATKINS LEWIS A 44 HEN B
WATKINS LOVELIS A 44 ISL B
WATKINS MANUEL A 28 7TH B
WATKINS N V A 44 SAS W
WATKINS REUBIN A 44 TOW B
WATKINS RICHARD A 37 PEN W
WATKINS RICHARD A 44 OXF B
WATKINS ROBERT A 44 SAS B
WATKINS ROBT P A 44 HEN B
WATKINS SAMUEL A 44 YXR W
WATKINS SMITH A 44 OXF B
WATKINS STEPHEN A 44 ISL B
WATKINS THOMAS A 44 SAS B
WATKINS THOS A 44 HEN B
WATKINS W W A 32 THO W
WATKINS WALTER A 44 HEN B
WATKINS WILLIAM A 46 KIN B
WATKINS WILLIAM A 46 SUM B
WATLINGTON ALLEN A 46 MON B
WATLINGTON CHARLES BA 46 MON W
WATLINGTON GILBERT A 46 MON B
WATLINGTON HENRY T A 46 GRE W
WATLINGTON L L A 46 MON W
WATLINGTON WM H A 46 GRE W
WATSON ASA A 28 7TH W
CERTIF GIVEN LIVES
AT BACHELOR'S CREEK
WATSON AUGUSTIN W A 53 LA1 W
WATSON BENJAMIN G A 53 FAI W
WATSON C B A 46 HIG W
WATSON C T A 28 04B W
WATSON CAROLINE A 28 7TH B
WATSON CHAS A 28 01B W
WATSON DANIEL H A 53 LA1 W

WATSON DAVID R A 35 KEN W
WATSON DORRIS A 37 PEN B
WATSON E W A 28 03A W
WATSON EDWARD S A 35 KEN W
WATSON ELIJAH A 35 FAI W
WATSON FABIUS H A 99 BUS W
WATSON FRANCIS A 28 7TH W
WATSON FRANCIS M A 46 ROS W
WATSON GEORGE A 37 ROC B
WATSON HENRY G A 53 LA1 W
WATSON ISAAC A 32 COT W
WATSON ISAAC B A 44 TOW W
WATSON ISHMAEL A 28 7TH B
CERTIF GIVEN LIVES
IN WILSON CO NOW
WATSON ISRAEL R A 53 LA1 W
WATSON J R 19 HAD W
WATSON JABEZ R A 53 LA1 W
WATSON JAMES A 28 10T B
WATSON JAMES A 44 HEN B
WATSON JAMES B A 53 LA1 W
WATSON JAMES H A 53 LA1 W
WATSON JEREMIAH A 19 HAD W
WATSON JNO A 29 FA1 B
WATSON JNO A A 29 FA1 W
WATSON JNO L A 29 FA1 W
WATSON JOE A 37 PIN B
WATSON JOHN A 44 HEN B
WATSON JOHN A 72 SWA W
WATSON JOHN H C A 46 RAG W
WATSON JONATHAN H A 19 NEW W
WATSON JORDAN A 32 DAV W
WATSON KIDDICK A 24 EDE W
WATSON LAWRENCE A 39 FRA B
WATSON LEVI JAMES A 28 7TH W
WATSON LEWIS A 28 05A B
WATSON MATHEW A 44 HEN B
WATSON MICHAEL A 35 FAI W
WATSON NATHAN A 28 7TH W
WATSON OMSTED A 37 TA1 B
WATSON R B A 29 FA1 W
WATSON ROBERT A A 37 ROC W
RES TARBORO
WATSON ROBERT F A 53 LA1 W
WATSON SELBY A 53 FAI W
WATSON THOMAS E A 53 SWA W
WATSON THOMAS H A 53 FAI W
WATSON THOMAS S A 35 KEN W
WATSON W A A 32 DAV W
WATSON WASHINGTON A 37 MAN B
WATSON WILLIAM B A 53 GER W
WATSON WILLIAM F A 37 EDW W
WATSON WILLIAM S A 53 SWA W
WATSON WILSON A 26 SHE B
WATSON WILSON A 37 TA1 B
WATSON WM M A 28 01A W
WATT FRANKLIN A 46 MON B
WATT GEORGE A 40 FER B
WATT LEWIS A 46 MON B
WATT R S 26 GOF B
WATTERSON JOHN A 26 GOF W
WATTERSON P H CHALR 26 GOF W
MILITIA OFFICER &
ENGAGED IN REB.
WATTERSON R N A 26 SHE W
MILITIA OFFICER &
ENGAGED IN REBELLION
WATTERSON V M A 26 GOF W
WATTS ALFRED A 53 GER B
WATTS ISAAC A 25 HAY W
WATTS JONAS A 26 BUR B
WATTS RICHARD A A 46 GRE W
WATTS WILLIAM A A 25 HAY W

WAYNE ARTHUR J A 28 11T W
WAYNE FREDRICK A 28 13T W
WAYNE JACOB A 28 11T B
WAYNE JOHN T A 28 13T W
WAYNE LEVI P A 28 11T W
WAYNE MOSES A 28 04A B
WAYNE SIMON A 28 04A B
WAYNE WM N A 28 13T W
WAYNICK LEWIS A 46 MCL W
WAYNICK TOBIAS A 46 MCL W
WEAR GILBERT A 26 SHE B
WEAR J W A 26 GOF W
WEAR JOHN A A 26 GOF W
WEAR JOHN A A 26 SHE W
WEAR M L A 26 GOF W
WEAR M O A 26 BOR W
WEAR NELSON A 26 SHE B
WEAR R H A 26 SWA W
WEAR T A A 26 GOF W
WEARE PHILLIP A 32 POS W
WEATHERINGTON A M A 28 6TH W
WEATHERINGTON
WILLIAM B A 28 6TH W
WEATHERLEY PINKNEY A 46 JAM B
WEATHERLY GEORGE D A 46 MON W
WEATHERLY HENRY A 46 MON B
WEATHERLY J A A 46 GRE W
WEATHERLY JAMES W A 46 ROS W
WEATHERLY JEREMIAH A 46 ROS B
WEATHERLY MARTIN B A 46 GRE W
WEATHERLY SOLOMON A 46 GRE B
WEATHERLY W JOHN A 46 GRE W
WEATHERLY WM A 46 GRE W
WEATHERS A G A 26 SHE W
WEATHERS BENJAMIN A 26 BLA B
WEATHERS C M A 26 SHE W
WEATHERS J D A 26 SHE W
MILITIA OFFICER &
ENGAGED IN REBELLION
WEATHERS J P A 44 FOR W
WEATHERS JAMES A 44 FOR W
WEATHERS JAMES A 99 BUS W
WEATHERS JAMES S A 39 HAR W
WEATHERS JOHN W A 99 BUS W
WEATHERS MARTIN A A 26 SHE W
WEATHERS R O A 44 BEA W
WEATHERS R Y 2ND A 26 SHE W
WEATHERS W S A 26 SHE W
WEATHERSBEE B A 28 6TH W
WEATHERSBEE F J A 28 6TH W
WEATHERSBEE
WILLIAM H A 37 EDW W
WEATHERSTON
FREDRICK A 37 TA1 B
WEATHES W P A 44 FOR W
WEAVER A A A 32 DAV W
WEAVER A D A 44 DUT W
WEAVER ANDREW J A 37 PIN W
WEAVER BENJAMIN H A 37 SHA W
WEAVER CALVIN A 37 HIG B
WEAVER CHARLES A 32 POS W
WEAVER D W A 44 HEN W
WEAVER DAVID A 32 SHE W
WEAVER DICK A 44 HEN B
WEAVER ELIAS A 32 SHE W
WEAVER GEO W A 44 HEN W
WEAVER GEORGE W A 32 SHE W
WEAVER H F A 32 SHE W
WEAVER HENRY A 37 WHI W
WEAVER ISAAC A 44 DUT W
WEAVER ISM A 37 HIG B
WEAVER JAMES A 32 THO W
WEAVER JAMES A 44 DUT B

WEAVER JNO E A 44 HEN W
WEAVER JOHN A 37 WHI W
WEAVER JOSEPH A 32 DAV W
WEAVER JOSEPH A 44 DUT W
WEAVER LEWIS A 26 BUR W
WEAVER NATHAN A 37 HIG B
WEAVER POWELL A 32 SHE W
WEAVER RICHD H A 28 01A B
WEAVER S J A 26 SHE W
WEAVER SAMUEL A 26 BUR W
WEAVER SPENCER A 44 FIS W
WEAVER STARLING A 26 BUR W
WEAVER T P A 44 FIS W
WEAVER W G A 44 FIS W
WEAVER W G JR A 44 FIS W
WEAVER W H A 44 HEN W
WEAVER WILLIAM A 32 SHE W
WEAVER WILLIAM A 32 SHE W
WEAVER WILLIAM A 37 HIG B
WEAVER WILLIAM A 37 SHA W
WEAVER WILLIAM A 37 WHI W
WEAVER WILLIAM D A 37 SHA W
WEAVER WILLIAM H A 37 HIG W
WEAVER WM A 44 DUT W
WEAVIL ANDREW A 32 BRO W
WEAVIL DANIEL A 32 BRO W
WEAVIL JOHN A 32 BRO W
WEAVIL JOHN C A 32 POS W
WEB HARDAMON A 44 SAS B
WEBB ABRAHAM A 44 OXF B
WEBB ABRAM A 37 WEB B
WEBB ALBERT A 37 WEB W
WEBB ALEXR A 44 YXS B
WEBB ALFORD A 39 DAV B
WEBB ALFORD A 39 DAV B
WEBB ANTHONY A 44 SAS B
WEBB ARCHABOLD A 39 LOU B
WEBB BENNETT A 37 WEB W
WEBB CIDNEY A 32 DAV B
WEBB COLLIN A 37 WEB W
WEBB D C A 26 SHE W
WAS MILITIA OFFICER &
DEPT POSTMASTER PRIO
TO THE WAR & AFTERWARD
ENGAGED IN REBELLION
WEBB DANIEL A 37 WEB W
WEBB DANL A 29 FA1 B
WEBB DAVID A 37 WEB W
WEBB DAVID A 37 WHI W
WEBB DEMPSEY A 37 WEB W
WEBB DENNIS A 44 TAR B
WEBB ELI A 37 WHI B
WEBB ELISHA A 37 WEB W
WEBB GASTON A 39 DAV W
TRANS FROM NASH CO
MAMMERS PRE
WEBB GEORGE A 28 04A B
WEBB GEORGE A 39 DAV B
WEBB GREY A 37 WEB W
WEBB H W A 40 STO W
WEBB HARRY A 44 LED B
WEBB HARRY B A 39 LOU B
WEBB HENRY A 44 KNA B
WEBB HENRY A 44 TAR B
WEBB ISAAC A 44 LED B
WEBB J H A 44 LED W
WEBB J J A 26 SHE W
WEBB J L A 40 STO W
WEBB J R A 25 HAY W
WEBB JACOB A 44 LED B
WEBB JAMES A 44 TAR B
WEBB JAMES H A 44 LED W
WEBB JAMES R A 46 FRI W

WEBB JAS D	A	24	MID	W
WEBB JEPTHA	A	37	WHI	W
WEBB JIM	A	39	DAV	B
WEBB JNO J	A	29	FA1	B
WEBB JOHN	A	37	WEB	W
WEBB JOHN	A	37	WEB	W
WEBB JOHN MC	A	26	SHE	W
WEBB JOSEPH	A	26	SHE	B
WEBB L D	A	26	SHE	W
WEBB L D SR	A	26	SHE	W
WEBB L J	A	39	DAV	W
WEBB LAMPLETT	A	46	MON	W
WEBB LANT	A	46	MON	B
WEBB LEWIS	A	28	01A	W
WEBB MOSES	A	28	14T	B
WEBB NELSON	A	44	YXS	B
WEBB NORMAN W	A	37	WEB	W
WEBB PRINCE	A	28	14T	B
WEBB RICHD	A	29	FA1	B
WEBB ROBERT B	A	19	BE1	B
WEBB ROBT T	A	39	DAV	W
WEBB SAML	A	44	LED	B
WEBB SILAS	A	19	MOR	W
WEBB SPRUEL	A	28	05A	B
WEBB SQUARE	A	44	KIT	B
WEBB STEPHEN	A	44	LED	B
WEBB TURNER	A	44	KIT	B
WEBB W D	A	39	DAV	W
WEBB W R	A	44	OXF	W
WEBB WILLIAM	A	37	WEB	W
WEBB WILLIAM	A	46	FRI	B
WEBB WILLIAM SR	A	37	WEB	W
WEBB WILLIE	A	37	WEB	W
WEBB WM	A	44	OXF	B
WEBB WM J	A	24	MID	W
WEBB WM R	A	29	FA1	B
WEBBER ADAM	A	40	DEC	B
WEBBER BERRY	A	40	DEC	B
WEBBER BOSTON	A	28	02N	B
WEBBER HENRY	A	28	01A	B
WEBBER LOUIS	A	28	02N	B
WEBBS JESSE R	A	37	HIG	B
(WHITE WRITTEN IN PENCIL)				
WEBBS VIRGIL	A	37	ROB	B
WEBSTER DANL	A	28	03A	B
WEBSTER G F	A	29	FA1	W
WEBSTER JOHN	A	28	6TH	B
WEBSTER PETER	A	46	SUM	B
WEBSTER TIMOTHY	A	29	FA1	W
WEBSTER WM	A	29	FA1	W
WEDDELL MATHEW	A	37	TA1	W
WEDLON D W	A	39	PUG	W
WEEKS DANIEL S	A	19	HAD	W
WEEKS E B	A	19	HAD	W
WEEKS GEO W	A	19	BE1	W
WEEKS GEO W	A	37	ROB	W
WEEKS HARROLD	A	19	HAD	W
WEEKS HENRY	A	37	ROB	W
WEEKS ISAAC	A	19	HAD	W
WEEKS ISAAC JR	A	19	HAD	W
WEEKS J B	A	19	HAD	W
WEEKS J E	A	19	HAD	W
WEEKS LILAS	A	37	ROB	W
WEEKS S R	A	19	HAD	W
WEEKS THOS J	A	28	6TH	W
WEEKS W W	A	19	HAD	W
WEEKS WILLIS	A	28	04A	B
WEEKS WM P P	A	19	HAD	W
WEER J C	A	26	BOR	W
WEER WILLEY	A	32	POS	W
WEERE WILLIAM	A	32	POS	W
WEESNER DANIEL	A	32	SHE	W
WEESNER E M	A	32	SHE	W
WEESNER JOHN	A	32	SHE	W
WEESNER W D	A	32	SHE	W
WEESNER WM J	A	32	THO	W
WEINSTEIN LEVI	A	28	01A	W
WEIR ALEX	A	46	GRE	B
WEIR HENRY	A	46	SUM	B
WEIR SILAS	A	46	GRE	B
WEIRE ISAAC	A	46	GRE	B
WEISEGAR J W	A	29	FA1	W
MILLITIA OFFICER HOISTED THE CONFEDERATE FLAG OVER U S ARSENAL AT FAYETTE-VILLE 1861 & AFTER ENGAGED IN REBELL LUMBERTON ROBESON CO CERT APL 11, 68				
WELBER JACOB	A	26	CAR	B
WELBORN C H	A	32	DAV	W
WELBORN JOHN	A	32	LEE	W
WELBORN JOHN H	A	32	DAV	W
WELBORN WILLIAM M	A	32	LEE	W
WELBORNE D G	A	32	THO	W
WELBORNE DAVID A	A	32	BRO	W
WELBORNE J C	A	32	BRO	W
WELBORNE JAMES M	A	32	BRO	W
WELBORNE JOHN T M	A	32	BRO	W
WELBORNE PHILIP H	A	32	BRO	W
WELCH A L	A	46	HIG	W
WELCH DANL	A	24	UPP	B
WELCH DAVIS	A	46	HIG	W
WELCH HENRY	A	24	UPP	B
WELCH ISAAC	A	24	UPP	B
WELCH ISAAC JR	A	24	UPP	B
WELCH JACOB	A	24	UPP	B
WELCH JOHN J	A	46	HIG	W
WELCH JONATHAN	R	46	HIG	W
NAME LINED OUT MAGISTRATE BEFORE THE WAR AND DURING THE WAR AIDED THE REBELION COULD NOT TAKE OATH WITH THE WORD VOLIONTARY OMITED REJ				
WELCH KADER	A	24	MID	B
WELCH MOSES	A	46	HIG	W
WELCH RANDALL	A	24	UPP	B
WELCH ROBT	A	24	EDE	B
WELCH STEPHEN	A	24	MID	B
WELCH W D	A	24	UPP	W
WELCH WM	A	46	HIG	W
WELCH WM A	A	46	HIG	W
WELDER TERREL	A	39	DAV	B
WELDER WM	A	39	DAV	W
WELDON A C	A	46	HIG	W
WELFARE E A	A	32	CLE	W
WELFARE REWBEN A	A	32	CLE	W
WELFORD L S	A	32	DAV	W
WELHER WM A	A	46	COB	W
WELKIN GABREL	A	32	DAV	B
WELKINS RICHARD	A	37	SHA	B
WELLEFORD BENTON B	A	37	TA2	W
WELLINGTON JAMES	A	24	EDE	B
WELLINGTON NED	A	29	FA1	B
WELLINGTON SOUTHEY	A	28	04A	B
WELLINGTON W A	A	28	11T	W
WELLINGTON W H	A	28	6TH	W
WELLINGTON WILLIS	A	28	6TH	W
WELLMAN ARTHUR	A	26	GRI	B
WELLMAN JOHN	A	26	GRI	B
WELLMAN W R	A	26	SHE	W
WELLMAN WILLIAM	A	26	GRI	W
WELLMON ALFRED	A	40	DEC	B
WELLON S JR	A	39	FRA	W
WELLS ADAM	A	26	WAR	B
WELLS ALEXANDER	A	37	SHA	B
WELLS ALFRED	A	26	PEE	B
WELLS B F	A	40	STO	W
WELLS BONEY	A	35	ROC	W
WELLS DANIEL D	A	35	MAG	W
WELLS DAVID	A	40	DA1	W
WELLS DELEMER	A	19	STR	W
WELLS DENNIS	A	37	SHA	B
WELLS FRANK	A	35	MAG	B
WELLS GEORGE	A	35	MAG	B
WELLS GEORGE	A	40	STO	B
WELLS ISAAC	A	26	WAR	B
WELLS ISIAIH	A	35	MAG	B
WELLS J K JR	A	26	PEE	W
WELLS J S	A	26	GOF	W
WELLS JACOB	A	35	MAG	W
WELLS JAMES	A	26	PEE	W
WELLS JAMES	A	26	WAR	B
WELLS JAMES	A	35	ROC	W
WELLS JAMES	A	40	DA2	W
WELLS JAMES R	A	37	ROC	W
WELLS JAMES W	A	35	MAG	W
WELLS JAS J	A	26	PEE	B
WELLS JERRY	A	40	CAN	B
WELLS JNO	A	44	SAS	B
WELLS JOHN	A	26	WAR	B
WELLS JOHN	A	40	DA1	B
WELLS JOSEPH	A	35	ROC	W
WELLS JULIUS J	A	35	MAG	W
WELLS MOSES	A	26	PEE	B
WELLS NEEDOM	A	72	SWA	W
WELLS PRESTO	A	35	MAG	B
WELLS R T	A	26	PEE	W
WELLS ROBERT H	A	35	MAG	W
WELLS SAM'L	A	26	PEE	B
WELLS SAMEUL	A	35	ROC	B
WELLS SAMEUL	A	35	ROC	B
WELLS STOKES	A	35	ISL	B
WELLS STOKES	A	35	ISL	W
WELLS T P	A	26	SHE	W
WAS ASSISTANT POST-MASTER PRIOR TO WAR GAVE AID TO REBELLION				
WELLS THEOPHILUS	A	37	MAN	W
WELLS WILERY	A	37	ROC	B
WELLS WILLIAM	A	19	STR	W
WELLS WILLIAM B	A	35	ROC	W
WELLS WILLIAM C	A	37	MAN	W
WELSH JNO W	A	29	FA1	W
WELSH S N	A	29	BLA	W
CERTIF. FAYETTEVILLE CUMBERLAND CO				
WELSH S N	A	29	FA1	W
WELSH WILY	A	46	FRI	W
WEMBERLY BILLY	A	37	HIC	B
WENLEY GEO E	A	28	05A	B
WENTRS JOHN A	A	28	04A	B
WENTS R C	A	40	STO	W
WERTHELI JAMES A	A	28	16T	W
WESCOTT GEORGE W	A	30	ROA	W
WESCOTT JOHN	A	30	ROA	B
WESCOTT JOHN	A	30	ROA	W
WESCOTT STEPHEN	A	30	ROA	W
WESKOTT JOHN M	A	28	16T	W
WESLEY HENRY G	A	37	ROC	W
WESLEY HENRY L	A	37	ROC	B
WESLEY JOHN	A	19	MOR	B
WESLEY LEVI	A	28	04A	B
WESLEY LEWIS	A	37	ROC	B
WESLEY-WILLIAM	A	37	ROC	B
WESSON E A	A	26	SHE	W
WESSON EDWARD	A	26	SHE	B
WESSON JAMES A	A	26	SWA	W

WESSON JESSE A 26 SHE B
WESSON L C A 26 SHE W
WESSON LUKE A 26 SHE W
WESSON WILLIAM A 26 SHE W
WEST A A 29 FA1 W
WEST A M A 29 CED W
WEST ABRAHAM A 28 8TH B
WEST ALEXR A 44 YXS W
WEST ANSON C A 28 13T W
WEST BLUNT C A 28 7TH W
WEST BRYANT A 35 ISL B
WEST C T A 44 LED W
WEST CAESAR A 28 9TH B
WEST CHAS H A 44 TAR W
WEST D H A 29 FLE W
WEST D H A 39 JOR B
WEST D J A 29 CED W
WEST DANIEL A 29 ROC W
WEST DANIEL A 35 MAG W
WEST DAVID A 29 BLA W
BUNN LEVEL HARNETT
WEST DENNIS A 30 TUL W
WEST E A 40 CAN W
WEST ELISHA A 44 OXF W
WEST FERNEY A 28 01A B
WEST FRANK A 29 FA1 B
WEST G A A 44 YXS W
WEST G W A 28 8TH W
WEST GABRIEL A 30 TUL B
WEST GEO A 29 FA1 B
WEST GEO A A 28 04A B
WEST GEO W A 29 CED W
WEST H J A 29 CED W
WEST HAMILTON A 19 BE1 B
WEST HARDY A 29 FA2 W
WEST ISAAC A 28 04A B
WEST ISAAC A 39 JOR B
WEST ISAAC W A 35 ISL W
WEST J B A 44 YXS W
WEST J EDWIN A 28 01A W
WEST JAMES A 28 9TH B
WEST JAMES M A 46 MCL W
WEST JAS P A 44 OXF W
WEST JAS R A 44 OXF W
WEST JEFFREY A 28 11T B
WEST JNO T A 29 ROC W
WEST JOHN A 37 MAN W
WEST JOHN A 44 YXR W
WEST JOHN C A 28 03B W
WEST JOHN R A 35 WAR W
WEST JOHN W A 35 MAG W
WEST JOSEPH A 29 BLA W
WEST JOSEPH A 30 TUL W
WEST JOSEPH A 40 SAN W
WEST JOSEPH S A 30 GIB W
WEST JOSHUA A 35 WAR W
WEST JOSHUA J A 35 MAG W
WEST MACK A 35 ISL B
WEST MOSSES A 44 KNA B
WEST NELSON A 19 HAR B
WEST NOAH A 35 WAR W
WEST NOAH F A 28 16T W
WEST OWEN A 35 MAG W
WEST R C A 39 JOR W
WEST ROBERT A 44 SAS W
WEST SAML A 29 FA1 W
WEST STEPHEN A 28 9TH B
WEST SYLVESTER A 53 LA1 B
WEST T L A 28 7TH W
WEST THOMAS A 25 PIN W
WEST THOS S A 44 TOW W
WEST TITUS A 28 9TH B
WEST W C A 29 FLE W
WEST W F A 40 CAN W
WEST WALTER G A 28 01A W
WEST WILLOUGHBY JR A 30 TUL W
WEST WILLOUGHBY SR A 30 TUL W
WEST WM C A 28 13T W
WEST WM O A 44 YXS W
WEST WM R A 28 13T W
WEST WM W A 28 01A W
WEST ZOREL B A 28 13T W
WESTBROOK J S A 46 SUM W
WESTBROOK N G A 46 FRI W
WESTBROOK SILAS A 28 7TH W
WESTBROOK WM A 29 FA1 B
WESTBROOKS CHARLES A 46 GRE W
WESTER A D A 39 FRA W
WESTER ALBERT A 28 05A B
WESTER AXUM A 39 SPE W
WESTER BENJAMIN A 39 DAV W
WESTER BENJAMIN A 39 SPE W
WESTER BERRY A 39 LOU B
WESTER DANIEL A 39 DAV W
WESTER ELIJAH A 39 SPE B
WESTER GEORGE A 53 SWA B
WESTER H H A 39 DAV W
WESTER J J A 39 SPE W
WESTER JAMES A 39 JOR W
WESTER JOHN D A 39 SPE W
WESTER L C A 39 SPE W
WESTER LOCKEY A 39 JOR W
WESTER SOLOMAN A 39 DAV W
WESTER T C A 39 DAV W
WESTER THOMAS A 37 ROC B
WESTER THOMAS N A 39 JOR W
WESTERN JAMES A 28 03A B
WESTERN ROBBIN 37 TA1 B
WESTLEY JOHN A 19 BE1 B
WESTMORELAND D S A 32 THO W
WESTMORELAND WM A 32 THO W
WESTON B F A 24 EDE W
WESTON BENJAMIN A 53 LA1 B
WESTON BENJAMIN L A 53 FA1 W
WESTON ISAAC A 35 LIM W
WESTON JAMES A 53 LA1 W
WESTON JAMES A A 53 LA1 W
WESTON JOHN G A 35 LIM W
WESTON JOHN W H A 53 LA1 W
WESTON LOUIS A 53 LA1 B
WESTON MALACHI A 37 ROC W
WESTON RILEY A 53 LA1 B
WESTON SAML A 30 IND B
WESTON SYLVESTER A 53 LA1 W
WESTON-JESSE A 37 ROC B
WETHERINGTON ABNER A 28 8TH W
WETHERINGTON J T A 28 8TH W
WETHERINGTON JOHN H A 28 7TH W
WETHERINGTON JOHN O A 28 11T W
WETHERINGTON LOUIS A 28 11T W
WETHERINGTON RICHARDA 28 11T W
WETHERINGTON S D A 28 6TH W
WETHERINGTON S S A 28 6TH W
WETHERINGTON S T A 28 6TH W
WETHERINGTON
THOMAS W A 28 11T W
WETHERINGTON WM A 53 CHI W
WETHRINGTON E S A 28 6TH W
WEYMSS DAVID A 29 FA1 W
WHALEY BRADDOCK A 35 KEN W
WHALEY CHARLES A 35 LIM W
WHALEY GEORGE W A 72 SWA W
WHALEY H A 29 FA1 W
WHALEY HENRY J A 35 LIM W
WHALEY J J A 35 LIM W
WHALEY JASON A 35 LIM W
WHALEY JERRY A 30 IND W
WHALEY JOHN A 28 01A W
WHALEY SAMUEL D A 35 LIM W
WHALEY SAMUEL JR A 35 LIM W
WHALEY SAMUEL SR A 35 LIM W
WHALEY SEBASTIAN A 35 LIM W
WHALEY WAXEL A 35 LIM W
WHALEY WILLIAM A 35 KEN W
WHALEY WILLIAM B A 35 LIM W
WHALEY WILSON A 30 IND W
WHARTON A GREEN A 46 MCL B
WHARTON ALX A 46 GRE B
WHARTON ANDERSON A 46 MCL B
WHARTON BENJ A 46 GRE B
WHARTON BENJ E A 46 GRE B
WHARTON CALVIN LEE A 46 MCL B
WHARTON DAVID B A 19 BE1 W
WHARTON DOCT A 46 MCL B
WHARTON GEORGE A 46 GRE B
WHARTON GEORGE W A 46 MCL W
WHARTON HENRY A 46 GRE B
WHARTON IRVIN A 46 GRE B
WHARTON IRVING A 46 GIB B
WHARTON JERRY A 32 CLE B
WHARTON JESSE R A 46 GRE W
WHARTON JOHN A 46 GIB W
WHARTON JOHN A 46 GRE B
WHARTON JOHN A 46 GRE W
NAME LINED OUT
WHARTON JOHN C A 46 GRE W
WHARTON JOHN E A 46 GRE W
WHARTON JOHN W A 46 GIB W
WHARTON JONAS A 32 CLE B
WHARTON JOSEPH A 46 GRE B
WHARTON JOSEPH A 46 GRE B
WHARTON LASSON A 32 CLE B
WHARTON MARRISON A 46 MCL B
WHARTON MILTON A 46 GRE B
WHARTON MOSES A 46 MON B
WHARTON NELSON A 46 FRI B
WHARTON RAPER A 46 GRE B
WHARTON SIP A 46 GRE B
WHARTON THOMAS A 46 GRE B
WHARTON THOMAS C A 46 MCL B
WHARTON W D A 46 GRE W
WHARTON WASHINGTON A 46 GRE B
WHARTON WM P A 46 GRE W
WHARTON WM P A 46 MCL W
WHEALAS BEN A 39 DAV B
WHEALER BENGAMIN A 44 DUT W
WHEALER C C A 44 DUT W
WHEALTON GEORGE A 28 17T W
WHEALTON JAMES A 28 17T W
WHEALTON LEVEN E A 28 17T W
WHEALTON STEPHEN A 28 17T W
WHEDBEE JAMES H A 53 HAT W
WHEDBEE JOHN B A 53 HAT W
WHEDBEE JOHN B SEN A 53 HAT W
WHEDBEE MAJOR A 53 HAT W
WHEEDBY ALBERT A 28 04A B
WHEEDBY AMBROSE A 28 04A B
WHEEDBY DENNIS A 28 04A B
WHEEDBY GEORGE A 28 04A B
WHEELAR JESSE S A 46 FRI W
WHEELAR O C A 46 FRI W
WHEELAR W S A 46 FRI W
WHEELAS PLUMMER A 39 DAV B
WHEELER A J A 29 CED W
WHEELER D W A 44 LED W
WHEELER DAVID A 46 HIG W
WHEELER FRANKLIN R 46 GRE W
CAME TO THE SATE
IN 11 M/66

WHEELER G W A 29 CED W
WHEELER HARRISON A 44 LED W
WHEELER J Y A 44 LED W
WHEELER JAMES A 44 LED W
WHEELER JESSE A 46 GRE W
WHEELER JNO A 39 HAR W
WHEELER JOHN C A 29 ROC W
WHEELER NATHAN A 28 7TH B
WHEELER OLIVER A 46 COB W
WHEELER SAMUEL A 46 FRI B
WHEELER W B A 39 HAR W
WHEELER W W A 46 HIG W
WHEELER WM H A 46 COB W
WHEETLEY GEO W A 19 BE1 W
WHELESS ALFORD A 39 DAV W
WHELESS JAMES H A 39 DAV W
WHERLE HENRY A 32 DAV W
WHERLE JOSEPH A 32 DAV W
WHIBBY ISAAC A 19 BE1 B
WHICHARD FRANK M A 37 TA2 W
WHIDBEE LEVIN B A 53 HAT W
WHIDBY ADISON A 53 LA1 B
WHIDBY ISAAC A 53 LA1 B
WHIDBY JARREMIAH A 53 LA1 W
WHILESS E L A 39 DAV W
WHILKINS GEORGE A 37 HIG B
WHIMONT DAVID A 26 BLA W
WHISENHUNT THOS W A 32 CLE W
WHISENHUNT W H A 32 SHE W
WHISLOW ALEX A 32 DAV W
WHISNANT A A 26 BOR W
WHISNANT ADAM A 26 BLA W
WHISNANT H A 26 PEE W
WHISNANT J A 26 CAR W
WHISNANT J C A 26 PEE W
WHISNANT J F A 26 PEE W
WHISNANT JOHN A 26 CAR W
WHISNANT REUBEN A 26 WAR B
WHISTON JAMES M A 30 NAR W
WHIT WILLIAM A 32 CLE W
WHITACE ANTHONY A 46 GRE B
WHITACE DABNEY A 46 GRE B
WHITACE HENRY A 46 GRE B
WHITACE JAMES A 46 GRE B
WHITACE MOSES A 46 GRE B
WHITAKER ALEXANDER A 37 MAN B
WHITAKER ANTHONY A 37 ROB B
WHITAKER KITT A 39 LOU B
WHITAKER MOSES A A 32 THO W
WHITAKER R D A 26 MOO W
WHITAKER SAMUEL A 32 THO W
WHITAKER WASHINGTON A 37 ROB B
WHITAKER WM A 32 COT W
WHITAKER WM H A 37 ROB W
WHITAS EPHRAIM A 46 GRE B
WHITBY ALBERT A 24 EDE B
WHITBY EDMOND A 24 EDE B
WHITBY JACK A 24 EDE B
WHITBY JAMES A 24 EDE B
WHITBY SIMEON A 24 EDE B
WHITE A J A 24 EDE W
WHITE A S A 26 WAR W
WHITE ALBERT A 39 HAY B
WHITE ALBERT A 40 DA1 B
WHITE ALFRED A 28 15T B
WHITE ALLEN A 28 04A B
WHITE ANDREW A 24 EDE B
WHITE ANDREW A 40 DA1 B
WHITE ARAMISTEAD A 30 COI W
WHITE ARCHD A 29 FA1 B
WHITE AUGUSTUS A 28 15T B
WHITE BENJ F A 46 GRE W
WHITE BENJAMIN A 37 HIG B
WHITE BENJAMIN A 37 WHI B
WHITE BENJAMIN H A 37 MAN W
WHITE BILL A 37 HIC B
WHITE C D A 30 KNO W
WHITE C J A 44 HEN W
WHITE CAESAR A 28 04A B
WHITE CALVIN A 44 BRA B
WHITE CALVIN A 46 HIG W
WHITE CAROLINE A 19 NEW B
WHITE CHARLES A 29 BLA X
BUNN LEVEL HARNETT CO
WHITE D C A 44 BEA W
WHITE D N A 26 GOF W
WHITE DAVID A 26 GRI W
WHITE DAVID A 26 WAR W
WHITE DAVID H A 46 HIG W
WHITE DEMPSEY A 37 EDW B
WHITE E J A 28 7TH W
WHITE EDMUND A 28 05A B
WHITE EDWARD A 28 04A B
WHITE EDWARD B A 53 LA1 W
WHITE ELI A 28 8TH W
WHITE ELIAS B R 24 EDE B
REJECTED BY THE BOARD
ONLY 4 MONTHS IN STATE
WHITE ELIJAH A 28 9TH B
WHITE ELISHA A 44 BRA B
WHITE ELLIS A 46 GRE W
WHITE EPHRIM A 37 HIG B
WHITE EVANS A 39 FRA B
WHITE EVETT A 37 MAN B
WHITE FRANK A 44 BRA B
WHITE FREDERICK A 28 8TH W
WHITE GEO W A 24 EDE W
WHITE GEORGE A 24 EDE B
WHITE GEORGE A 26 PEE W
WHITE GEORGE A 44 HEN B
WHITE GEORGE A 72 SWA B
WHITE GEORGE JR A 26 PEE W
WHITE GEORGE W A 28 6TH W
WHITE GIBBS A 53 LA1 B
WHITE GILBERT A 44 BRA B
WHITE H A 26 PEE W
WHITE H W A 39 FRA W
WHITE HARRIS A 53 SWA B
WHITE HARRY A 39 LOU B
WHITE HARRY A 44 FIS B
WHITE HAYWOOD A 28 03A B
WHITE HENDERSON A 32 THO W
WHITE HENRY A 24 EDE W
WHITE HENRY A 28 05A B
WHITE HENRY F A 40 DA2 W
A HIST CENSUS TAKER IN
1860 VOLUNTEERED AS A
LIEUT. IN CONFED ARMY
IS ACCEPTED
WHITE HENRY S A 28 01A B
WHITE HILLIARD A 39 FRA B
WHITE ISAAC A 24 MID B
WHITE ISHAM A 39 DAV B
WHITE ISHAM A 44 BRA B
WHITE J E A 44 FOR W
WHITE J H A 46 HIG W
WHITE J O A 26 GRI W
WHITE JACOB A 28 04A B
WHITE JAMES A 24 EDE W
WHITE JAMES A 24 UPP B
WHITE JAMES A 26 BLA W
WHITE JAMES A 30 KNO W
WHITE JAMES A 37 HOL W
WHITE JAMES A 37 ROC W
WHITE JAMES A 44 BEA B
WHITE JAMES A 46 FRI W
WHITE JAMES A 53 FAI B
WHITE JAMES B A 19 HAR W
WHITE JAMES F A 19 BE1 W
WHITE JAMES F A 40 DA1 W
WHITE JAMES G A 40 BLA W
WHITE JAMES H A 28 7TH W
WHITE JAMES S A 28 6TH W
ROADMASTER
WHITE JAMES SR A 44 BRA B
WHITE JAMES W A 46 MCL W
WHITE JARNETT A 37 HOL W
WHITE JAROME A 30 NAR B
WHITE JAS H A 44 YXR W
WHITE JASPER A 30 COI W
APRIL 10, 1868
WHITE JERRY A 28 8TH W
WHITE JESSE A 28 7TH W
WHITE JESSE A 28 8TH B
WHITE JESSEE A 30 KNO W
WHITE JESSEE SR A 30 KNO W
WHITE JESSY A 29 FLE B
WHITE JNO C A 39 GRI W
WHITE JNO K A 39 GRI W
WHITE JOE A 39 FRA B
WHITE JOEL H A 24 EDE W
WHITE JOHN A 28 8TH B
WHITE JOHN B A 28 04B B
WHITE JOHN B A 37 HIC A
WHITE JOHN B A 40 DA1 W
WHITE JOHN J A 37 TA1 W
WHITE JOHN W A 37 TA1 W
WHITE JONATHAN D A 46 GRE W
WHITE JOS M A 28 03A W
WHITE JOSEPH A 24 UPP W
WHITE JOSEPH A 37 HOL W
WHITE JOSEPH A 40 DA1 W
WHITE JOSEPH A 44 BEA B
WHITE JOSEPH H A 53 LA2 W
WHITE JOURDAN W A 24 UPP W
WHITE LAMB A 28 16T B
WHITE LE ROY M A 28 11T W
WHITE LEONARD A 28 8TH W
WHITE LEONIDAS A 39 FRA B
WHITE LEWIS A 19 NEW B
WHITE LEWIS A 24 EDE B
WHITE LEWIS A 26 GRI W
WHITE LEWIS A 29 FA1 B
WHITE LEWIS A 30 GIB B
WHITE LEWIS A 44 BRA B
WHITE LUKE A 30 GIB B
WHITE LUKE A 37 EDW B
WHITE M A 19 NEW W
WHITE MANUEL A 19 NEW B
WHITE MARSHAL A 29 SEV B
WHITE MARTIN A 53 LA1 B
WHITE MATTHEW A 28 04A B
WHITE MILES A 44 BRA B
WHITE MOSES W A 24 UPP W
WHITE MUNROE A 37 MAN B
WHITE NEEDHAM M A 28 11T W
WHITE NERIAH A 53 LA1 W
WHITE NORFLEET A 39 FRA B
WHITE OLIVER A 28 03A B
WHITE OWEN A 19 NEW B
WHITE P R A 26 WAR W
WHITE PATRICK A 46 HIG W
WHITE PERRY A 28 04A B
WHITE PERRY A 39 HAR B
WHITE PETER F R 24 EDE W
REJECTED BY THE BOARD
WAS SHERIFF BEFORE THE WAR
ALSO DURING THE WAR
WHITE PHAETON A 28 02N B

WHITE R C A 30 KNO W
WHITE REUBEN A 28 8TH W
WHITE RICHARD JR A 28 8TH W
WHITE RICHARD L A 28 8TH W
WHITE ROBERT A 24 MID B
WHITE ROBERT A 28 8TH W
WHITE ROBERT A 44 BRA B
WHITE ROBERT A 53 LA1 B
WHITE ROBERT A A 40 DEC W
WHITE ROBERT J A 30 KNO W
WHITE ROBT A 44 YXR B
WHITE ROWAN A 30 ROA B
WHITE S A A 44 FIS W
WHITE S J A 26 WAR W
WHITE SAML A 29 FA1 B
WHITE SAMUEL A 29 FA2 B
WHITE SAMUEL J A 28 8TH W
WHITE SIDNEY S A 40 DA2 W
WHITE SILAS A 39 LOU B
WHITE SOLOMAN A 44 KIT B
WHITE STEPHEN P A 46 GRE W
CERT GIVEN TO
BUSH HILL RANDOLPH CTY
WHITE STEPNEY A 28 01A B
WHITE STEPNEY JR A 28 01A B
WHITE STEVEN A 26 WAR W
WHITE THADDEUS J A 40 DA1 W
WHITE THEOPHALUS A 46 JAM W
WHITE THOMAS A 37 HOL W
WHITE THOMAS A 39 LOU W
WHITE THOMAS A 44 YXR B
WHITE THOMAS A 46 HIG W
WHITE THOMAS H A 40 DEC W
WHITE THOS A A 30 KNO W
WHITE VIRGIL A 24 EDE B
WHITE W C A 28 02N W
DECEASED
WHITE W G A 28 03A W
WHITE W H A 39 GRI W
WHITE W P A 26 SHE W
WHITE W P A 44 BRA W
WHITE WARREN J A 24 UPP W
WHITE WILLIAM A 24 EDE W
WHITE WILLIAM A 26 WAR W
WHITE WILLIAM A 28 7TH W
WHITE WILLIAM A 30 KNO W
WHITE WILLIAM A 32 POS W
WHITE WILLIAM H A 53 LA1 W
WHITE WILLIAMS A 28 8TH W
CERTIF GIVEN LIVES
NOW AT NEW BERN
WHITE WILLIE A 39 FRA B
WHITE WM A 29 SEV W
WHITE WM H A 44 KIT W
WHITE WM N A 24 UPP W
WHITEAKER BACKUS A 53 LA1 B
WHITEAS EDMOND A 46 GRE B
WHITECOTTON J C R 25 HAY W
NAME LINED OUT
NOT HAVING BEEN A CITIZEN
OF THE STATE 12 MONTHS.
MOVED TO GA
WHITEFIELD THOMAS S A 35 KEN W
WHITEHALL BRISTOE A 30 POP B
WHITEHALL THOMAS A 30 KNO W
WHITEHEAD ABNER A 28 10T W
WHITEHEAD ABNER P A 28 10T W
WHITEHEAD ALLEN A 35 KEN B
WHITEHEAD ANDERSON A 46 FRI B
WHITEHEAD ARCHY A 28 05A B
WHITEHEAD
AUGUSTIN J M A 37 MAN W
WHITEHEAD BEN A 35 CYP B
WHITEHEAD CHARLES A 37 MAN B
WHITEHEAD CYRUS A 35 CYP B
WHITEHEAD DANL A 28 6TH B
WHITEHEAD EDWARD A 28 9TH B
WHITEHEAD EPH A 29 CAR W
WHITEHEAD FREDERICK A 37 HOL W
WHITEHEAD GRANVILLE A 37 HIC B
WHITEHEAD HENRY A 29 CAR B
WHITEHEAD HORACE A 28 05A B
WHITEHEAD HORACE A 29 FA1 B
WHITEHEAD JAMES A 35 CYP B
WHITEHEAD JAMES A 37 SHA B
WHITEHEAD JERRY A 37 SHA W
WHITEHEAD JOHN A 19 BE2 W
WHITEHEAD JOHN A 28 10T W
CHAL FOR FELONY
WHITEHEAD JOHN A 37 MAN B
WHITEHEAD JOHN S A 28 10T W
CHALLENGED FOR FELONY
WHITEHEAD JOSEPH A 37 MAN B
CERT RES TARBORO
WHITEHEAD LOFAX A 37 ROB B
WHITEHEAD MOSES A 28 05A B
WHITEHEAD MOSES A 29 SEV B
WHITEHEAD MOSES A 35 KEN B
WHITEHEAD PHILLIP A 37 TA1 B
WHITEHEAD THADUS A 37 ROB W
WHITEHEAD WESTON A 37 MAN B
CERT RES TARBORO
WHITEHEAD WILEY W A 35 KEN W
WHITEHEAD
WILLIAM 1ST A 35 KEN B
WHITEHEAD
WILLIAM 2ND A 35 KEN B
WHITEHEAD WILLIFORD A 37 SHA W
WHITEHEAD WILLIS A 37 EDW B
WHITEHEAD WILLIS A 37 PIN B
WHITEHEAD WILSON A 37 PIN B
WHITEHEAD WM A 28 05A B
WHITEHEAD WM A A 29 FA2 W
WHITEHEART N W A 46 FRI W
WHITEHEART PAWED (?)A 32 THO W
WHITEHED MATHEW A 37 SHA W
WHITEHERST TRAVEY A 30 MOY W
WHITEHOUSE DANL A 28 05A B
WHITEHURST CALVIN A 37 HIC B
WHITEHURST DANIAL A 37 HIC B
WHITEHURST ELIJAH A 19 BE1 W
WHITEHURST GEO A 28 05A B
WHITEHURST H C A 28 02N W
WHITEHURST H P R 28 02N W
CONSTABLE PRIOR TO WAR
WHITEHURST HENRY A 37 HIC B
WHITEHURST JAMES A 37 HIC A
WHITEHURST JAMES A A 37 HIC A
WHITEHURST JAMES E A 19 BE1 W
WHITEHURST JOHN A A 19 STR W
WHITEHURST JOHN B A 19 STR W
WHITEHURST JOHN H A 37 EDW W
WHITEHURST JOHN M A 19 STR W
WHITEHURST JOSEPH B A 19 BE1 W
WHITEHURST LEVIN A 30 KNO W
WHITEHURST M E A 28 02N W
WHITEHURST OLIVER C A 19 STR W
WHITEHURST PETER H A 30 GIB W
WHITEHURST RICHARD A 19 BE1 W
WHITEHURST ROBERT A 37 TA1 W
WHITEHURST ROBERT H A 19 SMY W
WHITEHURST ROBERT SRA 19 BE1 W
WHITEHURST ROBERT STA 19 BE1 W
WHITEHURST SAMUEL A 19 BE1 W
WHITEHURST SAMUEL A 28 15T W
WHITEHURST WINFIELD A 37 TA2 W
WHITEHURST WM H A 19 STR W
WHITELY JOHN A 46 RAG W
WHITEMAN LAFAYETTE A 24 EDE W
WHITENER ANDERSON A 26 SHE B
WHITENS BRISTOE A 28 04A B
WHITESETT PETER A 46 GIB W
WHITESIDES EDWARD A 40 DA1 W
WHITESIDES EDWARD JRA 40 FER W
WHITESIDES ISAAC A 26 BLA W
WHITESIDES JAMES F A 40 DA2 W
WHITESIDES JAMES J A 40 DA1 W
WHITESIDES JOHN L A 40 DA1 W
WHITESIDES
JONATHAN M A 40 FER W
WHITESIDES PETER 40 DA1 B
WHITESIDES WILLIAM TA 40 FER W
WHITESILL JAMES A 46 GRE B
WHITETON ARTER A 37 MAN B
CERT RES TARBORO
WHITFIELD A H A 29 FA1 W
WHITFIELD ANDERSON A 26 SHE B
WHITFIELD AUGUSTIN A 37 ROB B
WHITFIELD B H A 35 WOL W
WHITFIELD BALTIMORE A 28 04A B
WHITFIELD CHARLES A 37 ROB B
WHITFIELD CHARLES A 37 ROB B
WHITFIELD CHAS A 28 04A B
WHITFIELD CHAS A 29 FA1 B
WHITFIELD CLAIBORN A 28 04A B
WHITFIELD D H A 44 FOR W
WHITFIELD DANL A 28 04A B
WHITFIELD GEORGE A 37 ROC B
WHITFIELD GEORGE C A 28 04B B
WHITFIELD GEORGE C A 53 LA1 B
WHITFIELD GRANISON A 53 SWA B
WHITFIELD HENRY A 46 GRE B
WHITFIELD J A 39 FRA W
WHITFIELD J T A 35 WOL W
WHITFIELD JACKSON A 37 ROB B
WHITFIELD JNO H A 39 FRA W
WHITFIELD JOHN A 28 05A B
WHITFIELD JOHN A 37 TA1 B
WHITFIELD JOHN A 53 SWA B
WHITFIELD JOSEPH A 35 WOL W
WHITFIELD L D H A 35 ALB W
WHITFIELD L H A 35 ALB W
WHITFIELD LEN A 46 MCL B
WHITFIELD N B A 35 GLI W
WHITFIELD N G A 44 FOR W
WHITFIELD ORNEL A 53 SWA B
WHITFIELD PETER A 35 FAI B
WHITFIELD SHEPPARD A 53 SWA B
WHITFIELD THOMAS A 28 7TH B
WHITFIELD THOS A 29 FA1 B
WHITFIELD THOS C JR A 29 FA2 B
WHITFIELD VIRGIL A 28 04A B
WHITFIELD WRIGHT A 28 6TH B
WHITFORD A P A 28 12T W
WHITFORD ALBERT A 28 04A B
WHITFORD ALONZO J A 28 12T W
WHITFORD BRYAN CHALA 28 12T W
FOR GIVING AID AND
COMFORT TO THE REBELLION
AFTER HAVING BEEN A
MAGISTRATE
WHITFORD CALEB A 28 7TH B
WHITFORD EDWARD A 28 11T W
WHITFORD HARDY A 28 01A W
WHITFORD ISAAC A 28 03A B
WHITFORD JOHN N A 28 01A W
WHITFORD JOSEPH A 39 FRA B
WHITFORD NELSON A 28 01A W
WHITFORD WILLIAM A 28 12T B

WHITFORD STEPHEN E A 28 12T W
CERTIFICATE GIVEN LIVES
NOW AT DURHAM'S CK
BEAUFORT CO
WHITHEAD WASHINGTON A 37 ROB B
WHITICAR WILLIS A 53 LA1 B
WHITING BRAXTON A 46 GRE B
WHITING JOHN A 28 7TH B
WHITINGTON DAVID A 19 NEW B
WHITINGTON JOSEPH A 46 GRE W
WHITINGTON M N A 19 NEW B
WHITINGTON PARKER A 19 NEW B
WHITINGTON
WASHINGTON A 19 NEW B
WHITIST FREDK A 28 6TH B
WHITLEY ALEXANDER T A 99 BUS W
WHITLEY DREW A 37 ROC B
WHITLEY JOHN A 37 ROB W
WHITLEY JOSIAH E A 99 BUS W
WHITLEY LEROY A 37 ROC B
WHITLEY R D A 39 LOU W
WHITLOW JESSE A 32 THO W
WHITLY DEMPSEY A 28 04A B
WHITLY MERRITT A 28 02N B
WHITLY PEN A 28 04A B
WHITLY R H A 39 LOU W
WHITLY S H A 39 FRA W
WHITMAN
NOTHING ELSE 35 MAG W
WHITMAN EDWARD A 28 04A W
WHITMAN RICHARD A 24 EDE W
WHITMAN RILEY A 35 GLI W
WHITMAN WILLIAM A 35 GLI W
WHITMAN WRIGHT A 35 GLI W
WHITNEY AUGUSTUS R A 53 SWA B
WHITNEY CORNELOUS A 53 SWA B
WHITNEY FRANCIS A 53 SWA B
WHITNEY HENRY A 19 BE1 W
WHITNEY NATHAN A 53 SWA B
WHITNEY SAMUEL A 37 EDW B
WHITNEY THOMAS A 53 SWA B
WHITNEY TIMOTHY P A 19 BE1 W
WHITSING PETER A 37 MAN B
WHITSITT JOSEPH B A 46 GIB W
WHITSON WILLIAM R A 53 HAT W
WHITT DAVID A 46 MCL W
WHITT EDWARD A 46 MCL W
WHITT JAMES A 46 GRE W
WHITT NEWTON A 46 GRE W
WHITT SAMUEL A 46 KIN W
WHITT SAMUEL A 46 SUM W
WHITTAKER JESSE A 99 BUS B
WHITTED JESSEE A 29 GRA B
WHITTINGTON ALFONSO R 46 GRE W
NAME LINED OUT
WAS AN OVERSEER OF HIGHWAY
BEFORE THE WARE AND WAS
JALER AND BOUGHT HORSES
FOR THE QUARTERMASTER ON
THE ACCOUNT NOT WILLING
TO TAKE THE OATH
HAS NOT QUALIFIED
WHITTINGTON ALFRED PA 46 MCL W
WHITTINGTON DAVID A 46 GRE B
WHITTINGTON ERVIN A 46 MCL W
WHITTINGTON
MADISON S A 46 MCL W
WHITTINGTON N G A 46 MCL W
WHITTINGTON THOMAS A 46 MCL W
WHITTINGTON THOMAS DA 46 MCL W
WHITTINGTON THOMAS HA 46 MCL W
WHITTINGTON THOMAS SA 46 MCL W
WHITTINGTON WM F A 46 GRE W
WHITTINTON ALPHONSO A 46 GRE W
WHITTLEY AARON A 19 BE1 B
WHITTY ABRAM A 19 HAD B
WHITWORTH BENJAMIN A 40 DEC B
WHITWORTH C A A 46 SUM W
WHITWORTH FENNEL R A 40 DEC W
WHITWORTH GEORGE A 40 DA1 B
WHITWORTH J R A 26 BOR B
WHITWORTH J W A 26 BOR W
WHITWORTH ROBERT A 40 BLA W
WHITWORTH STANFORD A 40 DA1 B
WHITWORTH TITUS A 26 BOR B
WHITWORTH WILLIAM R A 40 BLA W
WHORTON CHARLES C A 28 16T W
WHORTON DAVID A 28 16T W
WHORTON ROBERT P A 28 15T W
WHORTON WILEY A 28 15T W
WIATT BERRY A 26 CAR W
WICHARD STATEN A 37 HIC A
WICHT ABRAHAM A 37 TA2 B
WICKER ALBERT A 29 FA1 W
WICKER C W A 30 KNO W
WICKER JNO W A 30 KNO W
WICKER JOEL J A 30 KNO W
WICKER JOHN D A 30 POW W
WICKER OLIVER J A 30 KNO W
WICKER WILLIAM A 30 NOR W
WICKS BENJAMIN A 19 HAR W
WICKS BENJN A 28 02N B
WICKS JNO A A 19 HAR W
WICKS R M A 19 HAR W
WICKS THOMAS A 28 16T B
WIDDERFIED W A 29 FA1 W
WIDES WILLIAM S A 37 ROB W
WIDES WILLIAM S A 37 ROB W
WIDOP CHARLES A 46 FRI W
WIDOP W C A 46 FRI W
WIDOWS D A A 46 JAM W
WIGFALL MOSES A 19 BE1 B
WIGGANS HENRY A 19 BE1 B
WIGGINS ALBERT A 39 GRI B
WIGGINS ALFRED A 28 12T B
WIGGINS AMBROS A 39 GRI B
WIGGINS ASBURY G A 40 DEC W
WIGGINS BEN A 39 FRA B
WIGGINS BENJAMIN A 37 HIG B
WIGGINS C G A 44 RAG W
WIGGINS DANID W A 44 HEN W
WIGGINS DENNIS A 28 11T W
WIGGINS ELI A 37 PEN B
WIGGINS FRANKLIN A 38 FRE B
WIGGINS FREDERICK A 28 11T W
WIGGINS G H A 39 FRE W
WIGGINS GORDON A 28 03A B
WIGGINS HARRY A 39 FRE B
WIGGINS HARWARD A 38 FRE W
WIGGINS HENRY A 28 7TH B
WIGGINS HENRY A 39 FRE B
WIGGINS HINTON A 39 HAR W
WIGGINS ISAAC A 37 HIG B
WIGGINS J H A 44 HEN W
WIGGINS J T A 44 HEN W
WIGGINS JACK A 37 ROB B
WIGGINS JACOB A 28 12T B
WIGGINS JAMES A 28 6TH W
WIGGINS JAS D A 29 GRA W
WIGGINS JESSE A 28 10T B
WIGGINS JESSEE A 39 GRI B
WIGGINS JNO A 39 GRI B
WIGGINS JNO W A 44 HEN W
WIGGINS JOHN A 28 12T B
WIGGINS JOHN B A 25 HAY W
WIGGINS JOS A 39 HAR B
WIGGINS JOSEPH A 28 02N B
WIGGINS JOSEPH A 28 11T W
WIGGINS JOSEPH JR A 28 11T W
WIGGINS JOSEPHUS A 28 11T B
WIGGINS LONDON A 24 EDE B
WIGGINS LOUIS A 19 HAD B
WIGGINS NELSON A 28 8TH B
WIGGINS P H A 28 04A B
WIGGINS PERRY A 38 FRE W
WIGGINS PETER A 19 BE2 B
WIGGINS PETER A 37 PEN B
WIGGINS REDDEN A 39 GRI B
WIGGINS RICHARD A 39 HAR B
WIGGINS RICHARD M A 40 DEC W
WIGGINS SID A 39 FRE B
WIGGINS T A A 44 FIS W
WIGGINS THOS A 38 FRE B
WIGGINS WILLIAM A 26 BLA W
WIGGINS WM A 28 04A B
WIGGINS WM A 39 GRI B
WIGGS ALEXANDER A 39 SPE W
WIGGS JNO A 39 GRI W
WIGINTON CHARLES A 30 MOY B
WILB J G A 26 GRI W
WILB P B A 26 GRI W
WILBERN A G A 32 THO W
WILBERN A H A 32 THO W
WILBERN J L A 32 THO W
WILBERN T J A 32 THO W
WILBORN BARNABUS A 32 BRO W
WILBORN EVANS A 32 THO W
WILBORN J W A 32 THO W
WILBORN JESSE A 46 HIG W
WILBORN P W A 46 HIG W
WILBORN RICHARD P A 44 YXS W
WILBORN WM D A 46 HIG W
WILBORNE HENRY R A 46 FRI W
WILBORNE J R A 46 FRI W
WILBURN SAML A 44 KNA B
WILCOX ALEXANDER A 28 11T W
WILDER ABE A 39 FRA B
WILDER ABRAHAM A 39 HAR B
WILDER B F A 39 HAR W
WILDER BOSTON A 24 EDE B
WILDER BRITTON A 39 LOU B
WILDER BRYANT A 39 GRI W
WILDER CALVIN A 39 FRA W
WILDER CALVIN A 39 GRI W
WILDER CHARLES A 24 EDE B
WILDER GANSEY A 24 EDE B
WILDER GEORGE A 99 BUS W
WILDER GUILFORD A 39 FRA B
WILDER HANDY A 39 FRA B
WILDER HANDY A 39 HAR B
WILDER HENRY A 39 FRA B
WILDER ISAAC A 39 FRA B
WILDER J H A 39 DAV W
WILDER J J A 39 LOU W
WILDER J W A 39 FRA W
WILDER JACKSON A 39 FRA B
WILDER JACOB A 39 GRI B
WILDER JAMES A 39 FRA B
WILDER JAMES A 39 HAR B
WILDER JAMES SR A 39 FRA B
WILDER LOUIS A 39 FRA B
WILDER MAJOR A 39 FRA B
WILDER MICHAEL A 24 EDE B
WILDER NELSON A 39 FRA B
WILDER REUBEN A 39 FRA W
WILDER RICHARD A 24 EDE B
WILDER THOMAS A 24 EDE B
WILDER WILLIAM A 99 BUS W
WILEY ADISON A 46 MCL W

WILEY AZARIAH F A 28 13T W
WILEY B F A 46 HIG W
WILEY EDMOND A 46 GRE B
WILEY EMANUEL A 46 ROS B
WILEY HUGH F A 46 MCL W
WILEY J NEWTON A 46 GRE B
WILEY JACOB A 46 GRE B
WILEY JAMES C A 46 RAG W
WILEY JOSEPHUS A 28 13T W
WILEY P A A 29 FA1 W
WILEY P A A 29 FA1 W
WILEY PETER A 46 ROS B
WILEY REDDING A 28 13T W
WILEY ROBERT A 46 RAG B
WILEY SAMUEL A 46 GRE B
WILEY SAMUEL A 72 SWA W
WILEY SHANNON A 46 JAM W
WILEY THOMAS W A 46 GRE W
WILEY W M A 46 JAM W
WILEY WILLIAM A 46 HIG W
WILFORD WILLIAM L A 37 MAN W
WILHITE H Y A 39 JOR W
WILIAMS THOMAS A A 39 PUG W
WILIBA JORDAN A 37 MAN B
WILIFORD J C A 29 BLA W
WILIFORD JIM A 29 BLA W
WILKENS JARRETT A 39 DAV B
WILKENS W T A 39 DAV B
WILKERSON ALEXN A 44 YXS W
WILKERSON ANDERSON A 44 YXS B
WILKERSON ANDREW A 44 OXF B
WILKERSON AUGUSTUS A 28 05A B
WILKERSON DANIEL A 32 COT W
WILKERSON ELIJAH W A 44 YXS B
WILKERSON GEORGE A 44 YXS B
WILKERSON H L A 44 TAR W
WILKERSON JAMES A 19 MOR B
WILKERSON JAMES A 44 YXS B
WILKERSON JAS D A 44 SAS W
WILKERSON JAS N A 44 YXS W
WILKERSON JOHN A 44 YXS W
WILKERSON JOSIAH A 44 YXS B
WILKERSON PETER A 44 SAS W
WILKERSON RANDOL A 44 YXS B
WILKERSON SCOTT A 44 YXS B
WILKERSON SMITH A 44 YXS B
WILKERSON STEPHEN A 44 YXS B
WILKERSON STEPHEN W A 44 SAS W
WILKERSON THOS B A 44 YXS W
WILKERSON THOS R A 44 FIS W
OXFORD DIST
WILKERSON W L A 44 SAS W
WILKERSON WM H A 44 YXS W
WILKES JOHN A 40 DA1 B
WILKES SAMUEL A 44 YXS B
WILKINGS E W A 29 FA1 W
WILKINS ABNER A 44 DUT W
WILKINS ABRAM A 37 PEN B
WILKINS ANDREW A 37 SPA B
WILKINS BENJAMIN C A 30 COI W
WILKINS
BENJAMIN RICHARD A 37 PEN B
WILKINS DANIEL A 26 SHE B
WILKINS EATON A 37 HIG B
WILKINS EDMUND A 37 HIC B
WILKINS EPHRAIM A 37 HIG B
WILKINS EPHRAIM A 37 ROB B
WILKINS FREEMAN A 19 BE1 B
WILKINS H N A 35 LIM W
WILKINS ISAAC A 28 04A B
WILKINS J D A 35 LIM W
WILKINS JOHN A 24 EDE B
WILKINS JOHN A 39 FRA B

WILKINS JOHN L A 44 OXF B
WILKINS JOSEPH A 19 BE1 B
WILKINS JOSEPH A 26 SWA B
WILKINS JOSIAH A 24 EDE B
WILKINS MANUEL A 37 HIG B
WILKINS PETER A 37 PEN B
WILKINS ROBT A 24 EDE B
WILKINS SPENCER A 37 HIG B
WILKINS THOS A 26 SHE W
WILKINS W W A 26 SHE W
WILKINS WASHINGTON A 37 HIG B
WILKINS WILLIAM A 37 PEN B
WILKINS WM HENRY A 28 01A B
WILKINSON CHARLES P A 37 HOL W
WILKINSON DAVID P A 28 10T W
WILKINSON FRANK A 37 TA1 W
WILKINSON FRANK A 37 TA1 W
WILKINSON GEO A 29 FA1 B
WILKINSON JACOB A 28 9TH B
WILKINSON JAMES A 53 BUR W
WILKINSON LEVI A 53 BUR W
WILKINSON NATHAN A 37 TA1 B
WILKINSON PETER A 44 OXF B
WILKS A J A 29 CAR W
WILKS RUFUS A 46 GRE B
WILLARD DAVID H A 40 DA1 W
WILLARD HENRY T A 40 BLA W
WILLEFORD JOSEPH A 37 ROB W
WILLETT JNO A 29 FA1 W
WILLETT WILLIAM A 46 SUM W
WILLEY HENRY A 44 OXF B
WILLIAM AUGUSTUS A 37 ROB W
WILLIAM CHARLES A 24 EDE B
WILLIAM MANUEL A 29 FA2 B
WILLIAM RICHARD A 37 SPA B
WILLIAM SAMUEL A 44 ISL B
WILLIAMS IRVING A 37 EDW B
WILLIAMS A A A 39 FRE W
WILLIAMS A D A 38 FRE W
WILLIAMS A D A 39 JOR W
WILLIAMS A J A 30 IND W
WILLIAMS A M A 32 TYR W
WILLIAMS ABERDEEN A 29 FA1 B
WILLIAMS ABNER A 28 04A B
WILLIAMS ABNER A 35 WAR B
WILLIAMS ABRAM A 35 WAR B
WILLIAMS ABRAM A 37 EDW B
WILLIAMS ABSALOM A 28 05A B
WILLIAMS ADAM A 29 CAR B
WILLIAMS ADAM A 29 FA1 B
WILLIAMS ADAM A 35 WOL W
WILLIAMS ADAM A 37 HIG B
WILLIAMS ADAM A 37 HOL B
WILLIAMS ADAM A 39 LOU B
TRNS FROM WARRENS
TO FRANKLIN BY AFF
WILLIAMS ADARAN A 39 SPE B
WILLIAMS ADERAN A 39 HAY B
2ND REGIS BORD FRANKLIN
WILLIAMS ALBERT A 29 FA1 B
WILLIAMS ALBERT F A 35 KEN W
WILLIAMS ALBIN B A 53 FAI W
WILLIAMS ALEC A 19 NEW B
WILLIAMS ALEDAM A 29 LOC B
WILLIAMS ALEISHA A 37 SHA W
WILLIAMS ALEX A 29 FA1 B
WILLIAMS ALEX A 29 FA1 B
WILLIAMS ALEX A 29 LOC B
WILLIAMS ALEX A 39 GRI B
WILLIAMS ALEXANDRIA A 53 LA1 B
CERT RES SWAN QUARTER
WILLIAMS ALEXR A 28 04A B
WILLIAMS ALFORD A 32 TYR B

WILLIAMS ALFRED A 19 BE1 B
WILLIAMS ALFRED A 29 CAR B
WILLIAMS ALFRED A 35 ISL B
WILLIAMS ALFRED A 35 KEN B
WILLIAMS ALFRED A 37 HOL B
WILLIAMS ALLADIN A 29 FA1 B
WILLIAMS ALLEN A 28 04A B
WILLIAMS ALLEN A 35 KEN B
WILLIAMS ALLEN A 35 WAR B
WILLIAMS ALLEN A 37 PEN B
WILLIAMS ALPHEUS A 30 CUR B
WILLIAMS ALPHEUS A 38 FRE W
WILLIAMS ALSTON A 26 GRI W
WILLIAMS ALTIMORE A 28 05A B
WILLIAMS AMOS A 28 04A B
WILLIAMS ANDERSON A 32 CLE B
WILLIAMS ANDERSON B A 32 TYR W
WILLIAMS ANDREW A 28 02N B
WILLIAMS ANDREW A 29 GRA B
WILLIAMS ANDREW A 44 TOW B
WILLIAMS ANDREW J A 35 ROC B
WILLIAMS ANTHONY A 29 FA1 B
WILLIAMS ANTHONY A 29 FA1 B
WILLIAMS ANTHONY A 29 GRA B
AFFADA FAYETTEVILLE
WILLIAMS ARNOLD A 29 FA1 B
WILLIAMS ARNOLD A 35 KEN B
WILLIAMS ARNOLD A 37 PEN B
WILLIAMS ASA A 29 ROC B
WILLIAMS AUTREY A 37 HOL B
WILLIAMS BALAAM A 28 8TH B
WILLIAMS BALEM A W A 29 FA1 B
WILLIAMS BEDFORD A 29 CAR B
WILLIAMS BENJ A 19 BE1 B
WILLIAMS BENJ A 44 OXF B
WILLIAMS BENJ T A 28 9TH W
WILLIAMS BENJAMAN A 53 GER B
WILLIAMS BENJAMIN A 44 DUT B
WILLIAMS BENJAMIN A 53 SWA W
WILLIAMS BENJAMIN JRA 53 FAI W
WILLIAMS BENJAMIN P A 53 FAI W
WILLIAMS BENJAMINE A 26 SHE W
WILLIAMS BENJAMINE A 39 PUG B
WILLIAMS BENNETT A 37 SHA W
WILLIAMS BERRY A 39 HAY B
WILLIAMS BERRY A 44 OXF B
WILLIAMS BLOUNT A 35 KEN B
WILLIAMS BRANCH A 35 SMI W
WILLIAMS BRAXTON A 44 FOR B
WILLIAMS BRISTER A 35 MAG B
WILLIAMS BRISTER A 35 ROC B
WILLIAMS BRISTER A 35 ROC B
WILLIAMS BRISTO A 37 HIG B
WILLIAMS BRITTON A 39 SPE B
WILLIAMS BRYAN A 35 ROC W
WILLIAMS BUCKLEY A 19 BE1 B
WILLIAMS BURRELL A 39 SPE B
WILLIAMS BUSTER A 37 ROB B
WILLIAMS C C A 26 BLA W
WILLIAMS C H A 44 FIS W
WILLIAMS CAESAR A 28 04A B
WILLIAMS CALVIN A 28 6TH B
WILLIAMS CALVIN A 28 8TH W
WILLIAMS CALVIN A 29 GRA B
WILLIAMS CALVIN A 35 SMI W
WILLIAMS CALVIN A 35 WAR B
WILLIAMS CALVIN A 37 SPA B
WILLIAMS CANICHET A 44 ISL B
WILLIAMS CARY A 46 GRE B
WILLIAMS CATO A 19 BE1 B
WILLIAMS CHARLES A 28 7TH B
CERTIFICATE GIVEN LIVES
NOW AT NEW BERN APR 20

WILLIAMS CHARLES A 30 CUR B
WILLIAMS CHARLES A 35 KEN B
WILLIAMS CHARLES F A 35 KEN W
WILLIAMS CHARLES H A 30 IND B
WILLIAMS CHARLES J A 28 11T W
WILLIAMS CHAS A 28 03A B
WILLIAMS CHAS A 28 05A B
WILLIAMS CHAS A 29 FA1 B
WILLIAMS CHAS H A 24 EDE W
WILLIAMS CHAS J A 29 GRA W
WILLIAMS CHS A 29 FLE B
WILLIAMS COFFIELD A 37 PIN B
WILLIAMS COOPER A 37 MAN W
WILLIAMS CURTIS A 29 FA1 B
WILLIAMS D F A 26 WAR W
WILLIAMS DALLAS A 39 DAV B
WILLIAMS DANDY A 35 SMI B
WILLIAMS DANIEL A 28 16T B
WILLIAMS DANIEL A 28 9TH B
WILLIAMS DANIEL A 29 FLE B
WILLIAMS DANIEL A 35 KEN B
WILLIAMS DANIEL A 35 KEN B
WILLIAMS DANIEL A 35 LIM W
WILLIAMS DANIEL A 37 HOL B
WILLIAMS DANIEL A 39 JOR B
CERT SHOCCO WARREN CO
WILLIAMS DANIEL A 53 FAI B
WILLIAMS DANIEL H A 53 GER W
WILLIAMS DANIEL S A 35 LIM W
WILLIAMS DANIEL SR A 39 JOR B
CERT SHOCCO WARREN CO
WILLIAMS DAVID A 28 04A B
WILLIAMS DAVID A 29 CAR B
WILLIAMS DAVID A 29 FA1 B
WILLIAMS DAVID A 29 FLE B
WILLIAMS DAVID A 35 SMI W
WILLIAMS DAVID A 35 WAR B
WILLIAMS DAVID A 38 FRE W
WILLIAMS DAVID A 39 FRE W
WILLIAMS DAVID G A 53 SWA W
WILLIAMS DAVID H A 35 ROC W
WILLIAMS DAVID L A 37 TA1 W
WILLIAMS DAVID R A 28 01A W
WILLIAMS DAVID S A 35 ROC W
WILLIAMS DEMPSEY A 28 03A B
WILLIAMS DEMPSEY A 37 EDW B
WILLIAMS DEMSEY A 30 IND W
WILLIAMS DICK A 35 CYP B
WILLIAMS DONALD A 37 TA1 W
WILLIAMS DORSEY A 37 TA1 B
WILLIAMS DUGLESS A 39 JOR B
WILLIAMS DURANT A 35 SMI W
WILLIAMS E B A 39 FRE W
WILLIAMS E H A 35 ALB W
WILLIAMS E J A 29 CAR W
WILLIAMS E M A 28 04A B
WILLIAMS E R A 46 FRI W
WILLIAMS EDGAR A 35 SMI B
WILLIAMS EDMANUEL A 44 HEN B
WILLIAMS EDMOND A 28 04A B
WILLIAMS EDMUND C A 30 KNO W
WILLIAMS EDWARD A 19 BE1 B
WILLIAMS EDWARD A 19 HAR B
WILLIAMS EDWARD A 28 11T W
WILLIAMS EDWARD A 30 NAR W
WILLIAMS EDWARD A 35 SMI W
WILLIAMS EDWARD A 44 DUT B
WILLIAMS EDWARD A 44 HEN B
WILLIAMS EDWARD A 44 OXF B
WILLIAMS EDWD A 28 04A B
WILLIAMS EDWIN A 29 CAR B
WILLIAMS EFF A 39 JOR B
WILLIAMS ELI A 19 BE1 B
WILLIAMS ELI A 28 11T B
WILLIAMS ELIAS A 30 KNO W
WILLIAMS ELIAS A 39 HAR W
WILLIAMS ELIJAH A 37 ROC W
WILLIAMS ENOCH A 44 OXF B
WILLIAMS ERASMUS A 44 BRA B
WILLIAMS EUGENE M A 28 03A W
WILLIAMS EZEKIAH A 39 JOR B
WILLIAMS EZEKIEL A 28 04A B
WILLIAMS EZEKIEL A 29 CAR B
WILLIAMS F M A 99 BUS W
WILLIAMS FENNELL A 35 ROC B
WILLIAMS FENNELL A 35 ROC B
WILLIAMS FENNER A 39 GRI B
WILLIAMS FERRY A 44 FOR B
WILLIAMS FLOYD A 39 GRI W
WILLIAMS FRANCIS A 53 OCR W
WILLIAMS FRANK A 28 7TH B
WILLIAMS FRANKLIN A 46 MCL B
WILLIAMS FRIDAY A 37 PIN B
WILLIAMS FRIDAY JR A 35 KEN B
WILLIAMS FRIDAY SR A 35 KEN B
WILLIAMS G O A 26 SHE W
WILLIAMS G W A 32 LOF W
WILLIAMS G W JR A 46 HIG W
WILLIAMS GABREL A 39 JOR B
WILLIAMS GANDER A 37 HIG B
WILLIAMS GEO A 29 CAR B
WILLIAMS GEO A 29 FA1 B
WILLIAMS GEO A 29 FA1 B
WILLIAMS GEO A 39 GRI B
WILLIAMS GEO H A 29 FLE W
FROM DUPLICATE COPY
WILLIAMS GEO W A 28 11T W
WILLIAMS GEO W A 44 YXR W
WILLIAMS GEORGE A 24 EDE B
WILLIAMS GEORGE A 28 15T B
WILLIAMS GEORGE A 29 GRA B
WILLIAMS GEORGE A 32 TYR B
WILLIAMS GEORGE A 35 SMI B
WILLIAMS GEORGE A 37 EDW B
WILLIAMS GEORGE A 37 HIG B
WILLIAMS GEORGE A 37 PEN B
WILLIAMS GEORGE F A 37 TA1 W
WILLIAMS GEORGE M A 46 GRE W
WILLIAMS GEORGE R A 53 LA1 W
WILLIAMS GEORGE SR A 35 KEN B
WILLIAMS GEORGE W A 35 KEN B
WILLIAMS GEORGE W A 35 ROC W
WILLIAMS GEORGE W A 46 HIG W
WILLIAMS GILBERT A 37 SHA B
WILLIAMS GILFORD A 29 FLE B
WILLIAMS GRANVILLE A 19 HAR B
WILLIAMS GUILFERD A 37 PEN B
WILLIAMS GUIN A 37 HIG B
WILLIAMS H A 29 FA2 B
WILLIAMS H F A 32 POS W
WILLIAMS H H J A 28 03A W
WILLIAMS H W A 29 CED W
WILLIAMS HANDY A 29 FA1 B
WILLIAMS HARDY A 28 05A B
WILLIAMS HARDY A 39 GRI B
WILLIAMS HARMAN A 46 GRE W
WILLIAMS HARPER A 35 KEN W
WILLIAMS HARPER A 35 SMI W
WILLIAMS HARRISON A 29 FA1 B
WILLIAMS HARRY A 37 HOL B
WILLIAMS HARVEY A 35 MAG B
WILLIAMS HAYWOOD A 28 04B B
WILLIAMS HAYWOOD A 28 16T B
WILLIAMS HENDERSON A 28 04A B
CERTIFICATE GRANTED
ONSLOW CO
WILLIAMS HENRY A 19 BE1 B
WILLIAMS HENRY A 19 BE1 B
WILLIAMS HENRY A 28 03A B
WILLIAMS HENRY A 28 04A B
WILLIAMS HENRY A 28 04A B
WILLIAMS HENRY A 28 10T B
WILLIAMS HENRY A 29 FA1 B
WILLIAMS HENRY A 29 FA1 B
WILLIAMS HENRY A 29 FA1 B
WILLIAMS HENRY A 29 FLE B
WILLIAMS HENRY A 29 LOC B
WILLIAMS HENRY A 32 THO B
WILLIAMS HENRY A 32 TYR W
WILLIAMS HENRY A 35 KEN B
WILLIAMS HENRY A 37 HIG W
WILLIAMS HENRY A 37 TA1 B
WILLIAMS HENRY A 39 JOR B
WILLIAMS HENRY A 44 OXF B
WILLIAMS HENRY A 44 SAS B
WILLIAMS HENRY COL A 44 SAS W
WILLIAMS HENRY C A 35 WAR B
WILLIAMS HENRY J A 28 04B B
WILLIAMS HENRY M A 37 TA1 W
WILLIAMS HINEKE A 28 9TH B
WILLIAMS HOLLEY A 35 ROC B
WILLIAMS HOLLEY A 35 ROC B
WILLIAMS HORATIA A 53 OCR W
WILLIAMS HUGH A 46 GRE W
WILLIAMS HUMPHREY A 29 CAR B
WILLIAMS HYRAM A 32 TYR W
WILLIAMS ISAAC A 28 03B B
WILLIAMS ISAAC A 28 04A B
WILLIAMS ISAAC A 28 6TH W
WILLIAMS ISAAC A 35 KEN B
WILLIAMS ISAAC A 35 ROC B
WILLIAMS ISAAC A 37 TA1 B
WILLIAMS ISAAC A 37 TA1 B
WILLIAMS ISAAC A 44 BRA B
WILLIAMS ISAAC P A 53 KEN W
WILLIAMS ISAC A 46 FRI B
WILLIAMS ISERAL A 44 TOW B
WILLIAMS ISHAM A 29 GRA B
WILLIAMS ISHAM A 35 WAR B
WILLIAMS ISHMAIL A 37 HIC B
WILLIAMS ISIAH A 39 SPE B
WILLIAMS J A A 29 GRA W
WILLIAMS J C A 44 FOR W
WILLIAMS J D A 39 SPE W
WILLIAMS J D A 44 FIS W
WILLIAMS J F T A 29 CED W
WILLIAMS J M A 29 FLE W
FROM DUPLICATE COPY
WILLIAMS J P A 35 SMI W
WILLIAMS J T A 44 FIS W
WILLIAMS J W A 26 BLA W
WILLIAMS J W A 26 WAR W
WILLIAMS J W A 32 JAC W
WILLIAMS J W A 35 LIM W
WILLIAMS J W A 44 BEA W
WILLIAMS J W A 46 SUM W
WILLIAMS JACK A 37 EDW B
WILLIAMS JACK A 37 PEN B
WILLIAMS JACOB A 30 CUR B
WILLIAMS JACOB A 35 ISL B
WILLIAMS JACOB A 35 MAG B
WILLIAMS JACOB A 40 MAU W
WILLIAMS JACOB A 46 GRE B
WILLIAMS JAMES A 19 BE1 B
WILLIAMS JAMES A 28 04A B
WILLIAMS JAMES A 29 FA2 B
WILLIAMS JAMES A 29 MON B
WILLIAMS JAMES A 29 SEV B
WILLIAMS JAMES A 30 CUR W

WILLIAMS JAMES A 32 POS W
WILLIAMS JAMES A 35 KEN B
WILLIAMS JAMES A 35 MAG B
WILLIAMS JAMES A 35 ROC B
WILLIAMS JAMES A 35 ROC B
WILLIAMS JAMES A 37 SHA W
WILLIAMS JAMES A 37 TA1 B
WILLIAMS JAMES A 44 DUT B
WILLIAMS JAMES A 44 TAR W
WILLIAMS JAMES A A 32 TYR W
WILLIAMS JAMES B A 35 ROC W
WILLIAMS JAMES C A 35 ALB W
WILLIAMS JAMES C A 35 GLI W
WILLIAMS JAMES H A 37 SHA W
WILLIAMS JAMES HARDYA 37 TA1 W
WILLIAMS JAMES JR A 35 SMI W
WILLIAMS JAMES P A 30 NAR W
WILLIAMS JAMES R A 37 ROC W
WILLIAMS JAMES R A 46 GRE W
WILLIAMS JAMES SR A 35 SMI W
WILLIAMS JAMES W A 37 SHA W
WILLIAMS JAS A 29 FA1 B
WILLIAMS JAS W CHALA 32 DAV W
RECONSIDERED
WILLIAMS JEFF A 29 FLE B
WILLIAMS JEFFRY A 29 CAR B
WILLIAMS JERRY A 37 EDW B
WILLIAMS JESSE A 28 02N B
WILLIAMS JESSE A 53 LA1 W
WILLIAMS JESSE W A 37 SHA W
WILLIAMS JESSEE J A 29 GRA W
WILLIAMS JESSEY A 30 CUR W
WILLIAMS JESSY F A 39 HAR W
WILLIAMS JIM A 39 JOR B
WILLIAMS JNO A 29 FA1 B
WILLIAMS JNO A 29 FA1 B
WILLIAMS JNO A A 44 OXF W
WILLIAMS JNO C A 29 FA1 W
WILLIAMS JNO D A 29 FA1 W
WILLIAMS JOE A 39 PUG B
WILLIAMS JOE A A 39 PUG B
WILLIAMS JOE K A 39 PUG B
WILLIAMS JOHN A 19 BE1 B
WILLIAMS JOHN A 24 EDE B
WILLIAMS JOHN A 28 01A B
WILLIAMS JOHN A 28 04A B
WILLIAMS JOHN A 28 04A B
WILLIAMS JOHN A 28 15T B
WILLIAMS JOHN A 28 6TH W
WILLIAMS JOHN A 28 7TH W
WILLIAMS JOHN A 29 BLA W
WILLIAMS JOHN A 30 CUR B
WILLIAMS JOHN A 30 KNO W
WILLIAMS JOHN A 32 LOF W
WILLIAMS JOHN A 35 KEN B
WILLIAMS JOHN A 35 LIM W
WILLIAMS JOHN A 35 WAR B
WILLIAMS JOHN A 37 PEN W
WILLIAMS JOHN A 39 PUG B
WILLIAMS JOHN A 46 RAG W
WILLIAMS JOHN CHAL A 30 CUR B
MINORITY ABSCENCE OF
OF PROOF
WILLIAMS JOHN A R 28 11T W
DID NOT TAKE THE OATH
A CONSTABLE & OVERSEER
OF ROADS, AND GAVE AID &
COMFORT TO CONFEDERATES
WILLIAMS JOHN B A 19 BE1 W
WILLIAMS JOHN D A 37 HOL W
WILLIAMS JOHN F A 39 GRI W
WILLIAMS JOHN H A 19 BE1 B
WILLIAMS JOHN J A 32 TYR W

WILLIAMS JOHN J JR A 30 NAR W
WILLIAMS JOHN P A 32 TYR W
WILLIAMS JOHN R A 37 HIG W
WILLIAMS JOHN R A 39 LOU B
WILLIAMS JOHN SR A 30 NAR W
WILLIAMS JOHN W A 26 BOR W
WILLIAMS JOHN W A 46 GRE W
WILLIAMS JOHN Y A 53 LA1 W
WILLIAMS JONAS A 29 FA1 B
WILLIAMS JORDAN A 37 HIG B
WILLIAMS JOS A 39 GRI B
WILLIAMS JOSEPH A 28 04A B
WILLIAMS JOSEPH A 28 11T W
WILLIAMS JOSEPH A 28 9TH B
WILLIAMS JOSEPH A 29 FA1 B
WILLIAMS JOSEPH A 35 KEN B
WILLIAMS JOSEPH A 35 LIM W
WILLIAMS JOSEPH A 37 HIC B
WILLIAMS JOSEPH A 37 HIG B
WILLIAMS JOSEPH A 37 WHI B
WILLIAMS JOSEPH A 46 FRI B
WILLIAMS JOSEPH A 53 FAI W
WILLIAMS JOSEPH M A 53 KEN W
WILLIAMS JOSEPH R A 99 BUS W
WILLIAMS JOSEPH T A 24 EDE W
WILLIAMS JOSEPH T A 35 ROC W
WILLIAMS JOSEPHAS A 40 RHY B
WILLIAMS JOSEPHUS A 24 MID W
WILLIAMS JOSHUA A 29 CAR B
WILLIAMS JOSHUA A 29 FA1 B
WILLIAMS JOSHUA A 29 FA2 B
WILLIAMS JOSHUA A 44 KIT B
WILLIAMS JULIUS A 29 FA1 B
WILLIAMS KAY A 37 EDW B
WILLIAMS KILL A 35 MAG B
WILLIAMS KITT A 35 SMI B
WILLIAMS LABAN A 26 GRI W
WILLIAMS LANDERS A 46 JAM B
WILLIAMS LARRY A 28 05A B
WILLIAMS LAYFATETTE A 39 LOU B
WILLIAMS LEE A 99 BUS B
WILLIAMS LEON A A 37 TA1 W
WILLIAMS LEVY A 35 LIM B
WILLIAMS LEWIS A 28 03A W
WILLIAMS LEWIS A 28 04A B
WILLIAMS LEWIS A 28 05A B
WILLIAMS LEWIS A 29 FA1 B
WILLIAMS LEWIS A 29 FA1 B
WILLIAMS LEWIS A 29 FA2 B
WILLIAMS LEWIS A 29 FLE B
WILLIAMS LEWIS A 35 WAR B
WILLIAMS LEWIS A 35 WAR B
WILLIAMS LEWIS A 37 HIG B
WILLIAMS LEWIS A 37 SHA B
WILLIAMS LEWIS A 37 TA1 B
WILLIAMS LEWIS A 37 WHI B
WILLIAMS LONDON A 29 FA1 B
WILLIAMS LONDON A 29 FA1 B
WILLIAMS LORENZO D A 53 FAI W
WILLIAMS LOUIS A 35 SMI B
WILLIAMS LUKE A 35 WAR B
WILLIAMS M J A 28 6TH W
WILLIAMS MACK A 37 TA1 B
WILLIAMS MADISON A 44 TOW B
WILLIAMS MAJOR A 37 ROC B
WILLIAMS MARK A 30 CUR B
WILLIAMS MARSLEY A 37 SHA W
WILLIAMS MARTEN A 53 LA1 B
WILLIAMS MARTIN A 29 FA1 B
WILLIAMS MARTIN L A 46 GRE W
WILLIAMS MATTHEW A 39 SPE B
WILLIAMS MERRICA A 19 BE1 B
WILLIAMS MICHAEL A 35 CYP B

WILLIAMS MIKEL A 37 ROC W
WILLIAMS MILES A 37 HIG B
WILLIAMS MINGO A 37 HIG B
WILLIAMS MITCHEAL A 37 ROC W
WILLIAMS MORRIS A 29 FA1 B
WILLIAMS MOSES A 28 04A B
WILLIAMS MOSES JR A 35 WAR B
WILLIAMS MOSES SR A 35 WAR B
WILLIAMS MUNROE A 37 TA1 B
WILLIAMS NASH A 53 HAT W
WILLIAMS NATHAN A 35 KEN B
WILLIAMS NATHAN A 37 HIG B
WILLIAMS NATHAN A 44 SAS B
WILLIAMS NATHAN A 53 OCR W
WILLIAMS NAYMOND A 37 HIG B
WILLIAMS NEAL A 37 HOL B
WILLIAMS NED A 39 SPE B
WILLIAMS NEEDHAM A 28 7TH B
WILLIAMS NELSON A 19 BE1 B
WILLIAMS NELSON A 29 FA1 B
WILLIAMS NELSON A 39 LOU B
WILLIAMS NELSON A 53 LA1 B
WILLIAMS NEPTUNE A 28 7TH B
WILLIAMS NEPTUNE A 29 FA1 B
WILLIAMS NOAH A 19 HAD B
WILLIAMS NOAH A 28 03A B
WILLIAMS OLIVER A 28 05A B
WILLIAMS OLIVER A 28 11T W
WILLIAMS OLIVER A 44 TOW B
WILLIAMS ORSBOURN A 26 SHE W
WILLIAMS ORVILLE A 39 LOU B
WILLIAMS OSBORNE A 26 GRI W
WILLIAMS OWEN A 35 LIM W
WILLIAMS OWEN A 35 ROC B
WILLIAMS PAUL A 28 04B B
WILLIAMS PAUL A 28 05A B
WILLIAMS PERRY A 28 11T B
WILLIAMS PERRY J A 37 ROC W
WILLIAMS PETER A 28 02N B
WILLIAMS PETER A 29 BLA X
WILLIAMS PETER A 29 CED B
WILLIAMS PETER A 32 CLE B
WILLIAMS PETER A 37 EDW B
WILLIAMS PETER A 37 HIG B
ACKNOWLEDGE CONVICTED
WILLIAMS PETER A 37 PEN B
WILLIAMS PETER A 44 BRA B
WILLIAMS PETER 2ND A 37 EDW B
WILLIAMS PETERA A 35 WAR B
WILLIAMS PEYTON A 29 GRA B
WILLIAMS PHIL A 29 FLE B
WILLIAMS PHIL A 39 FRA B
WILLIAMS PHILL A 39 DAV B
WILLIAMS PHILLIP A 24 EDE B
WILLIAMS POMPEY A 39 JOR B
WILLIAMS PRESTON A 39 JOR B
WILLIAMS PRINCE A 29 FA2 B
WILLIAMS PRINCE A 53 SWA B
WILLIAMS R A A 44 OXF W
WILLIAMS R J A 39 FRA B
WILLIAMS RANSOM A 29 CAR B
WILLIAMS RANSOM A 29 FLE B
WILLIAMS RANSOM A 44 OXF B
WILLIAMS REDDING S A 37 TA1 W
WILLIAMS REUBEN A 44 FIS B
WILLIAMS RICHARD A 35 WAR B
WILLIAMS RICHARD A 39 SPE B
WILLIAMS RICHD A 29 CAR B
WILLIAMS RICHD A 29 FA1 B
WILLIAMS RICHD A 29 FA1 B
WILLIAMS RICHD A 29 FA1 W
WILLIAMS RICHD A 39 GRI B
WILLIAMS RILEY A 28 05A B

WILLIAMS ROBERT A 26 GRI W
WILLIAMS ROBERT A 28 10T B
WILLIAMS ROBERT A 30 KNO W
WILLIAMS ROBERT A 32 LOF W
WILLIAMS ROBERT A 35 KEN B
WILLIAMS ROBERT A 44 YXS W
WILLIAMS ROBERT A 53 LA1 W
WILLIAMS ROBERT J A 35 KEN W
WILLIAMS ROBERT R A 37 HIG W
WILLIAMS ROBT A 28 04A B
WILLIAMS ROBT A 28 05A B
WILLIAMS ROBT A 29 FA1 B
WILLIAMS ROBT A 29 FLE B
WILLIAMS ROBT A 29 FLE W
WILLIAMS ROBT A 39 FRA B
WILLIAMS ROBT A 44 FIS B
WILLIAMS ROBT A 46 ROS B
WILLIAMS ROGER A 35 ROC B
WILLIAMS S J A 29 BLA W
WILLIAMS S J A 39 GRI W
WILLIAMS S S A 39 FRA W
WILLIAMS S T A 44 OXF W
WILLIAMS SALTER A 35 ROC B
WILLIAMS SAM A 39 SPE B
WILLIAMS SAMEUL A 35 ROC B
WILLIAMS SAMEUL A 35 ROC B
WILLIAMS SAMEUL A 35 WAR W
WILLIAMS SAMEUL A A 35 ROC W
WILLIAMS SAML A 28 04A B
WILLIAMS SAML A 29 FA1 B
WILLIAMS SAML A 29 FA1 B
WILLIAMS SAMUEL A 37 PEN B
WILLIAMS SAMUEL A 37 TA2 B
WILLIAMS SAMUEL L A 53 FAI W
WILLIAMS SAMUEL W A 53 LA2 W
WILLIAMS SANDY A 29 FA1 B
WILLIAMS SANDY A 29 FA1 B
WILLIAMS SHADE A 35 KEN B
WILLIAMS SHARPER A 19 BE1 B
WILLIAMS SHARPER A 28 03A B
WILLIAMS SIMON A 29 FLE B
WILLIAMS SIMON A 35 KEN B
WILLIAMS SIMON A 35 KEN B
WILLIAMS SIMON A 44 LED B
WILLIAMS SOLOMAN A 37 PIN B
WILLIAMS SOLOMAN A 72 SWA B
WILLIAMS SOLOMON A 19 BE1 B
WILLIAMS SOLOMON A 37 EDW B
WILLIAMS SOLOMON A 46 GRE B
WILLIAMS SQUIRE JR A 35 SMI B
WILLIAMS SQUIRE NO 3A 35 SMI B
WILLIAMS SQUIRE SR A 35 SMI B
WILLIAMS STEPHEN A 19 BE1 B
WILLIAMS STEPHEN A 35 MAG W
WILLIAMS STEPHEN R 28 01A B
MARKED OUT
MOVED TO 2ND PRE
WILLIAMS STEPHN A 28 02N W
WILLIAMS STEPN A 28 02N B
WILLIAMS THEODORE A 28 04A B
WILLIAMS THOMAS A 35 ROC B
WILLIAMS THOMAS A 35 ROC B
WILLIAMS THOMAS A 35 ROC B
WILLIAMS THOMAS A 35 ROC B
WILLIAMS THOMAS A 35 ROC B
WILLIAMS THOMAS A 35 ROC B
WILLIAMS THOMAS A 35 WAR W
WILLIAMS THOMAS A 37 HIG W
WILLIAMS THOMAS A 37 TA1 B
WILLIAMS THOMAS 1 A 44 KIT B
WILLIAMS THOMAS 2 A 44 KIT B
WILLIAMS THOMAS E A 24 MID W
WILLIAMS THOS A 28 01A W

WILLIAMS THOS A 28 05A B
WILLIAMS THOS A 29 FLE W
WILLIAMS THOS R 26 SHE W
MASTER IN EQUITY PRIOR
TO WAR & GAVE VOLUNTARY
AID TO REBELLION
WILLIAMS THOS T A 44 FIS W
WILLIAMS TOBIAS A 29 FA1 B
WILLIAMS TOBY A 29 FA1 B
WILLIAMS TONEY A 35 KEN B
WILLIAMS TONEY A 44 HEN B
WILLIAMS V W A 39 FRA W
WILLIAMS VIRGIL A 19 NEW B
WILLIAMS VIRGIL A 29 FA1 B
WILLIAMS VIRGIL A 29 FLE B
WILLIAMS W A 39 FRA B
WILLIAMS W A A 39 JOR W
WILLIAMS W B A 29 FLE W
FROM DUPLICATE COPY
WILLIAMS W G A 44 OXF W
WILLIAMS W H A 26 GRI W
WILLIAMS W H A 39 FRA W
WILLIAMS W L A 29 CAR W
CERTIFICATE GIVEN
WILLIAMS W L A 39 GRI W
WILLIAMS W W A 39 HAR W
WILLIAMS WALLACE A 29 MON B
WILLIAMS WARREN A 39 JOR B
WILLIAMS WASHG A 29 FA1 B
WILLIAMS WILEY A 29 FA1 B
WILLIAMS WILEY JR A 35 KEN B
WILLIAMS WILEY SR A 35 KEN B
WILLIAMS WILLIAM A 26 GRI W
WILLIAMS WILLIAM A 35 KEN B
WILLIAMS WILLIAM A 35 LIM W
WILLIAMS WILLIAM A 35 MAG W
WILLIAMS WILLIAM A 35 ROC B
WILLIAMS WILLIAM A 37 EDW B
WILLIAMS WILLIAM A 37 TA1 B
WILLIAMS WILLIAM A 39 LOU B
WILLIAMS WILLIAM A 53 FAI W
WILLIAMS WILLIAM A 53 OCR W
WILLIAMS WILLIAM A A 37 TA1 W
WILLIAMS WILLIAM A A 53 FAI W
WILLIAMS WILLIAM D A 28 9TH W
WILLIAMS WILLIAM D A 37 ROC W
WILLIAMS WILLIAM H A 35 KEN W
WILLIAMS WILLIAM J A 35 SMI W
WILLIAMS WILLIAM R A 53 FAI W
WILLIAMS WILLIAM W A 30 COI W
WILLIAMS WILLIE A 39 JOR B
WILLIAMS WILLIS A 53 FAI W
WILLIAMS WM A 24 MID W
WILLIAMS WM A 28 04A B
WILLIAMS WM A 28 05A B
WILLIAMS WM A 28 6TH B
WILLIAMS WM A 29 CAR B
WILLIAMS WM A 29 CAR B
WILLIAMS WM A 29 FA1 B
WILLIAMS WM A 39 FRA B
WILLIAMS WM R A 44 HEN B
WILLIAMS WRIGHT A 35 ROC B
WILLIAMS WRIGHT A 35 ROC B
WILLIAMS WYATT A 99 BUS B
WILLIAMS YORK A 19 SMY B
WILLIAMS YORK A 28 03A B
WILLIAMS ZACHARIAH A 28 03A B
WILLIAMS-JOHN A 37 ROC B
LIVES IN NASH CO
WILLIAMSON A C A 26 BLA W
WILLIAMSON ANDREW A 39 FRA B
WILLIAMSON ANSON A 53 SWA W
WILLIAMSON B A 26 GRI W

WILLIAMSON BENJAMIN A 53 LA1 W
WILLIAMSON BUCK A 46 MON B
WILLIAMSON C T A 35 FAI W
WILLIAMSON CHARLES A 35 WAR B
WILLIAMSON D A 29 LOC W
WILLIAMSON DENIS A 39 HAY B
WILLIAMSON ELISHA A 72 SWA W
WILLIAMSON EPHRAIM A 39 LOU B
WILLIAMSON HANDY A 29 FA1 B
WILLIAMSON HARRY A 39 FRA B
WILLIAMSON HENRY A 46 MCL B
WILLIAMSON HENRY A 53 LA1 W
WILLIAMSON J G JR A 26 BLA W
WILLIAMSON J M A 29 LOC W
WILLIAMSON J N A 35 FAI W
WILLIAMSON JESSE R A 35 WAR W
WILLIAMSON JESSIE A A 37 TA1 W
WILLIAMSON JOHN A 19 MOR W
WILLIAMSON JOHN H A 39 LOU B
REGISTRAR
WILLIAMSON JOS A 29 LOC W
WILLIAMSON JOSH A 39 FRA B
WILLIAMSON K M C R 29 FLE W
COUNTY COURT CLERK HOME
GUARD DURING THE WAR
HUNTED DESERTERS
WILLIAMSON LUKE A 39 FRA B
WILLIAMSON LUMPKIN A 39 LOU B
WILLIAMSON MINGO A 39 HAR B
WILLIAMSON N A 29 FA1 W
WILLIAMSON NATHAN A 29 GRA W
WILLIAMSON NATHANIELA 53 FAI W
WILLIAMSON NEEDAM A 29 FA1 B
WILLIAMSON P D A 26 BLA W
WILLIAMSON PAGE A 35 FAI W
WILLIAMSON PAGE A 35 WAR W
WILLIAMSON PETER A 26 GRI B
WILLIAMSON PETER A 39 LOU B
WILLIAMSON ROBERT A 44 SAS B
WILLIAMSON RUBEN A 37 WEB B
WILLIAMSON SAML A 30 IND W
WILLIAMSON SAML A 39 LOU B
WILLIAMSON SOL A 39 FRA B
WILLIAMSON TALLY A 53 LA1 W
WILLIAMSON THOMAS G A 40 MAU W
WILLIAMSON WILLIAM A 39 FRE B
WILLIAMSON WM A 29 FA1 B
WILLIAMSON WM A 29 FA1 W
WILLIE L K A 44 OXF W
WILLIFOR ARTHER A 37 SPA B
WILLIFORD ALFRED A 37 ROC B
WILLIFORD ARMSTEAD JA 37 ROC W
WILLIFORD B S A 37 ROC W
WILLIFORD BERRY A 37 ROC B
WILLIFORD CHATMAN A 37 ROC B
WILLIFORD DAVID A 44 TAR W
WILLIFORD ELIJAH A 37 TA1 W
WILLIFORD ENGLISH A 29 FLE B
WILLIFORD ENGLISH A 29 FLE W
WILLIFORD GUSTIN A 44 OXF B
WILLIFORD H J A 29 BLA W
WILLIFORD J A A 29 FLE W
WILLIFORD JAMES A 44 TAR W
WILLIFORD JESSE A 44 TAR W
WILLIFORD JOHN D A 37 SHA W
WILLIFORD JOHN JR A 29 FLE W
WILLIFORD L D A 44 TAR W
WILLIFORD MEEDY B A 37 ROC W
WILLIFORD S JR A 29 BLA W
WILLIFORD S W A 44 TAR W
WILLIFORD W E A 29 FA1 W
WILLIFORD WM A 24 EDE W
WILLIMAS WILLIAM A 19 HAR B

WILLIS A A 28 11T W
WILLIS ABISHA M A 28 7TH W
WILLIS ABNER A 19 NEW W
WILLIS AMMY L A 19 DAV W
WILLIS AMOS A 19 BE1 W
WILLIS AMOS F A 19 SHA W
WILLIS ANDREW A 19 MOR W
WILLIS ANSON A 19 MOR W
WILLIS ANTHONY R A 19 SMY W
WILLIS ARMEDA L A 72 SWA W
WILLIS ASA A 19 SMY W
WILLIS ASA A 28 7TH W
WILLIS ASA J A 19 DAV W
WILLIS B W A 19 MOR W
WILLIS BALDWIN A 28 11T B
WILLIS BANISTER A 19 SMY W
WILLIS BARTLET A 19 MOR W
WILLIS BENJ D A 19 HUN W
WILLIS BRITTEN F A 19 SHA W
WILLIS BRITTON S A 19 HUN W
WILLIS BURGESS A 32 DAV W
WILLIS CAESAR A 28 04A B
WILLIS CICERO S A 19 SMY W
WILLIS DANIEL C A 19 SMY W
WILLIS DAVID W A 19 SMY W
WILLIS DUNN A 28 13T B
WILLIS E A A 19 SMY W
WILLIS EASON L A 19 SMY W
WILLIS EASON S A 19 HUN W
WILLIS EDGAR A 19 STR W
WILLIS EDWARD A 19 MOR W
WILLIS EDWARD M A 19 SHA W
WILLIS ELIJAH A 19 MOR W
WILLIS ELIJAH A 19 STR W
WILLIS ELVIN A 19 HUN W
WILLIS EPHRAIM L A 19 STR W
WILLIS FRANKLIN A 19 MOR W
AGE VERIFIED BY MARCUS C ADAMS ---- BLACK?? -----
WILLIS G W A 19 HAD W
WILLIS GEO A 29 ROC B
WILLIS GEO B A 28 02N B
WILLIS GEO L A 19 SMY W
WILLIS GEORGE A 19 POR W
WILLIS GEORGE A 28 15T B
WILLIS GEORGE M A 28 11T W
WILLIS GEORGE T A 19 SMY W
WILLIS GEORGE T R 28 10T W
WAS OVERSEER OF ROADS DURING WAR
WILLIS GEORGE T CHALR 28 10T W
WAS AN OVERSEER OF ROADS AND GAVE AID AND COMFORT
WILLIS GEORGE W A 19 SMY W
WILLIS GEORGE W R 28 11T W
WAS A MAGISTRATE BEFORE WAR AND DURING THE WAR
WILLIS HAISTY A 19 BE1 B
WILLIS HARATIO A 19 BE1 W
WILLIS HARDY B A 28 11T W
WILLIS HAYWOOD A 19 HUN W
WILLIS HENRY A 26 WAR W
WILLIS HENRY C A 46 GRE W
WILLIS HENRY F A 19 SHA W
WILLIS HENRY S A 19 HUN W
WILLIS HENRY T A 19 SMY W
WILLIS HEZEKIAH A 19 HUN W
WILLIS HEZEKIAH H A 19 BE1 W
WILLIS ILIJAH JR A 19 DAV W
WILLIS ISAAC A 28 04A B
WILLIS ISAIAH F A 19 DAV W
WILLIS J B A 19 MOR W
WILLIS J C A 26 WAR W

WILLIS J G A 26 PEE W
WILLIS J R A 26 GRI W
WILLIS J R A 26 PEE W
WILLIS J R A 26 WAR W
WILLIS JACOB A 26 WAR W
WILLIS JAMES A 19 BE1 W
WILLIS JAMES A 19 POR W
WILLIS JAMES A 19 SHA W
WILLIS JAMES A 28 01B W
WILLIS JAMES A 53 SWA B
WILLIS JAMES P A 19 HUN W
WILLIS JAMES W A 19 HUN W
WILLIS JAMES W A 19 SHA W
WILLIS JESPER P A 19 SMY W
WILLIS JNO T A 19 MOR W
WILLIS JOHN A 19 BE1 W
WILLIS JOHN A 26 WAR W
WILLIS JOHN D A 19 HUN W
WILLIS JOHN E A 19 SMY W
WILLIS JOHN F A 19 SMY W
WILLIS JOHN G A 19 SMY W
WILLIS JOHN M A 19 SHA W
WILLIS JOHN MARTIN A 19 MOR W
WILLIS JOHN R A 26 WAR W
WILLIS JOHN W A 19 HUN W
WILLIS JORDAN A 46 MON B
WILLIS JOSEPH A 19 HUN W
WILLIS JOSEPH A 26 WAR W
WILLIS JOSEPH A 28 11T W
WILLIS JOSEPH B A 19 HUN W
WILLIS JOSEPH B A 19 NEW W
WILLIS JOSEPH C A 19 HUN W
WILLIS JOSEPH F A 19 STR W
WILLIS JOSEPH S A 19 HUN W
WILLIS JOSEPH W A 19 HUN W
WILLIS JOSEPH W A 19 SMY W
WILLIS JOSEPHES A 19 MOR W
WILLIS JOSEPHUS A 19 POR W
WILLIS JOSEPHUS A 19 SHA W
WILLIS JOSEPHUS F A 19 SHA W
WILLIS JOSEPHUS S A 19 BE1 W
WILLIS JOSHUA A 29 ROC B
WILLIS JOSIAH A 19 NEW W
WILLIS KILBY F A 19 SMY W
WILLIS LEVY A 29 SEV B
WILLIS MACAGY A 19 SHA W
WILLIS MAJOR A 28 11T W
WILLIS MARSDEN C A 72 SWA W
WILLIS MARTIN A 19 HUN W
WILLIS MARTIN A 19 HUN W
WILLIS MARTIN A 19 SMY W
WILLIS MASON A 19 HUN W
WILLIS MELVIN D A 19 SMY W
WILLIS MITCHELL A 19 HUN W
WILLIS MOSES A 28 04A B
WILLIS NEEDHAM A 28 11T W
WILLIS NEILL A 29 ROC B
WILLIS NOA A 28 03A B
WILLIS NOAH A 28 14T W
WILLIS NORMAN A 28 11T W
WILLIS OSCAR F A 19 DAV W
WILLIS PETER A 26 WAR W
WILLIS PETER A 28 11T W
WILLIS PHILOMEN A 28 14T W
WILLIS R A A 28 02N W
WILLIS R H A 26 WAR W
WILLIS R L A 19 MOR W
WILLIS REUBEN A 28 04A B
WILLIS REUBEN F A 19 STR W
WILLIS RICHARD A 19 MOR W
WILLIS RILEY A 37 ROC B
WILLIS ROBERT A 26 WAR W
WILLIS ROBERT A 28 04B B

WILLIS RUFUS A 19 MOR W
WILLIS SAML L A 29 GRA W
WILLIS SAMUEL A 28 14T W
WILLIS SAMUEL H A 19 BE1 W
WILLIS SAMUEL S A 46 GRE W
WILLIS SAMUEL W A 28 10T W
WILLIS SIMEON A 19 SMY W
WILLIS SIMON A 28 02N W
WILLIS SIMON A 28 04A B
WILLIS SOLOMON A 26 GRI W
WILLIS SOLOMON A 26 WAR W
WILLIS STEPHEN A 28 11T W
WILLIS STPHEN A 37 EDW B
WILLIS THOMAS A 19 DAV W
WILLIS THOMAS W A 19 DAV W
WILLIS THOS C A 28 01A W
WILLIS TILLMAN N A 28 10T W
WILLIS TIMOTHY A 19 MOR W
WILLIS TIMOTHY A 53 HAT W
WILLIS W Q A 26 WAR W
WILLIS WALLACE A 28 04A W
WILLIS WALLACE F A 19 SHA W
WILLIS WALLACE H A 19 SMY W
WILLIS WALLACE M A 19 SHA W
WILLIS WALLACE W A 19 HUN W
WILLIS WILEY A 28 02N B
WILLIS WILLIAM A 19 MOR W
WILLIS WILLIAM A 28 6TH W
WILLIS WILLIAM M A 19 SMY W
WILLIS WILLIAM S A 19 SHA W
WILLIS WILLIAM S A 19 SMY W
TRANSFERRED TO SHACKLEFORD BANKS PRECINCT APR 9 1868
WILLIS WILSON A 30 IND W
WILLIS WM A 28 03A B
WILLIS WM F A 19 DAV W
WILLIS WM F A 19 SMY W
WILLIS WM M A 19 BE1 W
WILLIS WM T A 28 03A W
WILLIS WRIGHT A 28 11T B
WILLISTON FRANK P A 29 FA1 B
WILLISTON JAS A 29 FA1 B
WILLITT JAMES A 28 02N B
WILLITT WM A 29 FA1 W
WILLMAN EDOM A 26 BOR B
WILLMAN S C A 26 SHE W
WILLOBY ELIJAH A 28 16T B
WILLOUGHBY BARNEY A 28 9TH B
WILLOUGHBY CUTHBERT A 28 10T B
WILLOUGHBY ISAAC A 28 10T B
WILLOUGHBY LEWIS A 28 10T B
WILLOUGHBY WM A 30 GIB W
WILLS JACOB A 24 EDE B
WILLS JAMES A 24 EDE B
WILLS JOHN A 24 EDE B
WILLS MICHAEL A 26 SHE B
WILLS THOS A 24 EDE B
WILLSON PEYTON A 28 7TH B
WILMAN E R CHAL A 26 CAR W
WILON ALLEN A 30 MOY B
WILSON A A A 26 SHE W
WILSON A J A 32 YAD W
WILSON A W A 39 PUG W
WILSON AARON A 26 SHE B
WILSON ABRAM A 46 SUM B
WILSON ABRIHAM A 32 TYR W
WILSON ADAM A 29 SEV B
WILSON ALBERT A 30 MOY B
WILSON ALEX A 26 WAR W
WILSON ALEXANDER A 30 MOY B
WILSON ALEXANDER A 46 KIN B
WILSON ALEXR H A 28 04A B
WILSON ALFRED A 35 MAG B

WILSON ALLEN A 35 MAG B
WILSON ALLEN A 35 WAR W
WILSON ARON A 26 SHE B
WILSON ASA A 46 SUM W
WILSON B W A 39 PUG W
WILSON BOLIN A 44 DUT W
WILSON BUCK A 39 PUG B
WILSON C H A 46 SUM W
WILSON C O A 26 SHE W
WILSON CALVIN D A 35 ROC W
WILSON CARY A 28 05A B
WILSON CHARELS A 30 IND B
WILSON CHARLES A 24 MID B
WILSON CHARLES A 40 SAN B
WILSON CHORNELIUS A 46 RAG W
WILSON DANIEL A 29 QUW W
WILSON DANIEL A 39 PUG B
WILSON DANIEL J A 29 FA2 W
WILSON DAVID A 26 SHE B
WILSON DAVID A 28 04A B
WILSON DAVID A 39 PUG B
WILSON DAVID A 46 RAG W
WILSON DAVID G A 44 SAS W
WILSON DEMPSEY A 30 MOY W
WILSON E A 26 CAR B
WILSON E C A 26 SHE W
WILSON EDMUND A 30 MOY B
WILSON EDOM 30 MOY B
7-MONTH-RESIDENCE
WILSON EDWARD A 26 SHE B
WILSON EDWARD A A 28 16T W
CERT GIVEN RESIDENCE
GREEN COUNTY.
WILSON ELIAS A 35 MAG B
WILSON EPHRAM R 26 MOU W
MILITIA OFFICER &
ENGAGED IN REBELLION
WILSON EZRA A 40 FER W
NAME LINED OUT
JUSTICE OF THE PEACE
BEFORE THE REBELLION &
GAVE AID & COMFORT TO
ENEMY DID NOT QUALIFY
WILSON EZRA B R 40 FER W
NAME LINED OUT
JUSTICE OF THE PEACE
BEFORE THE WAR AND
AFTER WAR GAVE AID OR
COMFORT TO THE ENEMY
WILSON F J A 26 GRI W
WILSON F O A 35 WOL W
WILSON FELIX A 40 DA1 B
WILSON FRANCIS M A 35 MAG W
WILSON FRANK A 37 EDW B
WILSON G W A 35 LIM W
WILSON GABRIL A 32 TYR B
WILSON GEORGE A 28 04A B
WILSON GEORGE A 46 SUM B
WILSON GEORGE M A 32 YAD W
WILSON H A 32 POS W
WILSON H F A 32 YAD W
WILSON HARDY A 19 BE1 B
WILSON HARMON A 28 16T B
WILSON HARRY A 30 MOY B
WILSON HENDERSON A 32 TYR W
WILSON HENDERSON A 46 COB B
WILSON HENRY A 24 EDE W
WILSON HENRY A 28 05A B
WILSON HENRY A 29 FA1 B
WILSON HENRY A 30 MOY W
WILSON HENRY A 32 DAV W
WILSON HENRY A 32 SHE W
WILSON HENRY A 44 HEN B

WILSON HENRY J A 28 01A W
WILSON HOYL A 26 SHE B
WILSON HUGH A 32 THO W
WILSON HUGH A 46 COB W
WILSON IRELAND A 35 ROC B
WILSON ISAAC A 30 MOY B
WILSON ISAAC A 35 MAG B
WILSON J A A 26 WAR W
WILSON J A A 44 RAG W
WILSON J A A 46 SUM W
WILSON J B A 40 CAN W
WILSON J C A 30 KNO W
WILSON J F A 39 PUG W
WILSON J F A 40 RHY W
WILSON J F A 40 SAN W
WILSON J G A 26 GRI W
WILSON J G A 44 RAG W
WILSON J J A 37 ROC W
WILSON J J A 39 PUG W
WILSON J R A 29 FA2 W
WILSON J R A 44 RAG W
WILSON J S A 29 FLE W
WILSON J W A 32 THO W
WILSON J W A 44 FOR W
WILSON JACKSON A 24 MID B
WILSON JAMES A 24 EDE W
WILSON JAMES A 30 MOY B
WILSON JAMES A 35 ROC W
WILSON JAMES A 39 LOU W
WILSON JAMES A 39 PUG W
TRANS TO LOUISBURG
WILSON JAMES A 40 SAN B
WILSON JAMES A 99 BUS W
WILSON JAMES D SR A 35 MAG W
WILSON JAMES JR A 39 LOU W
TRNS FROM PUGHES HILL
WILSON JAMES M A 28 9TH B
CERTIF GIVEN NOW IN
ADAM'S CREEK PR
WILSON JAMES M A 46 MCL W
WILSON JERRY 40 DA1 B
STRICKEN OUT APR 10 1868
WILSON JNO A 29 FA1 B
WILSON JNO A 72 SWA W
WILSON JOHN A 26 SHE B
WILSON JOHN A 26 SHE W
WILSON JOHN A 30 KNO B
WILSON JOHN A 32 DAV B
WILSON JOHN A 32 TYR W
WILSON JOHN A 39 PUG B
WILSON JOHN A 53 FAI B
WILSON JOHN 1 A 29 GRA B
WILSON JOHN 2 A 29 GRA B
WILSON JOHN C A 19 SMY W
WILSON JOHN F A 46 GRE B
WILSON JOHN G A 25 HAY W
WILSON JOHN H A 32 TYR W
WILSON JOHN H A 35 MAG B
WILSON JOHN L A 24 MID B
WILSON JOHN M A 46 GRE W
WILSON JOHN W A 35 ROC W
WILSON JOHN W A 37 WHI W
WILSON JOHN W A 46 RAG W
WILSON JOHNTHAN A 32 POS W
WILSON JOSEPH A 26 SHE B
WILSON JOSEPH A 28 05A B
WILSON JOSEPH A 30 IND W
WILSON JOSEPH A 35 MAG B
WILSON JOSEPH A 46 HIG W
WILSON JOSEPH A 53 HAT W
WILSON JOSEPH J A 35 MAG W
WILSON JOSEPH K JR A 40 FER W
WILSON JOSHUA A 32 YAD W

WILSON JOURDAN A 28 02N B
WILSON L L A 40 SAN W
WILSON LATAN A 26 SHE B
WILSON LAWSON R 40 FER W
NAME LINED OUT
POST MASTER BEFORE THE
REBELLION & GAVE AID &
COMFORT TO THE ENEMY
DID NOT QUALIFY
WILSON LEWIS A 32 POS W
WILSON LEWIS A 44 BRA W
WILSON LEWIS P A 44 ISL W
WILSON M M A 44 ISL W
WILSON MALCOM A 29 QUW W
WILSON MARK A 30 MOY B
WILSON MARSHAL A 28 04A B
WILSON MINOR A 40 SAN B
WILSON MOSES A 29 FA1 B
ROCKFISH
WILSON MOSES A 29 ROC B
WILSON MOSES A 35 MAG B
WILSON N H D A 46 GRE W
WILSON N W A 29 FA1 W
WILSON NAT A 44 LED B
WILSON NED A 30 IND B
WILSON NEILL A 29 ROC W
WILSON NELSON A 26 SHE B
WILSON OFFICE A 40 SAN B
WILSON P D A 26 SHE W
WILSON PETER A 35 MAG B
WILSON PETER A 46 RAG W
WILSON PHILIP A 26 SHE B
WILSON PHILLIP A 46 RAG W
WILSON QUASH A 28 9TH B
WILSON R F A 32 TYR W
WILSON R N A 40 SAN W
WILSON R S A 44 ISL W
WILSON RANDELL A 30 MOY B
7-MONTH-RESIDENCE
WILSON ROBERT A 40 SAN W
WILSON ROBERT A 46 MCL W
WILSON ROBT A 24 EDE B
WILSON ROBT A 29 GRA B
WILSON ROBT A 39 PUG W
WILSON ROBT M A 40 SAN W
WILSON S A A 26 SHE W
WILSON S P A 44 RAG W
WILSON S P R 30 IND W
CHAL P.M.
WILSON SAM A 30 MOY B
WILSON SAMEUL A 35 MAG B
WILSON SAMEUL A 35 WAR B
WILSON SAML A 28 05A B
WILSON SAML A 44 RAG B
WILSON SAMUEL A 39 PUG B
WILSON SAMUEL A 40 FER W
WILSON SAMUEL A 46 GRE B
WILSON SAMUEL M A 40 FER W
WILSON SANDY A 32 TYR B
WILSON SANDY A 40 SAN B
WILSON SIMSON A 32 DAV W
WILSON STARLIN A 26 SHE B
WILSON STARLIN A 26 SHE B
WILSON STEPHIN A 24 EDE B
WILSON T J A 29 FA1 W
WILSON T P A 28 02N B
WILSON THADDEUS A 28 03A B
WILSON THOMAS A 26 SHE B
WILSON THOMAS A 30 TUL B
WILSON THOMAS A 30 MOY B
7-MONTH-RESIDENCE
WILSON THOMAS A 39 PUG B
WILSON THOMAS A 40 DA1 W

WILSON THOMAS A 46 SUM W
WILSON THOS A 26 SHE W
WILSON THOS A 44 HEN B
CERT TO VOTE OUT COUNTY
WILSON THOS J A 24 MID W
WILSON THOS T A 24 MID B
WILSON TURNER A 40 STO B
WILSON VOLUNTINE A 46 COB W
WILSON W M A 40 SAN W
WILSON W R A 44 TOW W
WILSON W W A 46 SUM W
WILSON WESLEY A 30 MOY B
WILSON WILEY A 37 TA1 B
WILSON WILLIAM A 26 SHE B
WILSON WILLIAM A 28 7TH W
WILSON WILLIAM A 32 LEE W
WILSON WILLIAM A 44 TOW W
WILSON WILLIAM A 44 ISL B
WILSON WILLIAM A 46 SUM W
WILSON WILLIAM B A 46 SUM W
WILSON WILLIAM G A 30 IND W
WILSON WILLIAM W A 40 FER W
WILSON WILLIAM W W A 35 MAG W
WILSON WM A 29 BLA W
WILSON WM A 46 MCL W
WILSON WM H A 29 FA1 W
WILSON WM M A 32 THO W
WILSON WM R A 46 GRE W
WILTY M A 46 HIG W
WIMBERLEY ALLEN A 37 PEN B
WIMBERLEY JOSEPH W A 37 TA1 W
WIMBERLEY MARK A 37 PEN B
WIMBERLEY NAT A 37 PEN B
WIMBERLEY TONEY A 37 PEN B
WIMBERLY GEORGE L A 37 MAN W
WIMBERLY GRANT A 37 PEN B
WIMBERLY VIRGIL A 37 PEN B
WIMBISH ALFRED A 44 SAS B
WIMBISH FED A 44 TOW B
WIMBISH GILES A 44 SAS B
WIMBISH JACK A 44 TOW B
WIMBISH JESSE A 44 TOW B
WIMBISH PETER JR A 44 TOW B
WIMBISH PETER SR A 44 TOW B
WIMBISH RANE A 44 SAS B
WIMBISH VINCENT A 44 HEN B
WIMBLEY JOSIAH A 37 MAN B
WIMBUSH GEORGE A 44 ISL B
WIMBUSH MOSSES A 44 ISL B
WIMBY JOHN S A 72 SWA W
WIMBY STEPHEN A 72 SWA W
WIMBY STEPHEN M A 72 SWA W
WIMERLY ELIAS A 37 HOL B
WIMERLY EVERETT A 37 HOL B
WIMERLY KISIMIR A 37 HOL B
WIMERLY RAIF A 37 ROC B
WINBISH RICHARD A 44 HEN B
WINBISH ROBT A 44 KIT B
WINBON BEN A 39 DAV B
WINBORN ABRAHAM A 37 ROB W
WINBORN R H A 24 MID W
WINCHESTER BASLEY A 46 GRE B
WINCHESTER DAVID A 46 GRE B
WINCHESTER GREEN A 46 SUM B
WINCHESTER J W A 46 SUM W
WINCHESTER S C A 46 SUM W
WINCHESTER SANDY A 46 GRE B
WINCHESTER SHEPARD A 46 SUM W
WINCHESTER THOMAS A 25 PIN W
WIND ARCHABLE A 28 16T B
WIND WONARD A 29 FA1 B
WINDBURN GEORGE L A 37 TA1 W
WINDER EDWARD A 35 WOL W
WINDER JOHN C A 35 MAG W
CERTIFICATE
GIVEN 10 APR 1868
WINDERS AUSTIN A 35 WOL W
WINDERS CHARLES A 35 WAR B
WINDERS CHARLES A 35 WAR W
WINDERS DOCTOR A 35 WOL W
WINDERS M B A 35 WOL W
WINDERS MOSES A 35 KEN B
WINDERS N J A 35 WOL W
WINDERS W D A 35 WOL W
WINDERS WILLIAM H A 35 WAR W
WINDLEY ARMSTRONG A 53 GER B
WINDLEY BARZILLAI A 53 FAI W
WINDLEY BENJ A 28 04A B
WINDLEY SAML C A 28 01A W
WINDLEY SAMUEL A A 53 LA2 W
WINDRICK JAMES D A 53 LA1 W
WINDS ISAAC A 28 02N B
WINDS THOS D A 28 02N B
WINDSOR WILSON A 46 MCL B
WINES AMOS A 28 01A B
WINFIELD
BENJ PATRICK A 28 03B W
WINFIELD HARRY A 28 05A B
WINFIELD HENDERSON A 44 TOW B
WINFIELD JAMES A 28 05A B
WINFIELD JOHN A 19 MOR B
WINFIELD JOHN R A 53 GER W
WINFIELD WILLIAM D A 53 BUR W
WINFREE J S A 46 SUM W
WINFREE W C A 46 SUM W
WINGATE ELIAS A 37 ROB B
WINGATE JOSIAH A 26 BLA W
WINGATE NATHAN A 28 03A B
WINLEY DAIRY A 28 03A B
WINLEY HARRY A 28 05A B
WINLEY ISAM A 28 05A B
WINLEY ISRAEL A 28 10T B
WINLEY JAMES A 40 DEC B
WINLEY JESSE A 28 10T B
WINLEY MALFORD A 28 05A B
WINLEY VIRGIN A 28 03A B
WINLY DAIRY A 28 05A B
WINN BAILEY A 28 12T B
WINN CHARLES A 46 ROS B
WINN DANIEL A 24 EDE B
WINN EDMUND A 28 04A B
WINN FREDERICK A 24 EDE B
WINN JOHN P A 37 SHA W
WINN JOSEPH A 24 EDE B
WINN R H A 39 HAY W
WINN RICHARD A 24 EDE B
WINN RICHD G A 39 HAY W
WINN RICHD JUGE A 39 LOU W
WINN ROBERT A 37 SHA W
WINN ROBT A 28 05A B
WINN STARKEY A A 53 LA2 W
WINN THOS H A 24 EDE W
WINN WALLACE A 26 HOL B
WINN WM A 26 HOL B
WINNE G W A 39 LOU W
TRNS TO WAKE CO
WINNE RICHARD A 39 HAY W
WINSAR ANANIAS A 19 BE1 B
WINSAR SAMUAL A 19 SHA B
WINSLOW E L A 29 FA1 W
WINSLOW HURDLE A 24 UPP W
WINSLOW J S A 24 UPP W
WINSLOW JOB B A 24 UPP W
WINSLOW JOHN L A 24 UPP W
WINSLOW K A 24 UPP W
WINSLOW OBED A 24 UPP W
WINSLOW RICHD A 29 FA1 B
WINSLOW TIMOTHY A A 24 UPP W
WINSOR HENRY C A 19 BE1 B
WINSTAD JERRY A 37 ROC B
WINSTEAD CHARLES A 44 YXR B
WINSTEAD RENCHEL A 37 ROC B
WINSTEAD TONEY A 37 SHA B
WINSTON ALFRED A 39 FRA B
WINSTON B H A 38 FRE W
WINSTON B H A 39 FRA W
WINSTON C A 44 BEA W
WINSTON E A 44 FOR W
WINSTON G W JR A 39 FRA W
WINSTON GEO A 19 HAR B
WINSTON GEO JR A 39 FRA W
WINSTON GEORGE A 39 FRA B
WINSTON H A A 39 FRA W
WINSTON HENRY A 39 FRA B
WINSTON HENRY A 39 FRA W
WINSTON ISAAC A 44 FOR B
WINSTON ISAAC H A 39 FRA W
WINSTON J M A 39 FRA W
WINSTON J W SR A 39 FRA W
WINSTON JACOB A 39 FRA B
WINSTON JACOB A 44 DUT B
WINSTON JAMES A 39 FRA B
WINSTON JOHN A 39 FRA B
WINSTON JOHN A 39 FRA W
WINSTON JOHN A 44 BEA B
WINSTON JOHN J A 37 HIG W
WINSTON JOS B A 39 FRE W
WINSTON KINCHEN A 44 BEA B
WINSTON M C A 39 FRA W
WINSTON MONROE A 38 FRE B
WINSTON NELSON A 38 FRE B
WINSTON NORPHLET A 39 FRA W
WINSTON PORTER A 39 FRA B
WINSTON R N A 39 FRA W
WINSTON R T A 44 YXR W
WINSTON REUBEN A 38 FRE B
WINSTON S H A 39 FRA W
WINSTON SIDNEY A 38 FRE W
WINSTON THOS A 39 FRE W
WINSTON THOS A 44 FOR B
WINSTON W A A 39 FRA W
WINSTON W J A 39 FRA W
WINSTON W T A 39 FRA W
WINSTON WM A 39 FRA B
WINTERS CASWELL A 99 BUS B
WINTERS J A A 26 BOR W
WINTERS JOHN W A 46 HIG W
WINTERS MEBAN A 46 HIG W
WINTFIELD WILLIAM A 37 ROC B
WINTFRY THOMAS A 46 FRI W
WIRICK ALFRED A 46 MCL W
WIRICK BENAJMIN A 46 MON B
WIRICK DANIEL A 46 MON W
WIRICK DAVID A 46 MON W
WIRICK GEORGE A 46 MON W
WIRICK ISRAEL A 46 MON W
WIRICK J M A 46 MON W
WIRICK JACOB A 46 MON W
WIRICK JOEL A 46 MON W
WIRICK JOEL W A 46 MON W
WIRICK JOHN A 46 MON W
WIRICK MARTIN W A 46 GRE W
WIRICK MILTON A 46 MON W
WIRICK N A 46 MON W
WIRICK SOLOMON R 46 MON W
NAME LINED OUT
PUNISHED FOR THEFT
REJ BY HIS REQUEST
WIRICK WM A 46 MON W

WIRICK WM A	A	46	MON	W
WISE BENJAMIN	A	28	10T	B
WISE CHANCY	A	28	10T	B
WISE EDWARD	A	30	ROA	B
WISE FRANKLIN A	A	40	MAU	W
WISE FREDK	A	28	05A	B
WISE FREEMAN	A	28	17T	W
WISE GEORGE	A	28	16T	B
WISE JAMES	A	28	7TH	B
WISE JOHN	A	28	05A	B
WISE LUKE	A	30	ROA	B
WISE SMITH J	A	28	17T	W
WISEMAN HENRY	A	32	DAV	B
WISEMEN PETER	A	32	DAV	B
WISHIT EDWIN	A	29	ROC	W
WISTER BEANJMIN D	A	39	DAV	W
WITCHARD RANDALL	A	37	HIC	B
WITE EPHRAM R	A	37	MAN	B
WITHERING JAMES	A	35	GLI	B
WITHERINGTON SOLM	A	28	6TH	W
WITHERS CYRUS C	A	40	DA1	W
WITHERS ELI H	A	40	DA1	W
WITHERS JOHN L	A	40	DA1	W
WITHERS MARCUS S	A	40	DA1	W
WITHERS MILES	A	40	DA1	W
WITHERS MORGAN	A	40	DA1	W
WITHERS W C	A	40	RHY	W
WITHERS WILLIAM	A	40	DA1	W
WITHERSPOON CAMERON	A	46	GRE	W
WITHERSPOON HARRY	A	46	GRE	B
WITHERSPOON HENRY R	A	46	GRE	W
WITHINGTON A R	A	32	THO	W
WITHINGTON J W	A	32	THO	W
WITHINGTON JOHN A	A	46	MON	W
WITLEY J A	A	46	FRI	W
WITTY LEVI R	A	46	ROS	W
WITTY WM B	A	46	ROS	W
WOLF JOHN B	A	19	BE1	W
WOLFE HORACE	A	46	ROS	W
WOLFE J M	A	32	DAV	W
WOLFENDEN J J	A	28	01A	W
WOLLARD JOSEPH C	A	53	GER	W
WOLZ W C	A	26	BLA	W
WOMACK EDMOND	A	99	BUS	B
WOMACK J C	A	32	DAV	W
WOMACK MOSES	A	29	FA1	B
WOMBLE NATHANIEL G	A	37	ROC	W
WOMMOCK CHARLES	A	32	CLE	B
WOMOUTH W W	A	39	FRA	W
WONSLEY JOHN	A	37	HIG	B
WOOD A B	A	29	CAR	W
WOOD A G	A	39	DAV	W
WOOD A J	A	46	FRI	W
WOOD ALFORD	A	32	YAD	W
WOOD ALFORD	A	39	DAV	B
WOOD ALFRED	A	44	SAS	B
WOOD BENNETT	A	39	DAV	W
WOOD BERRY	A	46	FRI	W
WOOD BUCK	A	39	HAY	B
WOOD CASWELL	A	28	6TH	W
WOOD CLEMENS	A	29	FA1	W
WOOD CULLIN	A	46	GRE	W
WOOD DAVID T	A	44	TAR	W
WOOD DUGLIS	A	44	YXR	B
WOOD EDWARD	A	24	EDE	W
WOOD EMANUEL	A	28	01B	B
WOOD FERNEY	A	29	FLE	W
WOOD FRANK	A	39	SPE	B
TRANS TO FRANKLINTON NC				
WOOD GEORGE	A	39	JOR	W
WOOD GOODMAN	A	29	CAR	W
WOOD GREGORS	A	72	SWA	B
WOOD HARRY	A	32	JAC	B
WOOD HENRY	A	29	CAR	W
WOOD HENRY	A	39	JOR	W
WOOD ISAAC	A	28	02N	B
WOOD J H	A	39	JOR	W
TRNS TO WARREN CO				
APRIL 19 1868				
WOOD J K	A	44	OXF	W
WOOD J M	A	44	OXF	W
WOOD J M	A	46	JAM	W
WOOD J S	A	28	02N	W
WOOD JACOB	A	28	03A	B
WOOD JOHN	A	32	YAD	W
WOOD JOHN	A	46	FRI	W
WOOD JOHN E	A	32	DAV	W
WOOD JOHN JR	A	29	CAR	W
WOOD JOHN N	A	39	JOR	W
WOOD JOHN SR	A	29	CAR	W
WOOD JOHN SR	A	39	JOR	W
WOOD JOSEPH	A	24	EDE	B
WOOD JOSEPH L	A	40	FER	W
WOOD JOSEPH P	A	44	DUT	W
WOOD JOSEPH T	A	26	MOU	W
WOOD LEVI	A	37	ROC	B
WOOD LOGAN	A	44	YXR	B
WOOD MARK	A	29	CAR	W
WOOD MATTHEW	A	46	RAG	B
WOOD MICHALES	A	19	MOR	W
WOOD MILTON	A	46	JAM	W
WOOD MURRELL	A	35	CYP	W
WOOD NAT	A	39	DAV	B
WOOD NELSON	A	32	JAC	B
WOOD OWEN A G	A	46	GRE	W
WOOD PLESANT	A	44	OXF	W
WOOD RICHARD L	A	46	FRI	W
WOOD ROBERT	A	37	PIN	B
WOOD SAML D	A	28	03A	W
WOOD SHARP R	A	28	16T	W
WOOD SPENCER	A	32	JAC	W
WOOD STEPHEN	A	35	CYP	W
WOOD T J	A	26	MOU	W
WOOD THOMAS D	A	39	JOR	W
WOOD THOS M	A	26	MOU	W
WOOD TOM	A	39	DAV	B
WOOD W A	A	32	TYR	W
WOOD W M	A	29	BLA	W
WOOD W S	A	26	MOU	W
WOOD WILLIAM	A	39	JOR	W
WOOD WILLIAM	A	44	FIS	B
WOOD WILLIAM	A	44	KNA	W
WOOD WILLIAM	A	46	FRI	W
WOOD WILLIAM C	A	24	EDE	W
WOOD WILLIS	A	39	DAV	W
WOOD WM	A	39	DAV	W
WOOD ZEBIDEE	A	46	ROS	W
WOODALL VAN B	A	29	FA1	W
WOODARD JAMES	A	44	FOR	W
WOODARD JOHN	A	32	LEE	W
WOODARD JOHN M	A	28	15T	W
WOODARD JOSHUA	A	37	PEN	W
WOODARD NATHANIEL	A	24	EDE	W
WOODARD RICHARD	A	24	EDE	W
WOODARD THOMAS	A	28	16T	W
WOODARD WM	A	39	HAR	W
WOODBERN DAVID N	A	46	ROS	W
WOODBURN J A	A	46	JAM	W
WOODBURN TENNESON M	A	46	RAG	W
WOODBURN WM A	A	46	RAG	W
WOODELL DAVID B	A	29	FA1	W
WOODELL NORRIS	A	29	FA1	W
WOODEN GEORGE	A	28	6TH	B
WOODEN GEORGE	A	44	HEN	B
WOODHOUSE JAMES M	A	30	NAR	W
WOODHOUSE JOHN	A	30	IND	B
WOODHOUSE JOHN	A	30	NAR	B
WOODHOUSE M C	A	30	TUL	W
WOODHOUSE MAJOR E	A	30	POP	W
WOODHOUSE MARTIN	A	30	CUR	B
WOODHOUSE MOSES	A	30	IND	B
WOODHOUSE POMPEY	A	30	ROA	B
WOODHOUSE SAMUEL	A	30	POP	B
WOODHOUSE SAMUEL F	A	30	COI	W
WOODHOUSE THOMAS	A	30	POP	B
WOODHOUSE THOMAS	A	30	POW	W
WOODHOUSE TILMAN	A	30	NAR	W
WOODIS EDMOND	A	28	04B	B
WOODIS JOHN	A	28	04A	B
CERTIFICATE GRANTED				
RUSSELL'S				
WOODLEY B H	A	44	KIT	W
WOODLEY B T	A	44	KIT	W
WOODLEY DAVID	A	44	KIT	W
WOODLEY J E	A	44	KIT	W
WOODLEY JOHN	A	19	NEW	B
WOODLEY JOHN	A	30	ROA	B
WOODLEY JOSEPH J	A	44	HEN	W
WOODLEY MARCUS	A	44	KIT	W
WOODLEY N C	A	44	KIT	W
WOODLEY P C	A	44	KIT	W
WOODLEY PATRICK	A	44	KIT	W
WOODLEY WM H	A	44	KIT	W
WOODLIEF DAWSON	A	44	FOR	W
WOODLIEF JNO O	A	44	FOR	W
WOODLIEF ROBT	A	39	FRA	W
WOODLIEF W B	A	44	FOR	W
WOODLIFF A O	A	39	HAY	W
WOODLIFF B H	A	39	HAY	W
NAME LINED OUT				
1ST REGIS BORD				
GRANVILL CO NC				
WOODLIFF BENJAMIN	A	39	HAY	W
WOODLIFF IRVIN E	A	39	HAY	W
WOODLIFF J B	A	39	HAY	W
WOODLIFF N H	A	39	HAY	W
WOODLIFF W A	A	39	HAY	W
WOODLY R C	A	39	FRA	W
WOODLY WILLIAM	A	37	MAN	B
WOODMANSEE SAMEUL B	A	35	KEN	W
WOODS CICERO	A	28	05A	B
WOODS COOPER	A	28	04A	B
WOODS D C	A	25	TUS	W
WOODS DANNIEL	A	44	DUT	B
WOODS FREDK	A	28	04A	B
WOODS JAMES R	A	46	COB	W
WOODS JOHN	A	28	05A	B
WOODS JOHN S	A	46	COB	W
WOODS LEML S	A	28	01B	W
WOODS M N	A	25	TUS	W
WOODS MATTHEW	A	28	04A	W
WOODS OLIVER	A	28	6TH	W
WOODS ROBERT	A	26	GOF	B
WOODS VENTER JR	A	28	9TH	B
WOODS VENTER SR	A	28	9TH	B
WOODS W F	A	25	TUS	W
WOODS WILLIAM	A	46	RAG	B
WOODSON DOWNEY	A	44	SAS	B
MISPLACED				
WOODWARD A J	A	29	FA1	W
WOODWARD DAVID J	A	35	WAR	W
WOODWARD FRANCIS T	A	28	15T	W
WOODWARD GEO W	A	29	FA1	W
WOODWARD JAMES R	A	35	WAR	W
WOODWARD JESSE	A	28	03A	B
WOODWARD TIGLMON F	A	28	15T	W
WOODWORD MILES	A	19	HAR	B
WOODY FRANCIS F	A	44	YXR	W
WOODY REUBIN J	A	44	YXR	W

WOODY WM H A 44 YXR W
WOODYARD ISAAC A 46 GRE W
WOODYARD STANFORD A 46 MCL W
WOOLCOTT WM A 28 03A W
WOOLEN C W A 29 FA1 W
WOOLEN JAS A A 46 HIG W
WOOLEN L P A 46 SUM W
WOOLIN JOHN A 46 HIG W
WOOLLARD W J A 28 04A B
WOOLLEN BENJAMIN E A 46 ROS W
WOOLRIDGE THOS A 24 EDE B
WOOSLEY DAVID A 32 SHE W
WOOSLEY SAMUEL A 32 SHE W
WOOSLEY THOMAS A 32 SHE W
WOOTEN ALLEN A 28 11T W
WOOTEN HENRY A 37 WEB W
WOOTEN JOHN B A 28 7TH W
WOOTEN LACY A 37 WEB B
WOOTEN MILES A 37 WEB B
WOOTEN THOMAS A 28 02N W
WOOTERS CALVIN H A 46 MCL W
WOOTERS EMERY P A 46 MCL W
WOOTERS HENRY C C A 46 MCL W
WOOTERS JACKSON A 46 MCL W
WOOTERS JAS P A 46 GRE W
WOOTERS JOHN T A 46 MCL W
WORELL JAMES D A 29 SEV W
WORELL LOUIS A 29 SEV W
WORK WM MCD A 46 MON W
WORKMAN ALFORD A 32 COT W
WORKMAN C C A 32 LOF W
WORKMAN C D A 32 LOF W
WORKMAN C J A 32 LOF W
WORKMAN CLARKSON H A 32 COT W
WORKMAN H A A 32 DAV W
WORKMAN H J A 32 LOF W
WORKMAN HENRY A 32 LOF W
WORKMAN J C A 26 PEE W
WORKMAN J E A 32 LOF W
WORKMAN J J A 26 PEE W
WORKMAN JAMES A 32 LOF W
WORKMAN JOHN A 26 PEE W
WORKMAN JOHN J A 32 LOF W
WORKMAN L F A 32 LOF W
WORKMAN L H A 26 PEE W
WORKMAN L W A 32 LOF W
WORKMAN NOAH A 32 LOF W
WORKMAN SAM'L A 26 PEE W
WORKMAN TONEY R 40 STO B
CHALLENGED & REJ
NOT BEEN IN THE STATE
TWELVE MONTHS
WORKMAN W F A 32 LOF W
WORKMAN WILLIAM A 32 LOF W
WORLD WASHINGTON A 29 FA1 B
WORLEY FREDRICK A 35 SMI W
WORLEY P B A 35 SMI W
WORLEY T H A 25 SHO W
WORLEY W P A 25 SHO W
WORLICK MICHAEL A 26 GRI W
WORLY JOHN A 25 SHO W
WORNER JAMES A 53 GER B
WORREL JOHN A 32 DAV W
WORRELL BARTON A 37 ROC W
WORRELL ELIJAH A 29 ROC W
WORRELL J R A 44 ISL W
WORRELL L L A 29 ROC W
WORRELL SAMUEL A 37 EDW B
WORSELEY FRANKLIN A 37 TA1 B
WORSELEY GEORGE A 37 PIN B
WORSELEY HAINY A 37 PIN B
WORSELEY JAMES A A 37 PIN W
WORSELEY JOSEPH A 37 PIN B

WORSELEY LITTLE B A 37 PIN W
WORSELEY MACK A 37 PIN B
WORSELEY MORGAN A 37 PIN B
WORSELEY READING A 37 PIN W
WORSELEY WARREN A 37 PIN B
WORSELEY WILLIAM A 37 PIN B
WORSELY ARDEN A 37 TA1 B
WORSELY GLASCON A 37 PIN B
WORSELY ROBERT A 37 TA1 B
WORSELY VIRGIN A 37 HIC B
WORSLEY BEN A 28 11T B
WORSLEY JACK A 37 ROC B
WORSLEY JOHN A 37 WHI B
WORSLEY ROBERT A 37 ROC B
WORTH HIRAM C A 46 GRE W
WORTH JAS A A 29 FA1 W
WORTH JAS S A 29 FA1 W
WORTH JOSEPH A 35 ISL B
WORTH LINGLE A 29 FA1 B
WORTH WM H A 29 FA1 W
WORTHAM E W A 44 HEN W
WORTHAM EDMOND A 44 TOW B
WORTHAM ERASMUS A 44 OXF B
WORTHAM GEORGE A 44 TOW B
WORTHAM GRANVILLE A 44 HEN B
WORTHAM HARRISON A 44 HEN B
WORTHAM HENDERSON A 44 HEN B
WORTHAM J D A 44 HEN W
WORTHAM JAMES A 44 HEN W
WORTHAM OLIVER A 44 TOW B
WORTHAM R H A 44 HEN W
WORTHAM R J JR A 44 HEN W
WORTHAM RUBIN A 44 TAR B
WORTHAM SAMUEL A 44 HEN B
WORTHAM SCOTT A 44 HEN B
WORTHAM STERLING A 44 TAR B
WORTHAM W D A 44 HEN W
WORTHAM WILLIS A 44 LED B
WORTHINGTON EMMET A 44 YXS B
WORTHY EPHRAIM A 29 MON B
WORTHY GLASGOW A 29 MON B
REMOVED TO MOORE CO
CERTIF GIVEN
WORTMON HENRY A 26 PEE W
WORTMON JOHNATHAN A 26 PEE W
WOTEN AMOS A 37 WEB W
WOTEN MARSHAL A 37 WEB W
WOTTEN BENJAMIN A 37 WEB B
WRATLY WM A 29 ROC W
WRAY G W A 26 HOL B
WRAY GEORGE A 26 BOR B
WRAY J A A 26 BOR W
WRAY J A L A 26 HOL B
WRAY JOHN S A 26 SHE W
WRAY LEWIS A 26 SHE B
WRAY SIDNEY A 26 SHE B
WRAY THOS CHAL A 26 BOR B
CHARGED WITH BREACH
OF TRUST
WRAY W A 26 BOR W
WREGHT W H A 26 GRI W
WREN JAMES A 46 MCL W
WREN JOHN A 44 KIT W
WREN ZACARY A 39 SPE W
WRENN HENRY M A 46 GRE W
WRENN HENRY R A 46 GRE W
WRENN PETER A A 46 GIB W
WRIGHT A J A 44 RAG W
WRIGHT A L A 46 HIG W
WRIGHT ABRAM A 46 GRE B
WRIGHT ADAM A 19 BE2 B
WRIGHT ALFORD A 39 PUG B
WRIGHT ALFRED A 29 GRA B

WRIGHT ALFRED A 46 MON B
WRIGHT ANDREW A 29 FA1 B
WRIGHT ANDREW A 29 GRA B
WRIGHT ANDY A 24 EDE B
WRIGHT ANTHONY A 24 EDE B
WRIGHT ARCHY A 29 FA1 B
WRIGHT B H A 26 GRI W
WRIGHT BEN A 39 PUG B
WRIGHT BENJ A 26 GRI W
WRIGHT BENJ A 29 FA1 B
WRIGHT BENJAMIN A 19 HAR B
WRIGHT CALVIN A 35 FAI B
WRIGHT CHARLES A 29 FA2 B
WRIGHT CHARLES A 46 HIG B
WRIGHT CHARLES A 46 MON B
WRIGHT CHARLES A 46 ROS B
WRIGHT CLARKSON A 46 JAM W
WRIGHT DANIEL A 39 SPE B
WRIGHT DAVID A 35 FAI W
WRIGHT E G A 44 HEN W
WRIGHT EDMOND A 29 GRA B
WRIGHT EDMUND A 24 EDE W
WRIGHT ELLIC A 44 HEN B
WRIGHT ELLIE A 44 HEN B
CERT TO VOTE OUT COUNTY
WRIGHT EMANUAL A 29 FA1 B
WRIGHT FRANK A 28 12T B
WRIGHT FRANK T A 44 OXF B
WRIGHT FRANKLIN A 39 PUG B
WRIGHT FRIDAY A 26 MOO B
WRIGHT G H A 26 MOO W
WRIGHT G W A 26 SWA W
WRIGHT GEO W A 44 RAG W
WRIGHT GEORGE A 26 GRI W
WRIGHT GEORGE A 39 PUG B
WRIGHT GEORGE A 40 DA2 B
WRIGHT GEORGE A 46 SUM W
WRIGHT GILLIS A 29 FA1 B
WRIGHT GREGORY A 24 EDE B
WRIGHT H N A 28 02N W
WRIGHT H T A 46 FRI W
WRIGHT HARRISON A 39 PUG B
WRIGHT HARRY A 24 EDE B
WRIGHT HARRY A 35 FAI B
WRIGHT HENRY A 28 16T B
WRIGHT HENRY A 39 PUG B
WRIGHT HENRY A 46 JAM W
WRIGHT J F A 32 LEE W
WRIGHT J F A 44 KNA W
WRIGHT J H A 44 RAG W
WRIGHT J J A 29 FA1 W
WRIGHT J L A 44 RAG W
WRIGHT J M A 40 STO W
WRIGHT J W A 46 JAM W
WRIGHT JACK A 24 EDE B
WRIGHT JAMES A 26 CAR W
WRIGHT JAMES A 28 04B B
WRIGHT JAMES A 44 HEN B
WRIGHT JAMES A 46 FRI B
WRIGHT JAS K A 44 FOR W
WRIGHT JIM A 39 PUG B
WRIGHT JIM A 39 PUG B
WRIGHT JOHN A 28 01A B
WRIGHT JOHN A 28 7TH B
WRIGHT JOHN A 40 SAN W
COPIED FROM DUPLICATE
WRIGHT JOHN A 44 KNA B
WRIGHT JOHN A 46 SUM W
WRIGHT JOHN M A 29 FA1 W
WRIGHT JOHN R A 46 GRE W
WRIGHT JOSIAH T A 46 MON W
WRIGHT L S A 26 GRI W
WRIGHT LAWSON A 44 OXF B

WRIGHT LEE	A 39	PUG	B
WRIGHT M	A 26	PEE	W
WRIGHT M	A 32	LOF	W
WRIGHT MAJOR	A 29	FA1	B
WRIGHT MAJOR B	A 30	CUR	W
WRIGHT MARCIUS	A 39	HAY	B
WRIGHT MARTIN	A 29	FA1	B
WRIGHT MICAJAH	A 46	HIG	W
WRIGHT MIMMS	A 44	TAR	B
WRIGHT N J	A 26	GRI	W
WRIGHT N M	A 46	JAM	W
WRIGHT NAT	A 46	GRE	B
WRIGHT NEWTON	A 26	CAR	W
WRIGHT NOAH	A 40	BLA	W
WRIGHT NORRIS	A 28	05A	B
WRIGHT P A	A 26	GRI	W
WRIGHT PERRY	A 26	CAR	W
WRIGHT PETER	A 28	11T	B
WRIGHT PHILIP	A 28	12T	B
WRIGHT R	A 26	CAR	W
WRIGHT R H	A 26	GRI	W
WRIGHT RALPH	A 32	THO	W
WRIGHT RANDLESON	A 35	FAI	B
WRIGHT RECHARD JR	A 46	HIG	W
WRIGHT ROBERT	A 26	GRI	W
WRIGHT ROBT R	A 28	04B	B
WRIGHT S M	A 26	WAR	W
WRIGHT SAMUEL	A 44	OXF	B
WRIGHT SHEPHERD	A 29	GRA	B
WRIGHT SIDNEY	A 28	01A	B
WRIGHT SILAS	A 32	LOF	W
WRIGHT SIMON	A 26	SHE	B
WRIGHT SOL	A 29	FA1	W
WRIGHT STEPHEN	A 24	EDE	B
WRIGHT STEPHEN	A 46	MON	B
WRIGHT T B	A 35	FAI	W
WRIGHT THOMAS	A 35	FAI	W
WRIGHT THOMAS	A 46	MON	B
WRIGHT THOS	A 44	HEN	B
WRIGHT WILEY	A 29	FA1	B
WRIGHT WILLIAM	A 26	MOO	W
WRIGHT WILLIAM	A 39	LOU	B
WRIGHT WILLOUGHBY	A 30	IND	W
WRIGHT WILSON	A 30	IND	W
WRIGHT WM	A 29	FA1	W
WRIGHT WM B	A 29	FA1	W
WRIGHT WM F	A 46	GRE	W
WRIGHT WM H	A 26	WAR	W
WRIGHT WM L	A 46	HIG	W
WRIGHT WODSON	A 44	KNA	B
WRIGHTENBURY ALFRED	A 46	JAM	W
WRIGHTIN PETER	A 24	EDE	B
WRITE ELIAS	A 53	FAI	B
WRITENBURY CHARLES	A 46	FRI	W
WROTEN JEREMIAH	A 30	POP	B
WST GEORGE R	A 28	13T	W
WYATT BLOUNT	A 53	LA1	B
WYATT JAMES	A 40	DAI	W
WYATT JAMES A	A 46	GRE	W
WYATT R G	A 44	HEN	W
WYCHE ALBERT	A 44	HEN	B
WYCHE BENJ	A 44	HEN	W
WYCHE GASTON	A 44	HEN	B
WYCHE GEO J	A 44	OXF	B
WYCHE GEORGE	A 44	OXF	B
WYCHE HILLIARD	A 44	HEN	B
WYCHE JNO J	A 44	HEN	W
WYCHE MATHEW	A 44	OXF	B
WYCHE NORAGE	A 44	HEN	B
WYCHE NORICE	A 44	HEN	B
WYCHE PARRY	A 44	OXF	B
WYCHE W E	A 44	FOR	W
GRANVILLE CO			

WYCHE WM	A 44	HEN	B
WYER SAMUEL	A 32	POS	W
WYLES AARON W	A 40	DEC	W
WYLIE JOHN W	A 26	SHE	W
WYLIE SAMUEL	A 26	BUR	W
WYLIE W G	A 26	BUR	W
WYNN CHAS H	A 29	FA1	W
WYNN WILLIAM L	A 28	9TH	W
WYNNE GEORGE W	A 30	POW	W
WYNNE JAMES C	A 39	LOU	W
WYNNE RICHD	A 39	FRA	B
WYNNE W W	A 39	LOU	W
WYNNE WILLIAM	A 30	POW	B
WYRE ADAM	A 32	POS	W
WYRE ADAM	A 32	POS	W
WYRE BARNEY	A 32	POS	W
WYRE H	A 32	POS	W
WYRE JACOB	A 32	POS	W
WYRICK MARTIN	A 46	MCL	W
- Y -			
YANCEY ABSALUM	A 44	YXR	W
YANCEY ALBERT	A 44	YXR	B
YANCEY CHARLES A	A 44	YXR	W
YANCEY GEO H	A 44	HEN	W
YANCEY HARRY	A 44	YXR	B
YANCEY HENRY	A 44	TAR	B
YANCEY HENRY	A 44	YXR	B
YANCEY JAMES E	A 44	YXR	W
YANCEY LEVIE	A 44	YXR	B
YANCEY MADISON	A 44	SAS	B
YANCEY MARROW	A 44	SAS	B
YANCEY PETER	A 44	HEN	B
YANCEY SOLOMAN	A 44	KNA	B
YANCEY TONEY	A 44	HEN	B
YANCEY WARREN	A 44	YXS	B
YANCY J A	A 29	FA2	W
YANCY RICHD E	A 44	YXR	W
YARBER JIM	A 37	TA2	B
YARBER THOMAS G	A 37	ROC	B
YARBORAUGH ALPHIUS	A 40	STO	W
YARBORO ISHAM CHAL	A 39	JOR	B
YARBORO JAMES H	A 26	MOO	W
YARBORO JOHN L	A 26	HOL	B
YARBORO JULY	A 38	FRE	B
YARBORO L H	A 26	HOL	B
YARBORO STARLING	A 39	FRE	B
YARBOROUGH AARON	A 39	LOU	B
YARBOROUGH ANDERSON	A 39	FRA	B
YARBOROUGH CARY	A 39	HAY	B
YARBOROUGH CHARLES	A 39	LOU	B
YARBOROUGH COOPER	A 39	LOU	B
YARBOROUGH DRED	A 44	OXF	B
YARBOROUGH FRANK	A 39	FRA	B
YARBOROUGH GEORGE	A 39	LOU	B
YARBOROUGH GREEN	A 39	FRA	B
YARBOROUGH HAMPTON	A 39	HAR	B
YARBOROUGH HENRY	A 39	HAY	B
YARBOROUGH HENRY	A 39	LOU	B
YARBOROUGH J	A 26	CAR	W
YARBOROUGH JACK	A 39	DAV	B
YARBOROUGH JACK	A 39	LOU	B
YARBOROUGH JACKSON	A 39	LOU	B
YARBOROUGH JOHN	A 39	FRA	B
YARBOROUGH JOHN	A 39	JOR	W
YARBOROUGH JOS	A 39	FRA	B
YARBOROUGH LINDCA	A 39	DAV	B
YARBOROUGH MILO	A 39	FRA	B
YARBOROUGH PLEASANT	A 39	LOU	B
YARBOROUGH R F	A 39	LOU	W
YARBOROUGH ROBERT	A 39	LOU	B
YARBOROUGH SAMUEL	A 39	LOU	B
YARBOROUGH TOBE	A 39	FRA	B

YARBOROUGH W H	A 39	LOU	W
TRNS TO DAVIS X ROADS			
YARBOROUGH WASHINGTON	A 39	LOU	B
YARBOROUGH WM	A 39	LOU	B
YARBORRO J A	A 40	STO	W
YARBROUGH CHARLES	A 32	DAV	W
YARBROUGH DAVID	A 39	SPE	W
YARBROUGH GEORGE	A 99	BUS	B
YARBROUGH GREEN	A 44	BRA	B
YARBROUGH JACOB	A 44	BRA	B
YARBROUGH JAMES M	A 39	SPE	W
YARBROUGH JOHN	A 32	DAV	W
YARBROUGH PETER	A 39	PUG	B
YARBROUGH ROBERT	A 44	YXS	B
YATES CHARLES	A 46	GRE	W
CERT GIVEN REMOVED TO WILMINGTON NC			
YATES FRANCIS	A 19	NEW	W
YATES HARRY	A 46	GRE	B
YATES J F	A 46	JAM	W
YATES JETHRO	A 46	JAM	W
YATES JOHNSON	A 46	JAM	W
YATES JONATHAN Y	A 29	FA1	W
YATES JOSIAH	A 30	IND	W
YATES S W	A 46	JAM	W
YATES SAMUEL	A 46	JAM	W
YATES SANDFORD	A 46	JAM	W
YATES THOMAS	A 28	10T	B
YATES WILLIAM	A 19	NEW	W
YATES WM	A 46	GRE	B
YEANTS PETER C	A 46	JAM	W
YEARGIN DAVID	A 44	FIS	W
YELVINGTON JACOB	A 39	DAV	W
YEOMANS ABRAHAM J	A 28	04A	W
YEOWS JAMES	A 46	JAM	B
YEOWS ROBERT	A 46	JAM	B
YERMON REUBIN	A 19	BE1	B
YOAKLY JOSEPH	A 32	DAV	B
YOKELEY DAVID P	A 32	POS	W
YOKELEY JACOB	A 32	POS	W
YOKELEY LEWIS	A 32	POS	B
YOKELY ALLEN	A 46	HIG	B
YOKELY AMOS	A 32	THO	W
YOKELY ANDREW	A 32	POS	W
YOKELY DAVID	A 32	BRO	W
YOKELY EDWARD	A 46	SUM	B
YOKELY J M	A 32	THO	W
"C" LEXINGTON N C			
YOKELY JEFFRY	A 32	POS	W
YOKELY JOSEPH	A 32	POS	W
YOKELY MARTIN	A 32	THO	B
YOKELY SAMUEL	A 32	THO	W
YOKELY SAMUL L	A 32	THO	W
"C" LEXINGTON N C			
YOKELY SOLOMON	A 32	THO	W
YOKLEY HARRIS M	A 32	POS	W
YOKLEY SAMUEL D	A 32	POS	W
YOMANS EDEN	A 72	SWA	W
YORK AMOS	A 28	04A	B
YORK BACCHUS	A 28	04A	B
YORK BRANTLEY	A 46	ROS	W
YORK E T	A 44	FOR	W
YORK ENOCH	A 19	BE1	B
YORK HIRAM	A 19	NEW	W
YORK J E	A 44	OXF	W
YORK J W JR	A 44	OXF	W
YORK J W SR	A 44	OXF	W
YORK JAMES	A 28	02N	B
YORK MATTHEW	A 28	03A	B
YORK MILES	A 28	03A	B
YORK MILES 2ND	A 28	03A	B
YORK WM M	A 46	JAM	W

YORKE NATHAN A 32 DAV W
YOUNG A J A 32 TYR W
YOUNG A J A 39 HAR W
YOUNG A Y A 26 WAR B
YOUNG ABRAHM A 29 FA1 B
YOUNG ADOLPHUS A 44 OXF B
YOUNG B B A 32 TYR W
YOUNG B S A 32 TYR W
YOUNG BARNA A 32 TYR W
YOUNG BARTLETT A 44 SAS B
YOUNG BENJ A 26 SHE B
YOUNG BENJN A 28 05A B
YOUNG BOSS A 46 RAG B
YOUNG BURGESS A 39 FRA B
YOUNG CALEB A 46 RAG B
YOUNG CALIA A 39 HAR B
YOUNG CHARLES A 44 HEN B
YOUNG COMADORE A 44 HEN B
YOUNG DANIEL A 38 FRE B
YOUNG DANIEL A 44 HEN B
YOUNG DAVID A 26 GRI B
YOUNG DAVID A 44 SAS B
YOUNG DAVID S A 35 ROC W
YOUNG DENIS A 38 FRE B
YOUNG DORREL A 39 GRI W
YOUNG DR P W A 44 OXF W
YOUNG DR S D A 44 HEN W
YOUNG DR W W A 44 HEN W
YOUNG EDMOND A 44 TOW B
YOUNG EDWARD J A 53 OCR W
YOUNG ELI A 53 LA1 B
YOUNG ELIJAH A 99 BUS W
YOUNG ENOCH A 35 ROC W
YOUNG FRANKLIN A 53 GER B
YOUNG FREDERICK A 32 DAV W
YOUNG G W A 28 01A W
CERTIFICATE GRANTED
TO RUSSELL'S
YOUNG GEO HAMILTON A 44 HEN B
YOUNG GEORGE A 32 DAV W
YOUNG GEORGE A 44 YXS B
YOUNG GRANDISON A 44 OXF B
YOUNG HANABAL A 44 OXF B
YOUNG HENDERSON A 39 HAR B
YOUNG HENERY A 29 ROC B
YOUNG HENRY A 39 FRA B
YOUNG HENRY A 39 FRE B
YOUNG HENRY A A 38 FRE W
YOUNG HENRY H A 39 FRA W
YOUNG HORACE A 44 KIT B
YOUNG HOSEA A 35 ROC W
YOUNG HUSAND A 39 HAR B
YOUNG ISAAC A 38 FRE B
YOUNG ISHAM A 39 HAY B
YOUNG J B A 44 HEN W
YOUNG J D H A 39 FRA W
YOUNG J H A 32 TYR W
YOUNG J J A 38 FRE W
YOUNG J W C A 39 FRA W
YOUNG JACOB A 26 BUR B
YOUNG JACOB A 32 DAV W
YOUNG JACOB A 35 ROC W
YOUNG JAMES A A 32 DAV W
YOUNG JARREL A 39 HAR W
YOUNG JAS A 29 FA1 B
YOUNG JNO H A 44 HEN W
YOUNG JOHN 29 FLE B
YOUNG JOHN A 28 04A B
YOUNG JOHN A 32 DAV W
YOUNG JOHN A 32 TYR W
YOUNG JOHN A 32 TYR W
YOUNG JOHN A 37 SHA W
YOUNG JOHN A 37 TA1 B
YOUNG JOHN A 39 FRE W
YOUNG JOHN A 44 HEN B
YOUNG JOHN A 46 JAM W
YOUNG JOHN W A 39 HAY W
YOUNG JOS A A 39 HAR W
YOUNG JOSEPH A 44 YXR B
YOUNG JOSEPH A 46 RAG B
YOUNG JOSEPH J A 99 BUS W
YOUNG JOSHUA A 46 FRI W
YOUNG L A 32 TYR W
YOUNG LAWSON A 44 HEN B
YOUNG LAWSON JR A 44 HEN B
YOUNG LEONARD A 38 FRE W
YOUNG LEWIS A 39 FRA B
YOUNG LINDSAY A 46 RAG B
YOUNG LOUIS O A 32 TYR W
YOUNG M N A 39 GRI W
YOUNG MACKLIN A 39 FRE W
YOUNG MAJOR A 53 LA1 B
YOUNG MARK A 32 DAV W
YOUNG MAT A 44 HEN B
YOUNG MILLS A 46 RAG B
YOUNG MINOR A 39 FRA B
YOUNG MORTON A 44 SAS B
YOUNG NELSON A 39 HAR B
YOUNG NEWTON A 46 MON B
YOUNG NOAH A 32 LOF W
YOUNG PETER A 26 MOO B
YOUNG PHIL A 44 OXF B
YOUNG POWEL A 28 05A B
YOUNG R E A 44 HEN W
YOUNG RANDELL A 44 OXF B
YOUNG RICHARD G A 53 LA1 B
YOUNG RICHD A 39 FRE B
YOUNG RICHD A 44 SAS B
YOUNG ROBT A 44 OXF B
YOUNG S P A 28 01B W
YOUNG S W A 39 HAY W
YOUNG SAMUEL A 26 MOU W
YOUNG SAMUEL A 32 DAV B
YOUNG SCOTT A 44 BRA B
YOUNG SIDNEY A 44 SAS B
YOUNG SOLOMAN A 44 HEN B
YOUNG SOLOMON A 26 WAR B
YOUNG STANHOPE A 46 JAM B
YOUNG STEPHEN A 39 HAR W
YOUNG STEPHEN A 44 HEN B
YOUNG STREET A 44 OXF B
YOUNG T A 26 BOR B
YOUNG TASWELL A 44 SAS B
YOUNG THOMAS A 26 PEE B
YOUNG THOMAS A 32 DAV W
YOUNG THOMAS A 39 HAR W
YOUNG THOMAS A 44 HEN B
YOUNG THOMAS A 44 OXF B
YOUNG THOS A 44 HEN B
YOUNG THOS A 44 SAS B
YOUNG THOS M A 44 KIT W
YOUNG W HAMILTON A 44 HEN W
YOUNG W R A 39 HAR W
YOUNG W S A 39 JOR W
YOUNG W S A 39 LOU W
TRNS FROM COOKS
YOUNG WALTER C A 39 LOU W
TRNS BY AFF FROM
WAKE CO TO FRANKLIN
YOUNG WASHINGTON A 44 HEN B
YOUNG WASHINGTON A 44 SAS B
YOUNG WASHINGTON M A 46 GRE W
YOUNG WESLEY A 39 FRE W
YOUNG WILLE A 39 FRE W
YOUNG WILLIAM A 44 SAS B
YOUNG WILLIS A 44 OXF B
YOUNG WM J A 44 HEN W
YOUNG WM P A 38 FRE W
YOUNG WM W A 46 GRE W
YOUNTS FRANKLIN A 32 DAV W
YOUNTS ISAIH L A 32 DAV W
YOUNTS J L A 32 DAV W
YOUNTS JACOB A 32 LEE W
YOUNTS JAMES F A 32 DAV W
YOUNTS JOHN P A 32 DAV W
YOUNTS R A 32 DAV W
YOUNTS SAMUEL A 32 DAV W
YOUNTZ CHRISTIAN A 32 SHE W
YOUNTZ ELI A 32 DAV W
YOUNTZ HIRAM A 32 SHE W
YOUNTZ JEFFERSON A 32 SHE W
YOUNTZ JOHN A 32 DAV W
YOUNTZ R A A 32 DAV W

- Z -

ZACHARY JOHN P A 35 WAR W
ZANG ADAM A 28 01A W
ZIMMER LEWIS A 46 GRE W
ZIMMERMAN DAVID A 32 SHE W
ZIMMERMAN DAVID A 46 GIB W
ZIMMERMAN E A 32 SHE W
ZIMMERMAN GEORGE A 25 HAY W
ZIMMERMAN GEORGE A 32 SHE W
ZIMMERMAN JOHN A 25 HAY W
ZIMMERMAN JOHN A 35 ISL W
ZIMMERMAN JOHN A 46 GIB W
ZIMMERMAN LOVIS A 28 01B W
ZIMMERMAN N A A 25 HAY W
ZIMMERMAN SIMEON A 46 GIB W
ZIMMERMAN W H A 25 HAY W
ZINK P E A 32 TYR W
ZINKARD CHAS A 28 01A W
ZINKARD WM A 28 01A W
ZOELLER CHARLES F R 37 TA1 W
NAME LINED OUT
ZOELLER EDWARD R 37 TA1 W
NAME LINED OUT
(VOTED)
ZOELLER EDWARD R 37 TA2 W

APPENDIX A

Chapter CLIII. -- An Act to provide for the more efficient Government of the Rebel States.

Whereas no legal State governments or adequate protection for life or property now exists in the rebel States of Virginia, North Carolina, South Carolina, Georgia, Mississippi, Alabama, Louisiana, Florida, Texas, and Arkansas; and whereas it is necessary that peace and good order should be enforced in said States until loyal and republican State governments can be legally established: Therefore,

Sec. 1. Be it enacted by the Senate and House of Representatives of the United States of America in Congress assembled, That said rebel States shall be divided into military districts and made subject to the military authority of the United States as hereinafter prescribed, and for that purpose Virginia shall constitute the first district; North Carolina and South Carolina the second district; Georgia, Alabama, and Florida the third district; Mississippi and Arkansas the fourth district; and Louisiana and Texas the fifth district.

Sec. 2. And be it further enacted, That it shall be the duty of the President to assign to the command of each of said districts an officer of the army, not below the rank of brigadier-general, and to detail a sufficient military force to enable such officer to perform his duties and enforce his authority within the district to which he is assigned.

Sec. 3. And be it further enacted, That it shall be the duty of each officer assigned as aforesaid, to protect all persons in their rights of person and property, to suppress insurrection, disorder and violence, and to punish, or cause to be punished, all disturbers of the public peace and criminals; and to this end he may allow local civil tribunals to take jurisdiction of and to try offenders, or, when in his judgment it may be necessary for the trial of offenders, he shall have power to organize military commissions or tribunals for that purpose, and all interference under color of State authority with the exercise of military authority under this act, shall be null and void.

Sec. 4. And be it further enacted, That all persons put under military arrest by virtue of this act shall be tried without unnecessary delay, and no cruel or unusual punishment shall be inflicted, and no sentence of any military commission or tribunal hereby authorized, affecting the life or liberty of any person, shall be executed until it is approved by the officer in command of the district, and the laws and regulations for the government of the army shall not be affected by this act, except in so far as they conflict with its provisions; Provided, That no sentence of death under the provisions of this act shall be carried into effect without the approval of the President.

Sec. 5. And be it further enacted, That when the people of any one of said rebel States shall have formed a constitution of government in conformity with the Constitution of the United States in all respects, framed by a convention of delegates elected by the male citizens of said State, twenty-one years old and upward, of whatever race, color, or previous condition, who have been resident in said State for one year previous to the day of such election, except such as may be disfranchised for participation in the rebellion or for felony at common law, and when such constitution shall provide that the elective franchise shall be enjoyed by all such persons as have the qualifications herein stated for electors of delegates, and when such constitution shall be ratified by a majority of the persons voting on the question of ratification who are qualified as electors for delegates, and when such constitution shall have been shall have been submitted to Congress for examina-tion and approval, and Congress shall have approved the same, and when said State, by a vote of its legislature elected under said constitution, shall have adopted the amendment to the Constitution of the United States, proposed by the Thirty-ninth Congress, and known as article fourteen, and when said article shall have become a part of the Constitution of the United States, said State shall be declared entitled to representation in Congress, and senators and representatives shall be admitted therefrom on their taking the oath prescribed by law, and then and thereafter the preceding sections of this act shall be inoperative in said State: Provided, That no person excluded from the privilege of holding office by said proposed amendment to the Constitution of the United States, shall be eligible to election as a member of the convention to frame a constitution for any of said rebel States, nor shall any such person vote for members of such convention.

Sec. 6. And be it further enacted, That, until the people of said rebel States shall be by law admitted to representation in the Congress of the United States, any civil governments which may exist therein shall be deemed provisional only, and in all respects subject to the paramount authority of the United States at any time to abolish, modify, control, or supersede the same; and in all elections to any office under such provisional governments all persons shall be entitled to vote, and none others, who are entitled to vote, under the provisions of the fifth section of this act; and no person shall be eligible to any office under any such provisional governments who would be disqualified from holding office under the provisions of the third article of said constitutional amendment.

SCHUYLER COLFAX,
Speaker of the House of Representatives

LA FAYETTE S. FOSTER
President of the Senate, pro tempore

In the House of Representatives,)
March 2, 1867.)

The President of the United States having returned to the House of Representatives, in which it originated, the bill entitled "An act to provide for the more efficient government of the rebel States," with his objections thereto, the House of Representatives proceeded, in pursuance of the Constitution, to reconsider the same; and

Resolved, That the said bill do pass, two thirds of the House of Representatives agreeing to pass the same.

Attest: EDWD. McPHERSON,
Clerk of H. R. U. S.

APPENDIX B

The following letters were copied at the National Archives from RG No. 393, found in Stack area 10W2, Row 11, Compartment 17, Shelf A, Inventory Part 1, Entry 4089, 1867 only. Copies of correspondence of the Second Military District of Charleston, S.C.

#1632 Headquarters Second Military District
Charleston, S.C. December 6, 1867

Mr. Jacob Sorrell
Sorrell's Store
Wake County, N.C.
Sir,

Your communication of the 26th ultimo petitioning for permission to retail liquor by the glass is received. I am instructed by the Commanding General to inform you that the subject is under consideration, and that an order will shortly be issued modifying those now in force.

Very Respectfully &
Louis V. Caziare A.D. C. A. A.

* * * * *

Headquarters 2nd Military District
Charleston, SC, Dec 12, 1867

Commanding Officer
Post of Raleigh, N.C.

Sir:---- Referring to your endorsement of Nov. 28, 1867 on the comm. of Jacob Sorrell, I am directed by the Comdg Genl to state that the Deed of Trust enclosed in the papers referred to is in effect a mortgage, and that as such, proceedings for the enforcement thereof are subject to the operation of the concluding clause of Par. III, G.O. No. 10 is from these Headquarters. You will cause the parties in interest to be so informed.

Very respectfully,

Louis V. Caziare

OATH PRESCRIBED BY ACT OF JULY 2, 1862

I ____ of _________________________ County of __________________ and State of _________________________, do solemnly ________________ that I have never voluntarily borne arms against the United States since I have been a citizen thereof; that I have voluntarily given no aid, countenance, counsel, or encouragement to persons engaged in armed hostility thereto; that I have neither sought, nor accepted, nor attempted to exercise the functions of any office whatever, under any authority, or pretended authority, in hostility to the United States; that I have not yielded a voluntary support of any pretended government, authority, power, or constitution, within the United States, hostile or inimical thereto. And I do further _________ that, to the best of my knowledge and ability, I will support and defend the Constitution of the United States against all enemies, foreign and domestic; that I will bear true faith and allegiance to the same; that I take this obligation freely, without any mental reservation or purpose of evasion; and that I will well and faithfully discharge the duties of the office on which I am about to enter; So help me God.

____

_______________________ and subscribed before me,[2]

this ________ day of ___________ A. C. 186_____.[2]

____

North Carolina Extant Voter Registrations of 1867
APPENDIX D

NORTH CAROLINA COUNTIES AND VOTING PRECINCTS

In the North Carolina Archives the voter registration precinct books are found in the papers of the Secretary of State and are numbered as follows with exceptions noted:

SS 991
Carteret County
Harlows Creek
Hadnots Creek
Smyrna
Straights
Morehead City
New Bank
Shackleford Banks

SS 992
Carteret County
Hunting Quarters
Davis Shore
Cedar Island
Beaufort (2)
Portsmouth

SS 993
Chowan County
Edenton
Upper Ground
Middle Ground

SS 994
Clay County
Hayesville
Pine Log
Tusquitee
Shooting Creek

SS 995
Cleveland County
Mooresboro
Blantons
Shelby
Mouth of Sandy River
Swans
Borders Store
Holland's Mill

SS 996
Cleveland County
Burtown
Peelers
Griggs
Warlick
Carpenters
Goforths

SS 997
Cumberland County
Fayetteville (2)
Quwhiffle
Rockfish
Grays Creek
Carvers Creek

SS 998
Cumberland County
Locks Creek
Flea Hill
Cedar Creek
Carvers Creek
John Monroes
Black River

SS 999
Craven County
11th 15th
13th 16th
14th 17th

SS 1000
Craven County
1st 9th
2nd 10th
7th 12th
8th

SS 1001
Craven County
1st 5th
3rd 6th
4th

SS 1002
Currituck County
Knot Island
Indian Ridge
Falls Creek
Currituck CH.
Coinjock
Gibbs Woods

SS 1003
Currituck County
Moyock
Roanoke Island
Poplar Branch
Powells Point
North Bank
Narrow Shore

SS 1004
Davidson County
Loflin
Jackson Hill
Yadkin Inst.
Lees
Lexington

SS 1005
Davidson County
Clemmonsville
Possumtown
Thomasville
Sheltons
Brownstown
Tyro
Cotton Grove

SS 1006
Davidson County
(Books inside are Duplin)
Limestone
Island Creek
Glissons
Smiths
Albertsons
Faisons

SS 1007
Duplin County
Warsaw
Rockfish
Kenanville
Magnolia
Wolfes Crape
Cypress Creek

North Carolina Extant Voter Registrations of 1867
APPENDIX D

SS 1008
Edgecombe County
- Robertsons Store
- Sparta
- Webbes
- Whitleys Shop
- High Level
- Holly Groves
- Manner Hill

SS 1009
Edgecombe County
- Rocky Mount
- Piney Grove
- Penders Mill
- Edwards
- Tarboro (2)
- Hickory Fork
- Sharpes Store

SS 1010
Franklin County
- Harris X Road
- Griffin
- Robt A. Speed's Store
- Franklinton
- Freeman's X Rds

SS 1011
Franklin County
- Pughe's Hill
- Jordan Cooks
- Davis X Roads
- Hayesville
- Louisburg

SS 1012
Gaston County
- Sanderfers
- Stowes
- Canslers
- Decks
- Blacks

SS 1013
Gaston County
- Fergusons
- Mauneys
- Dallas (2)
- Ryners [Rymers]

SS 1014
Gaston County (Books inside are Granville)
- Henderson
- Fishing Creek
- Ragland
- Tar River
- Knapp of Reeds
- Sassafras Fork
- Oxford
- Kittrell
- Beaver Dam

SS 1015
Granville County
- Ledge of Rock
- Dutchville
- Young's Store
- Young's X Road
- Island Creek
- Gownsville
- Brassfield (2)

SS 1016
Hyde County
- Kennekeek
- Hatteras
- Lake Landing (2)
- Ocracoke

SS 1017
Hyde County
- Germanton
- Fairfield
- Burgess Mill
- Swan Quarter
- Chickamacomico

SS 1018
Onslow and Wake Counties
- Swansboro
- Busbee
- (Also contains POLK (1904), WILKES (1890-1896), MECKLENBURG (1896 and 1899)

SS 1019
Guilford County
- McLeansville
- Ragans
- Greensboro (2)
- Monticello
- Kings

SS 1020
Guilford County
- Summerfield
- High Point
- Jamestown
- Friendship
- Ross
- Gibsonville
- Coble

TABLE OF POPULATION COMPARISON OF FREE BLACK AND WH'TE FROM THE 1860 AND 1870 FEDERAL CENSUSES

For every census year, statistics are available for everything one can imagine. For the purposes of this book, comparison of the free black and white populations is interesting. The figures for 1860 were compiled in 1864 under the direction of the Secretary of the Interior by Joseph C.G. Kennedy, Superintendent of Census. The figure given is a total of free colored, combined black and mulatto, male and female. The figure for white is a total of male and female.

By 1870 many of the voting precincts in these seventeen counties in the 1867 precincts had changed names, been absorbed into other countries through boundary changes, or combined with other districts within the same county. The Government Printing Office in Washington in 1872 published statistics of population derived from the ninth census of the United States. The breakdown in Table III of this report shows townships, their names and numbers, cities (first indentation) and towns (second indentation). Names of towns are placed under the names of the townships in which they are respectively situated. The population of each township includes that of all towns located in it. Indian population was footnoted in the black column, but it was not added in the black figure.

COUNTY/TOWNSHIP/CITY/TOWN	1860		1870	
CARTERET COUNTY-	WH	BL	WH	BL
Beaufort, No.4			1492	1358
Beaufort-			1180	1242
Fort Macon (garrison)			118	3
Hunter Quarter, No.7			938	7
Morehead, No.2			635	533
Morehead-			184	83
Newport, No.3-			597	371
Newport			106	18
Portsmouth, No.8			335	6
Smyrna, No.6			843	62
Strait's No.5			928	63
White Oak, No.1-			517	325
CARTERET TOTALS	6064	153	7873	4071

COUNTY/TOWNSHIP/CITY/TOWN	1860		1870	
CHOWAN COUNTY-	WH	BL	WH	BL
Edenton or Lower, No.1			1133	2531
Edenton			1243	
Middle, No.2			1086	524
Upper, No.3-			862	314
CHOWAN TOTALS	2979	150	4324	3369

APPENDIX E POPULATION COMPARISONS

COUNTY/TOWNSHIP/CITY/TOWN	1860 WH	1860 BL	1870 WH	1870 BL
CLAY COUNTY	WH	BL	WH	BL
Brasstown, No.1			394	1
Hayesville, No.2			816	68
Hayesville			32	3
Hiawassee, No.4			387	31
Shooting Creek, No.5			415	8
Tusquittee, No.3			307	34
CLAY TOTALS	--	--	2351	144

COUNTY/TOWNSHIP/CITY/TOWN	1860 WH	1860 BL	1870 WH	1870 BL
CLEVELAND COUNTY	WH	BL	WH	BL
Double Shoal, No.9			1190	220
Duncan & Hinton Ck., No.8			1067	175
King's Mountain No.4			1033	245
Knob Creek, No.10			605	33
Rich Mountain, No.11			731	20
Sandy Run, No.7			1048	143
Shelby, No.6			1377	472
Sulphur Spring, No.3			1020	202
Township No.1 (no name)			390	81
Township No.2 (no name)			1036	131
Township No.5 (no name)			1166	341
CLEVELAND TOTALS	10108	109	10663	2063

COUNTY/TOWNSHIP/CITY/TOWN	1860 WH	1860 BL	1870 WH	1870 BL
CRAVEN COUNTY	WH	BL	WH	BL
Adam's Creek, No.5			432	920
Croatan, No.6			148	508
Dover, No.9			931	1275
New Berne, No.8			225	1381
New Berne			2020	3829
1st Ward			530	146
2nd Ward			367	257
3rd Ward			345	293
4th Ward			231	226
5th Ward			402	1027
6th Ward			78	1396
7th Ward			67	484
Wildwood No.7			108	2133
Township No.1 (no name)			1527	920
Township No.2 (no name)			1349	317
Township No.3 (no name)			681	228
Township No.4 (no name)			979	605
CRAVEN TOTALS	8747	1332	10420	15945

North Carolina Extant Voter Registrations of 1867
APPENDIX E POPULATION COMPARISONS

COUNTY/TOWNSHIP/CITY/TOWN	1860		1870	
CUMBERLAND COUNTY	WH	BL	WH	BL
Black River, No.8			531	229
Carver's Creek, No.2			658	733
Cedar Creek, No.6			1668	690
Cross Creek, No.4 (ex. Fay.)			38	109
Fayetteville			2342	2318
Flea Hill, No.7			942	957
Quewhiffle, No.1			632	322
Rock Fish, No.5			1723	1259
Seventy-first, No.3			986	898
CUMBERLAND TOTALS	9554	985	9520	7515

COUNTY/TOWNSHIP/CITY/TOWN	1860		1870	
CURRITUCK COUNTY	WH	BL	WH	BL
Crawford, No.24			1286	581
Fruitville, No.3			583	17
Moyock, No.1			910	294
Nag's Head, No.5			303	17
Poplar Branch, No.4			909	231
CURRITUCK TOTALS	4669	223	3991	1140

COUNTY/TOWNSHIP/CITY/TOWN	1860		1870	
DAVIDSON COUNTY	WH	BL	WH	BL
Alleghany, No.8			397	39
Arcadia, No.10			682	38
Boone, No.16			670	641
Brownstown, No.1			887	100
Conrad Hill, No.3			1019	96
Clemmonsville, No.11			738	240
Cotton Grove, No.15			469	399
Emmon's, No.4			901	40
Healing Springs, No.6			560	115
Jackson's Hill, No.7			570	67
Lexington, No.14			1590	699
Lexington			324	151
Midway, No.9			881	145
Silver Hill, No.5			905	70
Thomasville, No.2			2073	444
Thomasville			146	68
Tyro, No.13			733	252
Yadkin, No.12			793	161
DAVIDSON TOTALS	13376	149	14338	3765

APPENDIX E POPULATION COMPARISONS

COUNTY/TOWNSHIP/CITY/TOWN	1860		1870	
DUPLIN COUNTY	WH	BL	WH	BL
Albertson's No.4			520	147
Cypress Creek, No.7			758	266
Faison's, No.1			650	1268
Glesson's, No.3			379	102
Hallsville			228	153
Island Creek, No.8			875	574
Kenansville, No.12			1298	1580
Limestone, No.6			605	104
Magnolia, No.10			875	731
Rock Fish, No.9			701	679
Smith's, No.5			449	213
Warsaw, No.11			708	654
Wolfscrape, No.2			730	295
DUPLIN TOTALS	8269	371	8776	6766

EDGECOMBE COUNTY	WH	BL	WH	BL
Deep Creek, No.4			322	1384
Lawntown Creek, No.10			471	466
Lower Coneto, No.2			572	1428
Lower Fishing Creek No. 5			468	1161
Otter's Creek, No.9			465	186
Pokey, No.13			454	827
Rocky Mount, No.12			1024	1134
Rocky Mount			190	167
Sparta, No.8			589	933
Swift Creek, No.7			456	1927
Tarboro, No.1			1008	2094
Tarboro			687	653
Town Creek, No.14			650	442
Upper Coneto, No.3			418	1019
Upper Fishing Creek, No.6			683	1381
Walnut Creek, No.11			278	730
EDGECOMBE TOTALS	6879	389	8735	15932

North Carolina Extant Voter Registrations of 1867
APPENDIX E POPULATION COMPARISONS

COUNTY/TOWNSHIP/CITY/TOWN	1860		1870	
FRANKLIN COUNTY	WH	BL	WH	BL
Cedar Rock No.4			631	481
Cypress Creek, No.9			596	401
Dunn's, No.10			512	326
Franklinton, No.6			765	1191
Franklinton			200	105
Freeman's, No.7			613	705
Harris', No.8			764	502
Hayesville, No.1			739	891
Louisburg, No.5			830	1712
Louisburg			350	400
Sandy Creek, No.2			739	714
The Gold Mines, No.3			444	488
FRANKLIN TOTALS	6465	566	7183	7916

COUNTY/TOWNSHIP/CITY/TOWN	1860		1870	
GASTON COUNTY	WH	BL	WH	BL
Cherryville, No.1			1658	345
Crowder's Mountain, No.5			1304	627
Dallas, No.2			2628	1378
Dallas			196	103
River Bend, No.3			1398	850
South Point, No.4			1442	972
GASTON TOTALS	6997	111	8626	4275

COUNTY/TOWNSHIP/CITY/TOWN	1860		1870	
GRANVILLE COUNTY	WH	BL	WH	BL
Brassfield's No.11			1815	1200
Dutchville, No.10			1110	642
Fishing Creek, No.8			1018	1395
Henderson, No.6			1247	1786
Henderson			244	301
Kittrell's No.7			909	920
Oak Hill, No.3			951	1232
Oxford, No.5			1101	1623
Oxford			463	453
Sassafras Fork, No.2			772	1087
Tally Ho, No.9			1240	898
Townsville, No.1			548	1639
Walnut Grove, No.4			765	933
GRANVILLE TOTALS	11187	1123	12183	14109

North Carolina Extant Voter Registrations of 1867
APPENDIX E POPULATION COMPARISONS

COUNTY/TOWNSHIP/CITY/TOWN	1860		1870	
GUILFORD COUNTY	WH	BL	WH	BL
Bruce No.13			681	353
Centre Grove, No.10			637	473
Clay, No.6			726	109
Deep River, No.17			861	210
Fentriss, No.9			705	161
Friendship, No.14			968	380
Gilmer, No.8 (280 in Gilmer &			1319	992
Greensboro (217 in Morehead)			369	128
Green, No.3			979	140
High Point, No.18			1343	284
Jamestown, No.15			1327	212
Jefferson, No.5			815	230
Madison, No.4			575	265
Monroe, No.7			484	356
Morehead, No.11			1209	895
Oak Ridge, No.16			778	244
Rock Creek, No.2			710	372
Sumner, No.12			904	216
Washington, No.1			635	188
GUILFORD TOTALS	15738	693	16025	6208

HYDE COUNTY	WH	BL	WH	BL
Currituck, No.1			1008	574
Fairfield, No.4			642	503
Lake Landing, No.3			1421	841
Ocracoke, No.5			361	7
Swan Quarter, No.2			635	480
HYDE TOTALS	4684	257	4067	2405

ONSLOW COUNTY	WH	BL	WH	BL
Jacksonville, No.1			860	306
Jacksonville			39	21
Richland, No.3			1296	837
Stump Sound, No.2			1138	377
Swansboro, No.4			992	483
Swansboro			129	12
White Oaks, No.5			887	393
ONSLOW TOTALS	5195	162	5341	2429

COUNTY/TOWNSHIP/CITY/TOWN	1860		1870	
WAKE COUNTY	WH	BL	WH	BL
Barton's Creek, No.4			1040	545
Buckhorn, No.14			1019	675
Cedar Ford, No.7			979	554
House's Creek, No.8			1183	908
Little River, No.6			796	519
Mark's Creek, No.10			742	645
Middle Creek, No.15			985	492
New Light, No.2			528	270
Oak Grove, No.3			1353	722
Panther Branch, No.16			600	321
Raleigh, No.1			962	1397
Raleigh			3696	4094
East Ward			1368	1901
Middle Ward			510	611
West Ward			1818	1582
St. Mary's, No.13			1182	942
St. Matthew's, No.9			704	1488
Swift Creek, No.12			949	496
Wake Forest, No.5			1554	1581
White Oak, No.11			1154	526
WAKE TOTALS	16448	1446	23122	20269

* * * * *

North Carolina Extant Voter Registrations of 1867
INDEX TO NAMES OTHER THAN VOTER REGISTRANTS

www.ingramcontent.com/pod-product-compliance
Lightning Source LLC
LaVergne TN
LVHW061238100826
845148LV00008B/984

* 9 7 8 1 5 8 5 4 9 6 4 6 4 *